Webster's Everyday Spanish-English Dictionary

Created in Cooperation with
the Editors of
MERRIAM-WEBSTER

FEDERAL
STREET
PRESS

A Division of Merriam-Webster, Incorporated
Springfield, Massachusetts

This 2002 edition published by
Federal Street Press
A Division of Merriam-Webster, Incorporated
P.O. Box 281
Springfield, MA 01102

Federal Street Press books are available for
bulk purchase for sales promotion and premium use.
For details write the manager of special sales,
Federal Street Press, P.O. Box 281, Springfield, MA 01102

ISBN 1-892859-33-5

Printed in the United States of America

06   5

Contents

Preface

This Spanish-English Dictionary is a concise reference to the core vocabulary of Spanish and English. Its 40,000 entries and over 50,000 translations provide up-to-date coverage of the basic vocabulary and idioms in both languages. In addition, the book includes many specifically Latin-American words and phrases.

IPA (International Phonetic Alphabet) pronunciations are given for all English words. Included as well are tables of irregular verbs in both languages and the most common Spanish and English abbreviations.

This book shares many details of presentation with larger Spanish-English Dictionaries, but for reasons of conciseness it also has a number of features uniquely its own. Users need to be familiar with the following major features of this dictionary.

Main entries follow one another in strict alphabetical order, without regard to intervening spaces or hyphens. The Spanish letter combinations *ch* and *ll* are alphabetized within the letters *C* and *L*; however, the Spanish letter *ñ* is alphabetized separately between *N* and *O*.

Homographs (words spelled the same but having different meanings or parts of speech) are run on at a single main entry if they are closely related. Run-on homograph entries are replaced in the text by a boldfaced swung dash (as **haber** . . . *v aux* . . . — ~ *nm* . . .). Homographs of distinctly different origin (as **date¹** and **date²**) are given separate entries.

Run-on entries for related words that are not homographs may also follow the main entry. Thus we have the main entry **calcular** *vt* followed by run-on entries for — **calculador, -dora** *adj* . . . — **calculadora** *nf* . . . and — **cálculo** *nm*. However, if a related word falls later in the alphabet than a following unrelated main entry, it will be entered at its own place; **ear** and its run-on — **eardrum** precede the main entry **earl** which is followed by the main entry **earlobe**.

Variant spellings appear at the main entry separated by *or* (as **judgment** *or* **judgement, paralyze** *or Brit* **paralyse,** and **cacahuate** *or* **cacahuete**).

Inflected forms of English verbs, adjectives, adverbs, and nouns are shown when they are irregular (as **wage** . . . **waged; waging; ride** . . . **rode; ridden; good** . . . **better, best;** and **fly** . . . *n, pl* **flies**) or when there might be doubt about their spelling (as **ego** . . . *n, pl* **egos**). Inflected forms of Spanish irregular verbs are shown in the section Conjugation of Spanish Verbs on page 6a; numerical references to this table are included at the main entry (as **poseer** {20} *vt*). Irregular plurals of Spanish nouns or adjectives are shown at the main entry (as **ladrón, -drona** *n, mpl* **-drones**).

Cross-references are provided to lead the user to the appropriate main entry (as **mice → mouse** and **sobrestimar → sobreestimar**).

Pronunciation information is either given explicitly or implied for all English words. Pronunciation of Spanish words is assumed to be regular and is generally omitted; it is included, however, for certain foreign borrowings (as **pizza** [ˈpitsa, ˈpisa]). A full list of the pronunciation symbols used appears on page 24a.

The grammatical function of entry words is indicated by an italic **functional label** (as *vt, adj,* and *nm*). Italic **usage labels** may be added at the entry or sense as well (as **timbre** *nm* . . . **4** *Lat* : postage stamp, **center** *or Brit* **centre** . . . *n* . . ., or **garra** *nf* . . . **2** *fam* : hand, paw). These labels are also included in the translations (**bag** *n* . . . **2** HANDBAG : bolso *m,* cartera *f Lat*).

Usage notes are occasionally placed before a translation to clarify meaning or use (as **que** *conj* . . . **2** (*in comparisons*) : than).

Synonyms may appear before the translation word(s) in order to provide context for the meaning of an entry word or sense (as **sitio** *nm* . . . **2** ESPACIO : room, space; or **meet** . . . *vt* . . . **2** SATISFY : satisfacer).

Bold notes are sometimes used before a translation to introduce a plural sense or a common phrase using the main entry word (as **mueble** *nm* . . . **2 ~s** *nmpl* : furniture, furnishings, or **call** . . . vt . . . **2 ~ off** : cancelar). Note that when an entry word is repeated in a bold note, it is replaced by a swung dash.

Conjugation of Spanish Verbs

Simple Tenses

Tense	Regular Verbs Ending in -AR hablar	
PRESENT INDICATIVE	hablo	hablamos
	hablas	habláis
	habla	hablan
PRESENT SUBJUNCTIVE	hable	hablemos
	hables	habléis
	hable	hablen
PRETERIT INDICATIVE	hablé	hablamos
	hablaste	hablasteis
	habló	hablaron
IMPERFECT INDICATIVE	hablaba	hablábamos
	hablabas	hablabais
	hablaba	hablaban
IMPERFECT SUBJUNCTIVE	hablara	habláramos
	hablaras	hablarais
	hablara	hablaran
	or	
	hablase	hablásemos
	hablases	hablaseis
	hablase	hablasen
FUTURE INDICATIVE	hablaré	hablaremos
	hablarás	hablaréis
	hablará	hablarán
FUTURE SUBJUNCTIVE	hablare	habláremos
	hablares	hablareis
	hablare	hablaren
CONDITIONAL	hablaría	hablaríamos
	hablarías	hablaríais
	hablaría	hablarían
IMPERATIVE		hablemos
	habla	hablad
	hable	hablen
PRESENT PARTICIPLE (GERUND)	hablando	
PAST PARTICIPLE	hablado	

Regular Verbs Ending in -ER		Regular Verbs Ending in -IR	
comer		vivir	
como	comemos	vivo	vivimos
comes	coméis	vives	vivís
come	comen	vive	viven
coma	comamos	viva	vivamos
comas	comáis	vivas	viváis
coma	coman	viva	vivan
comí	comimos	viví	vivimos
comiste	comisteis	viviste	vivisteis
comió	comieron	vivió	vivieron
comía	comíamos	vivía	vivíamos
comías	comíais	vivías	vivíais
comía	comían	vivía	vivían
comiera	comiéramos	viviera	viviéramos
comieras	comierais	vivieras	vivierais
comiera	comieran	viviera	vivieran
or		*or*	
comiese	comiésemos	viviese	viviésemos
comieses	comieseis	vivieses	vivieseis
comiese	comiesen	viviese	viviesen
comeré	comeremos	viviré	viviremos
comerás	comeréis	vivirás	viviréis
comerá	comerán	vivirá	vivirán
comiere	comiéremos	viviere	viviéremos
comieres	comiereis	vivieres	viviereis
comiere	comieren	viviere	vivieren
comería	comeríamos	viviría	viviríamos
comerías	comeríais	vivirías	viviríais
comería	comerían	viviría	vivirían
	comamos		vivamos
come	comed	vive	vivid
coma	coman	viva	vivan
comiendo		viviendo	
comido		vivido	

Compound Tenses

1. Perfect Tenses

The perfect tenses are formed with *haber* and the past participle:

PRESENT PERFECT
>he hablado, etc. (*indicative*);
>haya hablado, etc. (*subjunctive*)

PAST PERFECT
>había hablado, etc. (*indicative*);
>hubiera hablado, etc. (*subjunctive*)
>*or*
>hubiese hablado, etc. (*subjunctive*)

PRETERIT PERFECT
>hube hablado, etc. (*indicative*)

FUTURE PERFECT
>habré hablado, etc. (*indicative*)

CONDITIONAL PERFECT
>habría hablado, etc. (*indicative*)

2. Progressive Tenses

The progressive tenses are formed with *estar* and the present participle:

PRESENT PROGRESSIVE
>estoy llamando, etc. (*indicative*);
>esté llamando, etc. (*subjunctive*)

IMPERFECT PROGRESSIVE
>estaba llamando, etc. (*indicative*);
>estuviera llamando, etc. (*subjunctive*)
>*or*
>estuviese llamando, etc. (*subjunctive*)

PRETERIT PROGRESSIVE
>estuve llamando, etc. (*indicative*)

FUTURE PROGRESSIVE
>estaré llamando, etc. (*indicative*)

CONDITIONAL PROGRESSIVE
    estaría llamando, etc. (*indicative*)

PRESENT PERFECT PROGRESSIVE
    he estado llamando, etc. (*indicative*);
    haya estado llamando, etc. (*subjunctive*)

PAST PERFECT PROGRESSIVE
    había estado llamando, etc. (*indicative*);
    hubiera estado llamando, etc. (*subjunctive*)
    or
    hubiese estado llamando, etc. (*subjunctive*)

Irregular Verbs

The *imperfect subjunctive*, the *future subjunctive*, the *conditional*, and most forms of the *imperative* are not included in the model conjugations, but can be derived as follows:

The *imperfect subjunctive* and the *future subjunctive* are formed from the third person plural form of the preterit tense by removing the last syllable (*-ron*) and adding the appropriate suffix:

PRETERIT INDICATIVE, THIRD PERSON PLURAL (querer)	quisieron
IMPERFECT SUBJUNCTIVE (querer)	quisiera, quisieras, etc. *or* quisiese, quisieses, etc.
FUTURE SUBJUNCTIVE (querer)	quisiere, quisieres, etc.

The conditional uses the same stem as the future indicative:

FUTURE INDICATIVE (poner)	pondré, pondrás, etc.
CONDITIONAL (poner)	pondría, pondrías, etc.

The third person singular, first person plural, and third person plural forms of the *imperative* are the same as the corresponding forms of the present subjunctive.

The second person singular form of the *imperative* is generally the same as the third person singular of the present indicative. Exceptions are noted in the model conjugations list.

The second person plural *(vosotros)* form of the *imperative* is formed by removing the final *-r* of the infinitive form and adding a *-d* (ex.: *oír* → *oíd*).

Model Conjugations of Irregular Verbs

The model conjugations below include the following simple tenses: the *present indicative* (*IND*), the *present subjunctive* (*SUBJ*), the *preterit indicative* (*PRET*), the *imperfect indicative* (*IMPF*), the *future indicative* (*FUT*), the second person singular form of the *imperative* (*IMPER*) when it differs from the third person singular of the present indicative, the *gerund* or *present participle* (*PRP*), and the *past participle* (*PP*). Each set of conjugations is preceded by the corresponding infinitive form of the verb, shown in bold type. Only tenses containing irregularities are listed, and the irregular verb forms within each tense are displayed in bold type.

Each irregular verb entry in the Spanish-English section of this dictionary is cross-referenced by number to one of the following model conjugations. These cross-reference numbers are shown in curly braces { } immediately following the entry's functional label.

1 **abolir** *(defective verb)* : *IND* abolimos, abolís *(other forms not used); SUBJ (not used); IMPER (only second person plural is used)*

2 **abrir** : *PP* abierto

3 **actuar** : *IND* **actúo, actúas, actúa**, actuamos, actuáis, **actúan**; *SUBJ* **actúe, actúes, actúe**, actuemos, actuéis, **actúen**; *IMPER* **actúa**

4 **adquirir** : *IND* **adquiero, adquieres, adquiere**, adquirimos, adquirís, **adquieren**; *SUBJ* **adquiera, adquieras, adquiera**, adquiramos, adquiráis, **adquieran**; *IMPER* **adquiere**

5 **airar** : *IND* **aíro, aíras, aíra**, airamos, airáis, **aíran**; *SUBJ* **aíre, aíres, aíre**, airemos, airéis, **aíren**; *IMPER* **aíra**

6 **andar** : *PRET* **anduve, anduviste, anduvo, anduvimos, anduvisteis, anduvieron**

7 **asir** : *IND* **asgo**, ases, ase, asimos, asís, asen; *SUBJ* **asga, asgas, asga, asgamos, asgáis, asgan**

8 **aunar** : *IND* **aúno, aúnas, aúna**, aunamos, aunáis, **aúnan**; *SUBJ* **aúne, aúnes, aúne**, aunemos, aunéis, **aúnen**; *IMPER* **aúna**

9 **avergonzar** : *IND* **avergüenzo, avergüenzas, avergüenza**, avergonzamos, avergonzáis, **avergüenzan**; *SUBJ* **avergüence, avergüences, avergüence**, avergoncemos, avergoncéis, **avergüencen**; *PRET* **avergoncé**; *IMPER* **avergüenza**

10 **averiguar** : *SUBJ* **averigüe, averigües, averigüe, averigüe-mos, averigüéis, averigüen;** *PRET* **averigüé,** averiguaste, averiguó, averiguamos, averiguasteis, averiguaron

11 **bendecir** : *IND* **bendigo, bendices, bendice,** bendecimos, bendecís, **bendicen;** *SUBJ* **bendiga, bendigas, bendiga, bendigamos, bendigáis, bendigan;** *PRET* **bendije, bendijiste, bendijo, bendijimos, bendijisteis, bendijeron;** *IMPER* **bendice**

12 **caber** : *IND* **quepo,** cabes, cabe, cabemos, cabéis, caben; *SUBJ* **quepa, quepas, quepa, quepamos, quepáis, quepan;** *PRET* **cupe, cupiste, cupo, cupimos, cupisteis, cupieron;** *FUT* **cabré, cabrás, cabrá, cabremos, cabréis, cabrán**

13 **caer** : *IND* **caigo,** caes, cae, caemos, caéis, caen; *SUBJ* **caiga, caigas, caiga, caigamos, caigáis, caigan;** *PRET* **caí, caíste, cayó, caímos, caísteis, cayeron;** *PRP* **cayendo;** *PP* **caído**

14 **cocer** : *IND* **cuezo, cueces, cuece,** cocemos, cocéis, **cuecen;** *SUBJ* **cueza, cuezas, cueza, cozamos, cozáis, cuezan;** *IMPER* **cuece**

15 **coger** : *IND* **cojo,** coges, coge, cogemos, cogéis, cogen; *SUBJ* **coja, cojas, coja, cojamos, cojáis, cojan**

16 **colgar** : *IND* **cuelgo, cuelgas, cuelga,** colgamos, colgáis, **cuelgan;** *SUBJ* **cuelgue, cuelgues, cuelgue, colguemos, colguéis, cuelguen;** *PRET* **colgué,** colgaste, colgó, colgamos, colgasteis, colgaron; *IMPER* **cuelga**

17 **concernir** (*defective verb; used only in the third person singular and plural of the present indicative, present subjunctive, and imperfect subjunctive*) *see* 25 **discernir**

18 **conocer** : *IND* **conozco,** conoces, conoce, conocemos, conocéis, conocen; *SUBJ* **conozca, conozcas, conozca, conozcamos, conozcáis, conozcan**

19 **contar** : *IND* **cuento, cuentas, cuenta,** contamos, contáis, **cuentan;** *SUBJ* **cuente, cuentes, cuente,** contemos, contéis, **cuenten;** *IMPER* **cuenta**

20 **creer** : *PRET* creí, **creíste, creyó, creímos, creísteis, creyeron;** *PRP* **creyendo;** *PP* **creído**

21 **cruzar** : *SUBJ* **cruce, cruces, cruce, crucemos, crucéis, crucen;** *PRET* **crucé,** cruzaste, cruzó, cruzamos, cruzasteis, cruzaron

22 **dar** : *IND* **doy,** das, da, damos, **dais,** dan; *SUBJ* **dé,** des, **dé,** demos, **deis,** den; *PRET* **di, diste, dio, dimos, disteis, dieron**

23 **decir** : *IND* **digo, dices, dice,** decimos, decís, **dicen;** *SUBJ* **diga, digas, diga, digamos, digáis, digan;** *PRET* **dije, dijiste, dijo, dijimos, dijisteis, dijeron;** *FUT* **diré, dirás, dirá, diremos, diréis, dirán;** *IMPER* **di;** *PRP* **diciendo;** *PP* **dicho**

24 **delinquir** : *IND* **delinco,** delinques, delinque, delinquimos, delinquís, delinquen; *SUBJ* **delinca, delincas, delinca, delincamos, delincáis, delincan**

25 **discernir** : *IND* **discierno, disciernes, discierne,** discernimos, discernís, **disciernen;** *SUBJ* **discierna, disciernas, discierna,** discernamos, discernáis, **disciernan;** *IMPER* **discierne**

26 **distinguir** : *IND* **distingo,** distingues, distingue, distinguimos, distinguís, distinguen; *SUBJ* **distinga, distingas, distinga, distingamos, distingáis, distingan**

27 **dormir** : *IND* **duermo, duermes, duerme,** dormimos, dormís, **duermen;** *SUBJ* **duerma, duermas, duerma, durmamos, durmáis, duerman;** *PRET* dormí, dormiste, **durmió,** dormimos, dormisteis, **durmieron;** *IMPER* **duerme;** *PRP* **durmiendo**

28 **elegir** : *IND* **elijo, eliges, elige,** elegimos, elegís, **eligen;** *SUBJ* **elija, elijas, elija, elijamos, elijáis, elijan;** *PRET* elegí, elegiste, **eligió,** elegimos, elegisteis, **eligieron;** *IMPER* **elige;** *PRP* **eligiendo**

29 **empezar** : *IND* **empiezo, empiezas, empieza,** empezamos, empezáis, **empiezan;** *SUBJ* **empiece, empieces, empiece, empecemos, empecéis, empiecen;** *PRET* **empecé,** empezaste, empezó, empezamos, empezasteis, empezaron; *IMPER* **empieza**

30 **enraizar** : *IND* **enraízo, enraízas, enraíza,** enraizamos, enraizáis, **enraízan;** *SUBJ* **enraíce, enraíces, enraíce, enraicemos, enraicéis, enraícen;** *PRET* **enraicé,** enraizaste, enraizó, enraizamos, enraizasteis, enraizaron; *IMPER* **enraíza**

31 **erguir** : *IND* **irgo** *or* **yergo, irgues** *or* **yergues, irgue** *or* **yergue,** erguimos, erguís, **irguen** *or* **yerguen;** *SUBJ* **irga** *or* **yerga, irgas** *or* **yergas, irga** *or* **yerga, irgamos, irgáis, irgan** *or* **yergan;** *PRET* erguí, erguiste, **irguió,** erguimos, erguisteis, **irguieron;** *IMPER* **irgue** *or* **yergue;** *PRP* **irguiendo**

32 **errar** : *IND* **yerro, yerras, yerra,** erramos, erráis, **yerran;** *SUBJ* **yerre, yerres, yerre,** erremos, erréis, **yerren;** *IMPER* **yerra**

33 **escribir** : *PP* **escrito**

34 **estar** : *IND* **estoy, estás, está,** estamos, estáis, **están;** *SUBJ* **esté, estés, esté,** estemos, estéis, **estén;** *PRET* **estuve, estuviste, estuvo, estuvimos, estuvisteis, estuvieron;** *IMPER* **está**

35 **exigir** : *IND* **exijo,** exiges, exige, exigimos, exigís, exigen; *SUBJ* **exija, exijas, exija, exijamos, exijáis, exijan**

36 **forzar** : *IND* **fuerzo, fuerzas, fuerza,** forzamos, forzáis, **fuerzan;** *SUBJ* **fuerce, fuerces, fuerce, forcemos, forcéis, fuercen;** *PRET* **forcé,** forzaste, forzó, forzamos, forzasteis, forzaron; *IMPER* **fuerza**

37 **freír** : *IND* **frío, fríes, fríe,** freímos, freís, **fríen;** *SUBJ* **fría, frías, fría,** friamos, friáis, **frían;** *PRET* freí, **freíste, frió,** freímos, freísteis, frieron; *IMPER* **fríe;** *PRP* **friendo;** *PP* **frito**

38 **gruñir** : *PRET* gruñí, gruñiste, **gruñó,** gruñimos, gruñisteis, **gruñeron;** *PRP* **gruñendo**

39 **haber** : *IND* **he, has, ha,** hemos, habéis, **han;** *SUBJ* **haya, hayas, haya, hayamos, hayáis, hayan;** *PRET* **hube, hubiste, hubo, hubimos, hubisteis, hubieron;** *FUT* **habré, habrás, habrá, habremos, habréis, habrán;** *IMPER* **he**

40 **hacer** : *IND* **hago,** haces, hace, hacemos, hacéis, hacen; *SUBJ* **haga, hagas, haga, hagamos, hagáis, hagan;** *PRET* **hice, hiciste, hizo, hicimos, hicisteis, hicieron;** *FUT* **haré, harás, hará, haremos, haréis, harán;** *IMPER* **haz;** *PP* **hecho**

41 **huir** : *IND* **huyo, huyes, huye,** huimos, huís, **huyen;** *SUBJ* **huya, huyas, huya, huyamos, huyáis, huyan;** *PRET* **huí,** huiste, **huyó,** huimos, huisteis, **huyeron;** *IMPER* **huye;** *PRP* **huyendo**

42 **imprimir** : *PP* **impreso**

43 **ir** : *IND* **voy, vas, va, vamos, vais, van;** *SUBJ* **vaya, vayas, vaya, vayamos, vayáis, vayan;** *PRET* **fui, fuiste, fue, fuimos, fuisteis, fueron;** *IMPF* **iba, ibas, iba, íbamos, ibais, iban;** *IMPER* **ve;** *PRP* **yendo;** *PP* **ido**

44 **jugar** : *IND* **juego, juegas, juega,** jugamos, jugáis, **juegan;** *SUBJ* **juegue, juegues, juegue, juguemos, juguéis, jueguen;** *PRET* **jugué,** jugaste, jugó, jugamos, jugasteis, jugaron; *IMPER* **juega**

45 **lucir** : *IND* **luzco,** luces, luce, lucimos, lucís, lucen; *SUBJ* **luzca, luzcas, luzca, luzcamos, luzcáis, luzcan**

46 **morir** : *IND* **muero, mueres, muere,** morimos, morís,

mueren; *SUBJ* **muera, mueras, muera, muramos, muráis, mueran;** *PRET* morí, moriste, **murió,** morimos, moristeis, murieron; *IMPER* **muere;** *PRP* **muriendo;** *PP* **muerto**

47 **mover** : *IND* **muevo, mueves, mueve,** movemos, movéis, **mueven;** *SUBJ* **mueva, muevas, mueva,** movamos, mováis, **muevan;** *IMPER* **mueve**

48 **nacer** : *IND* **nazco,** naces, nace, nacemos, nacéis, nacen; *SUBJ* **nazca, nazcas, nazca, nazcamos, nazcáis, nazcan**

49 **negar** : *IND* **niego, niegas, niega,** negamos, negáis, **niegan;** *SUBJ* **niegue, niegues, niegue, neguemos, neguéis, nieguen;** *PRET* **negué,** negaste, negó, negamos, negasteis, negaron; *IMPER* **niega**

50 **oír** : *IND* **oigo, oyes, oye, oímos,** oís, **oyen;** *SUBJ* **oiga, oigas, oiga, oigamos, oigáis, oigan;** *PRET* **oí, oíste, oyó, oímos, oísteis, oyeron;** *IMPER* **oye;** *PRP* **oyendo;** *PP* **oído**

51 **oler** : *IND* **huelo, hueles, huele,** olemos, oléis, **huelen;** *SUBJ* **huela, huelas, huela,** olamos, oláis, **huelan;** *IMPER* **huele**

52 **pagar** : *SUBJ* **pague, pagues, pague, paguemos, paguéis, paguen;** *PRET* **pagué,** pagaste, pagó, pagamos, pagasteis, pagaron

53 **parecer** : *IND* **parezco,** pareces, parece, parecemos, parecéis, parecen; *SUBJ* **parezca, parezcas, parezca, parezcamos, parezcáis, parezcan**

54 **pedir** : *IND* **pido, pides, pide,** pedimos, pedís, **piden;** *SUBJ* **pida, pidas, pida, pidamos, pidáis, pidan;** *PRET* pedí, pediste, **pidió,** pedimos, pedisteis, **pidieron;** *IMPER* **pide;** *PRP* **pidiendo**

55 **pensar** : *IND* **pienso, piensas, piensa,** pensamos, pensáis, **piensan;** *SUBJ* **piense, pienses, piense,** pensemos, penséis, **piensen;** *IMPER* **piensa**

56 **perder** : *IND* **pierdo, pierdes, pierde,** perdemos, perdéis, **pierden;** *SUBJ* **pierda, pierdas, pierda,** perdamos, perdáis, **pierdan;** *IMPER* **pierde**

57 **placer** : *IND* **plazco,** places, place, placemos, placéis, placen; *SUBJ* **plazca, plazcas, plazca, plazcamos, plazcáis, plazcan;** *PRET* plací, placiste, plació *or* **plugo,** placimos, placisteis, placieron *or* **pluguieron**

58 **poder** : *IND* **puedo, puedes, puede,** podemos, podéis, **pueden;** *SUBJ* **pueda, puedas, pueda,** podamos, podáis, **puedan;** *PRET*

pude, pudiste, pudo, pudimos, pudisteis, pudieron; *FUT* **podré, podrás, podrá, podremos, podréis, podrán;** *IMPER* **puede;** *PRP* **pudiendo**

59 **podrir** *or* **pudrir** : *PP* **podrido** *(all other forms based on* pudrir*)*

60 **poner** : *IND* **pongo,** pones, pone, ponemos, ponéis, ponen; *SUBJ* **ponga, pongas, ponga, pongamos, pongáis, pongan;** *PRET* **puse, pusiste, puso, pusimos, pusisteis, pusieron;** *FUT* **pondré, pondrás, pondrá, pondremos, pondréis, pondrán;** *IMPER* **pon;** *PP* **puesto**

61 **producir** : *IND* **produzco,** produces, produce, producimos, producís, producen; *SUBJ* **produzca, produzcas, produzca, produzcamos, produzcáis, produzcan;** *PRET* **produje, produjiste, produjo, produjimos, produjisteis, produjeron**

62 **prohibir** : *IND* **prohíbo, prohíbes, prohíbe,** prohibimos, prohibís, **prohíben;** *SUBJ* **prohíba, prohíbas, prohíba,** prohibamos, prohibáis, **prohíban;** *IMPER* **prohíbe**

63 **proveer** : *PRET* **proveí, proveíste, proveyó, proveímos, proveísteis, proveyeron;** *PRP* **proveyendo;** *PP* **provisto**

64 **querer** : *IND* **quiero, quieres, quiere,** queremos, queréis, **quieren;** *SUBJ* **quiera, quieras, quiera,** queramos, queráis, **quieran;** *PRET* **quise, quisiste, quiso, quisimos, quisisteis, quisieron;** *FUT* **querré, querrás, querrá, querremos, querréis, querrán;** *IMPER* **quiere**

65 **raer** : *IND* **rao** *or* **raigo** *or* **rayo,** raes, rae, raemos, raéis, raen; *SUBJ* **raiga** *or* **raya, raigas** *or* **rayas, raiga** *or* **raya, raigamos** *or* **rayamos, raigáis** *or* **rayáis, raigan** *or* **rayan;** *PRET* **raí, raíste, rayó, raímos, raísteis, rayeron;** *PRP* **rayendo;** *PP* **raído**

66 **reír** : *IND* **río, ríes, ríe, reímos,** reís, **ríen;** *SUBJ* **ría, rías, ría, riamos, riáis, rían;** *PRET* **reí, reíste, rió, reímos, reísteis, rieron;** *IMPER* **ríe;** *PRP* **riendo;** *PP* **reído**

67 **reñir** : *IND* **riño, riñes, riñe,** reñimos, reñís, **riñen;** *SUBJ* **riña, riñas, riña, riñamos, riñáis, riñan;** *PRET* reñí, reñiste, **riñó,** reñimos, reñisteis, **riñeron;** *PRP* **riñendo**

68 **reunir** : *IND* **reúno, reúnes, reúne,** reunimos, reunís, **reúnen;** *SUBJ* **reúna, reúnas, reúna,** reunamos, reunáis, **reúnan;** *IMPER* **reúne**

69 **roer** : *IND* **roo** *or* **roigo** *or* **royo,** roes, roe, roemos, roéis, roen;

SUBJ roa *or* **roiga** *or* **roya**, roas *or* **roigas** *or* **royas**, roa *or* **roiga** *or* **roya**, roamos *or* **roigamos** *or* **royamos**, roáis *or* **roigáis** *or* **royáis**, roan *or* **roigan** *or* **royan**; *PRET* roí, **roíste, royó**, roímos, roísteis, **royeron**; *PRP* **royendo**; *PP* **roído**

70 **romper** : *PP* **roto**

71 **saber** : *IND* **sé**, sabes, sabe, sabemos, sabéis, saben; *SUBJ* **sepa, sepas, sepa, sepamos, sepáis, sepan**; *PRET* **supe, supiste, supo, supimos, supisteis, supieron**; *FUT* **sabré, sabrás, sabrá, sabremos, sabréis, sabrán**

72 **sacar** : *SUBJ* **saque, saques, saque, saquemos, saquéis, saquen**; *PRET* **saqué**, sacaste, sacó, sacamos, sacasteis, sacaron

73 **salir** : *IND* **salgo**, sales, sale, salimos, salís, salen; *SUBJ* **salga, salgas, salga, salgamos, salgáis, salgan**; *FUT* **saldré, saldrás, saldrá, saldremos, saldréis, saldrán**; *IMPER* **sal**

74 **satisfacer** : *IND* **satisfago**, satisfaces, satisface, satisfacemos, satisfacéis, satisfacen; *SUBJ* **satisfaga, satisfagas, satisfaga, satisfagamos, satisfagáis, satisfagan**; *PRET* **satisfice, satisficiste, satisfizo, satisficimos**, satificisteis, **satisficieron**; *FUT* **satisfaré, satisfarás, satisfará, satisfaremos, satisfaréis, satisfarán**; *IMPER* **satisfaz** *or* **satisface**; *PP* **satisfecho**

75 **seguir** : *IND* **sigo, sigues, sigue**, seguimos, seguís, **siguen**; *SUBJ* **siga, sigas, siga, sigamos, sigáis, sigan**; *PRET* seguí, seguiste, **siguió**, seguimos, seguisteis, **siguieron**; *IMPER* **sigue**; *PRP* **siguiendo**

76 **sentir** : *IND* **siento, sientes, siente**, sentimos, sentís, **sienten**; *SUBJ* **sienta, sientas, sienta, sintamos, sintáis, sientan**; *PRET* sentí, sentiste, **sintió**, sentimos, sentisteis, **sintieron**; *IMPER* **siente**; *PRP* **sintiendo**

77 **ser** : *IND* **soy, eres, es, somos, sois, son**; *SUBJ* **sea, seas, sea, seamos, seáis, sean**; *PRET* **fui, fuiste, fue, fuimos, fuisteis, fueron**; *IMPF* **era, eras, era, éramos, erais, eran**; *IMPER* **sé**; *PRP* **siendo**; *PP* **sido**

78 **soler** *(defective verb; used only in the present, preterit, and imperfect indicative, and the present and imperfect subjunctive) see 47* **mover**

79 **tañer** : *PRET* tañí, tañiste, **tañó**, tañimos, tañisteis, **tañeron**; *PRP* **tañendo**

80 **tener** : *IND* **tengo, tienes, tiene**, tenemos, tenéis, **tienen**; *SUBJ* **tenga, tengas, tenga, tengamos, tengáis, tengan**; *PRET* **tuve,**

tuviste, tuvo, tuvimos, tuvisteis, tuvieron; *FUT* tendré, tendrás, tendrá, tendremos, tendréis, tendrán; *IMPER* ten

81 **traer** : *IND* **traigo**, traes, trae, traemos, traéis, traen; *SUBJ* **traiga, traigas, traiga, traigamos, traigáis, traigan;** *PRET* **traje, trajiste, trajo, trajimos, trajisteis, trajeron;** *PRP* **trayendo;** *PP* **traído**

82 **trocar** : *IND* **trueco, truecas, trueca,** trocamos, trocáis, **truecan;** *SUBJ* **trueque, trueques, trueque, troquemos, troquéis, truequen;** *PRET* **troqué**, trocaste, trocó, trocamos, trocasteis, trocaron; *IMPER* **trueca**

83 **uncir** : *IND* **unzo**, unces, unce, uncimos, uncís, uncen; *SUBJ* **unza, unzas, unza, unzamos, unzáis, unzan**

84 **valer** : *IND* **valgo**, vales, vale, valemos, valéis, valen; *SUBJ* **valga, valgas, valga, valgamos, valgáis, valgan;** *FUT* **valdré, valdrás, valdrá, valdremos, valdréis, valdrán**

85 **variar** : *IND* **varío, varías, varía,** variamos, variáis, **varían;** *SUBJ* **varíe, varíes, varíe,** variemos, variéis, **varíen;** *IMPER* **varía**

86 **vencer** : *IND* **venzo**, vences, vence, vencemos, vencéis, vencen; *SUBJ* **venza, venzas, venza, venzamos, venzáis, venzan**

87 **venir** : *IND* **vengo, vienes, viene,** venimos, venís, **vienen;** *SUBJ* **venga, vengas, venga, vengamos, vengáis, vengan;** *PRET* **vine**, viniste, **vino**, vinimos, vinisteis, vinieron; *FUT* **vendré, vendrás, vendrá, vendremos, vendréis, vendrán;** *IMPER* **ven;** *PRP* **viniendo**

88 **ver** : *IND* **veo**, ves, ve, vemos, veis, ven; *PRET* **vi**, viste, vio, vimos, visteis, vieron; *IMPER* ve; *PRP* **viendo;** *PP* **visto**

89 **volver** : *IND* **vuelvo, vuelves, vuelve,** volvemos, volvéis, **vuelven;** *SUBJ* **vuelva, vuelvas, vuelva,** volvamos, volváis, **vuelvan;** *IMPER* **vuelve;** *PP* **vuelto**

90 **yacer** : *IND* **yazco** *or* **yazgo** *or* **yago,** yaces, yace, yacemos, yacéis, yacen; *SUBJ* **yazca** *or* **yazga** *or* **yaga, yazcas** *or* **yazgas** *or* **yagas, yazca** *or* **yazga** *or* **yaga, yazcamos** *or* **yazgamos** *or* **yagamos, yazcáis** *or* **yazgáis** *or* **yagáis, yazcan** *or* **yazgan** *or* **yagan;** *IMPER* yace *or* **yaz**

Irregular English Verbs

INFINITIVE	PAST	PAST PARTICIPLE
arise	arose	arisen
awake	awoke	awoken *or* awaked
be	was, were	been
bear	bore	borne
beat	beat	beaten *or* beat
become	became	become
befall	befell	befallen
begin	began	begun
behold	beheld	beheld
bend	bent	bent
beseech	beseeched *or* besought	beseeched *or* besought
beset	beset	beset
bet	bet	bet
bid	bade *or* bid	bidden *or* bid
bind	bound	bound
bite	bit	bitten
bleed	bled	bled
blow	blew	blown
break	broke	broken
breed	bred	bred
bring	brought	brought
build	built	built
burn	burned *or* burnt	burned *or* burnt
burst	burst	burst
buy	bought	bought
can	could	—
cast	cast	cast
catch	caught	caught
choose	chose	chosen
cling	clung	clung
come	came	come
cost	cost	cost
creep	crept	crept
cut	cut	cut
deal	dealt	dealt
dig	dug	dug
do	did	done
draw	drew	drawn

INFINITIVE	PAST	PAST PARTICIPLE
dream	dreamed *or* dreamt	dreamed *or* dreamt
drink	drank	drunk *or* drank
drive	drove	driven
dwell	dwelled *or* dwelt	dwelled *or* dwelt
eat	ate	eaten
fall	fell	fallen
feed	fed	fed
feel	felt	felt
fight	fought	fought
find	found	found
flee	fled	fled
fling	flung	flung
fly	flew	flown
forbid	forbade	forbidden
forecast	forecast	forecast
forego	forewent	foregone
foresee	foresaw	foreseen
foretell	foretold	foretold
forget	forgot	forgotten *or* forgot
forgive	forgave	forgiven
forsake	forsook	forsaken
freeze	froze	frozen
get	got	got *or* gotten
give	gave	given
go	went	gone
grind	ground	ground
grow	grew	grown
hang	hung	hung
have	had	had
hear	heard	heard
hide	hid	hidden *or* hid
hit	hit	hit
hold	held	held
hurt	hurt	hurt
keep	kept	kept
kneel	knelt *or* kneeled	knelt *or* kneeled
know	knew	known
lay	laid	laid
lead	led	led
lean	leaned	leaned
leap	leaped *or* leapt	leaped *or* leapt
learn	learned	learned

INFINITIVE	PAST	PAST PARTICIPLE
leave	left	left
lend	lent	lent
let	let	let
lie	lay	lain
light	lit *or* lighted	lit *or* lighted
lose	lost	lost
make	made	made
may	might	—
mean	meant	meant
meet	met	met
mow	mowed	mowed *or* mown
pay	paid	paid
put	put	put
quit	quit	quit
read	read	read
rend	rent	rent
rid	rid	rid
ride	rode	ridden
ring	rang	rung
rise	rose	risen
run	ran	run
saw	sawed	sawed *or* sawn
say	said	said
see	saw	seen
seek	sought	sought
sell	sold	sold
send	sent	sent
set	set	set
shake	shook	shaken
shall	should	—
shear	sheared	sheared *or* shorn
shed	shed	shed
shine	shone *or* shined	shone *or* shined
shoot	shot	shot
show	showed	shown *or* showed
shrink	shrank *or* shrunk	shrunk *or* shrunken
shut	shut	shut
sing	sang *or* sung	sung
sink	sank *or* sunk	sunk
sit	sat	sat
slay	slew	slain
sleep	slept	slept

INFINITIVE	PAST	PAST PARTICIPLE
slide	slid	slid
sling	slung	slung
smell	smelled *or* smelt	smelled *or* smelt
sow	sowed	sown *or* sowed
speak	spoke	spoken
speed	sped *or* speeded	sped *or* speeded
spell	spelled	spelled
spend	spent	spent
spill	spilled	spilled
spin	spun	spun
spit	spit *or* spat	spit *or* spat
split	split	split
spoil	spoiled	spoiled
spread	spread	spread
spring	sprang *or* sprung	sprung
stand	stood	stood
steal	stole	stolen
stick	stuck	stuck
sting	stung	stung
stink	stank *or* stunk	stunk
stride	strode	stridden
strike	struck	struck
swear	swore	sworn
sweep	swept	swept
swell	swelled	swelled *or* swollen
swim	swam	swum
swing	swung	swung
take	took	taken
teach	taught	taught
tear	tore	torn
tell	told	told
think	thought	thought
throw	threw	thrown
thrust	thrust	thrust
tread	trod	trodden *or* trod
wake	woke	woken *or* waked
waylay	waylaid	waylaid
wear	wore	worn
weave	wove *or* weaved	woven *or* weaved
wed	wedded	wedded
weep	wept	wept
will	would	—

INFINITIVE	PAST	PAST PARTICIPLE
win	won	won
wind	wound	wound
withdraw	withdrew	withdrawn
withhold	withheld	withheld
withstand	withstood	withstood
wring	wrung	wrung
write	wrote	written

Abbreviations in this Work

adj	adjective	*nmf*	masculine or feminine noun
adv	adverb		
adv	adverbial phrase	*nmfpl*	plural noun invariable for gender
algn	alguien (someone)		
art	article	*nmfs & pl*	noun invariable for both gender and number
Brit	Great Britain		
conj	conjunction	*nmpl*	masculine plural noun
conj phr	conjunctive phrase	*nms & pl*	invariable singular or plural masculine noun
esp	especially		
etc	et cetera	*npl*	plural noun
f	feminine	*ns & pl*	noun invariable for plural
fam	familiar or colloquial		
fpl	feminine plural	*pl*	plural
interj	interjection	*pp*	past participle
Lat	Latin America	*prep*	preposition
m	masculine	*prep phr*	prepositional phrase
mf	masculine or feminine	*pron*	pronoun
mpl	masculine plural	*s.o.*	someone
n	noun	*sth*	something
nf	feminine noun	*usu*	usually
nfpl	feminine plural noun	*v*	verb
nfs & pl	invariable singular or plural feminine noun	*v aux*	auxiliary verb
		vi	intransitive verb
nm	masculine noun	*v impers*	impersonal verb
		vr	reflexive verb
		vt	transitive verb

Pronunciation Symbols

VOWELS

æ	ask, bat, glad
ɑ	cot, bomb
a	*New England* aunt, *British* ask, glass, *Spanish* casa
ɛ	egg, bet, fed
ə	about, javelin, Alabama
ə	when italicized as in əl, əm, ən, indicates a syllabic pronunciation of the consonant as in bottle, prism, button
i	very, any, thirty, *Spanish* piña
iː	eat, bead, bee
ɪ	id, bid, pit
o	Ohio, yellower, potato, *Spanish* óvalo
oː	oats, own, zone, blow
ɔ	awl, maul, caught, paw
ʊ	sure, should, could
uː	boot, few, coo
ʌ	under, putt, bud
eɪ	eight, wade, bay
aɪ	ice, bite, tie
aʊ	out, gown, plow
ɔɪ	oyster, coil, boy
ː	indicates that the preceding vowel is long. Long vowels are almost always diphthongs in English, but not in Spanish.

STRESS MARKS

ˈ	high stress	penmanship
ˌ	low stress	penmanship

CONSONANTS

b	baby, labor, cab
d	day, ready, kid
dʒ	just, badger, fudge
ð	then, either, bathe
f	foe, tough, buff
g	go, bigger, bag
h	hot, aha
j	yes, vineyard
k	cat, keep, lacquer, flock
l	law, hollow, boil
m	mat, hemp, hammer, rim
n	new, tent, tenor, run
ŋ	rung, hang, swinger
p	pay, lapse, top
r	rope, burn, tar
s	sad, mist, kiss
ʃ	shoe, mission, slush
t	toe, button, mat
t̬	indicates that some speakers of English pronounce this sound as a voiced alveolar flap [ɾ], as in later, catty, battle
tʃ	choose, batch
θ	thin, ether, bath
v	vat, never, cave
w	wet, software
z	zoo, easy, buzz
ʒ	azure, beige
h, k, p, t	when italicized indicate sounds which are present in the pronunciation of some speakers of English but absent in the pronunciation of others, so that *whence* [ˈhwɛnt̬s] can be pronounced as [ˈhwɛns], [ˈhwɛnts], [ˈwɛnts], or [ˈwɛns]

Spanish-English
Dictionary

A

a¹ *nf* : a, first letter of the Spanish alphabet

a² *prep* **1** : to **2 ~ las dos** : at two o'clock **3 al día siguiente** : (on) the following day **4 ~ pied** : on foot **5 de lunes ~ viernes** : from Monday until Friday **6 tres veces ~ la semana** : three times per week **7 ~ la** : in the manner of, like

abadía *nf* : abbey

abajo *adv* **1** : down, below, downstairs **2 ~ de** *Lat* : under, beneath **3 de ~** : (at the) bottom **4 hacia ~** : downwards

abalanzarse {21} *vr* : hurl oneself, rush

abandonar *vt* **1** : abandon, leave **2** RENUNCIAR A : give up — **abandonarse** *vr* **1** : neglect oneself **2 ~ a** : give oneself over to — **abandonado, -da** *adj* **1** : abandoned, deserted **2** DESCUIDADO : neglected **3** DESALIÑADO : slovenly — **abandono** *nm* **1** : abandonment, neglect **2 por ~** : by default

abanico *nm* : fan — **abanicar** {72} *vt* : fan

abaratar *vt* : lower the price of — **abaratarse** *vr* : become cheaper

abarcar {72} *vt* **1** : cover, embrace **2** *Lat* : monopolize

abarrotar *vt* : pack, cram — **abarrotes** *nmpl Lat* **1** : groceries **2 tienda de ~** : grocery store

abastecer {53} *vt* : supply, stock — **abastecimiento** *nm* : supply, provisions — **abasto** *nm* **1** : supply **2 no dar ~** : be unable to cope with

abatir *vt* **1** : knock down, shoot down **2** DEPRIMIR : depress — **abatirse** *vr* **1** : get depressed **2 ~ sobre** : swoop down on — **abatido, -da** *adj* : dejected, depressed — **abatimiento** *nm* : depression, dejection

abdicar {72} *v* : abdicate — **abdicación** *nf, pl* **-ciones** : abdication

abdomen *nm, pl* **-dómenes** : abdomen — **abdominal** *adj* : abdominal

abecé *nm* : ABC — **abecedario** *nm* : alphabet

abedul *nm* : birch

abeja *nf* : bee — **abejorro** *nm* : bumblebee

aberración *nf, pl* **-ciones** : aberration

abertura *nf* : opening

abeto *nm* : fir (tree)

abierto, -ta *adj* : open

abigarrado, -da *adj* : multicolored

abismo *nm* : abyss, chasm — **abismal** *adj* : vast, enormous

abjurar *vi* **~ de** : abjure

ablandar *vt* : soften (up) — **ablandarse** *vr* : soften

abnegarse {49} *vr* : deny oneself — **abnegado, -da** *adj* : self-sacrificing — **abnegación** *nf, pl* **-ciones** : self-denial

abochornar *vt* : embarrass — **abochornarse** *vr* : get embarrassed

abofetear *vt* : slap

abogado, -da *n* : lawyer — **abogacía** *nf* : legal profession — **abogar** {52} *vi* **~ por** : plead for, defend

abolengo *nm* : lineage

abolir {1} *vt* : abolish — **abolición** *nf, pl* **-ciones** : abolition

abollar *vt* : dent — **abolladura** *nf* : dent

abominar *vt* : abominate — **abominable** *adj* : abominable — **abominación** *nf, pl* **-ciones** : abomination

abonar *vt* **1** : pay (a bill, etc.) **2** : fertilize (the soil) — **abonarse** *vr* : subscribe — **abonado, -da** *n* : subscriber — **abono** *nm* **1** : payment, installment **2** FERTILIZANTE : fertilizer **3** : season ticket (to the theater, etc.)

abordar *vt* **1** : tackle (a problem) **2** : accost, approach (a person) **3** *Lat* : board — **abordaje** *nm* : boarding

aborigen *nmf, pl* **-rígenes** : aborigine — *~ adj* : aboriginal, native

aborrecer {53} *vt* : abhor, detest — **aborrecible** *adj* : hateful — **aborrecimiento** *nm* : loathing

abortar *vi* : have a miscarriage — *vt* : abort — **aborto** *nm* : abortion, miscarriage

abotonar *vt* : button — **abotonarse** *vr* : button up

abovedado, -da *adj* : vaulted

abrasar *vt* : burn, scorch — **abrasarse** *vr* : burn up — **abrasador, -dora** *adj* : burning

abrasivo, -va *adj* : abrasive — **abrasivo** *nm* : abrasive

abrazar {21} *vt* : hug, embrace — **abrazarse** *vr* : embrace — **abraza-**

dera *nf* : clamp — **abrazo** *nm* : hug, embrace

abrebotellas *nms & pl* : bottle opener — **abrelatas** *nms & pl* : can opener

abrevadero *nm* : watering trough

abreviar *vt* **1** : shorten, abridge **2** : abbreviate (a word) — **abreviación** *nf, pl* **-ciones** : shortening — **abreviatura** *nf* : abbreviation

abridor *nm* : bottle opener, can opener

abrigar {52} *vt* **1** : wrap up (in clothing) **2** ALBERGAR : cherish, harbor — **abrigarse** *vr* : dress warmly — **abrigado, -da** *adj* **1** : sheltered **2** : warm, wrapped up (of persons) — **abrigo** *nm* **1** : coat, overcoat **2** REFUGIO : shelter, refuge

abril *nm* : April

abrillantar *vt* : polish, shine

abrir {2} *vt* **1** : open **2** : unlock, undo — *vi* : open up — **abrirse** *vr* **1** : open up **2** : clear up (of weather)

abrochar *vt* : button, fasten — **abrocharse** *vr* : fasten, do up

abrogar {52} *vt* : annul, repeal

abrumar *vt* : overwhelm — **abrumador, -dora** *adj* : overwhelming, oppressive

abrupto, -ta *adj* **1** ESCARPADO : steep **2** ÁSPERO : rugged, harsh **3** REPENTINO : abrupt

absceso *nm* : abscess

absolución *nf, pl* **-ciones 1** : absolution **2** : acquittal (in law)

absoluto, -ta *adj* **1** : absolute, unconditional **2 en absoluto** : not at all — **absolutamente** *adv* : absolutely

absolver {89} *vt* **1** : absolve **2** : acquit (in law)

absorber *vt* **1** : absorb **2** : take up (time, energy, etc.) — **absorbente** *adj* **1** : absorbent **2** INTERESANTE : absorbing — **absorción** *nf, pl* **-ciones** : absorption — **absorto, -ta** *adj* : absorbed, engrossed

abstemio, -mia *adj* : abstemious — **~** *n* : teetotaler

abstenerse {80} *vr* : abstain, refrain — **abstención** *nf, pl* **-ciones** : abstention — **abstinencia** *nf* : abstinence

abstracción *nf, pl* **-ciones** : abstraction — **abstracto, -ta** *adj* : abstract — **abstraer** {81} *vt* : abstract — **abstraerse** *vr* : lose oneself in thought — **abstraído, -da** *adj* : preoccupied

absurdo, -da *adj* : absurd, ridiculous — **absurdo** *nm* : absurdity

abuchear *vt* : boo, jeer — **abucheo** *nm* : booing

abuelo, -la *n* **1** : grandfather, grand-

mother **2 abuelos** *nmpl* : grandparents

abulia *nf* : apathy, lethargy

abultar *vi* : bulge, be bulky — *vt* : enlarge, expand — **abultado, -da** *adj* : bulky

abundar *vi* : abound, be plentiful — **abundancia** *nf* : abundance — **abundante** *adj* : abundant

aburrir *vt* : bore — **aburrirse** *vr* : get bored — **aburrido, -da** *adj* **1** : bored **2** TEDIOSO : boring — **aburrimiento** *nm* : boredom

abusar *vi* **1** : go too far **2 ~ de** : abuse — **abusivo, -va** *adj* : outrageous, excessive — **abuso** *nm* : abuse

abyecto, -ta *adj* : abject, wretched

acá *adv* : here, over here

acabar *vi* **1** : finish, end **2 ~ de** : have just (done something) **3 ~ con** : put an end to **4 ~ por** : end up (doing sth) — *vt* : finish — **acabarse** *vr* : come to an end — **acabado, -da** *adj* **1** : finished, perfect **2** AGOTADO : old, worn-out — **acabado** *nm* : finish

academia *nf* : academy — **académico, -ca** *adj* : academic

acaecer {53} *vi* : happen, occur

acallar *vt* : quiet, silence

acalorar *vt* : stir up, excite — **acalorarse** *vr* : get worked up — **acalorado, -da** *adj* : emotional, heated

acampar *vi* : camp — **acampada** *nf* **ir de ~** : go camping

acanalado, -da *adj* **1** : grooved **2** : corrugated (of iron, etc.)

acantilado *nm* : cliff

acaparar *vt* **1** : hoard **2** MONOPOLIZAR : monopolize

acápite *nm Lat* : paragraph

acariciar *vt* **1** : caress **2** : cherish (hopes, ideas, etc.)

ácaro *nm* : mite

acarrear *vt* **1** : haul, carry **2** OCASIONAR : give rise to — **acarreo** *nm* : transport

acaso *adv* **1** : perhaps, maybe **2 por si ~** : just in case

acatar *vt* : comply with, respect — **acatamiento** *nm* : compliance, respect

acatarrarse *vr* : catch a cold

acaudalado, -da *adj* : wealthy, rich

acaudillar *vt* : lead

acceder *vi* **1** : agree **2 ~ a** : gain access to, enter

acceso *nm* **1** : access **2** ENTRADA : entrance **3** : attack, bout (of an illness) — **accesible** *adj* : accessible

accesorio *nm* : accessory — **accesorio, -ria** *adj* : incidental

accidentado, -da *adj* **1** : eventful, turbulent **2** : rough, uneven (of land, etc.) **3** HERIDO : injured — ~ *n* : accident victim

accidental *adj* : accidental — **accidentarse** *vr* : have an accident — **accidente** *nm* **1** : accident **2** : unevenness (of land)

acción *nf, pl* **-ciones 1** : action **2** ACTO : act, deed **3** : share, stock (in finance) — **accionar** *vt* : activate — *vi* : gesticulate — **accionista** *nmf* : stockholder

acebo *nm* : holly

acechar *vt* : watch, stalk — **acecho** *nm* **estar al** ~ **por** : be on the lookout for

aceite *nm* : oil — **aceitar** *vt* : oil — **aceitera** *nf* **1** : oilcan **2** : cruet (in cookery) **3** *Lat* : oil refinery — **aceitoso, -sa** *adj* : oily

aceituna *nf* : olive

acelerar *v* : accelerate — **acelerarse** *vr* : hurry up — **aceleración** *nf, pl* **-ciones** : acceleration — **acelerador** *nm* : accelerator

acelga *nf* : (Swiss) chard

acentuar {3} *vt* **1** : accent **2** ENFATIZAR : emphasize, stress — **acentuarse** *vr* : stand out — **acento** *nm* **1** : accent **2** ÉNFASIS : stress, emphasis

acepción *nf, pl* **-ciones** : sense, meaning

aceptar *vt* : accept — **aceptable** *adj* : acceptable — **aceptación** *nf, pl* **-ciones 1** : acceptance **2** ÉXITO : success

acequia *nf* : irrigation ditch

acera *nf* : sidewalk

acerbo, -ba *adj* : harsh, caustic

acerca *prep* ~ **de** : about, concerning

acercar {72} *vt* : bring near or closer — **acercarse** *vr* : approach, draw near

acero *nm* **1** : steel **2** ~ **inoxidable** : stainless steel

acérrimo, -ma *adj* **1** : staunch, steadfast **2** : bitter (of an enemy)

acertar {55} *vt* : guess correctly — *vi* **1** ATINAR : be accurate **2** ~ **a** : manage to — **acertado, -da** *adj* : correct, accurate

acertijo *nm* : riddle

acervo *nm* : heritage

acetona *nf* : acetone, nail-polish remover

achacar {72} *vt* : attribute, impute

achacoso, -sa *adj* : sickly

achaparrado, -da *adj* : squat, stocky

achaque *nm* : aches and pains

achatar *vt* : flatten

achicar {72} *vt* **1** : make smaller **2** ACOBARDAR : intimidate **3** : bail out

(water) — **achicarse** *vr* : become intimidated

achicharrar *vt* : scorch, burn to a crisp

achicoria *nf* : chicory

aciago, -ga *adj* : fateful, unlucky

acicalar *vt* : dress up, adorn — **acicalarse** *vr* : get dressed up

acicate *nm* **1** : spur **2** INCENTIVO : incentive

ácido, -da *adj* : acid, sour — **acidez** *nf, pl* **-deces** : acidity — **ácido** *nm* : acid

acierto *nm* **1** : correct answer **2** HABILIDAD : skill, sound judgment

aclamar *vt* : acclaim — **aclamación** *nf, pl* **-ciones** : acclaim, applause

aclarar *vt* **1** CLARIFICAR : clarify, explain **2** : rinse (clothing) **3** ~ **la voz** : clear one's throat — *vi* : clear up — **aclararse** *vr* : become clear — **aclaración** *nf, pl* **-ciones** : explanation — **aclaratorio, -ria** *adj* : explanatory

aclimatar *vt* : acclimatize — **aclimatarse** *vr* ~ **a** : get used to — **aclimatación** *nf, pl* **-ciones** : acclimatization

acné *nm* : acne

acobardar *vt* : intimidate — **acobardarse** *vr* : become frightened

acodarse *vr* ~ **en** : lean (one's elbows) on

acoger {15} *vt* **1** REFUGIAR : shelter **2** RECIBIR : receive, welcome — **acogerse** *vr* **1** : take refuge **2** ~ **a** : resort to — **acogedor, -dora** *adj* : cozy, welcoming — **acogida** *nf* **1** : welcome **2** REFUGIO : refuge

acolchar *vt* : pad

acólito *nm* MONAGUILLO : altar boy

acometer *vt* **1** : attack **2** EMPRENDER : undertake — *vi* ~ **contra** : rush against — **acometida** *nf* : attack, assault

acomodar *vt* **1** ADAPTAR : adjust **2** COLOCAR : put, make a place for — **acomodarse** *vr* **1** : settle in **2** ~ **a** : adapt to — **acomodado, -da** *adj* : well-to-do — **acomodaticio, -cia** *adj* : accommodating, obliging — **acomodo** *nm* : job, position

acompañar *vt* **1** : accompany **2** ADJUNTAR : enclose — **acompañamiento** *nm* : accompaniment — **acompañante** *nmf* **1** COMPAÑERO : companion **2** : accompanist (in music)

acompasado, -da *adj* : rhythmic, measured

acondicionar *vt* : fit out, equip — **acondicionado, -da** *adj* : equipped

acongojar *vt* : distress, upset — **acongojarse** *vr* : get upset

aconsejar *vt* : advise — **aconsejable** *adj* : advisable

acontecer {53} *vi* : occur, happen — **acontecimiento** *nm* : event

acoplar *vt* : gather, collect — **acopio** *nm* : collection, stock

acoplar *vt* : couple, connect — **acoplarse** *vr* : fit together — **acoplamiento** *nm* : connection, coupling

acorazado, -da *adj* : armored — **acorazado** *nm* : battleship

acordar {19} *vt* 1 : agree (on) 2 *Lat* : award — **acordarse** *vr* : remember

acorde *adj* 1 : in agreement 2 ~ **con** : in keeping with — ~ *nm* : chord (in music)

acordeón *nm, pl* **-deones** : accordion

acordonar *vt* 1 : cordon off 2 : lace up (shoes)

acorralar *vt* : corner, corral

acortar *vt* : shorten, cut short — **acortarse** *vr* : get shorter

acosar *vt* : hound, harass — **acoso** *nm* : harassment

acostar {19} *vt* : put to bed — **acostarse** *vr* 1 : go to bed 2 TUMBARSE : lie down

acostumbrar *vt* : accustom — *vi* ~ **a** : be in the habit of — **acostumbrarse** *vr* ~ **a** : get used to — **acostumbrado, -da** *adj* 1 HABITUADO : accustomed 2 HABITUAL : usual

acotar *vt* 1 ANOTAR : annotate 2 DELIMITAR : mark off (land) — **acotación** *nf, pl* **-ciones** : marginal note — **acotado, -da** *adj* : enclosed

acre *adj* 1 : pungent 2 MORDAZ : harsh, biting

acrecentar {55} *vt* : increase — **acrecentamiento** *nm* : growth, increase

acreditar *vt* 1 : accredit, authorize 2 PROBAR : prove — **acreditarse** *vr* : prove oneself — **acreditado, -da** *adj* 1 : reputable 2 : accredited (in politics, etc.)

acreedor, -dora *adj* : worthy — ~ *n* : creditor

acribillar *vt* 1 : riddle, pepper 2 ~ **a** : harass with

acrílico *nm* : acrylic

acrimonia *nf or* **acritud** *nf* 1 : pungency 2 RESENTIMIENTO : bitterness, acrimony

acrobacia *nf* : acrobatics — **acróbata** *nmf* : acrobat — **acrobático, -ca** *adj* : acrobatic

acta *nf* 1 : certificate 2 : minutes *pl* (of a meeting)

actitud *nf* 1 : attitude 2 POSTURA : posture, position

activar *vt* 1 : activate 2 ESTIMULAR : stimulate, speed up — **actividad** *nf* : activity — **activo, -va** *adj* : active — **activo** *nm* : assets *pl*

acto *nm* 1 ACCIÓN : act, deed 2 : act (in theater) 3 **en el** ~ : right away

actor *nm* : actor — **actriz** *nf, pl* **-trices** : actress

actual *adj* : present, current — **actualidad** *nf* 1 : present time 2 ~**es** *nfpl* : current affairs — **actualizar** {21} *vt* : modernize — **actualización** *nf, pl* **-ciones** : modernization — **actualmente** *adv* : at present, nowadays

actuar {3} *vi* 1 : act, perform 2 ~ **de** : act as

acuarela *nf* : watercolor

acuario *nm* : aquarium

acuartelar *vt* : quarter (troops)

acuático, -ca *adj* : aquatic, water

acuchillar *vt* : knife, stab

acudir *vi* 1 : go, come 2 ~ **a** : be present at, attend 3 ~ **a** : turn to

acueducto *nm* : aqueduct

acuerdo *nm* 1 : agreement 2 **de** ~ : OK, all right 3 **de** ~ **con** : in accordance with 4 **estar de** ~ : agree

acumular *vt* : accumulate — **acumularse** *vr* : pile up — **acumulación** *nf, pl* **-ciones** : accumulation — **acumulador** *nm* : storage battery — **acumulativo, -va** *adj* : cumulative

acunar *vt* : rock

acuñar *vt* 1 : mint (money) 2 : coin (a word)

acuoso, -sa *adj* : watery

acupuntura *nf* : acupuncture

acurrucarse {72} *vr* : curl up, nestle

acusar *vt* 1 : accuse 2 MOSTRAR : reveal, show — **acusación** *nf, pl* **-ciones** : accusation, charge — **acusado, -da** *adj* : prominent, marked — ~ *n* : defendant

acuse *nm* ~ **de recibo** : acknowledgment of receipt

acústica *nf* : acoustics — **acústico, -ca** *adj* : acoustic

adagio *nm* 1 REFRÁN : adage, proverb 2 : adagio (in music)

adaptar *vt* 1 : adapt 2 AJUSTAR : adjust, fit — **adaptarse** *vr* ~ **a** : adapt to — **adaptable** *adj* : adaptable — **adaptación** *nf, pl* **-ciones** : adaptation — **adaptador** *nm* : adapter (in electricity)

adecuar {8} *vt* : adapt, make suitable — **adecuarse** *vr* ~ **a** : be appropriate for — **adecuado, -da** *adj* : suitable, appropriate

adelantar *vt* 1 : advance, move forward 2 PASAR : overtake 3 : pay in advance — **adelantarse** *vr* 1 : move forward, get ahead 2 : be fast (of a clock) — **adelantado, -da** *adj* 1 : advanced, ahead 2 : fast (of a clock) 3 **por ~** : in advance — **adelante** *adv* 1 : ahead, forward 2 **¡~!** : come in! 3 **más ~** : later on, further on — **adelanto** *nm* 1 : advance 2 *or* **~ de dinero** : advance payment

adelgazar {21} *vt* : make thin — *vi* : lose weight

ademán *nm, pl* **-manes** 1 GESTO : gesture 2 **~es** *nmpl* : manners 3 **en ~ de** : as if to

además *adv* 1 : besides, furthermore 2 **~ de** : in addition to, as well as

adentro *adv* : inside, within — **adentrarse** *vr* **~ en** : go into, get inside of

adepto, -ta *n* : follower, supporter

aderezar {21} *vt* : season, dress — **aderezo** *nm* : dressing, seasoning

adeudar *vt* 1 : debit 2 DEBER : owe — **adeudo** *nm* 1 DÉBITO : debit 2 *Lat* : debt

adherirse {76} *vr* : adhere, stick — **adherencia** *nf* : adherence — **adhesión** *nf, pl* **-siones** 1 : adhesion 2 APOYO : support — **adhesivo, -va** *adj* : adhesive — **adhesivo** *nm* : adhesive

adición *nf, pl* **-ciones** : addition — **adicional** *adj* : additional

adicto, -ta *adj* : addicted — **~** *n* : addict

adiestrar *vt* : train

adinerado, -da *adj* : wealthy

adiós *nm, pl* **adioses** 1 : farewell 2 **¡~!** : good-bye!

aditamento *nm* : attachment, accessory

aditivo *nm* : additive

adivinar *vt* 1 : guess 2 PREDECIR : foretell — **adivinación** *nf, pl* **-ciones** : guessing, prediction — **adivinanza** *nf* : riddle — **adivino, -na** *n* : fortune-teller

adjetivo *nm* : adjective

adjudicar {72} *vt* : award — **adjudicarse** *vr* : appropriate — **adjudicación** *nf, pl* **-ciones** : awarding

adjuntar *vt* : enclose (with a letter, etc.) — **adjunto, -ta** *adj* : enclosed, attached — **~** *n* : assistant

administración *nf, pl* **-ciones** 1 : administration 2 : administering (of a drug, etc.) 3 DIRECCIÓN : management — **administrador, -dora** *n* : administrator, manager — **administrar** *vt* 1 : manage, run 2 : administer (a drug, etc.) — **administrativo, -va** *adj* : administrative

admirar *vt* : admire — **admirarse** *vr* : be amazed — **admirable** *adj* : admirable — **admiración** *nf, pl* **-ciones** 1 : admiration 2 ASOMBRO : amazement — **admirador, -dora** *n* : admirer

admitir *vt* 1 : admit 2 ACEPTAR : accept — **admisible** *adj* : admissible, acceptable — **admisión** *nf, pl* **-siones** 1 : admission 2 ACEPTACIÓN : acceptance

ADN *nm* : DNA

adobe *nm* : adobe

adobo *nm* : marinade

adoctrinar *vt* : indoctrinate — **adoctrinamiento** *nm* : indoctrination

adolecer {53} *vi* **~ de** : suffer from

adolescente *adj & nmf* : adolescent — **adolescencia** *nf* : adolescence

adonde *conj* : where

adónde *adv* : where

adoptar *vt* : adopt (a child), take (a decision) — **adopción** *nf, pl* **-ciones** : adoption — **adoptivo, -va** *adj* : adopted, adoptive

adoquín *nm, pl* **-quines** : cobblestone

adorar *vt* : adore, worship — **adorable** *adj* : adorable — **adoración** *nf, pl* **-ciones** : adoration, worship

adormecer {53} *vt* 1 : make sleepy 2 ENTUMECER : numb — **adormecerse** *vr* : doze off — **adormecimiento** *nm* : drowsiness — **adormilarse** *vr* : doze

adornar *vt* : decorate, adorn — **adorno** *nm* : ornament, decoration

adquirir {4} *vt* 1 : acquire 2 COMPRAR : purchase — **adquisición** *nf, pl* **-ciones** 1 : acquisition 2 COMPRA : purchase

adrede *adv* : intentionally, on purpose

adscribir {33} *vt* : assign, appoint

aduana *nf* : customs (office) — **aduanero, -ra** *adj* : customs — **~** *n* : customs officer

aducir {61} *vt* : cite, put forward

adueñarse *vr* **~ de** : take possession of

adular *vt* : flatter — **adulación** *nf, pl* **-ciones** : adulation, flattery — **adulador, -dora** *adj* : flattering — **~** *n* : flatterer

adulterar *vt* : adulterate

adulterio *nm* : adultery — **adúltero, -ra** *n* : adulterer

adulto, -ta *adj & n* : adult

adusto, -ta *adj* : stern, severe

advenedizo, -za *n* : upstart

advenimiento *nm* : advent, arrival

adverbio *nm* : adverb — **adverbial** *adj* : adverbial

adversario, -ria *n* : adversary, opponent — **adverso, -sa** *adj* : adverse — **adversidad** *nf* : adversity

advertir {76} *vt* **1** AVISAR : warn **2** NOTAR : notice — **advertencia** *nf* : warning

adviento *nm* : Advent

adyacente *adj* : adjacent

aéreo, -rea *adj* : aerial, air

aerobic *nm* : aerobics *pl*

aerodinámico, -ca *adj* : aerodynamic

aeródromo *nm* : airfield

aerolínea *nf* : airline

aeromozo, -za *n* : flight attendant, steward *m*, stewardess *f*

aeronave *nf* : aircraft

aeropuerto *nm* : airport

aerosol *nm* : aerosol, spray

afable *adj* : affable — **afabilidad** *nf* : affability

afán *nm*, *pl* **afanes 1** ANHELO : eagerness **2** EMPEÑO : effort, hard work — **afanarse** *vr* : toil — **afanosamente** *adv* : industriously, busily — **afanoso, -sa** *adj* **1** : eager **2** TRABAJOSO : arduous

afear *vt* : make ugly, disfigure

afección *nf*, *pl* **-ciones** : ailment, complaint

afectar *vt* : affect — **afectación** *nf*, *pl* **-ciones** : affectation — **afectado, -da** *adj* : affected

afectivo, -va *adj* : emotional

afecto *nm* : affection — **afecto, -ta** *adj* **~ a** : fond of — **afectuoso, -sa** *adj* : affectionate, caring

afeitar *vt* : shave — **afeitarse** *vr* : shave — **afeitada** *nf* : shave

afeminado, -da *adj* : effeminate

aferrarse {55} *vr* : cling, hold on

afianzar {21} *vt* : secure, strengthen — **afianzarse** *vr* : become established

afiche *nm* *Lat* : poster

afición *nf*, *pl* **-ciones 1** : penchant, fondness **2** PASATIEMPO : hobby — **aficionado, -da** *n* **1** ENTUSIASTA : enthusiast, fan **2** AMATEUR : amateur — **aficionarse** *vr* **~ a** : become interested in

afilar *vt* : sharpen — **afilado, -da** *adj* : sharp — **afilador** *nm* : sharpener

afiliarse *vr* **~ a** : join, become a member of — **afiliación** *nf*, *pl* **-ciones** : affiliation — **afiliado, -da** *adj* : affiliated

afín *adj*, *pl* **afines** : related, similar — **afinidad** *nf* : affinity, similarity

afinar *vt* **1** : tune **2** PULIR : perfect, refine

afirmar *vt* **1** : state, affirm **2** REFORZAR : strengthen — **afirmación** *nf*, *pl* **-ciones** : statement, affirmation — **afirmativo, -va** *adj* : affirmative

afligir {35} *vt* **1** : afflict **2** APENAR : distress — **afligirse** *vr* : grieve — **aflicción** *nf*, *pl* **-ciones** : grief, sorrow — **afligido, -da** *adj* : sorrowful, distressed

aflojar *vt* : loosen, slacken — *vi* : ease up — **aflojarse** *vr* : become loose, slacken

aflorar *vi* : come to the surface, emerge — **afloramiento** *nm* : outcrop

afluencia *nf* : influx — **afluente** *nm* : tributary

afortunado, -da *adj* : fortunate, lucky — **afortunadamente** *adv* : fortunately

afrentar *vt* : insult — **afrenta** *nf* : affront, insult

africano, -na *adj* : African

afrontar *vt* : confront, face

afuera *adv* **1** : out **2** : outside, outdoors — **afueras** *nfpl* : outskirts

agachar *vt* : lower — **agacharse** *vr* : crouch, stoop

agalla *nf* **1** BRANQUIA : gill **2 tener ~s** *fam* : have guts

agarrar *vt* **1** ASIR : grasp **2** *Lat* : catch — **agarrarse** *vr* : hold on, cling — **agarradera** *nf* *Lat* : handle — **agarrado, -da** *adj* *fam* : stingy — **agarre** *nm* : grip, grasp — **agarrón** *nm*, *pl* **-rones** : tug, pull

agasajar *vt* : fête, wine and dine — **agasajo** *nm* : lavish attention

agave *nm* : agave

agazaparse *vr* : crouch down

agencia *nf* : agency, office — **agente** *nmf* : agent, officer

agenda *nf* **1** : agenda **2** LIBRETA : notebook

ágil *adj* : agile — **agilidad** *nf* : agility

agitar *vt* **1** : agitate, shake **2** : wave, flap (wings, etc.) **3** PERTURBAR : stir up — **agitarse** *vr* **1** : toss about **2** INQUIETARSE : get upset — **agitación** *nf*, *pl* **-ciones** : agitation, shaking **3** TRANQUILIDAD : restlessness — **agitado, -da** *adj* **1** : agitated, excited **2** : choppy, rough (of the sea)

aglomerar *vt* : amass — **aglomerarse** *vr* : crowd together

agnóstico, -ca *adj* & *n* : agnostic

agobiar *vt* **1** : oppress **2** ABRUMAR : overwhelm — **agobiado, -da** *adj* : weary, weighed down — **agobiante** *adj* : oppressing, oppressive

agonizar {21} *vi* : be dying — **agonía** *nf* **1** : death throes **2** PENA : agony — **agonizante** *adj* : dying

agorero, -ra *adj* : ominous

agostar *vt* : wither

agosto *nm* : August

agotar *vt* **1** : deplete, use up **2** CANSAR : exhaust, weary — **agotarse** *vr* **1**

: run out, give out 2 CANSARSE : get tired — **agotado, -da** *adj* 1 CANSADO : exhausted 2 : sold out — **agotador, -dora** *adj* : exhausting — **agotamiento** *nm* : exhaustion

agraciado, -da *adj* 1 : attractive 2 AFORTUNADO : fortunate

agradar *vi* : be pleasing — **agradable** *adj* : pleasant, agreeable — **agrado** *nm* 1 : taste, liking 2 **con** ~ : with pleasure

agradecer {53} *vt* : be grateful for, thank — **agradecido, -da** *adj* : grateful — **agradecimiento** *nm* : gratitude

agrandar *vt* : enlarge — **agrandarse** *vr* : grow larger

agrario, -ria *adj* : agrarian, agricultural

agravar *vt* : make heavier 2 EMPEORAR : aggravate, worsen — **agravarse** *vr* : get worse

agraviar *vt* : insult — **agravio** *nm* : insult

agredir {1} *vt* : attack

agregar {52} *vt* : add, attach — **agregado, -da** *n* : attaché — **agregado** *nm* : aggregate

agresión *nf*, *pl* **-siones** : aggression, attack — **agresividad** *nf* : aggressiveness — **agresivo, -va** *adj* : aggressive — **agresor, -sora** *n* : aggressor, attacker

agreste *adj* : rugged, wild

agriar *vt* : sour — **agriarse** *vr* 1 : turn sour (of milk, etc.) 2 : become embittered

agrícola *adj* : agricultural — **agricultura** *nf* : agriculture, farming — **agricultor, -tora** *n* : farmer

agridulce *adj* 1 : bittersweet 2 : sweet-and-sour (in cooking)

agrietar *vt* : crack — **agrietarse** *vr* 1 : crack 2 : chap

agrimensor, -sora *n* : surveyor

agrio, agria *adj* : sour

agrupar *vt* : group together — **agruparse** *vr* : form a group — **agrupación** *nf*, *pl* **-ciones** : group, association — **agrupamiento** *nm* : grouping

agua *nf* 1 : water 2 ~ **oxigenada** : hydrogen peroxide 3 ~**s negras** *or* ~**s residuales** : sewage

aguacate *nm* : avocado

aguacero *nm* : downpour

aguado, -da *adj* 1 : watery 2 *Lat fam* : soft, flabby — **aguar** {10} *vt* 1 : water down, dilute 2 ~ **la fiesta** *fam* : spoil the party

aguafuerte *nm* : etching

aguanieve *nf* : sleet

aguantar *vt* 1 SOPORTAR : bear, withstand 2 SOSTENER : hold — *vi* : hold out, last — **aguantarse** *vr* 1 : resign oneself 2 CONTENERSE : restrain oneself — **aguante** *nm* 1 : patience 2 RESISTENCIA : endurance

aguardar *vt* : await

aguardiente *nm* : clear brandy

aguarrás *nm* : turpentine

agudo, -da *adj* 1 : acute, sharp 2 : shrill, high-pitched (in music) — **agudeza** *nf* 1 : sharpness 2 : witticism

agüero *nm* : augury, omen

aguijón *nm*, *pl* **-jones** 1 : stinger (of an insect) 2 ESTÍMULO : goad, stimulus — **aguijonear** *vt* : goad

águila *nf* : eagle

aguja *nf* 1 : needle 2 : hand (of a clock) 3 : spire (of a church)

agujero *nm* : hole

agujeta *nf* 1 *Lat* : shoelace 2 ~**s** *nfpl* : (muscular) stiffness

aguzar {21} *vt* : sharpen 2 ~ **el oído** : prick up one's ears

ahí *adv* 1 : there 2 **por** ~ : somewhere, thereabouts

ahijado, -da *n* : godchild, godson *m*, goddaughter *f*

ahínco *nm* : eagerness, zeal

ahogar {52} *vt* 1 : drown 2 ASFIXIAR : smother — **ahogarse** *vr* : drown — **ahogo** *nm* : breathlessness

ahondar *vt* : deepen — *vi* : elaborate, go into detail

ahora *adv* 1 : now 2 ~ **mismo** : right now

ahorcar {72} *vt* : hang, kill by hanging — **ahorcarse** *vr* : hang oneself

ahorita *adv* *Lat fam* : right now

ahorrar *vt* : save, spare — *vi* : save up — **ahorrarse** *vr* : spare oneself — **ahorro** *nm* : saving

ahuecar {72} *vt* 1 : hollow out 2 : cup (one's hands)

ahumar {8} *vt* : smoke, cure — **ahumado, -da** *adj* : smoked

ahuyentar *vt* : scare away, chase away

airado, -da *adj* : irate, angry

aire *nm* 1 : air 2 ~ **acondicionado** : air-conditioning 3 **al** ~ **libre** : in the open air, outdoors — **airear** *vt* : air, air out

aislar {5} *vt* 1 : isolate 2 : insulate (in electricity) — **aislamiento** *nm* 1 : isolation 2 : (electrical) insulation

ajar *vt* 1 : crumple, wrinkle 2 ESTROPEAR : spoil

ajedrez *nm* : chess

ajeno, -na *adj* 1 : someone else's 2 EXTRAÑO : alien 3 ~ **a** : foreign to

ajetreado, -da *adj* : hectic, busy —

ajetrearse *vr* : bustle about — **ajetreo** *nm* : hustle and bustle
ají *nm, pl* **ajíes** *Lat* : chili pepper
ajo *nm* : garlic
ajustar *vt* **1** : adjust, adapt **2** ACORDAR : agree on **3** SALDAR : settle — **ajustarse** *vr* : fit, conform — **ajustable** *adj* : adjustable — **ajustado, -da** *adj* **1** : close, tight **2** CEÑIDO : tight-fitting — **ajuste** *nm* : adjustment
ajusticiar *vt* : execute, put to death
al (*contraction of a and* **el**) → **a²**
ala *nf* **1** : wing **2** : brim (of a hat)
alabanza *nf* : praise — **alabar** *vt* : praise
alacena *nf* : cupboard, larder
alacrán *nm, pl* **-cranes** : scorpion
alado, -da *adj* : winged
alambre *nm* : wire
alameda *nf* **1** : poplar grove **2** : tree-lined avenue — **álamo** *nm* : poplar
alarde *nm* : show, display — **alardear** *vi* : boast
alargar {52} *vt* **1** : extend, lengthen **2** PROLONGAR : prolong — **alargarse** *vr* : become longer — **alargador** *nm* : extension cord
alarido *nm* : howl, shriek
alarmar *vt* : alarm — **alarma** *nf* : alarm — **alarmante** *adj* : alarming
alba *nf* : dawn
albahaca *nf* : basil
albañil *nm* : bricklayer, mason
albaricoque *nm* : apricot
albedrío *nm* **libre ~** : free will
alberca *nf* **1** : reservoir, tank **2** *Lat* : swimming pool
albergar {52} *vt* : house, lodge — **albergue** *nm* **1** : lodging REFUGIO : shelter **3 ~ juvenil** : youth hostel
albóndiga *nf* : meatball
alborear *v impers* : dawn — **albor** *nm* : dawning — **alborada** *nf* : dawn
alborotar *vt* : excite, stir up — *vi* : make a racket — **alborotarse** *vr* : get excited — **alborotado, -da** *adj* : excited, agitated — **alborotador, -dora** *n* : agitator, rioter — **alboroto** *nm* : ruckus
alborozar {21} *vt* : gladden — **alborozo** *nm* : joy
álbum *nm* : album
alcachofa *nf* : artichoke
alcalde, -desa *n* : mayor
alcance *nm* **1** : reach **2** ÁMBITO : range, scope
alcancía *nf* : money box
alcantarilla *nf* : sewer, drain
alcanzar {21} *vt* **1** : reach **2** LLEGAR A : catch up with **3** LOGRAR : achieve, at-

tain — *vi* **1** : suffice, be enough **2 ~ a** : manage to
alcaparra *nf* : caper
alcázar *nm* : fortress, castle
alce *nm* : moose, European elk
alcoba *nf* : bedroom
alcohol *nm* : alcohol — **alcohólico, -ca** *adj & n* : alcoholic — **alcoholismo** *nm* : alcoholism
aldaba *nf* : door knocker
aldea *nf* : village — **aldeano, -na** *n* : villager
aleación *nf, pl* **-ciones** : alloy
aleatorio, -ria *adj* : random
aleccionar *vt* : instruct, teach
aledaño, -ña *adj* : bordering — **aledaños** *nmpl* : outskirts
alegar {52} *vt* : assert, allege — *vi Lat* : argue — **alegato** *nm* **1** : allegation (in law) **2** *Lat* : argument
alegoría *nf* : allegory — **alegórico, -ca** *adj* : allegorical
alegrar *vt* : make happy, cheer up — **alegrarse** *vr* : be glad — **alegre** *adj* **1** CONTENTO : glad, happy **2** : colorful, bright — **alegremente** *adv* : happily — **alegría** *nf* : joy, cheer
alejar *vt* **1** : remove, move away **2** ENAJENAR : estrange — **alejarse** *vr* : move away, drift apart — **alejado, -da** *adj* : remote — **alejamiento** *nm* **1** : removal **2** : estrangement (of persons)
alemán, -mana *adj, mpl* **-manes** : German — **alemán** *nm* : German (language)
alentar {55} *vt* : encourage — **alentador, -dora** *adj* : encouraging
alergia *nf* : allergy — **alérgico, -ca** *adj* : allergic
alero *nm* : eaves *pl*
alertar *vt* : alert — **alerta** *adv* : on the alert — **alerta** *adj & nf* : alert
aleta *nf* **1** : fin, flipper **2** : small wing
alevosía *nf* : treachery — **alevoso, -sa** *adj* : treacherous
alfabeto *nm* : alphabet — **alfabético, -ca** *adj* : alphabetical — **alfabetismo** *nm* : literacy — **alfabetizar** {21} *vt* **1** : teach literacy **2** : alphabetize
alfalfa *nf* : alfalfa
alfarería *nf* : pottery
alféizar *nm* : sill, windowsill
alfil *nm* : bishop (in chess)
alfiler *nm* **1** : pin **2** BROCHE : brooch — **alfiletero** *nm* : pincushion
alfombra *nf* : carpet, rug — **alfombrilla** *nf* : small rug, mat
alga *nf* : seaweed
álgebra *nf* : algebra

algo *pron* **1** : something **2** ~ **de** : some, a little — ~ *adv* : somewhat, rather
algodón *nm, pl* **-dones** : cotton
alguacil *nm* : constable, bailiff
alguien *pron* : somebody, someone
alguno, -na *adj* (**algún** *before masculine singular nouns*) **1** : some, any **2** (*in negative constructions*) : not any, not at all **3 algunas veces** : sometimes — ~ *pron* **1** : one, someone, somebody **2 algunos, -nas** *pron pl* : some, a few
alhaja *nf* : jewel
alharaca *nf* : fuss
aliado, -da *n* : ally — ~ *adj* : allied — **alianza** *nf* : alliance — **aliarse** {85} *vr* : form an alliance
alias *adv & nm* : alias
alicaído, -da *adj* : depressed
alicates *nmpl* : pliers
aliciente *nm* **1** : incentive **2** : attraction (to a place)
alienar *vt* : alienate — **alienación** *nf, pl* **-ciones** : alienation
aliento *nm* **1** : breath **2** ÁNIMO : encouragement, strength
aligerar *vt* **1** : lighten **2** APRESURAR : hasten, quicken
alimaña *nf* : pest, vermin
alimentar *vt* : feed, nourish — **alimentarse** *vr* ~ **con** : live on — **alimentación** *nf, pl* **-ciones 1** : feeding **2** NUTRICIÓN : nourishment — **alimenticio, -cia** *adj* : nourishing — **alimento** *nm* : food, nourishment
alinear *vt* : align, line up — **alinearse** *vr* ~ **con** : align oneself with — **alineación** *nf, pl* **-ciones 1** : alignment **2** : lineup (in sports)
aliño *nm* : dressing, seasoning — **aliñar** *vt* : season, dress
alisar *vt* : smooth
alistarse *vr* : join up, enlist — **alistamiento** *nm* : enlistment
aliviar *vt* : relieve, soothe — **aliviarse** *vr* : recover, get better — **alivio** *nm* : relief
aljibe *nm* : cistern, tank
allá *adv* **1** : there, over there **2 más** ~ : farther away **3 más** ~ **de** : beyond
allanar *vt* **1** : smooth, level out **2** *Spain* : break into (a house) **3** *Lat* : raid — **allanamiento** *nm* **1** *Spain* : breaking and entering **2** *Lat* : raid
allegado, -da *n* : close friend, relation
allí *adv* : there, over there
alma *nf* : soul
almacén *nm, pl* **-cenes 1** : warehouse **2** *Lat* : shop, store **3 grandes almacenes** : department store — **alma-**

cenamiento *or* **almacenaje** *nm* : storage — **almacenar** *vt* : store
almádena *nf* : sledgehammer
almanaque *nm* : almanac
almeja *nf* : clam
almendra *nf* **1** : almond **2** : kernel (of nuts, fruit, etc.)
almiar *nm* : haystack
almíbar *nm* : syrup
almidón *nm, pl* **-dones** : starch — **almidonar** *vt* : starch
almirante *nm* : admiral
almohada *nf* : pillow — **almohadilla** *nf* : small pillow, pad — **almohadón** *nm, pl* **-dones** : bolster, large cushion
almorranas *nfpl* : hemorrhoids, piles
almorzar {36} *vi* : have lunch — *vt* : have for lunch — **almuerzo** *nm* : lunch
alocado, -da *adj* : crazy, wild
áloe *or* **aloe** *nm* : aloe
alojar *vt* : house, lodge — **alojarse** *vr* : lodge, room — **alojamiento** *nm* : lodging, accommodations *pl*
alondra *nf* : lark
alpaca *nf* : alpaca
alpinismo *nm* : mountain climbing — **alpinista** *nmf* : mountain climber
alpiste *nm* : birdseed
alquilar *vt* : rent, lease — **alquilarse** *vr* : be for rent — **alquiler** *nm* : rent, rental
alquitrán *nm, pl* **-tranes** : tar
alrededor *adv* **1** : around, about **2** ~ **de** : approximately — **alrededor de** *prep phr* : around — **alrededores** *nmpl* : outskirts
alta *nf* : discharge (of a patient)
altanería *nf* : haughtiness — **altanero, -ra** *adj* : haughty
altar *nm* : altar
altavoz *nm, pl* **-voces** : loudspeaker
alterar *vt* **1** : alter, modify **2** PERTURBAR : disturb — **alterarse** *vr* : get upset — **alteración** *nf, pl* **-ciones 1** : alteration **2** ALBOROTO : disturbance — **alterado, -da** *adj* : upset
altercado *nm* : altercation, argument
alternar *vi* **1** : alternate **2** ~ **con** : socialize with — *vt* : alternate — **alternarse** *vr* : take turns — **alternativa** *nf* : alternative — **alternativo, -va** *adj* : alternating, alternative — **alterno, -na** *adj* : alternate
Alteza *nf* : Highness
altiplano *nm* : high plateau
altitud *nf* : altitude
altivez *nf, pl* **-veces** : haughtiness — **altivo, -va** *adj* : haughty
alto, -ta *adj* **1** : tall, high **2** RUIDOSO

: loud — **alto** *adv* **1** ARRIBA : high **2**
: loud, loudly — **~** *nm* **1** ALTURA
: height, elevation **2** : stop, halt — **~**
interj : halt!, stop! — **altoparlante** *nm*
Lat : loudspeaker
altruista *adj* : altruistic — **altruismo**
nm : altruism
altura *nf* **1** : height **2** ALTITUD : altitude
3 a la ~ de : near, up by
alubia *nf* : kidney bean
alucinar *vi* : hallucinate — **alucinación**
nf, pl **-ciones** : hallucination
alud *nm* : avalanche
aludir *vi* : allude, refer — **aludido, -da**
adj **darse por ~** : take it personally
alumbrar *vt* **1** : light, illuminate **2** PARIR
: give birth to — **alumbrado** *nm*
: (electric) lighting — **alumbramiento** *nm* : childbirth
aluminio *nm* : aluminum
alumno, -na *n* : pupil, student
alusión *nf, pl* **-siones** : allusion
aluvión *nm, pl* **-viones** : flood, barrage
alzar {21} *vt* : lift, raise — **alzarse** *vr*
: rise (up) — **alza** *nf* : rise — **alza-
miento** *nm* : uprising
ama → amo
amabilidad *nf* : kindness — **amable**
adj : kind, nice
amaestrar *vt* : train
amagar {52} *vt* **1** : show signs of **2**
AMENAZAR : threaten — *vi* : be imminent — **amago** *nm* **1** INDICIO : sign **2**
AMENAZA : threat
amainar *vi* : abate
amamantar *v* : breast-feed, nurse
amanecer {53}*v impers* : dawn — *vi*
: wake up — **~** *nm* : dawn, daybreak
amanerado *adj* : affected, mannered
amansar *vt* **1** : tame **2** APACIGUAR
: soothe — **amansarse** *vr* : calm down
amante *adj* **~ de** : fond of — **~** *nmf*
: lover
amañar *vt* : rig, tamper with
amapola *nf* : poppy
amar *vt* : love
amargar {52} *vt* : make bitter — **amar-
gado, -da** *adj* : embittered — **amargo, -ga** *adj* : bitter — **amargo** *nm*
: bitterness — **amargura** *nf* : bitterness, grief
amarillo, -lla *adj* : yellow — **amarillo**
nm : yellow
amarrar *vt* **1** : moor **2** ATAR : tie up
amasar *vt* **1** : knead **2** : amass (a fortune, etc.)
amateur *adj & nmf* : amateur
amatista *nf* : amethyst
ambages *nmpl* **sin ~** : without hesitation, straight to the point

ámbar *nm* : amber
ambición *nf, pl* **-ciones** : ambition —
ambicionar *vt* : aspire to — **ambicioso, -sa** *adj* : ambitious
ambiente *nm* **1** AIRE : atmosphere **2**
MEDIO : environment, surroundings *pl*
— **ambiental** *adj* : environmental
ambigüedad *nf* : ambiguity — **ambiguo, -gua** *adj* : ambiguous
ámbito *nm* : domain, sphere
ambos, -bas *adj & pron* : both
ambulancia *nf* : ambulance
ambulante *adj* : traveling, itinerant
ameba *nf* : amoeba
amedrentar *vt* : intimidate
amén *nm* **1** : amen **2 ~ de** : in addition
to
amenazar {21} *vt* : threaten — **amenaza** *nf* : threat, menace
amenizar {21} *vt* : make pleasant, enliven — **ameno, -na** *adj* : pleasant
americano, -na *adj* : American
ameritar *vt Lat* : deserve
ametralladora *nf* : machine gun
amianto *nm* : asbestos
amiba → ameba
amígdala *nf* : tonsil — **amigdalitis** *nf*
: tonsilitis
amigo, -ga *adj* : friendly, close — **~** *n*
: friend — **amigable** *adj* : friendly
amilanar *vt* : daunt — **amilanarse** *vr*
: lose heart
aminorar *vt* : diminish
amistad *nf* : friendship — **amistoso,
-sa** *adj* : friendly
amnesia *nf* : amnesia
amnistía *nf* : amnesty
amo, ama *n* **1** : master *m*, mistress *f* **2**
ama de casa : homemaker, house-
wife **3 ama de llaves** : housekeeper
amodorrado, -da *adj* : drowsy
amolar {19} *vt* **1** : grind, sharpen **2** MO-
LESTAR : annoy
amoldar *vt* : adapt, adjust —
amoldarse *vr* **~ a** : adapt to
amonestar *vt* : admonish, warn —
amonestación *nf, pl* **-ciones** : admo-
nition, warning
amoníaco *or* **amoniaco** *nm* : ammonia
amontonar *vt* : pile up — **amontonarse** *vr* : pile up (of things), form a
crowd (of persons)
amor *nm* : love
amordazar {21} *vt* : gag
amorío *nm* : love affair — **amoroso,
-sa** *adj* **1** : loving **2** *Lat* : sweet, lovable
amortado, -da *adj* : black-and-blue
amortiguar {10} *vt* : muffle, soften,
tone down — **amortiguador** *nm*
: shock absorber

amortizar {21} vt : pay off — **amortización** nf : repayment

amotinar vt : incite (to riot) — **amotinarse** vr : riot, rebel

amparar vt : shelter, protect — **ampararse** vr 1 ~ de : take shelter from 2 ~ en : have recourse to — **amparo** nm : refuge, protection

ampliar {85} vt 1 : expand 2 : enlarge (a photograph) — **ampliación** nf, pl **-ciones** 1 : expansion, enlargement 2 : extension (of a building)

amplificar {72} vt : amplify — **amplificador** nm : amplifier

amplio, -plia adj : broad, wide, ample — **amplitud** nf 1 : breadth, extent 2 ESPACIOSIDAD : spaciousness

ampolla nf 1 : blister 2 : vial, ampoule — **ampollarse** vr : blister

ampuloso, -sa adj : pompous

amputar vt : amputate — **amputación** nf, pl **-ciones** : amputation

amueblar vt : furnish (a house, etc.)

amurallar vt : wall in

anacardo nm : cashew nut

anaconda nf : anaconda

anacrónico, -ca adj : anachronistic — **anacronismo** nm : anachronism

ánade nmf : duck

anagrama nm : anagram

anales nmpl : annals

analfabeto, -ta adj & n : illiterate — **analfabetismo** nm : illiteracy

analgésico nm : painkiller, analgesic

analizar {21} vt : analyze — **análisis** nm : analysis — **analítico, -ca** adj : analytical, analytic

analogía nf : analogy — **análogo, -ga** adj : analogous

ananá or **ananás** nm, pl **-nás** : pineapple

anaquel nm : shelf

anaranjado, -da adj : orange-colored

anarquía nf : anarchy — **anarquista** adj & nmf : anarchist

anatomía nf : anatomy — **anatómico, -ca** adj : anatomic, anatomical

anca nf 1 : haunch 2 ~s de rana : frogs' legs

ancestral adj : ancestral

ancho, -cha adj : wide, broad, ample — **ancho** nm : width

anchoa nf : anchovy

anchura nf : width, breadth

anciano, -na adj : aged, elderly — ~ n : elderly person

ancla nf : anchor — **anclar** v : anchor

andadas nfpl 1 : tracks 2 **volver a las ~** : go back to one's old ways

andadura nf : walking, journey

andaluz, -luza adj & n, mpl **-luces** : Andalusian

andamio nm : scaffold

andanada nf 1 : volley 2 **soltar una ~** : reprimand

andanzas nfpl : adventures

andar {6} vi 1 CAMINAR : walk 2 IR : go, travel 3 FUNCIONAR : run, work 4 ~ en : rummage around in 5 ~ **por** : be approximately — vt : cover, travel — ~ nm : gait, walk

andén nm, pl **-denes** 1 : (train) platform 2 Lat : sidewalk

andino, -na adj : Andean

andorrano, -na adj : Andorran

andrajos nmpl : tatters — **andrajoso, -sa** adj : ragged

anécdota nf : anecdote

anegar {52} vt : flood — **anegarse** vr 1 : be flooded 2 AHOGARSE : drown

anemia nf : anemia — **anémico, -ca** adj : anemic

anestesia nf : anesthesia — **anestésico, -ca** adj : anesthetic — **anestésico** nm : anesthetic

anexar vt : annex, attach — **anexo, -xa** adj : attached — **anexo** nm : annex

anfibio, -bia adj : amphibious — **anfibio** nm : amphibian

anfiteatro nm : amphitheater

anfitrión, -triona n, mpl **-triones** : host, hostess f

ángel nm : angel — **angelical** adj : angelic, angelical

angloparlante adj : English-speaking

angiosajón, -jona adj, mpl **-jones** : Anglo-Saxon

angosto, -ta adj : narrow

anguila nf : eel

ángulo nm 1 : angle 2 ESQUINA : corner — **angular** adj : angular — **anguloso, -sa** adj : angular

angustiar vt 1 : anguish, distress 2 INQUIETAR : worry — **angustiarse** vr : get upset — **angustia** nf 1 : anguish 2 INQUIETUD : worry — **angustioso, -sa** adj 1 : anguished 2 INQUIETANTE : distressing

anhelar vt : yearn for, crave — **anhelante** adj : yearning, longing — **anhelo** nm : longing

anidar vi : nest

anillo nm : ring

ánima n : soul

animación nf, pl **-ciones** 1 VIVEZA : liveliness 2 BULLICIO : hustle and bustle — **animado, -da** adj : cheerful, animated — **animador, -dora** n 1 : (television) host 2 : cheerleader

animadversión *nf, pl* **-siones** : animosity

animal *nm* : animal — ~ *nmf* : brute, beast — ~ *adj* : brutish

animar *vt* 1 ALENTAR : encourage 2 ALEGAR : cheer up — **animarse** *vr* 1 : liven up 2 ~ **a** : get up the nerve to

ánimo *nm* 1 : spirit, soul 2 HUMOR : mood, spirits *pl* 3 ALIENTO : encouragement

animosidad *nf* : animosity, ill will

animoso, -sa *adj* : spirited, brave

aniquilar *vt* : annihilate — **aniquilación** *n, pl* **-ciones** : annihilation

anís *nm* : anise

aniversario *nm* : anniversary

ano *nm* : anus

anoche *adv* : last night

anochecer {53} *vi* : get dark — ~ *nm* : dusk, nightfall

anodino, -na *adj* : insipid, dull

anomalía *nf* : anomaly

anonadado, -da *adj* : dumbfounded

anónimo, -ma *adj* : anonymous — **anonimato** *nm* : anonymity

anorexia *nf* : anorexia

anormal *adj* : abnormal — **anormalidad** *nf* : abnormality

anotar *vt* 1 : annotate 2 APUNTAR : jot down — **anotación** *nf, pl* **-ciones** : annotation, note

anquilosarse *vr* 1 : become paralyzed 2 ESTANCARSE : stagnate — **anquilosamiento** *nm* 1 : paralysis 2 ESTANCAMIENTO : stagnation

ansiar {85} *vt* : long for — **ansia** *nf* 1 INQUIETUD : uneasiness 2 ANGUSTIA : anguish 3 ANHELO : longing — **ansiedad** *nf* : anxiety — **ansioso, -sa** *adj* 1 : anxious 2 DESEOSO : eager

antagónico, -ca *adj* : antagonistic — **antagonismo** *nm* : antagonism — **antagonista** *nmf* : antagonist

antaño *adv* : yesteryear, long ago

antártico, -ca *adj* : antarctic

ante[1] *nm* 1 : elk, moose 2 GAMUZA : suede

ante[2] *prep* 1 : before, in front of 2 : in view of 3 ~ **todo** : above all

anteanoche *adv* : the night before last

anteayer *adv* : the day before yesterday

antebrazo *nm* : forearm

anteceder *vt* : precede — **antecedente** *adj* : previous, prior — ~ *nm* : precedent — **antecesor, -sora** *n* 1 : ancestor 2 PREDECESOR : predecessor

antedicho, -cha *adj* : aforesaid

antelación *nf, pl* **-ciones** 1 : advance notice 2 **con** ~ : in advance

antemano *adv* **de** ~ : beforehand

antena *nf* : antenna

antenoche → anteanoche

anteojos *nmpl* 1 : glasses, eyeglasses 2 ~ **bifocales** : bifocals

antepasado, -da *n* : ancestor

antepecho *nm* : ledge

antepenúltimo, -ma *adj* : third from last

anteponer {60} *vt* 1 : place before 2 PREFERIR : prefer

anterior *adj* 1 : previous, earlier 2 DELANTERO : front — **anterioridad** *nf* **con** ~ : beforehand, in advance — **anteriormente** *adv* : previously

antes *adv* 1 : before, earlier 2 ANTERIORMENTE : previously 3 PRIMERO : first 4 MEJOR : rather 5 ~ **de** : before, previous to 6 ~ **que** : before

antesala *nf* : waiting room

antiaéreo, -rea *adj* : antiaircraft

antibiótico *nm* : antibiotic

anticipar *vt* 1 : move up (a date, etc.) 2 : pay in advance — **anticiparse** *vr* 1 : be early 2 ADELANTARSE : get ahead — **anticipación** *nf, pl* **-ciones** 1 : anticipation 2 **con** ~ : in advance — **anticipado, -da** *adj* 1 : advance, early 2 **por** ~ : in advance — **anticipo** *nm* 1 : advance (payment) 2 : foretaste

anticoncepción *nf, pl* **-ciones** : contraception — **anticonceptiva, -va** *adj* : contraceptive — **anticonceptivo** *nm* : contraceptive

anticongelante *nm* : antifreeze

anticuado, -da *adj* : antiquated, outdated

anticuario, -ria *n* : antique dealer — **anticuario** *nm* : antique shop

anticuerpo *nm* : antibody

antídoto *nm* : antidote

antier → anteayer

antiestético, -ca *adj* : unsightly

antifaz *nm, pl* **-faces** : mask

antífona *nf* : anthem

antigualla *nf* : relic, old thing

antiguo, -gua *adj* 1 : ancient, old 2 ANTERIOR : former 3 ANTICUADO : old-fashioned 4 **muebles antiguos** : antique furniture — **antiguamente** *adv* 1 : long ago 2 ANTES : formerly — **antigüedad** *nf* 1 : antiquity 2 : seniority (in the workplace) 3 ~**es** *nfpl* : antiques

antihigiénico, -ca *adj* : unsanitary

antihistamínico *nm* : antihistamine

antiinflamatorio, -ria *adj* : anti-inflammatory

antílope *nm* : antelope

antinatural *adj* : unnatural

antipatía *nf* : aversion, dislike — **antipático, -ca** *adj* : unpleasant

antirreglamentario, -ria *adj* : unlawful

antirrobo, -ba *adj* : antitheft

antisemita *adj* : anti-Semitic — **antisemitismo** *nm* : anti-Semitism

antiséptico, -ca *adj* : antiseptic — **antiséptico** *nm* : antiseptic

antisocial *adj* : antisocial

antítesis *nf* : antithesis

antojarse *vr* **1** APETECER : crave **2** PARECER : seem, appear — **antojadizo, -za** *adj* : capricious — **antojo** *nm* : whim, craving

antología *nf* : anthology

antorcha *nf* : torch

antro *nm* : dive, den

antropófago, -ga *nmf* : cannibal

antropología *nf* : anthropology

anual *adj* : annual, yearly — **anualidad** *nf* : annuity — **anuario** *nm* : yearbook, annual

anudar *vt* : knot — **anudarse** *vr* : tie, knot

anular *vt* : annul, cancel — **anulación** *nf, pl* -**ciones** : annulment, cancellation

anunciar *vt* **1** : announce **2** : advertise (products) — **anunciante** *nmf* : advertiser — **anuncio** *nm* **1** : announcement **2** *or* **publicitario** : advertisement

anzuelo *nm* **1** : fishhook **2 morder el ~** : take the bait

añadir *vt* : add — **añadidura** *nf* **1** : additive, addition **2 por ~** : in addition, furthermore

añejo, -ja *adj* : aged, vintage

añicos *nmpl* **hacer(se) ~** : smash to pieces

añil *adj & nm* : indigo (color)

año *nm* **1** : year **2 Año Nuevo** : New Year

añorar *vt* : long for, miss — **añoranza** *nf* : nostalgia

añoso, -sa *adj* : aged, old

aorta *nf* : aorta

apabullar *vt* : overwhelm

apacentar {55} *vt* : pasture, graze

apachurrar *vt Lat* : crush

apacible *adj* : gentle, mild

apaciguar {10} *vt* : appease, pacify — **apaciguarse** *vr* : calm down

apadrinar *vt* **1** : be a godparent to **2** : sponsor (an artist, etc.)

apagar {52} *vt* **1** : turn or switch off **2** EXTINGUIR : extinguish, put out — **apagarse** *vr* **1** EXTINGUIRSE : go out **2** : die down — **apagado, -da** *adj* **1** : off, out **2** : dull, subdued (of colors, sounds, etc.) — **apagador** *nm Lat*

: (light) switch — **apagón** *nm, pl* -**gones** : blackout

apalancar {72} *vt* **1** LEVANTAR : jack up **2** ABRIR : pry open — **apalancamiento** *nm* : leverage

apalear *vt* : beat up, thrash

aparador *nm* **1** : sideboard **2** *Lat* : shop window

aparato *nm* **1** : machine, appliance, apparatus **2** : system (in anatomy) **3** OSTENTACIÓN : ostentation — **aparatoso, -sa** *adj* **1** : ostentatious **2** ESPECTACULAR : spectacular

aparcar {72} *v Spain* : park — **aparcamiento** *nm Spain* **1** : parking **2** : parking lot

aparcero, -ra *n* : sharecropper

aparear *vt* : mate, pair up — **aparearse** *vr* : mate

aparecer {53} *vi* **1** : appear **2** PRESENTARSE : show up — **aparecerse** *vr* : appear

aparejar *vt* **1** : rig (a ship) **2** : harness (an animal) — **aparejado, -da** *adj* **llevar ~** : entail — **aparejo** *nm* **1** : equipment, gear **2** : harness (for an animal) **3** : rigging (for a ship)

aparentar *vt* **1** : seem **2** FINGIR : feign — **aparente** *adj* : apparent, seeming

aparición *nf, pl* -**ciones 1** : appearance **2** FANTASMA : apparition — **apariencia** *nf* **1** : appearance, look **2 en ~** : apparently

apartado *nm* **1** : section, paragraph **2 ~ postal** : post office box

apartamento *nm* : apartment

apartar *vt* **1** ALEJAR : move away **2** SEPARAR : set aside, separate — **apartarse** *vr* **1** : move away **2** DESVIARSE : stray — **aparte** *adv* **1** : apart, separately **2** ADEMÁS : besides

apasionar *vt* : excite, fascinate — **apasionarse** *vr* : get excited — **apasionado, -da** *adj* : passionate, excited — **apasionante** *adj* : exciting

apatía *nf* : apathy — **apático, -ca** *adj* : apathetic

apearse *vr* **1** : dismount **2** : get out of or off (a vehicle)

apedrear *vt* : stone

apegarse {52} *vr* **~ a** : become attached to, grow fond of — **apegado, -da** *adj* : devoted — **apego** *nm* : fondness

apelar *vi* **1** : appeal **2 ~ a** : resort to — **apelación** *nf, pl* -**ciones** : appeal

apellido *nm* : last name, surname — **apellidarse** *vr* : have for a last name

apenar *vt* : sadden — **apenarse** *vr* **1** : grieve **2** *Lat* : become embarrassed

apenas *adv* : hardly, scarcely — ~
conj : as soon as
apéndice *nm* : appendix — **apendicitis**
nf : appendicitis
apercibir *vt* **1** : warn **2** *Lat* : notice —
apercibirse *vr* ~ de : notice —
apercibimiento *nm* : warning
aperitivo *nm* **1** : appetizer **2** : aperitif
apero *nm* : tool, implement
apertura *nf* : opening
apesadumbrar *vt* : sadden — **apesa-**
dumbrarse *vr* : be weighed down
apestar *vi* : stink — **apestoso, -sa** *adj*
: stinking, foul
apetecer {53} *vt* : crave, long for —
apetecible *adj* : appealing
apetito *nm* : appetite — **apetitoso, -sa**
adj : appetizing
ápice *nm* **1** : apex, summit **2** PIZCA : bit,
smidgen
apilar *vt* : pile up — **apilarse** *vr* : pile
up
apiñar *vt* : pack, cram — **apiñarse** *vr*
: crowd together
apio *nm* : celery
apisonadora *nf* : steamroller
aplacar {72} *vt* : appease, placate —
aplacarse *vr* : calm down
aplanar *vt* : flatten, level
aplastar *vt* : crush — **aplastante** *adj*
: overwhelming
aplaudir *v* : applaud — **aplauso** *nm* **1**
: applause **2** : acclaim
aplazar {21} *vt* : postpone, defer —
aplazamiento *nm* : postponement
aplicar {72} *vt* : apply — **aplicarse** *vr*
: apply oneself — **aplicable** *adj* : applicable — **aplicación** *nf, pl* **-ciones**
: application — **aplicado, -da** *adj*
: diligent
aplomo *nm* : aplomb
apocarse {72} *vr* : belittle oneself —
apocado, -da *adj* : timid — **apo-**
camiento *nm* : timidity
apodar *vt* : nickname
apoderar *vt* : empower — **apoderarse**
vr ~ de : seize — **apoderado, -da** *n*
: agent, proxy
apodo *nm* : nickname
apogeo *nm* : peak, height
apología *nf* : defense, apology
apoplegía *nf* : stroke, apoplexy
aporrear *vt* : bang on, beat
aportar *vt* : contribute — **aportación**
nf, pl **-ciones** : contribution
apostar[1] {19} *v* : bet, wager
apostar[2] *vt* : station, post
apostillar *vt* : annotate — **apostilla** *nf*
: note
apóstol *nm* : apostle

apóstrofo *nm* : apostrophe
apostura *nf* : elegance, grace
apoyar *vt* **1** : support **2** INCLINAR : lean,
rest — **apoyarse** *vr* ~ en : lean on,
rest on — **apoyo** *nm* : support
apreciar *vt* **1** ESTIMAR : appreciate **2**
EVALUAR : appraise — **apreciable** *adj*
: considerable — **apreciación** *nf, pl*
-ciones 1 : appreciation **2** VALO-
RACIÓN : appraisal — **aprecio** *nm* **1**
: appraisal **2** ESTIMA : esteem
aprehender *vt* : apprehend — **apre-**
hensión *nf, pl* **-siones** : apprehension, capture
apremiar *vt* : urge — *vi* : be urgent —
apremiante *adj* : pressing, urgent —
apremio *nm* : urgency
aprender *v* : learn — **aprenderse** *vr*
: memorize
aprendiz, -diza *n, mpl* **-dices** : apprentice, trainee — **aprendizaje** *nm* : ap-
prenticeship
aprensión *nf, pl* **-siones** : apprehension, dread — **aprensivo, -va** *adj* : apprehensive
apresar *vt* : capture, seize — **apre-**
samiento *nm* : seizure, capture
aprestar *vt* : make ready — **aprestarse**
vr : get ready
apresurar *vt* : speed up — **apresurarse**
vr : hurry — **apresuradamente** *adv*
: hurriedly, hastily — **apresurado,**
-da *adj* : in a rush
apretar {55} *vt* **1** : press, push (a button) **2** : tighten (a knot, etc.) **3** ES-
TRECHAR : squeeze — *vi* **1** : press
(down) **2** : fit too tightly — **apretón**
nm, pl **-tones 1** : squeeze **2** ~ **de**
manos : handshake — **apretado, -da**
adj **1** : tight **2** *fam* : tightfisted
aprieto *nm* : predicament, jam
aprisa *adv* : quickly
aprisionar *vt* : imprison
aprobar {19} *vt* **1** : approve of **2** : pass
(an exam, etc.) — *vi* : pass —
aprobación *nf, pl* **-ciones** : approval
apropiarse *vr* ~ de : take possession
of, appropriate — **apropiación** *nf, pl*
-ciones : appropriation — **apropia-**
do, -da *adj* : appropriate
aprovechar *vt* : take advantage of,
make good use of — *vi* : be of use —
aprovecharse *vr* ~ de : take advantage of — **aprovechado, -da** *adj* **1**
: diligent **2** OPORTUNISTA : opportunis-
tic
aproximar *vt* : bring closer — **aproxi-**
marse *vr* : approach — **aproxi-**
mación *nf, pl* **-ciones** : approxima-
tion — **aproximadamente** *adv*

: approximately — **aproximado, -da** *adj* : approximate

apto, -ta *adj* **1** : suitable **2** CAPAZ : capable — **aptitud** *nf* : aptitude, capability

apuesta *nf* : bet, wager

apuesto, -ta *adj* : elegant, good-looking

apuntalar *vt* : prop up, shore up

apuntar *vt* **1** : aim, point **2** ANOTAR : jot down **3** SEÑALAR : point at **4** : prompt (in theater) — **apuntarse** *vr* **1** : sign up **2** : score, chalk up (a victory, etc.) — **apunte** *nm* : note

apuñalar *vt* : stab

apurar *vt* **1** : hurry, rush **2** AGOTAR : use up **3** PREOCUPAR : trouble — **apurarse** *vr* **1** : worry **2** *Lat* : hurry up — **apuradamente** *adv* : with difficulty — **apurado, -da** *adj* **1** : needy **2** DIFÍCIL : difficult **3** *Lat* : rushed — **apuro** *nm* **1** : predicament, jam **2** *Lat* : hurry

aquejar *vt* : afflict

aquel, aquella *adj, mpl* **aquellos** : that, those

aquél, aquélla *pron, mpl* **aquéllos 1** : that (one), those (ones) **2** : the former

aquello *pron* : that, that matter

aquí *adv* **1** : here **2** AHORA : now **3 por ～** : hereabouts

aquietar *vt* : calm — **aquietarse** *vr* : calm down

ara *nf* **1** : altar **2 en ～s de** : for the sake of

árabe *adj* : Arab, Arabic — **～** *nm* : Arabic (language)

arado *nm* : plow

arancel *nm* : tariff

arándano *nm* : blueberry

araña *nf* **1** : spider **2** LÁMPARA : chandelier

arañar *v* : scratch, claw — **arañazo** *nm* : scratch

arar *v* : plow

arbitrar *v* **1** : arbitrate **2** : referee, umpire (in sports) — **arbitraje** *nm* : arbitration — **arbitrario, -ria** *adj* : arbitrary — **arbitrio** *nm* **1** : (free) will **2** JUICIO : judgment — **árbitro, -tra** *n* **1** : arbitrator **2** : referee, umpire (in sports)

árbol *nm* : tree — **arboleda** *nf* : grove

arbusto *nm* : shrub, bush

arca *nf* **1** : ark **2** COFRE : chest

arcada *nf* **1** : arcade **2 ～s** *nfpl* : retching

arcaico, -ca *adj* : archaic

arcano, -na *adj* : arcane, secret

arce *nm* : maple tree

archipiélago *nm* : archipelago

archivar *vt* : file — **archivador** *nm* : filing cabinet — **archivo** *nm* **1** : file **2** : archives *pl*

arcilla *nf* : clay

arco *nm* **1** : arch **2** : bow (in sports, music, etc.) **3** : arc (in geometry) **4 ～ iris** : rainbow

arder *vi* : burn

ardid *nm* : scheme, ruse

ardiente *adj* **1** : burning **2** FOGOSO : ardent

ardilla *nf* **1** : squirrel **2 ～ listada** : chipmunk

ardor *nm* **1** : burning **2** ENTUSIASMO : passion, ardor

arduo, -dua *adj* : arduous

área *nf* : area

arena *nf* **1** : sand **2** PALESTRA : arena — **arenoso, -sa** *adj* : sandy, gritty

arenque *nm* : herring

arete *nm* *Lat* : earring

argamasa *nf* : mortar

argentino, -na *adj* : Argentinian, Argentine

argolla *nf* : hoop, ring

argot *nm* : slang

argüir {41} *vt* **1** : argue **2** DEMOSTRAR : prove, show — *vi* : argue

argumentar *vt* : argue, contend — **argumentación** *nf, pl* **-ciones** : (line of) argument — **argumento** *nm* **1** : argument, reasoning **2** TRAMA : plot, story line

árido, -da *adj* : dry, arid — **aridez** *nf, pl* **-deces** : aridity

arisco, -ca *adj* : surly

aristocracia *nf* : aristocracy — **aristócrata** *nmf* : aristocrat — **aristocrático, -ca** *adj* : aristocratic

aritmética *nf* : arithmetic — **aritmético, -ca** *adj* : arithmetic, arithmetical

armar *vt* **1** : arm **2** MONTAR : assemble — **arma** *nf* **1** : arm, weapon **2 ～ de fuego** : firearm — **armada** *nf* : navy — **armado, -da** *adj* : armed — **armadura** *nf* **1** : armor **2** ARMAZÓN : framework — **armamento** *nm* : armament, arms *pl*

armario *nm* **1** : (clothes) closet **2** : cupboard, cabinet

armazón *nmf, pl* **-zones** : frame, framework

armisticio *nm* : armistice

armonizar {21} *vt* **1** : harmonize **2** : reconcile (differences, etc.) — *vi* : harmonize, go together — **armonía** *nf* : harmony — **armónica** *nf* : harmonica — **armónico, -ca** *adj* : harmonic — **armonioso, -sa** *adj* : harmonious

arnés *nm, pl* **-neses** : harness

aro *nm* **1** : hoop, ring **2** *Lat* : earring

aroma *nm* : aroma, scent — **aromático, -ca** *adj* : aromatic

arpa *nf* : harp

arpón *nm, pl* **-pones** : harpoon

arquear *vt* : arch, bend — **arquearse** *vr* : bend, bow

arqueología *nf* : archaeology — **arqueológico, -ca** *adj* : archaeological — **arqueólogo, -ga** *n* : archaeologist

arquero, -ra *n* **1** : archer **2** PORTERO : goalkeeper, goalie

arquetipo *nm* : archetype

arquitectura *nf* : architecture — **arquitecto, -ta** *n* : architect — **arquitectónico, -ca** *adj* : architectural

arrabal *nm* **1** : slum **2 ~es** *nmpl* : outskirts

arracimarse *vr* : cluster together

arraigar {52} *vi* : take root, become established — **arraigarse** *vr* : settle down — **arraigado, -da** *adj* : deeply rooted, well established — **arraigo** *nm* : roots *pl*

arrancar {72} *vt* **1** : pull out, tear off **2** : start (an engine), boot (a computer) — *vi* **1** : start an engine **2** : get going — **arranque** *nm* **1** : starter (of a car) **2** ARREBATO : outburst **3 punto de ~** : starting point

arrasar *vt* **1** : destroy, devastate **2** LLENAR : fill to the brim

arrastrar *vt* **1** : drag **2** ATRAER : draw, attract — *vi* : hang down, trail — **arrastrarse** *vr* **1** : crawl, creep **2** HUMILLARSE : grovel — **arrastre** *nm* **1** : dragging **2** : trawling (for fish)

arrear *vt* : urge on

arrebatar *vt* **1** : snatch, seize **2** CAUTIVAR : captivate — **arrebatarse** *vr* : get carried away — **arrebatado, -da** *adj* : hotheaded, rash — **arrebato** *nm* : outburst

arreciar *vi* : intensify, worsen

arrecife *nm* : reef

arreglar *vt* **1** COMPONER : fix **2** ORDENAR : tidy up **3** SOLUCIONAR : solve, work out — **arreglarse** *vr* **1** : get dressed (up) **2 arreglárselas** *fam* : get by, manage — **arreglado, -da** *adj* **1** : fixed, repaired **2** ORDENADO : tidy **3** SOLUCIONADO : settled, sorted out **4** ATAVIADO : smart, dressed-up — **arreglo** *nm* **1** : arrangement **2** REPARACIÓN : repair **3** ACUERDO : agreement

arremangarse {52} *vr* : roll up one's sleeves

arremeter *vi* : attack, charge — **arremetida** *nf* : attack, onslaught

arremolinarse *vr* **1** : crowd around, mill about **2** : swirl (about)

arrendar {55} *vt* : rent, lease — **arrendador, -dora** *n* : landlord, landlady *f* — **arrendamiento** *nm* : rent, rental — **arrendatario, -ria** *n* : tenant, renter

arrepentirse {76} *vr* **1** : regret, be sorry **2** : repent (for one's sins) — **arrepentido, -da** *adj* : repentant — **arrepentimiento** *nm* : regret, repentance

arrestar *vt* : arrest, detain — **arresto** *nm* : arrest

arriar *vt* : lower

arriba *adv* **1** (*indicating position*) : above, overhead **2** (*indicating direction*) : up, upwards **3** : upstairs (of a house) **4 ~ de** : more than **5 de ~ abajo** : from top to bottom

arribar *vi* **1** : arrive **2** : dock, put into port — **arribista** *nmf* : parvenu, upstart — **arribo** *nm* : arrival

arriendo → arrendimiento

arriesgar {52} *vt* : risk, venture — **arriesgarse** *vr* : take a chance — **arriesgado, -da** *adj* : risky

arrimar *vt* : bring closer, draw near — **arrimarse** *vr* : approach

arrinconar *vt* **1** : corner, box in **2** ABANDONAR : push aside

arrobar *vt* : entrance — **arrobarse** *vr* : be enraptured — **arrobamiento** *nm* : rapture, ecstasy

arrodillarse *vr* : kneel (down)

arrogancia *nf* : arrogance — **arrogante** *adj* : arrogant

arrojar *vt* **1** : hurl, cast **2** EMITIR : give off, spew out **3** PRODUCIR : yield — **arrojarse** *vr* : throw oneself — **arrojado, -da** *adj* : daring — **arrojo** *nm* : boldness, courage

arrollar *vt* **1** : sweep away **2** DERROTAR : crush, overwhelm **3** : run over (with a vehicle) — **arrollador, -dora** *adj* : overwhelming

arropar *vt* : clothe, cover (up) — **arroparse** *vr* : wrap oneself up

arroyo *nm* **1** RIACHUELO : stream **2** : gutter (in a street)

arroz *nm, pl* **arroces** : rice

arrugar {52} *vt* : wrinkle, crease — **arrugarse** *vr* : get wrinkled — **arruga** *nf* : wrinkle, crease

arruinar *vt* : ruin, wreck — **arruinarse** *vr* **1** : be ruined **2** EMPOBRECERSE : go bankrupt

arrullar *vt* : lull to sleep — *vi* : coo — **arrullo** *nm* **1** : lullaby **2** : cooing (of doves)

arrumbar *vt* : lay aside

arsenal *nm* : arsenal

arsénico *nm* : arsenic
arte *nmf (usually m in singular, f in plural)* **1** : art **2** HABILIDAD : skill **3** ASTUCIA : cunning, cleverness **4** → **bello**
artefacto *nm* : artifact, device
arteria *nf* : artery
artesanía *nm* **1** : craftsmanship **2** : handicrafts — **artesanal** *adj* : handmade — **artesano, -na** *n* : artisan, craftsman
ártico, -ca *adj* : arctic
articular *vt* : articulate — **articulación** *nf, pl* **-ciones 1** : articulation, pronunciation **2** COYUNTURA : joint
artículo *nm* **1** : article **2** ~s de primera necesidad : essentials **3** ~s de tocador : toiletries
artífice *nmf* : artisan, craftsman
artificial *adj* : artificial
artificio *nm* **1** HABILIDAD : skill **2** APARATO : device **3** ARDID : artifice, ruse — **artificioso, -sa** *adj* : cunning, deceptive
artillería *nf* : artillery
artilugio *nm* : gadget
artimaña *nf* : ruse, trick
artista *nmf* **1** : artist **2** ACTOR : actor, actress *f* — **artístico, -ca** *adj* : artistic
artritis *nms & pl* : arthritis — **artrítico, -ca** *adj* : arthritic
arveja *nf Lat* : pea
arzobispo *nm* : archbishop
as *nm* : ace
asa *nf* : handle
asado, -da *adj* : roasted, grilled — **asado** *nm* : roast — **asador** *nm* : spit — **asaduras** *nfpl* : offal, entrails
asalariado, -da *n* : wage earner — ~ *adj* : salaried
asaltar *vt* **1** : assault **2** ROBAR : mug, rob — **asaltante** *nmf* **1** : assailant **2** ATRACADOR : mugger, robber — **asalto** *nm* **1** : assault **2** ROBO : mugging, robbery
asamblea *nf* : assembly, meeting
asar *vt* : roast, grill — **asarse** *vr fam* : roast, feel the heat
asbesto *nm* : asbestos
ascender {56} *vi* **1** : ascend, rise up **2** : be promoted (in a job) **3** ~ a : amount to — *vt* : promote — **ascendencia** *nf* : ancestry, descent — **ascendiente** *nmf* : ancestor — ~ *nm* : influence — **ascensión** *nf, pl* **-siones** : ascent — **ascenso** *nm* **1** : ascent, rise **2** : promotion (in a job) — **ascensor** *nm* : elevator
asco *nm* **1** : disgust **2** hacer ~s de : turn up one's nose at **3** me da ~ : it makes me sick

ascua *nf* **1** : ember **2** estar en ~s *fam* : be on edge
asear *vt* **1** : clean, tidy up — **asearse** *vr* : get cleaned up — **aseado, -da** *adj* : clean, tidy
asediar *vt* **1** : besiege **2** ACOSAR : harass — **asedio** *nm* **1** : siege **2** ACOSO : harassment
asegurar *vt* **1** : assure **2** FIJAR : secure **3** : insure (a car, house, etc.) — **asegurarse** *vr* : make sure
asemejarse *vr* **1** : be similar **2** ~ a : look like, resemble
asentar {55} *vt* **1** : set down **2** INSTALAR : set up, establish **3** *Lat* : state — **asentarse** *vr* **1** : settle **2** ESTABLECERSE : settle down — **asentado, -da** *adj* : settled, established
asentir {76} *vi* : assent, agree — **asentimiento** *nm* : assent
aseo *nm* : cleanliness
asequible *adj* : accessible, attainable
aserrar {55} *vt* : saw — **aserradero** *nm* : sawmill — **aserrín** *nm, pl* **-rrines** : sawdust
asesinar *vt* **1** : murder **2** : assassinate — **asesinato** *nm* **1** : murder **2** : assassination — **asesino, -na** *n* **1** : murderer, killer **2** : assassin
asesorar *vt* : advise, counsel — **asesorarse** *vr* ~ de : consult — **asesor, -sora** *n* : advisor, consultant — **asesoramiento** *nm* : advice, counsel
asestar {55} *vt* **1** : aim (a weapon) **2** : deal (a blow)
aseverar *vt* : assert — **aseveración** *nf, pl* **-ciones** : assertion
asfalto *nm* : asphalt
asfixiar *vt* : asphyxiate, suffocate — **asfixiarse** *vr* : suffocate — **asfixia** *nf* : asphyxiation, suffocation
así *adv* **1** : like this, like that, thus **2** ~ de : so, that (much) **3** ~ que : so, therefore **4** ~ que : as soon as **5** ~ como : as well as — ~ *adj* : such, like that — ~ *conj* AUNQUE : even though
asiático, -ca *adj* : Asian, Asiatic
asidero *nm* : handle
asiduo, -dua *adj* : frequent, regular
asiento *nm* : seat
asignar *vt* **1** : assign, allocate **2** DESTINAR : appoint — **asignación** *nf, pl* **-ciones 1** : assignment **2** SUELDO : salary, pay — **asignatura** *nf* : subject, course
asilo *nm* **1** : asylum, home **2** REFUGIO : refuge, shelter — **asilado, -da** *n* : inmate
asimilar *vt* : assimilate — **asimilarse** *vr* ~ a : resemble

asimismo *adv* **1** : similarly, likewise **2** TAMBIÉN : as well, also

asir {7} *vt* : seize, grasp — **asirse** *vr* ~ **a** : cling to

asistir *vi* ~ **a** : attend, be present at — *vt* : assist — **asistencia** *nf* **1** : attendance **2** AYUDA : assistance — **asistente** *nmf* **1** : assistant **2** los ~s : those present

asma *nf* : asthma — **asmático, -ca** *adj* : asthmatic

asno *nm* : ass, donkey

asociar *vt* : associate — **asociarse** *vr* : form a partnership **2** ~ **a** : join, become a member of — **asociación** *nf, pl* **-ciones** : association — **asociado, -da** *adj* : associate, associated — ~ *n* : associate, partner

asolar {19} *vt* : devastate

asomar *vt* : show, stick out — *vi* : appear, show — **asomarse** *vr* **1** : appear **2** : stick one's head out (of a window)

asombrar *vt* : amaze, astonish — **asombrarse** *vr* : be amazed — **asombro** *nm* : amazement, astonishment — **asombroso, -sa** *adj* : amazing, astonishing

asomo *nm* **1** : hint, trace **2** ni por ~ : by no means

aspaviento *nm* : exaggerated gestures, fuss

aspecto *nm* **1** : aspect **2** APARIENCIA : appearance, look

áspero, -ra *adj* : rough, harsh — **aspereza** *nf* : roughness, harshness

aspersión *nf, pl* **-siones** : sprinkling — **aspersor** *nm* : sprinkler

aspiración *nf, pl* **-ciones** **1** : breathing in **2** ANHELO : aspiration

aspiradora *nf* : vacuum cleaner

aspirar *vi* ~ **a** : aspire to — *vt* : inhale, breathe in — **aspirante** *nmf* : applicant, candidate

aspirina *nf* : aspirin

asquear *vt* : sicken, disgust

asquerosidad *nf* : filth, foulness — **asqueroso, -sa** *adj* : disgusting, sickening

asta *nf* **1** : flagpole **2** CUERNO : antler, horn **3** : shaft (of a spear) — **astado, -da** *adj* : horned

asterisco *nm* : asterisk

asteroide *nm* : asteroid

astigmatismo *nm* : astigmatism

astillar *vt* : splinter — **astilla** *nf* : splinter, chip

astillero *nm* : shipyard

astral *adj* : astral

astringente *adj & nm* : astringent

astro *nm* **1** : heavenly body **2** : star (of movies, etc.)

astrología *nf* : astrology

astronauta *nmf* : astronaut — **astronáutica** *nf* : astronautics

astronave *nf* : spaceship

astronomía *nf* : astronomy — **astronómico, -ca** *adj* : astronomical — **astrónomo, -ma** *n* : astronomer

astucia *nf* **1** : astuteness **2** ARDID : cunning, guile — **astuto, -ta** *adj* **1** : astute **2** TAIMADO : crafty

asueto *nm* : time off, break

asumir *vt* : assume — **asunción** *nf, pl* **-ciones** : assumption

asunto *nm* **1** : matter, affair **2** NEGOCIO : business

asustar *vt* : scare, frighten — **asustarse** *vr* ~ **de** : be frightened of — **asustadizo, -za** *adj* : jumpy, skittish — **asustado, -da** *adj* : frightened, afraid

atacar {72} *v* : attack — **atacante** *nmf* : attacker

atado *nm* : bundle

atadura *nf* : tie, bond

atajar *vt* : block, cut off — *vi* ~ **por** : take a shortcut through — **atajo** *nm* : shortcut

atañer {79} *vi* ~ **a** : concern, have to do with

ataque *nm* **1** : attack, assault **2** ACCESO : fit **3** ~ **de nervios** : nervous breakdown

atar *vt* : tie up, tie down — **atarse** *vr* : tie (up)

atardecer {53} *v impers* : get dark — ~ *nm* : late afternoon, dusk

atareado, -da *adj* : busy

atascar {72} *vt* **1** : block, clog **2** ESTORBAR : hinder — **atascarse** *vr* **1** OBSTRUIRSE : become obstructed **2** : get bogged down — **atasco** *nm* **1** : blockage **2** EMBOTELLAMIENTO : traffic jam

ataúd *nm* : coffin

ataviar {85} *vt* : dress (up) — **ataviarse** *vr* : dress up — **atavío** *nm* : attire

atemorizar {21} *vt* : frighten — **atemorizarse** *vr* : get scared

atención *nf, pl* **-ciones** **1** : attention **2** prestar ~ : pay attention **3** llamar la ~ : attract attention — ~ *interj* : attention!, watch out!

atender {56} *vt* **1** : attend to **2** CUIDAR : look after **3** : heed (advice, etc.) — *vi* : pay attention

atenerse {80} *vr* ~ **a** : abide by

atentamente *adv* **1** : attentively **2** le saluda ~ : sincerely yours

atentar {55} *vi* ~ **contra** : make an attempt on — **atentado** *nm* : attack
atento, -ta *adj* 1 : attentive, mindful 2 CORTÉS : courteous
atenuar {3} *vt* 1 : dim (lights), tone down (colors, etc.) 2 DISMINUIR : lessen — **atenuante** *nmf* : extenuating circumstances
ateo, atea *adj* : atheistic — ~ *n* : atheist
aterciopelado, -da *adj* : velvety, downy
aterido, -da *adj* : frozen stiff
aterrar {55} *vt* : terrify — **aterrador, -dora** *adj* : terrifying
aterrizar {21} *vi* : land — **aterrizaje** *nm* : landing
aterrorizar {21} *vt* : terrify
atesorar *vt* : hoard, amass
atestar {55} *vt* 1 : crowd, pack 2 : testify to (in law) — **atestado, -da** *adj* : stuffed, packed
atestiguar {10} *vt* : testify to
atiborrar *vt* : stuff, cram — **atiborrarse** *vr* : stuff oneself
ático *nm* 1 : penthouse 2 DESVÁN : attic
atildado, -da *adj* : smart, neat
atinar *vi* : be on target
atípico, -ca *adj* : atypical
atirantar *vt* : tighten
atisbar *vt* 1 : spy on 2 VISLUMBRAR : catch a glimpse of — **atisbo** *nm* : sign, hint
atizar {21} *vt* 1 : poke (a fire) 2 : rouse, stir up (passions, etc.) — **atizador** *nm* : poker
atlántico, -ca *adj* : Atlantic
atlas *nm* : atlas
atleta *nmf* : athlete — **atlético, -ca** *adj* : athletic — **atletismo** *nm* : athletics
atmósfera *nf* : atmosphere — **atmosférico, -ca** *adj* : atmospheric
atolondrado, -da *adj* 1 : scatterbrained 2 ATURDIDO : bewildered, dazed
átomo *nm* : atom — **atómico, -ca** *adj* : atomic — **atomizador** *nm* : atomizer
atónito, -ta *adj* : astonished, amazed
atontar *vt* : stun, daze
atorar *vt* : block — **atorarse** *vr* : get stuck
atormentar *vt* : torment, torture — **atormentarse** *vr* : torment oneself, agonize — **atormentor, -dora** *n* : tormenter
atornillar *vt* : screw
atorrante *nmf Lat* : bum, loafer
atosigar {52} *vt* : harass, annoy
atracar {72} *vi* : dock, land — *vt* : hold up, mug — **atracarse** *vr fam* ~ **de** : gorge oneself with — **atracadero**

nm : dock, pier — **atracador, -dora** *n* : robber, mugger
atracción *nf, pl* **-clones** : attraction
atraco *nm* : holdup, robbery
atractivo, -va *adj* : attractive — **atractivo** *nm* : attraction, appeal
atraer {81} *vt* : attract
atragantarse *vr* : choke
atrancar {72} *vt* : block, bar — **atrancarse** *vr* : get blocked, get stuck
atrapar *vt* : trap, capture
atrás *adv* 1 DETRÁS : back, behind 2 ANTES : before, earlier 3 **para** ~ *or* **hacia** ~ : backwards
atrasar *vt* 1 : put back (a clock) 2 DEMORAR : delay — *vi* : lose time — **atrasarse** *vr* : fall behind — **atrasado, -da** *adj* 1 : late, overdue 2 : backward (of countries, etc.) 3 : slow (of a clock) — **atraso** *nm* 1 RETRASO : delay 2 : backwardness 3 ~**s** *nmpl* : arrears
atravesar {55} *vt* 1 CRUZAR : cross 2 TRASPASAR : pierce 3 : lay across (a road, etc.) 4 : go through (a situation) — **atravesarse** *vr* : be in the way
atrayente *adj* : attractive
atreverse *vr* : dare — **atrevido, -da** *adj* 1 : bold 2 INSOLENTE : insolent — **atrevimiento** *nm* 1 : boldness 2 DESCARO : insolence
atribuir {41} *vt* 1 : attribute 2 : confer (powers, etc.) — **atribuirse** *vr* : take credit for
atribular *vt* : afflict, trouble
atributo *nm* : attribute
atrincherar *vt* : entrench — **atrincherarse** *vr* : dig oneself in
atrocidad *nf* : atrocity
atronador, -dora *adj* : thunderous
atropellar *vt* 1 : run over 2 : violate, abuse (a person) — **atropellarse** *vr* : rush — **atropellado, -da** *adj* : hasty — **atropello** *nm* : abuse, outrage
atroz *adj, pl* **atroces** : atrocious
atuendo *nm* : attire
atufar *vt* : vex — **atufarse** *vr* : get angry
atún *nm, pl* **atunes** : tuna
aturdir *vt* 1 : stun, shock 2 CONFUNDIR : bewilder — **aturdido, -da** *adj* : dazed, bewildered
audaz *adj, pl* **-daces** : bold, daring — **audacia** *nf* : boldness, audacity
audible *adj* : audible
audición *nf, pl* **-clones** 1 : hearing 2 : audition (in theater, etc.)
audiencia *nf* : audience
audífono *nm* 1 : hearing aid 2 ~**s** *nmpl Lat* : headphones, earphones
audiovisual *adj* : audiovisual

auditar *vt* : audit — **auditor, -tora** *n* : auditor

auditorio *nm* 1 : auditorium 2 PÚBLICO : audience

auge *nm* 1 : peak 2 : (economic) boom

augurar *vt* : predict, foretell — **augurio** *nm* : omen

augusto, -ta *adj* : august

aula *nf* : classroom

aullar {8} *vi* : howl — **aullido** *nm* : howl

aumentar *vt* : increase, raise — *vi* : increase, grow — **aumento** *nm* : increase, rise

aun *adv* 1 : even 2 ~ **así** : even so

aún *adv* 1 : still, yet 2 **más** ~ : furthermore

aunar {8} *vt* : join, combine — **aunarse** *vr* : unite

aunque *conj* 1 : though, although, even if 2 ~ **sea** : at least

aureola *nf* 1 : halo 2 FAMA : aura

auricular *nm* 1 : telephone receiver 2 ~ **es** *nmpl* : headphones

aurora *nf* : dawn

ausentarse *vr* : leave, go away — **ausencia** *nf* : absence — **ausente** *adj* : absent — ~ *nmf* 1 : absentee 2 : missing person (in law)

auspicios *nmpl* : sponsorship, auspices

austero, -ra *adj* : austere — **austeridad** *nf* : austerity

austral *adj* : southern

australiano, -na *adj* : Australian

austriaco *or* **austríaco, -ca** *adj* : Austrian

auténtico, -ca *adj* : authentic, genuine — **autenticidad** *nf* : authenticity

auto *nm* : auto, car

autoayuda *nf* : self-help

autobiografía *nf* : autobiography — **autobiográfico, -ca** *adj* : autobiographical

autobús *nm, pl* **-buses** : bus

autocompasión *nf* : self-pity

autocontrol *nm* : self-control

autocracia *nf* : autocracy

autóctono, -na *adj* : indigenous, native

autodefensa *nf* : self-defense

autodidacta *adj* : self-taught

autodisciplina *nf* : self-discipline

autoestop → **autostop**

autografiar *vt* : autograph — **autógrafo** *nm* : autograph

autómata *nm* : automaton

automático, -ca *adj* : automatic — **automatización** *nf, pl* **-ciones** : automation — **automatizar** {21} *vt* : automate

automotor, -triz *adj, fpl* **-trices** : self-propelled

automóvil *nm* : automobile — **automovilista** *nmf* : motorist — **automovilístico, -ca** *adj* : automobile, car

autonomía *nf* : autonomy — **autónomo, -ma** *adj* : autonomous

autopista *nf* : expressway, highway

autopropulsado, -da *adj* : self-propelled

autopsia *nf* : autopsy

autor, -tora *n* 1 : author 2 : perpetrator (of a crime)

autoridad *nf* : authority — **autoritario, -ria** *adj* : authoritarian

autorizar {21} *vt* : authorize, approve — **autorización** *nf, pl* **-ciones** : authorization — **autorizado, -da** *adj* 1 PERMITIDO : authorized 2 : authoritative

autorretrato *nm* : self-portrait

autoservicio *nm* 1 : self-service restaurant 2 SUPERMERCADO : supermarket

autostop *nm* 1 : hitchhiking 2 **hacer** ~ : hitchhike — **autostopista** *nmf* : hitchhiker

autosuficiente *adj* : self-sufficient

auxiliar *vt* : aid, assist — ~ *adj* : auxiliary — ~ *nmf* 1 : assistant, helper 2 ~ **de vuelo** : flight attendant — **auxilio** *nm* 1 : aid, assistance 2 **primeros** ~ **s** : first aid

avalancha *nf* : avalanche

avalar *vt* : guarantee, endorse — **aval** *nm* : guarantee, endorsement

avanzar {21} *v* : advance, move forward — **avance** *nm* : advance — **avanzado, -da** *adj* : advanced

avaricia *nf* : greed, avarice — **avaricioso, -sa** *adj* : avaricious, greedy — **avaro, -ra** *adj* : miserly — ~ *n* : miser

avasallar *vt* : overpower, subjugate — **avasallador, -dora** *adj* : overwhelming

ave *nf* : bird

avecinarse *vr* : approach

avecindarse *vr* : settle, take up residence

avellana *nf* : hazelnut

avena *nf* 1 : oats *pl* 2 *or* **harina de** ~ : oatmeal

avenida *nf* : avenue

avenir {87} *vt* : reconcile, harmonize — **avenirse** *vr* : agree, come to terms

aventajar *vt* : be ahead of, surpass

aventar {55} *vt* 1 : fan 2 : winnow (grain) 3 *Lat* : throw, toss

aventurar *vt* : venture, risk — **aventurarse** *vr* : take a risk — **aventura** *nf* 1 : adventure 2 RIESGO : risk 3 AMORÍO : love affair — **aventurado, -da** *adj*

: risky — **aventurero, -ra** *adj* : adventurous — **~** *n* : adventurer

avergonzar {9} *vt* : shame, embarrass — **avergonzarse** *vr* : be ashamed, be embarrassed

averiar {85} *vt* : damage — **averiarse** *vr* : break down — **avería** *nf* 1 : damage 2 : breakdown (of an automobile) — **averiado, -da** *adj* 1 : damaged, faulty 2 : broken down (of an automobile)

averiguar {10} *vt* 1 : find out 2 INVESTIGAR : investigate — **averiguación** *nf, pl* **-clones** : investigation, inquiry

aversión *nf, pl* **-siones** : aversion, dislike

avestruz *nm, pl* **-truces** : ostrich

aviación *nf, pl* **-clones** : aviation — **aviador, -dora** *n* : aviator

aviar {85} *vt* : prepare, make ready

ávido, -da *adj* : eager, avid — **avidez** *nf, pl* **-deces** : eagerness

avío *nm* 1 : preparation, provision 2 **~s** *nmpl* : gear, equipment

avión *nm, pl* **aviones** : airplane — **avioneta** *nf* : light airplane

avisar *vt* 1 : notify 2 ADVERTIR : warn — **aviso** *nm* 1 : notice 2 ADVERTENCIA : warning 3 *Lat* : advertisement, ad 4 **estar sobre ~** : be on the alert

avispa *nf* : wasp — **avispón** *nm, pl* **-pones** : hornet

avispado, -da *adj fam* : clever, sharp

avistar *vt* : catch sight of

avivar *vt* 1 : enliven, brighten 2 : arouse (desire, etc.) 3 : intensify (pain)

axila *nf* : underarm, armpit

axioma *nm* : axiom

ay *interj* 1 : oh! 2 : ouch!, ow!

ayer *adv* : yesterday — **~** *nm* : yesteryear, days gone by

ayote *nm Lat* : pumpkin

ayudar *vt* : help, assist — **ayudarse** *vr* **~ de** : make use of — **ayuda** *nf* : help, assistance — **ayudante** *nmf* : helper, assistant

ayunar *vi* : fast — **ayunas** *nfpl* **en ~** : fasting — **ayuno** *nm* : fast

ayuntamiento *nm* 1 : town hall, city hall (building) 2 : town or city council

azabache *nm* : jet

azada *nf* : hoe — **azadonar** *vt* : hoe

azafata *nf* : stewardess *f*

azafrán *nm, pl* **-franes** : saffron

azalea *nf* : azalea

azar *nm* 1 : chance 2 **al ~** : at random — **azaroso, -sa** *adj* : hazardous (of a journey, etc.), eventful (of a life)

azorar *vt* 1 : alarm 2 DESCONCERTAR : embarrass — **azorarse** *vr* : get embarrassed

azotar *vt* : beat, whip — **azote** *nm* 1 LÁTIGO : whip, lash 2 CALAMIDAD : scourge

azotea *nf* : flat or terraced roof

azteca *adj* : Aztec

azúcar *nmf* : sugar — **azucarado, -da** *adj* : sugary — **azucarera** *nf* : sugar bowl — **azucarero, -ra** *adj* : sugar

azufre *nm* : sulphur

azul *adj & nm* : blue — **azulado, -da** *adj* : bluish

azulejo *nm* 1 : ceramic tile 2 *Lat* : bluebird

azur *n* : azure, sky blue

azuzar {21} *vt* : incite, urge on

B

b *nf* : b, second letter of the Spanish alphabet

babear *vi* : drool, slobber — **baba** *nf* : saliva, drool

babel *nmf* : bedlam

babero *nm* : bib

babor *nm* : port (side)

babosa *nf* : slug — **baboso, -sa** *adj* 1 : slimy 2 *Lat fam* : silly

babucha *nf* : slipper

babuino *nm* : baboon

bacalao *nm* : cod

bache *nm* 1 : pothole, rut 2 DIFICULTADES : bad time

bachiller *nmf* : high school graduate — **bachillerato** *nm* : high school diploma

bacon *nm Spain* : bacon

bacteria *nf* : bacterium

bagaje *nm* : baggage, luggage

bagatela *nf* : trinket

bagre *nm* : catfish

bahía *nf* : bay

bailar *v* : dance — **bailarín, -rina** *n, mpl* **-rines** : dancer — **baile** *nm* 1 : dance 2 FIESTA : dance party, ball

bajar *vt* 1 : bring down, lower 2 DESCENDER : go down, come down — *vi* : descend, drop — **bajarse** *vr* **~ de** : get out of, get off — **baja** *nf* 1 : fall, drop 2 CESE : dismissal 3 PERMISO : sick leave 4 : (military) casualty — **bajada** *nf* 1 : descent, drop 2 PENDIENTE : slope

bajeza *nf* : lowness, meanness
bajío *nm* : sandbank, shoal
bajo, -ja *adj* **1** : low, lower **2** : short (in stature) **3** : soft, faint (of sounds) **4** VIL : base, vile — **bajo** *adv* **1** : low **2** habla más ~ : speak more softly — ~ *nm* **1** : ground floor **2** DOBLADILLO : hem **3** : bass (in music) — ~ *prep* : under, below — **bajón** *nm, pl* **-jones** : sharp drop, slump
bala *nf* **1** : bullet **2** : bale (of cotton, etc.)
balada *nf* : ballad
balancear *vt* **1** : balance **2** : swing (one's arms, etc.), rock (a boat) — **balancearse** *vr* : swing, sway — **balance** *nm* **1** : balance **2** : balance sheet — **balanceo** *nm* : swaying, rocking
balancín *nm, pl* **-cines 1** : seesaw **2** MECEDORA : rocking chair
balanza *nf* : scales *pl*, balance
balar *vi* : bleat
balaustrada *nf* : balustrade, banister
balazo *nm* **1** DISPARO : shot **2** : bullet wound
balbucear *vi* **1** : stammer, stutter **2** : babble (of a baby) — **balbuceo** *nm* : stammering, muttering, babbling
balcón *nm, pl* **-cones** : balcony
balde *nm* **1** : bucket, pail **2** en ~ : in vain
baldío, -día *adj* **1** : uncultivated **2** INÚTIL : useless — **baldío** *nm* : wasteland
baldosa *nf* : floor tile
balear *vt* *Lat* : shoot (at) — **baleo** *nm* *Lat* : shot, shooting
balido *nm* : bleat
balín *nm, pl* **-lines** : pellet
balística *nf* : ballistics — **balístico, -ca** *adj* : ballistic
baliza *nf* **1** : buoy **2** : beacon (for aircraft)
ballena *nf* : whale
ballesta *nf* **1** : crossbow **2** : spring (of an automobile)
ballet *nm* : ballet
balneario *nm* : spa
balompié *nm* : soccer
balón *nm, pl* **-lones** : ball — **baloncesto** *nm* : basketball — **balonvolea** *nm* : volleyball
balsa *nf* **1** : raft **2** ESTANQUE : pond, pool
bálsamo *nm* : balsam, balm — **balsámico, -ca** *adj* : soothing
baluarte *nm* : bulwark, bastion
bambolear *vi* : sway, swing — **bambolearse** *vr* : sway, rock
bambú *nm, pl* **-búes** *or* **-bús** : bamboo
banal *adj* : banal
banana *nf* *Lat* : banana — **banano** *nm* *Lat* : banana
banca *nf* **1** : banking **2** BANCO : bench — **bancario, -ria** *adj* : bank, banking

— **bancarrota** *nf* : bankruptcy —
banco *nm* **1** : bank **2** BANCA : stool, bench, pew **3** : school (of fish)
banda *nf* **1** : band, strip **2** : band (in music) **3** PANDILLA : gang **4** : flock (of birds) **5** ~ **sonora** : sound track — **bandada** *nf* : flock (of birds), school (of fish)
bandazo *nm* : lurch
bandeja *nf* : tray, platter
bandera *nf* : flag, banner
banderilla *nf* : banderilla
banderín *nm, pl* **-rines** : pennant, small flag
bandido, -da *n* : bandit
bando *nm* **1** : proclamation, edict **2** PARTIDO : faction, side
bandolero, -ra *n* : bandit
banjo *nm* : banjo
banquero, -ra *n* : banker
banqueta *nf* **1** : stool, footstool **2** *Lat* : sidewalk
banquete *nm* : banquet
bañar *vt* **1** : bathe, wash **2** SUMERGIR : immerse **3** CUBRIR : coat, cover — **bañarse** *vr* **1** : take a bath **2** : go swimming — **bañera** *nf* : bathtub — **bañista** *nmf* : bather — **baño** *nm* **1** : bath, swim **2** BAÑERA : bathtub **3** ¿donde está el ~? : where is the bathroom? **4** ~ **María** : double boiler
baqueta *nf* **1** : ramrod **2** ~s *nfpl* : drumsticks
bar *nm* : bar, tavern
barajar *vt* **1** : shuffle (cards) **2** CONSIDERAR : consider — **baraja** *nf* : deck of cards
baranda *nf* : rail, railing — **barandal** *nm* : handrail, banister
barato, -ta *adj* : cheap — **barato** *adv* : cheap, cheaply — **barata** *nf* *Lat* : sale, bargain — **baratija** *nf* : trinket — **baratillo** *nm* : secondhand store, flea market
barba *nf* **1** : beard, stubble **2** BARBILLA : chin
barbacoa *nf* : barbecue
barbaridad *nf* **1** : barbarity, cruelty **2** ¡qué ~! : that's outrageous! — **barbarie** *nf* : barbarism, savagery — **bárbaro, -ra** *adj* : barbaric
barbecho *nm* : fallow land
barbero, -ra *n* : barber — **barbería** *nf* : barbershop
barbilla *nf* : chin
barbudo, -da *adj* : bearded
barca *nf* **1** : boat **2** ~ **de pasaje** : ferryboat — **barcaza** *nf* : barge — **barco** *nm* : boat, ship
barítono *nm* : baritone

barman *nm* : bartender
barnizar {21} *vt* **1** : varnish **2** : glaze (ceramics) — **barniz** *nm, pl* **-nices 1** : varnish **2** : glaze (on ceramics)
barómetro *nm* : barometer
barón *nm, pl* **-rones** : baron — **baronesa** *nf* : baroness
barquero *nm* : boatman
barquillo *nm* : wafer, cone
barra *nf* **1** : bar, rod, stick **2** : counter (of a bar, etc.)
barraca *nf* **1** : hut, cabin **2** CASETA : booth, stall
barranco *nm or* **barranca** *nf* : ravine, gorge, gully
barredera *nf* : street-sweeping machine
barrenar *vt* : drill — **barrena** *nf* : drill, auger
barrer *v* : sweep
barrera *nf* : barrier
barreta *nf* : crowbar
barriada *nf* : district, quarter
barrica *nf* : cask, keg
barricada *nf* : barricade
barrido *nm* : sweep, sweeping
barriga *nf* : belly
barril *nm* **1** : barrel, keg **2 de ~** : draft
barrio *nm* **1** : neighborhood **2 ~ bajo** : slums *pl*
barro *nm* **1** : mud **2** ARCILLA : clay **3** GRANO : pimple, blackhead — **barroso, -sa** *adj* : muddy
barrote *nm* : bar (on a window)
barrunto *nm* **1** : suspicion **2** INDICIO : sign, indication
bártulos *nmpl* : things, belongings
barullo *nm* : racket, ruckus
basa *nf* : base, pedestal — **basar** *vt* : base — **basarse** *vr* **~ en** : be based on
báscula *nf* : scales *pl*
base *nf* **1** : base **2** FUNDAMENTO : basis, foundation **3 ~ de datos** : database — **básico, -ca** *adj* : basic
basquetbol *or* **básquetbol** *nm Lat* : basketball
bastar *vi* : be enough, suffice — **bastante** *adv* **1** : fairly, rather **2** SUFICIENTE : enough — **~** *adj* : enough, sufficient — **~** *pron* : enough
bastardo, -da *adj & n* : bastard
bastidor *nm* **1** : frame **2** : wing (in theater) **3 entre ~es** : behind the scenes, backstage
bastilla *nf* : hem
bastión *nf, pl* **-tiones** : bastion, stronghold
basto, -ta *adj* : coarse, rough
bastón *nm, pl* **-tones 1** : cane, walking stick **2** : baton (in parades)

basura *nf* : garbage, rubbish — **basurero, -ra** *n* : garbage collector
bata *nf* **1** : bathrobe, housecoat **2** : smock (of a doctor, laboratory worker, etc.)
batallar *vi* : battle, fight — **batalla** *nf* **1** : battle, fight, struggle **2 de ~** : ordinary, everyday — **batallón** *nm, pl* **-llones** : battalion
batata *nf* : yam, sweet potato
batear *v* : bat, hit — **bate** *nm* : baseball bat — **bateador, -dora** *n* : batter, hitter
batería *nf* **1** : battery **2** : drums *pl* **3 ~ de cocina** : kitchen utensils *pl*
batir *vt* **1** : beat, whip **2** DERRIBAR : knock down — **batirse** *vr* : fight — **batido** *nm* : milk shake — **batidor** *nm* : eggbeater, whisk — **batidora** *nf* : electric mixer
batuta *nf* : baton
baúl *nm* : trunk, chest
bautismo *nm* : baptism — **bautismal** *adj* : baptismal — **bautizar** {21} *vt* : baptize — **bautizo** *nm* : baptism, christening
baya *nf* : berry
bayeta *nf* : cleaning cloth
bayoneta *nf* : bayonet
bazar *nm* : bazaar
bazo *nm* : spleen
bazofia *nf fam* : rubbish, hogwash
beato, -ta *adj* : blessed
bebé *nm* : baby
beber *v* : drink — **bebedero** *nm* : watering trough — **bebedor, -dora** *n* : (heavy) drinker — **bebida** *nf* : drink, beverage — **bebido, -da** *adj* : drunk
beca *nf* : grant, scholarship
becerro, -rra *n* : calf
befa *nf* : jeer, taunt
beige *adj & nm* : beige
beisbol *or* **béisbol** *nm* : baseball — **beisbolista** *nmf* : baseball player
beldad *nf* : beauty
belén *nf, pl* **-lenes** : Nativity scene
belga *adj* : Belgian
beliceño, -ña *adj* : Belizean
bélico, -ca *adj* : military, war — **belicoso, -sa** *adj* : warlike
beligerancia *nf* : belligerence — **beligerante** *adj & nmf* : belligerent
belleza *nf* : beauty — **bello, -lla** *adj* **1** : beautiful **2 bellas artes** : fine arts
bellota *nf* : acorn
bemol *adj & nm* : flat (in music)
bendecir {11} *vt* **1** : bless **2 ~ la mesa** : say grace — **bendición** *nf, pl* **-ciones** : benediction, blessing — **bendito, -ta** *adj* **1** : blessed, holy **2** DI-

CHOSO : fortunate **3 ¡bendito sea Dios!** : thank goodness!
benefactor, -tora n : benefactor
beneficiar vt : benefit, assist — **beneficiarse** vr : benefit, profit — **beneficiario, -ria** n : beneficiary — **beneficio** nm **1** : gain, profit **2** BIEN : benefit — **beneficioso, -sa** adj : beneficial — **benéfico, -ca** adj : charitable
benemérito, -ta adj : worthy
beneplácito nm : approval, consent
benévolo, -la adj : benevolent, kind — **benevolencia** nf : benevolence, kindness
bengala nf or **luz de ~** : flare
benigno, -na adj **1** : mild **2** : benign (in medicine) — **benignidad** nf : mildness, kindness
benjamín, -mina n, mpl **-mines** : youngest child
beodo, -da adj & n : drunk
berenjena nf : eggplant
berrear vi **1** : bellow, low **2** : bawl, howl (of a person) — **berrido** nm **1** : bellowing **2** : howl, scream (of a person)
berro nm : watercress
berza nf : cabbage
besar vt : kiss — **besarse** vr : kiss (each other) — **beso** nm : kiss
bestia nf : beast, animal — **bestial** adj : bestial, brutal — **bestialidad** nf : brutality
betabel nm Lat : beet
betún nm, pl **-tunes** : shoe polish
bianual adj : biannual
biberón nm, pl **-rones** : baby's bottle
Biblia nf : Bible — **bíblico, -ca** adj : biblical
bibliografía nf : bibliography — **bibliográfico, -ca** adj : bibliographic, bibliographical
biblioteca nf : library — **bibliotecario, -ria** n : librarian
bicarbonato nm **~ de soda** : baking soda
bicentenario nm : bicentennial
bíceps nms & pl : biceps
bicho nm : small animal, bug
bicicleta nf : bicycle — **bici** nf fam : bike
bicolor adj : two-tone
bidón nm, pl **-dones** : large can, drum
bien adv **1** : well, good **2** CORRECTAMENTE : correctly, right **3** MUY : very, quite **4** DE BUENA GANA : willingly **5 ~ que** : although **6 más ~** : rather — **bien** adj **1** : all right, well **2** AGRADABLE : pleasant, nice **3** SATISFACTORIO : satisfactory **4** CORRECTO : correct, right — **bien** nm **1** : good **2 ~es** nmpl : property, goods

bienal adj & nf : biennial
bienaventurado, -da adj : blessed, fortunate
bienestar nm : welfare, well-being
bienhechor, -chora n : benefactor
bienintencionado, -da adj : well-meaning
bienvenido, -da adj : welcome — **bienvenida** nf **1** : welcome **2 dar la ~ a** : welcome (s.o.)
bife nm Lat : steak
bifocales nmpl : bifocals
bifurcarse {72} vr : fork — **bifurcación** nf, pl **-ciones** : fork, branch
bigamia nf : bigamy
bigote nm **1** : mustache **2 ~s** nmpl : whiskers (of an animal)
bikini nm : bikini
bilingüe adj : bilingual
bilis nf : bile
billar nm : pool, billiards
billete nm **1** : bill, banknote **2** BOLETO : ticket — **billetera** nf : billfold, wallet
billón nm, pl **-llones** : trillion
bimensual, -suale adj : twice a month — **bimestral** adj : bimonthly
binario, -ria adj : binary
bingo nm : bingo
binoculares nmpl : binoculars
biodegradable adj : biodegradable
biofísica nf : biophysics
biografía nf : biography — **biográfico, -ca** adj : biographical — **biógrafo, -fa** n : biographer
biología nf : biology — **biológico, -ca** adj : biological, biologic — **biólogo, -ga** n : biologist
biombo nm : folding screen
biomecánica nf : biomechanics
biopsia nf : biopsy
bioquímica nf : biochemistry — **bioquímico, -ca** adj : biochemical
biotecnología nf : biotechnology
bipartidista adj : bipartisan
bípedo nm : biped
biquini → bikini
birlar vt fam : swipe, pinch
bis adv **1** : twice (in music) **2** : A (in an address) — **~** nm : encore
bisabuelo, -la n : great-grandfather m, great-grandmother f
bisagra nf : hinge
bisecar {72} vt : bisect
biselar vt : bevel
bisexual adj : bisexual
bisiesto adj **año ~** : leap year
bisnieto, -ta n : great-grandson m, great-granddaughter f
bisonte nm : bison, buffalo
bisoño, -ña n : novice

bistec *nm* : steak

bisturí *nm* : scalpel

bisutería *nf* : costume jewelry

bit *nm* : bit (unit of information)

bizco, -ca *adj* : cross-eyed

bizcocho *nm* : sponge cake

bizquear *vi* : squint — **bizquera** *nf* : squint

blanco, -ca *adj* : white — **blanco, -ca** *n* : white person — **blanco** *nm* **1** : white **2** DIANA : target, bull's-eye **3** : blank (space) — **blancura** *nf* : whiteness

blandir {1} *vt* : wave, brandish

blando, -da *adj* **1** : soft, tender **2** DÉBIL : weak-willed **3** INDULGENTE : lenient — **blandura** *nf* **1** : softness, tenderness **2** DEBILIDAD : weakness **3** INDULGENCIA : leniency

blanquear *vt* **1** : whiten, bleach **2** : launder (money) — *vi* : turn white — **blanqueador** *nm Lat* : bleach

blasfemar *vi* : blaspheme — **blasfemia** *nf* : blasphemy — **blasfemo, -ma** *adj* : blasphemous

bledo *nm* **no me importa un ~** *fam* : I couldn't care less

blindaje *nm* : armor, armor plating — **blindado, -da** *adj* : armored

bloc *nm, pl* **blocs** : (writing) pad

bloquear *vt* **1** OBSTRUIR : block, obstruct **2** : blockade — **bloque** *nm* **1** : block **2** : bloc (in politics) — **bloqueo** *nm* **1** OBSTRUCCIÓN : blockage **2** : blockade

blusa *nf* : blouse — **blusón** *nm, pl* **-sones** : smock

boato *nm* : showiness

bobina *nf* : bobbin, reel

bobo, -ba *adj* : silly, stupid — **~** *n* : fool, simpleton

boca *nf* **1** : mouth **2** ENTRADA : entrance **3** **~ arriba** : faceup **4** **~ abajo** : facedown, prone **5** **~ de riego** : hydrant

bocacalle *nf* : entrance (to a street)

bocado *nm* **1** : bite, mouthful **2** : bit (of a bridle) — **bocadillo** *nm Spain* : sandwich

bocajarro *nm* **a ~** : point-blank

bocallave *nf* : keyhole

bocanada *nf* **1** : swallow, swig **2** : puff, gust (of smoke, wind, etc.)

boceto *nm* : sketch, outline

bochorno *nm* **1** VERGÜENZA : embarrassment **2** : muggy weather — **bochornoso, -sa** *adj* **1** VERGONZOSO : embarrassing **2** : muggy, sultry

bocina *nf* **1** : horn **2** : mouthpiece (of a telephone) — **bocinazo** *nm* : honk, toot

boda *nf* : wedding

bodega *nf* **1** : wine cellar **2** : warehouse

3 : hold (of a ship or airplane) **4** *Lat* : grocery store

bofetear *vt* : slap — **bofetada** *nf or* **bofetón** *nm* : slap (in the face)

boga *nf* : fashion, vogue

bohemio, -mia *adj & n* : bohemian

boicotear *vt* : boycott — **boicot** *nm, pl* **-cots** : boycott

boina *nf* : beret

bola *nf* **1** : ball **2** *fam* : fib

bolera *nf* : bowling alley

boleta *nf Lat* : ticket — **boletería** *nf Lat* : ticket office

boletín *nm, pl* **-tines** **1** : bulletin **2** **~ de noticias** : news release

boleto *nm* : ticket

boliche *nm* **1** : bowling **2** BOLERA : bowling alley

bolígrafo *nm* : ballpoint pen

bolillo *nm* : bobbin

boliviano, -na *adj* : Bolivian

bollo *nm* : bun, sweet roll

bolo *nm* **1** : bowling pin **2** **~s** *nmpl* : bowling

bolsa *nf* **1** : bag **2** *Lat* : pocketbook, purse **3** **la Bolsa** : the stock market — **bolsillo** *nm* : pocket — **bolso** *nm Spain* : pocketbook, handbag

bomba *nf* **1** : bomb **2** **~ de gasolina** : gas pump

bombachos *nmpl* : baggy trousers

bombardear *vt* : bomb, bombard — **bombardeo** *nm* : bombing, bombardment — **bombardero** *nm* : bomber (airplane)

bombear *vt* : pump — **bombero, -ra** *n* : firefighter

bombilla *nf* : lightbulb — **bombillo** *nm Lat* : lightbulb

bombo *nm* **1** : bass drum **2** **a ~s y platillos** : with a great fanfare

bombón *nm, pl* **-bones** : candy, chocolate

bonachón, -chona *adj, mpl* **-chones** *fam* : good-natured

bonanza *nf* **1** : fair weather (at sea) **2** PROSPERIDAD : prosperity

bondad *nf* : goodness, kindness — **bondadoso, -sa** *adj* : kind, good

boniato *nm* : sweet potato

bonificación *nf, pl* **-ciones** **1** : bonus, extra **2** DESCUENTO : discount

bonito, -ta *adj* : pretty, lovely

bono *nm* **1** : bond **2** VALE : voucher

boquear *vi* : gasp — **boqueada** *nf* : gasp

boquerón *nm, pl* **-rones** : anchovy

boquete *nm* : gap, opening

boquiabierto, -ta *adj* : open-mouthed, speechless

boquilla *nf* : mouthpiece (of a musical instrument)

borbollar *vi* : bubble

borbotar *or* **borbotear** *vi* : boil, bubble, gurgle — **borbotón** *nm, pl* **-tones** 1 : spurt 2 **salir a borbotones** : gush out

bordar *v* : embroider — **bordado** *nm* : embroidery, needlework

borde *nm* 1 : border, edge 2 **al ~ de** : on the verge of — **bordear** *vt* : border — **bordillo** *nm* : curb

bordo *nm* **a ~** : aboard, on board

borla *nf* 1 : pom-pom, tassel 2 : powder puff

borracho, -cha *adj & n* : drunk — **borrachera** *nf* : drunkenness

borrar *vt* : erase, blot out — **borrador** *nm* 1 : rough draft 2 : eraser (for a blackboard)

borrascoso, -sa *adj* : stormy

borrego, -ga *n* : lamb, sheep — **borrego** *nm Lat* : false rumor, hoax

borrón *nm, pl* **-rrones** 1 : smudge, blot 2 **~ y cuenta nueva** : let's forget about it — **borroso, -sa** *adj* 1 : blurry, smudgy 2 INDISTINTO : vague, hazy

bosque *nm* : woods, forest — **boscoso, -sa** *adj* : wooded

bosquejar *vt* : sketch (out) — **bosquejo** *nm* : outline, sketch

bostezar {21} *vi* : yawn — **bostezo** *nm* : yawn

bota *nf* : boot

botánica *nf* : botany — **botánico, -ca** *adj* : botanical

botar *vt* 1 : throw, hurl 2 *Lat* : throw away 3 : launch (a ship) — *vi* : bounce

bote *nm* 1 : small boat 2 *Spain* : can 3 TARRO : jar 4 SALTO : bounce, jump

botella *nf* : bottle

botín *nm, pl* **-tines** 1 : ankle boot 2 DESPOJOS : booty, plunder

botiquín *nm, pl* **-quines** 1 : medicine cabinet 2 : first-aid kit

botón *nm, pl* **-tones** 1 : button 2 YEMA : bud — **botones** *nmfs & pl* : bellhop

botulismo *nm* : botulism

boutique *nf* : boutique

bóveda *nf* : vault

boxear *vi* : box — **boxeador, -dora** *n* : boxer — **boxeo** *nm* : boxing

boya *nf* : buoy — **boyante** *adj* 1 : buoyant 2 PRÓSPERO : prosperous, thriving

bozal *nm* 1 : muzzle 2 : halter (for a horse)

bracear *vi* 1 : wave one's arms 2 NADAR : swim, crawl

bracero, -ra *n* : day laborer

bragas *nf Spain* : panties

bragueta *nf* : fly, pants zipper

braille *adj & nm* : braille

bramante *nm* : twine, string

bramar *vi* 1 : bellow, roar 2 : howl (of the wind) — **bramido** *nm* : bellow, roar

brandy *nm* : brandy

branquia *nf* : gill

brasa *nf* : ember

brasier *nm Lat* : brassiere

brasileño, -ña *adj* : Brazilian

bravata *nf* 1 : boast, bravado 2 AMENAZO : threat

bravo, -va *adj* 1 : fierce, savage 2 : rough (of the sea) 3 *Lat* : angry — **~** *interj* : bravo!, well done! — **bravura** *nf* 1 FEROCIDAD : fierceness 2 VALENTÍA : bravery

braza *nf* 1 : breaststroke 2 : fathom (measurement) — **brazada** *nf* : stroke (in swimming)

brazalete *nm* 1 : bracelet 2 : (cloth) armband

brazo *nm* 1 : arm 2 : branch (of a river, etc.) 3 **~ derecho** : right-hand man 4 **~s** *nmpl* : hands, laborers

brea *nf* : tar

brebaje *nm* : concoction

brecha *nf* : breach, gap

brécol *nm* : broccoli

bregar {52} *vi* 1 LUCHAR : struggle 2 TRABAJAR : work hard — **brega** *nf* **andar a la ~** : struggle

breña *nf or* **breñal** *nm* : scrubland, brush

breve *adj* 1 : brief, short 2 **en ~** : shortly, in short — **brevedad** *nf* : brevity, shortness — **brevemente** *adv* : briefly

brezal *nm* : moor, heath — **brezo** *nm* : heather

bricolaje *or* **bricolage** *nm* : do-it-yourself

brida *nf* : bridle

brigada *nf* 1 : brigade 2 EQUIPO : gang, team, squad

brillar *vi* : shine, sparkle — **brillante** *adj* : brilliant, shiny — **~** *nm* : diamond — **brillantez** *nf* : brilliance — **brillo** *nm* 1 : luster, shine 2 ESPLENDOR : splendor — **brilloso, -sa** *adj* : shiny

brincar {72} *vi* : jump about, frolic — **brinco** *nm* : jump, skip

brindar *vi* : drink a toast — *vt* : offer, provide — **brindarse** *vr* : offer one's assistance — **brindis** *nm* : drink, toast

brío *nm* 1 : force, determination 2 ÁNIMO : spirit, verve — **brioso, -sa** *adj* : spirited, lively

brisa *nf* : breeze

británico, -ca *adj* : British
brizna *nf* **1** : strand, thread **2** : blade (of grass)
brocado *nm* : brocade
brocha *nf* : paintbrush
broche *nm* **1** : fastener, clasp **2** ALFILER : brooch
brocheta *nf* : skewer
brócoli *nm* : broccoli
bromear *vi* : joke, fool around — **broma** *nf* : joke, prank — **bromista** *adj* : fun-loving, joking — ~ *nmf* : joker, prankster
bronca *nf fam* : fight, row
bronce *nm* : bronze — **bronceado, -da** *adj* : suntanned — **bronceado** *nm* : tan — **broncearse** *vr* : get a suntan
bronco, -ca *adj* **1** : harsh, rough **2** : untamed, wild (of a horse)
bronquitis *nf* : bronchitis
broqueta *nf* : skewer
brotar *vi* **1** : bud, sprout **2** : stream, gush (of a river, tears, etc.) **3** : arise (of feelings, etc.) **4** : break out (in medicine) — **brote** *nm* **1** : outbreak **2** : sprout, bud, shoot (of plants)
brujería *nf* : witchcraft — **bruja** *nf* **1** : witch **2** *fam* : old hag — **brujo** *nm* : warlock, sorcerer — **brujo, -ja** *adj* : bewitching
brújula *nf* : compass
bruma *nf* : haze, mist — **brumoso, -sa** *adj* : hazy, misty
bruñir {38} *vt* : burnish, polish
brusco, -ca *adj* **1** SÚBITO : sudden, abrupt **2** TOSCO : brusque, rough — **brusquedad** *nf* : abruptness, brusqueness
brutal *adj* : brutal — **brutalidad** *nf* : brutality
bruto, -ta *adj* **1** : brutish, stupid **2** : crude (of petroleum, etc.), uncut (of diamonds) **3 peso** ~ : gross weight — ~ *n* : brute
bucal *adj* : oral
bucear *vi* **1** : dive, swim underwater **2** ~ **en** : delve into — **buceo** *nm* : (underwater) diving
bucle *nm* : curl
budín *nm, pl* **-dines** : pudding
budismo *nm* : Buddhism — **budista** *adj & nmf* : Buddhist
buenamente *adv* **1** : easily **2** VOLUNTARIAMENTE : willingly
buenaventura *nf* **1** : good luck **2 decir la** ~ **a uno** : tell s.o.'s fortune
bueno, -na *adj* (**buen** *before masculine singular nouns*) **1** : good **2** AMABLE : kind **3** APROPIADO : appropriate **4** SALUDABLE : well, healthy **5** : nice,

fine (of weather) **6 buenos días** : hello, good day **7 buenas noches** : good night **8 buenas tardes** : good afternoon, good evening — **bueno** *interj* : OK!, all right!
buey *nm* : ox, steer
búfalo *nm* : buffalo
bufanda *nf* : scarf
bufar *vi* : snort — **bufido** *nm* : snort
bufet *or* **bufé** *nm* : buffet-style meal
bufete *nm* **1** : law practice **2** MESA : writing desk
bufo, -fa *adj* : comic — **bufón, -fona** *n, mpl* **-fones** : buffoon, jester — **bufonada** *nf* : wisecrack
buhardilla *nf* : attic, garret
búho *nm* : owl
buitre *nm* : vulture
bujía *nf* : spark plug
bulbo *nm* : bulb (of a plant)
bulevar *nm* : boulevard
búlgaro, -ra *adj* : Bulgarian
bulla *nf* : uproar, racket
bulldozer *nm* : bulldozer
bullicio *nm* **1** : uproar **2** AJETREO : hustle and bustle — **bullicioso, -sa** *adj* : noisy, boisterous
bullir {38} *vi* **1** : boil **2** AJETREARSE : bustle, stir
bulto *nm* **1** : package, bundle **2** VOLUMEN : bulk, size **3** FORMA : form, shape **4** PROTUBERANCIA : lump, swelling
bumerán *nm, pl* **-ranes** : boomerang
buñuelo *nm* : fried pastry
buque *nm* : ship
burbujear *vi* : bubble — **burbuja** *nf* : bubble
burdel *nm* : brothel
burdo, -da *adj* : coarse, rough
burgués, -guesa *adj & n, mpl* **-gueses** : bourgeois — **burguesía** *nf* : bourgeoisie
burlar *vt* : trick, deceive — **burlarse** *vr* ~ **de** : make fun of — **burla** *nf* **1** MOFA : mockery, ridicule **2** BROMA : joke, trick
burlesco, -ca *adj* : comic, funny
burlón, -lona *adj, mpl* **-lones** : mocking
burocracia *nf* : bureaucracy — **burócrata** *nmf* : bureaucrat — **burocrático, -ca** *adj* : bureaucratic
burro, -rra *n* **1** : donkey **2** *fam* : dunce — ~ *adj* : stupid — **burro** *nm* **1** : sawhorse **2** *Lat* : stepladder
bus *nm* : bus
buscar {72} *vt* **1** : look for, seek **2 ir a** ~ **a uno** : fetch s.o. — *vi* : search — **busca** *nf* : search — **búsqueda** *nf* : search

busto *nm* : bust (in sculpture)
butaca *nf* **1** : armchair **2** : (theater) seat
butano *nm* : butane

buzo *nm* : diver
buzón *nm*, *pl* **-zones** : mailbox
byte ['bait] *nm* : byte

C

c *nf* : c, third letter of the Spanish alphabet
cabal *adj* **1** : exact **2** COMPLETO : complete — **cabales** *nmpl* **no estar en sus ~** : not be in one's right mind
cabalgar {52} *vi* : ride — **cabalgata** *nf* : cavalcade
caballa *nf* : mackerel
caballería *nf* **1** : cavalry **2** CABALLO : horse, mount — **caballeriza** *nf* : stable
caballero *nm* **1** : gentleman **2** : knight (rank) — **caballerosidad** *nf* : chivalry — **caballeroso, -sa** *adj* : chivalrous
caballete *nm* **1** : ridge (of a roof) **2** : easel (for a canvas) **3** : bridge (of the nose)
caballito *nm* **1** : rocking horse **2 ~s** *nmpl* : merry-go-round
caballo *nm* **1** : horse **2** : knight (in chess) **3 ~ de fuerza** : horsepower
cabaña *nf* : cabin, hut
cabaret *nm*, *pl* **-rets** : nightclub, cabaret
cabecear *vi* **1** : shake one's head, nod **2** : pitch, lurch (of a boat)
cabecera *nf* **1** : head (of a bed, etc.) **2** : heading (in a text) **3 médico de ~** : family doctor
cabecilla *nmf* : ringleader
cabello *nm* : hair — **cabelludo, -da** *adj* : hairy
caber {12} *vi* **1** : fit, go (into) **2 no cabe duda** : there's no doubt
cabestro *nm* : halter
cabeza *nf* **1** : head **2 de ~** : head first — **cabezada** *nf* **1** : butt (of the head) **2 dar ~s** : nod off
cabezal *nm* : bolster, headrest
cabida *nf* **1** : room, capacity **2 dar ~ a** : accomodate, find room for
cabina *nf* **1** : booth **2** : cab (of a truck, etc.) **3** : cabin, cockpit (of an airplane)
cabizbajo, -ja *adj* : downcast
cable *nm* : cable
cabo *nm* **1** : end, stub **2** TROZO : bit **3** : corporal (in the military) **4** : cape (in geography) **5 al fin y al ~** : after all **6 llevar a ~** : carry out, do
cabra *nf* : goat

cabriola *nf* **1** : leap, skip **2 hacer ~s** : prance around
cabrito *nm* : kid (goat)
cacahuate *or* **cacahuete** *nm* : peanut
cacao *nm* **1** : cacao (tree) **2** : cocoa (drink)
cacarear *vi* : crow, cackle — *vt fam* : boast about
cacería *nf* : hunt
cacerola *nf* : pan, saucepan
cacharro *nm* **1** *fam* : thing, piece of junk **2** *fam* : jalopy **3 ~s** *nmpl* : pots and pans
cachear *vt* : search, frisk
cachemir *nm* *or* **cachemira** *nf* : cashmere
cachete *nm* *Lat* : cheek — **cachetada** *nf Lat* : slap
cacho *nm* **1** *fam* : piece, bit **2** *Lat* : horn
cachorro, -rra *n* **1** : cub **2** PERRITO : puppy
cactus *or* **cacto** *nm* : cactus
cada *adj* : each, every
cadalso *nm* : scaffold
cadáver *nm* : corpse
cadena *nf* **1** : chain **2** : (television) channel **3 ~ de montaje** : assembly line
cadencia *nf* : cadence
cadera *nf* : hip
cadete *nmf* : cadet
caducar {72} *vi* : expire — **caducidad** *nf* : expiration
caer {13} *vi* **1** : fall, drop **2 ~ bien a uno** : be to one's liking **3 dejar ~** : drop **4 me cae bien** : I like her, I like him — **caerse** *vr* : drop, fall (down)
café *nm* **1** : coffee **2** : café — *adj Lat* : brown — **cafetera** *nf* : coffeepot — **cafetería** *nf* : coffee shop, cafeteria — **cafeína** *nf* : caffeine
caída *nf* **1** : fall, drop **2** PENDIENTE : slope
caimán *nm*, *pl* **-manes** : alligator
caja *nf* **1** : box, case **2** : checkout counter, cashier's desk (in a store) **3 ~ fuerte** : safe **4 ~ registradora** : cash register — **cajero, -ra** *n* **1** : cashier **2** : (bank) teller — **cajetilla** *nf* : pack (of cigarettes) — **cajón** *nm*, *pl* **-jones 1**

: drawer (in furniture) **2** : large box, crate

cajuela *nf Lat* : trunk (of a car)

cal *nf* : lime

cala *nf* : cove

calabaza *nf* **1** : pumpkin, squash, gourd **2 dar —s a** *fam* : give the brush-off to — **calabacín** *nm, pl* **-cines** *or* **calabacita** *nf Lat* : zucchini

calabozo *nm* **1** : prison **2** CELDA : cell

calamar *nm* : squid

calambre *nm* **1** ESPASMO : cramp **2** : (electric) shock

calamidad *nf* : calamity

calar *vt* **1** : soak (through) **2** PERFORAR : pierce — **calarse** *vr* : get drenched

calavera *nf* : skull

calcar {72} *vt* **1** : trace **2** IMITAR : copy, imitate

calcetín *nm, pl* **-tines** : sock

calcinar *vt* : char

calcio *nm* : calcium

calcomanía *nf* : decal

calcular *vt* : calculate, estimate — **calculador, -dora** *adj* : calculating — **calculadora** *nf* : calculator — **cálculo** *nm* **1** : calculation **2** : calculus (in mathematics and medicine) **3 ~ biliar** : gallstone

caldera *nf* **1** : cauldron **2** : boiler (for heating, etc.) — **caldo** *nm* : broth, stock

calefacción *nf, pl* **-ciones** : heating, heat

calendario *nm* : calendar

calentar {55} *vt* : heat (up), warm (up) — **calentarse** *vr* : get warm, heat up — **calentador** *nm* : heater — **calentura** *nf* : temperature, fever

calibre *nm* **1** : caliber **2** DIÁMETRO : bore, diameter — **calibrar** *vt* : calibrate

calidad *nf* **1** : quality **2 en ~ de** : as, in the capacity of

cálido, -da *adj* : hot, warm

caidoscopio *nm* : kaleidoscope

caliente *adj* **1** : hot **2** ACALORADO : heated, fiery

calificar {72} *vt* **1** : qualify **2** EVALUAR : rate **3** : grade (an exam, etc.) — **calificación** *nf, pl* **-ciones** **1** : qualification **2** EVALUACIÓN : rating **3** NOTA : grade — **calificativo, -va** *adj* : qualifying — **calificativo** *nm* : qualifier, epithet

caligrafía *nf* : penmanship

calistenia *nf* : calisthenics

cáliz *nm, pl* **-lices** : chalice

caliza *nf* : limestone

callar *vi* : keep quiet, be silent — *vt* **1**

: silence, hush **2** OCULTAR : keep secret — **callarse** *vr* : remain silent — **callado, -da** *adj* : quiet, silent

calle *nf* : street, road — **callejear** *vi* : wander about the streets — **callejero, -ra** *adj* **1** : street **2 perro callejero** : stray dog — **callejón** *nm, pl* **-jones 1** : alley **2 ~ sin salida** : dead-end street

callo *nm* : callus, corn

calma *nf* : calm, quiet — **calmante** *adj* : soothing — ~ *nm* : tranquilizer — **calmar** *vt* : calm, soothe — **calmarse** *vr* : calm down — **calmo, -ma** *adj Lat* : calm — **calmoso, -sa** *adj* **1** : calm **2** LENTO : slow

calor *nm* **1** : heat, warmth **2 tener ~** : be hot — **caloría** *nf* : calorie

calumnia *nf* : slander, libel — **calumniar** *vt* : slander, libel

caluroso, -sa *adj* **1** : hot **2** : warm, enthusiastic (of applause, etc.)

calvo, -va *adj* : bald — **calvicie** *nf* : baldness

calza *nf* : wedge

calzada *nf* : roadway

calzado *nm* : footwear — **calzar** {21} *vt* **1** : wear (shoes) **2** : put shoes on (s.o.)

calzones *nmpl Lat* : panties — **calzoncillos** *nmpl* : underpants, briefs

cama *nf* : bed

camada *nf* : litter, brood

camafeo *nm* : cameo

cámara *nf* **1** : chamber **2** *or* **~ fotográfica** : camera **3** : house (in government)

camarada *nmf* : comrade — **camaradería** *nf* : camaraderie

camarero, -ra *n* **1** : waiter, waitress *f* **2** : steward *m*, stewardess *f* (on a ship, etc.) — **camarera** *nf* : chambermaid *f*

camarón *nm, pl* **-rones** : shrimp

camarote *nm* : cabin, stateroom

cambiar *vt* **1** : change **2** CANJEAR : exchange — *vi* **1** : change **2** : shift gears (of an automobile) — **cambiarse** *vr* **1** : change (clothing) **2** : move (to a new address) — **cambiable** *adj* : changeable — **cambio** *nm* **1** : change **2** CANJE : exchange **3 en ~** : on the other hand

camello *nm* : camel

camilla *nf* : stretcher — **camillero** *nm* : orderly (in a hospital)

caminar *vi* : walk — *vt* : cover (a distance) — **caminata** *nf* : hike

camino *nm* **1** : road, path **2** RUTA : way **3 a medio ~** : halfway (there) **4 ponerse en ~** : set out

camión *nm, pl* **-miones 1** : truck **2** *Lat*

: bus — **camionero, -ra** *n* 1 : truck driver 2 *Lat* : bus driver — **camioneta** *nm* : light truck, van

camisa *nf* 1 : shirt 2 ~ **de fuerza** : straitjacket — **camiseta** *nf* : T-shirt, undershirt — **camisón** *nm, pl* **-sones** : nightshirt, nightgown

camorra *nf fam* : fight, trouble

camote *nm Lat* : sweet potato

campamento *nm* : camp

campana *nf* : bell — **campanada** *nf* : stroke (of a bell), peal — **campanario** *nm* : bell tower — **campanilla** *nf* : (small) bell

campaña *nf* 1 : countryside 2 : (military or political) campaign

campeón, -peona *n, mpl* **-peones** : champion — **campeonato** *nm* : championship

campesino, -na *n* : peasant, farm laborer — **campestre** *adj* : rural, rustic

camping *nm* 1 : campsite 2 **hacer** ~ : go camping

campiña *nf* : countryside

campo *nm* 1 : field 2 CAMPIÑA : countryside, country 3 CAMPAMENTO : camp

camuflaje *nm* : camouflage — **camuflar** *vt* : camouflage

cana *nf* : gray hair

canadiense *adj* : Canadian

canal *nm* 1 : canal 2 MEDIO : channel 3 : (radio or television) channel — **canalizar** {21} *vt* : channel

canalete *nm* : paddle (of a canoe)

canalla *nf* : rabble — ~ *nmf fam* : swine, bastard

canapé *nm* 1 : canapé 2 SOFÁ : sofa, couch

canario *nm* : canary

canasta *nf* : basket — **canasto** *nm* : large basket

cancelar *vt* 1 : cancel 2 : pay off, settle (a debt) — **cancelación** *nf, pl* **-ciones** 1 : cancellation 2 : payment in full (of a debt)

cáncer *nm* : cancer — **canceroso, -sa** *adj* : cancerous

cancha *nf* : court, field (for sports)

canciller *nm* : chancellor

canción *nf, pl* **-ciones** 1 : song 2 ~ **de cuna** : lullaby — **cancionero** *nm* : songbook

candado *nm* : padlock

candela *nf* : candle — **candelabro** *nm* : candelabra — **candelero** *nm* 1 : candlestick 2 **estar en el** ~ : be in the limelight

candente *adj* : red-hot

candidato, -ta *n* : candidate — **candidatura** *nf* : candidacy

cándido, -da *adj* : naïve — **candidez** *nf* 1 : simplicity 2 INGENUIDAD : naïveté

candil *nm* : oil lamp — **candilejas** *nfpl* : footlights

candor *nm* : naïveté, innocence

canela *nf* : cinnamon

cangrejo *nm* : crab

canguro *nm* : kangaroo

caníbal *nmf* : cannibal — **canibalismo** *nm* : cannibalism

canicas *nfpl* : (game of) marbles

canino, -na *adj* : canine — **canino** *nm* : canine (tooth)

canjear *vt* : exchange — **canje** *nm* : exchange, trade

cano, -na *adj* : gray, gray-haired

canoa *nf* : canoe

canon *nm, pl* **cánones** : canon

canonizar {21} *vt* : canonize

canoso, -sa *adj* : gray, gray-haired

cansar *vt* : tire (out) — *vi* : be tiring — **cansarse** *vr* : get tired — **cansado, -da** *adj* 1 : tired 2 PESADO : tiresome — **cansancio** *nm* : fatigue, weariness

cantalupo *nm* : cantaloupe

cantar *v* : sing — ~ *nm* : song — **cantante** *nmf* : singer

cántaro *nm* 1 : pitcher, jug 2 **llover a** ~**s** *fam* : rain cats and dogs

cantera *nf* : quarry (excavation)

cantidad *nf* 1 : quantity, amount 2 **una** ~ **de** : lots of

cantimplora *nf* : canteen, water bottle

cantina *nf* 1 : canteen, cafeteria 2 *Lat* : tavern, bar

canto *nm* 1 : singing, song 2 BORDE, LADO : edge 3 **de** ~ : on end, sideways 4 ~ **rodado** : boulder — **cantor, -tora** *adj* 1 : singing 2 **pájaro** ~ : songbird — ~ *n* : singer

caña *nf* 1 : cane, reed 2 ~ **de pescar** : fishing pole

cáñamo *nm* : hemp

cañería *nf* : pipes, piping — **caño** *nm* 1 : pipe 2 : spout (of a fountain) — **cañón** *nm, pl* **-ñones** 1 : cannon 2 : barrel (of a gun) 3 : canyon (in geography)

caoba *nf* : mahogany

caos *nm* : chaos — **caótico, -ca** *adj* : chaotic

capa *nf* 1 : cape, cloak 2 : coat (of paint, etc.), coating (in cooking) 3 ESTRATO : layer, stratum 4 : (social) class

capacidad *nf* 1 : capacity 2 APTITUD : ability

capacitar *vt* : train, qualify — **capacitación** *nf, pl* **-ciones** : training

caparazón nm, pl **-zones** : shell
capataz nmf, pl **-taces** : foreman
capaz adj, pl **-paces 1** : capable, able **2** ESPACIOSO : spacious
capellán nm, pl **-llanes** : chaplain
capilla nf : chapel
capital adj **1** : capital **2** PRINCIPAL : chief, principal — ~ nm : capital (assets) — ~ nf : capital (city) — **capitalismo** nm : capitalism — **capitalista** adj & nmf : capitalist, capitalistic — **capitalizar** {21} vt : capitalize
capitán, -tana n, mpl **-tanes** : captain
capitolio nm : capitol
capitular vi : capitulate, surrender — **capitulación** nf, pl **-ciones** : surrender
capítulo nm : chapter
capó nm : hood (of a car)
capote nm : cloak, cape
capricho nm : whim, caprice — **caprichoso, -sa** adj : whimsical, capricious
cápsula nf : capsule
captar vt **1** : grasp **2** ATRAER : gain, attract (interest, etc.) **3** : harness (waters)
capturar vt : capture, seize — **captura** nf : capture, seizure
capucha nf : hood (of clothing)
capullo nm **1** : cocoon **2** : (flower) bud
caqui adj & nm : khaki
cara nf **1** : face **2** ASPECTO : appearance **3** fam : nerve, gall **4** ~ **a** or **de** ~ **a** : facing
carabina nf : carbine
caracol nm **1** : snail **2** Lat : conch **3** RIZO : curl
carácter nm, pl **-racteres 1** : character **2** ÍNDOLE : nature — **característica** nf : characteristic — **característico, -ca** adj : characteristic — **caracterizar** {21} vt : characterize
caramba interj : oh my!, good grief!
carámbano nm : icicle
caramelo nm **1** : caramel **2** DULCE : candy
carátula nf **1** CARETA : mask **2** : jacket (of a record, etc.) **3** Lat : face (of a watch)
caravana nf **1** : caravan **2** REMOLQUE : trailer
caray → **caramba**
carbohidrato nm : carbohydrate
carbón nm, pl **-bones 1** : coal **2** : charcoal (for drawing) — **carboncillo** nm : charcoal — **carbonero, -ra** adj : coal — **carbonizar** {21} vt : char — **carbono** nm : carbon — **carburador** nm : carburetor — **carburante** nm : fuel
carcajada nf : loud laugh, guffaw

cárcel nf : jail, prison — **carcelero, -ra** n : jailer
carcinógeno nm : carcinogen
carcomer vt : eat away at — **carcomido, -da** adj : worm-eaten
cardenal nm **1** : cardinal **2** CONTUSIÓN : bruise
cardíaco or **cardiaco, -ca** adj : cardiac, heart
cárdigan nm, pl **-gans** : cardigan
cardinal adj : cardinal
cardiólogo, -ga n : cardiologist
cardo nm : thistle
carear vt : bring face-to-face
carecer {53} vi ~ **de** : lack — **carencia** nf : lack, want — **carente** adj ~ **de** : lacking (in)
carestía nf **1** : high cost **2** ESCASEZ : dearth, scarcity
careta nf : mask
cargar {52} vt **1** : load **2** : charge (a battery, a purchase, etc.) **3** LLEVAR : carry **4** ~ **de** : burden with — vi **1** : load **2** ~ **con** : pick up, carry away — **carga** nf **1** : load **2** CARGAMENTO : freight, cargo **3** RESPONSABILIDAD : burden **4** : charge (in electricity, etc.) — **cargado, -da** adj **1** : loaded, burdened **2** PESADO : heavy, stuffy **3** : charged (of a battery) **4** FUERTE : strong, concentrated — **cargamento** nm : cargo, load — **cargo** nm **1** : charge **2** PUESTO : position, office
cariarse vr : decay (of teeth)
caribe adj : Caribbean
caricatura nf **1** : caricature **2** : (political) cartoon — **caricaturizar** vt : caricature
caricia nf : caress
caridad nf **1** : charity **2** LIMOSNA : alms pl
caries nfs & pl : cavity (in a tooth)
cariño nm : affection, love — **cariñoso, -sa** adj : affectionate, loving
carisma nf : charisma — **carismático, -ca** adj : charismatic
caritativo, -va adj : charitable
cariz nm, pl **-rices** : appearance, aspect
carmesí adj & nm : crimson
carmín nm, pl **-mines** or ~ **de labios** : lipstick
carnada nf : bait
carnal adj **1** : carnal **2 primo** ~ : first cousin
carnaval nm : carnival
carne nf **1** : meat **2** : flesh (of persons or fruits) **3** ~ **de cerdo** : pork **4** ~ **de gallina** : goose bumps **5** ~ **de ternera** : veal
carné nm → **carnet**

carnero nm 1 : ram, sheep 2 : mutton (in cooking)

carnet nm 1 ~ **de conducir** : driver's license 2 ~ **de identidad** : identification card, ID

carnicería nf 1 : butcher shop 2 MATANZA : slaughter — **carnicero, -ra** n : butcher

carnívoro, -ra adj : carnivorous — **carnívoro** nm : carnivore

carnoso, -sa adj : fleshy

caro, -ra adj 1 : expensive 2 QUERIDO : dear — **caro** adv : dearly

carpa nf 1 : carp 2 TIENDA : tent

carpeta nf : folder

carpintería nf : carpentry — **carpintero, -ra** n : carpenter

carraspear vi : clear one's throat — **carraspera** nf 1 : hoarseness 2 **tener** ~ : have a frog in one's throat

carrera nf 1 : running, run 2 COMPETICIÓN : race 3 : course (of studies) 4 PROFESIÓN : career, profession

carreta nf : cart, wagon

carrete nm : reel, spool

carretera nf : highway, road

carretilla nf : wheelbarrow

carril nm 1 : lane (of a road) 2 : rail (for a railroad)

carrillo nm : cheek

carrito nm : cart, trolley

carrizo nm : reed

carro nm 1 : wagon, cart 2 Lat : automobile, car — **carrocería** nf : body (of an automobile)

carroña nf : carrion

carroza nf 1 : carriage 2 : float (in a parade)

carruaje nm : carriage

carrusel nm : merry-go-round, carousel

carta nf 1 : letter 2 NAIPE : playing card 3 : charter (of an organization, etc.) 4 MENÚ : menu 5 MAPA : map, chart

cartel nm : poster, bill — **cartelera** nf : billboard

cartera nf 1 : briefcase 2 BILLETERA : wallet 3 Lat : pocketbook, handbag — **carterista** nmf : pickpocket

cartero, -ra nm : mail carrier, mailman m

cartílago nm : cartilage

cartilla nf 1 : primer, reader 2 : booklet, record (of a savings account, etc.)

cartón nm, pl **-tones** 1 : cardboard 2 : carton (of cigarettes, etc.)

cartucho nm : cartridge

casa nf 1 : house 2 HOGAR : home 3 EMPRESA : company, firm 4 ~ **flotante** : houseboat

casar vt : marry — vi : go together, match up — **casarse** vr 1 : get married 2 ~ **con** : marry — **casado, -da** adj : married — **casamiento** nm 1 : marriage 2 BODA : wedding

cascabel nm : small bell

cascada nf : waterfall

cascanueces nms & pl : nutcracker

cascar {72} vt : crack (a shell, etc.) — **cascarse** vr : crack, chip — **cáscara** nf : skin, peel, shell — **cascarón** nm, pl **-rones** : eggshell

casco nm 1 : helmet 2 : hull (of a boat) 3 : hoof (of a horse) 4 : fragment (of ceramics, etc.) 5 : center (of a town) 6 ENVASE : empty bottle

caserío nm 1 Spain : country house 2 POBLADO : hamlet

casero, -ra adj 1 : homemade 2 DOMÉSTICO : domestic, household — ~ n : landlord, landlady f

caseta nf : booth, stall

casete nm ~ **cassette**

casi adv 1 : almost, nearly 2 (in negative phrases) : hardly

casilla nf 1 : compartment, pigeonhole 2 CASETA : booth 3 : box (on a form)

casino nm 1 : casino 2 : (social) club

caso nm 1 : case 2 **en** ~ **de** : in the event of 3 **hacer** ~ : pay attention 4 **no venir al** ~ : be beside the point

caspa nf : dandruff

cassette nmf : cassette

casta nf 1 : lineage, descent 2 : breed (of animals) 3 : caste (in India)

castaña nf : chestnut

castañetear vi : chatter (of teeth)

castaño, -ña adj : chestnut (color)

castañuela nf : castanet

castellano nm : Spanish, Castilian (language)

castidad nf : chastity

castigar {52} vt 1 : punish 2 : penalize (in sports) — **castigo** nm 1 : punishment 2 : penalty (in sports)

castillo nm : castle

casto, -ta adj : chaste, pure — **castizo, -za** adj : pure, traditional (in style)

castor nm : beaver

castrar vt : castrate

castrense adj : military

casual adj : chance, accidental — **casualidad** nf 1 : coincidence 2 **por** ~ or **de** ~ : by chance — **casualmente** adv : by chance

cataclismo nm : cataclysm

catalán, -lana adj, mpl **-lanes** : Catalan — **catalán** nm : Catalan (language)

catalizador nm : catalyst

catalogar {52} vt : catalog, classify — **catálogo** nm : catalog

catapulta *nf* : catapult

catar *vt* : taste, sample

catarata *nf* **1** : waterfall **2** : cataract (in medicine)

catarro *nm* RESFRIADO : cold

catástrofe *nf* : catastrophe, disaster — **catastrófico, -ca** *adj* : catastrophic, disastrous

catecismo *nm* : catechism

cátedra *nf* : chair (at a university)

catedral *nf* : cathedral

catedrático, -ca *n* : professor

categoría *nf* **1** : category **2** RANGO : rank **3 de ~** : first-rate — **categórico, -ca** *adj* : categorical

católico, -ca *adj & n* : Catholic — **catolicismo** *nm* : Catholicism

catorce *adj & nm* : fourteen — **catorceavo** *nm* : fourteenth

catre *nm* : cot

cauce *nm* **1** : riverbed **2** VÍA : channel, means *pl*

caucho *nm* : rubber

caución *nf, pl* **-ciones** : security, guarantee

caudal *nm* **1** : volume of water, flow **2** RIQUEZA : wealth

caudillo *nm* : leader, commander

causar *vt* : cause, provoke — **causa** *nf* **1** : cause **2** RAZÓN : reason **3** : case (in law) **4 a ~ de** : because of

cáustico, -ca *adj* : caustic

cautela *nf* : caution — **cauteloso, -sa** *adj* : cautious — **cautelosamente** *adv* : cautiously, warily

cautivar *vt* **1** : capture **2** ENCANTAR : captivate — **cautiverio** *nm* : captivity — **cautivo, -va** *adj & n* : captive

cauto, -ta *adj* : cautious

cavar *v* : dig

caverna *nf* : cavern, cave

cavidad *nf* : cavity

cavilar *vi* : ponder

cayado *nm* : crook, staff

cazar {21} *vt* **1** : hunt **2** ATRAPAR : catch, bag — *vi* : go hunting — **caza** *nf* **1** : hunt, hunting **2** : game (animals) — **cazador, -dora** *n* : hunter

cazo *nm* **1** : saucepan **2** CUCHARÓN : ladle — **cazuela** *nf* : casserole

CD *nm* : CD, compact disc

cebada *nf* : barley

cebar *vt* **1** : bait **2** : feed, fatten (animals) **3** : prime (a firearm, etc.) — **cebo** *nm* **1** CARNADA : bait **2** : charge (of a firearm)

cebolla *nf* : onion — **cebolleta** *nf* : scallion, green onion — **cebollino** *nm* : chive

cebra *nf* : zebra

cecear *vi* : lisp — **ceceo** *nm* : lisp

cedazo *nm* : sieve

ceder *vi* **1** : yield, give way **2** DISMINUIR : diminish, abate — *vt* : cede, hand over

cedro *nm* : cedar

cédula *nf* : document, certificate

cegar {49} *vt* **1** : blind **2** TAPAR : block, stop up — *vi* : be blinded, go blind — **ceguera** *nf* : blindness

ceja *nf* : eyebrow

cejar *vi* : give in, back down

celada *nf* : trap, ambush

celador, -dora *n* : guard, warden

celda *nf* : cell (of a jail)

celebrar *vt* **1** : celebrate **2** : hold (a meeting), say (Mass) **3** ALEGRARSE DE : be happy about — **celebrarse** *vr* : take place — **celebración** *nf, pl* **-ciones** : celebration — **célebre** *adj* : famous, celebrated — **celebridad** *nf* : celebrity

celeridad *nf* : swiftness, speed

celeste *adj* **1** : celestial, heavenly **2** *or* **azul ~** : sky blue — **celestial** *adj* : celestial, heavenly

celibato *nm* : celibacy — **célibe** *adj* : celibate

celo *nm* **1** : zeal **2 en ~** : in heat **3 ~s** *nmpl* : jealousy **4 tener ~s** : be jealous

celofán *nm, pl* **-fanes** : cellophane

celoso, -sa *adj* **1** : jealous **2** DILIGENTE : zealous

célula *nf* : cell — **celular** *adj* : cellular

celulosa *nf* : cellulose

cementerio *nm* : cemetery

cemento *nm* **1** : cement **2 ~ armado** : reinforced concrete

cena *nf* : supper, dinner

cenagal *nm* : bog, quagmire — **cenagoso** *adj* : swampy

cenar *vi* : have dinner, have supper — *vt* : have for dinner or supper

cenicero *nm* : ashtray

cenit *nm* : zenith

ceniza *nf* : ash

censo *nm* : census

censurar *vt* **1** : censor **2** REPROBAR : censure, criticize — **censura** *nf* **1** : censorship **2** REPROBACIÓN : censure, criticism

centavo *nm* **1** : cent **2** : centavo (unit of currency)

centellear *vi* : sparkle, twinkle — **centella** *nf* **1** : flash **2** CHISPA : spark — **centelleo** *nm* : twinkling, sparkle

centenar *nm* : hundred — **centenario** *nm* : centennial

centeno *nm* : rye

centésimo, -ma *adj* : hundredth
centígrado *adj* : centigrade, Celsius
centigramo *nm* : centigram
centímetro *nm* : centimeter
centinela *nmf* : sentinel, sentry
central *adj* : central — ~ *nf* : main office, headquarters — **centralita** *nf* : switchboard — **centralizar** {21} *vt* : centralize
centrar *vt* : center — **centrarse** *vr* ~ **en** : focus on — **céntrico, -ca** *adj* : central — **centro** *nm* 1 : center 2 : downtown (of a city) 3 ~ **de mesa** : centerpiece
centroamericano, -na *adj* : Central American
ceñir {67} *vt* 1 : encircle 2 : fit (s.o.) tightly — **ceñirse** *vr* ~ **a** : limit oneself to — **ceñido, -da** *adj* : tight
ceño *nm* 1 : frown 2 **fruncir el** ~ : knit one's brow, frown
cepillo *nm* 1 : brush 2 : (carpenter's) plane 3 ~ **de dientes** : toothbrush — **cepillar** *vt* 1 : brush 2 : plane (wood)
cera *nf* 1 : wax, beeswax 2 : floor wax, furniture wax
cerámica *nf* 1 : ceramics *pl* 2 : (piece of) pottery
cerca¹ *nf* : fence — **cercado** *nm* : enclosure
cerca² *adv* 1 : close, near 2 ~ **de** : near, close to 3 ~ **de** : nearly, almost — **cercano, -na** *adj* : near, close — **cercanía** *nf* 1 : proximity 2 ~**s** *nfpl* : outskirts
cercar {72} *vt* 1 : fence in 2 RODEAR : surround
cerciorarse *vr* ~ **de** : make sure of
cerco *nm* 1 : circle, ring 2 ASEDIO : siege 3 *Lat* : fence
cerda *nf* : bristle
cerdo *nm* 1 : pig, hog 2 ~ **macho** : boar
cereal *adj & nm* : cereal
cerebro *nm* : brain — **cerebral** *adj* : cerebral
ceremonia *nf* : ceremony — **ceremonial** *adj* : ceremonial — **ceremonioso, -sa** *adj* : ceremonious
cereza *nf* : cherry
cerilla *nf* : match — **cerillo** *nm* *Lat* : match
cerner {56} *or* **cernir** *vt* : sift — **cernerse** *vr* 1 : hover 2 ~ **sobre** : loom over — **cernidor** *nm* : sieve
cero *nm* : zero
cerrar {55} *vt* 1 : close, shut 2 : turn off (a faucet, etc.) 3 : bring to an end — *vi* 1 : close up, lock up 2 : close down (a business, etc.) — **cerrarse** *vr* 1

: close, shut 2 TERMINAR : come to a close, end — **cerrado, -da** *adj* 1 : closed, shut, locked 2 : overcast (of weather) 3 : sharp (of a curve) 4 : thick, broad (of an accent) — **cerradura** *nf* : lock — **cerrajero, -ra** *n* : locksmith
cerro *nm* : hill
cerrojo *nm* : bolt, latch
certamen *nm, pl* **-támenes** : competition, contest
certero, -ra *adj* : accurate, precise
certeza *nf* : certainty — **certidumbre** *nf* : certainty
certificar {72} *vt* 1 : certify 2 : register (mail) — **certificado, -da** *adj* : certified, registered — **certificado** *nm* : certificate
cervato *nm* : fawn
cerveza *nf* 1 : beer 2 ~ **de barril** : draft beer — **cervecería** *nf* 1 : brewery 2 BAR : beer hall, bar
cesar *vi* : cease, stop — *vt* : dismiss, lay off — **cesación** *nf, pl* **-ciones** : cessation, suspension — **cesante** *adj* 1 : laid off 2 *Lat* : unemployed — **cesantía** *nf Lat* : unemployment
cesárea *nf* : cesarean (section)
cese *nm* 1 : cessation, stop 2 DESTITUCIÓN : dismissal
césped *nm* : lawn, grass
cesta *nf* : basket — **cesto** *nm* 1 : (large) basket 2 ~ **de basura** : wastebasket
cetro *nm* : scepter
chabacano *nm Lat* : apricot
chabola *nf Spain* : shack, shanty
chacal *nm* : jackal
cháchara *nf fam* : gabbing, chatter
chacra *nf Lat* : (small) farm
chafar *vt fam* : flatten, crush
chal *nm* : shawl
chaleco *nm* : vest
chalet *nm Spain* : house
chalupa *nf* 1 : small boat 2 *Lat* : small stuffed tortilla
chamarra *nf* : jacket
chamba *nf Lat fam* : job
champaña *or* **champán** *nm* : champagne
champiñón *nm, pl* **-ñones** : mushroom
champú *nm, pl* **-pús** *or* **-púes** : shampoo
chamuscar {72} *vt* : scorch
chance *nm Lat* : chance, opportunity
chancho *nm Lat* : pig
chanclos *nmpl* : galoshes
chantaje *nm* : blackmail — **chantajear** *vt* : blackmail
chanza *nf* : joke, jest
chapa *nf* 1 : sheet, plate 2 INSIGNIA : badge — **chapado, -da** *adj* 1 : plated

2 chapado a la antigua : old-fashioned

chaparrón *nm, pl* **-rrones** : downpour

chapotear *vi* : splash

chapucero, -ra *adj* : shoddy, sloppy — **chapuza** *nf* : botched job

chapuzón *nm, pl* **-zones** : dip, short swim

chaqueta *nf* : jacket

charca *nf* : pond — **charco** *nm* : puddle

charlar *vi* : chat — **charla** *nf* : chat, talk — **charlatán, -tana** *adj, mpl* **-tanes** : talkative — ~ *n* 1 : chatterbox 2 FARSANTE : charlatan

charol *nm* 1 : patent leather 2 BARNIZ : varnish

chasco *nm* 1 : trick, joke 2 DECEPCIÓN : disappointment

chasis *nms & pl* : chassis

chasquear *vt* 1 : click (the tongue), snap (one's fingers) 2 : crack (a whip) — **chasquido** *nm* 1 : click, snap 2 : crack (of a whip)

chatarra *nf* : scrap (metal)

chato, -ta *adj* 1 : pug-nosed 2 APLANADO : flat

chauvinismo *nm* : chauvinism — **chauvinista** *adj* : chauvinist, chauvinistic

chaval, -vala *n fam* : kid, boy *m*, girl *f*

checo, -ca *adj* : Czech — **checo** *nm* : Czech (language)

chef *nm* : chef

cheque *nm* : check — **chequera** *nf* : checkbook

chequear *vt Lat* 1 : check, inspect, verify 2 : check in (baggage) — **chequeo** *nm* 1 : (medical) checkup 2 *Lat* : check, inspection

chica → **chico**

chicano, -na *adj* : Chicano, Mexican-American

chícharo *nm Lat* : pea

chicharrón *nm, pl* **-rrones** : pork rind

chichón *nm, pl* **-chones** : bump

chicle *nm* : chewing gum

chico, -ca *adj* : little, small — ~ *n* : child, boy *m*, girl *f*

chiflar *vt* : whistle at, boo — *vi Lat* : whistle — **chiflado, -da** *adj fam* : crazy, nuts — **chiflido** *nm* : whistling

chile *nm* : chili pepper

chileno, -na *adj* : Chilean

chillar *vi* 1 : shriek, scream 2 CHIRRIAR : screech, squeal — **chillido** *nm* 1 : scream 2 CHIRRIDO : screech, squeal — **chillón, -llona** *adj, mpl* **-llones** : shrill, loud

chimenea *nf* 1 : chimney 2 HOGAR : fireplace

chimpancé *nm* : chimpanzee

chinche *nf* : bedbug

chino, -na *adj* : Chinese — **chino** *nm* : Chinese (language)

chiquillo, -lla *n* : kid, child

chiquito, -ta *adj* : tiny — ~ *n* : little child, tot

chiribita *nf* : spark

chiripa *nf* 1 : fluke 2 **de ~** : by sheer luck

chirivía *nf* : parsnip

chirriar {85} *vi* 1 : squeak, creak 2 : screech (of brakes, etc.) — **chirrido** *nm* 1 : squeak, creak 2 : screech (of brakes)

chisme *nm* : (piece of) gossip — **chismear** *vi* : gossip — **chismoso, -sa** *adj* : gossipy — ~ *n* : gossip

chispear *vi* : spark — **chispa** *nf* : spark

chisporrotear *vi* : crackle, sizzle — **chisporroteo** *nm* : crackle

chiste *nm* : joke, funny story — **chistoso, -sa** *adj* : funny, witty

chivo, -va *n* : kid, young goat

chocar {72} *vi* 1 : crash, collide 2 ENFRENTARSE : clash — **chocante** *adj* 1 : striking, shocking 2 *Lat* : unpleasant, rude

choclo *nm Lat* : ear of corn, corncob

chocolate *nm* : chocolate

chofer *or* **chófer** *nm* 1 : chauffeur 2 CONDUCTOR : driver

choque *nm* 1 : shock 2 : crash, collision (of vehicles) 3 CONFLICTO : clash

chorizo *nm* : chorizo, sausage

chorrear *vi* 1 : drip 2 BROTAR : pour out, gush — **chorro** *nm* 1 : stream, jet 2 HILO : trickle

chovinismo → **chauvinismo**

choza *nf* : hut, shack

chubasco *nm* : downpour, squall

chuchería *nf* 1 : knickknack, trinket 2 DULCE : sweet

chueco, -ca *adj Lat* : crooked

chuleta *nf* : cutlet, chop

chulo, -la *adj fam* : cute, pretty

chupar *vt* 1 : suck 2 ABSORBER : absorb 3 *fam* : guzzle — *vi* : suckle — **chupada** *nf* : suck, sucking — **chupete** *nm* 1 : pacifier 2 *Lat* : lollipop

churro *nm* 1 : fried dough 2 *fam* : botch, mess

chusco, -ca *adj* : funny

chusma *nf* : riffraff, rabble

chutar *vi* : shoot (in soccer)

cianuro *nm* : cyanide

cicatriz *nf, pl* **-trices** : scar — **cicatrizar** {21} *vi* : form a scar, heal

cíclico, -ca *adj* : cyclical

ciclismo *nm* : cycling — **ciclista** *nmf* : cyclist

ciclo *nm* : cycle

ciclón *nm, pl* **-clones** : cyclone

ciego, -ga *adj* : blind — **ciegamente** *adv* : blindly

cielo *nm* **1** : sky **2** : heaven (in religion)

ciempiés *nms & pl* : centipede

cien *adj* : a hundred, hundred — **~** *nm* : one hundred

ciénaga *nf* : swamp, bog

ciencia *nf* **1** : science **2 a ~ cierta** : for a fact

cieno *nm* : mire, mud, silt

científico, -ca *adj* : scientific — **~** *n* : scientist

ciento *adj (used in compound numbers)* : one hundred — **~** *nm* **1** : hundred, group of a hundred **2 por ~** : percent

cierre *nm* **1** : closing, closure **2** BROCHE : fastener, clasp

cierto, -ta *adj* **1** : true **2** SEGURO : certain **3 por ~** : as a matter of fact

ciervo, -va *n* : deer, stag *m*, hind *f*

cifra *nf* **1** : number, figure **2** : sum (of money, etc.) **3** CLAVE : code, cipher — **cifrar** *vt* **1** : write in code **2 ~ la esperanza en** : pin all one's hopes on

cigarrillo *nm* : cigarrette — **cigarro** *nm* **1** : cigarrette **2** PURO : cigar

cigüeña *nf* : stork

cilantro *nm* : cilantro, coriander

cilindro *nm* : cylinder — **cilíndrico, -ca** *adj* : cylindrical

cima *nf* : peak, summit

címbalo *nm* : cymbal

cimbrar *or* **cimbrear** *vt* : shake, rock — **cimbrarse** *or* **cimbrearse** *vr* : sway

cimentar {55} *vt* **1** : lay the foundation of **2** : cement, strengthen (relations, etc.) — **cimientos** *nmpl* : base, foundation(s)

cinc *nm* : zinc

cincel *nm* : chisel — **cincelar** *vt* : chisel

cinco *adj & nm* : five

cincuenta *adj & nm* : fifty — **cincuentavo, -va** *adj* : fiftieth — **cincuentavo** *nm* : fiftieth

cine *nm* : cinema, movies *pl* — **cinematográfico, -ca** *adj* : movie, film

cínico, -ca *adj* : cynical — **~** *n* : cynic — **cinismo** *nm* : cynicism

cinta *nf* **1** : ribbon, band **2 ~ adhesiva** : adhesive tape **3 ~ métrica** : tape measure **4 ~ magnetofónica** : magnetic tape

cinto *nm* : belt, girdle — **cintura** *nf* : waist — **cinturón** *nm, pl* **-rones 1** : belt **2 ~ de seguridad** : seat belt

ciprés *nm, pl* **-preses** : cypress

circo *nm* : circus

circuito *nm* : circuit

circulación *nf, pl* **-clones 1** : circulation **2** TRÁFICO : traffic — **circular** *vi* **1** : circulate **2** : drive (a vehicle) — **~** *adj* : circular

círculo *nm* : circle

circuncidar *vt* : circumcise — **circuncisión** *nf, pl* **-siones** : circumcision

circundar *vt* : surround

circunferencia *nf* : circumference

circunscribir {33} *vt* : confine, limit — **circunscribirse** *vr* **~ a** : limit oneself to — **circunscripción** *nf, pl* **-clones** : district, constituency

circunspecto, -ta *adj* : circumspect, cautious

circunstancia *nf* : circumstance — **circunstancial** *adj* : chance — **circunstante** *nmf* **1** : bystander **2 los ~s** : those present

circunvalación *nf, pl* **-clones 1** : encircling **2 carretera de ~** : bypass

cirio *nm* : candle

ciruela *nf* **1** : plum **2 ~ pasa** : prune

cirugía *nf* : surgery — **cirujano, -na** *n* : surgeon

cisma *nf* : schism

cisne *nm* : swan

cisterna *nf* : cistern

cita *nf* **1** : appointment, date **2** REFERENCIA : quote, quotation — **citación** *nf, pl* **-clones** : quote, cite **2** CONVOCAR : make an appointment with **3** : summon (in law) — **citarse** *vr* **~ con** : arrange to meet

cítrico *nm* : citrus (fruit)

ciudad *nf* : city, town — **ciudadano, -na** *n* **1** : citizen **2** HABITANTE : resident — **ciudadanía** *nf* : citizenship

cívico, -ca *adj* : civic

civil *adj* : civil — **~** *nmf* : civilian — **civilidad** *nf* : civility — **civilización** *nf, pl* **-clones** : civilization — **civilizar** {21} *vt* : civilize

cizaña *nf* : discord, rift

clamar *vi* : clamor, cry out — **clamor** *nm* : clamor, outcry — **clamoroso, -sa** *adj* : clamorous, loud

clan *nm* : clan

clandestino, -na *adj* : clandestine, secret

clara *nf* : egg white

claraboya *nf* : skylight

claramente *adv* : clearly

clarear *v impers* **1** : dawn **2** ACLARAR : clear up — *vi* : be transparent

claridad *nf* **1** : clarity, clearness **2** LUZ : light

clarificar {72} *vt* : clarify — **clarificación** *nf, pl* **-clones** : clarification

clarín *nm, pl* **-rines** : bugle

clarinete *nm* : clarinet
clarividente *adj* 1 : clairvoyant 2 PERSPICAZ : perspicacious — **clarividencia** *nf* 1 : clairvoyance 2 PERSPICACIA : farsightedness
claro *adv* 1 : clearly 2 POR SUPUESTO : of course, surely — ~ *nm* 1 : clearing, glade 2 ~ **de luna** : moonlight —
claro, -ra *adj* 1 : clear, bright 2 : light (of colors) 3 EVIDENTE : clear, evident
clase *nf* 1 : class 2 TIPO : sort, kind
clásico, -ca *adj* : classic, classical — **clásico** *nm* : classic
clasificar {72} *vt* 1 : classify, sort out 2 : rate, rank (a hotel, a team, etc.) — **clasificarse** *vr* : qualify (in competitions) — **clasificación** *nf, pl* -**ciones** 1 : classification 2 : league (in sports)
claudicar {72} *vi* : back down
claustro *nm* : cloister
claustrofobia *nf* : claustrophobia — **claustrofóbico, -ca** *adj* : claustrophobic
cláusula *nf* : clause
clausurar *vt* : close (down) — **clausura** *nf* : closure, closing
clavado *nm Lat* : dive
clavar *vt* 1 : nail, hammer 2 HINCAR : drive in, plunge
clave *nf* 1 CIFRA : code 2 SOLUCIÓN : key 3 : clef (in music) — ~ *adj* : key
clavel *nm* : carnation
clavicémbalo *nm* : harpsichord
clavícula *nf* : collarbone
clavija *nf* 1 : peg, pin 2 : (electric) plug
clavo *nm* 1 : nail 2 : clove (spice)
claxon *nm, pl* **cláxones** : horn (of an automobile)
clemencia *nf* : clemency, mercy — **clemente** *adj* : merciful
clerical *adj* : clerical — **clérigo, -ga** *n* : clergyman, cleric — **clero** *nm* : clergy
cliché *nm* 1 : cliché 2 : negative (of a photograph)
cliente, -ta *n* : customer, client — **clientela** *nf* : clientele, customers *pl*
clima *nm* 1 : climate 2 AMBIENTE : atmosphere — **climático, -ca** *adj* : climatic
climatizar {21} *vt* : air-condition — **climatizado, -da** *adj* : air-conditioned
clímax *nm* : climax
clínica *nf* : clinic — **clínico, -ca** *adj* : clinical
clip *nm, pl* **clips** : (paper) clip
cloaca *nf* : sewer
cloquear *vi* : cluck — **cloqueo** *nm* : cluck, clucking
cloro *nm* : chlorine

clóset *nm Lat, pl* **clósets** : (built-in) closet, cupboard
club *nm* : club
coacción *nf, pl* -**ciones** : coercion — **coaccionar** *vt* : coerce
coagular *v* : clot, coagulate — **coagularse** *vr* : coagulate — **coágulo** *nm* : clot
coalición *nf, pl* -**ciones** : coalition
coartada *nf* : alibi
coartar *vt* : restrict, limit
cobarde *nmf* : coward — ~ *adj* : cowardly — **cobardía** *nf* : cowardice
cobaya *nf* : guinea pig
cobertizo *nm* : shelter, shed
cobertor *nm* : bedspread
cobertura *nf* 1 : cover 2 : coverage (of news, etc.)
cobijar *vt* : shelter — **cobijarse** *vr* : take shelter — **cobija** *nf Lat* : blanket — **cobijo** *nm* : shelter
cobra *nf* : cobra
cobrar *vt* 1 : charge, collect 2 : earn (a salary, etc.) 3 ADQUERIR : acquire, gain 4 : cash (a check) — *vi* : be paid — **cobrador, -dora** *n* 1 : collector 2 : conductor (of a bus, etc.)
cobre *nm* : copper
cobro *nm* : collection (of money), cashing (of a check)
cocaína *nf* : cocaine
cocción *nf, pl* -**ciones** : cooking
cocear *vi* : kick
cocer {14} *vt* 1 : cook 2 HERVIR : boil
coche *nm* 1 : car, automobile 2 : coach (of a train) 3 or ~ **de caballos** : carriage 4 ~ **fúnebre** : hearse — **cochecito** *nm* : baby carriage, stroller — **cochera** *nf* : garage, carport
cochino, -na *n* : pig, hog — ~ *adj fam* : dirty, filthy — **cochinada** *nf fam* : dirty thing — **cochinillo** *nm* : piglet
cocido, -da *adj* 1 : boiled, cooked 2 **bien** ~ : well-done — **cocido** *nm* : stew
cociente *nm* : quotient
cocina *nf* 1 : kitchen 2 : (kitchen) stove 3 : (art of) cooking, cuisine — **cocinar** *v* : cook — **cocinero, -ra** *n* : cook, chef
coco *nm* : coconut
cocodrilo *nm* : crocodile
coctel *or* **cóctel** *nm* 1 : cocktail 2 FIESTA : cocktail party
codazo *nm* 1 : nudge 2 **dar un** ~ **a** : elbow, nudge
codicia *nf* : greed — **codiciar** *vt* : covet — **codicioso, -sa** *adj* : covetous, greedy

código *nm* **1** : code **2** ~ **postal** : zip code **3** ~ **morse** : Morse code

codo *nm* : elbow

codorniz *nf, pl* **-nices** : quail

coexistir *vi* : coexist

cofre *nm* : chest, coffer

coger {15} *vt* **1** : take (hold of) **2** ATRAPAR : catch **3** : pick up (from the ground) **4** : pick (fruit, etc.) — **cogerse** *vr* : hold on

cohechar *vt* : bribe — **cohecho** *nm* : bribe, bribery

coherencia *nf* : coherence — **coherente** *adj* : coherent — **cohesión** *nf, pl* **-siones** : cohesion

cohete *nm* : rocket

cohibir {62} *vt* **1** : restrict **2** : inhibit (a person) — **cohibirse** *vr* : feel inhibited — **cohibido, -da** *adj* : inhibited, shy

coincidir *vi* **1** : coincide **2** ~ **con** : agree with — **coincidencia** *nf* : coincidence

cojear *vi* **1** : limp **2** : wobble (of furniture, etc.) — **cojera** *nf* : limp

cojín *nm, pl* **-jines** : cushion — **cojinete** *nm* **1** : pad, cushion **2** : bearing (of a machine)

cojo, -ja *adj* **1** : lame **2** : wobbly (of furniture) — ~ *n* : lame person

col *nf* **1** : cabbage **2** ~ **de Bruselas** : Brussels sprout

cola *nf* **1** : tail **2** FILA : line (of people) **3** : end (of a line) **4** PEGAMENTO : glue **5** ~ **de caballo** : ponytail

colaborar *vi* : collaborate — **colaboración** *nf, pl* **-ciones** : collaboration — **colaborador, -dora** *n* **1** : collaborator **2** : contributor (to a periodical)

colada *nf Spain* **1** : laundry **2 hacer la** ~ : do the washing

colador *nm* : colander, strainer

colapso *nm* : collapse

colar {19} *vt* : strain, filter — **colarse** *vr* : sneak in, gate-crash

colcha *nf* : bedspread, quilt — **colchón** *nm, pl* **-chones** : mattress — **colchoneta** *nf* : mat

colear *vi* : wag its tail

colección *nf, pl* **-ciones** : collection — **coleccionar** *vt* : collect — **coleccionista** *nmf* : collector — **colecta** *nf* : collection (of donations)

colectividad *nf* : community — **colectivo, -va** *adj* : collective — **colectivo** *nm* **1** : collective **2** *Lat* : city bus

colector *nm* : sewer

colega *nmf* : colleague

colegio *nm* **1** : school **2** : (professional) college — **colegial, -giala** *n* : schoolboy *m*, schoolgirl *f*

colegir {28} *vt* : gather

cólera *nm* : cholera — ~ *nf* : anger, rage — **colérico, -ca** *adj* **1** : bad-tempered **2** FURIOSO : angry

colesterol *nm* : cholesterol

coleta *nf* : pigtail

colgar {16} *vt* **1** : hang **2** : hang up (a telephone) **3** : hang out (laundry) — *vi* : hang up — **colgante** *adj* : hanging — ~ *nm* : pendant

colibrí *nm* : hummingbird

cólico *nm* : colic

coliflor *nf* : cauliflower

colilla *nf* : (cigarette) butt

colina *nf* : hill

colindar *vi* ~ **con** : be adjacent to — **colindante** *adj* : adjacent

coliseo *nm* : coliseum

colisión *nf, pl* **-siones** : collision — **colisionar** *vi* ~ **contra** : collide with

collar *nm* **1** : necklace **2** : collar (for pets)

colmar *vt* **1** : fill to the brim **2** : fulfill (a wish, etc.) **3** ~ **de** : shower with — **colmado, -da** *adj* : heaping

colmena *nf* : beehive

colmillo *nm* **1** : canine (tooth) **2** : fang (of a dog, etc.), tusk (of an elephant)

colmo *nm* **1** : height, limit **2 ¡eso es el** ~ **!** : that's the last straw!

colocar {72} *vt* **1** PONER : place, put **2** : find a job for — **colocarse** *vr* **1** SITUARSE : position oneself **2** : get a job — **colocación** *nf, pl* **-ciones** : placement, placing **2** EMPLEO : position, job

colombiano, -na *adj* : Colombian

colon *nm* : (intestinal) colon

colonia *nf* **1** : colony **2** PERFUME : cologne **3** *Lat* : residential area — **colonial** *adj* : colonial — **colonizar** {21} *vt* : colonize — **colonización** *nf, pl* **-ciones** : colonization — **colono, -na** *n* : settler, colonist

coloquial *adj* : colloquial — **coloquio** *nm* **1** : talk, discussion **2** CONGRESO : conference

color *nm* : color — **colorado, -da** *adj* : red — **colorear** *vt* : color — **colorete** *nm* : rouge — **colorido** *nm* : colors *pl*, coloring

colosal *adj* : colossal

columna *nf* **1** : column **2** ~ **vertebral** : spine, backbone — **columnista** *nmf* : columnist

columpiar *vt* : push (on a swing) — **columpiarse** *vr* : swing — **columpio** *nm* : swing

coma[1] *nm* : coma

coma[2] *nf* : comma

comadre *nf* **1** : godmother of one's child, mother of one's godchild **2** *fam*

: (female) friend — **comadrear** *vi fam*
: gossip
comadreja *nf* : weasel
comadrona *nf* : midwife
comandancia *nf* : command headquarters, command — **comandante** *nmf* 1
: commander 2 : major (in the military) — **comando** *nm* 1 : commando
2 *Lat* : command
comarca *nf* : region, area
combar *vt* : bend, curve
combatir *vt* : combat, fight against — *vi*
: fight — **combate** *nm* 1 : combat 2
: fight (in boxing) — **combatiente**
nmf : combatant, fighter
combinar *vt* 1 : combine 2 : put together, match (colors, etc.) — **combinarse** *vr* : get together — **combinación**
nf, pl -**ciones** 1 : combination 2 : connection (in travel)
combustible *nm* : fuel — ~ *adj* : combustible — **combustión** *nf, pl* -**tiones**
: combustion
comedia *nf* : comedy
comedido, -da *adj* : moderate
comedor *nm* : dining room
comensal *nmf* : diner, dinner guest
comentar *vt* 1 : comment on, discuss 2
MENCIONAR : mention — **comentario**
nm 1 : comment, remark 2 ANÁLISIS
: commentary — **comentarista** *nmf*
: commentator
comenzar {29} *v* : begin, start
comer *vt* 1 : eat 2 *fam* : eat up, eat into
— *vi* 1 : eat 2 CENAR : have a meal 3
dar de ~ : feed — **comerse** *vr* : eat
up
comercio *nm* 1 : commerce, trade 2 NEGOCIO : business — **comercial** *adj*
: commercial — **comercializar** {21}
vt : market — **comerciante** *nmf* : merchant, dealer — **comerciar** *vi* : do
business, trade
comestible *adj* : edible — **comestibles** *nmpl* : groceries, food
cometa *nm* : comet — ~ *nf* : kite
cometer *vt* 1 : commit 2 ~ **un error**
: make a mistake — **cometido** *nm*
: assignment, task
comezón *nf, pl* -**zones** : itchiness, itching
comicios *nmpl* : elections
cómico, -ca *adj* : comic, comical — ~
n : comic, comedian
comida *nf* 1 ALIMENTO : food 2 *Spain*
: lunch 3 *Lat* : dinner 4 **tres** ~**s al día**
: three meals a day
comienzo *nm* : beginning
comillas *nfpl* : quotation marks
comino *nm* : cumin

comisario, -ria *n* : commissioner —
comisaría *nf* : police station
comisión *nf, pl* -**siones** 1 : commission
2 COMITÉ : committee
comité *nm* : committee
como *conj* 1 : as, since 2 **sí** : if — ~
prep 1 : like, as 2 **así** ~ : as well as —
~ *adv* 1 : as 2 APROXIMADAMENTE
: around, about
cómo *adv* 1 : how 2 ~ **no** : by all
means 3 ¿~ **te llamas?** : what's your
name?
cómoda *nf* : chest of drawers
comodidad *nf* : comfort, convenience
comodín *nm, pl* -**dines** : joker (in playing cards)
cómodo, -da *adj* 1 : comfortable 2 ÚTIL
: handy, convenient
comoquiera *adv* 1 : in any way 2 ~
que : however
compacto, -ta *adj* : compact
compadecer {53} *vt* : feel sorry for —
compadecerse *vr* ~ **de** : take pity on
compadre *nm* 1 : godfather of one's
child, father of one's godchild 2 *fam*
: buddy
compañero, -ra *n* : companion, partner
— **compañerismo** *nm* : companionship
compañía *nf* : company
comparar *vt* : compare — **comparable**
adj : comparable — **comparación** *nf,
pl* -**ciones** : comparison — **comparativo, -va** *adj* : comparative
comparecer *vt* : appear (before a court,
etc.)
compartimiento *or* **compartimento**
nm : compartment
compartir *vt* : share
compás *nm, pl* -**pases** 1 : compass 2
: rhythm, time (in music)
compasión *nf, pl* -**siones** : compassion, pity — **compasivo, -va** *adj*
: compassionate
compatible *adj* : compatible — **compatibilidad** *nf* : compatibility
compatriota *nmf* : compatriot, fellow
countryman
compeler *vt* : compel
compendiar *vt* : summarize — **compendio** *nm* : summary
compensar *vt* : compensate for —
compensación *nf, pl* -**ciones** : compensation
competir {54} *vi* : compete — **competencia** *nf* 1 : competition, rivalry 2 CAPACIDAD : competence — **competente**
adj : competent — **competición** *nf, pl*
-**ciones** : competition — **competidor,
-dora** *n* : competitor

compilar *vt* : compile

compinche *nmf fam* : friend, chum

complacer {57} *vt* : please — **complacerse** *vr* ~ **en** : take pleasure in — **complaciente** *adj* : obliging, helpful

complejidad *nf* : complexity — **complejo, -ja** *adj* : complex — **complejo** *nm* : complex

complementar *vt* : complement — **complementario, -ria** *adj* : complementary — **complemento** *nm* 1 : complement 2 : object (in grammar)

completar *vt* : complete — **completo, -ta** *adj* 1 : complete 2 PERFECTO : perfect 3 LLENO : full — **completamente** *adv* : completely

complexión *nf, pl* -**xiones** : constitution, build

complicar {72} *vt* 1 : complicate 2 IMPLICAR : involve — **complicación** *nf, pl* -**ciones** : complication — **complicado, -da** *adj* : complicated, complex

cómplice *nmf* : accomplice — ~ *adj* : conspiratorial, knowing

complot *nm, pl* -**plots** : conspiracy, plot

componer {60} *vt* 1 : make up, compose 2 : compose, write (a song) 3 ARREGLAR : fix, repair — **componerse** *vr* ~ **de** : consist of — **componente** *adj* ~ *nm* : component, constituent

comportarse *vr* : behave — **comportamiento** *nm* : behavior

composición *nf, pl* -**ciones** : composition — **compositor, -tora** *n* : composer, songwriter

compostura *nf* 1 : composure 2 REPARACIÓN : repair

comprar *vt* : buy, purchase — **compra** *nf* 1 : purchase 2 **ir de** ~**s** : go shopping — **comprador, -dora** *n* : buyer, shopper

comprender *vt* 1 : comprehend, understand 2 ABARCAR : cover, include — **comprensible** *adj* : understandable — **comprensión** *nf, pl* -**siones** : understanding — **comprensivo, -va** *adj* : understanding

compresa *nf* 1 : compress 2 *or* ~ **higiénica** : sanitary napkin

compresión *nf, pl* -**siones** : compression — **comprimido** *nm* : pill, tablet — **comprimir** *vt* : compress

comprobar {19} *vt* 1 VERIFICAR : check 2 DEMOSTRAR : prove — **comprobación** *nf, pl* -**ciones** : verification, check — **comprobante** *nm* 1 : proof 2 RECIBO : receipt, voucher

comprometer *vt* 1 : compromise 2 ARRIESGAR : jeopardize 3 OBLIGAR : commit, put under obligation — **comprometerse** *vr* 1 : commit oneself 2 ~ **con** : get engaged to — **comprometedor, -dora** *adj* : compromising — **comprometido, -da** *adj* 1 : compromising, awkward 2 : engaged (to be married) — **compromiso** *nm* 1 : obligation, commitment 2 : (marriage) engagement 3 ACUERDO : agreement 4 APURO : awkward situation

compuesto, -ta *adj* 1 : compound 2 ~ **de** : made up of, consisting of — **compuesto** *nm* : compound

compulsivo, -va *adj* : compelling, urgent

computar *vt* : compute, calculate — **computadora** *nf or* **computador** *nm* 1 : computer 2 ~ **portátil** : laptop computer — **cómputo** *nm* : calculation

comulgar {52} *vi* : receive Communion

común *adj, pl* -**munes** 1 : common 2 ~ **y corriente** : ordinary 3 **por lo** ~ : generally

comuna *nf* : commune — **comunal** *adj* : communal

comunicar {72} *vt* : communicate — **comunicarse** *vr* 1 : communicate 2 ~ **con** : get in touch with — **comunicación** *nf, pl* -**ciones** : communication — **comunicado** *nm* : communiqué — **comunicativo, -va** *adj* : communicative

comunidad *nf* : community

comunión *nf, pl* -**niones** : communion, Communion

comunismo *nm* : Communism — **comunista** *adj & nmf* : Communist

con *prep* 1 : with 2 A PESAR DE : in spite of 3 (*before an infinitive*) : by 4 ~ (**tal**) **que** : so long as

cóncavo, -va *adj* : concave

concebir {54} *v* : conceive — **concebible** *adj* : conceivable

conceder *vt* 1 : grant, bestow 2 ADMITIR : concede

concejal, -jala *n* : councilman, alderman

concentrar *vt* : concentrate — **concentrarse** *vr* : concentrate — **concentración** *nf, pl* -**ciones** : concentration

concepción *nf, pl* -**ciones** : conception — **concepto** *nm* 1 : concept 2 OPINIÓN : opinion

concernir {17} *vi* ~ **a** : concern — **concerniente** *adj* ~ **a** : concerning

concertar {55} *vt* 1 : arrange, coordinate 2 (*used before an infinitive*) : agree 3 : harmonize (in music) — *vi* : be in harmony

concesión *nf, pl* **-siones 1** : concession **2** : awarding (of prizes, etc.)
concha *nf* : shell
conciencia *nf* **1** : conscience **2** CONOCIMIENTO : consciousness, awareness — **concientizar** {21} *vt Lat* : make aware — **concientizarse** *vr Lat* ~ **de** : realize
concienzudo, -da *adj* : conscientious
concierto *nm* **1** : concert **2** : concerto (musical composition)
conciliar *vt* : reconcile — **conciliación** *nf, pl* **-ciones** : reconciliation
concilio *nm* : council
conciso, -sa *adj* : concise
conciudadano, -na *n* : fellow citizen
concluir {41} *vt* : conclude — *vi* : come to an end — **conclusión** *nf, pl* **-siones** : conclusion — **concluyente** *adj* : conclusive
concordar {19} *vi* : agree — *vt* : reconcile — **concordancia** *nf* : agreement — **concordia** *nf* : harmony, concord
concretar *vt* : make concrete, specify — **concretarse** *vr* : become definite, take shape — **concreto, -ta** *adj* **1** : concrete **2** DETERMINADO : specific **3** **en** ~ : specifically — **concreto** *nm Lat* : concrete
concurrir *vi* **1** : come together, meet **2** ~ **a** : take part in — **concurrencia** *nf* : audience, turnout — **concurrido, -da** *adj* : busy, crowded
concursar *vi* : compete, participate — **concursante** *nmf* : competitor — **concurso** *nm* **1** : competition **2** CONCURRENCIA : gathering **3** AYUDA : help, cooperation
condado *nm* : county
conde, -desa *n* : count *m*, countess *f*
condenar *vt* **1** : condemn, damn **2** : sentence (a criminal) — **condena** *nf* **1** : condemnation **2** SENTENCIA : sentence — **condenación** *nf, pl* **-ciones** : condemnation, damnation
condensar *vt* : condense — **condensación** *nf, pl* **-ciones** : condensation
condesa *nf* → **conde**
condescender {56} *vi* **1** : acquiesce, agree **2** ~ **a** : condescend to — **condescendiente** *adj* : condescending
condición *nf, pl* **-ciones 1** : condition, state **2** CALIDAD : capacity, position — **condicional** *adj* : conditional
condimento *nm* : condiment, seasoning
condolerse {47} *vr* : sympathize — **condolencia** *nf* : condolence
condominio *nm* **1** : joint ownership **2** *Lat* : condominium

condón *nm, pl* **-dones** : condom
conducir {61} *vt* **1** DIRIGIR : direct, lead **2** MANEJAR : drive — *vi* **1** : drive **2** ~ **a** : lead to — **conducirse** *vr* : behave
conducta *nf* : behavior, conduct
conducto *nm* : conduit, duct
conductor, -tora *n* : driver
conectar *vt* **1** : connect **2** ENCHUFAR : plug in — *vi* : connect
conejo, -ja *n* : rabbit — **conejera** *nf* : (rabbit) hutch
conexión *nf, pl* **-xiones** : connection — **conexo, -xa** *adj* : connected
confabularse *vr* : conspire, plot
confeccionar *vt* : make (up), prepare — **confección** *nf, pl* **-ciones 1** : making, preparation **2** : tailoring, dressmaking
confederación *nf, pl* **-ciones** : confederation
conferencia *nf* **1** : lecture **2** REUNIÓN : conference
conferir {76} *vt* : confer, bestow
confesar {55} *v* : confess — **confesarse** *vr* : go to confession — **confesión** *nf, pl* **-siones 1** : confession **2** CREDO : religion, creed
confeti *nm* : confetti
confiar {85} *vi* : trust — *vt* : entrust — **confiable** *adj* : trustworthy, reliable — **confiado, -da** *adj* **1** : confident **2** CRÉDULO : trusting — **confianza** *nf* **1** : trust **2** : confidence (in oneself)
confidencia *nf* : confidence, secret — **confidencial** *adj* : confidential — **confidencialidad** *nf* : confidentiality — **confidente** *nmf* **1** : confidant, confidante *f* **2** : (police) informer
configuración *nf, pl* **-ciones** : configuration, shape
confín *nm, pl* **-fines** : boundary, limit — **confinar** *vt* **1** : confine **2** DESTERRAR : exile
confirmar *vt* : confirm — **confirmación** *nf, pl* **-ciones** : confirmation
confiscar {72} *vt* : confiscate
confitería *nm* : candy store
confitura *nf* : jam
conflagración *nf, pl* **-ciones 1** : war, conflict **2** INCENDIO : fire
conflicto *nm* : conflict
confluencia *nf* : junction, confluence
conformar *vt* : shape, make up — **conformarse** *vr* **1** RESIGNARSE : resign oneself **2** ~ **con** : content oneself with — **conforme** *adj* **1** : content, satisfied **2** ~ **a** : in accordance with — ~ *conj* : as — **conformidad** *nf* **1** : agreement **2** RESIGNACIÓN : resignation

confortar *vt* : comfort — **confortable** *adj* : comfortable

confrontar *vt* **1** : confront **2** COMPARAR : compare — *vi* : border — **confrontarse** *vr* ~ **con** : face up to — **confrontación** *nf*, *pl* **-ciones** : confrontation

confundir *vt* : confuse, mix up — **confundirse** *vr* : make a mistake, be confused — **confusión** *nf*, *pl* **-siones** : confusion — **confuso, -sa** *adj* **1** : confused **2** INDISTINTO : hazy, indistinct — **congelar** *vt* : freeze — **congelarse** *vr* : freeze — **congelación** *nf*, *pl* **-ciones** : freezing — **congelado, -da** *adj* : frozen — **congelador** *nm* : freezer

congeniar *vi* : get along

congestión *nf*, *pl* **-tiones** : congestion — **congestionado, -da** *adj* : congested

congoja *nf* : anguish, grief

congraciarse *vr* : ingratiate oneself

congratular *vt* : congratulate

congregar {52} *vt* : bring together — **congregarse** *vr* : congregate — **congregación** *nf*, *pl* **-ciones** : congregation, gathering

congreso *nm* : congress — **congresista** *nmf* : member of congress

conjeturar *vt* : guess, conjecture — **conjetura** *nf* : guess, conjecture

conjugar {52} *vt* : conjugate — **conjugación** *nf*, *pl* **-ciones** : conjugation

conjunción *nf*, *pl* **-ciones** : conjunction

conjunto, -ta *adj* : joint — **conjunto** *nm* **1** : collection **2** : outfit (of clothing) **3** GRUPO : band **4 en ~** : as a whole

conjurar *vt* : ward off — *vi* : conspire, plot

conllevar *vt* : entail

conmemorar *vt* : commemorate — **conmemoración** *nf*, *pl* **-ciones** : commemoration — **conmemorativo, -va** *adj* : commemorative

conmigo *pron* : with me

conminar *vt* : threaten

conmiseración *nf*, *pl* **-ciones** : pity, commiseration

conmocionar *vt* : shock — **conmoción** *nf*, *pl* **-ciones** **1** : shock, upheaval **2** *or* ~ **cerebral** : concussion

conmover {47} *vt* **1** : move, touch **2** SACUDIR : shake (up) — **conmoverse** *vr* : be moved — **conmovedor, -dora** *adj* : moving, touching

conmutador *nm* **1** : (electric) switch **2** *Lat* : switchboard

cono *nm* : cone

conocer {18} *vt* **1** : know **2** : meet (a person), get to know (a city, etc.) **3** RECONOCER : recognize — **conocerse** *vr* **1** : meet, get to know each other **2** : know oneself — **conocedor, -dora** *adj* & *n* : expert — **conocido, -da** *adj* : well-known — ~ *n* : acquaintance — **conocimiento** *nm* **1** : knowledge **2** SENTIDO : consciousness

conque *conj* : so

conquistar *vt* : conquer — **conquista** *nf* : conquest — **conquistador, -dora** *adj* : conquering — **conquistador** *nm* : conqueror

consabido, -da *adj* **1** : well-known **2** HABITUEL : usual

consagrar *vt* **1** : consecrate DEDICAR : devote — **consagración** *nf*, *pl* **-ciones** : consecration

consciencia *nf* → **conciencia** — **consciente** *adj* : conscious, aware

consecución *nf*, *pl* **-ciones** : attainment

consecuencia *nf* **1** : consequence **2 en** ~ : accordingly — **consecuente** *adj* : consistent

consecutivo, -va *adj* : consecutive

conseguir {75} *vt* **1** : get, obtain **2** ~ **hacer algo** : manage to do sth

consejo *nm* **1** : advice, counsel **2** : council (assembly) — **consejero, -ra** *n* : adviser, counselor

consenso *nm* : consensus

consentir {76} *vt* **1** : allow, permit **2** MIMAR : pamper, spoil — *vi* : consent — **consentimiento** *nm* : consent, permission

conserje *nmf* : caretaker, janitor

conservar *vt* **1** : preserve **2** GUARDAR : keep, conserve — **conservarse** *vr* : keep — **conserva** *nf* **1** : preserve(s) **2** ~**s** *nfpl* : canned goods — **conservación** *nf*, *pl* **-ciones** : conservation, preservation — **conservador, -dora** *adj* & *n* : conservative — **conservatorio** *nm* : conservatory

considerar *vt* **1** : consider **2** RESPETAR : respect — **considerable** *adj* : considerable — **consideración** *nf*, *pl* **-ciones** **1** : consideration **2** RESPETO : respect — **considerado, -da** *adj* **1** : considerate **2** RESPETADO : respected

consigna *nf* **1** ESLOGAN : slogan **2** ORDEN : orders **3** : checkroom (for baggage)

consigo *pron* : with her, with him, with you, with oneself

consiguiente *adj* **1** : consequent **2 por** ~ : consequently

consistir *vi* ～ **en 1** : consist of **2** : lie in, consist in — **consistencia** *nf* : consistency — **consistente** *adj* **1** : firm, solid **2** ～ **en** : consisting of
consolar {19} *vt* : console, comfort — **consolarse** *vr* : console oneself — **consolación** *nf, pl* -**ciones** : consolation
consolidar *vt* : consolidate — **consolidación** *nf, pl* -**ciones** : consolidation
consomé *nm* : consommé
consonante *adj* : consonant, harmonious — ～ *nf* : consonant
consorcio *nm* : consortium
conspirar *vi* : conspire, plot — **conspiración** *nf, pl* -**ciones** : conspiracy — **conspirador, -dora** *n* : conspirator
constancia *nf* **1** : record, evidence **2** PERSEVERANCIA : perseverance — **constante** *adj* : constant — **constantemente** *adv* : constantly, continually
constar *vi* **1** : be evident, be clear **2** ～ **de** : consist of
constatar *vt* **1** : verify **2** AFIRMAR : state, affirm
constelación *nf, pl* -**ciones** : constellation
consternación *nf, pl* -**ciones** : consternation
constipado, -da *adj* estar ～ : have a cold — **constipado** *nm* : cold — **constiparse** *vr* : catch a cold
constituir {41} *vt* **1** FORMAR : constitute, form **2** FUNDAR : establish, set up — **constituirse** *vr* ～ **en** : set oneself up as — **constitución** *nf, pl* -**ciones** : constitution — **constitucional** *adj* : constitutional — **constitutivo, -va** *adj* : constituent — **constituyente** *adj & nm* : constituent
constreñir {67} *vt* **1** : force, compel **2** RESTRINGIR : restrict, limit
construir {41} *vt* : build, construct — **construcción** *nf, pl* -**ciones** : construction, building — **constructivo, -va** *adj* : constructive — **constructor, -tora** *n* : builder
consuelo *nm* : consolation, comfort
consuetudinario, -ria *adj* : customary
cónsul *nmf* : consul — **consulado** *nm* : consulate
consultar *vt* : consult — **consulta** *nf* : consultation — **consultor, -tora** *n* : consultant — **consultorio** *nm* : office (of a doctor or dentist)
consumar *vt* : consummate, complete **2** : commit (a crime)
consumir *vt* : consume — **consumirse** *vr* : waste away — **consumición** *nf, pl* -**ciones 1** : consumption **2** : drink

(in a restaurant) — **consumido, -da** *adj* : thin, emaciated — **consumidor, -dora** *n* : consumer — **consumo** *nm* : consumption
contabilidad *nf* **1** : accounting, bookkeeping **2** : accountancy (profession) — **contable** *nmf Spain* : accountant, bookkeeper
contactar *vi* ～ **con** : get in touch with, contact — **contacto** *nm* : contact
contado, -da *adj* : numbered, few — **contado** *nm* al ～ : (in) cash
contador, -dora *n Lat* : accountant — **contador** *nm* : meter
contagiar *vt* **1** : infect **2** : transmit (a disease) — **contagiarse** *vr* **1** : be contagious **2** : become infected (with a disease) — **contagio** *nm* : contagion, infection — **contagioso, -sa** *adj* : contagious, infectious
contaminar *vt* : contaminate, pollute — **contaminación** *nf, pl* -**ciones** : contamination, pollution
contar {19} *vt* **1** : count **2** NARRAR : tell — *vi* **1** : count **2** ～ **con** : rely on, count on
contemplar *vt* **1** MIRAR : look at, behold **2** CONSIDERAR : contemplate — **contemplación** *nf, pl* -**ciones** : contemplation
contemporáneo, -nea *adj & n* : contemporary
contender {56} *vi* : contend, compete — **contendiente** *nmf* : competitor
contener {80} *vt* **1** : contain **2** RESTRINGIR : restrain, hold back — **contenerse** *vr* : restrain oneself — **contenedor** *nm* : container — **contenido, -da** *adj* : restrained — **contenido** *nm* : contents *pl*
contentar *vt* : please, make happy — **contentarse** *vr* ～ **con** : be satisfied with — **contento, -ta** *adj* : glad, happy, contented
contestar *vt* : answer — *vi* : reply, answer back — **contestación** *nf, pl* -**ciones** : answer, reply
contexto *nm* : context
contienda *nf* **1** COMBATE : dispute, fight **2** COMPETICIÓN : contest
contigo *pron* : with you
contiguo, -gua *adj* : adjacent
continente *nm* : continent — **continental** *adj* : continental
contingencia *nf* : contingency — **contingente** *adj & nm* : contingent
continuar {3} *v* : continue — **continuación** *nf, pl* -**ciones 1** : continuation **2** a ～ : next, then — **continuidad** *nf* : continuity — **continuo, -nua** *adj* **1**

: continuous, steady **2** FRECUENTE
: continual

contorno *nm* **1** : outline **2 ~s** *nmpl*
: surrounding area

contorsión *nf, pl* **-siones** : contortion

contra *prep* **1** : against **2 en ~** : against
— **~** *nm* **los pros y los ~s** : the pros
and cons

contraatacar {72} *v* : counterattack —
contraataque *nm* : counterattack

contrabajo *nm* : double bass

contrabalancear *vt* : counterbalance

contrabandista *nmf* : smuggler —
contrabando *nm* **1** : smuggling **2**
: contraband (goods)

contracción *nf, pl* **-ciones** : contraction

contrachapado *nm* : plywood

contradecir {11} *vt* : contradict —
contradicción *nf, pl* **-ciones** : contradiction — **contradictorio, -ria** *adj*
: contradictory

contraer {81} *vt* **1** : contract **2 ~ matrimonio** : get married — **contraerse**
vr : contract, tighten up

contrafuerte *nm* : buttress

contragolpe *nm* : backlash

contralto *nmf* : contralto

contrapartida *nf* : compensation

contrapelo: a ~ *adv phr* : the wrong
way

contrapeso *nm* : counterbalance

contraponer {60} *vt* **1** : counter, oppose **2** COMPARAR : compare

contraproducente *adj* : counterproductive

contrariar {85} *vt* **1** : oppose **2** MO-
LESTAR : vex, annoy — **contrariedad**
nf **1** : obstacle **2** DISGUSTO : annoyance
— **contrario, -ria** *adj* **1** OPUESTO : opposite **2 al contrario** : on the contrary
3 ser ~ a : be opposed to

contrarrestar *vt* : counteract

contrasentido *nm* : contradiction (in
terms)

contraseña *nf* : password

contrastar *vt* **1** : check, verify **2** RESIS-
TIR : resist — *vi* : contrast — **contraste** *nm* : contrast

contratar *vt* **1** : contract for **2** : hire, engage (workers)

contratiempo *nm* **1** : mishap **2** DIFICUL-
TAD : setback

contrato *nm* : contract — **contratista**
nmf : contractor

contraventana *nf* : shutter

contribuir {41} *vi* **1** : contribute **2** : pay
taxes — **contribución** *nf, pl* **-ciones** **1**
: contribution **2** IMPUESTO : tax — **contribuyente** *nmf* **1** : contributor **2** : taxpayer

contrincante *nmf* : opponent

contrito, -ta *adj* : contrite

controlar *vt* **1** : control **2** COMPROBAR
: monitor, check — **control** *nm* **1**
: control **2** VERIFICACIÓN : inspection,
check — **controlador, -dora** *n* : con-
troller

controversia *nf* : controversy

contundente *adj* **1** : blunt **2** : forceful,
convincing (of arguments, etc.)

contusión *nf, pl* **-siones** : bruise

convalecencia *nf* : convalescence —
convaleciente *adj & nmf* : convalescent

convencer {86} *vt* : convince, persuade — **convencerse** *vr* : be convinced — **convencimiento** *nm* : conviction, belief

convención *nf, pl* **-ciones** : convention
— **convencional** *adj* : conventional

convenir {87} *vi* **1** : be suitable, be advisable **2 ~ en** : agree on — **conveniencia** *nf* **1** : convenience **2** : suitability (of an action, etc.) — **conveniente**
adj **1** : convenient **2** ACONSEJABLE
: suitable, advisable **3** PROVECHOSO
: useful — **convenio** *nm* : agreement,
pact

convento *nm* : convent, monastery

converger {15} *or* **convergir** *vi* : converge

conversar *vi* : converse, talk — **conversación** *nf, pl* **-ciones** : conversation

conversión *nf, pl* **-siones** : conversion
— **converso, -sa** *n* : convert

convertir {76} *vt* : convert — **convertirse** *vr* **~ en** : turn into — **convertible** *adj & nm* : convertible

convexo, -xa *adj* : convex

convicción *nf, pl* **-ciones** : conviction
— **convicto, -ta** *adj* : convicted

convidar *vt* : invite — **convidado, -da**
n : guest

convincente *adj* : convincing

convite *nm* **1** : invitation **2** : banquet

convivir *vi* : live together — **conviven-
cia** *nf* : coexistence, living together

convocar {72} *vt* : convoke, call together

convulsión *nf, pl* **-siones** **1** : convulsion **2** TRASTORNO : upheaval — **convulsivo, -va** *adj* : convulsive

conyugal *adj* : conjugal — **cónyuge**
nmf : spouse, partner

coñac *nm* : cognac, brandy

cooperar *vi* : cooperate — **cooperación** *nf, pl* **-ciones** : cooperation
— **cooperativa** *nf* : cooperative, coop — **cooperativo, -va** *adj* : cooperative

coordenada *nf* : coordinate

coordinar *vt* : coordinate — **coordinación** *nf, pl* -**ciones** : coordination — **coordinador, -dora** *n* : coordinator

copa *nf* **1** : glass, goblet **2** : cup (in sports) **3 tomar una ~** : have a drink

copia *nf* : copy — **copiar** *vt* : copy

copioso, -sa *adj* : copious, abundant

copla *nf* **1** : (popular) song **2** ESTROFA : verse, stanza

copo *nm* **1** : flake **2** *or* **~ de nieve** : snowflake

coquetear *vi* : flirt — **coqueteo** *nm* : flirting, flirtation — **coqueto, -ta** *adj* : flirtatious — **~** *n* : flirt

coraje *nm* **1** : valor, courage **2** IRA : anger

coral[1] *nm* : coral

coral[2] *adj* : choral — **~** *nf* : choir, chorale

Corán *nm* **el ~** : the Koran

coraza *nf* **1** : armor plating **2** : shell

corazón *nm, pl* -**zones 1** : heart **2** : core (of fruit) **3 mi ~** : my darling — **corazonada** *nf* **1** : hunch **2** IMPULSO : impulse

corbata *nf* : tie, necktie

corchete *nm* **1** : hook and eye, clasp **2** : square bracket (punctuation mark)

corcho *nm* : cork

cordel *nm* : cord, string

cordero *nm* : lamb

cordial *adj* : cordial — **cordialidad** *nf* : cordiality

cordillera *nf* : mountain range

córdoba *nf* : córdoba (Nicaraguan unit of currency)

cordón *nm, pl* -**dones 1** : cord **2 ~ policial** : (police) cordon **3 cordones** *nmpl* : shoelaces

cordura *nf* : sanity

corear *vt* : chant

coreografía *nf* : choreography

cornamenta *nf* : antlers *pl*

corneta *nf* : bugle

coro *nm* **1** : chorus **2** : (church) choir

corona *nf* **1** : crown **2** : wreath, garland (of flowers) — **coronación** *nf, pl* -**ciones** : coronation — **coronar** *vt* : crown

coronel *nm* : colonel

coronilla *nf* **1** : crown (of the head) **2 estar hasta la ~** : be fed up

corporación *nf, pl* -**ciones** : corporation

corporal *adj* : corporal, bodily

corporativo, -va *adj* : corporate

corpulento, -ta *adj* : stout

corral *nm* **1** : farmyard **2** : pen, corral (for animals) **3** *or* **corralito** : playpen

correa *nf* **1** : strap, belt **2** : leash (for a dog, etc.)

corrección *nf, pl* -**ciones 1** : correction **2** : correctness, propriety (of manners) — **correccional** *nm* : reformatory — **correctivo, -va** *adj* : corrective — **correcto, -ta** *adj* **1** : correct, right **2** CORTÉS : polite

corredizo, -za *adj* : sliding

corredor, -dora *n* **1** : runner, racer **2** AGENTE : agent, broker — **corredor** *nm* : corridor, hallway

corregir {28} *vt* : correct — **corregirse** *vr* : mend one's ways

correlación *nf, pl* -**ciones** : correlation

correo *nm* **1** : mail **2 ~ aéreo** : airmail

correr *vi* **1** : run, race **2** : flow (of a river, etc.) **3** : pass (of time) — *vt* **1** : run **2** RECORRER : travel over, cover **3** : draw (curtains) — **correrse** *vr* **1** : move along **2** : run (of colors)

corresponder *vi* **1** : correspond **2** PERTENECER : belong **3** ENCAJAR : fit **4 ~ a** : reciprocate, repay — **corresponderse** *vr* : write to each other — **correspondencia** *nf* **1** : correspondence **2** : connection (of a train, etc.) — **correspondiente** *adj* : corresponding, respective — **corresponsal** *nmf* : correspondent

corretear *vi* : run about, scamper

corrida *nf* **1** : run **2** *or* **~ de toros** : bullfight — **corrido, -da** *adj* **1** : straight, continuous **2** *fam* : worldly

corriente *adj* **1** : current **2** NORMAL : common, ordinary **3** : running (of water, etc.) — **~** *nf* **1** : current (of water, electricity, etc.), draft (of air) **2** TENDENCIA : tendency, trend — **~** *nm* **al ~ 1** : up-to-date **2** ENTERADO : aware, informed

corrillo *nm* : clique, circle — **corro** *nm* : ring, circle (of people)

corroborar *vt* : corroborate

corroer {69} *vt* **1** : corrode (of metals) **2** : erode, wear away — **corroerse** *vr* : corrode

corromper *vt* **1** : corrupt **2** PUDRIR : rot — **corrompido, -da** *adj* : corrupt

corrosión *nf, pl* -**siones** : corrosion — **corrosivo, -va** *adj* : corrosive

corrupción *nf, pl* -**ciones 1** : corruption **2** DESCOMPOSICIÓN : decay, rot — **corrupto, -ta** *adj* : corrupt

corsé *nm* : corset

cortar *vt* **1** : cut **2** RECORTAR : cut out **3** QUITAR : cut off — *vi* : cut — **cortarse** *vr* **1** : cut oneself **2** : be cut off (on the telephone) **3** : curdle (of milk) **4 ~ el pelo** : have one's hair cut — **cortada**

nf Lat : cut — **cortante** *adj* : cutting, sharp

cortauñas *nms & pl* : nail clippers

corte[1] *nm* **1** : cutting **2** ESTILO : cut, style **3 ~ de pelo** : haircut

corte[2] *nf* **1** : court **2 hacer la ~ a** : court, woo — **cortejar** *vt* : court, woo

cortejo *nm* **1** : entourage **2** NOVIAZGO : courtship **3 ~ fúnebre** : funeral procession

cortés *adj* : courteous, polite — **cortesía** *nf* : courtesy, politeness

corteza *nf* **1** : bark **2** : crust (of bread) **3** : rind, peel (of fruit)

cortina *nf* : curtain

corto, -ta *adj* **1** : short **2** ESCASO : scarce **3** *fam* : timid, shy **4 ~ de vista** : nearsighted — **cortocircuito** *nm* : short circuit

corvo, -va *adj* : curved, bent

cosa *nf* **1** : thing **2** ASUNTO : matter, affair **3 ~ de** : about **4 poca ~** : nothing much

cosechar *v* : harvest, reap — **cosecha** *nf* **1** : harvest, crop **2** : vintage (of wine)

coser *v* : sew

cosmético, -ca *adj* : cosmetic — **cosmético** *nm* : cosmetic

cósmico, -ca *adj* : cosmic

cosmopolita *adj* : cosmopolitan

cosmos *nm* : cosmos

cosquillas *nfpl* **1** : tickling **2 hacer ~** : tickle — **cosquilleo** *nm* : tickling sensation, tingle

costa *nf* **1** : coast, shore **2 a toda ~** : at any cost

costado *nm* **1** : side **2 al ~** : alongside

costar {19} *v* : cost

costarricense *or* **costarriqueño, -ña** *adj* : Costa Rican

coste *nm* → **costo** — **costear** *vt* : pay for

costero, -ra *adj* : coastal

costilla *nf* **1** : rib **2** CHULETA : chop, cutlet

costo *nm* : cost, price — **costoso, -sa** *adj* : costly

costra *nf* : scab

costumbre *nf* **1** : custom, habit **2 de ~** : usual

costura *nf* **1** : sewing, dressmaking **2** PUNTADAS : seam — **costurera** *nf* : dressmaker

cotejar *vt* : compare

cotidiano, -na *adj* : daily

cotizar {21} *vt* : quote, set a price on — **cotización** *nf, pl* **-ciones** : quotation, price — **cotizado, -da** *adj* : in demand

coto *nm* : enclosure, reserve

cotorra *nf* **1** : small parrot **2** *fam* : chatterbox — **cotorrear** *vi* *fam* : chatter, gab

coyote *nm* : coyote

coyuntura *nf* **1** : joint **2** SITUACIÓN : situation, moment

coz *nm, pl* **coces** : kick (of an animal)

cráneo *nf* : cranium, skull

cráter *nm* : crater

crear *vt* : create — **creación** *nf, pl* **-ciones** : creation — **creativo, -va** *adj* : creative — **creador, -dora** *n* : creator

crecer {53} *vi* **1** : grow **2** AUMENTAR : increase — **crecido, -da** *adj* **1** : full-grown **2** : large (of numbers) — **creciente** *adj* **1** : growing, increasing **2** : crescent (of the moon) — **crecimiento** *nm* **1** : growth **2** AUMENTO : increase

credenciales *nfpl* : credentials

credibilidad *nf* : credibility

crédito *nm* : credit

credo *nm* : creed

crédulo, -la *adj* : credulous, gullible

creer {20} *v* **1** : believe **2** SUPONER : suppose, think — **creerse** *vr* : regard oneself as — **creencia** *nf* : belief — **creíble** *adj* : believable, credible — **creído, -da** *adj fam* : conceited

crema *nf* : cream

cremación *nf, pl* **-ciones** : cremation

cremallera *nf* : zipper

cremoso, -sa *adj* : creamy

crepe *nmf* : crepe, pancake

crepitar *vi* : crackle

crepúsculo *nm* : twilight, dusk

crespo, -pa *adj* : curly, frizzy

crespón *nm, pl* **-pones** : crepe (fabric)

cresta *nf* **1** : crest **2** : comb (of a rooster)

cretino, -na *n* : cretin

creyente *nmf* : believer

criar {85} *vt* **1** : nurse (a baby) **2** EDUCAR : bring up, rear **3** : raise, breed (animals) — **cría** *nf* **1** : breeding, rearing **2** : young animal — **criadero** *nm* : farm, hatchery — **criado, -da** *n* : servant, maid *f* — **criador, -dora** *n* : breeder — **crianza** *nf* : upbringing, rearing

criatura *nf* **1** : creature **2** NIÑO : baby, child

crimen *nm, pl* **crímenes** : crime — **criminal** *adj & nmf* : criminal

críquet *nm* : cricket (game)

crin *nf* : mane

criollo, -lla *adj & n* : Creole

cripta *nf* : crypt

crisantemo *nm* : chrysanthemum

crisis *nf* **1** : crisis **2** ~ **nerviosa** : nervous breakdown

crispar *vt* **1** : tense (muscles), clench (one's fist) **2** IRRITAR : irritate, set on edge — **crisparse** *vr* : tense up

cristal *nm* **1** : crystal **2** VIDRIO : glass, piece of glass — **cristalería** *nf* : glassware — **cristalino, -na** *adj* : crystalline — **cristalino** *nm* : lens (of the eye) — **cristalizar** {21} *vi* : crystallize

cristiano, -na *adj & n* : Christian — **cristianismo** *nm* : Christianity — **Cristo** *nm* : Christ

criterio *nm* **1** : criterion **2** JUICIO : judgment, opinion

criticar {72} *vt* : criticize — **crítica** *nf* **1** : criticism **2** RESEÑA : review, critique — **crítico, -ca** *adj* : critical — ~ *n* : critic, reviewer

croar *vi* : croak

cromo *nm* : chromium, chrome

cromosoma *nm* : chromosome

crónica *nf* **1** : chronicle **2** : (news) report

crónico, -ca *adj* : chronic

cronista *nmf* : reporter, newscaster

cronología *nf* : chronology — **cronológico, -ca** *adj* : chronological

cronometrar *vt* : time, clock — **cronómetro** *nm* : chronometer, stopwatch

croqueta *nf* : croquette

croquis *nms & pl* : (rough) sketch

cruce *nm* **1** : crossing **2** : crossroads, intersection **3** ~ **peatonal** : crosswalk

crucero *nm* **1** : cruise **2** : cruiser (ship)

crucial *adj* : crucial

crucificar {72} *vt* : crucify — **crucifijo** *nm* : crucifix — **crucifixión** *nf, pl* **-fixiones** : crucifixion

crucigrama *nm* : crossword puzzle

crudo, -da *adj* **1** : harsh, crude **2** : raw (of food) — **crudo** *nm* : crude oil

cruel *adj* : cruel — **crueldad** *nf* : cruelty

crujir *vi* : rustle, creak, crackle, crunch — **crujido** *nm* : rustle, creak, crackle, crunch — **crujiente** *adj* : crunchy, crisp

cruzar {21} *vt* **1** : cross **2** : exchange (words) — **cruzarse** *vr* **1** : intersect **2** : pass each other — **cruz** *nf, pl* **cruces** : cross — **cruzada** *nf* : crusade — **cruzado, -da** *adj* : crossed — **cruzado** *nm* : crusader

cuaderno *nm* : notebook

cuadra *nf* **1** : stable **2** *Lat* : (city) block

cuadrado, -da *adj* : square — **cuadrado** *nm* : square

cuadragésimo, -ma *adj* : fortieth, forty- — ~ *n* : fortieth, forty- (in a series)

cuadrar *vi* **1** : conform, agree **2** : add up, tally (numbers) — *vt* : square — **cuadrarse** *vr* : stand at attention

cuadrilátero *nm* **1** : quadrilateral **2** : ring (in sports)

cuadrilla *nf* : gang, group

cuadro *nm* **1** : square **2** PINTURA : painting **3** DESCRIPCIÓN : picture, description **4** : staff, management (of an organization) **5** CUADRADO : check, square **6** : (baseball) diamond

cuadrúpedo *nm* : quadruped

cuádruple *adj* : quadruple — **cuadruplicar** {72} *vt* : quadruple

cuajar *vi* **1** : curdle **2** COAGULAR : clot, coagulate **3** : set (of pudding, etc.) **4** AFIANZARSE : catch on — *vt* **1** : curdle **2** ~ **de** : fill with

cual *pron* **1** **el** ~, **la** ~, **los** ~**es, las** ~**es** : who, whom, which **2** **lo** ~ : which **3** **cada** ~ : everyone, everybody — ~ *prep* : like, as

cuál *pron* : which (one), what (one) — ~ *adj* : which, what

cualidad *nf* : quality, trait

cualquiera (**cualquier** *before nouns*) *adj, pl* **cualesquiera** : any, whatever — ~ *pron, pl* **cualesquiera** : anyone, whatever

cuán *adv* : how

cuando *conj* **1** : when **2** SI : since, if **3** ~ **más** : at the most **4** **de vez en** ~ : from time to time — ~ *prep* : during, at the time of

cuándo *adv* **1** : when **2** **¿desde** ~? : since when?

cuantía *nf* **1** : quantity, extent **2** IMPORTANCIA : importance — **cuantioso, -sa** *adj* : abundant, considerable

cuanto *adv* **1** : as much as **2** ~ **antes** : as soon as possible **3** **en** ~ : as soon as **4** **en** ~ **a** : as for, as regards — **cuanto, -ta** *adj* : as many, whatever — ~ *pron* **1** : as much as, all that, everything **2** **unos cuantos, unas cuantas** : a few

cuánto *adv* : how much, how many — **cuánto, -ta** *adj* : how much, how many — ~ *pron* : how much, how many

cuarenta *adj & nm* : forty — **cuarentavo, -va** *adj* : fortieth — **cuarentavo** *nm* : fortieth

cuarentena *nf* : quarantine

Cuaresma *nf* : Lent

cuartear *vt* : quarter, divide up — **cuartearse** *vr* : crack, split

cuartel *nm* **1** : barracks *pl* **2** ~ **general** : headquarters **3** **no dar** ~ : show no mercy

cuarteto *nm* : quartet

cuarto, -ta *adj* : fourth — ~ *n* : fourth (in a series) — **cuarto** *nm* 1 : quarter, fourth 2 HABITACIÓN : room

cuarzo *nm* : quartz

cuatro *adj & nm* : four — **cuatrocientos, -tas** *adj* : four hundred — **cuatrocientos** *nms & pl* : four hundred

cuba *nf* : cask, barrel

cubano, -na *adj* : Cuban

cubeta *nf* 1 : keg, cask 2 *Lat* : pail, bucket

cúbico, -ca *adj* : cubic, cubed — **cubículo** *nm* : cubicle

cubierta *nf* 1 : cover, covering 2 : (automobile) tire 3 : deck (of a ship) — **cubierto** *nm* 1 : cutlery, place setting 2 a ~ : under cover

cubo *nm* 1 : cube 2 *Spain* : pail, bucket 3 : hub (of a wheel)

cubrecama *nm* : bedspread

cubrir {2} *vt* : cover — **cubrirse** *vr* 1 : cover oneself 2 : cloud over

cucaracha *nf* : cockroach

cuchara *nf* : spoon — **cucharada** *nf* : spoonful — **cucharilla** *or* **cucharita** *nf* : teaspoon — **cucharón** *nm, pl* **-rones** : ladle

cuchichear *vi* : whisper — **cuchicheo** *nm* : whisper

cuchilla *nf* 1 : (kitchen) knife 2 ~ **de afeitar** : razor blade — **cuchillada** *nf* : stab, knife wound — **cuchillo** *nm* : knife

cuclillas *nfpl* **en** ~ : squatting, crouching

cuco *nm* : cuckoo — **cuco, -ca** *adj fam* : pretty, cute

cucurucho *nm* : ice-cream cone

cuello *nm* 1 : neck 2 : collar (of clothing)

cuenca *nf* 1 : river basin 2 : (eye) socket — **cuenco** *nm* 1 : bowl 2 CONCAVIDAD : hollow

cuenta *nf* 1 : calculation, count 2 : (bank) account 3 FACTURA : check, bill 4 : bead (for a necklace, etc.) 5 **darse** ~ : realize 6 **tener en** ~ : bear in mind

cuento *nm* 1 : story, tale 2 ~ **de hadas** : fairy tale

cuerda *nf* 1 : cord, rope, string 2 ~**s vocales** : vocal cords 3 **dar** ~ **a** : wind up

cuerdo, -da *adj* : sane, sensible

cuerno *nm* 1 : horn 2 : antlers *pl* (of a deer)

cuero *nm* 1 : leather, hide 2 ~ **cabelludo** : scalp

cuerpo *nm* 1 : body 2 : corps (in the military, etc.)

cuervo *nm* : crow

cuesta *nf* 1 : slope 2 a ~**s** : on one's back 3 ~ **abajo** : downhill 4 ~ **arriba** : uphill

cuestión *nf, pl* **-tiones** : matter, affair — **cuestionar** *vt* : question — **cuestionario** *nm* 1 : questionnaire 2 : quiz (in school)

cueva *nf* : cave

cuidar *vt* 1 : take care of, look after 2 : pay attention to (details, etc.) — *vi* 1 ~ **de** : look after 2 ~ **de que** : make sure that — **cuidarse** *vr* : take care of oneself — **cuidado** *nm* 1 : care 2 PREOCUPACIÓN : worry, concern 3 **tener** ~ : be careful 4 **¡cuidado!** : watch out!, careful! — **cuidadoso, -sa** *adj* : careful — **cuidadosamente** *adv* : carefully

culata *nf* : butt (of a gun) — **culatazo** *nf* : kick, recoil

culebra *nf* : snake

culinario, -ria *adj* : culinary

culminar *vi* : culminate — **culminación** *nf, pl* **-ciones** : culmination

culo *nm fam* : backside, bottom

culpa *nf* 1 : fault, blame 2 PECADO : sin 3 **echar la** ~ **a** : blame 4 **tener la** ~ : be at fault — **culpabilidad** *nf* : guilt — **culpable** *adj* : guilty — ~ *nmf* : culprit, guilty party — **culpar** *vt* : blame

cultivar *vt* : cultivate — **cultivo** *nm* 1 : farming, cultivation 2 ~**s** : crops

culto, -ta *adj* : cultured, educated — **culto** *nm* 1 : worship 2 : (religious) cult — **cultura** *nf* : culture — **cultural** *adj* : cultural

cumbre *nf* : summit, top

cumpleaños *nms & pl* : birthday

cumplido, -da *adj* 1 : complete, full 2 CORTÉS : courteous — **cumplido** *nm* : compliment, courtesy

cumplimentar *vt* 1 : congratulate 2 CUMPLIR : carry out — **cumplimiento** *nm* : carrying out, performance

cumplir *vt* 1 : accomplish, carry out 2 : keep (a promise), observe (a law, etc.) 3 : reach (a given age) — *vi* 1 : expire, fall due 2 ~ **con el deber** : do one's duty — **cumplirse** *vr* 1 : expire 2 REALIZARSE : come true

cúmulo *nm* 1 : heap, pile 2 : cumulus (cloud)

cuna *nf* 1 : cradle 2 ORIGEN : birthplace

cundir *vi* 1 PROPAGARSE : spread, propagate 2 : go a long way

cuneta *nf* : ditch (in a road), gutter (in a street)

cuña *nf* : wedge

cuñado, -da *n* : brother-in-law *m*, sister-in-law *f*

cuota *nf* 1 : fee, dues 2 CUPO : quota 3 *Lat* : installment, payment

cupo *nm* 1 : quota, share 2 *Lat* : capacity, room

cupón *nm, pl* **-pones** : coupon

cúpula *nf* : dome, cupola

cura *nf* : cure, treatment — ~ *nm* : priest — **curación** *nf, pl* **-ciones** : healing — **curar** *vt* 1 : cure 2 : dress (a wound) 3 CURTIR : tan (hides) — **curarse** *vr* : get well

curiosear *vi* 1 : snoop, pry 2 : browse (in a store) — *vt* : look over — **curiosidad** *nf* : curiosity — **curioso, -sa** *adj* 1 : curious, inquisitive 2 RARO : unusual, strange

currículum *nm, pl* **-lums** *or* **currícule** *nm* : résumé, curriculum vitae

cursar *vt* 1 : take (a course), study 2 ENVIAR : send, pass on

cursi *adj fam* : affected, pretentious

cursiva *nf* : italics *pl*

curso *nm* 1 : course 2 : (school) year 3 en ~ : under way 4 en ~ : current

curtir *vt* 1 : tan 2 : harden (skin, features, etc.) — **curtiduría** *nf* : tannery

curva *nf* 1 : curve, bend 2 ~ **de nivel** : contour — **curvo, -va** *adj* : curved, bent

cúspide *nf* : apex, peak

custodia *nf* : custody — **custodiar** *vt* : guard, look after — **custodio, -dia** *n* : guardian

cutáneo, -nea *adj* : skin

cutícula *nf* : cuticle

cutis *nms & pl* : skin, complexion

cuyo, -ya *adj* 1 : whose, of whom, of which 2 **en cuyo caso** : in which case

D

d *nf* : d, fourth letter of the Spanish alphabet

dádiva *nf* : gift, handout — **dadivoso, -sa** *adj* : generous

dado, -da *adj* 1 : given 2 **dado que** : provided that, since — **dados** *nmpl* : dice

daga *nf* : dagger

daltónico, -ca *adj* : color-blind

dama *nf* 1 : lady 2 ~**s** *nfpl* : checkers

damnificar {72} *vt* : damage, injure

danés, -nesa *adj* : Danish — **danés** *nm* : Danish (language)

danzar {21} *v* : dance — **danza** *nf* : dance, dancing

dañar *vt* : damage, harm — **dañarse** *vr* 1 : be damaged 2 : hurt oneself — **dañino, -na** *adj* : harmful — **daño** *nm* 1 : damage, harm 2 ~**s y perjuicios** : damages

dar {22} *vt* 1 : give 2 PRODUCIR : yield, produce 3 : strike (the hour) 4 MOSTRAR : show — *vi* 1 ~ **como** : consider, regard as 2 ~ **con** : run into, meet 3 ~ **contra** : knock against 4 ~ **para** : be enough for — **darse** *vr* 1 : happen 2 ~ **contra** : bump into 3 ~ **por** : consider oneself 4 **dárselas de** : pose as

dardo *nm* : dart

dársena *nf* : dock

datar *vt* : date — *vi* ~ **de** : date from

dátil *nm* : date (fruit)

dato *nm* 1 : fact 2 ~**s** *nmpl* : data

de *prep* 1 : of 2 ~ **Managua** : from Managua 3 ~ **niño** : as a child 4 ~ **noche** : at night 5 **las tres** ~ **la mañana** : three o'clock in the morning 6 **más** ~ **10** : more than 10

deambular *vi* : wander about, stroll

debajo *adv* 1 : underneath 2 ~ **de** : under, underneath 3 **por** ~ : below, beneath

debatir *vt* : debate — **debatirse** *vr* : struggle — **debate** *nm* : debate

deber *vt* : owe — *v aux* 1 : have to, should 2 (*expressing probability*) : must — **deberse** *vr* ~ **a** : be due to — ~ *nm* 1 : duty 2 ~**es** *nmpl* : homework — **debido, -da** *adj* ~ **a** : due to, owing to

débil *adj* : weak, feeble — **debilidad** *nf* : weakness — **debilitar** *vt* : weaken — **debilitarse** *vr* : get weak — **débilmente** *adv* : weakly, faintly

débito *nm* 1 : debit 2 DEUDA : debt

debutar *vi* : debut — **debut** *nm, pl* ~**s** : debut — **debutante** *nf* : debutante *f*

década *nf* : decade

decadencia *nf* : decadence — **decadente** *adj* : decadent

decaer {13} *vi* : decline, weaken

decano, -na *n* : dean

decapitar *vt* : behead

decena *nf* : ten, about ten

decencia *nf* : decency

decenio *nm* : decade

decente *adj* : decent

decepcionar *vt* : disappoint — **decepción** *nf, pl* **-clones** : disappointment
decibelio *or* **decibel** *nm* : decibel
decidir *vt* : decide, determine — *vi* : decide — **decidirse** *vr* : make up one's mind — **decididamente** *adv* : definitely, decidedly — **decidido, -da** *adj* : determined, resolute
decimal *adj* : decimal
décimo, -ma *adj & n* : tenth
decimoctavo, -va *adj* : eighteenth — ~ *n* : eighteenth (in a series)
decimocuarto, -ta *adj* : fourteenth — ~ *n* : fourteenth (in a series)
decimonoveno, -na *or* **decimonono, -na** *adj* : nineteenth — ~ *n* : nineteenth (in a series)
decimoquinto, -ta *adj* : fifteenth — ~ *n* : fifteenth (in a series)
decimoséptimo, -ma *adj* : seventeenth — ~ *n* : seventeenth (in a series)
decimosexto, -ta *adj* : sixteenth — ~ *n* : sixteenth (in a series)
decimotercero, -ra *adj* : thirteenth — ~ *n* : thirteenth (in a series)
decir {23} *vt* 1 : say 2 CONTAR : tell 3 es ~ : that is to say 4 querer ~ : mean — **decirse** *vr* 1 : tell oneself 2 ¿cómo se dice…en español? : how do you say…in Spanish? — ~ *nm* : saying, expression
decisión *nf, pl* **-siones** : decision — **decisivo, -va** *adj* : decisive
declarar *vt* : declare — *vi* : testify — **declararse** *vr* 1 : declare oneself 2 : break out (of a fire, an epidemic, etc.) — **declaración** *nf, pl* **-clones** : statement
declinar *v* : decline
declive *nm* 1 : decline 2 PENDIENTE : slope
decolorar *vt* : bleach — **decolorarse** *vr* : fade
decoración *nf, pl* **-clones** : decoration — **decorado** *nm* : stage set — **decorar** *vt* : decorate — **decorativo, -va** *adj* : decorative
decoro *nm* : decency, decorum — **decoroso, -sa** *adj* : decent, proper
decrecer {53} *vi* : decrease
decrépito, -ta *adj* : decrepit
decretar *vt* : decree — **decreto** *nm* : decree
dedal *nm* : thimble
dedicar {72} *vt* : dedicate — **dedicarse** *vr* ~ a : devote oneself to — **dedicación** *nf, pl* **-clones** : dedication — **dedicatoria** *nf* : dedication, inscription
dedo *nm* 1 : finger 2 ~ del pie : toe

deducir {61} *vt* 1 INFERIR : deduce 2 DESCONTAR : deduct — **deducción** *nf, pl* **-clones** : deduction
defecar {72} *vi* : defecate
defecto *nm* : defect — **defectuoso, -sa** *adj* : defective, faulty
defender {56} *vt* : defend — **defenderse** *vr* : defend oneself — **defensa** *nf* : defense — **defensiva** *nf* : defensive — **defensivo, -va** *adj* : defensive — **defensor, -sora** *n* 1 : defender 2 *or* **abogado defensor** : defense counsel
deferencia *nf* : deference — **deferente** *adj* : deferential
deficiencia *nf* : deficiency — **deficiente** *adj* : deficient
déficit *nm, pl* **-cits** : deficit
definir *vt* : define — **definición** *nf, pl* **-clones** : definition — **definitivo, -va** *adj* 1 : definitive 2 en **definitiva** : in short
deformar *vt* 1 : deform 2 : distort (the truth, etc.) — **deformación** *nf, pl* **-clones** : distortion — **deforme** *adj* : deformed — **deformidad** *nf* : deformity
defraudar *vt* 1 : defraud 2 DECEPCIONAR : disappoint
degenerar *vi* : degenerate — **degenerado, -da** *adj* : degenerate
degradar *vt* 1 : degrade 2 : demote (in the military)
degustar *vt* : taste
dehesa *nf* : pasture
deidad *nf* : deity
dejar *vt* 1 : leave 2 ABANDONAR : abandon 3 PERMITIR : allow — *vi* ~ de : quit — **dejado, -da** *adj* : slovenly, careless
dejo *nm* 1 : aftertaste 2 : (regional) accent
delantal *nm* : apron
delante *adv* 1 : ahead 2 ~ de : in front of
delantera *nf* 1 : front 2 tomar la ~ : take the lead — **delantero, -ra** *adj* : front, forward — ~ *n* : forward (in sports)
delatar *vt* : denounce, inform against
delegar {52} *vt* : delegate — **delegación** *nf, pl* **-clones** : delegation — **delegado, -da** *n* : delegate, representative
deleitar *vt* : delight, please — **deleite** *nm* : delight
deletrear *vi* : spell (out)
delfín *nm, pl* **-fines** : dolphin
delgado, -da *adj* : thin
deliberar *vi* : deliberate — **deliberación** *nf, pl* **-clones** : deliberation

— **deliberado, -da** *adj* : deliberate, intentional

delicadeza *nf* **1** : delicacy, daintiness **2** SUAVIDAD : gentleness **3** TACTO : tact — **delicado, -da** *adj* **1** : delicate **2** SENSIBLE : sensible **3** DISCRETO : tactful

delicia *nf* : delight — **delicioso, -sa** *adj* **1** : delightful **2** RICO : delicious

delictivo, -va *adj* : criminal

delimitar *vt* : define, set the boundaries of

delincuencia *nf* : delinquency, crime — **delincuente** *adj & nmf* : delinquent, criminal — **delinquir** {24} *vi* : break the law

delirante *adj* : delirious — **delirar** *vi* **1** : be delirious **2** ~ **por** *fam* : rave about — **delirio** *nm* **1** : delirium **2** ~ **de grandeza** : delusions of grandeur

delito *nm* : crime

delta *nm* : delta

demacrado, -da *adj* : emaciated

demandar *vt* **1** : sue **2** PEDIR : demand **3** *Lat* : require — **demanda** *nf* **1** : lawsuit **2** PETICIÓN : request **3** **la oferta y la** ~ : supply and demand — **demandante** *nmf* : plaintiff

demás *adj* : rest of the, other — ~ *pron* **1** **lo (la, los, las)** ~ : the rest, others **2 por** ~ : extremely **3 por lo** ~ : otherwise **4 y** ~ : and so on

demasiado *adv* **1** : too **2** : too much — ~ *adj* : too much, too many

demencia *nf* : madness — **demente** *adj* : insane, mad

democracia *nf* : democracy — **demócrata** *nmf* : democrat — **democrático, -ca** *adj* : democratic

demoler {47} *vt* : demolish — **demolición** *nf, pl* **-ciones** : demolition

demonio *nm* : devil, demon

demorar *v* : delay — **demorarse** *vr* : take a long time — **demora** *nf* : delay

demostrar {19} *vt* **1** : demonstrate **2** MOSTRAR : show — **demostración** *nf, pl* **-ciones** : demonstration

demudar *vt* : change, alter

denegar {49} *vt* : deny, refuse — **denegación** *nf, pl* **-ciones** : denial, refusal

denigrar *vt* **1** : denigrate **2** INJURIAR : insult

denominador *nm* : denominator

denotar *vt* : denote, show

densidad *nf* : density — **denso, -sa** *adj* : dense

dental *adj* : dental — **dentado, -da** *adj* : toothed, notched — **dentadura** *nf* ~ **postiza** : dentures *pl* — **dentífrico** *nm* : toothpaste — **dentista** *nmf* : dentist

dentro *adv* **1** : in, inside **2** ~ **de poco** : soon, shortly **3 por** ~ : inside

denuedo *nm* : courage

denunciar *vt* **1** : denounce **2** : report (a crime) — **denuncia** *nf* **1** : accusation **2** : (police) report

departamento *nm* **1** : department **2** *Lat* : apartment

depender *vi* **1** : depend **2** ~ **de** : depend on — **dependencia** *nf* **1** : dependence, dependency **2** SUCURSAL : branch office — **dependiente** *adj* : dependent — **dependiente, -ta** *n* : clerk, salesperson

deplorar *vt* : deplore, regret

deponer {60} *vt* : remove from office, depose

deportar *vt* : deport — **deportación** *nf, pl* **-ciones** : deportation

deporte *nm* : sport, sports *pl* — **deportista** *nmf* : sportsman *m*, sportswoman *f* — **deportivo, -va** *adj* **1** : sporty **2 artículos deportivos** : sporting goods

depositar *vt* **1** : put, place **2** : deposit (in a bank, etc.) — **depósito** *nm* **1** : deposit **2** ALMACÉN : warehouse

depravado, -da *adj* : depraved

depreciarse *vr* : depreciate — **depreciación** *nf* : depreciation

depredador *nm* : predator

deprimir *vt* : depress — **deprimirse** *vr* : get depressed — **depresión** *nf, pl* **-siones** : depression

derecha *nf* **1** : right side **2** : right wing (in politics) — **derechista** *adj* : right-wing — **derecho** *nm* **1** : right **2** LEY : law — ~ *adv* : straight — **derecho, -cha** *adj* **1** : right, right-hand **2** VERTICAL : upright **3** RECTO : straight

deriva *nf* **1** : drift **2 a la** ~ : adrift — **derivación** *nf, pl* **-ciones** : derivation — **derivar** *vi* **1** : drift **2** ~ **de** : derive from

derramamiento *nm* ~ **de sangre** : bloodshed

derramar *vt* **1** : spill **2** : shed (tears, blood) — **derramarse** *vr* : overflow — **derrame** *nm* **1** : spilling **2** : discharge, hemorrhage

derrapar *vi* : skid — **derrape** *nm* : skid

derretir {54} *vt* : melt, thaw — **derretirse** *vr* **1** : melt, thaw **2** ~ **por** *fam* : be crazy about

derribar *vt* **1** : demolish **2** : bring down (a plane, a tree, etc.) **3** : overthrow (a government, etc.)

derrocar {72} *vt* : overthrow

derrochar *vt* : waste, squander — **der-**

rochador, -dora n : spendthrift — **derroche** nm : extravagance, waste

derrotar vt : defeat — **derrota** nf : defeat

derruir {41} vt : demolish, tear down

derrumbar vt : demolish, knock down — **derrumbarse** vr : collapse, break down — **derrumbamiento** nm : collapse — **derrumbe** nm : collapse

desabotonar vt : unbutton, undo

desabrido, -da adj : bland

desabrochar vt : unbutton, undo — **desabrocharse** vr : come undone

desacato nm 1 : disrespect 2 : contempt (of court) — **desacatar** vt : defy, disobey

desacertado, -da adj : mistaken, wrong — **desacertar** {55} vi : be mistaken — **desacierto** nm : mistake, error

desaconsejar vt : advise against — **desaconsejable** adj : inadvisable

desacreditar vt : discredit

desactivar vt : deactivate

desacuerdo nm : disagreement

desafiar {85} vt : defy, challenge — **desafiante** adj : defiant

desafilado, -da adj : blunt

desafinado, -da adj : out-of-tune, off-key

desafío nm : challenge, defiance

desafortunado, -da adj : unfortunate — **desafortunadamente** adv : unfortunately

desagradar vt : displease — **desagradable** adj : disagreeable, unpleasant

desagradecido, -da adj : ungrateful

desagrado nm 1 : displeasure 2 con ~ : reluctantly

desagravio nm : amends, reparation

desagregarse {52} vr : disintegrate

desaguar {10} vi : drain, empty — **desagüe** nm 1 : drainage 2 : drain (of a sink, etc.)

desahogar {52} vt 1 : relieve 2 : give vent to (anger, etc.) — **desahogarse** vr : let off steam, unburden oneself — **desahogado, -da** adj 1 : roomy 2 ADINERADO : comfortable, well-off — **desahogo** nm 1 : relief 2 con ~ : comfortably

desahuciar vt 1 : deprive of hope 2 DESALOJAR : evict — **desahucio** nm : eviction

desaire nm : snub, rebuff — **desairar** vt : snub, slight

desalentar {55} vt : discourage — **desaliento** nm : discouragement

desaliñado, -da adj : slovenly

desalmado, -da adj : heartless, cruel

desalojar vt 1 : evacuate 2 DESAHUCIAR : evict

desamparar vt : abandon — **desamparo** nm : abandonment, desertion

desamueblado, -da adj : unfurnished

desangrarse vr : lose blood, bleed to death

desanimar vt : discourage — **desanimarse** vr : get discouraged — **desanimado, -da** adj : downhearted, despondent — **desánimo** nm : discouragement

desanudar vt : untie

desaparecer {53} vi : disappear — **desaparecido, -da** n : missing person — **desaparición** nf, pl **-ciones** : disappearance

desapasionado, -da adj : dispassionate

desapego nm : indifference

desapercibido, -da adj : unnoticed

desaprobar {19} vt : disapprove of — **desaprobación** nf, pl **-ciones** : disapproval

desaprovechar vt : waste

desarmar vt 1 : disarm 2 DESMONTAR : dismantle, take apart — **desarme** nm : disarmament

desarraigar {52} vt : uproot, root out

desarreglar vt 1 : mess up 2 : disrupt (plans, etc.) — **desarreglado, -da** adj : disorganized — **desarreglo** nm : untidiness, disorder

desarrollar vt : develop — **desarrollarse** vr : take place — **desarrollo** nm : development

desarticular vt 1 : break up, dismantle 2 : dislocate (a bone)

desaseado, -da adj 1 : dirty 2 DESORDENADO : messy

desastre nm : disaster — **desastroso, -sa** adj : disastrous

desatar vt 1 : undo, untie 2 : unleash (passions) — **desatarse** vr 1 : come undone 2 DESENCADENARSE : break out, erupt

desatascar {72} vt : unclog

desatender {56} vt 1 : disregard 2 : neglect (an obligation, etc.) — **desatento, -ta** adj : inattentive

desatinado, -da adj : foolish, silly

desautorizado, -da adj : unauthorized

desavenencia nf : disagreement

desayunar vi : have breakfast — vt : have for breakfast — **desayuno** nm : breakfast

desbancar {72} vt : oust

desbarajuste nm : disorder, confusion

desbaratar vt : ruin, destroy — **desbaratarse** vr : fall apart

desbocarse {72} *vr* : run away, bolt
desbordar *vt* 1 : overflow 2 : exceed (limits) — **desbordarse** *vr* : overflow — **desbordamiento** *nm* : overflow
descabellado, -da *adj* : crazy
descafeinado, -da *adj* : decaffeinated
descalabrar *vt* : hit on the head — **descalabro** *nm* : misfortune, setback
descalificar {72} *vt* : disqualify — **descalificación** *nf, pl* -**ciones** : disqualification
descalzarse {21} *vr* : take off one's shoes — **descalzo, -za** *adj* : barefoot
descaminar *vt* : mislead, lead astray
descansar *v* : rest — **descanso** *nm* 1 : rest 2 : landing (of a staircase) 3 : intermission (in theater), halftime (in sports)
descapotable *adj & nm* : convertible
descarado, -da *adj* : insolent, shameless
descargar {52} *vt* 1 : unload 2 : discharge (a firearm, etc.) — **descarga** *nf* 1 : unloading 2 : discharge (of a firearm, of electricity, etc.) — **descargo** *nm* 1 : unloading 2 : discharge (of a duty, etc.) 3 : defense (in law)
descarnado, -da *adj* : scrawny, gaunt
descaro *nm* : insolence, nerve
descarrilar *vi* : derail — **descarrilarse** *vr* : be derailed
descartar *vt* : reject — **descartarse** *vr* : discard
descascarar *vt* : peel, shell, husk
descender {56} *vt* 1 : go down 2 BAJAR : lower — *vi* 1 : descend 2 ~ **de** : be descended from — **descendencia** *nf* 1 : descendants *pl* 2 LINAJE : lineage, descent — **descendiente** *nmf* : descendant — **descenso** *nm* 1 : descent 2 : drop, fall (in level, in temperature, etc.)
descifrar *vt* : decipher, decode
descolgar {16} *vt* 1 : take down 2 : pick up, answer (the telephone)
descolorarse *vr* : fade — **descolorido, -da** *adj* : faded, discolored
descomponer {60} *vt* : break down — **descomponerse** *vr* 1 : rot, decompose 2 *Lat* : break down — **descompuesto, -ta** *adj Lat* : out of order
descomunal *adj* : enormous
desconcertar {55} *vt* : disconcert, confuse — **desconcertante** *adj* : confusing — **desconcierto** *nm* : confusion, bewilderment
desconectar *vt* : disconnect
desconfiar {85} *vi* ~ **de** : distrust — **desconfiado, -da** *adj* : distrustful — **desconfianza** *nf* : distrust

descongelar *vt* 1 : thaw, defrost 2 : unfreeze (assets)
descongestionante *nm* : decongestant
desconocer {18} *vt* : not know, fail to recognize — **desconocido, -da** *adj* : unknown — ~ *n* : stranger
desconsiderado, -da *adj* : inconsiderate
desconsolar *vt* : distress — **desconsolado, -da** *adj* : heartbroken — **desconsuelo** *nm* : grief, sorrow
descontar {19} *vt* : discount
descontento, -ta *adj* : dissatisfied — **descontento** *nm* : discontent
descontinuar *vt* : discontinue
descorazonado, -da *adj* : discouraged
descorrer *vt* : draw back
descortés *adj, pl* -**teses** : rude — **descortesía** *nf* : discourtesy, rudeness
descoyuntar *vt* : dislocate
descrédito *nm* : discredit
descremado, -da *adj* : nonfat, skim
describir {33} *vt* : describe — **descripción** *nf, pl* -**ciones** : description — **descriptivo, -va** *adj* : descriptive
descubierto, -ta *adj* 1 : exposed, uncovered 2 **al descubierto** : in the open — **descubierto** *nm* : deficit, overdraft
descubrir {2} *vt* 1 : discover 2 REVELAR : reveal — **descubrimiento** *nm* : discovery
descuento *nm* : discount
descuidar *vt* : neglect — **descuidarse** *vr* 1 : be careless 2 ABANDONARSE : let oneself go — **descuidado, -da** *adj* 1 : careless, sloppy 2 DESATENDIDO : neglected — **descuido** *nm* : neglect, carelessness
desde *prep* 1 : from (a place), since (a time) 2 ~ **luego** : of course
desdén *nm* : scorn, disdain — **desdeñar** *vt* : scorn — **desdeñoso, -sa** *adj* : disdainful
desdicha *nf* 1 : misery 2 DESGRACIA : misfortune — **desdichado, -da** *adj* : unfortunate, unhappy
desear *vt* : wish, want — **deseable** *adj* : desirable
desecar *vt* : dry up
desechar *vt* 1 : throw away 2 RECHAZAR : reject — **desechable** *adj* : disposable — **desechos** *nmpl* : rubbish
desembarazarse {21} *vr* ~ **de** : get rid of
desembarcar {72} *vi* : disembark — *vt* : unload — **desembarcadero** *nm* : jetty, landing pier — **desembarco** *nm* : landing
desembocar {72} *vi* ~ **en** 1 : flow

into **2** : lead to (a result) — **desembo-cadura** *nf* **1** : mouth (of a river) **2** : opening, end (of a street)

desembolsar *vt* **1** : pay out — **desembolso** *nm* : payment, outlay

desembragar *vi* : disengage the clutch

desempacar {72} *v Lat* : unpack

desempate *nm* : tiebreaker

desempeñar *vt* **1** : play (a role) **2** : redeem (from a pawnshop) — **desempeñarse** *vr* : get out of debt

desempleo *nm* : unemployment — **desempleado, -da** *adj* : unemployed

desempolvar *vt* : dust

desencadenar *vt* : unchain **2** : trigger, unleash (protests, crises, etc.) — **desencadenarse** *vr* : break loose

desencajar *vt* **1** : dislocate **2** DESCONECTAR : disconnect

desencanto *nm* : disillusionment

desenchufar *vt* : disconnect, unplug

desenfadado, -da *adj* : carefree, confident — **desenfado** *nm* : confidence, ease

desenfrenado, -da *adj* : unrestrained — **desenfreno** *nm* : abandon, lack of restraint

desenganchar *vt* : unhook

desengañar *vt* : disillusion — **desengaño** *nm* : disappointment

desenlace *nm* : ending, outcome

desenmarañar *vt* : disentangle

desenmascarar *vt* : unmask

desenredar *vt* : untangle — **desenredarse** *vr* ~ **de** : extricate oneself from

desenrollar *vt* : unroll, unwind

desentenderse {56} *vr* ~ **de** : want nothing to do with

desenterrar {55} *vt* : dig up, disinter

desentonar *vi* **1** : be out of tune **2** : clash (of colors, etc.)

desenvoltura *nf* : confidence, ease

desenvolver {89} *vt* : unfold, unwrap — **desenvolverse** *vr* : unfold, develop

desenvuelto, -ta *adj* : confident, self-assured

deseo *nm* : desire — **deseoso, -sa** *adj* : eager, anxious

desequilibrar *vt* : throw off balance — **desequilibrado, -da** *adj* : unbalanced — **desequilibrio** *nm* : imbalance

desertar *vt* : desert — **deserción** *nf, pl* **-ciones** : desertion — **desertor, -tora** *n* : deserter

desesperar *vt* : exasperate — *vi* : despair — **desesperarse** *vr* : become exasperated — **desesperación** *nf, pl* **-ciones** : desperation, despair — **de-**

sesperado, -da *adj* : desperate, hopeless

desestimar *vt* : reject

desfalcar {72} *vt* : embezzle — **desfalco** *nm* : embezzlement

desfallecer {53} *vi* **1** : weaken **2** DESMAYARSE : faint

desfavorable *adj* : unfavorable

desfigurar *vt* **1** : disfigure, mar **2** : distort (the truth)

desfiladero *nm* : mountain pass, gorge

desfilar *vi* : march, parade — **desfile** *nm* : parade, procession

desfogar {52} *vt* : vent — **desfogarse** *vr* : let off steam

desgajar *vt* : tear off, break apart — **desgajarse** *vr* : come off

desgana *nf* **1** : lack of appetite **2** : lack of enthusiasm, reluctance

desgarbado, -da *adj* : gawky, ungainly

desgarrar *vt* : tear, rip — **desgarrador, -dora** *adj* : heartbreaking — **desgarro** *nm* : tear

desgastar *vt* : wear away, wear down — **desgaste** *nm* : deterioration, wear and tear

desgracia *nf* **1** : misfortune **2 caer en** ~ : fall into disgrace **3 por** ~ : unfortunately — **desgraciadamente** *adv* : unfortunately — **desgraciado, -da** *adj* : unfortunate

deshabitado, -da *adj* : uninhabited

deshacer {40} *vt* **1** : undo **2** DESTRUIR : destroy, ruin **3** DISOLVER : dissolve **4** : break (an agreement), cancel (plans, etc.) — **deshacerse** *vr* **1** : come undone **2** ~ **de** : get rid of **3** ~ **en** : lavish, heap (praise, etc.) — **deshecho, -cha** *adj* **1** : undone **2** DESTROZADO : destroyed, ruined

desheredar *vt* : disinherit

deshidratar *vt* : dehydrate

deshielo *nm* : thaw

deshilachar *vt* : unravel — **deshilacharse** *vr* : fray

deshonesto, -ta *adj* : dishonest

deshonrar *vt* : dishonor, disgrace — **deshonra** *nf* : dishonor — **deshonroso, -sa** *adj* : dishonorable

deshuesar *vt* **1** : pit (a fruit) **2** : bone, debone (meat)

desidia *nf* **1** : indolence **2** DESASEO : sloppiness

desierto, -ta *adj* : deserted, uninhabited — **desierto** *nm* : desert

designar *vt* : designate — **designación** *nf, pl* **-ciones** : appointment (to an office, etc.)

designio *nm* : plan

desigual *adj* **1** : unequal **2** DISPAREJO

: uneven — **desigualdad** *nf* : inequality

desilusionar *vt* : disappoint, disillusion — **desilusión** *nf, pl* **-siones** : disappointment, disillusionment

desinfectar *vt* : disinfect — **desinfectante** *adj & nm* : disinfectant

desinflar *vt* : deflate — **desinflarse** *vr* : deflate, go flat

desinhibido, -da *adj* : uninhibited

desintegrar *vt* : disintegrate — **desintegrarse** *vr* : disintegrate — **desintegración** *nf, pl* **-ciones** : disintegration

desinteresado, -da *adj* : unselfish, generous — **desinterés** *nm* : unselfishness

desistir *vi* ~ **de** : give up

desleal *adj* : disloyal — **deslealtad** *nf* : disloyalty

desleír {66} *vt* : dilute, dissolve

desligar {52} *vt* **1** : untie **2** SEPARAR : separate — **desligarse** *vr* : extricate oneself

desliz *nm, pl* **-lices** : slip, mistake — **deslizar** {21} *vt* : slide, slip — **deslizarse** *vr* : slide, glide

deslucido, -da *adj* : dingy, tarnished

deslumbrar *vt* : dazzle — **deslumbrante** *adj* : dazzling, blinding

deslustrar *vt* : tarnish, dull

desmán *nm, pl* **-manes** : outrage, excess

desmandarse *vr* : get out of hand

desmantelar *vt* : dismantle

desmañado, -da *adj* : clumsy

desmayar *vi* : lose heart — **desmayarse** *vr* : faint — **desmayo** *nm* : faint

desmedido, -da *adj* : excessive

desmejorar *vt* : impair — *vi* : deteriorate

desmemoriado, -da *adj* : forgetful

desmentir {76} *vt* : deny — **desmentido** *nm* : denial

desmenuzar {21} *vt* **1** : crumble **2** EXAMINAR : scrutinize — **desmenuzarse** *vr* : crumble

desmerecer {53} *vt* : be unworthy of — *vi* : decline in value

desmesurado, -da *adj* : excessive

desmigajar *vt* : crumble

desmontar *vt* **1** : dismantle, take apart **2** ALLANAR : level — *vi* : dismount

desmoralizar {21} *vt* : demoralize

desmoronarse *vr* : crumble

desnivel *nm* : unevenness

desnudar *vt* : undress, strip — **desnudarse** *vr* : get undressed — **desnudez** *nf, pl* **-deces** : nudity, nakedness — **desnudo, -da** *adj* : nude, naked — **desnudo** *nm* : nude

desnutrición *nf, pl* **-ciones** : malnutrition

desobedecer {53} *v* : disobey — **desobediencia** *nf* : disobedience — **desobediente** *adj* : disobedient

desocupar *vt* : empty, vacate — **desocupado, -da** *adj* **1** : vacant **2** DESEMPLEADO : unemployed

desodorante *adj & nm* : deodorant

desolado, -da *adj* **1** : desolate **2** DESCONSOLADO : devastated, distressed — **desolación** *nf, pl* **-ciones** : desolation

desorden *nm, pl* **desórdenes** : disorder, mess — **desordenado, -da** *adj* : untidy — **desordenadamente** *adv* : in a disorderly way

desorganizar {21} *vt* : disorganize — **desorganización** *nf, pl* **-ciones** : disorganization

desorientar *vt* : disorient, confuse — **desorientarse** *vr* : lose one's way

desovar *vi* : spawn

despachar *vt* **1** : deal with (a task, etc.) **2** ENVIAR : dispatch, send **3** : wait on, serve (customers) — **despacho** *nm* **1** : dispatch, shipment **2** OFICINA : office

despacio *adv* : slowly

desparramar *vt* : spill, scatter, spread

despavorido, -da *adj* : terrified

despecho *nm* **1** : spite **2 a** ~ **de** : despite, in spite of

despectivo, -va *adj* **1** : pejorative **2** DESPRECIATIVO : contemptuous

despedazar {21} *vt* : tear apart

despedir {54} *vt* **1** : see off **2** DESTITUIR : dismiss, fire **3** DESPRENDER : emit — **despedirse** *vr* : say good-bye — **despedida** *nf* : farewell, good-bye

despegar {52} *vt* : detach, unstick — *vi* : take off — **despegado, -da** *adj* : cold, distant — **despegue** *nm* : takeoff

despeinar *vt* : ruffle (hair) — **despeinado, -da** *adj* : disheveled, unkempt

despejar *vt* : clear, free — *vi* : clear up — **despejado, -da** *adj* **1** : clear, fair **2** LÚCIDO : clear-headed

despellejar *vt* : skin (an animal)

despensa *nf* : pantry, larder

despeñadero *nm* : precipice

desperdiciar *vt* : waste — **desperdicio** *nm* **1** : waste **2** ~**s** *nmpl* : scraps

desperfecto *nm* : flaw, defect

despertar {55} *vi* : awaken, wake up — *vt* : wake, rouse — **despertador** *nm* : alarm clock

despiadado, -da *adj* : pitiless, merciless

despido *nm* : dismissal, layoff
despierto, -ta *adj* : awake
despilfarrar *vt* : squander — **despilfarrador, -dora** *n* : spendthrift — **despilfarro** *nm* : extravagance, wastefulness
despistar *vt* : throw off the track, confuse — **despistarse** *vr* : lose one's way — **despistado, -da** *adj* 1 : absentminded 2 DESORIENTADO : confused — **despiste** *nm* 1 : absentmindedness 2 ERROR : mistake
desplazar {21} *vt* : displace — **desplazarse** *vr* : travel
desplegar {49} *vt* : unfold, spread out — **despliegue** *nm* : display
desplomarse *vr* : collapse
desplumar *vt* 1 : pluck 2 *fam* : fleece
despoblado, -da *adj* : uninhabited, deserted — **despoblado** *nm* : deserted area
despojar *vt* : strip, deprive — **despojos** *nmpl* 1 : plunder 2 RESTOS : remains, scraps
desportillar *vt* : chip — **desportillarse** *vr* : chip — **desportilladura** *nf* : chip, nick
despota *nmf* : despot
despotricar *vi* : rant (and rave)
despreciar *vt* : despise, scorn — **despreciable** *adj* 1 : despicable 2 **una cantidad ~** : a negligible amount — **desprecio** *nm* : disdain, scorn
desprender *vt* 1 : detach, remove 2 EMITIR : give off — **desprenderse** *vr* 1 : come off 2 DEDUCIRSE : be inferred, follow — **desprendimiento** *nm* **~ de tierras** : landslide
despreocupado, -da *adj* : carefree, unconcerned
desprestigiar *vt* : discredit — **desprestigiarse** *vr* : lose face
desprevenido, -da *adj* : unprepared
desproporcionado, -da *adj* : out of proportion
despropósito *nm* : (piece of) nonsense, absurdity
desprovisto, -ta *adj* **~ de** : lacking in
después *adv* 1 : afterward 2 ENTONCES : then, next 3 **~ de** : after 4 **después (de) que** : after 5 **~ de todo** : after all
despuntado, -da *adj* : blunt, dull
desquiciar *vt* : drive crazy
desquitarse *vr* 1 : retaliate 2 **~ con** : take it out on, get back at — **desquite** *nm* : revenge
destacar {72} *vt* : emphasize — *vi* : stand out — **destacado, -da** *adj* : outstanding
destapar *vt* : open, uncover — **destapador** *nm Lat* : bottle opener

destartalado, -da *adj* : dilapidated
destellar *vi* : flash, sparkle — **destello** *nm* : sparkle, twinkle, flash
destemplado, -da *adj* 1 : out of tune 2 MAL : out of sorts 3 : unpleasant (of weather)
desteñir {67} *vt* : fade, bleach — *vi* : run, fade — **desteñirse** *vr* : fade
desterrar {55} *vt* : banish, exile — **desterrado, -da** *n* : exile
destetar *vt* : wean
destiempo *adv a* **~** : at the wrong time
destierro *nm* : exile
destilar *vt* : distill — **destilería** *nf* : distillery
destinar *vt* 1 : assign, allocate 2 NOMBRAR : appoint — **destinado, -da** *adj* : destined — **destinatario, -ria** *n* : addressee — **destino** *nm* 1 : destiny 2 RUMBO : destination
destituir {41} *vt* : dismiss — **destitución** *nf, pl* **-ciones** : dismissal
destornillar *vt* : unscrew — **destornillador** *nm* : screwdriver
destreza *nf* : skill, dexterity
destrozar {21} *vt* : destroy, wreck — **destrozos** *nmpl* : damage, destruction
destrucción *nf, pl* **-ciones** : destruction — **destructivo, -va** *adj* : destructive — **destruir** {41} *vt* : destroy
desunir *vt* : split, divide
desusado, -da *adj* 1 : obsolete 2 INSÓLITO : unusual — **desuso** *nm* **caer en ~** : fall into disuse
desvaído, -da *adj* 1 : pale, washed-out 2 BORROSO : vague, blurred
desvalido, -da *adj* : destitute, needy
desvalijar *vt* : rob
desván *nm, pl* **-vanes** : attic
desvanecer {53} *vt* : make disappear — **desvanecerse** *vr* 1 : vanish 2 DESMAYARSE : faint
desvariar {85} *vi* : be delirious — **desvarío** *nm* : delirium
desvelar *vt* : keep awake — **desvelarse** *vr* : stay awake — **desvelo** *nm* 1 : sleeplessness 2 **~s** *nmpl* : efforts
desvencijado, -da *adj* : dilapidated, rickety
desventaja *nf* : disadvantage
desventura *nf* : misfortune
desvergonzado, -da *adj* : shameless — **desvergüenza** *nf* : shamelessness
desvestir {54} *vt* : undress — **desvestirse** *vr* : get undressed
desviación *nf, pl* **-ciones** 1 : deviation 2 : detour (in a road) — **desviar** {85} *vt* : divert, deflect — **desviarse** *vr* 1 : branch off 2 APARTARSE : stray — **desvío** *nm* : diversion, detour

detallar vt : detail — **detallado, -da** adj : detailed, thorough — **detalle** nm 1 : detail 2 **al ~** : retail — **detallista** adj : retail — **~** nmf : retailer

detectar vt : detect — **detective** nmf : detective

detener {80} vt 1 : arrest, detain 2 PARAR : stop 3 RETRASAR : delay — **detenerse** vr 1 : stop 2 DEMORARSE : linger — **detención** nf, pl **-ciones** : arrest, detention

detergente nm : detergent

deteriorar vt : damage — **deteriorarse** vr : wear out, deteriorate — **deteriorado, -da** adj : damaged, worn — **deterioro** nm : deterioration, damage

determinar vt 1 : determine 2 MOTIVAR : bring about 3 DECIDIR : decide — **determinarse** vr : decide — **determinación** nf, pl **-ciones** 1 : determination 2 **tomar una ~** : make a decision — **determinado, -da** adj 1 : determined 2 ESPECÍFICO : specific

detestar vt : detest

detonar vi : explode, detonate — **detonación** nf, pl **-ciones** : detonation

detrás adv 1 : behind 2 **~ de** : in back of 3 **por ~** : from behind

detrimento nm **en ~ de** : to the detriment of

deuda nf : debt — **deudor, -dora** n : debtor

devaluar {3} vt : devalue — **devaluarse** vr : depreciate

devastar vt : devastate — **devastador, -dora** adj : devastating

devenir {87} vi 1 : come about 2 **~ en** : become, turn into

devoción nf, pl **-ciones** : devotion

devolución nf, pl **-ciones** : return

devolver {89} vt 1 RESTITUIR : give back 2 : refund, pay back — vi : vomit — **devolverse** vr Lat : return, come back

devorar vt : devour

devoto, -ta adj : devout — **~** n : devotee

día nm 1 : day 2 : daytime 3 **al ~** : up-to-date 4 **en pleno ~** : in broad daylight

diabetes nf : diabetes — **diabético, -ca** adj & n : diabetic

diablo nm : devil — **diablillo** nm : imp, rascal — **diablura** nf : prank — **diabólico, -ca** adj : diabolic, diabolical

diafragma nm : diaphragm

diagnosticar {72} vt : diagnose — **diagnóstico, -ca** adj : diagnostic — **diagnóstico** nm : diagnosis

diagonal adj & nf : diagonal

diagrama nm : diagram

dial nm : dial (of a radio, etc.)

dialecto nm : dialect

dialogar {52} vi : have a talk — **diálogo** nm : dialogue

diamante nm : diamond

diámetro nm : diameter

diana nf 1 : reveille 2 BLANCO : target, bull's-eye

diario, -ria adj : daily — **diario** nm 1 : diary 2 PERIÓDICO : newspaper — **diariamente** adv : daily

diarrea nf : diarrhea

dibujar vt 1 : draw 2 DESCRIBIR : portray — **dibujante** nmf : draftsman m, draftswoman f — **dibujo** nm 1 : drawing 2 **~s animados** : (animated) cartoons

diccionario nm : dictionary

dicha nf 1 ALEGRÍA : happiness 2 SUERTE : good luck — **dicho** nm : saying, proverb — **dichoso, -sa** adj 1 : happy 2 AFORTUNADO : lucky

diciembre nm : December

dictar vt 1 : dictate 2 : pronounce (a sentence), deliver (a speech) — **dictado** nm : dictation — **dictador, -dora** n : dictator — **dictadura** nf : dictatorship

diecinueve adj & nm : nineteen — **diecinueveavo, -va** adj : nineteenth

dieciocho adj & nm : eighteen — **dieciochoavo, -va** or **dieciochavo, -va** adj : eighteenth

dieciséis adj & nm : sixteen — **dieciseisavo, -va** adj : sixteenth

diecisiete adj & nm : seventeen — **diecisieteavo, -va** adj : seventeenth

diente nm 1 : tooth 2 : prong, tine (of a fork, etc.) 3 **~ de ajo** : clove of garlic 4 **~ de león** : dandelion

diesel ['disɛl] adj & nm : diesel

diestra nf : right hand — **diestro, -tra** adj 1 : right 2 HÁBIL : skillful

dieta nf : diet — **dietético, -ca** adj : dietetic, dietary

diez adj & nm, pl **dieces** : ten

difamar vt : slander, libel — **difamación** nf, pl **-ciones** : slander, libel

diferencia nf : difference — **diferenciar** vt : distinguish between — **diferenciarse** vr : differ — **diferente** adj : different

diferir {76} vt : postpone — vi : differ

difícil adj : difficult — **dificultad** nf : difficulty — **dificultar** vt : hinder, obstruct

difteria nf : diphtheria

difundir vt 1 : spread (out) 2 : broadcast (television, etc.)

difunto, -ta *adj & n* : deceased
difusión *nf, pl* **-siones** : spreading
digerir {76} *vt* : digest — **digerible** *adj* : digestible — **digestión** *nf, pl* **-tiones** : digestion — **digestivo, -va** *adj* : digestive
dígito *nm* : digit — **digital** *adj* : digital
dignarse *vr* ~ **a** : deign to
dignatario, -ria *n* : dignitary — **dignidad** *nf* : dignity — **digno, -na** *adj* : worthy
digresión *nf, pl* **-ciones** : digression
dilapidar *vt* : waste, squander
dilatar *vt* **1** : expand, dilate **2** PROLONGAR : prolong **3** POSPONER : postpone
dilema *nm* : dilemma
diligencia *nf* **1** : diligence **2** TRÁMITE : procedure, task — **diligente** *adj* : diligent
diluir {41} *vt* : dilute
diluvio *nm* **1** : flood **2** LLUVIA : downpour
dimensión *nf, pl* **-siones** : dimension
diminuto, -ta *adj* : minute, tiny
dimitir *vi* : resign — **dimisión** *nf, pl* **-siones** : resignation
dinámico, -ca *adj* : dynamic
dinamita *nf* : dynamite
dínamo *or* **dinamo** *nmf* : dynamo
dinastía *nf* : dynasty
dineral *nm* : large sum, fortune
dinero *nm* : money
dinosaurio *nm* : dinosaur
diócesis *nfs & pl* : diocese
dios, diosa *n* : god, goddess *f* — **Dios** *nm* : God
diploma *nm* : diploma — **diplomado, -da** *adj* : qualified, trained
diplomacia *nf* : diplomacy — **diplomático, -ca** *adj* : diplomatic — ~ *n* : diplomat
diputación *nf, pl* **-ciones** : delegation — **diputado, -da** *n* : delegate
dique *nm* : dike
dirección *nf, pl* **-ciones** **1** : address **2** SENTIDO : direction **3** GESTIÓN : management **4** : steering (of an automobile) — **direccional** *nf Lat* : turn signal, blinker — **directa** *nf* : high gear — **directiva** *nf* : board of directors — **directivo, -va** *adj* : managerial — ~ *n* : manager, director — **directo, -ta** *adj* **1** : direct **2** DERECHO : straight — **director, -tora** *n* **1** : director, manager **2** : conductor (of an orchestra) — **directorio** *nm* : directory — **directriz** *nf, pl* **-trices** : guideline
dirigencia *nf* : leaders *pl*, leadership — **dirigente** *nmf* : director, leader
dirigible *nm* : dirigible, blimp

dirigir {35} *vt* **1** : direct, lead **2** : address (a letter, etc.) **3** ENCAMINAR : aim **4** : conduct (music) — **dirigirse** *vr* **1** ~ **a** : go towards **2** ~ **a algn** : speak to s.o., write to s.o.
discernir {25} *vt* : discern, distinguish — **discernimiento** *nm* : discernment
disciplinar *vt* : discipline — **disciplina** *nf* : discipline
discípulo, -la *n* : disciple, follower
disco *nm* **1** : disc, disk **2** : discus (in sports) **3** ~ **compacto** : compact disc
discordante *adj* : discordant — **discordia** *nf* : discord
discoteca *nf* : disco, discotheque
discreción *nf, pl* **-ciones** : discretion
discrepancia *nf* **1** : discrepancy **2** DESACUERDO : disagreement — **discrepar** *vi* : differ, disagree
discreto, -ta *adj* : discreet
discriminar *vt* **1** : discriminate against **2** DISTINGUIR : distinguish — **discriminación** *nf, pl* **-ciones** : discrimination
disculpar *vt* : excuse, pardon — **disculparse** *vr* : apologize — **disculpa** *nf* **1** : apology **2** EXCUSA : excuse
discurrir *vi* **1** : pass, go by **2** REFLEXIONAR : ponder, reflect
discurso *nm* : speech, discourse
discutir *vt* **1** : discuss **2** CUESTIONAR : dispute — *vi* : argue — **discusión** *nf, pl* **-siones** **1** : discussion **2** DISPUTA : argument — **discutible** *adj* : debatable
disecar {72} *vt* : dissect — **disección** *nf, pl* **-ciones** : dissection
diseminar *vt* : disseminate, spread
disentería *nf* : dysentery
disentir {76} *vi* ~ **de** : disagree with — **disentimiento** *nm* : disagreement, dissent
diseñar *vt* : design — **diseñador, -dora** *n* : designer — **diseño** *nm* : design
disertación *nf, pl* **-ciones** **1** : lecture **2** : (written) dissertation
disfrazar {21} *vt* : disguise — **disfrazarse** *vr* ~ **de** : disguise oneself as — **disfraz** *nm, pl* **-fraces** **1** : disguise **2** : costume (for a party, etc.)
disfrutar *vt* : enjoy — *vi* : enjoy oneself
disgustar *vt* : upset, annoy — **disgustarse** *vr* **1** : get annoyed **2** ENEMISTARSE : fall out (with s.o.) — **disgusto** *nm* **1** : annoyance, displeasure **2** RIÑA : quarrel
disidente *adj & nmf* : dissident
disimular *vt* : conceal, hide — *vi* : pretend — **disimulo** *nm* : pretense
disipar *vt* **1** : dispel **2** DERROCHAR : squander

diskette [dis'ket] *nm* : floppy disk, diskette

dislexia *nf* : dyslexia — **disléxico, -ca** *adj* : dyslexic

dislocar {72} *vt* : dislocate — **dislocarse** *vr* : become dislocated

disminuir {41} *vt* : reduce — *vi* : decrease, drop — **disminución** *nf, pl* **-ciones** : decrease

disociar *vt* : dissociate

disolver {89} *vt* : dissolve — **disolverse** *vr* : dissolve

disparar *vi* : shoot, fire — *vt* : shoot — **dispararse** *vr* : shoot up, skyrocket

disparatado, -da *adj* : absurd — **disparate** *nm* : nonsense, silly thing

disparejo, -ja *adj* : uneven — **disparidad** *nf* : difference, disparity

disparo *nm* : shot

dispensar *vt* 1 : dispense, distribute 2 DISCULPAR : excuse

dispersar *vt* : disperse, scatter — **dispersarse** *vr* : disperse — **dispersión** *nf, pl* **-siones** : scattering

disponer {60} *vt* 1 : arrange, lay out 2 ORDENAR : decide, stipulate — *vi* ~ **de** : have at one's disposal — **disponerse** *vr* ~ **a** : be ready to — **disponibilidad** *nf* : availability — **disponible** *adj* : available

disposición *nf, pl* **-ciones** 1 : arrangement 2 APTITUD : aptitude 3 : order, provision (in law) 4 **a** ~ **de** : at the disposal of

dispositivo *nm* : device, mechanism

dispuesto, -ta *adj* : prepared, ready

disputar *vi* 1 : argue COMPETIR : compete — *vt* : dispute — **disputa** *nf* : dispute, argument

disquete → **diskette**

distanciar *vt* : space out — **distanciarse** *vr* : grow apart — **distancia** *nf* : distance — **distante** *adj* : distant

distinguir {26} *vt* : distinguish — **distinguirse** *vr* : distinguish oneself, stand out — **distinción** *nf, pl* **-ciones** : distinction — **distintivo, -va** *adj* : distinctive — **distinto, -ta** *adj* 1 : different 2 CLARO : distinct, clear

distorsión *nf, pl* **-siones** : distortion

distraer {81} *vt* 1 : distract 2 DIVERTIR : entertain — **distraerse** *vr* 1 : get distracted 2 ENTRETENERSE : amuse oneself — **distracción** *nf, pl* **-ciones** 1 : amusement 2 DESPISTE : absentmindedness — **distraído, -da** *adj* : distracted, absentminded

distribuir {41} *vt* : distribute — **distribución** *nf, pl* **-ciones** : distribution — **distribuidor, -dora** *n* : distributor

distrito *nm* : district

disturbio *nm* : disturbance

disuadir *vt* : dissuade, discourage — **disuasivo, -va** *adj* : deterrent

diurno, -na *adj* : day, daytime

divagar {52} *vi* : digress

diván *nm, pl* **-vanes** : divan, couch

divergir {35} *vi* 1 : diverge 2 ~ **en** : differ on

diversidad *nf* : diversity

diversificar {72} *vt* : diversify

diversión *nf, pl* **-siones** : fun, entertainment

diverso, -sa *adj* : diverse

divertir {76} *vt* : entertain — **divertirse** *vr* : enjoy oneself, have fun — **divertido, -da** *adj* : entertaining

dividendo *nm* : dividend

dividir *vt* 1 : divide 2 REPARTIR : distribute

divinidad *nf* : divinity — **divino, -na** *adj* : divine

divisa *nf* 1 : currency 2 EMBLEMA : emblem

divisar *vt* : discern, make out

división *nf, pl* **-siones** : division — **divisor** *nm* : denominator

divorciar *vt* : divorce — **divorciarse** *vr* : get a divorce — **divorciado, -da** *n* : divorcé *m*, divorcée *f* — **divorcio** *nm* : divorce

divulgar {52} *vt* 1 : divulge, reveal 2 PROPAGAR : spread, circulate

dizque *adv Lat* : supposedly, apparently

doblar *vt* 1 : double 2 PLEGAR : fold 3 : turn (a corner) 4 : dub (a film) — *vi* : turn — **doblarse** *vr* 1 : double over 2 ~ **a** : give in to — **dobladillo** *nm* : hem — **doble** *adj & nm* : double — ~ *nmf* : stand-in, double — **doblemente** *adv* : doubly — **doblegar** {52} *vt* : force to yield — **doblegarse** *vr* : give in — **doblez** *nm, pl* **-bleces** : fold, crease

doce *adj & nm* : twelve — **doceavo, -va** *adj* : twelfth — **docena** *nf* : dozen

docente *adj* : teaching

dócil *adj* : docile

doctor, -tora *n* : doctor — **doctorado** *nm* : doctorate

doctrina *nf* : doctrine

documentar *vt* : document — **documentación** *nf, pl* **-ciones** : documentation — **documental** *adj & nm* : documentary — **documento** *nm* : document

dogma *nm* : dogma — **dogmático, -ca** *adj* : dogmatic

dólar *nm* : dollar

doler {47} *vi* 1 : hurt 2 **me duelen los pies** : my feet hurt — **dolerse** *vr* ~ **de** : complain about — **dolor** *nm* 1 : pain 2 PENA : grief 3 ~ **de cabeza** : headache 4 ~ **de estómago** : stomachache — **dolorido, -da** 1 : sore 2 AFLIGIDO : hurt — **doloroso, -sa** *adj* : painful

domar *vt* : tame, break in

domesticar {72} *vt* : domesticate, tame — **doméstico, -ca** *adj* : domestic

domicilio *nm* : home, residence

dominar *vt* 1 : dominate, control 2 : master (a subject, a language, etc.) — **dominarse** *vr* : control oneself — **dominación** *nf, pl* -**ciones** : domination — **dominante** *adj* : dominant

domingo *nm* : Sunday — **dominical** *adj* **periódico** ~ : Sunday newspaper

dominio *nm* 1 : authority 2 : mastery (of a subject) 3 TERRITORIO : domain

dominó *nm, pl* -**nós** : dominoes *pl* (game)

don[1] *nm* : courtesy title preceding a man's first name

don[2] *nm* 1 : gift 2 TALENTO : talent — **donación** *nf, pl* -**ciones** : donation — **donador, -dora** *n* : donor

donaire *nm* : grace, charm

donar *vt* : donate — **donante** *nmf* : donor — **donativo** *nm* : donation

donde *conj* : where — ~ *prep Lat* : over by

dónde *adv* 1 : where 2 **¿de ~ eres?** : where are you from? 3 **¿por ~?** : whereabouts?

dondequiera *adv* 1 : anywhere 2 ~ **que** : wherever, everywhere

doña *nf* : courtesy title preceding a woman's first name

doquier *adv* **por** ~ : everywhere

dorar *vt* 1 : gild 2 : brown (food) — **dorado, -da** *adj* : gold, golden

dormir {27} *vt* : put to sleep — *vi* : sleep — **dormirse** *vr* : fall asleep — **dormido, -da** *adj* 1 : asleep 2 ENTUMECIDO : numb — **dormilón, -lona** *n* : sleepyhead, late riser — **dormitar** *vi* : doze — **dormitorio** *nm* 1 : bedroom 2 : dormitory (in a college)

dorso *nm* : back

dos *adj & nm* : two — **doscientos, -tas** *adj* : two hundred — **doscientos** *nms & Lat* : two hundred

dosel *nm* : canopy

dosis *nfs & pl* : dose, dosage

dotar *vt* 1 : provide, equip 2 ~ **de** : endow with — **dotación** *nf, pl* -**ciones** 1 : endowment, funding 2 PERSONAL : personnel — **dote** *nf* 1 : dowry 2 ~**s** *nfpl* : gift, talent

dragar {52} *vt* : dredge — **draga** *nf* : dredge

dragón *nm, pl* -**gones** : dragon

drama *nm* : drama — **dramático, -ca** *adj* : dramatic — **dramatizar** {21} *vt* : dramatize — **dramaturgo, -ga** *n* : dramatist, playwright

drástico, -ca *adj* : drastic

drenar *vt* : drain — **drenaje** *nm* : drainage

droga *nf* : drug — **drogadicto, -ta** *n* : drug addict — **drogar** {52} *vt* : drug — **drogarse** *vr* : take drugs — **droguería** *nf* : drugstore

dromedario *nm* : dromedary

dual *adj* : dual

ducha *nf* : shower — **ducharse** *vr* : take a shower

ducho, -cha *adj* : experienced, skilled

duda *nf* : doubt — **dudar** *vt* : doubt — *vi* ~ **en** : hesitate to — **dudoso, -sa** *adj* 1 : doubtful 2 SOSPECHOSO : questionable

duelo *nm* 1 : duel 2 LUTO : mourning

duende *nm* : elf, imp

dueño, -na *n* 1 : owner 2 : landlord, landlady *f*

dulce *adj* 1 : sweet 2 : fresh (of water) 3 SUAVE : mild, gentle — ~ *nm* : candy, sweet — **dulzura** *nf* : sweetness

duna *nf* : dune

dúo *nm* : duo, duet

duodécimo, -ma *adj* : twelfth — ~ *n* : twelfth (in a series)

dúplex *nms & pl* : duplex (apartment)

duplicar {72} *vt* 1 : double 2 : duplicate, copy (a document, etc.) — **duplicado, -da** *adj* : duplicate — **duplicado** *nm* : copy

duque *nm* : duke — **duquesa** *nf* : duchess

durabilidad *nf* : durability

duración *nf, pl* -**ciones** : duration, length

duradero, -ra *adj* : durable, lasting

durante *prep* 1 : during 2 ~ **una hora** : for an hour

durar *vi* : endure, last

durazno *nm Lat* : peach

duro *adv* : hard — **duro, -ra** *adj* 1 : hard 2 SEVERO : harsh — **dureza** *nf* 1 : hardness 2 SEVERIDAD : harshness

E

e¹ *nf* : e, fifth letter of the Spanish alphabet

e² *conj* (*used instead of* **y** *before words beginning with i or hi*) : and

ebanista *nmf* : cabinetmaker

ébano *nm* : ebony

ebrio, -bria *adj* : drunk

ebullición *nf, pl* **-ciones** : boiling

echar *vt* **1** : throw, cast **2** EXPULSAR : expel, dismiss **3** : give off, emit (smoke, sparks, etc.) **4** BROTAR : sprout **5** PONER : put (on) **6** ~ **a perder** : spoil, ruin **7** ~ **de menos** : miss — **echarse** *vr* **1** : throw oneself **2** ACOSTARSE : lie down **3** ~ **a** : start (to)

eclesiástico, -ca *adj* : ecclesiastic — ~ *nm* : clergyman

eclipse *nm* : eclipse — **eclipsar** *vi* : eclipse

eco *nm* : echo

ecología *nf* : ecology — **ecológico, -ca** *adj* : ecological — **ecologista** *nmf* : ecologist

economía *nf* **1** : economy **2** : economics (science) — **económico, -ca** *adj* **1** : economic, economical **2** BARATO : inexpensive — **economista** *nmf* : economist — **economizar** {21} *v* : save

ecosistema *nm* : ecosystem

ecuación *nf, pl* **-ciones** : equation

ecuador *nm* : equator

ecuánime *adj* **1** : even-tempered **2** : impartial (in law)

ecuatoriano, -na *adj* : Ecuadorian, Ecuadorean, Ecuadoran

ecuestre *adj* : equestrian

edad *nf* **1** : age **2 Edad Media** : Middle Ages *pl* **3 ¿qué** ~ **tienes?** : how old are you?

edición *nf, pl* **-ciones 1** : publishing, publication **2** : edition (of a book, etc.)

edicto *nm* : edict

edificar {72} *vt* : build — **edificio** *nm* : building

editar *vt* **1** : publish **2** : edit (a film, a text, etc.) — **editor, -tora** *n* **1** : publisher **2** : editor — **editorial** *adj* : publishing — ~ *nm* : editorial — ~ *nf* : publishing house

edredón *nm, pl* **-dones** : (down) comforter, duvet

educar {72} *vt* **1** : educate **2** CRIAR : bring up, raise **3** : train (the body, the

voice, etc.) — **educación** *nf, pl* **-ciones 1** : education **2** MODALES : (good) manners *pl* — **educado, -da** *adj* : polite — **educador, -dora** *n* : educator — **educativo, -va** *adj* : educational

efectivo, -va *adj* **1** : effective **2** REAL : real — **efectivo** *nm* : cash — **efectivamente** *adv* **1** : really **2** POR SUPUESTO : yes, indeed — **efecto** *nm* **1** : effect **2 en** ~ : in fact **3** ~**s** *nmpl* : goods, property — **efectuar** {3} *vt* : effect, carry out

efervescente *adj* : effervescent — **efervescencia** *nf* : effervescence

eficaz *adj, pl* **-caces 1** : effective **2** EFICIENTE : efficient — **eficacia** *nf* **1** : effectiveness **2** EFICIENCIA : efficiency

eficiente *adj* : efficient — **eficiencia** *nf* : efficiency

efímero, -ra *adj* : ephemeral

efusivo, -va *adj* : effusive

egipcio, -cia *adj* : Egyptian

ego *nm* : ego — **egocéntrico, -ca** *adj* : egocentric — **egoísmo** *nm* : egoism — **egoísta** *adj* : egoistic — ~ *nmf* : egoist

egresar *vi* : graduate — **egresado, -da** *n* : graduate — **egreso** *nm* : graduation, commencement

eje *nm* **1** : axis **2** : axle (of a wheel, etc.)

ejecutar *vt* **1** : execute, put to death **2** REALIZAR : carry out — **ejecución** *nf, pl* **-ciones** : execution

ejecutivo, -va *adj & n* : executive

ejemplar *adj* : exemplary — ~ *nm* **1** : copy, issue **2** EJEMPLO : example — **ejemplificar** {72} *vt* : exemplify — **ejemplo** *nm* **1** : example **2 por** ~ : for example

ejercer {86} *vt* **1** : practice (a profession) **2** : exercise (a right, etc.) — *vi* ~ **de** : practice as, work as — **ejercicio** *nm* **1** : exercise **2** : practice (of a profession, etc.)

ejército *nm* : army

el, la *art, pl* **los, las** : the — **el** *pron* (*referring to masculine nouns*) **1** : the one **2** ~ **que** : he who, whoever, the one that

él *pron* : he, him

elaborar *vt* **1** : manufacture, produce **2** : draw up (a plan, etc.)

elástico, -ca *adj* : elastic — **elástico** *nm* : elastic — **elasticidad** *nf* : elasticity

elección *nf, pl* **-ciones 1** : election **2** SELECCIÓN : choice — **elector, -tora** *n* : voter — **electorado** *nm* : electorate — **electoral** *adj* : electoral

electricidad *nf* : electricity — **eléctrico, -ca** *adj* : electric, electrical — **electricista** *nmf* : electrician — **electrificar** {72} *vt* : electrify — **electrizar** {21} *vt* : electrify, thrill — **electrocutar** *vt* : electrocute

electrodo *nm* : electrode

electrodoméstico *nm* : electric appliance.

electromagnético, -ca *adj* : electromagnetic

electrón *nm, pl* **-trones** : electron — **electrónico, -ca** *adj* : electronic — **electrónica** *nf* : electronics

elefante, -ta *n* : elephant

elegante *adj* : elegant — **elegancia** *nf* : elegance

elegía *nf* : elegy

elegir {28} *vt* **1** : elect **2** ESCOGER : choose, select — **elegible** *adj* : eligible

elemento *nm* : element — **elemental** *adj* **1** : elementary, basic **2** ESENCIAL : fundamental

elenco *nm* : cast (of actors)

elevar *vt* **1** : raise, lift **2** ASCENDER : elevate (in a hierarchy), promote — **elevarse** *vr* : rise — **elevación** *nf, pl* **-ciones** : elevation — **elevador** *nm* **1** : hoist **2** *Lat* : elevator

eliminar *vt* : eliminate — **eliminación** *nf, pl* **-ciones** : elimination

elipse *nf* : ellipse — **elíptico, -ca** *adj* : elliptical, elliptic

elite *or* **élite** *nf* : elite

elixir *or* **elíxir** *nm* : elixir

ella *pron* : she, her — **ello** *pron* : it — **ellos, ellas** *pron pl* **1** : they, them **2 de ellos, de ellas** : theirs

elocuente *adj* : eloquent — **elocuencia** *nf* : eloquence

elogiar *vt* : praise — **elogio** *nm* : praise

eludir *vt* : avoid, elude

emanar *vi* **~ de** : emanate from

emancipar *vt* : emancipate — **emanciparse** *vr* : free oneself — **emancipación** *nf, pl* **-ciones** : emancipation

embadurnar *vt* : smear, daub

embajada *nf* : embassy — **embajador, -dora** *n* : ambassador

embalar *vt* : wrap up, pack — **embalaje** *nm* : packing

embaldosar *vt* : pave with tiles

embalsamar *vt* : embalm

embalse *nm* : dam, reservoir

embarazar {21} *vt* **1** : make pregnant **2** IMPEDIR : restrict, hamper — **embarazada** *adj* : pregnant — **embarazo** *nm* **1** : pregnancy **2** IMPEDIMENTO : hindrance, obstacle — **embarazoso, -sa** *adj* : embarrassing

embarcar {72} *vt* : load — **embarcarse** *vr* : embark, board — **embarcación** *nf, pl* **-ciones** : boat, craft — **embarcadero** *nm* : pier, jetty — **embarco** *nm* : embarkation

embargar {52} *vt* **1** : seize, impound **2** : overwhelm (with emotion, etc.) — **embargo** *nm* **1** : embargo **2** : seizure (in law) **3 sin ~** : nevertheless

embarque *nm* : loading (of goods), boarding (of passengers)

embarrancar {72} *vi* : run aground

embarullarse *vr fam* : get mixed up

embaucar {72} *vt* : trick, swindle — **embaucador, -dora** *n* : swindler

embeber *vt* : absorb — *vi* : shrink — **embeberse** *vr* : become absorbed

embelesar *vt* : enchant, delight — **embelesado, -da** *adj* : spellbound

embellecer {53} *vt* : embellish, beautify

embestir {54} *vt* : attack, charge at — *vi* : charge, attack — **embestida** *nf* **1** : attack **2** : charge (of a bull)

emblema *nm* : emblem

embobar *vt* : amaze, fascinate

embocadura *nf* **1** : mouth (of a river, etc.) **2** : mouthpiece (of an instrument)

émbolo *nm* : piston

embolsarse *vr* : put in one's pocket

emborracharse *vr* : get drunk

emborronar *vt* **1** : smudge, blot **2** GARABATEAR : scribble

emboscar {72} *vt* : ambush — **emboscada** *nf* : ambush

embotar *vt* : dull, blunt

embotellar *vt* : bottle (up) — **embotellamiento** *nm* : traffic jam

embrague *nm* : clutch — **embragar** {52} *vi* : engage the clutch

embriagarse {52} *vr* : get drunk — **embriagado, -da** *adj* : intoxicated, drunk — **embriagador, -dora** *adj* : intoxicating — **embriaguez** *nf* : drunkenness

embrión *nm, pl* **-briones** : embryo

embrollo *nm* : tangle, confusion

embrujar *vt* : bewitch — **embrujo** *nm* : spell, curse

embrutecer *vt* : brutalize

embudo *nm* : funnel

embuste *nm* : lie — **embustero, -ra** *adj* : lying — ~ *n* : liar, cheat

embutir *vt* : stuff — **embutido** *nm* : sausage, cold meat

emergencia *nf* : emergency

emerger {15} *vi* : emerge, appear

emigrar *vi* 1 : emigrate 2 : migrate (of animals) — **emigración** *nf, pl* -**ciones** 1 : emigration 2 : migration (of animals) — **emigrante** *adj & nmf* : emigrant

eminente *adj* : eminent — **eminencia** *nf* : eminence

emitir *vt* 1 : emit 2 EXPRESAR : express (an opinion, etc.) 3 : broadcast (on radio or television) 4 : issue (money, stamps, etc.) — **emisión** *nf, pl* -**siones** 1 : emission 2 : broadcast (on radio or television) 3 : issue (of money, etc.) — **emisora** *nf* : radio station

emoción *nf, pl* -**ciones** : emotion — **emocional** *adj* : emotional — **emocionante** *adj* 1 APASIONANTE : exciting, thrilling 2 **emocionar** *vt* 1 : move, touch 2 APASIONAR : excite, thrill — **emocionarse** *vr* 1 : be moved 2 APASIONARSE : get excited — **emotivo, -va** *adj* 1 : emotional 2 CONMOVEDOR : moving

empacar {72} *vt Lat* : pack

empachar *vt* : give indigestion to — **empacharse** *vr* : get indigestion — **empacho** *nm* : indigestion

empadronarse *vr* : register to vote

empalagoso, -sa *adj* : excessively sweet, cloying

empalizada *nf* : palisade (fence)

empalmar *vt* : connect, link — *vi* : meet, converge — **empalme** *nm* 1 : connection, link 2 : junction (of a railroad, etc.)

empanada *nf* : pie, turnover — **empanadilla** *nf* : meat or seafood pie

empanar *vt* : bread (in cooking)

empantanar *vt* : flood — **empantanarse** *vr* 1 : become flooded 2 : get bogged down

empañar *vt* 1 : steam (up) 2 : tarnish (one's reputation, etc.) — **empañarse** *vr* : fog up

empapar *vt* : soak — **empaparse** *vr* : get soaking wet

empapelar *vt* : wallpaper

empaquetar *vt* : pack, package

emparedado, -da *adj* : walled in, confined — **emparedado** *nm* : sandwich

emparejar *vt* : match up, pair — **emparejarse** *vr* : pair off

emparentado, -da *adj* : related, kindred

empastar *vt* : fill (a tooth) — **empaste** *nm* : filling

empatar *vi* : result in a draw, be tied — **empate** *nm* : draw, tie

empedernido, -da *adj* : inveterate, hardened

empedrar {55} *vt* : pave (with stones) — **empedrado** *nm* : paving, pavement

empeine *nm* : instep

empeñar *vt* : pawn — **empeñarse** *vr* 1 : insist, persist 2 ENDEUDARSE : go into debt 3 ~ **en** : make an effort to — **empeñado, -da** *adj* 1 : determined, committed 2 ENDEUDADO : in debt — **empeño** *nm* 1 : determination, effort 2 **casa de** ~**s** : pawnshop

empeorar *vi* : get worse — *vt* : make worse

empequeñecer {53} *vt* : diminish, make smaller

emperador *nm* : emperor — **emperatriz** *nf, pl* -**trices** : empress

empezar {29} *v* : start, begin

empinar *vt* : raise — **empinarse** *vr* : stand on tiptoe — **empinado, -da** *adj* : steep

empírico, -ca *adj* : empirical

emplasto *nm* : poultice

emplazar {21} *vt* 1 : summon, subpoena 2 SITUAR : place, locate — **emplazamiento** *nm* 1 : location, site 2 CITACIÓN : summons, subpoena

emplear *vt* 1 : employ 2 USAR : use — **emplearse** *vr* 1 : get a job 2 USARSE : be used — **empleado, -da** *n* : employee — **empleador, -dora** *n* : employer — **empleo** *nm* 1 : occupation, job 2 USO : use

empobrecer {53} *vt* : impoverish — **empobrecerse** *vr* : become poor

empollar *vi* : brood (eggs) — *vt* : incubate

empolvarse *vr* : powder one's face

empotrar *vt* : fit, build into — **empotrado, -da** *adj* : built-in

emprender *vt* : undertake, begin — **emprendedor, -dora** *adj* : enterprising

empresa *nf* 1 COMPAÑÍA : company, firm 2 TAREA : undertaking — **empresarial** *adj* : business, managerial — **empresario, -ria** *n* 1 : businessman *m*, businesswoman *f* 2 : impresario (in theater), promoter (in sports)

empujar *v* : push — **empuje** *nm* : impetus, drive — **empujón** *nm, pl* -**jones** : push, shove

empuñar *vt* : grasp, take hold of

emular *vt* : emulate

en *prep* 1 : in 2 DENTRO DE : into, inside

(of) **3** SOBRE : on **4** ~ **avión** : by plane **5** ~ **casa** : at home

enajenar *vt* : alienate — **enajenación** *nf*, *pl* **-ciones** : alienation

enagua *nf* : slip, petticoat

enaltecer {53} *vt* : praise, extol

enamorar *vt* : win the love of — **enamorarse** *vr* : fall in love — **enamorado, -da** *adj* : in love — ~ *n* : lover, sweetheart

enano, -na *adj & n* : dwarf

enarbolar *vt* **1** : hoist, raise **2** : brandish (arms, etc.)

enardecer {53} *vt* : stir up, excite

encabezar {21} *vt* **1** : head, lead **2** : put a heading on (an article, a list, etc.) — **encabezamiento** *nm* **1** : heading **2** : headline (in a newspaper)

encabritarse *vr* : rear up

encadenar *vt* **1** : chain, tie (up) **2** ENLAZAR : connect, link

encajar *vt* : fit (together) — *vi* **1** : fit **2** CUADRAR : conform, tally — **encaje** *nm* : lace

encalar *vt* : whitewash

encallar *vi* : run aground

encaminar *vt* : direct, aim — **encaminarse** *vr* ~ **a** : head for — **encaminado, -da** *adj* ~ **a** : aimed at, designed to

encandilar *vt* : dazzle

encanecer {53} *vi* : turn gray

encantar *vt* : enchant, bewitch — *vi* **me encanta esta canción** : I love this song — **encantado, -da** *adj* **1** : delighted **2** HECHIZADO : bewitched — **encantador, -dora** *adj* : charming, delightful — **encantamiento** *nm* : enchantment, spell — **encanto** *nm* **1** : charm, fascination **2** HECHIZO : spell

encapotarse *vr* : cloud over — **encapotado, -da** *adj* : overcast

encapricharse *vr* ~ **con** : be infatuated with

encapuchado, -da *adj* : hooded

encaramar *vt* : lift up — **encaramarse** *vr* ~ **a** : climb up on

encarar *vt* : face, confront

encarcelar *vt* : imprison — **encarcelamiento** *nm* : imprisonment

encarecer {53} *vt* : increase, raise (price, value, etc.) — **encarecerse** *vr* : become more expensive

encargar {52} *vt* **1** : put in charge of **2** PEDIR : order — **encargarse** *vr* ~ **de** : take charge of — **encargado, -da** *adj* : in charge — ~ *n* : manager, person in charge — **encargo** *nm* **1** : errand **2** TAREA : assignment, task **3** PEDIDO : order

encariñarse *vr* ~ **con** : become fond of

encarnar *vt* : embody — **encarnación** *nf*, *pl* **-ciones** : embodiment — **encarnado, -da** *adj* **1** : incarnate **2** ROJO : red

encarnizarse {21} *vr* ~ **con** : attack viciously — **encarnizado, -da** *adj* : bitter, bloody

encarrilar *vt* : put on the right track

encasillar *vt* : pigeonhole

encauzar {21} *vt* : channel

encender {56} *vt* **1** : light, set fire to **2** PRENDER : switch on, start **3** AVIVAR : arouse (passions, etc.) — **encenderse** *vr* **1** : get excited **2** RUBORIZARSE : blush — **encendedor** *nm* : lighter — **encendido, -da** *adj* : lit, on — **encendido** *nm* : ignition (switch)

encerar *vt* : wax, polish — **encerado, -da** *adj* : waxed — **encerado** *nm* : blackboard

encerrar {55} *vt* **1** : lock up, shut away **2** CONTENER : contain

encestar *vi* : score (in basketball)

enchilada *nf* : enchilada

enchufar *vt* : plug in, connect — **enchufe** *nm* : plug, socket

encía *nf* : gum (tissue)

encíclica *nf* : encyclical

enciclopedia *nf* : encyclopedia — **enciclopédico, -ca** *adj* : encyclopedic

encierro *nm* **1** : confinement **2** : sit-in (at a university, etc.)

encima *adv* **1** : on top **2** ADEMÁS : as well, besides **3** ~ **de** : on, over, on top of **4** **por** ~ **de** : above, beyond

encinta *adj* : pregnant

enclenque *adj* : weak, sickly

encoger {15} *v* : shrink — **encogerse** *vr* **1** : shrink **2** : cower, cringe **3** ~ **de hombros** : shrug (one's shoulders) — **encogido, -da** *adj* **1** : shrunken **2** TÍMIDO : shy

encolar *vt* : glue, stick

encolerizar {21} *vt* : enrage, infuriate — **encolerizarse** *vr* : get angry

encomendar {55} *vt* : entrust

encomienda *nf* **1** : charge, mission **2** *Lat* : parcel

encono *nm* : rancor, animosity

encontrar {19} *vt* **1** : find **2** : meet, encounter (difficulties, etc.) — **encontrarse** *vr* **1** : meet **2** HALLARSE : find oneself, be — **encontrado, -da** *adj* : contrary, opposing

encorvar *vt* : bend, curve — **encorvarse** *vr* : bend over, stoop

encrespar *vt* **1** : curl **2** IRRITAR : irritate — **encresparse** *vr* **1** : curl one's hair

2 IRRITARSE : get annoyed **3** : become choppy (of the sea)

encrucijada *nf* : crossroads

encuadernar *vt* 1 : bind (a book) — **encuadernación** *nf, pl* **-ciones** : bookbinding

encuadrar *vt* 1 : frame **2** ENCAJAR : fit **3** COMPRENDER : contain, include

encubrir {2} *vt* : conceal, cover (up) — **encubierto, -ta** *adj* : covert — **encubrimiento** *nm* : cover-up

encuentro *nm* : meeting, encounter

encuestar *vt* : poll, take a survey of — **encuesta** *nf* 1 : investigation, inquiry **2** SONDEO : survey — **encuestador, -dora** *n* : pollster

encumbrado, -da *adj* : eminent, distinguished

encurtir *vt* : pickle

endeble *adj* : weak, feeble — **endeblez** *nf* : weakness, frailty

endemoniado, -da *adj* : wicked

enderezar {21} *vt* 1 : straighten (out) **2** : put upright, stand on end

endeudarse *vr* : go into debt — **endeudado, -da** *adj* : indebted, in debt — **endeudamiento** *nm* : debt

endiablado, -da *adj* 1 : wicked, diabolical **2** : complicated, difficult

endibia *or* **endivia** *nf* : endive

endosar *vt* : endorse — **endoso** *nm* : endorsement

endulzar {21} *vt* 1 : sweeten **2** : soften, mellow (a tone, a response, etc.) — **endulzante** *nm* : sweetener

endurecer {53} *vt* : harden — **endurecerse** *vr* : become hardened

enema *nm* : enema

enemigo, -ga *adj* : hostile — **~** *n* : enemy — **enemistad** *nf* : enmity — **enemistar** *vt* : make enemies of — **enemistarse** *vr* **~ con** : fall out with

energía *nf* : energy — **enérgico, -ca** *adj* : energetic, vigorous, forceful

enero *nm* : January

enervar *vt* 1 : enervate, weaken **2** *fam* : get on one's nerves

enésimo, -ma *adj* **por enésima vez** : for the umpteenth time

enfadar *vt* : annoy, make angry — **enfadarse** *vr* : get annoyed — **enfado** *nm* : anger, annoyance — **enfadoso, -sa** *adj* : annoying

enfatizar {21} *vt* : emphasize — **énfasis** *nms & pl* : emphasis — **enfático, -ca** *adj* : emphatic

enfermar *vt* : make sick — *vi* : get sick — **enfermedad** *nf* : sickness, disease — **enfermería** *nf* : infirmary — **enfermero, -ra** *n* : nurse — **enfermizo, -za**

adj : sickly — **enfermo, -ma** *adj* : sick — **~** *n* : sick person, patient

enflaquecer {53} *vi* : lose weight

enfocar {72} *vt* 1 : focus (on) **2** : consider (a problem, etc.) — **enfoque** *nm* : focus

enfrascarse {72} *vr* **~ en** : immerse oneself in, get caught up in

enfrentar *vt* 1 : confront, face **2** : bring face to face — **enfrentarse** *vr* **~ con** : confront, clash with — **enfrente** *adv* 1 : opposite **2 ~ de** : in front of

enfriar {85} *vt* : chill, cool — **enfriarse** *vr* 1 : get cold **2** RESFRIARSE : catch a cold — **enfriamiento** *nm* 1 : cooling off **2** CATARRO : cold

enfurecer {53} *vt* : infuriate — **enfurecerse** *vr* : fly into a rage

enfurruñarse *vr fam* : sulk

engalanar *vt* : decorate — **engalanarse** *vr* : dress up

enganchar *vt* : hook, snag, catch — **engancharse** *vr* 1 : get caught **2** ALISTARSE : enlist

engañar *vt* 1 EMBAUCAR : trick, deceive **2** : cheat on, be unfaithful to — **engañarse** *vr* 1 : deceive oneself **2** EQUIVOCARSE : be mistaken — **engaño** *nm* : deception, deceit — **engañoso, -sa** *adj* : deceptive, deceitful

engatusar *vt* : coax, cajole

engendrar *vt* 1 : beget **2** : engender, give rise to (suspicions, etc.)

englobar *vt* : include, embrace

engomar *vt* : glue

engordar *vt* : fatten — *vi* : gain weight

engorroso, -sa *adj* : bothersome

engranar *v* : mesh, engage — **engranaje** *nm* : gears *pl*

engrandecer {53} *vt* 1 : enlarge **2** ENALTECER : exalt

engrapar *vt Lat* : staple — **engrapadora** *nf Lat* : stapler

engrasar *vt* : lubricate, grease — **engrase** *nm* : lubrication

engreído, -da *adj* : conceited

engrosar {19} *vt* : swell — *vi* : gain weight

engrudo *nm* : paste

engullir {38} *vt* : gulp down, gobble up

enhebrar *vt* : thread

enhorabuena *nf* : congratulations *pl*

enigma *nm* : enigma — **enigmático, -ca** *adj* : enigmatic

enjabonar *vt* : soap (up), lather

enjaezar {21} *vt* : harness

enjalbegar {52} *vt* : whitewash

enjambrar *vi* : swarm — **enjambre** *nm* : swarm

enjaular *vt* 1 : cage **2** *fam* : jail

enjuagar {52} *vt* : rinse — **enjuague** *nm* 1 : rinse 2 ~ **bucal** : mouthwash

enjugar {52} *vt* 1 : wipe away (tears) 2 : wipe out (debt)

enjuiciar *vt* 1 : prosecute 2 JUZGAR : try

enjuto, -ta *adj* : gaunt, lean

enlace *nm* 1 : bond, link 2 : junction (of a highway, etc.)

enlatar *vt* : can

enlazar {21} *vt* : join, link — *vi* ~ **con** : link up with

enlistarse *vr Lat* : enlist

enlodar *vt* : cover with mud

enloquecer {53} *vt* : drive crazy — **enloquecerse** *vr* : go crazy

enlosar *vt* : pave, tile

enlutarse *vr* : go into mourning

enmarañar *vt* 1 : tangle 2 COMPLICAR : complicate 3 CONFUNDIR : confuse — **enmarañarse** *vr* 1 : get tangled up 2 CONFUNDIRSE : become confused

enmarcar {72} *vt* : frame

enmascarar *vt* : mask

enmendar {55} *vt* 1 : amend 2 CORREGIR : emend, correct — **enmendarse** *vr* : mend one's ways — **enmienda** *nf* 1 : amendment 2 CORRECCIÓN : correction

enmohecerse {53} *vr* 1 : become moldy 2 OXIDARSE : rust

enmudecer {53} *vt* : silence — *vi* : fall silent

ennegrecer {53} *vt* : blacken

ennoblecer {53} *vt* : ennoble, dignify

enojar *vt* 1 : anger 2 MOLESTAR : annoy — **enojarse** *vr* ~ **con** : get upset with — **enojo** *nm* 1 : anger 2 MOLESTIA : annoyance — **enojoso, -sa** *adj* : annoying

enorgullecer {53} *vt* : make proud — **enorgullecerse** *vr* ~ **de** : pride oneself on

enorme *adj* : enormous — **enormemente** *adv* : enormously, extremely — **enormidad** *nf* : enormity

enraizar {30} *vi* : take root

enredadera *nf* : climbing plant, vine

enredar *vt* 1 : tangle up, entangle 2 CONFUNDIR : confuse 3 IMPLICAR : involve — **enredarse** *vr* 1 : become entangled 2 ~ **en** : get mixed up in — **enredo** *nm* 1 : tangle 2 EMBROLLO : confusion, mess — **enredoso, -sa** *adj* : tangled up, complicated

enrejado *nm* 1 : railing 2 REJILLA : grating, grille 3 : trellis (for plants)

enrevesado, -da *adj* : complicated

enriquecer {53} *vt* : enrich — **enriquecerse** *vr* : get rich

enrojecer {53} *vt* : redden — **enrojecerse** *vr* : blush

enrolar *vt* : enlist — **enrolarse** *vr* ~ **en** : enlist in

enrollar *vt* : roll up, coil

enroscar {72} *vt* 1 : roll up 2 ATORNILLAR : screw in

ensalada *nf* : salad

ensalzar {21} *vt* : praise

ensamblar *vt* : assemble, fit together

ensanchar *vt* 1 : widen 2 AMPLIAR : expand — **ensanche** *nm* 1 : widening 2 : (urban) expansion, development

ensangrentado, -da *adj* : bloody, bloodstained

ensañarse *vr* : act cruelly

ensartar *vt* : string, thread

ensayar *vi* : rehearse — *vt* : try out, test — **ensayo** *nm* 1 : essay 2 PRUEBA : trial, test 3 : rehearsal (in theater, etc.)

enseguida *adv* : right away, immediately

ensenada *nf* : inlet, cove

enseñar *vt* 1 : teach 2 MOSTRAR : show — **enseñanza** *nf* 1 EDUCACIÓN : education 2 INSTRUCCIÓN : teaching

enseres *nmpl* 1 : equipment 2 ~ **domésticos** : household goods

ensillar *vt* : saddle (up)

ensimismarse *vr* : lose oneself in thought

ensombrecer {53} *vt* : cast a shadow over, darken

ensoñación *nf, pl* **-ciones** : fantasy, daydream

ensordecer {53} *vt* : deafen — *vi* : go deaf — **ensordecedor, -dora** *adj* : deafening

ensortijar *vt* : curl

ensuciar *vt* : soil — **ensuciarse** *vr* : get dirty

ensueño *nm* : daydream, fantasy

entablar *vt* : initiate, start

entallar *vt* : tailor, fit (clothing) — *vi* : fit

entarimado *nm* : floorboards, flooring

ente *nm* 1 : being 2 ORGANISMO : body, organization

entender {56} *vt* 1 : understand 2 OPINAR : think, believe — *vi* 1 : understand 2 ~ **de** : know about, be good at — **entenderse** *vr* 1 : understand each other 2 LLEVARSE BIEN : get along well — ~ *nm* **a mi** ~ : in my opinion — **entendido, -da** *adj* 1 : understood 2 **eso se da por** ~ : that goes without saying 3 **tener** ~ : be under the impression — **entendimiento** *nm* 1 : understanding 2 INTELIGENCIA : intellect

enterar *vt* : inform — **enterarse** *vr* : find out, learn — **enterado, -da** *adj* : well-informed

entereza *nf* **1** HONRADEZ : integrity **2** FORTALEZA : fortitude **3** FIRMEZA : resolve

enternecer {53} *vt* : move, touch

entero, -ra *adj* **1** : whole **2** TOTAL : absolute, total **3** INTACTO : intact — **entero** *nm* : integer, whole number

enterrar {55} *vt* : bury

entibiar *vt* : cool (down) — **entibiarse** *vr* : become lukewarm

entidad *nf* **1** : entity **2** ORGANIZACIÓN : body, organization

entierro *nm* **1** : burial **2** : funeral (ceremony)

entomología *nf* : entomology — **entomólogo, -ga** *n* : entomologist

entonar *vt* : sing, intone — *vi* : be in tune

entonces *adv* **1** : then **2** desde ~ : since then

entornado, -da *adj* : half-closed, ajar

entorno *nm* : surroundings *pl*, environment

entorpecer {53} *vt* **1** : hinder, obstruct **2** : numb, dull (wits, reactions, etc.)

entrada *nf* **1** : entrance, entry **2** BILLETE : ticket **3** COMIENZO : beginning **4** : inning (in baseball) **5** ~s *nfpl* : income **6** tener ~s : have a receding hairline

entraña *nf* **1** : core, heart **2** ~s *nfpl* VÍSCERAS : entrails, innards — **entrañable** *adj* : close, intimate — **entrañar** *vt* : involve

entrar *vi* **1** : enter **2** EMPEZAR : begin — *vt* : introduce, bring in

entre *prep* **1** : between **2** : among

entreabrir {2} *vt* : leave ajar — **entreabierto, -ta** *adj* : half-open, ajar

entreacto *nm* : intermission

entrecejo *nm* fruncir el ~ : knit one's brows, frown

entrecortado, -da *adj* : faltering (of the voice), labored (of breathing)

entrecruzar {21} *vi* : intertwine

entredicho *nm* : doubt, question

entregar {52} *vt* : deliver, hand over — **entregarse** *vr* : surrender — **entrega** *nf* **1** : delivery **2** DEDICACIÓN : dedication, devotion **3** ~ inicial : down payment

entrelazar {21} *vt* : intertwine — **entrelazarse** *vr* : become intertwined

entremés *nm, pl* **-meses 1** : hors d'oeuvre **2** : short play (in theater)

entremeterse → **entrometerse**

entremezclar *vt* : mix (up)

entrenar *vt* : train, drill — **entrenarse**

vr : train — **entrenador, -dora** *n* : trainer, coach — **entranamiento** *nm* : training

entrepierna *nf* : crotch

entresacar {72} *vt* : pick out, select

entresuelo *nm* : mezzanine

entretanto *adv* : meanwhile — ~ *nm* en el ~ : in the meantime

entretener {80} *vt* **1** : entertain **2** DESPISTAR : distract **3** RETRASAR : delay, hold up — **entretenerse** *vr* **1** : amuse oneself **2** DEMORARSE : dawdle — **entretenido, -da** *adj* : entertaining — **entretenimiento** *nm* **1** : entertainment, amusement **2** PASATIEMPO : pastime

entrever {88} *vt* : catch a glimpse of, make out

entrevistar *vt* : interview — **entrevista** *nf* : interview — **entrevistador, -dora** *n* : interviewer

entristecer {53} *vt* : sadden

entrometerse *vr* : interfere — **entrometido, -da** *adj* : meddling, nosy — *n* : meddler

entroncar {72} *vi* : be related, be connected

entumecer {53} *vt* : make numb — **entumecerse** *vr* : go numb — **entumecido, -da** *adj* **1** : numb **2** : stiff (of muscles, etc.)

enturbiar *vt* : cloud — **enturbiarse** *vr* : become cloudy

entusiasmar *vt* : fill with enthusiasm — **entusiasmarse** *vr* : get excited — **entusiasmo** *nm* : enthusiasm — **entusiasta** *adj* : enthusiastic — ~ *nmf* : enthusiast

enumerar *vt* : enumerate, list — **enumeración** *nf, pl* **-ciones** : enumeration, count

enunciar *vt* : enunciate — **enunciación** *nf, pl* **-ciones** : enunciation

envalentonar *vt* : make bold, encourage — **envalentonarse** *vr* : be brave

envanecerse {53} *vr* : become vain

envasar *vt* **1** : package **2** : bottle, can — **envase** *nm* **1** : packaging **2** RECIPIENTE : container **3** : jar, bottle, can

envejecer {53} *v* : age — **envejecido, -da** *adj* : aged, old — **envejecimiento** *nm* : aging

envenenar *vt* : poison — **envenenamiento** *nm* : poisoning

envergadura *nf* **1** ALCANCE : scope **2** : span (of wings, etc.)

envés *nm, pl* **-veses** : reverse side

enviar {85} *vt* : send — **enviado, -da** *n* : envoy, correspondent

envidiar *vt* : envy — **envidia** *nf* : envy,

jealousy — **envidioso, -sa** adj : jealous, envious

envilecer {53} vt : degrade, debase — **envilecimiento** nm : degradation

envío nm 1 : sending, shipment 2 : remittance (of funds)

enviudar vi : be widowed

envolver {89} vt 1 : wrap 2 RODEAR : surround 3 IMPLICAR : involve — **envoltorio** nm or **envoltura** nf : wrapping, wrapper

enyesar vt 1 : plaster 2 ESCAYOLAR : put in a plaster cast

enzima nf : enzyme

épico, -ca adj : epic — **épica** nf : epic

epidemia nf : epidemic — **epidémico, -ca** adj : epidemic

epilepsia nf : epilepsy — **epiléptico, -ca** adj & n : epileptic

epílogo nm : epilogue

episodio nm : episode

epitafio nm : epitaph

epíteto nm : epithet

época nf 1 : epoch, period 2 ESTACIÓN : season

epopeya nf : epic poem

equidad nf : equity, justice

equilátero, -ra adj : equilateral

equilibrar vt : balance — **equilibrado, -da** adj : well-balanced — **equilibrio** nm 1 : balance, equilibrium 2 JUICIO : good sense

equinoccio nm : equinox

equipaje nm : baggage, luggage

equipar vt : equip

equiparar vt 1 IGUALAR : make equal 2 COMPARAR : compare — **equiparable** adj : comparable

equipo nm 1 : equipment 2 : team, crew (in sports, etc.)

equitación nf, pl **-ciones** : horseback riding

equitativo, -va adj : equitable, fair, just

equivaler {84} vi : be equivalent — **equivalencia** nf : equivalence — **equivalente** adj & nm : equivalent

equivocar {72} vt : mistake, confuse — **equivocarse** vr : make a mistake — **equivocación** nf, pl **-ciones** : error, mistake — **equivocado, -da** adj : mistaken, wrong

equívoco, -ca adj : ambiguous — **equívoco** nm : misunderstanding

era nf : era

erario nm : public treasury, funds pl

erección nf, pl **-ciones** : erection

erguir {31} vt : raise, lift — **erguirse** vr : rise (up) — **erguido, -da** adj : erect, upright

erigir {35} vt : build, erect — **erigirse** vr ~ **en** : set oneself up as

erizarse {21} vr : bristle, stand on end — **erizado, -da** adj : bristly

erizo nm 1 : hedgehog 2 ~ **de mar** : sea urchin

ermitaño, -ña n : hermit

erosionar vt : erode — **erosión** nf, pl **-siones** : erosion

erótico, -ca adj : erotic

erradicar {72} vt : eradicate

errar {32} vt : miss — vi 1 : be wrong, be mistaken 2 VAGAR : wander — **errado, -da** adj Lat : wrong, mistaken

errata nf : misprint

errático, -ca adj : erratic

error nm : error — **erróneo, -nea** adj : erroneous, mistaken

eructar vi : belch, burp — **eructo** nm : belch, burp

erudito, -ta adj : erudite, learned

erupción nf, pl **-ciones** 1 : eruption 2 SARPULLIDO : rash

esa, ésa → **ese, ése**

esbelto, -ta adj : slender, slim

esbozar {21} vt : sketch, outline — **esbozo** nm : sketch, outline

escabechar vt : pickle — **escabeche** nm : brine (for pickling)

escabel nm : footstool

escabroso, -sa adj 1 : rugged, rough 2 ESPINOSO : thorny, difficult 3 ATREVIDO : shocking, risqué

escabullirse {38} vr : slip away, escape

escalar vt : climb, scale — vi : escalate — **escala** nf 1 : scale 2 ESCALERA : ladder 3 : stopover (of an airplane, etc.) — **escalada** nf : ascent, climb — **escalador, -dora** n ALPINISTA : mountain climber

escaldar vt : scald

escalera nf 1 : stairs pl, staircase 2 ESCALA : ladder 3 ~ **mecánica** : escalator

escalfar vt : poach

escalinata nf : flight of stairs

escalofrío nm : shiver, chill — **escalofriante** adj : chilling, horrifying

escalonar vt 1 : stagger, spread out 2 : terrace (land) — **escalón** nm, pl **-lones** : step, rung

escama nf 1 : scale (of fish or reptiles) 2 : flake (of skin) — **escamoso, -sa** adj : scaly

escamotear vt 1 : conceal 2 ~ **algo a aign** : rob s.o. of sth

escandalizar {21} vt : scandalize — **escandalizarse** vr : be shocked — **escándalo** nm 1 : scandal 2 ALBOROTO : scene, commotion — **escandaloso,**

-sa *adj* **1** : shocking, scandalous **2** RUIDOSO : noisy

escandinavo, -va *adj* : Scandinavian

escáner *nm* : scanner

escaño *nm* **1** : seat (in a legislative body) **2** BANCO : bench

escapar *vi* : escape, run away — **escaparse** *vr* **1** : escape **2** : leak out (of gas, water, etc.) — **escapada** *nf* : escape

escaparate *nm* : store window

escapatoria *nf* : loophole, way out

escape *nm* **1** : leak (of gas, water, etc.) **2** : exhaust (from a vehicle)

escarabajo *nm* : beetle

escarbar *vt* **1** : dig, scratch, poke **2** ~ **en** : pry into

escarcha *nf* : frost (on a surface)

escarlata *adj & nf* : scarlet — **escarlatina** *nf* : scarlet fever

escarmentar {55} *vi* : learn one's lesson — **escarmiento** *nm* : lesson, punishment

escarnecer {53} *vt* : ridicule, mock — **escarnio** *nm* : ridicule, mockery

escarola *nf* : escarole, endive

escarpa *nf* : steep slope — **escarpado, -da** *adj* : steep

escasear *vi* : be scarce — **escasez** *nf, pl* **-seces** : shortage, scarcity — **escaso, -sa** *adj* **1** : scarce **2** ~ **de** : short of

escatimar *vt* : be sparing with, skimp on

escayolar *vt* : put in a plaster cast — **escayola** *nf* **1** : plaster (for casts) **2** : plaster cast

escena *nf* **1** : scene **2** ESCENARIO : stage — **escenario** *nm* **1** : setting, scene **2** ESCENA : stage — **escénico, -ca** *adj* : scenic

escepticismo *nm* : skepticism — **escéptico, -ca** *adj* : skeptical — ~ *n* : skeptic

esclarecer {53} *vt* : shed light on, clarify

esclavo, -va *n* : slave — **esclavitud** *nf* : slavery — **esclavizar** {21} *vt* : enslave

esclerosis *nf* ~ **múltiple** : multiple sclerosis

esclusa *nf* : floodgate, lock (of a canal)

escoba *nf* : broom

escocer {14} *vi* : sting

escocés, -cesa *adj, mpl* **-ceses 1** : Scottish **2** : tartan, plaid — **escocés** *nm, pl* **-ceses** : Scotch (whiskey)

escoger {15} *vt* : choose — **escogido, -da** *adj* : choice, select

escolar *adj* : school — ~ *nmf* : student, pupil

escolta *nmf* : escort — **escoltar** *vt* : escort, accompany

escombros *nmpl* : ruins, rubble

esconder *vt* : hide, conceal — **esconderse** *vr* : hide — **escondidas** *nfpl* **1** *Lat* : hide-and-seek **2 a** ~ : secretly, in secret — **escondite** *nm* **1** : hiding place **2** : hide-and-seek (game) — **escondrijo** *nm* : hiding place

escopeta *nf* : shotgun

escoplo *nm* : chisel

escoria *nf* **1** : slag **2** : dregs *pl* (of society, etc.)

escorpión *nm, pl* **-piones** : scorpion

escote *nm* **1** : (low) neckline **2 pagar a** ~ : go Dutch

escotilla *nf* : hatchway

escribir {33} *v* : write — **escribirse** *vr* **1** : write to one another, correspond **2** : be spelled — **escribiente** *nmf* : clerk — **escrito, -ta** *adj* : written — **escritos** *nmpl* : writings — **escritor, -tora** *n* : writer — **escritorio** *nm* : desk — **escritura** *nf* **1** : handwriting **2** : deed (in law)

escroto *nm* : scrotum

escrúpulo *nm* : scruple — **escrupuloso, -sa** *adj* : scrupulous

escrutar *vt* **1** : scrutinize **2** : count (votes) — **escrutinio** *nm* **1** : scrutiny **2** : count (of votes)

escuadra *nf* **1** : square (instrument) **2** : fleet (of ships), squad (in the military) — **escuadrón** *nm, pl* **-drones** : squadron

escuálido, -da *adj* **1** : skinny **2** SUCIO : squalid

escuchar *vt* **1** : listen to **2** *Lat* : hear — *vi* : listen

escudo *nm* **1** : shield **2** *or* ~ **de armas** : coat of arms

escudriñar *vt* : scrutinize, examine

escuela *nf* : school

escueto, -ta *adj* : plain, simple

esculpir *v* : sculpt — **escultor, -tora** *n* : sculptor — **escultura** *nf* : sculpture

escupir *v* : spit

escurrir *vt* **1** : drain **2** : wring out (clothes) — *vi* **1** : drain **2** : drip-dry (of clothes) — **escurrirse** *vr* **1** : drain **2** *fam* : slip away — **escurridizo, -da** *adj* : slippery, evasive — **escurridor** *nm* **1** : dish drainer **2** COLADOR : colander

ese, esa *adj, mpl* **esos** : that, those

ése, ésa *pron, mpl* **ésos** : that one, those ones *pl*

esencia *nf* : essence — **esencial** *adj* : essential

esfera *nf* **1** : sphere **2** : dial (of a watch) — **esférico, -ca** *adj* : spherical

esfinge *nf* : sphinx

esforzar {36} *vt* : strain — **esforzarse** *vr* : make an effort — **esfuerzo** *nm* : effort

esfumarse *vr* : fade away, vanish

esgrimir *vt* **1** : brandish, wield **2** : make use of (an argument, etc.) — **esgrima** *nf* **1** : fencing **2 hacer ~** : fence

esguince *nm* : sprain, strain

eslabonar *vt* : link, connect — **eslabón** *nm, pl* **-bones** : link

eslavo, -va *adj* : Slavic

eslogan *nm, pl* **-lóganes** : slogan

esmaltar *vt* : enamel — **esmalte** *nm* **1** : enamel **2 ~ de uñas** : nail polish

esmerado, -da *adj* : careful

esmeralda *nf* : emerald

esmerarse *vr* : take great care

esmeril *nm* : emery

esmoquin *nm, pl* **-móquines** : tuxedo

esnob *nmf, pl* **esnobs** : snob — **~** *adj* : snobbish

eso *pron (neuter)* **1** : that **2 ¡~ es!** : that's it!, that's right! **3 en ~** : at that point, then

esófago *nm* : esophagus

esos, ésos → ese, ése

espabilarse *vr* **1** : wake up **2 DARSE PRISA** : get moving — **espabilado, -da** *adj* **1** : awake **2 LISTO** : bright, clever

espaciar *vt* : space out, spread out — **espacial** *adj* : space — **espacio** *nm* **1** : space **2 ~ exterior** : outer space — **espacioso, -sa** *adj* : spacious

espada *nf* **1** : sword **2 ~s** *nfpl* : spades (in playing cards)

espagueti *nm or* **espaguetis** *nmpl* : spaghetti

espalda *nf* **1** : back **2 ~ s** *nfpl* : shoulders, back

espantar *vt* : scare, frighten — **espantarse** *vr* : become frightened — **espantajo** *nm or* **espantapájaros** *nms & pl* : scarecrow — **espanto** *nm* : fright, fear — **espantoso, -sa** *adj* **1** : frightening, horrific **2 TERRIBLE** : awful, terrible

español, -ñola *adj* : Spanish — **español** *nm* : Spanish (language)

esparadrapo *nm* : adhesive bandage

esparcir {83} *vt* : scatter, spread — **esparcirse** *vr* **1** : be scattered, spread out **2 DIVERTIRSE** : enjoy oneself

espárrago *nm* : asparagus

espasmo *nm* : spasm — **espasmódico, -ca** *adj* : spasmodic

espátula *nf* : spatula

especia *nf* : spice

especial *adj & nm* : special — **especialidad** *nf* : specialty — **especialista** *nmf* : specialist — **especializarse** {21} *vr* **~ en** : specialize in — **especialmente** *adv* : especially

especie *nf* **1** : species **2 CLASE** : type, kind

especificar {72} *vt* : specify — **especificación** *nf, pl* **-ciones** : specification — **específico, -ca** *adj* : specific

espécimen *nm, pl* **especímenes** : specimen

espectáculo *nm* **1** : show, performance **2 VISIÓN** : spectacle, view — **espectacular** *adj* : spectacular — **espectador, -dora** *n* : spectator

espectro *nm* **1** : spectrum **2 FANTASMA** : ghost

especulación *nf, pl* **-ciones** : speculation

espejo *nm* : mirror — **espejismo** *nm* **1** : mirage **2 ILUSIÓN** : illusion

espeluznante *adj* : terrifying, hair-raising

esperar *vt* **1** : wait for **2 CONTAR CON** : expect **3 ~ que** : hope (that) — *vi* : wait — **espera** *nf* : wait — **esperanza** *nf* : hope, expectation — **esperanzado, -da** *adj* : hopeful — **esperanzar** {21} *vt* : give hope to

esperma *nmf* **1** : sperm **2 ~ de ballena** : blubber

esperpento *nm* : (grotesque) sight, fright

espesar *vt* : thicken — **espesarse** *vr* : thicken — **espeso, -sa** *adj* : thick, heavy — **espesor** *nm* : thickness, density — **espesura** *nf* **1 ESPESOR** : thickness **2** : thicket

espetar *vt* : blurt out

espiar {85} *vt* : spy on — *vi* : spy — **espía** *nmf* : spy

espiga *nf* : ear (of wheat, etc.)

espina *nf* **1** : thorn **2** : (fish) bone **3 ~ dorsal** : spine, backbone

espinaca *nf* **1** : spinach (plant) **2 ~s** *nfpl* : spinach (food)

espinazo *nm* : spine, backbone

espinilla *nf* **1** : shin **2 GRANO** : blackhead, pimple

espinoso, -sa *adj* **1** : prickly **2** : bony (of fish) **3** : difficult, thorny (of problems, etc.)

espionaje *nm* : espionage

espiral *adj & nf* : spiral

espirar *v* : breathe out, exhale

espíritu *nm* **1** : spirit **2 Espíritu Santo** : Holy Spirit — **espiritual** *adj* : spiritual — **espiritualidad** *nf* : spirituality

espita *nf* : spigot, faucet

espléndido, -da *adj* **1** : splendid **2 GE-**

NEROSO : lavish — **esplendor** *nm* : splendor

espliego *nm* : lavender

espolear *vt* : spur on

espoleta *nf* : fuse

espolvorear *vt* : sprinkle, dust

esponja *nf* 1 : sponge 2 **tirar la ~** : throw in the towel — **esponjoso, -sa** *adj* : spongy

espontaneidad *nf* : spontaneity — **espontáneo, -nea** *adj* : spontaneous

espora *nf* : spore

esporádico, -ca *adj* : sporadic

esposo, -sa *n* : spouse, wife *f*, husband *m* — **esposar** *vt* : handcuff — **esposas** *nfpl* : handcuffs

esprintar *vi* : sprint (in sports) — **esprint** *nm* : sprint

espuela *nf* : spur

espumar *vt* : skim — **espuma** *nf* 1 : foam, froth 2 : (soap) lather 3 : head (on beer) — **espumoso, -sa** *adj* 1 : foamy, frothy 2 : sparkling (of wine)

esqueleto *nm* : skeleton

esquema *nf* : outline, sketch

esquí *nm* 1 : ski 2 : skiing (sport) 3 **~ acuático** : waterskiing — **esquiador, -dora** *n* : skier — **esquiar** {85} *vi* : ski

esquilar *vt* : shear

esquimal *adj* : Eskimo

esquina *nf* : corner

esquirol *nm* : strikebreaker, scab

esquivar *vt* 1 : evade, dodge (a blow) 2 EVITAR : avoid — **esquivo, -va** *adj* : shy, elusive

esquizofrenia *nf* : schizophrenia — **esquizofrénico, -ca** *adj & n* : schizophrenic

esta, ésta → **este¹, éste**

estable *adj* : stable — **estabilidad** *nf* : stability — **estabilizar** {21} *vt* : stabilize

establecer {53} *vt* : establish — **establecerse** *vr* : establish oneself, settle — **establecimiento** *nm* : establishment

establo *nm* : stable

estaca *nf* : stake — **estacada** *nf* 1 : (picket) fence 2 **dejar en la ~** : leave in a lurch

estación *nf, pl* **-ciones** 1 : season 2 **~ de servicio** : gas station — **estacionar** *v* : park — **estacionamiento** *nm* : parking — **estacionario, -ria** *adj* : stationary

estadía *nf Lat* : stay

estadio *nm* 1 : stadium 2 FASE : phase, stage

estadista *nmf* : statesman

estadística *nf* : statistics — **estadístico, -ca** *adj* : statistical

estado *nm* 1 : state 2 **~ civil** : marital status

estadounidense *adj & nmf* : American (from the United States)

estafar *vt* : swindle, defraud — **estafa** *nf* : swindle, fraud — **estafador, -dora** *n* : cheat, swindler

estallar *vi* 1 : explode 2 : break out (of war, an epidemic, etc.) 3 **~ en llamas** : burst into flames — **estallido** *nm* 1 : explosion 2 : report (of a gun) 3 : outbreak (of war, etc.)

estampar *vt* : stamp, print — **estampa** *nf* 1 : print, illustration 2 ASPECTO : appearance — **estampado, -da** *adj* : printed

estampida *nf* : stampede

estampilla *nf* : stamp

estancarse {72} *vr* 1 : stagnate 2 : come to a halt — **estancado, -da** *adj* : stagnant

estancia *nf* 1 : stay 2 HABITACIÓN : (large) room 3 *Lat* : (cattle) ranch

estanco, -ca *adj* : watertight

estándar *adj & nm* : standard — **estandarizar** {21} *vt* : standardize

estandarte *nm* : standard, banner

estanque *nm* 1 : pool, pond 2 : reservoir (for irrigation)

estante *nm* : shelf — **estantería** *nf* : shelves *pl*, bookcase

estaño *nm* : tin

estar {34} *v aux* : be — *vi* 1 : be 2 : be at home 3 QUEDARSE : stay, remain 4 **¿cómo estás?** : how are you? 5 **~ a** : cost 6 **~ bien (mal)** : be well (sick) 7 **~ para** : be in the mood for 8 **~ por** : be in favor of 9 **~ por** : be about to — **estarse** *vr* : stay, remain

estarcir {83} *vt* : stencil

estárter *nm* : choke (of an automobile)

estatal *adj* : state, national

estático, -ca *adj* 1 : static 2 INMÓVIL : unmoving, still — **estática** *nf* : static

estatua *nf* : statue

estatura *nf* : height

estatus *nms* : status, prestige

estatuto *nm* : statute — **estatutario, -ria** *adj* : statutory

este¹, esta *adj, mpl* **estos** : this, these

este² *adj* : eastern, east — **este** *nm* 1 : east 2 : east wind 3 **el Este** : the Orient

éste, ésta *pron, mpl* **éstos** 1 : this one, these ones *pl* 2 : the latter

estela *nf* 1 : wake (of a ship) 2 : trail (of smoke, etc.)

estera *nf* : mat

estéreo *adj & nm* : stereo — **estereofónico, -ca** *adj* : stereophonic

estereotipo *nm* : stereotype
estéril *adj* 1 : sterile 2 : infertile — **esterilidad** *nf* 1 : sterility 2 : infertility — **esterilizar** {21} *vt* : sterilize
estética *nf* : aesthetics — **estético, -ca** *adj* : aesthetic
estiércol *nm* : dung, manure
estigma *nm* : stigma — **estigmatizar** {21} *vt* : stigmatize
estilarse {21} *vr* : be in fashion
estilo *nm* 1 : style 2 MANERA : fashion, manner — **estilista** *nmf* : stylist
estima *nf* : esteem, regard — **estimación** *nf, pl* **-ciones** 1 : esteem 2 VALORACIÓN : estimate — **estimado, -da** *adj* **Estimado señor** : Dear Sir — **estimar** *vt* 1 : esteem, respect 2 VALORAR : value, estimate 3 CONSIDERAR : consider
estimular *vt* 1 : stimulate 2 ALENTAR : encourage — **estimulante** *adj* : stimulating — **~** *nm* : stimulant — **estímulo** *nm* : stimulus
estío *nm* : summertime
estipular *vt* : stipulate
estirar *vt* : stretch (out), extend — **estirado, -da** *adj* 1 : stretched, extended 2 ALTANERO : stuck-up, haughty — **estiramiento** *nm* **~ facial** : face-lift — **estirón** *nm, pl* **-rones** : pull, tug
estirpe *nf* : lineage, stock
estival *adj* : summer
esto *pron (neuter)* 1 : this 2 **en ~** : at this point 3 **por ~** : for this reason
estofa *nf* 1 : class, quality 2 **de baja ~** : low-class
estofar *vt* : stew — **estofado** *nm* : stew
estoicismo *nm* : stoicism — **estoico, -ca** *adj* : stoic, stoical — **~** *n* : stoic
estómago *nm* : stomach — **estomacal** *adj* : stomach
estorbar *vt* : obstruct — *vi* : get in the way — **estorbo** *nm* 1 : obstacle 2 MOLESTIA : nuisance
estornino *nm* : starling
estornudar *vi* : sneeze — **estornudo** *nm* : sneeze
estos, éstos → **este, éste**
estrabismo *nm* : squint
estrado *nm* : platform, stage
estrafalario, -ria *adj* : eccentric, bizarre
estragar {52} *vt* : devastate — **estragos** *nmpl* **~** : ravages 2 **hacer ~ en** *or* **causar ~ entre** : wreak havoc with
estragón *nm* : tarragon
estrangular *vt* : strangle — **estrangulación** *nf* : strangulation
estratagema *nf* : stratagem
estrategia *nf* : strategy — **estratégico, -ca** *adj* : strategic

estrato *nm* : stratum
estratosfera *nf* : stratosphere
estrechar *vt* 1 : narrow 2 : strengthen (a bond) 3 ABRAZAR : embrace 4 **~ la mano a uno** : shake s.o.'s hand — **estrecharse** *vr* : narrow — **estrechez** *nf, pl* **-checes** 1 : narrowness 2 **estrecheces** *nfpl* : financial problems — **estrecho, -cha** *adj* 1 : tight, narrow 2 ÍNTIMO : close — **estrecho** *nm* : strait
estrella *nf* 1 : star 2 DESTINO : destiny 3 **~ de mar** : starfish — **estrellado, -da** *adj* 1 : starry 2 : star-shaped
estrellar *v* : crash — **estrellarse** *vr* **~ contre** : smash into
estremecer {53} *vt* : cause to shudder — *vi* : tremble, shake — **estremecerse** *vr* : shudder, shiver (with emotion) — **estremecimiento** *nm* : shaking, shivering
estrenar *vt* 1 : use for the first time 2 : premiere, open (a film, etc.) — **estrenarse** *vr* : make one's debut — **estreno** *nm* : debut, premiere
estreñirse {67} *vr* : be constipated — **estreñimiento** *nm* : constipation
estrépito *nm* : clamor, din — **estrepitoso, -sa** *adj* : noisy, clamorous
estrés *nm, pl* **estreses** : stress — **estresante** *adj* : stressful — **estresar** *vt* : stress (out)
estría *nf* : groove
estribaciones *nfpl* : foothills
estribar *vi* **~ en** : stem from, lie in
estribillo *nm* : refrain, chorus
estribo *nm* 1 : stirrup 2 : running board (of a vehicle) 3 CONTRAFUERTE : buttress 4 **perder los ~s** : lose one's temper
estribor *nm* : starboard
estricto, -ta *adj* : strict
estridente *adj* : strident, shrill
estrofa *nf* : stanza, verse
estropajo *nm* : scouring pad
estropear *vt* 1 : ruin, spoil 2 DAÑAR : damage — **estropearse** *vr* 1 : go bad 2 AVERIARSE : break down — **estropicio** *nm* : damage, havoc
estructura *nf* : structure — **estructural** *adj* : structural
estruendo *nm* : din, roar — **estruendoso, -sa** *adj* : thunderous
estrujar *vt* : squeeze
estuario *nm* : estuary
estuche *nm* : kit, case
estuco *nm* : stucco
estudiar *v* : study — **estudiante** *nmf* : student — **estudiantil** *adj* : student — **estudio** *nm* 1 : study 2 OFICINA

: studio, office 3 ~s *nmpl* : studies, education — **estudioso, -sa** *adj* : studious

estufa *nf* : stove, heater

estupefaciente *adj & nm* : narcotic — **estupefacto, -ta** *adj* : astonished

estupendo, -da *adj* : stupendous, marvelous

estúpido, -da *adj* : stupid — **estupidez** *nf, pl* **-deces** : stupidity

estupor *nm* 1 : stupor 2 ASOMBRO : amazement

etapa *nf* : stage, phase

etcétera : et cetera, and so on

éter *nm* : ether

etéreo, -rea *adj* : ethereal

eterno, -na *adj* : eternal — **eternidad** *nf* : eternity — **eternizarse** {21} *vr* : take forever

ética *nf* : ethics — **ético, -ca** *adj* : ethical

etimología *nf* : etymology

etíope *adj* : Ethiopian

etiqueta *nf* 1 : tag, label 2 PROTOCOLO : etiquette 3 de ~ : formal, dressy — **etiquetar** *vt* : label

étnico, -ca *adj* : ethnic

eucalipto *nm* : eucalyptus

Eucaristía *nf* : Eucharist, communion

eufemismo *nm* : euphemism — **eufemístico, -ca** *adj* : euphemistic

euforia *nf* : euphoria — **eufórico, -ca** *adj* : euphoric

europeo, -pea *adj* : European

eutanasia *nf* : euthanasia

evacuar *vt* : evacuate, vacate — *vi* : have a bowel movement — **evacuación** *nf, pl* **-ciones** : evacuation

evadir *vt* : evade, avoid — **evadirse** *vr* : escape

evaluar {3} *vt* : evaluate — **evaluación** *nf, pl* **-ciones** : evaluation

evangelio *nm* : gospel — **evangélico, -ca** *adj* : evangelical — **evangelismo** *nm* : evangelism

evaporar *vt* : evaporate — **evaporarse** *vr* : evaporate, disappear — **evaporación** *nf, pl* **-ciones** : evaporation

evasión *nf, pl* **-siones** 1 : evasion 2 FUGA : escape — **evasiva** *nf* : excuse, pretext — **evasivo, -va** *adj* : evasive

evento *nm* : event

eventual *adj* 1 : temporary 2 POSIBLE : possible — **eventualidad** *nf* : possibility, eventuality

evidencia *nf* 1 : evidence, proof 2 poner en ~ : demonstrate — **evidenciar** *vt* : demonstrate, show — **evidente** *adj* : evident — **evidentemente** *adj* : evidently, apparently

evitar *vt* 1 : avoid 2 IMPEDIR : prevent — **evitable** *adj* : avoidable

evocar {72} *vt* : evoke

evolución *nf, pl* **-ciones** : evolution — **evolucionar** *vi* : evolve

exacerbar *vt* 1 : exacerbate 2 IRRITAR : irritate

exacto, -ta *adj* : precise, exact — **exactamente** *adv* : exactly — **exactitud** *nf* : precision, accuracy

exagerar *v* : exaggerate — **exageración** *nf, pl* **-ciones** : exaggeration — **exagerado, -da** *adj* : exaggerated

exaltar *vt* 1 : exalt, extol 2 EXCITAR : excite, arouse — **exaltarse** *vr* : get worked-up — **exaltado, -da** *adj* : worked up, hotheaded

examen *nm, pl* **exámenes** 1 : examination, test 2 ANÁLISIS : investigation — **examinar** *vt* 1 : examine 2 ESTUDIAR : study, inspect — **examinarse** *vr* : take an exam

exánime *adj* : lifeless

exasperar *vt* : exasperate, irritate — **exasperación** *nf, pl* **-ciones** : exasperation

excavar *v* : excavate — **excavación** *nf, pl* **-ciones** : excavation

exceder *vt* : exceed, surpass — **excederse** *vr* : go too far — **excedente** *adj & nm* : surplus, excess

excelente *adj* : excellent — **excelencia** *nf* 1 : excellence 2 Su Excelencia : His/Her Excellency

excéntrico, -ca *adj & n* : eccentric — **excentricidad** *nf* : eccentricity

excepción *nf, pl* **-ciones** : exception — **excepcional** *adj* : exceptional

excepto *prep* : except (for) — **exceptuar** {3} *vt* : exclude, except

exceso *nm* 1 : excess 2 ~ de velocidad : speeding — **excesivo, -va** *adj* : excessive

excitar *vt* : excite, arouse — **excitarse** *vr* : get excited — **excitable** *adj* : excitable — **excitación** *nf, pl* **-ciones** : excitement, agitation, arousal — **excitante** *adj* : exciting

exclamar *v* : exclaim — **exclamación** *nf, pl* **-ciones** : exclamation

excluir {41} *vt* : exclude — **exclusión** *nf, pl* **-siones** : exclusion — **exclusivo, -va** *adj* : exclusive

excomulgar {52} *vt* : excommunicate — **excomunión** *nf, pl* **-niones** : excommunication

excremento *nm* : excrement

exculpar *vt* : exonerate

excursión *nf, pl* **-siones** : excursion —

excursionista *nmf* 1 : tourist, sightseer 2 : hiker

excusar *vt* 1 : excuse 2 EXIMIR : exempt — **excusarse** *vr* : apologize — **excusa** *nf* 1 : excuse 2 DISCULPA : apology

exento, -ta *adj* : exempt

exequias *nfpl* : funeral rites

exhalar *vt* 1 : exhale 2 : give off (an odor, etc.)

exhaustivo, -va *adj* : exhaustive — **exhausto, -ta** *adj* : exhausted, worn-out

exhibir *vt* : exhibit, show — **exhibición** *nf, pl* -**ciones** : exhibition

exhortar *vt* : exhort, admonish

exigir {35} *vt* : demand, require — **exigencia** *nf* : demand, requirement — **exigente** *adj* : demanding

exiguo, -gua *adj* : meager

exiliar *vt* : exile — **exiliarse** *vr* : go into exile — **exiliado, -da** *adj* : exiled, in exile — ~ *n* : exile — **exilio** *nm* : exile

eximir *vt* : exempt

existir *vi* : exist — **existencia** *nf* 1 : existence 2 ~s *nfpl* MERCANCÍA : goods, stock — **existente** *adj* : existing

éxito *nm* 1 : success, hit 2 tener ~ : be successful — **exitoso, -sa** *adj* Lat : successful

éxodo *nm* : exodus

exorbitante *adj* : exorbitant

exorcizar {21} *vt* : exorcize — **exorcismo** *nm* : exorcism

exótico, -ca *adj* : exotic

expandir *vt* : expand — **expandirse** *vr* : spread — **expansión** *nf, pl* -**siones** : expansion — **expansivo, -va** *adj* : expansive

expatriarse {85} *vr* 1 : emigrate 2 EXILIARSE : go into exile — **expatriado, -da** *adj* & *n* : expatriate

expectativa *nf* 1 : expectation, hope 2 ~s *nfpl* : prospects

expedición *nf, pl* -**ciones** : expedition

expediente *nm* 1 : expedient 2 DOCUMENTOS : file, record 3 INVESTIGACIÓN : inquiry, proceedings

expedir {54} *vt* 1 : issue 2 ENVIAR : dispatch — **expedito, -ta** *adj* : free, clear

expeler *vt* : expel, eject

expendedor, -dora *n* : dealer, seller

expensas *nfpl* 1 : expenses 2 a ~ de : at the expense of

experiencia *nf* : experience

experimentar *vi* : experiment — *vt* 1 : experiment with, test out 2 SENTIR : experience, feel — **experimentado, -da** *adj* : experienced — **experimental** *adj* : experimental — **experimento** *nm* : experiment

experto, -ta *adj* & *n* : expert

expiar {85} *vt* : atone for

expirar *vi* 1 : expire 2 MORIR : die

explayar *vt* : extend — **explayarse** *vr* 1 : spread out 2 HABLAR : speak at length

explicar {72} *vt* : explain — **explicarse** *vr* : understand — **explicación** *nf, pl* -**ciones** : explanation — **explicativo, -va** *adj* : explanatory

explícito, -ta *adj* : explicit

explorar *vt* : explore — **exploración** *nf, pl* -**ciones** : exploration — **explorador, -dora** *n* : explorer, scout — **exploratorio, -ria** *adj* : exploratory

explosión *nf, pl* -**siones** 1 : explosion 2 : outburst (of anger, laughter, etc.) — **explosivo, -va** *adj* : explosive — **explosivo** *nm* : explosive

explotar *vt* 1 : exploit 2 : operate, run (a factory, etc.), work (a mine) — *vi* : explode — **explotación** *nf, pl* -**ciones** 1 : exploitation 2 : running (of a business), working (of a mine)

exponer {60} *vt* 1 : expose 2 : explain, set out (ideas, theories, etc.) 3 EXHIBIR : exhibit, display — *vi* : exhibit — **exponerse a** : expose oneself to

exportar *vt* : export — **exportaciones** *nfpl* : exports — **exportador, -dora** *n* : exporter

exposición *nf, pl* -**ciones** 1 : exposure 2 : exhibition (of objects, art, etc.) 3 : exposition, setting out (of ideas, etc.) — **expositor, -tora** *n* 1 : exhibitor 2 : exponent (of a theory, etc.)

exprés *nms & pl* 1 : express (train) 2 or café ~ : espresso

expresamente *adv* : expressly, on purpose

expresar *vt* : express — **expresarse** *vr* : express oneself — **expresión** *nf, pl* -**siones** : expression — **expresivo, -va** *adj* 1 : expressive 2 CARIÑOSO : affectionate

expreso, -sa *adj* : express — **expreso** *nm* : express train, express

exprimir *vt* 1 : squeeze 2 EXPLOTAR : exploit — **exprimidor** *nm* : squeezer, juicer

expuesto, -ta *adj* 1 : exposed 2 PELIGROSO : risky, dangerous

expulsar *vt* : expel, eject — **expulsión** *nf, pl* -**siones** : expulsion

exquisito, -ta *adj* 1 : exquisite 2 RICO : delicious — **exquisitez** *nf* 1 : exquisiteness 2 : delicacy, special dish

éxtasis *nms & pl* : ecstasy — **extático, -ta** *adj* : ecstatic

extender {56} *vt* 1 : spread out 2 : draw up (a document), write out (a check)

— **extenderse** *vr* **1** : extend, spread **2**
DURAR : last — **extendido, -da** *adj* **1**
: widespread **2** : outstretched (of arms,
wings, etc.)
extensamente *adv* : extensively
extensión *nf, pl* **-siones 1** : extension **2**
AMPLITUD : expanse **3** ALCANCE : range,
extent — **extenso, -sa** *adj* : extensive
extenuar {3} *vt* : exhaust, tire out
exterior *adj* **1** : exterior, external **2**
EXTRANJERO : foreign — ～ *nm* **1** : outside **2 en el** ～ : abroad — **exteri-
orizar** {21} *vt* : show, reveal — **exteriormente** *adv* : outwardly, externally
exterminar *vt* : exterminate — **exterminación** *nf, pl* **-ciones** : extermination
— **exterminio** *nm* : extermination
externo, -na *adj* : external
extinguir {26} *vt* **1** : extinguish (a fire)
2 : put an end to, wipe out — **extinguirse** *vr* **1** : go out (of fire, light, etc.)
2 : become extinct — **extinción** *nf, pl*
-ciones : extinction — **extinguidor**
nm Lat : fire extinguisher — **extinto,
-ta** *adj* : extinct — **extintor** *nm* : fire
extinguisher
extirpar *vt* : remove, eradicate
extorsión *nf, pl* **-siones 1** : extortion **2**
MOLESTIA : trouble
extra *adv* : extra — ～ *adj* **1** ADICIONAL
: additional **2** : top-quality — ～ *nmf*
: extra (in movies) — ～ *nm* : extra
(expense)
extraditar *vt* : extradite
extraer {81} *vt* : extract — **extracción**
nf, pl **-ciones** : extraction — **extracto**
nm **1** : extract **2** RESUMEN : abstract,
summary

extranjero, -ra *adj* : foreign — ～ *n*
: foreigner — **extranjero** *nm* : foreign
countries *pl*
extrañar *vt* : miss (someone) — **ex-
trañarse** *vr* : be surprised — **ex-
trañeza** *nf* : surprise — **extraño, -ña**
adj **1** : foreign **2** RARO : strange, odd
— ～ *n* : stranger
extraoficial *adj* : unofficial
extraordinario, -ria *adj* : extraordinary
extrasensorial *adj* : extrasensory
extraterrestre *adj & nmf* : extraterrestrial
extravagante *adj* : extravagant, outrageous — **extravagancia** *nf* : extravagance, outlandishness
extraviar {85} *vt* : lose, misplace — **extraviarse** *vr* : get lost — **extravío** *nm*
: loss
extremar *vt* : carry to extremes — **ex-
tremarse** *vr* : do one's utmost — **extremadamente** *adv* : extremely — **ex-
tremado, -da** *adj* : extreme —
extremidad *nf* **1** : tip, end **2** ～**es** *nfpl*
: extremities — **extremista** *adj & nmf*
: extremist — **extremo, -ma** *adj* **1**
: extreme **2 en caso** ～ : as a last resort — **extremo** *nm* **1** : end **2 en** ～
: in the extreme, extremely **3 en último** ～ : as a last resort
extrovertido -da *adj* : extroverted —
～ *n* : extrovert
exuberante *adj* : exuberant — **exuberancia** *nf* : exuberance
exudar *vt* : exude
eyacular *vi* : ejaculate — **eyaculación**
nf, pl **-ciones** : ejaculation

F

f *nf* : f, sixth letter of the Spanish alphabet
fabricar {72} *vt* **1** : manufacture **2** CON-
STRUIR : build, construct **3** INVENTAR
: fabricate — **fábrica** *nf* : factory —
fabricación *nf, pl* **-ciones** : manufacture — **fabricante** *nmf* : manufacturer
fábula *nf* **1** : fable **2** MENTIRA : story, lie
fabuloso, -sa *adj* : fabulous
facción *nf, pl* **-ciones 1** : faction **2**
～**es** *nfpl* RASGOS : features
faceta *nf* : facet
facha *nf* : appearance, look
fachada *nf* : façade
facial *adj* : facial
fácil *adj* **1** : easy **2** PROBABLE : likely —
facilemente *adv* : easily, readily —

facilidad *nf* **1** : facility, ease **2** ～**es**
nfpl : facilities, services — **facilitar** *vt*
1 : facilitate **2** PROPORCIONAR : provide, supply
facsímil *or* **facsímile** *nm* **1** COPIA : facsimile, copy **2** : fax
factible *adj* : feasible
factor *nm* : factor
factoría *nf* : factory
factura *nf* **1** : bill, invoice **2** HECHURA
: making, manufacture — **facturar** *vt*
1 : bill for **2** : check in (baggage, etc.)
facultad *nf* **1** : faculty, ability **2** AUTORI-
DAD : authority **3** : school (of a university) — **facultativo, -va** *adj* : optional
faena *nf* **1** : task, job **2** ～**s domésticas**
: housework

fagot *nm* : bassoon
faisán *nm, pl* **-sanes** : pheasant
faja *nf* **1** : sash **2** : girdle, corset **3** : strip (of land)
fajo *nm* : bundle, sheaf
falda *nf* **1** : skirt **2** : side, slope (of a mountain)
falible *adj* : fallible
fálico, -ca *adj* : phallic
fallar *vi* : fail, go wrong — *vt* **1** : pronounce judgment on **2** ERRAR : miss — **falla** *nf* **1** : flaw, defect **2** : (geological) fault
fallecer {53} *vi* : pass away, die — **fallecimiento** *nm* : demise, death
fallido, -da *adj* : failed, unsuccessful
fallo *nm* **1** : error **2** SENTENCIA : sentence, verdict
falo *nm* : phallus, penis
falsear *vt* : falsify, distort — **falsedad** *nf* **1** : falseness **2** MENTIRA : falsehood, lie — **falsificación** *nf, pl* **-ciones** : forgery, fake — **falsificador, -dora** *n* : forger — **falsificar** {72} *vt* **1** : counterfeit, forge **2** ALTERAR : falsify — **falso, -sa** *adj* **1** : false, untrue **2** FALSIFICADO : counterfeit, forged
falta *nf* **1** CARENCIA : lack **2** DEFECTO : defect, fault, error **3** AUSENCIA : absence **4** : offense, misdemeanor (in law) **5** : foul (in sports) **6 hacer ~** : be lacking, be needed **7 sin ~** : without fail — **faltar** *vi* **1** : be lacking, be needed **2** : be missing **3** QUEDAR : remain, be left **4 ¡no faltaba más!** : don't mention it! — **falto, -ta** *adj* **~ de** : lacking (in)
fama *nf* **1** : fame **2** REPUTACIÓN : reputation
famélico, -ca *adj* : starving
familia *nf* : family — **familiar** *adj* **1** : familial, family **2** CONOCIDO : familiar **3** : informal (of language, etc.) — *~ nmf* : relation, relative — **familiaridad** *nf* : familiarity — **familiarizarse** {21} *vr* **~ con** : familiarize oneself with
famoso, -sa *adj* : famous
fanático, -ca *adj* : fanatic, fanatical — *~ n* : fanatic — **fanatismo** *nm* : fanaticism
fanfarria *nf* : fanfare
fanfarrón, -rrona *adj, mpl* **-rrones** *fam* : boastful — *~ n fam* : braggart — **fanfarronear** *vi* : boast, brag
fango *nm* : mud, mire — **fangoso, -sa** *adj* : muddy
fantasear *vi* : fantasize, daydream — **fantasía** *nf* **1** : fantasy **2** IMAGINACIÓN : imagination
fantasma *nm* : ghost, phantom — **fantasmal** *adj* : ghostly

fantástico, -ca *adj* : fantastic
fardo *nm* : bundle
farfullar *v* : jabber, gabble
farmacéutico, -ca *adj* : pharmaceutical — *~ n* : pharmacist — **farmacia** *nf* : drugstore, pharmacy
faro *nm* **1** : lighthouse **2** : headlight (of an automobile) — **farol** *nm* **1** LINTERNA : lantern **2** FAROLA : streetlight — **farola** *nf* **1** : lamppost **2** FAROL : streetlight
farsa *nf* : farce — **farsante** *nmf* : charlatan, fraud
fascículo *nm* : installment, part (of a publication)
fascinar *vt* : fascinate — **fascinación** *nf, pl* **-ciones** : fascination — **fascinante** *adj* : fascinating
fascismo *nm* : fascism — **fascista** *adj* & *nmf* : fascist
fase *nf* : phase
fastidiar *vt* : annoy, bother — *vi* : be annoying or bothersome — **fastidio** *nm* : annoyance — **fastidioso, -sa** *adj* : annoying, bothersome
fatal *adj* **1** : fateful **2** MORTAL : fatal **3** *fam* : awful, terrible — **fatalidad** *nf* **1** : fate, destiny **2** DESGRACIA : misfortune
fatídico, -ca *adj* : fateful, momentous
fatiga *nf* : fatigue — **fatigado, -da** *adj* : weary, tired — **fatigar** {52} *vt* : tire — **fatigarse** *vr* : get tired — **fatigoso, -sa** *adj* : fatiguing, tiring
fatuo, -tua *adj* **1** : fatuous **2** PRESUMIDO : conceited
fauna *nf* : fauna
favor *nm* **1** : favor **2 a ~ de** : in favor of **3 por ~** : please — **favorable** *adj* **1** : favorable **2 ser ~ a** : be in favor of — **favorecedor, -dora** *adj* : flattering — **favorecer** {53} *vt* **1** AYUDAR : favor **2** : look well on, suit — **favoritismo** *nm* : favoritism — **favorito, -ta** *adj* & *n* : favorite
fax *nm* : fax — **faxear** *vt* : fax
faz *nf, pl* **faces** : face, countenance
fe *nf* **1** : faith **2 dar ~ de** : bear witness to **3 de buena ~** : in good faith
fealdad *nf* : ugliness
febrero *nm* : February
febril *adj* : feverish
fecha *nf* **1** : date **2 ~ de caducidad** *or* **~ de vencimiento** : expiration date **3 ~ límite** : deadline — **fechar** *vt* : date, put on date
fechoría *nf* : misdeed
fécula *nf* : starch (in food)
fecundar *vt* **1** : fertilize (an egg) **2** : make fertile — **fecundo, -da** *adj* : fertile

federación *nf, pl* **-ciones** : federation — **federal** *adj* : federal

felicidad *nf* 1 : happiness 2 ¡~es! : best wishes!, congratulations!, happy birthday! — **felicitación** *nf, pl* **-ciones** : congratulation — **felicitar** *vt* : congratulate — **felicitarse** *vr* ~ **de** : be glad about

feligrés, -gresa *n, mpl* **-greses** : parishioner

felino, -na *adj & n* : feline

feliz *adj, pl* **-lices** 1 : happy 2 AFORTUNADO : fortunate 3 **Feliz Navidad** : Merry Christmas

felpa *nf* 1 : plush 2 : terry cloth (for towels, etc.)

felpudo *nm* : doormat

femenino, -na *adj* 1 : feminine 2 : female (in biology) — **femenino** *nm* : feminine (in grammar) — **feminelidad** *nf* : femininity — **feminismo** *nm* : feminism — **feminista** *adj & nmf* : feminist

fenómeno *nm* : phenomenon — **fenomenal** *adj* 1 : phenomenal 2 *fam* : fantastic, terrific

feo, fea *adj* 1 : ugly 2 DESAGRADABLE : unpleasant, nasty

féretro *nm* : coffin

feria *nf* 1 : fair, market 2 FIESTA : festival, holiday 3 *Lat fam* : small change — **feriado, -da** *adj* **día feriado** : public holiday

fermentar *v* : ferment — **fermentación** *nf, pl* **-ciones** : fermentation — **fermento** *nm* : ferment

feroz *adj, pl* **-roces** : ferocious, fierce — **ferocidad** *nf* : ferocity, fierceness

férreo, -rrea *adj* 1 : iron 2 **vía férrea** : railroad track

ferretería *nf* : hardware store

ferrocarril *nm* : railroad, railway — **ferroviario, -ria** *adj* : rail, railroad

ferry *nm, pl* **ferrys** : ferry

fértil *adj* : fertile, fruitful — **fertilidad** *nf* : fertility — **fertilizante** *nm* : fertilizer — **fertilizar** *vt* : fertilize

fervor *nm* : fervor, zeal — **ferviente** *adj* : fervent

festejar *vt* 1 : celebrate 2 AGASAJAR : entertain, wine and dine — **festejo** *nm* : celebration, festivity

festín *nm, pl* **-tines** : banquet, feast

festival *nm* : festival — **festividad** *nf* : festivity — **festivo, -va** *adj* 1 : festive 2 **día festivo** : holiday

fetiche *nm* : fetish

fétido, -da *adj* : foul-smelling, fetid

feto *nm* : fetus — **fetal** *adj* : fetal

feudal *adj* : feudal

fiable *adj* : reliable — **fiabilidad** *nf* : reliability

fiado, -da *adj* : on credit — **fiador, -dora** *n* : bondsman, guarantor

fiambres *nfpl* : cold cuts

fianza *nf* 1 : bail, bond 2 **dar** ~ : pay a deposit

fiar {85} *vt* 1 : guarantee 2 : sell on credit — *vi* **ser de** ~ : be trustworthy — **fiarse** *vr* ~ **de** : place trust in

fiasco *nm* : fiasco

fibra *nf* 1 : fiber 2 ~ **de vidrio** : fiberglass

ficción *nf, pl* **-ciones** : fiction

ficha *nf* 1 : token 2 TARJETA : index card 3 : counter, chip (in games) — **fichar** *vt* : file, index — **fichero** *nm* 1 : card file 2 : filing cabinet

ficticio, -cia *adj* : fictitious

fidedigno, -na *adj* : reliable, trustworthy

fidelidad *nf* : fidelity, faithfulness

fideo *nm* : noodle

fiebre *nf* 1 : fever 2 ~ **del heno** : hay fever 3 ~ **palúdica** : malaria

fiel *adj* 1 : faithful, loyal 2 PRECISO : accurate, reliable — ~ *nm* 1 : pointer (of a scale) 2 **los** ~**es** : the faithful — **fielmente** *adv* : faithfully

fieltro *nm* : felt

fiero, -ra *adj* : fierce, ferocious — **fiera** *nf* : wild animal, beast

fierro *nm Lat* : iron (bar)

fiesta *nf* 1 : party 2 DIA FESTIVO : holiday, feast day

figura *nf* 1 : figure 2 FORMA : shape, form — **figurar** *vi* 1 : figure (in), be included (among) 2 DESTACAR : stand out — *vt* : represent — **figurarse** *vr* : imagine

fijar *vt* 1 : fasten, affix 2 CONCRETAR : set, fix — **fijarse** *vr* 1 : settle 2 ~ **en** : notice, pay attention to — **fijo, -ja** *adj* 1 : fixed, firm 2 PERMANENTE : permanent

fila *nf* 1 : line, file, row 2 **ponerse en** ~ : line up

filantropía *nf* : philanthropy — **filantrópico, -ca** *adj* : philanthropic — **filántropo, -pa** *n* : philanthropist

filatelia *nf* : philately, stamp collecting

filete *nm* : fillet

filial *adj* : filial — ~ *nf* : affiliate, subsidiary

filigrana *nf* 1 : filigree 2 : watermark (on paper)

filipino, -na *adj* : Filipino

filmar *vt* : film, shoot — **filme** *or* **film** *nm* : film, movie

filo *nm* 1 : edge 2 **dar** ~ **a** : sharpen

filón *nm, pl* **-lones** 1 : vein (of minerals) 2 *fam* : gold mine

filoso, -sa *adj Lat* : sharp

filosofía *nf* : philosophy — **filosófico, -ca** *adj* : philosophical — **filósofo, -fa** *n* : philosopher

filtrar *v* : filter — **filtrarse** *vr* : leak out, seep through — **filtro** *nm* : filter

fin *nm* 1 : end 2 OBJETIVO : purpose, aim 3 en ～ : well, in short 4 ～ **de semana** : weekend 5 por ～ : finally, at last

final *adj* : final — ～ *nm* : end, conclusion — ～ *nf* : final (in sports) — **finalidad** *nf* : purpose, aim — **finalista** *nmf* : finalist — **finalizar** {21} *v* : finish, end — **finalmente** *adv* : finally

financiar *vt* : finance, fund — **financiero, -ra** *adj* : financial — ～ *n* : financier — **finanzas** *nfpl* : finance

finca *nf* 1 : farm, ranch 2 *Lat* : country house

fingir {35} *v* : feign, pretend — **fingido, -da** *adj* : false, feigned

finito, -ta *adj* : finite

finlandés, -desa *adj* : Finnish

fino, -na *adj* 1 : fine 2 DELGADO : slender 3 REFINADO : refined 4 AGUDO : sharp, keen — **finura** *nf* 1 : fineness 2 REFINAMIENTO : refinement

firma *nf* 1 : signature 2 : (act of) signing 3 EMPRESA : firm, company

firmamento *nm* : firmament, sky

firmar *v* : sign

firme *adj* 1 : firm, resolute 2 ESTABLE : steady, stable — **firmeza** *nf* 1 : strength, resolve 2 ESTABILIDAD : firmness, stability

fiscal *adj* : fiscal — ～ *nmf* : district attorney — **fisco** *nm* : (national) treasury

fisgar {52} *vt* : pry into — *vi* : pry — **fisgón, -gona** *n, mpl* **-gones** : snoop, busybody

física *nf* : physics — **físico, -ca** *adj* : physical — ～ *n* : physicist — **físico** *nm* : physique

fisiología *nf* : physiology — **fisiológico, -ca** *adj* : physiological — **fisiólogo, -ga** *n* : physiologist

fisioterapia *nf* : physical therapy — **fisioterapeuta** *nmf* : physical therapist

fisonomía *nf* : features *pl*, appearance

fisura *nf* : fissure

fláccido, -da *or* **flácido, -da** *adj* : flaccid, flabby

flaco, -ca *adj* 1 : thin, skinny 2 DÉBIL : weak

flagrante *adj* : flagrant

flamante *adj* 1 : bright, brilliant 2 NUEVO : brand-new

flamenco, -ca *adj* 1 : flamenco (of music or dance) 2 : Flemish — **fla-**

menco *nm* 1 : flamingo 2 : flamenco (music or dance)

flaquear *vi* : weaken, flag — **flaqueza** *nf* 1 : thinness 2 DEBILIDAD : weakness

flash *nm* : flash

flatulencia *nf* : flatulence

flauta *nf* 1 : flute 2 ～ **dulce** : recorder — **flautín** *nm, pl* **-tines** : piccolo — **flautista** *nmf* : flutist

flecha *nf* : arrow

fleco *nm* 1 : fringe 2 *Lat* : bangs *pl*

flema *nf* : phlegm — **flemático, -ca** *adj* : phlegmatic

flequillo *nm* : bangs *pl*

fletar *vt* 1 : charter, rent 2 *Lat* : transport — **flete** *nm* 1 : charter 2 : shipping (charges) 3 *Lat* : transport, freight

flexible *adj* : flexible — **flexibilidad** *nf* : flexibility

flirtear *vi* : flirt

flojo, -ja *adj* 1 SUELTO : loose, slack 2 DÉBIL : weak 3 PEREZOSO : lazy — **flojera** *nf fam* : lethargy

flor *nf* : flower — **flora** *nf* : flora — **floral** *adj* : floral — **floreado, -da** *adj* : flowered — **florear** *vi Lat* : flower, bloom — **florecer** {53} *vi* 1 : bloom, blossom 2 PROSPERAR : flourish — **floreciente** *adj* : flourishing — **florero** *nm* : vase — **florido, -da** *adj* : flowery — **florista** *nmf* : florist — **floritura** *nf* : frill, flourish

flota *nf* : fleet

flotar *vi* : float — **flotador** *nm* 1 : float 2 : life preserver (for a swimmer) — **flotante** *adj* : floating, buoyant — **flote: a** ～ *adv phr* : afloat

flotilla *nf* : flotilla, fleet

fluctuar {3} *vi* : fluctuate — **fluctuación** *nf, pl* **-ciones** : fluctuation

fluir {41} *vi* : flow — **fluidez** *nf* 1 : fluidity 2 : fluency (of language, etc.) — **fluido, -da** *adj* 1 : fluid 2 : fluent (of language) — **fluido** *nm* : fluid — **flujo** *nm* : flow

fluorescente *adj* : fluorescent

fluoruro *nm* : fluoride

fluvial *adj* : river

fobia *nf* : phobia

foca *nf* : seal (animal)

foco *nm* 1 : focus 2 : spotlight, floodlight (in theater, etc.) 3 *Lat* : lightbulb

fofo, -fa *adj* : flabby

fogata *nf* : bonfire

fogón *nm, pl* **-gones** : burner

fogoso, -sa *adj* : ardent

folklore *nm* : folklore — **folklórico, -ca** *adj* : folk, traditional

follaje *nm* : foliage

folleto *nm* : pamphlet, leaflet

fomentar *vt* : promote, encourage — **fomento** *nm* : promotion, encouragement

fonda *nf* : boarding house

fondear *vt* : sound out, examine — *vi* : anchor

fondillos *nmpl* : seat (of pants, etc.)

fondo *nm* **1** : bottom **2** : rear, back, end **3** PROFUNDIDAD : depth **4** : background (of a painting, etc.) **5** *Lat* : slip, petticoat **6** ~s *nmpl* : funds, resources **7 a** ~ : thoroughly, in depth **8 en el** ~ : deep down

fonético, -ca *adj* : phonetic — **fonética** *nf* : phonetics

fontanería *nf Spain* : plumbing — **fontanero, -ra** *n Spain* : plumber

footing ['fuˌtɪŋ] *nm* **1** : jogging **2 hacer** ~ : jog

forajido, -da *n* : bandit, outlaw

foráneo, -nea *adj* : foreign, strange

forastero, -ra *n* : stranger, outsider

forcejear *vi* : struggle — **forcejeo** *nm* : struggle

forense *adj* : forensic

forja *nf* : forge — **forjar** *vt* **1** : forge **2** CREAR, FORMAR : build up, create

forma *nf* **1** : form, shape **2** MANERA : manner, way **3 en** ~ : fit, healthy **4** ~s *nfpl* : appearances, conventions — **formación** *nf, pl* **-ciones 1** : formation **2** EDUCACIÓN : training

formal *adj* **1** : formal **2** SERIO : serious **3** FIABLE : dependable, reliable — **formalidad** *nf* **1** : formality **2** SERIEDAD : seriousness **3** FIABILIDAD : reliability

formar *vt* **1** : form, shape **2** CONSTITUIR : constitute **3** EDUCAR : train, educate — **formarse** *vr* **1** DESARROLLARSE : develop, take shape **2** EDUCARSE : be educated

formato *nm* : format

formidable *adj* **1** : tremendous **2** *fam* : fantastic, terrific

fórmula *nf* : formula

formular *vt* **1** : formulate, draw up **2** : make, lodge (a complaint, etc.)

formulario *nm* : form

fornido, -da *adj* : well-built, burly

foro *nm* : forum

forraje *nm* : forage, fodder — **forrajear** *vi* : forage

forrar *vt* **1** : line (a garment) **2** : cover (a book) — **forro** *nm* **1** : lining **2** CUBIERTA : book cover

fortalecer {53} *vt* : strengthen — **fortaleza** *nf* **1** : fortress **2** FUERZA : strength **3** : (moral) fortitude

fortificar {72} *vt* : fortify — **fortificación** *nf, pl* **-ciones** : fortification

fortuito, -ta *adj* : fortuitous, chance

fortuna *nf* **1** SUERTE : fortune, luck **2** RIQUEZA : wealth, fortune **3 por** ~ : fortunately

forzar {36} *vt* **1** : force **2** : strain (one's eyes) — **forzosamente** *adv* : necessarily — **forzoso, -sa** *adj* : necessary, inevitable

fosa *nf* **1** : pit, ditch **2** TUMBA : grave **3** ~s nasales : nostrils

fósforo *nm* **1** : phosphorus **2** CERILLA : match — **fosforescente** *adj* : phosphorescent

fósil *nm* : fossil

foso *nm* **1** : ditch **2** : pit (of a theater) **3** : moat (of a castle)

foto *nf* : photo

fotocopia *nf* : photocopy — **fotocopiadora** *nf* : photocopier — **fotocopiar** *vt* : photocopy

fotogénico, -ca *adj* : photogenic

fotografía *nf* **1** : photography **2** : photograph, picture — **fotografiar** {85} *vt* : photograph — **fotográfico, -ca** *adj* : photographic — **fotógrafo, -fa** *n* : photographer

fotosíntesis *nf* : photosynthesis

fracasar *vi* : fail — **fracaso** *nm* : failure

fracción *nf, pl* **-ciones 1** : fraction **2** : faction (in politics) — **fraccionamiento** *nm Lat* : housing development

fractura *nf* : fracture — **fracturarse** *vr* : fracture, break (a bone)

fragancia *nf* : fragrance, scent — **fragante** *adj* : fragrant

fragata *nf* : frigate

frágil *adj* **1** : fragile **2** DÉBIL : frail, delicate — **fragilidad** *nf* **1** : fragility **2** DEBILIDAD : frailty

fragmento *nm* : fragment

fragor *nm* : clamor, din

fragoso, -sa *adj* : rough, rugged

fragua *nf* : forge — **fraguar** {10} *vt* **1** : forge **2** IDEAR : concoct — *vi* : harden, solidify

fraile *nm* : friar, monk

frambuesa *nf* : raspberry

francés, -cesa *adj, mpl* **-ceses** : French — **francés** *nm* : French (language)

franco, -ca *adj* **1** : frank, candid **2** : free (in commerce) — **franco** *nm* : franc

francotirador, -dora *n* : sniper

franela *nf* : flannel

franja *nf* **1** : stripe, band **2** FLECO : fringe

franquear *vt* **1** : clear (a path, etc.) **2** : cross over (a doorstep, etc.) **3** : pay postage on (mail) — **franqueo** *nm* : postage

franqueza *nf* : frankness
frasco *nm* : small bottle, vial, flask
frase *nf* **1** : phrase **2** ORACIÓN : sentence
fraternal *adj* : brotherly, fraternal —
  fraternidad *nf* : brotherhood, fraternity — **fraternizar** {21} *vi* : fraternize
  — **fraterno, -na** *adj* : brotherly, fraternal
fraude *nm* : fraud — **fraudulento, -ta** *adj* : fraudulent
fray *nm* (*used in titles*) : brother, friar
frazada *nf Lat* : blanket
frecuencia *nf* **1** : frequency **2 con ~** : often, frequently — **frecuentar** *vt* : frequent, haunt — **frecuente** *adj* : frequent
fregadero *nm* : kitchen sink
fregar {49} *vt* **1** : scrub, wash **2** *Lat fam* : annoy — *vi Lat fam* : be a pest
freír {37} *vt* : fry
fregona *nf Spain* : mop
frenar *vt* **1** : brake **2** RESTRINGIR : curb, check
frenesí *nm* : frenzy — **frenético, -ca** *adj* : frantic, frenzied
freno *nm* **1** : brake **2** : bit (of a bridle) **3** CONTROL : check, restraint
frente *nm* **1** : front **2** : facade (of a building) **3 al ~ de** : at the head of **4 ~ a** : opposite **5 de ~** : (facing) forward **6 hacer ~ a** : face up to, brave — **~** *nf* : forehead
fresa *nf* : strawberry
fresco, -ca *adj* **1** : fresh **2** FRÍO : cool **3** *fam* : insolent, nervy — **fresco** *nm* **1** : fresh air **2** FRESCOR : coolness **3** : fresco (art or painting) — **frescor** *nm* : coolness, cool air — **frescura** *nf* **1** : freshness **2** FRÍO : coolness **3** *fam* : nerve, insolence
fresno *nm* : ash (tree)
frialdad *nf* **1** : coldness **2** INDIFERENCIA : indifference
fricción *nf, pl* **-ciones 1** : friction **2** MASAJE : rubbing, massage — **friccionar** *vt* : rub
frigidez *nf* : frigidity
frigorífico *nm Spain* : refrigerator
frijol *nm Lat* : bean
frío, fría *adj* **1** : cold **2** INDIFERENTE : cool, indifferent — **frío** *nm* **1** : cold **2** INDIFERENCIA : coldness, indifference **3 hacer ~** : be cold (outside) **4 tener ~** : be cold, feel cold
frito, -ta *adj* **1** : fried **2** *fam* : fed up
frívolo, -la *adj* : frivolous — **frivolidad** *nf* : frivolity
fronda *nf* **1** : frond **2** *or* **~s** *nfpl* : foliage — **frondoso, -sa** *adj* : leafy
frontera *nf* : border, frontier — **fronter-**

izo, -za *adj* : border, on the border —
frontero, -ra *adj* : facing, opposite
frotar *vt* : rub — **frotarse** *vr* **~ las manos** : rub one's hands
fructífero, -ra *adj* : fruitful
frugal *adj* : frugal, thrifty — **frugalidad** *adj* : frugality
fruncir {83} *vt* **1** : gather (in pleats) **2 ~ el ceño** : frown **3 ~ la boca** : purse one's lips
frustrar *vt* : frustrate — **frustrarse** *vr* : fail — **frustración** *nf, pl* **-ciones** : frustration — **frustrado, -da** *adj* : frustrated **2** FRACASADO : failed, unsuccessful — **frustrante** *adj* : frustrating
fruta *nf* : fruit — **frutilla** *nf Lat* : strawberry — **fruto** *nm* **1** : fruit **2** RESULTADO : result, consequence
fucsia *adj & nm* : fuchsia
fuego *nm* **1** : fire **2** : flame, burner (on a stove) **3 ~s artificiales** *nmpl* : fireworks **4 ¿tienes fuego?** : have you got a light?
fuelle *nm* : bellows
fuente *nf* **1** : fountain **2** MANANTIAL : spring **3** ORIGEN : source **4** PLATO : platter, serving dish
fuera *adv* **1** : outside, out **2** : abroad, away **3 ~ de** : outside of, beyond **4 ~ de** : aside from, in addition to
fuerte *adj* **1** : strong **2** : bright (of colors), loud (of sounds) **3** EXTREMO : intense **4** DURO : hard — **~** *adv* **1** : strongly, hard **2** : loudly **3** MUCHO : abundantly, a lot — **~** *nm* **1** : fort **2** ESPECIALIDAD : strong point
fuerza *nf* **1** : strength **2** VIOLENCIA : force **3** PODER : power, might **4 ~s armadas** *nfpl* : armed forces **5 a ~ de** : by dint of **6 a la ~** : necessarily
fuga *nf* **1** : flight, escape **2** : fugue (in music) **3** ESCAPE : leak — **fugarse** {52} *vr* : flee, run away — **fugaz** *adj, pl* **-gaces** : fleeting — **fugitivo, -va** *adj & n* : fugitive
fulano, -na *n* : so-and-so, what's-his-name, what's-her-name
fulgor *nm* : brilliance, splendor
fulminar *vt* **1** : strike with lightning **2** : strike down (with an illness, etc.) — **fulminante** *adj* : devastating
fumar *v* : smoke — **fumarse** *vr* **1** : smoke **2** *fam* : squander — **fumador, -dora** *n* : smoker
funámbulo, -la *n* : tightrope walker
función *nf, pl* **-ciones 1** : function **2** TRABAJOS : duties *pl* **3** : performance, show (in theater) — **funcional** *adj* : functional — **funcionamiento** *nm* **1**

: functioning **2 en ~** : in operation —
funcionar *vi* **1** : function, run, work
2 no funciona : out of order —
funcionario, -ria *n* : civil servant, official
funda *nf* **1** : cover, sheath **2** *or* **~ de almohada** : pillowcase
fundar *vt* **1** ESTABLECER : found, establish **2** BASAR : base — **fundarse** *vr* **~ en** : be based on — **fundación** *nf, pl* **-ciones** : foundation — **fundador, -dora** *n* : founder — **fundamental** *adj* : fundamental, basic — **fundamentalmente** *adv* : basically — **fundamentar** *vt* **1** : lay the foundations for **2** BASAR : base — **fundamento** *nm* **1** : foundation **2 ~s** *nmpl* : fundamentals
fundir *vt* **1** : melt down, smelt **2** FUSIONAR : fuse, merge — **fundirse** *vr* **1** : blend, merge **2** DERRETIRSE : melt **3** : burn out (of a lightbulb) — **fundición** *nf, pl* **-ciones 1** : smelting **2** : foundry
fúnebre *adj* **1** : funeral **2** LÚGUBRE : gloomy
funeral *adj* : funeral, funerary — **~** *nm* **1** : funeral **2 ~es** *nmpl* EXEQUIAS : funeral (rites) — **funeraria** *nf* : funeral home
funesto, ta *adj* : terrible, disastrous
fungir {35} *vi Lat* : act, function
furgón *nm, pl* **-gones 1** : van, truck **2** : freight car (of a train) **3 ~ de cola** : caboose — **furgoneta** *nf* : van
furia *nf* **1** CÓLERA : fury, rage **2** VIOLENCIA : violence — **furibundo, -da** *adj* : furious — **furioso, -sa** *adj* **1** : furious, irate **2** INTENSO : intense, violent — **furor** *nm* : fury
furtivo, -va *adj* : furtive
furúnculo *nm* : boil
fuselaje *nm* : fuselage
fusible *nm* : fuse
fusil *nm* : rifle — **fusilar** *vt* : shoot (by firing squad)
fusión *nf, pl* **-siones 1** : fusion **2** UNIÓN : union, merger — **fusionar** *vt* **1** : fuse **2** UNIR : merge — **fusionarse** *vr* : merge
futbol *or* **fútbol** *nm* **1** : soccer **2 ~ americano** : football — **futbolista** *nmf* : soccer player, football player
fútil *adj* : trifling, trivial
futuro, -ra *adj* : future — **futuro** *nm* : future

G

g *nf* : g, seventh letter of the Spanish alphabet
gabán *nm, pl* **-banes** : topcoat, overcoat
gabardina *nf* **1** : trench coat, raincoat **2** : gabardine (fabric)
gabinete *nm* **1** : cabinet (in government) **2** : (professional) office
gacela *nf* : gazelle
gaceta *nf* : gazette
gachas *nfpl* : porridge
gacho, -cha *adj* : drooping
gaélico, -ca *adj* : Gaelic
gafas *nfpl* **1** : eyeglasses **2 ~ de sol** : sunglasses
gaita *nf* : bagpipes *pl*
gajo *nm* : segment (of fruit)
gala *nf* **1** : gala **2 de ~** : formal **3 hacer ~ de** : display, show off **4 ~s** *nfpl* : finery
galáctico, -ca *adj* : galactic
galán *nm, pl* **-lanes 1** : leading man (in theater) **2** *fam* : boyfriend
galante *adj* : gallant — **galantear** *vt* : court, woo — **galantería** *nf* **1** : gallantry **2** CUMPLIDO : compliment
galápago *nm* : (aquatic) turtle
galardón *nm, pl* **-dones** : reward
galaxia *nf* : galaxy
galera *nf* : galley
galería *nf* **1** : corridor **2** : gallery, balcony (in a theater)
galés, -lesa *adj, mpl* **-leses** : Welsh
galgo *nm* : greyhound
galimatías *nms & pl* : gibberish
gallardía *nf* **1** : bravery **2** ELEGANCIA : elegance — **gallardo, -da** *adj* **1** : brave **2** APUESTO : elegant, good-looking
gallego, -ga *adj* : Galician
galleta *nf* **1** : (sweet) cookie **2** : (salted) cracker
gallina *nf* **1** : hen **2 ~ de Guinea** : guinea fowl — **gallinero** *nm* : henhouse, (chicken) coop — **gallo** *nm* : rooster, cock
galón *nm, pl* **-lones 1** : gallon **2** : stripe (military insignia)
galopar *vi* : gallop — **galope** *nm* : gallop
galvanizar {21} *vt* : galvanize
gama *nf* **1** : range, spectrum **2** : scale (in music)
gamba *nf* : large shrimp, prawn

gamuza *nf* **1** : chamois (animal) **2** : chamois (leather), suede

gana *nf* **1** : desire, wish **2** APETITO : appetite **3 de buena ~** : willingly, heartily **de mala ~** : unwillingly **5 no me da la ~** : I don't feel like it **6 tener ~s de** : feel like, be in the mood for

ganado *nm* **1** : cattle *pl*, livestock **2 ~ ovino** : sheep *pl* **3 ~ porcino** : swine *pl* — **ganadería** *nf* **1** : cattle raising **2** GANADO : livestock

ganador, -dora *adj* : winning — *~ n* : winner

ganancia *nf* : profit

ganar *vt* **1** : earn **2** : win (in games, etc.) **3** CONSEGUIR : gain **4** ADQUIRIR : get, obtain **5 ~ a algn** : win over s.o., beat s.o. — *vi* : win — **ganarse** *vr* **1** : win, gain **2 ~ la vida** : make a living

gancho *nm* **1** : hook **2** HORQUILLA : hairpin **3** *Lat* : (clothes) hanger

gandul, -dula *adj & n fam* : good-for-nothing — **gandul** *nm Lat* : pigeon pea

ganga *nf* : bargain

gangrena *nf* : gangrene

gángster *nmf* : gangster

ganso, -sa *n* : goose, gander *m* — **gansada** *nf* : silly thing, nonsense

gañir {38} *vi* : yelp — **gañido** *nm* : yelp

garabatear *v* : scribble — **garabato** *nm* : scribble

garaje *nm* : garage

garantizar {21} *vt* : guarantee — **garante** *nmf* : guarantor — **garantía** *nf* **1** : guarantee, warranty **2** FIANZA : surety

garapiñar *vt* : candy (fruits, etc.)

garbanzo *nm* : chickpea, garbanzo

garbo *nm* : grace, elegance — **garboso, -sa** *adj* : graceful, elegant

gardenia *nf* : gardenia

garfio *nm* : hook, gaff

garganta *nf* **1** : throat **2** CUELLO : neck **3** DESFILADERO : ravine, gorge — **gargantilla** *nf* : necklace

gárgara *nf* **1** : gargling, gargle **2 hacer ~s** : gargle

gárgola *nf* : gargoyle

garita *nf* **1** : sentry box **2** CABAÑA : cabin, hut

garito *nm* : gambling den

garra *nf* **1** : claw, talon **2** *fam* : hand, paw

garrafa *nf* : decanter, carafe — **garrafón** *nm, pl* **-fones** : large decanter or bottle

garrapata *nf* : tick

garrocha *nf* **1** : lance, pike **2** *Lat* : pole (in sports)

garrote *nm* : club, cudgel

garúa *nf Lat* : drizzle

garza *nf* : heron

gas *nm* **1** : gas **2 ~ lacrimógeno** : tear gas

gasa *nf* : gauze

gaseosa *nf* : soda, soft drink

gasolina *nf* : gasoline, gas — **gasoil** *or* **gasóleo** *nm* : diesel fuel — **gasolinera** *nf* : gas station, service station

gastar *vt* **1** : spend **2** CONSUMIR : consume, use up **3** DESPERDICIAR : squander, waste — **gastarse** *vr* **1** : spend **2** DETERIORARSE : wear out — **gastado, -da** *adj* **1** : spent **2** : worn-out (of clothing, etc.) — **gastador, -dora** *n* : spendthrift — **gasto** *nm* **1** : expense, expenditure **2 ~s generales** : overhead

gástrico, -ca *adj* : gastric

gastronomía *nf* : gastronomy — **gastrónomo, -ma** *n* : gourmet

gatas: a ~ *adv phr* : on all fours

gatear *vi* : crawl, creep

gatillo *nm* : trigger — **gatillero** *nm Mex* : gunman

gato, -ta *n* : cat — **gatito, -ta** *n* : kitten — **gato** *nm* : jack (for an automobile)

gaucho *nm* : gaucho

gaveta *nf* : drawer

gavilla *nf* **1** : sheaf **2** PANDILLA : gang

gaviota *nf* : gull, seagull

gay ['ge, 'gai] *adj* : gay (homosexual)

gaza *nf* : loop

gazpacho *nm* : gazpacho

géiser *nm* : geyser

gelatina *nf* : gelatin

gema *nf* : gem

gemelo, -la *adj & n* : twin — **gemelo** *nm* **1** : cuff link **2 ~s** *nmpl* : binoculars

gemir {54} *vi* : moan, groan, whine — **gemido** *nm* : moan, groan, whine

gen *or* **gene** *nm* : gene

genealogía *nf* : genealogy — **genealógico, -ca** *adj* : genealogical

generación *nf, pl* **-ciones** : generation

generador *nm* : generator

general *adj* **1** : general **2 en ~** *or* **por lo ~** : in general, generally — *~ nmf* : general — **generalidad** *nf* **1** : generalization **2** MAYORÍA : majority — **generalizar** {21} *vi* : generalize — *vt* : spread (out) — **generalizarse** *vr* : become widespread — **generalmente** *adv* : usually, generally

generar *vt* : generate

género *nm* **1** : kind, sort **2** : gender (in

grammar) **3 ~ humano** : human race
— **genérico, -ca** *adj* : generic
generoso, -sa *adj* **1** : generous, unselfish **2** : ample (in quantity) — **generosidad** *nf* : generosity
génesis *nfs & pl* : genesis
genética *nf* : genetics — **genético, -ca**
adj : genetic
genial *adj* **1** : brilliant **2** ESTUPENDO
: great, terrific
genio *nm* **1** : genius **2** CARÁCTER : temper, disposition **3** : genie (in mythology)
genital *adj* : genital — **genitales** *nmpl*
: genitals
genocidio *nm* : genocide
gente *nf* **1** : people **2** *fam* : relatives *pl*,
folks *pl* **3 ser buena ~** : be nice, be
kind
gentil *adj* **1** AMABLE : kind **2** : gentile
(in religion) — **gentileza** *nf* : kindness, courtesy
gentío *nm* : crowd, mob
gentuza *nf* : riffraff, rabble
genuflexión *nf, pl* **-xiones** : genuflec-
tion
genuino, -na *adj* : genuine
geografía *nf* : geography — **geográfico, -ca** *adj* : geographic, geographical
geología *nf* : geology — **geológico,
-ca** *adj* : geologic, geological
geometría *nf* : geometry — **geométrico, -ca** *adj* : geometric, geometrical
geranio *nm* : geranium
gerencia *nf* : management — **gerente**
nmf : manager
geriatría *nf* : geriatrics — **geriátrico,
-ca** *adj* : geriatric
germen *nm, pl* **gérmenes** : germ
germinar *vi* : germinate, sprout
gestación *nf, pl* **-ciones** : gestation
gesticular *vi* : gesticulate, gesture —
gesticulación *nf, pl* **-ciones** : gestic-
ulation
gestión *nf, pl* **-tiones** **1** : procedure, step
2 ADMINISTRACIÓN : management —
gestionar *vt* **1** : negotiate, work towards **2** ADMINISTRAR : manage, handle
gesto *nm* **1** : gesture **2** : (facial) expression **3** MUECA : grimace
gigante *adj & nm* : giant — **gigantesco, -ca** *adj* : gigantic
gimnasia *nf* : gymnastics — **gimnasio**
nm : gymnasium, gym — **gimnasta**
nmf : gymnast
gimotear *vi* : whine, whimper
ginebra *nf* : gin
ginecología *nf* : gynecology — **gine-
cólogo, -ga** *n* : gynecologist
gira *nf* : tour

girar *vi* : turn (around), revolve — *vt* **1**
: turn, twist, rotate **2** : draft (checks) **3**
: transfer (funds)
girasol *nm* : sunflower
giratorio, -ria *adj* : revolving
giro *nm* **1** : turn, rotation **2** LOCUCIÓN
: expression **3 ~ bancario** : bank
draft **4 ~ postal** : money order
giroscopio *nm* : gyroscope
gis *nm Lat* : chalk
gitano, -na *adj & n* : Gypsy
glaciar *nm* : glacier — **glacial** *adj* : glacial, icy
gladiador *nm* : gladiator
glándula *nf* : gland
glasear *vt* : glaze, ice (cake, etc.) —
glaseado *nm* : icing
glicerina *nf* : glycerin
globo *nm* **1** : globe **2** : balloon **3 ~ ocular** : eyeball — **global** *adj* **1** : global
2 TOTAL : total, overall
glóbulo *nm* : blood cell, corpuscle
gloria *nf* : glory
glorieta *nf* **1** : bower, arbor **2** *Spain* : rotary, traffic circle
glorificar {72} *vt* : glorify
glorioso, -sa *adj* : glorious
glosario *nm* : glossary
glotón, -tona *adj, mpl* **-tones** : gluttonous — **~** *n* : glutton — **glotonería** *nf*
: gluttony
glucosa *nf* : glucose
gnomo ['nomo] *nm* : gnome
gobernar {55} *v* **1** : govern, rule **2** DIRI-
GIR : direct, manage **3** : steer (a boat,
etc.) — **gobernación** *nf, pl* **-ciones**
: governing, government — **gobernador, -dora** *n* : governor — **gobernante** *adj* : ruling, governing — **~** *n*
: ruler, leader — **gobierno** *nm* : government
goce *nm* : enjoyment
gol *nm* : goal (in sports)
golf *nm* : golf — **golfista** *nmf* : golfer
golfo *nm* : gulf
golondrina *nf* **1** : swallow **2 ~ de mar**
: tern
golosina *nf* : sweet, candy — **goloso,
-sa** *adj* : fond of sweets
golpe *nm* **1** : blow **2** PUÑETAZO : punch
3 : knock (on a door, etc.) **4 de ~**
: suddenly **5 de un ~** : all at once **6
~ de estado** : coup d'etat — **gol-
pear** *vt* **1** : hit, punch **2** : slam, bang (a
door, etc.) — *vi* : knock (at a door)
goma *nf* **1** CAUCHO : rubber **2** PEGAMEN-
TO : glue **3** *or* **~ elástica** : rubber
band **4 ~ de mascar** : chewing gum
5 ~ de borrar : eraser
gong *nm* : gong

gordo, -da *adj* **1** : fat, plump **2** GRUESO
: thick **3** : fatty (of meat) **4** *fam* : big,
serious — ∼ *n* : fat person — **gorda**
nf Lat : thick corn tortilla — **gordo** *nm*
1 GRASA : fat **2** : jackpot (in a lottery)
— **gordura** *nf* : fatness, flab
gorgotear *vi* : gurgle, bubble
gorila *nm* : gorilla
gorjear *vi* **1** : chirp, tweet **2** : gurgle (of
a baby) — **gorjeo** *nm* : chirping
gorra *nf* **1** : cap, bonnet **2** de ∼ *fam*
: for free
gorrear *vt fam* : bum, scrounge
gorrión *nm, pl* **-rriones** : sparrow
gorro *nm* **1** : cap, bonnet **2** de ∼ *fam*
: for free
gota *nf* **1** : drop **2** : gout (in medicine)
— **gotear** *vi* : drip, leak — **goteo** *nm*
: drip, dripping — **gotera** *nf* : leak
gótico, -ca *adj* : Gothic
gozar {21} *vi* **1** : enjoy oneself **2** ∼ **de**
algo : enjoy sth
gozne *nm* : hinge
gozo *nm* **1** : joy **2** PLACER : enjoyment,
pleasure — **gozoso, -sa** *adj* : joyful,
glad
grabar *vt* **1** : engrave **2** : record, tape —
grabación *nf, pl* **-ciones** : recording
— **grabado** *nm* : engraving — **grabadora** *nf* : tape recorder
gracia *nf* **1** : grace **2** FAVOR : favor, kindness **3** HUMOR : humor, wit **4** ∼**s** *nfpl*
: thanks **5** ¡(muchas) ∼**s**! : thank you
(very much)! — **gracioso, -sa** *adj*
: funny, amusing
grada *nf* **1** : step, stair **2** : row (in a theater, etc.) **3** ∼**s** *nfpl* : bleachers,
grandstand — **gradación** *nf, pl*
-ciones : gradation, scale — **gradería**
nf : rows *pl*, stands *pl* — **grado** *nm* **1**
: degree **2** : grade (in school) **3 de
buen** ∼ : willingly
graduar {3} *vt* **1** : regulate, adjust **2**
MARCAR : calibrate **3** : confer a degree
on (in education) — **graduarse** *vr*
: graduate (from a school) — **grad-
uación** *nf, pl* **-ciones** **1** : graduation **2**
: alcohol content, proof — **graduado,
-da** *n* : graduate — **gradual** *adj* : gradual — **gradualmente** *adv* : little by
little, gradually
gráfico, -ca *adj* : graphic — **gráfica** *nf*
: graph — **gráfico** *nm* **1** : graph **2**
: graphic (in computers)
gragea *nf* : pill, tablet
grajo *nm* : rook (bird)
gramática *nf* : grammar — **gramatical**
adj : grammatical
gramo *nm* : gram

gran → **grande**
grana *nf* : scarlet
granada *nf* **1** : pomegranate **2** : grenade
(in the military)
granate *nm* : garnet
grande *adj* (**gran** *before singular
nouns*) **1** : large, big **2** ALTO : tall **3**
: great (in quality, intensity, etc.) **4** *Lat*
: grown-up — **grandeza** *nf* **1** : greatness **2** NOBLEZA : nobility — **grandiosidad** *nf* : grandeur — **grandioso, -sa**
adj : grand, magnificent
granel: a ∼ *adv phr* **1** : in bulk **2** : in
abundance
granero *nm* : barn, granary
granito *nm* : granite
granizar {21} *v impers* : hail — **grani-
zada** *nf* : hailstorm — **granizado** *nm*
: iced drink — **granizo** *nm* : hail
granja *nf* : farm — **granjero, -ra** *n*
: farmer
grano *nm* **1** : grain **2** SEMILLA : seed **3**
: (coffee) bean **4** BARRO : pimple
granuja *nmf* : rascal
grapa *nf* : staple — **grapadora** *nf* : stapler — **grapar** *vt* : staple
grasa *nf* **1** : grease **2** : fat (in cooking,
etc.) — **grasiento, -ta** *adj* : greasy, oily
— **graso, -sa** *adj* : fatty, greasy, oily —
grasoso, -sa *adj Lat* : greasy, oily
gratificar {72} *vt* **1** : give a tip or bonus
to **2** SATISFACER : gratify, satisfy —
gratificación *nf, pl* **-ciones** **1** : bonus,
tip, reward **2** SATISFACCIÓN : gratifica-
tion
gratis *adv & adj* : free
gratitud *nf* : gratitude
grato, -ta *adj* : pleasant, agreeable
gratuito, -ta *adj* **1** : gratuitous, unwarranted **2** GRATIS : free
grava *nf* : gravel
gravar *vt* **1** : tax **2** CARGAR : burden —
gravamen *nm, pl* **-vámenes** **1** : burden, obligation **2** IMPUESTO : tax
grave *adj* **1** : grave, serious **2** : deep,
low (of a voice, etc.) — **gravedad** *nf*
: gravity
gravilla *nf* : gravel
gravitar *vi* **1** : gravitate **2** ∼ **sobre**
: weigh on — **gravitación** *nf, pl*
-ciones : gravitation
gravoso, -sa *adj* : costly, burdensome
graznar *vi* : caw, quack, honk —
graznido *nm* : caw, quack, honk
gregario, -ria *adj* : gregarious
gremio *nm* : guild, (trade) union
greñas *nfpl* : shaggy hair, mop
griego, -ga *adj* : Greek — **griego** *nm*
: Greek (language)
grieta *nf* : crack, crevice

grifo *nm Spain* : faucet, tap
grillete *nm* : shackle
grillo *nm* 1 : cricket 2 ~s *nmpl* : fetters, shackles
grima *nf* dar ~ : annoy, irritate
gringo, -ga *adj & n Lat fam* : Yankee, gringo
gripe *nf or* **gripa** *nf Lat* : flu, influenza
gris *adj & nm* : gray
gritar *v* : shout, scream, cry — **grito** *nm* 1 : shout, scream, cry 2 dar ~s : shout
grosella *nf* : currant
grosería *nf* 1 : vulgar remark 2 DESCORTESÍA : rudeness — **grosero, -ra** *adj* 1 : coarse, vulgar 2 DESCORTÉS : rude
grosor *nm* : thickness
grotesco, -ca *adj* : grotesque, hideous
grúa *nf* : crane, derrick
grueso, -sa *adj* 1 : thick 2 CORPULENTO : stout, heavy — **gruesa** *nf* : gross — **grueso** *nm* 1 GROSOR : thickness 2 : main body, mass 3 en ~ : wholesale
grulla *nf* : crane (bird)
grumo *nm* : lump, clot — **grumoso, -sa** *adj* : lumpy
gruñir {38} *vi* 1 : growl, grunt 2 *fam* : grumble — **gruñido** *nm* 1 : growl, grunt 2 *fam* : grumble — **gruñón, -ñona** *adj, mpl* -ñones *fam* : grumpy, grouchy — ~ *n fam* : grouch
grupa *nf* : rump, hindquarters *pl*
grupo *nm* : group
gruta *nf* : grotto
guacamayo *nm or* **guacamaya** *nf Lat* : macaw
guacamole *nm* : guacamole
guadaña *nf* : scythe
guagua *nf Lat* 1 : baby 2 AUTOBÚS : bus
guajolote, -ta *or* **guajolote, -ta** *n Lat* : turkey
guante *nm* : glove
guapo, -pa *adj* : handsome, good-looking
guaraní *nm* : Guarani (language of Paraguay)
guarda *nmf* 1 : keeper, custodian 2 GUARDIÁN : security guard — **guardabarros** *nms & pl* : fender — **guardabosque** *nmf* : forest ranger — **guardacostas** *nmfs & pl* : coast guard vessel — **guardaespaldas** *nmfs & pl* : bodyguard — **guardameta** *nmf* : goalkeeper — **guardapolvo** *nm* : overalls *pl* — **guardar** *vt* 1 : keep 2 PROTEGER : guard, protect 3 RESERVAR : save — **guardarse** *vr* ~ de 1 : refrain from 2 : guard against — **guardarropa** *nm* 1

: cloakroom, checkroom 2 ARMARIO : wardrobe
guardería *nf* : nursery, day-care center
guardia *nf* 1 : guard, vigilence 2 TURNO : duty, watch — ~ *nmf* 1 : guard 2 or ~ **municipal** : police officer — **guardián, -diana** *n, mpl* -dianes 1 : guardian, keeper 2 GUARDA : security guard
guarecer {53} *vt* : shelter, protect — **guarecerse** *vr* : take shelter
guarida *nf* 1 : den, lair (of animals) 2 : hideout (of persons)
guarnecer {53} *vt* 1 : adorn, garnish 2 : garrison (an area) — **guarnición** *nf, pl* -ciones 1 : garnish, trimming 2 : (military) garrison
guasa *nf fam* 1 : joke 2 de ~ : in jest — **guasón, -sona** *adj, mpl* -sones *fam* : joking, witty — ~ *n fam* : joker
guatemalteco, -ca *adj* : Guatemalan
guayaba *nf* : guava
gubernamental *or* **gubernativo, -va** *adj* : governmental
guepardo *nm* : cheetah
güero, -ra *adj Lat* : blond, fair
guerra *nf* 1 : war, warfare 2 LUCHA : conflict, struggle — **guerrear** *vi* : wage war — **guerrero, -ra** *adj* 1 : war, fighting 2 BELICOSO : warlike — ~ *n* : warrior — **guerrilla** *nf* : guerrilla warfare — **guerrillero, -ra** *adj & n* : guerrilla
gueto *nm* : ghetto
guiar {85} *vt* 1 : guide, lead 2 ACONSEJAR : advise — **guiarse** *vr* : be guided by, go by — **guía** *nf* 1 : guidebook 2 ORIENTACIÓN : guidance — ~ *nmf* : guide, leader
guijarro *nm* : pebble
guillotina *nf* : guillotine
guinda *nf* : morello (cherry)
guiñar *vi* : wink — **guiño** *nm* : wink
guion *nm, pl* **guiones** 1 : script, screenplay 2 : hyphen, dash (in punctuation) — **guionista** *nmf* : scriptwriter, screenwriter
guirnalda *nf* : garland
guisa *nf* 1 : manner, fashion 2 a ~ de : by way of 3 de tal ~ : in such a way
guisado *nm* : stew
guisante *nm* : pea
guisar *vt* : cook — **guiso** *nm* : stew, casserole
guitarra *nf* : guitar — **guitarrista** *nmf* : guitarist
gula *nf* : gluttony
gusano *nm* 1 : worm 2 : maggot (larva)
gustar *vt* 1 : taste 2 *Lat* : like — *vi* 1 : be pleasing 2 como guste : as you like 3

me gustan los dulces : I like sweets
— **gusto** *nm* **1** : taste **2** PLACER : pleasure, liking **3 a ~** : comfortable, at ease **4 al ~** : to taste **5 mucho ~**
: pleased to meet you — **gustoso, -sa** *adj* **1** : tasty **2** AGRADABLE : pleasant **3 hacer algo ~** : do sth willingly

gutural *adj* : guttural

H

h *nf* : h, eighth letter of the Spanish alphabet

haba *nf* : broad bean

habanero, -ra *adj* : Havanan — **habano** *nm* : Havana cigar

haber {39} *v aux* **1** : have, has **2 ~ de** : must — *v impers* **1 hay** : there is, there are **2 hay que** : it is necessary (to) **3 ¿qué hay?** *or* **¿qué hubo?** : how's it going? — **~** *nm* **1** : assets *pl* **2** : credit side (in accounting) **3 ~es** *nmpl* : income, earnings

habichuela *nf* **1** : bean **2 ~ verde** : string bean

hábil *adj* **1** : able, skillful **2** LISTO : clever **3 horas ~es** : business hours — **habilidad** *nf* : ability, skill

habilitar *vt* **1** : equip, furnish **2** AUTORIZAR : authorize

habitar *vt* : inhabit — *vi* : reside, dwell — **habitable** *adj* : habitable, inhabitable — **habitación** *nf*, *pl* **-ciones 1** : room, bedroom **2** MORADA : dwelling, abode **3** : habitat (in biology) — **habitante** *nmf* : inhabitant, resident — **hábitat** *nm* : habitat

hábito *nm* : habit — **habitual** *adj* : habitual, usual — **habituar** {3} *vt* : accustom, habituate — **habituarse** *vr* **~ a** : get used to

hablar *vi* **1** : speak, talk **2 ~ de** : mention, talk about **3 ~ con** : talk to, speak with — *vt* **1** : speak (a language) **2** DISCUTIR : discuss — **hablarse** *vr* **1** : speak to each other **2 se habla inglés** : English spoken — **habla** *nf* **1** : speech **2** IDIOMA : language, dialect **3 de ~ inglesa** : English-speaking — **hablador, -dora** *adj* : talkative — **~** *n* : chatterbox — **habladuría** *nf* **1** : rumor **2 ~s** *nfpl* : gossip — **hablante** *nmf* : speaker

hacedor, -dora *n* : creator, maker

hacendado, -da *n* : landowner, rancher

hacer {40} *vt* **1** : do, perform **2** CONSTRUIR, CREAR : make **3** OBLIGAR : force, oblige — *vi* : act — *v impers* **1 ~ calor/viento** : be hot/be windy **2 ~ falta** : be necessary **3 hace mucho tiempo** : a long time ago **4 no lo hace** : it doesn't matter — **hacerse** *vr* **1**

VOLVERSE : become **2** : pretend (to be) **3 ~ a** : get used to **4 se hace tarde** : it's getting late

hacha *nf* **1** : hatchet, ax **2** ANTORCHA : torch

hachís *nm* : hashish

hacia *prep* **1** : toward, towards **2** CERCA DE : near, around, about **3 ~ abajo** : downward **4 ~ adelante** : forward

hacienda *nf* **1** : estate, ranch **2** BIENES : property **3** *Lat* : livestock **4 Hacienda** : department of revenue

hacinar *vt* : stack

hada *nf* : fairy

hado *nm* : fate

halagar {52} *vt* : flatter — **halagador, -dora** *adj* : flattering — **halago** *nm* : flattery — **halagüeño, -ña** *adj* **1** : flattering **2** PROMETEDOR : promising

halcón *nm*, *pl* **-cones** : hawk, falcon

halibut *nm*, *pl* **-buts** : halibut

hálito *nm* : breath

hallar *vt* **1** : find **2** DESCUBRIR : discover, find out — **hallarse** *vr* : be, find oneself — **hallazgo** *nm* : discovery, find

halo *nm* : halo

hamaca *nf* : hammock

hambre *nf* **1** : hunger **2** INANICIÓN : starvation, famine **3 tener ~** : be hungry — **hambriento, -ta** *adj* : hungry, starving — **hambruna** *nf* : famine

hamburguesa *nf* : hamburger

hampa *nf* : underworld — **hampón, -pona** *n*, *mpl* **-pones** : criminal, thug

hámster *nm* : hamster

hándicap *nm* : handicap (in sports)

hangar *nm* : hangar

haragán, -gana *adj*, *mpl* **-ganes** : lazy, idle — **~** *n* : slacker, idler — **haraganear** : be lazy, loaf

harapiento, -ta *adj* : ragged, in rags — **harapos** *nmpl* : rags, tatters

harina *nf* : flour

hartar *vt* **1** : glut, satiate **2** FASTIDIAR : annoy — **hartarse** *vr* **1** : gorge oneself **2** CANSARSE : get fed up — **harto, -ta** *adj* **1** : full, satiated **2** CANSADO : tired, fed up — **harto** *adv* : extremely, very — **hartura** *nf* **1** : surfeit **2** ABUNDANCIA : abundance, plenty

hasta *prep* **1** : until, up until (in time) **2**

: as far as, up to (in space) **3** ¡~
luego! : see you later! **4** — **que** : until
— ~ *adv* : even
hastiar {85} *vt* **1** : make weary, bore **2**
ASQUEAR : sicken — **hastiarse** *vr* ~
de : get tired of — **hastío** *nm* **1** : weariness, tedium **2** REPUGNANCIA : disgust
hato *nm* **1** : flock, herd **2** : bundle (of
possessions)
haya *nf* : beech
haz *nm, pl* **haces 1** : bundle, sheaf **2**
: beam (of light)
hazaña *nf* : feat, exploit
hazmerreír *nm fam* : laughingstock
he {39} *v impers* ~ **aquí** : here is, here
are, behold
hebilla *nf* : buckle
hebra *nf* : strand, thread
hebreo, -brea *adj* : Hebrew — **hebreo**
nm : Hebrew (language)
hecatombe *nm* : disaster
hechizo *nm* **1** : spell **2** ENCANTO : charm,
fascination — **hechicería** *nf* : sorcery,
witchcraft — **hechicero, -ra** *n* : sorcerer, sorceress *f* — **hechizar** {21} *vt* **1**
: bewitch **2** CAUTIVAR : charm
hecho, -cha *adj* **1** : made, done **2**
: ready-to-wear (of clothing) **3** — **y**
derecho : full-fledged, mature —
hecho *nm* **1** : fact **2** SUCESO : event **3**
ACTO : act, deed **4 de** ~ : in fact —
hechura *nf* **1** : making, creation **2**
FORMA : shape, form **3** : build (of the
body) **4** ARTESANÍA : workmanship
heder {56} *vi* : stink, reek — **hedion-**
dez *nf, pl* **-deces** : stench — **hedion-**
do, -da *adj* : stinking — **hedor** *nm*
: stench
helar {55} *v* : freeze — **helarse** *vr*
: freeze up, freeze over — **helado, -da**
adj **1** : freezing cold **2** CONGELADO
: frozen — **helada** *nf* : frost —
heladería *nf* : ice-cream parlor —
helado *nm* : ice cream — **heladora** *nf*
: freezer
helecho *nm* : fern
hélice *nf* **1** : propeller **2** ESPIRAL : spiral,
helix
helicóptero *nm* : helicopter
helio *nm* : helium
hembra *nf* **1** : female **2** MUJER : woman
hemisferio *nm* : hemisphere
hemorragia *nf* **1** : hemorrhage **2** —
nasal : nosebleed
hemorroides *nfpl* : hemorrhoids, piles
henchir {54} *vt* : stuff, fill
hender {56} *vt* : cleave, split — **hen-**
didura *nf* : crevice, fissure
henequén *nm, pl* **-quenes** : sisal
heno *nm* : hay

hepatitis *nf* : hepatitis
heraldo *nm* : herald
herbolario, -ria *n* : herbalist
heredar *vt* : inherit — **heredad** *nm*
: rural property, estate — **heredero,**
-ra *n* : heir, heiress *f* — **hereditario,**
-ria *adj* : hereditary
hereje *nmf* : heretic — **herejía** *nf*
: heresy
herencia *nf* **1** : inheritance **2** : heredity
(in biology)
herir {76} *vt* **1** : injure, wound **2** : hurt
(feelings, pride, etc.) — **herida** *nf* : injury, wound — **herido, -da** *adj* **1** : injured, wounded **2** : hurt (of feelings,
pride, etc.) — ~ *n* : injured person,
casualty
hermano, -na *n* : brother *m*, sister *f* —
hermanastro, -tra *n* : half brother *m*,
half sister *f* — **hermandad** *nf* : brotherhood
hermético, -ca *adj* : hermetic, watertight
hermoso, -sa *adj* : beautiful, lovely —
hermosura *nf* : beauty
hernia *nf* : hernia
héroe *nm* : hero — **heroico, -ca** *adj*
: heroic — **heroína** *nf* **1** : heroine **2**
: heroin (narcotic) — **heroísmo** *nm*
: heroism
herradura *nf* : horseshoe
herramienta *nf* : tool
herrero, -ra *n* : blacksmith
herrumbre *nf* : rust
hervir {76} *v* : boil — **hervidero** *nm* **1**
: mass, swarm **2** : hotbed (of intrigue,
etc.) — **hervidor** *nm* : kettle — **hervor**
nm **1** : boiling **2** ENTUSIASMO : fervor,
ardor
heterogéneo, -nea *adj* : heterogeneous
heterosexual *adj & nmf* : heterosexual
hexágono *nm* : hexagon — **hexagonal**
adj : hexagonal
hez *nf, pl* **heces** : dregs *pl*, scum
hiato *nm* : hiatus
hibernar *vi* : hibernate — **hibernación**
nf, pl **-ciones** : hibernation
híbrido, -da *adj* : hybrid — **híbrido** *nm*
: hybrid
hidalgo, -ga *n* : nobleman *m*, noble-
woman *f*
hidratante *adj* : moisturizing
hidrato *nm* ~ **de carbono** : carbohydrate
hidráulico, -ca *adj* : hydraulic
hidroavión *nm, pl* **-aviones** : seaplane
hidroeléctrico, -ca *adj* : hydroelectric
hidrofobia *nf* : rabies
hidrógeno *nm* : hydrogen
hidroplano *nm* : hydroplane

hiedra *nf* 1 : ivy 2 ~ **venenosa** : poison ivy

hiel *nm* 1 : bile 2 AMARGURA : bitterness

hielo *nm* 1 : ice 2 FRIALDAD : coldness 3 **romper el** ~ : break the ice

hiena *nf* : hyena

hierba *nf* 1 : herb 2 CÉSPED : grass 3 **mala** ~ : weed — **hierbabuena** *nf* : mint

hierro *nm* 1 : iron 2 ~ **fundido** : cast iron

hígado *nm* : liver

higiene *nf* : hygiene — **higiénico, -ca** *adj* : hygienic

higo *nm* : fig

hijo, -ja *n* 1 : son *m*, daughter *f* 2 **hijos** *nmpl* : children, offspring — **hijastro, -tra** *n* : stepson *m*, stepdaughter *f*

hilar *v* 1 : spin 2 ~ **delgado** : split hairs — **hilado** *nm* : yarn, thread

hilaridad *nf* : hilarity

hilera *nf* : file, row

hilo *nm* 1 : thread 2 LINO : linen 3 ALAMBRE : wire 4 : trickle (of water, etc.) 5 ~ **dental** : dental floss

hilvanar *vt* 1 : baste, tack 2 : put together (ideas, etc.)

himno *nm* 1 : hymn 2 ~ **nacional** : national anthem

hincapié *nm* **hacer** ~ **en** : emphasize, stress

hincar {72} *vt* : drive in, plunge — **hincarse** *vr* ~ **de rodillas** : kneel (down)

hinchar *vt Spain* : inflate, blow up — **hincharse** *vr* 1 : swell (up) 2 *Spain fam* : stuff oneself — **hinchado, -da** *adj* 1 : swollen 2 POMPOSO : pompous — **hinchazón** *nf, pl* **-zones** : swelling

hindú *adj & nmf* : Hindu — **hinduismo** *nm* : Hinduism

hinojo *nm* : fennel

hiperactivo, -va *adj* : hyperactive

hipersensible *adj* : oversensitive

hipertensión *nf, pl* **-siones** : hypertension, high blood pressure

hípico, -ca *adj* : equestrian, horse

hipil → huipil

hipnosis *nfs & pl* : hypnosis — **hipnótico, -ca** *adj* : hypnotic — **hipnotismo** *nm* : hypnotism — **hipnotizador, -dora** *n* : hypnotist — **hipnotizar** {21} *vt* : hypnotize

hipo *nm* 1 : hiccup, hiccups *pl* 2 **tener** ~ : have hiccups

hipocondríaco, -ca *adj* : hypochondriacal — ~ *n* : hypochondriac

hipocresía *nf* : hypocrisy — **hipócrita** *adj* : hypocritical — ~ *nmf* : hypocrite

hipodérmico, -ca *adj* : hypodermic

hipódromo *nm* : racetrack

hipopótamo *nm* : hippopotamus

hipoteca *nf* : mortgage — **hipotecar** {72} *vt* : mortgage

hipótesis *nfs & pl* : hypothesis — **hipotético, -ca** *adj* : hypothetical

hiriente *adj* : hurtful, offensive

hirsuto, -ta *adj* 1 : hairy 2 : bristly, wiry (of hair)

hirviente *adj* : boiling

hispano, -na *or* **hispánico, -ca** *adj & n* : Hispanic — **hispanoamericano, -na** *adj* : Latin-American — ~ *n* : Latin American — **hispanohablante** *or* **hispanoparlante** *adj* : Spanish-speaking

histeria *nf* : hysteria — **histérico, -ca** *adj* : hysterical — **histerismo** *nm* : hysteria

historia *nf* 1 : history 2 CUENTO : story — **historiador, -dora** *n* : historian — **historial** *nm* : record, background — **histórico, -ca** *adj* 1 : historical 2 IMPORTANTE : historic, important — **historieta** *nf* : comic strip

hito *nm* : milestone, landmark

hocico *nm* : snout, muzzle

hockey ['hɔke, -ki] *nm* : hockey

hogar *nm* 1 : home 2 CHIMENEA : hearth, fireplace — **hogareño, -ña** *adj* 1 : home-loving 2 DOMÉSTICO : home, domestic

hoguera *nf* : bonfire

hoja *nf* 1 : leaf 2 : sheet (of paper) 3 ~ **de afeitar** : razor blade — **hojalata** *nf* : tinplate — **hojaldre** *nm* : puff pastry — **hojear** *vt* : leaf through — **hojuela** *nf Lat* : flake

hola *interj* : hello!, hi!

holandés, -desa *adj, mpl* **-deses** : Dutch

holgado, -da *adj* 1 : loose, baggy 2 : comfortable (of an economic situation, a victory, etc.) — **holgazán, -zana** *adj, mpl* **-zanes** : lazy — ~ *n* : slacker, idler — **holgazanear** *vi* : laze about, loaf — **holgura** *nf* 1 : looseness 2 BIENESTAR : comfort, ease

hollín *nm, pl* **-llines** : soot

holocausto *nm* : holocaust

hombre *nm* 1 : man 2 **el** ~ : mankind 3 ~ **de estado** : statesman 4 ~ **de negocios** : businessman

hombrera *nf* 1 : shoulder pad 2 : epaulet (of a uniform)

hombría *nf* : manliness

hombro *nm* : shoulder

hombruno, -na *adj* : mannish

homenaje *nm* 1 : homage 2 **rendir ~ a** : pay tribute to

homeopatía *nf* : homeopathy

homicidio *nm* : homicide, murder — **homicida** *adj* : homicidal, murderous — *~ nmf* : murderer

homogéneo, -nea *adj* : homogeneous

homólogo, -ga *adj* : equivalent — *~ n* : counterpart

homosexual *adj & nmf* : homosexual — **homosexualidad** *nf* : homosexuality

hondo, -da *adj* : deep — **hondo** *adv* : deeply — **hondonada** *nf* : hollow — **hondura** *nf* : depth

hondureño, -ña *adj* : Honduran

honesto, -ta *adj* : decent, honorable — **honestidad** *nf* : honesty, integrity

hongo *nm* 1 : mushroom 2 : fungus (in botany and medicine)

honor *nm* : honor — **honorable** *adj* : honorable — **honorario, -ria** *adj* : honorary — **honorarios** *nmpl* : payment, fee — **honra** *nf* : honor — **honradez** *nf, pl* **-deces** : honesty, integrity — **honrado, -da** *adj* : honest, upright — **honrar** *vt* : honor — **honrarse** *vr* : be honored — **honroso, -sa** *adj* : honorable

hora *nf* 1 : hour 2 : (specific) time 3 CITA : appointment 4 **a la última ~** : at the last minute 5 **~ punta** : rush hour 6 **media ~** : half an hour 7 **¿qué ~ es?** : what time is it? 8 **~s de oficina** : office hours 9 **~s extraordinarias** : overtime

horario *nm* : schedule, timetable

horca *nf* 1 : gallows *pl* 2 : pitchfork (in agriculture)

horcajadas: a ~ *adv phr* : astride

horda *nf* : horde

horizonte *nm* : horizon — **horizontal** *adj* : horizontal

horma *nf* 1 : form, mold, last 2 : shoe tree

hormiga *nf* : ant

hormigón *nm, pl* **-gones** : concrete

hormigueo *nm* : tingling, pins and needles

hormiguero *nm* 1 : anthill 2 : swarm (of people)

hormona *nf* : hormone

horno *nm* 1 : oven (for cooking) 2 : small furnace, kiln — **hornada** *nf* : batch — **hornear** *vt* : bake — **hornillo** *nf* : portable stove

horóscopo *nm* : horoscope

horquilla *nf* 1 : hairpin, bobby pin 2 HORCA : pitchfork

horrendo, -da *adj* : horrendous, awful

— **horrible** *adj* : horrible — **horripilante** *adj* : horrifying — **horror** *nm* 1 : horror, dread 2 ATROCIDAD : atrocity — **horrorizar** {21} *vt* : horrify, terrify — **horrorizarse** *vr* : be horrified — **horroroso, -sa** *adj* : horrifying, dreadful

hortaliza *nf* : (garden) vegetable — **hortelano, -na** *n* : truck farmer — **horticultura** *nf* : horticulture

hosco, -ca *adj* : sullen, gloomy

hospedar *vt* : put up, lodge — **hospedarse** *vr* : stay, lodge — **hospedaje** *nm* : lodging

hospital *nm* : hospital — **hospitalario, -ria** *adj* : hospitable — **hospitalidad** *nf* : hospitality — **hospitalizar** {21} *vt* : hospitalize

hostería *nf* : small hotel, inn

hostia *nf* : host (in religion)

hostigar {52} *vt* 1 : whip 2 ACOSAR : harass, pester

hostil *adj* : hostile — **hostilidad** *nf* : hostility

hotel *nm* : hotel — **hotelero, -ra** *adj* : hotel — *~ n* : hotel manager, hotelier

hoy *adv* 1 : today 2 **de ~ en adelante** : from now on 3 **~ (en) día** : nowadays 4 **~ mismo** : this very day

hoyo *nm* : hole — **hoyuelo** *nm* : dimple

hoz *nf, pl* **hoces** : sickle

huarache *nm* : huarache (sandal)

hueco, -ca *adj* 1 : hollow, empty 2 ESPONJOSO : soft, spongy 3 RESONANTE : resonant — **hueco** *nm* 1 : hollow, cavity 2 : recess (in a wall, etc.) 3 **~ de escalera** : stairwell

huelga *nf* 1 : strike 2 **declararse en ~** : go on strike — **huelguista** *nmf* : striker

huella *nf* 1 : footprint 2 VESTIGIO : track, mark 3 **~ digital** *or* **~ dactilar** : fingerprint

huérfano, -na *n* : orphan — *~ adj* : orphaned

huerta *nf* : truck farm — **huerto** *nm* 1 : vegetable garden 2 : (fruit) orchard

hueso *nm* 1 : bone 2 : pit, stone (of a fruit)

huésped, -peda *n* : guest — **huésped** *nm* : host (organism)

huesudo, -da *adj* : bony

huevo *nm* 1 : egg 2 **~s estrellados** : fried eggs 3 **~s revueltos** : scrambled eggs — **hueva** *nf* : roe

huida *nf* : flight, escape — **huidizo, -za** *adj* 1 : shy 2 FUGAZ : fleeting

huipil *nm Lat* : traditional embroidered blouse or dress

huir {41} *vi* **1** : escape, flee **2** ~ **de** : shun, avoid

hule *nm* **1** : oilcloth **2** *Lat* : rubber

humano, -na *adj* **1** : human **2** COMPASIVO : humane — **humano** *nm* : human (being) — **humanidad** *nf* **1** : humanity, mankind **2** BENEVOLENCIA : humaneness **3** ~**es** *nfpl* : humanities — **humanismo** *nm* : humanism — **humanista** *nmf* : humanist — **humanitario, -ria** *adj & n* : humanitarian

humear *vi* : smoke, steam — **humareda** *nf* : cloud of smoke

humedad *nf* **1** : dampness **2** : humidity (in meteorology) — **humedecer** {53} *vt* : moisten, dampen — **humedecerse** *vr* : become moist — **húmedo, -da** *adj* **1** : moist, damp **2** : humid (in meteorology)

humildad *nf* : humility — **humilde** *adj* : humble — **humillación** *nf, pl* -**ciones** : humiliation — **humillante** *adj* : humiliating — **humillar** *vt* : humiliate — **humillarse** *vr* : humble oneself

humo *nm* **1** : smoke, steam, fumes **2** ~**s** *nmpl* : airs, conceit

humor *nm* **1** : mood, temper **2** GRACIA : humor **3 de buen** ~ : in a good mood — **humorismo** *nm* : humor, wit — **humorista** *nmf* : humorist, comedian — **humorístico, -ca** *adj* : humorous

hundir *vt* **1** : sink **2** : destroy, ruin (a building, plans, etc.) — **hundirse** *vr* **1** : sink **2** DERRUMBARSE : collapse — **hundido, -da** *adj* : sunken — **hundimiento** *nm* **1** : sinking **2** DERRUMBE : collapse

húngaro, -ra *adj* : Hungarian

huracán *nm, pl* -**canes** : hurricane

huraño, -ña *adj* : unsociable

hurgar {52} *vi* ~ **en** : rummage around in

hurón *nm, pl* -**rones** : ferret

hurra *interj* : hurrah!, hooray!

hurtadillas: a ~ *adv phr* : stealthily, on the sly

hurtar *vt* : steal — **hurto** *nm* **1** ROBO : theft **2** : stolen property

husmear *vt* : sniff out, pry into — *vi* : nose around

huy *interj* : ow!, ouch!

I

i *nf* : i, ninth letter of the Spanish alphabet

ibérico, -ca *adj* : Iberian — **ibero, -ra** *or* **íbero, -ra** *adj* : Iberian

iceberg *nm, pl* -**bergs** : iceberg

icono *nm* : icon

ictericia *nf* : jaundice

ida *nf* **1** : outward journey **2** ~ **y vuelta** : round-trip **3** ~**s y venidas** : comings and goings

idea *nf* **1** : idea **2** OPINIÓN : opinion

ideal *adj & nm* : ideal — **idealismo** *nm* : idealism — **idealista** *adj* : idealistic — ~ *nmf* : idealist — **idealizar** {21} *vt* : idealize

idear *vt* : devise, think up

ídem *nm* : the same, ditto

identidad *nf* : identity — **idéntico, -ca** *adj* : identical — **identificar** {72} *vt* : identify — **identificarse** *vr* **1** : identify oneself **2** ~ **con** : identify with — **identificación** *nf, pl* -**ciones** : identification

ideología *nf* : ideology — **ideológico, -ca** *adj* : ideological

idílico, -ca *adj* : idyllic

idioma *nm* : language — **idiomático, -ca** *adj* : idiomatic

idiosincrasia *nf* : idiosyncrasy — **idiosincrásico, -ca** *adj* : idiosyncratic

idiota *adj* : idiotic — ~ *nmf* : idiot — **idiotez** *nf* : idiocy

ídolo *nm* : idol — **idolatrar** *vt* : idolize — **idolatría** *nf* : idolatry

idóneo, -nea *adj* : suitable, fitting — **idoneidad** *nf* : fitness, suitability

iglesia *nf* : church

iglú *nm* : igloo

ignición *nf, pl* -**ciones** : ignition

ignífugo, -ga *adj* : fire-resistant, fireproof

ignorar *vt* **1** : ignore **2** DESCONOCER : be unaware of — **ignorancia** *nf* : ignorance — **ignorante** *adj* : ignorant — ~ *nmf* : ignorant person

igual *adv* **1** : in the same way **2 por** ~ : equally — ~ *adj* **1** : equal **2** IDÉNTICO : the same **3** LISO : smooth, even **4** SEMEJANTE : similar — ~ *nmf* : equal, peer — **igualar** *vt* **1** : make equal **2** : be equal to **3** NIVELAR : level (off) — **igualdad** *nf* **1** : equality **2** UNIFORMI-

DAD : uniformity — **igualmente** *adv* : likewise

iguana *nf* : iguana

ijada *nf* : flank

ilegal *adj* : illegal

ilegible *adj* : illegible

ilegítimo, -ma *adj* : illegitimate — **ilegitimidad** *nf* : illegitimacy

ileso, -sa *adj* : unharmed

ilícito, -ta *adj* : illicit

ilimitado, -da *adj* : unlimited

ilógico, -ca *adj* : illogical

iluminar *vt* : illuminate — **iluminarse** *vr* : light up — **iluminación** *nf, pl* **-ciones 1** : illumination **2** ALUMBRADO : lighting

ilusionar *vt* : excite — **ilusionarse** *vr* : get one's hopes up — **ilusión** *nf, pl* **-siones 1** : illusion **2** ESPERANZA : hope — **ilusionado, -da** *adj* : excited

iluso -sa *adj* : naïve, gullible — ~ *n* : dreamer, visionary — **ilusorio, -ria** *adj* : illusory

ilustrar *vt* **1** : illustrate **2** ACLARAR : explain — **ilustración** *nf, pl* **-ciones 1** : illustration **2** SABER : learning **3 la ilustración** : the Enlightenment — **ilustrado, -da** *adj* **1** : illustrated **2** ERUDITO : learned — **ilustrador, -dora** *n* : illustrator

ilustre *adj* : illustrious

imagen *nf, pl* **imágenes** : image, picture

imaginar *vt* : imagine — **imaginarse** *vr* : imagine — **imaginación** *nf, pl* **-ciones** : imagination — **imaginario, -ria** *adj* : imaginary — **imaginativo, -va** *adj* : imaginative

imán *nm, pl* **imanes** : magnet — **imantar** *vt* : magnetize

imbécil *adj* : stupid, idiotic — ~ *nmf* : idiot

imborrable *adj* : indelible

imbuir {41} *vt* ~ **de** : imbue with

imitar *vt* **1** COPIAR : imitate, copy **2** : impersonate — **imitación** *nf, pl* **-ciones 1** COPIA : imitation, copy **2** : impersonation — **imitador, -dora** *n* : impersonator

impaciencia *nf* : impatience — **impacientar** *vt* : make impatient, exasperate — **impacientarse** *vr* : grow impatient — **impaciente** *adj* : impatient

impacto *nm* : impact

impar *adj* : odd — ~ *nm* : odd number

imparcial *adj* : impartial — **imparcialidad** *nf* : impartiality

impartir *vt* : impart, give

impasible *adj* : impassive

impasse *nm* : impasse

impávido, -da *adj* : fearless

impecable *adj* : impeccable, spotless

impedir {54} *vt* **1** : prevent **2** DIFICULTAR : impede, hinder — **impedido, -da** *adj* : disabled — **impedimento** *nm* : obstacle, impediment-

impeler *vt* : drive, propel

impenetrable *adj* : impenetrable

impenitente *adj* : unrepentant

impensable *adj* : unthinkable — **impensado, -da** *adj* : unexpected

imperar *vi* : reign, rule **2** PREDOMINAR : prevail — **imperante** *adj* : prevailing

imperativo, -va *adj* : imperative — **imperativo** *nm* : imperative

imperceptible *adj* : imperceptible

imperdible *nm* : safety pin

imperdonable *adj* : unforgivable

imperfección *nf, pl* **-ciones** : imperfection — **imperfecto, -ta** *adj* : imperfect — **imperfecto** *nm* : imperfect (tense)

imperial *adj* : imperial — **imperialismo** *nm* : imperialism — **imperialista** *adj & nmf* : imperialist

impericia *nf* : lack of skill

imperio *nm* **1** : empire **2** DOMINIO : rule — **imperioso, -sa** *adj* **1** : imperious **2** URGENTE : pressing, urgent

impermeable *adj* **1** : waterproof **2** ~ **a** : impervious to — ~ *nm* : raincoat

impersonal *adj* : impersonal

impertinente *adj* : impertinent — **impertinencia** *nf* : impertinence

ímpetu *nm* **1** : impetus **2** ENERGÍA : energy, vigor **3** VIOLENCIA : force — **impetuoso, -sa** *adj* : impetuous — **impetuosidad** *nf* : impetuosity

impío, -pía *adj* : impious, ungodly

implacable *adj* : implacable

implantar *vt* **1** : implant **2** ESTABLECER : establish, introduce

implemento *nm Lat* : implement, tool

implicar {72} *vt* **1** : involve, implicate **2** SIGNIFICAR : imply — **implicación** *nf, pl* **-ciones** : implication

implícito, -ta *adj* : implicit

implorar *vt* : implore

imponer {60} *vt* **1** : impose **2** : command (respect, etc.) — *vi* : be imposing — **imponerse** *vr* **1** : assert oneself, command respect **2** PREVALECER : prevail — **imponente** *adj* : imposing, impressive — **imponible** *adj* : taxable

impopular *adj* : unpopular — **impopularidad** *nf* : unpopularity

importación *nf, pl* **-ciones 1** : importation **2 importaciones** *nfpl* : imports — **importado, -da** *adj* : imported — **importador, -dora** *adj* : importing — ~ *n* : importer

importancia *nf* : importance — **importante** *adj* : important — **importar** *vi* 1 : matter, be important 2 **no me importa** : I don't care — *vt* 1 : import 2 ASCENDER A : amount to, cost

importe *nm* 1 : price 2 CANTIDAD : sum, amount

importunar *vt* : bother — **importuno, -na** *adj* 1 : inopportune 2 MOLESTO : bothersome

imposible *adj* : impossible — **imposibilidad** *nf* : impossibility

imposición *nf*, *pl* **-ciones** 1 : imposition 2 IMPUESTO : tax

impostor, -tora *n* : impostor

impotente *adj* : powerless, impotent — **impotencia** *nf* : impotence

impracticable *adj* 1 : impracticable 2 INTRANSITABLE : impassable

impreciso, -sa *adj* : vague, imprecise — **imprecisión** *nf*, *pl* **-siones** 1 : vagueness 2 ERROR : inaccuracy

impredecible *adj* : unpredictable

impregnar *vt* : impregnate

imprenta *nf* 1 : printing 2 : printing shop, press

imprescindible *adj* : essential, indispensable

impresión *nf*, *pl* **-siones** 1 : impression 2 IMPRENTA : printing — **impresionable** *adj* : impressionable — **impresionante** *adj* : impressive — **impresionar** *vt* 1 : impress 2 CONMOVER : affect, move — *vi* : make an impression — **impresionarse** *vr* 1 : be impressed 2 CONMOVERSE : be affected

impreso, -sa *adj* : printed — **impreso** *nm* 1 FORMULARIO : form 2 **~s** *nmpl* : printed matter — **impresor, -sora** *n* : printer — **impresora** *nf* : (computer) printer

imprevisible *adj* : unforeseeable — **imprevisto, -ta** *adj* : unexpected, unforeseen

imprimir {42} *vt* 1 : print 2 DAR : impart, give

improbable *adj* : improbable — **improbabilidad** *nf* : improbability

improcedente *adj* : inappropriate

improductivo, -va *adj* : unproductive

improperio *nm* : insult

impropio, -pia *adj* 1 : inappropriate 2 INCORRECTO : incorrect

improvisar *v* : improvise — **improvisado, -da** *adj* 1 : improvised, impromptu — **improvisación** *nf*, *pl* **-ciones** : improvisation — **improviso: de ~** *adv phr* : suddenly

imprudente *adj* : imprudent, rash —

imprudencia *nf* : imprudence, carelessness

impúdico, -ca *adj* : shameless, indecent

impuesto *nm* 1 : tax 2 **~ sobre la renta** : income tax

impugnar *vt* : challenge, contest

impulsar *vt* : propel, drive — **impulsividad** *nf* : impulsiveness — **impulsivo, -va** *adj* : impulsive — **impulso** *nm* 1 : drive, thrust 2 MOTIVACIÓN : impulse

impune *adj* : unpunished — **impunidad** *nf* : impunity

impuro, -ra *adj* : impure — **impureza** *nf* : impurity

imputar *vt* : impute, attribute

inacabable *adj* : interminable, endless

inaccesible *adj* : inaccessible

inaceptable *adj* : unacceptable

inactivo, -va *adj* : inactive — **inactividad** *nf* : inactivity

inadaptado, -da *adj* : maladjusted — **~** *n* : misfit

inadecuado, -da *adj* 1 : inadequate 2 INAPROPIADO : inappropriate

inadmisible *adj* : inadmissible

inadvertido, -da *adj* 1 : unnoticed 2 DISTRAÍDO : distracted — **inadvertencia** *nf* : oversight

inagotable *adj* : inexhaustible

inaguantable *adj* : unbearable

inalámbrico, -ca *adj* : wireless, cordless

inalcanzable *adj* : unreachable, unattainable

inalterable *adj* 1 : unchangeable 2 : impassive (of character) 3 : fast (of colors)

inanición *nf*, *pl* **-ciones** : starvation, famine

inanimado, -da *adj* : inanimate

inaplicable *adj* : inapplicable

inapreciable *adj* : imperceptible

inapropiado, -da *adj* : inappropriate

inarticulado, -da *adj* : inarticulate

inasequible *adj* : unattainable

inaudito, -ta *adj* : unheard-of, unprecedented

inaugurar *vt* : inaugurate — **inauguración** *nf*, *pl* **-ciones** : inauguration — **inaugural** *adj* : inaugural

inca *adj* : Inca, Incan

incalculable *adj* : incalculable

incandescencia *nf* : incandescence — **incandescente** *adj* : incandescent

incansable *adj* : tireless

incapacitar *vt* : incapacitate, disable — **incapacidad** *nf* : incapacity, inability — **incapaz** *adj*, *pl* **-paces** : incapable

incautar *vt* : confiscate, seize

incendiar *vt* : set fire to, burn (down) — **incendiarse** *vr* : catch fire — **incendiario, -ria** *adj* : incendiary — ~ *n* : arsonist — **incendio** *nm* 1 : fire 2 ~ **premeditado** : arson

incentivo *nm* : incentive

incertidumbre *nf* : uncertainty

incesante *adj* : incessant

incesto *nm* : incest — **incestuoso, -sa** *adj* : incestuous

incidencia *nf* 1 : impact 2 SUCESO : incident — **incidental** *adj* : incidental — **incidente** *nm* : incident

incidir *vi* ~ **en** 1 : fall into (a habit, mistake, etc.) 2 INFLUIR EN : affect, influence

incienso *nm* : incense

incierto, -ta *adj* : uncertain

incinerar *vt* 1 : incinerate 2 : cremate (a corpse) — **incineración** *nf, pl* -**ciones** 1 : incineration 2 : cremation (of a corpse) — **incinerador** *nm* : incinerator

incipiente *adj* : incipient

incisión *nf, pl* -**siones** : incision

incisivo, -va *adj* : incisive — **incisivo** *nm* : incisor

incitar *vt* : incite, rouse

incivilizado, -da *adj* : uncivilized

inclinar *vt* : tilt, lean — **inclinarse** *vr* 1 : lean (over) 2 ~ **a** : be inclined to — **inclinación** *nf, pl* -**ciones** 1 : inclination 2 LADEAR : incline, tilt

incluir {41} *vt* 1 : include 2 ADJUNTAR : enclose — **inclusión** *nf, pl* -**siones** : inclusion — **inclusive** *adv* : up to and including — **inclusivo, -va** *adj* : inclusive — **incluso** *adv* : even, in fact — **incluso, -sa** *adj* : enclosed

incógnito, -ta *adj* 1 : unknown 2 **de** ~ : incognito

incoherente *adj* : incoherent — **incoherencia** *nf* : incoherence

incoloro, -ra *adj* : colorless

incombustible *adj* : fireproof

incomible *adj* : inedible

incomodar *vt* 1 : inconvenience 2 ENFADAR : bother, annoy — **incomodarse** *vr* 1 : take the trouble 2 ENFADARSE : get annoyed — **incomodidad** *nf* : discomfort — **incómodo, -da** *adj* 1 : uncomfortable 2 INCONVENIENTE : inconvenient, awkward

incomparable *adj* : incomparable

incompatible *adj* : incompatible — **incompatibilidad** *nf* : incompatibility

incompetente *adj* : incompetent — **incompetencia** *nf* : incompetence

incompleto, -ta *adj* : incomplete

incomprendido, -da *adj* : misunderstood — **incomprensible** *adj* : incomprehensible — **incomprensión** *nf, pl* -**siones** : lack of understanding

incomunicado, -da *adj* 1 : isolated 2 : in solitary confinement

inconcebible *adj* : inconceivable

inconcluso, -sa *adj* : unfinished

incondicional *adj* : unconditional

inconformista *adj & nmf* : nonconformist

inconfundible *adj* : unmistakable

incongruente *adj* : incongruous

inconmensurable *adj* : vast, immeasurable

inconsciente *adj* 1 : unconscious, unaware 2 IRREFLEXIVO : reckless — ~ *nm* **el** ~ : the unconscious — **inconsciencia** *nf* 1 : unconsciousness 2 INSENSATEZ : thoughtlessness

inconsecuente *adj* : inconsistent — **inconsecuencia** *nf* : inconsistency

inconsiderado, -da *adj* : inconsiderate

inconsistente *adj* 1 : flimsy 2 : watery (of a sauce, etc.) 3 : inconsistent (of an argument) — **inconsistencia** *nf* : inconsistency

inconsolable *adj* : inconsolable

inconstante *adj* : changeable, unreliable — **inconstancia** *nf* : inconstancy

inconstitucional *adj* : unconstitutional

incontable *adj* : countless

incontenible *adj* : irrepressible

incontestable *adj* : indisputable

incontinente *adj* : incontinent — **incontinencia** *nf* : incontinence

inconveniente *adj* 1 : inconvenient 2 INAPROPIADO : inappropriate — ~ *nm* : obstacle, problem — **inconveniencia** *nf* 1 : inconvenience 2 : tactless remark

incorporar *vt* 1 AGREGAR : incorporate, add 2 : mix (in cooking) — **incorporarse** *vr* 1 : sit up 2 ~ **a** : join — **incorporación** *nf, pl* -**ciones** : incorporation

incorrecto, -ta *adj* 1 : incorrect 2 DESCORTÉS : impolite

incorregible *adj* : incorrigible

incrédulo, -la *adj* : incredulous — **incredulidad** *nf* : incredulity, disbelief

increíble *adj* : incredible, unbelievable

incrementar *vt* : increase — **incremento** *nm* : increase

incriminar *vt* 1 : incriminate 2 ACUSAR : accuse

incrustar *vt* : set, inlay — **incrustarse** *vr* : become embedded

incubar *vt* : incubate — **incubadora** *nf* : incubator

incuestionable *adj* : unquestionable
inculcar {72} *vt* : instill
inculpar *vt* : accuse, charge
inculto, -ta *adj* 1 : uneducated 2 : uncultivated (of land)
incumplimiento *nm* 1 : noncompliance 2 ~ **de contrato** : breach of contract
incurable *adj* : incurable
incurrir *vi* ~ **en** 1 : incur (expenses, etc.) 2 : fall into, commit (crimes)
incursión *nf, pl* -**siones** : raid
indagar {52} *vt* : investigate — **indagación** *nf, pl* -**ciones** : investigation
indebido, -da *adj* : undue
indecente *adj* : indecent, obscene — **indecencia** *nf* : indecency, obscenity
indecible *adj* : inexpressible
indecisión *nf, pl* -**siones** : indecision — **indeciso, -sa** *adj* 1 : undecided 2 IRRESOLUTO : indecisive
indefenso, -sa *adj* : defenseless, helpless
indefinido, -da *adj* : indefinite — **indefinidamente** *adv* : indefinitely
indeleble *adj* : indelible
indemnizar {21} *vt* : indemnify, compensate — **indemnización** *nf, pl* -**ciones** : compensation
independiente *adj* : independent — **independencia** *nf* : independence — **independizarse** {21} *vr* : become independent
indescifrable *adj* : indecipherable
indescriptible *adj* : indescribable
indeseable *adj* : undesirable
indestructible *adj* : indestructible
indeterminado, -da *adj* : indeterminate
indicar {72} *vt* 1 : indicate 2 MOSTRAR : show — **indicación** *nf, pl* -**ciones** 1 : sign, indication 2 **indicaciones** *nfpl* : directions — **indicador** *nm* 1 : sign, signal 2 : gauge, dial, meter — **indicativo, -va** *adj* : indicative — **indicativo** *nm* : indicative (mood)
índice *nm* 1 : indication 2 : index (of a book, etc.) 3 : index finger 4 ~ **de natalidad** : birth rate
indicio *nm* : indication, sign
indiferente *adj* 1 : indifferent 2 **me es** ~ : it doesn't matter to me — **indiferencia** *nf* : indifference
indígena *adj* : indigenous, native — ~ *nmf* : native
indigente *adj & nmf* : indigent — **indigencia** *nf* : poverty
indigestión *nf, pl* -**tiones** : indigestion — **indigesto, -ta** *adj* : indigestible
indignar *vt* : outrage, infuriate — **indignarse** *vr* : become indignant — **indignación** *nf, pl* -**ciones** : indignation

— **indignado, -da** *adj* : indignant —
indignidad *nf* : indignity — **indigno, -na** *adj* : unworthy
indio, -dia *adj* 1 : American Indian 2 : Indian (from India)
indirecta *nf* 1 : hint 2 **lanzar una** ~ : drop a hint — **indirecto, -ta** *adj* : indirect
indisciplina *nf* : lack of discipline — **indisciplinado, -da** *adj* : undisciplined
indiscreto, -ta *adj* : indiscreet — **indiscreción** *nf, pl* -**ciones** 1 : indiscretion 2 : tactless remark
indiscriminado, -da *adj* : indiscriminate
indiscutible *adj* : indisputable
indispensable *adj* : indispensable
indisponer {60} *vt* 1 : upset, make ill 2 ENEMISTAR : set against, set at odds — **indisponerse** *vr* 1 : become ill 2 ~ **con** : fall out with — **indisposición** *nf, pl* -**ciones** : indisposition, illness — **indispuesto, -ta** *adj* : unwell, indisposed
indistinto, -ta *adj* : indistinct
individual *adj* : individual — **individualidad** *nf* : individuality — **individualizar** {21} *vt* : individualize — **individuo** *nm* : individual
indivisible *adj* : indivisible
índole *nf* 1 : nature, character 2 TIPO : type, kind
indolente *adj* : indolent, lazy — **indolencia** *nf* : indolence, laziness
indoloro, -ra *adj* : painless
indómito, -ta *adj* : indomitable
indonesio, -sia *adj* : Indonesian
inducir {61} *vt* 1 : induce 2 DEDUCIR : infer
indudable *adj* : beyond doubt — **indudablemente** *adv* : undoubtedly
indulgente *adj* : indulgent — **indulgencia** *nf* : indulgence
indultar *vt* : pardon, reprieve — **indulto** *nm* : pardon, reprieve
industria *nf* : industry — **industrial** *adj* : industrial — ~ *nmf* : industrialist, manufacturer — **industrialización** *nf, pl* -**ciones** : industrialization — **industrializar** {21} *vt* : industrialize — **industrioso, -sia** *adj* : industrious
inédito, -ta *adj* : unpublished
inefable *adj* : inexpressible
ineficaz *adj, pl* -**caces** 1 : ineffective 2 INEFICIENTE : inefficient
ineficiente *adj* : inefficient — **ineficiencia** *nf* : inefficiency
inelegible *adj* : ineligible

ineludible *adj* : unavoidable, inescapable

inepto, -ta *adj* : inept — **ineptitud** *nf* : ineptitude

inequívoco, -ca *adj* : unequivocal

inercia *nf* : inertia

inerme *adj* : unarmed, defenseless

inerte *adj* : inert

inesperado, -da *adj* : unexpected

inestable *adj* : unstable — **inestabilidad** *nf* : instability

inevitable *adj* : inevitable

inexacto, -ta *adj* 1 : inexact 2 INCORRECTO : incorrect, wrong

inexistente *adj* : nonexistent

inexorable *adj* : inexorable

inexperiencia *nf* : inexperience — **inexperto, -ta** *adj* : inexperienced, unskilled

inexplicable *adj* : inexplicable

infalible *adj* : infallible

infame *adj* 1 : infamous, vile 2 *fam* : horrible — **infamia** *nf* : infamy, disgrace

infancia *nf* : infancy — **infanta** *nf* : infanta, princess — **infante** *nm* 1 : infante, prince 2 : infantryman (in the military) — **infantería** *nf* : infantry — **infantil** *adj* 1 : child's, children's 2 INMADURO : childish

infarto *nm* : heart attack

infatigable *adj* : tireless

infectar *vt* : infect — **infectarse** *vr* : become infected — **infección** *nf, pl* -**ciones** : infection — **infeccioso, -sa** *adj* : infectious — **infecto, -ta** *adj* 1 : infected 2 : foul, sickening

infecundo, -da *adj* : infertile

infeliz *adj, pl* -**lices** : unhappy — **infelicidad** *nf* : unhappiness

inferior *adj & nmf* : inferior — **inferioridad** *nf* : inferiority

inferir {76} *vt* 1 DEDUCIR : infer 2 : cause (harm or injury)

infernal *adj* : infernal, hellish

infestar *vt* : infest

infiel *adj* : unfaithful — **infidelidad** *nf* : infidelity

infierno *nm* 1 : hell 2 **el quinto** ~ *fam* : the middle of nowhere

infiltrar *vt* : infiltrate — **infiltrarse** *vr* : infiltrate

infinidad *nf* 1 : infinity 2 **una** ~ **de** : countless — **infinitivo** *nm* : infinitive — **infinito, -ta** *adj* : infinite — **infinito** *nm* : infinity

inflación *nf, pl* -**ciones** : inflation — **inflacionario, -ria** *or* **inflacionista** *adj* : inflationary

inflamar *vt* : inflame — **inflamable** *adj* : flammable, inflammable — **inflamación** *nf, pl* -**ciones** : inflammation — **inflamatorio, -ria** *adj* : inflammatory

inflar *vt* 1 : inflate 2 EXAGERAR : exaggerate — **inflarse** *vr* ~ **de** : swell (up) with

inflexible *adj* : inflexible — **inflexión** *nf, pl* -**xiones** : inflection

infligir {35} *vt* : inflict

influencia *nf* : influence — **influenciar** → **influir**

influenza *nf* : influenza

influir {41} *vt* : influence — *vi* ~ **en** *or* ~ **sobre** : have an influence on — **influjo** *nm* : influence — **influyente** *adj* : influential

información *nf, pl* -**ciones** 1 : information 2 NOTICIAS : news 3 : directory assistance (on the telephone)

informal *adj* 1 : informal 2 IRRESPONSABLE : unreliable

informar *v* : inform — **informarse** *vr* : get information, find out — **informante** *nmf* : informant — **informática** *nf* : information technology — **informativo, -va** *adj* : informative — **informatizar** {21} *vt* : computerize

informe *adj* : shapeless — ~ *nm* 1 : report 2 ~**s** *nmpl* : information, data 3 ~**s** *nmpl* : references (for employment)

infortunado, -da *adj* : unfortunate — **infortunio** *nm* : misfortune

infracción *nf, pl* -**ciones** : violation, infraction

infraestructura *nf* : infrastructure

infrahumano, -na *adj* : subhuman

infranqueable *adj* 1 : impassable 2 INSUPERABLE : insurmountable

infrarrojo, -ja *adj* : infrared

infrecuente *adj* : infrequent

infringir {35} *vt* : infringe

infructuoso, -sa *adj* : fruitless

infundado, -da *adj* : unfounded, baseless

infundir *vt* : instill, infuse — **infusión** *nf, pl* -**siones** : infusion

ingeniar *vt* : invent, think up

ingeniería *nf* : engineering — **ingeniero, -ra** *n* : engineer

ingenio *nm* 1 : ingenuity 2 AGUDEZA : wit 3 MÁQUINA : device, apparatus 4 ~ **azucarero** *Lat* : sugar refinery — **ingenioso, -sa** *adj* 1 : ingenious 2 AGUDO : clever, witty — **ingeniosamente** *adv* : cleverly

ingenuidad *nf* : naïveté, ingenuousness — **ingenuo, -nua** *adj* : naive

ingerir {76} *vt* : ingest, consume

ingle *nf* : groin
inglés, -glesa *adj, mpl* **-gleses** : English — **inglés** *nm* : English (language)
ingrato, -ta *adj* **1** : ungrateful **2 un trabajo ingrato** : a thankless task — **ingratitud** *nf* : ingratitude
ingrediente *nm* : ingredient
ingresar *vt* : deposit — *vi* **~ en** : enter, be admitted into, join — **ingreso** *nm* **1** : entrance, entry **2** : admission (into a hospital, etc.) **3 ~s** *nmpl* : income, earnings
inhábil *adj* **1** : unskillful, clumsy **2 ~ para** : unsuited for — **inhabilidad** *nf* : unskillfulness
inhabitable *adj* : uninhabitable — **inhabitado, -da** *adj* : uninhabited
inhalar *vt* : inhale — **inhalación** *nf* : inhalation
inherente *adj* : inherent
inhibir *vt* : inhibit — **inhibición** *nf, pl* **-ciones** : inhibition
inhóspito, -ta *adj* : inhospitable
inhumano, -na *adj* : inhuman, inhumane — **inhumanidad** *nf* : inhumanity
iniciar *vt* : initiate, begin — **iniciación** *nf, pl* **-ciones 1** : initiation **2** COMIENZO : beginning — **inicial** *adj & nf* : initial — **iniciativa** *nf* : initiative — **inicio** *nm* : start, beginning
inigualado, -da *adj* : unequaled
ininterrumpido, -da *adj* : uninterrupted
injerirse {76} *vr* : interfere — **injerencia** *nf* : interference
injertar *vt* : graft — **injerto** *nm* : graft
injuriar *vt* : insult — **injuria** *nf* : insult — **injurioso, -sa** *adj* : insulting, abusive
injusticia *nf* : injustice, unfairness — **injusto, -ta** *adj* : unfair, unjust
inmaculado, -da *adj* : immaculate
inmaduro, -ra *adj* **1** : immature **2** : unripe (of fruit) — **inmadurez** *nf* : immaturity
inmediaciones *nfpl* : surrounding area
inmediato, -ta *adj* **1** : immediate **2** CONTIGUO : adjoining **3 de ~** : immediately, right away **4 ~ a** : next to, close to — **inmediatamente** *adv* : immediately
inmejorable *adj* : excellent
inmenso, -sa *adj* : immense, vast — **inmensidad** *nf* : immensity
inmerecido, -da *adj* : undeserved
inmersión *nf, pl* **-siones** : immersion
inmigrar *vi* : immigrate — **inmigración** *nf, pl* **-ciones** : immigration — **inmigrante** *adj & nmf* : immigrant
inminente *adj* : imminent, impending — **inminencia** *nf* : imminence

inmiscuirse {41} *vr* : interfere
inmobiliario, -ria *adj* : real estate, property
inmodesto, -ta *adj* : immodest
inmoral *adj* : immoral — **inmoralidad** *nf* : immorality
inmortal *adj & nmf* : immortal — **inmortalidad** *nf* : immortality
inmóvil *adj* : motionless, still — **inmovilizar** {21} *vt* : immobilize
inmueble *nm* : building, property
inmundicia *nf* : filth, trash — **inmundo, -da** *adj* : dirty, filthy
inmunizar {21} *vt* : immunize — **inmune** *adj* : immune — **inmunidad** *nf* : immunity — **inmunización** *nf, pl* **-ciones** : immunization
inmutable *adj* : unchangeable
innato, -ta *adj* : innate
innecesario, -ria *adj* : unnecessary, needless
innegable *adj* : undeniable
innoble *adj* : ignoble
innovar *vt* : introduce — *vi* : innovate — **innovación** *nf, pl* **-ciones** : innovation — **innovador, -dora** *adj* : innovative — **~ n** : innovator
innumerable *adj* : innumerable
inocencia *nf* : innocence — **inocente** *adj & nmf* : innocent — **inocentón, -tona** *adj, mpl* **-tones** : naive — **~ n** : simpleton, dupe
inocular *vt* : inoculate — **inoculación** *nf, pl* **-ciones** : inoculation
inocuo, -cua *adj* : innocuous
inodoro, -ra *adj* : odorless — **inodoro** *nm* : toilet
inofensivo, -va *adj* : inoffensive, harmless
inolvidable *adj* : unforgettable
inoperable *adj* : inoperable
inoperante *adj* : ineffective
inopinado, -da *adj* : unexpected
inoportuno, -na *adj* : untimely, inopportune
inorgánico, -ca *adj* : inorganic
inoxidable *adj* **1** : rustproof **2 acero ~** : stainless steel
inquebrantable *adj* : unwavering
inquietar *vt* : disturb, worry — **inquietarse** *vr* : worry — **inquietante** *adj* : disturbing, worrisome — **inquieto, -ta** *adj* : anxious, worried — **inquietud** *nf* : anxiety, worry
inquilino, -na *n* : tenant
inquirir {4} *vi* : make inquiries — *vt* : investigate
insaciable *adj* : insatiable
insalubre *adj* : unhealthy

insatisfecho, -cha *adj* **1** : unsatisfied **2** DESCONTENTO : dissatisfied

inscribir {33} *vt* **1** : enroll, register **2** GRABAR : inscribe, engrave — **inscribirse** *vr* : register — **inscripción** *nf, pl* **-ciones 1** : inscription **2** REGISTRO : registration

insecto *nm* : insect — **insecticida** *nm* : insecticide

inseguro, -ra *adj* **1** : insecure **2** PELIGROSO : unsafe **3** DUDOSO : uncertain — **inseguridad** *nf* **1** : insecurity **2** PELIGRO : lack of safety **3** DUDA : uncertainty

inseminar *vt* : inseminate — **inseminación** *nf, pl* **-ciones** : insemination

insensato, -ta *adj* : senseless, foolish — **insensatez** *nf* : foolishness, thoughtlessness

insensible *adj* **1** : insensitive, unfeeling **2** : numb (in medicine) **3** IMPERCEPTIBLE : imperceptible — **insensibilidad** *nf* : insensitivity

inseparable *adj* : inseparable

insertar *vt* : insert

insidia *nf* : snare, trap — **insidioso, -sa** *adj* : insidious

insigne *adj* : noted, famous

insignia *nf* **1** : insignia, badge **2** BANDERA : flag

insignificante *adj* : insignificant, negligible

insincero, -ra *adj* : insincere

insinuar {3} *vt* : insinuate — **insinuarse** *vr* ~ **en** : worm one's way into — **insinuación** *nf, pl* **-ciones** : insinuation — **insinuante** *adj* : insinuating, suggestive

insípido, -da *adj* : insipid

insistir *v* : insist — **insistencia** *nf* : insistence — **insistente** *adj* : insistent

insociable *adj* : unsociable

insolación *nf, pl* **-ciones** : sunstroke

insolencia *nf* : insolence — **insolente** *adj* : insolent

insólito, -ta *adj* : rare, unusual

insoluble *adj* : insoluble

insolvencia *nf* : insolvency, bankruptcy — **insolvente** *adj* : insolvent, bankrupt

insomnio *nm* : insomnia — **insomne** *nmf* : insomniac

insondable *adj* : unfathomable

insonorizado, -da *adj* : soundproof

insoportable *adj* : unbearable

insospechado, -da *adj* : unexpected

insostenible *adj* : untenable

inspeccionar *vt* : inspect — **inspección** *nf, pl* **-ciones** : inspection — **inspector, -tora** *n* : inspector

inspirar *vt* : inspire — *vi* : inhale — **inspirarse** *vr* : be inspired — **inspiración** *nf, pl* **-ciones 1** : inspiration **2** RESPIRACIÓN : inhalation — **inspirador, -dora** *adj* : inspirational

instalar *vt* : install — **instalarse** *vr* : settle — **instalación** *nf, pl* **-ciones** : installation

instancia *nf* **1** : request **2 en última** ~ : ultimately, as a last resort

instantáneo, -nea *adj* : instantaneous, instant — **instantánea** *nf* : snapshot — **instante** *nm* **1** : instant **2 a cada** ~ : frequently, all the time **3 al** ~ : immediately

instar *vt* : urge, press

instaurar *vt* : establish — **instauración** *nf, pl* **-ciones** : establishment

instigar {52} *vt* : incite, instigate — **instigador, -dora** *n* : instigator

instinto *nm* : instinct — **instintivo, -va** *adj* : instinctive

institución *nf, pl* **-ciones** : institution — **institucional** *adj* : institutional — **institucionalizar** {21} *vt* : institutionalize — **instituir** {41} *vt* : institute, establish — **instituto** *nm* : institute — **institutriz** *nf, pl* **-trices** : governess

instruir {41} *vt* : instruct — **instrucción** *nf, pl* **-ciones 1** : instruction **2 instrucciones** *nfpl* : instructions, directions — **instructivo, -va** *adj* : instructive — **instructor, -tora** *n* : instructor

instrumento *nm* : instrument — **instrumental** *adj* : instrumental

insubordinarse *vr* : rebel — **insubordinado, -da** *adj* : insubordinate — **insubordinación** *nf, pl* **-ciones** : insubordination

insuficiente *adj* : insufficient, inadequate — **insuficiencia** *nf* **1** : insufficiency, inadequacy **2** ~ **cardíaca** : heart failure

insufrible *adj* : insufferable

insular *adj* : insular, island

insulina *nf* : insulin

insulso, -sa *adj* **1** : insipid, bland **2** SOSO : dull

insultar *vt* : insult — **insultante** *adj* : insulting — **insulto** *nm* : insult

insuperable *adj* : insurmountable

insurgente *adj & nmf* : insurgent

insurrección *nf, pl* **-ciones** : insurrection, uprising

intachable *adj* : irreproachable

intacto, -ta *adj* : intact

intangible *adj* : intangible

integrar *vt* : integrate — **integrarse** *vr* : become integrated — **integración**

nf, pl **-ciones** : integration — **integral**
adj 1 : integral 2 **pan ~** : whole grain
bread — **íntegro, -gra** *adj* 1 : honest,
upright 2 ENTERO : whole, complete —
integridad *nf* 1 RECTITUD : integrity 2
TOTALIDAD : wholeness
intelecto *nm* : intellect — **intelectual**
adj & nmf : intellectual
inteligencia *nf* : intelligence — **inteligente** *adj* : intelligent — **inteligible** *adj* : intelligible
intemperie *nf* **a la ~** : in the open air,
outside
intempestivo, -va *adj* : untimely, inopportune
intención *nf, pl* **-ciones** : intention, intent — **intencionado, -da** *adj* 1 : intended 2 **bien ~** : well-meaning 3
mal ~ : malicious — **intencional**
: intentional
intensidad *nf* : intensity — **intensificar**
{72} *vt* : intensify — **intensificarse** *vr*
: intensify — **intensivo, -va** *adj* : intensive — **intenso, -sa** *adj* : intense
intentar *vt* : attempt, try — **intento** *nm*
1 : intention 2 TENTATIVA : attempt
interactuar {3} *vi* : interact — **interacción** *nf, pl* **-ciones** : interaction — **interactivo, -va** *adj* : interactive
intercalar *vt* : insert, intersperse
intercambio *nm* : exchange — **intercambiable** *adj* : interchangeable —
intercambiar *vt* : exchange, trade
interceder *vi* : intercede
interceptar *vt* : intercept — **intercepción** *nf, pl* **-ciones** : interception
intercesión *nf, pl* **-siones** : intercession
interés *nm, pl* **-reses** : interest — **interesado, -da** *adj* 1 : interested 2 EGOISTA : selfish — **interesante** *adj* : interesting — **interesar** *vt* : interest —
vi : be of interest — **interesarse** *vr*
: take an interest
interfaz *nf, pl* **-faces** : interface
interferir {76} *vi* : interfere — *vt* : interfere with — **interferencia** *nf* : interference
interino, -na *adj* : temporary, interim —
interiormente *adv* : inwardly
interior *adj* : interior, inner — **~** *nm*
: interior, inside — **interiormente** *adv*
: inwardly
interjección *nf, pl* **-ciones** : interjection
interlocutor, -tora *n* : speaker
intermediario, -ria *adj & n* : intermediary
intermedio, -dia *adj* : intermediate —
intermedio *nm* : intermission

interminable *adj* : interminable, endless
intermisión *nf, pl* **-siones** : intermission, pause
intermitente *adj* : intermittent — **~**
nm : blinker, turn signal
internacional *adj* : international
internar *vt* : commit, confine — **internarse** *vr* : penetrate — **internado**
nm : boarding school — **interno, -na**
adj : internal — **~** *n* 1 : boarder 2 : inmate (in a jail, etc.)
interponer {60} *vt* : interpose — **interponerse** *vr* : intervene
interpretar *vt* 1 : interpret 2 : play, perform (in theater, etc.) — **interpretación** *nf, pl* **-ciones** : interpretation — **intérprete** *nmf* 1 TRADUCTOR
: interpreter 2 : performer (of music)
interrogar {52} *vt* : interrogate, question — **interrogación** *nf, pl* **-ciones**
: interrogation 2 **signo de ~** : question mark — **interrogativo, -va** *adj*
: interrogative — **interrogatorio** *nm*
: interrogation, questioning
interrumpir *v* : interrupt — **interrupción** *nf, pl* **-ciones** : interruption —
interruptor *nm* : (electrical) switch
intersección *nf, pl* **-ciones** : intersection
intervalo *nm* : interval
intervenir {87} *vi* 1 : take part 2 MEDIAR : intervene — *vt* 1 : tap (a telephone) 2 INSPECCIONAR : audit 3 OPERAR : operate on — **intervención** *nf, pl*
-ciones 1 : intervention 2 : audit (in
business) 3 *or* **~ quirúrgica** : operation — **interventor, -tora** *n* : inspector, auditor
intestino *nm* : intestine — **intestinal**
adj : intestinal
intimar *vi* **~ con** : become friendly
with — **intimidad** *nf* 1 : private life 2
AMISTAD : intimacy
intimidar *vt* : intimidate
íntimo, -ma *adj* 1 : intimate, close 2 PRIVADO : private
intolerable *adj* : intolerable — **intolerancia** *nf* : intolerance — **intolerante**
adj : intolerant
intoxicar {72} *vt* : poison — **intoxicación** *nf, pl* **-ciones** : poisoning
intranquilizar {21} *vt* : make uneasy —
intranquilizarse *vr* : be anxious — **intranquilidad** *nf* : uneasiness, anxiety
— **intranquilo, -la** *adj* : uneasy, worried
intransigente *adj* : unyielding, intransigent
intransitable *adj* : impassable

intransitivo, -va *adj* : intransitive
intrascendente *adj* : unimportant, insignificant
intravenoso, -sa *adj* : intravenous
intrépido, -da *adj* : intrepid, fearless
intrigar {52} *v* : intrigue — **intriga** *nf* : intrigue — **intrigante** *adj* : intriguing
intrincado, -da *adj* : intricate, involved
intrínseco, -ca *adj* : intrinsic — **intrínsecament** *adv* : intrinsically, inherently
introducción *nf, pl* **-ciones** : introduction — **introducir** {61} *vt* **1** : introduce **2** METER : insert — **introducirse** *vr* ~ **en** : penetrate, get into — **introductorio, -ria** *adj* : introductory
intromisión *nf, pl* **-siones** : interference
introvertido, -da *adj* : introverted — ~ *n* : introvert
intrusión *nf, pl* **-siones** : intrusion — **intruso, -sa** *adj* : intrusive — ~ *n* : intruder
intuir {41} *vt* : sense — **intuición** *nf, pl* **-ciones** : intuition — **intuitivo, -va** *adj* : intuitive
inundar *vt* : flood — **inundarse** *vr* ~ **de** : be inundated with — **inundación** *nf, pl* **-ciones** : flood
inusitado, -da *adj* : unusual, uncommon
inútil *adj* **1** : useless **2** INVÁLIDO : disabled — **inutilidad** *nf* : uselessness — **inutilizar** {21} *vt* **1** : make useless **2** INCAPACITAR : disable
invadir *vt* : invade
invalidez *nf, pl* **-deces 1** : invalidity **2** : disability (in medicine) — **inválido, -da** *adj & n* : invalid
invalorable *adj Lat* : invaluable
invariable *adj* : invariable
invasión *nf, pl* **-siones** : invasion — **invasor, -sora** *adj* : invading — ~ *n* : invader
invencible *adj* : invincible
inventar *vt* **1** : invent **2** : fabricate, make up (a word, an excuse, etc.) — **invención** *nf, pl* **-ciones 1** : invention **2** MENTIRA : lie, fabrication
inventario *nm* : inventory
inventiva *nf* : inventiveness — **inventivo, -va** *adj* : inventive — **inventor, -tora** *n* : inventor
invernadero *nm* : greenhouse
invernal *adj* : winter
inverosímil *adj* : unlikely
inversión *nf, pl* **-siones 1** : inversion, reversal **2** : investment (of money, time, etc.)

inverso, -sa *adj* **1** : inverse **2** CONTRARIO : opposite **3 a la inversa** : the other way around, inversely
inversor, -sora *n* : investor
invertebrado, -da *adj* : invertebrate — **invertebrado** *nm* : invertebrate
invertir {76} *vt* **1** : invert, reverse **2** : invest (money, time, etc.) — *vi* : make an investment
investidura *nf* : investiture
investigar {52} *vt* **1** : investigate **2** ESTUDIAR : research — *vi* ~ **sobre** : do research into — **investigación** *nf, pl* **-ciones 1** : investigation **2** ESTUDIO : research — **investigador, -dora** *n* : investigator, researcher
investir {54} *vt* : invest
inveterado, -da *adj* : deep-seated, inveterate
invicto, -ta *adj* : undefeated
invierno *nm* : winter
invisible *adj* : invisible — **invisibilidad** *nf* : invisibility
invitar *vt* : invite — **invitación** *nf, pl* **-ciones** : invitation — **invitado, -da** *n* : guest
invocar {72} *vt* : invoke — **invocación** *nf, pl* **-ciones** : invocation
involuntario, -ria *adj* : involuntary
invulnerable *adj* : invulnerable
inyectar *vt* : inject — **inyección** *nf, pl* **-ciones** : injection, shot — **inyectado, -da** *adj* **ojos inyectados** : bloodshot eyes
ion *nm* : ion — **ionizar** {21} *vt* : ionize
ir {43} *vi* **1** : go **2** FUNCIONAR : work, function **3** CONVENIR : suit **4 ¿cómo te va?** : how are you? **5** ~ **con prisa** : be in a hurry **6** ~ **por** : follow, go along **7 vamos** : let's go — *v aux* **1** ~ **a** : be going to, be about to **2** ~ **caminando** : take a walk **3 vamos a ver** : we shall see — **irse** *vr* : go away, be gone
ira *nf* : rage, anger — **iracundo, -da** *adj* : irate, angry
iraní *adj* : Iranian
iraquí *adj* : Iraqi
iris *nms & pl* **1** : iris (of the eye) **2 arco** ~ : rainbow
irlandés, -desa *adj, mpl* **-deses** : Irish
ironía *nf* : irony — **irónico, -ca** *adj* : ironic, ironical
irracional *adj* : irrational
irradiar *vt* : radiate, irradiate
irrazonable *adj* : unreasonable
irreal *adj* : unreal
irreconciliable *adj* : irreconcilable
irreconocible *adj* : unrecognizable
irrecuperable *adj* : irretrievable

irreductible *adj* : unyielding
irreemplazable *adj* : irreplaceable
irreflexivo, -va *adj* : rash, unthinking
irrefutable *adj* : irrefutable
irregular *adj* : irregular — **irregularidad** *nf* : irregularity
irrelevante *adj* : irrelevant
irreparable *adj* : irreparable
irreprimible *adj* : irrepressible
irreprochable *adj* : irreproachable
irresistible *adj* : irresistible
irresoluto, -ta *adj* : indecisive, irresolute
irrespetuoso, -sa *adj* : disrespectful
irresponsable *adj* : irresponsible — **irresponsabilidad** *nf* : irresponsibility
irreverente *adj* : irreverent
irreversible *adj* : irreversible
irrevocable *adj* : irrevocable
irrigar {52} *vt* : irrigate — **irrigación** *nf, pl* **-ciones** : irrigation

irrisorio, -ria *adj* : laughable, ridiculous
irritar *vt* : irritate — **irritarse** *vr* : get annoyed — **irritable** *adj* : irritable — **irritación** *nf, pl* **-ciones** : irritation — **irritante** *adj* : irritating
irrompible *adj* : unbreakable
irrumpir *vi* ~ **en** : burst into
isla *nf* : island
islámico, -ca *adj* : Islamic, Muslim
islandés, -desa *adj, mpl* **-deses** : Icelandic
isleño, -ña *n* : islander
israelí *adj* : Israeli
istmo *nm* : isthmus
italiano, -na *adj* : Italian — **italiano** *nm* : Italian (language)
itinerario *nm* : itinerary
izar {21} *vt* : hoist, raise
izquierda *nf* : left — **izquierdista** *adj & nmf* : leftist — **izquierdo, -da** *adj* : left

J

j *nf* : j, tenth letter of the Spanish alphabet
jabalí *nm, pl* **-líes** : wild boar
jabalina *nf* : javelin
jabón *nm, pl* **-bones** : soap — **jabonar** *vt* : soap (up) — **jabonera** *nf* : soap dish — **jabonoso, -sa** *adj* : soapy
jaca *nf* : pony
jacinto *nm* : hyacinth
jactarse *vr* : boast, brag — **jactancia** *nf* : boastfulness, bragging — **jactancioso, -sa** *adj* : boastful
jadear *vi* : pant, gasp — **jadeante** *adj* : panting, breathless — **jadeo** *nm* : gasp, panting
jaez *nm, pl* **jaeces 1** : harness **2 jaeces** *nmpl* : trappings
jaguar *nm* : jaguar
jaiba *nf Lat* : crab
jalapeño *nm Lat* : jalapeño pepper
jalar *v Lat* : pull, tug
jalea *nf* : jelly
jaleo *nm* **1** : uproar, racket **2 armar un** ~ : raise a ruckus
jalón *nm, pl* **-lones** *Lat* : pull, tug
jamaicano, -na *or* **jamaiquino, -na** *adj* : Jamaican
jamás *adv* **1** : never **2 para siempre** ~ : for ever and ever
jamelgo *nm* : nag (horse)
jamón *nm, pl* **-mones 1** : ham **2** ~ **serrano** : cured ham
Januká *nmf* : Hanukkah

japonés, -nesa *adj, mpl* **-neses** : Japanese — **japonés** *nm* : Japanese (language)
jaque *nm* **1** : check (in chess) **2** ~ **mate** : checkmate
jaqueca *nf* : headache, migraine
jarabe *nm* : syrup
jardín *nm, pl* **-dines 1** : garden **2** ~ **infantil** *or* ~ **de niños** *Lat* : kindergarten — **jardinería** *nf* : gardening — **jardinero, -ra** *n* : gardener
jarra *nf* : pitcher, jug — **jarro** *nm* : pitcher — **jarrón** *nm, pl* **-rrones** : vase
jaula *nf* : cage
jauría *nf* : pack of hounds
jazmín *nm, pl* **-mines** : jasmine
jazz ['jas, 'dʒas] *nm* : jazz
jeans ['jins, 'dʒins] *nmpl* : jeans
jefe, -fa *fam* **1** : chief, leader PATRÓN : boss **3** ~ **de cocina** : chef — **jefatura** *nf* **1** : leadership **2** SEDE : headquarters
jengibre *nm* : ginger
jeque *nm* : sheikh, sheik
jerarquía *nf* **1** : hierarchy **2** RANGO : rank — **jerárquico, -ca** *adj* : hierarchical
jerez *nm, pl* **-reces** : sherry
jerga *nf* **1** : coarse cloth **2** ARGOT : jargon, slang
jerigonza *nf* **1** : jargon **2** GALIMATÍAS : gibberish

jeringa or **jeringuilla** nf : syringe — **jeringar** {52} vt fam : annoy, pester

jeroglífico nm : hieroglyphic

jersey nm, pl **-seys** : jersey

jesuita adj & nm : Jesuit

Jesús nm : Jesus

jilguero nm : goldfinch

jinete nmf : horseman, horsewoman f, rider

jirafa nf : giraffe

jirón nm, pl **-rones** : shred, tatter

jitomate nm Lat : tomato

jockey ['joki, 'dʒo-] nmf, pl **-keys** [-kis] : jockey

jocoso, -sa adj : humorous, jocular

jofaina nf : washbowl

jolgorio nm : merrymaking

jornada nf 1 : day's journey 2 : working day — **jornal** nm : day's pay — **jornalero, -ra** n : day laborer

joroba nf : hump — **jorobado, -da** adj : hunchbacked, humpbacked — ~ n : hunchback — **jorobar** vt fam : annoy

jota nf 1 : iota, jot 2 **no veo ni** ~ : I can't see a thing

joven adj, pl **jóvenes** : young — ~ nmf : young man m, young woman f, youth

jovial adj : jovial, cheerful

joya nf : jewel — **joyería** nf : jewelry store — **joyero, -ra** n : jeweler — **joyero** nm : jewelry box

juanete nm : bunion

jubilación nf, pl **-ciones** : retirement — **jubilado, -da** adj : retired — ~ nmf : retiree — **jubilar** vt : retire, pension off — **jubilarse** vr : retire — **jubileo** nm : jubilee

júbilo nm : joy, jubilation — **jubiloso, -sa** adj : joyous, jubilant

judaísmo nm : Judaism

judía nf 1 : bean 2 or ~ **verde** : green bean, string bean

judicial adj : judicial

judío, -día adj : Jewish — ~ n : Jew

judo ['juðo, 'dʒu-] nm : judo

juego nm 1 : game 2 : playing (of children, etc.) 3 or ~**s de azar** : gambling 4 CONJUNTO : set 5 **estar en** ~ : be at stake 6 **fuera de** ~ : offside (in sports) 7 **hacer** ~ : go together, match 8 ~ **de manos** : conjuring trick 9 **poner en** ~ : bring into play

juerga nf fam : spree, binge

jueves nms & pl : Thursday

juez nmf, pl **jueces** 1 : judge 2 ÁRBITRO : umpire, referee

jugar {44} vi 1 : play 2 : gamble (in a casino, etc.) 3 APOSTAR : bet 4 ~ **(al) tenis** : play tennis — vt : play — **jugarse** vr : risk, gamble (away) — **jugada** nf 1 : play, move 2 TRETA : (dirty) trick — **jugador, -dora** n 1 : player 2 : gambler

juglar nm : minstrel

jugo nm 1 : juice 2 SUSTANCIA : substance, essence — **jugoso, -sa** adj 1 : juicy 2 SUSTANCIAL : substantial, important

juguete nm : toy — **juguetear** vi : play — **juguetería** nf : toy store — **juguetón, -tona** adj, mpl **-tones** : playful

juicio nm 1 : judgment 2 RAZÓN : reason, sense 3 **a mi** ~ : in my opinion — **juicioso, -sa** adj : wise, sensible

julio nm : July

junco nm : reed, rush

jungla nf : jungle

junio nm : June

juntar vt 1 UNIR : join, unite 2 REUNIR : collect — **juntarse** vr 1 : join (together) 2 REUNIRSE : meet, get together — **junta** nf 1 : board, committee 2 REUNIÓN : meeting 3 : (political) junta 4 : joint, gasket — **junto, -ta** adj 1 : joined 2 PRÓXIMO : close, adjacent 3 (used adverbially) : together 4 ~ **a** : next to 5 ~ **con** : together with — **juntura** nf : joint

Júpiter nm : Jupiter

jurar v 1 : swear 2 ~ **en falso** : commit perjury — **jurado** nm 1 : jury 2 : juror, member of a jury — **juramento** nm : oath

jurídico, -ca adj : legal

jurisdicción nf, pl **-ciones** : jurisdiction

jurisprudencia nf : jurisprudence

justamente adv 1 : fairly, justly 2 PRECISAMENTE : precisely, exactly

justicia nf : justice, fairness

justificar {72} vt 1 : justify 2 DISCULPAR : excuse, vindicate — **justificación** nf, pl **-ciones** : justification

justo, -ta adj 1 : just, fair 2 EXACTO : exact 3 APRETADO : tight — **justo** adv 1 : just, exactly 2 ~ **a tiempo** : just in time

juvenil adj : youthful — **juventud** nf 1 : youth 2 JÓVENES : young people

juzgar {52} vt 1 : try (a case in court) 2 ESTIMAR : judge, consider 3 **a** ~ **por** : judging by — **juzgado** nm : court, tribunal

K

k *nf* : k, eleventh letter of the Spanish alphabet
kaki → caqui
karate *or* **kárate** *nm* : karate
kilo *nm* : kilo — **kilogramo** *nm* : kilogram

kilómetro *nm* : kilometer — **kilometraje** *nm* : distance in kilometers, mileage — **kilométrico, -ca** *adj fam* : endless
kilovatio *nm* : kilowatt
kiosco *nm* → **quiosco**

L

l *nf* : l, twelfth letter of the Spanish alphabet
la *pron* **1** : her, it **2** (*formal*) : you **3** ~ **que** : the one who — ~ *art* → **el**
laberinto *nm* : labyrinth, maze
labia *nf fam* : gift of gab
labio *nm* : lip
labor *nf* **1** : work, labor **2** TAREA : task **3** ~**es domésticas** : housework — **laborable** *adj* **día** ~ : business day — **laborar** *vi* : work — **laboratorio** *nm* : laboratory, lab — **laborioso, -sa** *adj* : laborious
labrar *vt* **1** : cultivate, till **2** : work (metals), carve (stone, wood) **3** CAUSAR : cause, bring about — **labrado, -da** *adj* **1** : cultivated, tilled **2** : carved, wrought — **labrador, -dora** *n* : farmer — **labranza** *nf* : farming
laca *nf* **1** : lacquer **2** : hair spray
lacayo *nm* **1** : lackey
lacerar *vt* : lacerate
lacio, -cia *adj* **1** : limp **2** : straight (of hair)
lacónico, -ca *adj* : laconic
lacra *nf* : scar
lacrar *vt* : seal — **lacre** *nm* : sealing wax
lacrimógeno, -na *adj* **gas lacrimógeno** : tear gas — **lacrimoso, -sa** *adj* : tearful
lácteo, -tea *adj* **1** : dairy **2 Vía Láctea** : Milky Way
ladear *vt* : tilt — **ladearse** *vr* : lean
ladera *nf* : slope, hillside
ladino, -na *adj* : crafty
lado *nm* **1** : side **2 al** ~ : next door, nearby **3 al** ~ **de** : beside, next to **4 de** ~ : sideways **5 por otro** ~ : on the other hand **6 por todos** ~**s** : everywhere, all around
ladrar *vi* : bark — **ladrido** *nm* : bark
ladrillo *nm* : brick

ladrón, -drona *n, mpl* **-drones** : thief
lagarto *nm* : lizard — **lagartija** *nf* : (small) lizard
lago *nm* : lake
lágrima *nf* : tear
laguna *nf* **1** : lagoon **2** VACÍO : gap
laico, -ca *adj* : lay, secular — ~ *n* : layman *m*, layperson
lamentar *vt* **1** : regret, be sorry about **2 lo lamento** : I'm sorry — **lamentarse** *vr* : lament — **lamentable** *adj* **1** : deplorable **2** TRISTE : sad, pitiful — **lamento** *nm* : lament, moan
lamer *vt* **1** : lick **2** : lap (against) — **lamida** *nf* : lick
lámina *nf* **1** PLANCHA : sheet **2** DIBUJO : plate, illustration — **laminar** *vt* : laminate
lámpara *nf* : lamp
lampiño, -ña *adj* : beardless, hairless
lana *nf* **1** : wool **2 de** ~ : woolen
lance *nm* **1** : event, incident **2** : throw (of dice, etc.) **3** RIÑA : quarrel
lanceta *nf* : lancet
lancha *nf* **1** : boat, launch **2** ~ **motora** : motorboat
langosta *nf* **1** : lobster **2** : locust (insect) — **langostino** *nm* : prawn, crayfish
languidecer {53} *vi* : languish — **languidez** *nf, pl* **-deces** : languor — **lánguido, -da** *adj* : languid, listless
lanilla *nf* : nap (of fabric)
lanudo, -da *adj* : woolly
lanza *nf* : spear, lance
lanzar {21} *vt* **1** : throw **2** : shoot (a glance), give (a sigh, etc.) **3** : launch (a missile, a project) — **lanzarse** *vr* : throw oneself — **lanzamiento** *nm* : throwing, launching
lapicero *nm* : (mechanical) pencil
lápida *nf* : tombstone

lapidar *vt* : stone
lápiz *nm, pl* **-pices 1** : pencil **2 ~ de labios** : lipstick
lapso *nm* : lapse (of time) — **lapsus** *nms & pl* : lapse, slip (of the tongue)
largar {52} *vt* **1** AFLOJAR : loosen, slacken **2** *fam* : give — **largarse** *vr fam* : go away, beat it — **largo, -ga** *adj* **1** : long **2 a la larga** : in the long run **3 a lo largo** : lengthwise **4 a lo largo de** : along — **largo** *nm* : length — **largometraje** *nm* : feature film — **largueza** *nf* : generosity
laringe *nf* : larynx — **laringitis** *nfs & pl* : laryngitis
larva *nf* : larva
las → **el**
lascivo, -va *adj* : lascivious, lewd
láser *nm* : laser
lastimar *vt* : hurt — **lastimarse** *vr* : hurt oneself — **lástima** *nf* **1** : pity **2 dar ~** : be pitiful **3 me dan ~** : I feel sorry for them **4 ¡qué ~!** : what a shame! — **lastimero, -ra** *adj* : pitiful, wretched — **lastimoso, -sa** *adj* : pitiful, terrible
lastre *nm* : ballast
lata *nf* **1** : tinplate **2** : (tin) can **3** *fam* : nuisance, bore **4 dar (la) lata a** *fam* : bother, annoy
latente *adj* : latent
lateral *adj* : side, lateral
latido *nm* **1** : beat, throb **2 ~ del corazón** : heartbeat
latifundio *nm* : large estate
látigo *nm* : whip — **latigazo** *nm* : lash
latín *nm* : Latin (language)
latino, -na *adj* **1** : Latin **2** : Latin-American — **~** *n* : Latin American — **latinoamericano, -na** *adj* : Latin-American — **~** *n* : Latin American
latir *vi* : beat, throb
latitud *nf* : latitude
latón *nm, pl* **-tones** : brass
latoso, -sa *adj fam* : annoying
laúd *nm* : lute
laudable *adj* : laudable
laureado, -da *adj* : prize-winning
laurel *nm* **1** : laurel **2** : bay leaf (in cooking)
lava *nf* : lava
lavar *vt* : wash — **lavarse** *vr* **1** : wash oneself **2 ~ las manos** : wash one's hands — **lavable** *adj* : washable — **lavabo** *nm* **1** : sink **2** RETRETE : lavatory, toilet — **lavadero** *nm* : laundry room — **lavado** *nm* : wash, washing — **lavadora** *nf* : washing machine — **lavamanos** *nms & pl* : washbowl — **lavandería** *nf* : laundry (service) — **lavaplatos** *nms & pl* **1** : dishwasher **2**

Lat : kitchen sink — **lavativa** *nf* : enema — **lavatorio** *nm* : lavatory, washroom — **lavavajillas** *nms & pl* : dishwasher
laxante *adj & nm* : laxative — **laxo, -xa** *adj* : loose
lazo *nm* **1** VÍNCULO : link, bond **2** LAZADA : bow **3** : lasso, lariat — **lazada** *nf* : bow, loop
le *pron* **1** : (to) her, (to) him, (to) it **2** *(formal)* : (to) you **3** *(as direct object)* : him, you
leal *adj* : loyal, faithful — **lealtad** *nf* : loyalty, allegiance
lebrel *nm* : hound
lección *nf, pl* **-ciones 1** : lesson **2** : lecture (in a classroom)
leche *nf* **1** : milk **2 ~ descremada** or **~ desnatada** : skim milk **3 ~ en polvo** : powdered milk — **lechera** *nf* : milk jug — **lechería** *nf* : dairy store — **lechero, -ra** *adj* : dairy — **~** *n* : milkman *m*, milk dealer
lecho *nm* : bed
lechón, -chona *n, mpl* **-chones** : suckling pig
lechoso, -sa *adj* : milky
lechuga *nf* : lettuce
lechuza *nf* : owl
lector, -tora *n* : reader — **lectura** *nf* **1** : reading **2** ESCRITOS : reading matter
leer {20} *v* : read
legación *nf, pl* **-ciones** : legation
legado *nm* **1** : legacy **2** ENVIADO : legate, emissary
legajo *nm* : dossier, file
legal *adj* : legal — **legalidad** *nf* : legality — **legalizar** {21} *vt* : legalize — **legalización** *nf, pl* **-ciones** : legalization
legar {52} *vt* : bequeath
legendario, -ria *adj* : legendary
legible *adj* : legible
legión *nf, pl* **-giones** : legion — **legionario, -ria** *n* : legionnaire
legislar *vi* : legislate — **legislación** *nf, pl* **-ciones** : legislation — **legislador, -dora** *n* : legislator — **legislatura** *nf* : legislature
legítimo, -ma *adj* **1** : legitimate **2** GENUINO : authentic — **legitimidad** *nf* : legitimacy
lego, -ga *adj* **1** : secular, lay **2** IGNORANTE : ignorant — **~** *n* : layman *m*, layperson
legua *nf* : league
legumbre *nf* : vegetable
leído, -da *adj* : well-read
lejano, -na *adj* : distant, far away — **lejanía** *nf* : distance
lejía *nf* : bleach

lejos *adv* **1** : far (away) **2 a lo ~** : in the distance **3 de ~** *or* **desde ~** : from afar **4 ~ de** : far from

lelo, -la *adj* : silly, stupid

lema *nm* : motto

lencería *nf* **1** : linen **2** : (women's) lingerie

lengua *nf* **1** : tongue **2** IDIOMA : language **3 morderse la ~** : hold one's tongue

lenguado *nm* : sole, flounder

lenguaje *nm* : language

lengüeta *nf* **1** : tongue (of a shoe) **2** : reed (of a musical instrument)

lengüetada *nf* **beber a ~s** : lap (up)

lente *nmf* **1** : lens **2 ~s** *nmpl* : eyeglasses **3 ~s de contacto** : contact lenses

lenteja *nf* : lentil — **lentejuela** *nf* : sequin

lento, -ta *adj* : slow — **lento** *adv* : slowly — **lentitud** *nf* : slowness

leña *nf* : firewood — **leñador, -dora** *n* : lumberjack, woodcutter — **leño** *nm* : log

león, -ona *n, mpl* **leones** : lion, lioness *f*

leopardo *nm* : leopard

leotardo *nm* : leotard, tights *pl*

lepra *nf* : leprosy — **leproso, -sa** *n* : leper

lerdo, -da *adj* **1** TORPE : clumsy **2** TONTO : slow-witted

les *pron* **1** : (to) them, (to) you **2** (*as direct object*) : them, you

lesbiano, -na *adj* : lesbian — **lesbiana** *nf* : lesbian — **lesbianismo** *nm* : lesbianism

lesión *nf, pl* **-siones** : lesion, wound — **lesionado, -da** *adj* : injured, wounded — **lesionar** *vt* **1** : injure, wound **2** DAÑAR : damage

letal *adj* : lethal

letanía *nf* : litany

letárgico, -ca *adj* : lethargic — **letargo** *nm* : lethargy

letra *nf* **1** : letter **2** ESCRITURA : handwriting **3** : lyrics *pl* (of a song) **4 ~ de cambio** : bill of exchange **5 ~s** *nfpl* : arts — **letrado, -da** *adj* : learned — **letrero** *nm* : sign, notice

letrina *nf* : latrine

leucemia *nf* : leukemia

levadizo, -za *adj* **puente levadizo** : drawbridge

levadura *nf* **1** : yeast **2 ~ en polvo** : baking powder

levantar *vt* **1** : lift, raise **2** RECOGER : pick up **3** CONSTRUIR : erect, put up **4** ENCENDER : rouse, stir up **5 ~ la mesa** *Lat* : clear the table — **levan-**

-tarse *vr* **1** : rise, stand up **2** : get out of bed **3** SUBLEVARSE : rise up — **levantamiento** *nm* **1** : raising, lifting **2** SUBLEVACIÓN : uprising

levante *nm* **1** : east **2** : east wind

levar *vt* **~ anclas** : weigh anchor

leve *adj* **1** : light, slight **2** : minor, trivial (of wounds, sins, etc.) — **levedad** *nf* : lightness — **levemente** *adv* : lightly, slightly

léxico *nm* : vocabulary, lexicon

ley *nf* **1** : law **2 de (buena) ~** : genuine, pure (of metals)

leyenda *nf* **1** : legend **2** : caption (of an illustration, etc.)

liar {85} *vt* **1** : bind, tie (up) **2** : roll (a cigarette) **3** CONFUNDIR : confuse, muddle — **liarse** *vr* : get mixed up

libanés, -nesa *adj, mpl* **-neses** : Lebanese

libelo *nm* **1** : libel **2** : petition (in court)

libélula *nf* : dragonfly

liberación *nf, pl* **-ciones** : liberation, deliverance

liberal *adj & nmf* : liberal — **liberalidad** *nf* : generosity, liberality

liberar *vt* : liberate, free — **libertad** *nf* **1** : freedom, liberty **2 ~ bajo fianza** : bail **3 ~ condicional** : parole **4 en ~** : free — **libertar** *vt* : set free

libertinaje *nm* : licentiousness — **libertino, -na** *n* : libertine

libido *nf* : libido

libio, -bia *adj* : Libyan

libra *nf* **1** : pound **2 ~ esterlina** : pound sterling

librar *vt* **1** : free, save **2** : wage, fight (a battle) **3** : draw, issue (a check, etc.) — **librarse** *vr* **~ de** : free oneself from, get rid of

libre *adj* **1** : free **2** : unoccupied (of space), spare (of time) **3 al aire ~** : in the open air **4 ~ de impuestos** : tax-free

librea *nf* : livery

libro *nm* **1** : book **2 ~ de bolsillo** : paperback — **librería** *nf* : bookstore — **librero, -ra** *n* : bookseller — **librero** *nm Lat* : bookcase — **libreta** *nf* : notebook

licencia *nf* **1** : license, permit **2** PERMISO : permission **3** : (military) leave — **licenciado, -da** *n* **1** : graduate **2** *Lat* : lawyer — **licenciar** *vt* : dismiss, discharge — **licenciarse** *vr* : graduate — **licenciatura** *nf* : degree

licencioso, -sa *adj* : licentious

liceo *nm* : high school

licitar *vt* : bid for

lícito, -ta *adj* **1** : lawful, legal **2** JUSTO : just, fair

licor *nm* **1** : liquor **2** : liqueur — **licorera** *nf* : decanter

licuadora *nf* : blender — **licuado** *nm* : milk shake — **licuar** {3} *vt* : liquefy

lid *nf* **1** : fight **2 en buena ~** : fair and square

líder *adj* : leading — **~** *nmf* : leader — **liderato** *or* **liderazgo** *nm* : leadership

lidia *nf* : bullfight — **lidiar** *v* : fight

liebre *nf* : hare

lienzo *nm* **1** : cotton or linen cloth **2** : canvas (for a painting) **3** PARED : wall

liga *nf* **1** : league **2** *Lat* : rubber band **3** : garter (for stockings) — **ligadura** *nf* **1** ATADURA : tie, bond **2** : ligature (in medicine or music) — **ligamento** *nm* : ligament — **ligar** {52} *vt* : bind, tie (up)

ligero, -ra *adj* **1** : light, lightweight **2** LEVE : slight **3** ÁGIL : agile **4** FRÍVOLO : lighthearted, superficial — **ligeramente** *adv* : lightly, slightly — **ligereza** *nf* **1** : lightness **2** : flippancy (of character), thoughtlessness (of actions) **3** AGILIDAD : agility

lija *nf* : sandpaper — **lijar** *vt* : sand

lila *nf* : lilac

lima *nf* **1** : file **2** : lime (fruit) **3 ~ para uñas** : nail file — **limar** *vt* : file

limbo *nm* : limbo

limitar *vt* : limit — *vi* **~ con** : border on — **limitación** *nf, pl* **-ciones** : limitation, limit — **límite** *nm* **1** : limit **2** CONFÍN : boundary, border **3 ~ de velocidad** : speed limit **4 fecha ~** : deadline — **limítrofe** *adj* : bordering

limo *nm* : slime, mud

limón *nm, pl* **-mones 1** : lemon **2 ~ verde** *Lat* : lime — **limonada** *nf* : lemonade

limosna *nf* **1** : alms **2 pedir ~** : beg — **limosnero, -ra** *n* : beggar

limpiabotas *nmfs & pl* : bootblack

limpiaparabrisas *nms & pl* : windshield wiper

limpiar *vt* **1** : clean, wipe (away) **2 ~ en seco** : dry-clean — **limpieza** *nf* **1** : cleanliness **2** : (act of) cleaning — **limpio** *adv* : cleanly, fairly — **limpio, -pia** *adj* **1** : clean, neat **2** HONRADO : honest **3** NETO : net, clear

limusina *nf* : limousine

linaje *nm* : lineage, ancestry

linaza *nf* : linseed

lince *nm* : lynx

linchar *vt* : lynch

lindar *vi* **~ con** : border on — **lindante** *adj* : bordering — **linde** *nmf or* **lindero** *nm*: boundary

lindo, -da *adj* **1** : pretty, lovely **2 de lo lindo** *fam* : a lot

línea *nf* **1** : line **2 ~ de conducta** : course of action **3 en ~** : on-line **4 guardar la ~** : watch one's figure — **lineal** *adj* : linear

lingote *nm* : ingot

lingüista *nmf* : linguist — **lingüística** *nf* : linguistics — **lingüístico, -ca** *adj* : linguistic

linimento *nm* : liniment

lino *nm* **1** : flax (plant) **2** : linen (fabric)

linóleo *nm* : linoleum

linterna *nf* **1** FAROL : lantern **2** : flashlight

lío *nm* **1** : bundle **2** *fam* : mess, trouble **3** *fam* : (love) affair

liofilizar {21} *vt* : freeze-dry

liquen *nm* : lichen

liquidar *vt* **1** : liquefy **2** : liquidate (merchandise, etc.) **3** : settle, pay off (a debt, etc.) — **liquidación** *nf, pl* **-ciones 1** : liquidation **2** REBAJA : clearance sale — **líquido, -da** *adj* **1** : liquid **2** NETO : net — **líquido** *nm* : liquid

lira *nf* : lyre

lírico, -ca *adj* : lyric, lyrical — **lírica** *nf* : lyric poetry

lirio *nm* : iris

lisiado, -da *adj* : disabled — **~** *n* : disabled person — **lisiar** *vt* : disable, cripple

liso, -sa *adj* **1** : smooth **2** PLANO : flat **3** SENCILLO : plain **4 pelo ~** : straight hair

lisonjear *vt* : flatter — **lisonja** *nf* : flattery

lista *nf* **1** : stripe **2** ENUMERACIÓN : list **3** : menu (in a restaurant) — **listado, -da** *adj* : striped

listo, -ta *adj* **1** : clever, smart **2** PREPARADO : ready

listón *nm, pl* **-tones 1** : ribbon **2** : strip (of wood)

lisura *nf* : smoothness

litera *nf* : bunk bed, berth

literal *adj* : literal

literatura *nf* : literature — **literario, -ria** *adj* : literary

litigar {52} *vi* : litigate — **litigio** *nm* **1** : litigation **2 en ~** : in dispute

litografía *nf* **1** : lithography **2** : lithograph (picture)

litoral *adj* : coastal — **~** *nm* : shore, seaboard

litro *nm* : liter

liturgia *nf* : liturgy — **litúrgico, -ca** *adj* : liturgical

liviano, -na *adj* **1** LIGERO : light **2** INCONSTANTE : fickle

lívido, -da *adj* : livid

llaga *nf* : sore, wound

llama *nf* **1** : flame **2** : llama (animal)

llamar *vt* **1** : call **2** : call up (on the telephone) — *vi* **1** : phone, call **2** : knock, ring (at the door) — **llamarse** *vr* **1** : be called **2 ¿cómo te llamas?** : what's your name? — **llamada** *nf* : call — **llamado, -da** *adj* : named, called — **llamamiento** *nm* : call, appeal

llamarada *nf* **1** : blaze **2** : flushing (of the face)

llamativo, -va *adj* : flashy, showy

llamear *vi* : flame, blaze

llano, -na *adj* **1** : flat **2** : straightforward (of a person, a message, etc.) **3** SENCILLO : plain, simple — **llano** *nm* : plain — **llaneza** *nf* : simplicity

llanta *nf* **1** : rim (of a wheel) **2** *Lat* : tire

llanto *nm* : crying, weeping

llanura *nf* : plain

llave *nf* **1** : key **2** *Lat* : faucet **3** INTERRUPTOR : switch **4 cerrar con ~** : lock **5 ~ inglesa** : monkey wrench — **llavero** *nm* : key chain

llegar {52} *vi* **1** : arrive, come **2** ALCANZAR : reach **3** BASTAR : be enough **4 ~ a** : manage to **5 ~ a ser** : become — **llegada** *nf* : arrival

llenar *vt* : fill (up), fill in — **lleno, -na** *adj* **1** : full **2 de lleno** : completely — **lleno** *nm* : full house

llevar *vt* **1** : take, carry **2** CONDUCIR : lead **3** : wear (clothing, etc.) **4** TENER : have **5 llevo una hora aquí** : I've been here for an hour — **llevarse** *vr* **1** : take (away) **2 ~ bien** : get along well — **llevadero, -ra** *adj* : bearable

llorar *vi* : cry, weep — **lloriquear** *vi* : whimper, whine — **lloro** *nm* : crying — **llorón, -rona** *n*, *mpl* **-rones** : crybaby, whiner — **lloroso, -sa** *adj* : tearful

llover {47} *v impers* : rain — **llovizna** *nf* : drizzle — **lloviznar** *v impers* : drizzle

lluvia *nf* : rain — **lluvioso, -sa** *adj* : rainy

lo *pron* **1** : him, it **2** (*formal, masculine*) : you **3 ~ que** : what, that which — *~ art* **1** : the **2 ~ mejor** : the best (part) **3 sé ~ bueno que eres** : I know how good you are

loa *nf* : praise — **loable** *adj* : praiseworthy — **loar** *vt* : praise

lobo, -ba *n* : wolf

lóbrego, -ga *adj* : gloomy

lóbulo *nm* : lobe

local *adj* : local — *~ nm* : premises *pl* — **localidad** *nf* : town, locality — **localizar** {21} *vt* **1** : localize **2** ENCONTRAR : locate — **localizarse** *vr* : be located

loción *nf*, *pl* **-ciones** : lotion

loco, -ca *adj* **1** : crazy, insane **2 a lo loco** : wildly, recklessly **3 volverse ~** : go mad — *~ n* **1** : crazy person, lunatic **2 hacerse el loco** : act the fool

locomoción *nf*, *pl* **-ciones** : locomotion — **locomotora** *nf* : engine, locomotive

locuaz *adj*, *pl* **-cuaces** : talkative, loquacious

locución *nf*, *pl* **-ciones** : expression, phrase

locura *nf* **1** : insanity, madness **2** INSENSATEZ : crazy act, folly

locutor, -tora *n* : announcer

locutorio *nm* : phone booth

lodo *nm* : mud — **lodazal** *nm* : quagmire

logaritmo *nm* : logarithm

lógica *nf* : logic — **lógico, -ca** *adj* : logical — **logística** *nf* : logistics *pl*

logotipo *nm* : logo

lograr *vt* **1** : achieve, attain **2** CONSEGUIR : get, obtain **3 ~ hacer** : manage to do — **logro** *nm* : achievement, success

loma *nf* : hill, hillock

lombriz *nf*, *pl* **-brices** : worm

lomo *nm* **1** : back (of an animal) **2** : spine (of a book) **3 ~ de cerdo** : pork loin

lona *nf* : canvas

loncha *nf* : slice (of bacon, etc.)

lonche *nm* *Lat* : lunch — **lonchería** *nf* *Lat* : luncheonette

longaniza *nf* : sausage

longevidad *nf* : longevity — **longevo, -va** *adj* : long-lived

longitud *nf* **1** : longitude **2** LARGO : length

lonja → loncha

loro *nm* : parrot

los, las *pron* **1** : them **2** : you **3 los que, las que** : those who, the ones who — **los** *art* **→ el**

losa *nf* **1** : flagstone **2** *or* **~ sepulcral** : tombstone

lote *nm* **1** : batch, lot **2** *Lat* : plot of land

lotería *nf* : lottery

loto *nm* : lotus

loza *nf* : crockery, earthenware

lozano, -na *adj* **1** : healthy-looking, vigorous **2** : luxuriant (of plants) — **lozanía** *nf* **1** : (youthful) vigor **2** : luxuriance (of plants)

lubricar {72} *vt* : lubricate — **lubri-**

cante adj : lubricating — ~ nm : lubricant
lucero nm : bright star
luchar vi 1 : fight, struggle 2 : wrestle (in sports) — **lucha** nf 1 : struggle, fight 2 : wrestling (sport) — **luchador, -dora** n : fighter, wrestler
lucidez nf, pl **-deces** : lucidity — **lúcido, -da** adj : lucid
lucido, -da adj : magnificent, splendid
luciérnaga nf : firefly, glowworm
lucir {45} vi 1 : shine 2 Lat : appear, seem — vt 1 : wear, sport 2 OSTENTAR : show off — **lucirse** vr 1 : shine, excel 2 PRESUMIR : show off — **lucimiento** nm 1 : brilliance 2 ÉXITO : brilliant performance, success
lucrativo, -va adj : lucrative — **lucro** nm : profit
luego adv 1 : then 2 : later (on) 3 desde ~ : of course 4 ¡hasta ~! : see you later! 5 ~ que : as soon as — ~ conj : therefore
lugar nm 1 : place 2 ESPACIO : space, room 3 dar ~ a : give rise to 4 en ~ de : instead of 5 tener ~ : take place

lugarteniente nmf : deputy
lúgubre adj : gloomy
lujo nm 1 : luxury 2 de ~ : deluxe — **lujoso, -sa** adj : luxurious
lujuria nf : lust
lumbre nf 1 : fire 2 poner en la ~ : put on the stove
luminoso, -sa adj : shining, luminous
luna nf 1 : moon 2 : (window) glass 3 ESPEJO : mirror 4 ~ de miel : honeymoon — **lunar** adj : lunar — ~ nm : mole, beauty spot
lunes nms & pl : Monday
lupa nf : magnifying glass
lúpulo nm : hops
lustrar vt : shine, polish — **lustre** nm 1 BRILLO : luster, shine 2 ESPLENDOR : glory — **lustroso, -sa** adj : lustrous, shiny
luto nm 1 : mourning 2 estar de ~ : be in mourning
luxación nf, pl **-ciones** : dislocation
luz nf, pl **luces** 1 : light 2 : lighting (in a room, etc.) 3 fam : electricity 4 a la ~ de : in light of 5 dar a ~ : give birth 6 sacar a la ~ : bring to light

M

m nf : m, 13th letter of the Spanish alphabet
macabro, -bra adj : macabre
macarrón nm, pl **-rrones** 1 : macaroon 2 **macarrones** nmpl : macaroni
maceta nf : flowerpot
machacar {72} vt : crush, grind — vi ~ sobre : go on about — **machacón, -cona** adj, mpl **-cones** : tiresome, boring
machete nm : machete — **machetear** vt : hack with a machete
macho adj 1 : male 2 fam : macho — ~ nm 1 : male 2 fam : he-man — **machista** nm : male chauvinist
machucar {72} vt 1 : beat, crush 2 : bruise (fruit)
macizo, -za adj : solid — **macizo** nm ~ de flores : flower bed
mácula nf : stain
madeja nf : skein, hank
madera nf 1 : wood 2 : lumber (for construction) 3 ~ dura : hardwood — **madero** nm : piece of lumber, plank
madre nf 1 : mother 2 ~ política : mother-in-law — **madrastra** nf : stepmother
madreselva nf : honeysuckle

madriguera nf : burrow, den
madrileño, -ña adj : of or from Madrid
madrina nf 1 : godmother 2 : bridesmaid (at a wedding)
madrugada nf : dawn, daybreak — **madrugador, -dora** n : early riser
madurar v 1 : mature 2 : ripen (of fruit) — **madurez** nf, pl **-reces** 1 : maturity 2 : ripeness (of fruit) — **maduro, -ra** adj 1 : mature 2 : ripe (of fruit)
maestría nf : mastery, skill — **maestro, -tra** adj : masterly, skilled — ~ n 1 : teacher (in grammar school) 2 EXPERTO : expert, master
Mafia nf : Mafia
magia nf : magic — **mágico, -ca** adj : magic, magical
magisterio nm : teachers pl, teaching profession
magistrado, -da n : magistrate, judge
magistral adj 1 : masterful 2 : magisterial (of an attitude, etc.)
magnánimo, -ma adj : magnanimous — **magnanimidad** nf : magnanimity
magnate nmf : magnate, tycoon
magnesia nf : magnesia — **magnesio** nm : magnesium
magnético, -ca adj : magnetic — **mag-**

netismo *nm* : magnetism — **magneti-zar** {21} *vt* : magnetize

magnetófono *nm* : tape recorder

magnificencia *nf* : magnificence — **magnífico, -ca** *adj* : magnificent

magnitud *nf* : magnitude

magnolia *nf* : magnolia

mago, -ga *n* 1 : magician 2 **los Reyes Magos** : the Magi

magro, -gra *adj* 1 : lean 2 MEZQUINO : poor, meager

magullar *vt* : bruise — **magulladura** *nf* : bruise

mahometano, -na *adj* : Islamic, Muslim — ~ *n* : Muslim

maicena *nf* : cornstarch

maíz *nm* : corn

maja *nf* : pestle

majadero, -ra *adj* : foolish, silly — ~ *n* : fool

majar *vt* : crush

majestad *nf* 1 : majesty 2 **Su Majestad** : His/Her Majesty — **majestuoso, -sa** *adj* : majestic

majo, -ja *adj* 1 : nice 2 GUAPO : good-looking

mal *adv* 1 : badly, poorly 2 INCORRECTA-MENTE : incorrectly 3 DIFÍCILMENTE : with difficulty, hardly 4 **de ~ en peor** : from bad to worse 5 **menos ~** : it's just as well — ~ *nm* 1 : evil 2 DAÑO : harm, damage 3 ENFERMEDAD : illness — ~ *adj* → **malo**

malabarismo *nm* : juggling — **malabarista** *nmf* : juggler

malacostumbrar *vt* : spoil, pamper — **malacostumbrado, -da** *adj* : spoiled

malaria *nf* : malaria

malasio, -sia *adj* : Malaysian

malaventura *nf* : misfortune — **malaventurado, -da** *adj* : unfortunate

malayo, -ya *adj* : Malay, Malayan

malcriado, -da *adj* : bad-mannered, spoiled

maldad *nf* 1 : evil 2 : evil deed

maldecir {11} *vt* : curse, damn — *vi* 1 : curse, swear 2 ~ **de** : speak ill of — **maldición** *nf, pl* **-ciones** : curse — **maldito, -ta** *adj fam* : damned

maleable *adj* : malleable

maleante *nmf* : crook

malecón *nm, pl* **-cones** : jetty

maleducado, -da *adj* : rude

maleficio *nm* : curse — **maléfico, -ca** *adj* : evil, harmful

malentendido *nm* : misunderstanding

malestar *nm* 1 : discomfort 2 INQUI-ETUD : uneasiness

maleta *nf* 1 : suitcase 2 **hacer la ~** : pack one's bags — **maletero, -ra** *n*

: porter — **maletero** *nm* : trunk (of an automobile) — **maletín** *nm, pl* **-tines** 1 PORTAFOLIO : briefcase 2 : overnight bag

malévolo, -la *adj* : malevolent — **malevolencia** *nf* : malevolence

maleza *nf* 1 : underbrush 2 MALAS HIERBAS : weeds *pl*

malgastar *vt* : waste, squander

malhablado, -da *adj* : foul-mouthed

malhechor, -chora *n* : criminal, delinquent

malhumorado, -da *adj* : bad-tempered, cross

malicia *nf* : malice — **malicioso, -sa** *adj* : malicious

maligno, -na *adj* 1 : malignant 2 PERNICIOSO : harmful, evil

malla *nf* 1 : mesh 2 ~**s** *nfpl* : tights

malo, -la *adj* (**mal** *before masculine singular nouns*) 1 : bad 2 : poor (in quality) 3 ENFERMO : unwell 4 **estar de malas** : be in a bad mood — ~ *n* : villain, bad guy (in movies, etc.)

malograr *vt* : waste — **malograrse** *vr* 1 FRACASAR : fail 2 : die young — **malogro** *nm* : failure

maloliente *adj* : smelly

malpensado, -da *adj* : malicious, nasty

malsano, -na *adj* : unhealthy

malsonante *adj* : rude

malta *nf* : malt

maltratar *vt* : mistreat

maltrecho, -cha *adj* : battered

malvado, -da *adj* : evil, wicked

malvavisco *nm* : marshmallow

malversar *vt* : embezzle — **malversación** *nf, pl* **-ciones** : embezzlement

mama *nf* : teat (of an animal), breast (of a woman)

mamá *nf fam* : mom, mama

mamar *vi* 1 : suckle 2 **dar de ~ a** : breast-feed — *vt* 1 : suckle, nurse 2 : learn from childhood, grow up with — **mamario, -ria** *adj* : mammary

mamarracho *nm fam* : mess, sight

mambo *nm* : mambo

mamífero, -ra *adj* : mammalian — **mamífero** *nm* : mammal

mamografía *nf* : mammogram

mampara *nf* : screen, room divider

mampostería *nf* : masonry

manada *nf* 1 : flock, herd, pack 2 **en ~** : in droves

manar *vi* 1 : flow 2 ~ **en** : be rich in — **manantial** *nm* 1 : spring 2 ORIGEN : source

manchar *vt* 1 : stain, spot, mark 2 : tarnish (a reputation, etc.) — **mancharse** *vr* : get dirty — **mancha** *nf* : stain

mancillar *vt* : sully, stain

manco, -ca *adj* : one-armed, one-handed

mancomunar *vt* : combine, join — **mancomunarse** *vr* : unite — **mancomunidad** *nf* : union

mandar *vt* 1 : command, order 2 ENVIAR : send 3 *Lat* : hurl, throw — *vi* 1 : be in charge 2 ¿**mande?** *Lat* : yes?, pardon? — **mandadero, -ra** *nm* : messenger — **mandado** *nm* : errand — **mandamiento** *nm* 1 : order, warrant 2 : commandment (in religion)

mandarina *nf* : mandarin orange, tangerine

mandato *nm* 1 : term of office 2 ORDEN : mandate — **mandatario, -ria** *n* 1 : leader (in politics) 2 : agent (in law)

mandíbula *nf* : jaw, jawbone

mandil *nm* : apron

mando *nm* 1 : command, leadership 2 **al ~ de** : in charge of 3 **~ a distancia** : remote control

mandolina *nf* : mandolin

mandón, -dona *adj, mpl* **-dones** : bossy

manecilla *nf* : hand (of a clock), pointer

manejar *vt* 1 : handle, operate 2 : manage (a business, etc.) 3 : manipulate (a person) 4 *Lat* : drive (a car) — **manejarse** *vr* 1 : manage, get by 2 *Lat* : behave — **manejo** *nm* 1 : handling, use 2 : management (of a business, etc.)

manera *nf* 1 : way, manner 2 **de ~ que** : so that 3 **de ninguna ~** : by no means 4 **de todas ~s** : anyway

manga *nf* 1 : sleeve 2 MANGUERA : hose

mango *nm* 1 : hilt, handle 2 : mango (fruit)

mangonear *vt fam* : boss around — *vi* 1 : be bossy 2 HOLGAZANEAR : loaf, fool around

manguera *nf* : hose

maní *nm, pl* **-níes** *Lat* : peanut

manía *nf* 1 : mania, obsession 2 MODA PASAJERA : craze, fad 3 ANTIPATÍA : dislike — **maníaco, -ca** *adj* : maniacal — **~** *n* : maniac

maniatar *vt* : tie the hands of

maniático, -ca *adj* : obsessive, fussy — **~** *n* : fussy person, fanatic

manicomio *nm* : insane asylum

manicura *nf* : manicure — **manicuro, -ra** *n* : manicurist

manido, -da *adj* : stale, hackneyed

manifestar {55} *vt* 1 : demonstrate, show 2 DECLARAR : express, declare — **manifestarse** *vr* 1 : become evident 2 : demonstrate (in politics) — **mani-**

festación *nf, pl* **-ciones** 1 : manifestation, sign 2 : demonstration (in politics) — **manifestante** *nmf* : protester, demonstrator — **manifiesto, -ta** *adj* : manifest, evident — **manifiesto** *nm* : manifesto

manija *nf* : handle

manillar *nm* : handlebars *pl*

maniobra *nf* : maneuver — **maniobrar** *v* : maneuver

manipular *vt* 1 : manipulate 2 MANEJAR : handle — **manipulación** *nf, pl* **-ciones** : manipulation

maniquí *nmf, pl* **-quíes** : mannequin, model — **~** *nm* : mannequin, dummy

manirroto, -ta *adj* : extravagant — **~** *n* : spendthrift

manivela *nf* : crank

manjar *nm* : delicacy, special dish

mano *nf* 1 : hand 2 : coat (of paint, etc.) 3 **a ~** *or* **a la ~** : at hand, nearby 4 **dar la ~** : shake hands 5 **de segunda ~** : secondhand 6 **~ de obra** : labor, manpower

manojo *nm* : bunch

manopla *nf* : mitten

manosear *vt* 1 : handle excessively 2 : fondle (a person)

manotazo *nm* : slap

mansalva: a ~ *adv phr* : at close range, without risk

mansarda *nf* : attic

mansedumbre *nf* 1 : gentleness 2 : tameness (of an animal)

mansión *nf, pl* **-siones** : mansion

manso, -sa *adj* 1 : gentle 2 : tame (of an animal)

manta *nf* 1 : blanket 2 *Lat* : poncho

manteca *nf* : lard, fat — **mantecoso, -sa** *adj* : greasy

mantel *nm* : tablecloth — **mantelería** *nf* : table linen

mantener {80} *vt* 1 : support 2 CONSERVAR : preserve 3 : keep up, maintain (relations, correspondence, etc.) 4 AFIRMAR : affirm — **mantenerse** *vr* 1 : support oneself 2 **~ firme** : hold one's ground — **mantenimiento** *nm* 1 : maintenance 2 SUSTENTO : sustenance

mantequilla *nf* : butter — **mantequera** *nf* : churn — **mantequería** *nf* : dairy

mantilla *nf* : mantilla

manto *nm* : cloak

mantón *nm, pl* **-tones** : shawl

manual *adj* : manual — **~** *nm* : manual, handbook

manubrio *nm* 1 : handle, crank 2 *Lat* : handlebars *pl*

manufactura *nf* 1 : manufacture 2
FÁBRICA : factory
manuscrito *nm* : manuscript — **manuscrito, -ta** *adj* : handwritten
manutención *nf, pl* **-ciones** : maintenance
manzana *nf* 1 : apple 2 : (city) block —
manzanar *nm* : apple orchard —
manzano *nm* : apple tree
maña *nf* 1 : skill 2 ASTUCIA : cunning,
guile
mañana *adv* : tomorrow — ~ *nm* **el** ~
: the future — ~ *nf* : morning
mañoso, -sa *adj* 1 : skillful 2 *Lat*
: finicky
mapa *nm* : map — **mapamundi** *nm*
: map of the world
mapache *nm* : raccoon
maqueta *nf* : model, mock-up
maquillaje *nm* : makeup — **maquil-
larse** *vr* : put on makeup
máquina *nf* 1 : machine 2 LOCOMOTORA
: locomotive 3 **a toda** ~ : at full
speed 4 ~ **de escribir** : typewriter —
maquinación *nf, pl* **-ciones** : machi-
nation — **maquinal** *adj* : mechanical
— **maquinaria** *nf* 1 : machinery 2
: mechanism, works *pl* (of a watch,
etc.) — **maquinilla** *nf* : small machine
— **maquinista** *nmf* 1 : machinist 2
: (railroad) engineer
mar *nmf* 1 : sea 2 **alta** ~ : high seas *pl*
maraca *nf* : maraca
maraña *nf* 1 : thicket ENREDO : tangle,
mess
maratón *nm, pl* **-tones** : marathon
maravilla *nf* 1 : wonder, marvel 2
: marigold (flower) — **maravillar** *vt*
: astonish — **maravillarse** *vr* : be
amazed — **maravilloso, -sa** *adj* : marvelous
marca *nf* 1 : mark 2 : brand (on livestock) 3 *or* ~ **de fábrica** : trademark
4 : record (in sports) — **marcado, -da**
adj : marked — **marcador** *nm* 1
: scoreboard 2 *Lat* : marker, felt-
tipped pen
marcapasos *nms & pl* : pacemaker
marcar {72} *vt* 1 : mark 2 : brand (livestock) 3 INDICAR : indicate, show 4
: dial (a telephone, etc.) 5 : score (in
sports) — *vi* 1 : score 2 : dial (on the
telephone, etc.)
marchar *vi* 1 : go 2 CAMINAR : walk 3
FUNCIONAR : work, run — **marcharse**
vr : leave, go — **marcha** *nf* 1 : march 2
PASO : pace, speed 3 : gear (of an automobile) 4 **poner en** ~ : put in motion
marchitarse *vr* : wither, wilt — **mar-
chito, -ta** *adj* : withered

marcial *adj* : martial, military
marco *nm* 1 : frame 2 : goalposts *pl* (in
sports) 3 ENTORNO : setting, framework
marea *nf* : tide — **marear** *vt* 1 : make
nauseous or dizzy 2 CONFUNDIR : confuse — **marearse** *vr* 1 : become nau-
seated or dizzy 2 CONFUNDIRSE : get
confused — **mareado, -da** *adj* 1 : sick,
nauseous 2 ATURDIDO : dazed, dizzy
maremoto *nm* : tidal wave
mareo *nm* 1 : nausea, seasickness 2
VÉRTIGO : dizziness
marfil *nm* : ivory
margarina *nf* : margarine
margarita *nf* : daisy
margen *nm, pl* **márgenes** 1 : edge,
border 2 : margin (of a page, etc.) —
marginado, -da *adj* 1 : alienated 2
clases marginadas : underclass —
~ *n* : outcast — **marginal** *adj* : marginal — **marginar** *vt* : ostracize, exclude
mariachi *nm* : mariachi musician or
band
maridaje *nm* : marriage, union — **marido** *nm* : husband
marihuana *or* **mariguana** *or* **marijuana** *nf* : marijuana
marimba *nf* : marimba
marina *nf* 1 : coast 2 *or* ~ **de guerra**
: navy, fleet
marinada *nf* : marinade — **marinar** *vt*
: marinate
marinero, -ra *adj* 1 : sea, marine 2
: seaworthy (of a ship) — **marinero**
nm : sailor — **marino, -na** *adj* : marine — **marino** *nm* : seaman, sailor
marioneta *nf* : puppet, marionette
mariposa *nf* 1 : butterfly 2 ~ **noctur-
na** : moth
mariquita *nf* : ladybug
marisco *nm* 1 : shellfish 2 ~**s** *nmpl*
: seafood
marisma *nf* : salt marsh
marítimo, -ma *adj* : maritime, shipping
mármol *nm* : marble
marmota *nf* ~ **de América** : groundhog
marquesina *nf* : marquee, (glass)
canopy
marrano, -na *n* 1 : pig, hog 2 *fam* : slob
marrar *vt* : miss (a target) — *vi* : fail
marrón *adj & nm, pl* **-rrones** : brown
marroquí *adj* : Moroccan
marsopa *nf* : porpoise
marsupial *nm* : marsupial
Marte *nm* : Mars
martes *nms & pl* : Tuesday
martillo *nm* 1 : hammer 2 ~ **neumáti-**

co : jackhammer — **martillar** *or* **martillear** *v* : hammer

mártir *nmf* : martyr — **martirio** *nm* : martyrdom — **martirizar** {21} *vt* 1 : martyr 2 ATORMENTAR : torment

marxismo *nm* : Marxism — **marxista** *adj & nmf* : Marxist

marzo *nm* : March

mas *conj* : but

más *adv* 1 : more 2 **el/la/lo ~** : (the) most 3 (*in negative constructions*) : (any) longer 4 **¡qué día ~ bonito!** : what a beautiful day! — **~** *adj* : more 2 : most 3 **¿quién ~?** : who else? — **~** *prep* : plus — **~** *pron* 1 **a lo ~** : at most 2 **de ~** : extra, spare 3 **~ o menos** : more or less 4 **¿tienes ~?** : do you have more?

masa *nf* 1 : mass, volume 2 : dough (in cooking) 3 **~s** *nfpl* : people, masses

masacre *nf* : massacre

masaje *nm* : massage — **masajear** *vt* : massage

mascar {72} *v* : chew

máscara *nf* : mask — **mascarada** *nf* : masquerade — **mascarilla** *nf* : mask (in medecine, etc.)

mascota *nf* : mascot

masculino, -na *adj* 1 : masculine, male 2 VARONIL : manly 3 : masculine (in grammar) — **masculinidad** *nf* : masculinity

mascullar *v* : mumble

masilla *nf* : putty

masivo, -va *adj* : mass, large-scale

masón *nm, pl* **-sones** : Mason, Freemason — **masónico, -ca** *adj* : Masonic

masoquismo *nm* : masochism — **masoquista** *adj* : masochistic — **~** *nmf* : masochist

masticar {72} *v* : chew

mástil *nm* 1 : mast 2 ASTA : flagpole 3 : neck (of a stringed instrument)

mastín *nm, pl* **-tines** : mastiff

masturbarse *vr* : masturbate — **masturbación** *nf, pl* **-ciones** : masturbation

mata *nf* : bush, shrub

matadero *nm* : slaughterhouse

matador *nm* : matador, bullfighter

matamoscas *nms & pl* : flyswatter

matar *vt* 1 : kill 2 : slaughter (animals) — **matarse** *vr* 1 : be killed 2 SUICIDARSE : commit suicide — **matanza** *nf* : slaughter, killing

matasanos *nms & pl fam* : quack

matasellos *nms & pl* : postmark

mate *adj* : matte, dull — **~** *nm* 1 : maté 2 **jaque ~** : checkmate

matemáticas *nfpl* : mathematics — **matemático, -ca** *adj* : mathematical — **~** *n* : mathematician

materia *nf* 1 ASUNTO : matter 2 MATERIAL : material — **material** *adj* 1 : material 2 **daños ~es** : property damage — **~** *nm* 1 : material 2 EQUIPO : equipment, gear — **materialismo** *nm* : materialism — **materialista** *adj* : materialistic — **materializar** {21} *vt* : bring to fruition — **materializarse** *vr* : materialize — **materialmente** *adv* : absolutely

maternal *adj* : maternal — **maternidad** *nf* 1 : motherhood 2 : maternity hospital — **materno, -na** *adj* 1 : maternal 2 **lengua materna** : mother tongue

matinal *adj* : morning

matinée *or* **matiné** *nf* : matinee

matiz *nm, pl* **-tices** 1 : nuance 2 : hue, shade (of colors) — **matizar** {21} *vt* 1 : blend (colors) 2 : qualify (a statement, etc.) 3 **~ de** : tinge with

matón *nm, pl* **-tones** 1 : bully 2 CRIMINAL : gangster, hoodlum

matorral *nm* : thicket

matraca *nf* 1 : rattle, noisemaker 2 **dar la ~ a** : pester

matriarcado *nm* : matriarchy

matrícula *nf* 1 : list, roll, register 2 INSCRIPCIÓN : registration 3 : license plate (of an automobile) — **matricular** *vt* : register — **matricularse** *vr* : register, matriculate

matrimonio *nm* 1 : marriage 2 PAREJA : (married) couple — **matrimonial** *adj* : marital

matriz *nf, pl* **-trices** 1 : matrix 2 : uterus, womb (in anatomy)

matrona *nf* : matron

matutino, -na *adj* : morning

maullar {8} *vi* : meow — **maullido** *nm* : meow

maxilar *nm* : jaw, jawbone

máxima *nf* : maxim

máxime *adv* : especially

máximo, -ma *adj* : maximum, highest — **máximo** *nm* 1 : maximum 2 **al ~** : to the full

maya *adj* : Mayan

mayo *nm* : May

mayonesa *nf* : mayonnaise

mayor *adj* 1 (*comparative of* **grande**) : bigger, larger, greater, older 2 (*superlative of* **grande**) : biggest, largest, greatest, oldest 3 **al por ~** : wholesale 4 **~ de edad** : of (legal) age — **~** *nmf* 1 : major (in the military) 2 ADULTO : adult 3 **~es** *nmfpl* : grown-ups — **mayoral** *nm* : foreman

mayordomo *nm* : butler

mayoreo *nm Lat* : wholesale

mayoría *nf* : majority

mayorista *adj* : wholesale — ~ *nmf* : wholesaler

mayormente *adv* : primarily

mayúscula *nf* : capital letter — **mayúsculo, -la** *adj* **1** : capital, uppercase **2 un fallo mayúsculo** : a terrible mistake

maza *nf* : mace (weapon)

mazapán *nm, pl* **-panes** : marzipan

mazmorra *nf* : dungeon

mazo *nm* **1** : mallet **2** MAJA : pestle

mazorca *nf* ~ **de maíz** : corncob

me *pron* **1** (*direct object*) : me **2** (*indirect object*) : to me, for me, from me **3** (*reflexive*) : myself, to myself, for myself, from myself

mecánica *nf* : mechanics — **mecánico, -ca** *adj* : mechanical — ~ *n* : mechanic

mecanismo *nm* : mechanism — **mecanización** *nf, pl* **-ciones** : mechanization — **mecanizar** {21} *vt* : mechanize

mecanografiar {85} *vt* : type — **mecanografía** *nf* : typing — **mecanógrafo, -fa** *n* : typist

mecate *nm Lat* : rope

mecedora *nf* : rocking chair

mecenas *nmfs & pl* : patron, sponsor — **mecenazgo** *nm* : patronage, sponsorship

mecer {86} *vt* **1** : rock **2** : push (on a swing) — **mecerse** *vr* : rock, swing

mecha *nf* **1** : fuse (of a bomb, etc.) **2** : wick (of a candle)

mechero *nm* **1** : burner **2** *Spain* : cigarette lighter

mechón *nm, pl* **-chones** : lock (of hair)

medalla *nf* : medal — **medallón** *nm, pl* **-llones** **1** : medallion **2** : locket (jewelry)

media *nf* **1** : average **2** ~**s** *nfpl* : stockings **3** **a** ~**s** : by halves, halfway

mediación *nf, pl* **-ciones** : mediation

mediado, -da *adj* **1** : half full, half empty, half over **2** : halfway through — **mediados** *nmpl* **a** ~ **de** : halfway through, in the middle of

mediador, -dora *n* : mediator

medialuna *nf* **1** : crescent **2** : croissant (pastry)

medianamente *adv* : fairly

medianero, -ra *adj* **pared medianera** : dividing wall

mediano, -na *adj* **1** : medium, average **2** MEDIOCRE : mediocre

medianoche *nf* : midnight

mediante *prep* : through, by means of

mediar *vi* **1** : be in the middle **2** INTERVENIR : mediate **3** ~ **entre** : be between

medicación *nf, pl* **-ciones** : medication — **medicamento** *nm* : medicine — **medicar** {72} *vt* : medicate — **medicarse** *vr* : take medicine — **medicina** *nf* : medicine — **medicinal** *adj* : medicinal

medición *nf, pl* **-ciones** : measurement

médico, -ca *adj* : medical — ~ *n* : doctor, physician

medida *nf* **1** : measurement, measure **2** MODERACIÓN : moderation **3** GRADO : extent, degree **4 tomar** ~**s** : take steps — **medidor** *nm Lat* : meter, gauge

medieval *adj* : medieval

medio, -dia *adj* **1** : half **2** MEDIANO : average **3 una media hora** : half an hour **4 la clase media** : the middle class — **medio** *adv* : half — ~ *nm* **1** : half **2** MANERA : means *pl*, way **3 en** ~ **de** : in the middle of **4** ~ **ambiente** : environment **5** ~**s** *nmpl* : means, resources

mediocre *adj* : mediocre, average — **mediocridad** *nf* : mediocrity

mediodía *nm* : noon, midday

medioevo *nm* : Middle Ages

medir {54} *vt* **1** : measure **2** CONSIDERAR : weigh, consider — **medirse** *vr* : be moderate

meditar *vi* : meditate, contemplate — *vt* **1** : think over, consider **2** PLANEAR : plan, work out — **meditación** *nf, pl* **-ciones** : meditation

mediterráneo, -nea *adj* : Mediterranean

medrar *vt* : flourish, thrive

medroso, -sa *adj* : fearful

médula *nf* **1** : marrow **2** ~ **espinal** : spinal cord

medusa *nf* : jellyfish

megabyte *nm* : megabyte

megáfono *nm* : megaphone

mejicano → **mexicano**

mejilla *nf* : cheek

mejillón *nm, pl* **-llones** : mussel

mejor *adv* **1** (*comparative*) : better **2** (*superlative*) : best **3 a lo** ~ : maybe, perhaps — ~ *adj* **1** (*comparative of* **bueno** *or* **bien**) : better **2** (*superlative of* **bueno** *or* **bien**) : best **3 lo** ~ : the best thing **4 tanto** ~ : so much the better — **mejora** *nf* : improvement

mejorana *nf* : marjoram

mejorar *vt* : improve — *vi* : improve, get better

mejunje *nm* : concoction, brew

melancolía *nf* : melancholy — **melan-cólico, -ca** *adj* : melancholic, melancholy

melaza *nf* : molasses

melena *nf* 1 : long hair 2 : mane (of a lion)

melindroso, -sa *adj* 1 : affected 2 *Lat* : finicky

mella *nf* : chip, nick — **mellado, -da** *adj* : chipped, jagged

mellizo, -za *adj & n* : twin

melocotón *nm, pl* **-tones** : peach

melodía *nf* : melody — **melódico, -ca** *adj* : melodic

melodrama *nm* : melodrama — **melo-dramático, -ca** *adj* : melodramatic

melón *nm, pl* **-lones** : melon

meloso, -sa *adj* 1 : sweet, honeyed 2 EMPALAGOSO : cloying

membrana *nf* : membrane

membrete *nm* : letterhead, heading

membrillo *nm* : quince

membrudo, -da *adj* : muscular, burly

memorable *adj* : memorable

memorándum *or* **memorando** *nm, pl* **-dums** *or* **-dos** 1 : memorandum 2 AGENDA : notebook

memoria *nf* 1 : memory 2 RECUERDO : remembrance 3 INFORME : report 4 **de ~** : by heart 5 **~s** *nfpl* : memoirs — **memorizar** {21} *vt* : memorize

mena *nf* : ore

menaje *nm* : household goods *pl*, furnishings *pl*

mencionar *vt* : mention, refer to — **mención** *nf, pl* **-ciones** : mention

mendaz *adj, pl* **-daces** : lying

mendigar {52} *vi* : beg — *vt* : beg for — **mendicidad** *nf* : begging — **mendigo, -ga** *n* : beggar

mendrugo *nm* : crust (of bread)

menear *vt* : move, shake 2 : sway (one's hips) 3 : wag (a tail) — **menearse** *vr* 1 : sway, shake, move 2 *fam* : hurry up

menester *nm* ser **~** : be necessary — **menestroso, -sa** *adj* : needy

menguar *vt* : diminish, lessen — *vi* 1 : decline, decrease 2 : wane (of the moon) — **mengua** *nf* : decrease, decline

menopausia *nf* : menopause

menor *adj* 1 (*comparative of* **pequeño**) : smaller, lesser, younger 2 (*superlative of* **pequeño**) : smallest, least, youngest 3 : minor (in music) 4 **al por ~** : retail — **~** *nmf* : minor, juvenile

menos *adv* 1 (*comparative*) : less 2 (*superlative*) : least 3 **~ de** : fewer than — **~** *adj* 1 (*comparative*) : less, fewer

2 (*superlative*) : least, fewest — **~** *prep* 1 : minus 2 EXCEPTO : except — **~** *pron* 1 : less, fewer 2 **al ~** *or* **por lo ~** : at least 3 **a ~ que** : unless —

menoscabar *vt* 1 : lessen 2 ESTRO-PEAR : harm, damage — **menospre-ciar** *vt* 1 DESPRECIAR : scorn 2 SUBES-TIMAR : undervalue — **menosprecio** *nm* : contempt

mensaje *nm* : message — **mensajero, -ra** *n* : messenger

menso, -sa *adj Lat fam* : foolish, stupid

menstruar {3} *vi* : menstruate — **men-struación** *nf* : menstruation

mensual *adj* : monthly — **mensuali-dad** *nf* 1 : monthly payment 2 : monthly salary

mensurable *adj* : measurable

menta *nf* 1 : mint, peppermint 2 **~ verde** : spearmint

mental *adj* : mental — **mentalidad** *nf* : mentality

mentar {55} *vt* : mention, name

mente *nf* : mind

mentir {76} *vi* : lie — **mentira** *nf* : lie — **mentirilla** *nf* : fib — **mentiroso, -sa** *adj* : lying — **~** *n* : liar

mentís *nms & pl* : denial

mentol *nm* : menthol

mentón *nm, pl* **-tones** : chin

menú *nm, pl* **-nús** : menu

menudear *vi* : occur frequently — **menudeo** *nm Lat* : retail, retailing

menudillos *nmpl* : giblets

menudo, -da *adj* 1 : small, insignificant 2 **a ~** : often

meñique *nm or* **dedo ~** : little finger, pinkie

meollo *nm* 1 : marrow 2 ESENCIA : essence, core

mercado *nm* 1 : market 2 **~ de va-lores** : stock market — **mercadería** *nf* : merchandise, goods *pl*

mercancía *nf* : merchandise, goods *pl* — **mercante** *nmf* : merchant, dealer — **mercantil** *adj* : commercial

mercenario, -ria *adj & n* : mercenary

mercería *nf* : notions store

mercurio *nm* : mercury

Mercurio *nm* : Mercury (planet)

merecer {53} *vt* : deserve — *vi* : be worthy — **merecedor, -dora** *adj* : deserving, worthy — **merecido** *nm* **recibir su ~** : get one's just deserts

merendar {55} *vi* : have an afternoon snack — *vt* : have as an afternoon snack — **merendero** *nm* 1 : snack bar 2 : picnic area

merengue *nm* 1 : meringue 2 : me-rengue (dance)

meridiano, -na *adj* 1 : midday 2 CLARO : crystal-clear — **meridiano** *nm* : meridian — **meridional** *adj* : southern

merienda *nf* : afternoon snack, tea

mérito *nm* : merit, worth — **meritorio, -ria** *adj* : deserving — ～ *n* : intern, trainee

mermar *vi* : decrease — *vt* : reduce, cut down — **merma** *nf* : decrease

mermelada *nf* : marmalade, jam

mero, -ra *adj* 1 : mere, simple 2 *Lat fam* (*used as an intensifier*) : very, real — **mero** *adv Lat fam* 1 : nearly, almost 2 **aquí** ～ : right here

merodear *vi* 1 : maraud 2 ～ **por** : prowl about (a place)

mes *nm* : month

mesa *nf* 1 : table 2 COMITÉ : committee, board

mesarse *vr* ～ **los cabellos** : tear one's hair

meseta *nf* : plateau

Mesías *nm* : Messiah

mesilla *nf* : small table

mesón *nm, pl* **-sones** : inn — **mesonero, -ra** *nm* : innkeeper

mestizo, -za *adj* 1 : of mixed ancestry 2 HÍBRIDO : hybrid — ～ *n* : person of mixed ancestry

mesura *nf* : moderation — **mesurado, -da** *adj* : moderate, restrained

meta *nf* : goal, objective

metabolismo *nm* : metabolism

metafísica *nf* : metaphysics — **metafísico, -ca** *adj* : metaphysical

metáfora *nf* : metaphor — **metafórico, -ca** *adj* : metaphoric, metaphorical

metal *nm* 1 : metal 2 : brass section (in an orchestra) — **metálico, -ca** *adj* : metallic, metal — **metalurgia** *nf* : metallurgy

metamorfosis *nfs & pl* : metamorphosis

metano *nm* : methane

metedura *nf* ～ **de pata** *fam* : blunder

meteoro *nm* : meteor — **meteórico, -ca** *adj* : meteoric — **meteorito** *nm* : meteorite — **meteorología** *nf* : meteorology — **meteorólogo, -ga** *adj* : meteorological, meteorologic — ～ *n* : meteorologist

meter *vt* 1 : put (in) 2 : place (in a job, etc.) 3 ENREDAR : involve 4 CAUSAR : make, cause 5 : spread (a rumor) 6 *Lat* : strike (a blow) — **meterse** *vr* 1 : get in, enter 2 ～ **en** : get involved in, meddle in 3 ～ **con** *fam* : pick a fight with

meticuloso, -sa *adj* : meticulous

método *nm* : method — **metódico, -ca** *adj* : methodical — **metodología** *nf* : methodology

metomentodo *nmf fam* : busybody

metralla *nf* : shrapnel — **metralleta** *nf* : submachine gun

métrico, -ca *adj* : metric, metrical

metro *nm* 1 : meter 2 : subway (train)

metrópoli *nf or* **metrópolis** *nfs & pl* : metropolis — **metropolitano, -na** *adj* : metropolitan

mexicano, -na *adj* : Mexican — **mexicoamericano, -na** *adj* : Mexican-American

mezcla *nf* 1 : mixture 2 ARGAMASA : mortar — **mezclar** *vt* 1 : mix, blend 2 CONFUNDIR : mix up, muddle 3 INVOLUCRAR : involve — **mezclarse** *vr* 1 : get mixed up 2 : mingle (socially) — **mezcolanza** *nf* : mixture

mezclilla *nf Lat* : denim

mezquino, -na *nms adj* 1 : mean, petty 2 ESCASO : meager — **mezquindad** *nf* : meanness, stinginess

mezquita *nf* : mosque

mezquite *nm* : mesquite

mi *adj* : my

mí *pron* 1 : me 2 *or* ～ **mismo,** ～ **misma** : myself 3 **a** ～ **no me importa** : it doesn't matter to me

miajas → **migajas**

miau *nm* : meow

mica *nf* : mica

mico *nm* : (long-tailed) monkey

microbio *nm* : microbe, germ — **microbiología** *nf* : microbiology

microbús *nm, pl* **-buses** : minibus

microcosmos *nms & pl* : microcosm

microfilm *nm, pl* **-films** : microfilm

micrófono *nm* : microphone

microondas *nms & pl* : microwave (oven)

microorganismo *nm* : microorganism

microscopio *nm* : microscope — **microscópico, -ca** *adj* : microscopic

miedo *nm* 1 : fear 2 **dar** ～ : be frightening — **miedoso, -sa** *adj* : fearful

miel *nf* : honey

miembro *nm* 1 : member 2 EXTREMIDAD : limb, extremity

mientras *adv or* ～ **tanto** : meanwhile, in the meantime — *conj* 1 : while, as 2 ～ **que** : while, whereas 3 ～ **viva** : as long as I live

miércoles *nms & pl* : Wednesday

mies *nf* : (ripe) corn, grain

miga *nf* : crumb — **migajas** *nfpl* 1 : breadcrumbs 2 SOBRAS : leftovers

migración *nf, pl* **-ciones** : migration

migraña *nf* : migraine

migrar *vi* : migrate

mijo *nm* : millet

mil *adj & nm* : thousand

milagro *nm* : miracle — **milagroso, -sa** *adj* : miraculous

milenio *nm* : millennium

milésimo, -ma *adj* : thousandth

milicia *nf* 1 : militia 2 : military (service)

miligramo *nm* : milligram

mililitro *nm* : milliliter

milímetro *nm* : millimeter

militante *adj & nmf* : militant

militar *adj* : military — **~** *nmf* : soldier — **militarizar** {21} *vt* : militarize

milla *nf* : mile

millar *nm* : thousand

millón *nm, pl* **-llones** 1 : million 2 **mil millones** : billion — **millonario, -ria** *n* : millionaire — **millonésimo, -ma** *adj* : millionth

mimar *vt* : pamper, spoil

mimbre *nm* : wicker

mímica *nf* 1 : mime, sign language 2 IMITACIÓN : mimicry

mimo *nm* : pampering — **~** *nmf* : mime

mina *nf* 1 : mine 2 : lead (for pencils) — **minar** *vt* 1 : mine 2 DEBILITAR : undermine

mineral *adj* : mineral — **~** *nm* 1 : mineral 2 : ore (of a metal)

minería *nf* : mining — **minero, -ra** *adj* : mining — **~** *n* : miner

miniatura *nf* : miniature

minifalda *nf* : miniskirt

minifundio *nm* : small farm

minimizar {21} *vt* : minimize

mínimo, -ma *adj* 1 : minimum 2 MINÚSCULO : minute 3 **en lo más ~** : in the slightest — **mínimo** *nm* : minimum

minino, -na *n fam* : pussycat

ministerio *nm* : ministry — **ministro, -tra** *n* 1 : minister, secretary 2 **primer ministro** : prime minister

minoría *nf* : minority

minorista *adj* : retail — **~** *nmf* : retailer

minoritario, -ria *adj* : minority

minucia *nf* : trifle, small detail — **minucioso, -sa** *adj* 1 : detailed 2 METICULOSO : thorough

minué *nm* : minuet

minúsculo, -la *adj* : minuscule, tiny

minusvalía *nf* : handicap, disability — **minusválido, -da** *adj* : disabled

minuta *nf* 1 : bill, fee 2 BORRADOR : rough draft

minuto *nm* : minute — **minutero** *nm* : minute hand

mío, mía *adj* 1 : mine 2 **una amiga mía** : a friend of mine — **~** *pron* **el mío, la mía** : mine, my own

miope *adj* : nearsighted

mirar *vt* 1 : look at 2 OBSERVAR : watch 3 CONSIDERAR : consider — *vi* 1 : look 2 **~ a** : face, overlook 3 **~ por** : look after — **mirarse** *vr* 1 : look at oneself 2 : look at each other — **mira** *nf* 1 : sight (of a firearm or instrument) 2 INTENCIÓN : aim, objective — **mirada** *nf* : look — **mirado, -da** *adj* 1 : careful 2 CONSIDERADO : considerate 3 **bien ~** : well thought of — **mirador** *nm* 1 BALCÓN : balcony 2 : lookout, vantage point — **miramiento** *nm* : consideration

mirlo *nm* : blackbird

misa *nf* : Mass

miscelánea *nf* : miscellany

miserable *adj* 1 : poor 2 LASTIMOSO : miserable, wretched — **miseria** *nf* 1 : poverty 2 DESGRACIA : misfortune, misery

misericordia *nf* : mercy — **misericordioso, -sa** *adj* : merciful

mísero, -ra *adj* : wretched, miserable

misil *nm* : missile

misión *nf, pl* **-siones** : mission — **misionero, -ra** *adj & n* : missionary

mismo, -ma *adv* (used for emphasis) : right, exactly — **mismo, -ma** *adj* 1 : same 2 (used for emphasis) : very 3 : -self 4 **por lo ~** : for that reason

misoginia *nf* : misogyny — **misógino** *nm* : misogynist

misterio *nm* : mystery — **misterioso, -sa** *adj* : mysterious

mística *nf* : mysticism — **místico, -ca** *adj* : mystic, mystical — **~** *n* : mystic

mitad *nf* 1 : half 2 MEDIO : middle

mítico, -ca *adj* : mythical, mythic

mitigar {52} *vt* : mitigate

mitin *nm, pl* **mítines** : (political) meeting

mito *nm* : myth — **mitología** *nm* : mythology — **mitológico, -ca** *adj* : mythological

mixto, -ta *adj* 1 : mixed, joint 2 : coeducational (of a school)

mnemónico, -ca *adj* : mnemonic

mobiliario *nm* : furniture

mocasín *nm, pl* **-sines** : moccasin

mochila *nf* : backpack, knapsack

moción *nf, pl* **-ciones** : motion

moco *nm* 1 : mucus 2 **limpiarse los ~s** : wipe one's nose — **mocoso, -sa** *n fam* : kid, brat

moda *nf* 1 : fashion, style 2 **a la ~ or de ~** : in style, fashionable 3 **~ pasajera** : fad — **modal** *adj* : modal — **modales** *nmpl* : manners — **modalidad** *nf* : type, kind

modelar *vt* : model, mold — **modelo** *adj* : model — ~ *nm* : model, pattern — ~ *nmf* : model, mannequin

módem *or* **modem** ['moðem] *nm* : modem

moderar *vt* 1 : moderate 2 : reduce (speed, etc.) 3 PRESIDIR : chair (a meeting) — **moderarse** *vr* : restrain oneself — **moderación** *nf, pl* -ciones : moderation — **moderado, -da** *adj & n* : moderate — **moderador, -dora** *n* : moderator, chairperson

moderno, -na *adj* : modern — **modernismo** *nm* : modernism — **modernizar** {21} *vt* : modernize

modesto, -ta *adj* : modest — **modestia** *nf* : modesty

modificar {72} *vt* : modify, alter — **modificación** *nf, pl* -ciones : alteration

modismo *nm* : idiom

modista *nmf* 1 : dressmaker 2 : (fashion) designer

modo *nm* 1 : way, manner 2 : mood (in grammar) 3 : mode (in music) 4 a ~ de : by way of 5 de ~ que : so (that) 6 de todos ~s : in any case, anyway

modorra *nf* : drowsiness

modular *vt* : modulate — **modulación** *nf, pl* -ciones : modulation

módulo *nm* : module, unit

mofa *nf* : ridicule, mockery — **mofarse** *vr* ~ de : make fun of

mofeta *nf* : skunk

moflete *nm fam* : fat cheek — **mofletudo, -da** *adj fam* : fat-cheeked, chubby

mohín *nm, pl* -hines : grimace — **mohíno, -na** *adj* : sulky

moho *nm* 1 : mold, mildew 2 ÓXIDO : rust — **mohoso, -sa** *adj* 1 : moldy 2 OXIDADO : rusty

moisés *nm, pl* -seses : bassinet, cradle

mojar *vt* 1 : wet, moisten 2 : dunk (food) — **mojarse** *vr* : get wet — **mojado, -da** *adj* : wet, damp

mojigato, -ta *adj* : prudish — ~ *n* : prude

mojón *nm, pl* -jones : boundary stone, marker

molar *nm* : molar

moldear *vt* : mold, shape — **molde** *nm* : mold, form — **moldura** *nf* : molding

mole[1] *nf* : mass, bulk

mole[2] *nm* 1 : Mexican chili sauce 2 : meat served with mole

molécula *nf* : molecule — **molecular** *adj* : molecular

moler {47} *vt* : grind, crush

molestar *vt* 1 : annoy, bother 2 no ~ : do not disturb — *vi* : be a nuisance — **molestarse** *vr* 1 : bother 2 OFENDERSE

: take offense — **molestia** *nf* 1 : annoyance, nuisance 2 MALESTAR : discomfort — **molesto, -ta** *adj* 1 : annoyed 2 FASTIDIOSO : annoying 3 INCÓMODO : in discomfort — **molestoso, -sa** *adj* : bothersome, annoying

molido, -da *adj* 1 : ground (of meat, etc.) 2 *fam* : worn out, exhausted

molino *nm* 1 : mill 2 ~ de viento : windmill — **molinero, -ra** *n* : miller — **molinillo** *nm* : grinder, mill

mollera *nf* 1 : crown (of the head) 2 *fam* : brains *pl*

molusco *nm* : mollusk

momento *nm* 1 : moment, instant 2 : (period of) time 3 : momentum (in physics) 4 de ~ : for the moment 5 de un ~ a otro : any time now — **momentáneamente** *adv* : momentarily — **momentáneo, -nea** *adj* 1 : momentary 2 PASAJERO : temporary

momia *nf* : mummy

monaguillo *nm* : altar boy

monarca *nmf* : monarch — **monarquía** *nf* : monarchy

monasterio *nm* : monastery — **monástico, -ca** *adj* : monastic

mondadientes *nms & pl* : toothpick

mondar *vt* : peel

mondongo *nm* : innards *pl*, guts *pl*

moneda *nf* 1 : coin 2 : currency (of a country) — **monedero** *nm* : change purse

monetario, -ria *adj* : monetary

monitor *nm* : monitor

monja *nf* : nun — **monje** *nm* : monk

mono, -na *n* : monkey — ~ *adj fam* : lovely, cute

monogamia *nf* : monogamy — **monógamo -ma** *adj* : monogamous

monografía *nf* : monograph

monograma *nm* : monogram

monolingüe *adj* : monolingual

monólogo *nm* : monologue

monopatín *nm, pl* -tines : scooter, skateboard

monopolio *nm* : monopoly — **monopolizar** {21} *vt* : monopolize

monosílabo *nm* : monosyllable — **monosilábico, -ca** *adj* : monosyllabic

monoteísmo *nm* : monotheism — **monoteísta** *adj* : monotheistic

monotonía *nf* : monotony — **monótono, -na** *adj* : monotonous

monóxido *nm* ~ de carbono : carbon monoxide

monstruo *nm* : monster — **monstruosidad** *nf* : monstrosity — **monstruoso, -sa** *adj* : monstrous

monta *nf* : importance, value

montaje *nm* **1** : assembly **2** ~ : staging (in theater), editing (of films)

montaña *nf* **1** : mountain **2** ~ **rusa** : roller coaster — **montañero, -ra** *n* : mountain climber — **montañoso, -sa** *adj* : mountainous

montar *vt* **1** : mount **2** ESTABLECER : establish **3** ENSAMBLAR : assemble, put together **4** : stage (a performance) **5** : cock (a gun) — *vi* **1** ~ **a caballo** : ride horseback **2** ~ **en bicicleta** : get on a bicycle

monte *nm* **1** : mountain **2** BOSQUE : woodland **3** *or* ~ **bajo** : scrubland **4** ~ **de piedad** : pawnshop

montés *adj, pl* **-teses** : wild (of animals or plants)

montículo *nm* : mound, hillock

montón *nm, pl* **-tones 1** : heap, pile **2** **un** ~ **de** *fam* : lots of

montura *nf* **1** : mount (horse) **2** SILLA : saddle **3** : frame (of glasses)

monumento *nm* : monument — **monumental** *adj fam* : monumental, huge

monzón *nm, pl* **-zones** : monsoon

moño *nm* **1** : bun (of hair) **2** *Lat* : bow (knot)

mora *nf* **1** : mulberry **2** ZARZAMORA : blackberry

morada *nf* : residence, dwelling

morado, -da *adj* : purple — **morado** *nm* : purple

moral *adj* : moral — ~ *nf* **1** : ethics, morals *pl* **2** ÁNIMO : morale — **moraleja** *nf* : moral (of a story) — **moralidad** *nf* : morality — **moralista** *adj* : moralistic — ~ *nmf* : moralist

morar *vi* : live, reside

morboso, -sa *adj* : morbid

mordaz *adj* : caustic, scathing — **mordacidad** *nf* : bite, sharpness

mordaza *nf* : gag

morder {47} *v* : bite — **mordedura** *nf* : bite (of an animal)

mordisquear *vt* : nibble (on) — **mordisco** *nm* : nibble, bite

moreno, -na *adj* **1** : dark-haired, brunette **2** : dark-skinned — ~ *n* **1** : brunette **2** : dark-skinned person

moretón *nm, pl* **-tones** : bruise

morfina *nf* : morphine

morir {46} *vi* **1** : die **2** APAGARSE : die out, go out — **morirse** *vr* **1** ~ **de** : die of **2** ~ **por** : be dying for — **moribundo, -da** *adj* : dying

moro, -ra *adj* : Moorish — ~ *n* : Moor

moroso, -sa *adj* : delinquent, in arrears — **morosidad** *nf* : delinquency (in payment)

morral *nm* : backpack

morriña *nf* : homesickness

morro *nm* : snout

morsa *nf* : walrus

morse *nm* : Morse code

mortaja *nf* : shroud

mortal *adj* **1** : mortal **2** : deadly (of a wound, an enemy, etc.) — ~ *nmf* : mortal — **mortalidad** *nf* : mortality — **mortandad** *nf* : death toll

mortero *nm* : mortar

mortífero, -ra *adj* : deadly, lethal

mortificar {72} *vt* **1** : mortify **2** ATORMENTAR : torment — **mortificarse** *vr* : be distressed

mosaico *nm* : mosaic

mosca *nf* : fly

moscada *adj* → **nuez**

mosquearse *vr fam* **1** : become suspicious **2** ENFADARSE : get annoyed

mosquito *nm* : mosquito — **mosquitero** *nm* **1** : (window) screen **2** : mosquito net

mostachón *nm, pl* **-chones** : macaroon

mostaza *nf* : mustard

mostrador *nm* : counter (in a store)

mostrar {19} *vt* : show — **mostrarse** *vr* : show oneself, appear

mota *nf* : spot, speck — **moteado, -da** *adj* : speckled, spotted

mote *nm* : nickname

motel *nm* : motel

motín *nm, pl* **-tines 1** : riot, uprising **2** : mutiny (of troops)

motivo *nm* **1** : motive, cause **2** : motif (in art, music, etc.) — **motivación** *nf, pl* **-ciones** : motivation — **motivar** *vt* **1** : cause **2** IMPULSAR : motivate

moto *nf* : motorcycle, motorbike — **motocicleta** *nf* : motorcycle — **motociclista** *nmf* : motorcyclist

motor, -triz *or* **-tora** *adj* : motor — **motor** *nm* : motor, engine — **motorista** *nmf* **1** : motorcyclist **2** *Lat* : motorist

mover {47} *vt* **1** : move, shift **2** : shake (the head) **3** PROVOCAR : provoke — **moverse** *vr* **1** : move (over) **2** APRESURARSE : get a move on — **movedizo, -za** *adj* : movable, shifting — **movible** *adj* : movable

móvil *adj* : mobile — ~ *nm* **1** MOTIVO : motive **2** : mobile — **movilidad** *nf* : mobility — **movilizar** {21} *vt* : mobilize

movimiento *nm* **1** : movement, motion **2** ~ **sindicalista** : labor movement

mozo, -za *adj* : young — ~ *n* **1** : young man *m*, young woman *f* **2** *Lat* : waiter *m*, waitress *f*

muchacho, -cha *n* : kid, boy *m*, girl *f*
muchedumbre *nf* : crowd
mucho *adv* **1** : very much, a lot **2** : long, a long time — **mucho, -cha** *adj* **1** : a lot of, many, much **2 muchas veces** : often — **~** *pron* : a lot, many, much
mucosidad *nf* : mucus
muda *nf* **1** : molting (of animals) **2** : change (of clothing) — **mudanza** *nf* **1** : change **2** TRASLADO : move, change of residence — **mudar** *v* **1** : molt, shed **2** CAMBIAR : change — **mudarse** *vr* **1** : change (one's clothes) **2** TRASLA-DARSE : move (one's residence)
mudo, -da *adj* **1** : mute **2** SILENCIOSO : silent
mueble *nm* **1** : piece of furniture **2** **~s** *nmpl* : furniture, furnishings
mueca *nf* **1** : grimace, face **2 hacer ~s** : makes faces
muela *nf* **1** : tooth, molar **2 ~ de juicio** : wisdom tooth
muelle *adj* : soft — **~** *nm* **1** : wharf, jetty **2** RESORTE : spring
muérdago *nm* : mistletoe
muerte *nf* : death — **muerto, -ta** *adj* **1** : dead **2** : dull (of colors, etc.) — **~** *nm* : dead person, deceased
muesca *nf* : nick, notch
muestra *nf* **1** : sample **2** SEÑAL : sign, show
mugir {35} *vi* : moo, bellow — **mugido** *nm* : mooing, bellowing
mugre *nf* : grime, filth — **mugriento, -ta** *adj* : filthy, grimy
muguete *nm* : lily of the valley
mujer *nf* **1** : woman **2** ESPOSA : wife **3** **~ de negocios** : businesswoman
mulato, -ta *adj & n* : mulatto
muleta *nf* **1** : crutch **2** APOYO : prop, support
mullido, -da *adj* : soft, spongy
mulo, -la *n* : mule
multa *nf* : fine — **multar** *vt* : fine
multicolor *adj* : multicolored
multicultural *adj* : multicultural
multimedia *adj* : multimedia
multinacional *adj* : multinational
multiplicar {72} *v* : multiply — **multiplicarse** *vr* : multiply, reproduce — **múltiple** *adj* : multiple — **multipli-**cación *nf, pl* **-ciones** : multiplication — **múltiplo** *nm* : multiple
multitud *nf* : crowd, multitude
mundo *nm* **1** : world **2 todo el ~** : everyone, everybody — **mundanal** *adj* : worldly — **mundano, -na** *adj* **1** : worldly, earthly **2 la vida mundana** : high society — **mundial** *adj* : world, worldwide
municiones *nfpl* : ammunition
municipal *adj* : municipal — **munici-pio** *nm* **1** : municipality **2** AYUN-TAMIENTO : town council
muñeca *nf* **1** : doll **2** : wrist (in anato-my) — **muñeco** *nm* **1** : boy doll **2** MANIQUÍ : dummy, puppet
muñon *nm, pl* **-ñones** : stump (of an arm or leg)
mural *adj & nm* : mural — **muralla** *nf* : wall, rampart
murciélago *nm* : bat (animal)
murmullo *nm* **1** : murmur, murmuring **2** : rustling (of leaves, etc.)
murmurar *vi* **1** : murmur, whisper **2** CRITICAR : gossip
muro *nm* : wall
musa *nf* : muse
musaraña *nf* : shrew
músculo *nm* : muscle — **muscular** *adj* : muscular — **musculatura** *nf* : mus-cles *pl* — **musculoso, -sa** *adj* : mus-cular
muselina *nf* : muslin
museo *nm* : museum
musgo *nm* : moss — **musgoso, -sa** *adj* : mossy
música *nf* : music — **musical** *adj* : mu-sical — **músico, -ca** *adj* : musical — **~** *n* : musician
musitar *vt* : mumble
muslo *nm* : thigh
musulmán, -mana *adj & n, mpl* **-manes** : Muslim
mutar *v* : mutate — **mutación** *nf, pl* **-ciones** : mutation — **mutante** *adj & nmf* : mutant
mutilar *vt* : mutilate — **mutilación** *nf, pl* **-ciones** : mutilation
mutuo, -tua *adj* : mutual
muy *adv* **1** : very, quite **2** DEMASIADO : too

N

n *nf* : n, 14th letter of the Spanish alphabet

nabo *nm* : turnip

nácar *nm* : mother-of-pearl

nacer {48} *vi* 1 : be born 2 — : hatch (of an egg), sprout (of a plant) 3 SURGIR : arise, spring up — **nacido, -da** *adj & n* **recién ~** : newborn — **naciente** *adj* 1 : new, growing 2 : rising (of the sun) — **nacimiento** *nm* 1 : birth 2 : source (of a river) 3 ORIGEN : beginning 4 BELÉN : Nativity scene

nación *nf, pl* **-ciones** : nation, country — **nacional** *adj* : national — **~** *nmf* : national, citizen — **nacionalidad** *nf* : nationality — **nacionalismo** *nm* : nationalism — **nacionalista** *adj & nmf* : nationalist — **nacionalizar** {21} *vt* 1 : nationalize 2 : naturalize (as a citizen) — **nacionalizarse** *vr* : become naturalized

nada *pron* 1 : nothing 2 **de ~** : you're welcome 3 **~ más** : nothing else, nothing more — **~** *adv* : not at all — **~ nf la ~** : nothingness

nadar *v* : swim — **nadador, -dora** *n* : swimmer

nadería *nf* : small thing, trifle

nadie *pron* : nobody, no one

nado: a ~ *adv phr* : swimming

nafta *nf Lat* : gasoline

naipe *nm* : playing card

nalgas *nfpl* : buttocks, bottom

nana *nf* : lullaby

naranja *adj & nm* : orange (color) — **~** *nf* : orange (fruit) — **naranjal** *nm* : orange grove — **naranjo** *nm* : orange tree

narciso *nm* : narcissus, daffodil

narcótico, -ca *adj* : narcotic — **narcótico** *nm* : narcotic — **narcotizar** {21} *vt* : drug — **narcotraficante** *nmf* : drug trafficker — **narcotráfico** *nm* : drug trafficking

nariz *nf, pl* **-rices** 1 : nose 2 OLFATO : sense of smell 3 **narices** *nfpl* : nostrils

narrar *vt* : narrate, tell — **narración** *nf, pl* **-ciones** : narration — **narrador, -dora** *n* : narrator — **narrativa** *nf* : narrative, storytelling

nasal *adj* : nasal

nata *nf Spain* : cream

natación *nf, pl* **-ciones** : swimming

natal *adj* : native, birth — **natalicio** *nm* : birthday — **natalidad** *nf* : birthrate

natillas *nfpl* : custard

natividad *nf* : birth, nativity

nativo, -va *adj & n* : native

natural *adj* 1 : natural 2 NORMAL : normal 3 **~ de** : native of, from — **~** *nm* 1 : temperament 2 NATIVO : native — **naturaleza** *nf* : nature — **naturalidad** *nf* : naturalness — **naturalista** *adj* : naturalistic — **naturalización** *nf, pl* **-ciones** : naturalization — **naturalizar** {21} *vt* : naturalize — **naturalizarse** *vr* : become naturalized — **naturalmente** *adv* 1 : naturally 2 POR SUPUESTO : of course

naufragar {52} *vi* 1 : be shipwrecked 2 FRACASAR : fail — **naufragio** *nm* : shipwreck — **náufrago, -ga** *adj* : shipwrecked — **~** *n* : castaway

náusea *nf* 1 : nausea 2 **dar ~s** : nauseate 3 **~s matutinas** : morning sickness — **nauseabundo, -da** *adj* : nauseating

náutico, -ca *adj* : nautical

navaja *nf* : pocketknife, penknife

naval *adj* : naval

nave *nf* 1 : ship 2 : nave (of a church) 3 **~ espacial** : spaceship

navegar {52} *v* : navigate, sail — **navegable** *adj* : navigable — **navegación** *nf, pl* **-ciones** : navigation — **navegante** *adj* : sailing, seafaring — **~** *nmf* : navigator

Navidad *nf* 1 : Christmas 2 **feliz ~** : Merry Christmas — **navideño, -ña** *adj* : Christmas

naviero, -ra *adj* : shipping

nazi *adj & nmf* : Nazi — **nazismo** *nm* : Nazism

neblina *nf* : mist

nebuloso, -sa *adj* 1 : hazy, misty, foggy 2 VAGO : vague, nebulous

necedad *nf* 1 : stupidity 2 **decir ~es** : talk nonsense

necesario, -ria *adj* : necessary — **necesariamente** *adv* : necessarily — **necesidad** *nf* 1 : need, necessity 2 POBREZA : poverty 3 **~es** *nfpl* : hardships — **necesitado, -da** *adj* : needy — **necesitar** *vt* : need — *vi* **~ de** : have need of

necio, -cia *adj* : silly, dumb
necrología *nf* : obituary
néctar *nm* : nectar
nectarina *nf* : nectarine
neerlandés, -desa *adj, mpl* **-deses** : Dutch — **neerlandés** *nm* : Dutch (language)
nefasto, -ta *adj* **1** : ill-fated **2** *fam* : terrible, awful
negar {49} *vt* **1** : deny **2** REHUSAR : refuse **3** : disown (a person) — **negarse** *vr* : refuse — **negación** *nf, pl* **-ciones** **1** : denial **2** : negative (in grammar) — **negativa** *nf* **1** : denial **2** RECHAZO : refusal — **negativo, -va** *adj* : negative — **negativo** *nm* : negative (of a photograph)
negligente *adj* : negligent — **negligencia** *nf* : negligence
negociar *vt* : negotiate — *vi* : deal, do business — **negociable** *adj* : negotiable — **negociación** *nf, pl* **-ciones** : negotiation — **negociante** *nmf* : businessman *m*, businesswoman *f* — **negocio** *nm* **1** : business **2** TRANSACCIÓN : deal **3** **~s** : business, commerce
negro, -gra *adj* : black, dark — **~** *n* : dark-skinned person — **negro** *nm* : black (color) — **negrura** *nf* : blackness — **negruzco, -ca** *adj* : blackish
nene, -na *n fam* : baby, small child
nenúfar *nm* : water lily
neón *nm* : neon
neoyorquino, -na *adj* : of or from New York
nepotismo *nm* : nepotism
Neptuno *nm* : Neptune
nervio *nm* **1** : nerve **2** : sinew (in meat) **3** VIGOR : vigor, energy **4 tener ~s** : be nervous — **nerviosismo** *nf* : nervousness — **nervioso, -sa** *adj* **1** : nervous, anxious **2 sistema nervioso** : nervous system
nervudo, -da *adj* : sinewy
neto, -ta *adj* **1** : clear, distinct **2** : net (of weight, salaries, etc.)
neumático *nm* : tire
neumonía *nf* : pneumonia
neurología *nf* : neurology — **neurológico, -ca** *adj* : neurological, neurologic — **neurólogo, -ga** *n* : neurologist
neurosis *nfs & pl* : neurosis — **neurótico, -ca** *adj & n* : neurotic
neutral *adj* : neutral — **neutralidad** *nf* : neutrality — **neutralizar** {21} *vt* : neutralize — **neutro, -tra** *adj* **1** : neutral **2** : neuter (in biology and grammar)
neutrón *nm, pl* **-trones** : neutron
nevar {55} *v impers* : snow — **nevada**

nf : snowfall — **nevado, -da** *adj* **1** : snow-covered, snowy **2** : snow-white — **nevasca** *nf* : snowstorm
nevera *nf* : refrigerator
nevisca *nf* : light snowfall, flurry
nexo *nm* : link, connection
ni *conj* **1** : neither, nor **2** **~ que** : as if **3** **~ siquiera** : not even
nicaragüense *adj* : Nicaraguan
nicho *nm* : niche
nicotina *nf* : nicotine
nidada *nf* : brood (of chicks, etc.)
nido *nm* **1** : nest **2** GUARIDA : hiding place, den
niebla *nf* : fog, mist
nieto, -ta *n* **1** : grandson *m*, granddaughter *f* **2 nietos** *nmpl* : grandchildren
nieve *nf* : snow
nigeriano, -na *adj* : Nigerian
nilón *or* **nilon** *nm, pl* **-lones** : nylon
nimio, -mia *adj* : insignificant, trivial — **nimiedad** *nf* **1** : trifle **2** INSIGNIFICANCIA : triviality
ninfa *nf* : nymph
ninguno, -na (**ningún** *before masculine singular nouns*) *adj* : no, not any — **~** *pron* **1** : neither, none **2** : no one, nobody
niña *nf* **1** : pupil (of the eye) **2 la ~ de los ojos** : the apple of one's eye
niño, -ña *n* : child, boy *m*, girl *f* — **~** *adj* **1** : young **2** INFANTIL : immature, childish — **niñero, -ra** *n* : baby-sitter, nanny — **niñez** *nf, pl* **-ñeces** : childhood
nipón, -pona *adj* : Japanese
níquel *nm* : nickel
nítido, -da *adj* : clear, sharp — **nitidez** *nf, pl* **-deces** : clarity, sharpness
nitrato *nm* : nitrate
nitrógeno *nm* : nitrogen
nivel *nm* **1** : level, height **2** **~ de vida** : standard of living — **nivelar** *vt* : level (out)
no *adv* **1** : not **2** (*in answer to a question*) : no **3** ¡**como ~!** : of course! **4** **~ bien** : as soon as **5** **~ fumador** : non-smoker — **~** *nm* : no
noble *adj & nmf* : noble — **nobleza** *nf* : nobility
noche *nf* **1** : night, evening **2 buenas ~s** : good evening, good night **3 de ~** *or* **por la ~** : at night **4 hacerse de ~** : get dark — **Nochebuena** *nf* : Christmas Eve — **nochecita** *nf* : dusk — **Nochevieja** *nf* : New Year's Eve
noción *nf, pl* **-ciones** **1** : notion, concept **2 nociones** *nfpl* : rudiments
nocivo, -va *adj* : harmful, noxious

nocturno, -na *adj* **1** : night **2** : nocturnal (of animals, etc.) — **nocturno** *nm* : nocturne

nogal *nm* **1** : walnut tree **2** ~ **americano** : hickory

nómada *nmf* : nomad — ~ *adj* : nomadic

nomás *adv Lat* : only, just

nombrar *vt* **1** : appoint **2** CITAR : mention — **nombrado, -da** *adj* : famous, well-known — **nombramiento** *nm* : appointment, nomination — **nombre** *nm* **1** : name **2** SUSTANTIVO : noun **3** FAMA : fame, renown **4** ~ **de pila** : first name

nómina *nf* : payroll

nominal *adj* : nominal

nominar *vt* : nominate — **nominación** *nf*, *pl* **-ciones** : nomination

nomo *nm* : gnome

non *adj* : odd, not even — ~ *nm* : odd number

nonagésimo, -ma *adj & n* : ninetieth

nopal *nm* : nopal, prickly pear

nordeste *or* **noreste** *adj* **1** : northeastern **2** : northeasterly (of wind, etc.) — ~ *nm* : northeast

nórdico, -ca *adj* : Scandinavian

noreste → **nordeste**

noria *nf* **1** : waterwheel **2** : Ferris wheel (at a fair, etc.)

norma *nf* : rule, norm, standard — **normal** *adj* **1** : normal **2 escuela** ~ : teacher-training college — **normalidad** *nf* : normality — **normalizar** {21} *vt* **1** : normalize **2** ESTANDARIZAR : standardize — **normalizarse** *vr* : return to normal — **normalmente** *adv* : ordinarily, generally

noroeste *adj* **1** : northwestern **2** : northwesterly (of wind, etc.) — ~ *nm* : northwest

norte *adj* : north, northern — ~ *nm* **1** : north **2** : north wind

norteamericano, -na *adj* : North American

norteño, -ña *adj* : northern

noruego, -ga *adj* : Norwegian — **noruego** *nm* : Norwegian (language)

nos *pron* **1** (*direct object*) : us **2** (*indirect object*) : to us, for us, from us **3** (*reflexive*) : ourselves **4** : each other, one another

nosotros, -tras *pron* **1** (*subject*) : we **2** (*object*) : us **3** *or* ~ **mismos** : ourselves

nostalgia *nf* **1** : nostalgia **2 sentir** ~ **por** : be homesick for — **nostálgico, -ca** *adj* : nostalgic

nota *nf* **1** : note **2** : grade, mark (in school) **3** CUENTA : bill, check — **notable** *adj* : noteworthy, notable — **notar** *vt* : notice — **notarse** *vr* : be evident, seem

notario, -ria *n* : notary (public)

noticia *nf* **1** : news item, piece of news **2** ~ **s** *nfpl* : news — **noticiario** *nm* : newscast — **noticiero** *nm Lat* : newscast

notificar {72} *vt* : notify — **notificación** *nf*, *pl* **-ciones** : notification

notorio, -ria *adj* **1** : obvious **2** CONOCIDO : well-known — **notoriedad** *nf* : fame, notoriety

novato, -ta *adj* : inexperienced — ~ *n* : beginner, novice

novecientos, -tas *adj* : nine hundred — **novecientos** *nms & pl* : nine hundred

novedad *nf* **1** : newness, innovation **2** NOTICIAS : news **3** ~ **es** : novelties, latest news — **novedoso, -sa** *adj* : original, novel

novela *nf* **1** : novel **2** : soap opera (on television) — **novelesco, -ca** *adj* **1** : fictional **2** FANTÁSTICO : fabulous — **novelista** *nmf* : novelist

noveno, -na *adj* : ninth — **noveno** *nm* : ninth

noventa *adj & nm* : ninety — **noventavo, -va** *adj* : ninetieth — **noventavo** *nm* : ninetieth

novia → **novio**

noviazgo *nm* : engagement

novicio, -cia *n* : novice

noviembre *nm* : November

novillo, -lla *n* : young bull *m*, heifer *f*

novio, -via *n* **1** : boyfriend *m*, girlfriend *f* **2** PROMETIDO : fiancé *m*, fiancée *f* **3** : bridegroom *m*, bride *f* (at a wedding)

novocaína *nf* : novocaine

nube *nf* : cloud — **nubarrón** *nm*, *pl* **-rrones** : storm cloud — **nublado, -da** *adj* **1** : cloudy **2** ENTURBIADO : clouded, dim — **nublado** *nm* : storm cloud — **nublar** *vt* **1** : cloud **2** OSCURECER : obscure — **nublarse** *vr* : get cloudy — **nuboso, -sa** *adj* : cloudy

nuca *nf* : nape, back of the neck

núcleo *nm* **1** : nucleus **2** CENTRO : center, core — **nuclear** *adj* : nuclear

nudillo *nm* : knuckle

nudismo *nm* : nudism — **nudista** *adj & nmf* : nudist

nudo *nm* **1** : knot **2** : crux, heart (of a problem, etc.) — **nudoso, -sa** *adj* : knotty, gnarled

nuera *nf* : daughter-in-law

nuestro, -tra *adj* : our — ~ *pron* (*with definite article*) : ours, our own

nuevamente *adv* : again, anew

nueve *adj & nm* : nine
nuevo, -va *adj* **1** : new **2 de nuevo** : again, once more
nuez *nf, pl* **nueces 1** : nut **2** *or* ∼ **de nogal** : walnut **3** ∼ **de Adán** : Adam's apple **4** ∼ **moscada** : nutmeg
nulo, -la *adj* **1** *or* ∼ **y sin efecto** : null and void **2** INCAPAZ : useless, inept — **nulidad** *nf* **1** : nullity **2 es una** ∼ *fam* : he's a total loss
numerar *vt* : number — **numeración** *nf, pl* **-ciones 1** : numbering **2** NÚMEROS : numbers *pl*, numerals — **numeral** *adj* : numeral — **número** *nm* **1** : number, numeral **2** : issue (of a publication) **3 sin** ∼ : countless —
numérico, -ca *adj* : numerical — **numeroso, -sa** *adj* : numerous
nunca *adv* **1** : never, ever **2** ∼ **más** : never again **3** ∼ **jamás** : never ever
nupcial *adj* : nuptial, wedding — **nupcias** *nfpl* : nuptials, wedding
nutria *nf* : otter
nutrir *vt* **1** ALIMENTAR : feed, nourish **2** FOMENTAR : fuel, foster — **nutrición** *nf, pl* **-ciones** : nutrition — **nutrido, -da** *adj* **1** : nourished **2** ABUNDANTE : considerable, abundant — **nutriente** *nm* : nutrient — **nutritivo, -va** *adj* : nourishing, nutritious

O

o¹ *nf* : o, 16th letter of the Spanish alphabet
o² *conj* (u *before words beginning with* o- *or* ho-) **1** : or, either **2** ∼ **sea** : in other words
oasis *nms & pl* : oasis
obcecar {72} *vt* : blind (by emotions) — **obcecarse** *vr* : become stubborn
obedecer {53} *vt* : obey — *vi* **1** : obey **2** ∼ **a** : respond to **3** ∼ **a** : be due to — **obediencia** *nf* : obedience — **obediente** *adj* : obedient
obertura *nf* : overture
obeso, -sa *adj* : obese — **obesidad** *nf* : obesity
obispo *nm* : bishop
objetar *v* : object — **objeción** *nf, pl* **-ciones** : objection
objeto *nm* : object — **objetivo, -va** *adj* : objective — **objetivo** *nm* **1** : objective, goal **2** : lens (in photography, etc.)
objetor, -tora *n* ∼ **de conciencia** : conscientious objector
oblicuo, -cua *adj* : oblique
obligar {52} *vt* : require, oblige — **obligarse** *vr* : commit oneself (to do something) — **obligación** *nf, pl* **-ciones** : obligation — **obligado, -da** *adj* **1** : obliged **2** FORZOSO : obligatory — **obligatorio, -ria** *adj* : mandatory
oblongo, -ga *adj* : oblong
oboe *nm* : oboe — ∼ *nmf* : oboist
obra *nf* **1** : work, deed **2** : work (of art, literature, etc.) **3** CONSTRUCCIÓN : construction work **4** ∼ **maestra** : masterpiece **5** ∼ **s públicas** : public works — **obrar** *vt* : work, produce — *vi* : act, behave — **obrero, -ra** *adj* **la clase obrera** : the working class — ∼ *n* : worker, laborer

obsceno, -na *adj* : obscene — **obscenidad** *nf* : obscenity
obsequiar *vt* : give, present — **obsequio** *nm* : gift, present
observar *vt* **1** : observe, watch **2** ADVERTIR : notice **3** ACATAR : observe, obey **4** COMENTAR : remark — **observación** *nf, pl* **-ciones** : observation — **observador, -dora** *adj* : observant — ∼ *n* : observer — **observancia** *nf* : observance — **observatorio** *nm* : observatory
obsesionar *vt* : obsess — **obsesionarse** *vr* : be obsessed — **obsesión** *nf, pl* **-siones** : obsession — **obsesivo, -va** *adj* : obsessive — **obseso, -sa** *adj* : obsessed
obsoleto, -ta *adj* : obsolete
obstaculizar {21} *vt* : hinder — **obstáculo** *nm* : obstacle
obstante: no ∼ *conj phr* : nevertheless, however — ∼ *prep phr* : in spite of, despite
obstar {21} *vi* ∼ **a** *or* ∼ **para** : stop, prevent
obstetricia *nf* : obstetrics — **obstetra** *nmf* : obstetrician
obstinarse *vr* : be stubborn — **obstinado, -da** *adj* **1** : obstinate, stubborn **2** TENAZ : persistent
obstruir {41} *vt* : obstruct — **obstrucción** *nf, pl* **-ciones** : obstruction
obtener {80} *vt* : obtain, get
obtuso, -sa *adj* : obtuse
obviar *vt* : get around, avoid
obvio, -via *adj* : obvious — **obviamente** *adv* : obviously, clearly
oca *nf* : goose
ocasión *nf, pl* **-siones 1** : occasion **2** OPORTUNIDAD : opportunity **3** GANGA

: bargain — **ocasional** *adj* 1 : occasional 2 ACCIDENTAL : accidental, chance — **ocasionar** *vt* : cause

ocaso *nm* 1 : sunset 2 DECADENCIA : decline

occidente *nm* 1 : west 2 el Occidente : the West — **occidental** *adj* : western, Western

océano *nm* : ocean — **oceanografía** *nf* : oceanography

ochenta *adj & nm* : eighty

ocho *adj & nm* : eight — **ochocientos, -tas** *adj* : eight hundred — **ochocientos** *nms & pl* : eight hundred

ocio *nm* 1 : free time, leisure 2 INACTIVIDAD : idleness — **ociosidad** *nf* : idleness, inactivity — **ocioso, -sa** *adj* 1 : idle, inactive 2 INÚTIL : useless

ocre *adj & nm* : ocher

octágono *nm* : octagon — **octagonal** *adj* : octagonal

octava *nf* : octave

octavo, -va *adj & n* : eighth

octeto *nm* : byte

octogésimo, -ma *adj & n* : eightieth

octubre *nm* : October

ocular *adj* : ocular, eye — **oculista** *nmf* : ophthalmologist

ocultar *vt* : conceal, hide — **ocultarse** *vr* : hide — **oculto, -ta** *adj* : hidden, occult

ocupar *vt* 1 : occupy 2 : hold (a position, etc.) 3 : provide work for — **ocuparse** *vr* 1 ~ **de** : concern oneself with 2 ~ **de** : take care of (children, etc.) — **ocupación** *nf, pl* **-ciones** 1 : occupation 2 EMPLEO : job — **ocupado, -da** *adj* 1 : busy 2 : occupied (of a place) 3 **señal de ocupado** : busy signal — **ocupante** *nmf* : occupant

ocurrir *vi* : occur, happen — **ocurrirse** *vr* ~ **a** : occur to — **ocurrencia** *nf* 1 : occurrence, event 2 SALIDA : witty remark, quip

oda *nf* : ode

odiar *vt* : hate — **odio** *nm* : hatred — **odioso, -sa** *adj* : hateful

odisea *nf* : odyssey

odontología *nf* : dentistry, dental surgery — **odontólogo, -ga** *n* : dentist, dental surgeon

oeste *adj* : west, western — ~ *nm* 1 : west 2 **el Oeste** : the West

ofender *v* 1 : offend — **ofenderse** *vr* : take offense — **ofensa** *nf* : offense, insult — **ofensiva** *nf* : offensive — **ofensivo, -va** *adj* : offensive

oferta *nf* 1 : offer 2 **de** ~ : on sale 3 ~ **y demanda** : supply and demand

oficial *adj* : official — ~ *nmf* 1 : skilled worker 2 : officer (in the military)

oficina *nf* : office — **oficinista** *nmf* : office worker

oficio *nm* : trade, profession — **oficioso, -sa** *adj* : unofficial

ofrecer {53} *vt* 1 : offer 2 : provide, present (an opportunity, etc.) — **ofrecerse** *vr* : volunteer — **ofrecimiento** *nm* : offer

ofrenda *nf* : offering

oftalmología *nf* : ophthalmology — **oftalmólogo, -ga** *n* : ophthalmologist

ofuscar {72} *vt* 1 : blind, dazzle 2 CONFUNDIR : confuse — **ofuscarse** *vr* ~ **con** : be blinded by — **ofuscación** *nf, pl* **-ciones** 1 : blindness 2 CONFUSIÓN : confusion

ogro *nm* : ogre

oír {50} *vi* : hear — *vt* 1 : hear 2 ESCUCHAR : listen to 3 ¡**olga!** *or* ¡**oye!** : excuse me!, listen! — **oídas: de** ~ *adv phr* : by hearsay — **oído** *nm* 1 : ear 2 : (sense of) hearing 3 **duro de** ~ : hard of hearing

ojal *nm* : buttonhole

ojalá *interj* : I hope so!, if only!

ojear *vt* : eye, look at — **ojeada** *nf* : glimpse, glance

ojeriza *nf* 1 : ill will 2 **tener** ~ **a** : have a grudge against

ojo *nm* 1 : eye 2 PERSPICACIA : shrewdness 3 : span (of a bridge) 4 ¡~! : look out!, pay attention!

ola *nf* : wave — **oleada** *nf* : wave, surge — **oleaje** *nm* : swell (of the sea)

olé *interj* : bravo!

oleada *nf* : wave, swell — **oleaje** *nm* : waves *pl*, surf

óleo *nm* 1 : oil 2 CUADRO : oil painting — **oleoducto** *nm* : oil pipeline

oler {51} *vt* : smell — *vi* 1 : smell 2 ~ **a** : smell of — **olerse** *vr fam* : have a hunch about

olfatear *vt* 1 : sniff 2 OLER : sense, sniff out — **olfato** *nm* 1 : sense of smell 2 PERSPICACIA : nose, instinct

Olimpíada *or* **Olimpíada** *nf* : Olympics *pl*, Olympic Games *pl* — **olímpico, -ca** *adj* : Olympic

oliva *nf* : olive — **olivo** *nm* : olive tree

olla *nf* 1 : pot 2 ~ **podrida** : (Spanish) stew

olmo *nm* : elm

olor *nm* : smell — **oloroso, -sa** *adj* : fragrant

olvidar *vt* 1 : forget 2 DEJAR : leave (behind) — **olvidarse** *vr* : forget — **olvidadizo, -za** *adj* : forgetful — **olvido** *nm* 1 : forgetfulness 2 DESCUIDO : oversight

ombligo *nm* : navel

omelette *nmf Lat* : omelet

ominoso, -sa *adj* : ominous

omitir *vt* : omit — **omisión** *nf, pl* **-siones** : omission

ómnibus *nm, pl* **-bus** *or* **-buses** : bus

omnipotente *adj* : omnipotent

omóplato *or* **omoplato** *nm* : shoulder blade

once *adj & nm* : eleven — **onceavo, -va** *adj & n* : eleventh

onda *nf* : wave — **ondear** *vi* : ripple — **ondulación** *nf, pl* **-ciones** : undulation — **ondulado, -da** *adj* : wavy — **ondular** *vt* : wave (hair) — *vi* : undulate, ripple

ónice *nmf or* **ónix** *nm* : onyx

onza *nf* : ounce

opaco, -ca *adj* 1 : opaque 2 DESLUSTRADO : dull

ópalo *nm* : opal

opción *nf, pl* **-ciones** : option — **opcional** *adj* : optional

ópera *nf* : opera

operar *vt* 1 : operate on 2 *Lat* : operate, run (a machine) — *vi* 1 : operate 2 NEGOCIAR : deal, do business — **operarse** *vr* 1 : have an operation 2 OCURRIR : take place — **operación** *nf, pl* **-ciones** 1 : operation 2 TRANSACCIÓN : transaction, deal — **operacional** *adj* : operational — **operador, -dora** *n* 1 : operator 2 : cameraman (for television, etc.)

opereta *nf* : operetta

opinar *vt* : think — *vi* : express an opinion — **opinión** *nf, pl* **-niones** : opinion

opio *nm* : opium

oponer {60} *vt* 1 : raise, put forward (arguments, etc.) 2 ∼ **resistencia** : put up a fight — **oponerse** *vr* ∼ **a** : oppose, be against — **oponente** *nmf* : opponent

oporto *nm* : port (wine)

oportunidad *nf* : opportunity — **oportunista** *nmf* : opportunist — **oportuno, -na** *adj* 1 : opportune, timely 2 APROPIADO : suitable

opositor, -tora *n* 1 : opponent 2 : candidate (for a position) — **oposición** *nf, pl* **-ciones** : opposition

oprimir *vt* 1 : press, squeeze 2 TIRANIZAR : oppress — **opresión** *nf, pl* **-siones** 1 : oppression 2 ∼ **de pecho** : tightness in the chest — **opresivo, -va** *adj* : oppressive — **opresor, -sora** *n* : oppressor

optar *vi* 1 ∼ **a** : apply for 2 ∼ **por** : choose, opt for

óptica *nf* 1 : optics 2 : optician's (shop) — **óptico, -ca** *adj* : optical — ∼ *n* : optician

optimismo *nm* : optimism — **optimista** *adj* : optimistic — ∼ *nmf* : optimist

optometría *nf* : optometry — **optometrista** *nmf* : optometrist

opuesto *adj* 1 : opposite 2 CONTRADICTORIO : opposed, conflicting

opulencia *nf* : opulence — **opulento, -ta** *adj* : opulent

oración *nf, pl* **-ciones** 1 : prayer 2 FRASE : sentence, clause

oráculo *nm* : oracle

orador, -dora *n* : speaker

oral *adj* : oral

orar *vi* : pray

órbita *nf* 1 : orbit (in astronomy) 2 : eye socket — **orbitar** *vi* : orbit

orden *nm, pl* **órdenes** 1 : order 2 ∼ **del día** : agenda (at a meeting) 3 ∼ **público** : law and order — ∼ *nf, pl* **órdenes** 1 : order (of food) 2 ∼ **religiosa** : religious order 3 ∼ **de compra** : purchase order

ordenador *nm Spain* : computer

ordenar *vt* 1 : order, command 2 ARREGLAR : put in order 3 : ordain (a priest) — **ordenanza** *nm* : orderly (in the armed forces) — ∼ *nf* : ordinance, regulation

ordeñar *vt* : milk

ordinal *adj & nm* : ordinal

ordinario, -ria *adj* 1 : ordinary 2 GROSERO : common, vulgar

orear *vt* : air

orégano *nm* : oregano

oreja *nf* : ear

orfanato *or* **orfelinato** *nm* : orphanage

orfebre *nmf* : goldsmith, silversmith

orgánico, -ca *adj* : organic

organigrama *nm* : flowchart

organismo *nm* 1 : organism 2 ORGANIZACIÓN : agency, organization

organista *nmf* : organist

organizar {21} *vt* : organize — **organizarse** *vr* : get organized — **organización** *nf, pl* **-ciones** : organization — **organizador, -dora** *n* : organizer

órgano *nm* : organ

orgasmo *nm* : orgasm

orgía *nf* : orgy

orgullo *nm* : pride — **orgulloso, -sa** *adj* : proud

orientación *nf, pl* **-ciones** 1 : orientation 2 DIRECCIÓN : direction 3 CONSEJO : guidance

oriental *adj* 1 : eastern 2 : oriental — ∼ *nmf* : Oriental

orientar *vt* 1 : orient, position 2 GUIAR : guide, direct — **orientarse** *vr* 1 : orient oneself 2 ∼ **hacia** : turn towards

oriente *nm* **1** : east, East **2 el Oriente** : the Orient

orificio *nm* : orifice, opening

origen *nm, pl* **orígenes** : origin — **original** *adj & nm* : original — **originalidad** *nf* : originality — **originar** *vt* : give rise to — **originarse** *vr* : originate, arise — **originario, -ria** *adj* ~ **de** : native of

orilla *nf* **1** : border, edge **2** : bank (of a river), shore (of the sea)

orinar *vi* : urinate — **orina** *nf* : urine

oriol *nm* : oriole

oriundo, -da *adj* ~ **de** : native of

orla *nf* : border

ornamental *adj* : ornamental — **ornamento** *nm* : ornament

ornar *vt* : adorn

ornitología *nf* : ornithology

oro *nm* : gold

orquesta *nf* : orchestra — **orquestar** *vt* : orchestrate

orquídea *nf* : orchid

ortiga *nf* : nettle

ortodoxia *nf* : orthodoxy — **ortodoxo, -xa** *adj* : orthodox

ortografía *nf* : spelling

ortopedia *nf* : orthopedics — **ortopédico, -ca** *adj* : orthopedic

oruga *nf* : caterpillar

orzuelo *nm* : sty (in the eye)

os *pron pl Spain* **1** (*direct or indirect object*) : you, to you **2** (*reflexive*) : yourselves, to yourselves **3** : each other, to each other

osado, -da *adj* : bold, daring — **osadía** *nf* **1** : boldness, daring **2** DESCARO : audacity, nerve

osamenta *nf* : skeleton

osar *vi* : dare

oscilar *vi* **1** : swing, sway **2** FLUCTUAR : fluctuate — **oscilación** *nf, pl* **-ciones** **1** : swinging **2** FLUCTUACIÓN : fluctuation

oscuro, -ra *adj* **1** : dark **2** : obscure (of ideas, persons, etc.) **3 a oscuras** : in the dark — **oscurecer** {53} *vt* **1** : darken **2** : confuse, cloud (the mind)

3 al ~ : at nightfall — *v impers* : get dark — **oscurecerse** *vr* : grow dark — **oscuridad** *nf* **1** : darkness **2** : obscurity (of ideas, persons, etc.)

óseo, ósea *adj* : skeletal, bony

oso, osa *n* **1** : bear **2** ~ **de peluche** *or* ~ **de felpa** : teddy bear

ostensible *adj* : evident, obvious

ostentar *vt* **1** : flaunt, display **2** POSEER : have, hold — **ostentación** *nf, pl* **-ciones** : ostentation — **ostentoso, -sa** *adj* : ostentatious, showy

osteopatía *n* : osteopathy — **osteópata** *nmf* : osteopath

osteoporosis *nf* : osteoporosis

ostra *nf* : oyster

ostracismo *nm* : ostracism

otear *vt* : scan, survey

otoño *nm* : autumn, fall — **otoñal** *adj* : autumn, fall

otorgar {52} *vt* **1** : grant, award **2** : draw up (a legal document)

otro, otra *adj* **1** : another, other **2 otra vez** : again — ~ *pron* **1** : another (one), other (one) **2 los otros, las otras** : the others, the rest

ovación *nf, pl* **-ciones** : ovation

óvalo *nm* : oval — **oval** *or* **ovalado, -da** *adj* : oval

ovario *nm* : ovary

oveja *nf* **1** : sheep, ewe **2** ~ **negra** : black sheep

overol *nm Lat* : overalls *pl*

ovillo *nm* **1** : ball (of yarn) **2 hacerse un** ~ : curl up (into a ball)

ovni *or* **OVNI** *nm* (*objeto volador no identificado*) : UFO

ovular *vi* : ovulate — **ovulación** *nf, pl* **-ciones** : ovulation

oxidar *vi* : rust — **oxidarse** *vr* : get rusty — **oxidación** *nf, pl* **-ciones** : rusting — **oxidado, -da** *adj* : rusty — **óxido** *nm* : rust

oxígeno *nm* : oxygen

oye → **oír**

oyente *nmf* **1** : listener **2** : auditor (student)

ozono *nm* : ozone

P

p *nf* : p, 17th letter of the Spanish alphabet

pabellón *nm, pl* **-llones** **1** : pavilion **2** : block, building (in a hospital complex, etc.) **3** : summerhouse (in a garden, etc.) **4** BANDERA : flag

pabilo *nm* : wick

pacer {48} *v* : graze

paces → **paz**

paciencia *nf* : patience — **paciente** *adj & nmf* : patient

pacificar {72} *vt* : pacify, calm — **paci-**

ficarse *vr* : calm down — **pacífico, -ca** *adj* : peaceful, pacific — **pacifismo** *nm* : pacifism — **pacifista** *adj* & *nmf* : pacifist

pacotilla *nf* **de ~** : second-rate, trashy

pacto *nm* : pact, agreement — **pactar** *vt* : agree on — *vi* : come to an agreement

padecer {53} *vt* : suffer, endure — *vi* **~ de** : suffer from — **padecimiento** *nm* : suffering

padre *nm* **1** : father **2 ~s** *nmpl* : parents — *~ adj Lat fam* : great, fantastic — **padrastro** *nm* : stepfather — **padrino** *nm* **1** : godfather **2** : best man (at a wedding)

padrón *nm*, *pl* **-drones** : register, roll

paella *nf* : paella

paga *nf* : pay, wages *pl* — **pagadero, -ra** *adj* : payable

pagano, -na *adj* & *n* : pagan, heathen

pagar {52} *vt* : pay, pay for — *vi* : pay — **pagaré** *nm* : IOU

página *nf* : page

pago *nm* : payment

país *nm* **1** : country, nation **2** REGIÓN : region, land — **paisaje** *nm* : scenery, landscape — **paisano, -na** *n* : compatriot

paja *nf* **1** : straw **2** *fam* : nonsense

pájaro *nm* **1** : bird **2 ~ carpintero** : woodpecker — **pajarera** *nf* : aviary

pajita *nf* : (drinking) straw

pala *nf* **1** : shovel, spade **2** : blade (of an oar or a rotor) **3** : paddle, racket (in sports)

palabra *nf* **1** : word **2** HABLA : speech **3 tener la ~** : have the floor — **palabrota** *nf* : swearword

palacio *nm* **1** : palace, mansion **2 ~ de justicia** : courthouse

paladar *nm* : palate — **paladear** *vt* : savor

palanca *nf* **1** : lever, crowbar **2** *fam* : leverage, influence **3 ~ de cambio** *or* **~ de velocidades** : gearshift

palangana *nf* : washbowl

palco *nm* : box (in a theater)

palestino, -na *adj* : Palestinian

paleta *nf* **1** : small shovel, trowel **2** : palette (in art) **3** : paddle (in sports, etc.)

paletilla *nf* : shoulder blade

paliar *vt* : alleviate, ease — **paliativo, -va** *adj* : palliative

pálido, -da *adj* : pale — **palidecer** {53} *vi* : turn pale — **palidez** *nf*, *pl* **-deces** : paleness, pallor

palillo *nm* **1** : small stick **2** *or* **~ de dientes** : toothpick

paliza *nf* : beating

palma *nf* **1** : palm (of the hand) **2** : palm (tree or leaf) **3 batir ~s** : clap, applaud — **palmada** *nf* **1** : pat, slap **2 ~s** *nfpl* : clapping

palmera *nf* : palm tree

palmo *nm* **1** : span, small amount **2 ~ a ~** : bit by bit

palmotear *vi* : applaud — **palmoteo** *nm* : clapping, applause

palo *nm* **1** : stick **2** MANGO : shaft, handle **3** MÁSTIL : mast **4** POSTE : pole **5** GOLPE : blow **6** : suit (of cards)

paloma *nf* : pigeon, dove — **palomilla** *nf* : moth — **palomitas** *nfpl* : popcorn

palpar *vt* : feel, touch — **palpable** *adj* : palpable

palpitar *vi* : palpitate, throb — **palpitación** *nf*, *pl* **-ciones** : palpitation

palta *nf Lat* : avocado

paludismo *nm* : malaria

pampa *nf* : pampa

pan *nm* **1** : bread **2** : loaf (of bread, etc.) **3 ~ tostado** : toast

pana *nf* : corduroy

panacea *nf* : panacea

panadería *nf* : bakery, bread shop — **panadero, -ra** *n* : baker

panal *nm* : honeycomb

panameño, -ña *adj* : Panamanian

pancarta *nf* : placard, banner

pancito *nm Lat* : (bread) roll

páncreas *nms* & *pl* : pancreas

panda *nmf* : panda

pandemonio *nm* : pandemonium

pandero *nm* : tambourine — **pandereta** *nf* : (small) tambourine

pandilla *nf* : gang

panecillo *nm Spain* : (bread) roll

panel *nm* : panel

panfleto *nm* : pamphlet

pánico *nm* : panic

panorama *nm* : panorama — **panorámico, -ca** *adj* : panoramic

panqueque *nm Lat* : pancake

pantaletas *nfpl Lat* : panties

pantalla *nf* **1** : screen **2** : lampshade

pantalón *nm*, *pl* **-lones 1** *or* **pantalones** *nmpl* : pants *pl*, trousers *pl* **2 pantalones vaqueros** : jeans

pantano *nm* **1** : swamp, marsh **2** EMBALSE : reservoir — **pantanoso, -sa** *adj* : marshy, swampy

pantera *nf* : panther

pantimedias *nfpl Lat* : panty hose

pantomima *nf* : pantomime

pantorrilla *nf* : calf (of the leg)

pantufla *nf* : slipper

panza *nf* : belly, paunch — **panzón, -zona** *adj*, *mpl* **-zones** : potbellied

pañal *nm* : diaper
paño *nm* **1** : cloth **2** TRAPO : rag, dust cloth **3** ~ **de cocina** : dishcloth **4** ~ **higiénico** : sanitary napkin **5** ~**s menores** : underwear
pañuelo *nm* **1** : handkerchief **2** : scarf, kerchief
papa¹ *nm* : pope
papa² *nf Lat* **1** : potato **2** ~**s fritas** : potato chips, french fries
papá *nm fam* **1** : dad, pop **2** ~**s** *nmpl* : parents, folks
papada *nf* : double chin
papagayo *nm* : parrot
papal *adj* : papal
papalote *nm Lat* : kite
papanatas *nmfs & pl fam* : simpleton
papaya *nf* : papaya
papel *nm* **1** : paper, sheet of paper **2** : role, part (in theater, etc.) **3** ~ **de aluminio** : aluminum foil **4** ~ **higiénico** *or* ~ **de baño** : toilet paper **5** ~ **de lija** : sandpaper **6** ~ **pintado** : wallpaper — **papeleo** *nm* : paperwork, red tape — **papelera** *nf* : wastebasket — **papelería** *nf* : stationery store — **papeleta** *nf* **1** : ticket, slip **2** : ballot (paper)
paperas *nfpl* : mumps
papilla *nf* **1** : baby food, pap **2 hacer** ~ : smash to bits
paquete *nm* **1** : package, parcel **2** : pack (of cigarettes, etc.)
paquistaní *adj* : Pakistani
par *nm* **1** : pair, couple **2** : par (in golf) **3** NOBLE : peer **4 abierto de** ~ **en** ~ : wide open **5 sin** ~ : without equal — ~ *adj* : even (in number) — ~ *nf* **1** : par **2 a la** ~ **que** : at the same time as
para *prep* **1** : for **2** HACIA : towards **3** : (in order) to **4** : around, by (a time) **5** ~ **adelante** : forwards **6** ~ **atrás** : backwards **7** ~ **que** : so (that), in order that
parabienes *nmpl* : congratulations
parábola *nf* : parable
parabrisas *nms & pl* : windshield
paracaídas *nms & pl* : parachute — **paracaidista** *nmf* **1** : parachutist **2** : paratrooper (in the military)
parachoques *nms & pl* : bumper
parada *nf* **1** : pair (up) **2** : (act of) stopping **3** DESFILE : parade — **paradero** *nm* **1** : whereabouts **2** *Lat* : bus stop — **parado, -da** *adj* **1** : stopped **2** *Lat* : standing (up) **3 bien (mal) parado** : in good (bad) shape
paradoja *nf* : paradox
parafernalia *nf* : paraphernalia

parafina *nf* : paraffin
parafrasear *vt* : paraphrase — **paráfrasis** *nfs & pl* : paraphrase
paraguas *nms & pl* : umbrella
paraguayo, -ya *adj* : Paraguayan
paraíso *nm* : paradise
paralelo, -la *adj* : parallel — **paralelo** *nm* : parallel — **paralelismo** *nm* : similarity
parálisis *nfs & pl* : paralysis — **paralítico, -ca** *adj* : paralytic — **paralizar** {21} *vt* : paralyze
parámetro *nm* : parameter
páramo *nm* : barren plateau
parangón *nm, pl* **-gones 1** : comparison **2 sin** ~ : matchless
paraninfo *nm* : auditorium, hall
paranoia *nf* : paranoia — **paranoico, -ca** *adj & n* : paranoid
parapeto *nm* : parapet, rampart
parapléjico, -ca *adj & n* : paraplegic
parar *vt* **1** : stop **2** *Lat* : stand, prop — *vi* **1** : stop **2 ir a** ~ : end up, wind up — **pararse** *vr* **1** : stop **2** *Lat* : stand up
pararrayos *nms & pl* : lightning rod
parásito, -ta *adj* : parasitic — **parásito** *nm* : parasite
parasol *nm* : parasol
parcela *nf* : parcel, tract (of land) — **parcelar** *vt* : parcel (up)
parche *nm* : patch
parcial *adj* **1** : partial **2 a tiempo** ~ : part-time — **parcialidad** *nf* : partiality, bias
parco, -ca *adj* : sparing, frugal
pardo, -da *adj* : brownish grey
parear *vt* : pair (up)
parecer {53} *vi* **1** : seem, look **2** ASEMEJARSE A : look like, seem like **3 me parece que** : I think that, in my opinion **4 ¿qué te parece?** : what do you think? **5 según parece** : apparently — **parecerse** *vr* ~ **a** : resemble — ~ *nm* **1** : opinion **2** ASPECTO : appearance **3 al** ~ : apparently — **parecido, -da** *adj* **1** : similar **2 bien parecido** : good-looking — **parecido** *nm* : resemblance, similarity
pared *nf* : wall
parejo, -ja *adj* **1** : even, smooth **2** SEMEJANTE : similar — **pareja** *nf* **1** : couple, pair **2** : partner (person)
parentela *nf* : relatives *pl*, kin — **parentesco** *nm* : relationship, kinship
paréntesis *nms & pl* **1** : parenthesis **2** DIGRESIÓN : digression **3 entre** ~ : by the way
paria *nmf* : outcast
paridad *nf* : equality
pariente *nmf* : relative, relation

parir *vi* : give birth, have a baby — *vt* : give birth to

parking *nm* : parking lot

parlamentar *vi* : discuss — **parlamentario, -ria** *adj* : parliamentary — **~** *n* : member of parliament — **parlamento** *nm* : parliament

parlanchín, -china *adj, mpl* **-chines** : talkative, chatty — **~** *n* : chatterbox

parlotear *vi fam* : chatter — **parloteo** *nm fam* : chatter

paro *nm* 1 : stoppage, shutdown 2 DESEMPLEO : unemployment 3 *Lat* : strike 4 **~ cardíaco** : cardiac arrest

parodia *nf* : parody — **parodiar** *vt* : parody

párpado *nm* : eyelid — **parpadear** *vi* 1 : blink 2 : flicker (of light), twinkle (of stars) — **parpadeo** *nm* 1 : blink 2 : flicker (of light), twinkling (of stars)

parque *nm* 1 : park 2 **~ de atracciones** : amusement park

parqué *nm* : parquet

parquear *vt Lat* : park

parquedad *nf* : frugality, moderation

parquímetro *nm* : parking meter

parra *nf* : grapevine

párrafo *nm* : paragraph

parranda *nf fam* : party, spree

parrilla *nf* 1 : broiler, grill 2 : grate (of a chimney, etc.) — **parrillada** *nf* : barbecue

párroco *nm* : parish priest — **parroquia** *nf* 1 : parish 2 : parish church — **parroquial** *adj* : parochial — **parroquiano, -na** *nm* 1 : parishioner 2 CLIENTE : customer

parsimonia *nf* 1 : calm 2 FRUGALIDAD : thrift — **parsimonioso, -sa** *adj* 1 : calm, unhurried 2 FRUGAL : thrifty

parte *nf* 1 : part 2 PORCIÓN : share 3 LADO : side 4 : party (in negotiations, etc.) 5 **de ~ de** : on behalf of 6 **¿de ~ de quién?** : who is speaking? 7 **en alguna ~** : somewhere 8 **en todas ~s** : everywhere 9 **tomar ~** : take part — **~** *nm* 1 : report 2 **~ meteorológico** : weather forecast

partero, -ra *n* : midwife

partición *nf, pl* **-ciones** : division, sharing

participar *vi* 1 : participate, take part 2 **~ en** : have a share in — *vt* : notify — **participación** *nf, pl* **-ciones** 1 : participation 2 : share, interest (in a fund, etc.) 3 NOTICIA : notice — **participante** *adj* : participating — **~** *nmf* : participant — **partícipe** *nmf* : participant

participio *nm* : participle

partícula *nf* : particle

particular *adj* 1 : particular 2 PRIVADO : private — **~** *nm* 1 : matter 2 PERSONA : individual — **particularidad** *nf* : peculiarity — **particularizar** {21} *vt* : distinguish, characterize — *vi* : go into details

partir *vt* 1 : split, divide 2 ROMPER : break, crack 3 REPARTIR : share (out) — *vi* 1 : depart 2 **~ de** : start from 3 **a ~ de** : as of, from — **partirse** *vr* 1 : split (open) 2 RAJARSE : crack — **partida** *nf* 1 : departure 2 : entry, item (in a register, etc.) 3 JUEGO : game 4 : group (of persons) 5 **mala ~** : dirty trick 6 **~ de nacimiento** : birth certificate — **partidario, -ria** *n* : follower, supporter — **partido** *nm* 1 : (political) party 2 : game, match (in sports) 3 PARTIDARIOS : following 4 **sacar ~ de** : make the most of

partitura *nf* : (musical) score

parto *nm* 1 : childbirth 2 **estar de ~** : be in labor

parvulario *nm* : nursery school

pasa *nf* 1 : raisin 2 **~ de Corinto** : currant

pasable *adj* : passable

pasada *nf* 1 : pass, wipe, coat (of paint, etc.) 2 **de ~** : in passing 3 **mala ~** : dirty trick — **pasadizo** *nm* : corridor — **pasado, -da** *adj* 1 : past 2 PODRIDO : bad, spoiled 3 ANTICUADO : out-of-date 4 **el año pasado** : last year — **pasado** *nm* : past

pasador *nm* 1 CERROJO : bolt 2 : barrette (for the hair)

pasaje *nm* 1 : passage 2 BILLETE : ticket, fare 3 PASILLO : passageway 4 PASAJEROS : passengers *pl* — **pasajero, -ra** *adj* : passing — **~** *n* : passenger

pasamanos *nms & pl* : handrail, banister

pasaporte *nm* : passport

pasar *vi* 1 : pass, go (by) 2 ENTRAR : come in 3 SUCEDER : happen 4 TERMINARSE : be over, end 5 **~ de** : exceed 6 **¿qué pasa?** : what's the matter? — *vt* 1 : pass 2 : spend (time) 3 CRUZAR : cross 4 TOLERAR : tolerate 5 SUFRIR : go through, suffer 6 : show (a movie, etc.) 7 **pasarlo bien** : have a good time 8 **~ por alto** : overlook, omit — **pasarse** *vr* 1 : pass, go away 2 ESTROPEARSE : spoil, go bad 3 OLVIDARSE : slip one's mind 4 EXCEDERSE : go too far

pasarela *nf* 1 : footbridge 2 : gangway (on a ship)

pasatiempo *nm* : pastime, hobby
Pascua *nf* 1 : Easter (Christian feast) 2 : Passover (Jewish feast) 3 NAVIDAD : Christmas
pase *nm* : pass
pasear *vi* : take a walk, go for a ride — *vt* 1 : take for a walk 2 EXHIBIR : parade, show off — **pasearse** *vr* : go for a walk, go for a ride — **paseo** *nm* 1 : walk, ride 2 *Lat* : outing
pasillo *nm* : passage, corridor
pasión *nf, pl* -siones : passion
pasivo, -va *adj* : passive — **pasivo** *nm* : liabilities *pl*
pasmar *vt* : astonish, amaze — **pasmarse** *vr* : be astonished — **pasmado, -da** *adj* : stunned, flabbergasted — **pasmo** *nm* : astonishment — **pasmoso, -sa** *adj* : astonishing
paso¹, -sa *adj* : dried (of fruit)
paso² *nm* 1 : step 2 HUELLA : footprint 3 RITMO : pace 4 CRUCE : crossing 5 PASAJE : passage, way through 6 : (mountain) pass 7 de ~ : in passing
pasta *nf* 1 : paste 2 MASA : dough 3 *or* ~s : pasta 4 ~ de dientes *or* ~ dentífrica : toothpaste
pastar *v* : graze
pastel *nm* 1 : cake 2 EMPANADA : pie 3 : pastel (crayon) — **pastelería** *nf* : pastry shop
pasteurizar {21} *vt* : pasteurize
pastilla *nf* 1 : pill, tablet 2 : bar (of chocolate, soap, etc.) 3 ~ para la tos : lozenge, cough drop
pasto *nm* 1 : pasture 2 *Lat* : grass, lawn — **pastor, -tora** *n* 1 : shepherd 2 : pastor (in religion) — **pastoral** *adj* : pastoral
pata *nf* 1 : paw, leg (of an animal) 2 : foot, leg (of furniture) 3 meter la ~ *fam* : put one's foot in it — **patada** *nf* 1 : kick 2 : stamp (of the foot) — **patalear** *vi* 1 : kick 2 : stamp (one's feet)
patata *nf Spain* : potato
patear *vt* : kick — *vi* 1 : kick 2 : stamp (one's feet)
patentar *vt* : patent — **patente** *adj* : obvious, patent — ~ *nf* : patent
paternal *adj* : fatherly, paternal — **paternidad** *nf* 1 : fatherhood 2 : paternity (in law) — **paterno, -na** *adj* : paternal
patético, -ca *adj* : pathetic, moving
patillas *nfpl* : sideburns
patinar *vi* 1 : skate 2 RESBALAR : slip, slide — **patín** *nm, pl* -tines : skate — **patinador, -dora** *n* : skater — **patinaje** *nm* : skating — **patinazo** *nm* 1 : skid 2 *fam* : blunder — **patinete** *nm* : scooter

patio *nm* 1 : courtyard, patio 2 *or* ~ de recreo : playground
pato, -ta *n* 1 : duck 2 pagar el pato *fam* : take the blame — **patito, -ta** *n* : duckling
patología *nf* : pathology — **patológico, -ca** *adj* : pathological
patraña *nf* : hoax
patria *nf* : native land
patriarca *nm* : patriarch
patrimonio *nm* 1 : inheritance 2 : (historical or cultural) heritage
patriota *adj* : patriotic — ~ *nmf* : patriot — **patriótico, -ca** *adj* : patriotic — **patriotismo** *nm* : patriotism
patrocinador, -dora *n* : sponsor — **patrocinar** *vt* : sponsor — **patrocinio** *nm* : sponsorship
patrón, -trona *n, mpl* -trones 1 : patron 2 JEFE : boss 3 : landlord, landlady *f* (of a boarding house, etc.) — **patrón** *nm, pl* -trones : pattern (in sewing) — **patronato** *nm* 1 : patronage 2 FUNDACIÓN : foundation, trust
patrulla *nf* 1 : patrol 2 : (police) cruiser — **patrullar** *v* : patrol
paulatino, -na *adj* : gradual
pausa *nf* : pause, break — **pausado, -da** *adj* : slow, deliberate
pauta *nf* : guideline
pavimento *nm* : pavement — **pavimentar** *vt* : pave
pavo, -va *n* 1 : turkey 2 pavo real : peacock
pavonearse *vr* : strut, swagger
pavor *nm* : dread, terror — **pavoroso, -sa** *adj* : terrifying
payaso, -sa *n* : clown — **payasada** *nf* : antic, buffoonery — **payasear** *vi Lat fam* : clown (around)
paz *nf, pl* paces 1 : peace 2 dejar en ~ : leave alone 3 hacer las paces : make up, reconcile
peaje *nm* : toll
peatón *nm, pl* -tones : pedestrian
peca *nf* : freckle
pecado *nm* : sin — **pecador, -dora** *adj* : sinful — ~ *n* : sinner — **pecaminoso, -sa** *adj* : sinful — **pecar** {72} *vi* : sin
pecera *nf* : fishbowl, fish tank
pecho *nm* 1 : chest 2 MAMA : breast 3 CORAZÓN : heart, courage 4 dar el ~ : breast-feed 5 tomar a ~ : take to heart — **pechuga** *nf* : breast (of fowl)
pecoso, -sa *adj* : freckled
pectoral *adj* : pectoral
peculiar *adj* 1 : particular 2 RARO : peculiar, odd — **peculiaridad** *nf* : peculiarity

pedagogía *nf* : education, pedagogy —
pedagogo, -ga *n* : educator, teacher
pedal *nm* : pedal — **pedalear** *vi* : pedal
pedante *adj* : pedantic, pompous
pedazo *nm* 1 : piece, bit 2 **hacerse ~s**
: fall to pieces
pedernal *nm* : flint
pedestal *nm* : pedestal
pediatra *nmf* : pediatrician
pedigrí *nm* : pedigree
pedir {54} *vt* 1 : ask for, request 2
: order (food, merchandise, etc.) — *vi*
1 : ask 2 ~ **prestado** : borrow — **pedido** *nm* 1 : order 2 **hacer un ~**
: place an order
pedregoso, -sa *adj* : rocky, stony
pedrería *nf* : precious stones *pl*
pegar {52} *vt* 1 : stick, glue, paste 2
: sew on (a button, etc.) 3 JUNTAR
: bring together 4 GOLPEAR : hit, strike
5 PROPINAR : deal (a blow, etc.) 6
: transmit (an illness) 7 ~ **un grito**
: let out a scream — *vi* 1 : adhere, stick
2 GOLPEAR : hit — **pegarse** *vr* 1 : hit
oneself, hit each other 2 ADHERIRSE
: stick, adhere 3 CONTAGIARSE : be
transmitted — **pegadizo, -za** *adj* 1
: catchy 2 CONTAGIOSO : contagious —
pegajoso, -sa *adj* 1 : sticky 2 *Lat*
: catchy — **pegamento** *nm* : glue
peinar *vt* : comb — **peinarse** *vr* : comb
one's hair — **peinado** *nm* : hairstyle,
hairdo — **peine** *nm* : comb — **peine-
ta** *nf* : ornamental comb
pelado, -da *adj* 1 : shorn, hairless 2
: peeled (of fruit, etc.) 3 *fam* : bare 4
fam : broke, penniless
pelaje *nm* : coat (of an animal), fur
pelar *vt* 1 : cut the hair of (a person) 2
MONDAR : peel (fruit) 3 : pluck (a
chicken, etc.), skin (an animal) —
pelarse *vr* : peel 2 *fam* : get a haircut
peldaño *nm* 1 : step (of stairs) 2 : rung
(of a ladder)
pelear *vi* 1 : fight 2 DISCUTIR : quarrel
— **pelearse** *vr* : have a fight — **pelea**
nf 1 : fight 2 DISCUSIÓN : quarrel
peletería *nf* : fur shop
peliagudo, -da *adj* : tricky, difficult
pelícano *nm* : pelican
película *nf* : movie, film
peligro *nm* 1 : danger 2 RIESGO : risk —
peligroso, -sa *adj* : dangerous
pelirrojo, -ja *adj* : red-haired — ~ *n*
: redhead
pellejo *nm* : skin, hide
pellizcar {72} *vt* : pinch — **pellizco** *nm*
: pinch
pelo *nm* 1 : hair 2 : coat, fur (of an animal) 3 : pile, nap (of fabric) 4 **con ~s**

y **señales** : in great detail 5 **no tener
~ en la lengua** *fam* : not to mince
words 6 **tomar el ~ a algn** *fam* : pull
someone's leg — **pelón, -lona** *adj
fam, mpl* **-lones** : bald
pelota *nf* : ball
pelotón *nm, pl* **-tones** : squad, detach-
ment
peltre *nm* : pewter
peluca *nf* : wig
peluche *nm* 1 : plush 2 **oso de ~**
: teddy bear
peludo, -da *adj* : hairy, furry
peluquería *nf* : hairdresser's, barber
shop — **peluquero, -ra** *n* : barber,
hairdresser
pelusa *nf* : fuzz, lint
pelvis *nfs & pl* : pelvis
pena *nf* 1 : penalty 2 TRISTEZA : sorrow
3 DOLOR : suffering, pain 4 *Lat* : embarrassment 5 **a duras ~s** : with
great difficulty 6 **¡qué ~!** : what a
shame! 7 **valer la ~** : be worthwhile
penacho *nm* 1 : crest, tuft 2 : plume
(ornament)
penal *adj* : penal — ~ *nm* : prison,
penitentiary — **penalidad** *nf* 1 : hardship 2 : penalty (in law) — **penalizar**
{21} *vt* : penalize
penalty *nm* : penalty (in sports)
penar *vt* : punish — *vi* : suffer
pendenciero, -ra *adj* : quarrelsome
pender *vi* : hang — **pendiente** *adj* 1
: pending 2 **estar ~ de** : be watching
out for — ~ *nf* : slope — ~ *nm Spain*
: earring
pendón *nm, pl* **-dones** : banner
péndulo *nm* : pendulum
pene *nm* : penis
penetrar *vi* 1 : penetrate 2 ~ **en** : go
into — *vt* 1 : penetrate 2 : pierce (one's
heart, etc.) 3 ENTENDER : fathom,
grasp — **penetración** *nf, pl* **-ciones** 1
: penetration 2 PERSPICACIA : insight
— **penetrante** *adj* 1 : penetrating 2
: sharp (of odors, etc.), piercing (of
sounds) 3 : deep (of a wound, etc.)
penicilina *nf* : penicillin
península *nf* : peninsula — **peninsular**
adj : peninsular
penitencia *nf* 1 : penitence 2 CASTIGO
: penance — **penitenciaría** *nf* : penitentiary — **penitente** *adj & nmf* : pen-
itent
penoso, -sa *adj* 1 : painful, distressing
2 TRABAJOSO : difficult 3 *Lat* : shy
pensar {55} *vi* 1 : think 2 ~ **en** : think
about — *vt* 1 : think 2 CONSIDERAR
: think about 3 ~ **hacer algo** : intend
to do sth — **pensador, -dora** *n*

: thinker — **pensamiento** *nm* **1**
: thought **2** : pansy (flower) — **pensativo, -va** *adj* : pensive, thoughtful
pensión *nf*, *pl* **-siones 1** : boarding house **2** : (retirement) pension **3** ~ **alimenticia** : alimony — **pensionista** *nmf* **1** : lodger **2** JUBILADO : retiree
pentágono *nm* : pentagon
pentagrama *nm* : staff (in music)
penúltimo, -ma *adj* : next to last, penultimate
penumbra *nf* : half-light
penuria *nf* : dearth, shortage
peña *nf* : rock, crag — **peñasco** *nm* : crag, large rock — **peñón** *nm*, *pl* **-ñones** : craggy rock
peón *nm*, *pl* **peones 1** : laborer, peon **2** : pawn (in chess)
peonía *nf* : peony
peor *adv* **1** (*comparative of* **mal**) : worse **2** (*superlative of* **mal**) : worst — ~ *adj* **1** (*comparative of* **malo**) : worse **2** (*superlative of* **malo**) : worst
pepino *nm* : cucumber — **pepinillo** *nm* : pickle, gherkin
pepita *nf* **1** : seed, pip **2** : nugget (of gold, etc.)
pequeño, -ña *adj* : small, little — **pequeñez** *nf*, *pl* **-ñeces 1** : smallness **2** NIMIEDAD : trifle
pera *nf* : pear — **peral** *nm* : pear tree
percance *nm* : mishap, setback
percatarse *vr* ~ **de** : notice
percepción *nf*, *pl* **-ciones** : perception — **perceptible** *adj* : perceptible
percha *nf* **1** : perch (for birds) **2** : (coat) hanger **3** : coatrack (on a wall)
percibir *vt* **1** : perceive **2** : receive (a salary, etc.)
percusión *nf*, *pl* **-siones** : percussion
perder {56} *vt* **1** : lose **2** : miss (an opportunity, etc.) **3** DESPERDICIAR : waste (time) — *vi* : lose — **perderse** *vr* **1** : get lost **2** DESAPARECER : disappear **3** DESPERDICIARSE : be wasted — **perdedor, -dora** *n* : loser — **pérdida** *nf* **1** : loss **2** ESCAPE : leak **3** ~ **de tiempo** : waste of time — **perdido, -da** *adj* **1** : lost **2 un caso perdido** *fam* : a hopeless case
perdigón *nm*, *pl* **-gones** : shot, pellet
perdiz *nf*, *pl* **-dices** : partridge
perdón *nm*, *pl* **-dones** : forgiveness, pardon — **perdón** *interj* : sorry! — **perdonar** *vt* **1** DISCULPAR : forgive **2** : pardon (in law)
perdurar *vi* : last, endure — **perdurable** *adj* : lasting
perecer {53} *vi* : perish, die — **perecedero, -ra** *adj* : perishable

peregrinación *nf*, *pl* **-ciones** *or* **peregrinaje** *nm* : pilgrimage — **peregrino, -na** *adj* **1** : migratory **2** RARO : unusual, odd — ~ *n* : pilgrim
perejil *nm* : parsley
perenne *adj* & *nm* : perennial
pereza *nf* : laziness — **perezoso, -sa** *adj* : lazy
perfección *nf*, *pl* **-ciones** : perfection — **perfeccionar** *vt* **1** : perfect **2** MEJORAR : improve — **perfeccionista** *nmf* : perfectionist — **perfecto, -ta** *adj* : perfect
perfidia *nf* : treachery — **pérfido, -da** *adj* : treacherous
perfil *nm* **1** : profile **2** CONTORNO : outline **3** ~**es** *nmpl* RASGOS : features — **perfilar** *vt* : outline — **perfilarse** *vr* **1** : be outlined **2** CONCRETARSE : take shape
perforar *vt* **1** : perforate **2** : drill, bore (a hole) — **perforación** *nf*, *pl* **-ciones** : perforation — **perforadora** *nf* : (paper) punch
perfume *nm* : perfume, scent — **perfumar** *vt* : perfume — **perfumarse** *vr* : put perfume on
pergamino *nm* : parchment
pericia *nf* : skill
periferia *nf* : periphery, outskirts (of a city, etc.) — **periférico, -ca** *adj* : peripheral
perilla *nf* **1** : goatee **2** *Lat* : knob **3 venir de** ~**s** *fam* : come in handy
perímetro *nm* : perimeter
periódico, -ca *adj* : periodic — **periódico** *nm* : newspaper — **periodismo** *nm* : journalism — **periodista** *nmf* : journalist
período *or* **periodo** *nm* : period
periquito *nm* : parakeet
periscopio *nm* : periscope
perito, -ta *adj* & *n* : expert
perjudicar {72} *vt* : harm, damage — **perjudicial** *adj* : harmful — **perjuicio** *nm* **1** : harm, damage **2 en** ~ **de** : to the detriment of
perjurar *vi* : perjure oneself — **perjurio** *nm* : perjury
perla *nf* **1** : pearl **2 de** ~**s** *fam* : great, just fine
permanecer {53} *vi* : remain — **permanencia** *nf* **1** : permanence **2** : stay, staying (in a place) — **permanente** *adj* : permanent — ~ *nf* : permanent (wave)
permeable *adj* : permeable
permitir *vt* **1** : permit, allow **2 ¿me permite?** : may I? — **permitirse** *vr* : allow oneself — **permisible** *adj*

: permissible, allowable — **permisi-vo, -va** adj : permissive — **permiso** nm 1 : permission 2 : permit, license (document) 3 : leave (in the military) 4 con — : excuse me

permuta nf : exchange

pernicioso, -sa adj : pernicious, destructive

pero conj : but — ~ nm 1 : fault 2 REPARO : objection

perorar vi : make a speech — **perorata** nf : (long-winded) speech

perpendicular adj & nf : perpendicular

perpetrar vt : perpetrate

perpetuar {3} vt : perpetuate — **perpetuo, -tua** adj : perpetual

perplejo, -ja adj : perplexed — **perplejidad** nf : perplexity

perro, -rra n 1 : dog, bitch f 2 **perro caliente** : hot dog — **perrera** nf : kennel

perseguir {75} vt 1 : pursue, chase 2 ACOSAR : persecute — **persecución** nf, pl **-ciones** 1 : pursuit, chase 2 ACOSO : persecution

perseverar vi : persevere — **perseverancia** nf : perseverance

persiana nf : (venetian) blind

persistir vi : persist — **persistencia** nf : persistence — **persistente** adj : persistent

persona nf : person — **personaje** nm 1 : character (in literature, etc.) 2 : important person, celebrity — **personal** adj : personal — ~ nm : personnel, staff — **personalidad** nf : personality — **personificar** {72} vt : personify

perspectiva nf 1 : perspective 2 VISTA : view 3 POSIBILIDAD : prospect, outlook

perspicacia nf : shrewdness, insight — **perspicaz** adj, pl **-caces** : shrewd, discerning

persuadir vt : persuade — **persuadirse** vr : become convinced — **persuasión** nf, pl **-siones** : persuasion — **persuasivo, -va** adj : persuasive

pertenecer {53} vi ~ a : belong to — **perteneciente** adj ~ a : belonging to — **pertenencia** nf 1 : ownership 2 ~s nfpl : belongings

pertinaz adj, pl **-naces** 1 OBSTINADO : obstinate 2 PERSISTENTE : persistent

pertinente adj : pertinent, relevant — **pertinencia** nf : relevance

perturbar vt : disturb — **perturbación** nf, pl **-ciones** : disturbance

peruano, -na adj : Peruvian

pervertir {76} vt : pervert — **perversión** nf, pl **-siones** : perversion —

perverso, -sa adj : perverse — **pervertido, -da** adj : perverted, depraved — ~ n : pervert

pesa nf 1 : weight 2 ~s : weights (in sports) — **pesadez** nf, pl **-deces** 1 : heaviness 2 fam : tediousness, drag

pesadilla nf : nightmare

pesado, -da adj 1 : heavy 2 LENTO : sluggish 3 MOLESTO : annoying 4 ABURRIDO : tedious 5 DURO : tough, difficult — ~ n fam : bore, pest — **pesadumbre** nf : grief, sorrow

pésame nm : condolences pl

pesar vt : weigh — vi 1 : weigh, be heavy 2 INFLUIR : carry weight 3 **pese a** : despite — ~ nm 1 : sorrow, grief 2 REMORDIMIENTO : remorse 3 a ~ de : in spite of

pescado nm : fish — **pesca** nf 1 : fishing 2 PECES : fish pl, catch 3 **ir de** ~ : go fishing — **pescadería** nf : fish market — **pescador, -dora** n, mpl **-dores** : fisherman — **pescar** {72} vt 1 : fish for 2 fam : catch (a cold, etc.) 3 fam : catch hold of, nab — vi : fish

pescuezo nm : neck (of an animal)

pese a → **pesar**

pesebre nm : manger

pesero nm Lat : minibus

peseta nf : peseta

pesimismo nm : pessimism — **pesimista** adj : pessimistic — ~ nmf : pessimist

pésimo, -ma adj : awful

peso nm 1 : weight 2 CARGA : burden 3 : peso (currency) 4 ~ **pesado** : heavyweight

pesquero, -ra adj : fishing

pesquisa nf : inquiry

pestaña nf : eyelash — **pestañear** vi : blink — **pestañeo** nm : blink

peste nf 1 : plague 2 fam : stench, stink 3 Lat fam : cold, bug — **pesticida** nm : pesticide — **pestilencia** nf 1 : stench 2 PLAGA : pestilence

pestillo nm : bolt, latch

petaca nf Lat : suitcase

pétalo nm : petal

petardo nm : firecracker

petición nf, pl **-ciones** : petition, request

petirrojo nm : robin

petrificar {72} vt : petrify

petróleo nm : oil, petroleum — **petrolero, -ra** adj : oil — **petrolero** nm : oil tanker

petulante adj : insolent, arrogant

peyorativo, -va adj : pejorative

pez nm, pl **peces** 1 : fish 2 ~ **de col-**

ores : goldfish 3 ~ **espada** : swordfish 4 ~ **gordo** *fam* : big shot
pezón *nm, pl* **-zones** : nipple
pezuña *nf* : hoof
piadoso, -sa *adj* 1 : compassionate 2 DEVOTO : pious, devout
piano *nm* : piano — **pianista** *nmf* : pianist, piano player
piar {85} *vi* : chirp, tweet
pibe, -ba *n Lat fam* : kid, child
pica *nf* 1 : pike, lance 2 : spade (in playing cards)
picado, -da *adj* 1 : perforated 2 : minced, chopped (of meat, etc.) 3 : decayed (of teeth) 4 : choppy (of the sea) 5 *fam* : annoyed — **picada** *nf* 1 : bite, sting 2 *Lat* : sharp descent — **picadillo** *nm* : minced meat — **picadura** *nf* 1 : sting, bite 2 : (moth) hole
picante *adj* : hot, spicy
picaporte *nm* 1 : door handle 2 ALDABA : door knocker 3 PESTILLO : latch
picar {72} *vt* 1 : sting, bite 2 : peck at, nibble on (food) 3 PERFORAR : prick, puncture 4 TRITURAR : chop, mince — *vi* 1 : bite, take the bait 2 ESCOCER : sting, itch 3 COMER : nibble 4 : be spicy (of food) — **picarse** *vr* 1 : get a cavity 2 ENFADARSE : take offense
picardía *nf* 1 : craftiness 2 TRAVESURA : prank — **picaresco, -ca** *adj* 1 : picaresque 2 TRAVIESO : roguish — **pícaro, -ra** *adj* 1 : mischievous 2 MALICIOSO : villainous — ~ *n* : rascal, scoundrel
picazón *nf, pl* **-zones** : itch
pichón, -chona *n, mpl* **-chones** : (young) pigeon
picnic *nm, pl* **-nics** : picnic
pico *nm* 1 : beak 2 CIMA : peak 3 PUNTA : (sharp) point 4 : pick, pickax (tool) 5 **las siete y** ~ : a little after seven — **picotazo** *nm* : peck — **picotear** *vt* : peck — *vi fam* : nibble, pick — **picudo, -da** *adj* : pointy
pie *nm* 1 : foot (in anatomy) 2 : base, bottom, stem 3 **al** ~ **de la letra** : word for word 4 **dar** ~ **a** : give rise to 5 **de** ~ : standing (up) 6 **de** ~**s a cabeza** : from top to bottom
piedad *nf* 1 : pity, mercy 2 DEVOCIÓN : piety
piedra *nf* 1 : stone 2 : flint (of a lighter) 3 GRANIZO : hailstone 4 ~ **angular** : cornerstone 5 → **pómez**
piel *nf* 1 : skin 2 CUERO : leather 3 PELO : fur, pelt
pienso *nm* : feed, fodder
pierna *nf* : leg
pieza *nf* 1 : piece, part 2 *or* ~ **de teatro** : play 3 HABITACIÓN : room

pigmento *nm* : pigment — **pigmentación** *nf, pl* **-ciones** : pigmentation
pigmeo, -mea *adj* : pygmy
pijama *nm* : pajamas *pl*
pila *nf* 1 : battery 2 MONTÓN : pile 3 FREGADERO : sink 4 : basin (of a fountain, etc.)
pilar *nm* : pillar
píldora *nf* : pill
pillar *vt* 1 : catch 2 : get (a joke, etc.) — **pillaje** *nm* : pillage — **pillo, -lla** *adj* : crafty — ~ *n* : rascal, scoundrel
piloto *nmf* : pilot — **pilotar** *vt* : pilot
pimienta *nf* : pepper (condiment) — **pimiento** *nm* : pepper (fruit) — **pimentero** *nm* : pepper shaker — **pimentón** *nm, pl* **-tones** 1 : paprika 2 : cayenne pepper
pináculo *nm* : pinnacle
pincel *nm* : paintbrush
pinchar *vt* 1 : pierce, prick 2 : puncture (a tire, etc.) 3 INCITAR : goad — **pinchazo** *nm* 1 : prick 2 : puncture (of a tire, etc.)
pingüino *nm* : penguin
pino *nm* : pine (tree)
pintar *v* : paint — **pintarse** *vr* : put on makeup — **pinta** *nf* 1 : spot 2 : pint (measure) 3 *fam* : appearance — **pintada** *nf* : graffiti — **pinto, -ta** *adj* : speckled, spotted — **pintor, -tora** *n, mpl* **-tores** : painter — **pintoresco, -ca** *adj* : picturesque, quaint — **pintura** *nf* 1 : paint 2 CUADRO : painting
pinza *nf* 1 : clothespin 2 : claw, pincer (of a crab, etc.) 3 ~**s** *nfpl* : tweezers
pinzón *nm, pl* **-zones** : finch
piña *nf* 1 : pine cone 2 ANANÁS : pineapple
piñata *nf* : piñata
piñón *nm, pl* **-ñones** : pine nut
pío[1], pía *adj* 1 : pious 2 : piebald (of a horse)
pío[2] *nm* : peep, chirp
piojo *nm* : louse
pionero, -ra *n* : pioneer
pipa *nf* 1 : pipe (for smoking) 2 *Spain* : seed, pip
pique *nm* 1 : grudge 2 RIVALIDAD : rivalry 3 **irse a** ~ : sink, founder
piqueta *nf* : pickax
piquete *nm* : picket (line) — **piquetear** *v* : picket
piragua *nf* : canoe
pirámide *nf* : pyramid
piraña *nf* : piranha
pirata *adj* : bootleg, pirated — ~ *nmf* : pirate — **piratear** *vt* 1 : bootleg, pirate 2 : hack into (a computer)

piropo *nm* : (flirtatious) compliment
pirueta *nf* : pirouette
pirulí *nm* : (cone-shaped) lollipop
pisada *nf* 1 : footstep 2 HUELLA : footprint
pisapapeles *nms & pl* : paperweight
pisar *vt* 1 : step on 2 HUMILLAR : walk all over, abuse — *vi* : step, tread
piscina *nf* 1 : swimming pool 2 : (fish) pond
piso *nm* 1 : floor, story 2 *Lat* : floor (of a room) 3 *Spain* : apartment
pisotear *vt* : trample (on)
pista *nf* 1 : trail, track 2 INDICIO : clue 3 ~ **de aterrizaje** : runway, airstrip 4 ~ **de baile** : dance floor 5 ~ **de hielo** : ice-skating rink
pistacho *nm* : pistachio
pistola *nf* 1 : pistol, gun 2 PULVERIZADOR : spray gun — **pistolera** *nf* : holster — **pistolero** *nm* : gunman
pistón *nm, pl* **-tones** : piston
pito *nm* 1 SILBATO : whistle 2 CLAXON : horn — **pitar** *vi* 1 : blow a whistle 2 : beep, honk (of a horn) — *vt* : whistle at — **pitido** *nm* 1 : whistle, whistling 2 : beep (of a horn) — **pitillo** *nm fam* : cigarette
pitón *nm, pl* **-tones** *nm* : python
pitorro *nm* : spout
pivote *nm* : pivot
piyama *nmf Lat* : pajamas *pl*
pizarra *nf* 1 : slate 2 ENCERADO : blackboard — **pizarrón** *nm, pl* **-rrones** *Lat* : blackboard
pizca *nf* 1 : pinch (of salt) 2 ÁPICE : speck, tiny bit 3 *Lat* : harvest
pizza ['pitsa, 'pisa] *nf* : pizza — **pizzería** *nf* : pizzeria
placa *nf* 1 : sheet, plate 2 INSCRIPCIÓN : plaque 3 : (police) badge
placenta *nf* : placenta
placer {57} *vt* : please — ~ *nm* : pleasure — **placentero, -ra** *adj* : pleasant, agreeable
plácido, -da *adj* : placid, calm
plaga *nf* 1 : plague 2 CALAMIDAD : disaster — **plagar** {52} *vt* : plague, infest
plagiar *vt* : plagiarize — **plagio** *nm* : plagiarism
plan *nm* 1 : plan 2 **en** ~ **de** : as 3 **no te pongas en ese** ~ *fam* : don't be that way
plana *nf* 1 : page 2 **en primera** ~ : on the front page
plancha *nf* 1 : iron (for ironing) 2 : grill (for cooking) 3 LÁMINA : sheet, plate — **planchar** *v* : iron — **planchado** *nm* : ironing

planear *vt* : plan — *vi* : glide — **planeador** *nm* : glider
planeta *nm* : planet
planicie *nf* : plain
planificar {72} *vt* : plan — **planificación** *nf, pl* **-ciones** : planning
planilla *nf Lat* : list, roster
plano, -na *adj* : flat — **plano** *nm* 1 : map, plan 2 : plane (surface) 3 NIVEL : level 4 **de** ~ : flatly, outright 5 **primer** ~ : foreground, close-up (in photography)
planta *nf* 1 : plant 2 PISO : floor, story 3 : sole (of the foot) — **plantación** *nf, pl* **-ciones** 1 : plantation 2 : (action of) planting — **plantar** *vt* 1 : plant 2 *fam* : deal, land — **plantarse** *vr* : stand firm
plantear *vt* 1 : expound, set forth 2 : raise (a question) 3 CAUSAR : create, pose (a problem) — **plantearse** *vr* : think about, consider
plantel *nm* 1 : staff, team 2 *Lat* : educational institution
plantilla *nf* 1 : insole 2 PATRÓN : pattern, template 3 : staff (of a business, etc.)
plasma *nm* : plasma
plástico, -ca *adj* : plastic — **plástico** *nm* : plastic
plata *nf* 1 : silver 2 *Lat fam* : money 3 ~ **de ley** : sterling silver
plataforma *nf* 1 : platform 2 ~ **petrolífera** : oil rig 3 ~ **de lanzamiento** : launching pad
plátano *nm* 1 : banana 2 : plantain
platea *nf* : orchestra, pit (in a theater)
plateado, -da *adj* 1 : silver, silvery (color) 2 : silver-plated
platicar {72} *vi* : talk, chat — **plática** *nf* : chat, conversation
platija *nf* : flatfish, flounder
platillo *nm* 1 : saucer 2 CÍMBALO : cymbal 3 *Lat* : dish, course
platino *nm* : platinum
plato *nm* 1 : plate, dish 2 : course (of a meal) 3 ~ **principal** : entrée
platónico, -ca *adj* : platonic
playa *nf* 1 : beach, seashore 2 ~ **de estacionamiento** *Lat* : parking lot
plaza *nf* 1 : square, plaza 2 : seat (in transportation) 3 PUESTO : post, position 4 MERCADO : market, marketplace 5 ~ **de toros** : bullring
plazo *nm* 1 : period, term 2 PAGO : installment 3 **a largo** ~ : long-term
plazoleta *or* **plazuela** *nf* : small square
pleamar *nf* : high tide
plebe *nf* : common people — **plebeyo, -ya** *adj & nm* : plebeian
plegar {49} *vt* : fold, bend — **plegarse** *vr* 1 : give in, yield 2 : jackknife (of a

truck) — **plegable** *or* **plegadizo, -za** *adj* : folding, collapsible
plegaria *nf* : prayer
pleito *nm* **1** : lawsuit **2** *Lat* : dispute, fight
plenilunio *nm* : full moon
pleno, -na *adj* **1** : full, complete **2 en plena forma** : in top form **3 en pleno día** : in broad daylight — **plenitud** *nf* : fullness, abundance
pleuresía *nf* : pleurisy
pliego *nm* : sheet (of paper) — **pliegue** *nm* **1** : crease, fold **2** : pleat (in fabric)
plisar *vt* : pleat
plomería *nf Lat* : plumbing — **plomero, -ra** *n Lat* : plumber
plomo *nm* **1** : lead **2** FUSIBLE : fuse
pluma *nf* **1** : feather **2** : (fountain) pen — **plumaje** *nm* : plumage — **plumero** *nm* : feather duster — **plumilla** *nf* : nib — **plumón** *nm, pl* **-mones** : down
plural *adj & nm* : plural — **pluralidad** *nf* : plurality
pluriempleo *nm* **hacer** ~ : have more than one job
plus *nm* : bonus
plusvalía *nf* : appreciation, capital gain
plutocracia *nf* : plutocracy
Plutón *nm* : Pluto
plutonio *nm* : plutonium
pluvial *adj* : rain
poblar {19} *vt* **1** : settle, colonize **2** HABITAR : inhabit — **poblarse** *vr* : become crowded — **población** *nf, pl* **-ciones 1** : city, town, village **2** HABITANTES : population — **poblado, -da** *adj* **1** : populated **2** : thick, bushy (of a beard, eyebrows, etc.) — **poblado** *nm* : village
pobre *adj* **1** : poor **2** ¡~ **de mí!** : poor me! — ~ *nmf* **1** : poor person **2 los** ~**s** : the poor **3** ¡**pobre!** : poor thing! — **pobreza** *nf* : poverty
pocilga *nf* : pigsty
poción *nf, pl* **-ciones** *or* **pócima** *nf* : potion
poco, -ca *adj* **1** : little, not much, (a) few **2 pocas veces** : rarely — ~ *pron* **1** : little, few **2 hace poco** : not long ago **3 poco a poco** : bit by bit, gradually **4 por poco** : nearly, just about **5 un poco** : a little, a bit — **poco** *adv* : little, not much
podar *vt* : prune
poder {58} *v aux* **1** : be able to, can **2** (*expressing possibility*) : might, may **3** (*expressing permission*) : can, may **4** ¿**cómo puede ser?** : how can it be? **5** ¿**puedo pasar?** : may I come in? — *vi* **1** : be possible **2** ~ **con** : cope with, manage **3 no puedo más** : I've

had enough — ~ *nm* **1** : power **2** POSESIÓN : possession — **poderío** *nm* : power — **poderoso, -sa** *adj* : powerful
podólogo, -ga *n* : chiropodist
podrido, -da *adj* : rotten
poema *nm* : poem — **poesía** *nf* **1** : poetry **2** POEMA : poem — **poeta** *nmf* : poet — **poético, -ca** *adj* : poetic
póker *nm* → **póquer**
polaco, -ca *adj* : Polish
polar *adj* : polar — **polarizar** {21} *vt* : polarize
polea *nf* : pulley
polémica *nf* : controversy — **polémico, -ca** *adj* : controversial — **polemizar** *vt* : argue
polen *nm, pl* **pólenes** : pollen
policía *nf* : police — ~ *nmf* : police officer, policeman *m*, policewoman *f* — **policíaco, -ca** *adj* **1** : police **2 novela policíaca** : detective story
poliéster *nm* : polyester
poligamia *nf* : polygamy — **polígamo, -ma** *n* : polygamist
polígono *nm* : polygon
polilla *nf* : moth
polio *or* **poliomielitis** *nf* : polio, poliomyelitis
politécnico, -ca *adj* : polytechnic
política *nf* **1** : politics **2** POSTURA : policy — **político, -ca** *adj* **1** : political **2 hermano político** : brother-in-law — ~ *n* : politician
póliza *nf or* ~ **de seguros** : insurance policy
polizón *nm, pl* **-zones** : stowaway
pollo, -lla *n* **1** : chicken, chick **2** : chicken (for cooking) — **pollera** *nf Lat* : skirt — **pollería** *nf* : poultry shop — **pollito, -ta** *n* : chick
polo *nm* **1** : pole **2** : polo (sport) **3** ~ **norte** : North Pole
poltrona *nf* : easy chair
polución *nf, pl* **-ciones** : pollution
polvo *nm* **1** : powder **2** SUCIEDAD : dust **3** ~**s** *nmpl* : face powder **4 hacer** ~ *fam* : crush, shatter — **polvareda** *nf* : cloud of dust — **polvera** *nf* : compact (for powder) — **pólvora** *nf* : gunpowder — **polvoriento, -ta** *adj* : dusty
pomada *nf* : ointment
pomelo *nm* : grapefruit
pómez *nm or* **piedra** ~ *nf* : pumice
pomo *nm* : knob, doorknob
pompa *nf* **1** : (soap) bubble **2** ESPLENDOR : pomp **3** ~**s fúnebres** : funeral — **pomposo, -sa** *adj* **1** : pompous **2** ESPLÉNDIDO : splendid
pómulo *nm* : cheekbone

ponchar *vt Lat* : puncture — **ponchadura** *nf Lat* : puncture
ponche *nm* : punch (drink)
poncho *nm* : poncho
ponderar *vt* **1** : consider **2** ALABAR : speak highly of
poner {60} *vt* **1** : put **2** AGREGAR : add **3** CONTRIBUIR : contribute **4** SUPONER : suppose **5** DISPONER : arrange, set out **6** : give (a name), call **7** ENCENDER : turn on **8** ESTABLECER : set up, establish **9** : lay (eggs) — *vi* : lay eggs — **ponerse** *vr* **1** : move (into a position) **2** : put on (clothing, etc.) **3** : set (of the sun) **4** ~ **furioso** : become angry
poniente *nm* **1** OCCIDENTE : west **2** : west wind
pontífice *nm* : pontiff
pontón *nm, pl* **-tones** : pontoon
ponzoña *nf* : poison, venom
popa *nf* **1** : stern **2 a** ~ : astern
popelín *nm, pl* **-lines** : poplin
popote *nm Lat* : (drinking) straw
populacho *nm* : rabble, masses *pl*
popular *adj* **1** : popular **2** : colloquial (of language) — **popularidad** *nf* : popularity — **popularizar** {21} *vt* : popularize — **populoso, -sa** *adj* : populous
póquer *nm* : poker (card game)
por *prep* **1** : for **2** (*indicating an approximate time*) : around, during **3** (*indicating an approximate place*) : around, about **4** A TRAVÉS DE : through, along **5** A CAUSA DE : because of **6** (*indicating rate or ratio*) : per **7** *or* ~ **medio de** : by means of **8** : times (in mathematics) **9** SEGÚN : as for, according to **10 estar** ~ : be about to **11** ~ **ciento** : percent **12** ~ **favor** : please **13** ~ **lo tanto** : therefore **14 ¿por qué?** : why?
porcelana *nf* : porcelain, china
porcentaje *nm* : percentage
porción *nf, pl* **-ciones** : portion, piece
pordiosero, -ra *n* : beggar
porfiar {85} *vi* : insist — **porfiado, -da** *adj* : obstinate, persistent
pormenor *nm* : detail
pornografía *nf* : pornography — **pornográfico, -ca** *adj* : pornographic
poro *nm* : pore — **poroso, -sa** *adj* : porous
poroto *nm Lat* : bean
porque *conj* **1** : because **2** *or* **por que** : in order that — **porqué** *nm* : reason
porquería *nf* **1** SUCIEDAD : filth **2** : shoddy thing, junk
porra *nf* : nightstick, club — **porrazo** *nm* : blow, whack

portaaviones *nms & pl* : aircraft carrier
portada *nf* **1** : facade **2** : title page (of a book), cover (of a magazine)
portador, -dora *n* : bearer
portaequipajes *nms & pl* : luggage rack
portafolio *or* **portafolios** *nm, pl* **-lios 1** : portfolio **2** MALETÍN : briefcase
portal *nm* **1** : doorway **2** VESTÍBULO : hall, vestibule
portamonedas *nms & pl* : purse
portar *vt* : carry, bear — **portarse** *vr* : behave
portátil *adj* : portable
portaviones *nm* → **portaaviones**
portavoz *nmf, pl* **-voces** : spokesperson, spokesman *m*, spokeswoman *f*
portazo *nm* **dar un** ~ : slam the door
porte *nm* **1** : transport, freight **2** ASPECTO : bearing, appearance **3** ~ **pagado** : postage paid
portento *nm* : marvel, wonder — **portentoso, -sa** *adj* : marvelous
porteño, -ña *adj* : of or from Buenos Aires
portería *nf* **1** : superintendent's office **2** : goal, goalposts *pl* (in sports) — **portero, -ra** *n* **1** : goalkeeper, goalie **2** CONSERJE : janitor, superintendent
portezuela *nf* : door (of an automobile)
pórtico *nm* : portico
portilla *nf* : porthole
portugués, -guesa *adj, mpl* **-gueses** : Portuguese — **portugués** *nm* : Portuguese (language)
porvenir *nm* : future
pos: en ~ **de** *adv phr* : in pursuit of
posada *nf* : inn
posaderas *nfpl fam* : backside, bottom
posar *vi* : pose — *vt* : place, lay — **posarse** *vr* : settle, rest
posavasos *nms & pl* : coaster
posdata *nf* : postscript
pose *nf* : pose
poseer {20} *vt* : possess, own — **poseedor, -dora** *n* : possessor, owner — **poseído, -da** *adj* : possessed — **posesión** *nf, pl* **-siones** : possession — **posesionarse** *vr* ~ **de** : take possession of, take over — **posesivo, -va** *adj* : possessive
posguerra *nf* : postwar period
posibilidad *nf* : possibility — **posibilitar** *vt* : make possible — **posible** *adj* **1** : possible **2 de ser** ~ : if possible
posición *nf, pl* **-ciones** : position — **posicionar** *vt* : position — **posicionarse** *vr* : take a stand
positivo, -va *adj* : positive
poso *nm* : sediment, (coffee) grounds

posponer {60} *vt* **1** : postpone **2** RELE-GAR : put behind, subordinate

postal *adj* : postal — **~** *nf* : postcard

postdata → **posdata**

poste *nm* : post, pole

póster *nm, pl* **-ters** : poster

postergar {52} *vt* **1** : pass over **2** APLAZAR : postpone

posteridad *nf* : posterity — **posterior** *adj* **1** : later, subsequent **2** TRASERO : back, rear — **posteriormente** *adv* : subsequently, later

postigo *nm* **1** : small door **2** CONTRA-VENTANA : shutter

postizo, -za *adj* : artificial, false

postrarse *vr* : prostrate oneself — **postrado, -da** *adj* : prostrate

postre *nm* : dessert

postular *vt* **1** : advance, propose **2** *Lat* : nominate — **postulado** *nm* : postulate

póstumo, -ma *adj* : posthumous

postura *nf* : position, stance

potable *adj* : drinkable, potable

potaje *nm* : thick vegetable soup

potasio *nm* : potassium

pote *nm* : jar

potencia *nf* : power — **potencial** *adj & nm* : potential — **potente** *adj* : powerful

potro, -tra *n* : colt *m*, filly *f* — **potro** *nm* : horse (in gymnastics)

pozo *nm* **1** : well **2** : shaft (in a mine)

práctica *nf* **1** : practice **2 en la ~** : in practice **2** PRUDENCIA : caution, care **3 con ~** : cautiously

precaver *vt* : guard against — **precavido, -da** *adj* : prudent, cautious

preceder *v* : precede — **precedencia** *nf* : precedence, priority — **precedente** *adj* : preceding, previous — **~** *nm* : precedent

precepto *nm* : precept

preciado, -da *adj* : prized, valuable — **preciarse** *vr* **~ de** : pride oneself on, boast about

precinto *nm* : seal

precio *nm* : price, cost — **preciosidad** *nf* **1** VALOR : value **2** : beautiful thing — **precioso, -sa** *adj* **1** HERMOSO : beautiful **2** VALIOSO : precious

precipicio *nm* : precipice

precipitar *vt* **1** : hasten, speed up **2** ARROJAR : hurl — **precipitarse** *vr* **1** APRESURARSE : rush **2** : act rashly **3** ARROJARSE : throw oneself — **precipitación** *nf, pl* **-ciones 1** : precipitation **2** PRISA : haste — **precipitadamente** *adv* : in a rush, hastily — **precipitado, -da** *adj* : hasty

preciso, -sa *adj* **1** : precise **2** NECESARIO : necessary — **precisamente** *adv* : precisely, exactly — **precisar** *vt* **1** : specify, determine **2** NECESITAR : require — **precisión** *nf, pl* **-siones 1** : precision **2** NECESIDAD : necessity

preconcebido *adj* : preconceived

precoz *adj, pl* **-coces 1** : early **2** : precocious (of children)

precursor, -sora *n* : forerunner

predecesor, -sora *n* : predecessor

predecir {11} *vt* : foretell, predict

predestinado, -da *adj* : predestined

predeterminar *vt* : predetermine

prédica *nf* : sermon

predicado *nm* : predicate

predicar {72} *v* : preach — **predicador, -dora** *n* : preacher

predicción *nf, pl* **-ciones 1** : prediction **2** PRONÓSTICO : forecast

predilección *nf, pl* **-ciones** : preference — **predilecto, -ta** *adj* : favorite

predisponer {60} *vt* : predispose — **predisposición** *nf, pl* **-ciones** : predisposition

predominar *vi* : predominate — **predominante** *adj* : predominant, prevailing — **predominio** *nm* : predominance

preeminente *adj* : preeminent

prefabricado, -da *adj* : prefabricated

prefacio *nm* : preface

preferir {76} *vt* : prefer — **preferencia** *nf* **1** : preference **2 de ~** : preferably — **preferente** *adj* : preferential — **preferible** *adj* : preferable — **preferido, -da** *adj* : favorite

prefijo *nm* **1** : prefix **2** *Spain* : area code

pregonar *vt* : proclaim, announce

pregunta *nf* **1** : question **2 hacer ~s** : ask questions — **preguntar** *v* : ask — **preguntarse** *vr* : wonder

prehistórico, -ca *adj* : prehistoric

prejuicio *nm* : prejudice

preliminar *adj & nm* : preliminary

preludio *nm* : prelude

prematrimonial *adj* : premarital

---

práctica *nf* **1** : practice **2 en la ~** : in practice — **practicable** *adj* : practicable, feasible — **practicante** *adj* : practicing — **~** *nmf* : practitioner — **practicar** {72} *vt* **1** : practice **2** REALIZAR : perform, carry out — *vi* : practice — **práctico, -ca** *adj* : practical

pradera *nf* : grassland, prairie — **prado** *nm* : meadow

pragmático, -ca *adj* : pragmatic

preámbulo *nm* : preamble

precario, -ria *adj* : precarious

precaución *nf, pl* **-ciones 1** : precaution **2** PRUDENCIA : caution, care **3 con ~** : cautiously

prematuro, -ra *adj* : premature
premeditar *vt* : premeditate — **premeditación** *nf, pl* **-ciones** : premeditation
premenstrual *adj* : premenstrual
premio *nm* **1** : prize **2** RECOMPENSA : reward **3** ~ **gordo** : jackpot — **premiado, -da** *adj* : prizewinning — **premiar** *vt* **1** : award a prize to **2** RECOMPENSAR : reward
premisa *nf* : premise
premonición *nf, pl* **-ciones** : premonition
premura *nf* : haste, urgency
prenatal *adj* : prenatal
prenda *nf* **1** : piece of clothing **2** GARANTÍA : pledge **3** : forfeit (in a game) — **prendar** *vt* : captivate — **prendarse** *vr* ~ **de** : fall in love with
prender *vt* **1** SUJETAR : pin, fasten **2** APRESAR : capture **3** : light (a match, etc.) **4** *Lat* : turn on (a light, etc.) — *vi* **1** : take root **2** ARDER : catch, burn (of fire) — **prenderse** *vr* : catch fire — **prendedor** *nm Lat* : brooch, pin
prensa *nf* : press — **prensar** *vt* : press
preñado, -da *adj* **1** : pregnant **2** ~ **de** : filled with
preocupar *vt* : worry — **preocuparse** *vr* **1** : worry **2** ~ **de** : take care of — **preocupación** *nf, pl* **-ciones** : worry
preparar *vt* : prepare — **prepararse** *vr* : get ready — **preparación** *nf, pl* **-ciones** : preparation — **preparado, -da** *adj* : prepared, ready — **preparado** *nm* : preparation — **preparativo, -va** *adj* : preparatory, preliminary — **preparativos** *nmpl* : preparations — **preparatorio, -ria** *adj* : preparatory
preposición *nf, pl* **-ciones** : preposition
prepotente *adj* : arrogant, domineering
prerrogativa *nf* : prerogative
presa *nf* **1** : catch, prey **2** DIQUE : dam **3** **hacer** ~ **en** : seize
presagiar *vt* : presage, forebode — **presagio** *nm* **1** : omen **2** PREMONICIÓN : premonition
presbítero *nm* : presbyter, priest
prescindir *vi* ~ **de 1** : do without **2** OMITIR : dispense with
prescribir {33} *vt* : prescribe — **prescripción** *nf, pl* **-ciones** : prescription
presencia *nf* **1** : presence **2** ASPECTO : appearance — **presenciar** *vt* : be present at, witness
presentar *vt* **1** : present **2** OFRECER : offer, give **3** MOSTRAR : show **4** : introduce (persons) — **presentarse** *vr* **1** : show up **2** : arise, come up (of a

problem, etc.) **3** : introduce oneself — **presentación** *nf, pl* **-ciones 1** : presentation **2** : introduction (of persons) **3** ASPECTO : appearance — **presentador, -dora** *n* : presenter, host (of a television program, etc.)
presente *adj* **1** : present **2 tener** ~ : keep in mind — ~ *nm* **1** : present **2 entre los** ~**s** : among those present
presentir {76} *vt* : have a presentiment of — **presentimiento** *nm* : premonition
preservar *vt* : preserve, protect — **preservación** *nf, pl* **-ciones** : preservation — **preservativo** *nm* : condom
presidente, -ta *n* **1** : president **2** : chair, chairperson (of a meeting) — **presidencia** *nf* **1** : presidency **2** : chairmanship (of a meeting) — **presidencial** *adj* : presidential
presidio *nm* : prison — **presidiario, -ria** *n* : convict
presidir *vt* **1** : preside over, chair **2** PREDOMINAR : dominate
presión *nf, pl* **-siones 1** : pressure **2** ~ **arterial** : blood pressure **3 hacer** ~ : press — **presionar** *vt* **1** : press **2** COACCIONAR : put pressure on
preso, -sa *adj* : imprisoned — ~ *n* : prisoner
prestar *vt* **1** : lend, loan **2** : give (aid) **3** ~ **atención** : pay attention — **prestado, -da** *adj* **1** : borrowed, on loan **2 pedir** ~ : borrow — **prestamista** *nmf* : moneylender — **préstamo** *nm* : loan
prestidigitación *nf, pl* **-ciones** : sleight of hand — **prestidigitador, -dora** *n* : magician
prestigio *nm* : prestige — **prestigioso, -sa** *adj* : prestigious
presto, -ta *adj* : prompt, ready — **presto** *adv* : promptly, right away
presumir *vt* : presume — *vi* : boast, show off — **presumido, -da** *adj* : conceited, vain — **presunción** *nf, pl* **-ciones 1** : presumption **2** VANIDAD : vanity — **presunto, -ta** *adj* : presumed, alleged — **presuntuoso, -sa** *adj* : conceited
presuponer {60} *vt* : presuppose — **presupuesto** *nm* **1** : budget, estimate **2** SUPUESTO : assumption
presuroso, -sa *adj* : hasty, quick
pretender *vt* **1** : try to **2** AFIRMAR : claim **3** CORTEJAR : court, woo **4** ~ **que** : expect — **pretencioso, -sa** *adj* : pretentious — **pretendido** *adj* : supposed — **pretendiente** *nmf* **1** : candidate **2** : pretender (to a throne) — ~

nm : suitor — **pretensión** *nf, pl* **-siones 1** INTENCIÓN : intention, aspiration **2** : claim (to a throne, etc.) **3 pretensiones** *nfpl* : pretensions

pretérito *nm* : past (in grammar)

pretexto *nm* : pretext, excuse

prevalecer {53} *vi* : prevail — **prevaleciente** *adj* : prevailing, prevalent

prevenir {87} *vt* **1** : prevent **2** AVISAR : warn — **prevenirse** {87} *vr* ~ **contra** *or* ~ **de** : take precautions against — **prevención** *nf, pl* **-ciones 1** : prevention **2** PRECAUCIÓN : precaution **3** PREJUICIO : prejudice — **prevenido, -da** *adj* **1** : prepared, ready **2** PRECAVIDO : cautious — **preventivo, -va** *adj* : preventive

prever {88} *vt* **1** : foresee **2** PLANEAR : plan

previo, -via *adj* : previous, prior

previsible *adj* : foreseeable — **previsión** *nf, pl* **-siones 1** : foresight **2** PREDICCIÓN : prediction, forecast — **previsor, -sora** *adj* : farsighted, prudent

prieto, -ta *adj* **1** CEÑIDO : tight **2** *Lat fam* : dark-skinned

prima *nf* **1** : bonus **2** : (insurance) premium **3** → **primo**

primario, -ria *adj* **1** : primary **2 escuela primaria** : elementary school

primate *nm* : primate

primavera *nf* **1** : spring (season) **2** : primrose (flower) — **primaveral** *adj* : spring

primero, -ra *adj* (**primer** *before masculine singular nouns*) **1** : first **2** MEJOR : top, leading **3** PRINCIPAL : main, basic **4 de primera** : first-rate — ~ *n* : first (person or thing) — **primero** *adv* **1** : first **2** MÁS BIEN : rather, sooner

primitivo, -va *adj* : primitive

primo, -ma *n* : cousin

primogénito, -ta *adj & n* : firstborn

primor *nm* : beautiful thing

primordial *adj* : basic, fundamental

primoroso, -sa *adj* **1** : exquisite, fine **2** HÁBIL : skillful

princesa *nf* : princess

principado *nm* : principality

principal *adj* : main, principal

príncipe *nm* : prince

principio *nm* **1** : principle **2** COMIENZO : beginning, start **3** ORIGEN : origin **4 al** ~ : at first **5 a** ~ **s de** : at the beginning of — **principiante** *nmf* : beginner

pringar {52} *vt* : spatter (with grease) — **pringoso, -sa** *adj* : greasy

prioridad *nf* : priority

prisa *nf* **1** : hurry, rush **2 a** ~ *or* **de** ~ : quickly **3 a toda** ~ : as fast as possible **4 darse** ~ : hurry **5 tener** ~ : be in a hurry

prisión *nf, pl* **-siones 1** : prison **2** ENCARCELAMIENTO : imprisonment — **prisionero, -ra** *n* : prisoner

prisma *nm* : prism — **prismáticos** *nmpl* : binoculars

privar *vt* **1** : deprive **2** PROHIBIR : forbid **3** *Lat* : knock out — **privarse** *vr* : deprive oneself — **privación** *nf, pl* **-ciones** : deprivation — **privado, -da** *adj* : private — **privativo, -va** *adj* : exclusive

privilegio *nm* : privilege — **privilegiado, -da** *adj* : privileged

pro *prep* : for, in favor of — ~ *nm* **1** : pro, advantage **2 en** ~ **de** : for, in support of **3 los pros y los contras** : the pros and cons

proa *nf* : bow, prow

probabilidad *nf* : probability — **probable** *adj* : probable, likely — **probablemente** *adv* : probably

probar {19} *vt* **1** : try, test **2** : try on (clothing) **3** DEMOSTRAR : prove **4** DEGUSTAR : taste — *vi* : try — **probarse** *vr* : try on (clothing) — **probeta** *nf* : test tube

problema *nm* : problem — **problemático, -ca** *adj* : problematic

proceder *vi* **1** : proceed, act **2** : be appropriate **3** ~ **de** : come from — **procedencia** *nf* : origin — **procedente** *adj* ~ **de** : coming from, originating in — **procedimiento** *nm* **1** : procedure, method **2** : proceedings *pl* (in law)

procesar *vt* **1** : prosecute **2** : process (data) — **procesador** *nm* ~ **de textos** : word processor — **procesamiento** *nm* : processing — **procesión** *nf, pl* **-siones** : procession — **proceso** *nm* **1** : process **2** : trial, proceedings *pl* (in law)

proclamar *vt* : proclaim — **proclama** *nf* : proclamation — **proclamación** *nf, pl* **-ciones** : proclamation

procrear *vi* : procreate — **procreación** *nf, pl* **-ciones** : procreation

procurar *vt* **1** : try, endeavor **2** CONSEGUIR : obtain, procure — **procurador, -dora** *n* : attorney

prodigar {52} *vt* : lavish — **prodigio** *nm* : wonder, prodigy — **prodigioso, -sa** *adj* : prodigious

pródigo, -ga *adj* : extravagant, prodigal

producir {61} *vt* **1** : produce **2** CAUSAR : cause **3** : yield, bear (interest, fruit, etc.) — **producirse** *vr* : take place —

producción *nf, pl* **-ciones** : production — **productividad** *nf* : productivity — **productivo, -va** *adj* : productive — **producto** *nm* : product — **productor, -tora** *n* : producer

proeza *nf* : exploit

profanar *vt* : profane, desecrate — **profanación** *nf, pl* **-ciones** : desecration — **profano, -na** *adj* : profane

profecía *nf* : prophecy

proferir {76} *vt* 1 : utter 2 : hurl (insults)

profesar *vt* 1 : profess 2 : practice (a profession, etc.) — **profesión** *nf, pl* **-siones** : profession — **profesional** *adj & nmf* : professional — **profesor, -sora** *n* 1 : teacher 2 : professor (at a university, etc.) — **profesorado** *nm* 1 : teaching profession 2 PROFESORES : faculty

profeta *nm* : prophet — **profético, -ca** *adj* : prophetic — **profetista** *nf* : (female) prophet — **profetizar** {21} *vt* : prophesy

prófugo, -ga *adj & n* : fugitive

profundo, -da *adj* 1 HONDO : deep 2 : profound (of thoughts, etc.) — **profundamente** *adv* : deeply, profoundly — **profundidad** *nf* : depth — **profundizar** {21} *vt* : study in depth

profuso, -sa *adj* : profuse — **profusión** *nf, pl* **-siones** : profusion

progenie *nf* : progeny, offspring

programa *nm* 1 : program 2 : curriculum (in education) — **programación** *nf, pl* **-ciones** : programming — **programador, -dora** *n* : programmer — **programar** *vt* 1 : schedule 2 : program (a computer, etc.)

progreso *nm* : progress — **progresar** *vi* : (make) progress — **progresión** *nf, pl* **-ciones** : progression — **progresista** *adj & nmf* : progressive — **progresivo, -va** *adj* : progressive, gradual

prohibir {62} *vt* : prohibit, forbid — **prohibición** *nf, pl* **-ciones** : ban, prohibition — **prohibido, -da** *adj* : forbidden — **prohibitivo, -va** *adj* : prohibitive

prójimo *nm* : neighbor, fellow man

prole *nf* : offspring

proletariado *nm* : proletariat — **proletario, -ria** *adj & n* : proletarian

proliferar *vi* : proliferate — **proliferación** *nf, pl* **-ciones** : proliferation — **prolífico, -ca** *adj* : prolific

prolijo, -ja *adj* : wordy, long-winded

prólogo *nm* : prologue, foreword

prolongar {52} *vt* 1 : prolong 2 ALARGAR : lengthen — **prolongarse** *vr* : last, continue — **prolongación** *nf, pl* **-ciones** : extension

promedio *nm* : average

promesa *nf* : promise — **prometedor, -dora** *adj* : promising, hopeful — **prometer** *vt* : promise — *vi* : show promise — **prometerse** *vr* : get engaged — **prometido, -da** *adj* : engaged — ~ *n* : fiancé *m*, fiancée *f*

prominente *adj* : prominent — **prominencia** *nf* : prominence

promiscuo, -cua *adj* : promiscuous — **promiscuidad** *nf* : promiscuity

promocionar *vt* : promote — **promoción** *nf, pl* **-ciones** : promotion

promontorio *nm* : promontory

promover {47} *vt* 1 : promote 2 CAUSAR : cause — **promotor, -tora** *n* : promoter

promulgar {52} *vt* 1 : proclaim 2 : enact (a law)

pronombre *nm* : pronoun

pronosticar {72} *vt* : predict, forecast — **pronóstico** *nm* 1 : prediction, forecast 2 : (medical) prognosis

pronto, -ta *adj* 1 : quick, prompt 2 PREPARADO : ready — **pronto** *adv* 1 : soon 2 RAPIDAMENTE : quickly, promptly 3 de ~ : suddenly 4 por lo ~ : for the time being 5 tan ~ como : as soon as

pronunciar *vt* 1 : pronounce 2 : give, deliver (a speech) — **pronunciarse** *vr* 1 : declare oneself 2 SUBLEVARSE : revolt — **pronunciación** *nf, pl* **-ciones** : pronunciation

propagación *nf, pl* **-ciones** : propagation

propaganda *nf* 1 : propaganda 2 PUBLICIDAD : advertising

propagar {52} *vt* : propagate, spread — **propagarse** *vr* : propagate

propano *nm* : propane

propasarse *vr* : go too far

propensión *nf, pl* **-siones** : inclination, propensity — **propenso, -sa** *adj* : prone, inclined

propiamente *adv* : exactly

propicio, -cia *adj* : favorable, propitious

propiedad *nf* 1 : property 2 PERTINENCIA : ownership, possession — **propietario, -ria** *n* : owner, proprietor

propina *nf* : tip

propinar *vt* : give, deal (a blow, etc.)

propio, -pia *adj* 1 : own 2 APROPIADO : proper, appropriate 3 CARACTERÍSTICO : characteristic, typical 4 MISMO : himself, herself, oneself

proponer {60} *vt* 1 : propose 2 : nominate (a person) — **proponerse** *vr* : propose, intend

proporción *nf, pl* **-clones** : proportion — **proporcionado, -da** *adj* : proportionate — **proporcional** *adj* : proportional — **proporcionar** *vt* 1 : provide 2 AJUSTAR : adapt, proportion

proposición *nf, pl* **-ciones** : proposal, proposition

propósito *nm* 1 : purpose, intention 2 a ~ : incidentally, by the way 3 a ~ : on purpose, intentionally

propuesta *nf* 1 : proposal 2 : offer (of employment, etc.)

propulsar *vt* 1 : propel, drive 2 PROMOVER : promote — **propulsión** *nf, pl* **-siones** : propulsion

prorrogar {52} *vt* 1 : extend 2 APLAZAR : postpone — **prórroga** *nf* 1 : extension, deferment 2 : overtime (in sports)

prorrumpir *vi* : burst forth, break out

prosa *nf* : prose

proscribir {33} *vt* 1 : prohibit, ban 2 DESTERRAR : exile — **proscripción** *nf, pl* **-ciones** 1 : ban 2 DESTIERRO : banishment — **proscrito, -ta** *adj* : banned — ~ *n* : exile, outlaw

proseguir {75} *v* : continue — **prosecución** *nf, pl* **-ciones** : continuation

prospección *nf, pl* **-ciones** : prospecting, exploration

prospecto *nm* : prospectus

prosperar *vi* : prosper, thrive — **prosperidad** *nf* : prosperity — **próspero, -ra** *adj* : prosperous, fluorishing

prostituir {41} *vt* : prostitute — **prostitución** *nf, pl* **-ciones** : prostitution — **prostituta** *nf* : prostitute

protagonista *nmf* : protagonist — **protagonizar** *vt* : star in

proteger {15} *vt* : protect — **protegerse** *vr* : protect oneself — **protección** *nf, pl* **-ciones** : protection — **protector, -tora** *adj* : protective — ~ *n* : protector — **protegido, -da** *n* : protégé

proteína *nf* : protein

protestar *v* : protest — **protesta** *nf* : protest — **protestante** *adj & nmf* : Protestant

protocolo *nm* : protocol

prototipo *nm* : prototype

protuberancia *nf* : protuberance — **protuberante** *adj* : protuberant

provecho *nm* 1 : benefit, advantage 2 ¡buen ~! : enjoy your meal! — **provechoso, -sa** *adj* : profitable, beneficial

proveer {63} *vt* : provide, supply — **proveedor, -dora** *n* : supplier

provenir {87} *vi* ~ de : come from

proverbio *nm* : proverb — **proverbial** *adj* : proverbial

providencia *nf* 1 : providence 2 PRE-CAUCIÓN : precaution — **providencial** *adj* : providential

provincia *nf* : province — **provincial** *adj* : provincial — **provinciano, -na** *adj* : provincial, parochial

provisión *nf, pl* **-siones** : provision — **provisional** *adj* : provisional

provocar {72} *vt* 1 : provoke, cause 2 IRRITAR : irritate — **provocación** *nf, pl* **-ciones** : provocation — **provocativo, -va** *adj* : provocative

próximo, -ma *adj* 1 CERCANO : near 2 SIGUIENTE : next — **próximamente** *adv* : shortly, soon — **proximidad** *nf* 1 : proximity 2 ~es *nfpl* : vicinity

proyectar *vt* 1 : plan 2 LANZAR : throw, hurl 3 : cast (light) 4 : show (a film) — **proyección** *nf, pl* **-ciones** : projection — **proyectil** *nm* : missile — **proyecto** *nm* : plan, project — **proyector** *nm* : projector

prudencia *nf* : prudence, care — **prudente** *adj* : prudent, sensible

prueba *nf* 1 : proof, evidence 2 : test (in education, medicine, etc.) 3 : event (in sports) 4 a ~ de agua : waterproof

psicoanálisis *nm* : psychoanalysis — **psicoanalista** *nmf* : psychoanalyst — **psicoanalizar** {21} *vt* : psychoanalyze

psicología *nf* : psychology — **psicológico, -ca** *adj* : psychological — **psicólogo, -ga** *n* : psychologist

psicópata *nmf* : psychopath

psicosis *nfs & pl* : psychosis

psicoterapia *nf* : psychotherapy — **psicoterapeuta** *nmf* : psychotherapist

psicótico, -ca *adj & n* : psychotic

psiquiatría *nf* : psychiatry — **psiquiatra** *nmf* : psychiatrist — **psiquiátrico, -ca** *adj* : psychiatric

psíquico, -ca *adj* : psychic

púa *nf* 1 : sharp point 2 : tooth (of a comb) 3 : thorn (of a plant), quill (of a porcupine, etc.) 4 : (guitar) pick

pubertad *nf* : puberty

publicar {72} *vt* 1 : publish 2 DIVULGAR : divulge, disclose — **publicación** *nf, pl* **-ciones** : publication

publicidad *nf* 1 : publicity 2 : advertising (in marketing) — **publicista** *nmf* : publicist — **publicitar** *vt* 1 : publicize 2 : advertise (a product, etc.) — **publicitario, -ria** *adj* : advertising

público, -ca *adj* : public — **público** *nm* 1 : public 2 : audience (of theater, etc.), spectators *pl* (of sports)

puchero *nm* 1 : (cooking) pot 2 GUISADO : stew 3 hacer ~s : pout

púdico, -ca *adj* : modest

pudiente *adj* : wealthy

pudín *nm, pl* **-dines** : pudding
pudor *nm* : modesty — **pudoroso, -sa**
  adj : modest
pudrir {59} *vt* **1** : rot **2** *fam* : annoy —
  pudrirse *vr* : rot
pueblo *nm* **1** : town, village **2** NACIÓN
  : people, nation
puente *nm* **1** : bridge **2 hacer** ~ : have
  a long weekend **3** ~ **levadizo** : drawbridge
puerco, -ca *n* **1** : pig **2 puerco espín**
  : porcupine — ~ *adj* : dirty, filthy
pueril *adj* : childish
puerro *nm* : leek
puerta *nf* **1** : door, gate **2 a** ~ **cerrada**
  : behind closed doors
puerto *nm* **1** : port **2** : (mountain) pass **3**
  REFUGIO : haven
puertorriqueño, -ña *adj* : Puerto Rican
pues *conj* **1** : since, because **2 POR LO**
  TANTO : so, therefore **3** (*used interjec-
  tionally*) : well, then
puesta *nf* **1** ~ **a punto** : tune-up **2** ~ **de**
  sol : sunset **3** ~ **en marcha** : starting
  up — **puesto, -ta** *adj* **1** : put, set **2** VESTI-
  DO : dressed — **puesto** *nm* **1** : place **2**
  EMPLEO : position, job **3** : stand, stall (in
  a market) **4** ~ **avanzado** : outpost —
  ~ **que** *conj* : since, given that
púgil *nm* : boxer
pugnar *vi* : fight — **pugna** *nf* : fight,
  battle
pulcro, -cra *adj* : tidy, neat
pulga *nf* **1** : flea **2 tener malas** ~**s**
  : have a bad temper
pulgada *nf* : inch — **pulgar** *nm* **1**
  : thumb **2** : big toe
pulir *vt* **1** : polish **2** REFINAR : touch up,
  perfect
pulla *nf* : cutting remark, gibe
pulmón *nm, pl* **-mones** : lung — **pul-
  monar** *adj* : pulmonary — **pulmonía**
  nf : pneumonia
pulpa *nf* : pulp
pulpería *nf Lat* : grocery store
púlpito *nm* : pulpit
pulpo *nm* : octopus
pulsar *vt* **1** : press (a button), strike (a
  key) **2** : play (music) — **pulsación** *nf,
  pl* **-ciones 1** : beat, throb **2** : keystroke
  (on a typewriter, etc.)
pulsera *nf* : bracelet
pulso *nm* **1** : pulse **2** : steadiness (of hand)
pulular *vi* : swarm
pulverizar {21} *vt* **1** : pulverize, crush **2**
  : spray (a liquid) — **pulverizador** *nm*
  : atomizer, spray
puma *nf* : puma
punitivo, -va *adj* : punitive
punta *nf* **1** : tip, end **2** : point (of a nee-

dle, etc.) **3** ~ **del dedo** : fingertip **4**
  sacar ~ **a** : sharpen
puntada *nf* **1** : stitch **2** ~**s** *nfpl* : seam
puntal *nm* : prop, support
puntapié *nm* : kick
puntear *vt* : pluck (a guitar)
puntería *nf* : aim, marksmanship
puntiagudo, -da *adj* : sharp, pointed
puntilla *nf* **1** : lace edging **2 de** ~**s** : on
  tiptoe
punto *nm* **1** : dot, point **2** : period (in
  punctuation) **3** ASUNTO : item, question **4** LUGAR : spot, place **5** MOMENTO
  : moment **6** : point (in a score) **7** PUN-
  TADA : stitch **8 a las dos en** ~ : at
  two o'clock sharp **9 dos** ~**s** : colon
  10 hasta cierto ~ : up to a point **11**
  ~ **de partida** : starting point **12** ~
  muerto : deadlock **13** ~ **y coma**
  : semicolon
puntuación *nf, pl* **-ciones 1** : punctuation **2** : scoring, score (in sports)
puntual *adj* **1** : prompt, punctual **2** EX-
  ACTO : accurate, detailed — **puntualidad** *nf* **1** : punctuality **2** EXACTITUD
  : accuracy
puntuar {3} *vt* : punctuate — *vi* : score
  (in sports)
punzar {21} *vt* : prick, puncture —
  punzada *nf* **1** PINCHAZO : prick **2**
  : sharp pain — **punzante** *adj* **1** : sharp
  2 MORDAZ : biting, caustic
puñado *nm* **1** : handful **2 a** ~**s** : by the
  handful
puñal *nm* : dagger — **puñalada** *nf* : stab
puño *nm* **1** : fist **2** : cuff (of a shirt) **3**
  : handle, hilt (of a sword, etc.) —
  puñetazo *nm* : punch (with the fist)
pupila *nf* : pupil (of the eye)
pupitre *nm* : desk
puré *nm* **1** : purée **2** ~ **de papas** *or* ~
  de patatas *Spain* : mashed potatoes
pureza *nf* : purity
purga *nf* : purge — **purgar** {52} *vt*
  : purge — **purgatorio** *nm* : purgatory
purificar {72} *vt* : purify — **purificación** *nf, pl* **-ciones** : purification
puritano, -na *adj* : puritanical — ~ *n*
  : puritan
puro, -ra *adj* **1** : pure **2** SIMPLE : plain,
  simple **3** *Lat fam* : only, just — **puro**
  nm : cigar
púrpura *nf* : purple — **purpúreo, -rea**
  adj : purple
pus *nm* : pus
pusilánime *adj* : cowardly
puta *nf* : whore
putrefacción *nf, pl* **-ciones** : putrefac-
  tion, rot — **pútrido, -da** *adj* : putrid,
  rotten

Q

q *nf* : q, 18th letter of the Spanish alphabet

que *conj* 1 : that 2 *(in comparisons)* : than 3 *(introducing a reason or cause)* : so that, or else 4 es ~ : the thing is that 5 yo ~ tú : if I were you — ~ *pron* 1 *(referring to persons)* : who, whom 2 *(referring to things)* : that, which 3 el (la, lo, las, los) ~ : he (she, it, they) who, whoever, the one(s) that

qué *adv* 1 : how, what 2 ¡~ lindo! : how lovely! — ~ *adj* : what, which — ~ *pron* 1 : what 2 ¿~ crees? : what do you think?

quebrar {55} *vt* : break — *vi* : go bankrupt — quebrarse *vr* : break — quebrada *nf* : ravine, gorge — quebradizo, -za *adj* : breakable, fragile — quebrado, -da *adj* 1 : bankrupt 2 : rough, uneven (of land, etc.) 3 ROTO : broken — quebrado *nm* : fraction — quebradura *nf* : crack, fissure — quebrantar *vt* 1 : break 2 DEBILITAR : weaken — quebranto *nm* 1 : harm, damage 2 AFLICCIÓN : grief, pain

queda *nf* → toque

quedar *vi* 1 PERMANECER : remain, stay 2 ESTAR : be 3 FALTAR : be left 4 : fit, look (of clothing, etc.) 5 no queda lejos : it's not far 6 ~ en : agree to, agree on — quedarse *vr* 1 : stay 2 ~ con : keep

quedo, -da *adj* : quiet, still — quedo *adv* : softly, quietly

quehacer *nm* 1 : task 2 ~es *nmpl* : chores

queja *nf* : complaint — quejarse *vr* 1 : complain 2 GEMIR : moan, groan — quejido *nm* : moan, whimper — quejoso, -sa *adj* : complaining, whining

quemar *vt* 1 : burn 2 MALGASTAR : squander — *vi* : burn — quemarse *vr* 1 : burn oneself 2 : burn (up) 3 : get sunburned — quemado, -da *adj* 1 : burned 2 AGOTADO : burned-out 3 estar ~ : be fed up — quemador *nm* : burner — quemadura *nf* : burn — quemarropa : a ~ *adj & adv phr* : point-blank

querella *nf* 1 : dispute, quarrel 2 : charge (in law)

querer {64} *vt* 1 : want 2 AMAR : love 3

~ decir : mean 4 ¿quieres pasarme la leche? : please pass the milk 5 sin ~ : unintentionally — ~ *nm* : love — querido, -da *adj* : dear, beloved — ~ *n* 1 : darling 2 AMANTE : lover

queroseno *nm* : kerosene

querubín *nm*, *pl* -bines : cherub

queso *nm* : cheese — quesadilla *nf Lat* : quesadilla

quicio *nm* 1 estar fuera de ~ : be beside oneself 2 sacar de ~ : drive crazy

quiebra *nf* 1 : break 2 BANCARROTA : bankruptcy

quien *pron*, *pl* quienes 1 *(subject)* : who 2 *(object)* : whom 3 *(indefinite)* : whoever, anyone, some people

quién *pron*, *pl* quiénes 1 *(subject)* : who 2 *(object)* : whom 3 ¿de ~ es este lápiz? : whose pencil is this?

quienquiera *pron*, *pl* quienesquiera : whoever, whomever

quieto, -ta *adj* 1 : calm, quiet 2 INMÓVIL : still — quietud *nf* : stillness

quijada *nf* : jaw, jawbone (of an animal)

quilate *nm* : carat, karat

quilla *nf* : keel

quimera *nf* : illusion — quimérico, -ca *adj* : fanciful

química *nf* : chemistry — químico, -ca *adj* : chemical — *n* : chemist

quince *adj & nm* : ~ : fifteen — quinceañero, -ra *n* : fifteen-year-old, teenager — quincena *nf* : two-week period, fortnight — quincenal *adj* : semimonthly, twice a month

quincuagésimo, -ma *adj & n* : fiftieth

quinientos, -tas *adj* : five hundred — quinientos *nms & pl* : five hundred

quinina *nf* : quinine

quinqué *nm* : oil lamp

quinta *nf* : country house, villa

quintaesencia *nf* : quintessence

quinteto *nm* : quintet

quinto, -ta *adj & n* : fifth — quinto *nm* : fifth

quiosco *nm* : kiosk, newsstand

quiropráctico, -ca *n* : chiropractor

quirúrgico, -ca *adj* : surgical

quisquilloso, -sa *adj* : fastidious, fussy

quiste *nm* : cyst

quitar *vt* 1 : remove, take away 2 : take off (clothes) 3 : get rid of, relieve (pain, etc.) — quitarse *vr* 1 : withdraw, leave **2** : take off (one's clothes) **3 ~ de** : give up (a habit) **4 ~ de encima** : get rid of — **quitaesmalte** *nm* : nail-polish remover — **quita-**

manchas *nms & pl* : stain remover — **quitanieves** *nm* : snowplow — **quitasol** *nm* : parasol

quizá *or* **quizás** *adv* : maybe, perhaps

R

r *nf* : r, 19th letter of the Spanish alphabet

rábano *nm* **1** : radish **2 ~ picante** : horseradish

rabí *nmf, pl* **-bíes** : rabbi

rabia *nf* **1** : rage, anger **2** : rabies (disease) — **rabiar** *vi* **1** : be furious **2** : be in great pain **3 ~ por** : be dying for — **rabioso, -sa** *adj* **1** : enraged, furious **2** : rabid, having rabies

rabino, -na *n* : rabbi

rabo *nm* **1** : tail **2 el ~ del ojo** : the corner of one's eye

racha *nf* **1** : gust of wind **2** SERIE : series, string — **racheado, -da** *adj* : gusty

racial *adj* : racial

racimo *nm* : bunch, cluster

raciocinio *nm* : reason, reasoning

ración *nf, pl* **-ciones 1** : share, ration **2** : helping (of food)

racional *adj* : rational — **racionalizar** {21} *vt* : rationalize

racionar *vt* : ration — **racionamiento** *nm* : rationing

racismo *nm* : racism — **racista** *adj & nmf* : racist

radar *nm* : radar

radiación *nf, pl* **-ciones** : radiation

radiactivo, -va *adj* : radioactive — **radiactividad** *nf* : radioactivity

radiador *nm* : radiator

radiante *adj* : radiant

radical *adj & nmf* : radical

radicar {72} *vi* **~ en** : lie in, be rooted in

radio *nm* **1** : radius **2** : spoke (of a wheel) **3** : radium (element) — **~** *nmf* : radio

radioactivo, -va *adj* : radioactive — **radioactividad** *nf* : radioactivity

radiodifusión *nf, pl* **-siones** : broadcasting — **radioemisora** *nf* : radio station — **radioescucha** *nmf* : listener — **radiofónico, -ca** *adj* : radio

radiografía *nf* : X ray — **radiografiar** {85} *vt* : x-ray

radiología *nf* : radiology — **radiólogo, -ga** *n* : radiologist

raer {65} *vt* : scrape off

ráfaga *nf* **1** : gust (of wind) **2** : flash (of light)

raído, -da *adj* : worn, shabby

raíz *nf, pl* **raíces 1** : root **2** ORIGEN : origin, source **3 echar raíces** : take root

raja *nf* **1** : crack, slit **2** RODAJA : slice — **rajar** *vt* : crack, split — **rajarse** *vr* **1** : crack, split open **2** *fam* : back out

rajatabla: a ~ *adv phr* : strictly, to the letter

ralea *nf* : sort, kind

ralentí *nm* : neutral (gear)

rallar *vt* : grate — **rallador** *nm* : grater

rama *nf* : branch — **ramaje** *nm* : branches *pl* — **ramal** *nm* : branch (of a railroad, etc.) — **ramificarse** {72} *vr* : branch (off) — **ramillete** *nm* **1** : bouquet **2** GRUPO : cluster, bunch — **ramo** *nm* **1** : branch **2** RAMILLETE : bouquet

rampa *nf* : ramp, incline

rana *nf* **1** : frog **2 ~ toro** : bullfrog

rancho *nm* : ranch, farm — **ranchero, -ra** *n* : rancher, farmer

rancio, -cia *adj* **1** : rancid **2** : aged (of wine)

rango *nm* **1** : rank **2** : (social) standing

ranúnculo *nm* : buttercup

ranura *nf* : groove, slot

rapar *vt* **1** : shave **2** : crop (hair)

rapaz *adj, pl* **-paces** : rapacious, predatory

rápido, -da *adj* : rapid, quick — **rápidamente** *adv* : rapidly, fast — **rapidez** *nf* : speed — **rápido** *adv* : quickly, fast — **~** *nm* **1** : express train **2 ~s** *nmpl* : rapids

rapiña *nf* **1** : plunder **2 ave de ~** : bird of prey

rapsodia *nf* : rhapsody

raptar *vt* : kidnap — **rapto** *nm* : kidnapping — **raptor, -tora** *n* : kidnapper

raqueta *nf* : racket (in sports)

raro, -ra *adj* **1** : rare **2** EXTRAÑO : odd, strange — **raramente** *adv* : rarely, infrequently — **rareza** *nf* : rarity

ras *nm* **a ~ de** : level with

rascacielos *nms & pl* : skyscraper

rascar {72} *vt* **1** : scratch **2** RASPAR : scrape — **rascarse** *vr* : scratch oneself

rasgar {52} *vt* : rip, tear — **rasgarse** *vr* : rip

rasgo *nm* **1** : stroke (of a pen) **2** CARAC-
TERÍSTICA : trait, characteristic **3 ~s**
nmpl FACCIONES : features

rasguear *vt* : strum

rasguñar *vt* : scratch — **rasguño** *nm*
: scratch

raso, -sa *adj* **1** : level, flat **2** : low (of a
flight) **3 soldado raso** : private (in the
army) — **raso** *nm* : satin

raspar *vt* **1** : scrape **2** LIMAR : file down,
smooth — *vi* : be rough — **raspadura**
nf **1** : scratch **2 ~s** *nfpl* : scrapings

rastra *nf* **1** : rake **2 a ~s** : unwillingly
— **rastrear** *vt* : track, trace — **ras-
trero, -ra** *adj* **1** : creeping **2** DESPRE-
CIABLE : despicable — **rastrillar** *vt*
: rake — **rastrillo** *nm* : rake — **rastro**
nm **1** : trail, track **2** SEÑAL : sign

rasurar *vt* *Lat* : shave — **rasurarse** *vr*
Lat : shave

rata *nf* : rat

ratear *vt* : steal — **ratero, -ra** *n* : thief

ratificar {72} *vt* : ratify — **ratificación**
nf, pl **-ciones** : ratification

rato *nm* **1** : while **2 al poco ~** : shortly after **3 pasar el ~** : pass the time

ratón *nm, pl* **-tones** : mouse — **ratonera** *nf* : mousetrap

raudal *nm* **1** : torrent **2 a ~es** : in
abundance — **raudo, -da** *adj* : swift

raya *nf* **1** : line **2** LISTA : stripe **3** : part
(in the hair) — **rayar** *vt* : scratch — *vi*
1 al ~ el día : at daybreak **2 ~ en**
: border on — **rayarse** *vr* : get
scratched

rayo *nm* **1** : ray, beam **2** : bolt of lightning **3 ~s X** : X rays

rayón *nm* : rayon

raza *nf* **1** : (human) race **2** : breed (of
animals) **3 de ~** : thoroughbred,
pedigreed

razón *nf, pl* **-zones** **1** : reason **2 dar ~**
: inform **3 en ~ de** : because of **4
tener ~** : be right — **razonable** *adj*
: reasonable — **razonamiento** *nm*
: reasoning — **razonar** *v* : reason,
think

reacción *nf, pl* **-ciones** : reaction —
reaccionar *vi* : react — **reaccionario,
-ria** *adj & n* : reactionary

reacio, -cia *adj* : resistant, stubborn

reactivar *vt* : reactivate, revive

reactor *nm* **1** : jet (airplane) **2 ~ nuclear** : nuclear reactor

reajustar *vt* : readjust — **reajuste** *nm*
: readjustment

real *adj* **1** : royal **2** VERDADERO : real,
true

realce *nm* **1** : relief **2 dar ~** : highlight

realeza *nf* : royalty

realidad *nf* **1** : reality **2 en ~** : actually, in fact

realismo *nm* : realism — **realista** *adj*
: realistic — *nmf* : realist

realizar {21} *vt* **1** : carry out **2** : achieve
(a goal) **3** : produce (a film or play) **4**
: realize (a profit) — **realizarse** *vr* **1**
: fulfill oneself **2** : come true (of a
dream, etc.) — **realización** *nf, pl*
-ciones : execution, realization

realmente *adv* : really, actually

realzar {21} *vt* : highlight, enhance

reanimar *vt* : revive

reanudar *vt* : resume, renew — **reanudarse** *vr* : resume

reaparecer {53} *vi* : reappear — **rea-
parición** *nf, pl* **-ciones** : reappearance

reavivar *vt* : revive

rebajar *vt* **1** : lower, reduce **2** HUMILLAR
: humiliate — **rebajarse** *vr* **1** : humble
oneself **2 ~ a** : stoop to — **rebaja** *nf*
1 : reduction **2** DESCUENTO : discount **3
~s** *nfpl* : sales

rebanada *nf* : slice

rebaño *nm* **1** : herd **2** : flock (of sheep)

rebasar *vt* : surpass, exceed

rebatir *vt* : refute

rebelarse *vr* : rebel — **rebelde** *adj* : rebellious — *nmf* : rebel — **rebeldía**
nf : rebelliousness — **rebelión** *nf, pl*
-liones : rebellion

reblandecer *vt* : soften

rebobinar *vt* : rewind

rebosar *vi* **1** : overflow **2 ~ de** : be
bursting with — *vt* : overflow with

rebotar *vi* : bounce, rebound — **rebote**
nm **1** : bounce **2 de ~** : on the rebound

rebozar {21} *vt* : coat in batter

rebuscado, -da *adj* : pretentious

rebuznar *vi* : bray

recabar *vt* **1** : obtain, collect **2 ~ fondos** : raise money

recado *nm* **1** MENSAJE : message **2**
Spain : errand

recaer {13} *vi* **1** : relapse **2 ~ sobre**
: fall on — **recaída** *nf* : relapse

recalcar {72} *vt* : emphasize, stress

recalcitrante *adj* : recalcitrant

recalentar {55} *vt* **1** : overheat **2** : re-
heat, warm up (food) — **recalentarse**
vr : overheat

recámara *nf* **1** : chamber (of a firearm)
2 *Lat* : bedroom

recambio *nm* **1** : spare part **2** : refill (for
a pen), etc.)

recapitular *vt* : recapitulate, sum up —
recapitulación *nf, pl* **-ciones** : reca-
pitulation

recargar {52} *vt* **1** : overload **2**

: recharge (a battery), reload (a firearm, etc.) — **recargado, -da** adj : overly elaborate — **recargo** nm : surcharge

recato nm : modesty — **recatado, -da** adj : modest, demure

recaudar vt : collect — **recaudación** nf, pl **-ciones** : collection — **recaudador, -dora** n ~ **de impuestos** : tax collector

recelar vt : distrust, fear — **recelo** nm : distrust, suspicion — **receloso, -sa** adj : distrustful, suspicious

recepción nf, pl **-ciones** : reception — **recepcionista** nmf : receptionist

receptáculo nm : receptacle

receptivo, -va adj : receptive — **receptor, -tora** n : recipient — **receptor** nm : receiver (of a radio, etc.)

recesión nf, pl **-siones** : recession

receso nm Lat : recess, adjournment

receta nf 1 : recipe 2 : prescription (in medicine)

rechazar {21} vt 1 : reject, refuse 2 REPELER : repel 3 : reflect (light) — **rechazo** nm : rejection

rechinar vi 1 : squeak, creak 2 : grind, gnash (one's teeth)

rechoncho, -cha adj fam : chubby

recibir vt 1 : receive 2 ACOGER : welcome — vi : receive visitors — **recibidor** nm : vestibule, entrance hall — **recibimiento** nm : reception, welcome — **recibo** nm : receipt

reciclar vt 1 : recycle 2 : retrain (workers) — **reciclaje** nm : recycling

recién adv 1 : newly, recently 2 ~ **casados** : newlyweds — **reciente** adj : recent — **recientemente** adv : recently

recinto nm 1 : enclosure 2 ÁREA : area, site

recio, -cia adj : tough, strong

recipiente nm : container, receptacle — ~ nmf : recipient

recíproco, -ca adj : reciprocal, mutual

recitar vt : recite — **recital** nm : recital

reclamar vt : demand, ask for — vi : complain — **reclamación** nf, pl **-ciones** 1 : claim, demand 2 QUEJA : complaint — **reclamo** nm 1 : lure (in hunting) 2 Lat : inducement, attraction

reclinar vt : rest, lean — **reclinarse** vr : recline, lean back

recluir {41} vt : confine, lock up — **recluirse** vr : shut oneself away — **reclusión** nf, pl **-siones** : imprisonment — **recluso, -sa** n : prisoner

recluta nmf : recruit — **reclutamiento**

nm : recruitment — **reclutar** vt : recruit, enlist

recobrar vt : recover, regain — **recobrarse** vr ~ **de** : recover from

recodo nm : bend

recoger {15} vt 1 : collect, gather 2 COGER : pick up 3 LIMPIAR, ORDENAR : clean up, tidy (up) — **recogerse** vr : retire, withdraw — **recogedor** nm : dustpan — **recogido, -da** adj : quiet, secluded

recolección nf, pl **-ciones** 1 : collection 2 COSECHA : harvest

recomendar {55} vt : recommend — **recomendación** nf, pl **-ciones** : recommendation

recompensar vt : reward — **recompensa** nf : reward

reconciliar vt : reconcile — **reconciliarse** vr : be reconciled — **reconciliación** nf, pl **-ciones** : reconciliation

recóndito, -ta adj : hidden

reconfortar vt : comfort

reconocer {18} vt 1 : recognize 2 ADMITIR : admit 3 EXAMINAR : examine — **reconocible** adj : recognizable — **reconocido, -da** adj 1 : recognized, accepted 2 AGRADECIDO : grateful — **reconocimiento** nm 1 : recognition 2 AGRADECIMIENTO : gratitude 3 : (medical) examination

reconsiderar vt : reconsider

reconstruir {41} vt : reconstruct — **reconstrucción** nf, pl **-ciones** : reconstruction

recopilar vt 1 RECOGER : collect, gather 2 : compile — **recopilación** nf, pl **-ciones** : collection, compilation

récord nm, pl **-cords** : record

recordar {19} vt 1 ACORDARSE DE : remember 2 : remind — vi : remember — **recordatorio** nm : reminder

recorrer vt 1 : travel through 2 : cover (a distance) — **recorrido** nm 1 : journey, trip 2 TRAYECTO : route, course

recortar vt 1 : reduce 2 CORTAR : cut (out) 3 : trim (hair) — **recortarse** vr : stand out — **recorte** nm 1 : cut, cutting 2 ~**s de periódicos** : newspaper clippings

recostar {19} vt : lean, rest — **recostarse** vr : lie down

recoveco nm 1 : bend 2 RINCÓN : nook, corner

recrear vt 1 : recreate 2 ENTRETENER : entertain — **recrearse** vr : to enjoy oneself — **recreativo, -va** adj : recreational — **recreo** nm 1 : recreation, amusement 2 : recess, break (at school)

recriminar *vt* : reproach

recrudecer {53} *vi* : worsen — **recrudecerse** *vr* : intensify, get worse

rectángulo *nm* : rectangle — **rectangular** *adj* : rectangular

rectificar {72} *vt* 1 : rectify, correct 2 AJUSTAR : straighten (out) — **rectitud** *nf* 1 : straightness 2 : (moral) rectitude — **recto, -ta** *adj* 1 : straight 2 INTEGRO : upright, honorable — **recto** *nm* : rectum

rector, -tora *adj* : governing, managing — ~ *n* : rector — **rectoría** *nf* : rectory

recubrir {2} *vt* : cover, coat

recuento *nm* : count, recount

recuerdo *nm* 1 : memory 2 : souvenir, remembrance (of a journey, etc.) 3 ~s *nmpl* SALUDOS : regards

recuperar *vt* 1 : recover, retrieve 2 ~ el tiempo perdido : make up for lost time — **recuperarse** *vr* ~ de : recover from — **recuperación** *nf, pl* -ciones 1 : recovery 2 ~ de datos : data retrieval

recurrir *vi* ~ a : turn to (a person), resort to (force, etc.) — **recurso** *nm* 1 : recourse, resort 2 : appeal (in law) 3 ~s *nmpl* : resources

red *nf* 1 : net 2 SISTEMA : network, system 3 la Red : the Internet

redactar *vt* : write (up), draft — **redacción** *nf, pl* -ciones 1 : writing, drafting 2 : editing (of a newspaper, etc.) — **redactor, -tora** *n* : editor

redada *nf* 1 : (police) raid 2 : catch (in fishing)

redescubrir {2} *vt* : rediscover

redención *nf, pl* -ciones : redemption — **redentor, -tora** *adj* : redeeming

redil *nm* : fold, pen

rédito *nm* : interest, yield

redoblar *vt* : redouble

redomado, -da *adj* : out-and-out

redondear *vt* 1 : make round 2 : round off (a number, etc.) — **redonda** *nf* 1 : whole note (in music) 2 a la ~ : in the surrounding area — **redondel** *nm* 1 : ring, circle 2 : bullring — **redondo, -da** *adj* 1 : round 2 PERFECTO : excellent

reducir {61} *vt* : reduce — **reducirse** *vr* ~ a : come down to, amount to — **reducción** *nf, pl* -ciones : reduction — **reducido, -da** *adj* 1 : reduced, limited 2 PEQUEÑO : small

redundante *adj* : redundant — **redundancia** *nf* : redundancy

reedición *nf, pl* -ciones : reprint

reembolsar *vt* : refund, reimburse, repay — **reembolso** *nm* : refund, reimbursement

reemplazar {21} *vt* : replace — **reemplazo** *nm* : replacement

reencarnación *nf, pl* -ciones : reincarnation

reencuentro *nm* : reunion

reestructurar *vt* : restructure

refaccionar *vt* Lat : repair, renovate — **refacciones** *nfpl* Lat : repairs, renovations

referir {76} *vt* 1 : tell 2 REMITIR : refer — **referirse** *vr* ~ a : refer to — **referencia** *nf* 1 : reference 2 hacer ~ a : refer to — **referéndum** *nm, pl* -dums : referendum — **referente** *adj* ~ a : concerning

refinar *vt* : refine — **refinado, -da** *adj* : refined — **refinamiento** *nm* : refinement — **refinería** *nf* : refinery

reflector *nm* 1 : reflector 2 : spotlight, searchlight, floodlight

reflejar *vt* : reflect — **reflejarse** *vr* : be reflected — **reflejo** *nm* 1 : reflection 2 : (physical) reflex 3 ~s *nmpl* : highlights (in hair)

reflexionar *vi* : reflect, think — **reflexión** *nf, pl* -xiones : reflection, thought — **reflexivo, -va** *adj* 1 : reflective, thoughtful 2 : reflexive (in grammar)

reflujo *nm* : ebb (tide)

reforma *nf* 1 : reform 2 ~s *nfpl* : renovations — **reformador, -dora** *n* : reformer — **reformar** *vt* 1 : reform 2 : renovate, repair (a house, etc.) — **reformarse** *vr* : mend one's ways — **reformatorio** *nm* : reformatory

reforzar {36} *vt* : reinforce

refrán *nm, pl* -franes : proverb, saying

refregar {49} *vt* : scrub

refrenar *vt* 1 : rein in (a horse) 2 CONTENER : restrain — **refrenarse** *vr* : restrain oneself

refrendar *vt* : approve, endorse

refrescar {72} *vt* 1 : refresh, cool 2 : brush up on (knowledge) — *vi* : turn cooler — **refrescante** *adj* : refreshing — **refresco** *nm* : soft drink

refriega *nf* : scuffle, skirmish

refrigerar *vt* 1 : refrigerate 2 CLIMATIZAR : air-condition — **refrigeración** *nf, pl* -ciones 1 : refrigeration 2 AIRE ACONDICIONADO : air-conditioning — **refrigerador** *nmf* Lat : refrigerator — **refrigerio** *nm* : refreshments *pl*

refrito, -ta *adj* : refried — **refrito** *nm* : rehash

refuerzo *nm* : reinforcement

refugiar *vt* : shelter — **refugiarse** *vr* : take refuge — **refugiado, -da** *n*

: refugee — **refugio** *nm* : refuge, shelter

refulgir {35} *vi* : shine brightly

refunfuñar *vi* : grumble, groan

refutar *vt* : refute

regadera *nf* 1 : watering can 2 *Lat* : shower head, shower

regalar *vt* : give (as a gift) — **regalarse** *vr* ~ **con** : treat oneself to

regaliz *nm, pl* -**lices** : licorice

regalo *nm* 1 : gift, present 2 PLACER : pleasure, delight

regañadientes: a ~ *adv phr* : reluctantly, unwillingly

regañar *vt* : scold — *vi* 1 QUEJARSE : grumble 2 *Spain* : quarrel — **regañón, -ñona** *adj, mpl* -**ñones** *fam* : grumpy, irritable

regar {49} *vt* 1 : irrigate, water 2 ESPARCIR : scatter

regatear *vt* 1 : haggle over 2 ESCATIMAR : skimp on — *vi* : bargain, haggle

regazo *nm* : lap (of a person)

regenerar *vt* : regenerate

regentar *vt* : run, manage

régimen *nm, pl* **regímenes** 1 : regime 2 DIETA : diet 3 ~ **de vida** : lifestyle

regimiento *nm* : regiment

regio, -gia *adj* : royal, regal

región *nf, pl* -**giones** : region, area — **regional** *adj* : regional

regir {28} *vt* 1 : rule 2 ADMINISTRAR : manage, run 3 DETERMINAR : govern, determine — *vi* : apply, be in force — **regirse** *vr* ~ **por** : be guided by

registrar *vt* 1 : register 2 GRABAR : record, tape 3 : search (a house, etc.), frisk (a person) — **registrarse** *vr* 1 : register 2 : be recorded (of temperatures, etc.) — **registrador, -dora** *adj* **caja registradora** : cash register — ~ *n* : registrar — **registro** *nm* 1 : registration 2 : register (book) 3 : registry (office) 4 : range (of a voice, etc.) 5 INSPECCIÓN : search

regla *nf* 1 : rule, regulation 2 : ruler (for measuring) 3 MENSTRUACIÓN : period — **reglamentación** *nf, pl* -**ciones** 1 : regulation 2 REGLAS : rules *pl* — **reglamentar** *vt* : regulate — **reglamentario, -ria** *adj* : regulation, official — **reglamento** *nm* : regulations *pl*, rules *pl*

regocijar *vt* : gladden, delight — **regocijarse** *vr* : rejoice — **regocijo** *nm* : delight, rejoicing

regodearse *vr* : be delighted — **regodeo** *nm* : delight

regordete *adj fam* : chubby

regresar *vi* : return, come back, go back — *vt Lat* : give back — **regresión** *nf, pl* -**siones** : regression — **regresivo, -va** *adj* : regressive — **regreso** *nm* 1 : return 2 **estar de** ~ : be back, be home again

reguero *nm* 1 : irrigation ditch 2 SEÑAL : trail, trace 3 **correr como un** ~ **de pólvora** : spread like wildfire

regular *adj* 1 : regular 2 MEDIANO : medium, average 3 **por lo** ~ : in general — ~ *vt* : regulate, control — **regulación** *nf, pl* -**ciones** : regulation, control — **regularidad** *nf* : regularity — **regularizar** {21} *vt* : normalize, make regular

rehabilitar *vt* 1 : rehabilitate 2 : reinstate (s.o. in a position) 3 : renovate (a building, etc.) — **rehabilitación** *nf* 1 : rehabilitation 2 : reinstatement (in a position) 3 : renovation (of a building, etc.)

rehacer {40} *vt* 1 : redo 2 REPARAR : repair — **rehacerse** *vr* 1 : recover 2 ~ **de** : get over

rehén *nm, pl* -**henes** : hostage

rehuir {41} *vt* : avoid, shun

rehusar {8} *v* : refuse

reimprimir *vt* : reprint — **reimpresión** *nf, pl* -**siones** : reprinting, reprint

reina *nf* : queen — **reinado** *nm* : reign — **reinante** *adj* : reigning — **reinar** *vi* 1 : reign 2 PREVALECER : prevail

reincidir *vi* : backslide, relapse

reino *nm* : kingdom, realm

reintegrar *vt* 1 : reinstate 2 : refund (money), reimburse (expenses, etc.) — **reintegrarse** *vr* ~ **a** : return to — **reintegro** *nm* : reimbursement

reír {66} *vi* : laugh — *vt* : laugh at — **reírse** *vr* : laugh

reiterar *vt* : repeat, reiterate

reivindicar {72} *vt* 1 : claim 2 RESTAURAR : restore

reja *nf* : grille, grating — **rejilla** *nf* : grille, grate, screen

rejuvenecer {53} *vt* : rejuvenate — **rejuvenecerse** *vr* : be rejuvenated

relación *nf, pl* -**ciones** 1 : relation, connection 2 COMUNICACIÓN : relationship, relations *pl* 3 RELATO : account 4 LISTA : list 5 **con** ~ **a** *or* **en** ~ **a** : in relation to — **relacionar** *vt* : relate, connect — **relacionarse** *vr* ~ **con** : be connected to, interact with

relajar *vt* : relax — **relajarse** *vr* : relax — **relajación** *nf, pl* -**ciones** : relaxation — **relajado, -da** *adj* 1 : relaxed 2 : dissolute, lax (in behavior)

relamerse *vr* : smack one's lips, lick its chops

relámpago *nm* : flash of lightning — **relampaguear** *vi* : flash
relatar *vt* : relate, tell
relativo, -va *adj* 1 : relative 2 **en lo relativo a** : with regard to — **relatividad** *nf* : relativity
relato *nm* 1 : account, report 2 CUENTO : story, tale
releer {20} *vt* : reread
relegar {52} *vt* : relegate
relevante *adj* : outstanding, important
relevar *vt* 1 : relieve, take over from 2 ~ **de** : exempt from — **relevo** *nm* 1 : relief, replacement 2 **carrera de ~s** : relay race
relieve *nm* 1 : relief (in art, etc.) 2 IMPORTANCIA : prominence, importance 3 **poner en ~** : emphasize
religión *nf, pl* -**giones** : religion — **religioso, -sa** *adj* : religious — ~ *n* : monk *m*, nun *f*
relinchar *vi* : neigh, whinny — **relincho** *nm* : neigh, whinny
reliquia *nf* 1 : relic 2 ~ **de familia** : family heirloom
rellenar *vt* 1 : refill 2 : stuff, fill (in cooking) — **relleno, -na** *adj* : stuffed, filled — **relleno** *nm* : stuffing, filling
reloj *nm* 1 : clock 2 ~ **de pulsera** : wristwatch 3 ~ **de arena** : hourglass 4 **como un** ~ : like clockwork
relucir {45} *vi* 1 : glitter, shine 2 **sacar a** ~ : bring up, mention — **reluciente** *adj* : brilliant, shining
relumbrar *vi* : shine brightly
remachar *vt* 1 : rivet 2 RECALAR : stress, drive home — **remache** *nm* : rivet
remanente *nm* : remainder, surplus
remanso *nm* : pool
remar *vi* : row
rematar *vt* 1 : conclude, finish up 2 MATAR : finish off 3 LIQUIDAR : sell off cheaply 4 *Lat* : auction — *vi* 1 : shoot (in sports) 2 TERMINAR : end — **rematado, -da** *adj* : utter, complete — **remate** *nm* 1 : shot (in sports) 2 FIN : end
remedar *vt* : imitate, mimic
remediar *vt* 1 : remedy, repair 2 : solve (a problem) 3 EVITAR : avoid — **remedio** *nm* 1 : remedy, cure 2 SOLUCIÓN : solution 3 **sin** ~ : hopeless
rememorar *vi* : recall
remendar {55} *vt* : mend
remesa *nf* 1 : remittance 2 : shipment (of merchandise)
remezón *nm, pl* -**zones** *Lat* : mild earthquake, tremor
remiendo *nm* : mend, patch
remilgado, -da *adj* 1 : prudish 2 AFEC-

TADO : affected — **remilgo** *nm* : primness, affectation
reminiscencia *nf* : reminiscence
remisión *nf, pl* -**siones** : remission
remiso, -sa *adj* 1 : reluctant 2 NEGLIGENTE : remiss
remitir *vt* 1 : send, remit 2 ~ **a** : refer to, direct to — *vi* : subside, let up — **remite** *nm* : return address — **remitente** *nmf* : sender (of a letter, etc.)
remo *nm* : paddle, oar
remodelar *vt* 1 : remodel 2 : restructure (an organization)
remojar *vt* : soak, steep — **remojo** *nm* **poner en** ~ : soak
remolacha *nf* : beet
remolcar {72} *vt* : tow, tug — **remolcador** *nm* : tugboat
remolino *nm* 1 : whirlwind, whirlpool 2 : crowd (of people) 3 : cowlick (of hair)
remolque *nm* 1 : towing, tow 2 : trailer (vehicle)
remontar *vt* 1 : overcome 2 SUBIR : go up — **remontarse** *vr* 1 : soar 2 ~ **a** : date from, go back to
rémora *nf* : hindrance
remorder {47} *vt* : trouble, worry — **remordimiento** *nm* : remorse
remoto, -ta *adj* : remote — **remotamente** *adv* : remotely, slightly
remover {47} *vt* 1 : stir 2 : move around, turn over (earth, embers, etc.) 3 REAVIVIR : bring up again 4 DESPEDIR : fire, dismiss
remunerar *vt* : remunerate
renacer {48} *vi* : be reborn, revive — **renacimiento** *nm* 1 : rebirth, revival 2 **el Renacimiento** : the Renaissance
renacuajo *nm* : tadpole, pollywog
rencilla *nf* : quarrel
renco, -ca *adj Lat* : lame
rencor *nm* 1 : rancor, hostility 2 **guardar** ~ : hold a grudge — **rencoroso, -sa** *adj* : resentful
rendición *nf, pl* -**ciones** : surrender — **rendido, -da** *adj* 1 : submissive 2 AGOTADO : exhausted
rendija *nf* : crack, split
rendir {54} *vt* 1 : render, give 2 PRODUCIR : yield, produce 3 CANSAR : exhaust — *vi* : make progress, go a long way — **rendirse** *vr* : surrender, give up — **rendimiento** *nm* 1 : performance 2 : yield, return (in finance, etc.)
renegar {49} *vt* : deny — *vi* 1 QUEJARSE : grumble 2 ~ **de** ABJURAR : renounce, disown — **renegado, -da** *n* : renegade

renglón *nm, pl* **-glones 1** : line (of writing) **2** *Lat* : line (of products)

reno *nm* : reindeer

renombre *nm* : renown — **renombrado, -da** *adj* : famous, renowned

renovar {19} *vt* **1** : renew, restore **2** : renovate (a building, etc.) — **renovación** *nf, pl* **-ciones 1** : renewal **2** : renovation (of a building, etc.)

renquear *vi* : limp, hobble

rentar *vt* **1** : produce, yield **2** *Lat* : rent — **renta** *nf* **1** : income **2** ALQUILER : rent **3 impuesto sobre la ~** : income tax — **rentable** *adj* : profitable

renunciar *vi* **1** : resign **2 ~ a** : renounce, relinquish — **renuncia** *nf* **1** : renunciation **2** DIMISIÓN : resignation

reñir {67} *vi* **~ con** : argue with, fall out with — *vt* **1** : scold **2** DISPUTAR : fight — **reñido, -da** *adj* **1** : hardfought **2 ~ con** : on bad terms with

reo, rea *n* **1** : accused, defendant **2** CULPABLE : culprit

reojo *nm* **de ~** : out of the corner of one's eye

reorganizar {21} *vt* : reorganize

repantigarse {52} *vr* : sprawl out

reparar *vt* **1** : repair, fix **2** : make amends for (an offense, etc.) — *vi* **1 ~ en** ADVERTIR : take notice of **2 ~ en** CONSIDERAR : consider — **reparación** *nf, pl* **-ciones 1** : reparation, amends **2** ARREGLO : repair — **reparo** *nm* **1** : reservation, objection **2 poner ~s a** : object to

repartir *vt* **1** : allocate **2** DISTRIBUIR : distribute **3** ESPARCIR : spread — **repartición** *nf, pl* **-ciones** : distribution — **repartidor, -dora** *n* : delivery person, distributor — **reparto** *nm* **1** : allocation **2** DISTRIBUCIÓN : delivery **3** : cast (of characters)

repasar *vt* **1** : review, go over **2** ZURCIR : mend — **repaso** *nm* **1** : review **2** : mending (of clothes)

repeler *vt* **1** : repel **2** REPUGNAR : disgust — **repelente** *adj* : repellent, repulsive

repente *nm* **1** : fit, outburst **2 de ~** : suddenly — **repentino, -na** *adj* : sudden

repercutir *vi* **1** : reverberate **2 ~ en** : have repercussions on — **repercusión** *nf, pl* **-siones** : repercussion

repertorio *nm* : repertoire

repetir {54} *vt* **1** : repeat **2** : have a second helping of (food) — **repetirse** *vr* **1** : repeat oneself **2** : recur (of an event, etc.) — **repetición** *nf, pl* **-ciones 1** : repetition **2** : rerun, repeat (of a program, etc.) — **repetido, -da**

adj **1** : repeated **2 repetidas veces** : repeatedly, time and again — **repetitivo, -va** *adj* : repetitive, repetitious

repicar {72} *vt* : ring — *vi* : ring out, peal — **repique** *nm* : ringing, pealing

repisa *nf* **1** : shelf, ledge **2 ~ de ventana** : windowsill

replegar {49} *vt* : fold — **replegarse** *vr* : retreat, withdraw

repleto, -ta *adj* **1** : replete, full **2 ~ de** : packed with

replicar {72} *vt* : reply, retort — *vi* : answer back — **réplica** *nf* **1** RESPUESTA : reply **2** COPIA : replica, reproduction

repliegue *nm* **1** : fold **2** : (military) withdrawal

repollo *nm* : cabbage

reponer {60} *vt* **1** : replace **2** REPLICAR : reply — **reponerse** *vr* : recover

reportar *vt* **1** : yield, bring **2** *Lat* : report — **reportaje** *nm* : article, (news) report — **reporte** *nm* *Lat* : report — **reportero, -ra** *n* : reporter

reposar *vi* **1** DESCANSAR : rest **2** : stand, settle (of liquids, dough, etc.) — **reposado, -da** *adj* : calm, relaxed — **reposición** *nf, pl* **-ciones 1** : replacement **2** : rerun, repeat (of a program, etc.) — **reposo** *nm* : rest

repostar *vi* **1** : stock up on **2** : refuel (an airplane, etc.) — *vi* : fill up, refuel

reprender *vt* : reprimand, scold — **reprensible** *adj* : reprehensible

represalia *nf* **1** : reprisal **2 tomar ~s** : retaliate

represar *vt* : dam

representar *vt* **1** : represent **2** : perform (a play, etc.) **3** APARENTAR : look, appear as — **representación** *nf, pl* **-ciones 1** : representation **2** : performance (of a play, etc.) **3 en ~ de** : on behalf of — **representante** *nmf* **1** : representative **2** ACTOR : performer — **representativo, -va** *adj* : representative

represión *nf, pl* **-siones** : repression

reprimenda *nf* : reprimand

reprimir *vt* **1** : repress **2** : suppress (a rebellion, etc.)

reprobar {19} *vt* **1** : reprove, condemn **2** *Lat* : fail (an exam, etc.)

reprochar *vt* : reproach — **reprocharse** *vr* : reproach oneself — **reproche** *nm* : reproach

reproducir {61} *vt* : reproduce — **reproducirse** *vr* **1** : breed, reproduce **2** : recur (of an event, etc.) — **reproducción** *nf, pl* **-ciones** : reproduction — **reproductor, -tora** *adj* : reproductive

reptil *nm* : reptile

república *nf* : republic — **republicano, -na** *adj & n* : republican
repudiar *vt* : repudiate
repuesto *nm* : spare (auto) part
repugnar *vt* : disgust — **repugnancia** *nf* : disgust — **repugnante** *adj* : disgusting
repujar *vt* : emboss
repulsivo, -va *adj* : repulsive
reputar *vt* : consider, deem — **reputación** *nf, pl* **-ciones** : reputation
requerir {76} *vt* 1 : require 2 : summon, send for (a person)
requesón *nm, pl* **-sones** : cottage cheese
réquiem *nm* : requiem
requisito *nm* 1 : requirement 2 ~ **previo** : prerequisite
res *nf* 1 : beast, animal 2 *Lat or* **carne de** ~ : beef
resabio *nm* 1 VICIO : bad habit, vice 2 DEJO : aftertaste
resaca *nf* 1 : undertow 2 **tener** ~ : have a hangover
resaltar *vi* 1 : stand out 2 **hacer** ~ : bring out, highlight — *vt* : emphasize
resarcir {83} *vt* : compensate, repay — **resarcirse** *vr* ~ **de** : make up for
resbalar *vi* 1 : slip, slide 2 : skid (of an automobile) — **resbalarse** *vr* : slip, skid — **resbaladizo, -za** *adj* : slippery — **resbalón** *nm, pl* **-lones** : slip — **resbaloso, -sa** *adj Lat* : slippery
rescatar *vt* 1 : rescue, ransom 2 RECUPERAR : recover, get back — **rescate** *nm* 1 : rescue 2 : ransom (money) 3 RECUPERACIÓN : recovery
rescindir *vt* : cancel — **rescisión** *nf, pl* **-siones** : cancellation
rescoldo *nm* : embers *pl*
resecar {72} *vt* : dry (out) — **resecarse** *vr* : dry up — **reseco, -ca** *adj* : dry, dried-up
resentirse {76} *vr* 1 : suffer, be weakened 2 OFENDERSE : be offended 3 ~ **de** : feel the effects of — **resentido, -da** *adj* : resentful — **resentimiento** *nm* : resentment
reseñar *vt* 1 : review 2 DESCRIBIR : describe — **reseña** *nf* 1 : review, report 2 DESCRIPCIÓN : description
reservar *vt* 1 : reserve 2 GUARDAR : keep, save — **reservarse** *vr* 1 : save oneself 2 : keep for oneself — **reserva** *nf* 1 : reservation 2 PROVISIÓN : reserve 3 **de** ~ : spare, in reserve — **reservación** *nf, pl* **-ciones** : reservation — **reservado, -da** *adj* 1 : reserved 2 : confidential (of a document, etc.)
resfriar {85} *vt* : spare, in reserve — **resfriarse** *vr* 1

: cool off 2 CONSTIPARSE : catch a cold — **resfriado** *nm* CATARRO : cold — **resfrío** *nm Lat* : cold
resguardar *vt* : protect — **resguardarse** *vr* : protect oneself — **resguardo** *nm* 1 : protection 2 RECIBO : receipt
residir *vi* 1 : reside, live 2 ~ **en** : lie in — **residencia** *nf* 1 : residence 2 *or* ~ **universitaria** : dormitory — **residencial** *adj* : residential — **residente** *adj & nmf* : resident
residuo *nm* 1 : residue 2 ~**s** *nmpl* : waste — **residual** *adj* : residual
resignar *vt* : resign — **resignarse** *vr* ~ **a** : resign oneself to — **resignación** *nf, pl* **-ciones** : resignation
resina *nf* 1 : resin 2 ~ **epoxídica** : epoxy
resistir *vt* 1 AGUANTAR : stand, bear 2 : withstand (temptation, etc.) — *vi* : resist — **resistirse** *vr* ~ **a** : be resistant to — **resistencia** *nf* 1 : resistance 2 AGUANTE : endurance, stamina — **resistente** *adj* : resistant, strong, tough
resma *nf* : ream
resollar {19} *vi* : breathe heavily, pant
resolver {89} *vt* 1 : resolve 2 DECIDIR : decide — **resolverse** *vr* : make up one's mind — **resolución** *nf, pl* **-ciones** : resolution 2 DECISIÓN : decision 3 FIRMEZA : determination, resolve
resonar {19} *vi* : resound — **resonancia** *nf* 1 : resonance 2 CONSECUENCIAS : impact, repercussions *pl* — **resonante** *adj* : resonant, resounding
resoplar *vi* 1 : puff, pant 2 : snort (with annoyance)
resorte *nm* MUELLE : spring 2 **tocar** ~**s** : pull strings
respaldar *vt* : back, endorse — **respaldarse** *vr* : lean back — **respaldo** *nm* 1 : back (of a chair, etc.) 2 APOYO : support, backing
respectar *vt* : concern, relate to — **respectivo, -va** *adj* : respective — **respecto** *nm* 1 **al** ~ : in this respect 2 ~ **a** : in regard to, concerning
respetar *vt* : respect — **respetable** *adj* : respectable — **respeto** *nm* 1 : respect 2 **presentar sus** ~**s** : pay one's respects — **respetuoso, -sa** *adj* : respectful
respingo *nm* : start, jump
respirar *v* : breathe — **respiración** *nf, pl* **-ciones** : respiration, breathing — **respiratorio, -ria** *adj* : respiratory — **respiro** *nm* 1 : breath 2 DESCANSO : respite, break

resplandecer {53} *vi* : shine — **resplandeciente** *adj* : shining, gleaming — **resplandor** *nm* **1** : brilliance, gleam **2** : flash (of lightning, etc.)

responder *vt* : answer, reply — *vi* **1** : answer **2** REPLICAR : answer back **3** ~ **a** : respond to **4** ~ **de** : answer for (something)

responsable *adj* : responsible — **responsabilidad** *nf* : responsibility

respuesta *nf* **1** : answer, reply **2** REACCIÓN : response

resquebrajar *vt* : split, crack — **resquebrajarse** *vr* : crack

resquicio *nm* **1** : crack, crevice **2** VESTIGIO : trace, glimmer

resta *nf* : subtraction

restablecer {53} *vt* : reestablish, restore — **restablecerse** *vr* : recover — **restablecimiento** *nm* : restoration, recovery

restallar *vi* : crack, crackle

restar *vt* **1** : deduct, subtract **2** DISMINUIR : minimize — *vi* : be left — **restante** *adj* **1** : remaining **2 lo** ~ : the rest

restauración *nf, pl* **-ciones** : restoration

restaurante *nm* : restaurant

restaurar *vt* : restore

restituir {41} *vt* : return, restore — **restitución** *nf, pl* **-ciones** : restitution

resto *nm* **1** : rest, remainder **2** ~**s** *nmpl* : leftovers **3** *or* ~**s mortales** : mortal remains

restregar {49} *vt* : rub, scrub — **restregarse** *vr* : rub

restringir {35} *vt* : restrict, limit — **restricción** *nf, pl* **-ciones** : restriction, limitation — **restrictivo, -va** *adj* : restrictive

resucitar *vt* : resuscitate, revive — *vi* : come back to life

resuelto, -ta *adj* : determined, resolved

resuello *nm* : heavy breathing, panting

resultar *vi* **1** : succeed, work out **2** SALIR : turn out (to be) **3** ~ **de** : be the result of **4** ~ **en** : result in — **resultado** *nm* : result, outcome

resumir *v* : summarize, sum up — **resumen** *nm, pl* **-súmenes 1** : summary **2 en** ~ : in short

resurgir {35} *vi* : reappear, revive — **resurgimiento** *nm* : resurgence — **resurrección** *nf, pl* **-ciones** : resurrection

retahíla *nf* : string, series

retal *nm* : remnant

retardar *vt* **1** RETRASAR : delay **2** POSPONER : postpone

retazo *nm* **1** : remnant, scrap **2** : fragment (of a text, etc.)

retener {80} *vt* **1** : retain, keep **2** : withhold (funds, etc.) **3** DETENER : detain — **retención** *nf, pl* **-ciones 1** : retention **2** : deduction, withholding (of funds)

reticente *adj* : reluctant — **reticencia** *nf* : reluctance

retina *nf* : retina

retintín *nm, pl* **-tines 1** : tinkling, jingle **2 con** ~ : sarcastically

retirar *vt* **1** : remove, take away **2** : withdraw (funds, statements, etc.) — **retirarse** *vr* **1** : retreat, withdraw **2** JUBILARSE : retire — **retirada** *nf* **1** : withdrawal **2 batirse en** ~ : beat a retreat — **retirado, -da** *adj* **1** : remote, secluded **2** JUBILADO : retired — **retiro** *nm* **1** : retreat **2** JUBILACIÓN : retirement **3** *Lat* : withdrawal

reto *nm* : challenge, dare

retocar {72} *vt* : touch up

retoño *nm* : sprout, shoot

retoque *nm* **1** : retouching **2 el último** ~ : the finishing touch

retorcer {14} *vt* **1** : twist, contort **2** : wring out (clothes, etc.) — **retorcerse** *vr* **1** : get twisted up **2** : squirm, writhe (in pain) — **retorcijón** *nm, pl* **-jones** : cramp, spasm — **retorcimiento** *nm* : twisting, wringing out

retórica *nf* : rhetoric — **retórico, -ca** *adj* : rhetorical

retornar *v* : return — **retorno** *nm* : return

retozar {21} *vi* : frolic, romp — **retozón, -zona** *adj* : playful, frisky

retractarse *vr* **1** : withdraw, back down **2** ~ **de** : take back, retract

retraer {81} *vt* : retract — **retraerse** *vr* : withdraw — **retraído, -da** *adj* : withdrawn, shy

retrasar *vt* **1** : delay, hold up **2** APLAZAR : postpone **3** : set back (a clock) — **retrasarse** *vr* **1** : be late **2** : fall behind (in work, etc.) — **retrasado, -da** *adj* **1** : retarded **2** : in arrears (of payments) **3** : backward (of a country) **4** : slow (of a clock) — **retraso** *nm* **1** : delay **2** SUBDESARROLLO : backwardness **3** ~ **mental** : mental retardation

retratar *vt* **1** : portray **2** FOTOGRAFIAR : photograph **3** DIBUJAR : paint a portrait of — **retrato** *nm* **1** : portrayal **2** DIBUJO : portrait **3** FOTOGRAFÍA : photograph

retrete *nm* : restroom, toilet

retribuir {41} *vt* **1** : pay **2** RECOMPENSAR : reward — **retribución** *nf, pl*

-ciones 1 : payment **2** RECOMPENSA : reward
retroactivo, -va adj : retroactive
retroceder vi : go back, turn back **2** CEDER : back down — **retroceso** nm **1** : backward movement **2** : backing down
retrógrado, -da adj & nmf : reactionary
retrospectiva nf : hindsight — **retrospectivo, -va** adj : retrospective
retrovisor nm : rearview mirror
retumbar vi : resound, reverberate, rumble
reumatismo nm : rheumatism
reunir {68} vt **1** : unite, join **2** TENER : have, possess **3** RECOGER : gather, collect — **reunirse** vr : meet, gather — **reunión** nf, pl **-niones 1** : meeting **2** : (social) gathering, reunion
revalidar vt : confirm, ratify
revancha nf **1** : revenge **2** : rematch (in sports)
revelar vt **1** : reveal, disclose **2** : develop (film) — **revelación** nf, pl **-ciones** : revelation — **revelado** nm : developing (of film) — **revelador, -dora** adj : revealing
reventar {55} v : burst, blow up — **reventarse** vr : burst — **reventón** nm, pl **-tones** : blowout, flat tire
reverberar vi : reverberate — **reverberación** nf, pl **-ciones** : reverberation
reverenciar vt : revere — **reverencia** nf **1** : bow, curtsy **2** VENERACIÓN : reverence — **reverendo, -da** adj & nmf : reverend — **reverente** adj : reverent
reversa nf Lat : reverse (gear)
reverso nm **1** : back, reverse **2 el ~ de la medalla** : the complete opposite — **reversible** adj : reversible
revertir {76} vi **1** : revert **2 ~ en** : result in
revés nm, pl **-veses 1** : back, wrong side **2** CONTRATIEMPO : setback **3** BOFETADA : slap **4** : backhand (in sports) **5 al ~** : the other way around, upside down, inside out
revestir {54} vt **1** : coat, cover **2** ASUMIR : take on, assume — **revestimiento** nm : covering, coating
revisar vt **1** : examine, inspect **2** : check over, overhaul (machinery, etc.) **3** MODIFICAR : revise — **revisión** nf, pl **-siones 1** : revision **2** INSPECCIÓN : inspection, check — **revisor, -sora** n : inspector
revistar vt : review, inspect (troops, etc.) — **revista** nf **1** : magazine, jour-

nal **2** : revue (in theater) **3 pasar ~** : review, inspect
revivir vi : revive, come alive again — vt : relive
revocar {72} vt : revoke
revolcar {82} vt : knock over, knock down — **revolcarse** vr : roll around
revolotear vi : flutter, flit — **revoloteo** nm : fluttering, flitting
revoltijo nm : mess, jumble
revoltoso, -sa adj : rebellious
revolución nf, pl **-ciones** : revolution — **revolucionar** vt : revolutionize — **revolucionario, -ria** adj & n : revolutionary
revolver {89} vt **1** : mix, stir **2** : upset (one's stomach) **3** DESORGANIZAR : mess up — **revolverse** vr **1** : toss and turn **2** VOLVERSE : turn around
revólver nm : revolver
revuelo nm : commotion
revuelta nf : uprising, revolt — **revuelto, -ta** adj **1** : choppy, rough **2** DESORDENADO : messed up **3 huevos revueltos** : scrambled eggs
rey nm : king
reyerta nf : brawl, fight
rezagarse {52} vr : fall behind, lag
rezar {21} vi **1** DECIR : pray **2** DECIR : say — vt : say, recite — **rezo** nm : prayer
rezongar {52} vi : gripe, grumble
rezumar v : ooze
ría nf : estuary
riachuelo nm : brook, stream
riada nf : flood
ribera nf : bank, shore
ribetear vt : border, trim — **ribete** nm **1** : border, trim **2** : embellishment
rico, -ca adj **1** : rich, wealthy **2** ABUNDANTE : abundant **3** SABROSO : rich, tasty — **~** n : rich person
ridiculizar {21} vt : ridicule — **ridículo, -la** adj : ridiculous — **ridículo** nm **1 hacer el ~** : make a fool of oneself **2 poner en ~** : ridicule
riego nm : irrigation
riel nm : rail
rienda nf **1** : rein **2 dar ~ suelta a** : give free rein to
riesgo nm : risk
rifa nf : raffle — **rifar** vt : raffle (off) — **rifarse** vr fam : fight over
rifle nm : rifle
rígido, -da adj **1** : rigid, stiff **2** SEVERO : harsh, strict — **rigidez** nf, pl **-deces 1** : rigidity, stiffness **2** SEVERIDAD : harshness, strictness
rigor nm **1** : rigor, harshness **2** EXACTITUD : precision **3 de ~** : essential,

obligatory — **riguroso, -sa** *adj* : rigorous

rima *nf* 1 : rhyme 2 **~s** *nfpl* : verse, poetry — **rimar** *vi* : rhyme

rimbombante *adj* : showy, pompous

rímel *nm* : mascara

rincón *nm*, *pl* **-cones** : corner, nook

rinoceronte *nm* : rhinoceros

riña *nf* 1 : fight, brawl 2 DISPUTA : dispute, quarrel

riñón *nm*, *pl* **-ñones** : kidney

río *nm* 1 : river 2 TORRENTE : torrent, stream

riqueza *nf* 1 : wealth 2 ABUNDANCIA : richness 3 **~s naturales** : natural resources

risa *nf* 1 : laughter, laugh 2 **dar ~ a algn** : make s.o. laugh 3 **morirse de la ~** *fam* : die laughing

risco *nm* : crag, cliff

risible *adj* : laughable

ristra *nf* : string, series

risueño, -ña *adj* : cheerful, smiling

ritmo *nm* 1 : rhythm 2 VELOCIDAD : pace, speed — **rítmico, -ca** *adj* : rhythmical

rito *nm* : rite, ritual — **ritual** *adj & nm* : ritual

rival *adj & nmf* : rival — **rivalidad** *nf* : rivalry, competition — **rivalizar** {21} *vi* **~ con** : rival, compete with

rizar {21} *vt* 1 : curl 2 : ripple (a surface) — **rizarse** *vr* : curl — **rizado, -da** *adj* 1 : curly 2 : choppy (of water) — **rizo** *nm* 1 : curl 2 : ripple (in water) 3 : loop (in aviation)

róbalo *nm* : bass (fish)

robar *vt* 1 : steal 2 : burglarize (a house, etc.) 3 SECUESTRAR : kidnap — **robo** *nm* : robbery, theft

roble *nm* : oak

robot *nm*, *pl* **-bots** : robot — **robótica** *nf* : robotics

robustecer {53} *vt* : make stronger, strengthen — **robusto, -ta** *adj* : robust, sturdy

roca *nf* : rock, boulder

roce *nm* 1 : rubbing, chafing 2 RASGUÑO : graze, scratch 3 **tener un ~ con** : have a brush with

rociar {85} *vt* : spray, sprinkle — **rocío** *nm* : dew

rocoso, -sa *adj* : rocky

rodaja *nf* : slice

rodar {19} *vi* 1 : roll, roll down, roll along 2 GIRAR : turn, go around 3 : travel (of a vehicle) 4 : film (of movies, etc.) — *vt* 1 : film, shoot 2 : break in (a vehicle) — **rodaje** *nm* 1 : filming, shooting 2 : breaking in (of a vehicle)

rodear *vt* 1 : surround, encircle 2 *Lat* : round up (cattle) — **rodearse** *vr* **~ de** : surround oneself with — **rodeo** *nm* 1 : rodeo, roundup 2 DESVÍO : detour 3 **andar con ~s** : beat around the bush

rodilla *nf* : knee

rodillo *nm* 1 : roller 2 : rolling pin (for pastry)

roer {69} *vt* 1 : gnaw 2 ATORMENTAR : eat away at, torment — **roedor** *nm* : rodent

rogar {16} *vt* : beg, request — *vi* : pray

rojo, -ja *adj* 1 : red 2 **ponerse ~** : blush — **rojo** *nm* : red — **rojez** *nf* : redness — **rojizo, -za** *adj* : reddish

rollizo, -za *adj* : plump, chubby

rollo *nm* 1 : roll, coil 2 *fam* : boring speech, lecture

romance *nm* 1 : romance 2 : Romance (language)

romano, -na *adj & n* : Roman

romántico, -ca *adj* : romantic — **romanticismo** *nm* : romanticism

romería *nf* : pilgrimage, procession

romero *nm* : rosemary

romo, -ma *adj* : blunt, dull

rompecabezas *nms & pl* : puzzle

romper {70} *vt* 1 : break 2 RASGAR : rip, tear 3 : break off (relations), break (a contract) — *vi* 1 : break (of the day, waves, etc.) 2 **~ a** : begin to, burst out with 3 **~ con** : break off with — **romperse** *vr* : break

ron *nm* : rum

roncar {72} *vi* : snore — **ronco, -ca** *adj* : hoarse

ronda *nf* 1 : rounds *pl*, patrol 2 : round (of drinks, etc.) — **rondar** *vt* 1 : patrol 2 : hang around (a place) 3 : be approximately (an age, a number, etc.) — *vi* 1 : be on patrol 2 MERODEAR : prowl about

ronquera *nf* : hoarseness

ronquido *nm* : snore

ronronear *vi* : purr — **ronroneo** *nm* : purr, purring

ronzar {21} *vt* : munch, crunch

roña *nf* 1 : mange 2 SUCIEDAD : dirt, filth — **roñoso, -sa** *adj* 1 : mangy 2 SUCIO : dirty 3 *fam* : stingy

ropa *nf* 1 : clothes *pl*, clothing 2 **~ interior** : underwear — **ropaje** *nm* : robes *pl*, regalia — **ropero** *nm* : wardrobe, closet

rosa *nf* : rose (flower) — **~** *adj* : rose-colored — **~** *nm* : rose (color) — **rosado, -da** *adj* 1 : pink 2 **vino rosado** : rosé — **rosado** *nm* : pink (color) — **rosal** *nm* : rosebush

rosario *nm* : rosary
rosbif *nm* : roast beef
rosca *nf* **1** : thread (of a screw) **2** ESPIRAL : ring, coil
roseta *nf* : rosette
rosquilla *nf* : doughnut
rostro *nm* : face
rotación *nf*, *pl* **-ciones** : rotation — **rotativo, -va** *adj* : rotary, revolving
roto, -ta *adj* : broken, torn
rotonda *nf* : traffic circle, rotary
rótula *nf* : kneecap
rótulo *nm* **1** : heading, title **2** ETIQUETA : label, sign
rotundo, -da *adj* : categorical, absolute
rotura *nf* : break, tear, fracture
rozar {21} *vt* **1** : graze, touch lightly **2** APROXIMARSE DE : touch on, border on — *vi* : scrape, rub — **rozarse** *vr* **1** : rub, chafe **2 ~ con** *fam* : rub elbows with — **rozadura** *nf* : scratch
rubí *nm*, *pl* **rubíes** : ruby
rubicundo, -da *adj* : ruddy
rubio, -bia *adj & n* : blond
rubor *nm* : flush, blush — **ruborizarse** {21} *vr* : blush
rúbrica *nf* **1** : flourish (in writing) **2** TÍTULO : title, heading
rudeza *nf* : roughness, coarseness
rudimentos *nmpl* : rudiments, basics — **rudimentario, -ria** *adj* : rudimentary
rudo, -da *adj* **1** : rough, harsh **2** GROSERO : coarse, unpolished
rueda *nf* **1** : wheel **2** CORRO : circle, ring **3** RODAJA : (round) slice **4 ir sobre ~s** : go smoothly — **ruedo** *nm* : bullring

ruego *nm* : request
rugir {35} *vi* : roar — **rugido** *nm* : roar
rugoso, -sa *adj* **1** : rough **2** ARRUGADO : wrinkled
ruibarbo *nm* : rhubarb
ruido *nm* : noise — **ruidoso, -sa** *adj* : loud, noisy
ruina *nf* **1** : ruin, destruction **2** COLAPSO : collapse **3 ~s** *nfpl* : ruins, remains — **ruinoso, -sa** *adj* : run-down, dilapidated
ruiseñor *nm* : nightingale
ruleta *nf* : roulette
rulo *nm* : curler, roller
rumano, -na *adj* : Romanian, Rumanian
rumba *nf* : rumba
rumbo *nm* **1** : direction, course **2** ESPLENDIDEZ : lavishness **3 con ~ a** : bound for, heading for **4 perder el ~** : go off course
rumiar *vt* : mull over — *vi* : chew the cud — **rumiante** *adj & nm* : ruminant
rumor *nm* **1** : rumor **2** MURMULLO : murmur — **rumorearse** *or* **rumorarse** *vr* : be rumored — **rumoroso, -sa** *adj* : murmuring, babbling
ruptura *nf* **1** : break, rupture **2** : breach (of a contract) **3** : breaking off (of relations)
rural *adj* : rural
ruso, -sa *adj* : Russian — **ruso** *nm* : Russian (language)
rústico, -ca *adj* **1** : rural, rustic **2 en rústica** : in paperback
ruta *nf* : route
rutina *nf* : routine — **rutinario, -ria** *adj* : routine

S

s *nf* : s, 20th letter of the Spanish alphabet
sábado *nm* : Saturday
sábana *nf* : sheet
sabandija *nf* : bug
saber {71} *vt* **1** : know **2** SER CAPAZ DE : know how to, be able to **3** ENTERARSE : learn, find out **4 a ~** : namely — *vi* **1** : taste **2 ~ de** : know about — *~ nm* : knowledge — **sabelotodo** *nmf fam* : know-it-all — **sabido, -da** *adj* : well-known — **sabiduría** *nf* **1** : wisdom **2** CONOCIMIENTO : learning, knowledge — **sabiendas: a ~** *adv phr* : knowingly — **sabio, -bia** *adj* **1** : learned **2** PRUDENTE : wise, sensible

sabor *nm* : flavor, taste — **saborear** *vt* : savor
sabotaje *nm* : sabotage — **saboteador, -dora** *n* : saboteur — **sabotear** *vt* : sabotage
sabroso, -sa *adj* : delicious, tasty
sabueso *nm* **1** : bloodhound **2** *fam* : sleuth
sacacorchos *nms & pl* : corkscrew
sacapuntas *nms & pl* : pencil sharpener
sacar {72} *vt* **1** : take out **2** OBTENER : get, obtain **3** EXTRAER : extract, withdraw **4** : bring out (a book, a product, etc.) **5** : take (photos), make (copies) **6** QUITAR : remove **7 ~ adelante** : bring up (children), carry out (a project,

etc.) 8 ~ **la lengua** : stick out one's tongue — *vi* : serve (in sports)
sacarina *nf* : saccharin
sacerdote, -tisa *n* : priest *m*, priestess *f* — **sacerdocio** *nm* : priesthood — **sacerdotal** *adj* : priestly
saciar *vt* : satisfy
saco *nm* 1 : bag, sack 2 : sac (in anatomy) 3 *Lat* : jacket
sacramento *nm* : sacrament — **sacramental** *adj* : sacramental
sacrificar {72} *vt* : sacrifice — **sacrificarse** *vr* : sacrifice oneself — **sacrificio** *nm* : sacrifice
sacrilegio *nm* : sacrilege — **sacrílego, -ga** *adj* : sacrilegious
sacro, -cra *adj* : sacred — **sacrosanto, -ta** *adj* : sacrosanct
sacudir *vt* 1 : shake 2 GOLPEAR : beat 3 CONMOVER : shake up, shock — **sacudirse** *vr* : shake off — **sacudida** *nf* 1 : shaking 2 : jolt (of a train, etc.), tremor (of an earthquake) 3 : (emotional) shock
sádico, -ca *adj* : sadistic — ~ *n* : sadist — **sadismo** *nm* : sadism
saeta *nf* : arrow
safari *nm* : safari
sagaz *adj*, *pl* **-gaces** : shrewd, sagacious — **sagacidad** *nf* : shrewdness
sagrado, -da *adj* : sacred, holy
sal *nf* : salt
sala *nf* 1 : room, hall 2 : living room (of a house) 3 ~ **de espera** : waiting room
salar *vt* : salt — **salado, -da** *adj* 1 : salty 2 GRACIOSO : witty 3 **agua salada** : salt water
salario *nm* : salary, wage
salchicha *nf* : sausage — **salchichón** *nf*, *pl* **-chones** : salami-like cold cut
saldar *vt* 1 : settle, pay off 2 VENDER : sell off — **saldo** *nm* 1 : balance (of an account) 2 ~s *nmpl* : remainders, sale items
salero *nm* : saltshaker
salir {73} *vi* 1 : go out, come out 2 PARTIR : leave 3 APARECER : appear 4 RESULTAR : turn out 5 : rise (of the sun) 6 ~ **adelante** : get by 7 ~ **con** : go out with, date 8 ~ **de** : come from — **salirse** *vr* 1 : leave 2 ESCAPARSE : leak out, escape 3 SOLTARSE : come off 4 ~ **con la suya** : get one's own way — **salida** *nf* 1 : exit 2 : (action of) leaving, departure 3 SOLUCIÓN : way out 4 : leak (of gas, liquid, etc.) 5 OCURRENCIA : witty remark 6 ~ **de emergencia** : emergency exit 7 ~ **del sol** : sunrise — **saliente** *adj* 1 : departing, outgoing 2 DESTACADO : outstanding

saliva *nf* : saliva
salmo *nm* : psalm
salmón *nm*, *pl* **-mones** : salmon
salmuera *nf* : brine
salón *nm*, *pl* **-lones** 1 : lounge, sitting room 2 ~ **de belleza** : beauty salon 3 ~ **de clase** : classroom
salpicar {72} *vt* 1 : splash, spatter 2 ~ **de** : pepper with — **salpicadera** *nf* *Lat* : fender — **salpicadura** *nf* : splash
salsa *nf* 1 : sauce 2 : (meat) gravy 3 : salsa (music)
saltamontes *nms & pl* : grasshopper
saltar *vi* 1 : jump, leap 2 REBOTAR : bounce 3 : come off (of a button, etc.) 4 ROMPERSE : shatter 5 ESTALLAR : explode, blow up — *vt* 1 : jump (over) 2 OMITIR : skip, miss — **saltarse** *vr* 1 : come off 2 OMITIR : skip, miss
saltear *vt* : sauté
saltimbanqui *nmf* : acrobat
salto *nm* 1 : jump, leap 2 : dive (into water) 3 ~ **de agua** : waterfall — **saltón, -tona** *adj*, *mpl* **-tones** : bulging, protruding
salud *nf* 1 : health 2 ¡**salud**! : here's to your health! 3 ¡**salud**! *Lat* : bless you! (when someone sneezes) — **saludable** *adj* : healthy
saludar *vt* 1 : greet, say hello to 2 : salute (in the military) — **saludo** *nm* 1 : greeting 2 : (military) salute 3 ~s : best wishes, regards
salva *nf* ~ **de aplausos** : round of applause
salvación *nf*, *pl* **-ciones** : salvation
salvado *nm* : bran
salvador, -dora *n* : savior, rescuer
salvadoreño, -ña *adj* : (El) Salvadoran
salvaguardar *vt* : safeguard
salvaje *adj* 1 : wild 2 PRIMITIVO : savage, primitive — ~ *nmf* : savage
salvar *vt* 1 : save, rescue 2 RECORRER : cover, travel 3 SUPERAR : overcome — **salvarse** *vr* : save oneself — **salvavidas** *nms & pl* 1 : life preserver 2 **bote** ~ : lifeboat
salvia *nf* : sage (plant)
salvo, -va *adj* : safe — **salvo** *prep* 1 : except (for), save 2 ~ **que** : unless
samba *nf* : samba
San → **santo**
sanar *vt* : heal, cure — *vi* : recover — **sanatorio** *nm* 1 : sanatorium 2 HOSPITAL : clinic, hospital
sanción *nf*, *pl* **-ciones** : sanction — **sancionar** *vt* : sanction
sandalia *nf* : sandal
sándalo *nm* : sandalwood
sandía *nf* : watermelon

sandwich ['sandwitʃ, 'saŋgwitʃ] *nm, pl* **-wiches** [-dwitʃes, -gwi-] : sandwich
saneamiento *nm* : sanitation
sangrar *vt* 1 : bleed 2 : indent (a paragraph) — *vi* : bleed — **sangrante** *adj* : bleeding — **sangre** *nf* 1 : blood 2 **a ~ fría** : in cold blood — **sangriento, -ta** *adj* : bloody
sanguijuela *nf* : leech
sanguinario, -ria *adj* : bloodthirsty — **sanguíneo, -nea** *adj* : blood
sano, -na *adj* 1 : healthy 2 : (morally) wholesome 3 ENTERO : intact 4 **sano y salvo** : safe and sound — **sanidad** *nf* 1 : health 2 : public health, sanitation — **sanitario, -ria** *adj* : sanitary, health — **sanitario** *nm Lat* : toilet
santiamén *nm* **en un ~** : in no time at all
santo, -ta *adj* 1 : holy 2 **Santo, Santa** (**San** *before masculine names except those beginning with D or T*) : Saint — **~** *n* : saint — **santo** *nm* 1 : saint's day 2 *Lat* : birthday — **santidad** *nf* : holiness, sanctity — **santiguarse** {10} *vr* : cross oneself — **santuario** *nm* : sanctuary
saña *nf* 1 : fury 2 BRUTALIDAD : viciousness
sapo *nm* : toad
saque *nm* : serve (in tennis, etc.), throw-in (in soccer)
saquear *vt* : sack, loot — **saqueador, -dora** *n* : looter — **saqueo** *nm* : sacking, looting
sarampión *nm* : measles *pl*
sarape *nm Lat* : serape
sarcasmo *nm* : sarcasm — **sarcástico, -ca** *adj* : sarcastic
sardina *nf* : sardine
sardónico, -ca *adj* : sardonic
sargento *nm* : sergeant
sarpullido *nm* : rash
sartén *nmf, pl* **-tenes** : frying pan
sastre, -tra *n* : tailor — **sastrería** *nf* 1 : tailoring 2 : tailor's shop
Satanás *nm* : Satan — **satánico, -ca** *adj* : satanic
satélite *nm* : satellite
sátira *nf* : satire — **satírico, -ca** *adj* : satirical
satisfacer {74} *vt* 1 : satisfy 2 CUMPLIR : fulfill, meet 3 PAGAR : pay — **satisfacerse** *vr* 1 : be satisfied 2 VENGARSE : take revenge — **satisfacción** *nf, pl* **-ciones** : satisfaction — **satisfactorio, -ria** *adj* : satisfactory — **satisfecho, -cha** *adj* : satisfied
saturar *vt* : saturate — **saturación** *nf, pl* **-ciones** : saturation

Saturno *nm* : Saturn
sauce *nm* : willow
sauna *nmf* : sauna
savia *nf* : sap
saxofón *nm, pl* **-fones** : saxophone
sazón *nf, pl* **-zones** 1 : seasoning 2 MADUREZ : ripeness 3 **a la ~** : at that time, then 4 **en ~** : ripe, in season — **sazonar** *vt* : season
se *pron* 1 (*reflexive*) : himself, herself, itself, oneself, yourself, yourselves, themselves 2 (*indirect object*) : (to) him, (to) her, (to) you, (to) them 3 : each other, one another 4 **~ dice que** : it is said that 5 **~ habla inglés** : English spoken
sebo *nm* 1 : fat 2 : tallow (for candles, etc.) 3 : suet (for cooking)
secar {72} *v* : dry — **secarse** *vr* : dry (up) — **secador** *nm* : hair dryer — **secadora** *nf* : (clothes) dryer
sección *nf, pl* **-ciones** : section
seco, -ca *adj* 1 : dry 2 : dried (of fruits, etc.) 3 TAJANTE : sharp, brusque 4 *fam* : thin, skinny 5 **a secas** : simply, just 6 **en seco** : suddenly
secretar *vt* : secrete — **secreción** *nf, pl* **-ciones** : secretion
secretario, -ria *n* : secretary — **secretaría** *nf* : secretariat
secreto, -ta *adj* : secret — **secreto** *nm* 1 : secret 2 **en ~** : in confidence
secta *nf* : sect
sector *nm* : sector
secuaz *nmf, pl* **-cuaces** : follower, henchman
secuela *nf* : consequence
secuencia *nf* : sequence
secuestrar *vt* 1 : kidnap 2 : hijack (an airplane, etc.) 3 EMBARGAR : confiscate, seize — **secuestrador, -dora** *n* 1 : kidnapper 2 : hijacker (of an airplane, etc.) — **secuestro** *nm* 1 : kidnapping 2 : hijacking (of an airplane, etc.) 3 : seizure (of goods)
secular *adj* : secular
secundar *vt* : support, second — **secundario, -ria** *adj* : secondary
sed *nf* 1 : thirst 2 **tener ~** : be thirsty
seda *nf* : silk
sedal *nm* : fishing line
sedar *vt* : sedate — **sedante** *adj & nm* : sedative
sede *nf* 1 : seat, headquarters 2 **Santa Sede** : Holy See
sedentario, -ria *adj* : sedentary
sedición *nf, pl* **-ciones** : sedition — **sedicioso, -sa** *adj* : seditious
sediento, -ta *adj* : thirsty
sedimento *nm* : sediment

sedoso, -sa *adj* : silky, silken
seducir {61} *vt* **1** : seduce **2** ATRAER : captivate, charm — **seducción** *nf, pl* **-ciones** : seduction — **seductor, -tora** *adj* **1** : seductive **2** ENCANTADOR : charming — **~** *n* : seducer
segar {49} *vt* : reap — **segador, -dora** *n* : reaper, harvester
seglar *adj* : lay, secular — **~** *nm* : layperson, layman *m*, laywoman *f*
segmento *nm* : segment
segregar {52} *vt* : segregate — **segregación** *nf, pl* **-ciones** : segregation
seguir {75} *vt* : follow — *vi* : go on, continue — **seguida: en — ~** *adv phr* : right away — **seguido** *adv* **1** : straight (ahead) **2** *Lat* : often — **seguido, -da** *adj* **1** : continuous **2** CONSECUTIVO : consecutive — **seguidor, -dora** *n* : follower
según *prep* : according to — **~** *adv* : it depends — **~** *conj* : as, just as
segundo, -da *adj* : second — **~** *n* : second (one) — **segundo** *nm* : second (unit of time)
seguro, -ra *adj* **1** : safe **2** FIRME : secure **3** CIERTO : sure, certain **4** FIABLE : reliable — **seguramente** *adv* : for sure, surely — **seguridad** *nf* **1** : safety **2** GARANTÍA : security **3** CERTEZA : certainty **4** CONFIANZA : confidence — **seguro** *adv* : certainly — **~** *nm* **1** : insurance **2** : safety (device)
seis *adj & nm* : six — **seiscientos, -tas** *adj* : six hundred — **seiscientos** *nms & pl* : six hundred
seísmo *nm* : earthquake
selección *nf, pl* **-ciones** : selection — **seleccionar** *vt* : select, choose — **selectivo, -va** *adj* : selective — **selecto, -ta** *adj* : choice, select
sellar *vt* **1** : seal **2** TIMBRAR : stamp — **sello** *nm* **1** : seal **2** TIMBRE : stamp **3** *or* **~ distintivo** : hallmark
selva *nf* **1** : jungle **2** BOSQUE : forest
semáforo *nm* : traffic light
semana *nf* : week — **semanal** *adj* : weekly — **semanario** *nm* : weekly
semántica *nf* : semantics — **semántico, -ca** *adj* : semantic
semblante *nm* **1** : countenance, face **2** APARIENCIA : look
sembrar {55} *vt* **1** : sow **2 ~ de** : strew with
semejar *vi* : resemble — **semejarse** *vr* : look alike — **semejante** *adj* **1** : similar **2** TAL : such — **~** *nm* : fellowman — **semejanza** *nf* : similarity
semen *nm* : semen — **semental** *nm* **1** : stud **2 caballo ~** : stallion

semestre *nm* : semester
semiconductor *nm* : semiconductor
semifinal *nf* : semifinal
semilla *nf* : seed — **semillero** *nm* **1** : nursery (for plants) **2** HERVIDERO : hotbed, breeding ground
seminario *nm* **1** : seminary **2** CURSO : seminar, course
sémola *nf* : semolina
senado *nm* : senate — **senador, -dora** *n* : senator
sencillo, -lla *adj* **1** : simple **2** ÚNICO : single — **sencillez** *nf* : simplicity
senda *nf* *or* **sendero** *nm* : path, way
sendos, -das *adj pl* : each, both
senil *adj* : senile
seno *nm* **1** : breast, bosom **2** : sinus (in anatomy) **3 ~ materno** : womb
sensación *nf, pl* **-ciones** : feeling, sensation — **sensacional** *adj* : sensational — **sensacionalista** *adj* : sensationalistic, lurid
sensato, -ta *adj* : sensible — **sensatez** *nf* : good sense
sensible *adj* **1** : sensitive **2** APRECIABLE : considerable, significant — **sensibilidad** *nf* : sensitivity — **sensitivo, -va** *or* **sensorial** *adj* : sense, sensory
sensual *adj* : sensual, sensuous — **sensualidad** *nf* : sensuality
sentar {55} *vt* **1** : seat, sit **2** ESTABLECER : establish, set — *vi* **1** : suit **2 ~ bien a** : agree with (of food or drink) — **sentarse** *vr* : sit (down) — **sentado, -da** *adj* **1** : sitting, seated **2 dar por sentado** : take for granted
sentencia *nf* **1** FALLO : sentence, judgment **2** MÁXIMA : saying — **sentenciar** *vt* : sentence
sentido, -da *adj* **1** : heartfelt, sincere **2** SENSIBLE : touchy, sensitive — **sentido** *nm* **1** : sense **2** CONOCIMIENTO : consciousness **3** DIRECCIÓN : direction **4 doble ~** : double entendre **5 ~ común** : common sense **6 ~ del humor** : sense of humor **7 ~ único** : one-way
sentimiento *nm* **1** : feeling, emotion **2** PESAR : regret — **sentimental** *adj* : sentimental — **sentimentalismo** *nm* : sentimentality
sentir {76} *vt* **1** : feel **2** OÍR : hear **3** LAMENTAR : be sorry for **4 lo siento** : I'm sorry — *vi* : feel — **sentirse** *vr* : feel
seña *nf* **1** : sign **2 ~s** *nfpl* DIRECCIÓN : address **3 ~s particulares** : distinguishing marks
señal *nf* **1** : signal **2** AVISO, INDICIO : sign **3** DEPÓSITO : deposit **4 dar ~es**

de : show signs of **5 en ~ de** : as a
token of — **señalado, -da** adj : notable — **señalar** vt 1 INDICAR : indicate, point out 2 MARCAR : mark 3
FIJAR : fix, set — **señalarse** vr : distinguish oneself
señor, -ñora n 1 : gentleman m, man m,
lady f, woman f 2 : Sir m, Madam f 3
: Mr. m, Mrs. f 4 **señora** : wife f 5 **el
Señor** : the Lord — **señorial** adj
: stately — **señorita** nf 1 : young lady,
young woman 2 : Miss
señuelo nm 1 : decoy 2 TRAMPA : bait,
lure
separar vt 1 : separate 2 QUITAR : detach, remove 3 APARTAR : move away
4 DESTITUIR : dismiss — **separarse** vr
1 APARTARSE : separate 2 : part company — **separación** nf, pl **-ciones** : separation — **separado, -da** adj 1 : separate 2 : separated (of persons) 3 **por
separado** : separately
septentrional adj : northern
séptico, -ca adj : septic
septiembre nm : September
séptimo, -ma adj : seventh — **~** n
: seventh
sepulcro nm : tomb, sepulchre —
sepultar vt : bury — **sepultura** nf 1
: burial 2 TUMBA : grave
sequedad nf : dryness — **sequía** nf
: drought
séquito nm : retinue, entourage
ser {77} vi 1 : be 2 **a no ~ que** : unless 3 **¿cuánto es?** : how much is it?
4 **es más** : what's more 5 **~ de** : belong to 6 **~ de** : come from 7 **son las
diez** : it's ten o'clock — **~** nm 1 ENTE
: being 2 **~ humano** : human being
serbio, -bia adj : Serb, Serbian
serenar vt : calm — **serenarse** vr
: calm down — **serenata** nf : serenade
— **serenidad** nf : serenity — **sereno,
-na** adj 1 : serene, calm 2 : fair, clear
(of weather) — **sereno** nm : night
watchman
serie nf 1 : series 2 **fabricación en ~**
: mass production 3 **fuera de ~** : extraordinary — **serial** nm : serial
serio, -ria adj 1 : serious 2 RESPONS-
ABLE : reliable 3 **en serio** : seriously
— **seriedad** nf : seriousness
sermón nm, pl **-mones** : sermon —
sermonear vt : lecture, reprimand
serpentear vi : twist, wind — **serpiente** nf 1 : serpent, snake 2 **~ de cascabel** : rattlesnake
serrado, -da adj : serrated
serrano, -na adj 1 : mountain 2 **jamón
serrano** : cured ham

serrar {55} vt : saw — **serrín** nm, pl
-rrines : sawdust — **serrucho** nm
: saw, handsaw
servicio nm 1 : service 2 **~s** nmpl
: restroom — **servicial** adj : obliging,
helpful — **servidor, -dora** n 1 : servant 2 **su seguro servidor** : yours
truly — **servidumbre** nf 1 : servitude
2 CRIADOS : help, servants pl — **servil**
adj : servile
servilleta nf : napkin
servir {54} vt : serve — vi 1 : work,
function 2 VALER : be of use —
servirse vr 1 : help oneself 2 **sírvase
sentarse** : please have a seat
sesenta adj & nm : sixty
sesgo nm : bias, slant
sesión nf, pl **-siones** 1 : session 2
: showing (of a film), performance (of
a play)
seso nm : brain — **sesudo, -da** adj 1
: sensible 2 fam : brainy
seta nf : mushroom
setecientos, -tas adj : seven hundred
— **setecientos** nms & pl : seven hundred
setenta adj & nm : seventy
setiembre nm → **septiembre**
seto nm 1 : fence 2 **~ vivo** : hedge
seudónimo nm : pseudonym
severo, -ra adj 1 : harsh, severe 2
: strict (of a teacher, etc.) — **severidad** nf : severity
sexagésimo, -ma adj & n : sixtieth
sexo nm : sex — **sexismo** nm : sexism
— **sexista** adj & nmf : sexist
sexteto nm : sextet
sexto, -ta adj & n : sixth
sexual adj : sexual — **sexualidad** nf
: sexuality
sexy adj, pl **sexy** or **sexys** : sexy
si conj 1 : if 2 (in indirect questions)
: whether 3 **~ bien** : although 4 **~
no** : otherwise, or else
sí¹ adv 1 : yes 2 **creo que ~** : I think
so 3 **porque ~** fam : (just) because —
~ nm : consent
sí² pron 1 **de por ~** or **en ~** : by itself, in itself, per se 2 **fuera de ~**
: beside oneself 3 **para ~ (mismo)**
: to himself, to herself, for himself, for
herself 4 **entre ~** : among themselves
sico- → **psico-**
SIDA or **sida** nm : AIDS
siderurgia nf : iron and steel industry
sidra nf : (hard) cider
siega nf 1 : harvesting 2 : harvest (time)
siembra nf 1 : sowing 2 : sowing season

siempre *adv* **1** : always **2** *Lat* : still **3 para ~** : forever, for good **4 ~ que** : whenever, every time **5 ~ que** *or* **~ y cuando** : provided that
sien *nf* : temple
sierra *nf* **1** : saw **2** CORDILLERA : mountain range **3 la ~** : the mountains *pl*
siervo, -va *n* : slave
siesta *nf* : nap, siesta
siete *adj & nm* : seven
sífilis *nf* : syphilis
sifón *nm, pl* **-fones** : siphon
sigilo *nm* : secrecy
sigla *nf* : acronym, abbreviation
siglo *nm* **1** : century **2 hace ~s** : for ages
significar {72} *vt* **1** : mean, signify **2** EXPRESAR : express — **significación** *nf, pl* **-ciones** **1** : significance, importance **2** : meaning (of a word, etc.) — **significado, -da** *adj* : well-known — **significado** *nm* : meaning — **significativo, -va** *adj* : significant
signo *nm* **1** : sign **2 ~ de admiración** : exclamation point **3 ~ de interrogación** : question mark
siguiente *adj* : next, following
sílaba *nf* : syllable
silbar *v* **1** : whistle **2** ABUCHEAR : hiss, boo — **silbato** *nm* : whistle — **silbido** *nm* **1** : whistle, whistling **2** ABUCHEO : hiss, booing
silenciar *vt* : silence — **silenciador** *nm* : muffler — **silencio** *nm* : silence — **silencioso, -sa** *adj* : silent, quiet
silicio *nm* : silicon
silla *nf* **1** : chair **2** *or* **~ de montar** : saddle **3 ~ de ruedas** : wheelchair — **sillón** *nm, pl* **-llones** : armchair, easy chair
silo *nm* : silo
silueta *nf* **1** : silhouette **2** CONTORNO : outline, shape
silvestre *adj* : wild
silvicultura *nf* : forestry
símbolo *nm* : symbol — **simbólico, -ca** *adj* : symbolic — **simbolismo** *nm* : symbolism — **simbolizar** {21} *vt* : symbolize
simetría *nf* : symmetry — **simétrico, -ca** *adj* : symmetrical, symmetric
simiente *nf* : seed
símil *nm* **1** : simile **2** COMPARACIÓN : comparison — **similar** *adj* : similar, alike
simio *nm* : ape
simpatía *nf* **1** : liking, affection **2** AMABILIDAD : friendliness — **simpático, -ca** *adj* **1** : nice, likeable **2** AMABLE : pleasant, kind — **simpatizante** *nmf*

: sympathizer — **simpatizar** {21} *vi* **1** : get along, hit it off **2 ~ con** : sympathize with
simple *adj* **1** SENCILLO : simple **2** MERO : pure, sheer **3** TONTO : simpleminded — **~** *n* : fool, simpleton — **simpleza** *nf* **1** : simpleness **2** TONTERÍA : silly thing — **simplicidad** *nf* : simplicity — **simplificar** {72} *vt* : simplify
simposio *or* **simposium** *nm* : symposium
simular *vt* **1** : simulate **2** FINGIR : feign — **simulacro** *nm* : simulation, drill
simultáneo, -nea *adj* : simultaneous
sin *prep* **1** : without **2 ~ que** : without
sinagoga *nf* : synagogue
sincero, -ra *adj* : sincere — **sinceramente** *adv* : sincerely — **sinceridad** *nf* : sincerity
síncopa *nf* : syncopation
sincronizar {21} *vt* : synchronize
sindicato *nm* : (labor) union — **sindical** *adj* : union, labor
síndrome *nm* : syndrome
sinfín *nm* **1** : endless number **2 un ~ de** : no end of
sinfonía *nf* : symphony — **sinfónico, -ca** *adj* : symphonic
singular *adj* **1** : exceptional, outstanding **2** PECULIAR : peculiar **3** : singular (in grammar) — **~** *nm* : singular — **singularizar** {21} *vt* : single out — **singularizarse** *vr* : stand out
siniestro, -tra *adj* **1** : sinister **2** IZQUIERDO : left — **siniestro** *nm* : disaster
sinnúmero *nm* → **sinfín**
sino *conj* **1** : but, rather **2** EXCEPTO : except, save
sinónimo, -ma *adj* : synonymous — **sinónimo** *nm* : synonym
sinopsis *nfs & pl* : synopsis
sinrazón *nf, pl* **-zones** : wrong
sintaxis *nfs & pl* : syntax
síntesis *nfs & pl* : synthesis — **sintético, -ca** *adj* : synthetic — **sintetizar** {21} *vt* **1** : synthesize **2** RESUMIR : summarize
síntoma *nm* : symptom — **sintomático, -ca** *adj* : symptomatic
sintonía *nf* **1** : tuning in (of a radio) **2 en ~ con** : in tune with — **sintonizar** {21} *vt* : tune (in) to
sinuoso, -sa *adj* : winding
sinvergüenza *nmf* : scoundrel
sionismo *nm* : Zionism
siquiera *adv* **1** : at least **2 ni ~** : not even — **~** *conj* : even if
sirena *nf* **1** : mermaid **2** : siren (of an ambulance, etc.)
sirio, -ria *adj* : Syrian

sirviente, -ta *n* : servant, maid *f*
sisear *vi* : hiss — **siseo** *nm* : hiss
sismo *nm* : earthquake — **sísmico, -ca** *adj* : seismic
sistema *nm* **1** : system **2 por ~** : systematically — **sistemático, -ca** *adj* : systematic
sitiar *vt* : besiege
sitio *nm* **1** : place, site **2** ESPACIO : room, space **3** CERCO : siege **4 en cualquier ~** : anywhere
situar {3} *vt* : situate, place — **situarse** *vr* **1** : be located **2** ESTABLECERSE : get oneself established — **situación** *nf, pl* **-ciones** : situation, position — **situado, -da** *adj* : situated, placed
slip *nm* : briefs *pl*, underpants *pl*
smoking *nm* : tuxedo
so *prep* : under
sobaco *nm* : armpit
sobar *vt* **1** : finger, handle **2** : knead (dough) — **sobado, -da** *adj* : worn, shabby
soberanía *nf* : sovereignty — **soberano, -na** *adj & n* : sovereign
soberbia *nf* : pride, arrogance — **soberbio, -bia** *adj* : proud, arrogant
sobornar *vt* : bribe — **soborno** *nm* **1** : bribe **2** : (action of) bribery
sobrar *vi* **1** : be more than enough **2** RESTAR : be left over — **sobra** *nf* **1** : surplus **2 de ~** : to spare **3 ~s** *nfpl* : leftovers — **sobrado, -da** *adj* : more than enough — **sobrante** *adj* : remaining
sobre[1] *nm* : envelope
sobre[2] *prep* **1** : on, on top of **2** POR ENCIMA DE : over, above **3** ACERCA DE : about **4 ~ todo** : especially, above all
sobrecama *nmf Lat* : bedspread
sobrecargar {52} *vt* : overload, overburden
sobrecoger {15} *vt* : startle — **sobrecogerse** *vr* : be startled
sobrecubierta *nf* : dust jacket
sobredosis *nfs & pl* : overdose
sobreentender {56} *vt* : infer, understand — **sobreentenderse** *vr* : be understood
sobreestimar *vt* : overestimate
sobregiro *nm* : overdraft
sobrellevar *vt* : endure, bear
sobremesa *nf* **de ~** : after-dinner
sobrenatural *adj* : supernatural
sobrenombre *nm* : nickname
sobrentender → **sobreentender**
sobrepasar *vt* : exceed
sobreponer {60} *vt* **1** : superimpose **2** ANTEPONER : put before — **sobreponerse** *vr* **~ a** : overcome

sobresalir {73} *vi* **1** : protrude **2** DESTACARSE : stand out — **sobresaliente** *adj* : outstanding
sobresaltar *vt* : startle — **sobresaltarse** *vr* : start, jump up — **sobresalto** *nm* : fright
sobrestimar → **sobreestimar**
sobretodo *nm* : overcoat
sobrevenir {87} *vi* : happen, ensue
sobrevivencia *nf* → **supervivencia**
sobreviviente *adj & nmf* → **superviviente**
sobrevivir *vi* : survive — *vt* : outlive
sobrevolar {19} *vt* : fly over
sobriedad *nf* **1** : sobriety **2** MODERACIÓN : restraint
sobrino, -na *n* : nephew *m*, niece *f*
sobrio, -bria *adj* : sober
socarrón, -rrona *adj, mpl* **-rrones** : sarcastic
socavar *vt* : undermine
sociable *adj* : sociable — **social** *adj* : social — **socialismo** *nm* : socialism — **socialista** *adj & nmf* : socialist — **sociedad** *nf* **1** : society **2** EMPRESA : company **3 ~ anónima** : incorporated company — **socio, -cia** *n* **1** : partner **2** MIEMBRO : member — **sociología** *nf* : sociology — **sociólogo, -ga** *n* : sociologist
socorrer *vt* : help — **socorrista** *nmf* : lifeguard — **socorro** *nm* : help
soda *nf* : soda (water)
sodio *nf* : sodium
sofá *nm* : couch, sofa
sofisticación *nf, pl* **-ciones** : sophistication — **sofisticado, -da** *adj* : sophisticated
sofocar {72} *vt* **1** : suffocate, smother **2** : put out (a fire), stifle (a rebellion, etc.) — **sofocarse** *vr* **1** : suffocate **2** *fam* : get upset — **sofocante** *adj* : suffocating, stifling
sofreír {66} *vt* : sauté
soga *nf* : rope
soja *nf* → **soya**
sojuzgar *vt* : subdue, subjugate
sol *nm* **1** : sun **2 hacer ~** : be sunny
solamente *adv* : only, just
solapa *nf* **1** : lapel (of a jacket) **2** : flap (of an envelope) — **solapado, -da** *adj* : secret, underhanded
solar[1] *adj* : solar, sun
solar[2] *nm* : lot, site
solariego, -ga *adj* : ancestral
solaz *nm, pl* **-laces 1** : solace **2** DESCANSO : relaxation — **solazarse** {21} *vr* : relax
soldado *nm* **1** : soldier **2 ~ raso** : private
soldar {19} *vt* : weld, solder — **solda-**

dor *nm* : soldering iron — **soldador, -dora** *n* : welder
soleado, -da *adj* : sunny
soledad *nf* : loneliness, solitude
solemne *adj* : solemn — **solemnidad** *nf* : solemnity
soler {78} *vi* 1 : be in the habit of 2 **suele llegar tarde** : he usually arrives late
solicitar *vt* 1 : request, solicit 2 : apply for (a job, etc.) — **solicitante** *nmf* : applicant — **solícito, -ta** *adj* : solicitous, obliging — **solicitud** *nf* 1 : concern 2 PETICIÓN : request 3 : application (for a job, etc.)
solidaridad *nf* : solidarity
sólido, -da *adj* 1 : solid 2 : sound (of an argument, etc.) — **sólido** *nm* : solid — **solidez** *nf* : solidity — **solidificar** {72} *vt* : solidify — **solidificarse** *vr* : solidify, harden
soliloquio *nm* : soliloquy
solista *nmf* : soloist
solitario, -ria *adj* 1 : solitary 2 AISLADO : lonely, deserted — ~ *n* : recluse — **solitaria** *nf* : tapeworm — **solitario** *nm* : solitaire
sollozar {21} *vi* : sob — **sollozo** *nm* : sob
solo, -la *adj* 1 : alone 2 AISLADO : lonely 3 **a solas** : alone, by oneself — **solo** *nm* : solo
sólo *adv* : just, only
solomillo *nm* : sirloin
solsticio *nm* : solstice
soltar {19} *vt* 1 : release 2 DEJAR CAER : let go of, drop 3 DESATAR : unfasten, undo — **soltarse** *vr* 1 : break free 2 DESATARSE : come undone
soltero, -ra *adj* : single, unmarried — ~ *n* 1 : bachelor *m*, single woman *f* 2 **apellido de soltera** : maiden name
soltura *nf* 1 : looseness 2 : fluency (in language) 3 AGILIDAD : agility, ease
soluble *adj* : soluble
solución *nf*, *pl* **-ciones** : solution — **solucionar** *vt* : solve, resolve
solventar *vt* 1 : settle, pay 2 RESOLVER : resolve — **solvente** *adj* & *nm* : solvent
sombra *nf* 1 : shadow 2 : shade (of a tree, etc.) 3 ~**s** *nfpl* : darkness, shadows — **sombreado, -da** *adj* : shady
sombrero *nm* : hat
sombrilla *nf* : parasol, umbrella
sombrío, -bría *adj* : dark, somber, gloomy
somero, -ra *adj* : superficial
someter *vt* 1 : subjugate 2 SUBORDINAR : subordinate 3 : subject (to treatment,

etc.) 4 PRESENTAR : submit, present — **someterse** *vr* 1 : submit, yield 2 ~ **a** : undergo
somnífero, -ra *adj* : soporific — **somnífero** *nm* : sleeping pill — **somnoliento, -ta** *adj* : drowsy, sleepy
somos → **ser**
son[1] → **ser**
son[2] *nm* 1 : sound 2 **en** ~ **de** : as, in the manner of
sonajero *nm* : (baby's) rattle
sonámbulo, -la *n* : sleepwalker
sonar {19} *vi* 1 : sound 2 : ring (as a bell) 3 : look or sound familiar 4 ~ **a** : sound like — **sonarse** *vr or* ~ **las narices** : blow one's nose
sonata *nf* : sonata
sondear *vt* 1 : sound, probe 2 : survey, sound out (opinions, etc.) — **sondeo** *nm* 1 : sounding, probing 2 ENCUESTA : survey, poll
soneto *nm* : sonnet
sónico, -ca *adj* : sonic
sonido *nm* : sound
sonoro, -ra *adj* 1 : resonant, sonorous 2 RUIDOSO : loud
sonreír {66} *vi* : smile — **sonreírse** *vr* : smile — **sonriente** *adj* : smiling — **sonrisa** *nf* : smile
sonrojar *vt* : cause to blush — **sonrojarse** *vr* : blush — **sonrojo** *nm* : blush
sonrosado, -da *adj* : rosy, pink
sonsacar {72} *vt* : wheedle (out)
soñar {19} *v* 1 : dream 2 ~ **con** : dream about 3 ~ **despierto** : daydream — **soñador, -dora** *adj* : dreamy — ~ *n* : dreamer — **soñoliento, -ta** *adj* : sleepy, drowsy
sopa *nf* : soup
sopesar *vt* : weigh, consider
soplar *vi* : blow — *vt* : blow out, blow off, blow up — **soplete** *nm* : blowtorch — **soplo** *nm* : puff, gust
soplón, -plona *n*, *pl* **-plones** *fam* : sneak
sopor *nm* : drowsiness — **soporífero, -ra** *adj* : soporific
soportar *vt* 1 SOSTENER : support 2 AGUANTAR : bear — **soporte** *nm* : support
soprano *nmf* : soprano
sor *nf* : Sister (in religion)
sorber *vt* 1 : sip 2 ABSORBER : absorb 3 CHUPAR : suck up — **sorbete** *nm* : sherbet — **sorbo** *nm* 1 : sip, swallow 2 **beber a** ~**s** : sip
sordera *nf* : deafness
sórdido, -da *adj* : sordid, squalid
sordo, -da *adj* 1 : deaf 2 : muted (of a

sound) — **sordomudo, -da** *n* : deaf-mute

sorna *nf* : sarcasm

sorprender *vt* : surprise — **sorprenderse** *vr* : be surprised — **sorprendente** *adj* : surprising — **sorpresa** *nf* : surprise

sortear *vt* 1 : raffle off, draw lots for 2 ESQUIVAR : dodge — **sorteo** *nm* : drawing, raffle

sortija *nf* 1 : ring 2 : ringlet (of hair)

sortilegio *nm* 1 HECHIZO : spell 2 HECHICERÍA : sorcery

sosegar {49} *vt* : calm, pacify — **sosegarse** *vr* : calm down — **sosegado, -da** *adj* : calm, tranquil — **sosiego** *nm* : calm

soslayo: de ~ *adv phr* : obliquely, sideways

soso, -sa *adj* 1 : insipid, tasteless 2 ABURRIDO : dull

sospechar *vt* : suspect — **sospecha** *nf* : suspicion — **sospechoso, -sa** *adj* : suspicious — **~** *n* : suspect

sostener {80} *vt* 1 : support 2 SUJETAR : hold 3 MANTENER : sustain, maintain — **sostenerse** *vr* 1 : stand (up) 2 CONTINUAR : remain 3 SUSTENTARSE : support oneself — **sostén** *nm, pl* **-tenes** 1 APOYO : support 2 SUSTENTO : sustenance 3 : brassiere, bra — **sostenido, -da** *adj* 1 : sustained 2 : sharp (in music) — **sostenido** *nm* : sharp

sótano *nm* : basement

soterrar {55} *vt* 1 : bury 2 ESCONDER : hide

soto *nm* : grove

soviético, -ca *adj* : Soviet

soy → **ser**

soya *nf* : soy

Sr. *nm* : Mr. — **Sra.** *nf* : Mrs., Ms. — **Srta.** *or* **Srita.** *nf* : Miss, Ms.

su *adj* 1 : his, her, its, their, one's 2 (*formal*) : your

suave *adj* 1 : soft LISO : smooth 3 APACIBLE : gentle, mild — **suavidad** *nf* 1 : softness, smoothness 2 APACIBILIDAD : mildness, gentleness — **suavizar** {21} *vt* : soften, smooth

subalimentado, -da *adj* : undernourished, underfed

subalterno, -na *adj* 1 SUBORDINADO : subordinate 2 SECUNDARIO : secondary — **~** *n* : subordinate

subarrendar {55} *vt* : sublet

subasta *nf* : auction — **subastar** *vt* : auction (off)

subcampeón, -peona *n, mpl* **-peones** : runner-up

subcomité *nm* : subcommittee

subconsciente *adj & nm* : subconscious

subdesarrollado, -da *adj* : underdeveloped

subdirector, -tora *n* : assistant manager

súbdito, -ta *n* : subject

subdividir *vt* : subdivide — **subdivisión** *nf, pl* **-siones** : subdivision

subestimar *vt* : underestimate

subir *vt* 1 : climb, go up 2 LLEVAR : bring up, take up 3 AUMENTAR : raise — *vi* 1 : go up, come up 2 **~ a** : get in (a car), get on (a bus, etc.) — **subirse** *vr* 1 : climb (up) 2 **~ a** : get in (a car), get on (a bus, etc.) 3 **~ a la cabeza** : go to one's head — **subida** *nf* 1 : ascent, climb 2 AUMENTO : rise 3 PENDIENTE : slope — **subido, -da** *adj* 1 : bright, strong 2 **~ de tono** : risqué

súbito, -ta *adj* 1 : sudden 2 **de súbito** : all of a sudden, suddenly

subjetivo, -va *adj* : subjective

subjuntivo, -va *adj* : subjunctive — **subjuntivo** *nm* : subjunctive (case)

sublevar *vt* : stir up, incite to rebellion — **sublevarse** *vr* : rebel — **sublevación** *nf, pl* **-ciones** : uprising, rebellion

sublime *adj* : sublime

submarino, -na *adj* : underwater — **submarino** *nm* : submarine — **submarinismo** *nm* : scuba diving

subordinar *vt* : subordinate — **subordinado, -da** *adj & n* : subordinate

subproducto *nm* : by-product

subrayar *vt* 1 : underline 2 ENFATIZAR : emphasize, stress

subrepticio, -cia *adj* : surreptitious

subsanar *vt* 1 : rectify, correct 2 : make up for (a deficiency), overcome (an obstacle)

subscribir → **suscribir**

subsidio *nm* : subsidy, benefit

subsiguiente *adj* : subsequent

subsistir *vi* 1 : live, subsist 2 SOBREVIVIR : survive — **subsistencia** *nf* : subsistence

substancia *nf* → **sustancia**

subterfugio *nm* : subterfuge

subterráneo, -nea *adj* : underground, subterranean — **subterráneo** *nm* : underground passage

subtítulo *nm* : subtitle

suburbio *nm* 1 : suburb 2 : slum (outside a city) — **suburbano, -na** *adj* : suburban

subvencionar *vt* : subsidize — **sub-**

vención *nf, pl* **-ciones** : subsidy, grant
subvertir {76} *vt* : subvert — **subversión** *nf, pl* **-siones** : subversion — **subversivo, -va** *adj & n* : subversive
subyacente *adj* : underlying
subyugar {52} *vt* : subjugate, subdue
succión *nf, pl* **-ciones** : suction — **succionar** *vt* : suck up, draw in
sucedáneo *nm* : substitute
suceder *vi* **1** : happen, occur **2** ~ **a** : follow **3 suceda lo que suceda** : come what may — **sucesión** *nf, pl* **-siones** : succession — **sucesivo, -va** *adj* : successive — **suceso** *nm* **1** : event **2** INCIDENTE : incident — **sucesor, -sora** *n* : successor
suciedad *nf* **1** : dirtiness **2** MUGRE : dirt, filth
sucinto, -ta *adj* : succinct, concise
sucio, -cia *adj* : dirty, filthy
suculento, -ta *adj* : succulent
sucumbir *vi* : succumb
sucursal *nf* : branch (of a business)
sudadera *nf* : sweatshirt — **sudado, -da** *adj* : sweaty
sudafricano, -na *adj* : South African
sudamericano, -na *adj* : South American
sudar *vi* : sweat
sudeste → **sureste**
sudoeste → **suroeste**
sudor *nm* : sweat — **sudoroso, -sa** *adj* : sweaty
sueco, -ca *adj* : Swedish — **sueco** *nm* : Swedish (language)
suegro, -gra *n* **1** : father-in-law *m*, mother-in-law *f* **2 suegros** *nmpl* : in-laws
suela *nf* : sole (of a shoe)
sueldo *nm* : salary, wage
suelo *nm* **1** : ground **2** : floor (in a house) **3** TIERRA : soil, land
suelto, -ta *adj* : loose, free — **suelto** *nm* : loose change
sueño *nm* **1** : dream **2 coger el** ~ : get to sleep **3 tener** ~ : be sleepy
suero *nm* **1** : whey **2** : serum (in medicine)
suerte *nf* **1** : luck, fortune **2** AZAR : chance **3** DESTINO : fate **4** CLASE : sort, kind **5 por** ~ : luckily **6 tener** ~ : be lucky
suéter *nm* : sweater
suficiencia *nf* **1** CAPACIDAD : competence, proficiency **2** PRESUNCIÓN : smugness — **suficiente** *adj* **1** : enough, sufficient **2** PRESUNTUOSO : smug — **suficientemente** *adv* : enough

sufijo *nm* : suffix
sufragio *nm* : suffrage, vote
sufrir *vt* **1** : suffer **2** SOPORTAR : bear, stand — *vi* : suffer — **sufrido, -da** *adj* **1** : long-suffering **2** : sturdy, serviceable (of clothing) — **sufrimiento** *nm* : suffering
sugerir {76} *vt* : suggest — **sugerencia** *nf* : suggestion — **sugestión** *nf, pl* **-tiones** : suggestion — **sugestionable** *adj* : impressionable — **sugestionar** *vt* : influence — **sugestivo, -va** *adj* **1** : suggestive **2** ESTIMULANTE : interesting, stimulating
suicidio *nm* : suicide — **suicida** *adj* : suicidal — ~ *nmf* : suicide (victim) — **suicidarse** *vr* : commit suicide
suite *nf* : suite
suizo, -za *adj* : Swiss
sujetar *vt* **1** : hold (on to) **2** FIJAR : fasten **3** DOMINAR : subdue — **sujetarse** *vr* **1** ~ **a** : hold on to, cling to **2** ~ **a** : abide by — **sujeción** *nf, pl* **-ciones 1** : fastening **2** DOMINACIÓN : subjection — **sujetador** *nm Spain* : brassiere, bra — **sujetapapeles** *nms & pl* : paper clip — **sujeto, -ta** *adj* **1** : fastened **2** ~ **a** : subject to — **sujeto** *nm* **1** : individual **2** : subject (in grammar)
sulfuro *nm* : sulfur — **sulfúrico, -ca** *adj* : sulfuric
sultán *nm, pl* **-tanes** : sultan
suma *nf* **1** : sum, total **2** : addition (in mathematics) **3 en** ~ : in short — **sumamente** *adv* : extremely — **sumar** *vt* **1** : add (up) **2** TOTALIZAR : add up to, total — *vi* : add up — **sumarse** *vr* ~ **a** : join
sumario, -ria *adj* : concise — **sumario** *nm* **1** : summary **2** : indictment (in law)
sumergir {35} *vt* : submerge, plunge — **sumergirse** *vr* : be submerged — **sumergible** *adj* : waterproof (of a watch, etc.)
sumidero *nm* : drain
suministrar *vt* : supply, provide — **suministro** *nm* : supply, provision
sumir *vt* : plunge, immerse — **sumirse** *vr* ~ **en** : sink into
sumisión *nf, pl* **-siones** : submission — **sumiso, -sa** *adj* : submissive
sumo, -ma *adj* **1** : highest, supreme **2 de suma importancia** : of great importance
suntuoso, -sa *adj* : sumptuous, lavish
super *or* **súper** *nm fam* : supermarket
superabundancia *nf* : overabundance
superar *vt* **1** : surpass, outdo **2** VENCER : overcome — **superarse** *vr* : improve oneself

superávit *nm* : surplus
superestructura *nf* : superstructure
superficie *nf* 1 : surface 2 ÁREA : area
— **superficial** *adj* : superficial
superfluo, -flua *adj* : superfluous
superintendente *nmf* : supervisor, superintendent
superior *adj* 1 : superior 2 : upper (of a floor, etc.) 3 ~ **a** : above, higher than — ~ *nm* : superior — **superioridad** *nf* : superiority
superlativo, -va *adj* : superlative — **superlativo** *nm* : superlative
supermercado *nm* : supermarket
superpoblado, -da *adj* : overpopulated
supersónico, -ca *adj* : supersonic
superstición *nf, pl* -**ciones** : superstition — **supersticioso, -sa** *adj* : superstitious
supervisar *vt* : supervise, oversee — **supervisión** *nf, pl* -**siones** : supervision — **supervisor, -sora** *n* : supervisor
supervivencia *nf* : survival — **superviviente** *adj* : surviving — ~ *nmf* : survivor
suplantar *vt* : supplant, replace
suplemento *nm* : supplement — **suplementario, -ria** *adj* : supplementary
suplente *adj & nmf* : substitute
suplicar {72} *vt* : beg, entreat — **súplica** *nf* : plea, entreaty
suplicio *nm* : ordeal, torture
suplir *vt* 1 : make up for 2 REEMPLAZAR : replace
supo, etc. → **saber**
suponer {60} *vt* 1 : suppose, assume 2 SIGNIFICAR : mean 3 IMPLICAR : involve, entail — **suposición** *nf, pl* -**ciones** : supposition
supositorio *nm* : suppository
supremo, -ma *adj* : supreme — **supremacía** *nf* : supremacy
suprimir *vt* 1 : suppress, eliminate 2 : delete (text) — **supresión** *nf, pl* -**siones** 1 : suppression, elimination 2 : deletion (of text)
supuesto, -ta *adj* 1 : supposed, alleged 2 **por supuesto** : of course — **supuesto** *nm* : assumption — **supuestamente** *adv* : allegedly
sur *nm* 1 : south, South 2 : south wind 3 **del** ~ : south, southerly
surafricano, -na → **sudafricano**
suramericano, -na → **sudamericano**
surcar {72} *vt* 1 : plow (earth) 2 : cut through (air, water, etc.) — **surco** *nm* : groove, furrow, rut
sureño, -ña *adj* : southern, Southern — ~ *n* : Southerner

sureste *adj* 1 : southeast, southeastern 2 : southeasterly (of wind, etc.) — ~ *nm* : southeast, Southeast
surf *or* **surfing** *nm* : surfing
surgir {35} *vi* 1 : arise 2 APARECER : appear — **surgimiento** *nm* : rise, emergence
suroeste *adj* 1 : southwest, southwestern 2 : southwesterly (of wind, etc.) — ~ *nm* : southwest, Southwest
surtir *vt* 1 : supply, provide 2 ~ **efecto** : have an effect — **surtirse** *vr* ~ **de** : stock up on — **surtido, -da** *adj* 1 : assorted, varied 2 : stocked (with merchandise) — **surtido** *nm* 1 : assortment, selection — **surtidor** *nm* : gas pump
susceptible *adj* 1 : susceptible, sensitive 2 ~ **de** : capable of — **susceptibilidad** *nf* : sensitivity
suscitar *vt* : provoke, arouse
suscribir {33} *vt* 1 : sign (a formal document) 2 RATIFICAR : endorse — **suscribirse** *vr* ~ **a** : subscribe to — **suscripción** *nf, pl* -**ciones** : subscription — **suscriptor, -tora** *n* : subscriber
susodicho, -cha *adj* : aforementioned
suspender *vt* 1 : suspend 2 COLGAR : hang 3 *Spain* : fail (an exam, etc.) — **suspensión** *nf, pl* -**siones** : suspension — **suspenso** *nm* 1 *Spain* : failure (in an exam, etc.) 2 *Lat* : suspense
suspicaz *adj, pl* -**caces** : suspicious
suspirar *vi* : sigh — **suspiro** *nm* : sigh
sustancia *nf* 1 : substance 2 **sin** ~ : shallow, lacking substance — **sustancial** *adj* : substantial, significant — **sustancioso, -sa** *adj* : substantial, solid
sustantivo *nm* : noun
sustentar *vt* 1 : support 2 ALIMENTAR : sustain, nourish 3 MANTENER : maintain — **sustentarse** *vr* : support oneself — **sustentación** *nf, pl* -**ciones** : support — **sustento** *nm* 1 : means of support, livelihood 2 ALIMENTO : sustenance
sustituir {41} *vt* : replace, substitute — **sustitución** *nf, pl* -**ciones** : replacement, substitution — **sustituto, -ta** *n* : substitute
susto *nm* : fright, scare
sustraer {81} *vt* 1 : remove, take away 2 : subtract (in mathematics) — **sustraerse** *vr* ~ **a** : avoid, evade — **sustracción** *nf, pl* -**ciones** : subtraction
susurrar *vi* 1 : whisper 2 : murmur (of water) 3 : rustle (of leaves, etc.) — *vt* : whisper — **susurro** *nm* 1 : whisper 2

: murmur (of water) **3** : rustle, rustling (of leaves, etc.)
sutil *adj* **1** : delicate, fine **2** : subtle (of fragrances, differences, etc.) — **sutileza** *nf* : subtlety
sutura *nf* : suture

suyo, -ya *adj* **1** : his, her, its, one's, theirs **2** (*formal*) : yours **3 un primo suyo** : a cousin of his/hers — **~** *pron* **1** : his, hers, its (own), one's own, theirs **2** (*formal*) : yours
switch *nm Lat* : switch

T

t *nf* : t, 21st letter of the Spanish alphabet
taba *nf* : anklebone
tabaco *nm* : tobacco — **tabacalero, -ra** *adj* : tobacco
tábano *nm* : horsefly
taberna *nf* : tavern
tabicar {72} *vt* : wall up — **tabique** *nm* : thin wall, partition
tabla *nf* **1** : board, plank **2** LISTA : table, list **3 ~ de planchar** : ironing board **4 ~s** *nfpl* : stage, boards *pl* — **tablado** *nm* **1** : flooring **2** PLATAFORMA : platform **3** : (theater) stage — **tablero** *nm* **1** : bulletin board **2** : board (in games) **3** PIZARRA : blackboard **4 ~ de instrumentos** : dashboard, instrument panel
tableta *nf* **1** : tablet, pill **2** : bar (of chocolate)
tablilla *nf* : slat — **tablón** *nm, pl* **-lones** **1** : plank, beam **2 ~ de anuncios** : bulletin board
tabú *adj* : taboo — **tabú** *nm, pl* **-búes** or **-bús** : taboo
tabular *vt* : tabulate
taburete *nm* : stool
tacaño, -na *adj* : stingy, miserly
tacha *nf* **1** : flaw, defect **2 sin ~** : flawless
tachar *vt* **1** : cross out, delete **2 ~ de** : accuse of, label as
tachón *nm, pl* **-chones** : stud, hobnail — **tachuela** *nf* : tack, hobnail
tácito, -ta *adj* : tacit
taciturno, -na *adj* : taciturn
taco *nm* **1** : stopper, plug **2** *Lat* : heel (of a shoe) **3** : cue (in billiards) **4** : taco (in cooking)
tacón *nm, pl* **-cones** **1** : heel (of a shoe) **2 de ~ alto** : high-heeled
táctica *nf* : tactic, tactics *pl* — **táctico, -ca** *adj* : tactical
tacto *nm* **1** : (sense of) touch, feel **2** DELICADEZA : tact
tafetán *nm, pl* **-tanes** : taffeta
tailandés, -desa *adj* : Thai
taimado, -da *adj* : crafty, sly
tajar *vt* : cut, slice — **tajada** *nf* **1** : slice **2 sacar ~** *fam* : get one's share — **tajante** *adj* : categorical — **tajo** *nm* **1** : cut, gash **2** ESCARPA : steep cliff
tal *adv* **1** : so, in such a way **2 con ~ que** : provided that, as long as **3 ¿qué ~?** : how are you?, how's it going? — **~** *adj* **1** : such, such a **2 ~ vez** : maybe, perhaps — **~** *pron* **1** : such a one, such a thing **2 ~ para cual** : two of a kind
taladrar *vt* : drill — **taladro** *nm* : drill
talante *nm* **1** HUMOR : mood **2** VOLUNTAD : willingness
talar *vt* : cut down, fell
talco *nm* : talcum powder
talego *nm* : sack
talento *nm* : talent — **talentoso, -sa** *adj* : talented
talismán *nm, pl* **-manes** : talisman, charm
talla *nf* **1** : sculpture, carving **2** ESTATURA : height **3** : size (in clothing) — **tallar** *vt* **1** : sculpt, carve **2** : measure (someone's height)
tallarín *nf, pl* **-rines** : noodle
talle *nm* **1** : waist, waistline **2** FIGURA : figure **3** : measurements *pl* (of clothing)
taller *nm* **1** : workshop **2** : studio (of an artist)
tallo *nm* : stalk, stem
talón *nm, pl* **-lones** **1** : heel (of the foot) **2** : stub (of a check) — **talonario** *nm* : checkbook
taltuza *nf* : gopher
tamal *nm* : tamale
tamaño, -ña *adj* : such a, such a big — **tamaño** *nm* **1** : size **2 de ~ natural** : life-size
tambalearse *vr* **1** : teeter, wobble **2** : stagger, totter (of persons)
también *adv* : too, as well, also
tambor *nm* : drum — **tamborilear** *vi* : drum
tamiz *nm* : sieve — **tamizar** {21} *vt* : sift
tampoco *adv* : neither, not either
tampón *nm, pl* **-pones** **1** : tampon **2** : ink pad (for stamping)
tan *adv* **1** : so, so very **2 ~ pronto como** : as soon as **3 ~ sólo** : only, merely

tanda *nf* 1 TURNO : turn, shift 2 GRUPO : batch, lot, series

tangente *nf* : tangent

tangible *adj* : tangible

tango *nm* : tango

tanque *nm* : tank

tantear *vt* 1 : feel, grope 2 SOPESAR : size up, weigh — *vi* : feel one's way — **tanteador** *nm* : scoreboard — **tanteo** *nm* 1 : weighing, sizing up 2 PUNTUACIÓN : scoring (in sports)

tanto *adv* 1 : so much 2 (*in expressions of time*) : so long — ~ *nm* 1 : certain amount 2 : goal, point (in sports) 3 **en** ~ : somewhat, rather — **tanto, -ta** *adj* 1 : so much, so many 2 (*in comparisons*) : as much, as many 3 *fam* : however many — ~ *pron* 1 : so much, so many 2 **entre** ~ : meanwhile 3 **por lo** ~ : therefore

tañer {79} *vt* 1 : ring (a bell) 2 : play (a musical instrument)

tapa *nf* 1 : cover, top, lid 2 *Spain* : snack

tapacubos *nms & pl* : hubcap

tapar *vt* 1 : cover, put a lid on 2 OCULTAR : block out 3 ENCUBRIR : cover up — **tapadera** *nf* 1 : cover, lid 2 : front (to hide a deception)

tapete *nm* 1 : small rug, mat 2 : cover (for a table)

tapia *nf* : (adobe) wall, garden wall — **tapiar** *vt* 1 : wall in 2 : block off (a door, etc.)

tapicería *nf* 1 : upholstery 2 TAPIZ : tapestry — **tapicero, -ra** *n* : upholsterer

tapioca *nf* : tapioca

tapiz *nm, pl* **-pices** : tapestry — **tapizar** {21} *vt* : upholster

tapón *nm, pl* **-pones** 1 : cork 2 : cap (for a bottle, etc.) 3 : plug, stopper (for a sink)

tapujo *nm* **sin** ~**s** : openly, outright

taquigrafía *nf* : stenography, shorthand — **taquígrafo, -fa** *n* : stenographer

taquilla *nf* 1 : box office 2 RECAUDACIÓN : earnings *pl*, take — **taquillero, -ra** *adj* **un éxito taquillero** : a box-office hit

tarántula *nf* : tarantula

tararear *vt* : hum

tardar *vi* 1 : take a long time, be late 2 **a más** ~ : at the latest — *vt* : take (time) — **tardanza** *nf* : lateness, delay — **tarde** *adv* 1 : late 2 ~ **o temprano** : sooner or later — ~ *nf* 1 : afternoon, evening 2 **¡buenas** ~**s!** : good afternoon!, good evening! 3 **en la** ~ **or por la** ~ : in the afternoon, in the evening — **tardío, -día** *adj* : late, tardy — **tardo, -da** *adj* : slow

tarea *nf* 1 : task, job 2 : homework (in education)

tarifa *nf* 1 : fare, rate 2 LISTA : price list 3 ARANCEL : duty, tariff

tarima *nf* : platform, stage

tarjeta *nf* 1 : card 2 ~ **de crédito** : credit card 3 ~ **postal** : postcard

tarro *nm* : jar, pot

tarta *nf* 1 : cake 2 TORTA : tart

tartamudear *vi* : stammer, stutter — **tartamudeo** *nm* : stutter, stammer

tartán *nm, pl* **-tanes** : tartan, plaid

tártaro *nm* : tartar

tarugo *nm* 1 : block (of wood) 2 *fam* : blockhead, dunce

tasa *nf* 1 : rate 2 IMPUESTO : tax 3 VALORACIÓN : appraisal — **tasación** *nf, pl* **-ciones** : appraisal — **tasar** *vt* 1 : set the price of 2 VALORAR : appraise, value

tasca *nf* : cheap bar, dive

tatuar {3} *vt* : tattoo — **tatuaje** *nm* : tattoo, tattooing

taurino, -na *adj* : bull, bullfighting — **tauromaquia** *nf* : (art of) bullfighting

taxi *nm, pl* **taxis** : taxi, taxicab — **taxista** *nmf* : taxi driver

taza *nf* 1 : cup 2 : (toilet) bowl — **tazón** *nm, pl* **-zones** : bowl

te *pron* 1 (*direct object*) : you 2 (*indirect object*) : for you, to you, from you 3 (*reflexive*) : yourself, for yourself, to yourself, from yourself

té *nm* : tea

teatro *nm* : theater — **teatral** *adj* : theatrical

techo *nm* 1 : roof 2 : ceiling (of a room) 3 LÍMITE : upper limit, ceiling — **techumbre** *nf* : roofing

tecla *nf* : key (of a musical instrument or a machine) — **teclado** *nm* : keyboard — **teclear** *vt* : type in, enter

técnica *nf* 1 : technique, skill 2 TECNOLOGÍA : technology — **técnico, -ca** *adj* : technical — ~ *n* : technician

tecnología *nf* : technology — **tecnológico, -ca** *adj* : technological

tecolote *nm Lat* : owl

tedio *nm* : boredom — **tedioso, -sa** *adj* : tedious, boring

teja *nf* : tile — **tejado** *nm* : roof

tejer *v* 1 : knit, crochet 2 : weave (on a loom)

tejido *nm* 1 : fabric, cloth 2 : tissue (of the body)

tejón *nm, pl* **-jones** : badger

tela *nf* 1 : fabric, material 2 ~ **de araña** : spiderweb — **telar** *nm* : loom — **telaraña** *nf* : spiderweb, cobweb

tele *nf fam* : TV, television

telecomunicación *nf, pl* **-ciones** : telecommunication

teledifusión *nf, pl* **-siones** : television broadcasting

teledirigido, -da *adj* : remote-controlled

telefonear *v* : telephone, call — **telefónico, -ca** *adj* : telephone — **telefonista** *nmf* : telephone operator — **teléfono** *nm* 1 : telephone 2 **llamar por ~** : make a phone call

telegrafiar {85} *v* : telegraph — **telegráfico, -ca** *adj* : telegraphic — **telégrafo** *nm* : telegraph

telegrama *nm* : telegram

telenovela *nf* : soap opera

telepatía *nf* : telepathy — **telepático, -ca** *adj* : telepathic

telescopio *nm* : telescope — **telescópico, -ca** *adj* : telescopic

telespectador, -dora *n* : (television) viewer

telesquí *nm, pl* **-squís** : ski lift

televidente *nmf* : (television) viewer

televisión *nf, pl* **-siones** : television, TV — **televisar** *vt* : televise — **televisor** *nm* : television set

telón *nm, pl* **-lones** 1 : curtain (in theater) 2 **~ de fondo** : backdrop, background

tema *nm* : theme

temblar {55} *vi* 1 : tremble, shiver 2 : shake (of a building, the ground, etc.) — **temblor** *nm* 1 : shaking, trembling 2 *or* **~ de tierra** : tremor, earthquake — **tembloroso, -sa** *adj* : trembling, shaky

temer *vt* : fear, dread — *vi* : be afraid — **temerario, -ria** *adj* : reckless — **temeridad** *nf* 1 : recklessness 2 : rash act — **temeroso, -sa** *adj* : fearful — **temor** *nm* : fear, dread

temperamento *nm* : temperament — **temperamental** *adj* : temperamental

temperatura *nf* : temperature

tempestad *nf* : storm — **tempestuoso, -sa** *adj* : stormy

templar *vt* 1 : temper (steel) 2 : moderate (temperature) 3 : tune (a musical instrument) — **templarse** *vr* : warm up, cool down — **templado, -da** *adj* 1 : temperate, mild 2 TIBIO : lukewarm 3 VALIENTE : courageous — **templanza** *nf* 1 : moderation 2 : mildness (of weather)

templo *nm* : temple, synagogue

tempo *nm* : tempo

temporada *nf* 1 : season, time 2 PERÍODO : period, spell — **temporal** *adj* 1 : temporal 2 PROVISIONAL : temporary — **~ *nm*** : storm — **temporero, -ra** *n* : temporary or seasonal worker

temporizador *nm* : timer

temprano, -na *adj* : early — **temprano** *adv* : early

tenaz *adj, pl* **-naces** : tenacious — **tenaza** *nf or* **tenazas** *nfpl* 1 : pliers 2 : tongs (for the fireplace, etc.) 3 : claw (of a crustacean)

tendedero *nm* : clothesline

tendencia *nf* : tendency, trend

tender {56} *vt* 1 : spread out, stretch out 2 : hang out (clothes) 3 : lay (cables, etc.) 4 : set (a trap) — *vi* **~ a** : have a tendency towards — **tenderse** *vr* : stretch out, lie down

tendero, -ra *n* : shopkeeper

tendido *nm* 1 : laying (of cables, etc.) 2 : seats *pl*, stand (at a bullfight)

tendón *nm, pl* **-dones** : tendon

tenebroso, -sa *adj* 1 : gloomy, dark 2 SINIESTRO : sinister

tenedor, -dora *n* 1 : holder 2 **~ de libros** : bookkeeper — **tenedor** *nm* : table fork — **teneduría** *nf* **~ de libros** : bookkeeping

tener {80} *vt* 1 : have, possess 2 SUJETAR : hold 3 TOMAR : take 4 **~ frío** (**hambre,** *etc.*) : be cold (hungry, etc.) 5 **~ ... años** : be ... years old 6 **~ por** : think, consider — *v aux* 1 **~ que** : have to, ought to 2 **tenía pensado escribirte** : I've been thinking of writing to you — **tenerse** *vr* 1 : stand up 2 **~ por** : consider oneself

teneduría *nf* : tannery

tengo → tener

tenia *nf* : tapeworm

teniente *nmf* : lieutenant

tenis *nms & pl* 1 : tennis 2 **~** *nmpl* : sneakers — **tenista** *nmf* : tennis player

tenor *nm* 1 : tenor 2 : tone, sense (in style)

tensar *vt* 1 : tense, make taut 2 : draw (a bow) — **tensarse** *vr* : become tense — **tensión** *nf, pl* **-siones** 1 : tension 2 **~ arterial** : blood pressure — **tenso, -sa** *adj* : tense

tentación *nf, pl* **-ciones** : temptation

tentáculo *nm* : tentacle

tentar {55} *vt* 1 : feel, touch 2 ATRAER : tempt — **tentador, -dora** *adj* : tempting

tentativa *nf* : attempt

tentempié *nm fam* : snack

tenue *adj* 1 : tenuous 2 : faint, weak (of sounds) 3 : light, fine (of thread, rain, etc.)

teñir {67} *vt* 1 : dye 2 **~ de** : tinge with

teología *nf* : theology — **teólogo, -ga** *n* : theologian

teorema *nm* : theorem
teoría *nf* 1 : theory — **teórico, -ca** *adj* : theoretical
tequila *nm* : tequila
terapia *nf* 1 : therapy 2 ~ **ocupacional** : occupational therapy — **terapeuta** *nmf* : therapist — **terapéutico, -ca** *adj* : therapeutic
tercermundista *adj* : third-world
tercero, -ra *adj* (**tercer** *before masculine singular nouns*) 1 : third 2 **el Tercer Mundo** : the Third World — ~ *n* : third (in a series)
terciar *vt* : sling (sth over one's shoulders), tilt (a hat) — *vi* 1 : intervene 2 ~ **en** : take part in
tercio *nm* : third
terciopelo *nm* : velvet
terco, -ca *adj* : obstinate, stubborn
tergiversar *vt* : distort, twist
termal *adj* : thermal, hot — **termas** *nfpl* : hot springs
terminar *vt* : conclude, finish — *vi* 1 : finish 2 ACABARSE : come to an end — **terminarse** *vr* 1 : run out 2 ACABARSE : come to an end — **terminación** *nf, pl* **-ciones** : termination, conclusion — **terminal** *adj* : terminal, final — ~ *nm* (*in some regions f*) : (electric or electronic) terminal — ~ *nf* (*in some regions m*) : terminal, station — **término** *nm* 1 : end 2 PLAZO : period, term 3 ~ **medio** : happy medium 4 ~**s** *nmpl* : terms — **terminología** *nf* : terminology
termita *nf* : termite
termo *nm* : thermos
termómetro *nm* : thermometer
termóstato *nm* : thermostat
ternero, -ra *n* : calf — **ternera** *nf* : veal
ternura *nf* : tenderness
terquedad *nf* : obstinacy, stubbornness
terracota *nf* : terra-cotta
terraplén *nm, pl* **-plenes** : embankment
terráqueo, -quea *adj* : earth, terrestrial
terrateniente *nmf* : landowner
terraza *nf* 1 : terrace 2 BALCÓN : balcony
terremoto *nm* : earthquake
terreno *nm* 1 : terrain 2 SUELO : earth, ground 3 SOLAR : plot, tract of land — **terreno, -na** *adj* : earthly — **terrestre** *adj* : terrestrial
terrible *adj* : terrible
terrier *nmf* : terrier
territorio *nm* : territory — **territorial** *adj* : territorial
terrón *nm, pl* **-rones** 1 : clod (of earth) 2 ~ **de azúcar** : lump of sugar
terror *nm* : terror — **terrorífico, -ca** *adj*

: terrifying — **terrorismo** *nm* : terrorism — **terrorista** *adj & nmf* : terrorist
terroso, -sa *adj* : earthy
terso, -sa *adj* 1 : smooth 2 : polished, flowing (of a style) — **tersura** *nf* : smoothness
tertulia *nf* : gathering, group
tesis *nfs & pl* : thesis
tesón *nm* : persistence, tenacity
tesoro *nm* 1 : treasure 2 : thesaurus (book) 3 **el Tesoro** : the Treasury — **tesorero, -ra** *n* : treasurer
testaferro *nm* : figurehead
testamento *nm* : testament, will — **testamentario, -ria** *n* : executor, executrix *f* — **testar** *vi* : draw up a will
testarudo, -da *adj* : stubborn
testículo *nm* : testicle
testificar {72} *v* : testify — **testigo** *nmf* 1 : witness 2 ~ **ocular** : eyewitness — **testimoniar** *vi* : testify — **testimonio** *nm* : testimony
tétano *or* **tétanos** *nm* : tetanus
tetera *nf* : teapot
tetilla *nf* 1 : teat, nipple (of a man) 2 : nipple (of a baby bottle) — **tetina** *nf* : nipple (of a baby bottle)
tétrico, -ca *adj* : somber, gloomy
textil *adj & nm* : textile
texto *nm* : text — **textual** *adj* 1 : textual 2 EXACTO : literal, exact
textura *nf* : texture
tez *nf, pl* **teces** : complexion
ti *pron* 1 : you 2 ~ **mismo, ~ misma** : yourself
tía → tío
tianguis *nms & pl Lat* : open-air market
tibio, -bia *adj* : lukewarm
tiburón *nm, pl* **-rones** : shark
tic *nm* : tic
tiempo *nm* 1 : time 2 ÉPOCA : age, period 3 : weather (in meteorology) 4 : halftime (in sports) 5 : tempo (in music) 6 : tense (in grammar)
tienda *nf* 1 : store, shop 2 *or* ~ **de campaña** : tent
tiene → tener
tienta *nf* **andar a ~s** : feel one's way, grope around
tierno, -na *adj* 1 : tender, fresh, young 2 CARIÑOSO : affectionate
tierra *nf* 1 : land 2 SUELO : ground, earth 3 *or* ~ **natal** : native land 4 **la Tierra** : the Earth 5 **por** ~ : overland 6 ~ **adentro** : inland
tieso, -sa *adj* 1 : stiff, rigid 2 ERGUIDO : erect 3 ENGREÍDO : haughty
tiesto *nm* : flowerpot
tifoideo, -dea *adj* **fiebre tifoidea** : typhoid fever

tifón *nm, pl* **-fones** : typhoon

tifus *nm* : typhus

tigre, -gresa *n* **1** : tiger, tigress *f* **2** *Lat* : jaguar

tijera *nf or* **tijeras** *nfpl* : scissors — **tijeretada** *nf* : cut, snip

tildar *vt* ~ **de** : brand as, call

tilde *nf* **1** : tilde **2** ACENTO : accent mark

tilo *nm* : linden (tree)

timar *vt* : swindle, cheat

timbre *nm* **1** : bell **2** : tone, timbre (of a voice, etc.) **3** SELLO : seal, stamp **4** *Lat* : postage stamp — **timbrar** *vt* : stamp

tímido, -da *adj* : timid, shy — **timidez** *nf* : timidity, shyness

timo *nm fam* : swindle, hoax

timón *nm, pl* **-mones** **1** : rudder **2** **coger el** ~ : take the helm, take charge

tímpano *nm* **1** : eardrum **2** ~**s** *nmpl* : timpani, kettledrums

tina *nf* **1** : vat **2** BAÑERA : bathtub

tinieblas *nfpl* **1** : darkness **2 estar en** ~ **sobre** : be in the dark about

tino *nm* **1** : good judgment, sense **2** TACTO : tact

tinta *nf* **1** : ink **2 saberlo de buena** ~ : have it on good authority — **tinte** *nm* **1** : dye, coloring **2** MATIZ : overtone — **tintero** *nm* : inkwell

tintinear *vi* : jingle, tinkle, clink — **tintineo** *nm* : jingle, tinkle, clink

tinto, -ta *adj* **1** : dyed, stained **2** : red (of wine)

tintorería *nf* : dry cleaner (service)

tintura *nf* **1** : dye, tint **2** ~ **de yodo** : tincture of iodine

tiña *nf* : ringworm

tío, tía *n* : uncle *m*, aunt *f*

tiovivo *nm* : merry-go-round

típico, -ca *adj* : typical

tiple *nm* : soprano

tipo *nm* **1** : type, kind **2** FIGURA : figure (of a woman), build (of a man) **3** : rate (of interest, etc.) **4** : (printing) type, typeface — **tipo, -pa** *n fam* : guy *m*, gal *f*

tipografía *nf* : typography, printing — **tipográfico, -ca** *adj* : typographical — **tipógrafo, -fa** *n* : printer

tique *or* **tiquet** *nm* : ticket — **tiquete** *nm Lat* : ticket

tira *nf* **1** : strip, strap **2** ~ **cómica** : comic strip

tirabuzón *nf, pl* **-zones** **1** : corkscrew **2** RIZO : curl, coil

tirada *nf* **1** : throw **2** DISTANCIA : distance **3** IMPRESIÓN : printing, issue — **tirador** *nm* : handle, knob — **tirador, -dora** *n* : marksman *m*, markswoman *f*

tiranía *nf* : tyranny — **tiránico, -ca** *adj* : tyrannical — **tiranizar** {21} *vt* : tyrannize — **tirano, -na** *adj* : tyrannical — ~ *n* : tyrant

tirante *adj* **1** : taut, tight **2** : tense (of a situation, etc.) — ~ *nm* **1** : (shoulder) strap **2** ~**s** *nmpl* : suspenders

tirar *vt* **1** : throw **2** DESECHAR : throw away **3** DERRIBAR : knock down **4** DISPARAR : shoot, fire **5** IMPRIMIR : print — *vi* **1** : pull **2** DISPARAR : shoot **3** ATRAER : attract **4** *fam* : get by, manage **5** ~ **a** : tend towards — **tirarse** *vr* **1** : throw oneself **2** *fam* : spend (time)

tiritar *vi* : shiver

tiro *nm* **1** : shot, gunshot **2** : shot, kick (in sports) **3** : team (of horses, etc.) **4 a** ~ : within range

tiroides *nmf* : thyroid (gland)

tirón *nm, pl* **-rones** **1** : pull, yank **2 de un** ~ : in one go

tirotear *vt* : shoot at — **tiroteo** *nm* : shooting

tisis *nfs & pl* : tuberculosis

títere *nm* : puppet

titilar *vi* : flicker

titiritero, -ra *n* **1** : puppeteer **2** ACRÓBATA : acrobat

titubear *vi* **1** : hesitate **2** BALBUCEAR : stutter, stammer — **titubeante** *adj* : hesitant, faltering — **titubeo** *nm* : hesitation

titular *vt* : title, call — **titularse** *vr* **1** : be called, be titled **2** LICENCIARSE : receive a degree — ~ *adj* : titular, official — ~ *nm* : headline — ~ *nmf* : holder, incumbent — **título** *nm* **1** : title **2** : degree, qualification (in education)

tiza *nf* : chalk

tiznar *vt* : blacken (with soot, etc.) — **tizne** *nm* : soot

toalla *nf* : towel — **toallero** *nm* : towel rack

tobillo *nm* : ankle

tobogán *nm, pl* **-ganes** **1** : toboggan, sled **2** : slide (in a playground, etc.)

tocadiscos *nms & pl* : record player

tocado, -da *adj fam* : touched, not all there — **tocado** *nm* : headgear, headdress

tocador *nm* : dressing table

tocar {72} *vt* **1** : touch, feel **2** MENCIONAR : touch on, refer to **3** : play (a musical instrument) — *vi* **1** : knock, ring **2** ~ **en** : touch on, border on

tocayo, -ya *n* : namesake

tocino *nm* **1** : bacon **2** : salt pork (for cooking) — **tocineta** *nf Lat* : bacon

tocólogo, -ga *n* : obstetrician

tocón *nm, pl* **-cones** : stump (of a tree)

todavía *adv* 1 AÚN : still 2 (*in comparisons*) : even 3 ~ **no** : not yet
todo, -da *adj* 1 : all 2 CADA, CUALQUIER : every, each 3 **a toda velocidad** : at top speed 4 **todo el mundo** : everyone, everybody — ~ *pron* 1 : everything, all 2 **todos, -das** *pl* : everybody, everyone, all — **todo** *nm* : whole — **todopoderoso, -sa** *adj* : almighty, all-powerful
toga *nf* 1 : toga 2 : gown, robe (of a judge, etc.)
toldo *nm* : awning, canopy
tolerar *vt* : tolerate — **tolerancia** *nf* : tolerance — **tolerante** *adj* : tolerant
toma *nf* 1 : capture 2 DOSIS : dose 3 : take (in film) 4 ~ **de corriente** : wall socket, outlet 5 ~ **y daca** : give-and-take — **tomar** *vt* 1 : take 2 : have (food or drink) 3 CAPTURAR : capture, seize 4 ~ **el sol** : sunbathe 5 ~ **tierra** : land — *vi* : drink (alcohol) — **tomarse** *vr* 1 : take (time, etc.) 2 : drink, eat, have (food, drink)
tomate *nm* : tomato
tomillo *nm* : thyme
tomo *nm* : volume
ton *nm* **sin ~ ni son** : without rhyme or reason
tonada *nf* : tune
tonel *nm* : barrel, cask
tonelada *nf* : ton — **tonelaje** *nm* : tonnage
tónica *nf* 1 : tonic (water) 2 TENDENCIA : trend, tone — **tónico, -ca** *adj* : tonic — **tónico** *nm* : tonic (in medicine)
tono *nm* 1 : tone 2 : shade (of colors) 3 : key (in music)
tontería *nf* 1 : silly thing or remark 2 ESTUPIDEZ : foolishness 3 **decir ~s** : talk nonsense — **tonto, -ta** *adj* 1 : stupid, silly 2 **a tontas y a locas** : haphazardly — ~ *n* : fool, idiot
topacio *nm* : topaz
toparse *vr* ~ **con** : run into, come across
tope *nm* 1 : limit, end 2 *or* ~ **de puerta** : doorstop 3 *Lat* : bump — ~ *adj* : maximum
tópico, -ca *adj* 1 : topical, external 2 MANIDO : trite — **tópico** *nm* : cliché
topo *nm* : mole (animal)
toque *nm* 1 : (light) touch 2 : ringing, peal (of a bell) 3 ~ **de queda** : curfew 4 ~ **de diana** : reveille — **toquetear** *vt* : finger, handle
tórax *nms & pl* : thorax
torbellino *nm* : whirlwind
torcer {14} *vt* 1 : twist, bend 2 : turn (a corner) 3 : wring (out) — *vi* : turn —

torcerse *vr* 1 : twist, sprain 2 FRUSTRARSE : go wrong 3 DESVIARSE : go astray — **torcedura** *nf* 1 : twisting 2 ESGUINCE : sprain — **torcido, -da** *adj* : twisted, crooked
tordo, -da *adj* : dappled — **tordo** *nm* : thrush (bird)
torear *vt* 1 : fight (bulls) 2 ELUDIR : dodge, sidestep — *vi* : fight bulls — **toreo** *nm* : bullfighting — **torero, -ra** *n* : bullfighter
tormenta *nf* : storm — **tormento** *nm* 1 : torture 2 ANGUSTIA : torment, anguish — **tormentoso, -sa** *adj* : stormy
tornado *nm* : tornado
tornar *vt* CONVERTIR : render, turn — *vi* : go back, return — **tornarse** *vr* : become, turn into
torneo *nm* : tournament
tornillo *nm* : screw
torniquete *nm* 1 : turnstile 2 : tourniquet (in medicine)
torno *nm* 1 : winch 2 : (carpenter's) lathe 3 ~ **de alfarero** : (potter's) wheel 4 ~ **de banco** : vise 5 **en** ~ **a** : around, about
toro *nm* 1 : bull 2 ~**s** *nmpl* : bullfight
toronja *nf* : grapefruit
torpe *adj* 1 : clumsy, awkward 2 ESTÚPIDO : stupid, dull
torpedear *vt* : torpedo — **torpedo** *nm* : torpedo
torpeza *nf* 1 : clumsiness, awkwardness 2 ESTUPIDEZ : slowness, stupidity
torre *nf* 1 : tower 2 : turret (on a ship, etc.) 3 : rook, castle (in chess)
torrente *nm* 1 : torrent 2 ~ **sanguíneo** : bloodstream — **torrencial** *adj* : torrential
tórrido, -da *adj* : torrid
torsión *nf, pl* **-siones** : twisting
torta *nf* 1 : torte, cake 2 *Lat* : sandwich
tortazo *nm fam* : blow, wallop
tortícolis *nfs & pl* : stiff neck
tortilla *nf* 1 : tortilla 2 *or* ~ **de huevo** : omelet
tórtola *nf* : turtledove
tortuga *nf* 1 : turtle, tortoise 2 ~ **de agua dulce** : terrapin
tortuoso, -sa *adj* : tortuous, winding
tortura *nf* : torture — **torturar** *vt* : torture
tos *nf* 1 : cough 2 ~ **ferina** : whooping cough
tosco, -ca *adj* : rough, coarse
toser *vi* : cough
tosquedad *nf* : coarseness
tostar {19} *vt* 1 : toast 2 BRONCEAR : tan — **tostarse** *vr* : get a tan — **tostada**

nf **1** : piece of toast **2** *Lat* : tostada —
tostador *nm* : toaster
tostón *nm, pl* **-tones** *Lat* : fried plantain chip
total *adj & nm* : total — **~** *adv* : so,
after all — **totalidad** *nf* : whole — **totalitario, -ria** *adj & n* : totalitarian —
totalitarismo *nm* : totalitarianism —
totalizar {21} *vt* : total, add up to
tóxico, -ca *adj* : toxic, poisonous —
tóxico *nm* : poison — **toxicomanía** *nf*
: drug addiction — **toxicómano, -na** *n*
: drug addict — **toxina** *nf* : toxin
tozudo, -da *adj* : stubborn
traba *nf* : obstacle, hindrance
trabajar *vi* **1** : work **2** : act, perform (in
theater, etc.) — *vt* **1** : work (metal) **2**
: knead (dough) **3** MEJORAR : work on,
work at — **trabajador, -dora** *adj*
: hard-working — **~** *n* : worker —
trabajo *nm* **1** : work **2** EMPLEO : job **3**
TAREA : task **4** ESFUERZO : effort **5**
costar ~ : be difficult **6** **~** **en**
equipo : teamwork **7** **~s** *nmpl*
: hardships, difficulties — **trabajoso,
-sa** *adj* : hard, laborious
trabalenguas *nms & pl* : tongue twister
trabar *vt* **1** : join, connect **2** OBSTACULIZAR : impede **3** : strike up (a conversation, etc.) **4** : thicken (sauces) —
trabarse *vr* **1** : jam **2** ENREDARSE : become entangled **3** **se le traba la**
lengua : he gets tongue-tied
trabucar {72} *vt* : mix up
tracción *nf* : traction
tractor *nm* : tractor
tradición *nf, pl* **-ciones** : tradition —
tradicional *adj* : traditional
traducir {61} *vt* : translate — **traducción** *nf, pl* **-ciones** : translation — **traductor, -tora** *n* : translator
traer {81} *vt* **1** : bring **2** CAUSAR : cause,
bring about **3** CONTENER : carry, have **4**
LLEVAR : wear — **traerse** *vr* **1** : bring
along **2** **traérselas** : be difficult
traficar {72} *vi* **~ en** : traffic in —
traficante *nmf* : dealer, trafficker —
tráfico *nm* **1** : trade (of merchandise)
2 : traffic (of vehicles)
tragaluz *nf, pl* **-luces** : skylight
tragar {52} *vt* **1** : swallow **2** *fam* : put up
with — *vi* : swallow — **tragarse** *vr* **1**
: swallow **2** ABSORBER : absorb, swallow up
tragedia *nf* : tragedy — **trágico, -ca** *adj*
: tragic
trago *nm* **1** : swallow, swig **2** *fam*
: drink, liquor — **tragón, -gona** *adj*
fam : greedy — **~** *nmf fam* : glutton
traicionar *vt* : betray — **traición** *nf, pl*

-ciones 1 : betrayal **2** : treason (in
law) — **traidor, -dora** *adj* : traitorous,
treacherous — **~** *n* : traitor
trailer *nm* : trailer
traje *nm* **1** : dress, costume **2** : (man's)
suit **3** **~ de baño** : bathing suit
trajinar *vi fam* : rush around — **trajín**
nm, pl **-jines** *fam* : hustle and bustle
trama *nf* **1** : plot **2** : weave, weft (of fabric) — **tramar** *vt* **1** : plot, plan **2**
: weave (fabric)
tramitar *vt* : negotiate — **trámite** *nm*
: procedure, step
tramo *nm* **1** : stretch, section **2** : flight
(of stairs)
trampa *nf* **1** : trap **2 hacer ~s** : cheat
— **trampear** *vt* : cheat
trampilla *nf* : trapdoor
trampolín *nm, pl* **-lines 1** : diving board
2 : trampoline (in a gymnasium, etc.)
tramposo, -sa *adj* : crooked, cheating
— **~** *n* : cheat, swindler
tranca *nf* **1** : cudgel, club **2** : bar (for a
door or window)
trance *nm* **1** : critical juncture **2** : (hypnotic) trance **3 en ~ de** : in the
process of
tranquilo, -la *adj* : calm, tranquil —
tranquilidad *nf* : tranquility, peace —
tranquilizante *nm* : tranquilizer —
tranquilizar {21} *vt* : calm, soothe —
tranquilizarse *vr* : calm down
trans- *see also* **tras-**
transacción *nf, pl* **-ciones** : transaction
transatlántico, -ca *adj* : transatlantic
— **transatlántico** *nm* : ocean liner
transbordador *nm* **1** : ferry **2 ~ espacial** : space shuttle — **transbordar** *vt*
: transfer — *vi* : change (of trains, etc.)
— **transbordo** *nm* **hacer ~** : change
(trains, etc.)
transcribir {33} *vt* : transcribe —
transcripción *nf, pl* **-ciones** : transcription
transcurrir *vi* : elapse, pass — **transcurso** *nm* : course, progression
transeúnte *nmf* : passerby
transferir {76} *vt* : transfer — **transferencia** *nf* : transfer, transference
transformar *vt* **1** : transform, change **2**
CONVERTIR : convert — **transformarse** *vr* : be transformed — **transformación** *nf, pl* **-ciones** : transformation — **transformador** *nm*
: transformer
transfusión *nf, pl* **-siones** : transfusion
transgredir {1} *vt* : transgress —
transgresión *nf* : transgression
transición *nf, pl* **-ciones** : transition
transido, -da *adj* : overcome, stricken

transigir {35} *vi* : give in, compromise

transistor *nm* : transistor

transitar *vi* : go, travel — **transitable** *adj* : passable

transitivo, -va *adj* : transitive

tránsito *nm* 1 : transit 2 TRÁFICO : traffic 3 **hora de máximo ~** : rush hour — **transitorio, -ria** *adj* : transitory

transmitir *vt* 1 : transmit 2 : broadcast (radio, TV, etc.) 3 CEDER : pass on — **transmisión** *nf, pl* **-siones** 1 : broadcast 2 TRANSFERENCIA : transfer 3 : transmission (of an automobile) — **transmisor** *nm* : transmitter

transparentarse *vr* : be transparent — **transparente** *adj* : transparent

transpirar *vi* : perspire, sweat — **transpiración** *nf, pl* **-ciones** : perspiration, sweat

transponer {60} *vt* : transpose, move — **transponerse** *vr* 1 : set (of the sun, etc.) 2 DORMITAR : doze off

transportar *vt* : transport, carry — **transportarse** *vr* : get carried away — **transporte** *nm* : transport, transportation

transversal *adj* **corte ~** : cross section

tranvía *nm* : streetcar, trolley

trapear *vt Lat* : mop

trapecio *nm* : trapeze

trapisonda *nf* : scheme, plot

trapo *nm* 1 : cloth, rag 2 **~s** *nmpl fam* : clothes

tráquea *nf* : trachea, windpipe

traquetear *vi* : rattle around, shake — **traqueteo** *nm* : rattling

tras *prep* 1 DESPUÉS DE : after 2 DÉTRAS DE : behind

tras- *see also* **trans-**

trascender {56} *vi* 1 : leak out, become known 2 EXTENDERSE : spread 3 **~ de** : transcend — **trascendencia** *nf* : importance — **trascendental** *adj* 1 : transcendental 2 IMPORTANTE : important

trasegar *vt* : move around

trasero, -ra *adj* : rear, back — **trasero** *nm* : buttocks *pl*

trasfondo *nm* 1 : background 2 : undercurrent (of suspicion, etc.)

trasladar *vt* 1 : transfer, move 2 POSPONER : postpone — **trasladarse** *vr* : move, relocate — **traslado** *nm* 1 : transfer, move 2 COPIA : copy

traslapar *vt* : overlap — **traslaparse** *vr* : overlap

traslucirse {45} *vr* 1 : be translucent 2 REVELARSE : be revealed — **traslúcido, -da** : translucent

trasnochar *vi* : stay up all night

traspasar *vt* 1 : pierce, go through 2 EXCEDER : go beyond 3 ATRAVESAR : cross, go across 4 : transfer (a business, etc.) — **traspaso** *nm* : transfer, sale

traspié *nm* 1 : stumble, trip 2 ERROR : blunder

trasplantar *vt* : transplant — **trasplante** *nm* : transplant

trasquilar *vt* : shear

traste *nm* 1 : fret (on a guitar, etc.) 2 *Lat* : (kitchen) utensil 3 **dar al ~ con** : ruin 4 **irse al ~** : fall through

trastos *nmpl fam* : pieces of junk, stuff

trastornar *vt* 1 : disturb, disrupt 2 VOLVER LOCO : drive crazy — **trastornarse** *vr* : go crazy — **trastornado, -da** *adj* : disturbed, deranged — **trastorno** *nm* 1 : disturbance, disruption 2 : (medical or psychological) disorder

trastrocar *vt* : change, switch around

tratable *adj* : friendly, sociable

tratar *vi* 1 **~ con** : deal with 2 **~ de** : try to 3 **~ de** *or* **sobre** : be about, concern 4 **~ en** : deal in — *vt* 1 : treat 2 MANEJAR : deal with, handle — **tratarse** *vr* **~ de** : be about, concern — **tratado** *nm* 1 : treatise 2 CONVENIO : treaty — **tratamiento** *nm* : treatment — **trato** *nm* 1 : treatment 2 ACUERDO : deal, agreement 3 **~s** *nmpl* : dealings

trauma *nm* : trauma — **traumático, -ca** *adj* : traumatic

través *nm* 1 **a ~ de** : across, through 2 **de ~** : sideways

travesaño *nm* : crosspiece

travesía *nf* : voyage, crossing (of the sea)

travesura *nf* 1 : prank 2 **~s** *nfpl* : mischief — **travieso, -sa** *adj* : mischievous, naughty

trayecto *nm* 1 : trajectory, path 2 VIAJE : journey 3 RUTA : route — **trayectoria** *nf* : path, trajectory

traza *nf* 1 : design, plan 2 ASPECTO : appearance — **trazado** *nm* 1 : outline, sketch 2 DISEÑO : plan, layout — **trazar** {21} *vt* 1 : trace, outline 2 : draw up (a plan, etc.) — **trazo** *nm* : stroke, line

trébol *nm* 1 : clover, shamrock 2 **~es** *nmpl* : clubs (in playing cards)

trece *adj & nm* : thirteen — **treceavo, -va** *adj* : thirteenth — **treceavo** *nm* : thirteenth (fraction)

trecho *nm* 1 : stretch, period 2 DISTANCIA : distance 3 **de ~ a ~** : at intervals

tregua *nf* **1** : truce **2 sin ~** : without respite

treinta *adj & nm* : thirty — **treintavo, -va** *adj* : thirtieth — **treintavo** *nm* : thirtieth (fraction)

tremendo, -da *adj* : tremendous, enormous

trementina *nf* : turpentine

trémulo, -la *adj* : trembling, flickering

tren *nm* **1** : train **2 ~ de aterrizaje** : landing gear

trenza *nf* : braid, pigtail — **trenzar** {21} *vt* : braid — **trenzarse** *vr Lat* : get involved

trepar *vi* **1** : climb **2** : creep, spread (of a plant) — **treparse** *vr* : climb (up) — **trepador, -dora** *adj* : climbing — **trepadora** *nf* **1** : climbing plant **2** *fam* : social climber

trepidar *vi* : shake, vibrate

tres *adj & nm* : three — **trescientos, -tas** *adj* : three hundred — **trescientos** *nms & pl* : three hundred

treta *nf* : trick

triángulo *nm* : triangle — **triangular** *adj* : triangular

tribu *nf* : tribe — **tribal** *adj* : tribal

tribulación *nf, pl* **-ciones** : tribulation

tribuna *nf* **1** : dais, platform **2** : grandstand, bleachers *pl* (in a stadium)

tribunal *nm* : court, tribunal

tributar *vt* : pay, render — *vi* : pay taxes — **tributo** *nm* **1** : tribute **2** IMPUESTO : tax

triciclo *nm* : tricycle

tricolor *adj* : tricolored

tridimensional *adj* : three-dimensional

trigésimo, -ma *adj & n* : thirtieth

trigo *nm* : wheat

trigonometría *nf* : trigonometry

trillado, -da *adj* : trite

trillar *vt* : thresh — **trilladora** *nf* : threshing machine

trillizo, -za *n* : triplet

trilogía *nf* : trilogy

trimestral *adj* : quarterly

trinar *vi* : warble

trinchar *vt* : carve

trinchera *nf* **1** : trench, ditch **2** IMPERMEABLE : trench coat

trineo *nm* : sled, sleigh

trinidad *nf* : trinity

trino *nm* : trill, warble

trío *nm* : trio

tripa *nf* **1** : gut, intestine **2 ~s** *nfpl fam* : belly, tummy

triple *adj & nm* : triple — **triplicar** {72} *vt* : triple

trípode *nm* : tripod

tripular *vt* : man — **tripulación** *nf, pl*

-ciones : crew — **tripulante** *nmf* : crew member

tris *nm* **estar en un ~ de** : be within an inch of

triste *adj* **1** : sad **2** SOMBRÍO : dismal, gloomy **3** MISERABLE : sorry, miserable — **tristeza** *nf* : sadness, grief

tritón *nm, pl* **-tones** : newt

triturar *vt* : crush, grind

triunfar *vi* : triumph, win — **triunfal** *adj* : triumphal — **triunfante** *adj* : triumphant — **triunfo** *nm* : triumph, victory

trivial *adj* : trivial

triza *nf* **1** : shred, bit **2 hacer ~s** : smash to pieces

trocar {82} *vt* **1** CONVERTIR : change **2** INTERCAMBIAR : exchange

trocha *nf* : path, trail

trofeo *nm* : trophy

trombón *nm, pl* **-bones** **1** : trombone **2** : trombonist (musician)

trombosis *nf* : thrombosis

trompa *nf* **1** : trunk (of an elephant), snout **2** : horn (musical instrument) **3** : tube (in anatomy)

trompeta *nf* : trumpet — **trompetista** *nmf* : trumpet player

trompo *nm* : top (toy)

tronada *nf* : thunderstorm — **tronar** {19} *vi* : thunder, rage — *vt Lat fam* : shoot — *v impers* : thunder

tronchar *vt* **1** : snap **2** TRUNCAR : cut short

tronco *nm* **1** : trunk (of a tree) **2** : torso (of a person) **3 dormir como un ~** : sleep like a log

trono *nm* : throne

tropa *nf* : troops *pl*, soldiers *pl*

tropel *nm* : mob

tropezar {29} *vi* **1** : trip, stumble **2 ~ con** : come up against, run into — **tropezón** *nm, pl* **-zones** **1** : stumble **2** EQUIVOCACIÓN : mistake, slip

trópico *nm* : tropic — **tropical** *adj* : tropical

tropiezo *nm* **1** CONTRATIEMPO : snag, setback **2** EQUIVOCACIÓN : mistake, slip

trotar *vi* **1** : trot **2** *fam* : rush about — **trote** *nm* **1** : trot **2** *fam* : rush, bustle **3 al ~** : at a trot, quickly

trozo *nm* : piece, bit, chunk

trucha *nf* : trout

truco *nm* **1** : knack **2** ARDID : trick

trueno *nm* : thunder

trueque *nm* : barter, exchange

trufa *nf* : truffle

truncar {72} *vt* **1** : cut short **2** : thwart, spoil (plans, etc.)

tu *adj* : your
tú *pron* : you
tuba *nf* : tuba
tuberculosis *nf* : tuberculosis
tubo *nm* 1 : tube, pipe 2 ~ **de escape**
: exhaust pipe (of a vehicle) 3 ~ **de**
desagüe : drainpipe — **tubería** *nf*
: pipes *pl*, tubing
tuerca *nf* : nut (for a screw)
tuerto, -ta *adj* : one-eyed, blind in one
eye
tuétano *nm* : marrow
tufo *nm* 1 : vapor 2 *fam* : stench, stink
tugurio *nm* : hovel
tulipán *nm, pl* **-panes** : tulip
tullido, -da *adj* : crippled, paralyzed
tumba *nf* : tomb, grave
tumbar *vt* : knock down, knock over —
tumbarse *vr* : lie down — **tumbo** *nm*
dar ~**s** : jolt, bump around
tumor *nm* : tumor
tumulto *nm* 1 : commotion, tumult 2
MOTÍN : riot — **tumultuoso, -sa** *adj*
: tumultuous
tuna *nf* : prickly pear
túnel *nm* : tunnel
túnica *nf* : tunic
tupé *nm* : toupee
tupido, -da *adj* : dense, thick
turba *nf* 1 : peat 2 MUCHEDUMBRE
: mob, throng

turbación *nf, pl* **-ciones** 1 : disturbance
2 CONFUSIÓN : confusion
turbante *nm* : turban
turbar *vt* 1 : disturb, upset 2 CONFUNDIR
: confuse, bewilder
turbina *nf* : turbine
turbio, -bia *adj* 1 : cloudy, murky 2
: blurred (of vision, etc.) — **turbión**
nm, pl **-biones** : squall
turbulencia *nf* : turbulence — **turbulento, -ta** *adj* : turbulent
turco, -ca *adj* : Turkish — **turco** *nm*
: Turkish (language)
turista *nmf* : tourist — **turismo** *nm*
: tourism, tourist industry — **turístico, -ca** *adj* : tourist, travel
turnarse *vr* : take turns, alternate —
turno *nm* 1 : turn 2 ~ **de noche**
: night shift
turquesa *nf* : turquoise
turrón *nm, pl* **-rrones** : nougat
tutear *vt* : address as *tú*
tutela *nf* 1 : guardianship (in law) 2
bajo la ~ **de** : under the protection of
tuteo *nm* : addressing as *tú*
tutor, -tora *n* 1 : guardian 2 : tutor (in
education)
tuyo, -ya *adj* : yours, of yours — ~
pron 1 **el tuyo, la tuya, lo tuyo, los
tuyos, las tuyas** : yours 2 **los tuyos**
: your family, your friends

U

u¹ *nf* : u, 22d letter of the Spanish alphabet
u² *conj* (*used before words beginning
with o- or ho-*) : or
uapití *nm* : American elk, wapiti
ubicar {72} *vt Lat* 1 COLOCAR : place,
position 2 LOCALIZAR : find — **ubi-
carse** *vr* : be located
ubre *nf* : udder
Ud., Uds. → **usted**
ufanarse *vr* ~ **de** : boast about —
ufano, -na *adj* 1 : proud 2 ENGREÍDO
: self-satisfied
ujier *nm* : usher
úlcera *nf* : ulcer
ulterior *adj* : later, subsequent — **ulteri-
ormente** *adv* : subsequently
últimamente *adv* : lately, recently
ultimar *vt* 1 : complete, finish 2 *Lat*
: kill — **ultimátum** *nm, pl* **-tums** : ultimatum
último, -ma *adj* 1 : last 2 : latest, most

recent (in time) 3 : farthest (in space)
4 **por último** : finally
ultrajar *vt* : outrage, insult — **ultraje** *nm*
: outrage, insult
ultramar *nm* **de** ~ **or en** ~ : overseas
— **ultramarino, -na** *adj* : overseas —
ultramarinos *nmpl* **tienda de** ~
: grocery store
ultranza: a ~ *adv phr* : to the extreme
— **a** ~ *adj phr* : out-and-out, complete
ultrasonido *nm* : ultrasound
ultravioleta *adj* : ultraviolet
ulular *vi* 1 : hoot (of an owl) 2 : howl (of
a wolf, etc.) — **ululato** *nm*
: hoot (of an owl)
umbilical *adj* : umbilical
umbral *nm* : threshold
un, una *art, mpl* **unos** 1 : a, an 2 **unos**
or **unas** *pl* : some, a few 3 **unos** *or*
unas *pl* : about, approximately — **un**
adj → **uno**

unánime *adj* : unanimous — **unanimidad** *nf* : unanimity
uncir {83} *vt* : yoke
undécimo, -ma *adj & n* : eleventh
ungir {35} *vt* : anoint — **ungüento** *nm* : ointment
único, -ca *adj* 1 : only, sole 2 EXCEPCIONAL : unique — ~ *n* : only one — **únicamente** *adv* : only
unicornio *nm* : unicorn
unidad *nf* 1 : unit 2 ARMONÍA : unity — **unido, -da** *adj* 1 : united 2 : close (of friends, etc.)
unificar {72} *vt* : unify — **unificación** *nf, pl* **-ciones** : unification
uniformar *vt* 1 : standardize 2 : put into uniform — **uniformado, -da** *adj* : uniformed — **uniforme** *adj & nm* : uniform — **uniformidad** *nf* : uniformity
unilateral *adj* : unilateral
unir *vt* 1 : unite, join 2 COMBINAR : combine, mix together — **unirse** *vr* 1 : join together 2 ~ a : join — **unión** *nf, pl* **uniones** 1 : union 2 JUNTURA : joint, coupling
unísono *nm* al ~ : in unison
unitario, -ria *adj* : unitary
universal *adj* : universal
universidad *nf* : university, college — **universitario, -ria** *adj* : university, college
universo *nm* : universe
uno, una (un *before masculine singular nouns*) *adj* : one — ~ *pron* 1 : one 2 **unos, unas** *pl* : some 3 **uno(s) a otro(s)** : one another, each other 4 **uno y otro** : both — **uno** *nm* : one (number)
untar *vt* 1 : smear, grease 2 *fam* : bribe — **untuoso, -sa** *adj* : greasy, sticky
uña *nf* 1 : nail, fingernail 2 : claw (of a cat, etc.), hoof (of a horse, etc.)
uranio *nm* : uranium

Urano *nm* : Uranus
urbano, -na *adj* : urban, city — **urbanidad** *nf* : politeness, courtesy — **urbanización** *nf, pl* **-ciones** : housing development — **urbanizar** *vt* : develop, urbanize — **urbe** *nf* : large city
urdir *vt* 1 : warp 2 PLANEAR : plot — **urdimbre** *nf* : warp (of a fabric)
urgir {35} *v impers* : be urgent, be pressing — **urgencia** *nf* 1 : urgency 2 EMERGENCIA : emergency — **urgente** *adj* : urgent
urinario, -ria *adj* : urinary — **urinario** *nm* : urinal (place)
urna *nf* 1 : urn 2 : ballot box (for voting)
urraca *nf* : magpie
uruguayo, -ya *adj* : Uruguayan
usar *vt* 1 : use 2 LLEVAR : wear — **usarse** 1 EMPLEARSE : be used 2 : be worn, be in fashion — **usado, -da** *adj* 1 : used 2 GASTADO : worn, worn-out — **usanza** *nf* : custom, usage — **uso** *nm* 1 : use 2 DESGASTE : wear and tear 3 USANZA : custom, usage
usted *pron* 1 (*used in formal address; often written as Ud. or Vd.*) : you 2 ~es *pl* (*often written as Uds. or Vds.*) : you (all)
usual *adj* : usual
usuario, -ria *n* : user
usura *nf* : usury — **usurero, -ra** *n* : usurer
usurpar *vt* : usurp
utensilio *nm* : utensil, tool
útero *nm* : uterus, womb
utilizar {21} *vt* : use, utilize — **útil** *adj* : useful — **útiles** *nmpl* : implements, tools — **utilidad** *nf* : utility, usefulness — **utilitario, -ria** *adj* : utilitarian — **utilización** *nf, pl* **-ciones** : utilization, use
uva *nf* : grape

V

v *nf* : v, 23d letter of the Spanish alphabet
va → ir
vaca *nf* : cow
vacaciones *nfpl* 1 : vacation 2 **estar de** ~ : be on vacation 3 **irse de** ~ : go on vacation
vacante *adj* : vacant — ~ *nf* : vacancy
vaciar {85} *vt* 1 : empty (out) 2 AHUECAR : hollow out 3 : cast, mold (a statue, etc.)

vacilar *vi* 1 : hesitate, waver 2 : flicker (of light) 3 TAMBALEARSE : be unsteady, wobble 4 *fam* : joke, fool around — **vacilación** *nf, pl* **-ciones** : hesitation — **vacilante** *adj* 1 : hesitant 2 OSCILANTE : unsteady
vacío, -cía *adj* : empty — **vacío** *nm* 1 : void 2 : vacuum (in physics) 3 HUECO : space, gap
vacuna *nf* : vaccine — **vacunación** *nf,*

pl **-ciones** : vaccination — **vacunar** *vt*
: vaccinate
vacuno, -na *adj* : bovine
vadear *vt* : ford — **vado** *nm* : ford
vagabundear *vi* : wander — **vagabundo, -da** *adj* 1 : vagrant 2 : stray (of a
dog, etc.) — ~ *n* : hobo, bum — **va-
gancia** *nf* 1 : vagrancy 2 PEREZA : laziness, idleness — **vagar** {52} *vi*
: roam, wander
vagina *nf* : vagina
vago, -ga *adj* 1 : vague 2 PEREZOSO
: lazy, idle — ~ *n* : idler, loafer
vagón *nm, pl* **-gones** : car (of a train)
vahído *nm* : dizzy spell
vaho *nm* 1 : breath 2 VAPOR : vapor,
steam
vaina *nf* 1 : sheath, scabbard 2 : pod (in
botany) 3 *Lat fam* : bother, pain
vainilla *nf* : vanilla
vaivén *nm, pl* **-venes** 1 : swinging,
swaying 2 : coming and going (of
people, etc.) 3 **vaivenes** *nmpl* : ups
and downs
vajilla *nf* : dishes *pl*
vale *nm* 1 : voucher 2 PAGARÉ : IOU —
valedero, -ra *adj* : valid
valentía *nf* : courage, bravery
valer {84} *vt* 1 : be worth 2 COSTAR
: cost 3 GANAR : gain, earn 4 EQUI-
VALER A : be equal to — *vi* 1 : have
value, cost 2 SER VÁLIDO : be valid,
count 3 SERVIR : be of use 4 **hacerse**
~ : assert oneself 5 **más vale** : it's
better — **valerse** *vr* 1 ~ **de** : take advantage of 2 ~ **solo** *or* ~ **por sí
mismo** : look after oneself
valeroso, -sa *adj* : courageous
valga, etc. → **valer**
valía *nf* : worth
validar *vt* : validate — **validez** *nf* : validity — **válido, -da** *adj* : valid
valiente *adj* 1 : brave 2 (*used ironical-
ly*) : fine, great
valija *nf* : case, valise
valioso, -sa *adj* : valuable
valla *nf* 1 : fence 2 : hurdle (in sports)
— **vallar** *vt* : put a fence around
valle *nm* : valley
valor *nm* 1 : value, worth 2 VALENTÍA
: courage, valor 3 **objetos de** ~
: valuables 4 **sin** ~ : worthless 5
~**es** *nmpl* : values, principles 6 ~**es**
nmpl : securities, bonds — **valoración**
nf, pl **-ciones** : valuation — **valorar** *vt*
: evaluate, assess
vals *nm* : waltz
válvula *nf* : valve
vamos → **ir**
vampiro *nm* : vampire

van → **ir**
vanagloriarse *vr* : boast, brag
vándalo *nm* : vandal — **vandalismo**
: vandalism
vanguardia *nf* 1 : vanguard 2 : avant-
garde (in art, music, etc.) 3 **a la** ~
: at/in the forefront
vanidad *nf* : vanity — **vanidoso, -sa**
adj : vain, conceited
vano, -na *adj* 1 INÚTIL : vain, useless 2
SUPERFICIAL : empty, hollow 3 **en
vano** : in vain
vapor *nm* 1 : steam, vapor 2 **al** ~
: steamed — **vaporizador** *nm* : vapor-
izer — **vaporizar** {21} *vt* : vaporize
vaquero, -ra *n* : cowboy *m*, cowgirl *f* —
vaqueros *nmpl* : jeans
vara *nf* 1 : stick, rod 2 : staff (of office)
varado, -da *adj* : stranded
variar {85} *vt* 1 : vary 2 CAMBIAR
: change, alter — *vi* : vary, change —
variable *adj & nf* : variable — **variación** *nf, pl* **-ciones** : variation —
variado, -da *adj* : varied — **variante**
nf : variant
varicela *nf* : chicken pox
varicoso, -sa *adj* : varicose
variedad *nf* : variety
varilla *nf* : rod, stick
vario, -ria *adj* 1 : varied 2 ~**s** *pl* : several
varita *nf* : wand
variz *nf, pl* **-rices** *or* **várices** : varicose
vein
varón *nm, pl* **-rones** 1 : man, male 2
NIÑO : boy — **varonil** *adj* : manly
vas → **ir**
vasco, -ca *adj* : Basque — **vasco** *nm*
: Basque (language)
vasija *nf* : container, vessel
vaso *nm* 1 : glass 2 : vessel (in anatomy)
vástago *nm* 1 : offspring, descendent 2
BROTE : shoot 3 VARILLA : rod
vasto, -ta *adj* : vast
vaticinar *vt* : prophesy, predict —
vaticinio *nm* : prophecy
vatio *nm* : watt
vaya, etc. → **ir**
Vd., Vds. → **usted**
ve, etc. → **ir, ver**
vecinal *adj* : local
vecino, -na *n* 1 : neighbor 2 HABITANTE
: resident, inhabitant — ~ *adj*
: neighboring — **vecindad** *nf* : neighborhood, vicinity — **vecindario** *nm* 1
: neighborhood 2 VECINOS : community, residents *pl*
vedar *vt* : prohibit — **veda** *nf* 1 : prohibition, ban 2 : closed season (for hunt-

ing and fishing) — **vedado** *nm* : preserve (for game, etc.)

vega *nf* : fertile lowland

vegetal *nm* : vegetable, plant — ~ *adj* : vegetable — **vegetación** *nf*, *pl* **-ciones** : vegetation — **vegetar** *vi* : vegetate — **vegetariano, -na** *adj* & *n* : vegetarian

vehemente *adj* : vehement

vehículo *nm* : vehicle

veinte *adj* & *nm* : twenty — **veinteavo, -va** *adj* : twentieth — **veinteavo** *nm* : twentieth — **veintena** *nf* : group of twenty, score

vejar *vt* : mistreat, humiliate — **vejación** *nf*, *pl* **-ciones** : humiliation

vejez *nf* : old age

vejiga *nf* **1** : bladder **2** AMPOLLA : blister

vela *nf* **1** : candle **2** : sail (of a ship) **3** VIGILIA : vigil **4 pasar la noche en** ~ : have a sleepless night

velada *nf* : evening (party)

velar *vt* **1** : hold a wake over **2** CUIDAR : watch over **3** : blur (a photograph) **4** OCULTAR : veil, mask — *vi* **1** : stay awake **2** ~ **por** : watch over — **velado, -da** *adj* **1** : veiled, hidden **2** : blurred (of a photograph)

velero *nm* : sailing ship

veleta *nf* : weather vane

vello *nm* **1** : body hair **2** PELUSA : down, fuzz — **vellón** *nm*, *pl* **-llones** : fleece — **velloso, -sa** *adj* : downy, fluffy — **velludo, -da** *adj* : hairy

velo *nm* : veil

veloz *adj*, *pl* **-loces** : fast, quick — **velocidad** *nf* **1** : speed, velocity **2** MARCHA : gear (of an automobile) — **velocímetro** *nm* : speedometer

vena *nf* **1** : vein **2** : grain (of wood) **3** DISPOSICIÓN : mood **4 tener** ~ **de** : have a talent for

venado *nm* **1** : deer **2** : venison (in cooking)

vencer {86} *vt* **1** : beat, defeat **2** SUPERAR : overcome — *vi* **1** : win **2** CADUCAR : expire — **vencerse** *vr* : collapse, give way — **vencedor, -dora** *adj* : winning — ~ *n* : winner — **vencido, -da** *adj* **1** : beaten, defeated **2** CADUCADO : expired **3** : due, payable (in finance) **4 darse por** ~ : give up — **vencimiento** *nm* **1** : expiration **2** : maturity (of a loan)

venda *nf* : bandage — **vendaje** *nm* : bandage, dressing — **vendar** *vt* **1** : bandage **2** ~ **los ojos** : blindfold

vendaval *nm* : gale

vender *vt* : sell — **venderse** *vr* **1** : be sold **2 se vende** : for sale — **vendedor, -dora** *n* **1** : seller **2** : salesman *m*, saleswoman *f* (in a store)

vendimia *nf* : grape harvest

vendrá, etc. → **venir**

veneno *nm* **1** : poison **2** : venom (of a snake, etc.) — **venenoso, -sa** *adj* : poisonous

venerar *vt* : venerate, revere — **venerable** *adj* : venerable — **veneración** *nf*, *pl* **-ciones** : veneration, reverence

venéreo, -rea *adj* : venereal

venezolano, -na *adj* : Venezuelan

venga → **venir**

vengar {52} *vt* : avenge — **vengarse** *vr* : get even, take revenge — **venganza** *nf* : vengeance, revenge — **vengativo, -va** *adj* : vindictive, vengeful

venia *nf* **1** : permission **2** : pardon (in law)

venial *adj* : venial, petty

venir {87} *vi* **1** : come **2** LLEGAR : arrive **3** HALLARSE : be, appear **4** QUEDAR : fit **5 que viene** : coming, next **6** ~ **a ser** : turn out to be **7** ~ **bien** : be suitable — **venirse** *vr* **1** : come **2** ~ **abajo** : fall apart, collapse — **venida** *nf* **1** : arrival, coming **2** REGRESO : return — **venidero, -ra** *adj* : coming

venta *nf* **1** : sale, selling **2 en** ~ : for sale

ventaja *nf* : advantage — **ventajoso, -sa** *adj* : advantageous

ventana *nf* **1** : window **2** ~ **de la nariz** : nostril — **ventanilla** *nf* **1** : window (of a vehicle or airplane) **2** : ticket window, box office (of a theater, etc.)

ventilar *vt* : ventilate, air (out) — **ventilación** *nf*, *pl* **-ciones** : ventilation — **ventilador** *nm* : fan, ventilator

ventisca *nf* : blizzard — **ventisquero** *nm* : snowdrift

ventoso, -sa *adj* : windy — **ventosidad** *nf* : wind, flatulence

ventrílocuo, -cua *n* : ventriloquist

ventura *nf* **1** : fortune, luck **2** SATISFACCIÓN : happiness **3 a la** ~ : at random — **venturoso, -sa** *adj* : fortunate, happy

ver {88} *vt* **1** : see **2** : watch (television, etc.) — *vi* **1** : see **2 a** ~ **or vamos a** ~ : let's see **3 no tener nada que** ~ **con** : have nothing to do with **4 ya veremos** : we'll see — **verse** *vr* **1** : see oneself **2** HALLARSE : find oneself **3** ENCONTRARSE : see each other, meet

vera *nf* **1** : side, edge **2** : bank (of a river)

veracidad *nf* : truthfulness

verano *nm* : summer — **veraneante** *nmf* : summer vacationer — **veranear**

vi : spend the summer — **veraniego, -ga** *adj* : summer
veras *nfpl* **de ~** : really
veraz *adj, pl* **-races** : truthful
verbal *adj* : verbal
verbena *nf* : festival, fair
verbo *nm* : verb — **verboso, -sa** *adj* : verbose
verdad *nf* 1 : truth 2 **de ~** : really, truly 3 **¿verdad?** : right?, isn't that so? — **verdaderamente** *adv* : really, truly — **verdadero, -dera** *adj* : true, real
verde *adj* 1 : green 2 : dirty, risqué (of a joke, etc.) — **~** *nm* : green — **verdor** *nm* : greenness
verdugo *nm* 1 : executioner, hangman 2 : cruel person, tyrant
verdura *nf* : vegetable(s), green(s)
vereda *nf* 1 : path, trail 2 *Lat* : sidewalk
veredicto *nm* : verdict
vergüenza *nf* 1 : shame 2 TIMIDEZ : bashfulness, shyness — **vergonzoso, -sa** *adj* 1 : shameful 2 TÍMIDO : bashful, shy
verídico, -ca *adj* : true, truthful
verificar {72} *vt* 1 : verify, confirm 2 EXAMINAR : test, check out — **verificarse** *vr* 1 : take place 2 : come true (of a prophecy, etc.) — **verificación** *nf, pl* **-ciones** : verification
verja *nf* 1 : (iron) gate 2 : rails *pl* (of a fence) 3 ENREJADO : grating, grille
vermut *nm, pl* **-muts** : vermouth
vernáculo, -la *adj* : vernacular
verosímil *adj* 1 : probable, likely 2 CREÍBLE : credible
verraco *nm* : boar
verruga *nf* : wart
versar *vi* **~ sobre** : deal with, be about — **versado, -da** *adj* **~ en** : versed in
versátil *adj* 1 : versatile 2 VOLUBLE : fickle
versión *nf, pl* **-siones** 1 : version 2 TRADUCCIÓN : translation
verso *nm* 1 : poem, verse 2 : line (of poetry)
vértebra *nf* : vertebra
verter {56} *vt* 1 : pour (out) 2 DERRAMAR : spill 3 TIRAR : dump — *vi* : flow — **vertedero** *nm* 1 : dump, landfill 2 DESAGÜE : drain, outlet
vertical *adj & nf* : vertical
vértice *nm* : vertex, apex
vertiente *nf* : slope
vértigo *nm* : vertigo, dizziness — **vertiginoso, -sa** *adj* : dizzy
vesícula *nf* 1 : blister 2 **~ biliar** : gallbladder
vestíbulo *nm* : vestibule, hall, foyer

vestido *nm* 1 : dress 2 ROPA : clothing, clothes *pl*
vestigio *nm* : vestige, trace
vestir {54} *vt* 1 : dress, clothe 2 LLEVAR : wear — *vi* : dress — **vestirse** *vr* : get dressed — **vestimenta** *nf* : clothing
vestuario *nm* 1 : wardrobe, clothes *pl* 2 : dressing room (in a theater), locker room (in sports)
veta *nf* 1 : vein, seam 2 : grain (of wood)
vetar *vt* : veto
veteado, -da *adj* : streaked, veined
veterano, -na *adj & n* : veteran
veterinaria *nf* : veterinary medicine — **veterinario, -ria** *adj* : veterinary — **~** *n* : veterinarian
veto *nm* : veto
vetusto, -ta *adj* : ancient
vez *nf, pl* **veces** 1 : time 2 TURNO : turn 3 **a la ~** : at the same time 4 **a veces** : sometimes 5 **de una ~** : all at once 6 **de una ~ para siempre** : once and for all 7 **de ~ en cuando** : from time to time 8 **dos veces** : twice 9 **en ~ de** : instead of 10 **una ~** : once
vía *nf* 1 : way, road, route 2 MEDIO : means 3 : track, line (of a railroad) 4 : (anatomical) tract 5 **en ~ de** : in the process of — **~** *prep* : via
viable *adj* : viable, feasible — **viabilidad** *nf* : viability
viaducto *nm* : viaduct
viajar *vi* : travel — **viajante** *nmf* : traveling salesperson — **viaje** *nm* : trip, journey — **viajero, -ra** *adj* : traveling — **~** *n* 1 : traveler 2 PASAJERO : passenger
vial *adj* : road, traffic
víbora *nf* : viper
vibrar *vi* : vibrate — **vibración** *nf, pl* **-ciones** : vibration — **vibrante** *adj* : vibrant
vicario, -ria *n* : vicar
vicepresidente, -ta *n* : vice president
viceversa *adv* : vice versa
vicio *nm* 1 : vice 2 MALA COSTUMBRE : bad habit 3 DEFECTO : defect — **viciado, -da** *adj* 1 : corrupt 2 : stuffy, stale (of air, etc.) — **viciar** *vt* 1 : corrupt 2 ESTROPEAR : spoil, pollute — **vicioso, -sa** *adj* : depraved, corrupt
vicisitud *nf* : vicissitude
víctima *nf* : victim
victoria *nf* : victory — **victorioso, -sa** *adj* : victorious
vid *nf* : vine, grapevine
vida *nf* 1 : life 2 DURACIÓN : lifetime 3 **de por ~** : for life 4 **estar con ~** : be alive

video or **vídeo** nm **1** : video **2** : VCR, videocassette recorder

vidrio nm : glass — **vidriado** nm : glaze — **vidriar** vt : glaze — **vidriera** nf **1** : stained-glass window **2** : glass door **3** Lat : shopwindow — **vidrioso, -sa** adj **1** : delicate (of a subject, etc.) **2** **ojos vidriosos** : glassy eyes

vieira nf : scallop

viejo, -ja adj : old — ~ n **1** : old man m, old woman f **2 hacerse** ~ : get old

viene, etc. → **venir**

viento nm : wind

vientre nm **1** : abdomen, belly **2** MATRIZ : womb **3** INTESTINO : bowels pl

viernes nms & pl **1** : Friday **2 Viernes Santo** : Good Friday

vietnamita adj & nm : Vietnamese

viga nf : beam, girder

vigencia nf **1** : validity **2 entrar en** ~ : go into effect — **vigente** adj : valid, in force

vigésimo, -ma adj & n : twentieth

vigía nmf : lookout

vigilar vt : look after, watch over — vi : keep watch — **vigilancia** nf **1** : vigilance **2 bajo** ~ : under surveillance — **vigilante** adj : vigilant — ~ nmf : watchman, guard — **vigilia** nf **1** : wakefulness **2** : vigil (in religion)

vigor nm **1** : vigor **2 entrar en** ~ : go into effect — **vigorizante** adj : invigorating — **vigoroso, -sa** adj : vigorous

VIH nm : HIV

vil adj : vile, despicable — **vileza** nf **1** : vileness **2** : despicable act — **vilipendiar** vt : revile

villa nf **1** : town, village **2** : villa (house)

villancico nm : (Christmas) carol

villano, -na n : villain

vilo nm **en** ~ : suspended, in the air

vinagre nm : vinegar — **vinagrera** nf : cruet — **vinagreta** nf : vinaigrette

vincular vt : tie, link — **vínculo** nm : link, tie, bond

vindicar vt **1** : vindicate **2** VENGAR : avenge

vino[1], etc. → **venir**

vino[2] nm : wine

viña nf or **viñedo** nm : vineyard

vio, etc. → **ver**

viola nf : viola

violar vt **1** : violate (a law, etc.) **2** : rape (a person) — **violación** nf, pl **-ciones 1** : violation, offense **2** : rape (of a person)

violencia nf : violence, force — **violentar** vt **1** : force **2** : break into (a house, etc.) — **violentarse** vr **1** : force one-self **2** AVERGONZARSE : be embarrassed — **violento, -ta** adj **1** : violent **2** INCÓMODO : awkward, embarrassing

violeta adj & nm : violet (color) — ~ nf : violet (flower)

violín nm, pl **-lines** : violin — **violinista** nmf : violinist — **violoncelista** or **violonchelista** nmf : cellist — **violoncelo** or **violonchelo** nm : cello, violoncello

virar vi : turn, change direction — **viraje** nm **1** : turn, swerve **2** CAMBIO : change

virgen adj & nmf, pl **vírgenes** : virgin — **virginal** adj : virginal — **virginidad** nf : virginity

viril adj : virile — **virilidad** nf : virility

virtual adj : virtual

virtud nf **1** : virtue **2 en** ~ **de** : by virtue of — **virtuoso, -sa** adj : virtuous — ~ n : virtuoso

viruela nf **1** : smallpox **2 picado de** ~**s** : pockmarked

virulento, -ta adj : virulent

virus nms & pl : virus

visa nf Lat : visa — **visado** nm Spain : visa

vísceras nfpl : entrails — **visceral** adj : visceral

viscoso, -sa adj : viscous — **viscosidad** nf : viscosity

visera nf : visor

visible adj : visible — **visibilidad** nf : visibility

visión nf, pl **-siones 1** : eyesight **2** APARICIÓN : vision, illusion **3** PUNTO DE VISTA : view, perspective — **visionario, -ria** adj & n : visionary

visitar vt : visit — **visita** nf **1** : visit **2 tener** ~ : have company — **visitante** adj : visiting — ~ nmf : visitor

vislumbrar vt : make out, discern — **vislumbre** nf **1** : glimpse, sign **2** RESPLANDOR : glimmer, gleam

viso nm **1** : sheen **2 tener** ~**s de** : seem, show signs of

visón nm : mink

víspera nf : eve, day before

vista nf **1** : vision, eyesight **2** MIRADA : look, gaze **3** PANORAMA : view, vista **4** : hearing (in court) **5 a primera** ~ or **a simple** ~ : at first sight **6 hacer la** ~ **gorda** : turn a blind eye **7 perder de** ~ : lose sight of — **vistazo** nm **1** : glance **2 echar un** ~ : have a look

visto, -ta adj **1** : clear, obvious **2** COMÚN : commonly seen **3 estar bien** ~ : be approved of **4 estar mal** ~ : be frowned upon **5 nunca** ~ : unheard-of **6 por lo visto** : apparently **7 visto que** : since, given that — **visto** *nm* ~ **bueno** : approval — ~ *pp* → **ver**

vistoso, -sa *adj* : colorful, bright

visual *adj* : visual — **visualizar** {21} *vt* : visualize

vital *adj* : vital — **vitalicio, -cia** *adj* : life, for life — **vitalidad** *nf* : vitality

vitamina *nf* : vitamin

viticultor, -tora *n* : winegrower — **viticultura** *nf* : wine growing

vitorear *vt* : cheer, acclaim

vítreo, -trea *adj* : glassy

vitrina *nf* **1** : showcase, display case **2** *Lat* : shopwindow

vituperar *vt* : censure — **vituperio** *nm* : censure

viudo, -da *n* : widower *m*, widow *f* — ~ *adj* : widowed — **viudez** *nf* : widowerhood, widowhood

viva *nm* **dar** ~**s** : cheer

vivacidad *nf* : vivacity, liveliness

vivamente *adv* **1** : vividly **2** PROFUNDAMENTE : deeply, acutely

vivaz *adj, pl* **-vaces 1** : lively, vivacious **2** AGUDO : vivid, sharp

víveres *nmpl* : provisions, supplies

vivero *nm* **1** : nursery (for plants) **2** : (fish) hatchery, (oyster) bed

viveza *nf* **1** : liveliness **2** : vividness (of colors, descriptions, etc.) **3** ASTUCIA : sharpness (of mind) — **vívido, -da** *adj* : vivid

vividor, -dora *n* : freeloader

vivienda *nf* **1** : housing **2** MORADA : dwelling

viviente *adj* : living

vivificar {72} *vt* : enliven

vivir *vi* **1** : live, be alive **2** ~ **de** : live on — *vt* : experience, live (through) — ~ *nm* **1** : life, lifestyle **2 de mal** ~ : disreputable — **vivo, -va** *adj* **1** : alive **2** INTENSO : intense, bright **3** ANIMADO : lively **4** ASTUTO : sharp, quick **5 en vivo** : live

vocablo *nm* : word — **vocabulario** *nm* : vocabulary

vocación *nf, pl* **-ciones** : vocation — **vocacional** *adj* : vocational

vocal *adj* : vocal — ~ *nmf* : member (of a committee, etc.) — ~ *nf* : vowel — **vocalista** *nmf* : singer, vocalist

vocear *v* : shout — **vocerío** *nm* : shouting

vociferar *vi* : shout

vodka *nmf* : vodka

volar {19} *vi* **1** : fly **2** : blow away (of papers, etc.) **3** *fam* : disappear **4 irse volando** : rush off — *vt* : blow up — **volador, -dora** *adj* : flying — **volan-**

das: **en** ~ *adv phr* : in the air

volante *adj* : flying — ~ *nm* **1** : steering wheel **2** : shuttlecock (in badminton) **3** : flounce (of fabric) **4** *Lat* : flier, circular

volátil *adj* : volatile

volcán *nm, pl* **-canes** : volcano — **volcánico, -ca** *adj* : volcanic

volcar {82} *vt* **1** : upset, knock over **2** VACIAR : empty out — *vi* : overturn — **volcarse** *vr* **1** : overturn, tip over **2** ~ **en** : throw oneself into

voleibol *nm* : volleyball

voltaje *nm* : voltage

voltear *vt* : turn over, turn upside down — **voltearse** *vr* *Lat* : turn (around) — **voltereta** *nf* : somersault

voltio *nm* : volt

voluble *adj* : fickle

volumen *nm, pl* **-lúmenes** : volume — **voluminoso, -sa** *adj* : voluminous

voluntad *nf* **1** : will **2** DESEO : wish **3** INTENCIÓN : intention **4 a** ~ : at will **5 buena** ~ : goodwill **6 mala** ~ : ill will **7 fuerza de** ~ : willpower — **voluntario, -ria** *adj* : voluntary — ~ *n* : volunteer — **voluntarioso, -sa** *adj* **1** : willing **2** TERCO : stubborn, willful

voluptuoso, -sa *adj* : voluptuous

volver {89} *vi* **1** : return, come or go back **2** ~ **a** : return to, do again **3** ~ **en sí** : come to — *vt* **1** : turn, turn over, turn inside out **2** CONVERTIR EN : turn (into) **3** ~ **loco** : drive crazy — **volverse** *vr* **1** : turn (around) **2** HACERSE : become

vomitar *vi* : vomit — *vt* **1** : vomit **2** : spew (out) — **vómito** *nm* **1** : (action of) vomiting **2** : vomit

voraz *adj, pl* **-races** : voracious

vos *pron* *Lat* : you

vosotros, -tras *pron* *Spain* : you, yourselves

votar *vi* : vote — *vt* : vote for — **votación** *nf, pl* **-ciones** : vote, voting — **votante** *nmf* : voter — **voto** *nm* **1** : vote **2** : vow (in religion)

voy → **ir**

voz *nf, pl* **voces 1** : voice **2** GRITO : shout, yell **3** VOCABLO : word, term **4** RUMOR : rumor **5 dar voces** : shout **6 en** ~ **alta** : loudly **7 en** ~ **baja** : softly

vuelco *nm* : upset, overturning

vuelo *nm* **1** : flight **2** : (action of) flying **3** : flare (of clothing) **4 al** ~ : on the wing

vuelta *nf* **1** : turn **2** REVOLUCIÓN : circle, revolution **3** CURVA : bend, curve **4** REGRESO : return **5** : round, lap (in sports)

6 PASEO : walk, drive, ride **7** REVÉS : back, other side **8** *Spain* : change **9** **dar ~s** : spin **10 estar de ~** : be back — **vuelto** *nm Lat* : change

vuestro, -tra *adj Spain* : your, of yours — **~** *pron Spain* (*with definite article*) : yours

vulgar *adj* **1** : vulgar **2** CORRIENTE : common — **vulgaridad** *nf* **1** : vulgarity **2** BANALIDAD : banality — **vulgo** *nm* **el ~** : the masses, common people

vulnerable *adj* : vulnerable — **vulnerabilidad** *nf* : vulnerability

WXYZ

w *nf* : w, 24th letter of the Spanish alphabet

wáter *nm Spain* : toilet

whisky *nm*, *pl* **-skys** *or* **-skies** : whiskey

x *nf* : x, 25th letter of the Spanish alphabet

xenofobia *nf* : xenophobia

xilófono *nm* : xylophone

y[1] *nf* : y, 26th letter of the Spanish alphabet

y[2] *conj* : and

ya *adv* **1** : already **2** AHORA : (right) now **3** MÁS TARDE : later, soon **4 ~ no** : no longer **5 ~ que** : now that, since, inasmuch as

yacer {90} *vi* : lie (on or in the ground) — **yacimiento** *nm* : bed, deposit

yanqui *adj & nmf* : Yankee

yate *nm* : yacht

yegua *nf* : mare

yelmo *nm* : helmet

yema *nf* **1** : bud, shoot **2** : yolk (of an egg) **3** *or* **~ del dedo** : fingertip

yerba *nf* **1** *or* **~ mate** : maté **2 → hierba**

yermo, -ma *adj* : barren, deserted — **yermo** *nm* : wasteland

yerno *nm* : son-in-law

yerro *nm* : blunder, mistake

yerto, -ta *adj* : stiff

yesca *nf* : tinder

yeso *nm* **1** : gypsum **2** : plaster (for art, construction)

yo *pron* **1** (*subject*) : I **2** (*object*) : me **3 soy ~** : it is I, it's me — **~** *nm* : ego, self

yodo *nm* : iodine

yoga *nm* : yoga

yogurt *or* **yogur** *nm* : yogurt

yuca *nf* : yucca

yugo *nm* : yoke (of oxen)

yugoslavo, -va *adj* : Yugoslavian

yugular *adj* : jugular

yunque *nm* : anvil

yunta *nf* : yoke

yuxtaponer {60} *vt* : juxtapose — **yuxtaposición** *nf*, *pl* **-ciones** : juxtaposition

z *nf* : z, 27th letter of the Spanish alphabet

zacate *nm Lat* : grass

zafar *vt Lat* : loosen, untie — **zafarse** *vr* **1** : come undone **2** : get free of (an obligation, etc.)

zafio, -fia *adj* : coarse

zafiro *nm* : sapphire

zaga *nf* **a la ~** *or* **en ~** : behind, in the rear

zaguán *nm*, *pl* **-guanes** : (entrance) hall

zaherir {76} *vt* : hurt (s.o.'s feelings)

zaino, -na *adj* : chestnut (color)

zalamería *nf* : flattery — **zalamero, -ra** *adj* : flattering — **~** *n* : flatterer

zambullirse {38} *vr* : dive, plunge — **zambullida** *nf* : dive, plunge

zanahoria *nf* : carrot

zancada *nf* : stride, step — **zancadilla** *nf* **1** : trip, stumble **2 hacer una ~ a algn** : trip s.o. up

zancos *nmpl* : stilts

zancudo *nm Lat* : mosquito

zángano, -na *n fam* : lazy person, slacker — **zángano** *nm* : drone (bee)

zanja *nf* : ditch, trench — **zanjar** *vt* : settle, resolve

zapallo *nm Lat* : pumpkin — **zapallito** *nm Lat* : zucchini

zapapico *nm* : pickax

zapato *nm* : shoe — **zapatería** *nf* : shoe store — **zapatero, -ra** *n* : shoemaker, cobbler — **zapatilla** *nf* **1** : slipper **2** : sneaker (for sports, etc.)

zar *nm* : czar

zarandear *vt* **1** : sift **2** SACUDIR : shake

zarcillo *nm* : earring

zarpa *nf* : paw

zarpar *vi* : set sail, raise anchor

zarza *nf* : bramble — **zarzamora** *nf* : blackberry

zigzag *nm*, *pl* **-zags** *or* **-zagues** : zigzag — **zigzaguear** *vi* : zigzag

zinc *nm* : zinc
zíper *nm Lat* : zipper
zircón *nm, pl* **-cones** : zircon
zócalo *nm* **1** : base (of a column, etc.) **2** : baseboard (of a wall) **3** *Lat* : main square, plaza
zodíaco *nm* : zodiac
zona *nf* : zone, area
zoo *nm* : zoo — **zoología** *nf* : zoology — **zoológico, -ca** *adj* : zoological — **zoológico** *nm* : zoo — **zoólogo, -ga** *n* : zoologist
zopilote *nm Lat* : buzzard
zoquete *nmf fam* : oaf, blockhead

zorrillo *nm Lat* : skunk
zorro, -rra *n* : fox, vixen *f* — ~ *adj* : foxy, sly
zozobra *nf* : anxiety, worry — **zozobrar** *vi* : capsize
zueco *nm* : clog (shoe)
zumbar *vi* : buzz — *vt fam* : hit, beat — **zumbido** *nm* : buzzing
zumo *nf* : juice
zurcir {83} *vt* : darn, mend
zurdo, -da *adj* : left-handed — ~ *n* : left-handed person — **zurda** *nf* : left hand
zutano, -na → **fulano**

English-Spanish
Dictionary

A

a¹ ['eɪ] *n, pl* **a's** *or* **as** ['eɪz] : a *f*, primera letra del alfabeto inglés

a² [ə, 'eɪ] *art* (**an** [ən, æn] *before vowel or silent h*) **1** : un *m*, una *f* **2** PER : por, a la, al

aback [ə'bæk] *adv* **be taken ~** : quedarse desconcertado

abacus ['æbəkəs] *n, pl* **abaci** ['æbə,saɪ, -,kiː] *or* **abacuses** : ábaco *m*

abandon [ə'bændən] *vt* **1** DESERT : abandonar **2** GIVE UP : renunciar a — **~** *n* : desenfreno *m* — **abandonment** [ə'bændənmənt] *n* : abandono *m*

abashed [ə'bæʃt] *adj* : avergonzado

abate [ə'beɪt] *vi* **abated; abating** : amainar, disminuir

abattoir ['æbə,twar] *n* : matadero *m*

abbey ['æbi] *n, pl* **-beys** : abadía *f* — **abbot** ['æbət] *n* : abad *m*

abbreviate [ə'briːvi,eɪt] *vt* **-ated; -ating** : abreviar — **abbreviation** [ə,briːvi'eɪʃən] *n* : abreviatura *f*, abreviación *f*

abdicate ['æbdɪ,keɪt] *v* **-cated; -cating** : abdicar — **abdication** [,æbdɪ'keɪæən] *n* : abdicación *f*

abdomen ['æbdəmən, æb'doːmən] *n* : abdomen *m*, vientre *m* — **abdominal** [æb'dɑmənəl] *adj* : abdominal

abduct [æb'dʌkt] *vt* : secuestrar — **abduction** [æb'dʌkʃən] *n* : secuestro *m*

aberration [,æbə'reɪʃən] *n* : aberración *f*

abet [ə'bet] *vt* **abetted; abetting** *or* **aid and ~** : ser cómplice de

abeyance [ə'beɪəns] *n* : desuso *m*

abhor [əb'hɔr, æb-] *vt* **-horred; -horring** : aborrecer

abide [ə'baɪd] *v* **abode** [ə'boːd] *or* **abided; abiding** *vt* : soportar, tolerar — *vi* **1** DWELL : morar **2 ~ by** : atenerse a

ability [ə'bɪləti] *n, pl* **-ties 1** CAPABILITY : aptitud *f*, capacidad *f* **2** SKILL : habilidad *f*

abject ['æb,dʒekt, æb'-] *adj* : miserable, desdichado

ablaze [ə'bleɪz] *adj* : en llamas

able ['eɪbəl] *adj* **abler; ablest 1** CAPABLE : capaz, hábil **2** COMPETENT : competente

abnormal [æb'nɔrməl] *adj* : anormal — **abnormality** [,æbnər'mæləti, -nɔr-] *n, pl* **-ties** : anormalidad *f*

aboard [ə'bord] *adv* : a bordo — **~** *prep* : a bordo de

abode *n* : morada *f*, domicilio *m*

abolish [ə'bɑlɪʃ] *vt* : abolir, suprimir — **abolition** [,æbə'lɪʃən] *n* : abolición *f*

abominable [ə'bɑmənəbəl] *adj* : abominable, aborrecible — **abomination** [ə,bɑmə'neɪʃən] *n* : abominación *f*

aborigine [,æbə'rɪdʒəni] *n* : aborigen *mf*

abort [ə'bɔrt] *vt* : abortar — **abortion** [ə'bɔrʃən] *n* : aborto *m* — **abortive** [ə'bɔrtɪv] *adj* UNSUCCESSFUL : malogrado

abound [ə'baund] *vi* **~ in** : abundar en

about [ə'baut] *adv* **1** APPROXIMATELY : aproximadamente, más o menos **2** AROUND : alrededor **3 be ~ to** : estar a punto de **4 be up and ~** : estar levantado — **~** *prep* **1** AROUND : alrededor de **2** CONCERNING : acerca de, sobre

above [ə'bʌv] *adv* : arriba — **~** *prep* **1** : encima de **2 ~ all** : sobre todo — **aboveboard** *adj* : honrado

abrasive [ə'breɪsɪv] *adj* **1** : abrasivo **2** BRUSQUE : brusco, mordaz

abreast [ə'brest] *adv* **1** : al lado **2 keep ~ of** : mantenerse al corriente de

abridge [ə'brɪdʒ] *vt* **abridged; abridging** : abreviar

abroad [ə'brɔd] *adv* **1** : en el extranjero **2** WIDELY : por todas partes **3 go ~** : ir al extranjero

abrupt [ə'brʌpt] *adj* **1** SUDDEN : repentino **2** BRUSQUE : brusco

abscess ['æb,ses] *n* : absceso *m*

absence ['æbsəns] *n* **1** : ausencia *f* **2** LACK : falta *f*, carencia *f* — **absent** ['æbsənt] *adj* : ausente — **absentee** [,æbsən'tiː] *n* : ausente *mf* — **absentminded** [,æbsənt'maɪndəd] *adj* : distraído, despistado

absolute ['æbsə,luːt, ,æbsə'luːt] *adj* : absoluto — **absolutely** [,æbsə'luːtli] *adv* : absolutamente

absolve [əb'zɑlv, æb-, -'sɑlv] *vt* **-solved; -solving** : absolver

absorb [əb'zɔrb, æb-, -'sɔrb] *vt* : absorber — **absorbent** [əb'zɔrbənt, æb-, -'sɔr-] *adj* : absorbente — **absorption** [əb'zɔrpʃən, æb-, -'sɔrp-] *n* : absorción *f*

abstain [əb'steɪn, æb-] *vi* **~ from** : abstenerse de — **abstinence** ['æbstənənts] *n* : abstinencia *f*

abstract ['æb,strækt, ,æb'-] *adj* : abstracto — **~** *vt* : extraer — **~** ['æb,strækt] *n* : resumen *m* — **abstraction** [æb'strækʃən] *n* : abstracción *f*

absurd [əb'sərd, -'zərd] *adj* : absurdo — **absurdity** [əb'sərdəti, -'zərdəti] *n, pl* **-ties** : absurdo *m*

abundant [ə'bʌndənt] *adj* : abundante — **abundance** [ə'bʌndənts] *n* : abundancia *f*

abuse [ə'bju:z] *vt* **abused; abusing 1** MISUSE : abusar de **2** MISTREAT : maltratar **3** REVILE : insultar — **~** [ə'bju:s] *n* **1** : abuso *m* **2** INSULTS : insultos *mpl* — **abusive** [ə'bju:sɪv] *adj* : injurioso

abut [ə'bʌt] *vi* **abutted; abutting ~ on** : colindar con

abyss [ə'bɪs, 'æbɪs] *n* : abismo *m* — **abysmal** [ə'bɪzməl] *adj* : atroz, pésimo

academy [ə'kædəmi] *n, pl* **-mies** : academia *f* — **academic** [,ækə'dɛmɪk] *adj* **1** : académico **2** THEORETICAL : teórico

accelerate [ɪk'sɛlə,reɪt, æk-] *v* **-ated; -ating** : acelerar — **acceleration** [ɪk,sɛlə'reɪʃən, æk-] *n* : aceleración *f*

accent ['æk,sɛnt, æk'sɛnt] *vt* : acentuar — **~** ['æk,sɛnt, sənt] *n* : acento *m* — **accentuate** [ɪk'sɛntʃu,eɪt, æk-] *vt* **-ated; -ating** : acentuar, subrayar

accept [ɪk'sɛpt, æk-] *vt* : aceptar — **acceptable** [ɪk'sɛptəbəl, æk-] *adj* : aceptable — **acceptance** [ɪk'sɛptənts, æk-] *n* **1** : aceptación *f* **2** APPROVAL : aprobación *f*

access ['æk,sɛs] *n* : acceso *m* — **accessible** [ɪk'sɛsəbəl, æk-] *adj* : accesible, asequible

accessory *n, pl* **-ries 1** : accesorio *m* **2** ACCOMPLICE : cómplice *mf*

accident ['æksədənt] *n* **1** MISHAP : accidente *m* **2** CHANCE : casualidad *f* — **accidental** [,æksə'dɛntəl] *adj* : accidental — **accidentally** [,æksə'dɛntəli, -'dɛntli] *adv* **1** BY CHANCE : por casualidad **2** UNINTENTIONALLY : sin querer

acclaim [ə'kleɪm] *vt* : aclamar — **~** *n* : aclamación *f*

acclimatize [ə'klaɪmə,taɪz] *vt* **-tized; -tizing** : aclimatar

accommodate [ə'kɑmə,deɪt] *vt* **-dated; -dating 1** ADAPT : acomodar, adaptar **2** SATISFY : complacer, satisfacer **3** HOLD : tener cabida para — **accomodation** [ə,kɑmə'deɪʃən] *n* **1** : adaptación *f* **2 ~s** *npl* LODGING : alojamiento *m*

accompany [ə'kʌmpəni, -'kʌm-] *vt* **-nied; -nying** : acompañar

accomplice [ə'kʌmpləs, -'kʌm-] *n* : cómplice *mf*

accomplish [ə'kʌmplɪʃ, -'kʌm-] *vt* : realizar, llevar a cabo — **accomplishment** [ə'kʌmplɪʃmənt, -'kʌm-] *n* **1** COMPLETION : realización *f* **2** ACHIEVEMENT : logro *m*, éxito *m*

accord *n* **1** AGREEMENT : acuerdo *m* **2 of one's own ~** : voluntariamente — **accordance** [ə'kɔrdənts] *n* **in ~ with** : conforme a, de acuerdo con — **accordingly** [ə'kɔrdɪŋli] *adv* : en consecuencia — **according to** [ə'kɔrdɪŋ] *prep* : según

accordion [ə'kɔrdiən] *n* : acordeón *m*

accost [ə'kɔst] *vt* : abordar

account [ə'kaʊnt] *n* **1** : cuenta *f* **2** REPORT : relato *m*, informe *m* **3** WORTH : importancia *f* **4 on ~ of** : a causa de, debido a **5 on no ~** : de ninguna manera — **~** *vi* **~ for** : dar cuenta de, explicar — **accountable** [ə'kaʊntəbəl] *adj* : responsable — **accountant** [ə'kaʊntənt] *n* : contador *m*, -dora *f Lat;* contable *mf Spain* — **accounting** [ə'kaʊntɪŋ] *n* : contabilidad *f*

accrue [ə'kru:] *vi* **-crued; -cruing** : acumularse

accumulate [ə'kju:mjə,leɪt] *v* **-lated; -lating** *vt* : acumular — *vi* : acumularse — **accumulation** [ə,kju:mjə'leɪʃən] *n* : acumulación *f*

accurate ['ækjərət] *adj* : exacto, preciso — **accuracy** ['ækjərəsi] *n* : exactitud *f*, precisión *f*

accuse [ə'kju:z] *vt* **-cused; -cusing** : acusar — **accusation** [,ækjə'zeɪʃən] *n* : acusación *f*

accustomed [ə'kʌstəmd] *adj* **1** : acostumbrado **2 become ~ to** : acostumbrarse a

ace ['eɪs] *n* : as *m*

ache ['eɪk] *vi* **ached; aching** : doler — **~** *n* : dolor *m*

achieve [ə'tʃi:v] *vt* **achieved; achieving** : lograr, realizar — **achievement** [ə'tʃi:vmənt] *n* : logro *m*, éxito *m*

acid ['æsəd] *adj* : ácido — **~** *n* : ácido *m*

acknowledge [ɪk'nɑlɪdʒ, æk-] *vt* **-edged; -edging 1** ADMIT : admitir **2** RECOGNIZE : reconocer **3 ~ receipt of** : acusar recibo de — **acknowledgment** [ɪk'nɑlɪdʒmənt, æk-] *n* **1** : reconocimiento *m* **2** THANKS : agradecimiento *m* **3 ~ of receipt** : acuse *m* de recibo

acne ['ækni] *n* : acné *m*

acorn ['eɪ,kɔrn, -kərn] *n* : bellota *f*

acoustic [ə'ku:stɪk] *or* **acoustical** [-stɪkəl] *adj* : acústico — **acoustics** [ə'ku:stɪks] *ns & pl* : acústica *f*

acquaint [ə'kweɪnt] *vt* **1 ~ s.o. with**

: poner a algn al corriente de **2 be ~ed with** : conocer a (una persona), saber (un hecho) — **acquaintance** [ə'kweıntənts] n : conocimiento m **2** : conocido m, -da f (persona)

acquire [ə'kwaır] vt **-quired; -quiring** : adquirir — **acquisition** [ˌækwə'zıʃən] n : adquisición f

acquit [ə'kwıt] vt **-quitted; -quitting** : absolver

acre ['eıkər] n : acre m — **acreage** ['eıkərıdʒ] n : superficie f en acres

acrid ['ækrəd] adj : acre

acrobat ['ækrəˌbæt] n : acróbata mf — **acrobatic** [ˌækrə'bætık] adj : acrobático

acronym ['ækrəˌnım] n : siglas fpl

across [ə'krɔs] adv **1** : de un lado a otro **2** CROSSWISE : a través **3 go ~** : atravesar — ~ prep **1** : a través de **2 ~ the street** : al otro lado de la calle

acrylic [ə'krılık] n : acrílico m

act ['ækt] vi **1** : actuar **2** PRETEND : fingir **3** FUNCTION : funcionar **4 ~ as** : servir de — vt : interpretar (un papel) — ~ n **1** ACTION : acto m, acción f **2** DECREE : ley f **3** : acto m (en una obra de teatro), número m (en un espectáculo) — **acting** adj : interino

action ['ækʃən] n **1** : acción f **2** LAWSUIT : demanda f **3 take ~** : tomar medidas

activate ['æktəˌveıt] vt **-vated; -vating** : activar

active ['æktıv] adj **1** : activo **2** LIVELY : enérgico **3 ~ volcano** : volcán m en actividad — **activity** [æk'tıvəţi] n, pl **-ties** : actividad f

actor ['æktər] n : actor m — **actress** ['æktrəs] n : actriz f

actual ['æktʃʊəl] adj : real, verdadero — **actually** ['æktʃʊəli, -əli] adv : realmente, en realidad

acupuncture ['ækjʊˌpʌŋktʃər] n : acupuntura f

acute [ə'kjuːt] adj **acuter; acutest 1** : agudo **2** PERCEPTIVE : perspicaz

ad ['æd] → **advertisement**

adamant ['ædəmənt, -ˌmænt] adj : inflexible

adapt [ə'dæpt] vt : adaptar — vi : adaptarse — **adaptable** [ə'dæptəbəl] adj : adaptable — **adaptation** [ˌæˌdæp'teıʃən, -dəp-] n : adaptación f — **adapter** [ə'dæptər] n : adaptador m

add ['æd] vt **1** : añadir **2 or ~ up** : sumar — vi : sumar

addict ['ædıkt] n **1** : adicto m, -ta f **2 or drug ~** : drogadicto m, -ta f; toxicómano m, -na f — **addiction** [ə'dıkʃən] n : dependencia f

addition [ə'dıʃən] n **1** : suma f (en matemáticas) **2** ADDING : adición f **3 in ~** : además — **additional** [ə'dıʃənəl] adj : adicional — **additive** ['ædəţıv] n : aditivo m

address [ə'drɛs] vt **1** : dirigirse a (una persona) **2** : ponerle la dirección a (una carta) **3** : tratar (un asunto) — ~ [ə'drɛs, 'æˌdrɛs] n **1** : dirección f, domicilio m **2** SPEECH : discurso m

adept [ə'dɛpt] adj : experto, hábil

adequate ['ædıkwət] adj : adecuado, suficiente

adhere [æd'hır, əd-] vi **-hered; -hering 1** STICK : adherirse **2 ~ to** : observar — **adherence** [æd'hırənts, əd-] n **1** : adhesión f **2** : observancia f (de una regla, etc.) — **adhesive** [æd'hiːsıv, əd-, -zıv] adj : adhesivo — ~ n : adhesivo m

adjacent [ə'dʒeısənt] adj : adyacente, contiguo

adjective ['ædʒıktıv] n : adjetivo m

adjoining [ə'dʒɔınıŋ] adj : contiguo, vecino

adjourn [ə'dʒərn] vt : aplazar, suspender — vi : suspenderse

adjust [ə'dʒʌst] vt : ajustar, arreglar — vi : adaptarse — **adjustable** [ə'dʒʌstəbəl] adj : ajustable — **adjustment** [ə'dʒʌstmənt] n : ajuste m (a una máquina, etc.), adaptación f (de una persona)

ad-lib ['æd'lıb] v **-libbed; -libbing** : improvisar

administer [æd'mınəstər, əd-] vt : administrar — **administration** [ˌædmınə'streıʃən, əd-] n : administración f — **administrative** [æd'mınəˌstreıţıv, əd-] adj : administrativo — **administrator** [æd'mınəˌstreıţər, əd-] n : administrador m, -dora f

admirable ['ædmərəbəl] adj : admirable

admiral ['ædmərəl] n : almirante m

admire [æd'maır] vt **-mired; -miring** : admirar — **admiration** [ˌædmə'reıʃən] n : admiración f — **admirer** [æd'maırər] n : admirador m, -dora f

admit [æd'mıt, əd-] vt **-mitted; -mitting 1** : admitir, dejar entrar **2** ACKNOWLEDGE : reconocer — **admission** [æd'mıʃən] n **1** ADMITTANCE : entrada f, admisión f **2** ACKNOWLEDGMENT : reconocimiento m — **admittance** [æd'mıtənts, əd-] n : admisión f, entrada f

admonish [æd'manıʃ, əd-] vt : amonestar, reprender

ado ['duː] n **1** : alboroto m, bulla f **2 without further ~** : sin más (preámbulos)

adolescent [‚ædəl'esənt] *n* : adolescente *mf* — **adolescence** [‚ædəl'esənts] *n* : adolescencia *f*

adopt [ə'dɑpt] *vt* : adoptar — **adoption** [ə'dɑpʃən] *n* : adopción *f*

adore [ə'dor] *vt* **adored; adoring 1** : adorar **2** LIKE, LOVE : encantarle (algo a uno) — **adorable** [ə'dorəbəl] *adj* : adorable — **adoration** [‚ædə'reɪæn] *n* : adoración *f*

adorn [ə'dorn] *vt* : adornar — **adornment** [ə'dornmənt] *n* : adorno *m*

adrift [ə'drɪft] *adj & adv* : a la deriva

adroit [ə'drɔɪt] *adj* : diestro, hábil

adult [ə'dʌlt, 'æˌdʌlt] *adj* : adulto — ~ *n* : adulto *m*, -ta *f*

adultery [ə'dʌltəri] *n, pl* **-teries** : adulterio *m*

advance [æd'vænts, əd-] *v* **-vanced; -vancing** *vt* : adelantar — *vi* : avanzar, adelantarse — ~ *n* **1** : avance *m* **2** PROGRESS : adelanto *m* **3** in ~ : por adelantado — **advancement** [æd'væntsmənt, əd-] *n* : adelanto *m*, progreso *m*

advantage [əd'væntɪdʒ, æd-] *n* **1** : ventaja *f* **2** take ~ of : aprovecharse de — **advantageous** [‚ædˌvæn'teɪdʒəs, -vən-] *adj* : ventajoso

advent ['æd‚vent] *n* **1** ARRIVAL : llegada *f* **2** Advent : Adviento *m*

adventure [æd'ventʃər, əd-] *n* : aventura *f* — **adventurous** [æd'ventʃərəs, əd-] *adj* **1** RISKY : arriesgado

adverb ['æd‚vərb] *n* : adverbio *m*

adversary ['ædvər‚seri] *n, pl* **-saries** : adversario *m*, -ria *f*

adverse [æd'vərs, 'æd-] *adj* : adverso, desfavorable — **adversity** [æd'vərsəti, əd-] *n, pl* **-ties** : adversidad *f*

advertise ['ædvər‚taɪz] *v* **-tised; -tising** *vt* : anunciar — *vi* : hacer publicidad — **advertisement** [‚ædvər'taɪzmənt] *n* : anuncio *m* — **advertiser** ['ædvər‚taɪzər] *n* : anunciante *mf* — **advertising** ['ædvər‚taɪzɪŋ] *n* : publicidad *f*

advice [æd'vaɪs] *n* : consejo *m*

advise [æd'vaɪz, əd-] *vt* **-vised; -vising 1** COUNSEL : aconsejar, asesorar **2** RECOMMEND : recomendar **3** INFORM : informar — **advisable** [æd'vaɪzəbəl, əd-] *adj* : aconsejable — **adviser** [æd'vaɪzər, əd-] *n* : consejero *m*, -ra *f*; asesor *m*, -sora *f* — **advisory** [æd'vaɪzəri, əd-] *adj* : consultivo

advocate ['ædvə‚keɪt] *vt* **-cated; -cating** : recomendar — ~ ['ædvəkət] *n* : defensor *m*, -sora *f*

aerial ['æriəl] *adj* : aéreo — ~ *n* : antena *f*

aerobics [‚æro:bɪks] *ns & pl* : aeróbic *m*

aerodynamic [‚æro:daɪr'næmɪk] *adj* : aerodinámico

aerosol ['ærə‚sɑl] *n* : aerosol *m*

aesthetic [es'θetɪk] *adj* : estético

afar [ə'fɑr] *adv* : lejos

affable ['æfəbəl] *adj* : afable

affair [ə'fær] *n* **1** : asunto *m*, cuestión *f* **2** *or* love ~ : amorío *m*, aventura *f*

affect [ə'fekt, æ-] *vt* **1** : afectar **2** FEIGN : fingir — **affection** [ə'fekʃən] *n* : afecto *m*, cariño *m* — **affectionate** [ə'fekʃənət] *adj* : afectuoso, cariñoso

affinity [ə'fɪnəti] *n, pl* **-ties** : afinidad *f*

affirm [ə'fərm] *vt* : afirmar — **affirmative** [ə'fərmətɪv] *adj* : afirmativo

affix [ə'fɪks] *vt* : fijar, pegar

afflict [ə'flɪkt] *vt* : afligir — **affliction** [ə'flɪkʃən] *n* : aflicción *f*

affluent ['æˌfluənt; æ'flu:-, ə-] *adj* : próspero, adinerado

afford [ə'ford] *vt* **1** : tener los recursos para, permitirse (el lujo de) **2** PROVIDE : brindar

affront [ə'frʌnt] *n* : afrenta *f*

afloat [ə'flo:t] *adv & adj* : a flote

afoot [ə'fut] *adj* : en marcha

afraid [ə'freɪd] *adj* **1** be ~ : tener miedo **2** I'm ~ not : me temo que no

African ['æfrɪkən] *adj* : africano

after ['æftər] *adv* **1** AFTERWARD : después **2** BEHIND : detrás, atrás — ~ *conj* : después de (que) — ~ *prep* **1** : después de **2** ~ all : después de todo **3** it's ten ~ five : son las cinco y diez

aftereffect ['æftərə‚fekt] *n* : efecto *m* secundario

aftermath ['æftər‚mæθ] *n* : consecuencias *fpl*

afternoon [‚æftər'nu:n] *n* : tarde *f*

afterward ['æftərwərd] *or* **afterwards** [-wərdz] *adv* : después, más tarde

again [ə'gen, -'gɪn] *adv* **1** : otra vez, de nuevo **2** ~ and ~ : una y otra vez **3** then ~ : por otra parte

against [ə'gentst, -'gɪntst] *prep* : contra, en contra de

age ['eɪdʒ] *n* **1** : edad *f* **2** ERA : era *f*, época *f* **3** be of ~ : ser mayor de edad **4** for ~s : hace siglos **5** old ~ : vejez *f* — ~ *vi* **aged; aging** : envejecer — **aged** *adj* **1** ['eɪdʒəd, 'eɪdʒd] OLD : anciano, viejo **2** ['eɪdʒd] children ~ 10 to 17 : niños de 10 a 17 años

agency ['eɪdʒəntsi] *n, pl* **-cies** : agencia *f*

agenda [ə'dʒendə] *n* : orden *m* del día

agent ['eɪdʒənt] *n* : agente *mf*, representante *mf*

aggravate ['ægrə‚veɪt] *vt* **-vated; -vating**

1 WORSEN : agravar, empeorar **2** AN-
NOY : irritar
aggregate ['ægrɪgət] *adj* : total, global
— **∼** *n* : total *m*
aggression [ə'greʃən] *n* : agresión *f* —
aggressive [ə'gresɪv] *adj* : agresivo —
aggressor [ə'gresər] *n* : agresor *m*,
-sora *f*
aghast [ə'gæst] *adj* : horrorizado
agile ['ædʒəl] *adj* : ágil — **agility** [ə-
'dʒɪləti] *n*, *pl* -**ties** : agilidad *f*
agitate ['ædʒə,teɪt] *v* -**tated; -tating** *vt* **1**
SHAKE : agitar **2** TROUBLE : inquietar —
agitation [ˌædʒə'teɪʃən] *n* : agitación *f*,
inquietud *f*
agnostic [æg'nɑstɪk] *n* : agnóstico *m*,
-ca *f*
ago [ə'goː] *adv* **1** : hace **2** long **∼** : hace
mucho tiempo
agony ['ægəni] *n*, *pl* -**nies 1** PAIN : dolor
m **2** ANGUISH : angustia *f* — **agonize**
['ægə,naɪz] *vi* -**nized; -nizing** : atormentarse — **agonizing** ['ægə,naɪzɪŋ]
adj : angustioso
agree [ə'griː] *v* **agreed; agreeing** *vt* **1**
: acordar **2 ∼ that** : estar de acuerdo
de que — *vi* **1** : estar de acuerdo **2**
CORRESPOND : concordar **3 ∼ to** : acceder a **4** this climate **∼s** with me
: este climate me sienta bien — **agreeable** [ə'griːəbəl] *adj* **1** PLEASING
: agradable **2** WILLING : dispuesto —
agreement [ə'griːmənt] *n* : acuerdo *m*
agriculture ['ægrɪ,kʌltʃər] *n* : agricultura
f — **agricultural** [ˌægrɪ'kʌltʃərəl] *adj*
: agrícola
aground [ə'graʊnd] *adv* run **∼** : encallar
ahead [ə'hed] *adv* **1** IN FRONT : delante,
adelante **2** BEFOREHAND : por adelantado **3** LEADING : a la delantera **4** get **∼**
: adelantar — **ahead of** *prep* **1** : delante de, antes de **2** get **∼ of** : adelantarse
aid ['eɪd] *vt* : ayudar — **∼** *n* : ayuda *f*,
asistencia *f*
AIDS ['eɪdz] *n* : SIDA *m*, sida *m*
ail ['eɪl] *vi* : estar enfermo — **ailment**
['eɪlmənt] *n* : enfermedad *f*
aim ['eɪm] *vt* : apuntar (un arma), dirigir
(una observación) — *vi* **1** : apuntar **2**
ASPIRE : aspirar — **∼** *n* **1** : puntería *f*ma **2**
GOAL : propósito *m*, objetivo *m* —
aimless ['eɪmləs] *adj* : sin objetivo
air ['ær] *vt or* **∼ out** : airear **2** EXPRESS
: expresar **3** BROADCAST : emitir — **∼**
n **1** : aire *m* **2** be on the **∼** : estar en
el aire — **air—conditioning** [ˌærkən-
'dɪʃənɪŋ] *n* : aire *m* acondicionado —
air conditioned ['ærkən,dɪʃənd] *n*

: climatizado — **aircraft** ['ær,kræft] *ns*
& pl **1** : avión *m*, aeronave *f* **2 ∼ carrier** : portaaviones *m* — **air force** *n*
: fuerza *f* aérea — **airline** ['ær,laɪn] *n*
: aerolínea *f*, línea *f* aérea — **airliner**
['ær,laɪnər] *n* : avión *m* de pasajeros —
airmail *n* : correo *m* aéreo — **airplane**
['ær,pleɪn] *n* : avión *m* — **airport** ['ær-
,port] *n* : aeropuerto *m* — **airstrip** ['ær-
,strɪp] *n* : pista *f* de aterrizaje — **air-
tight** ['ær'taɪt] *adj* : hermético — **airy**
['æri] *adj* **airier** [-iər]; -**est** : aireado,
bien ventilado
aisle ['aɪl] *n* **1** : pasillo *m* **2** : nave *f* lateral (de una iglesia)
ajar [ə'dʒɑr] *adj* : entreabierto
akin [ə'kɪn] *adj* **∼ to** : semejante a
alarm [ə'lɑrm] *n* **1** : alarma *f* **2** ANXIETY
: inquietud *f* — *vt* : alarmar, asustar —
alarm clock *n* : despertador *m*
alas [ə'læs] *interj* : ¡ay!
album ['ælbəm] *n* : álbum *m*
alcohol ['ælkə,hɔl] *n* : alcohol *m* — **alcoholic** [ˌælkə'hɔlɪk] *adj* : alcohólico
— **∼** *n* : alcohólico *m*, -ca *f* — **alcoholism** ['ælkəhɔ,lɪzəm] *n* : alcoholismo *m*
alcove ['æl,koːv] *n* : nicho *m*, hueco *m*
ale ['eɪl] *n* : cerveza *f*
alert [ə'lərt] *adj* **1** WATCHFUL : alerta,
atento **2** LIVELY : vivo — *n* : alerta *f*
— **∼** *vt* : alertar, poner sobre aviso
alfalfa [æl'fælfə] *n* : alfalfa *f*
alga ['ælgə] *n*, *pl* -**gae** ['æl,dʒiː] : alga *f*
algebra ['ældʒəbrə] *n* : álgebra *f*
alias ['eɪliəs] *adv* : alias — **∼** *n* : alias *m*
alibi ['ælə,baɪ] *n* : coartada *f*
alien ['eɪliən] *adj* : extranjero — **∼** *n* **1**
FOREIGNER : extranjero *m*, -ra *f* **2** EX-
TRATERRESTRIAL : extraterrestre *mf* —
alienate ['eɪliə,neɪt] *vt* -**ated; -ating**
: enajenar — **alienation** [ˌeɪliə'neɪæən]
n : enajenación *f*
alight [ə'laɪt] *vi* **1** LAND : posarse **2 ∼
from** : apearse de
align [ə'laɪn] *vt* : alinear — **alignment**
[ə'laɪnmənt] *n* : alineación *f*
alike [ə'laɪk] *adv* : igual, del mismo
modo — **∼** *adj* : parecido
alimony ['ælə,moːni] *n*, *pl* -**nies** : pensión *f* alimenticia
alive [ə'laɪv] *adj* **1** LIVING : vivo,
viviente **2** LIVELY : animado, activo
all ['ɔl] *adv* **1** COMPLETELY : todo, completamente **2 ∼ the better** : tanto
mejor **3 ∼ the more** : aún más, todavía más — **∼** *adj* : todo — **∼** *pron*
1 : todo, -da **2 ∼ in ∼** : en general **3**
not at **∼** : de ninguna manera —

all–around [ˌɔlə'raʊnd] *adj* VERSATILE : completo

allay [ə'leɪ] *vt* **1** ALLEVIATE : aliviar **2** CALM : aquietar

allege [ə'lɛdʒ] *vt* **-leged; -leging** : alegar — **allegation** [ˌælɪ'geɪʃən] *n* : alegato *m*, acusación *f* — **alleged** [ə'lɛdʒd, ə'lɛdʒəd] *adj* : presunto — **allegedly** [ə'lɛdʒədli] *adv* : supuestamente

allegiance [ə'liːdʒənts] *n* : lealtad *f*

allegory ['æləˌgori] *n, pl* **-ries** : alegoría *f* — **allegorical** [ˌælə'gorɪkəl] *adj* : alegórico

allergy ['ælərdʒi] *n, pl* **-gies** : alergia *f* — **allergic** [ə'lərdʒɪk] *adj* : alérgico

alleviate [ə'liːviˌeɪt] *vt* **-ated; -ating** : aliviar

alley ['æli] *n, pl* **-leys** : callejón *m*

alliance [ə'laɪənts] *n* : alianza *f*

alligator ['æləˌgeɪtər] *n* : caimán *m*

allocate ['æləˌkeɪt] *vt* **-cated; -cating** : asignar — **allocation** [ˌælə'keɪʃən] *n* : asignación *f*, reparto *m*

allot [ə'lat] *vt* **-lotted; -lotting** : asignar — **allotment** [ə'latmənt] *n* : reparto *m*, asignación *f*

allow [ə'laʊ] *vt* **1** PERMIT : permitir **2** GRANT : dar, conceder **3** ADMIT : admitir **4** CONCEDE : reconocer — *vi* **~ for** : tener en cuenta — **allowance** [ə'laʊənts] *n* **1** : pensión *f*, subsidio *m* **2 make ~s for** : tener en cuenta, disculpar

alloy ['æˌlɔɪ, ə'lɔɪ] *n* : aleación *f*

all right *adv* **1** YES : sí, de acuerdo **2** WELL : bien **3** DEFINITELY : bien, sin duda — **~** *adj* : bien, bueno

allude [ə'luːd] *vi* **-luded; -luding** : aludir

allure [ə'lʊr] *vt* **-lured; -luring** : atraer — **alluring** [ə'lʊrɪŋ] *adj* : atrayente, seductor

allusion [ə'luːʒən] *n* : alusión *f*

ally [ə'laɪ, 'æˌlaɪ] *vi* **-lied; -lying ~ oneself with** : aliarse con — **~** ['æˌlaɪ, ə'laɪ] *n* : aliado *m*, **-da** *f*

almanac ['ɔlmənæk, 'æl-] *n* : almanaque *m*

almighty [ɔl'maɪti] *adj* : omnipotente, todopoderoso

almond ['amənd, 'al-, 'æ-, 'æl-] *n* : almendra *f*

almost ['ɔlˌmoːst, ɔl'moːst] *adv* : casi

alms ['amz, 'almz, 'ælmz] *ns & pl* : limosna *f*

alone [ə'loːn] *adv* : sólo, solamente, únicamente — **~** *adj* : solo

along [ə'lɔŋ] *adv* **1** FORWARD : adelante **2 ~ with** : con, junto con **3 all ~** : desde el principio — **~** *prep* : por, a lo largo de — **alongside** [ə'lɔŋˌsaɪd]

adv : al costado — **~** *or* **~ of** *prep* : al lado de

aloof [ə'luːf] *adj* : distante, reservado

aloud [ə'laʊd] *adv* : en voz alta

alphabet ['ælfəˌbɛt] *n* : alfabeto *m* — **alphabetical** [ˌælfə'bɛtɪkəl] *or* **alphabetic** [-'bɛtɪk] *adj* : alfabético

already [ɔl'rɛdi] *adv* : ya

also ['ɔlˌsoː] *adv* : también, además

altar ['ɔltər] *n* : altar *m*

alter ['ɔltər] *vt* : alterar, modificar — **alteration** [ˌɔltə'reɪʃən] *n* : alteración *f*, modificación *f*

alternate ['ɔltərnət] *adj* : alterno — **~** ['ɔltərˌneɪt] *v* **-nated; -nating** : alternar — **alternating current** *n* : corriente *f* alterna — **alternative** [ɔl'tərnətɪv] *adj* : alternativo — **~** *n* : alternativa *f*

although [ɔl'ðoː] *conj* : aunque

altitude ['æltəˌtuːd, -ˌtjuːd] *n* : altitud *f*

altogether [ˌɔltə'gɛðər] *adv* **1** COMPLETELY : completamente, del todo **2** ON THE WHOLE : en suma, en general

aluminum [ə'luːmənəm] *n* : aluminio *m*

always ['ɔlwiz, -ˌweɪz] *adv* **1** : siempre **2** FOREVER : para siempre

am → be

amass [ə'mæs] *vt* : amasar, acumular

amateur ['æmətʃər, -tər, -tʊr, -tjʊr] *adj* : amateur — **~** *n* : amateur *mf*; aficionado *m*, **-da** *f*

amaze [ə'meɪz] *vt* **amazed; amazing** : asombrar — **amazement** [ə'meɪzmənt] *n* : asombro *m* — **amazing** [ə'meɪzɪŋ] *adj* : asombroso

ambassador [æm'bæsədər] *n* : embajador *m*, **-dora** *f*

amber ['æmbər] *n* : ámbar *m*

ambiguous [æm'bɪgjʊəs] *adj* : ambiguo — **ambiguity** [ˌæmbə'gjuːəʈi] *n, pl* **-ties** : ambigüedad *f*

ambition [æm'bɪʃən] *n* : ambición *f* — **ambitious** [æm'bɪʃəs] *adj* : ambicioso

ambivalence [æm'bɪvələnts] *n* : ambivalencia *f* — **ambivalent** [æm'bɪvələnt] *adj* : ambivalente

amble ['æmbəl] *vi* *or* **~ along** : andar sin prisa

ambulance ['æmbjələnts] *n* : ambulancia *f*

ambush ['æmˌbʊʃ] *vt* : emboscar — **~** *n* : emboscada *f*

amen ['eɪ'mɛn, 'a-] *interj* : amén

amenable [ə'miːnəbəl, -'mɛ-] *adj* **~ to** : receptivo

amend [ə'mɛnd] *vt* : enmendar — **amendment** [ə'mɛndmənt] *n* : enmienda *f* — **amends** [ə'mɛndz] *ns & pl* **make ~ for** : reparar

amenities [ə'menətiz, -'mi:-] *npl* : servicios *mpl*, comodidades *fpl*
American [ə'merɪkən] *adj* : americano
amethyst ['æməθəst] *n* : amatista *f*
amiable ['eɪmiəbəl] *adj* : amable, agradable
amicable ['æmɪkəbəl] *adj* : amigable, amistoso
amid [ə'mɪd] *or* **amidst** [ə'mɪdst] *prep* : en medio de, entre
amiss [ə'mɪs] *adv* 1 ~ : mal 2 **take sth** ~ : tomar algo a mal — ~ *adj* 1 **WRONG** : malo 2 **something is** ~ : algo anda mal
ammonia [ə'mo:njə] *n* : amoníaco *m*
ammunition [æmjə'nɪʃən] *n* : municiones *fpl*
amnesia [æm'ni:ʒə] *n* : amnesia *f*
amnesty ['æmnəsti] *n, pl* **-ties** : amnistía *f*
among [ə'mʌŋ] *prep* : entre
amorous ['æmərəs] *adj* : amoroso
amount [ə'maʊnt] *vi* 1 ~ **to** : equivaler a 2 ~ **to** TOTAL : sumar, ascender a — ~ *n* : cantidad *f*
amphibian [æm'fɪbiən] *n* : anfibio *m* — **amphibious** [æm'fɪbiəs] *adj* : anfibio
amphitheater ['æmfə,θiətər] *n* : anfiteatro *m*
ample ['æmpəl] *adj* **-pler; -plest** 1 SPACIOUS : amplio, extenso 2 ABUNDANT : abundante
amplify ['æmplə,faɪ] *vt* **-fied; -fying** : amplificar — **amplifier** ['æmplə,faɪər] *n* : amplificador *m*
amputate ['æmpjə,teɪt] *vt* **-tated; -tating** : amputar — **amputation** [æmpjə'teɪʃən] *n* : amputación *f*
amuse [ə'mju:z] *vt* **amused; amusing** 1 : hacer reír, divertir 2 ENTERTAIN : entretener — **amusement** [ə'mju:zmənt] *n* : diversión *f* — **amusing** *adj* : divertido
an → **a²**
analogy [ə'nælədʒi] *n, pl* **-gies** : analogía *f* — **analogous** [ə'næləgəs] *adj* : análogo
analysis [ə'næləsəs] *n, pl* **-yses** [-,si:z] : análisis *m* — **analytic** [æneə'lɪtɪk] *or* **analytical** [-tɪkəl] *adj* : analítico — **analyze** ['ænə,laɪz] *vt* **-lyzed; -lyzing** : analizar
anarchy ['ænərki, -nɑr-] *n* : anarquía *f*
anatomy [ə'næṱəmi] *n, pl* **-mies** : anatomía *f* — **anatomic** [ænə'tɑmɪk] *or* **anatomical** [-mɪkəl] *adj* : anatómico
ancestor ['æn,sestər] *n* : antepasado *m*, -da *f* — **ancestral** [æn'sestrəl] *adj* : ancestral — **ancestry** ['æn,sestri] *n* 1 DE-

SCENT : linaje *m*, abolengo *m* 2 ANCESTORS : antepasados *mpl*, -das *fpl*
anchor ['æŋkər] *n* 1 : ancla *f* 2 : presentador *m*, -dora *f* (en televisión) — ~ *vt* 1 : anclar 2 FASTEN : sujetar — *vi* : anclar
anchovy ['æn,tʃo:vi, æn'tʃo:-] *n, pl* **-vies** *or* **-vy** : anchoa *f*
ancient ['eɪnʃənt] *adj* : antiguo, viejo
and ['ænd] *conj* 1 : y (e *before words beginning with i- or hi-*) 2 **come** ~ **see** : ven a ver 3 **more** ~ **more** : cada vez más 4 **try** ~ **finish it soon** : trata de terminarlo pronto
anecdote ['ænɪk,do:t] *n* : anécdota *f*
anemia [ə'ni:miə] *n* : anemia *f* — **anemic** [ə'ni:mɪk] *adj* : anémico
anesthesia [ænəs'θi:ʒə] *n* : anestesia *f* — **anesthetic** [ænəs'θeṱɪk] *adj* : anestésico — ~ *n* : anestésico *m*
anew [ə'nu:, -'nju:] *adv* : de nuevo, nuevamente
angel ['eɪndʒəl] *n* : ángel *m* — **angelic** [æn'dʒelɪk] *or* **angelical** [-lɪkəl] *adj* : angélico
anger ['æŋgər] *vt* : enojar, enfadar — ~ *n* : ira *f*, enojo *m*, enfado *m*
angle *n* 1 : ángulo *m* 2 POINT OF VIEW : perspectiva *f*, punto *m* de vista — **angler** ['æŋglər] *n* : pescador *m*, -dora *f*
Anglo–Saxon [æŋglo'sæksən] *adj* : anglosajón
angry ['æŋgri] *adj* **-grier; -est** : enojado, enfadado
anguish ['æŋgwɪʃ] *n* : angustia *f*
angular ['æŋgjələr] *adj* 1 : angular 2 ~ **features** : rasgos *mpl* angulosos
animal ['ænəməl] *n* : animal *m*
animate ['ænəmət] *adj* : animado — ~ ['ænə,meɪt] *vt* **-mated; -mating** : animar — **animated** *adj* 1 : animado 2 ~ **cartoon** : dibujos *mpl* animados — **animation** [ænə'meɪʃən] *n* : animación *f*
animosity [ænə'mɑsəṱi] *n, pl* **-ties** : animosidad *f*
anise ['ænəs] *n* : anís *m*
ankle ['æŋkəl] *n* : tobillo *m*
annals ['ænəlz] *npl* : anales *mpl*
annex [ə'neks, 'æ,neks] *vt* : anexar — ~ ['æ,neks, -nɪks] *n* : anexo *m*
annihilate [ə'naɪə,leɪt] *vt* **-lated; -lating** : aniquilar — **annihilation** [ə,naɪə'leɪʃən] *n* : aniquilación *f*
anniversary [ænə'vərsəri] *n, pl* **-ries** : aniversario *m*
annotate ['ænə,teɪt] *vt* **-tated; -tating** : anotar — **annotation** [ænə'teɪʃən] *n* : anotación *f*
announce [ə'naʊnts] *vt* **-nounced;**

-nouncing : anunciar — **announcement** [ə'naʊntsmənt] n : anuncio m — **announcer** [ə'naʊntsər] n : locutor m, -tora f

annoy [ə'nɔɪ] vt : fastidiar, molestar — **annoyance** [ə'nɔɪənts] n : fastidio m, molestia f — **annoying** [ə'nɔɪɪŋ] adj : molesto, fastidioso

annual ['ænjuəl] adj : anual — ~ n : anuario m

annuity [ə'nu:əti] n, pl **-ties** : anualidad f

annul [ə'nʌl] vt **annulled; annulling** : anular — **annulment** [ə'nʌlmənt] n : anulación f

anoint [ə'nɔɪnt] vt : ungir

anomaly [ə'nɑməli] n, pl **-lies** : anomalía f

anonymous [ə'nɑnəməs] adj : anónimo — **anonymity** [,ænə'nɪməti] n : anonimato m

another [ə'nʌðər] adj 1 : otro 2 **in** ~ **minute** : en un minuto más — ~ pron : otro, otra

answer ['æntsər] n 1 REPLY : respuesta f, contestación f 2 SOLUTION : solución f — ~ vt 1 : contestar a, responder a 2 ~ **the door** : abrir la puerta — vi : contestar, responder

ant ['ænt] n : hormiga f

antagonize [æn'tægə,naɪz] vt **-nized; -nizing** : provocar la enemistad de — **antagonism** [æn'tægə,nɪzəm] n : antagonismo m

antarctic [æn'tɑrktɪk, -'ɑrṭɪk] adj : antártico

antelope ['æntəl,o:p] n, pl **-lope** or **-lopes** : antílope m

antenna [æn'tenə] n, pl **-nae** [-,ni:, -,naɪ] or **-nas** : antena f

anthem ['ænθəm] n : himno m

anthology [æn'θɑlədʒi] n, pl **-gies** : antología f

anthropology [,ænθrə'pɑlədʒi] n : antropología f

antibiotic [,æntɪbaɪ'ɑṭɪk, ,æntaɪ-, -bi-] adj : antibiótico — ~ n : antibiótico m

antibody ['æntɪ,bɑdi] n, pl **-bodies** : anticuerpo m

anticipate [æn'tɪsə,peɪt] vt **-pated; -pating** 1 FORESEE : anticipar, prever 2 EXPECT : esperar — **anticipation** [æn,tɪsə'peɪʃən] n : anticipación f, expectación f

antics ['æntɪks] npl : payasadas fpl

antidote ['æntɪ,do:t] n : antídoto m

antifreeze ['ænti,fri:z] n : anticongelante m

antipathy [æn'tɪpəθi] n, pl **-thies** : antipatía f

antiquated ['æntə,kweɪṭəd] adj : anticuado

antique [æn'ti:k] adj : antiguo — ~ n : antigüedad f — **antiquity** [æn'tɪkwə-ṭi] n, pl **-ties** : antigüedad f

anti–Semitic [,æntisə'mɪṭɪk, ,æntaɪ-] adj : antisemita

antiseptic [,æntə'septɪk] adj : antiséptico — ~ n : antiséptico m

antisocial [,ænti'so:ʃəl, ,æntaɪ-] adj 1 : antisocial 2 UNSOCIABLE : poco sociable

antithesis [æn'tɪθəsɪs] n, pl **-eses** [-,si:z] : antítesis f

antlers ['æntlərz] npl : cornamenta f

antonym ['æntə,nɪm] n : antónimo m

anus ['eɪnəs] n : ano m

anvil ['ænvəl, -vɪl] n : yunque m

anxiety [æŋk'zaɪəti] n, pl **-eties** 1 APPREHENSION : inquietud f, ansiedad f 2 EAGERNESS : anhelo m — **anxious** ['æŋkʃəs] adj 1 WORRIED : inquieto, preocupado 2 EAGER : ansioso — **anxiously** ['æŋkʃəsli] adv : con ansiedad

any ['eni] adv 1 SOMEWHAT : algo, un poco 2 **it's not** ~ **good** : no sirve para nada 3 **we can't wait** ~ **longer** : no podemos esperar más — ~ adj 1 : alguno 2 (in negative constructions) : ningún 3 WHATEVER : cualquier 4 **in** ~ **case** : en todo caso — ~ pron 1 : alguno, -na 2 : ninguno, -na 3 **do you want** ~ **more rice?** : ¿quieres más arroz?

anybody ['eni,bʌdi, -,bɑ-] → **anyone**

anyhow ['eni,haʊ] adv 1 : de todas formas 2 HAPHAZARDLY : de cualquier modo

anymore [,eni'mor] adv **not** ~ : ya no

anyone ['eni,wʌn] pron 1 SOMEONE : alguien 2 WHOEVER : quienquiera 3 **I don't see** ~ : no veo a nadie

anyplace ['eni,pleɪs] → **anywhere**

anything ['eni,θɪŋ] pron 1 SOMETHING : algo, alguna cosa 2 (in negative constructions) : nada 3 WHATEVER : cualquier cosa, lo que sea

anytime ['eni,taɪm] adv : en cualquier momento

anyway ['eni,weɪ] → **anyhow**

anywhere ['eni,hwer] adv 1 : en cualquier parte, dondequiera 2 (used in questions) : en algún sitio 3 **I can't find it** ~ : no lo encuentro por ninguna parte

apart [ə'pɑrt] adv 1 : aparte 2 ~ **from** : excepto, aparte de 3 **fall** ~ : deshacerse, hacerse pedazos 4 **live** ~ : vivir separados 5 **take** ~ : desmontar, desmantelar

apartment [ə'partmənt] *n* : apartamento *m*

apathy ['æpəθi] *n* : apatía *f* — **apathetic** [ˌæpə'θetɪk] *adj* : apático, indiferente

ape *n* : simio *m*

aperture ['æpərtʃər, -tʃʊr] *n* : abertura *f*

apex ['eɪpɛks] *n*, *pl* **apexes** *or* **apices** ['eɪpəˌsiz, 'æ-] : ápice *m*, cumbre *f*

apiece [ə'pis] *adv* : cada uno

aplomb [ə'plam, -'plʌm] *n* : aplomo *m*

apology [ə'palədʒi] *n*, *pl* **-gies** : disculpa *f* — **apologetic** [əˌpalə'dʒetɪk] *adj* : lleno de disculpas — **apologize** [ə'palədʒaɪz] *vi* **-gized; -gizing** : disculparse, pedir perdón

apostle [ə'pasəl] *n* : apóstol *m*

apostrophe [ə'pastrəˌfi] *n* : apóstrofo *m*

appall [ə'pɔl] *vt* : horrorizar — **appalling** [ə'pɔlɪŋ] *adj* : horroroso

apparatus [ˌæpə'rætəs, -'reɪ-] *n*, *pl* **-tuses** *or* **-tus** : aparato *m*

apparel [ə'pærəl] *n* : ropa *f*

apparent [ə'pærənt] *adj* **1** OBVIOUS : claro, evidente **2** SEEMING : aparente — **apparently** [ə'pærəntli] *adv* : al parecer, por lo visto

apparition [ˌæpə'rɪʃən] *n* : aparición *f*

appeal [ə'pil] *vi* **1** ~ **for** : solicitar **2** ~ **to** : apelar a (la bondad de algn, etc.) **3** ~ **to** ATTRACT : atraer a — *n* **1** : apelación *f* (en derecho) **2** REQUEST : llamamiento *m* **3** ATTRACTION : atractivo *m* — **appealing** [ə'pilɪŋ] *adj* : atractivo

appear [ə'pɪr] *vi* **1** : aparecer **2** : comparecer (ante un tribunal), actuar (en el teatro) **3** SEEM : parecer — **appearance** [ə'pɪrənts] *n* **1** : aparición *f* **2** LOOK : apariencia *f*, aspecto *m*

appease [ə'piz] *vt* **-peased; -peasing** : apaciguar, aplacar

appendix [ə'pɛndɪks] *n*, *pl* **-dixes** *or* **-dices** [-dəˌsiz] : apéndice *m* — **appendicitis** [əˌpɛndə'saɪtəs] *n* : apendicitis *f*

appetite ['æpəˌtaɪt] *n* : apetito *m* — **appetizer** ['æpəˌtaɪzər] *n* : aperitivo *m* — **appetizing** ['æpəˌtaɪzɪŋ] *adj* : apetitoso

applaud [ə'plɔd] *v* : aplaudir — **applause** [ə'plɔz] *n* : aplauso *m*

apple ['æpəl] *n* : manzana *f*

appliance [ə'plaɪənts] *n* : aparato *m*

apply [ə'plaɪ] *v* **-plied; -plying** *vt* **1** : aplicar **2** ~ **oneself** : aplicarse — *vi* **1** : aplicarse **2** ~ **for** : solicitar, pedir — **applicable** ['æplɪkəbəl, ə'plɪkə-] *adj* : aplicable — **applicant** ['æplɪkənt] *n* : solicitante *mf*; candidato *m*, -ta *f* — **application** [ˌæplə'keɪʃən] *n* **1** : apli-

cación *f* **2** : solicitud *f* (para un empleo, etc.)

appoint [ə'pɔɪnt] *vt* **1** NAME : nombrar **2** FIX, SET : fijar, señalar — **appointment** [ə'pɔɪntmənt] *n* **1** APPOINTING : nombramiento *m* **2** ENGAGEMENT : cita *f*

apportion [ə'porʃən] *vt* : distribuir, repartir

appraise [ə'preɪz] *vt* **-praised; -praising** : evaluar, valorar — **appraisal** [ə'preɪzəl] *n* : evaluación *f*

appreciate [ə'priʃiˌeɪt, -prɪ-] *v* **-ated; -ating** *vt* **1** VALUE : apreciar **2** UNDERSTAND : darse cuenta de **3** I ~ **your help** : te agradezco tu ayuda — *vi* : aumentar en valor — **appreciation** [əˌpriʃi'eɪʃən, -prɪ-] *n* **1** GRATITUDE : agradecimiento *m* **2** VALUING : apreciación *f*, valoración *f* — **appreciative** [ə'priʃəˌtɪv, -prɪ-; ə'priʃiˌeɪ-] *adj* **1** : apreciativo **2** GRATEFUL : agradecido

apprehend [ˌæprɪ'hɛnd] *vt* **1** ARREST : aprehender, detener **2** DREAD : temer **3** COMPREHEND : comprender — **apprehension** [ˌæprɪ'hɛntʃən] *n* **1** ARREST : detención *f*, aprehensión *f* **2** ANXIETY : aprensión *f*, temor *m* — **apprehensive** [ˌæprɪ'hɛntsɪv] *adj* : aprensivo, inquieto

apprentice [ə'prɛntɪs] *n* : aprendiz *m*, -diza *f*

approach [ə'protʃ] *vt* **1** NEAR : acercarse a **2** : dirigirse a (algn), abordar (un problema, etc.) — *vi* : acercarse — *n* **1** NEARING : acercamiento *m* **2** POSITION : enfoque *m* **3** ACCESS : acceso *m* — **approachable** [ə'protʃəbəl] *adj* : accesible, asequible

appropriate [ə'proˌpriˌeɪt] *vt* **-ated; -ating** : apropiarse de — ~ [ə'proˌpriət] *adj* : apropiado

approve [ə'pruv] *vt* **-proved; -proving** : aprobar — **approval** [ə'pruvəl] *n* : aprobación *f*

approximate [ə'praksəmət] *adj* : aproximado — ~ [ə'praksəˌmeɪt] *vt* **-mated; -mating** : aproximarse a — **approximately** [ə'praksəmətli] *adv* : aproximadamente

apricot ['æprəˌkat, 'eɪ-] *n* : albaricoque *m*, chabacano *m* Lat

April ['eɪprəl] *n* : abril *m*

apron ['eɪprən] *n* : delantal *m*

apropos [ˌæprə'po, 'æprəˌpo] *adv* : a propósito

apt ['æpt] *adj* **1** FITTING : apto, apropiado **2** LIABLE : propenso — **aptitude** ['æptəˌtud, -ˌtjud] *n* : aptitud *f*

aquarium [əˈkwæriəm] *n, pl* **-iums** *or* **-ia** [-iə] : acuario *m*
aquatic [əˈkwɑtɪk, -ˈkwæ-] *adj* : acuático
aqueduct [ˈækwəˌdʌkt] *n* : acueducto *m*
Arab [ˈærəb] *adj* : árabe — **Arabic** [ˈærəbɪk] *adj* : árabe — ~ *n* : árabe *m* (idioma)
arbitrary [ˈɑrbəˌtreri] *adj* : arbitrario
arbitrate [ˈɑrbəˌtreɪt] *v* **-trated; -trating** : arbitrar — **arbitration** [ˌɑrbəˈtreɪʃən] *n* : arbitraje *m*
arc [ˈɑrk] *n* : arco *m*
arcade [ɑrˈkeɪd] *n* **1** : arcada *f* **2 shopping** ~ : galería *f* comercial
arch [ˈɑrtʃ] *n* : arco *m* — ~ *vt* : arquear — *vi* : arquearse
archaeology *or* **archeology** [ˌɑrkiˈɑlədʒi] *n* : arqueología *f* — **archaeological** [ˌɑrkiəˈlɑdʒɪkəl] *adj* : arqueológico — **archaeologist** [ˌɑrkiˈɑlədʒɪst] *n* : arqueólogo *m*, -ga *f*
archaic [ɑrˈkeɪɪk] *adj* : arcaico
archbishop [ɑrtʃˈbɪʃəp] *n* : arzobispo *m*
archery [ˈɑrtʃəri] *n* : tiro *m* al arco
archipelago [ˌɑrkəˈpeləˌgoː, ˌɑrtʃə-] *n, pl* **-goes** *or* **-gos** [-goːz] : archipiélago *m*
architecture [ˈɑrkəˌtektʃər] *n* : arquitectura *f* — **architect** [ˈɑrkəˌtekt] *n* : arquitecto *m*, -ta *f* — **architectural** [ˌɑrkəˈtektʃərəl] *adj* : arquitectónico
archives [ˈɑrˌkaɪvz] *npl* : archivo *m*
archway [ˈɑrtʃˌweɪ] *n* : arco *m* (de entrada)
arctic [ˈɑrktɪk, ˈɑrt-] *adj* : ártico
ardent [ˈɑrdənt] *adj* : ardiente, fervoroso — **ardor** [ˈɑrdər] *n* : ardor *m*, fervor *m*
arduous [ˈɑrdʒuəs] *adj* : arduo
are → **be**
area [ˈæriə] *n* **1** REGION : área *f*, zona *f* **2** FIELD : campo *m* **3** ~ **code** : código *m* de la zona *Lat*, prefijo *m Spain*
arena [əˈriːnə] *n* : arena *f*, ruedo *m*
aren't [ˈɑrnt, ˈɑrənt] (*contraction of* **are not**) → **be**
Argentine [ˈɑrdʒənˌtaɪn, -ˌtiːn] *or* **Argentinean** *or* **Argentinian** [ˌɑrdʒənˈtɪniən] *adj* : argentino
argue [ˈɑrˌgjuː] *v* **-gued; -guing** *vi* **1** QUARREL : discutir **2** ~ **against** : argumentar contra — *vt* : argumentar, sostener — **argument** [ˈɑrgjəmənt] *n* **1** QUARREL : disputa *f*, discusión *f* **2** REASONING : argumentos *mpl*
arid [ˈærəd] *adj* : árido — **aridity** [əˈrɪdəˌʃi, æ-] *n* : aridez *f*
arise [əˈraɪz] *vi* **arose** [əˈroːz]; **arisen** [əˈrɪzən]; **arising 1** : levantarse **2** ~ **from** : surgir de
aristocracy [ˌærəˈstɑkrəsi] *n, pl* **-cies** : aristocracia *f* — **aristocrat** [əˈrɪstə-

ˌkræt] *n* : aristócrata *mf* — **aristocratic** [əˌrɪstəˈkrætɪk] *adj* : aristocrático
arithmetic [əˈrɪθməˌtɪk] *n* : aritmética *f*
ark [ˈɑrk] *n* : arca *f*
arm [ˈɑrm] *n* **1** : brazo *m* **2** WEAPON : arma *f* — ~ *vt* : armar — **armament** [ˈɑrməmənt] *n* : armamento *m* — **armchair** [ˈɑrmˌtʃer] *n* : sillón *m* — **armed** [ˈɑrmd] *adj* **1** ~ **forces** : fuerzas *fpl* armadas **2** ~ **robbery** : robo *m* a mano armada
armistice [ˈɑrməstɪs] *n* : armisticio *m*
armor *or Brit* **armour** [ˈɑrmər] *n* : armadura *f* — **armored** *or Brit* **armoured** [ˈɑrmərd] *adj* : blindado, acorazado — **armory** *or Brit* **armoury** [ˈɑrmri, ˈɑrməri] *n* : arsenal *m*
armpit [ˈɑrmˌpɪt] *n* : axila *f*, sobaco *m*
army [ˈɑrmi] *n, pl* **-mies** : ejército *m*
aroma [əˈroːmə] *n* : aroma *m* — **aromatic** [ˌærəˈmætɪk] *adj* : aromático
around [əˈraund] *adv* **1** : de circunferencia **2** NEARBY : por ahí **3** APPROXIMATELY : más o menos, aproximadamente **4 all** ~ : por todos lados, todo alrededor **5 turn** ~ : voltearse — ~ *prep* **1** SURROUNDING : alrededor de **2** THROUGHOUT : por **3** NEAR : cerca de **4** ~ **the corner** : a la vuelta de la esquina
arouse [əˈrauz] *vt* **aroused; arousing 1** AWAKE : despertar **2** EXCITE : excitar
arrange [əˈreɪndʒ] *vt* **-ranged; -ranging** : arreglar, poner en orden — **arrangement** [əˈreɪndʒmənt] *n* **1** ORDER : arreglo *m* **2** ~ **s** *npl* : preparativos *mpl*
array [əˈreɪ] *n* : selección *f*, surtido *m*
arrears [əˈrɪrz] *npl* **1** : atrasos *mpl* **2 be in** ~ : estar atrasado en pagos
arrest [əˈrest] *vt* : detener — ~ *n* **1** : arresto *m*, detención *f* **2 under** ~ : detenido
arrive [əˈraɪv] *vi* **-rived; -riving** : llegar — **arrival** [əˈraɪvəl] *n* : llegada *f*
arrogance [ˈærəgənts] *n* : arrogancia *f* — **arrogant** [ˈærəgənt] *adj* : arrogante
arrow [ˈæroː] *n* : flecha *f*
arsenal [ˈɑrsənəl] *n* : arsenal *m*
arsenic [ˈɑrsənɪk] *n* : arsénico *m*
arson [ˈɑrsən] *n* : incendio *m* premeditado
art [ˈɑrt] *n* **1** : arte *m* **2** ~ **s** *npl* : letras *fpl* (en educación) **3 fine** ~ **s** : bellas artes *fpl*
artefact *Brit* → **artifact**
artery [ˈɑrtəri] *n, pl* **-teries** : arteria *f*
artful [ˈɑrtfəl] *adj* : astuto, taimado
arthritis [ɑrˈθraɪtəs] *n, pl* **-tides** [ɑrˈθrɪtəˌdiːz] : artritis *f* — **arthritic** [ɑrˈθrɪtɪk] *adj* : artrítico

artichoke [ˈɑrtəˌtʃoːk] n : alcachofa f

article [ˈɑrtɪkəl] n : artículo m

articulate [ɑrˈtɪkjəˌleɪt] vt **-lated; -lating** : articular — [ɑrˈtɪkjələt] adj be ~ : expresarse bien

artifact or Brit **artefact** [ˈɑrtəˌfækt] n : artefacto m

artificial [ˌɑrtəˈfɪʃəl] adj : artificial

artillery [ɑrˈtɪləri] n, pl **-leries** : artillería f

artisan [ˈɑrtəzən, -sən] n : artesano m, -na f

artist [ˈɑrtɪst] n : artista mf — **artistic** [ɑrˈtɪstɪk] adj : artístico

as [ˈæz] adv 1 : tan, tanto 2 ~ **much** : tanto como 3 ~ **tall** ~ : tan alto como 4 ~ **well** : también — ~ conj 1 WHILE : mientras 2 (referring to manner) : como 3 SINCE : ya que 4 THOUGH : por más que — ~ prep 1 : de 2 LIKE : como — ~ pron : que

asbestos [æzˈbestəs, æs-] n : asbesto m, amianto m

ascend [əˈsend] vi : ascender, subir — vt : subir (a) — **ascent** [əˈsent] n : ascensión f, subida f

ascertain [ˌæsərˈteɪn] vt : averiguar, determinar

ascribe [əˈskraɪb] vt **-cribed; -cribing** : atribuir

as for prep : en cuanto a

ash[1] [ˈæʃ] n : ceniza f

ash[2] n : fresno m (árbol)

ashamed [əˈʃeɪmd] adj : avergonzado, apenado Lat

ashore [əˈʃor] adv 1 : en tierra 2 go ~ : desembarcar

ashtray [ˈæʃˌtreɪ] n : cenicero m

Asian [ˈeɪʒən, -ʃən] adj : asiático

aside [əˈsaɪd] adv 1 : a un lado 2 APART : aparte 3 set ~ : guardar — **aside from** prep 1 BESIDES : además de 2 EXCEPT : aparte de, menos

as if conj : como si

ask [ˈæsk] vt 1 : preguntar 2 REQUEST : pedir 3 INVITE : invitar — vi : preguntar

askance [əˈskænts] adv look ~ : mirar de soslayo

askew [əˈskjuː] adj : torcido, ladeado

asleep [əˈsliːp] adj 1 : dormido 2 fall ~ : dormirse, quedarse dormido

as of prep : desde, a partir de

asparagus [əˈspærəgəs] n : espárrago m

aspect [ˈæˌspekt] n : aspecto m

asphalt [ˈæsˌfɔlt] n : asfalto m

asphyxiate [æsˈfɪksiˌeɪt] v **-ated; -ating** vt : asfixiar — **asphyxiation** [æsˌfɪksiˈeɪʃən] n : asfixia f

aspire [əˈspaɪr] vi **-pired; -piring** : aspirar — **aspiration** [ˌæspəˈreɪʃən] n : aspiración f

aspirin [ˈæsprən, ˈæspə-] n, pl **aspirin** or **aspirins** : aspirina f

ass [ˈæs] n 1 : asno m 2 IDIOT : imbécil mf, idiota mf

assail [əˈseɪl] vt : atacar, asaltar — **assailant** [əˈseɪlənt] n : asaltante mf, atacante mf

assassin [əˈsæsən] n : asesino m, -na f — **assassinate** [əˈsæsəˌneɪt] vt **-nated; -nating** : asesinar — **assassination** [əˌsæsənˈeɪʃən] n : asesinato m

assault [əˈsɔlt] n 1 : ataque m, asalto m 2 : agresión f (contra algn) — ~ vt : atacar, asaltar

assemble [əˈsembəl] v **-bled; -bling** vt 1 GATHER : reunir, juntar 2 CONSTRUCT : montar — vi : reunirse — **assembly** [əˈsembli] n, pl **-blies** 1 MEETING : reunión f, asamblea f 2 CONSTRUCTING : montaje m

assent [əˈsent] vi : asentir, consentir — ~ n : asentimiento m

assert [əˈsərt] vt 1 : afirmar 2 ~ **oneself** : hacerse valer — **assertion** [əˈsərʃən] n : afirmación f — **assertive** [əˈsərtɪv] adj : firme, enérgico

assess [əˈses] vt : evaluar, valorar — **assessment** [əˈsesmənt] n : evaluación f, valoración f

asset [ˈæˌset] n 1 : ventaja f, recurso m 2 ~**s** npl : bienes mpl, activo m

assiduous [əˈsɪdʒʊəs] adj : asiduo

assign [əˈsaɪn] vt 1 APPOINT : designar, nombrar 2 ALLOT : asignar — **assignment** [əˈsaɪnmənt] n 1 TASK : misión f 2 HOMEWORK : tarea f 3 ASSIGNING : asignación f

assimilate [əˈsɪməˌleɪt] vt **-lated; -lating** : asimilar

assist [əˈsɪst] vt : ayudar — **assistance** [əˈsɪstənts] n : ayuda f — **assistant** [əˈsɪstənt] n : ayudante mf

associate [əˈsoːʃiˌeɪt, -siˌeɪt] v **-ated; -ating** vt : asociar — vi : asociarse — ~ [əˈsoːʃiət, -siət] n : asociado m, -da f; socio m, -cia f — **association** [əˌsoːʃiˈeɪʃən, -si-] n : asociación f

as soon as conj : tan pronto como

assorted [əˈsɔrtəd] adj : surtido — **assortment** [əˈsɔrtmənt] n : surtido m, variedad f

assume [əˈsuːm] vt **-sumed; -suming** 1 SUPPOSE : suponer 2 UNDERTAKE : asumir 3 TAKE ON : adquirir, tomar — **assumption** [əˈsʌmpʃən] n : suposición f

assure [əˈʃur] vt **-sured; -suring** : asegurar — **assurance** [əˈʃurənts] n 1

CERTAINTY : certeza *f*, garantía *f* 2 CON-
FIDENCE : confianza *f*, seguridad *f* (de
sí mismo)

asterisk ['æstə,rɪsk] *n* : asterisco *m*

asthma ['æzmə] *n* : asma *m*

as though → as if

as to *prep* : sobre, acerca de

astonish [ə'stɑnɪʃ] *vt* : asombrar — **astonishing** [ə'stɑnɪʃɪŋ] *adj* : asombroso
— **astonishment** [ə'stɑnɪʃmənt] *n*
: asombro *m*

astound [ə'staʊnd] *vt* : asombrar, pasmar — **astounding** [ə'staʊndɪŋ] *adj*
: asombroso, pasmoso

astray [ə'streɪ] *adv* 1 **go ~** : extraviarse
2 **lead ~** : llevar por mal camino

astrology [ə'strɑlədʒi] *n* : astrología *f*

astronaut ['æstrə,nɔt] *n* : astronauta *mf*

astronomy [ə'strɑnəmi] *n, pl* **-mies**
: astronomía *f* — **astronomer** [ə-
'strɑnəmər] *n* : astrónomo *m*, -ma *f* —
astronomical [,æstrə'nɑmɪkəl] *adj* : astronómico

astute [ə'stuːt, -'stjuːt] *adj* : astuto, sagaz
— **astuteness** [ə'stuːtnəs, -'stjuːt-] *n*
: astucia *f*

as well as *conj* : tanto como — **~** *prep*
: además de, aparte de

asylum [ə'saɪləm] *n* 1 : asilo *m* 2 **insane
~** : manicomio *m*

at ['æt] *prep* 1 : a 2 **~ home** : en casa 3
~ night : en la noche, por la noche 4
~ two o'clock : a las dos 5 **be angry
~** : estar enojado con 6 **laugh ~**
: reírse de — **at all** *adv* **not ~** : en absoluto, nada

ate → eat

atheist ['eɪθiːɪst] *n* : ateo *m*, atea *f* —
atheism *n* ['eɪθi,ɪzəm] : ateísmo *m*

athlete ['æθ,liːt] *n* : atleta *mf* — **athletic**
[æθ'lɛʈɪk] *adj* : atlético — **athletics**
[æθ'lɛʈɪks] *ns & pl* : atletismo *m*

atlas ['ætləs] *n* : atlas *m*

atmosphere ['ætmə,sfɪr] *n* 1 : atmósfera
f 2 AMBIENCE : ambiente *m* — **atmospheric** [,ætmə'sfɪrɪk, -'sfɛr-] *adj* : atmosférico

atom ['æʈəm] *n* : átomo *m* — **atomic** [ə-
'tɑmɪk] *adj* : atómico

atomizer ['æʈə,maɪzər] *n* : atomizador *m*

atone [ə'toʊn] *vi* **atoned; atoning ~ for**
: expiar

atrocity [ə'trɑsəʈi] *n, pl* **-ties** : atrocidad
f — **atrocious** [ə'troːʃəs] *adj* : atroz

atrophy ['ætrəfi] *vi* **-phied; -phying**
: atrofiarse

attach [ə'tætʃ] *vt* 1 : sujetar, atar 2 : adjuntar (un documento, etc.) 3 **~ importance to** : atribuir importancia a 4
become ~ed to s.o. : encariñarse

con algn — **attachment** [ə'tætʃmənt] *n*
1 ACCESSORY : accesorio *m* 2 FOND-
NESS : cariño *m*

attack [ə'tæk] *v* : atacar — **~** *n* : ataque
m — **attacker** [ə'tækər] *n* : agresor *m*,
-sora *f*

attain [ə'teɪn] *vt* : lograr, alcanzar — **attainment** [ə'teɪnmənt] *n* : logro *m*

attempt [ə'tɛmpt] *vt* : intentar — **~** *n*
: intento *m*

attend [ə'tɛnd] *vt* : asistir a — *vi* 1 : asistir 2 **~ to** : ocuparse de — **attendance** [ə'tɛndənts] *n* 1 : asistencia *f* 2
TURNOUT : concurrencia *f* — **attendant** *n* : encargado *m*, -da *f*; asistente
mf

attention [ə'tɛntʃən] *n* 1 : atención *f* 2
pay ~ : prestar atención, hacer caso
— **attentive** [ə'tɛntɪv] *adj* : atento

attest [ə'tɛst] *vt* : atestiguar

attic ['æʈɪk] *n* : desván *m*

attire [ə'taɪr] *n* : atavío *m*

attitude ['æʈə,tuːd, -,tjuːd] *n* 1 : actitud *f* 2
POSTURE : postura *f*

attorney [ə'tərni] *n, pl* **-neys** : abogado
m, -da *f*

attract [ə'trækt] *vt* : atraer — **attraction**
[ə'trækʃən] *n* 1 : atracción *f* 2 APPEAL
: atractivo *m* — **attractive** [ə'træktɪv]
adj : atractivo, atrayente

attribute ['ætrə,bjuːt] *n* : atributo *m* — **~**
[ə'trɪ,bjuːt] *vt* **-tributed; -tributing**
: atribuir, imputar

auburn ['ɔbərn] *adj* : castaño rojizo

auction ['ɔkʃən] *n* : subasta *f* — **~** *vt* or
~ off : subastar

audacious [ɔ'deɪʃəs] *adj* : audaz — **audacity** [ɔ'dæsəʈi] *n, pl* **-ties** : audacia *f*,
atrevimiento *m*

audible ['ɔdəbəl] *adj* : audible

audience ['ɔdiənts] *n* 1 INTERVIEW : audiencia *f* 2 PUBLIC : público *m*

audiovisual [,ɔdiˈvɪʒuəl] *adj* : audiovisual

audition [ɔ'dɪʃən] *n* : audición *f*

auditor ['ɔdəʈər] *n* 1 : auditor *m*, -tora *f*
(de finanzas) 2 STUDENT : oyente *mf*

auditorium [,ɔdə'toriəm] *n, pl* **-riums** or
-ria [-riæ] : auditorio *m*

augment [ɔg'mɛnt] *vt* : aumentar

augur ['ɔgər] *vi* **~ well** : ser de buen
agüero

August ['ɔgəst] *n* : agosto *m*

aunt ['ænt, 'ant] *n* : tía *f*

aura ['ɔrə] *n* : aura *f*

auspices ['ɔspəsəz, -,siːz] *npl* : auspicios
mpl

auspicious [ɔ'spɪʃəs] *adj* : propicio,
prometedor

austere [ɔ'stɪr] *adj* : austero — **austerity** [ɔ'sterəti] *n, pl* **-ties** : austeridad *f*
Australian [ɔ'streɪljən] *adj* : australiano
authentic [ə'θentɪk, ɔ-] *adj* : auténtico
author ['ɔθər] *n* : autor *m*, -tora *f*
authority [ə'θorəti, ɔ-] *n, pl* **-ties** : autoridad *f* — **authoritarian** [ə,θorə-'teriən, ə-] *adj* : autoritario — **authoritative** [ə'θorə,teɪtɪv, ɔ-] *adj* **1** RELIABLE : autorizado **2** DICTATORIAL : autoritario — **authorization** [,ɔθərə'zeɪʃən] *n* : autorización *f* — **authorize** ['ɔθə,raɪz] *vt* **-rized; -rizing** : autorizar
autobiography [,ɔtəbaɪ'agrəfi] *n, pl* **-phies** : autobiografía *f* — **autobiographical** [,ɔtə,baɪə'græfɪkəl] *adj* : autobiográfico
autograph ['ɔtə,græf] *n* : autógrafo *m* — ~ *vt* : autografiar
automatic [,ɔtə'mætɪk] *adj* : automático — **automate** ['ɔtə,meɪt] *vt* **-mated; -mating** : automatizar — **automation** [,ɔtə'meɪʃən] *n* : automatización *f*
automobile [,ɔtəmo'biːl, -'moː,biːl] *n* : automóvil *m*
autonomy [ɔ'tɑnəmi] *n, pl* **-mies** : autonomía *f* — **autonomous** [ɔ'tɑnəməs] *adj* : autónomo
autopsy ['ɔ,tɑpsi, -təp-] *n, pl* **-sies** : autopsia *f*
autumn ['ɔtəm] *n* : otoño *m*
auxiliary [ɔg'zɪljəri, -'zɪləri] *adj* : auxiliar — ~ *n, pl* **-ries** : auxiliar *mf*
avail [ə'veɪl] *vt* ~ **oneself of** : aprovecharse de — ~ *n* **to no** ~ : en vano — **available** [ə'veɪləbəl] *adj* : disponible — **availability** [ə,veɪlə'bɪləti] *n, pl* **-ties** : disponibilidad *f*
avalanche ['ævə,læntʃ] *n* : avalancha *f*
avarice ['ævərəs] *n* : avaricia *f*
avenge [ə'vendʒ] *vt* **avenged; avenging** : vengar
avenue ['ævə,nuː, -,njuː] *n* **1** : avenida *f* **2** MEANS : vía *f*
average ['ævrɪdʒ, 'ævə-] *n* : promedio *m* — ~ *adj* **1** MEAN : medio **2** ORDINARY : regular, ordinario — ~ *vt* **-aged; -aging 1** : hacer un promedio de **2** *or* ~ **out** : calcular el promedio de
averse [ə'vərs] *adj* **be** ~ **to** : sentir aversión por — **aversion** [ə'vərʒən] *n* : aversión *f*
avert [ə'vərt] *vt* **1** AVOID : evitar, prevenir **2** ~ **one's eyes** : apartar los ojos
aviation [,eɪvi'eɪʃən] *n* : aviación *f* — **aviator** ['eɪvi,eɪtər] *n* : aviador *m*, -dora *f*
avid ['ævɪd] *adj* : ávido — **avidly** *adv* : con avidez
avocado [,ævə'kɑdo, ,ɑvə-] *n, pl* **-dos** : aguacate *m*
avoid [ə'vɔɪd] *vt* : evitar — **avoidable** [ə'vɔɪdəbəl] *adj* : evitable
await [ə'weɪt] *vt* : esperar
awake [ə'weɪk] *v* **awoke** [ə'woːk]; **awoken** [ə'woːkən] *or* **awaked; awaking** : despertar — ~ *adj* : despierto — **awaken** [ə'weɪkən] *v* → **awake**
award [ə'wɔrd] *vt* **1** : otorgar, conceder (un premio, etc.) **2** : adjudicar (daños y perjuicios) — ~ *n* **1** PRIZE : premio *m* **2** : adjudicación *f*
aware [ə'wær] *adj* **be** ~ **of** : estar consciente de — **awareness** [ə'wærnəs] *n* : conciencia *f*
away [ə'weɪ] *adv* **1** (*referring to distance*) : de aquí, de distancia **2 far** ~ : lejos **3 give** ~ : regalar **4 go** ~ : irse **5 right** ~ : en seguida **6 take** ~ : quitar — ~ *adj* **1** ABSENT : ausente **2** ~ **game** : partido *m* fuera de casa
awe ['ɔ] *n* : temor *m* reverencial — **awesome** ['ɔsəm] *adj* : imponente, formidable
awful ['ɔfəl] *adj* **1** : terrible, espantoso **2** **an** ~ **lot** : muchísimo — **awfully** ['ɔfəli] *adv* : terriblemente
awhile [ə'hwaɪl] *adv* : un rato
awkward ['ɔkwərd] *adj* **1** CLUMSY : torpe **2** EMBARRASSING : embarazoso, delicado **3** DIFFICULT : difícil — **awkwardly** *adv* **1** : con dificultad **2** CLUMSILY : de manera torpe
awning ['ɔnɪŋ] *n* : toldo *m*
awry [ə'raɪ] *adj* **1** ASKEW : torcido **2 go** ~ : salir mal
ax *or* **axe** ['æks] *n* : hacha *f*
axiom ['æksiəm] *n* : axioma *m*
axis ['æksɪs] *n, pl* **axes** [-,siːz] : eje *m*
axle ['æksəl] *n* : eje *m*

B

b ['bi:] *n, pl* **b's** *or* **bs** ['bi:z] : b, segunda letra del alfabeto inglés

babble ['bæbəl] *vi* **-bled; -bling 1** : balbucear **2** MURMUR : murmurar — **~** *n* : balbuceo *m* (de bebé), murmullo *m* (de voces, de un arroyo)

baboon [bæ'bu:n] *n* : babuino *m*

baby ['beɪbi] *n, pl* **-bies** : bebé *m;* niño *m*, -ña *f* — **baby** *vt* **-bied; -bying** : mimar, consentir — **babyish** ['beɪbiɪʃ] *adj* : infantil — **baby-sit** ['beɪbi-,sɪt] *vi* **-sat** [-,sæt]; **-sitting** : cuidar a los niños

bachelor ['bætʃələr] *n* **1** : soltero *m* **2** GRADUATE : licenciado *m*, -da *f*

back ['bæk] *n* **1** : espalda *f* **2** REVERSE : reverso *m*, dorso *m*, revés *m* **3** REAR : fondo *m*, parte *f* trasera **4** : defensa *mf* (en deportes) — **~** *adv* **1** : atrás — **be ~** : estar de vuelta **3 go ~** : volver **4 two years ~** : hace dos años — **~** *adj* **1** REAR : de atrás, trasero **2** OVERDUE : atrasado — **~** *vt* **1** SUPPORT : apoyar **2** *or* **~ up** : darle marcha atrás a (un vehículo) — *vi* **1 ~ down** : volverse atrás **2 ~ up** : retroceder — **backache** ['bæk,eɪk] *n* : dolor *m* de espalda — **backbone** ['bæk,bon] *n* : columna *f* vertebral — **backfire** ['bæk,faɪr] *vi* **-fired; -firing** : petardear — **background** ['bæk-,graund] *n* **1** : fondo *m* (de un cuadro, etc.), antecedentes *mpl* (de una situación) **2** EXPERIENCE : formación *f* — **backhand** ['bæk,hænd] *adv* : de revés, con el revés — **backhanded** ['bæk,hændəd] *adj* : indirecto — **backing** ['bækɪŋ] *n* : apoyo *m*, respaldo *m* — **backlash** ['bæk,læʃ] *n* : reacción *f* violenta — **backlog** ['bæk,lɔg] *n* : atrasos *mpl* — **backpack** ['bæk,pæk] *n* : mochila *f* — **backstage** [,bæk'steɪdʒ, 'bæk,-] *adv & adj* : entre bastidores — **backtrack** ['bæk,træk] *vi* : dar marcha atrás — **backup** ['bæk,ʌp] *n* **1** SUPPORT : respaldo *m*, apoyo *m* **2** : copia *f* de seguridad (para computadoras) — **backward** ['bækwərd] *or* **backwards** [-wərdz] *adv* **1** : hacia atrás **2 do it ~** : hacerlo al revés **3 fall ~** : caer de espaldas **4 bend over ~s** : hacer todo lo posible — **backward** *adj* **1** : hacia atrás **2** RETARDED : retrasado

3 SHY : tímido **4** UNDERDEVELOPED : atrasado

bacon ['beɪkən] *n* : tocino *m*, tocineta *f Lat*, bacon *m Spain*

bacteria [bæk'tɪriə] : bacterias *fpl*

bad ['bæd] *adj* **worse** ['wərs]; **worst** ['wərst] **1** : malo **2** ROTTEN : podrido **3** SEVERE : grave **4 from ~ to worse** : de mal en peor **5 too ~!** : ¡qué lástima! — **~** *adv* → **badly**

badge ['bædʒ] *n* : insignia *f*, chapa *f*

badger ['bædʒər] *n* : tejón *m* — **~** *vt* : acosar

badly ['bædli] *adv* **1** : mal **2** SEVERELY : gravemente **3 want ~** : desear mucho

baffle ['bæfəl] *vi* **-fled; -fling** : desconcertar

bag ['bæg] *n* **1** : bolsa *f*, saco *m* **2** HANDBAG : bolso *m*, cartera *f Lat* **3** SUITCASE : maleta *f* — **~** *vt* **bagged; bagging** : ensacar, poner en una bolsa

baggage ['bægɪdʒ] *n* : equipaje *m*

baggy ['bægi] *adj* **-gier; -est** : holgado

bail ['beɪl] *n* : fianza *f* — **~** *vt* **1** : achicar (agua de un bote) **2 ~ out** RELEASE : poner en libertad bajo fianza **3 ~ out** EXTRICATE : sacar de apuros

bailiff ['beɪləf] *n* : alguacil *mf*

bait ['beɪt] *vt* **1** : cebar **2** HARASS : acosar — **~** *n* : cebo *m*, carnada *f*

bake ['beɪk] *v* **baked; baking** *vt* : cocer al horno — *vi* : cocerse (al horno) — **baker** ['beɪkər] *n* : panadero *m*, -ra *f* — **bakery** ['beɪkəri] *n, pl* **-ries** : panadería *f*

balance ['bælənts] *n* **1** SCALES : balanza *f* **2** COUNTERBALANCE : contrapeso *m* **3** EQUILIBRIUM : equilibrio *m* **4** REMAINDER : resto *m* **5** *or* **bank ~** : saldo *m* — **~** *v* **-anced; -ancing** *vt* **1** : hacer el balance de (una cuenta) **2** EQUALIZE : equilibrar **3** WEIGH : sopesar — *vi* **1** : sostenerse en equilibrio **2** : cuadrar (dícese de una cuenta)

balcony ['bælkəni] *n, pl* **-nies 1** : balcón *m* **2** : galería *f* (de un teatro)

bald ['bɔld] *adj* **1** : calvo **2** WORN : pelado **3 the ~ truth** : la pura verdad

bale *n* : bala *f*, fardo *m*

baleful ['beɪlfəl] *adj* : siniestro

balk ['bɔk] *vi* **~ at** : resistirse a

ball ['bɔl] *n* **1** : pelota *f*, bola *f*, balón *m* **2** DANCE : baile *m* **3** ~ **of string** : ovillo *m* de cuerda
ballad ['bæləd] *n* : balada *f*
ballast *n* : lastre *m*
ball bearing *n* : cojinete *m* de bola
ballerina [,bælə'rimə] *n* : bailarina *f*
ballet [bæ'leɪ, 'bæ,leɪ] *n* : ballet *m*
ballistic [bə'lɪstɪk] *adj* : balístico
balloon *n* : globo *m*
ballot *n* **1** : papeleta *f* (de voto) **2** VOTING : votación *f*
ballpoint pen ['bɔl,pɔɪnt] *n* : bolígrafo *m*
ballroom ['bɔl,rum, -,rum] *n* : sala *f* de baile
balm ['bam, 'balm] *n* : bálsamo *m* — **balmy** ['bami, 'bal-] *adj* **balmier; -est** : templado, agradable
baloney [bə'loːni] *n* NONSENSE : tonterías *fpl*
bamboo [bæm'buː] *n* : bambú *m*
bamboozle [bæm'buːzəl] *vt* **-zled; -zling** : engañar, embaucar
ban ['bæn] *vt* **banned; banning** : prohibir — ~ *n* : prohibición *f*
banal [bə'nɑl, bə'næl, 'beɪnəl] *adj* : banal
banana [bə'nænə] *n* : plátano *m*, banana *f Lat*, banano *m Lat*
band ['bænd] *n* **1** STRIP : banda *f* **2** GROUP : banda *f*, grupo *m*, conjunto *m* — ~ *vi* ~ **together** : unirse, juntarse
bandage ['bændɪdʒ] *n* : vendaje *m*, venda *f* — ~ *vt* **-daged; -daging** : vendar
bandit ['bændət] *n* : bandido *m*, -da *f*
bandy ['bændi] *vt* **-died; -dying** ~ **about** : circular, repetir
bang ['bæŋ] *vt* **1** STRIKE : golpear **2** SLAM : cerrar de un golpe — *vi* **1** SLAM : cerrarse de un golpe **2** ~ **on** : golpear — ~ *n* **1** BLOW : golpe *m* **2** NOISE : estrépito *m* **3** SLAM : portazo *m*
bangle ['bæŋgəl] *n* : brazalete *m*, pulsera *f*
bangs ['bæŋz] *npl* : flequillo *m*
banish ['bænɪʃ] *vt* : desterrar
banister ['bænəstər] *n* : pasamanos *m*, barandal *m*
bank ['bæŋk] *n* **1** : banco *m* **2** : orilla *f*, ribera *f* (de un río) **3** EMBANKMENT : terraplén *m* — ~ *vt* : depositar — *vi* **1** : ladearse (dícese de un avión) **2** : tener una cuenta (en un banco) **3** ~ **on** : contar con — **banker** ['bæŋkər] *n* : banquero *m*, -ra *f* — **banking** ['bæŋkɪŋ] *n* : banca *f*
bankrupt ['bæŋ,krʌpt] *adj* : en bancarrota, en quiebra — **bankruptcy** ['bæŋ,krʌptsi] *n, pl* **-cies** : quiebra *f*, bancarrota *f*

banner ['bænər] *n* : bandera *f*, pancarta *f*
banquet ['bæŋkwət] *n* : banquete *m*
banter ['bæntər] *n* : bromas *fpl* — ~ *vi* : hacer bromas
baptize [bæp'taɪz, 'bæp,taɪz] *vt* **-tized; -tizing** : bautizar — **baptism** ['bæp,tɪzəm] *n* : bautismo *m*
bar ['bar] *n* **1** : barra *f* **2** BARRIER : barrera *f*, obstáculo *m* **3** COUNTER : mostrador *m*, barra *f* **4** TAVERN : bar *m* **5 behind** ~**s** : entre rejas **6** ~ **of soap** : pastilla *f* de jabón — ~ *vt* **barred; barring 1** OBSTRUCT : obstruir, bloquear **2** EXCLUDE : excluir **3** PROHIBIT : prohibir — ~ *prep* **1** : excepto **2** ~ **none** : sin excepción
barbarian [bar'bæriən] *n* : bárbaro *m*, -ra *f*
barbecue ['barbɪ,kjuː] *vt* **-cued; -cuing** : asar a la parrilla — ~ *n* : barbacoa *f*
barbed wire ['barbd'waɪr] *n* : alambre *m* de púas
barber ['barbər] *n* : barbero *m*, -ra *f*
bare ['bær] *adj* **1** : desnudo **2** EMPTY : vacío **3** MINIMUM : mero, esencial — **barefaced** ['bær,feɪst] *adj* : descarado — **barefoot** ['bær,fʊt] *or* **barefooted** [-,fʊtəd] *adv* & *adj* : descalzo — **barely** ['bærli] *adv* : apenas, por poco
bargain ['bargən] *n* **1** AGREEMENT : acuerdo *m* **2** BUY : ganga *f* — ~ *vi* **1** : regatear, negociar **2** ~ **for** : contar con
barge ['bardʒ] *n* : barcaza *f* — ~ *vi* **barged; barging** ~ **in** : entrometerse, interrumpir
baritone ['bærə,toʊn] *n* : barítono *m*
bark[1] ['bark] *vi* : ladrar — ~ *n* : ladrido *m* (de un perro)
bark[2] *n* : corteza *f* (de un árbol)
barley ['barli] *n* : cebada *f*
barn ['barn] *n* : granero *m* — **barnyard** ['barn,jard] *n* : corral *m*
barometer [bə'ramətər] *n* : barómetro *m*
baron ['bærən] *n* : barón *m* — **baroness** ['bærənɪs, -nəs, -,nɛs] *n* : baronesa *f*
barracks ['bærəks] *ns* & *pl* : cuartel *m*
barrage [bə'raʒ, -radʒ] *n* **1** : descarga *f* (de artillería) **2** : aluvión *m* (de preguntas, etc.)
barrel ['bærəl] *n* **1** : barril *m*, tonel *m* **2** : cañón *m* (de un arma de fuego)
barren ['bærən] *adj* : estéril
barricade ['bærə,keɪd, ,bærə'-] *vt* **-caded; -cading** : cerrar con barricadas — ~ *n* : barricada *f*
barrier ['bæriər] *n* : barrera *f*
barring ['barɪŋ] *prep* : salvo
barrio ['bario, 'bær-] *n* : barrio *m*

bartender ['bɑr,tɛndər] *n* : camarero *m*, -ra *f*

barter ['bɑrtər] *vt* : cambiar, trocar — ~ *n* : trueque *m*

base ['beɪs] *n*, *pl* **bases** : base *f* — ~ *vt* **based; basing** : basar, fundamentar — ~ *adj* **baser; basest** : vil

baseball ['beɪs,bɔl] *n* : beisbol *m*, béisbol *m*

basement ['beɪsmənt] *n* : sótano *m*

bash ['bæʃ] *vt* : golpear violentamente — ~ *n* 1 BLOW : golpe *m* 2 PARTY : fiesta *f*

bashful ['bæʃfəl] *adj* : tímido, vergonzoso

basic ['beɪsɪk] *adj* : básico, fundamental — **basically** ['beɪsɪkli] *adv* : fundamentalmente

basil ['beɪzəl, 'bæzəl] *n* : albahaca *f*

basin ['beɪsən] *n* 1 WASHBOWL : palangana *f*, lavabo *m* 2 : cuenca *f* (de un río)

basis ['beɪsəs] *n*, *pl* **bases** [-,siːz] : base *f*

bask ['bæsk] *vi* ~ **in the sun** : tostarse al sol

basket ['bæskət] *n* : cesta *f*, cesto *m* — **basketball** ['bæskət,bɔl] *n* : baloncesto *m*, basquetbol *m Lat*

bass¹ ['bæs] *n*, *pl* **bass** *or* **basses** : róbalo *m* (pesca)

bass² ['beɪs] *n* : bajo *m* (tono, voz, instrumento)

bassoon [bə'suːn, bæ-] *n* : fagot *m*

bastard ['bæstərd] *n* : bastardo *m*, -da *f*

baste ['beɪst] *vt* **basted; basting** 1 STITCH : hilvanar 2 : bañar (carne)

bat¹ ['bæt] *n* : murciélago *m* (animal)

bat² *n* : bate *m* — ~ *vt* **batted; batting** : batear

batch ['bætʃ] *n* : hornada *f* (de pasteles, etc.), lote *m* (de mercancías), montón *m* (de trabajo), grupo *m* (de personas)

bath ['bæθ, 'bɑθ] *n*, *pl* **baths** ['bæðz, 'bæθs, 'bɑðz, 'bɑθs] 1 : baño *m* 2 BATHROOM : baño *m*, cuarto *m* de baño 3 **take a** ~ : bañarse — **bathe** ['beɪð] *v* **bathed; bathing** *vt* : bañar, lavar — *vi* : bañarse — **bathrobe** ['bæθ,roːb] *n* : bata *f* (de baño) — **bathroom** ['bæθ,ruːm, -rʊm] *n* : baño *m*, cuarto *m* de baño — **bathtub** ['bæθ,tʌb] *n* : bañera *f*, tina *f* (de baño)

baton [bə'tɑn] *n* : batuta *f*

battalion [bə'tæljən] *n* : batallón *m*

batter ['bætər] *vt* 1 BEAT : golpear 2 MISTREAT : maltratar — ~ *n* 1 : masa *f* para rebozar 2 HITTER : bateador *m*, -dora *f*

battery ['bætəri] *n*, *pl* **-teries** : batería *f*, pila *f* (de electricidad)

battle ['bætəl] *n* 1 : batalla *f* 2 STRUGGLE : lucha *f* — ~ *vi* **-tled; -tling** : luchar — **battlefield** ['bætəl,fiːld] *n* : campo *m* de batalla — **battleship** ['bætəl,ʃɪp] *n* : acorazado *m*

bawl ['bɔl] *vi* : llorar a gritos

bay¹ ['beɪ] *n* INLET : bahía *f*

bay² *n or* ~ **leaf** : laurel *m*

bay³ *vi* : aullar — ~ *n* : aullido *m*

bayonet [,beɪə'nɛt, 'beɪə,nɛt] *n* : bayoneta *f*

bay window *n* : ventana *f* en saliente

bazaar [bə'zɑr] *n* 1 : bazar *m* 2 SALE : venta *f* benéfica

be ['biː] *v* **was** ['wəz, 'wɑz], **were** ['wər]; **been** ['bɪn]; **being; am** ['æm], **is** ['ɪz], **are** ['ɑr] *vi* 1 : ser 2 (*expressing location*) : estar 3 (*expressing existence*) : ser, existir 4 (*expressing a state of being*) : estar, tener — *v impers* 1 (*indicating time*) : ser 2 (*indicating a condition*) : hacer, estar — *v aux* 1 (*expressing occurrence*) : ser 2 (*expressing possibility*) : poderse 3 (*expressing obligation*) : deber 4 (*expressing progression*) : estar

beach ['biːtʃ] *n* : playa *f*

beacon ['biːkən] *n* : faro *m*

bead ['biːd] *n* 1 : cuenta *f* 2 DROP : gota *f* 3 ~**s** *npl* NECKLACE : collar *m*

beak ['biːk] *n* : pico *m*

beam ['biːm] *n* 1 : viga *f* (de madera, etc.) 2 RAY : rayo *m* — ~ *vi* SHINE : brillar — *vt* BROADCAST : transmitir, emitir

bean ['biːn] *n* 1 : habichuela *f*, frijol *m* 2 **coffee** ~ : grano *m* 3 **string** ~ : judía *f*

bear¹ ['bær] *n*, *pl* **bears** *or* **bear** : oso *m*, osa *f*

bear² *v* **bore** ['bor]; **borne** ['born]; **bearing** *vt* 1 CARRY : portar 2 ENDURE : soportar — *vi* **right/left** : doble a la derecha/a la izquierda — **bearable** ['bærəbəl] *adj* : soportable

beard ['bɪrd] *n* : barba *f*

bearer ['bærər] *n* : portador *m*, -dora *f*

bearing ['bærɪŋ] *n* 1 MANNER : comportamiento *m* 2 SIGNIFICANCE : relación *f*, importancia *f* 3 **get one's** ~**s** : orientarse

beast ['biːst] *n* : bestia *f*

beat¹ ['biːt] *v* **beat**; **beaten** ['biːtən] *or* **beat**; **beating** *vt* 1 HIT : golpear 2 : batir (huevos, etc.) 3 DEFEAT : derrotar — *vi* : latir (dícese del corazón) — ~ *n* 1 : golpe *m* 2 : latido *m* (del corazón) 3 RHYTHM : ritmo *m*, tiempo *m* — **beating** ['biːtɪŋ] *n* 1 : paliza *f* 2 DEFEAT : derrota *f*

beauty ['bjuːṭi] *n*, *pl* **-ties** : belleza *f* —
beautiful ['bjuːṭɪfəl] *adj* : hermoso,
lindo — **beautifully** ['bjuːṭɪfəli] *adv*
WONDERFULLY : maravillosamente —
beautify ['bjuːṭɪfaɪ] *vt* **-fied; -fying**
: embellecer
beaver ['biːvər] *n* : castor *m*
because [br'kʌz, -'kɔz] *conj* : porque —
because of *prep* : por, a causa de, debido a
beckon ['bɛkən] *vt* : llamar, hacer señas
a — *vi* : hacer una seña
become [br'kʌm] *v* **-came** [-'keɪm];
-come; -coming *vi* : hacerse, ponerse
— *vt* SUIT : favorecer — **becoming**
[br'kʌmɪŋ] *adj* **1** SUITABLE : apropiado **2**
FLATTERING : favorecedor
bed ['bɛd] *n* **1** : cama *f* **2** : cauce *m* (de
un río), fondo *m* (del mar) **3** : macizo
m (de flores) **4 go to ~** : irse a
la cama — **bedclothes** ['bɛd,kloz,
-,kloːðz] *npl* : ropa *f* de cama
bedlam ['bɛdləm] *n* : confusión *f*, caos
m
bedraggled [br'drægəld] *adj* : desaliñado, sucio
bedridden ['bɛd,rɪdən] *adj* : postrado en
cama
bedroom ['bɛd,ruːm, -,rʊm] *n* : dormitorio *m*, recámara *f Lat*
bedspread ['bɛd,sprɛd] *n* : colcha *f*
bedtime ['bɛd,taɪm] *n* : hora *f* de acostarse
bee ['biː] *n* : abeja *f*
beech ['biːtʃ] *n*, *pl* **beeches** *or* **beech**
: haya *f*
beef ['biːf] *n* : carne *f* de vaca, carne *f* de
res *Lat* — **beefsteak** ['biːf,steɪk] *n*
: bistec *m*
beehive ['biː,haɪv] *n* : colmena *f*
beeline ['biː,laɪn] *n* **make a ~ for** : irse
derecho a
beep ['biːp] *n* : pitido *m* — **~** *v* : pitar
beer ['bɪr] *n* : cerveza *f*
beet ['biːt] *n* : remolacha *f*
beetle ['biːtəl] *n* : escarabajo *m*
before [br'for] *adv* **1** : antes **2 the
month ~** : el mes anterior — **~** *prep*
1 (*in space*) : delante de, ante **2** (*in
time*) : antes de — **~** *conj* : antes de
que — **beforehand** [br'for,hænd] *adv*
: antes
befriend [br'frɛnd] *vt* : hacerse amigo de
beg ['bɛg] *v* **begged; begging** *vt* **1**
: pedir, mendigar **2** ENTREAT : suplicar
— *vi* : mendigar, pedir limosna —
beggar ['bɛgər] *n* : mendigo *m*, -ga *f*
begin [br'gɪn] *v* **-gan** [-'gæn]; **-gun**
[-'gʌn]; **-ginning** : empezar, comenzar
— **beginner** [br'gɪnər] *n* : principiante

mf — **beginning** [br'gɪnɪŋ] *n* : principio *m*, comienzo *m*
begrudge [br'grʌdʒ] *vt* **-grudged;
-grudging 1** : dar de mala gana **2**
ENVY : envidiar
behalf [br'hæf, -'haf] *n* **on ~ of** : de
parte de, en nombre de
behave [br'heɪv] *vi* **-haved; -having**
: comportarse, portarse — **behavior**
[br'heɪvjər] *n* : comportamiento *m*,
conducta *f*
behind [br'haɪnd] *adv* **1** : detrás **2 fall ~**
: atrasarse — **~** *prep* **1** : atrás de, detrás de **2 be ~ schedule** : ir retrasado **3 her friends are ~ her** : tiene el
apoyo de sus amigos
behold [br'hoːld] *vt* **-held; -holding**
: contemplar
beige ['beɪʒ] *adj & nm* : beige
being ['biːɪŋ] *n* **1** : ser *m* **2 come into ~**
: nacer
belated [br'leɪṭəd] *adj* : tardío
belch ['bɛltʃ] *vi* : eructar — **~** *n* : eructo *m*
Belgian ['bɛldʒən] *adj* : belga
belie [br'laɪ] *vt* **-lied; -lying** : contradecir, desmentir
belief [bə'liːf] *n* **1** TRUST : confianza *f* **2**
CONVICTION : creencia *f*, convicción *f* **3**
FAITH : fe *f* — **believable** [bə'liːvəbəl]
adj : creíble — **believe** [bə'liːv] *v*
-lieved; -lieving : creer — **believer**
[bə'liːvər] *n* : creyente *mf*
belittle [br'lɪṭəl] *vt* **-littled; -littling**
: menospreciar
Belizean [bə'liːziən] *adj* : beliceño *m*,
-ña *f*
bell ['bɛl] *n* **1** : campana *f* **2** : timbre *m*
(de teléfono, de la puerta, etc.)
belligerent [bə'lɪdʒərənt] *adj* : beligerante
bellow ['bɛ,loː] *vi* : bramar, mugir — *vt*
or **~ out** : gritar
bellows ['bɛ,loːz] *ns & pl* : fuelle *m*
belly ['bɛli] *n*, *pl* **-lies** : vientre *m*
belong [br'lɔŋ] *vi* **1 ~ to** : pertenecer a,
ser propiedad de **2 ~ to** : ser miembro de (un club, etc.) **3 where does it
~** : ¿dónde va? — **belongings** [br-
'lɔŋɪŋz] *npl* : pertenencias *fpl*, efectos
mpl personales
beloved [br'lʌvəd, -'lʌvd] *adj* : querido,
amado — **~** *n* : querido *m*, -da *f*
below [br'loː] *adv* : abajo — **~** *prep* **1**
: abajo de, debajo de **2 ~ average**
: por debajo del promedio **3 ~ zero**
: bajo cero
belt ['bɛlt] *n* **1** : cinturón *m* **2** BAND,
STRAP : cinta *f*, correa *f* **3** AREA : frente

m, zona *f* — ~ *vt* **1** : ceñir con un cinturón **2** THRASH : darle una paliza a

bench ['bentʃ] *n* **1** : banco *m* **2** WORKBENCH : mesa *f* de trabajo **3** COURT : tribunal *m*

bend ['bend] *v* **bent** ['bent]; **bending** *vt* : doblar, torcer — *vi* **1** : torcerse **2** ~ **over** : inclinarse — ~ *n* : curva *f*, ángulo *m*

beneath [bɪ'ni:θ] *adv* : abajo, debajo — ~ *prep* : bajo, debajo de

benediction [,benə'dɪkʃən] *n* : bendición *f*

benefactor ['benə,fæktər] *n* : benefactor *m*, -tora *f*

benefit ['benəfɪt] *n* **1** ADVANTAGE : ventaja *f*, provecho *m* **2** AID : asistencia *f*, beneficio *m* — ~ *vt* : beneficiar — *vi* : beneficiarse — **beneficial** [,benə'fɪʃəl] *adj* : beneficioso — **beneficiary** [,benə'fɪʃi,eri, -'fɪʃəri] *n, pl* -**ries** : beneficiario *m*, -ria *f*

benevolent [bə'nevələnt] *adj* : benévolo

benign [bɪ'naɪn] *adj* **1** KIND : benévolo, amable **2** : benigno (en medicina)

bent ['bent] *adj* **1** : encorvado **2** be ~ **on** : estar empeñado en — ~ *n* : aptitud *f*, inclinación *f*

bequeath [bɪ'kwi:θ, -'kwi:ð] *vt* : legar — **bequest** [bɪ'kwest] *n* : legado *m*

berate [bɪ'reɪt] *vt* -**rated**; -**rating** : reprender, regañar

bereaved [bɪ'ri:vd] *adj* : desconsolado, a luto

beret [bə'reɪ] *n* : boina *f*

berry ['beri] *n, pl* -**ries** : baya *f*

berserk [bər'sərk, -'zərk] *adj* **1** : enloquecido **2** go ~ : volverse loco

berth ['bərθ] *n* **1** MOORING : atracadero *m* **2** BUNK : litera *f*

beseech [bɪ'si:tʃ] *vt* -**sought** [-'sɔt] *or* -**seeched**; -**seeching** : suplicar, implorar

beset [bɪ'set] *vt* -**set**; -**setting** **1** HARASS : acosar **2** SURROUND : rodear

beside [bɪ'saɪd] *prep* **1** : al lado de, junto a **2** be ~ **oneself** : estar fuera de sí — **besides** [bɪ'saɪdz] *adv* : además — ~ *prep* **1** : además de **2** EXCEPT : excepto

besiege [bɪ'si:dʒ] *vt* -**sieged**; -**sieging** : asediar

best ['best] *adj* (*superlative of* **good**) : mejor — ~ *adv* (*superlative of* **well**) : mejor — ~ *n* **1** at ~ : a lo más **2 do one's** ~ : hacer todo lo posible **3 the** ~ : lo mejor — **best man** *n* : padrino *m* (de boda)

bestow [bɪ'stoː] *vt* : otorgar, conceder

bet ['bet] *n* : apuesta *f* — ~ *v* **bet**; **bet-** ting *vt* : apostar — *vi* ~ **on sth** : apostarle a algo

betray [bɪ'treɪ] *vt* : traicionar — **betrayal** [bɪ'treɪəl] *n* : traición *f*

better ['betər] *adj* (*comparative of* **good**) **1** : mejor **2 get** ~ : mejorar — ~ *adv* (*comparative of* **well**) **1** : mejor **2 all the** ~ : tanto mejor — ~ *n* **1 the** ~ : el mejor, la mejor **2 get the** ~ **of** : vencer a — ~ *vt* **1** IMPROVE : mejorar **2** SURPASS : superar

between [bɪ'twin] *prep* : entre — ~ *adv or* **in** ~ : en medio

beverage ['bevrɪdʒ, 'bevə-] *n* : bebida *f*

beware [bɪ'wær] *vi* ~ **of** : tener cuidado con

bewilder [bɪ'wɪldər] *vt* : desconcertar — **bewilderment** [bɪ'wɪldərmənt] *n* : desconcierto *m*

bewitch [bɪ'wɪtʃ] *vt* : hechizar, encantar

beyond [bi'jɑnd] *adv* : más allá, más lejos (en el espacio), más adelante (en el tiempo) — ~ *prep* : más allá de

bias ['baɪəs] *n* **1** PREJUDICE : prejuicio *m* **2** TENDENCY : inclinación *f*, tendencia *f* — **biased** ['baɪəst] *adj* : parcial

bib ['bɪb] *n* : babero *m* (para niños)

Bible ['baɪbəl] *n* : Biblia *f* — **biblical** ['bɪblɪkəl] *adj* : bíblico

bibliography [,bɪbli'ɑgrəfi] *n, pl* -**phies** : bibliografía *f*

bicarbonate of soda [baɪ'kɑrbənət, ,neɪt] *n* : bicarbonato *m* de soda

biceps ['baɪseps] *ns & pl* : bíceps *m*

bicker ['bɪkər] *vi* : reñir

bicycle ['baɪsɪkəl, -ˌsɪ-] *n* : bicicleta *f* — ~ *vi* -**cled**; -**cling** : ir en bicicleta

bid ['bɪd] *vt* **bade** ['bæd, 'beɪd] *or* **bid**; **bidden** ['bɪdən] *or* **bid**; **bidding 1** OFFER : ofrecer **2** ~ **farewell** : decir adiós — ~ *n* **1** OFFER : oferta *f* **2** ATTEMPT : intento *m*, tentativa *f*

bide ['baɪd] *vt* **bode** ['bo:d] *or* **bided**; **bided**; **biding** ~ **one's time** : esperar el momento oportuno

bifocals [baɪ'fo:kəlz] *npl* : anteojos *mpl* bifocales

big ['bɪg] *adj* **bigger**; **biggest** : grande

bigamy ['bɪgəmi] *n* : bigamía *f*

bigot ['bɪgət] *n* : intolerante *mf* — **bigotry** ['bɪgətri] *n, pl* -**tries** : intolerancia *f*, fanatismo *m*

bike ['baɪk] *n* **1** BICYCLE : bici *f fam* **2** MOTORCYCLE : moto *f*

bikini [bə'ki:ni] *n* : bikini *m*

bile ['baɪl] *n* : bilis *f*

bilingual [baɪ'lɪŋgwəl] *adj* : bilingüe

bill ['bɪl] *n* **1** BEAK : pico *m* **2** INVOICE : cuenta *f*, factura *f* **3** BANKNOTE : billete *m* **4** LAW : proyecto *m* de ley, ley *f*

— ~ *vt* : pasarle la cuenta a — **billboard** ['bɪl,bord] *n* : cartelera *f* — **billfold** ['bɪl,fo:ld] *n* : billetera *f*, cartera *f*
billiards ['bɪljərdz] *n* : billar *m*
billion ['bɪljən] *n, pl* **billions** *or* **billion**
: mil millones *mpl*
billow ['bɪlo] *vi* : ondular, hincharse
billy goat ['bɪli,go:t] *n* : macho *m* cabrío
bin ['bɪn] *n* : cubo *m*, cajón *m*
binary ['baɪnəri, -ˌneri] *adj* : binario *m*
bind ['baɪnd] *vt* **bound** ['baʊnd]; **bind-
ing 1** TIE : atar **2** OBLIGATE : obligar **3**
UNITE : unir **4** BANDAGE : vendar **5**
: encuadernar (un libro) — **binder**
['baɪndər] *n* FOLDER : carpeta *f* — **bind-
ing** ['baɪndɪŋ] *n* : encuadernación *f* (de
libros)
binge ['bɪndʒ] *n* : juerga *f fam*
bingo ['bɪŋgo:] *n, pl* **-gos** : bingo *m*
binoculars [bə'nɑkjələrz, baɪ-] *npl*
: binoculares *mpl*, gemelos *mpl*
biochemistry [ˌbaɪo'kemɪstri] *n* : bioquímica *f*
biography [baɪ'ɑgrəfi, bi:-] *n, pl* **-phies**
: biografía *f* — **biographer** [baɪ-
'ɑgrəfər] *n* : biógrafo *m*, -fa *f* — **biographical** [ˌbaɪə'græfɪkəl] *adj* : biográfico
biology [baɪ'ɑlədʒi] *n* : biología *f* — **biological** [-dʒɪkəl] *adj* : biológico — **biologist** [baɪ'ɑlədʒɪst] *n* : biólogo *m*, -ga
f
birch ['bərtʃ] *n* : abedul *m*
bird ['bərd] *n* : pájaro *m* (pequeño), ave *f*
(grande)
birth ['bərθ] *n* **1** : nacimiento *m*, parto *m*
2 give ~ **to** : dar a luz a — **birthday**
['bərθ,deɪ] *n* : cumpleaños *m* — **birth-
mark** ['bərθ,mɑrk] *n* : mancha *f* de
nacimiento — **birthplace** ['bərθ,pleɪs]
n : lugar *m* de nacimiento — **birthrate**
['bərθ,reɪt] *n* : índice *m* de natalidad
biscuit ['bɪskət] *n* : bizcocho *m*
bisect ['baɪ,sekt, ˌbaɪ-] *vt* : bisecar
bisexual [ˌbaɪ'sekʃəwəl, -'sekʃəl] *adj* : bisexual
bishop ['bɪʃəp] *n* : obispo *m*
bison ['baɪzən, -sən] *n & pl* : bisonte *m*
bit[1] ['bɪt] *n* : bocado *m* (de una brida)
bit[2] **1** : trozo *m*, pedazo *m* **2** : bit *m* (de
información) **3 a** ~ : un poco
bitch ['bɪtʃ] *n* : perra *f* — ~ *vi* COMPLAIN
: quejarse, reclamar
bite ['baɪt] *v* **bit** ['bɪt]; **bitten** ['bɪtən]; **biting** *vt* **1** : morder **2** STING : picar — *vi*
: morder — *n* **1** : picadura *f* (de un insecto), mordedura *f* (de un animal) **2**
SNACK : bocado *m* — **biting** *adj* **1** PEN-
ETRATING : cortante, penetrante **2**
CAUSTIC : mordaz

bitter ['bɪtər] *adj* **1** : amargo **2 it's** ~
cold : hace un frío glacial **3 to the** ~
end : hasta el final — **bitterness**
['bɪtərnəs] *n* : amargura *f*
bizarre [bə'zɑr] *adj* : extraño
black ['blæk] *adj* : negro — ~ *n* **1**
: negro *m* (color) **2** : negro *m*, -gra *f*
(persona) — **black–and–blue**
[ˌblækən'blu:] *adj* : amoratado — **blackberry** ['blæk,beri] *n, pl* **-ries** : mora *f* —
blackbird ['blæk,bərd] *n* : mirlo *m* —
blackboard ['blæk,bord] *n* : pizarra *f*,
pizarrón *m Lat* — **blacken** ['blækən] *vt*
: ennegrecer — **blackmail** ['blæk,meɪl]
n : chantaje *m* — ~ *vt* : chantajear —
black market *n* : mercado *m* negro —
blackout ['blæk,aʊt] *n* **1** : apagón *m* (de
poder eléctrico) **2** FAINT : desmayo *m*
— **blacksmith** ['blæk,smɪθ] *n* : herrero
m — **blacktop** ['blæk,tɑp] *n* : asfalto *m*
bladder ['blædər] *n* : vejiga *f*
blade ['bleɪd] *n* **1** : hoja *f* (de un cuchillo), cuchilla *f* (de un patín) **2** : pala *f*
(de un remo, una hélice, etc.) **3** ~ **of
grass** : brizna *f* (de hierba)
blame ['bleɪm] *vt* **blamed**; **blaming**
: culpar, echar la culpa a — ~ *n*
: culpa *f* — **blameless** ['bleɪmləs] *adj*
: inocente
bland ['blænd] *adj* : soso, insulso
blank ['blæŋk] *adj* **1** : en blanco (dícese
de un papel), liso (dícese de una
pared) **2** EMPTY : vacío — ~ *n* : espacio *m* en blanco
blanket ['blæŋkət] *n* **1** : manta *f*, cobija *f*
Lat **2** ~ **of snow** : manto *m* de nieve
— ~ *vt* : cubrir
blare ['blær] *vi* **blared**; **blaring** : resonar
blasphemy ['blæsfəmi] *n, pl* **-mies**
: blasfemia *f*
blast ['blæst] *n* **1** GUST : ráfaga *f* **2** EX-
PLOSION : explosión *f* **3** : toque *m* (de
trompeta, etc.) — ~ *vt* BLOW UP
: volar — **blast-off** ['blæst,ɔf] *n* : despegue *m*
blatant ['bleɪtənt] *adj* : descarado
blaze ['bleɪz] *n* **1** FIRE : fuego *m* **2**
BRIGHTNESS : resplandor *m*, brillantez *f*
3 ~ **of anger** : arranque *m* de cólera
— *v* **blazed**; **blazing** *vi* : arder, brillar — *vt* ~ **a trail** : abrir un camino
blazer ['bleɪzər] *n* : chaqueta *f* deportiva
bleach ['bli:tʃ] *vt* : blanquear, decolorar
— ~ *n* : lejía *f*, blanqueador *m Lat*
bleachers ['bli:tʃərz] *ns & pl* : gradas *fpl*
bleak ['bli:k] *adj* **1** DESOLATE : desolado
2 GLOOMY : triste, sombrío
bleary–eyed ['blɪriˌaɪd] *adj* : con los
ojos nublados
bleat ['bli:t] *vi* : balar — ~ *n* : balido *m*

bleed ['bliːd] v **bled** ['blɛd]; **bleeding** : sangrar

blemish ['blɛmɪʃ] vt : manchar, marcar — ~ n 1 : mancha f, marca f

blend ['blɛnd] vt : mezclar, combinar — ~ n : mezcla f, combinación f — **blender** ['blɛndər] n : licuadora f

bless ['blɛs] vt **blessed** ['blɛst]; **blessing** : bendecir — **blessed** ['blɛsəd] or **blest** ['blɛst] adj : bendito — **blessing** ['blɛsɪŋ] n : bendición f

blew → **blow**

blind ['blaɪnd] adj : ciego — ~ vt 1 : cegar, dejar ciego 2 DAZZLE : deslumbrar — ~ n 1 : persiana f (para una ventana) 2 the ~ : los ciegos — **blindfold** ['blaɪndˌfoːld] vt : vendar los ojos — ~ n : venda f (para los ojos) — **blindly** ['blaɪndli] adv : ciegamente — **blindness** ['blaɪndnəs] n : ceguera f

blink ['blɪŋk] vi 1 : parpadear 2 FLICKER : brillar intermitentemente — ~ n : parpadeo m — **blinker** ['blɪŋkər] n : intermitente m, direccional f Lat

bliss ['blɪs] n : dicha f, felicidad f (absoluta) — **blissful** ['blɪsfəl] adj : feliz

blister ['blɪstər] n : ampolla f — ~ vi : ampollarse

blitz ['blɪts] n : bombardeo m aéreo

blizzard ['blɪzərd] n : ventisca f (de nieve)

bloated ['bloːtəd] adj : hinchado

blob ['blɑb] n 1 DROP : gota f 2 SPOT : mancha f

block ['blɑk] n 1 : bloque m 2 OBSTRUCTION : obstrucción f 3 : manzana f, cuadra f Lat (de edificios) 4 or **building ~** : cubo m de construcción — ~ vt : obstruir, bloquear — **blockade** [blɑˈkeɪd] n : bloqueo m — **blockage** ['blɑkɪdʒ] n : obstrucción f

blond or **blonde** ['blɑnd] adj : rubio — ~ n : rubio m, -bia f

blood ['blʌd] n : sangre f — **bloodhound** ['blʌdˌhaʊnd] n : sabueso m — **blood pressure** n : tensión f (arterial) — **bloodshed** ['blʌdˌʃɛd] n : derramamiento m de sangre — **bloodshot** ['blʌdˌʃɑt] adj : inyectado de sangre — **bloodstained** ['blʌdˌsteɪnd] adj : manchado de sangre — **bloodstream** ['blʌdˌstriːm] n : sangre f, torrente m sanguíneo — **bloody** ['blʌdi] adj **bloodier; -est** : ensangrentado, sangriento

bloom ['bluːm] n 1 : flor f 2 in full ~ : en plena floración — ~ vi : florecer

blossom ['blɑsəm] n : flor f — ~ vi : florecer

blot ['blɑt] n 1 : borrón m (de tinta, etc.) 2 BLEMISH : mancha f — ~ vt **blotted; blotting** 1 : emborronar 2 DRY : secar

blotch ['blɑtʃ] n : mancha f, borrón m — **blotchy** ['blɑtʃi] adj **blotchier; -est** : lleno de manchas

blouse ['blaʊs, 'blaʊz] n : blusa f

blow ['bloː] v **blew** ['bluː]; **blown** ['bloːn]; **blowing** vi 1 : soplar 2 SOUND : sonar 3 or ~ **out** : fundirse (dícese de un fusible eléctrico), reventarse (dícese de una llanta) — vt 1 : soplar 2 SOUND : tocar, sonar 3 BUNGLE : echar a perder — ~ n : golpe m — **blowout** ['bloːˌaʊt] n : reventón m — **blow up** vi : estallar, hacer explosión — vt 1 EXPLODE : volar 2 INFLATE : inflar

blubber ['blʌbər] n : esperma f de ballena

bludgeon ['blʌdʒən] vt : aporrear

blue ['bluː] adj **bluer; bluest** 1 : azul 2 MELANCHOLY : triste — ~ n : azul m — **blueberry** ['bluːˌbɛri] n, pl -**ries** : arándano m — **bluebird** ['bluːˌbərd] n : azulejo m — **blue cheese** n : queso m azul — **blueprint** ['bluːˌprɪnt] n PLAN : proyecto m — **blues** ['bluːz] npl 1 SADNESS : tristeza f 2 : blues m (en música)

bluff ['blʌf] vi : hacer un farol — ~ n : farol m

blunder ['blʌndər] vi : meter la pata fam — ~ n : metedura f de pata fam

blunt ['blʌnt] adj 1 DULL : desafilado 2 DIRECT : directo, franco

blur ['blər] n : imágen f borrosa — ~ vt **blurred; blurring** : hacer borroso

blurb ['blərb] n : nota f publicitaria

blurt ['blərt] vt or ~ **out** : espetar

blush ['blʌʃ] n : rubor m — ~ vi : ruborizarse

blustery ['blʌstəri] adj : borrascoso, tempestuoso

boar ['bor] n : cerdo m macho

board ['bord] n 1 PLANK : tabla f, tablón m 2 COMMITTEE : junta f, consejo m 3 : tablero m (de juegos) 4 **room and ~** : comida y alojamiento — ~ vt 1 : subir a bordo de (una nave, un avión, etc.), subir a (un tren) 2 LODGE : hospedar 3 ~ **up** : cerrar con tablas — **boarder** ['bordər] n : huésped mf

boast ['boːst] n : jactancia f — ~ vi : alardear, jactarse — **boastful** ['boːstfəl] adj : jactancioso

boat ['boːt] n : barco m (grande), barca f (pequeña)

bob ['bɑb] vi **bobbed; bobbing** or ~ **up and down** : subir y bajar

bobbin ['bɑbən] n : bobina f, carrete m

bobby pin ['bɑbiˌpɪn] n : horquilla f

body ['badi] *n, pl* **bodies 1** : cuerpo *m* **2** CORPSE : cadáver *m* **3** : carrocería (de un automóvil, etc.) **4** COLLECTION : conjunto *m* **5** ~ **of water** : masa *f* de agua — **bodily** *adj* : corporal — **bodyguard** ['badi,gard] *n* : guardaespaldas *mf*

bog ['bag, 'bɔg] *n* : ciénaga *f* — *vt* **bogged; bogging** *or* ~ **down** : empantanarse

bogus ['bo:gəs] *adj* : falso

boil ['bɔil] *v* : hervir — **boiler** ['bɔilər] *n* : caldera *f*

bold ['bo:ld] *adj* **1** DARING : audaz **2** IMPUDENT : descarado — **boldness** ['bo:ldnəs] *n* : audacia *f*

Bolivian [bə'lıviən] *adj* : boliviano *m*, -na *f*

bologna [bə'lo:ni] *n* : salchicha *f* ahumada

bolster ['bo:lstər] *vt* **-stered; -stering** *or* ~ **up** : reforzar

bolt ['bo:lt] *n* **1** LOCK : cerrojo *m* **2** SCREW : tornillo *m* **3** ~ **of lightning** : relámpago *m*, rayo *m* — ~ *vt* **1** FASTEN : atornillar **2** LOCK : echar el cerrojo a — *vi* FLEE : salir corriendo

bomb ['bam] *n* : bomba *f* — ~ *vt* : bombardear — **bombard** [bam'bard, bəm-] *vt* : bombardear — **bombardment** [bam'bardmənt] *n* : bombardeo *m* — **bomber** ['bamər] *n* : bombardero *m*

bond ['band] *n* **1** TIE : vínculo *m*, lazo *m* **2** SURETY : fianza *f* **3** : bono *m* (en finanzas) — ~ *vi* STICK : adherirse

bondage ['bandıdʒ] *n* : esclavitud *f*

bone ['bo:n] *n* : hueso *m* — ~ *vt* **boned; boning** : deshuesar

bonfire ['ban,faır] *n* : hoguera *f*

bonus ['bo:nəs] *n* **1** PAY : prima *f* **2** BENEFIT : beneficio *m* adicional

bony ['bo:ni] *adj* **bonier; -est 1** : huesudo **2** : lleno de espinas (dícese de pescados)

boo ['bu:] *n, pl* **boos** : abucheo *m* — ~ *vt* : abuchear

book ['bʊk] *n* **1** : libro *m* **2** NOTEBOOK : libreta *f*, cuaderno *m* — ~ *vt* : reservar — **bookcase** ['bʊk,keıs] *n* : estantería *f* — **bookkeeping** ['bʊk,ki:pıŋ] *n* : teneduría *f* de libros, contabilidad *f* — **booklet** ['bʊklət] *n* : folleto *m* — **bookmark** ['bʊk,mark] *n* : marcador *m* de libros — **bookseller** ['bʊk,selər] *n* : librero *m*, -ra *f* — **bookshelf** ['bʊk,ʃelf] *n, pl* **-shelves** : estante *m* — **bookstore** ['bʊk,stor] *n* : librería *f*

boom ['bu:m] *vi* **1** : tronar, resonar **2** PROSPER : estar en auge, prosperar —

~ *n* **1** : bramido *m*, estruendo *m* **2** : auge *m* (económico)

boon ['bu:n] *n* : ayuda *f*, beneficio *m*

boost ['bu:st] *vt* **1** LIFT : levantar **2** INCREASE : aumentar — ~ *n* **1** INCREASE : aumento *m* **2** ENCOURAGEMENT : estímulo *m*

boot ['bu:t] *n* : bota *f*, botín *m* — ~ *vt* **1** : dar una patada a **2** *or* ~ **up** : cargar (un ordenador)

booth ['bu:θ] *n, pl* **booths** ['bu:ðz, 'bu:θs] : cabina *f* (de teléfono, de votar), caseta *f* (de información)

booty ['bu:ti] *n, pl* **-ties** : botín *m*

booze ['bu:z] *n* : trago *m*, bebida *f* (alcohólica)

border ['bordər] *n* **1** EDGE : borde *m*, orilla *f* **2** TRIM : ribete *m* **3** FRONTIER : frontera *f*

bore[1] ['bor] *vt* **bored; boring** DRILL : taladrar

bore[2] *vt* TIRE : aburrir — ~ *n* : pesado *m*, -da *fam f* (persona), lata *f fam* (cosa, situación) — **boredom** ['bordəm] *n* : aburrimiento *m* — **boring** ['borıŋ] *adj* : aburrido, pesado

born ['born] *adj* **1** : nacido **2 be** ~ : nacer

borough ['bəro] *n* : distrito *m* municipal

borrow ['baro] *vt* : pedir prestado, tomar prestado

Bosnian ['baznıən, 'boz-] *adj* : bosnio *m*, -nia *f*

bosom ['buzəm, 'bu:-] *n* BREAST : pecho *m*, seno *m* — ~ *adj* ~ **friend** : amigo *m* íntimo

boss ['bos] *n* : jefe *m*, -fa *f*; patrón *m*, -trona *f* — ~ *vt* SUPERVISE : dirigir — **bossy** ['bosi] *adj* **bossier; -est** : autoritario

botany ['batəni] *n* : botánica *f* — **botanical** [bə'tænıkəl] *adj* : botánico

botch ['batʃ] *vt* : hacer una chapuza de, estropear

both ['bo:θ] *adj* : ambos, los dos, las dos — ~ *pron* : ambos *m*, -bas *f*; los dos, las dos

bother ['baðər] *vt* **1** TROUBLE : preocupar **2** PESTER : molestar, fastidiar — *vi* ~ **to** : molestarse en — ~ *n* : molestia *f*

bottle ['batəl] *n* **1** : botella *f*, frasco *m* **2** *or* **baby** ~ : biberón *m* — ~ *vt* **bottled; bottling** : embotellar — **bottleneck** ['batəl,nek] *n* : embotellamiento *m*

bottom ['batəm] *n* **1** : fondo *m* (de una caja, del mar, etc.), pie *m* (de una escalera, una montaña, etc.), final *m* (de una lista) **2** BUTTOCKS : nalgas *fpl*, trasero *m* — ~ *adj* : más bajo, inferi-

or, de abajo — **bottomless** ['batəmləs]
adj : sin fondo
bough ['baʊ] *n* : rama *f*
bought → **buy**
bouillon ['buːjan; 'buljan, -jən] *n* : caldo
m
boulder ['boːldər] *n* : canto *m* rodado
boulevard ['bʊlə,vard, 'buː-] *n* : bulevar *m*
bounce ['baʊnts] *v* **bounced; bounc-
ing** *vt* : hacer rebotar — *vi* : rebotar —
~ *n* : rebote *m*
bound[1] ['baʊnd] *adj* **be ~ for** : ir rumbo
a
bound[2] *adj* **1** OBLIGED : obligado **2** DE-
TERMINED : decidido **3 be ~ to** : te-
ner que
bound[3] *n* **out of ~s** : (en) zona pro-
hibida — **boundary** ['baʊndri, -dəri] *n*,
pl **-aries** : límite *m* — **boundless**
['baʊndləs] *adj* : sin límites
bouquet ['boːkeɪ, buː-] *n* : ramo *m*
bourgeois ['bʊrʒ,wa, bʊrʒ'wa] *adj* : burgués
bout ['baʊt] *n* **1** : combate *m* (en deportes) **2** : ataque *m* (de una enfermedad) **3** : período *m* (de actividad)
bow[1] ['baʊ] *vi* : inclinarse — *vt* **~
one's head** : inclinar la cabeza —
['baʊ] *n* : reverencia *f*, inclinación *f*
bow[2] ['boː] *n* **1** : arco *m* **2 tie a ~**
: hacer un lazo
bow[3] ['baʊ] *n* : proa *f* (de un barco)
bowels ['baʊəls] *npl* **1** : intestinos *mpl* **2**
DEPTHS : entrañas *fpl*
bowl[1] ['boːl] *n* : tazón *m*, cuenco *m*
bowl[2] *vi* : jugar a los bolos — **bowling**
['boːlɪŋ] *n* : bolos *mpl*
box[1] ['baks] *vi* FIGHT : boxear — **boxer**
['baksər] *n* : boxeador *m*, -dora *f* —
boxing ['baksɪŋ] *n* : boxeo *m*
box[2] *n* **1** : caja *f*, cajón *m* **2** : palco *m* (en
el teatro) — ~ *vt* : empaquetar — **box
office** *n* : taquilla *f*, boletería *f Lat*
boy ['bɔɪ] *n* : niño *m*, chico *m*
boycott ['bɔɪ,kat] *vt* : boicotear — ~ *n*
: boicot *m*
boyfriend ['bɔɪ,frend] *n* : novio *m*
bra ['bra] → **brassiere**
brace ['breɪs] *n* **1** SUPPORT : abrazadera *f*
2 ~s *npl* : aparatos *mpl* (para dientes)
— ~ *vi* **~ oneself for** : prepararse
para
bracelet ['breɪslət] *n* : brazalete *m*
bracket ['brækət] *n* **1** SUPPORT : soporte
m **2** : corchete *m* (marca de puntuación) **3** CATEGORY : categoría *f* —
~ *vt* **1** : poner entre corchetes **2** CATE-
GORIZE : catalogar
brag ['bræg] *vi* **bragged; bragging**
: jactarse

braid ['breɪd] *vt* : trenzar — ~ *n* : trenza *f*
braille ['breɪl] *n* : braille *m*
brain ['breɪn] *n* **1** : cerebro *m* **2 ~s** *npl*
: inteligencia *f* — **brainstorm** ['breɪn-
,stɔrm] *n* : idea *f* genial — **brainwash**
['breɪn,wɔʃ, -,waʃ] *vt* : lavar el cerebro
— **brainy** ['breɪni] *adj* **brainier; -est**
: inteligente, listo
brake ['breɪk] *n* : freno *m* — ~ *v*
braked; braking : frenar
bramble ['bræmbəl] *n* : zarza *f*
bran ['bræn] *n* : salvado *m*
branch ['bræntʃ] *n* **1** : rama *f* (de una
planta) **2** DIVISION : ramal *m* (de un
camino, etc.), sucursal *f* (de una empresa), agencia *f* (del gobierno) — ~
vi **~ off** : ramificarse, bifurcarse
brand ['brænd] *n* **1** : marca *f* (de ganado)
2 or ~ name : marca *f* de fábrica —
~ *vt* **1** : marcar (ganado) **2** LABEL
: tachar, tildar
brandish ['brændɪʃ] *vt* : blandir
brand–new ['brænd'nuː, -'njuː] *adj* : flamante
brandy ['brændi] *n*, *pl* **-dies** : brandy *m*,
coñac *m*
brass ['bræs] *n* **1** : latón *m* **2** : metales
mpl (de una orquesta)
brassiere [brə'zɪr, bra-] *n* : sostén *m*,
brasier *m Lat*
brat ['bræt] *n* : mocoso *m*, -sa *f fam*
bravado [brə'vado] *n*, *pl* **-does** *or* **-dos**
: bravuconadas *fpl*
brave ['breɪv] *adj* **braver; bravest** : valiente, valeroso — ~ *vt* **braved;
braving** : afrontar, hacer frente a —
~ *n* : guerrero *m* indio — **bravery**
['breɪvəri] *n* : valor *m*, valentía *f*
brawl ['brɔl] *n* : pelea *f*, reyerta *f*
brawn ['brɔn] *n* : músculos *mpl* —
brawny ['brɔni] *adj* **brawnier; -est**
: musculoso
bray ['breɪ] *vi* : rebuznar
brazen ['breɪzən] *adj* : descarado
Brazilian [brə'zɪljən] *adj* : brasileño *m*,
-ña *f*
breach ['briːtʃ] *n* **1** VIOLATION : infracción *f*, violación *f* **2** GAP : brecha *f*
bread ['bred] *n* **1** : pan *m* **2 ~ crumbs**
: migajas *fpl*
breadth ['bretθ] *n* : anchura *f*
break ['breɪk] *v* **broke** ['broːk]; **broken**
['broːkən]; **breaking** *vt* **1** : romper,
quebrar **2** VIOLATE : infringir, violar **3**
INTERRUPT : interrumpir **4** SURPASS
: batir (un récord, etc.) **5 ~ a habit**
: quitarse una costumbre **6 ~ the
news** : dar la noticia — *vi* **1**
: romperse, quebrarse **2 ~ away** : es-

capar 3 ~ **down** : estropearse (dícese de una máquina), fallar (dícese de un sistema, etc.) 4 ~ **into** : entrar en 5 ~ **off** : interrumpirse 6 ~ **out of** : escaparse de 7 ~ **up** SEPARATE : separarse — ~ *n* 1 : ruptura *f*, fractura *f* 2 GAP : interrupción *f*, claro *m* (entre las nubes) 3 **lucky** ~ : golpe *m* de suerte 4 **take a** ~ : tomar(se) un descanso — **breakable** ['breɪkəbəl] *adj* : quebradizo, frágil — **breakdown** ['breɪk-,daʊn] *n* 1 : avería *f* (de máquinas), interrupción *f* (de comunicaciones), fracaso *m* (de negociaciones) 2 *or* **nervous** ~ : crisis *f* nerviosa

breakfast ['brɛkfəst] *n* : desayuno *m*

breast ['brɛst] *n* 1 : seno *m* (de una mujer) 2 CHEST : pecho *m* — **breast–feed** ['brɛst,fiːd] *vt* -**fed** [-,fɛd]; -**feeding** : amamantar

breath ['brɛθ] *n* : aliento *m*, respiración *f* — **breathe** ['briːð] *v* **breathed**; **breathing** : respirar — **breathless** ['brɛθləs] *adj* : sin aliento, jadeante — **breathtaking** ['brɛθ,teɪkɪŋ] *adj* : impresionante

breed ['briːd] *v* **bred** ['brɛd]; **breeding** *vt* 1 : criar (animales) 2 ENGENDER : engendrar, producir — *vi* : reproducirse — ~ *n* 1 : raza *f* 2 CLASS : clase *f*, tipo *m*

breeze ['briːz] *n* : brisa *f* — **breezy** ['briːzi] *adj* **breezier**; -**est** 1 WINDY : ventoso 2 NONCHALANT : despreocupado

brevity ['brɛvəṭi] *n*, *pl* -**ties** : brevedad *f*

brew ['bruː] *vt* : hacer (cerveza, etc.), preparar (té) — *vi* 1 : fabricar cerveza 2 : amenazar (dícese de una tormenta) — **brewery** ['bruːəri, 'bruri] *n*, *pl* -**eries** : cervecería *f*

bribe ['braɪb] *n* : soborno *m* — ~ *vt* **bribed**; **bribing** : sobornar — **bribery** ['braɪbəri] *n*, *pl* -**eries** : soborno *m*

brick ['brɪk] *n* : ladrillo *m* — **bricklayer** ['brɪk,leɪər] *n* : albañil *mf*

bride ['braɪd] *n* : novia *f* — **bridal** ['braɪdəl] *adj* : nupcial, de novia — **bridegroom** ['braɪd,gruːm] *n* : novio *m* — **bridesmaid** ['braɪdz,meɪd] *n* : dama *f* de honor

bridge ['brɪdʒ] *n* 1 : puente *m* 2 : caballete *m* (de la nariz) 3 : bridge *m* (juego de naipes) — ~ *vt* **bridged**; **bridging** 1 : tender un puente sobre 2 ~ **the gap** : salvar las diferencias

bridle ['braɪdəl] *n* : brida *f* — ~ *vt* -**dled**; -**dling** : embridar

brief ['briːf] *adj* : breve — ~ *n* 1 : resumen *m*, sumario *m* 2 ~**s** *npl* UN-

DERPANTS : calzoncillos *mpl* — ~ *vt* : dar órdenes a, instruir — **briefcase** ['briːf,keɪs] *n* : portafolio *m*, maletín *m* — **briefly** ['briːfli] *adv* : brevemente

bright ['braɪt] *adj* 1 : brillante, claro 2 CHEERFUL : alegre, animado 3 INTELLIGENT : listo, inteligente — **brighten** ['braɪtən] *vi* 1 : hacerse más brillante 2 *or* ~ **up** : animarse, alegrarse — *vt* 1 ILLUMINATE : iluminar 2 ENLIVEN : alegrar, animar

brilliant ['brɪljənt] *adj* : brillante — **brilliance** ['brɪljənts] *n* 1 BRIGHTNESS : resplandor *m*, brillantez *f* 2 INTELLIGENCE : inteligencia *f*

brim ['brɪm] *n* 1 : borde *m* (de una taza, etc.) 2 : ala *f* (de un sombrero) — ~ *vi* **brimmed**; **brimming** *or* ~ **over** : desbordarse, rebosar

brine ['braɪn] *n* : salmuera *f*

bring ['brɪŋ] *vt* **brought** ['brɔt]; **bringing** 1 : traer 2 ~ **about** : ocasionar 3 ~ **around** PERSUADE : convencer 4 ~ **back** : devolver 5 ~ **down** : derribar 6 ~ **on** CAUSE : provocar 7 ~ **out** : sacar 8 ~ **to an end** : terminar (con) 9 ~ **up** REAR : criar 10 ~ **up** MENTION : sacar

brink ['brɪŋk] *n* : borde *m*

brisk ['brɪsk] *adj* 1 FAST : rápido 2 LIVELY : enérgico

bristle ['brɪsəl] *n* : cerda *f* (de un animal), pelo *m* (de una planta) — ~ *vi* -**tled**; -**tling** : erizarse

British ['brɪtɪʃ] *adj* : británico

brittle ['brɪtəl] *adj* -**tler**; -**tlest** : frágil, quebradizo

broach ['broːtʃ] *vt* : abordar

broad ['brɔd] *adj* 1 WIDE : ancho 2 GENERAL : general 3 **in** ~ **daylight** : en pleno día

broadcast ['brɔd,kæst] *vt* -**cast**; -**casting** : emitir — ~ *n* : emisión *f*

broaden ['brɔdən] *vt* : ampliar, ensanchar — *vi* : ensancharse — **broadly** ['brɔdli] *adv* : en general — **broad–minded** ['brɔd'maɪndəd] *adj* : de miras amplias, tolerante

broccoli ['brɑkəli] *n* : brócoli *m*, brécol *m*

brochure [bro'ʃur] *n* : folleto *m*

broil ['brɔɪl] *vt* : asar a la parrilla

broke ['broːk] → **break** — ~ *adj* : pelado *fam* — **broken** ['broːkən] *adj* : roto, quebrado — **brokenhearted** [,broːkən-'hɑrṭəd] *adj* : desconsolado, con el corazón destrozado

broker ['broːkər] *n* : corredor *m*, -dora *f*

bronchitis [brɑn'kaɪṭəs, brɑŋ-] *n* : bronquitis *f*

bronze ['brɑnz] *n* : bronce *m*

brooch ['broːtʃ, 'bruːtʃ] *n* : broche *m*

brood ['bruːd] *n* : nidada *f* (de pájaros), camada *f* (de mamíferos) — ~ *vi* 1 INCUBATE : empollar 2 ~ **about** : dar vueltas a, pensar demasiado en

brook ['bruk] *n* : arroyo *m*

broom ['bruːm, 'brum] *n* : escoba *f* — **broomstick** ['bruːmˌstɪk, 'brum-] *n* : palo *m* de escoba

broth ['brɔθ] *n*, *pl* **broths** ['brɔθs, 'brɔðz] : caldo *m*

brothel ['brɑθəl, 'brɔ-] *n* : burdel *m*

brother ['brʌðər] *n* : hermano *m* — **brotherhood** ['brʌðərˌhud] *n* : fraternidad *f* — **brother–in–law** ['brʌðərɪnˌlɔ] *n*, *pl* **brothers–in–law**: cuñado *m* — **brotherly** ['brʌðərli] *adj* : fraternal

brought → **bring**

brow ['brau] *n* 1 EYEBROW : ceja *f* 2 FOREHEAD : frente *f* 3 : cima *f* (de una colina)

brown ['braun] *adj* : marrón, castaño (dícese del pelo), moreno (dícese de la piel) — ~ *n* : marrón *m* — ~ *vt* : dorar (en cocinar)

browse ['brauz] *vi* **browsed; browsing** : mirar, echar un vistazo

bruise ['bruːz] *vt* **bruised; bruising** : contusionar, magullar (a una persona) 2 : machucar (frutas) — ~ *n* : cardenal *m*, magulladura *f*

brunch ['brʌntʃ] *n* : brunch *m*

brunet *or* **brunette** [bruːˈnet] *adj* : moreno — ~ *n* : moreno *m*, -na *f*

brunt ['brʌnt] *n* **bear the** ~ **of** : aguantar el mayor impacto de

brush ['brʌʃ] *n* 1 : cepillo *m*, pincel *m* (de artista), brocha *f* (de pintor) 2 UNDERBRUSH : maleza *f* — ~ *vt* 1 : cepillar 2 GRAZE : rozar 3 ~ **aside** : rechazar 4 ~ **off** DISREGARD : hacer caso omiso de — *vi* ~ **up on** : repasar — **brush–off** ['brʌʃˌɔf] *n* **give the ~ to** : dar calabazas a

brusque ['brʌsk] *adj* : brusco

brutal ['bruːtəl] *adj* : brutal — **brutality** [bruːˈtæləti] *n*, *pl* **-ties** : brutalidad *f*

brute ['bruːt] *adj* : bruto — ~ *n* : bestia *f*; bruto *m*, -ta *f*

bubble ['bʌbəl] *n* : burbuja *f* — ~ *vi* **-bled; -bling** : burbujear

buck ['bʌk] *n*, *pl* **buck** *or* **bucks** 1 : animal *m* macho, ciervo *m* (macho) 2 DOLLAR : dólar *m* — ~ *vi* 1 : corcovear (dícese de un caballo) 2 ~ **up** : animarse, levantar el ánimo — *vt* OPPOSE : oponerse a, ir en contra de

bucket ['bʌkət] *n* : cubo *m*

buckle ['bʌkəl] *n* : hebilla *f* — ~ *v* **-led;**

-ling *vt* 1 FASTEN : abrochar 2 BEND : combar, torcer — *vi* 1 : combarse, torcerse 2 : doblarse (dícese de las rodillas)

bud ['bʌd] *n* 1 : brote *m* 2 *or* **flower** ~ : capullo *m* — ~ *vi* **budded; budding** : brotar, hacer brotes

Buddhism ['buːˌdɪzəm, 'bu-] *n* : budismo *m* — **Buddhist** ['buːdɪst, 'bu-] *adj* : budista — ~ *n* : budista *mf*

buddy ['bʌdi] *n*, *pl* **-dies** : compañero *m*, -ra *f*

budge ['bʌdʒ] *vi* **budged; budging** 1 MOVE : moverse 2 YIELD : ceder

budget ['bʌdʒət] *n* : presupuesto *m* — ~ *vi* : presupuestar — **budgetary** ['bʌdʒəˌteri] *adj* : presupuestario

buff ['bʌf] *n* 1 : beige *m*, color *m* de ante 2 ENTHUSIAST : aficionado *m*, -da *f* — ~ *adj* : beige — ~ *vt* POLISH : pulir

buffalo ['bʌfəˌloː] *n*, *pl* **-lo** *or* **-loes** : búfalo *m*

buffet [bʌˈfei, buː-] *n* 1 : bufé *m* (comida) 2 SIDEBOARD : aparador *m*

bug ['bʌg] *n* 1 INSECT : bicho *m*, insecto *m* 2 FLAW : defecto *m* 3 GERM : microbio *m* 4 MICROPHONE : micrófono *m* (oculto) — ~ *vt* **bugged; bugging** 1 PESTER : fastidiar, molestar 2 : ocultar micrófonos en (una habitación, etc.)

buggy ['bʌgi] *n*, *pl* **-gies** 1 CARRIAGE : calesa *f* 2 *or* **baby** ~ : cochecito *m* (para niños)

bugle ['bjuːgəl] *n* : clarín *m*, corneta *f*

build ['bɪld] *v* **built** ['bɪlt]; **building** *vt* 1 : construir 2 DEVELOP : desarrollar — *vi* 1 *or* ~ **up** INTENSIFY : aumentar, intensificar 2 *or* ~ **up** ACCUMULATE : acumularse — ~ *n* PHYSIQUE : físico *m*, complexión *f* — **builder** ['bɪldər] *n* : constructor *m*, -tora *f* — **building** ['bɪldɪŋ] *n* 1 STRUCTURE : edificio *m* 2 CONSTRUCTION : construcción *f* — **built–in** ['bɪltˌɪn] *adj* : empotrado

bulb ['bʌlb] *n* 1 : bulbo *m* (de una planta) 2 LIGHTBULB : bombilla *f*

bulge ['bʌldʒ] *vi* **bulged; bulging** : sobresalir — ~ *n* : bulto *m*, protuberancia *f*

bulk ['bʌlk] *n* 1 VOLUME : volumen *m*, bulto *m* 2 **in** ~ : en grandes cantidades — **bulky** ['bʌlki] *adj* **bulkier; -est** : voluminoso

bull ['bul] *n* 1 : toro *m* 2 MALE : macho *m*

bulldog ['bulˌdɔg] *n* : buldog *m*

bulldozer ['bulˌdoːzər] *n* : bulldozer *m*

bullet ['bulət] *n* : bala *f*

bulletin ['bulətən, -lətən] *n* : boletín *m* — **bulletin board** *n* : tablón *m* de anuncios

bulletproof ['bulətpru:f] *adj* : a prueba de balas

bullfight ['bul,fait] *n* : corrida *f* (de toros) — **bullfighter** ['bul,faitər] *n* : torero *m*, -ra *f*; matador *m*

bullion ['buljən] *n* : oro *m* en lingotes, plata *f* en lingotes

bull's-eye ['bulz,ai] *n*, *pl* **bull's-eyes** : diana *f*

bully ['buli] *n*, *pl* **-lies** : matón *m* — *vt* **-lied; -lying** : intimidar

bum ['bʌm] *n* : vagabundo *m*, -da *f*

bumblebee ['bʌmbəl,bi:] *n* : abejorro *m*

bump ['bʌmp] *n* **1** BULGE : bulto *m*, protuberancia *f* **2** IMPACT : golpe *m* **3** JOLT : sacudida *f* — *vt* : chocar contra — *vi* ~ **into** MEET : encontrarse con — **bumper** ['bʌmpər] *n* : parachoques *mpl* — ~ *adj* : extraordinario, récord — **bumpy** ['bʌmpi] *adj* **bumpier; -est** **1** : desigual, lleno de baches (dícese de un camino) **2 a** ~ **flight** : un vuelo agitado

bun ['bʌn] *n* : bollo *m*

bunch ['bʌntʃ] *n* : grupo *m* (de personas), racimo *m* (de frutas, etc.), ramo *m* (de flores), manojo *m* (de llaves) — ~ *vi* or ~ **up** : amontonarse, agruparse

bundle ['bʌndəl] *n* **1** : lío *m*, bulto *m*, atado *m*, haz *m* (de palos) **2** PARCEL : paquete *m* **3** ~ **of nerves** : manojo *m* de nervios — ~ *vt* **-dled; -dling** or ~ **up** : liar, atar

bungalow ['bʌngə,lo:] *n* : casa *f* de un solo piso

bungle ['bʌngəl] *vt* **-gled; -gling** : echar a perder

bunion ['bʌnjən] *n* : juanete *m*

bunk ['bʌŋk] *n* or **bunk bed** : litera *f*

bunny ['bʌni] *n*, *pl* **-nies** : conejo *m*, -ja *f*

buoy ['bu:i, 'bɔi] *n* : boya *f* — ~ *vt* or ~ **up** HEARTEN : animar, levantar el ánimo a — **buoyant** ['bɔiənt, 'bu:jənt] *adj* **1** : boyante, flotante **2** LIGHT-HEARTED : alegre, optimista

burden ['bərdən] *n* : carga *f* — ~ *vt* ~ **s.o. with** : cargar a algn con — **burdensome** ['bərdənsəm] *adj* : oneroso

bureau ['bjuro] *n* **1** : cómoda *f* (mueble) **2** : departamento *m* (del gobierno) **3** AGENCY : agencia *f* — **bureaucracy** [bju'rokrəsi] *n*, *pl* **-cies** : burocracia *f* — **bureaucrat** ['bjurə,kræt] *n* : burócrata *mf* — **bureaucratic** [,bjurə'krætɪk] *adj* : burocrático

burglar ['bərglər] *n* : ladrón *m*, -drona *f* — **burglarize** ['bərglə,raiz] *vt* **-ized; -izing** : robar — **burglary** ['bərgləri] *n*, *pl* **-glaries** : robo *m*

burgundy ['bərgəndi] *n*, *pl* **-dies** : borgoña *m*, vino *m* de Borgoña

burial ['beriəl] *n* : entierro *m*

burly ['bərli] *adj* **-lier; -liest** : fornido

burn ['bərn] *v* **burned** ['bərnd, 'bərnt] or **burnt** ['bərnt]; **burning** *vt* **1** : quemar **2** or ~ **down** : incendiar **3** or ~ **up** : consumir — *vi* **1** : arder (dícese de un fuego), quemarse (dícese de la comida, etc.) **2** : estar encendido (dícese de una luz) **3** ~ **out** : apagarse — ~ *n* : quemadura *f* — **burner** ['bərnər] *n* : quemador *m*

burnish ['bərniʃ] *vt* : pulir

burp ['bərp] *vi* : eructar — ~ *n* : eructo *m*

burro ['bʌro, 'bur-] *n*, *pl* **-os** : burro *m*

burrow ['bʌro] *n* : madriguera *f* — ~ *vi* **1** : cavar **2** ~ **into** : hurgar en

bursar ['bərsər] *n* : tesorero *m*, -ra *f*

burst ['bərst] *v* **burst** or **bursted; bursting** *vi* : reventarse — *vt* : reventar — ~ *n* **1** EXPLOSION : estallido *m*, explosión *f* **2** OUTBURST : arranque *m*, arrebato *m* **3** ~ **of laughter** : carcajada *f*

bury ['beri] *vt* **buried; burying** **1** INTER : enterrar **2** HIDE : esconder

bus ['bʌs] *n*, *pl* **buses** or **busses** : autobús *m*, bus *m* — ~ *v* **bused** or **bussed** ['bʌst]; **busing** or **bussing** ['bʌsɪŋ] *vt* : transportar en autobús — *vi* : viajar en autobús

bush ['buʃ] *n* SHRUB : arbusto *m*, mata *f*

bushel ['buʃəl] *n* : medida *f* de áridos igual a 35.24 litros

bushy ['buʃi] *adj* **bushier; -est** : poblado, espeso

busily ['bɪzəli] *adv* : afanosamente

business ['bɪznəs, -nəz] *n* **1** COMMERCE : negocios *mpl*, comercio *m* **2** COMPANY : empresa *f*, negocio *m* **3** ~ **it's none of your** ~ : no es asunto tuyo — **businessman** ['bɪznəs,mæn, -nəz-] *n*, *pl* **-men** [-mən, -,men] : empresario *m*, hombre *m* de negocios — **businesswoman** ['bɪznəs,wumən, -nəz-] *n*, *pl* **-women** [-,wɪmən] : empresaria *f*, mujer *f* de negocios

bust[1] ['bʌst] *vt* BREAK : romper

bust[2] *n* **1** : busto *m* (en la escultura) **2** BREASTS : pecho *m*, senos *mpl*

bustle ['bʌsəl] *vi* **-tled; -tling** or ~ **about** : ir y venir, ajetrearse — ~ *n* or **hustle and** ~ : bullicio *m*, ajetreo *m*

busy ['bɪzi] *adj* **busier; -est** **1** : ocupado **2** BUSTLING : concurrido

but ['bʌt] *conj* **1** : pero **2 not one** ~ **two** : no uno sino dos — ~ *prep* : excepto, menos

butcher ['bʊtʃər] n : carnicero m, -ra f — ~ vt 1 : matar 2 BOTCH : hacer una carnicería de
butler ['bʌtlər] n : mayordomo m
butt ['bʌt] vt : embestir (con los cuernos), darle un cabezazo a — vi — **in** : interrumpir — ~ n 1 BUTTING : embestida f (de cuernos) 2 TARGET : blanco m 3 : extremo m, culata f (de un rifle), colilla f (de un cigarillo)
butter ['bʌtər] n : mantequilla f — ~ vt : untar con mantequilla
buttercup ['bʌtərˌkʌp] n : ranúnculo m
butterfly ['bʌtərˌflaɪ] n, pl -**flies** : mariposa f
buttocks ['bʌtəks, -ˌtɑks] npl : nalgas fpl
button ['bʌtən] n : botón m — ~ vt : abotonar — vi or — **up** : abotonarse — **buttonhole** ['bʌtənˌhoːl] n : ojal m — ~ vt -**holed; -holing** : acorralar
buy ['baɪ] vt **bought** ['bɔt]; **buying** : comprar — ~ n 1 : compra f — **buyer** ['baɪər] n : comprador m, -dora f

buzz ['bʌz] vi : zumbar — ~ n : zumbido m
buzzard ['bʌzərd] n : buitre m
buzzer ['bʌzər] n : timbre m
by ['baɪ] prep 1 NEAR : cerca de 2 VIA : por 3 PAST : por, por delante de 4 DURING : de, durante 5 (in expressions of time) : para 6 (indicating cause or agent) : por, de, a — ~ adv 1 ~ **and** ~ : poco después 2 ~ **and large** : en general 3 go ~ : pasar 4 stop ~ : pasar por casa
bygone ['baɪˌgɔn] adj : pasado — ~ n let ~s be ~s : lo pasado, pasado está
bypass ['baɪˌpæs] n : carretera f de circunvalación — ~ vt : evitar
by-product ['baɪˌprɑdəkt] n : subproducto m
bystander ['baɪˌstændər] n : espectador m, -dora f
byte ['baɪt] n : byte m, octeto m
byword ['baɪˌwərd] n be a ~ for : estar sinónimo de

C

c ['siː] n, pl **c's** or **cs** : c, tercera letra del alfabeto inglés
cab ['kæb] n 1 : taxi m 2 : cabina f (de un camión, etc.)
cabbage ['kæbɪdʒ] n : col f, repollo m
cabin ['kæbən] n 1 : cabaña f 2 : cabina f (de un avión, etc.), camarote m (de un barco)
cabinet ['kæbnət] n 1 CUPBOARD : armario m 2 : gabinete m (del gobierno) 3 or **medicine** ~ : botiquín m
cable ['keɪbəl] n : cable m — **cable television** n : televisión f por cable
cackle ['kækəl] vi -**led; -ling** 1 CLUCK : cacarear 2 LAUGH : reírse a carcajadas
cactus ['kæktəs] n, pl **cacti** [-ˌtaɪ] or -**tuses** : cactus m
cadence ['keɪdənts] n : cadencia f, ritmo m
cadet [kə'dɛt] n : cadete mf
café ['kæˌfeɪ, kə-] n : café m, cafetería f — **cafeteria** [ˌkæfə'tɪriə] n : restaurante m autoservicio, cantina f
caffeine ['kæˌfiːn] n : cafeína f
cage ['keɪdʒ] n : jaula f — ~ vt **caged; caging** : enjaular
cajole [kə'dʒoːl] vt -**joled; -joling** : engatusar
cake ['keɪk] n 1 : pastel m, torta f 2 : pastilla f (de jabón) 3 take the ~

: ser el colmo — **caked** ['keɪkt] adj ~ **with** : cubierto de
calamity [kə'læməti] n, pl -**ties** : calamidad f
calcium ['kælsiəm] n : calcio m
calculate ['kælkjəˌleɪt] v -**lated; -lating** : calcular — **calculating** ['kælkjəˌleɪtɪŋ] adj : calculador — **calculation** [ˌkælkjə'leɪʃən] n : cálculo m — **calculator** ['kælkjəˌleɪtər] n : calculadora f
calendar ['kæləndər] n : calendario m
calf[1] ['kæf, 'kaf] n, pl **calves** ['kævz, 'kavz] 1 : becerro m, -rra f; ternero m, -ra f (de vacunos) 2 : cría f (de otros mamíferos)
calf[2] n, pl **calves** : pantorrilla f (de la pierna)
caliber or **calibre** ['kæləbər] n : calibre m
call ['kɔl] vi 1 : llamar 2 VISIT : pasar, hacer (una) visita 3 ~ **for** : requerir — vt 1 : llamar 2 ~ **off** : cancelar — ~ n 1 : llamada f 2 SHOUT : grito m 3 VISIT : visita f 4 DEMAND : petición f — **calling** ['kɔlɪŋ] n : vocación f
callous ['kæləs] adj : insensible, cruel
calm ['kɑm, 'kɑlm] n : calma f, tranquilidad f — ~ vt : calmar — vi or — **down** : calmarse — ~ adj : tranquilo, en calma — **calmly** ['kɑmli, 'kɑlm-] adv : con calma

calorie ['kæləri] *n* : caloría *f*
came → **come**
camel ['kæməl] *n* : camello *m*
camera ['kæmrə, 'kæmərə] *n* : cámara *f*
camouflage ['kæməˌflɑʒ, -ˌflɑdʒ] *n* : camuflaje *m* — ~ *vt* **-flaged; -flaging** : camuflar
camp ['kæmp] *n* 1 : campamento *m* 2 FACTION : bando *m* — ~ *vi* : acampar, ir de camping
campaign [kæm'peɪn] *n* : campaña *f* — ~ *vi* : hacer (una) campaña
camping ['kæmpɪŋ] *n* : camping *m*
campus ['kæmpəs] *n* : ciudad *f* universitaria
can¹ ['kæn] *v aux, past* **could** ['kʊd]; *present s & pl* **can** 1 (*expressing possibility or permission*) : poder 2 (*expressing knowledge or ability*) : saber 3 **that cannot be!** : ¡no puede ser!
can² ['kæn] *n* : lata *f* — ~ *vt* **canned; canning** : enlatar
Canadian [kə'neɪdiən] *adj* : canadiense
canal [kə'næl] *n* : canal *m*
canary [kə'neri] *n, pl* **-naries** : canario *m*
cancel ['kænsəl] *vt* **-celed** *or* **-celled; -celing** *or* **-celling** : cancelar — **cancellation** [ˌkænsə'leɪʃən] *n* : cancelación *f*
cancer ['kænsər] *n* : cáncer *m* — **cancerous** ['kænsərəs] *adj* : canceroso
candelabra [ˌkændə'lɑbrə, -'læ-] *n, pl* **-bra** *or* **-bras** : candelabro *m*
candid ['kændɪd] *adj* : franco
candidate ['kændəˌdeɪt, -dət] *n* : candidato *m*, -ta *f* — **candidacy** ['kændədəsi] *n, pl* **-cies** : candidatura *f*
candle ['kændəl] *n* : vela *f* — **candlestick** ['kændəlˌstɪk] *n* : candelero *m*
candor *or Brit* **candour** ['kændər] *n* : franqueza *f*
candy ['kændi] *n, pl* **-dies** : dulce *m*, caramelo *m*
cane ['keɪn] *n* 1 : bastón *m* (para andar), vara *f* (para castigar) 2 REED : caña *f*, mimbre *m* — ~ *vt* **caned; caning** 1 : tapizar con mimbre 2 FLOG : azotar
canine ['keɪˌnaɪn] *n or* ~ **tooth** : colmillo *m*, diente *m* canino — ~ *adj* : canino
canister ['kænəstər] *n* : lata *f*, bote *m* Spain
cannibal ['kænəbəl] *n* : caníbal *mf*
cannon ['kænən] *n, pl* **-nons** *or* **-non** : cañón *m*
cannot (can not) ['kænˌɑt, kə'nɑt] → **can¹**
canny ['kæni] *adj* **cannier; -est** : astuto
canoe [kə'nuː] *n* : canoa *f*, piragua *f* — ~ *vi* **-noed; -noeing** : ir en canoa

canon ['kænən] *n* : canon *m* — **canonize** ['kænəˌnaɪz] *vt* **-ized; -izing** : canonizar
can opener *n* : abrelatas *m*
canopy ['kænəpi] *n, pl* **-pies** : dosel *m*
can't ['kænt, 'kant] (*contraction of* **can not**) → **can¹**
cantaloupe ['kæntəlˌoːp] *n* : melón *m*, cantalupo *m*
cantankerous [kæn'tæŋkərəs] *adj* : irritable, irascible
canteen [kæn'tiːn] *n* 1 FLASK : cantimplora *f* 2 CAFETERIA : cantina *f*
canter ['kæntər] *vi* : ir a medio galope — ~ *n* : medio galope *m*
canvas ['kænvəs] *n* 1 : lona *f* (tela) 2 : lienzo *m* (de pintar)
canvass ['kænvəs] *vt* 1 : solicitar votos de, hacer campaña entre 2 POLL : sondear — ~ *n* 1 : solicitación *f* (de votos) 2 POLL : sondeo *m*
canyon ['kænjən] *n* : cañón *m*
cap *n* 1 : gorra *f*, gorro *m* 2 TOP : tapa *f*, tapón *m* (de botellas) 3 LIMIT : tope *m* — ~ ['kæp] *vt* **capped; capping** 1 COVER : tapar, cubrir 2 OUTDO : superar
capable ['keɪpəbəl] *adj* : capaz, competente — **capability** [ˌkeɪpə'bɪləti] *n, pl* **-ties** : capacidad *f*
capacity [kə'pæsəti] *n, pl* **-ties** 1 : capacidad *f* 2 ROLE : calidad *f*
cape¹ ['keɪp] *n* : cabo *m* (en geografía)
cape² *n* CLOAK : capa *f*
caper¹ ['keɪpər] *n* : alcaparra *f*
caper² *n* PRANK : broma *f*, travesura *f*
capital ['kæpətəl] *adj* 1 : capital 2 : mayúsculo (dícese de las letras) — ~ *n* 1 *or* ~ **city** : capital *f* 2 WEALTH : capital *m* 3 *or* ~ **letter** : mayúscula *f* — **capitalism** ['kæpətəlˌɪzəm] *n* : capitalismo *m* — **capitalist** ['kæpətəlɪst] *or* **capitalistic** [ˌkæpətəl'ɪstɪk] *adj* : capitalista — **capitalize** ['kæpətəlˌaɪz] *vt* **-ized; -izing** 1 FINANCE : capitalizar 2 : escribir con mayúscula — *vi* ~ **on** : sacar partido de
capitol ['kæpətəl] *n* : capitolio *m*
capitulate [kə'pɪtʃəˌleɪt] *vi* **-lated; -lating** : capitular
capsize ['kæpˌsaɪz, kæp'saɪz] *v* **-sized; -sizing** *vt* : hacer volcar — *vi* : zozobrar, volcar(se)
capsule ['kæpsəl, -ˌsuːl] *n* : cápsula *f*
captain ['kæptən] *n* : capitán *m*, -tana *f*
caption ['kæpʃən] *n* 1 : leyenda *f* (al pie de una ilustración) 2 SUBTITLE : subtítulo *m*
captivate ['kæptəˌveɪt] *vt* **-vated; -vating** : cautivar, encantar

captive ['kæptɪv] *adj* : cautivo — ~ *n* : cautivo *m*, -va *f* — **captivity** [kæp-'tɪvəṭi] *n* : cautiverio *m*
capture ['kæpʃər] *n* : captura *f*, apresamiento *m* — ~ *vt* **-tured; -turing 1** SEIZE : capturar, apresar **2** ~ **one's interest** : captar el interés de uno
car ['kɑr] *n* **1** : automóvil *m*, coche *m*, carro *m* *Lat* **2** *or* **railroad** ~ : vagón *m*
carafe [kə'ræf, -'rɑf] *n* : garrafa *f*
caramel ['kɑrməl; 'kærəməl, -ˌmɛl] *n* : caramelo *m*, azúcar *f* quemada
carat ['kærət] *n* : quilate *m*
caravan ['kærəˌvæn] *n* : caravana *f*
carbohydrate [ˌkɑrbo'haɪˌdreɪt, -drət] *n* : carbohidrato *m*, hidrato *m* de carbono
carbon ['kɑrbən] *n* : carbono *m* — **carbon copy** *n* : copia *f*, duplicado *m*
carburetor ['kɑrbəˌreɪṭər, -bjə-] *n* : carburador *m*
carcass ['kɑrkəs] *n* : cuerpo *m* (de un animal muerto)
card ['kɑrd] *n* **1** : tarjeta *f* **2** *or* **playing** ~ : carta *f*, naipe *m* — **cardboard** ['kɑrd,bord] *n* : cartón *m*
cardiac ['kɑrdiˌæk] *adj* : cardíaco
cardigan ['kɑrdɪgən] *n* : cárdigan *m*
cardinal ['kɑrdənəl] *n* : cardenal *m* — ~ *adj* : cardinal, fundamental
care ['kær] *n* **1** : cuidado *m* **2** WORRY : preocupación **3** take ~ of : cuidar (de) — ~ *vi* **cared; caring 1** : preocuparse, inquietarse **2** ~ **for** TEND : cuidar (de), atender **3** ~ **for** LIKE : querer **4 I don't** ~ : no me importa
career [kə'rɪr] *n* : carrera *f* — ~ *vi* : ir a toda velocidad
carefree ['kær,fri, ,kær-] *adj* : despreocupado
careful ['kærfəl] *adj* : cuidadoso — **carefully** ['kærfəli] *adv* : con cuidado, cuidadosamente — **careless** ['kærləs] *adj* : descuidado — **carelessness** ['kærləsnəs] *n* : descuido *m*
caress [kə'rɛs] *n* : caricia *f* — ~ *vt* : acariciar
cargo ['kɑrˌgoː] *n, pl* **-goes** *or* **-gos** : cargamento *m*, carga *f*
caricature ['kærɪkətˌʃʊr] *n* : caricatura *f* — ~ *vt* **-tured; -turing** : caricaturizar
caring ['kærɪŋ] *adj* : solícito, afectuoso
carnage ['kɑrnɪdʒ] *n* : matanza *f*, carnicería *f*
carnal ['kɑrnəl] *adj* : carnal
carnation [kɑr'neɪʃən] *n* : clavel *m*
carnival ['kɑrnəvəl] *n* : carnaval *m*
carol ['kærəl] *n* : villancico *m*
carp ['kɑrp] *vi* ~ **at** : quejarse de
carpenter ['kɑrpəntər] *n* : carpintero *m*,

-ra *f* — **carpentry** ['kɑrpəntri] *n* : carpintería *f*
carpet ['kɑrpət] *n* : alfombra *f*
carriage ['kærɪdʒ] *n* **1** : transporte *m* (de mercancías) **2** BEARING : porte *m* **3** *or* **baby** ~ : cochecito *m* **4** *or* **horse-drawn** ~ : carruaje *m*, coche *m*
carrier ['kæriər] *n* **1** : transportista *mf*, empresa *f* de transportes **2** : portador *m*, -dora *f* (de una enfermedad)
carrot ['kærət] *n* : zanahoria *f*
carry ['kæri] *v* **-ried; -rying** *vt* **1** : llevar **2** TRANSPORT : transportar **3** STOCK : vender **4** ENTAIL : acarrear, implicar **5** ~ **oneself** : portarse — *vi* : oírse (dícese de sonidos) — **carry away** *vt* **get carried away** : exaltarse, entusiasmarse — **carry on** *vt* CONDUCT : realizar — *vi* **1** : portarse inapropiadamente **2** CONTINUE : seguir, continuar — **carry out** *vt* **1** PERFORM : llevar a cabo, realizar **2** FULFILL : cumplir
cart ['kɑrt] *n* : carreta *f*, carro *m* — ~ *vt* *or* ~ **around** : acarrear
cartilage ['kɑrṭəlɪdʒ] *n* : cartílago *m*
carton ['kɑrtən] *n* : caja *f* (de cartón)
cartoon [kɑr'tuːn] *n* **1** : caricatura *f* **2** COMIC STRIP : historieta *f* **3** *or* **animated** ~ : dibujos *mpl* animados
cartridge ['kɑrtrɪdʒ] *n* : cartucho *m*
carve ['kɑrv] *vt* **carved; carving 1** : tallar, esculpir **2** : trinchar (carne)
case *n* **1** : caso *m* **2** BOX : caja *f* **3 in any** ~ : en todo caso **4 in** ~ **of** : en caso de **5 just in** ~ : por si acaso
cash ['kæʃ] *n* : efectivo *m*, dinero *m* en efectivo — ~ *vt* : convertir en efectivo, cobrar
cashew ['kæˌʃuː, kə'ʃuː] *n* : anacardo *m*
cashier [kæ'ʃɪr] *n* : cajero *m*, -ra *f*
cashmere ['kæʒˌmɪr, 'kæʃ-] *n* : cachemira *f*
cash register *n* : caja *f* registradora
casino [kə'siːˌnoː] *n, pl* **-nos** : casino *m*
cask ['kæsk] *n* : barril *m*
casket ['kæskət] *n* : ataúd *m*
casserole ['kæsəˌroːl] *n* **1** *or* ~ **dish** : cazuela *f* **2** : guiso *m* (comida)
cassette [kə'sɛt, kæ-] *n* : cassette *mf*
cast ['kæst] *vt* **cast; casting 1** THROW : arrojar, lanzar **2** : depositar (un voto) **3** : repartir (papeles dramáticos) **4** MOLD : fundir — ~ *n* **1** : elenco *m*, reparto *m* (de actores) **2** *or* **plaster** ~ : molde *m* de yeso, escayola *f*
castanets [ˌkæstə'nɛts] *npl* : castañuelas *fpl*
castaway ['kæstəˌweɪ] *n* : náufrago *m*, -ga *f*
cast iron *n* : hierro *m* fundido

castle ['kæsəl] *n* **1** : castillo *m* **2** : torre *f* (en ajedrez)

castrate ['kæs,treɪt] *vt* **-trated; -trating** : castrar

casual ['kæʒuəl] *adj* **1** CHANCE : casual, fortuito **2** INDIFFERENT : despreocupado **3** INFORMAL : informal — **casually** ['kæʒuəli, 'kæʒəli] *adv* **1** : de manera despreocupada **2** INFORMALLY : informalmente

casualty ['kæʒuəlti, 'kæʒəl-] *n, pl* **-ties 1** : accidente *m* **2** VICTIM : víctima *f*; herido *m*, -da *f* **3** **casualties** *npl* : bajas *fpl* (militares)

cat ['kæt] *n* : gato *m*, -ta *f*

catalog *or* **catalogue** ['kætə,log] *n* : catálogo *m* — ~ *vt* **-loged** *or* **-logued; -loging** *or* **-loguing** : catalogar

catapult ['kætə,pʌlt, -,pʊlt] *n* : catapulta *f*

cataract ['kætə,rækt] *n* : catarata *f*

catastrophe [kə'tæstrə,fi:] *n* : catástrofe *f* — **catastrophic** [,kætə'strɑfɪk] *adj* : catastrófico

catch ['kætʃ, 'ketʃ] *v* **caught** ['kɔt]; **catching** *vt* **1** CAPTURE, TRAP : capturar, atrapar **2** SURPRISE : sorprender **3** GRASP : agarrar, captar **4** SNAG : enganchar **5** : tomar (un tren, etc.) **6** ~ **a cold** : resfriarse — *vi* **1** SNAG : engancharse **2** ~ **fire** : prender fuego — **catching** ['kætʃɪŋ, 'ke-] *adj* : contagioso — **catchy** ['kætʃi, 'ke-] *adj* **catchier; -est** : pegadizo, pegajoso *Lat*

category ['kætə,gori] *n, pl* **-ries** : categoría *f* — **categorical** [,kætə'gorɪkəl] *adj* : categórico

cater ['keɪtər] *vi* **1** : proveer comida **2** ~ **to** : atender a — **caterer** ['keɪtərər] *n* : proveedor *m*, -dora *f* de comida

caterpillar ['kætər,pɪlər] *n* : oruga *f*

catfish ['kæt,fɪʃ] *n* : bagre *m*

cathedral [kə'θiːdrəl] *n* : catedral *f*

catholic ['kæθəlɪk] *adj* **1** : universal **2** **Catholic** : católico — **catholicism** [kə'θɑlə,sɪzəm] *n* : catolicismo *m*

cattle ['kætəl] *npl* : ganado *m* (vacuno)

caught → **catch**

cauldron ['kɔldrən] *n* : caldera *f*

cauliflower ['kɑlɪ,flaʊər, 'kɔ-] *n* : coliflor *f*

cause ['kɔz] *n* **1** : causa *f* **2** REASON : motivo *m* — ~ *vt* **caused; causing** : causar

caustic ['kɔstɪk] *adj* : cáustico

caution ['kɔʃən] *n* **1** WARNING : advertencia *f* **2** CARE : precaución *f*, cautela *f* — ~ *vt* : advertir — **cautious** ['kɔʃəs] *adj* : cauteloso, precavido —

cautiously ['kɔʃəsli] *adv* : con precaución

cavalier [,kævə'lɪr] *adj* : arrogante, desdeñoso

cavalry ['kævəlri] *n, pl* **-ries** : caballería *f*

cave ['keɪv] *n* : cueva *f* — ~ *vi* **caved; caving** *or* ~ **in** : hundirse

cavern ['kævərn] *n* : caverna *f*

cavity ['kævəti] *n, pl* **-ties 1** : cavidad *f* **2** : caries *f* (dental)

cavort [kə'vɔrt] *vi* : brincar

CD [,si'di:] *n* : CD *m*, disco *m* compacto

cease ['si:s] *v* **ceased; ceasing** *vt* : dejar de — *vi* : cesar — **cease-fire** ['si:s'faɪr] *n* : alto *m* al fuego — **ceaseless** ['si:sləs] *adj* : incesante

cedar ['si:dər] *n* : cedro *m*

ceiling ['si:lɪŋ] *n* : techo *m*

celebrate ['selə,breɪt] *v* **-brated; -brating** *vt* : celebrar — *vi* : divertirse — **celebrated** ['selə,breɪtəd] *adj* : célebre — **celebration** [,selə'breɪʃən] *n* **1** : celebración *f* **2** FESTIVITY : fiesta *f* — **celebrity** [sə'lebrəti] *n, pl* **-ties** : celebridad *f*

celery ['seləri] *n, pl* **-eries** : apio *m*

cell ['sel] *n* **1** : célula *f* **2** : celda *f* (en una cárcel, etc.)

cellar ['selər] *n* **1** BASEMENT : sótano *m* **2** : bodega *f* (de vinos)

cello ['tʃe,lo] *n, pl* **-los** : violoncelo *m*

cellular ['seljələr] *adj* : celular

cement [sɪ'ment] *n* : cemento *m* — ~ *vt* : cementar

cemetery ['semə,teri] *n, pl* **-teries** : cementerio *m*

censor ['sensər] *vt* : censurar — **censorship** ['sensər,ʃɪp] *n* : censura *f* — **censure** ['sensər] *n* : censura *f* — ~ *vt* **-sured; -suring** : censurar, criticar

census ['sensəs] *n* : censo *m*

cent ['sent] *n* : centavo *m*

centennial [sen'teniəl] *n* : centenario *m*

center *or Brit* **centre** ['sentər] *n* : centro *m* — ~ *v* **centered** *or Brit* **centred; centering** *or Brit* **centring** *vt* : centrar — *vi* ~ **on** : centrarse en

centigrade ['sentə,greɪd, 'san-] *adj* : centígrado

centimeter ['sentə,miːtər, 'san-] *n* : centímetro *m*

centipede ['sentə,piːd] *n* : ciempiés *m*

central ['sentrəl] *adj* **1** : central **2** **a** ~ **location** : un lugar céntrico — **centralize** ['sentrə,laɪz] *vt* **-ized; -izing** : centralizar

centre ['sentər] → **center**

century ['sentʃəri] *n, pl* **-ries** : siglo *m*

ceramics [sə'ræmɪks] *npl* : cerámica *f*

cereal ['sɪriəl] *n* : cereal *m*

ceremony ['serəˌmoni] *n, pl* **-nies** : ceremonia *f* — **ceremonial** [ˌserə'moniəl] *adj* : ceremonial

certain ['sərtən] *adj* **1** : cierto **2 be ~ of** : estar seguro de **3 for ~** : seguro, con toda seguridad **4 make ~ of** : asegurarse de — **certainly** ['sərtənli] *adv* : desde luego, por supuesto — **certainty** ['sərtənti] *n, pl* **-ties** : certeza *f*, seguridad *f*

certify ['sərtəˌfaɪ] *vt* **-fied; -fying** : certificar — **certificate** [sər'tɪfɪkət] *n* : certificado *m*, partida *f*, acta *f*

chafe ['tʃeɪf] *v* **chafed; chafing** *vi* : rozarse — *vt* : rozar

chain ['tʃeɪn] *n* **1** : cadena *f* **2 ~ of events** : serie *f* de acontecimientos — **~** *vt* : encadenar

chair ['tʃer] *n* **1** : silla *f* **2** : cátedra *f* (en una universidad) — **~** *vt* : presidir — **chairman** ['tʃermən] *n, pl* **-men** [-mən, -men] : presidente *m* — **chairperson** ['tʃerˌpərsən] *n* : presidente *m*, -ta *f*

chalk ['tʃɔk] *n* : tiza *f*, gis *m Lat*

challenge ['tʃæləndʒ] *vt* **-lenged; -lenging 1** DISPUTE : disputar, poner en duda **2** DARE : desafiar — **~** *n* : reto *m*, desafío *m* — **challenging** ['tʃæləndʒɪŋ] *adj* : estimulante

chamber ['tʃeɪmbər] *n* : cámara *f* — **chambermaid** ['tʃeɪmbərˌmeɪd] *n* : camarera *f*

champagne [ʃæm'peɪn] *n* : champaña *m*, champán *m*

champion ['tʃæmpiən] *n* : campeón *m*, -peona *f* — **~** *vt* : defender — **championship** ['tʃæmpiənˌʃɪp] *n* : campeonato *m*

chance ['tʃænts] *n* **1** LUCK : azar *m*, suerte *f* **2** OPPORTUNITY : oportunidad *f* **3** LIKELIHOOD : probabilidad *f* **4 by ~** : por casualidad **5 take a ~** : arriesgarse — **~** *vt* **chanced; chancing** RISK : arriesgar — **~** *adj* : fortuito

chandelier [ˌʃændə'lɪr] *n* : araña *f* (de luces)

change ['tʃeɪndʒ] *v* **changed; changing** *vt* **1** : cambiar **2** SWITCH : cambiar de — *vi* **1** : cambiar **2** *or* **~ clothes** : cambiarse (de ropa) — **~** *n* : cambio *m* — **changeable** ['tʃeɪndʒəbəl] *adj* : cambiable

channel ['tʃænəl] *n* **1** : canal *m* **2** : cauce *m* (de un río) **3** MEANS : vía *f*, medio *m*

chant ['tʃænt] *v* : cantar — **~** *n* : canto *m*

chaos ['keɪˌɑs] *n* : caos *m* — **chaotic** [keɪ'ɑtɪk] *adj* : caótico

chap¹ ['tʃæp] *vi* **chapped; chapping** : agrietarse

chap² *n* : tipo *m fam*

chapel ['tʃæpəl] *n* : capilla *f*

chaperon *or* **chaperone** ['ʃæpəˌroːn] *n* : acompañante *mf*

chaplain ['tʃæplɪn] *n* : capellán *m*

chapter ['tʃæptər] *n* : capítulo *m*

char ['tʃɑr] *vt* **charred; charring** : carbonizar

character ['kærɪktər] *n* **1** : carácter *m* **2** : personaje *m* (en una novela, etc.) — **characteristic** [ˌkærɪktə'rɪstɪk] *adj* : característico — **~** *n* : característica *f* — **characterize** ['kærɪktəˌraɪz] *vt* **-ized; -izing** : caracterizar

charcoal ['tʃɑrˌkoɪl] *n* : carbón *m*

charge ['tʃɑrdʒ] *n* **1** : carga *f* (eléctrica) **2** COST : precio *m* **3** BURDEN : carga *f*, peso *m* **4** ACCUSATION : cargo *m*, acusación *f* **5 in ~ of** : encargado de **6 take ~ of** : hacerse cargo de — **~** *v* **charged; charging** *vt* **1** : cargar ENTRUST : encargar **3** COMMAND : ordenar, mandar **4** ACCUSE : acusar — *vi* **1** : cargar **2 ~ too much** : cobrar demasiado

charisma [kə'rɪzmə] *n* : carisma *m* — **charismatic** [ˌkærəz'mætɪk] *adj* : carismático

charity ['tʃærəti] *n, pl* **-ties 1** : organización *f* benéfica **2** GOODWILL : caridad *f*

charlatan ['ʃɑrlətən] *n* : charlatán *m*, -tana *f*

charm ['tʃɑrm] *n* **1** : encanto *m* **2** SPELL : hechizo *m* — **~** *vt* : encantar, cautivar — **charming** ['tʃɑrmɪŋ] *adj* : encantador

chart ['tʃɑrt] *n* **1** MAP : carta *f* **2** DIAGRAM : gráfico *m*, tabla *f* — **~** *vt* : trazar un mapa de

charter ['tʃɑrtər] *n* : carta *f* — **~** *vt* : alquilar, fletar

chase ['tʃeɪs] *n* : persecución *f* — **~** *vt* **chased; chasing 1** PURSUE : perseguir **2** *or* **~ away** : ahuyentar

chasm ['kæzəm] *n* : abismo *m*

chaste ['tʃeɪst] *adj* **chaster; -est** : casto — **chastity** ['tʃæstəti] *n* : castidad *f*

chat ['tʃæt] *v* **chatted; chatting** : charlar — **~** *n* : charla *f* — **chatter** ['tʃætər] *vi* **1** : parlotear *fam* **2** : castañetear (dícese de los dientes) — **~** *n* : parloteo *m*, cháchara *f* — **chatterbox** ['tʃætərˌbɑks] *n* : parlanchín *m*, -china *f* — **chatty** ['tʃæti] *adj* **chattier; chattiest 1** : parlanchín **2** INFORMAL : familiar

chauffeur ['ʃoːfər, ʃo'fər] *n* : chofer *mf*

chauvinist ['ʃoːvənɪst] *or* **chauvinistic**

[ʃoːvəˈnɪstɪk] *adj* : chauvinista, patriotero

cheap ['tʃiːp] *adj* **1** INEXPENSIVE : barato **2** SHODDY : de baja calidad — ~ *adv* : barato — **cheapen** ['tʃiːpən] *vt* : rebajar — **cheaply** ['tʃiːpli] *adv* : barato, a precio bajo

cheat ['tʃiːt] *vt* : defraudar, estafar — *vi* **1** : hacer trampa(s) **2** ~ **on s.o.** : engañar a algn — ~ *or* **cheater** ['tʃiːtər] *n* : tramposo *m*, -sa *f*

check ['tʃek] *n* **1** RESTRAINT : freno *m* **2** INSPECTION : inspección *f*, comprobación *f* **3** DRAFT : cheque *m* **4** BILL : cuenta *f* **5** : jaque *m* (en ajedrez) **6** : tela a cuadros — ~ *vt* **1** RESTRAIN : frenar, contener **2** INSPECT : revisar **3** VERIFY : comprobar **4** : dar jaque (en ajedrez) **5** ~ **in** : enregistrarse (en un hotel) **6** ~ **out** : irse (de un hotel) **7** ~ **out** VERIFY : verificar, comprobar

checkers ['tʃekərz] *n* : damas *fpl*

checkmate ['tʃek,meit] *n* : jaque *m* mate

checkpoint ['tʃek,pɔint] *n* : puesto *m* de control

checkup ['tʃek,ʌp] *n* : chequeo *m*, examen *m* médico

cheek ['tʃiːk] *n* : mejilla *f*

cheer ['tʃɪr] *n* **1** CHEERFULNESS : alegría *f* **2** APPLAUSE : aclamación *f* **3** ~**s!** : ¡salud! — ~ *vt* **1** GLADDEN : alegrar **2** APPLAUD, SHOUT : aclamar, aplaudir — **cheerful** ['tʃɪrfəl] *adj* : alegre

cheese ['tʃiːz] *n* : queso *m*

cheetah ['tʃiːt̬ə] *n* : guepardo *m*

chef ['ʃef] *n* : chef *m*

chemical ['kemɪkəl] *adj* : químico — ~ *n* : sustancia *f* química — **chemist** ['kemɪst] *n* : químico *m*, -ca *f* — **chemistry** ['kemɪstri] *n*, *pl* **-tries** : química *f*

cheque ['tʃek] *Brit* → **check**

cherish ['tʃerɪʃ] *vt* **1** : querer, apreciar **2** HARBOR : abrigar (un recuerdo, una esperanza, etc.)

cherry ['tʃeri] *n*, *pl* **-ries** : cereza *f*

chess ['tʃes] *n* : ajedrez *m*

chest ['tʃest] *n* **1** BOX : cofre *m* **2** : pecho *m* (del cuerpo) **3** *or* ~ **of drawers** : cómoda *f*

chestnut ['tʃes,nʌt] *n* : castaña *f*

chew ['tʃuː] *vt* : masticar, mascar — **chewing gum** *m* : chicle *m*

chic ['ʃik] *adj* : elegante

chick ['tʃik] *n* : polluelo *m*, -la *f* — **chicken** ['tʃikən] *n* : pollo *m* — **chicken pox** *n* : varicela *f*

chicory ['tʃikəri] *n*, *pl* **-ries** **1** : endivia *f* (para ensaladas) **2** : achicoria *f* (aditivo de café)

chief ['tʃiːf] *adj* : principal — ~ *n* : jefe

m, -fa *f* — **chiefly** ['tʃiːfli] *adv* : principalmente

child ['tʃaild] *n*, *pl* **children** ['tʃildrən] **1** : niño *m*, -ña *f* **2** OFFSPRING : hijo *m*, -ja *f* — **childbirth** ['tʃaild,bərθ] *n* : parto *m* — **childhood** ['tʃaild,hud] *n* : infancia *f*, niñez *f* — **childish** ['tʃaildɪʃ] *adj* : infantil — **childlike** ['tʃaild,laik] *adj* : infantil, inocente — **childproof** ['tʃaild,pruːf] *adj* : a prueba de niños

Chilean ['tʃilion, tʃiˈleiən] *adj* : chileno

chili *or* **chile** *or* **chilli** ['tʃili] *n*, *pl* **chilies** *or* **chiles** *or* **chillies 1** *or* ~ **pepper** : chile *m* **2** : chile *m* con carne

chill ['tʃil] *n* **1** CHILLINESS : frío *m* **2** **catch a** ~ : resfriarse **3 there's a** ~ **in the air** : hace fresco — ~ *adj* : frío — ~ *v* : enfriar — **chilly** ['tʃili] *adj* **chillier; -est** : fresco, frío

chime ['tʃaim] *vi* **chimed; chiming** : repicar, sonar — ~ *n* : carillón *m*

chimney ['tʃimni] *n*, *pl* **-neys** : chimenea *f*

chimpanzee [,tʃimˌpænˈziː, ˌʃim-; tʃimˈpænzi, ʃim-] *n* : chimpancé *m*

chin ['tʃin] *n* : barbilla *f*

china ['tʃainə] *n* : porcelana *f*, loza *f*

Chinese ['tʃainiːz, -niːs] *adj* : chino — ~ *n* : chino *m* (idioma)

chink ['tʃiŋk] *n* : grieta *f*

chip ['tʃip] *n* **1** : astilla *f* (de madera o vidrio), lasca *f* (de piedra) **2** : ficha *f* (de póker, etc.) **3** NICK : desportilladura *f* **4** *or* **computer** ~ : chip *m* **5** *or* **potato chips** — ~ *v* **chipped; chipping** *vt* : desportillar — *vi* **1** : desportillarse **2** ~ **in** : contribuir

chipmunk ['tʃip,mʌŋk] *n* : ardilla *f* listada

chiropodist [kəˈrapədist, ʃə-] *n* : podólogo *m*, -ga *f*

chiropractor ['kairəˌpræktər] *n* : quiropráctico *m*, -ca *f*

chirp ['tʃərp] *vi* : piar, gorjear

chisel ['tʃizəl] *n* : cincel *m* (para piedras, etc.), formón *m*, escoplo *m* (para madera) — ~ *vt* **-eled** *or* **-elled; -eling** *or* **-elling** : cincelar, tallar

chit ['tʃit] *n* : nota *f*

chitchat ['tʃit,tʃæt] *n* : cháchara *f fam*

chivalrous ['ʃivəlrəs] *adj* : caballeroso — **chivalry** ['ʃivəlri] *n*, *pl* **-ries** : caballerosidad *f*

chive ['tʃaiv] *n* : cebollino *m*

chlorine ['klor,iːn] *n* : cloro *m*

chock-full ['tʃak,ful, 'tʃʌk-] *adj* : repleto, atestado

chocolate ['tʃakələt, 'tʃɔk-] *n* : chocolate *m*

choice ['tʃɔis] *n* **1** : elección *f*, selección

f 2 PREFERENCE : preferencia *f* — ~ *adj* **choicer; -est** : selecto

choir ['kwaɪr] *n* : coro *m*

choke ['tʃok] *v* **choked; choking** *vt* 1 : asfixiar, estrangular 2 BLOCK : atascar — *vi* : asfixiarse, atragantarse (con comida) — ~ *n* : estárter *m* (de un motor)

choose ['tʃuːz] *v* **chose** ['tʃoz]; **chosen** ['tʃozən]; **choosing** *vt* 1 SELECT : escoger, elegir 2 DECIDE : decidir — *vi* : escoger — **choosy** *or* **choosey** ['tʃuːzi] *adj* **choosier; -est** : exigente

chop ['tʃɑp] *vt* **chopped; chopping** 1 : cortar, picar (carne, etc.) 2 ~ **down** : talar — ~ *n* : chuleta *f* (de cerdo, etc.) — **choppy** ['tʃɑpi] *adj* **-pier; -est** : picado, agitado

chopsticks ['tʃɑp,stɪks] *npl* : palillos *mpl*

chord ['kɔrd] *n* : acorde *m* (en música)

chore ['tʃor] *n* 1 : tarea *f* 2 **household** ~**s** : faenas *fpl* domésticas

choreography [ˌkori'ɑgrəfi] *n, pl* **-phies** : coreografía *f*

chortle ['tʃɔrtəl] *vi* **-tled; -tling** : reírse (con satisfacción o júbilo)

chorus ['korəs] *n* 1 : coro *m* (grupo de personas) 2 REFRAIN : estribillo *m*

chose, chosen → **choose**

christen ['krɪsən] *vt* : bautizar — **christening** ['krɪsənɪŋ] *n* : bautizo *m*

Christian ['krɪstʃən] *n* : cristiano *m*, -na *f* — ~ *adj* : cristiano — **Christianity** [ˌkrɪstʃi'ænəti, ˌkrɪs'tʃæ-] *n* : cristianismo *m*

Christmas ['krɪsməs] *n* : Navidad *f*

chrome ['krom] *n* : cromo *m*

chronic ['krɑnɪk] *adj* : crónico

chronicle ['krɑnɪkəl] *n* : crónica *f*

chronology [krə'nɑlədʒi] *n, pl* **-gies** : cronología *f* — **chronological** [ˌkrɑnəl'ɑdʒɪkəl] *adj* : cronológico

chrysanthemum [krɪ'sænθəməm] *n* : crisantemo *m*

chubby ['tʃʌbi] *adj* **-bier; -est** : regordete *fam*, rechoncho *fam*

chuck ['tʃʌk] *vt* : tirar, arrojar

chuckle ['tʃʌkəl] *vi* **-led; -ling** : reírse (entre dientes) — ~ *n* : risa *f* ahogada

chum ['tʃʌm] *n* : amigo *m*, -ga *f*; compinche *mf fam* — **chummy** ['tʃʌmi] *adj* **-mier; -est** : muy amigable

chunk ['tʃʌŋk] *n* : trozo *m*, pedazo *m*

church ['tʃərtʃ] *n* : iglesia *f*

churn ['tʃərn] *n* : mantequera *f* — *vt* 1 : agitar 2 ~ **out** : producir en grandes cantidades

chute ['ʃuːt] *n* 1 : vertedor *m* 2 SLIDE : tobogán *m*

cider ['saɪdər] *n* : sidra *f*

cigar [sɪ'gɑr] *n* : puro *m* — **cigarette** [ˌsɪgə'rɛt, 'sɪgəˌrɛt] *n* : cigarrillo *m*, cigarro *m*

cinch ['sɪntʃ] *n* **it's a** ~ : es pan comido

cinema ['sɪnəmə] *n* : cine *m*

cinnamon ['sɪnəmən] *n* : canela *f*

cipher ['saɪfər] *n* 1 ZERO : cero *m* 2 CODE : cifra *f*

circa ['sərkə] *prep* : hacia

circle ['sərkəl] *n* : círculo *m* — ~ *v* **-cled; -cling** *vt* 1 : dar vueltas alrededor de 2 : trazar un círculo alrededor de (un número, etc.) — *vi* : dar vueltas

circuit ['sərkət] *n* : circuito *m* — **circuitous** [ˌsər'kjuətəs] *adj* : tortuoso

circular ['sərkjələr] *adj* : circular — ~ *n* LEAFLET : circular *f*

circulate ['sərkjəˌleɪt] *v* **-lated; -lating** *vt* : hacer circular — *vi* : circular — **circulation** [ˌsərkjə'leɪʃən] *n* 1 : circulación *f* 2 : tirada *f* (de una publicación)

circumcise ['sərkəmˌsaɪz] *vt* **-cised; -cising** : circuncidar — **circumcision** [ˌsərkəm'sɪʒən, 'sərkəm-] *n* : circuncisión *f*

circumference [sər'kʌmfrənts] *n* : circunferencia *f*

circumspect ['sərkəmˌspɛkt] *adj* : circunspecto, prudente

circumstance ['sərkəmˌstænts] *n* 1 : circunstancia *f* 2 **under no** ~**s** : bajo ningún concepto

circus ['sərkəs] *n* : circo *m*

cistern ['sɪstərn] *n* : cisterna *f*

cite ['saɪt] *vt* **cited; citing** : citar — **citation** [saɪ'teɪʃən] *n* : citación *f*

citizen ['sɪtəzən] *n* : ciudadano *m*, -na *f* — **citizenship** ['sɪtəzənˌʃɪp] *n* : ciudadanía *f*

citrus ['sɪtrəs] *n, pl* **-rus** *or* **-ruses** *or* **fruit** : cítrico *m*

city ['sɪti] *n, pl* **cities** : ciudad *f*

civic ['sɪvɪk] *adj* : cívico — **civics** ['sɪvɪks] *ns & pl* : civismo *m*

civil ['sɪvəl] *adj* : civil — **civilian** [sə'vɪljən] *n* : civil *mf* — **civility** [sə'vɪləti] *n, pl* **-ties** : cortesía *f* — **civilization** [ˌsɪvələ'zeɪʃən] *n* : civilización *f* — **civilize** ['sɪvəˌlaɪz] *vt* **-lized; -lizing** : civilizar

clad ['klæd] *adj* ~ **in** : vestido de

claim ['kleɪm] *vt* 1 DEMAND : reclamar 2 MAINTAIN : afirmar, sostener 3 ~ **responsibility** : atribuirse la responsabilidad — ~ *n* 1 DEMAND : demanda *f*, reclamación *f* 2 ASSERTION : afirmación *f*

clam ['klæm] *n* : almeja *f*

clamber ['klæmbər] *vi* : trepar (con torpeza)

clammy ['klæmi] *adj* **-mier; -est** : húmedo y algo frío

clamor ['klæmər] *n* : clamor *m* — *vi* : clamar

clamp ['klæmp] *n* : abrazadera *f* — *vt* : sujetar con abrazaderas — *vi* ~ **down** *on* : reprimir

clan ['klæn] *n* : clan *m*

clandestine [klæn'destɪn] *adj* : clandestino

clang ['klæŋ] *n* : ruido *m* metálico

clap ['klæp] *v* **clapped; clapping** *vt* 1 : aplaudir 2 ~ **one's hands** : dar palmadas — *vi* : aplaudir — ~ *n* : palmada *f*

clarify ['klærə,faɪ] *vt* **-fied; -fying** : aclarar — **clarification** [,klærəfə'keɪʃən] *n* : clarificación *f*

clarinet [,klærə'net] *n* : clarinete *m*

clarity ['klærəti] *n* : claridad *f*

clash ['klæʃ] *vi* 1 : chocar, enfrentarse 2 CONFLICT : estar en conflicto — ~ *n* 1 CRASH : choque *m* 2 CONFLICT : conflicto *m*

clasp ['klæsp] *n* : broche *m*, cierre — ~ *vt* 1 : abrazar (a una persona), agarrar (una cosa) 2 FASTEN : abrochar

class ['klæs] *n* : clase *f*

classic ['klæsɪk] *or* **classical** ['klæsɪkəl] *adj* : clásico — **classic** *n* : clásico *m*

classify ['klæsə,faɪ] *vt* **-fied; -fying** : clasificar — **classification** [,klæsəfə'keɪʃən] *n* : clasificación *f* — **classified** ['klæsə,faɪd] *adj* RESTRICTED : secreto

classmate ['klæs,meɪt] *n* : compañero *m*, -ra *f* de clase

classroom ['klæs,ruːm] *n* : aula *f*, salón *m* de clase

clatter ['klæt̬ər] *vi* : hacer ruido — ~ *n* : estrépito *m*

clause ['klɔz] *n* : cláusula *f*

claustrophobia [,klɔstrə'foːbiə] *n* : claustrofobia *f*

claw ['klɔ] *n* : garra *f*, uña *f* (de un gato), pinza *f* (de un crustáceo) — ~ *v* : arañar

clay ['kleɪ] *n* : arcilla *f*

clean ['kliːn] *adj* 1 : limpio 2 UNADULTERATED : puro 3 SPOTLESS : impecable — ~ *vt* : limpiar — ~ *adv* : limpio — **cleaner** ['kliːnər] *n* 1 : limpiador *m*, -dora *f* 2 DRY CLEANER : tintorería *f* — **cleanliness** ['klenlinəs] *n* : limpieza *f* — **cleanse** ['klenz] *vt* **cleansed; cleansing** : limpiar, purificar

clear ['klɪr] *adj* 1 : claro 2 TRANSPARENT : transparente 3 UNOBSTRUCTED : despejado, libre — ~ *vt* 1 : despejar (una superficie), desatascar (un tubo, etc.) 2 EXONERATE : absolver 3 : saltar por encima de (un obstáculo) 4 ~ **the table** : levantar la mesa 5 ~ **up** RESOLVE : aclarar, resolver — *vi* 1 ~ **up** BRIGHTEN : despejarse (dícese del tiempo, etc.) 2 ~ **up** VANISH : desaparecer (dícese de una infección, etc.) — ~ *adv* 1 **make oneself** ~ : explicarse 2 **stand** ~ ! : ¡aléjate! — **clearance** ['klɪrənts] *n* 1 SPACE : espacio *m* (libre) 2 AUTHORIZATION : autorización *f* 3 ~ **sale** : liquidación *f* — **clearing** ['klɪrɪŋ] *n* : claro *m* — **clearly** ['klɪrli] *adv* 1 DISTINCTLY : claramente 2 OBVIOUSLY : obviamente

cleaver ['kliːvər] *n* : cuchillo *m* de carnicero

clef ['klef] *n* : clave *f*

cleft ['kleft] *n* : hendidura *f*, grieta *f*

clement ['klemənt] *adj* : clemente — **clemency** ['kleməntsi] *n* : clemencia *f*

clench ['klentʃ] *vt* : apretar

clergy ['klərdʒi] *n, pl* **-gies** : clero *m* — **clergyman** ['klərdʒimən] *n, pl* **-men** [-mən, -,men] : clérigo *m* — **clerical** ['klerɪkəl] *adj* 1 : clerical 2 ~ **work** : trabajo *m* de oficina

clerk ['klərk, *Brit* 'klɑrk] *n* 1 : oficinista *mf*; empleado *m*, -da *f* de oficina 2 SALESPERSON : dependiente *m*, -ta *f*

clever ['klevər] *adj* 1 SKILLFUL : ingenioso, hábil 2 SMART : listo, inteligente — **cleverly** ['klevərli] *adv* : ingeniosamente — **cleverness** ['klevərnəs] *n* 1 SKILL : ingenio *m* 2 INTELLIGENCE : inteligencia *f*

cliché [kli'ʃeɪ] *n* : cliché *m*

click ['klɪk] *vt* : chasquear — *vi* 1 : chasquear 2 GET ALONG : llevarse bien — ~ *n* : chasquido *m*

client ['klaɪənt] *n* : cliente *m*, -ta *f* — **clientele** [,klaɪən'tel, ,kliː-] *n* : clientela *f*

cliff ['klɪf] *n* : acantilado *m*

climate ['klaɪmət] *n* : clima *m*

climax ['klaɪ,mæks] *n* : clímax *m*, punto *m* culminante

climb ['klaɪm] *vt* : escalar, subir a, trepar a — *vi* 1 RISE : subir 2 *or* ~ **up** : subirse, treparse — ~ *n* : subida *f*

clinch ['klɪntʃ] *vt* : cerrar (un acuerdo, etc.)

cling ['klɪŋ] *vi* **clung** ['klʌŋ]; **clinging** : adherirse, pegarse

clinic ['klɪnɪk] *n* : clínica *f* — **clinical** ['klɪnɪkəl] *adj* : clínico

clink ['klɪŋk] *vi* : tintinear

clip ['klɪp] *vt* **clipped; clipping** 1 CUT

: cortar, recortar **2** FASTEN : sujetar (con un clip) — **~** *n* **1** FASTENER : clip *m* **2** at a good **~** : a buen trote **3** → paper clip — **clippers** ['klɪpərz] *npl* **1** : maquinilla *f* para cortar el pelo **2** *or* nail **~** : cortauñas *m*

cloak ['kloːk] *n* : capa *f*

clock ['klɑk] **1** : reloj *m* (de pared) **2** around the **~** : las veinticuatro horas — **clockwise** ['klɑk,waɪz] *adv* & *adj* : en el sentido de las agujas del reloj — **clockwork** ['klɑk,wərk] *n* **1** : mecanismo *m* de relojería **2** like **~** : con precisión

clog ['klɑg] *n* : zueco *m* — **~** *v* **clogged; clogging** *vt* : atascar, obstruir — *vi or* **~** up : atascarse

cloister ['klɔɪstər] *n* : claustro *m*

close¹ ['kloːz] *v* **closed; closing** *vt* : cerrar — *vi* **1** : cerrarse **2** TERMINATE : terminar **3** **~** in : acercarse — **~** *n* : final *m*

close² ['kloːs] *adj* **closer; closest 1** NEAR : cercano, próximo **2** INTIMATE : íntimo **3** STRICT : estricto **4** STUFFY : sofocante **5** a **~** game : un juego reñido — **~** *adv* : cerca, de cerca — **closely** ['kloːsli] *adv* : cerca, de cerca — **closeness** ['kloːsnəs] *n* **1** NEARNESS : cercanía *f* **2** INTIMACY : intimidad *f*

closet ['klɑzət] *n* : armario *m*, clóset *m Lat*

closure ['kloːʒər] *n* : cierre *m*

clot ['klɑt] *n* : coágulo *m* — **~** *v* **clotted; clotting** *vt* : coagular, cuajar — *vi* : coagularse

cloth ['klɔθ] *n, pl* **cloths** ['klɔðz, 'klɔθs] **1** FABRIC : tela *f* **2** RAG : trapo *m*

clothe ['kloːð] *vt* **clothed** *or* **clad** ['klæd]; **clothing** : vestir — **clothes** ['kloːz, 'kloːðz] *npl* **1** : ropa *f* **2** put on one's **~** : vestirse — **clothespin** ['kloːz,pɪn] *n* : pinza *f* (para la ropa) — **clothing** ['kloːðɪŋ] *n* : ropa *f*

cloud ['klaʊd] *n* : nube *f* — **~** *vt* : nublar — *vi or* **~** over : nublarse — **cloudy** ['klaʊdi] *adj* **cloudier; -est** : nublado

clout ['klaʊt] *n* **1** BLOW : golpe *m*, tortazo *m fam* **2** INFLUENCE : influencia *f*

clove ['kloːv] *n* **1** : clavo *m* **2** : diente *m* (de ajo)

clover ['kloːvər] *n* : trébol *m*

clown ['klaʊn] *n* : payaso *m*, -sa *f* — *or* **~** around *vi* : payasear — **cloying** ['klɔɪɪŋ] *adj* : empalagoso

club ['klʌb] *n* **1** : garrote *m*, porra *f* **2** ASSOCIATION : club *m* **3** **~**s *mpl* : tréboles *mpl* (en los naipes) — **~** *vt* **clubbed; clubbing** : aporrear

cluck ['klʌk] *vi* : cloquear

clue ['kluː] *n* **1** : pista *f*, indicio *m* **2** I haven't got a **~** : no tengo la menor idea

clump ['klʌmp] *n* : grupo *m* (de arbustos)

clumsy ['klʌmzi] *adj* **-sier; -est** : torpe — **clumsiness** ['klʌmzinəs] *n* : torpeza *f*

cluster ['klʌstər] *n* : grupo *m*, racimo *m* (de uvas, etc.) — **~** *vi* : agruparse

clutch ['klʌtʃ] *vt* : agarrar, asir — *vi* **~** at : tratar de agarrarse de — **~** *n* : embrague *m*, clutch *m Lat* (de un automóvil)

clutter ['klʌtər] *vt* : llenar desordenadamente — **~** *n* : desorden *m*, revoltijo *m*

coach ['koːtʃ] *n* **1** CARRIAGE : carruaje *m*, carroza *f* **2** : vagón *m* de pasajeros (de un tren) **3** BUS : autobús *m* **4** : pasaje *m* aéreo de segunda clase **5** TRAINER : entrenador *m*, -dora *f* — *vt* : entrenar (un atleta), dar clases particulares a (un alumno)

coagulate [ko'ægjə,leɪt] *v* **-lated; -lating** *vt* : coagular — *vi* : coagularse

coal ['koːl] *n* : carbón *m*

coalition [,koːə'lɪʃən] *n* : coalición *f*

coarse ['kors] *adj* **coarser; -est 1** : tosco, basto **2** CRUDE, VULGAR : grosero, ordinario — **coarseness** ['korsnəs] *n* : aspereza *f*, tosquedad *f*

coast ['koːst] *n* : costa *f* — **~** *vi* : ir en punto muerto (dícese de un automóvil), deslizarse (dícese de una bicicleta) — **coastal** ['koːstəl] *adj* : costero

coaster ['koːstər] *n* : posavasos *m*

coast guard *n* : guardacostas *mpl*

coastline ['koːst,laɪn] *n* : litoral *m*

coat ['koːt] *n* **1** : abrigo *m* **2** : pelaje *m* (de un animal) **3** : mano *f* (de pintura) — **~** *vt* : cubrir, revestir — **coating** ['koːtɪŋ] *n* : capa *f* — **coat of arms** *n* : escudo *m* de armas

coax ['koːks] *vt* : engatusar

cob ['kɑb] → **corncob**

cobblestone ['kɑbəl,stoːn] *n* : adoquín *m*

cobweb ['kɑb,web] *n* : telaraña *f*

cocaine [ko'keɪn, 'ko,keɪn] *n* : cocaína *f*

cock ['kɑk] *n* **1** ROOSTER : gallo *m* **2** FAUCET : grifo *m* **3** : martillo *m* (de un arma de fuego) — **~** *vt* **1** : amartillar (un arma de fuego) **2** **~** one's head : ladear la cabeza — **cockeyed** ['kɑk,aɪd] *adj* **1** ASKEW : ladeado **2** ABSURD : absurdo

cockpit ['kɑk,pɪt] *n* : cabina *f*

cockroach ['kɑk,roːtʃ] *n* : cucaracha *f*

cocktail ['kɑk,teɪl] *n* : coctel *m*, cóctel *m*

cocky ['kɑki] *adj* **cockier; -est** : engreído, arrogante

cocoa ['ko:,ko:] *n* **1** : cacao *m* **2** : chocolate *m* (bebida)

coconut ['ko:kə,nʌt] *n* : coco *m*

cocoon [kə'ku:n] *n* : capullo *m*

cod ['kɑd] *ns & pl* : bacalao *m*

coddle ['kɑdəl] *vt* **-dled; -dling** : mimar

code ['ko:d] *n* : código *m*

coeducational [,ko:,edʒə'keɪʃənəl] *adj* : mixto

coerce [ko'ərs] *vt* **-erced; -ercing** : coaccionar, forzar — **coercion** [ko'ərʒən, -ʃən] *n* : coacción *f*

coffee ['kɔfi] *n* : café *m* — **coffeepot** ['kɔfi,pɑt] *n* : cafetera *f*

coffer ['kɔfər] *n* : cofre *m*

coffin ['kɔfən] *n* : ataúd *m*, féretro *m*

cog ['kɑg] *n* : diente *m* (de una rueda)

cogent ['ko:dʒənt] *adj* : convincente, persuasivo

cognac ['ko:n,jæk] *n* : coñac *m*

cogwheel ['kɑg,hwi:l] *n* : rueda *f* dentada

coherent [ko'hɪrənt] *adj* : coherente

coil ['kɔɪl] *vt* : enrollar — *vi* : enrollarse — ~ *n* **1** ROLL : rollo *m* **2** : tirabuzón *m* (de pelo), espiral *f* (de humo)

coin ['kɔɪn] *n* : moneda *f* — ~ *vt* : acuñar

coincide [,ko:ɪn'saɪd, 'ko:ɪn,saɪd] *vi* **-cided; -ciding** : coincidir — **coincidence** [ko'ɪntsədənts] *n* : coincidencia *f*, casualidad *f* — **coincidental** [ko-,ɪntsə'dentəl] *adj* : casual, fortuito

coke ['ko:k] *n* : coque *m* (combustible)

colander ['kɑləndər, 'kʌ-] *n* : colador *m*

cold ['ko:ld] *adj* **1** : frío **2 be ~** : tener frío **3 it's ~ today** : hace frío hoy — ~ *n* **1** : frío *m* **2** : resfriado *m* (en medicina) **3 catch a ~** : resfriarse

coleslaw ['ko:l,slɔ] *n* : ensalada *f* de col

colic ['kɑlɪk] *n* : cólico *m*

collaborate [kə'læbə,reɪt] *vi* **-rated; -rating** : colaborar — **collaboration** [kə,læbə'reɪʃən] *n* : colaboración *f* — **collaborator** [kə'læbə,reɪtər] *n* : colaborador *m*, -dora *f*

collapse [kə'læps] *vi* **-lapsed; -lapsing** **1** : derrumbarse, hundirse **2** : sufrir un colapso (físico o mental) — ~ *n* **1** FALL : derrumbamiento *m* **2** BREAKDOWN : colapso *m* — **collapsible** [kə-'læpsəbəl] *adj* : plegable

collar ['kɑlər] *n* : cuello *m* (de camisa, etc.), collar *m* (para animales) — **collarbone** ['kɑlər,bo:n] *n* : clavícula *f*

colleague ['kɑ,li:g] *n* : colega *mf*

collect [kə'lekt] *vt* **1** GATHER : reunir **2** : coleccionar, juntar (timbres, etc.) **3** : recaudar (fondos, etc.) — *vi* **1** ACCUMULATE : acumularse, juntarse **2** CONGREGATE : congregarse, reunirse — ~ *adv* **call ~** : llamar a cobro revertido, llamar por cobrar *Lat* — **collection** [kə'lekʃən] *n* **1** : colección *f* **2** : colecta *f* (de contribuciones) — **collective** [kə'lektɪv] *adj* : colectivo — **collector** [kə'lektər] *n* **1** : coleccionista *mf* **2** : cobrador *m*, -dora *f* (de deudas)

college ['kɑlɪdʒ] *n* **1** : instituto *m* (a nivel universitario) **2** : colegio *m* (electoral, etc.)

collide [kə'laɪd] *vi* **-lided; -liding** : chocar, colisionar — **collision** [kə'lɪʒən] *n* : choque *m*, colisión *f*

colloquial [kə'lo:kwiəl] *adj* : coloquial, familiar

cologne [kə'lo:n] *n* : colonia *f*

Colombian [kə'lʌmbiən] *adj* : colombiano

colon[1] ['ko:lən] *n, pl* **colons** or **cola** [-lə] : colon *m* (en anatomía)

colon[2] *n, pl* **colons** : dos puntos *mpl* (signo de puntuación)

colonel ['kərnəl] *n* : coronel *m*

colony ['kɑləni] *n, pl* **-nies** : colonia *f* — **colonial** [kə'lo:niəl] *adj* : colonial — **colonize** ['kɑlə,naɪz] *vt* **-nized; -nizing** : colonizar

color or Brit **colour** ['kʌlər] *n* : color *m* — ~ *vt* : colorear, pintar — *vi* BLUSH : sonrojarse — **color-blind** or Brit **colour-blind** ['kʌlər,blaɪnd] *adj* : daltónico — **colored** or Brit **coloured** ['kʌlərd] *adj* : de color — **colorful** or Brit **colourful** ['kʌlərfəl] *adj* **1** : de vivos colores **2** PICTURESQUE : pintoresco — **colorless** or Brit **colourless** ['kʌlərləs] *adj* : incoloro

colossal [kə'lɑsəl] *adj* : colosal

colt ['ko:lt] *n* : potro *m*

column ['kɑləm] *n* : columna *f* — **columnist** ['kɑləmnɪst, -ləmɪst] *n* : columnista *mf*

coma ['ko:mə] *n* : coma *m*

comb ['ko:m] *n* **1** : peine *m* **2** : cresta *f* (de un gallo) — ~ *vt* : peinar

combat ['kɑm,bæt] *n* : combate *m* — ~ [kəm'bæt, 'kɑm,bæt] *vt* **-bated** or **-batted; -bating** or **-batting** : combatir — **combatant** [kəm'bætənt] *n* : combatiente *mf*

combine [kəm'baɪn] *v* **-bined; -bining** *vt* : combinar — *vi* : combinarse — ~ ['kɑm,baɪn] *n* HARVESTER : cosechadora *f* — **combination** [kɑmbə'neɪʃən] *n* : combinación *f*

combustion [kəm'bʌstʃən] *n* : combustión *f*

come ['kʌm] *vi* **came** ['keɪm]; **come**; **coming 1 ~** ARRIVE : llegar 2 **~ about** : suceder 4 **~ back** : regresar, volver 5 **~ from** : venir de, provenir de 6 **~ in** : entrar 7 **~ out** : salir 8 **~ to** REVIVE : volver en sí 9 **~ on!** : ¡ándale! 10 **~ up** OCCUR : surgir 11 **how ~?** : ¿por qué? — **comeback** ['kʌm‚bæk] *n* 1 RETURN : retorno *m* 2 RETORT : réplica *f*

comedy ['kɑmədi] *n, pl* **-dies** : comedia *f* — **comedian** [kə'miːdiən] *n* : cómico *m*, -ca *f*

comet ['kɑmət] *n* : cometa *m*

comfort ['kʌmfərt] *vt* : consolar — **~** *n* 1 : comodidad *f* 2 SOLACE : consuelo *m* — **comfortable** ['kʌmfərt̬əbəl, 'kʌmft̬ə-] *adj* : cómodo

comic ['kɑmɪk] *or* **comical** ['kɑmɪkəl] *adj* : cómico — **~** *n* 1 COMEDIAN : cómico *m*, -ca *f* 2 *or* **~ book** : revista *f* de historietas, cómic *m* — **comic strip** *n* : tira *f* cómica, historieta *f*

coming ['kʌmɪŋ] *adj* : próximo, que viene

comma ['kɑmə] *n* : coma *f*

command [kə'mænd] *vt* 1 ORDER : ordenar, mandar 2 : estar al mando de (un barco, etc.) 3 **~** RESPECT : inspirar (el) respeto — *vi* : dar órdenes — **~** *n* 1 ORDER : orden *f* 2 LEADERSHIP : mando *m* 3 MASTERY : maestría *f*, dominio *m* — **commander** [kə'mændər] *n* : comandante *mf* — **commandment** [kə'mændmənt] *n* : mandamiento *m*

commemorate [kə'memə‚reɪt] *vt* **-rated; -rating** : conmemorar — **commemoration** [kə‚memə'reɪʃən] *n* : conmemoración *f*

commence [kə'ments] *v* **-menced; -mencing** : comenzar, empezar — **commencement** [kə'mentsmənt] *n* 1 BEGINNING : comienzo *m* 2 GRADUATION : ceremonia *f* de graduación

commend [kə'mend] *vt* 1 ENTRUST : encomendar 2 PRAISE : alabar — **commendable** [kə'mendəbəl] *adj* : loable

comment ['kɑ‚ment] *n* : comentario *m*, observación *f* — **~** *vi* : hacer comentarios — **commentary** ['kɑmən‚teri] *n, pl* **-taries** : comentario *m* — **commentator** ['kɑmən‚teɪt̬ər] *n* : comentarista *mf*

commerce ['kɑmərs] *n* : comercio *m* — **commercial** [kə'mərʃəl] *adj* : comercial — **~** *n* : anuncio *m*, aviso *m* *Lat* — **commercialize** [kə'mərʃə‚laɪz] *vt* **-ized; -izing** : comercializar

commiserate [kə'mɪzə‚reɪt] *vi* **-ated; -ating** : compadecerse

commission [kə'mɪʃən] *n* : comisión *f* — **~** *vt* : encargar (una obra de arte) — **commissioner** [kə'mɪʃənər] *n* : comisario *m*, -ria *f*

commit [kə'mɪt] *vt* **-mitted; -mitting** 1 ENTRUST : confiar 2 : cometer (un crimen) 3 : internar (a algn en un hospital) 4 **~ oneself** : comprometerse 5 **~ to memory** : aprender de memoria — **commitment** [kə'mɪtmənt] *n* : compromiso *m*

committee [kə'mɪt̬i] *n* : comité *m*, comisión *f*

commodity [kə'mɑdət̬i] *n, pl* **-ties** : artículo *m* de comercio, producto *m*

common ['kɑmən] *adj* 1 : común 2 ORDINARY : ordinario, común y corriente — **~** *n* : en común — **commonly** ['kɑmənli] *adv* : comúnmente — **commonplace** ['kɑmən‚pleɪs] *adj* : común, banal — **common sense** *n* : sentido *m* común

commotion [kə'moːʃən] *n* : alboroto *m*, jaleo *m*

commune[1] ['kɑ‚mjuːn, kə'mjuːn] *n* : comuna *f* — **communal** [kə'mjuːnəl] *adj* : comunal

commune[2] [kə'mjuːn] *vi* **-muned; -muning ~ with** : comunicarse con

communicate [kə'mjuːnə‚keɪt] *v* **-cated; -cating** *vt* : comunicar — *vi* : comunicarse — **communicable** [kə'mjuːnɪkəbəl] *adj* : transmisible — **communication** [kə‚mjuːnə'keɪʃən] *n* : comunicación *f* — **communicative** [kə'mjuːnɪ‚keɪt̬ɪv, -kət̬ɪv] *adj* : comunicativo

communion [kə'mjuːnjən] *n* : comunión *f*

Communism ['kɑmjə‚nɪzəm] *n* : comunismo *m* — **Communist** ['kɑmjə‚nɪst] *adj* : comunista — **~** *n* : comunista *mf*

community [kə'mjuːnət̬i] *n, pl* **-ties** : comunidad *f*

commute [kə'mjuːt] *v* **-muted; -muting** *vt* : conmutar, reducir (una sentencia) — *vi* : viajar de la residencia al trabajo

compact [kəm'pækt, 'kɑm‚pækt] *adj* : compacto — **~** *n* 1 *or* **~ car** : auto *m* compacto 2 *or* **powder ~** : polvera *f* — **compact disc** ['kɑm‚pækt‚dɪsk] *n* : disco *m* compacto

companion [kəm'pænjən] *n* : compañero *m*, -ra *f* — **companionship** [kəm'pænjən‚ʃɪp] *n* : compañerismo *m*

company ['kʌmpəni] *n, pl* **-nies** 1 : compañía *f* 2 GUESTS : visita *f*

compare [kəm'pær] *v* **-pared; -paring**

vt : comparar — *vi* ~ **with** : poderse comparar con — **comparable** ['kɑmpərəbəl] *adj* : comparable — **comparative** [kəm'pærətɪv] *adj* : comparativo, relativo — **comparison** [kəm'pærəsən] *n* : comparación *f*

compartment [kəm'pɑrtmənt] *n* : compartimento *m*

compass ['kʌmpəs, 'kɑm-] *n* 1 : compás *m* 2 **points of the** ~ : puntos *mpl* cardinales

compassion [kəm'pæʃən] *n* : compasión *f* — **compassionate** [kəm'pæʃənət] *adj* : compasivo

compatible [kəm'pæt̬əbəl] *adj* : compatible, afín — **compatibility** [kəm,pæt̬ə'bɪlət̬i] *n* : compatibilidad *f*

compel [kəm'pɛl] *vt* **-pelled; -pelling** : obligar — **compelling** [kəm'pɛlɪŋ] *adj* : convincente

compensate ['kɑmpən,seɪt] *v* **-sated; -sating** *vi* ~ **for** : compensar — *vt* : indemnizar, compensar — **compensation** [kɑmpən'seɪʃən] *n* : compensación *f*, indemnización *f*

compete [kəm'piːt] *vi* **-peted; -peting** : competir — **competent** ['kɑmpət̬ənt] *adj* : competente — **competition** [kɑmpə'tɪʃən] *n* 1 : competencia *f* 2 CONTEST : concurso *m* — **competitor** [kəm'pɛt̬ət̬ər] *n* : competidor *m*, -dora *f*

compile [kəm'paɪl] *vt* **-piled; -piling** : compilar, recopilar

complacency [kəm'pleɪsəntsi] *n* : satisfacción *f* consigo mismo — **complacent** [kəm'pleɪsənt] *adj* : satisfecho de sí mismo

complain [kəm'pleɪn] *vi* : quejarse — **complaint** [kəm'pleɪnt] *n* 1 : queja *f* 2 AILMENT : enfermedad *f*

complement ['kɑmpləmənt] *n* : complemento *m* — ['kɑmplə,mɛnt] *vt* : complementar — **complementary** [kɑmplə'mɛntəri] *adj* : complementario

complete [kəm'pliːt] *adj* **-pleter; -est** 1 WHOLE : completo, entero 2 FINISHED : terminado 3 TOTAL : total — ~ *vt* **-pleted; -pleting** : completar — **completion** [kəm'pliːʃən] *n* : conclusión *f*

complex [kɑm'plɛks, kəm-; 'kɑm,plɛks] *adj* : complejo — ~ ['kɑm,plɛks] *n* : complejo *m*

complexion [kəm'plɛkʃən] *n* : cutis *m*, tez *f*

complexity [kəm'plɛksət̬i, kɑm-] *n*, *pl* **-ties** : complejidad *f*

compliance [kəm'plaɪənts] *n* 1 : acatamiento *m* 2 **in** ~ **with** : conforme a — **compliant** [kəm'plaɪənt] *adj* : sumiso

complicate ['kɑmplə,keɪt] *vt* **-cated; -cating** : complicar — **complicated** ['kɑmplə,keɪt̬əd] *adj* : complicado — **complication** [kɑmplə'keɪʃən] *n* : complicación *f*

compliment ['kɑmpləmənt] *n* 1 : cumplido *m* 2 ~**s** *npl* : saludos *mpl* — ['kɑmplə,mɛnt] *vt* : felicitar — **complimentary** [kɑmplə'mɛntəri] *adj* 1 FLATTERING : halagador, halagueño 2 FREE : de cortesía, gratis

comply [kəm'plaɪ] *vi* **-plied; -plying** ~ **with** : cumplir, obedecer

component [kəm'poːnənt, 'kɑm,poː-] *n* : componente *m*

compose [kəm'poːz] *vt* **-posed; -posing** 1 : componer 2 ~ **oneself** : serenarse — **composer** [kəm'poːzər] *n* : compositor *m*, -tora *f* — **composition** [kɑmpə'zɪʃən] *n* 1 : composición *f* 2 ESSAY : ensayo *m* — **composure** [kəm'poːʒər] *n* : calma *f*

compound[1] [kɑm'paʊnd, kəm-; 'kɑm,paʊnd] *vt* 1 COMPOSE : componer 2 : agravar (un problema, etc.) — ~ ['kɑm,paʊnd; kɑm'paʊnd, kəm-] *adj* : compuesto — ~ ['kɑm,paʊnd] *n* : compuesto *m*

compound[2] ['kɑm,paʊnd] *n* ENCLOSURE : recinto *m*

comprehend [kɑmprɪ'hɛnd] *vt* : comprender — **comprehension** [kɑmprɪ'hɛntʃən] *n* : comprensión *f* — **comprehensive** [kɑmprɪ'hɛntsɪv] *adj* 1 INCLUSIVE : inclusivo 2 BROAD : amplio

compress [kəm'prɛs] *vt* : comprimir — **compression** [kəm'prɛʃən] *n* : compresión *f*

comprise [kəm'praɪz] *vt* **-prised; -prising** : comprender

compromise ['kɑmprə,maɪz] *n* : acuerdo *m*, arreglo *m* — ~ *v* **-mised; -mising** *vi* : llegar a un acuerdo — *vt* : comprometer

compulsion [kəm'pʌlʃən] *n* 1 COERCION : coacción *f* 2 URGE : impulso *m* — **compulsive** [kəm'pʌlsɪv] *adj* : compulsivo — **compulsory** [kəm'pʌlsəri] *adj* : obligatorio

compute [kəm'pjuːt] *vt* **-puted; -puting** : computar — **computer** [kəm'pjuːt̬ər] *n* : computadora *f*, computador *m*, ordenador *m* Spain — **computerize** [kəm'pjuːt̬ə,raɪz] *vt* **-ized; -izing** : informatizar

comrade ['kɑm,ræd] *n* : camarada *mf*

con ['kɑn] *vt* **conned; conning** : estafar — ~ *n* 1 SWINDLE : estafa *f* 2 **the pros and** ~**s** : los pros y los contras

concave [kɑn'keɪv, 'kɑn,keɪv] *adj* : cóncavo

conceal [kən'si:l] vt : ocultar

concede [kən'si:d] vt -ceded; -ceding : conceder, admitir

conceit [kən'si:t] n : vanidad f — conceited [kən'si:t̬əd] adj : engreído

conceive [kən'si:v] v -ceived; -ceiving vt : concebir — vi ~ of : concebir — conceivable [kən'si:vəbəl] adj : concebible

concentrate ['kɑntsən,treɪt] v -trated; -trating vt : concentrar — vi : concentrarse — concentration [,kɑntsən'treɪʃən] n : concentración f

concept ['kɑn,sɛpt] n : concepto m — conception [kən'sɛpʃən] n : concepción f

concern [kən'sərn] vt 1 : concernir 2 ~ oneself about : preocuparse por — ~ n 1 AFFAIR : asunto m 2 WORRY : preocupación f 3 BUSINESS : negocio m — concerned [kən'sərnd] adj 1 ANXIOUS : ansioso 2 as far as I'm ~ : en cuanto a mí — concerning [kən'sərnɪŋ] prep : con respecto a

concert ['kɑn,sərt] n : concierto m — concerted [kən'sərt̬əd] adj : concertado

concession [kən'sɛʃən] n : concesión f

concise [kən'saɪs] adj : conciso

conclude [kən'klu:d] v -cluded; -cluding : concluir — conclusion [kən'klu:ʒən] n : conclusión f — conclusive [kən'klu:sɪv] adj : concluyente

concoct [kən'kɑkt, kɑn-] vt 1 PREPARE : confeccionar 2 DEVISE : inventarse, tramar — concoction [kən'kɑkʃən] n : mezcla f, brebaje m

concourse ['kɑn,kors] n : vestíbulo m, salón m

concrete [kɑn'kri:t, 'kɑn,kri:t] adj : concreto — ~ ['kɑn,kri:t, kɑn'kri:t] n : hormigón m, concreto m Lat

concur [kən'kər] vi concurred; concurring AGREE : estar de acuerdo

concussion [kən'kʌʃən] n : conmoción f cerebral

condemn [kən'dɛm] vt : condenar — condemnation [,kɑndɛm'neɪʃən] n : condenación f

condense [kən'dɛnts] v -densed; -densing vt : condensar — vi : condensarse — condensation [,kɑndɛn'seɪʃən, -dən-] n : condensación f

condescending [,kɑndɪ'sɛndɪŋ] adj : condescendiente

condiment ['kɑndəmənt] n : condimento m

condition [kən'dɪʃən] n 1 : condición f 2 in good ~ : en buen estado — conditional [kən'dɪʃənəl] adj : condicional

condolences [kən'do:ləntsəz] npl : pésame m

condom ['kɑndəm] n : condón m

condominium [,kɑndə'mɪniəm] n, pl -ums : condominio m Lat

condone [kən'do:n] vt -doned; -doning : aprobar

conducive [kən'du:sɪv, -'dju:-] adj : propicio, favorable

conduct ['kɑn,dʌkt] n : conducta f — ~ [kən'dʌkt] vt 1 DIRECT, GUIDE : conducir, dirigir 2 CARRY OUT : llevar a cabo 3 ~ oneself : conducirse, comportarse — conductor [kən'dʌktər] n : revisor m, -sora f (en un tren); cobrador m, -dora f (en un autobús); director m, -tora f (de una orquesta)

cone ['ko:n] n 1 : cono m 2 or icecream ~ : cucurucho m, barquillo m Lat

confection [kən'fɛkʃən] n : dulce m

confederation [kən,fɛdə'reɪʃən] n : confederación f

confer [kən'fər] v -ferred; -ferring vt : conferir, otorgar — vi ~ with : consultar — conference ['kɑnfərəns, -fərənts] n : conferencia f

confess [kən'fɛs] vt : confesar — vi 1 : confesarse 2 ~ to : confesar, admitir — confession [kən'fɛʃən] n : confesión f

confetti [kən'fɛt̬i] n : confeti m

confide [kən'faɪd] v -fided; -fiding : confiar — confidence ['kɑnfədənts] n 1 TRUST : confianza f 2 SELF-ASSURANCE : confianza f en sí mismo 3 SECRET : confidencia f — confident ['kɑnfədənt] adj 1 SURE : seguro 2 SELF-ASSURED : confiado, seguro de sí mismo — confidential [,kɑnfə'dɛntʃəl] adj : confidencial

confine [kən'faɪn] vt -fined; -fining 1 LIMIT : confinar, limitar 2 IMPRISON : encerrar — confines ['kɑn,faɪnz] npl : confines mpl

confirm [kən'fərm] vt : confirmar — confirmation [,kɑnfər'meɪʃən] n : confirmación f — confirmed [kən'fərmd] adj : inveterado

confiscate ['kɑnfə,skeɪt] vt -cated; -cating : confiscar

conflict ['kɑn,flɪkt] n : conflicto m — ~ [kən'flɪkt] vi : estar en conflicto, oponerse

conform [kən'fɔrm] vi 1 COMPLY : ajustarse 2 ~ with : corresponder a — conformity [kən'fɔrmət̬i] n, pl -ties : conformidad f

confound [kən'faʊnd, kɑn-] vt : confundir, desconcertar

confront [kən'frʌnt] *vt* : afrontar, encarar — **confrontation** [ˌkɑnfrən'teɪʃən] *n* : confrontación *f*

confuse [kən'fjuːz] *vt* **-fused; -fusing** : confundir — **confusing** [kən'fjuːzɪŋ] *adj* : confuso, desconcertante — **confusion** [kən'fjuːʒən] *n* : confusión *f*, desconcierto *m*

congeal [kən'dʒiːl] *vi* : coagularse

congenial [kən'dʒiːniəl] *adj* : agradable

congested [kən'dʒɛstəd] *adj* : congestionado — **congestion** [kən'dʒɛstʃən] *n* : congestión *f*

congratulate [kən'grædʒəˌleɪt, -'grætʃə-] *vt* **-lated; -lating** : felicitar — **congratulations** [kənˌgrædʒə'leɪʃən, -ˌgrætʃə-] *npl* : felicitaciones *fpl*

congregate ['kɑŋgrɪˌgeɪt] *vi* **-gated; -gating** : congregarse — **congregation** [ˌkɑŋgrɪ'geɪʃən] *n* : feligreses *mpl* (en religión)

congress ['kɑŋgrəs] *n* : congreso *m* — **congressional** [kən'grɛʃənəl, kɑn-] *adj* : del congreso — **congressman** ['kɑŋgrəsmən] *n*, *pl* **-men** [-mən, -ˌmɛn] : congresista *mf*

conjecture [kən'dʒɛktʃər] *n* : conjetura *f*, presunción *f* — ~ *vt* **-tured; -turing** *vt* : conjeturar — *vi* : hacer conjeturas

conjugal ['kɑndʒɪgəl, kən'dʒuː-] *adj* : conyugal

conjugate ['kɑndʒəˌgeɪt] *vt* **-gated; -gating** : conjugar — **conjugation** [ˌkɑndʒə'geɪʃən] *n* : conjugación *f*

conjunction [kən'dʒʌŋkʃən] *n* **1** : conjunción *f* **2 in ~ with** : en combinación con

conjure ['kɑndʒər, 'kʌn-] *v* **-jured; -juring** *vi* : hacer juegos de manos — ~ *vt or* ~ **up** : evocar

connect [kə'nɛkt] *vi* : conectarse — *vt* **1** JOIN : conectar, juntar **2** ASSOCIATE : asociar — **connection** [kə'nɛkʃən] *n* **1** : conexión *f* **2** : enlace *m* (con un tren, etc.) **3 ~s** *npl* : relaciones *fpl* (personas)

connoisseur [ˌkɑnə'sər, -'sʊr] *n* : conocedor *m*, -dora *f*

connote [kə'noːt] *vt* **-noted; -noting** : connotar, implicar

conquer ['kɑŋkər] *vt* : conquistar — **conqueror** ['kɑŋkərər] *n* : conquistador *m*, -dora *f* — **conquest** ['kɑnˌkwɛst, 'kɑŋ-] *n* : conquista *f*

conscience ['kɑntʃənts] *n* : conciencia *f* — **conscientious** [ˌkɑntʃi'ɛntʃəs] *adj* : concienzudo

conscious ['kɑntʃəs] *adj* **1** AWARE : consciente **2** INTENTIONAL : intencional — **consciously** *adv* : deliberadamente

— consciousness ['kɑntʃəsnəs] *n* **1** AWARENESS : conciencia *f* **2 lose ~** : perder el conocimiento

consecrate ['kɑntsəˌkreɪt] *vt* **-crated; -crating** : consagrar — **consecration** [ˌkɑntsər'kreɪʃən] *n* : consagración *f*

consecutive [kən'sɛkjətɪv] *adj* : consecutivo, sucesivo

consensus [kən'sɛntsəs] *n* : consenso *m*

consent [kən'sɛnt] *vi* : consentir — ~ *n* : consentimiento *m*

consequence ['kɑntsəˌkwɛnts, -kwənts] *n* **1** : consecuencia *f* **2 of no ~** : sin importancia — **consequent** ['kɑntsəkwənt, -ˌkwɛnt] *adj* : consiguiente — **consequently** ['kɑntsəkwəntli, -ˌkwɛnt-] *adv* : por consiguiente

conserve [kən'sərv] *vt* **-served; -serving** : conservar, preservar — **conservation** [ˌkɑntsər'veɪʃən] *n* : conservación *f* — **conservative** [kən'sərvətɪv] *adj* **1** : conservador **2** CAUTIOUS : moderado, prudente — ~ *n* : conservador *m*, -dora *f* — **conservatory** [kən'sərvəˌtori] *n*, *pl* **-ries** : conservatorio *m*

consider [kən'sɪdər] *vt* **1** : considerar **2 all things considered** : teniéndolo todo en cuenta — **considerable** [kən'sɪdərəbəl] *adj* : considerable — **considerate** [kən'sɪdərət] *adj* : considerado — **consideration** [kənˌsɪdə'reɪʃən] *n* **1** : consideración *f* **2 take into ~** : tener en cuenta — **considering** [kən'sɪdərɪŋ] *prep* : teniendo en cuenta

consign [kən'saɪn] *vt* **1** : relegar **2** SEND : enviar — **consignment** [kən'saɪnmənt] *n* : envío *m*

consist [kən'sɪst] *vi* **1 ~ in** : consistir en **2 ~ of** : constar de, componerse de — **consistency** [kən'sɪstəntsi] *n*, *pl* **-cies 1** TEXTURE : consistencia *f* **2** COHERENCE : coherencia *f* **3** UNIFORMITY : regularidad *f* — **consistent** [kən'sɪstənt] *adj* **1** UNCHANGING : constante, regular **2 ~ with** : consecuente con

console [kən'soːl] *vt* **-soled; -soling** : consolar — **consolation** [ˌkɑntsə'leɪʃən] *n* **1** : consuelo *m* **2 ~ prize** : premio *m* de consolación

consolidate [kən'sɑləˌdeɪt] *vt* **-dated; -dating** : consolidar — **consolidation** [kənˌsɑlə'deɪʃən] *n* : consolidación *f*

consonant ['kɑntsənənt] *n* : consonante *f*

conspicuous [kən'spɪkjuəs] *adj* **1** OBVIOUS : visible, evidente **2** STRIKING : llamativo — **conspicuously** [kən'spɪkjuəsli] *adv* : de manera llamativa

conspire [kən'spaɪr] *vi* **-spired; -spiring** : conspirar — **conspiracy** [kən'spɪrəsi] *n, pl* **-cies** : conspiración *f*

constant ['kɑntstənt] *adj* : constante — **constantly** ['kɑntstəntli] *adv* : constantemente

constellation [ˌkɑntstə'leɪʃən] *n* : constelación *f*

constipated ['kɑntstəˌpeɪtəd] *adj* : estreñido — **constipation** [ˌkɑntstə'peɪʃən] *n* : estreñimiento *m*

constituent [kən'stɪtʃuənt] *n* **1** COMPONENT : componente *m* **2** VOTER : elector *m*, -tora *f*; votante *mf*

constitute ['kɑntstəˌtuːt, -ˌtjuːt] *vt* **-tuted; -tuting** : constituir — **constitution** [ˌkɑntstə'tuːʃən, -'tjuː-] *n* : constitución *f* — **constitutional** [ˌkɑntstə'tuːʃənəl, -'tjuː-] *adj* : constitucional

constraint [kən'streɪnt] *n* : restricción *f*, limitación *f*

construct [kən'strʌkt] *vt* : construir — **construction** [kən'strʌkʃən] *n* : construcción *f* — **constructive** [kən'strʌktɪv] *adj* : constructivo

construe [kən'struː] *vt* **-strued; -struing** : interpretar

consul ['kɑntsəl] *n* : cónsul *mf* — **consulate** ['kɑntsələt] *n* : consulado *m*

consult [kən'sʌlt] *v* : consultar — **consultant** [kən'sʌltənt] *n* : asesor *m*, -sora *f*; consultor *m*, -tora *f* — **consultation** [ˌkɑntsəl'teɪʃən] *n* : consulta *f*

consume [kən'suːm] *vt* **-sumed; -suming** : consumir — **consumer** [kən'suːmər] *n* : consumidor *m*, -dora *f* — **consumption** [kən'sʌmpʃən] *n* : consumo *m*

contact ['kɑnˌtækt] *n* : contacto *m* — ['kɑnˌtækt, kən'-] *vt* : ponerse en contacto con — **contact lens** ['kɑnˌtæktˈlenz] *n* : lente *mf* (de contacto)

contagious [kən'teɪdʒəs] *adj* : contagioso

contain [kən'teɪn] *vt* **1** : contener **2** ~ **oneself** : contenerse — **container** [kən'teɪnər] *n* : recipiente *m*, envase *m*

contaminate [kən'tæməˌneɪt] *vt* **-nated; -nating** : contaminar — **contamination** [kənˌtæmə'neɪʃən] *n* : contaminación *f*

contemplate ['kɑntəmˌpleɪt] *v* **-plated; -plating** *vt* **1** : contemplar **2** CONSIDER : considerar, pensar en — *vi* : reflexionar — **contemplation** [ˌkɑntəm'pleɪʃən] *n* : contemplación *f*

contemporary [kən'tempəˌreri] *adj* : contemporáneo — ~ *n, pl* **-raries** : contemporáneo *m*, -nea *f*

contempt [kən'tempt] *n* : desprecio *m* —

contemptible [kən'temptəbəl] *adj* : despreciable — **contemptuous** [kən'temptʃuəs] *adj* : desdeñoso

contend [kən'tend] *vi* **1** COMPETE : contender, competir **2** ~ **with** : enfrentarse a — *vt* : sostener, afirmar — **contender** [kən'tendər] *n* : contendiente *mf*

content¹ ['kɑnˌtent] *n* **1** : contenido *m* **2 table of** ~ **s** : índice *m* de materias

content² [kən'tent] *adj* : contento — ~ *vt* ~ **oneself with** : contentarse con — **contented** [kən'tentəd] *adj* : satisfecho, contento

contention [kən'tentʃən] *n* **1** DISPUTE : disputa *f* **2** OPINION : argumento *m*, opinión *f*

contentment [kən'tentmənt] *n* : satisfacción *f*

contest [kən'test] *vt* : disputar — ~ ['kɑnˌtest] *n* **1** STRUGGLE : contienda *f* **2** COMPETITION : concurso *m*, competencia *f* — **contestant** [kən'testənt] *n* : concursante *mf*, contendiente *mf*

context ['kɑnˌtekst] *n* : contexto *m*

continent ['kɑntənənt] *n* : continente *m* — **continental** [ˌkɑntən'entəl] *adj* : continental

contingency [kən'tɪndʒəntsi] *n, pl* **-cies** : contingencia *f*

continue [kən'tɪnjuː] *v* **-tinued; -tinuing** : continuar — **continual** [kən'tɪnjuəl] *adj* : continuo, constante — **continuation** [kənˌtɪnju'eɪʃən] *n* : continuación *f* — **continuity** [ˌkɑntən'uːəti, -'juː-] *n, pl* **-ties** : continuidad *f* — **continuous** [kən'tɪnjuəs] *adj* : continuo

contort [kən'tort] *vt* : retorcer — **contortion** [kən'torʃən] *n* : contorsión *f*

contour ['kɑnˌtur] *n* **1** : contorno *m* **2 or** ~ **line** : curva *f* de nivel

contraband ['kɑntrəˌbænd] *n* : contrabando *m*

contraception [ˌkɑntrə'sepʃən] *n* : anticoncepción *f* — **contraceptive** [ˌkɑntrə'septɪv] *adj* : anticonceptivo — ~ *n* : anticonceptivo *m*

contract ['kɑnˌtrækt] *n* : contrato *m* — ~ [kən'trækt] *vt* : contraer — *vi* : contraerse — **contraction** [kən'trækʃən] *n* : contracción *f* — **contractor** ['kɑnˌtræktər, kən'træk-] *n* : contratista *mf*

contradiction [ˌkɑntrə'dɪkʃən] *n* : contradicción *f* — **contradict** [ˌkɑntrə'dɪkt] *vt* : contradecir — **contradictory** [ˌkɑntrə'dɪktəri] *adj* : contradictorio

contraption [kən'træpʃən] *n* : artilugio *m*, artefacto *m*

contrary ['kɑnˌtreri] *n, pl* **-traries 1** : contrario **2 on the** ~ : al contrario

— ~ ['kɑn,treri] *adj* 1 : contrario, opuesto 2 ~ **to** : en contra de
contrast [kən'træst] *v* : contrastar — ~ ['kɑn,træst] *n* : contraste *m*
contribute [kən'trɪbjət] *v* **-uted; -uting** : contribuir — **contribution** [ˌkɑntrə'bjuːʃən] *n* : contribución *f* — **contributor** [kən'trɪbjətər] *n* 1 : contribuyente *mf* 2 : colaborador *m*, -dora *f* (en periodismo)
contrite ['kɑn,traɪt, kən'traɪt] *adj* : arrepentido
contrive [kən'traɪv] *vt* **-trived; -triving** 1 DEVISE : idear 2 ~ **to do sth** : lograr hacer algo
control [kən'troːl] *vt* **-trolled; -trolling** : controlar — ~ *n* 1 : control *m* 2 ~**s** *npl* : mandos *mpl*
controversy ['kɑntrə,vərsi] *n, pl* **-sies** : controversia — **controversial** [ˌkɑntrə'vərʃəl, -siəl] *adj* : polémico
convalescence [ˌkɑnvə'lesənts] *n* : convalecencia *f* — **convalescent** [ˌkɑnvə'lesənt] *adj* : convaleciente — ~ *n* : convaleciente *mf*
convene [kən'viːn] *v* **-vened; -vening** *vt* : convocar — *vi* : reunirse
convenience [kən'viːnjənts] *n* : conveniencia *f*, comodidad *f* — **convenient** [kən'viːnjənt] *adj* : conveniente
convent ['kɑnvənt, -,vent] *n* : convento *m*
convention [kən'vɛntʃən] *n* : convención *f* — **conventional** [kən'vɛntʃənəl] *adj* : convencional
converge [kən'vərdʒ] *vi* **-verged; -verging** : converger, convergir
converse[1] [kən'vərs] *vi* **-versed; -versing** : conversar — **conversation** [ˌkɑnvər'seɪʃən] *n* : conversación *f* — **conversational** [ˌkɑnvər'seɪʃənəl] *adj* : familiar
converse[2] [kən'vərs, 'kɑn,vərs] *adj* : contrario, opuesto — **conversely** [kən'vərsli, 'kɑn,vərs-] *adv* : a la inversa
conversion [kən'vərʒən] *n* : conversión *f* — **convert** [kən'vərt] *vt* : convertir — *vi* : convertirse — **convertible** [kən'vərtəbəl] *adj* : convertible — ~ *n* : descapotable *m*, convertible *m Lat*
convex [kɑn'veks, 'kɑn-, kən'-] *adj* : convexo
convey [kən'veɪ] *vt* 1 TRANSPORT : llevar, transportar 2 TRANSMIT : comunicar
convict [kən'vɪkt] *vt* : declarar culpable a — ~ ['kɑn,vɪkt] *n* : presidiario *m*, -ria *f* — **conviction** [kən'vɪkʃən] *n* 1 : condena *f* (de un acusado) 2 BELIEF : convicción *f*

convince [kən'vɪnts] *vt* **-vinced; -vincing** : convencer — **convincing** [kən'vɪntsɪŋ] *adj* : convincente
convoke [kən'voːk] *vt* **-voked; -voking** : convocar
convoluted ['kɑnvə,luːtəd] *adj* : complicado
convulsion [kən'vʌlʃən] *n* : convulsión *f* — **convulsive** [kən'vʌlsɪv] *adj* : convulsivo
cook ['kʊk] *n* : cocinero *m*, -ra *f* — ~ *vi* : cocinar, guisar — *vt* : preparar (comida) — **cookbook** ['kʊk,bʊk] *n* : libro *m* de cocina
cookie *or* **cooky** ['kʊki] *n, pl* **-ies** : galleta *f* (dulce)
cooking *n* : cocina *f*
cool ['kuːl] *adj* 1 : fresco 2 CALM : tranquilo 3 UNFRIENDLY : frío — ~ *vt* : enfriar — *vi* : enfriarse — ~ *n* 1 : fresco *m* 2 COMPOSURE : calma *f* — **cooler** ['kuːlər] *n* : nevera *f* portátil — **coolness** ['kuːlnəs] *n* : frescura *f*
coop ['kuːp, 'kʊp] *n* : gallinero *m* — ~ *vt or* ~ **up** : encerrar
cooperate [koʊ'ɑpə,reɪt] *vi* **-ated; -ating** : cooperar — **cooperation** [koˌɑpə'reɪʃən] *n* : cooperación *f* — **cooperative** [koʊ'ɑpərəˌtɪv, -'ɑpərə,reɪtɪv] *adj* : cooperativo
coordinate [koʊ'ordən,eɪt] *v* **-nated; -nating** *vt* : coordinar — **coordination** [koˌordən'eɪʃən] *n* : coordinación *f*
cop ['kɑp] *n* 1 : poli *mf fam* 2 **the** ~**s** : la poli *fam*
cope ['koːp] *vi* **coped; coping** 1 : arreglárselas 2 ~ **with** : hacer frente a, poder con
copier ['kɑpiər] *n* : fotocopiadora *f*
copious ['koːpiəs] *adj* : copioso
copper ['kɑpər] *n* : cobre *m*
copy ['kɑpi] *n, pl* **copies** 1 : copia *f* 2 : ejemplar *m* (de un libro), número *m* (de una revista) — ~ *vt* **copied; copying** 1 DUPLICATE : hacer una copia de 2 IMITATE : copiar — **copyright** ['kɑpi,raɪt] *n* : derechos *mpl* de autor
coral ['korəl] *n* : coral *m*
cord ['kord] *n* 1 : cuerda *f* 2 *or* **electric** ~ : cable *m* (eléctrico)
cordial ['kordʒəl] *adj* : cordial
corduroy ['kordə,rɔɪ] *n* : pana *f*
core ['kor] *n* 1 : corazón *m* (de una fruta) 2 CENTER : núcleo *m*, centro *m*
cork ['kork] *n* : corcho *m* — **corkscrew** ['kork,skruː] *n* : sacacorchos *m*
corn ['korn] *n* 1 : grano *m* 2 *or* **indian** ~ : maíz *m* 3 : callo *m* (del pie) — **corncob** ['korn,kɑb] *n* : mazorca *f*

corner ['kɔrnər] *n* : ángulo *m*, rincón *m* (en una habitación), esquina *f* (de una intersección) — ~ *vt* **1** TRAP : acorralar **2** MONOPOLIZE : acaparar (un mercado) — **cornerstone** ['kɔrnər,stoːn] *n* : piedra *f* angular

cornmeal ['kɔrn,miːl] *n* : harina *f* de maíz — **cornstarch** ['kɔrn,stɑrtʃ] *n* : maicena *f*

corny ['kɔrni] *adj* : cursi, sentimental

coronary ['kɔrə,neri] *n*, *pl* **-naries** : trombosis *f* coronaria

coronation [,kɔrə'neɪʃən] *n* : coronación *f*

corporal ['kɔrpərəl] *n* : cabo *m*

corporation [,kɔrpə'reɪʃən] *n* : sociedad *f* anónima, compañía *f* — **corporate** ['kɔrpərət] *adj* : corporativo

corps ['kor] *n*, *pl* **corps** ['korz] : cuerpo *m*

corpse ['korps] *n* : cadáver *m*

corpulent ['kɔrpjələnt] *adj* : obeso, gordo

corpuscle ['kɔr,pʌsəl] *n* : glóbulo *m*

corral [kə'ræl] *n* : corral *m* — ~ *vt* **-ralled; -ralling** : acorralar

correct [kə'rɛkt] *vt* : corregir — ~ *adj* : correcto — **correction** [kə'rɛkʃən] *n* : corrección *f*

correlation [,kɔrə'leɪʃən] *n* : correlación *f*

correspond [,kɔrə'spɑnd] *vi* **1** WRITE : corresponderse **2** ~ **to** : corresponder a — **correspondence** [,kɔrə'spɑndənts] *n* : correspondencia *f*

corridor ['kɔrədər, -,dɔr] *n* : pasillo *m*

corroborate [kə'rɑbə,reɪt] *vt* **-rated; -rating** : corroborar

corrode [kə'roːd] *v* **-roded; -roding** *vt* : corroer — *vi* : corroerse — **corrosion** [kə'roʒən] *n* : corrosión *f* — **corrosive** [kə'roːsɪv] *adj* : corrosivo

corrugated ['kɔrə,geɪtəd] *adj* : ondulado

corrupt [kə'rʌpt] *vt* : corromper — ~ *adj* : corrupto, corrompido — **corruption** [kə'rʌpʃən] *n* : corrupción *f*

corset ['kɔrsət] *n* : corsé *m*

cosmetic [kɑz'mɛtɪk] *n* : cosmético *m* — ~ *adj* : cosmético

cosmic ['kɑzmɪk] *adj* : cósmico

cosmopolitan [,kɑzmə'pɑlətən] *adj* : cosmopolita

cosmos ['kɑzməs, -,moːs, -,mɑs] *n* : cosmos *m*

cost ['kɔst] *n* : costo *m*, coste *m* — ~ *vi* **cost; costing 1** : costar **2 how much does it** ~? : ¿cuánto cuesta?, ¿cuánto vale?

Costa Rican [,kɔstə'riːkən] *adj* : costarricense

costly ['kɔstli] *adj* : costoso

costume ['kɑs,tuːm, -,tjuːm] *n* **1** OUTFIT : traje *m* **2** DISGUISE : disfraz *m*

cot ['kɑt] *n* : catre *m*

cottage ['kɑtɪdʒ] *n* : casita *f* (de campo) — **cottage cheese** *n* : requesón *m*

cotton ['kɑtən] *n* : algodón *m*

couch ['kautʃ] *n* : sofá *m*

cough ['kɔf] *vi* : toser — ~ *n* : tos *f*

could ['kud] → **can¹**

council ['kauntsəl] *n* **1** : concejo *m* **2** *or* **city** ~ : ayuntamiento *m* — **councilor** *or* **councilor** ['kauntsələr] *n* : concejal *m*, -jala *f*

counsel *n* **1** ADVICE : consejo *m* **2** LAWYER : abogado *m*, -da *f* — ~ ['kauntsəl] *vt* **-seled** *or* **-selled; -seling** *or* **-selling** : aconsejar — **counselor** *or* **counsellor** ['kauntsələr] *n* : consejero *m*, -ra *f*

count¹ ['kaunt] *vt* : contar — *vi* **1** : contar **2** ~ **on** : contar con **3 that doesn't** ~ : eso no vale — ~ *n* **1** : recuento *m* **2 keep** ~ **of** : llevar la cuenta de

count² *n* : conde *m* (noble)

counter¹ ['kauntər] *n* **1** : mostrador *m* (de un negocio) **2** TOKEN : ficha *f* (de un juego)

counter² *vt* : oponerse a — *vi* : contraatacar — ~ *adv* ~ **to** : contrario a — **counteract** [,kauntər'ækt] *vt* : contrarrestar — **counterattack** ['kauntər,tæk] *n* : contraataque *m* — **counterbalance** [,kauntər'bælənts] *n* : contrapeso *m* — **counterclockwise** [,kauntər'klɑk,waɪz] *adv & adj* : en sentido opuesto a las agujas del reloj — **counterfeit** ['kauntər,fɪt] *vt* : falsificar — ~ *adj* : falsificado — ~ *n* : falsificación *f* — **counterpart** ['kauntər,part] *n* : homólogo *m* (de una persona), equivalente *m* (de una cosa) — **counterproductive** [,kauntərprə'dʌktɪv] *adj* : contraproducente

countess ['kauntɪs] *n* : condesa *f*

countless ['kauntləs] *adj* : incontable, innumerable

country ['kʌntri] *n*, *pl* **-tries 1** NATION : país *m* **2** COUNTRYSIDE : campo *m* — ~ *adj* : campestre, rural — **countryman** ['kʌntrimən] *n*, *pl* **-men** [-mən, -,men] *or* **fellow** ~ : compatriota *mf* — **countryside** ['kʌntri,saɪd] *n* : campo *m*, campiña *f*

county ['kaunti] *n*, *pl* **-ties** : condado *m*

coup ['kuː] *n*, *pl* **coups** ['kuːz] *or* ~ **d'etat** : golpe *m* (de estado)

couple ['kʌpəl] *n* **1** : pareja *f* (de per-

sonas) **2 a ~ of** : un par de — **~** vt
-pled; -pling : acoplar, unir
coupon ['ku:ˌpɑn, 'kju:-] n : cupón m
courage ['kərɪdʒ] n : valor m — **courageous** [kə'reɪdʒəs] adj : valiente
courier ['kuriər, 'kəriər] n : mensajero m,
-ra f
course ['kors] n 1 : curso m 2 : plato m
(de una cena) 3 : campo m
de golf 4 **in the ~ of** : en el transcurso de 5 **of ~** : desde luego, por
supuesto
court ['kort] n 1 : corte f (de un rey, etc.)
2 : cancha f, pista f (en deportes) 3 TRI-
BUNAL : corte f, tribunal m — **~** vt
: cortejar
courteous ['kərtiəs] adj : cortés —
courtesy ['kərtəsi] n, pl **-sies** : cortesía f
courthouse ['korthaus] n : palacio m de
justicia, juzgado m — **courtroom**
['kortˌru:m] n : sala f (de un tribunal)
courtship ['kortˌʃɪp] n : cortejo m, noviazgo m
courtyard ['kortjɑrd] n : patio m
cousin ['kʌzən] n : primo m, -ma f
cove ['ko:v] n : ensenada f, cala f
covenant ['kʌvənənt] n : pacto m, convenio m
cover ['kʌvər] vt 1 : cubrir 2 or **~ up**
: encubrir, ocultar 3 TREAT : tratar —
~ n 1 : cubierta f 2 SHELTER : abrigo
m, refugio m 3 LID : tapa f 4 : cubierta
f (de un libro), portada f (de una revista) 5 **~s** npl BEDCLOTHES : mantas
fpl, cobijas fpl Lat 6 **take ~** : ponerse
a cubierto 7 **under ~ of** : al amparo
de — **coverage** ['kʌvərɪdʒ] n : cobertura f — **covert** ['ko:ˌvərt, 'kʌvər] adj
: encubierto — **cover-up** ['kʌvərˌʌp] n
: encubrimiento m
covet ['kʌvət] vt : codiciar — **covetous**
['kʌvətəs] adj : codicioso
cow ['kau] n : vaca f — **~** vt : intimidar,
acobardar
coward ['kauərd] n : cobarde mf —
cowardice ['kauərdɪs] n : cobardía f —
cowardly ['kauərdli] adj : cobarde
cowboy ['kauˌbɔɪ] n : vaquero m
cower ['kauər] vi : encogerse (de miedo)
coy ['kɔɪ] adj : tímido y coqueto
coyote [ˌkaɪˈoːṭi, ˈkaɪˌoːt] n, pl **coyotes**
or **coyote** : coyote m
cozy ['ko:zi] adj **-zier; -est** : acogedor
crab ['kræb] n : cangrejo m, jaiba f Lat
crack ['kræk] vi 1 SPLIT : rajar, partir
2 : cascar (nueces, huevos) 3 : chasquear (un látigo, etc.) 4 **~ down on**
: tomar medidas enérgicas contra —
vi 1 SPLIT : rajarse, agrietarse 2

: chasquear (dícese de un látigo) 3 **~
up** : sufrir una crisis nerviosa — **~** n
1 CRACKING : chasquido m, crujido m 2
CREVICE : raja f, grieta f 3 **have a ~ at**
: intentar
cracker ['krækər] n : galleta f (de soda,
etc.)
crackle ['krækəl] vi **-led; -ling** : crepitar,
chisporrotear — **~** n : crujido m,
chisporroteo m
cradle ['kreɪdəl] n : cuna f — **~** vt
-dled; -dling : acunar
craft ['kræft] n 1 TRADE : oficio m 2 CUN-
NING : astucia f 3 → **craftsmanship** 4
pl usually **craft** BOAT : embarcación f
— **craftsman** ['kræftsmən] n, pl **-men**
[-mən, -ˌmen] : artesano m, -na f —
craftsmanship ['kræftsmənˌʃɪp] n
: artesanía f, destreza f — **crafty**
['kræfti] adj **craftier; -est** : astuto,
taimado
crag ['kræg] n : peñasco m
cram ['kræm] v **crammed; cramming**
vt 1 STUFF : embutir 2 **~ with** : atiborrar de — vi : estudiar a última hora
cramp ['kræmp] n 1 : calambre m, espasmo m (de los músculos) 2 **~s** npl
: retorcijones mpl
cranberry ['krænˌbɛri] n, pl **-berries**
: arándano m (rojo y agrio)
crane ['kreɪn] n 1 : grulla f (ave) 2 : grúa
f (máquina) — **~** vt **craned; craning**
: estirar (el cuello)
crank ['kræŋk] n 1 : manivela f 2 ECCEN-
TRIC : excéntrico m, -ca f — **cranky**
['kræŋki] adj **crankier; -est** : malhumorado
crash ['kræʃ] vi 1 : caerse con estrépito
2 COLLIDE : estrellarse, chocar — vt
: estrellar — **~** n 1 DIN : estrépito m 2
COLLISION : choque m
crass ['kræs] adj : burdo, grosero
crate ['kreɪt] n : cajón m (de madera)
crater ['kreɪtər] n : cráter m
crave ['kreɪv] vt **craved; craving** : ansiar — **craving** ['kreɪvɪŋ] n : ansia f
crawl ['krɔl] vi : arrastrarse, gatear
(dícese de un bebé) — **~** n at a **~** : a
paso lento
crayon ['kreɪˌɑn, -ən] n : lápiz m de cera
craze ['kreɪz] n : moda f pasajera, manía
f
crazy ['kreɪzi] adj **-zier; -est 1** : loco 2
go ~ : volverse loco — **craziness**
['kreɪzinəs] n : locura f
creak ['kri:k] vi : chirriar, crujir — **~** n
: chirrido m, crujido m
cream ['kri:m] n : crema f, nata f Spain
— **cream cheese** n : queso m crema

— **creamy** ['kri:mi] *adj* **creamier; -est** : cremoso

crease ['kri:s] *n* : pliegue *m*, raya *f* (del pantalón) — ~ *vt* **creased; creasing** : plegar, poner una raya en (el pantalón)

create [kri'eɪt] *vt* **-ated; -ating** : crear — **creation** [kri'eɪʃən] *n* : creación *f* — **creative** [kri'eɪtɪv] *adj* : creativo — **creator** [kri'eɪtər] *n* : creador *m*, -dora *f*

creature ['kri:tʃər] *n* : criatura *f*, animal *m*

credence ['kri:dənts] *n* **lend ~ to** : dar crédito a

credentials [krɪ'dentʃəlz] *npl* : credenciales *fpl*

credible ['kredəbəl] *adj* : creíble — **credibility** [ˌkredə'bɪləti] *n* : credibilidad *f*

credit ['kredɪt] *n* **1** : crédito *m* **2** RECOGNITION : reconocimiento *m* **3 be a ~ to** : ser el orgullo de — ~ *vt* **1** BELIEVE : creer **2** : abonar (en una cuenta) **3** ~ **s.o. with sth** : atribuir algo a algn — **credit card** *n* : tarjeta *f* de crédito

credulous ['kredʒələs] *adj* : crédulo

creed ['kri:d] *n* : credo *m*

creek ['kri:k, 'krɪk] *n* : arroyo *m*, riachuelo *m*

creep ['kri:p] *vi* **crept** ['krept]; **creeping 1** CRAWL : arrastrarse **2** SLINK : ir a hurtadillas — ~ *n* **1** CRAWL : paso *m* lento **2 the ~s** : escalofríos *mpl* — **creeping** *adj* : **~ plant** : planta *f* trepadora

cremate ['kri:ˌmeɪt] *vt* **-mated; -mating** : incinerar

crescent ['kresənt] *n* : media luna *f*

cress ['kres] *n* : berro *m*

crest ['krest] *n* : cresta *f* — **crestfallen** ['krest,fɔlən] *adj* : alicaído

crevice ['krevɪs] *n* : grieta *f*

crew ['kru:] *n* **1** : tripulación *f* (de una nave) **2** TEAM : equipo *m*

crib ['krɪb] *n* : cuna *f* (de un bebé)

cricket ['krɪkət] *n* **1** : grillo *m* (insecto) **2** : críquet *m* (juego)

crime ['kraɪm] *n* : crimen *m* — **criminal** ['krɪmənəl] *adj* : criminal — ~ *n* : criminal *mf*

crimp ['krɪmp] *vt* : rizar

crimson ['krɪmzən] *n* : carmesí *m*

cringe ['krɪndʒ] *vi* **cringed; cringing** : encogerse

crinkle ['krɪŋkəl] *vt* **-kled; -kling** : arrugar

cripple ['krɪpəl] *vt* **-pled; -pling 1** DISABLE : lisiar, dejar inválido **2** INCAPACITATE : inutilizar, paralizar

crisis ['kraɪsɪs] *n, pl* **crises** [-ˌsi:z] : crisis *f*

crisp ['krɪsp] *adj* **1** CRUNCHY : crujiente **2** : frío y vigorizante (dícese del aire) — **crispy** ['krɪspi] *adj* **crispier; -est** : crujiente

crisscross ['krɪsˌkrɔs] *vt* : entrecruzar

criterion [kraɪ'tɪriən] *n, pl* **-ria** [-iə] : criterio *m*

critic ['krɪtɪk] *n* : crítico *m*, -ca *f* — **critical** ['krɪtɪkəl] *adj* : crítico — **criticism** ['krɪtəˌsɪzəm] *n* : crítica *f* — **criticize** ['krɪtəˌsaɪz] *vt* **-cized; -cizing** : criticar

croak ['kroːk] *vi* : croar

crock ['krak] *n* : vasija *f* de barro — **crockery** ['krakəri] *n* : vajilla *f*, loza *f*

crocodile ['krakəˌdaɪl] *n* : cocodrilo *m*

crony ['kroːni] *n, pl* **-nies** : amigote *m fam*

crook ['krʊk] *n* **1** STAFF : cayado *m* **2** THIEF : ratero *m*, -ra *f*; ladrón *m*, -drona *f* **3** BEND : pliegue *m* — **crooked** ['krʊkəd] *adj* **1** BENT : torcido, chueco *Lat* **2** DISHONEST : deshonesto

crop ['krap] *n* **1** WHIP : fusta *f* **2** HARVEST : cosecha *f* **3** : cultivo *m* (de maíz, tabaco, etc.) — ~ *v* **cropped; cropping** *vt* TRIM : recortar, cortar — *vi* ~ **up** : surgir

cross ['krɔs] *n* **1** : cruz *f* **2** HYBRID : cruce *m* — ~ *vt* **1** : cruzar, atravesar **2** CROSSBREED : cruzar **3** *or* ~ **out** : tachar — ~ *adj* **1** : que atraviesa **2** ANGRY : enojado — **crossbreed** ['krɔsˌbri:d] *vt* **-bred** [-bred]; **-breeding** : cruzar — **cross-examine** *vt* : interrogar — **cross-eyed** ['krɔsˌaɪd] *adj* : bizco — **cross fire** *n* : fuego *m* cruzado — **crossing** ['krɔsɪŋ] *n* **1** INTERSECTION : cruce *m*, paso *m* **2** VOYAGE : travesía *f* (del mar) — **cross-reference** [ˌkrɔs'refrənts, -'refərənts] *n* : referencia *f* — **crossroads** ['krɔsˌroːdz] *n* : cruce *m* — **cross section** *n* **1** : corte *m* transversal **2** SAMPLE : muestra *f* representativa — **crosswalk** ['krɔsˌwɔk] *n* : cruce peatonal, paso *m* de peatones — **crossword puzzle** ['krɔsˌwərd] *n* : crucigrama *m*

crotch ['kratʃ] *n* : entrepierna *f*

crouch ['kraʊtʃ] *vi* : agacharse

crouton ['kru:ˌtan] *n* : crutón *m*

crow ['kroː] *n* : cuervo *m* — ~ *vi* **crowed** *or Brit* **crew; crowing** : cacarear

crowbar ['kroːˌbar] *n* : palanca *f*

crowd ['kraʊd] *vi* : amontonarse — *vt* : atestar, llenar — ~ *n* : multitud *f*, muchedumbre *f*

crown ['kraʊn] *n* **1** : corona *f* **2** : cima *f* (de una colina) — ~ *vt* : coronar
crucial ['kruːʃəl] *adj* : crucial
crucify ['kruːsəˌfaɪ] *vt* **-fied; -fying** : crucificar — **crucifix** ['kruːsəˌfɪks] *n* : crucifijo *m* — **crucifixion** [ˌkruːsə'fɪkʃən] *n* : crucifixión *f*
crude ['kruːd] *adj* **cruder; -est** **1** RAW : crudo **2** VULGAR : grosero **3** ROUGH : tosco, rudo
cruel ['kruːəl] *adj* **-eler** *or* **-eller; -elest** *or* **-ellest** : cruel — **cruelty** ['kruːəlti] *n, pl* **-ties** : crueldad *f*
cruet ['kruːɪt] *n* : vinagrera *f*
cruise ['kruːz] *vi* **cruised; cruising** **1** : hacer un crucero **2** : ir a velocidad de crucero — ~ *n* : crucero *m* — **cruiser** ['kruːzər] *n* **1** WARSHIP : crucero *m* **2** : patrulla *f* (de policía)
crumb ['krʌm] *n* : miga *f*, migaja *f*
crumble ['krʌmbəl] *v* **-bled; -bling** *vt* : desmenuzar — *vi* : desmenuzarse, desmoronarse
crumple ['krʌmpəl] *vt* **-pled; -pling** : arrugar
crunch ['krʌntʃ] *vt* : ronzar (con los dientes), hacer crujir (con los pies, etc.) — **crunchy** ['krʌntʃi] *adj* **crunchier; -est** : crujiente
crusade [kruː'seɪd] *n* : cruzada *f*
crush ['krʌʃ] *vt* : aplastar, apachurrar *Lat* — ~ *n* **have a ~ on** : estar chiflado por
crust ['krʌst] *n* : corteza *f*
crutch ['krʌtʃ] *n* : muleta *f*
crux ['krʌks, 'krʊks] *n* : quid *m*
cry ['kraɪ] *vi* **cried; crying** **1** SHOUT : gritar **2** WEEP : llorar — ~ *n, pl* **cries** : grito *m*
crypt ['krɪpt] *n* : cripta *f*
crystal ['krɪstəl] *n* : cristal *m*
cub ['kʌb] *n* : cachorro *m*, -rra *f*
Cuban ['kjuːbən] *adj* : cubano
cube ['kjuːb] *n* : cubo *m* — **cubic** ['kjuːbɪk] *adj* : cúbico
cubicle ['kjuːbɪkəl] *n* : cubículo *m*
cuckoo ['kuːkuː, 'kʊ-] *n* : cuco *m*, cuclillo *m*
cucumber ['kjuːˌkʌmbər] *n* : pepino *m*
cuddle ['kʌdəl] *v* **-dled; -dling** *vi* : acurrucarse, abrazarse — *vt* : abrazar
cudgel ['kʌdʒəl] *n* : porra *f* — ~ *vt* **-geled** *or* **-gelled; -geling** *or* **-gelling** : aporrear
cue¹ ['kjuː] *n* SIGNAL : señal *f*
cue² *n* : taco *m* (de billar)
cuff¹ ['kʌf] **1** : puño *m* (de una camisa) **2** ~**s** *npl* → **handcuffs**
cuff² *vt* : bofetear — ~ *n* SLAP : bofetada *f*

cuisine [kwɪ'ziːn] *n* : cocina *f*
culinary ['kʌləˌneri, 'kjuːlə-] *adj* : culinario
cull ['kʌl] *vt* : seleccionar, entresacar
culminate ['kʌlməˌneɪt] *vi* **-nated; -nating** : culminar — **culmination** [ˌkʌlmə'neɪʃən] *n* : culminación *f*
culprit ['kʌlprɪt] *n* : culpable *mf*
cult ['kʌlt] *n* : culto *m*
cultivate ['kʌltəˌveɪt] *vt* **-vated; -vating** : cultivar — **cultivation** [ˌkʌltə'veɪʃən] *n* : cultivo *m*
culture ['kʌltʃər] *n* **1** : cultura *f* **2** : cultivo *m* (en biología) — **cultural** ['kʌltʃərəl] *adj* : cultural — **cultured** ['kʌltʃərd] *adj* : culto
cumbersome ['kʌmbərsəm] *adj* : torpe (y pesado), difícil de manejar
cumulative ['kjuːmjələˌtɪv, -ˌleɪtɪv] *adj* : acumulativo
cunning ['kʌnɪŋ] *adj* : astuto, taimado — ~ *n* : astucia *f*
cup ['kʌp] *n* **1** : taza *f* **2** TROPHY : copa *f*
cupboard ['kʌbərd] *n* : alacena *f*, armario *m*
curator ['kjʊrˌeɪtər, kjʊ'reɪtər] *n* : conservador *m*, -dora *f*; director *m*, -tora *f*
curb ['kərb] *n* **1** RESTRAINT : freno *m* **2** : borde *m* de la acera — ~ *vt* : refrenar
curdle ['kərdəl] *v* **-dled; -dling** *vi* : cuajarse — *vt* : cuajar
cure ['kjʊr] *n* : cura *f*, remedio *m* — ~ *vt* **cured; curing** : curar
curfew ['kərˌfjuː] *n* : toque *m* de queda
curious ['kjʊriəs] *adj* : curioso — **curio** ['kjʊriˌoː] *n, pl* **-rios** : curiosidad *f* — **curiosity** [ˌkjʊri'asəti] *n, pl* **-ties** : curiosidad *f*
curl ['kərl] *vt* **1** : rizar **2** COIL : enrollar, enroscar — *vi* **1** : rizarse **2** ~ **up** : acurrucarse — ~ *n* : rizo *m* — **curler** ['kərlər] *n* : rulo *m* — **curly** ['kərli] *adj* **curlier; -est** : rizado
currant ['kərənt] *n* **1** : grosella *f* (fruta) **2** RAISIN : pasa *f* de Corinto
currency ['kərəntsi] *n, pl* **-cies** **1** MONEY : moneda *f* **2** **gain** ~ : ganar aceptación
current ['kərənt] *adj* **1** PRESENT : actual **2** PREVALENT : corriente — ~ *n* : corriente *f*
curriculum [kə'rɪkjələm] *n, pl* **-la** [-lə] : plan *m* de estudios
curry ['kəri] *n, pl* **-ries** : curry *m*
curse ['kərs] *n* : maldición *f* — ~ *v* **cursed; cursing** : maldecir
cursor ['kərsər] *n* : cursor *m*
cursory ['kərsəri] *adj* : superficial
curt ['kərt] *adj* : corto, seco

curtail [kər'teɪl] vt : acortar
curtain ['kərtən] n : cortina f (de una ventana), telón m (en un teatro)
curtsy ['kərtsi] vi **-sied** or **-seyed**; **-sying** or **-seying** : hacer una reverencia — ~ n : reverencia f
curve ['kərv] v **curved**; **curving** vi : hacer una curva — vt : encorvar — ~ n : curva f
cushion ['kʊʃən] n : cojín m — ~ vt : amortiguar
custard ['kʌstərd] n : natillas fpl
custody ['kʌstədi] n, pl **-dies** 1 : custodia f 2 **be in** ~ : estar detenido — **custodian** [kʌ'stodiən] n : custodio m, -dia f; guardián, -diana f
custom ['kʌstəm] n : costumbre f — **customary** ['kʌstə,meri] adj : habitual, acostumbrado — **customer** ['kʌstəmər] n : cliente m, -ta f — **customs** ['kʌstəmz] npl : aduana f
cut ['kʌt] v **cut**; **cutting** vt 1 : cortar 2 REDUCE : reducir, rebajar 3 ~ **oneself** : cortarse 4 ~ **up** : cortar en pedazos — vi 1 : cortar 2 ~ **in** : interrumpir —

~ n 1 : corte m 2 REDUCTION : rebaja f, reducción f
cute ['kjuːt] adj **cuter**; **-est** : mono fam, lindo
cutlery ['kʌtləri] n : cubiertos mpl
cutlet ['kʌtlət] n : chuleta f
cutting ['kʌtɪŋ] adj : cortante, mordaz
cyanide ['saɪə,naɪd, -nɪd] n : cianuro m
cycle ['saɪkəl] n 1 : ciclo m 2 BICYCLE : bicicleta f — ~ vi **-cled**; **-cling** : ir en bicicleta — **cyclic** ['saɪklɪk, 'sɪ-] or **cyclical** [-klɪkəl] adj : cíclico — **cyclist** ['saɪklɪst] n : ciclista mf
cyclone ['saɪkloɪn] n : ciclón m
cylinder ['sɪləndər] n : cilindro m — **cylindrical** [sə'lɪndrɪkəl] adj : cilíndrico
cymbal ['sɪmbəl] n : platillo m, címbalo m
cynic ['sɪnɪk] n : cínico m, -ca f — **cynical** ['sɪnɪkəl] adj : cínico — **cynicism** ['sɪnə,sɪzəm] n : cinismo m
cypress ['saɪprəs] n : ciprés m
cyst ['sɪst] n : quiste m
czar ['zɑr, 'sɑr] n : zar m
Czech ['tʃɛk] adj : checo — ~ n : checo m (idioma)

D

d ['diː] n, pl **d's** or **ds** ['diːz] : d f, cuarta letra del alfabeto inglés
dab ['dæb] n : toque m — ~ vt **dabbed**; **dabbing** : dar toques ligeros a, aplicar suavemente
dabble ['dæbəl] vi **-bled**; **-bling** ~ **in** : interesarse superficialmente en — **dabbler** n : aficionado m, -da f
dad ['dæd] n : papá m fam — **daddy** ['dædi] n, pl **-dies** : papá m fam
daffodil ['dæfə,dɪl] n : narciso m
dagger ['dægər] n : daga f, puñal m
daily ['deɪli] adj : diario — ~ adv : diariamente
dainty ['deɪnti] adj **-tier**; **-est** : delicado
dairy ['dæri] n, pl **-ies** 1 : lechería f (tienda) — ~ **farm** : granja f lechera
daisy ['deɪzi] n, pl **-sies** : margarita f
dam ['dæm] n : presa f — ~ vt **dammed**; **damming** : represar
damage ['dæmɪdʒ] n 1 : daño m, perjuicio m 2 ~**s** npl : daños y perjuicios mpl — ~ vt **-aged**; **-aging** : dañar
damn ['dæm] vt 1 CONDEMN : condenar 2 CURSE : maldecir — ~ **not give a** ~ or **damned** : no importarse un comino fam — ~ or **damned** ['dæmd] adj : maldito fam
damp ['dæmp] adj : húmedo — **dampen** ['dæmpən] vt 1 MOISTEN : humede-

cer 2 DISCOURAGE : desalentar, desanimar — **dampness** ['dæmpnəs] n : humedad f
dance ['dæns] v **danced**; **dancing** : bailar — ~ n : baile m — **dancer** ['dænsər] n : bailarín m, -rina f
dandelion ['dændə,laɪən] n : diente m de león
dandruff ['dændrəf] n : caspa f
dandy ['dændi] adj **-dier**; **-est** : de primera, excelente
danger ['deɪndʒər] n : peligro m — **dangerous** ['deɪndʒərəs] adj : peligroso
dangle ['dæŋgəl] v **-gled**; **-gling** vi HANG : colgar, pender — vt : hacer oscilar
Danish ['deɪnɪʃ] adj : danés — ~ n : danés m (idioma)
dank ['dæŋk] adj : frío y húmedo
dare ['dær] v **dared**; **daring** vt : desafiar — vi : osar — ~ n : desafío m — **daredevil** ['dær,dɛvəl] n : persona f temeraria — **daring** ['dærɪŋ] adj : atrevido, audaz — ~ n : audacia f
dark ['dɑrk] adj 1 : oscuro 2 : moreno (dícese del pelo o de la piel) 3 GLOOMY : sombrío 4 **get** ~ : hacerse de noche — **darken** ['dɑrkən] vt : oscurecer — vi : oscurecerse — **darkness** ['dɑrknəs] n : oscuridad f

darling ['dɑrlɪŋ] *n* BELOVED : querido *m*,
-da *f* — ~ *adj* : querido
darn ['dɑrn] *vt* : zurcir — ~ *adj*
: maldito *fam*
dart ['dɑrt] *n* **1** : dardo *m* **2** ~s *npl*
: juego *m* de dardos — ~ *vi* : precipitarse
dash ['dæʃ] *vt* **1** SMASH : romper **2** HURL
: lanzar **3** ~ **off** : hacer (algo) rápidamente — *vi* : lanzarse, irse corriendo
— ~ *n* **1** : guión *m* largo (signo de
puntuación) **2** PINCH : poquito *m*, pizca
f **3** RACE : carrera *f* — **dashboard**
['dæʃ,bord] *n* : tablero *m* de instrumentos — **dashing** ['dæʃɪŋ] *adj* : gallardo,
apuesto
data ['deɪtə, 'dæ-, 'dɑ-] *ns & pl* : datos
mpl — **database** ['deɪtə,beɪs, 'dæ-, 'dɑ-]
n : base *f* de datos
date¹ ['deɪt] *n* : dátil *m* (fruta)
date² *n* **1** : fecha *f* **2** APPOINTMENT : cita
f — ~ *v* dated; dating *vt* **1** : fechar
(una carta, etc.) **2** : salir con (algn) —
vi ~ **from** : datar de — **dated** ['deɪtəd]
adj : pasado de moda
daub ['dɔb] *vt* : embadurnar
daughter ['dɔtər] *n* : hija *f* — **daughter-in-law** ['dɔtərɪn,lɔ] *n*, *pl* **daugh-
ters-in-law** : nuera *f*
daunt ['dɔnt] *vt* : intimidar
dawdle ['dɔdəl] *vi* -dled; -dling : entretenerse, perder tiempo
dawn ['dɔn] *vi* **1** : amanecer **2 it** ~ed
on him that : cayó en la cuenta de que
— ~ *n* : amanecer *m*
day ['deɪ] *n* **1** : día *m* **2** *or* **working** ~
: jornada *f* **3 the** ~ **before** : el día anterior **4 the** ~ **before yesterday** : anteayer **5 the** ~ **after** : el día siguiente
6 the ~ **after tomorrow** : pasada
mañana — **daybreak** ['deɪ,breɪk] *n*
: amanecer *m* — **daydream** ['deɪ,drim]
n : ensueño *m* — *vi* : soñar despierto — **daylight** ['deɪ,laɪt] *n* : luz *f* del día
— **daytime** ['deɪ,taɪm] *n* : día *m*
daze ['deɪz] *vt* **dazed; dazing** : aturdir
— ~ *n* **in a** ~ : aturdido
dazzle ['dæzəl] *vt* -zled; -zling : deslumbrar
dead ['dɛd] *adj* **1** LIFELESS : muerto **2**
NUMB : entumecido — ~ *n* **1 in the**
~ **of night** : en plena noche **2 the** ~
: los muertos — ~ *adv* ABSOLUTELY
: absolutamente — **deaden** ['dɛdən] *vt*
1 : atenuar (dolores) **2** MUFFLE : amortiguar — **dead end** ['dɛd'ɛnd] *n* : callejón *m* sin salida — **deadline** ['dɛd,laɪn]
n : fecha *f* límite — **deadlock** ['dɛd-
,lɑk] *n* : punto *m* muerto — **deadly**

['dɛdli] *adj* -lier; -est **1** : mortal, letal **2**
ACCURATE : certero, preciso
deaf ['dɛf] *adj* : sordo — **deafen** ['dɛfən]
vt : ensordecer — **deafness** ['dɛfnəs] *n*
: sordera *f*
deal ['diːl] *n* **1** TRANSACTION : trato *m*,
transacción *f* **2** : reparto *m* (de naipes)
3 a good ~ : mucho — ~ *v* dealt;
dealing *vt* **1** : repartir, dar
(naipes) **3** ~ **a blow** : asestar un
golpe — *vi* **1** : dar, repartir (en juegos
de naipes) **2** ~ **in** : comerciar en **3** ~
with CONCERN : tratar de **4** ~ **with**
s.o. : tratar con algn — **dealer** ['diːlər]
n : comerciante *mf* — **dealings** *npl*
: trato *m*, relaciones *fpl*
dean ['diːn] *n* : decano *m*, -na *f*
dear ['dɪr] *adj* : querido *m* **1** ~ : querido *m*, -da *f* — **dearly** ['dɪrli] *adv* **1**
: mucho **2 pay** ~ : pagar caro
death ['dɛθ] *n* : muerte *f*
debar [di'bɑr] *vt* : excluir
debate [di'beɪt] *n* : debate *m*, discusión *f*
— ~ *vt* -bated; -bating : debatir, discutir
debit ['dɛbɪt] *vt* : adeudar, cargar — ~ *n*
: débito *m*, debe *m*
debris [də'briː, deɪ-; 'deɪ,briː] *n*, *pl* -bris
[-'briːz, -,briːz] : escombros *mpl*
debt ['dɛt] *n* : deuda *f* — **debtor** ['dɛtər]
n : deudor *m*, -dora *f*
debunk [di'bʌŋk] *vt* : desmentir
debut [deɪ'bjuː, 'deɪ,bjuː] *n* : debut *m* —
~ *vi* : debutar
decade ['dɛ,keɪd, dɛ'keɪd] *n* : década *f*
decadence ['dɛkədənts] *n* : decadencia *f*
— **decadent** ['dɛkədənt] *adj* : decadente
decal ['diː,kæl, di'kæl] *n* : calcomanía *f*
decanter [di'kæntər] *n* : licorera *f*
decapitate [di'kæpə,teɪt] *vt* -tated;
-tating : decapitar
decay [di'keɪ] *vi* **1** DECOMPOSE : descomponerse **2** DETERIORATE : deteriorarse **3** : cariarse (dícese de los dientes) — ~ *n* **1** : descomposición *f* **2**
: deterioro *m* (de un edificio, etc.) **3**
: caries *f* (de los dientes)
deceased [di'siːst] *adj* : difunto — ~ *n*
the ~ : el difunto, la difunta
deceive [di'siːv] *vt* -ceived; -ceiving
: engañar — **deceit** [di'siːt] *n* : engaño
m — **deceitful** [di'siːtfəl] *adj* : engañoso
December [di'sɛmbər] *n* : diciembre *m*
decent ['diːsənt] *adj* **1** : decente **2** KIND
: bueno, amable — **decency** ['diːsəntsi]
n, *pl* -cies : decencia *f*
deception [di'sɛpʃən] *n* : engaño *m* —
deceptive [di'sɛptɪv] *adj* : engañoso

decide [dɪ'saɪd] v **-cided; -ciding** vt : decidir — vi : decidirse — **decided** [dɪ'saɪdəd] adj **1** UNQUESTIONABLE : indudable **2** RESOLUTE : decidido — **decidedly** [dɪ'saɪdədli] adv **1** DEFINITELY : decididamente **2** RESOLUTELY : con decisión

decimal ['desəməl] adj : decimal — ~ n : número m decimal — **decimal point** n : coma f decimal

decipher [dɪ'saɪfər] vt : descifrar

decision [dɪ'sɪʒən] n : decisión f — **decisive** [dɪ'saɪsɪv] adj **1** RESOLUTE : decidido **2** CONCLUSIVE : decisivo

deck ['dɛk] n **1** : cubierta f (de un barco) **2** or **~ of cards** : baraja f (de naipes) **3** TERRACE : entarimado m

declare [dɪ'klær] vt **-clared; -claring** : declarar — **declaration** [,dɛklə'reɪʃən] n : declaración f

decline [dɪ'klaɪn] v **-clined; -clining** vt REFUSE : declinar, rehusar — vi DECREASE : declinar — ~ n **1** DETERIORATION : decadencia f, deterioro m **2** DECREASE : disminución f

decode [dɪ'koːd] vt **-coded; -coding** : descodificar

decompose [,diːkəm'poːz] vt **-posed; -posing** : descomponer — vi : descomponerse

decongestant [,diːkən'dʒɛstənt] n : descongestionante m

decorate ['dɛkəreɪt] vt **-rated; -rating** : decorar — **decor** or **décor** [derˈkɔr, 'derˌkɔr] n : decoración f — **decoration** [,dɛkə'reɪʃən] n : decoración f — **decorator** ['dɛkəˌreɪtər] n : decorador m, -dora f

decoy ['diːˌkɔɪ, dɪ'-] n : señuelo m

decrease [dɪ'kriːs] v **-creased; -creasing** : disminuir — ~ ['diːˌkriːs] n : disminución f

decree [dɪ'kriː] n : decreto m — ~ vt **-creed; -creeing** : decretar

decrepit [dɪ'krɛpɪt] adj **1** FEEBLE : decrépito **2** DILAPIDATED : ruinoso

dedicate ['dɛdɪˌkeɪt] vt **-cated; -cating** : dedicar **2** ~ **oneself to** : consagrarse a — **dedication** [,dɛdɪ'keɪʃən] n **1** DEVOTION : dedicación f **2** INSCRIPTION : dedicatoria f

deduce [dɪ'duːs, -'djuːs] vt **-duced; -ducing** : deducir — **deduct** [dɪ'dʌkt] vt : deducir — **deduction** [dɪ'dʌkʃən] n : deducción f

deed ['diːd] n : acción f, hecho m

deem ['diːm] vt : considerar, juzgar

deep ['diːp] adj : hondo, profundo — ~ adv **1** DEEPLY : profundamente **2** ~ **down** : en el fondo **3** dig ~ : cavar hondo — **deepen** ['diːpən] vt : ahondar — vi : hacerse más profundo — **deeply** ['diːpli] adv : hondo, profundamente

deer ['dɪr] ns & pl : ciervo m

deface [dɪ'feɪs] vt **-faced; -facing** : desfigurar

default [dɪ'fɔlt, 'diːˌfɔlt] n **by ~** : en rebeldía — ~ vi **1** ~ **on** : no pagar (una deuda) **2** : no presentarse (en deportes)

defeat [dɪ'fiːt] vt **1** BEAT : vencer, derrotar **2** FRUSTRATE : frustrar — ~ n : derrota f

defect ['diːˌfɛkt, dɪ'fɛkt] n : defecto m — ~ [dɪ'fɛkt] vi : desertar — **defective** [dɪ'fɛktɪv] adj : defectuoso

defend [dɪ'fɛnd] vt : defender — **defendant** [dɪ'fɛndənt] n : acusado m, -da f — **defense** or Brit **defence** [dɪ'fɛns, 'diːˌfɛns] n : defensa f — **defenseless** or Brit **defenceless** adj : indefenso — **defensive** [dɪ'fɛnsɪv] adj : defensivo — ~ n **on the ~** : a la defensiva

defer [dɪ'fər] v **-ferred; -ferring** vt : diferir, aplazar — vi ~ **to** : deferir a — **deference** ['dɛfərəns] n : deferencia f — **deferential** [,dɛfə'rɛnʃəl] adj : deferente

defiance [dɪ'faɪəns] n **1** : desafío m **2** in ~ **of** : a despecho de — **defiant** [dɪ'faɪənt] adj : desafiante

deficiency [dɪ'fɪʃənsi] n, pl **-cies** : deficiencia f — **deficient** [dɪ'fɪʃənt] adj : deficiente

deficit ['dɛfəsɪt] n : déficit m

defile [dɪ'faɪl] vt **-filed; -filing 1** DIRTY : ensuciar **2** DESECRATE : profanar

define [dɪ'faɪn] vt **-fined; -fining** : definir — **definite** ['dɛfənɪt] adj **1** : definido **2** CERTAIN : seguro, incuestionable — **definition** [,dɛfə'nɪʃən] n : definición f — **definitive** [dɪ'fɪnətɪv] adj : definitivo

deflate [dɪ'fleɪt] v **-flated; -flating** vt : desinflar (una llanta, etc.) — vi : desinflarse

deflect [dɪ'flɛkt] vt : desviar — vi : desviarse

deform [dɪ'fɔrm] vt : deformar — **deformity** [dɪ'fɔrməti] n, pl **-ties** : deformidad f

defraud [dɪ'frɔd] vt : defraudar

defrost [dɪ'frɔst] vt : descongelar — vi : descongelarse

deft ['dɛft] adj : hábil, diestro

defy [dɪ'faɪ] vt **-fied; -fying 1** CHALLENGE : desafiar **2** RESIST : resistir

degenerate [dɪ'dʒɛnəˌreɪt] vi : degenerar — ~ [dɪ'dʒɛnərət] adj : degenerado

degrade [dɪ'greɪd] *vt* **-graded; -grading** : degradar — **degrading** *adj* : degradante

degree [dɪ'griː] *n* 1 : grado *m* 2 *or* **academic ~** : título *m*

dehydrate [dɪ'haɪˌdreɪt] *vt* **-drated; -drating** : deshidratar

deign ['deɪn] *vi* **~ to** : dignarse (a)

deity ['diːəti, 'deɪ-] *n, pl* **-ties** : deidad *f*

dejected [dɪ'dʒɛktəd] *adj* : abatido — **dejection** [dɪ'dʒɛkʃən] *n* : abatimiento *m*

delay [dɪ'leɪ] *n* : retraso *m* — **~** *vt* 1 POSTPONE : aplazar 2 HOLD UP : retrasar — *vi* : demorar

delectable [dɪ'lɛktəbəl] *adj* : delicioso

delegate ['dɛlɪgət, -ˌgeɪt] *n* : delegado *m*, -da *f* — **~** ['dɛlɪgeɪt] *v* **-gated; -gating** : delegar — **delegation** [ˌdɛlɪ'geɪʃən] *n* : delegación *f*

delete [dɪ'liːt] *vt* **-leted; -leting** : borrar

deliberate [dɪ'lɪbəˌreɪt] *v* **-ated; -ating** *vt* : deliberar sobre — *vi* : deliberar — **~** [dɪ'lɪbərət] *adj* : deliberado — **deliberately** [dɪ'lɪbərətli] *adv* INTENTIONALLY : a propósito — **deliberation** [dɪˌlɪbə'reɪʃən] *n* : deliberación *f*

delicacy ['dɛlɪkəsi] *n, pl* **-cies** 1 : delicadeza *f* 2 FOOD : manjar *m*, exquisitez *f* — **delicate** ['dɛlɪkət] *adj* : delicado

delicatessen [ˌdɛlɪkə'tɛsən] *n* : charcutería *f*

delicious [dɪ'lɪʃəs] *adj* : delicioso

delight [dɪ'laɪt] *n* : placer *m*, deleite *m* — **~** *vt* : deleitar, encantar — *vi* **~ in** : deleitarse con — **delightful** [dɪ'laɪtfəl] *adj* : delicioso, encantador

delinquent [dɪ'lɪŋkwənt] *adj* : delincuente — **~** *n* : delincuente *mf*

delirious [dɪ'lɪriəs] *adj* : delirante — **delirium** [dɪ'lɪriəm] *n* : delirio *m*

deliver [dɪ'lɪvər] *vt* 1 DISTRIBUTE : entregar, repartir 2 FREE : liberar 3 : asistir en el parto de (un niño) 4 : pronunciar (un discurso, etc.) 5 DEAL : asestar (un golpe, etc.) — **delivery** [dɪ'lɪvəri] *n, pl* **-eries** 1 DISTRIBUTION : entrega *f*, reparto *m* 2 LIBERATION : liberación *f* 3 CHILDBIRTH : parto *m*, alumbramiento *m*

delude [dɪ'luːd] *vt* **-luded; -luding** 1 : engañar 2 **~ oneself** : engañarse

deluge ['dɛlˌjuːdʒ, -ˌjuːʒ] *n* : diluvio *m*

delusion [dɪ'luːʒən] *n* : ilusión *f*

deluxe [dɪ'lʌks, -'lʊks] *adj* : de lujo

delve ['dɛlv] *vi* **delved; delving** 1 : escarbar 2 **~ into** PROBE : investigar

demand [dɪ'mænd] *n* 1 REQUEST : petición *f* 2 CLAIM : reclamación *f*, exigencia *f* 3 **→ supply** — **~** *vt* : exigir — **demanding** *adj* : exigente

demean [dɪ'miːn] *vt* **~ oneself** : rebajarse

demeanor [dɪ'miːnər] *n* : comportamiento *m*

demented [dɪ'mɛntəd] *adj* : demente, loco

demise [dɪ'maɪz] *n* : fallecimiento *m*

democracy [dɪ'mɑkrəsi] *n, pl* **-cies** : democracia *f* — **democrat** ['dɛməˌkræt] *n* : demócrata *mf* — **democratic** [ˌdɛmə'krætɪk] *adj* : democrático

demolish [dɪ'mɑlɪʃ] *vt* : demoler — **demolition** [ˌdɛmə'lɪʃən, ˌdiː-] *n* : demolición *f*

demon ['diːmən] *n* : demonio *m*

demonstrate ['dɛmənˌstreɪt] *v* **-strated; -strating** *vt* : demostrar — *vi* RALLY : manifestarse — **demonstration** [ˌdɛmən'streɪʃən] *n* 1 : demostración *f* 2 RALLY : manifestación *f*

demoralize [dɪ'mɔrəˌlaɪz] *vt* **-ized; -izing** : desmoralizar

demote [dɪ'moʊt] *vt* **-moted; -moting** : bajar de categoría

demure [dɪ'mjʊr] *adj* : recatado

den ['dɛn] *n* LAIR : guarida *f*

denial [dɪ'naɪəl] *n* 1 : negación *f*, rechazo *m* 2 REFUSAL : denegación *f*

denim ['dɛnəm] *n* : tela *f* vaquera, mezclilla *f Lat*

denomination [dɪˌnɑmə'neɪʃən] *n* 1 : confesión *f* (religiosa) 2 : valor *m* (de una moneda)

denounce [dɪ'naʊnts] *vt* **-nounced; -nouncing** : denunciar

dense ['dɛnts] *adj* **denser; -est** 1 THICK : denso 2 STUPID : estúpido — **density** ['dɛntsəti] *n, pl* **-ties** : densidad *f*

dent ['dɛnt] *vt* : abollar — **~** *n* : abolladura *f*

dental ['dɛntəl] *adj* : dental — **dental floss** *n* : hilo *m* dental — **dentist** ['dɛntɪst] *n* : dentista *mf* — **dentures** ['dɛntʃərz] *npl* : dentadura *f* postiza

deny [dɪ'naɪ] *vt* **-nied; -nying** 1 : negar 2 REFUSE : denegar

deodorant [diː'oʊdərənt] *n* : desodorante *m*

depart [dɪ'pɑrt] *vi* 1 : salir 2 **~ from** : apartarse de (la verdad, etc.)

department [dɪ'pɑrtmənt] *n* : sección *f* (de una tienda, etc.), departamento *m* (de una empresa, etc.), ministerio *m* (del gobierno) — **department store** *n* : grandes almacenes *mpl*

departure [dɪ'pɑrtʃər] *n* 1 : salida *f* 2 DEVIATION : desviación *f*

depend [dɪ'pɛnd] *vi* 1 **~ on** : depender

de 2 ~ on s.o. : contar con algn 3
that ~s : eso depende — **dependable** [dɪ'pendəbəl] *adj* : digno de confianza — **dependence** [dɪ'pendənts] *n* : dependencia *f* — **dependent** [dɪ'pendənt] *adj* : dependiente

depict [dɪ'pɪkt] *vt* 1 PORTRAY : representar 2 DESCRIBE : describir

deplete [dɪ'pliːt] *vt* **-pleted; -pleting** : agotar, reducir

deplore [dɪ'plor] *vt* **-plored; -ploring** : deplorar, lamentar — **deplorable** [dɪ'plorəbəl] *adj* : lamentable

deploy [dɪ'plɔɪ] *vt* : desplegar

deport [dɪ'port] *vt* : deportar, expulsar (de un país) — **deportation** [ˌdiːpor'teɪʃən] *n* : deportación *f*

depose [dɪ'poːz] *vt* **-posed; -posing** : deponer

deposit [dɪ'pazət] *vt* **-ited; -iting** : depositar — ~ *n* 1 : depósito *m* 2 DOWN PAYMENT : entrega *f* inicial

depot [*in sense 1 usu* 'deˌpoː, *2 usu* 'diː-] *n* 1 WAREHOUSE : almacén *m*, depósito *m* 2 STATION : terminal *mf*

depreciate [dɪ'priːʃiˌeɪt] *vi* **-ated; -ating** : depreciarse — **depreciation** [dɪˌpriːʃi'eɪʃən] *n* : depreciación *f*

depress [dɪ'pres] *vt* 1 : deprimir 2 PRESS : apretar — **depressed** [dɪ'prest] *adj* : abatido, deprimido — **depressing** [dɪ'presɪŋ] *adj* : deprimente — **depression** [dɪ'preʃən] *n* : depresión *f*

deprive [dɪ'praɪv] *vt* **-prived; -priving** : privar

depth ['depθ] *n, pl* **depths** ['depθs, 'deps] 1 : profundidad *f* 2 **in the ~s of night** : en lo más profundo de la noche

deputy ['depjʊti] *n, pl* **-ties** : suplente *mf*; sustituto *m*, -ta *f*

derail [dɪ'reɪl] *vt* : hacer descarrilar

deranged [dɪ'reɪndʒd] *adj* : trastornado

derelict ['derəˌlɪkt] *adj* : abandonado

deride [dɪ'raɪd] *vt* **-rided; -riding** : burlarse de — **derision** [dɪ'rɪʒən] *n* : mofa *f*

derive [dɪ'raɪv] *vi* **-rived; -riving** : derivar — **derivation** [ˌderə'veɪʃən] *n* : derivación *f*

derogatory [dɪ'ragəˌtori] *adj* : despectivo

descend [dɪ'send] *v* : descender, bajar — **descendant** [dɪ'sendənt] *n* : descendiente *mf* — **descent** [dɪ'sent] *n* 1 : descenso *m* 2 LINEAGE : descendencia *f*

describe [dɪ'skraɪb] *vt* **-scribed; -scribing** : describir — **description** [dɪ'skrɪpʃən] *n* : descripción *f* — **descriptive** [dɪ'skrɪptɪv] *adj* : descriptivo

desecrate ['desɪˌkreɪt] *vt* **-crated; -crating** : profanar

desert ['dezərt] *n* : desierto *m* — ~ *adj* **~ island** : isla *f* desierta — ~ [dɪ'zərt] *vt* : abandonar — *vi* : desertar — **deserter** [dɪ'zərtər] *n* : desertor *m*, -tora *f*

deserve [dɪ'zərv] *vt* **-served; -serving** : merecer

design [dɪ'zaɪn] *vt* 1 DEVISE : diseñar 2 PLAN : proyectar — ~ *n* 1 : diseño *m* 2 PLAN : plan *m*, proyecto *m*

designate ['dezɪɡˌneɪt] *vt* **-nated; -nating** : nombrar, designar

designer [dɪ'zaɪnər] *n* : diseñador *m*, -dora *f*

desire [dɪ'zaɪr] *vt* **-sired; -siring** : desear — ~ *n* : deseo *m* — **desirable** [dɪ'zaɪrəbəl] *adj* : deseable

desk ['desk] *n* : escritorio *m*, pupitre *m* (en la escuela)

desolate ['desələt, -zə-] *adj* : desolado

despair [dɪ'spær] *vi* : desesperar — ~ *n* : desesperación *f*

desperate ['despərət] *adj* : desesperado — **desperation** [ˌdespə'reɪʃən] *n* : desesperación *f*

despise [dɪ'spaɪz] *vt* **-spised; -spising** : despreciar — **despicable** [dɪ'spɪkəbəl, 'despɪ-] *adj* : despreciable

despite [də'spaɪt] *prep* : a pesar de

despondent [dɪ'spandənt] *adj* : desanimado

dessert [dɪ'zərt] *n* : postre *m*

destination [ˌdestə'neɪʃən] *n* : destino *m* — **destined** ['destənd] *adj* 1 : destinado 2 **~ for** : con destino a — **destiny** ['destəni] *n, pl* **-nies** : destino *m*

destitute ['destəˌtuːt, -ˌtjuːt] *adj* : indigente

destroy [dɪ'strɔɪ] *vt* : destruir — **destruction** [dɪ'strʌkʃən] *n* : destrucción *f* — **destructive** [dɪ'strʌktɪv] *adj* : destructivo

detach [dɪ'tætʃ] *vt* : separar — **detached** [dɪ'tætʃt] *adj* 1 : separado 2 IMPARTIAL : objetivo

detail [dɪ'teɪl, 'diːˌteɪl] *n* 1 : detalle *m* 2 **go into ~** : entrar en detalles — ~ *vt* : detallar — **detailed** *adj* : detallado

detain [dɪ'teɪn] *vt* 1 : detener (un prisionero) 2 DELAY : entretener

detect [dɪ'tekt] *vt* : detectar — **detection** [dɪ'tekʃən] *n* : detección *f*, descubrimiento *m* — **detective** [dɪ'tektɪv] *n* : detective *mf*

detention [dɪ'tentʃən] *n* : detención *m*

deter [dɪ'tər] *vt* **-terred; -terring** : disuadir

detergent [dɪ'tərdʒənt] *n* : detergente *m*

deteriorate [dɪ'tɪriə,reɪt] vi **-rated; -rating** : deteriorarse — **deterioration** [dɪ,tɪriə'reɪʃən] n : deterioro m

determine [dɪ'tərmən] vt **-mined; -mining** : determinar — **determined** [dɪ'tərmənd] adj RESOLUTE : decidido — **determination** [dɪ,tərmə'neɪʃən] n : determinación f

deterrent [dɪ'tərənt] n : medida f disuasiva

detest [dɪ'tɛst] vt : detestar — **detestable** [dɪ'tɛstəbəl] adj : odioso

detonate ['dɛtən,eɪt] v **-nated; -nating** vt : hacer detonar — vi EXPLODE : detonar, estallar — **detonation** [,dɛtə'neɪʃən, ,dɛtə-] n : detonación f

detour ['di:,tur, dɪ'tur] n 1 : desviación f 2 **make a ~** : dar un rodeo — **~** vi : desviarse

detract [dɪ'trækt] vi **~ from** : aminorar, restar importancia a

detrimental [,dɛtrə'mɛntəl] adj : perjudicial

devalue [di'væl,ju:] vt **-ued; -uing** : devaluar

devastate ['dɛvə,steɪt] vt **-tated; -tating** : devastar — **devastating** adj : devastador — **devastation** [,dɛvə'steɪʃən] n : devastación f

develop [dɪ'vɛləp] vt 1 : desarrollar 2 **~ an illness** : contraer una enfermedad — vi 1 GROW : desarrollarse 2 HAPPEN : aparecer — **development** [dɪ'vɛləpmənt] n : desarrollo m

deviate [di:vi,eɪt] v **-ated; -ating** vi : desviarse — **deviation** [,di:vi'eɪʃən] n : desviación f

device [dɪ'vaɪs] n : dispositivo m, mecanismo m

devil ['dɛvəl] n : diablo m, demonio m — **devilish** ['dɛvəlɪʃ] adj : diabólico

devious ['di:viəs] adj 1 CRAFTY : taimado 2 WINDING : tortuoso

devise [dɪ'vaɪz] vt **-vised; -vising** : idear, concebir

devoid [dɪ'vɔɪd] adj **~ of** : desprovisto de

devote [dɪ'vo:t] vt **-voted; -voting** : consagrar, dedicar — **devoted** [dɪ'vo:təd] adj : leal — **devotee** [,dɛvə'ti:, -'teɪ] n : devoto m, -ta f — **devotion** [dɪ'vo:ʃən] n 1 : devoción f, dedicación f 2 : oración f (en religión)

devour [dɪ'vauər] vt : devorar

devout [dɪ'vaut] adj : devoto

dew ['du:, 'dju:] n : rocío m

dexterity [dɛk'stɛrəţi] n, pl **-ties** : destreza f

diabetes [,daɪə'bi:ţiz] n : diabetes f —

diabetic [,daɪə'bɛţɪk] adj : diabético — **~** n : diabético m, -ca f

diabolic [,daɪə'bɑlɪk] or **diabolical** [-lɪkəl] adj : diabólico

diagnosis [,daɪɪg'no:sɪs] n, pl **-noses** [-'no:,si:z] : diagnóstico m — **diagnose** ['daɪɪg,no:s, ,daɪɪg'no:s] vt **-nosed; -nosing** : diagnosticar — **diagnostic** [,daɪɪg'nɑstɪk] adj : diagnóstico

diagonal [daɪ'ægənəl] adj : diagonal, en diagonal — **~** n : diagonal f

diagram ['daɪə,græm] n : diagrama m

dial ['daɪl] n 1 : esfera f (de un reloj), dial m (de un radio, etc.) — **~** v **dialed** or **dialled; dialing** or **dialling** : marcar

dialect ['daɪə,lɛkt] n : dialecto m

dialogue ['daɪə,lɔg] n : diálogo m

diameter [daɪ'æmətər] n : diámetro m

diamond ['daɪmənd, 'daɪə-] n 1 : diamante m 2 : rombo m (forma) 3 or **baseball ~** : cuadro m, diamante m

diaper ['daɪpər, 'daɪə-] n : pañal m

diaphragm ['daɪə,fræm] n : diafragma m

diarrhea [,daɪə'ri:ə] n : diarrea f

diary ['daɪəri] n, pl **-ries** : diario m

dice ['daɪs] ns & pl : dados mpl (juego)

dictate ['dɪk,teɪt, dɪk'teɪt] vt **-tated; -tating** : dictar — **dictation** [dɪk'teɪʃən] n : dictado m — **dictator** ['dɪk,teɪtər] n : dictador m, -dora f — **dictatorship** [dɪk'teɪtər,ʃɪp, 'dɪk,teɪ-, 'dɪk,-] n : dictadura f

dictionary ['dɪkʃə,nɛri] n, pl **-naries** : diccionario m

did → do

die¹ ['daɪ] vi **died** ['daɪd]; **dying** ['daɪɪŋ] 1 : morir 2 **~ down** : aminar, disminuir 3 **~ out** : extinguirse 4 **be dying for** : morirse por

die² ['daɪ] n 1 pl **dice** ['daɪs] : dado m (para jugar) 2 pl **dies** ['daɪz] MOLD : molde m

diesel ['di:zəl, -səl] n : diesel m

diet ['daɪət] n 1 FOOD : alimentación f 2 **go on a ~** : ponerse a régimen — **~** vi : estar a régimen

differ ['dɪfər] vi **-ferred; -ferring** 1 : diferir, ser distinto 2 DISAGREE : no estar de acuerdo — **difference** ['dɪfrənts, 'dɪfərənts] n : diferencia f — **different** ['dɪfrənt, 'dɪfərənt] adj : distinto, diferente — **differentiate** [,dɪfə'rɛntʃi,eɪt] v **-ated; -ating** vt : diferenciar — vi : distinguir — **differently** ['dɪfrəntli, 'dɪfərənt-] adv : de otra manera

difficult ['dɪfɪ,kʌlt] adj : difícil — **difficulty** ['dɪfɪ,kʌlti] n, pl **-ties** : dificultad f

diffident ['dɪfədənt] adj : tímido, que falta confianza

dig ['dɪg] v **dug** ['dʌg]; **digging** vt 1 : cavar 2 ~ **up** : desenterrar — vi : cavar — ~ n 1 GIBE : pulla f 2 EXCAVATION : excavación f

digest ['daɪ,dʒɛst] n : resumen m — ~ [daɪ'dʒɛst] vt 1 : digerir 2 SUMMARIZE : resumir — **digestible** [daɪ'dʒɛstəbəl, dɪ-] adj : digerible — **digestion** [daɪ'dʒɛstʃən, dɪ-] n : digestión f — **digestive** [daɪ'dʒɛstɪv, dɪ-] adj : digestivo

digit ['dɪdʒət] n 1 NUMERAL : dígito m, número m 2 FINGER, TOE : dedo m — **digital** ['dɪdʒət̬əl] adj : digital

dignity ['dɪgnət̬i] n, pl **-ties** : dignidad f — **dignified** ['dɪgnə,faɪd] adj : digno, decoroso

digress [daɪ'grɛs, də-] vi : desviarse del tema, divagar — **digression** [daɪ'grɛʃən, də-] n : digresión f

dike ['daɪk] n : dique m

dilapidated [də'læpə,deɪt̬əd] adj : ruinoso

dilate [daɪ'leɪt, 'daɪ,leɪt] v **-lated; -lating** vt : dilatar — vi : dilatarse

dilemma [dɪ'lɛmə] n : dilema m

diligence ['dɪlədʒənts] n : diligencia f — **diligent** ['dɪlədʒənt] adj : diligente

dilute [daɪ'luːt, də-] vt **-luted; -luting** : diluir

dim ['dɪm] v **dimmed; dimming** vt : atenuar — vi : irse atenuando — ~ adj **dimmer; dimmest** 1 DARK : oscuro 2 FAINT : débil, tenue

dime ['daɪm] n : moneda f de diez centavos

dimension [də'mɛntʃən, daɪ-] n : dimensión f

diminish [də'mɪnɪʃ] v : disminuir

diminutive [də'mɪnjət̬ɪv] adj : diminuto

dimple ['dɪmpəl] n : hoyuelo m

din ['dɪn] n : estrépito m

dine ['daɪn] vi **dined; dining** : cenar — **diner** ['daɪnər] n 1 : comensal mf (persona) 2 : cafetería f (restaurante)

dingy ['dɪndʒi] adj **-gier; -est** : sucio, deslucido

dinner ['dɪnər] n : cena f, comida f

dinosaur ['daɪnə,sɔr] n : dinosaurio m

dint ['dɪnt] n **by** ~ **of** : a fuerza de

dip ['dɪp] v **dipped; dipping** vt : mojar — vi : bajar, descender — ~ n 1 DROP : descenso m, caída f 2 SWIM : chapuzón m 3 SAUCE : salsa f

diploma [də'ploːmə] n, pl **-mas** : diploma m

diplomacy [də'ploːməsi] n : diplomacia f — **diplomat** ['dɪplə,mæt] n : diplomático m, -ca f — **diplomatic** [dɪplə'mæt̬ɪk] adj : diplomático

dire ['daɪr] adj **direr; direst** 1 : grave, terrible 2 EXTREME : extremo

direct [də'rɛkt, daɪ-] vt 1 : dirigir 2 ORDER : mandar — ~ adj 1 STRAIGHT : directo 2 FRANK : franco — ~ adv : directamente — **direct current** n : corriente f continua — **direction** [də'rɛkʃən, daɪ-] n 1 : dirección f 2 **ask** ~s : pedir indicaciones — **directly** [də'rɛktli, daɪ-] adv 1 STRAIGHT : directamente 2 IMMEDIATELY : en seguida — **director** [də'rɛktər, daɪ-] n 1 : director m, -tora f 2 **board of** ~s : directorio m — **directory** [də'rɛktəri, daɪ-] n, pl **-ries** : guía f (telefónica)

dirt ['dərt] n 1 : suciedad f 2 SOIL : tierra f — **dirty** ['dərt̬i] adj **dirtier; -est** 1 : sucio 2 INDECENT : obsceno, cochino fam

disability [dɪsə'bɪlət̬i] n, pl **-ties** : minusvalía f, invalidez f — **disable** [dɪs'eɪbəl] vt **-abled; -abling** : incapacitar — **disabled** [dɪs'eɪbəld] adj : minusválido

disadvantage [dɪsəd'væntɪdʒ] n : desventaja f

disagree [dɪsə'griː] vi 1 : no estar de acuerdo (con algn) 2 CONFLICT : no coincidir — **disagreeable** [dɪsə'griːəbəl] adj : desagradable — **disagreement** [dɪsə'griːmənt] n 1 : desacuerdo m 2 ARGUMENT : discusión f

disappear [dɪsə'pɪr] vi : desaparecer — **disappearance** [dɪsə'pɪrənts] n : desaparición f

disappoint [dɪsə'pɔɪnt] vt : decepcionar, desilusionar — **disappointment** [dɪsə'pɔɪntmənt] n : decepción f, desilusión f

disapprove [dɪsə'pruːv] vi **-proved; -proving** ~ **of** : desaprobar — **disapproval** [dɪsə'pruːvəl] n : desaprobación f

disarm [dɪs'ɑrm] vt : desarmar — **disarmament** [dɪs'ɑrməmənt] n : desarme m

disarray [dɪsə'reɪ] n : desorden m

disaster [dɪ'zæstər] n : desastre m — **disastrous** [dɪ'zæstrəs] adj : desastroso

disbelief [dɪsbɪ'liːf] n : incredulidad f

disc → **disk**

discard [dɪs'kɑrd, 'dɪs,kɑrd] vt : desechar, deshacerse de

discern [dɪ'sərn, -'zərn] vt : percibir, discernir — **discernible** [dɪ'sərnəbəl, -'zər-] adj : perceptible

discharge [dɪs'tʃɑrdʒ, 'dɪs,-] vt **-charged; -charging** 1 UNLOAD : descargar 2 RELEASE : liberar, poner en libertad 3 DISMISS : despedir 4

CARRY OUT : cumplir con (una obligación) — ~ ['dɪstʃɑrdʒ, dɪs'-] *n* **1** : descarga *f* (de electricidad), emisión *f* (de humo, etc.) **2** DISMISSAL : despido *m* **3** RELEASE : alta *f* (de un paciente), puesta *f* en libertad (de un preso) **4** : supuración *f* (en medicina)

disciple [dɪ'saɪpəl] *n* : discípulo *m*, -la *f*

discipline ['dɪsəplən] *n* **1** : disciplina *f* **2** PUNISHMENT : castigo *m* — ~ *vt* **-plined; -plining 1** CONTROL : disciplinar **2** PUNISH : castigar

disclaim [dɪs'kleɪm] *vt* : negar

disclose [dɪs'kloːz] *vt* **-closed; -closing** : revelar — **disclosure** [dɪs'kloːʒər] *n* : revelación *f*

discomfort [dɪs'kʌmfərt] *n* **1** : incomodidad *f* **2** PAIN : malestar *m* **3** UNEASINESS : inquietud *f*

disconcert [,dɪskən'sərt] *vt* : desconcertar

disconnect [,dɪskə'nekt] *vt* : desconectar

disconsolate [dɪs'kɑntsələt] *adj* : desconsolado

discontented [,dɪskən'tentəd] *adj* : descontento

discontinue [,dɪskən'tɪnjuː] *vt* **-ued; -uing** : suspender, descontinuar

discount ['dɪs,kaʊnt, dɪs'-] *n* : descuento *m*, rebaja *f* — ~ *vt* **1** : descontar (precios) **2** DISREGARD : descartar

discourage [dɪs'kərɪdʒ] *vt* **-aged; -aging** : desalentar, desanimar — **discouragement** [dɪs'kərɪdʒmənt] *n* : desánimo *m*, desaliento *m*

discover [dɪs'kʌvər] *vt* : descubrir — **discovery** [dɪs'kʌvəri] *n, pl* **-ries** : descubrimiento *m*

discredit [dɪs'kredət] *vt* : desacreditar — ~ *n* : descrédito *m*

discreet [dɪs'kriːt] *adj* : discreto

discrepancy [dɪs'krepəntsi] *n, pl* **-cies** : discrepancia *f*

discretion [dɪs'kreʃən] *n* : discreción *f*

discriminate [dɪs'krɪmə,neɪt] *vi* **-nated; -nating 1** ~ **against** : discriminar **2** ~ **between** : distinguir entre — **discrimination** [dɪs,krɪmə'neɪʃən] *n* **1** PREJUDICE : discriminación *f* **2** DISCERNMENT : discernimiento *m*

discuss [dɪs'kʌs] *vt* : hablar de, discutir — **discussion** [dɪs'kʌʃən] *n* : discusión *f*

disdain [dɪs'deɪn] *n* : desdén *m* — ~ *vt* : desdeñar

disease [dɪ'ziːz] *n* : enfermedad *f* — **diseased** [dɪ'ziːzd] *adj* : enfermo

disembark [,dɪsɪm'bɑrk] *vi* : desembarcar

disengage [,dɪsɪn'geɪdʒ] *vt* **-gaged;**

-gaging 1 RELEASE : soltar **2** ~ **the clutch** : desembragar

disentangle [,dɪsɪn'tæŋgəl] *vt* **-gled; -gling** : desenredar

disfavor [dɪs'feɪvər] *n* : desaprobación *f*

disfigure [dɪs'fɪgjər] *vt* **-ured; -uring** : desfigurar

disgrace [dɪs'kreɪs] *vt* **-graced; -gracing** : deshonrar — ~ *n* **1** DISHONOR : deshonra *f* **2** SHAME : vergüenza *f* — **disgraceful** [dɪs'kreɪsfəl] *adj* : vergonzoso, deshonroso

disgruntled [dɪs'grʌntəld] *adj* : descontento

disguise [dɪs'kaɪz] *vt* **-guised; -guising** : disfrazar — ~ *n* : disfraz *m*

disgust [dɪs'kʌst] *n* : asco *m*, repugnancia *f* — ~ *vt* : asquear — **disgusting** [dɪs'kʌstɪŋ] *adj* : asqueroso

dish ['dɪʃ] *n* **1** : plato *m* **2** *or* **serving** ~ : fuente *f* **3 wash the** ~**es** : lavar los platos — ~ *vt or* ~ **up** : servir — **dishcloth** ['dɪʃ,klɔθ] *n* : paño *m* de cocina (para secar), trapo *m* de fregar (para lavar)

dishearten [dɪs'hɑrtən] *vt* : desanimar

disheveled *or* **dishevelled** [dɪ'ʃevəld] *adj* : desaliñado, despeinado (dícese del pelo)

dishonest [dɪs'ɑnəst] *adj* : deshonesto — **dishonesty** [dɪs'ɑnəsti] *n, pl* **-ties** : falta *f* de honradez

dishonor [dɪs'ɑnər] *n* : deshonra *f* — ~ *vt* : deshonrar — **dishonorable** [dɪ'sɑnərəbəl] *adj* : deshonroso

dishwasher ['dɪʃ,wɔʃər] *n* : lavaplatos *m*, lavavajillas *m*

disillusion [,dɪsɪ'luːʒən] *vt* : desilusionar — **disillusionment** [,dɪsə'luːʒənmənt] *n* : desilusión *f*

disinfect [,dɪsɪn'fekt] *vt* : desinfectar — **disinfectant** [,dɪsɪn'fektənt] *n* : desinfectante *m*

disintegrate [dɪs'ɪntə,greɪt] *vi* **-grated; -grating** : desintegrarse

disinterested [dɪs'ɪntərəstəd, -,res-] *adj* : desinteresado

disk *or* **disc** ['dɪsk] *n* : disco *m*

dislike [dɪs'laɪk] *n* : aversión *f*, antipatía *f* — ~ *vt* **-liked; -liking 1** : tener aversión a **2 I** ~ **dancing** : no me gusta bailar

dislocate ['dɪslo,keɪt, dɪs'lo:-] *vt* **-cated; -cating** : dislocar

dislodge [dɪs'lɑdʒ] *vt* **-lodged; -lodging** : sacar, desalojar

disloyal [dɪs'lɔɪəl] *adj* : desleal — **disloyalty** [dɪs'lɔɪəlti] *n, pl* **-ties** : deslealtad *f*

dismal ['dɪzməl] *adj* : sombrío, deprimente

dismantle [dɪs'mæntəl] *vt* **-tled; -tling** : desmontar, desarmar

dismay [dɪs'meɪ] *vt* : consternar — ~ *n* : consternación *f*

dismiss [dɪs'mɪs] *vt* **1** DISCHARGE : despedir, destituir **2** REJECT : descartar, rechazar — **dismissal** [dɪs'mɪsəl] *n* **1** : despido *m* (de un empleado), destitución *f* (de un funcionario) **2** REJECTION : rechazo *m*

dismount [dɪs'maʊnt] *vi* : desmontar

disobey [ˌdɪsə'beɪ] *v* : desobedecer — **disobedience** [ˌdɪsə'biːdiənts] *n* : desobediencia *f* — **disobedient** [-ənt] *adj* : desobediente

disorder [dɪs'ɔrdər] *n* **1** : desorden *m* **2** AILMENT : afección *f*, problema *m* — **disorderly** [dɪs'ɔrdərli] *adj* : desordenado

disorganize [dɪs'ɔrgənaɪz] *vt* **-nized; -nizing** : desorganizar

disown [dɪs'oːn] *vt* : renegar de

dispassionate [dɪs'pæʃənət] *adj* : desapasionado

dispatch [dɪs'pætʃ] *vt* : despachar, enviar

dispel [dɪs'pel] *vt* **-pelled; -pelling** : disipar

dispensation [ˌdɪspen'seɪʃən] *n* EXEMPTION : exención *m*, dispensa *f*

dispense [dɪs'pents] *v* **-pensed; -pensing** *vt* : repartir, distribuir — *vi* ~ **with** : prescindir de

disperse [dɪs'pərs] *v* **-persed; -persing** *vt* : dispersar — *vi* : dispersarse

displace [dɪs'pleɪs] *vt* **-placed; -placing** **1** : desplazar **2** REPLACE : reemplazar

display [dɪs'pleɪ] *vt* **1** EXHIBIT : exponer, exhibir **2** ~ **anger** : manifestar la ira — ~ *n* : muestra *f*, exposición *f*

displease [dɪs'pliːz] *vt* **-pleased; -pleasing** : desagradar — **displeasure** [dɪs'pleʒər] *n* : desagrado *m*

dispose [dɪs'poːz] *v* **-posed; -posing** *vt* : disponer — *vi* ~ **of** : deshacerse de — **disposable** [dɪs'poːzəbəl] *adj* : desechable — **disposal** [dɪs'poːzəl] *n* **1** REMOVAL : eliminación *f* **2 have at one's** ~ : tener a su disposición — **disposition** [ˌdɪspə'zɪʃən] *n* **1** ARRANGEMENT : disposición *f* **2** TEMPERAMENT : temperamento *m*, carácter *m*

disprove [dɪs'pruːv] *vt* **-proved; -proving** : refutar

dispute [dɪs'pjuːt] *v* **-puted; -putting** *vt* QUESTION : cuestionar — *vi* ARGUE : discutir — ~ *n* : disputa *f*, conflicto *m*

disqualification [dɪsˌkwɑləfə'keɪʃən] *n* : descalificación *f* — **disqualify** [dɪs'kwɑlə,faɪ] *vt* **-fied; -fying** : descalificar

disregard [ˌdɪsrɪ'gɑrd] *vt* : ignorar, hacer caso omiso de — ~ *n* : indiferencia *f*

disrepair [ˌdɪsrɪ'pær] *n* : mal estado *m*

disreputable [dɪs'repjʊtəbəl] *adj* : de mala fama

disrespect [ˌdɪsrɪ'spekt] *n* : falta *f* de respeto — **disrespectful** [ˌdɪsrɪ'spektfəl] *adj* : irrespetuoso

disrupt [dɪs'rʌpt] *vt* : trastornar, perturbar — **disruption** [dɪs'rʌpʃən] *n* : trastorno *m*

dissatisfaction [dɪsˌsætəs'fækʃən] *n* : descontento *m* — **dissatisfied** [dɪs'sætəs,faɪd] *adj* : descontento

dissect [dɪ'sekt] *vt* : disecar

disseminate [dɪ'semə,neɪt] *vt* **-nated; -nating** : diseminar, difundir

dissent [dɪ'sent] *vi* : disentir — ~ *n* : disentimiento *m*

dissertation [ˌdɪsər'teɪʃən] THESIS : tesis *f*

disservice [dɪs'sərvɪs] *n* **do a** ~ **to** : no hacer justicia a

dissident ['dɪsədənt] *n* : disidente *mf*

dissimilar [dɪ'sɪmələr] *adj* : distinto

dissipate ['dɪsə,peɪt] *vt* **-pated; -pating** **1** DISPEL : disipar **2** SQUANDER : desperdiciar

dissolve [dɪ'zɑlv] *v* **-solved; -solving** *vt* : disolver — *vi* : disolverse

dissuade [dɪ'sweɪd] *vt* **-suaded; -suading** : disuadir

distance ['dɪstənts] *n* **1** : distancia *f* **2 in the** ~ : a lo lejos — **distant** ['dɪstənt] *adj* : distante

distaste [dɪs'teɪst] *n* : desagrado *m* — **distasteful** [dɪs'teɪstfəl] *adj* : desagradable

distend [dɪs'tend] *vt* : dilatar — *vi* : dilatarse

distill [dɪ'stɪl] *or Brit* **distil** *vt* **-tilled; -tilling** : destilar

distinct [dɪ'stɪŋkt] *adj* **1** DIFFERENT : distinto **2** CLEAR : claro — **distinction** [dɪ'stɪŋkʃən] *n* : distinción *f* — **distinctive** [dɪ'stɪŋktɪv] *adj* : distintivo

distinguish [dɪs'tɪŋgwɪʃ] *vt* : distinguir — **distinguished** [dɪs'tɪŋgwɪʃt] *adj* : distinguido

distort [dɪ'stɔrt] *vt* : deformar, distorsionar — **distortion** [dɪ'stɔrʃən] *n* : deformación *f*

distract [dɪ'strækt] *vt* : distraer — **distraction** [dɪ'strækʃən] *n* : distracción *f*

distraught [dɪ'strɔt] *adj* : muy afligido

distress [dɪ'stres] *n* **1** : angustia *f*, aflicción *f* **2 in** ~ : en peligro — ~ *vt*

: afligir — **distressing** [dɪ'stresɪŋ] *adj*
: penoso
distribute [dɪ'strɪ,bju:t, -bjut] *vt* **-uted;**
-uting : distribuir, repartir — **distribu-**
tion [,dɪstrə'bju:ʃən] *n* : distribución *f* —
distributor [dɪ'strɪbjutər] *n* : distribuidor *m*, -dora *f*
district ['dɪs,trɪkt] *n* **1** REGION : región *f*,
zona *f*, barrio *m* (de una ciudad) **2**
: distrito *m* (zona política)
distrust [dɪs'trʌst] *n* : desconfianza *f* —
∼ *vt* : desconfiar de
disturb [dɪ'stərb] *vt* **1** BOTHER : molestar,
perturbar **2** WORRY : inquietar — **dis-**
turbance [dɪ'stərbənts] *n* **1** COMMOTION
: alboroto *m*, disturbio *m* **2** INTERRUP-
TION : interrupción *f*
disuse [dɪs'ju:s] *n* fall into ∼ : caer en
desuso
ditch ['dɪtʃ] *n* : zanja *f*, cuneta *f* — ∼ *vt*
DISCARD : deshacerse de, botar
ditto ['dɪ,to:] *n, pl* **-tos 1** : ídem *m* **2** ∼
marks : comillas *fpl*
dive ['daɪv] *vi* **dived** *or* **dove** ['do:v];
dived; diving 1 : zambullirse, tirarse
al agua **2** DESCEND : bajar en picada
(dícese de un avión, etc.) — ∼ *n* **1**
: zambullida *f*, clavado *m* Lat **2** DE-
SCENT : descenso *m* en picada — **diver**
['daɪvər] *n* : saltador *m*, -dora *f*
diverge [də'vərdʒ, daɪ-] *vi* **-verged;**
-verging : divergir
diverse [daɪ'vərs, də-, 'daɪ,vərs] *adj* : diverso — **diversify** [daɪ'vərsə,faɪ, də-] *v*
-fied; -fying *vt* : diversificar — *vi* : di-
versificarse
diversion [daɪ'vərʒən, də-] *n* **1**
: desviación *f* **2** AMUSEMENT : diversión *f*, distracción *f*
diversity [daɪ'vərsəti, də-] *n, pl* **-ties**
: diversidad *f*
divert [də'vərt, daɪ-] *vt* **1** : desviar **2** DIS-
TRACT : distraer **3** AMUSE : divertir
divide [də'vaɪd] *v* **-vided; -viding** *vt* : dividir — *vi* : dividirse
dividend ['dɪvə,dend, -dənd] *n* : dividendo *m*
divine [də'vaɪn] *adj* **-viner; -est** : divino
— **divinity** [də'vɪnəti] *n, pl* **-ties** : divinidad *f*
division [dɪ'vɪʒən] *n* : división *f*
divorce [də'vors] *n* : divorcio *m* — ∼ *v*
-vorced; -vorcing *vt* : divorciar — *vi*
: divorciarse — **divorcée** [dɪ,vor'seɪ,
-'si:; -'vor,-] *n* : divorciada *f*
divulge [də'vʌldʒ, daɪ-] *vt* **-vulged;**
-vulging : revelar, divulgar
dizzy ['dɪzi] *adj* **dizzier; -est 1** : mareado **2 a** ∼ **speed** : una velocidad ver-

tiginosa — **dizziness** ['dɪzinəs] *n*
: mareo *m*, vértigo *m*
DNA [,di:,ɛn'eɪ] *n* : AND *m*
do ['du:] *v* **did** ['dɪd]; **done** ['dʌn]; **doing;**
does ['dʌz] *vt* **1** : hacer **2** PREPARE
: preparar — *vi* **1** BEHAVE : hacer **2**
FARE : estar, ir, andar **3** SUFFICE : ser
suficiente **4** ∼ **away with** : abolir,
eliminar **5 how are you doing?**
: ¿cómo estás? — *v aux* **1** (*used in in-*
terrogative sentences) **do you know**
her? : ¿la conoces? **2** (*used in nega-*
tive statements) **I don't know** : yo no
se **3** (*used as a substitute verb to*
avoid repetition) **do you speak Eng-**
lish? yes, I do : ¿habla inglés? sí
dock ['dak] *n* : muelle *m* — ∼ *vt* : descontar dinero de (un sueldo) — *vi*
ANCHOR : fondear, atracar
doctor ['daktər] *n* **1** : doctor *m*, -tora *f*
(en derecho, etc.) **2** PHYSICIAN : médi-
co *m*, -ca; doctor *m*, -tora *f* — ∼ *vt*
ALTER : alterar, falsificar
doctrine ['daktrɪn] *n* : doctrina *f*
document ['dakjumənt] *n* : documento
m — ∼ ['dakju,ment] *vt* : documentar
— **documentary** [,dakju'mentəri] *n, pl*
-ries : documental *m*
dodge ['dadʒ] *n* : artimaña *f*, truco *m* —
∼ *v* **dodged; dodging** *vt* : esquivar,
eludir — *vi* : echarse a un lado
doe ['do:] *n, pl* **does** *or* **doe** : gama *f*,
cierva *f*
does → **do**
dog ['dɔg, 'dag] *n* : perro *m*, -rra *f* — ∼
vt **dogged; dogging** : perseguir —
dogged ['dɔgəd] *adj* : tenaz
dogma ['dɔgmə] *n* : dogma *m* — **dog-**
matic [dɔg'mætɪk] *adj* : dogmático
doily ['dɔɪli] *n, pl* **-lies** : tapete *m*
doings ['du:ɪŋz] *npl* : actividades *fpl*
doldrums ['do:ldrəmz, 'dal-] *npl* **be in**
the ∼ : estar abatido
dole ['do:l] *n* : subsidio *m* de desempleo
— ∼ *vt* **doled; doling** *or* ∼ **out**
: repartir
doleful ['do:lfəl] *adj* : triste, lúgubre
doll ['dal, 'dɔl] *n* : muñeco *m*, -ca *f*
dollar ['dalər] *n* : dólar *m*
dolphin ['dalfən, 'dɔl-] *n* : delfín *m*
domain [do'meɪn, də-] *n* **1** TERRITORY
: dominio *m* **2** FIELD : campo *m*, esfera
f
dome ['do:m] *n* : cúpula *f*
domestic [də'mestɪk] *adj* **1** : doméstico
2 INTERNAL : nacional — ∼ *n* SERVANT
: empleado *m* doméstico, empleada *f*
doméstica — **domesticate** [də'mestɪ-
,keɪt] *vt* **-cated; -cating** : domesticar
domination [,dɑmə'neɪʃən] *n* : domi-

nación *f* — **dominant** ['dɑmənənt] *adj* : dominante — **dominate** ['dɑmə,neɪt] *v* **-nated; -nating** : dominar — **domineer** [,dɑmə'nɪr] *vi* : dominar, tiranizar

dominos ['dɑmə,noːz] *n* : dominó *m* (juego)

donate ['doː,neɪt, doː'-] *vt* **-nated; -nating** : donar, hacer un donativo de — **donation** [doː'neɪʃən] *n* : donativo *m*

done ['dʌn] → **do** — *adj* **1** FINISHED : terminado, hecho **2** COOKED : cocido

donkey ['dɑŋki, 'dʌŋ-] *n, pl* **-keys** : burro *m*

donor ['doːnər] *n* : donante *mf*

don't ['doːnt] (*contraction of* **do not**) → **do**

doodle ['duːdəl] *v* **-dled; -dling** : garabatear — ~ *n* : garabato *m*

doom ['duːm] *n* : perdición *f*, fatalidad *f* — ~ *vt* : condenar

door ['dor] *n* **1** : puerta *f* **2** ENTRANCE : entrada *f* — **doorbell** ['dor,bɛl] *n* : timbre *m* — **doorknob** ['dor,nɑb] *n* : pomo *m* — **doorman** ['dormən] *n, pl* **-men** [-mən, -,mɛn] : portero *m* — **doormat** ['dor,mæt] *n* : felpudo *m* — **doorstep** ['dor,stɛp] *n* : umbral *m* — **doorway** ['dor,weɪ] *n* : entrada *f*, portal *m*

dope ['doːp] *n* **1** DRUG : droga *f* **2** IDIOT : idiota *mf* — ~ *vt* **doped; doping** : drogar

dormant ['dormənt] *adj* : inactivo, latente

dormitory ['dormə,tori] *n, pl* **-ries** : dormitorio *m*

dose ['doːs] *n* : dosis *f* — **dosage** ['doːsɪdʒ] *n* : dosis *f*

dot ['dɑt] *n* **1** : punto *m* **2 on the** ~ : en punto

dote ['doːt] *vi* **doted; doting** ~ **on** : adorar

double ['dʌbəl] *adj* : doble — ~ *v* **-bled; -bling** *vt* : doblar — *vi* : doblarse — ~ *adv* : (el) doble — ~ *n* : doble *mf* — **double bass** *n* : contrabajo *m* — **double-cross** [,dʌbəl'krɔs] *vt* : traicionar — **doubly** ['dʌbli] *adv* : doblemente

doubt ['daʊt] *vt* **1** : dudar **2** DISTRUST : desconfiar de, dudar de — ~ *n* : duda *f* — **doubtful** ['daʊtfəl] *adj* : dudoso — **doubtless** ['daʊtləs] *adv* : sin duda

dough ['doː] *n* : masa *f* — **doughnut** ['doː,nʌt] *n* : rosquilla *f*, dona *f Lat*

douse ['daʊs, 'daʊz] *vt* **doused; dousing 1** DRENCH : empapar, mojar **2** EXTINGUISH : apagar

dove[1] ['dʌv] → **dive**

dove[2] ['dʌv] *n* : paloma *f*

dowdy ['daʊdi] *adj* **dowdier; -est** : poco elegante

down ['daʊn] *adv* **1** DOWNWARD : hacia abajo **2 come/go** ~ : bajar **3** ~ **here** : aquí abajo **4 fall** ~ : caer **5 lie** ~ : acostarse **6 sit** ~ : sentarse — ~ *prep* **1** ALONG : a lo largo de **2** THROUGH : a través de **3** ~ **the hill** : cuesta abajo — ~ *adj* **1** DESCENDING : de bajada **2** DOWNCAST : abatido — ~ *n* : plumón *m* — **downcast** ['daʊn,kæst] *adj* : triste, abatido — **downfall** ['daʊn,fɔl] *n* : ruina *f* — **downhearted** ['daʊn,hɑrtəd] *adj* : desanimado — **downhill** ['daʊn,hɪl] *adv & adj* : cuesta abajo — **down payment** *n* : entrega *f* inicial — **downpour** ['daʊn,por] *n* : chaparrón *m* — **downright** ['daʊn,raɪt] *adv* : absolutamente — ~ *adj* : absoluto, categórico — **downstairs** ['daʊn,stærz] *adv* : abajo — ~ ['daʊn,stærz] *adj* : de abajo — **downstream** ['daʊn,striːm] *adv* : río abajo — **down-to-earth** [,daʊntu'ərθ] *adj* : realista — **downtown** [,daʊn'taʊn, 'daʊn,taʊn] *n* : centro *m* (de la ciudad) — ~ [,daʊn'taʊn] *adv* : al centro, en el centro — ~ *adj* : del centro — **downward** ['daʊnwərd] *or* **downwards** [-wərdz] *adv & adj* : hacia abajo

dowry ['daʊri] *n, pl* **-ries** : dote *f*

doze ['doːz] *vi* **dozed; dozing** : dormitar

dozen ['dʌzən] *n, pl* **dozens** *or* **dozen** : docena *f*

drab ['dræb] *adj* **drabber; drabbest** : monótono, apagado

draft ['dræft, 'draft] *n* **1** : corriente *f* de aire **2** *or* **rough** ~ : borrador *m* **3** : conscripción *f* (military) **4** *or* ~ **beer** : cerveza *f* de barril — ~ *vt* **1** SKETCH : hacer el borrador de **2** CONSCRIPT : reclutar — **drafty** ['dræfti] *adj* **draftier; -est** : con corrientes de aire

drag ['dræg] *v* **dragged; dragging** *vt* **1** : arrastrar **2** DREDGE : dragar — *vi* : arrastrar(se) — ~ *n* **1** RESISTANCE : resistencia *f* (aerodinámica) **2** BORE : pesadez *f*, plomo *m fam*

dragon ['drægən] *n* : dragón *m* — **dragonfly** ['drægən,flaɪ] *n, pl* **-flies** : libélula *f*

drain ['dreɪn] *vt* **1** EMPTY : vaciar, drenar **2** EXHAUST : agotar — *vi* **1** : escurrir(se) (se dice de los platos) **2** *or* ~ **away** : desaparecer poco a poco — ~ *n* **1** : desagüe *m* **2** SEWER : alcantarilla *f* **3** DEPLETION : agotamiento *m* — **drainage** ['dreɪnɪdʒ] *n* : drenaje *m* — **drainpipe** ['dreɪn,paɪp] *n* : tubo *m* de desagüe

drama ['drɑmə, 'dræ-] *n* : drama *m* —

dramatic [drə'mætɪk] *adj* : dramático — **dramatist** ['dræmətɪst, 'drɑ-] *n* : dramaturgo *m*, -ga *f* — **dramatize** ['dræmə,taɪz, 'drɑ-] *vt* **-tized; -tizing** : dramatizar

drank → **drink**

drape ['dreɪp] *vt* **draped; draping 1** COVER : cubrir (con tela) **2** HANG : drapear — **drapes** *npl* CURTAINS : cortinas *fpl*

drastic ['dræstɪk] *adj* : drástico

draught ['dræft, 'draft] → **draft**

draw ['drɔ] *v* **drew** ['druː]; **drawn** ['drɔn]; **drawing** *vt* **1** PULL : tirar de **2** ATTRACT : atraer **3** SKETCH : dibujar, trazar **4** : sacar (una espada, etc.) **5** ~ **a conclusion** : llegar a una conclusión **6** ~ **up** DRAFT : redactar — *vi* **1** SKETCH : dibujar **2** ~ **near** : acercarse — ~ *n* **1** DRAWING : sorteo *m* **2** TIE : empate *m* **3** ATTRACTION : atracción *f* — **drawback** ['drɔ,bæk] *n* : desventaja *f* — **drawer** ['drɔr, 'drɔər] *n* : gaveta *f*, cajón *m* (en un mueble) — **drawing** ['drɔɪŋ] *n* **1** LOTTERY : sorteo *m* **2** SKETCH : dibujo *m*

drawl ['drɔl] *n* : habla *f* lenta y con vocales prolongadas

dread ['drɛd] *vt* : temer — ~ *n* : pavor *m*, temor *m* — **dreadful** ['drɛdfəl] *adj* : espantoso, terrible

dream ['driːm] *n* : sueño *m* — ~ *v* **dreamed** ['drɛmt, 'driːmd] *or* **dreamt** ['drɛmt]; **dreaming** *vi* : soñar — *vt* **1** : soñar **2** ~ **up** : idear — **dreamer** ['driːmər] *n* : soñador *m*, -dora *f* — **dreamy** ['driːmi] *adj* **dreamier; -est** : soñador

dreary ['drɪri] *adj* **-rier; -est** : sombrío, deprimente

dredge ['drɛdʒ] *vt* **dredged; dredging** : dragar — ~ *n* : draga *f*

dregs ['drɛgz] *npl* : heces *fpl*

drench ['drɛntʃ] *vt* : empapar

dress ['drɛs] *vt* **1** : vestir **2** : preparar (pollo o pescado), aliñar (ensalada) — *vi* **1** : vestirse **2** ~ **up** : ponerse elegante — ~ *n* **1** CLOTHING : ropa *f* **2** : vestido *m* (de mujer) — **dresser** ['drɛsər] *n* : cómoda *f* con espejo — **dressing** ['drɛsɪŋ] *n* **1** : aliño *m* (de ensalada), relleno *m* (de pollo) **2** BANDAGE : vendaje *m* — **dressmaker** ['drɛs,meɪkər] *n* : modista *mf* — **dressy** ['drɛsi] *adj* **dressier; -est** : elegante

drew → **draw**

dribble ['drɪbəl] *vi* **-bled; -bling 1** DRIP : gotear **2** DROOL : babear **3** : driblar (en basquetbol) — ~ *n* **1** TRICKLE : goteo *m*, hilo *m* **2** DROOL : baba *f*

drier, driest → **dry**

drift ['drɪft] *n* **1** MOVEMENT : movimiento *m* **2** HEAP : montón *m* (de arena, etc.), ventisquero *m* (de nieve) **3** MEANING : sentido *m* — ~ *vi* **1** : ir a la deriva **2** ACCUMULATE : amontonarse

drill ['drɪl] *n* **1** : taladro *m* **2** : ejercicio *m* (en educación), simulacro *m* (de incendio, etc.) — ~ *vt* **1** : perforar, taladrar **2** TRAIN : instruir por repetición — *vi* ~ **for** : perforar en busca de

drink ['drɪŋk] *v* **drank** ['dræŋk]; **drunk** ['drʌŋk] *or* **drank; drinking** : beber — ~ *n* : bebida *f*

drip ['drɪp] *vi* **dripped; dripping** : gotear — ~ *n* **1** DROP : gota *f* **2** DRIPPING : goteo *m*

drive ['draɪv] *v* **drove** ['droːv]; **driven** ['drɪvən]; **driving** *vt* **1** : manejar **2** IMPEL : impulsar **3** ~ **crazy** : volver loco **4** ~ **s.o. to (do sth)** : llevar a algn a (hacer algo) — *vi* : manejar, conducir — ~ *n* **1** : paseo *m* (en coche) **2** CAMPAIGN : campaña *f* **3** VIGOR : energía *f* **4** NEED : instinto *m* — **drivel** ['drɪvəl] *n* : tonterías *fpl* — **driver** ['draɪvər] *n* : conductor *m*, -tora *f*; chofer *m* — **driveway** ['draɪv,weɪ] *n* : camino *m* de entrada

drizzle ['drɪzəl] *n* : llovizna *f* — ~ *vi* **-zled; -zling** : lloviznar

drone ['droːn] *n* **1** BEE : zángano *m* **2** HUM : zumbido *m* — ~ *vi* **droned; droning 1** BUZZ : zumbar **2** *or* ~ **on** : hablar con monotonía

drool ['druːl] *vi* : babear — ~ *n* : baba *f*

droop ['druːp] *vi* : inclinarse (dícese de la cabeza), encorvarse (dícese de los escombros), marchitarse (dícese de las flores)

drop ['drɑp] *n* **1** : gota *f* (de líquido) **2** DECLINE, FALL : caída *f* — ~ *v* **dropped; dropping** *vt* **1** : dejar caer **2** LOWER : bajar **3** ABANDON : abandonar, dejar **4** ~ **off** LEAVE : dejar — *vi* **1** FALL : caer(se) **2** DECREASE : bajar, descender **3** ~ **by** *or* ~ **in** : pasar

drought ['draut] *n* : sequía *f*

drove → **drive**

droves ['droːvz] *n* **in** ~ : en manada

drown ['draun] *vt* : ahogar — *vi* : ahogarse

drowsy ['drauzi] *adj* **drowsier; -est** : somnoliento

drudgery ['drʌdʒəri] *n, pl* **-eries** : trabajo *m* pesado

drug ['drʌg] *n* **1** MEDICATION : medicamento *m* **2** NARCOTIC : droga *f*, estupefaciente *m* — ~ *vt* **drugged; drugging** : drogar — **drugstore** ['drʌg,stor] *n* : farmacia *f*

drum ['drʌm] n 1 : tambor m 2 or **oil ~** : bidón m (de petróleo) — ~ v **drummed; drumming** vi : tocar el tambor — vt : tamborilear con (los dedos, etc.) — **drumstick** ['drʌm,stɪk] n 1 : palillo m (de tambor) 2 : muslo m (de pollo)

drunk ['drʌŋk] → **drink** — ~ adj : borracho — ~ or **drunkard** ['drʌŋkərd] n : borracho m, -cha f — **drunken** ['drʌŋkən] adj : borracho, ebrio

dry ['draɪ] adj **drier; driest** : seco — ~ v **dried; drying** vt : secar — vi : secarse — **dry-clean** ['draɪ,kliːn] vt : limpiar en seco — **dry cleaner** n : tintorería f (servicio) — **dry cleaning** n : limpieza f en seco — **dryer** ['draɪər] n : secadora f — **dryness** ['draɪnəs] n : sequedad f, aridez f

dual ['duːəl, 'djuː-] adj : doble

dub ['dʌb] vt **dubbed; dubbing** 1 CALL : apodar 2 : doblar (una película)

dubious ['duːbiəs, 'djuː-] adj 1 UNCERTAIN : dudoso 2 QUESTIONABLE : sospechoso

duchess ['dʌtʃəs] n : duquesa f

duck ['dʌk] n, pl **duck** or **ducks** : pato m, -ta f — ~ vt 1 LOWER : agachar, bajar 2 EVADE : eludir, esquivar — vi : agacharse — **duckling** ['dʌklɪŋ] n : patito m, -ta f

duct ['dʌkt] n : conducto m

due ['duː, 'djuː] adj 1 PAYABLE : pagadero 2 APPROPRIATE : debido, apropiado 3 EXPECTED : esperado 4 **~ to** : debido a — ~ n 1 **give s.o. their ~** : hacer justicia a algn 2 **~s** npl : cuota f — ~ adv **~ east** : justo al este

duel ['duːəl, 'djuː-] n : duelo m

duet ['duːet, djuː-] n : dúo m

dug → **dig**

duke ['duːk, 'djuːk] n : duque m

dull ['dʌl] adj 1 STUPID : torpe 2 BLUNT : desafilado 3 BORING : aburrido 4 LACKLUSTER : apagado — ~ vt : entorpecer (los sentidos), aliviar (el dolor)

dumb ['dʌm] adj 1 MUTE : mudo 2 STUPID : estúpido

dumbfound or **dumfound** [,dʌm'faʊnd] vt : dejar sin habla

dummy ['dʌmi] n, pl **-mies** 1 SHAM : imitación f 2 MANNEQUIN : maniquí m 3 IDIOT : tonto m, -ta f

dump ['dʌmp] vt : descargar, verter — ~ n 1 : vertedero m, tiradero m Lat 2 **down in the ~s** : triste, deprimido

dumpling ['dʌmplɪŋ] n : bola f de masa hervida

dumpy ['dʌmpi] adj **dumpier; -est** : regordete

dunce ['dʌnts] n : burro m, -rra f fam

dune ['duːn, 'djuːn] n : duna f

dung ['dʌŋ] n 1 : excrementos mpl 2 MANURE : estiércol m

dungarees [,dʌŋɡə'riːz] npl JEANS : vaqueros mpl, jeans mpl

dungeon ['dʌndʒən] n : calabozo m

dunk ['dʌŋk] vt : mojar

duo ['duːoː, 'djuː-] n, pl **duos** : dúo m

dupe ['duːp, 'djuːp] vt **duped; duping** : engañar — ~ n : inocentón m, -tona f

duplex ['duː,pleks, 'djuː-] n : casa f de dos viviendas, dúplex m

duplicate ['duː,plɪkət, 'djuː-] adj : duplicado — ~ ['duː,plɪkeɪt, 'djuː-] vt **-cated; -cating** : duplicar, hacer copias de — ~ ['duː,plɪkət, 'djuː-] n : duplicado m, copia f

durable ['dʊrəbəl, 'djʊr-] adj : duradero

duration [dʊ'reɪʃən, dju-] n : duración f

duress [dʊ'res, dju-] n : coacción f

during ['dʊrɪŋ, 'djʊr-] prep : durante

dusk ['dʌsk] n : anochecer m, crepúsculo m

dust ['dʌst] n : polvo m — ~ vt 1 : quitar el polvo a 2 SPRINKLE : espolvorear — **dustpan** ['dʌst,pæn] n : recogedor m — **dusty** ['dʌsti] adj **dustier; -est** : polvoriento

Dutch ['dʌtʃ] adj : holandés — ~ n 1 : holandés m (idioma) 2 **the ~** : los holandeses

duty ['duːti, 'djuː-] n, pl **-ties** 1 OBLIGATION : deber m 2 TAX : impuesto m 3 **on ~** : de servicio — **dutiful** ['duːtɪfəl, 'djuː-] adj : obediente

dwarf ['dwɔrf] n, pl **dwarfs** ['dwɔrfs] or **dwarves** ['dwɔrvz] : enano m, -na f — ~ vt : hacer parecer pequeño

dwell ['dwel] vi **dwelled** or **dwelt** ['dwelt]; **dwelling** 1 RESIDE : morar, vivir 2 **~ on** : pensar demasiado en — **dweller** ['dwelər] n : habitante mf — **dwelling** ['dwelɪŋ] n : morada f, vivienda f

dwindle ['dwɪndəl] vi **-dled; -dling** : disminuir

dye ['daɪ] n : tinte m — ~ vt **dyed; dyeing** : teñir

dying → **die**[1]

dynamic [daɪ'næmɪk] adj : dinámico

dynamite ['daɪnə,maɪt] n : dinamita f

dynamo ['daɪnə,moː] n, pl **-mos** : dínamo m

dynasty ['daɪnəsti, -,næs-] n, pl **-ties** : dinastía f

dysentery ['dɪsən,teri] n, pl **-teries** : disentería f

E

e ['iː] *n, pl* **e's** *or* **es** ['iːz] : e *f*, quinta letra del alfabeto inglés

each ['iːtʃ] *adj* : cada — *pron* **1** : cada uno *m*, cada una *f* **2** ~ **other** : el uno al otro **3 they hate** ~ **other** : se odian — ~ *adv* : cada uno, por persona

eager ['iːgər] *adj* **1** ENTHUSIASTIC : entusiasta **2** IMPATIENT : impaciente — **eagerness** ['iːgərnəs] *n* : entusiasmo *m*, impaciencia *f*

eagle ['iːgəl] *n* : águila *f*

ear ['ɪr] *n* **1** : oreja *f* **2** ~ **of corn** : mazorca *f*, choclo *m* *Lat* — **eardrum** ['ɪr,drʌm] *n* : tímpano *m*

earl ['ərl] *n* : conde *m*

earlobe ['ɪr,loːb] *n* : lóbulo *m* de la oreja

early ['ərli] *adv* **earlier; -est 1** : temprano **2 as** ~ **as possible** : lo más pronto posible **3 ten minutes** ~ : diez minutos de adelanto — ~ *adj* **earlier; -est 1** FIRST : primero **2** ANCIENT : primitivo, antiguo **3 an** ~ **death** : una muerte prematura **4 be** ~ : llegar temprano **5 in the** ~ **spring** : a principios de la primavera

earmark ['ɪr,mɑrk] *vt* : destinar

earn ['ərn] *vt* **1** : ganar **2** DESERVE : merecer

earnest ['ərnəst] *adj* : serio — ~ *n* **in** ~ : en serio

earnings ['ərnɪŋz] *npl* **1** WAGES : ingresos *mpl* **2** PROFITS : ganancias *fpl*

earphone ['ɪr,foːn] *n* : audífono *m*

earring ['ɪr,rɪŋ] *n* : pendiente *m*, arete *m* *Lat*

earshot ['ɪr,ʃɑt] *n* **within** ~ : al alcance del oído

earth ['ərθ] *n* **1** : tierra *f* — **earthenware** ['ərθən,wær, -ðən-] *n* : loza *f* — **earthly** ['ərθli] *adj* : terrenal — **earthquake** ['ərθ,kweɪk] *n* : terremoto *m* — **earthworm** ['ərθ,wərm] *n* : lombriz *f* (de tierra) — **earthy** ['ərθi] *adj* **earthier; -est 1** : terroso **2** COARSE, CRUDE : grosero

ease ['iːz] *n* **1** FACILITY : facilidad *f* **2** COMFORT : comodidad *f* **3 feel at** ~ : sentir cómodo — ~ *v* **eased; easing 1** ALLEVIATE : aliviar, calmar **2** FACILITATE : facilitar — *vi* **1** : calmarse **2** ~ **up** : disminuir

easel ['iːzəl] *n* : caballete *m*

easily ['iːzəli] *adv* **1** : fácilmente, con facilidad **2** UNQUESTIONABLY : con mucho, de lejos *Lat*

east ['iːst] *adv* : al este — ~ *adj* : este, del este — ~ *n* **1** : este *m* **2 the East** : el Oriente

Easter ['iːstər] *n* : Pascua *f*

easterly ['iːstərli] *adv & adj* : del este

eastern ['iːstərn] *adj* **1** : del este **2 Eastern** : oriental, del este

easy ['iːzi] *adj* **easier; -est 1** : fácil **2** RELAXED : relajado — **easygoing** [,iːzi'goːɪŋ] *adj* : tolerante, relajado

eat ['iːt] *v* **ate** ['eɪt]; **eaten** ['iːtən]; **eating** *vt* : comer — *vi* **1** : comer **2** ~ **into** CORRODE : corroer **3** ~ **into** DEPLETE : comerse — **eatable** ['iːtəbəl] *adj* : comestible

eaves ['iːvz] *npl* : alero *m* — **eavesdrop** ['iːvz,drɑp] *vi* -**dropped; -dropping** : escuchar a escondidas

ebb ['ɛb] *n* : reflujo *m* — ~ *vi* **1** : bajar (dícese de la marea) **2** DECLINE : decaer

ebony ['ɛbəni] *n, pl* -**nies** : ébano *m*

eccentric [ɪk'sɛntrɪk] *adj* : excéntrico — ~ *n* : excéntrico *m*, -ca *f* — **eccentricity** [,ɛksən'trɪsəti] *n, pl* -**ties** : excentricidad *f*

echo ['ɛ,koː] *n, pl* **echoes** : eco *m* — ~ *v* **echoed; echoing** *vt* : repetir — *vi* : hacer eco, resonar

eclipse [ɪ'klɪps] *n* : eclipse *m* — ~ *vt* **eclipsed; eclipsing** : eclipsar

ecology [i'kɑlədʒi, ɛ-] *n, pl* -**gies** : ecología *f* — **ecological** *adj* [,iːkə'lɑdʒɪkəl, ,ɛkə-] : ecológico

economy [i'kɑnəmi] *n, pl* -**mies** : economía *f* — **economic** [,iːkə'nɑmɪk, ,ɛkə-] *or* **economical** [,iːkə'nɑmɪkəl, ,ɛkə-] *adj* : económico — **economics** [,iːkə'nɑmɪks, ,ɛkə-] *n* : economía *f* — **economist** [i'kɑnəmɪst] *n* : economista *mf* — **economize** [i'kɑnə,maɪz] *v* -**mized; -mizing** : economizar

ecstasy ['ɛkstəsi] *n, pl* -**sies** : éxtasis *m* — **ecstatic** [ɛk'stætɪk, ɪk-] *adj* : extático

Ecuadoran [,ɛkwə'dorən] *or* **Ecuadorean** *or* **Ecuadorian** [,ɛkwə'doriən] *adj* : ecuatoriano

edge ['ɛdʒ] *n* **1** BORDER : borde *m* **2** : filo *m* (de un cuchillo) **3** ADVANTAGE : ventaja *f* — ~ *v* **edged; edging** *vt* : bordear, ribetear — *vi* : avanzar poco a poco — **edgewise** ['edʒwaız] *adv* : de lado — **edgy** ['edʒi] *adj* **edgier; -est** : nervioso

edible ['edəbəl] *adj* : comestible

edit ['edɪt] *vt* **1** : editar, redactar, corregir **2 — out** : suprimir, cortar — **edition** ['rdɪʃən] *n* : edición — **editor** ['edɪtər] *n* : director *m*, -tora *f* (de un periódico); redactor *m*, -tora *f* (de un libro) — **editorial** [,edɪ'toriəl] *n* : editorial *m*

educate ['edʒəˌkeɪt] *vt* **-cated; -cating 1** TEACH : educar, instruir **2** INFORM : informar — **education** [,edʒə'keɪʃən] *n* : educación — **educational** [,edʒə-'keɪʃənəl] *adj* **1** : educativo, instructivo **2** TEACHING : docente — **educator** ['edʒəˌkeɪtər] *n* : educador *m*, -dora *f*

eel ['i:l] *n* : anguila *f*

eerie ['ɪri] *adj* **-rier; -est** : extraño e inquietante, misterioso

effect [ɪ'fekt] *n* **1** : efecto *m* **2 go into —** : entrar en vigor — **~** *vt* : efectuar, llevar a cabo — **effective** [ɪ'fektɪv] *adj* **1** : eficaz **2** ACTUAL : efectivo, vigente — **effectiveness** [ɪ'fektɪvnəs] *n* : eficacia *f*

effeminate [ə'femənət] *adj* : afeminado

effervescent [,efər'vesənt] *adj* : efervescente

efficient [ɪ'fɪʃənt] *adj* : eficiente — **efficiency** [ɪ'fɪʃəntsi] *n*, *pl* **-cies** : eficiencia *f*

effort ['efərt] *n* **1** : esfuerzo *m* **2 it's not worth the ~** : no vale la pena — **effortless** ['efərtləs] *adj* : fácil, sin esfuerzo

egg ['eg] *n* : huevo *m* — **~** *vt* **~ on** : incitar — **eggplant** ['egˌplænt] *n* : berenjena *f* — **eggshell** ['egˌʃel] *n* : cascarón *m*

ego ['i:goː] *n*, *pl* **egos 1** SELF : ego *m*, yo *m* **2** SELF-ESTEEM : amor *m* propio — **egotism** ['i:gəˌtɪzəm] *n* : egotismo *m* — **egotist** ['i:gətɪst] *n* : egotista *mf* — **egotistic** [,i:gə'tɪstɪk] *or* **egotistical** [-'tɪstɪkəl] *adj* : egotista

eiderdown ['aɪdərˌdaʊn] *n* **1** DOWN : plumón *m* **2** COMFORTER : edredón *m*

eight ['eɪt] *n* : ocho *m* — **~** *adj* : ocho — **eight hundred** *n* : ochocientos *m*

eighteen [eɪt'ti:n] *n* : dieciocho *m* — **~** *adj* : dieciocho — **eighteenth** [eɪt-'ti:nθ] *adj* : decimoctavo — **~** *n* **1** : decimoctavo *m*, -va *f* (en una serie) **2** : dieciochoavo *m*, dieciochoava parte *f*

eighth ['eɪtθ] *n* **1** : octavo *m*, -va *f* (en una serie) **2** : octavo *m*, octava parte *f* — **~** *adj* : octavo

eighty ['eɪti] *n*, *pl* **eighties** : ochenta *m* — **~** *adj* : ochenta

either ['iːðər, 'aɪ-] *adj* **1** : cualquiera (de los dos) **2** (*in negative constructions*) : ninguno (de los dos) **3** EACH : cada — **~** *pron* **1** : cualquiera *mf* (de los dos) **2** (*in negative constructions*) : ninguno *m*, -na *f* (de los dos) **3** *or* **~ one** : algún *m*, alguna *f* — **~** *conj* **1** : o **2** (*in negative constructions*) : ni

eject [ɪ'dʒekt] *vt* : expulsar, expeler

eke ['i:k] *vt* **eked; eking** *or* **~ out** : ganar a duras penas

elaborate [ɪ'læbərət] *adj* **1** DETAILED : detallado **2** COMPLEX : complicado — **~** [ɪ'læbəˌreɪt] *v* **-rated; -rating** *vt* : elaborar — *vi* : entrar en detalles

elapse [ɪ'læps] *vi* **elapsed; elapsing** : transcurrir

elastic [ɪ'læstɪk] *adj* : elástico — **~** *n* **1** : elástico *m* **2** RUBBER BAND : goma *f* (elástica) — **elasticity** [ɪˌlæs'tɪsəti, ˌiːˌlæs-] *n*, *pl* **-ties** : elasticidad *f*

elated [ɪ'leɪtəd] *adj* : regocijado

elbow ['elˌboː] *n* : codo *m*

elder ['eldər] *adj* : mayor — **~** *n* **1** : mayor *mf* **2** : anciano *m*, -na *f* (de un tribu, etc.) — **elderly** ['eldərli] *adj* : mayor, anciano

elect [ɪ'lekt] *vt* : elegir — **~** *adj* : electo — **election** [ɪ'lekʃən] *n* : elección *f* — **electoral** [ɪ'lektərəl] *adj* : electoral — **electorate** [ɪ'lektərət] *n* : electorado *m*

electricity [ɪˌlek'trɪsəti] *n*, *pl* **-ties** : electricidad *f* — **electric** [ɪ'lektrɪk] *or* **electrical** [-trɪkəl] *adj* : eléctrico — **electrician** [ɪˌlek'trɪʃən] *n* : electricista *mf* — **electrify** [ɪ'lektrəˌfaɪ] *vt* **-fied; -fying** : electrificar — **electrocute** [ɪ'lektrəˌkjuːt] *vt* **-cuted; -cuting** : electrocutar

electron [ɪ'lektrɑn] *n* : electrón *m* — **electronic** [ɪˌlek'trɑnɪk] *adj* : electrónico — **electronic mail** *n* : correo *m* electrónico — **electronics** [ɪˌlek'trɑnɪks] *n* : electrónica *f*

elegant ['eləgənt] *adj* : elegante — **elegance** ['eləgənts] *n* : elegancia *f*

element ['eləmənt] *n* **1** : elemento *m* **2 ~s** *npl* BASICS : elementos *mpl*, rudimentos *mpl* — **elementary** [,elə'mentri] *adj* : elemental — **elementary school** *n* : escuela *f* primaria

elephant ['eləfənt] *n* : elefante *m*, -ta *f*

elevate ['eləˌveɪt] *vt* **-vated; -vating** : elevar — **elevator** ['eləˌveɪtər] *n* : ascensor *m*

eleven [ɪ'levən] *n* : once *m* — **~** *adj* : once — **eleventh** [ɪ'levənθ] *adj* : undécimo — **~** *n* **1** : undécimo *m*, -ma *f*

(en una serie) 2 : onceavo *m*, onceava
parte *f*
elf ['elf] *n, pl* **elves** ['elvz] : duende *m*
elicit [ɪ'lɪsət] *vt* : provocar
eligible ['eləʤəbəl] *adj* : elegible
eliminate [ɪ'lɪməˌneɪt] *vt* **-nated; -nating**
: eliminar — **elimination** [ɪˌlɪmə'neɪ-
ʃən] *n* : eliminación *f*
elite [eɪ'liːt, i-] *n* : elite *f*
elk ['elk] *n* : alce *m* (de Europa), uapití
m (de América)
elliptical [ɪ'lɪptɪkəl, ɛ-] *or* **elliptic** [-tɪk]
adj : elíptico
elm ['elm] *n* : olmo *m*
elongate [i'lɔŋgeɪt] *vt* **-gated; -gating**
: alargar
elope [i'loːp] *vi* **eloped; eloping** : fugarse — **elopement** [i'loːpmənt] *n*
: fuga *f*
eloquence ['eləkwənts] *n* : elocuencia *f*
— **eloquent** ['eləkwənt] *adj* : elocuente
else ['els] *adv* **1 how ~ ?** : ¿de qué otro
modo? **2 where ~ ?** : ¿en qué otro
sitio? **3 or ~** : si no, de lo contrario —
~ *adj* **1 everyone ~** : todos los
demás **2 nobody ~** : ningún otro,
nadie más **3 nothing ~** : nada más **4
what ~ ?** : ¿qué más? — **elsewhere**
['els,hwer] *adv* : en otra parte
elude [i'luːd] *vt* **eluded; eluding**
: eludir, esquivar — **elusive** [i'luːsɪv]
adj : esquivo
elves → elf
emaciated [i'meɪʃiˌeɪtəd] *adj* : esquáli-
do, demacrado
E—mail ['iˌmeɪl] → **electronic mail**
emanate ['eməˌneɪt] *vi* **-nated; -nating**
: emanar
emancipate [i'mæntsəˌpeɪt] *vt* **-pated;
-pating** : emancipar — **emancipation**
[iˌmæntsə'peɪʃən] *n* : emancipación *f*
embalm [ɪm'bɑm, ɛm-, -'bɑlm] *vt* : embalsamar
embankment [ɪm'bæŋkmənt, ɛm-] *n*
: terraplén *m*, dique *m* (de un río)
embargo [ɪm'bɑrgo, ɛm-] *n, pl* **-goes**
: embargo *m*
embark [ɪm'bɑrk, ɛm-] *vt* : embarcar —
vi **1** : embarcarse **2 ~ upon** : emprender — **embarkation** [ˌɛm,bɑr-
'keɪʃən] *n* : embarque *m*, embarco *f*
embarrass [ɪm'bærəs, ɛm-] *vt* : avergonzar — **embarrassing** [ɪm'bærəsɪŋ,
ɛm-] *adj* : embarazoso — **embarrassment** [ɪm'bærəsmənt, ɛm-] *n* : vergüenza *f*
embassy ['embəsi] *n, pl* **-sies** : embajada *f*
embed [ɪm'bed, ɛm-] *vt* **-bedded;
-bedding** : incrustar, enterrar

embellish [ɪm'belɪʃ, ɛm-] *vt* : adornar,
embellecer — **embellishment** [ɪm-
'belɪʃmənt, ɛm-] *n* : adorno *m*
embers ['embəz] *npl* : ascuas *fpl*
embezzle [ɪm'bezəl, ɛm-] *vt* **-zled;
-zling** : desfalcar, malversar — **embezzlement** [ɪm'bezəlmənt, ɛm-] *n*
: desfalco *m*, malversación *f*
emblem ['embləm] *n* : emblema *m*
embody [ɪm'bɑdi, ɛm-] *vt* **-bodied;
-bodying** : encarnar, personificar
emboss [ɪm'bɑs, ɛm-, -'bɔs] *vt* : repujar,
grabar en relieve
embrace [ɪm'breɪs, ɛm-] *v* **-braced;
-bracing** *vt* : abrazar — *vi* : abrazarse
— **~** *n* : abrazo *m*
embroider [ɪm'brɔɪdər, ɛm-] *vt* : bordar
— **embroidery** [ɪm'brɔɪdəri, ɛm-] *n, pl*
-deries : bordado *m*
embryo ['embriˌoː] *n, pl* **embryos** : embrión *m*
emerald ['emrəld, 'emə-] *n* : esmeralda *f*
emerge [i'mərʤ] *vi* **emerged; emerg-
ing** : salir, aparecer — **emergence**
[i'mərʤənts] *n* : aparición *f*
emergency [i'mərʤəntsi] *n, pl* **-cies 1**
: emergencia *f* **2 ~ exit** : salida *f* de
emergencia **3 ~ room** : sala *f* de ur-
gencias, sala *f* de guardia
emery ['eməri] *n, pl* **-eries 1** : esmeril *m*
2 ~ board : lima *f* de uñas
emigrant ['emigrənt] *n* : emigrante *mf*
— **emigrate** ['eməˌgreɪt] *vi* **-grated;
-grating** : emigrar — **emigration**
[ˌeməˈgreɪʃən] *n* : emigración *f*
eminence ['emənənts] *n* : eminencia *f* —
eminent ['emənənt] *adj* : eminente
emission [i'mɪʃən] *n* : emisión *f* — **emit**
[i'mɪt] *vt* **emitted; emitting** : emitir
emotion [i'moːʃən] *n* : emoción *f* —
emotional [i'moːʃənəl] *adj* **1** : emocional **2** MOVING : emotivo
emperor ['empərər] *n* : emperador *m*
emphasis ['emfəsɪs] *n, pl* **-phases**
[-ˌsiːz] : énfasis *m* — **emphasize** ['em-
fəˌsaɪz] *vt* **-sized; -sizing** : subrayar,
hacer hincapié en — **emphatic** [ɪm-
'fætɪk, ɛm-] *adj* : enérgico, categórico
empire ['emˌpaɪr] *n* : imperio *m*
employ [ɪm'plɔɪ, ɛm-] *vt* : emplear —
employee [ɪmˌplɔɪˈiː, ɛm-, -'plɔɪˌiː] *n*
: empleado *m*, -da *f* — **employer** [ɪm-
'plɔɪər, ɛm-] *n* : patrón *m*, -trona *f*; empleador *m*, -dora *f* — **employment**
[ɪm'plɔɪmənt, ɛm-] *n* : trabajo *m*, empleo *m*
empower [ɪm'paʊər, ɛm-] *vt* : autorizar
empress ['emprəs] *n* : emperatriz *f*
empty ['empti] *adj* **emptier; -est 1**
: vacío **2** MEANINGLESS : vano — **~** *v*

-tied; -tying *vt* : vaciar — *vi* : vaciarse — **emptiness** ['emptinəs] *n* : vacío *m*

emulate ['emjəˌleɪt] *vt* **-lated; -lating** : emular

enable [ɪˈneɪbəl, ε-] *vt* **-abled; -abling** : hacer posible, permitir

enact [ɪˈnækt, ε-] *vt* **1** : promulgar (un ley o un decreto) **2** PERFORM : representar

enamel [ɪˈnæməl] *n* : esmalte *m*

encampment [ɪnˈkæmpmənt, εn-] *n* : campamento *m*

encase [ɪnˈkeɪs, εn-] *vt* **-cased; -casing** : encerrar, revestir

enchant [ɪnˈtʃænt, εn-] *vt* : encantar — **enchanting** [ɪnˈtʃæntɪŋ, εn-] *adj* : encantador — **enchantment** [ɪnˈtʃæntmənt, εn-] *n* : encanto *m*

encircle [ɪnˈsərkəl, εn-] *vt* **-cled; -cling** : rodear

enclose [ɪnˈkloːz, εn-] *vt* **-closed; -closing 1** SURROUND : encerrar, cercar **2** INCLUDE : adjuntar (a una carta) — **enclosure** [ɪnˈkloːʒər, εn-] *n* **1** AREA : recinto *m* **2** : anexo *m* (con una carta)

encompass [ɪnˈkʌmpəs, εn-, -ˈkɑm-] *vt* **1** ENCIRCLE : cercar **2** INCLUDE : abarcar

encore [ˈɑnˌkor] *n* : bis *m*

encounter [ɪnˈkaʊntər, εn-] *vt* : encontrar — *~ n* : encuentro *m*

encourage [ɪnˈkərɪdʒ, εn-] *vt* **-aged; -aging 1** : animar, alentar **2** FOSTER : promover, fomentar — **encouragement** [ɪnˈkərɪdʒmənt, εn-] *n* **1** : aliento *m* **2** PROMOTION : fomento *m*

encroach [ɪnˈkroːtʃ, εn-] *vi ~ on* : invadir, usurpar, quitar (el tiempo)

encyclopedia [ɪnˌsaɪkləˈpiːdiə, εn-] *n* : enciclopedia *f*

end [ˈend] *n* **1** : fin **2** EXTREMITY : extremo *m*, punta *f* **3 come to an ~** : llegar a su fin **4 in the ~** : por fin — *~ vt* : terminar, poner fin a — *vi* : terminar(se)

endanger [ɪnˈdeɪndʒər, εn-] *vt* : poner en peligro

endearing [ɪnˈdɪrɪŋ, εn-] *adj* : simpático

endeavor *or Brit* **endeavour** [ɪnˈdεvər, εn-] *vt ~ to* : esforzarse por — *~ n* : esfuerzo *m*

ending [ˈendɪŋ] *n* : final *m*, desenlace *m*

endive [ˈenˌdaɪv, ˌɑnˈdiːv] *n* : endibia *f*, endivia *f*

endless [ˈendləs] *adj* **1** INTERMINABLE : interminable **2** INNUMERABLE : innumerable **3 ~ possibilities** : posibilidades *fpl* infinitas

endorse [ɪnˈdors, εn-] *vt* **-dorsed; -dorsing 1** SIGN : endosar **2** APPROVE

: aprobar — **endorsement** [ɪnˈdorsmənt, εn-] *n* APPROVAL : aprobación *f*

endow [ɪnˈdaʊ, εn-] *vt* : dotar

endure [ɪnˈdʊr, εn-, -ˈdjʊr] *v* **-dured; -during** *vt* : soportar, aguantar — *vi* LAST : durar — **endurance** [ɪnˈdʊrəns, εn-, -ˈdjʊr-] *n* : resistencia *f*

enemy [ˈenəmi] *n, pl* **-mies** : enemigo *m*, -ga *f*

energy [ˈenərdʒi] *n, pl* **-gies** : energía *f* — **energetic** [ˌenərˈdʒεtɪk] *adj* : enérgico

enforce [ɪnˈfors, εn-] *vt* **-forced; -forcing 1** : hacer cumplir (un ley, etc.) **2** IMPOSE : imponer — **enforced** *adj* : forzoso — **enforcement** [ɪnˈforsmənt, εn-] *n* : imposición *f* del cumplimiento

engage [ɪnˈgeɪdʒ, εn-] *v* **-gaged; -gaging** *vt* : captar, atraer (la atención, etc.) **2 ~ the clutch** : embragar — *vi ~ in* : dedicarse a, entrar en — **engagement** [ɪnˈgeɪdʒmənt, εn-] *n* **1** APPOINTMENT : cita *f*, hora *f* **2** BETROTHAL : compromiso *m* — **engaging** [ɪnˈgeɪdʒɪŋ, εn-] *adj* : atractivo

engine [ˈendʒən] *n* **1** : motor *m* **2** LOCOMOTIVE : locomotora *f* — **engineer** [ˌendʒəˈnɪr] *n* **1** : ingeniero *m*, -ra *f* **2** : maquinista *mf* (de locomotoras) — *~ vt* **1** CONSTRUCT : construir **2** CONTRIVE : tramar — **engineering** [ˌendʒəˈnɪrɪŋ] *n* : ingeniería *f*

English [ˈɪŋglɪʃ, ˈɪŋlɪʃ] *adj* : inglés — *~ n* : inglés *m* (idioma) — **Englishman** [ˈɪŋglɪʃmən, ˈɪŋlɪʃ-] *n* : inglés *m* — **Englishwoman** [ˈɪŋglɪʃˌwʊmən, ˈɪŋlɪʃ-] *n* : inglesa *f*

engrave [ɪnˈgreɪv, εn-] *vt* **-graved; -graving** : grabar — **engraving** [ɪnˈgreɪvɪŋ, εn-] *n* : grabado *m*

engross [ɪnˈgroːs, εn-] *vt* : absorber

engulf [ɪnˈgʌlf, εn-] *vt* : envolver

enhance [ɪnˈhæns, εn-] *vt* **-hanced; -hancing** : aumentar, mejorar

enjoy [ɪnˈdʒɔɪ, εn-] *vt* **1** : disfrutar, gozar de **2 ~ oneself** : divertirse — **enjoyable** [ɪnˈdʒɔɪəbəl, εn-] *adj* : agradable — **enjoyment** [ɪnˈdʒɔɪmənt, εn-] *n* : placer *m*

enlarge [ɪnˈlɑrdʒ, εn-] *v* **-larged; -larging** *vt* : agrandar, ampliar — *vi* **1** : agrandarse **2 ~ upon** : extenderse sobre — **enlargement** [ɪnˈlɑrdʒmənt, εn-] *n* : ampliación *f*

enlighten [ɪnˈlaɪtən, εn-] *vt* : aclarar, iluminar

enlist [ɪnˈlɪst, εn-] *vt* **1** ENROLL : alistar **2** OBTAIN : conseguir — *vi* : alistarse

enliven [ɪnˈlaɪvən, εn-] *vt* : animar

enmity ['enməṭi] *n*, *pl* **-ties** : enemistad *f*

enormous [ɪ'nɔrməs] *adj* : enorme

enough [ɪ'nʌf] *adj* : bastante, suficiente — ~ *adv* : bastante — ~ *pron* **1** : (lo) suficiente, (lo) bastante **2 it's not ~** : no basta **3 I've had ~** ! : ¡estoy harto!

enquire [ɪn'kwaɪr, ɛn-], **enquiry** ['ɪn,kwaɪri, 'ɛn-, -kwəri; ɪn'kwaɪri, ɛn'-] → **inquire, inquiry**

enrage [ɪn'reɪdʒ, ɛn-] *vt* **-raged; -raging** : enfurecer

enrich [ɪn'rɪtʃ, ɛn-] *vt* : enriquecer

enroll *or* **enrol** [ɪn'roːl, ɛn-] *v* **-rolled; -rolling** *vt* : matricular, inscribir — *vi* : matricularse, inscribirse

ensemble [ɑn'sɑmbəl] *n* : conjunto *m*

ensign ['ɛnsən, 'ɛn,saɪn] *n* **1** FLAG : enseña *f* **2** : alférez *mf* (de fragata)

enslave [ɪn'sleɪv, ɛn-] *vt* **-slaved; -slaving** : esclavizar

ensue [ɪn'suː, ɛn-] *vi* **-sued; -suing** : seguir, resultar

ensure [ɪn'ʃʊr, ɛn-] *vt* **-sured; -suring** : asegurar

entail [ɪn'teɪl, ɛn-] *vt* : suponer, conllevar

entangle [ɪn'tæŋɡəl, ɛn-] *vt* **-gled; -gling** : enredar — **entanglement** [ɪn'tæŋɡəlmənt, ɛn-] *n* : enredo *m*

enter ['ɛntər] *vt* **1** : entrar en **2** RECORD : inscribir — *vi* **1** : entrar **2 ~ into** : firmar (un acuerdo), entablar (negociaciones, etc.)

enterprise ['ɛntər,praɪz] *n* **1** : empresa *f* **2** INITIATIVE : iniciativa *f* — **enterprising** ['ɛntər,praɪzɪŋ] *adj* : emprendedor

entertain [,ɛntər'teɪn] *vt* **1** AMUSE : entretener, divertir **2** CONSIDER : considerar **3 ~ guests** : recibir invitados — **entertainment** [,ɛntər'teɪnmənt] *n* : entretenimiento *m*, diversión *f*

enthrall *or* **enthral** [ɪn'θrɔl, ɛn-] *vt* **-thralled; -thralling** : cautivar, embelesar

enthusiasm [ɪn'θuːzi,æzəm, ɛn-, -'θjuː-] *n* : entusiasmo *m* — **enthusiast** [ɪn'θuːzi,æst, ɛn-, -'θjuː-, -əst] *n* : entusiasta *mf* — **enthusiastic** [ɪn,θuːzi'æstɪk, ɛn-, -,θjuː-] *adj* : entusiasta

entice [ɪn'taɪs, ɛn-] *vt* **-ticed; -ticing** : atraer, tentar

entire [ɪn'taɪr, ɛn-] *adj* : entero, completo — **entirely** [ɪn'taɪrli, ɛn-] *adv* : completamente — **entirety** [ɪn'taɪrti, ɛn-, -'taɪrəṭi] *n*, *pl* **-ties** : totalidad *f*

entitle [ɪn'taɪṭəl, ɛn-] *vt* **-tled; -tling 1** NAME : titular **2** AUTHORIZE : dar derecho a — **entitlement** [ɪn'taɪṭəlmənt, ɛn-] *n* : derecho *m*

entity ['ɛnṭəṭi] *n*, *pl* **-ties** : entidad *f*

entrails ['ɛn,treɪlz, -trəlz] *npl* : entrañas *fpl*, vísceras *fpl*

entrance¹ [ɪn'trænts, ɛn-] *vt* **-tranced; -trancing** : encantar, fascinar

entrance² ['ɛntrənts] *n* : entrada *f* — **entrant** ['ɛntrənt] *n* : participante *mf*

entreat [ɪn'triːt, ɛn-] *vt* : suplicar

entrée *or* **entree** ['ɑn,treɪ, ,ɑn'-] *n* : plato *m* principal

entrepreneur [,ɑntrəprə'nər, -'njʊr] *n* : empresario *m*, -ria *f*

entrust [ɪn'trʌst, ɛn-] *vt* : confiar

entry ['ɛntri] *n*, *pl* **-tries 1** ENTRANCE : entrada *f* **2** NOTATION : entrada *f*, anotación *f*

enumerate [ɪ'nuːmə,reɪt, ɛ-, -'njuː-] *vt* **-ated; -ating** : enumerar

enunciate [ɪ'nʌntsi,eɪt, ɛ-] *vt* **-ated; -ating 1** STATE : enunciar **2** PRONOUNCE : articular

envelop [ɪn'vɛləp, ɛn-] *vt* : envolver — **envelope** ['ɛnvə,loːp, 'ɑn-] *n* : sobre *m*

envious ['ɛnviəs] *adj* : envidioso — **enviously** *adv* : con envidia

environment [ɪn'vaɪrənmənt, ɛn-, -'vaɪərn-] *n* : medio *m* ambiente — **environmental** [ɪn,vaɪrən'mentəl, ɛn-, -,vaɪərn-] *adj* : ambiental — **environmentalist** [ɪn,vaɪrən'mentəlɪst, ɛn-, -,vaɪərn-] *n* : ecologista *mf*

envision [ɪn'vɪʒən, ɛn-] *vt* : prever, imaginar

envoy ['ɛn,vɔɪ, 'ɑn-] *n* : enviado *m*, -da *f*

envy ['ɛnvi] *n*, *pl* **envies** : envidia *f* — ~ *vt* **-vied; -vying** : envidiar

enzyme ['ɛn,zaɪm] *n* : enzima *f*

epic ['ɛpɪk] *adj* : épico — ~ *n* : epopeya *f*

epidemic [,ɛpə'dɛmɪk] *n* : epidemia *f* — ~ *adj* : epidémico

epilepsy ['ɛpə,lɛpsi] *n*, *pl* **-sies** : epilepsia *f* — **epileptic** [,ɛpə'lɛptɪk] *adj* : epiléptico — ~ *n* : epiléptico *m*, -ca *f*

episode ['ɛpə,soːd] *n* : episodio *m*

epitaph ['ɛpə,tæf] *n* : epitafio *m*

epitome [ɪ'pɪṭəmi] *n* : personificación *f* — **epitomize** [ɪ'pɪṭə,maɪz] *vt* **-mized; -mizing** : ser la personificación de, personificar

epoch ['ɛpək, 'ɛ,pɑk, 'iː,pɑk] *n* : época *f*

equal ['iːkwəl] *adj* **1** SAME : igual **2 be ~ to** : estar a la altura de (una tarea, etc.) — ~ *n* : igual *mf* — ~ *vt* **equaled** *or* **equalled; equaling** *or* **equalling 1** : igualar **2** : ser igual a (en matemáticas) — **equality** [ɪ'kwɑləṭi] *n*, *pl* **-ties** : igualdad *f* — **equalize** ['iːkwə,laɪz] *vt* **-ized; -izing** : igualar — **equally** ['iːkwəli] *adv* **1** : igualmente 2 ~ **important** : igual de importante

equate [r'kweɪt] *vt* **equated; equating** ~ **with** : equiparar con — **equation** [r'kweɪʒən] *n* : ecuación *f*

equator [r'kweɪtər] *n* : ecuador *m*

equilibrium [,i:kwə'lıbrıəm, ,ε-] *n, pl* **-riums** *or* **-ria** [-brıə] : equilibrio *m*

equinox ['i:kwənɑks, 'ε-] *n* : equinoccio *m*

equip [r'kwɪp] *vt* **equipped; equipping** : equipar — **equipment** [r'kwɪpmənt] *n* : equipo *m*

equity ['ɛkwəţi] *n, pl* **-ties 1** FAIRNESS : equidad *f* **2 equities** *npl* STOCKS : acciones *fpl* ordinarias

equivalent [r'kwɪvələnt] *adj* : equivalente — ~ *n* : equivalente *m*

era ['ɪrə, 'εrə, 'i:rə] *n* : era *f*, época *f*

eradicate [r'rædɪ,keɪt] *vt* **-cated; -cating** : erradicar

erase [r'reɪs] *vt* **erased; erasing** : borrar — **eraser** [r'reɪsər] *n* : goma *f* de borrar, borrador *f*

erect [r'rεkt] *adj* : erguido — ~ *vt* : erigir, levantar — **erection** [r'rεkʃən] *n* **1** BUILDING : construcción *f* **2** : erección *f* (en fisiología)

erode [r'roːd] *vt* **eroded; eroding** : erosionar (el suelo), corroer (metales) — **erosion** [r'roʒən] *n* : erosión *f*, corrosión *f*

erotic [r'rɑţɪk] *adj* : erótico

err ['εr, 'ər] *vi* : equivocarse, errar

errand ['εrənd] *n* : mandado *m*, recado *m* Spain

erratic [r'ræţɪk] *adj* : errático, irregular

error ['εrər] *n* : error *m* — **erroneous** [r'roːnıəs, ε-] *adj* : erróneo

erupt [r'rʌpt] *vi* **1** : hacer erupción (dícese de un volcán) **2** : estallar (dícese de la cólera, la violencia, etc.) — **eruption** [r'rʌpʃən] *n* : erupción *f*

escalate ['εskə,leɪt] *vi* **-lated; -lating** : intensificarse

escalator ['εskə,leɪtər] *n* : escalera *f* mecánica

escapade ['εskə,peɪd] *n* : aventura *f*

escape [r'skeɪp, ε-] *v* **-caped; -caping** *vt* : escapar a, evitar — *vi* : escaparse, fugarse — ~ *n* **1** : fuga *f* **2** ~ **from reality** : evasión *f* de la realidad — **escapee** [ɪ,skeɪ'pi:, ,ε-] *n* : fugitivo *m*, -va *f*

escort ['εs,kɔrt] *n* **1** GUARD : escolta *f* **2** COMPANION : acompañante *mf* — ~ [ɪs'kɔrt, ε-] *vt* **1** : escoltar **2** ACCOMPANY : acompañar

Eskimo ['εskə,moː] *adj* : esquimal

especially [r'spεʃəli] *adv* : especialmente

espionage ['εspiə,nɑʒ, -,nɑdʒ] *n* : espionaje *m*

espresso [ε'sprε,soː] *n, pl* **-sos** : café *m* exprés

essay ['ε,seɪ] *n* : ensayo *m* (literario), composición *f* (académica)

essence ['εsənts] *n* : esencia *f* — **essential** [r'sεntʃəl] *adj* : esencial — ~ *n* **1** : elemento *m* esencial **2 the** ~**s** : lo indispensable

establish [r'stæblɪʃ, ε-] *vt* : establecer — **establishment** [r'stæblɪʃmənt, ε-] *n* : establecimiento *m*

estate [r'steɪt, ε-] *n* **1** POSSESSIONS : bienes *mpl* **2** LAND, PROPERTY : finca *f*

esteem [r'stiːm, ε-] *n* : estima *f* — ~ *vt* : estimar

esthetic [εs'θεţɪk] → **aesthetic**

estimate ['εstə,meɪt] *vt* **-mated; -mating** : calcular, estimar — ~ ['εstəmət] *n* **1** : cálculo *m* (aproximado) **2** *or* ~ **of costs** : presupuesto *m* — **estimation** [,εstə'meɪʃən] *n* **1** JUDGMENT : juicio *m* **2** ESTEEM : estima *f*

estuary ['εstʃu,wεri] *n, pl* **-aries** : estuario *m*, ría *f*

eternal [r'tərnəl, iː-] *adj* : eterno — **eternity** [r'tərnəţi, iː-] *n, pl* **-ties** : eternidad *f*

ether ['iːθər] *n* : éter *m*

ethical ['εθɪkəl] *adj* : ético — **ethics** ['εθɪks] *ns & pl* : ética *f*, moralidad *f*

ethnic ['εθnɪk] *adj* : étnico

etiquette ['εţɪkət, -,kεt] *n* : etiqueta *f*

Eucharist ['juːkərɪst] *n* : Eucaristía *f*

eulogy ['juːlədʒi] *n, pl* **-gies** : elogio *m*, panegírico *m*

euphemism ['juːfə,mɪzəm] *n* : eufemismo *m*

euphoria [jʊ'foriə] *n* : euforia *f*

European [,jʊrə'piən, -,piːn] *adj* : europeo

evacuate [r'vækju,eɪt] *vt* **-ated; -ating** : evacuar — **evacuation** [ɪ,vækju'eɪʃən] *n* : evacuación *f*

evade [r'veɪd] *vt* **evaded; evading** : evadir, eludir

evaluate [r'vælju,eɪt] *vt* **-ated; -ating** : evaluar

evaporate [r'væpə,reɪt] *vi* **-rated; -rating** : evaporarse

evasion [r'veɪʒən] *n* : evasión *f* — **evasive** [r'veɪsɪv] *adj* : evasivo

eve ['iːv] *n* : víspera *f*

even ['iːvən] *adj* **1** REGULAR, STEADY : regular, constante **2** LEVEL : plano, llano **3** SMOOTH : liso **4** EQUAL : igual **5** ~ **number** : número *m* par **6 get** ~ **with** : desquitarse con — ~ *adv* **1** : hasta, incluso **2** ~ **better** : aún

mejor, todavía mejor **3 ~ if** : aunque
4 ~ so : aun así — **~ vt** : igualar —
vi or **out** : nivelarse
evening ['iːvnɪŋ] *n* : tarde *f*, noche *f*
event [ɪ'vɛnt] *n* **1** : acontecimiento *m*,
suceso *m* **2** : prueba *f* (en deportes) **3**
in the ~ of : en caso de — **eventful**
[ɪ'vɛntfəl] *adj* : lleno de incidentes
eventual [ɪ'vɛntʃʊəl] *adj* : final — **eventuality** [ɪ,vɛntʃʊ'æləti] *n, pl* **-ties**
: eventualidad *f* — **eventually** [ɪ-
'vɛntʃʊəli] *adv* : al fin, finalmente
ever ['ɛvər] *adv* **1** ALWAYS : siempre **2 ~
since** : desde entonces **3 hardly ~**
: casi nunca **4 have you ~ done it?**
: ¿lo has hecho alguna vez?
evergreen ['ɛvər,griːn] *n* : planta *f* de
hoja perenne
everlasting [,ɛvər'læstɪŋ] *adj* : eterno
every ['ɛvri] *adj* **1** EACH — **cada 2 ~
month** : todos los meses **3 ~ other
day** : cada dos días — **everybody**
['ɛvri,bʌdi, -bɑ-] *pron* : todos *mpl*, -das
fpl; todo el mundo — **everyday** [,ɛvri-
'deɪ, 'ɛvri,-] *adj* : cotidiano, de todos los
días — **everyone** ['ɛvri,wʌn] — **everybody** — **everything** ['ɛvri ,θɪŋ] *pron*
: todo — **everywhere** ['ɛvri ,hwɛr] *adv*
: en todas partes, por todas partes
evict [ɪ'vɪkt] *vt* : desahuciar, desalojar —
eviction [ɪ'vɪkʃən] *n* : desahucio *m*
evidence ['ɛvədənts] *n* **1** PROOF : prue-
bas *fpl* **2** TESTIMONY : testimonio *m*,
declaración *f* — **evident** ['ɛvɪdənt] *adj*
: evidente — **evidently** ['ɛvɪdəntli, ,ɛvɪ-
'dɛntli] *adv* **1** OBVIOUSLY : obviamente
2 APPARENTLY : evidentemente, al
parecer
evil ['iːvəl, -vɪl] *adj* **eviler** *or* **eviller;
evilest** *or* **evillest** : malvado, malo —
~ n : mal *m*, maldad *f*
evoke [i'voːk] *vt* **evoked; evoking**
: evocar
evolution [,ɛvə'luːʃən, ,iː-] *n* : evolución
f, desarrollo *m* — **evolve** [i'vɑlv] *vi*
evolved; evolving : evolucionar, desarrollarse
exact [ɪg'zækt, ɛg-] *adj* : exacto, preciso
— **~ vt** : exigir — **exacting** [ɪg-
'zæktɪŋ, ɛg-] *adj* : exigente — **exactly**
[ɪg'zæktli, ɛg-] *adv* : exactamente
exaggerate [ɪg'zædʒə,reɪt, ɛg-] *v* **-ated;
-ating** : exagerar — **exaggeration** [ɪg-
,zædʒə'reɪʃən, ɛg-] *n* : exageración *f*
examine [ɪg'zæmən, ɛg-] *vt* **-ined;
-ining 1** : examinar **2** INSPECT : revisar
3 QUESTION : interrogar — **exam** [ɪg-
'zæm, ɛg-] *n* : examen *m* — **examination** [ɪg,zæmə'neɪʃən, ɛg-] *n* : examen
m

example [ɪg'zæmpəl, ɛg-] *n* : ejemplo *m*
exasperate [ɪg'zæspə,reɪt, ɛg-] *vt* **-ated;
-ating** : exasperar — **exasperation**
[ɪg,zæspə'reɪʃən, ɛg-] *n* : exasperación *f*
excavate ['ɛkskə,veɪt] *vt* **-vated; -vating**
: excavar — **excavation** [,ɛkskə'veɪʃən]
n : excavación *f*
exceed [ɪk'siːd, ɛk-] *vt* : exceder, sobrepasar — **exceedingly** [ɪk'siːdɪŋli,
ɛk-] *adv* : extremadamente
excel [ɪk'sɛl, ɛk-] *v* **-celled; -celling** *vi*
: sobresalir — *vt* SURPASS : superar —
excellence ['ɛksələnts] *n* : excelencia *f*
— **excellent** ['ɛksələnt] *adj* : excelente
except [ɪk'sɛpt] *prep or* **~ for** : excepto, menos, salvo — **~ vt** : exceptuar
— **exception** [ɪk'sɛpʃən] *n* : excepción
f — **exceptional** [ɪk'sɛpʃənəl] *adj* : excepcional
excerpt ['ɛk,sərpt, 'ɛg,zərpt] *n* : extracto
m
excess [ɪk'sɛs, 'ɛk,sɛs] *n* : exceso *m* —
~ ['ɛk,sɛs, ɪk'sɛs] *adj* : excesivo, de
sobra — **excessive** [ɪk'sɛsɪv, ɛk-] *adj*
: excesivo
exchange [ɪks'tʃeɪndʒ, ɛks-; 'ɛks,tʃeɪndʒ]
n **1** : intercambio *m* **2** : cambio *m* (en
finanzas) — **~ vt -changed; -chang-
ing** : cambiar, intercambiar
excise [ɪk'saɪz, ɛk-] *n* **~ tax** : impuesto
m interno, impuesto *m* sobre el consumo
excite [ɪk'saɪt, ɛk-] *vt* **-cited; -citing**
: excitar, emocionar — **excited** [ɪk-
'saɪtəd, ɛk-] *adj* : excitado, entusias-
mado — **excitement** [ɪk'saɪtmənt, ɛk-]
n : entusiasmo *m*, emoción *f*
exclaim [ɪks'kleɪm, ɛk-] *v* : exclamar —
exclamation [,ɛksklə'meɪʃən] *n* : exclamación *f* — **exclamation point** *n*
: signo *m* de admiración
exclude [ɪks'kluːd, ɛks-] *vt* **-cluded;
-cluding** : excluir — **excluding** [ɪks-
'kluːdɪŋ, ɛks-] *prep* : excepto, con excepción de — **exclusion** [ɪks'kluːʒən,
ɛks-] *n* : exclusión *f* — **exclusive** [ɪks-
'kluːsɪv, ɛks-] *adj* : exclusivo
excrement ['ɛkskrəmənt] *n* : excremento *m*
excruciating [ɪk'skruːʃi,eɪtɪŋ, ɛk-] *adj*
: insoportable, atroz
excursion [ɪk'skərʒən, ɛk-] *n* : excursión *f*
excuse [ɪk'skjuːz, ɛk-] *vt* **-cused;
-cusing 1** : perdonar **2 ~ me**
: perdóne, perdón — **~** [ɪk'skjuːs, ɛk-]
n : excusa *f*
execute ['ɛksɪ,kjuːt] *vt* **-cuted; -cuting**
: ejecutar — **execution** [,ɛksɪ'kjuːʃən] *n*
: ejecución *f* — **executioner** [,ɛksɪ-
'kjuːʃənər] *n* : verdugo *m*

executive [ɪg'zɛkjət̮ɪv, ɛg-] *adj* : ejecutivo — ~ *n* **1** MANAGER : ejecutivo *m*, -va *f* **2** *or* ~ **branch** : poder *m* ejecutivo

exemplify [ɪg'zɛmplə͵faɪ, ɛg-] *vt* **-fied; -fying** : ejemplificar — **exemplary** [ɪg'zɛmpləri, ɛg-] *adj* : ejemplar

exempt [ɪg'zɛmpt, ɛg-] *adj* : exento — ~ *vt* : dispensar — **exemption** [ɪg'zɛmpʃən, ɛg-] *n* : exención *f*

exercise ['ɛksər͵saɪz] *n* : ejercicio *m* — ~ *v* **-cised;** USE **-cising** *vt* : ejercer, hacer uso de — *vi* : hacer ejercicio

exert [ɪg'zərt, ɛg-] *vt* **1** : ejercer **2** ~ **oneself** : esforzarse — **exertion** [ɪg'zərʃən, ɛg-] *n* : esfuerzo *m*

exhale [ɛks'heɪl] *v* **-haled; -haling** : exhalar

exhaust [ɪg'zɔst, ɛg-] *vt* : agotar — ~ *n* **1** *or* ~ **fumes** : gases *mpl* de escape **2** *or* ~ **pipe** : tubo *m* de escape — **exhaustion** [ɪg'zɔstʃən, ɛg-] *n* : agotamiento *m* — **exhaustive** [ɪg'zɔstɪv, ɛg-] *adj* : exhaustivo

exhibit [ɪg'zɪbət, ɛg-] *vt* **1** DISPLAY : exponer **2** SHOW : mostrar — ~ *n* **1** : objeto *m* expuesto **2** EXHIBITION : exposición *f* — **exhibition** [͵ɛksə'bɪʃən] *n* : exposición *f*

exhilarate [ɪg'zɪlə͵reɪt, ɛg-] *vt* **-rated; -rating** : alegrar — **exhilaration** [ɪg͵zɪlə'reɪʃən] *n* : regocijo *m*

exile ['ɛg͵zaɪl, 'ɛk͵saɪl] *n* **1** : exilio *m* **2** OUTCAST : exiliado *m*, -da *f* — ~ *vt* **exiled; exiling** : exiliar

exist [ɪg'zɪst, ɛg-] *vi* : existir — **existence** [ɪg'zɪstənts, ɛg-] *n* : existencia *f* — **existing** *adj* : existente

exit ['ɛg͵zət, 'ɛksət] *n* : salida *f* — ~ *vi* : salir

exodus ['ɛksədəs] *n* : éxodo *m*

exonerate [ɪg'zɑnə͵reɪt, ɛg-] *vt* **-ated; -ating** : exonerar, disculpar

exorbitant [ɪg'zɔrbətənt, ɛg-] *adj* : exorbitante, excesivo

exotic [ɪg'zɑtɪk, ɛg-] *adj* : exótico

expand [ɪk'spænd, ɛk-] *vt* **1** : ampliar, extender **2** : dilatar (metales, etc.) — *vi* **1** : ampliarse, extenderse **2** : dilatarse (dícese de metales, etc.) — **expanse** [ɪk'spænts, ɛk-] *n* : extensión *f* — **expansion** [ɪk'spæntʃən, ɛk-] *n* : expansión *f*

expatriate [ɛks'peɪtriət, -͵eɪt] *n* : expatriado *m*, -da *f* — ~ *adj* : expatriado

expect [ɪk'spɛkt, ɛk-] *vt* **1** : esperar **2** REQUIRE : contar con — *vi* **be expecting** : estar embarazada — **expectancy** [ɪk'spɛktəntsi, ɛk-] *n, pl* **-cies** : esperanza *f* — **expectant** [ɪk'spɛktənt, ɛk-] *adj* **1**

: expectante **2** ~ **mother** : futura madre *f* — **expectation** [͵ɛkspɛk'teɪʃən] *n* : esperanza *f*

expedient [ɪk'spiːdiənt, ɛk-] *adj* : conveniente — ~ *n* : expediente *m*, recurso *m*

expedition [͵ɛkspə'dɪʃən] *n* : expedición *f*

expel [ɪk'spɛl, ɛk-] *vt* **-pelled; -pelling** : expulsar (a una persona), expeler (humo, etc.)

expend [ɪk'spɛnd, ɛk-] *vt* : gastar — **expendable** [ɪk'spɛndəbəl, ɛk-] *adj* : prescindible — **expenditure** [ɪk'spɛndɪtʃər, ɛk-, -dɪtʃʊr] *n* : gasto *m* — **expense** [ɪk'spɛnts, ɛk-] *n* **1** : gasto *m* **2** ~ **s** *npl* : gastos *mpl*, expensas *fpl* **3** **at the** ~ **of** : a expensas de — **expensive** [ɪk'spɛntsɪv, ɛk-] *adj* : caro

experience [ɪk'spɪriənts, ɛk-] *n* : experiencia *f* — ~ *vt* **-enced; -encing** : experimentar — **experienced** [ɪk'spɪriəntst, ɛk-] *adj* : experimentado — **experiment** [ɪk'spɛrəmənt, ɛk-, -'spɪr-] *n* : experimento *m* — ~ *vi* : experimentar — **experimental** [ɪk͵spɛrə'mɛntəl, ɛk-, -͵spɪr-] *adj* : experimental

expert ['ɛk͵spərt, ɪk'spərt] *adj* : experto — ~ *n* ['ɛk͵spərt] *n* : experto *m*, -ta *f* — **expertise** [͵ɛkspər'tiːz] *n* : pericia *f*, competencia *f*

expire [ɪk'spaɪr, ɛk-] *vi* **-pired; -piring 1** : caducar, vencer **2** DIE : expirar, morir — **expiration** [͵ɛkspə'reɪʃən] *n* : vencimiento *m*, caducidad *f*

explain [ɪk'spleɪn, ɛk-] *vt* : explicar — **explanation** [͵ɛksplə'neɪʃən] *n* : explicación *f* — **explanatory** [ɪk'splænə͵tori, ɛk-] *adj* : explicativo

explicit [ɪk'splɪsət, ɛk-] *adj* : explícito

explode [ɪk'sploːd, ɛk-] *v* **-ploded; -ploding** *vt* : hacer explotar — *vi* : explotar, estallar

exploit ['ɛk͵splɔɪt] *n* : hazaña *f*, proeza *f* — ~ [ɪk'splɔɪt, ɛk-] *vt* : explotar — **exploitation** [͵ɛksplɔɪ'teɪʃən] *n* : explotación *f*

exploration [͵ɛksplə'reɪʃən] *n* : exploración *f* — **explore** [ɪk'splor, ɛk-] *vt* **-plored; -ploring** : explorar — **explorer** [ɪk'splorər, ɛk-] *n* : explorador *m*, -dora *f*

explosion [ɪk'sploːʒən, ɛk-] *n* : explosión *f* — **explosive** [ɪk'sploːsɪv, ɛk-] *adj* : explosivo — ~ *n* : explosivo *m*

export [ɛk'sport, 'ɛk͵sport] *vt* : exportar — ~ ['ɛk͵sport] *n* : exportación *f*

expose [ɪk'spoːz, ɛk-] *vt* **-posed; -posing 1** : exponer **2** REVEAL : descubrir, revelar — **exposed** [ɪk'spoːzd, ɛk-] *adj*

: expuesto, al descubierto — **exposure** [ɪk'spoːʒər, ɛk-] *n* : exposición *f*

express [ɪk'sprɛs, ɛk-] *adj* **1** SPECIFIC : expreso, específico **2** FAST : expreso, rápido — **~** *adv* : por correo urgente — **~** *n or* **~ train** : expreso *m* — **~** *vt* : expresar — **expression** [ɪk-'sprɛʃən, ɛk-] *n* : expresión *f* — **expressive** [ɪk'sprɛsɪv, ɛk-] *adj* : expresivo — **expressly** [ɪk'sprɛsli, ɛk-] *adv* : expresamente — **expressway** [ɪk-'sprɛs,weɪ, ɛk-] *n* : autopista *f*

expulsion [ɪk'spʌlʃən, ɛk-] *n* : expulsión *f*

exquisite [ɛk'skwɪzət, 'ɛk,skwɪ-] *adj* : exquisito

extend [ɪk'stɛnd, ɛk-] *vt* **1** STRETCH : extender **2** LENGTHEN : prolongar **3** ENLARGE : ampliar **4 ~ one's hand** : tender la mano — *vi* : extenderse — **extension** [ɪk'stɛntʃən, ɛk-] *n* **1** : extensión *f* **2** LENGTHENING : prolongación *f* **3** ANNEX : ampliación *f*, anexo *m* **4 ~ cord** : alargador *m* — **extensive** [ɪk'stɛntsɪv, ɛk-] *adj* : extenso — **extent** [ɪk'stɛnt, ɛk-] *n* **1** SIZE : extensión *f* **2** DEGREE : alcance *m*, grado *m* **3 to a certain ~** : hasta cierto punto

extenuating [ɪk'stɛnjə,weɪtɪŋ, ɛk-] *adj* **~ circumstances** : circunstancias *fpl* atenuantes

exterior [ɛk'stɪriər] *adj* : exterior — **~** *n* : exterior *m*

exterminate [ɪk'stərmə,neɪt, ɛk-] *vt* **-nated; -nating** : exterminar — **extermination** [ɪk,stərmə'neɪʃən, ɛk-] *n* : exterminación *f*

external [ɪk'stərnəl, ɛk-] *adj* : externo — **externally** [ɪk'stərnəli, ɛk-] *adv* : exteriormente

extinct [ɪk'stɪŋkt, ɛk-] *adj* : extinto — **extinction** [ɪk'stɪŋkʃən, ɛk-] *n* : extinción *f*

extinguish [ɪk'stɪŋgwɪʃ, ɛk-] *vt* : extinguir, apagar — **extinguisher** [ɪk-'stɪŋgwɪʃər, ɛk-] *n* : extintor *m*

extol [ɪk'stoːl, ɛk-] *vt* **-tolled; -tolling** : ensalzar, alabar

extort [ɪk'stɔrt, ɛk-] *vt* : arrancar (algo a algn) por la fuerza — **extortion** [ɪk-'stɔrʃən, ɛk-] *n* : extorsión *f*

extra ['ɛkstrə] *adj* : suplementario, de

más — **~** *n* : extra *m* — **~** *adv* **1** : extra, más **2 ~ special** : super especial

extract [ɪk'strækt, ɛk-] *vt* : extraer, sacar — **~** ['ɛk,strækt] *n* : extracto *m* — **extraction** [ɪk'strækʃən, ɛk-] *n* : extracción *f*

extracurricular [,ɛkstrəkə'rɪkjələr] *adj* : extracurricular

extradite ['ɛkstrə,daɪt] *vt* **-dited; -diting** : extraditar

extraordinary [ɪk'strɔrdən,ɛri, ,ɛkstrə-'ɔrd-] *adj* : extraordinario

extraterrestrial [,ɛkstrətə'rɛstriəl] *adj* : extraterrestre — **~** *n* : extraterrestre *mf*

extravagant [ɪk'strævɪgənt, ɛk-] *adj* **1** WASTEFUL : despilfarrador, derrochador **2** EXAGGERATED : extravagante, exagerado — **extravagance** [ɪk-'strævɪgənts, ɛk-] *n* **1** WASTEFULNESS : derroche *m*, despilfarro *m* **2** LUXURY : lujo *m* **3** EXAGGERATION : extravagancia *f*

extreme [ɪk'striːm, ɛk-] *adj* : extremo — **~** *n* : extremo *m* — **extremely** [ɪk-'striːmli, ɛk-] *adv* : extremadamente — **extremity** [ɪk'strɛməti, ɛk-] *n, pl* **-ties** : extremidad *f*

extricate ['ɛkstrə,keɪt] *vt* **-cated; -cating** : librar, (lograr) sacar

extrovert ['ɛkstrə,vərt] *n* : extrovertido *m*, **-da** *f* — **extroverted** ['ɛkstrə,vərtəd] *adj* : extrovertido

exuberant [ɪg'zuːbərənt, ɛg-] *adj* **1** JOYOUS : eufórico **2** LUSH : exuberante — **exuberance** [ɪg'zuːbərənts, ɛg-] *n* **1** JOYOUSNESS : euforia *f* **2** VIGOR : exuberancia *f*

exult [ɪg'zʌlt, ɛg-] *vi* : exultar

eye ['aɪ] *n* **1** : ojo *m* **2** VISION : visión *f*, vista *f* **3** GLANCE : mirada *f* — **~** *vt* **eyed; eyeing** *or* **eying** : mirar — **eyeball** ['aɪ,bɔl] *n* : globo *m* ocular — **eyebrow** ['aɪ,braʊ] *n* : ceja *f* — **eyeglasses** ['aɪ,glæsəz] *npl* : anteojos *mpl*, lentes *mpl* — **eyelash** ['aɪ,læʃ] *n* : pestaña *f* — **eyelid** ['aɪ,lɪd] *n* : párpado *m* — **eyesight** ['aɪ,saɪt] *n* : vista *f*, visión *f* — **eyesore** ['aɪ,sor] *n* : monstruosidad *f* — **eyewitness** ['aɪ'wɪtnəs] *n* : testigo *mf* ocular

F

f ['ɛf] *n, pl* **f's** *or* **fs** ['ɛfs] : f, sexta letra del alfabeto inglés
fable ['feɪbəl] *n* : fábula *f*
fabric ['fæbrɪk] *n* : tela *f*, tejido *m*
fabulous ['fæbjələs] *adj* : fabuloso
facade [fə'sɑd] *n* : fachada *f*
face ['feɪs] *n* **1** : cara *f*, rostro *m* (de una persona) **2** APPEARANCE : fisonomía *f*, aspecto *m* **3** : cara *f* (de una moneda), fachada *f* (de un edificio) **4** ~ **value** : valor *m* nominal **5 in the** ~ **of** : en medio de, ante **6 lose** ~ : desprestigiarse **7 make** ~**s** : hacer muecas — ~ **faced; facing** *vt* **1** : estar frente a **2** CONFRONT : enfrentarse a **3** OVERLOOK : dar a — *vi* ~ **to the north** : mirar hacia el norte — **facedown** ['feɪs,daʊn] *adv* : boca abajo — **faceless** ['feɪsləs] *adj* : anónimo — **face-lift** ['feɪs,lɪft] *n* : estiramiento *m* facial
facet ['fæsət] *n* : faceta *f*
face-to-face *adv & adj* : cara a cara
facial ['feɪʃəl] *adj* : de la cara, facial — ~ *n* : limpieza *f* de cutis
facetious [fə'siːʃəs] *adj* : gracioso, burlón
facility [fə'sɪləti] *n, pl* **-ties 1** EASE : facilidad *f* **2** CENTER : centro *m* **3 facilities** *npl* : comodidades *fpl*, servicios *mpl*
facsimile [fæk'sɪməli] *n* : facsímile *m*, facsímil *m*
fact ['fækt] *n* **1** : hecho *m* **2 in** ~ : en realidad, de hecho
faction ['fækʃən] *n* : facción *m*, bando *m*
factor ['fæktər] *n* : factor *m*
factory ['fæktəri] *n, pl* **-ries** : fábrica *f*
factual ['fæktʃʊəl] *adj* : basado en hechos
faculty ['fækəlti] *n, pl* **-ties** : facultad *f*
fad ['fæd] *n* : moda *f* pasajera, manía *f*
fade ['feɪd] *v* **faded; fading** *vi* **1** WITHER : marchitarse **2** DISCOLOR : desteñirse, decolorarse **3** DIM : apagarse **4** VANISH : desvanecerse — *vt* : desteñir
fail ['feɪl] *vi* **1** : fracasar (dícese de una empresa, un matrimonio, etc.) **2** BREAK DOWN : fallar a ~ **in** : faltar a, no cumplir con **4** FLUNK : suspender *Spain*, ser reprobado *Lat* **5** ~ **to do sth** : no hacer algo — *vt* **1** DISAPPOINT : fallar **2** FLUNK : suspender *Spain*, reprobar *Lat* — ~ *n* **without** ~ : sin

falta — **failing** ['feɪlɪŋ] *n* : defecto *m* — **failure** ['feɪljər] *n* **1** : fracaso *m* **2** BREAKDOWN : falla *f*
faint ['feɪnt] *adj* **1** WEAK : débil **2** INDISTINCT : tenue, indistinto **3 feel** ~ : estar mareado — ~ *vi* : desmayarse — ~ *n* : desmayo *m* — **fainthearted** ['feɪnt'hɑrtəd] *adj* : cobarde, pusilánime — **faintly** ['feɪntli] *adv* **1** WEAKLY : débilmente **2** SLIGHTLY : ligeramente, levemente
fair¹ ['fær] *n* : feria *f*
fair² *adj* **1** BEAUTIFUL : bello, hermoso **2** : bueno (dícese del tiempo) **3** JUST : justo **4** : rubio (dícese del pelo), blanco (dícese de la tez) **5** ADEQUATE : adecuado — ~ *adv* **play** ~ : jugar limpio — **fairly** ['færli] *adv* **1** JUSTLY : justamente **2** QUITE : bastante — **fairness** ['færnəs] *n* : justicia *f*
fairy ['færi] *n, pl* **fairies 1** : hada *f* **2** ~ **tale** : cuento *m* de hadas
faith ['feɪθ] *n, pl* **faiths** ['feɪθs, 'feɪðz] : fe *f* — **faithful** ['feɪθfəl] *adj* : fiel — **faithfully** *adv* : fielmente — **faithfulness** ['feɪθfəlnəs] *n* : fidelidad *f*
fake ['feɪk] *v* **faked; faking** *vt* **1** FALSIFY : falsificar, falsear **2** FEIGN : fingir — *vi* PRETEND : fingir — ~ *adj* : falso — ~ *n* **1** IMITATION : falsificación *f* **2** IMPOSTOR : impostor *m*, -tora *f*
falcon ['fælkən, 'fɔl-] *n* : halcón *m*
fall ['fɔl] *vi* **fell** ['fɛl]; **fallen** ['fɔlən]; **falling 1** : caer, bajar (dícese de los precios), descender (dícese de la temperatura) **2** ~ **asleep** : dormirse **3** ~ **back** : retirarse **4** ~ **back on** : recurrir a **5** ~ **down** : caerse **6** ~ **in love** : enamorarse **7** ~ **out** QUARREL : pelearse **8** ~ **through** : fracasar — ~ *n* **1** : caída *f*, bajada *f* (de precios), descenso *m* (de temperatura) **2** AUTUMN : otoño *m* **3** ~**s** *npl* WATERFALL : cascada *f*, catarata *f*
fallacy ['fæləsi] *n, pl* **-cies** : concepto *m* erróneo
fallible ['fæləbəl] *adj* : falible
fallow ['fælo] *adj* **lie** ~ : estar en barbecho
false ['fɔls] *adj* **falser; falsest 1** : falso **2** ~ **alarm** : falsa alarma *f* **3** ~ **teeth** : dentadura *f* postiza — **falsehood** ['fɔls,hʊd] *n* : mentira — **falseness**

['fɔlsnəs] *n* : falsedad *f* — **falsify**
['fɔlsə,faɪ] *vt* **-fied; fying** : falsificar,
falsear

falter ['fɔltər] *vi* **-tered; -tering 1** STUM-
BLE : tambalearse **2** WAVER : vacilar

fame ['feɪm] *n* : fama *f*

familiar [fə'mɪljər] *adj* **1** : familiar **2 be
~ with** : estar familiarizado con —
familiarity [fə,mɪli'ærəṭi, -mɪl'jær-] *n,
pl* **-ties** : familiaridad *f* — **familiarize**
[fə'mɪljə,raɪz] *vt* **-ized; -izing ~ oneself** : familiarizarse

family ['fæmli, 'fæmə-] *n, pl* **-lies** : familia *f*

famine ['fæmən] *n* : hambre *f*, hambruna
f

famished ['fæmɪʃt] *adj* : famélico

famous ['feɪməs] *adj* : famoso

fan ['fæn] *n* **1** : ventilador *m*, abanico *m*
2 : aficionado *m*, -da *f* (a un pasatiempo); admirador *m*, -dora *f* (de una persona) — **~** *vt* **fanned; fanning**
: abanicar (a una persona), avivar (un
fuego)

fanatic [fə'næṭɪk] *or* **fanatical** [-ṭɪkəl]
adj : fanático — **~** *n* : fanático *m*, -ca
f — **fanaticism** [fə'næṭə,sɪzəm] *n* : fanatismo *m*

fancy ['fæntsi] *vt* **-cied; -cying 1** IMAG-
INE : imaginarse **2** DESIRE : apetecerle
(algo a uno) — **~** *adj* **-cier; -est 1**
ELABORATE : elaborado **2** LUXURIOUS
: lujoso, elegante — **~** *n, pl* **-cies 1**
WHIM : capricho *m* **2** IMAGINATION
: imaginación *f* **3 take a ~ to** : aficionarse a (una cosa), tomar cariño a
(una persona) — **fanciful** ['fæntsɪfəl]
adj **1** CAPRICIOUS : caprichoso **2** IMAG-
INATIVE : imaginativo

fanfare ['fæn,fær] *n* : fanfarria *f*

fang ['fæŋ] *n* : colmillo *m* (de un animal), diente *m* (de una serpiente)

fantasy ['fæntəsi] *n, pl* **-sies** : fantasía *f*
— **fantasize** ['fæntə,saɪz] *vi* **-sized;
-sizing** : fantasear — **fantastic** [fæn-
'tæstɪk] *adj* : fantástico

far ['fɑr] *adv* **farther** ['fɑrðər] *or* **further**
['fər-]; **farthest** *or* **furthest** [-ðəst] **1**
: lejos **2** MUCH : muy, mucho **3 as ~
as** : hasta (un lugar), con respecto a
(un tema) **4 by ~** : con mucho **5 ~
and wide** : por todas partes **6 ~ away**
: a lo lejos **7 ~ from it!** : ¡todo lo contrario! **8 so ~** : hasta ahora, todavía
— **~** *adj* **farther** *or* **further; farthest**
or **furthest 1** REMOTE : lejano **2** EX-
TREME : extremo — **faraway** ['fɑrə,weɪ]
adj : remoto, lejano

farce ['fɑrs] *n* : farsa *f*

fare ['fær] *vi* **fared; faring** : irle a uno —

~ *n* **1** : precio *m* del pasaje **2** FOOD
: comida *f*

farewell [fær'wel] *n* : despedida *f* — **~**
adj : de despedida

far—fetched ['fɑr'fetʃt] *adj* : improbable,
exagerado

farm ['fɑrm] *n* : granja *f*, hacienda *f* —
~ *vt* : cultivar (la tierra), criar (animales) — *vi* : ser agricultor — **farmer**
['fɑrmər] *n* : agricultor *m*, -tora *f*;
granjero *m*, -jera *f* — **farmhand**
['fɑrm,hænd] *n* : peón *m* — **farmhouse**
['fɑrm,haʊs] *n* : granja *f*, casa *f* de hacienda — **farming** ['fɑrmɪŋ] *n* : agricultura *f*, cultivo *m* (de plantas), crianza *f* (de animales) — **farmyard**
['fɑrm,jɑrd] *n* : corral *m*

far—off ['fɑr,ɔf, -'ɔf] *adj* : lejano

far—reaching ['fɑr'riːtʃɪŋ] *adj* : de gran
alcance

farsighted ['fɑr,saɪṭəd] *adj* **1** : hiper-
métrope **2** PRUDENT : previsor

farther ['fɑrðər] *adv* **1** : más lejos **2**
MORE : más — *adj* : más lejano — **farthest** *adv* **1** : lo más lejos **2** MOST
: más — *adj* : más lejano

fascinate ['fæsən,eɪt] *vt* **-nated; -nating**
: fascinar — **fascination** [,fæsən'eɪʃən]
n : fascinación *f*

fascism ['fæ,ʃɪzəm] *n* : fascismo *m* —
fascist ['fæʃɪst] *adj* : fascista — **~** *n*
: fascista *mf*

fashion ['fæʃən] *n* **1** MANNER : manera *f*
2 STYLE : moda *f* **3 out of ~** : pasada
de moda — **fashionable** ['fæʃənəbəl]
adj : de moda

fast[1] ['fæst] *vi* : ayunar — **~** *n* : ayuno
m

fast[2] ['fæst] *adj* **1** SWIFT : rápido **2** SECURE
: firme, seguro **3** : adelantado (dícese
de un reloj) **4 ~ friends** : amigos *mpl*
leales — **~** *adv* **1** SECURELY : firmemente **2** SWIFTLY : rápidamente **3 ~
asleep** : profundamente dormido

fasten ['fæsən] *vt* : sujetar (papeles,
etc.), abrochar (una blusa, etc.), cerrar
(una maleta, etc.) — *vi* : abrocharse,
cerrar — **fastener** ['fæsənər] *n* : cierre
m

fat ['fæt] *adj* **fatter; fattest 1** : gordo **2**
THICK : grueso — **~** *n* : grasa *f*

fatal ['feɪṭəl] *adj* **1** : mortal **2** FATEFUL
: fatal, fatídico — **fatality** [feɪ'tæləṭi,
fə-] *n, pl* **-ties** : víctima *f* mortal

fate ['feɪt] *n* **1** : destino *m* **2** LOT : suerte
f — **fateful** ['feɪtfəl] *adj* : fatídico

father ['fɑðər] *n* : padre *m* — *vt* : engendrar — **fatherhood** ['fɑðər,hʊd] *n*
: paternidad *f* — **father—in—law**
['fɑðərɪn,lɔ] *n, pl* **fathers—in—law** : sue-

gro *m* — **fatherly** ['foðərli] *adj* : paternal

fathom ['fæðəm] *vt* : comprender

fatigue [fə'tiːg] *n* : fatiga *f* — ~ *vt* -tigued; -tiguing : fatigar

fatten ['fætən] *vt* : engordar — **fattening** *adj* : que engorda

fatty ['fæti] *adj* **fattier; -est** : graso

faucet ['fɔsət] *n* : llave *f* *Lat*, grifo *m* *Spain*

fault ['fɔlt] *n* **1** FLAW : defecto *m* **2** RESPONSIBILITY : culpa *f* **3** : falla *f* (geológica) — *vt* : encontrar defectos a — **faultless** ['fɔltləs] *adj* : impecable — **faulty** ['fɔlti] *adj* **faultier; -est** : defectuoso

fauna ['fɔnə] *n* : fauna *f*

favor *or Brit* **favour** ['feɪvər] *n* **1** : favor *m* **2 in** ~ **of** : a favor de — ~ *vt* **1** : favorecer **2** SUPPORT : estar a favor de **3** PREFER : preferir — **favorable** *or Brit* **favourable** ['feɪvərəbəl] *adj* : favorable — **favorite** *or Brit* **favourite** ['feɪvərət] *n* : favorito *m*, -ta *f* — ~ *adj* : favorito — **favoritism** *or Brit* **favouritism** ['feɪvərəˌtɪzəm] *n* : favoritismo *m*

fawn[1] ['fɔn] *vi* ~ **over** : adular

fawn[2] *n* : cervato *m*

fax ['fæks] *n* : fax *m* — ~ *vt* : faxear, enviar por fax

fear ['fɪr] *v* : temer — ~ *n* **1** : miedo *m*, temor *m* **2 for** ~ **of** : por temor a — **fearful** ['fɪrfəl] *adj* **1** FRIGHTENING : espantoso **2** AFRAID : temeroso

feasible ['fiːzəbəl] *adj* : viable, factible

feast ['fiːst] *n* **1** BANQUET : banquete *m*, festín *m* **2** FESTIVAL : fiesta *f* — ~ *vi* **1** : banquetear **2** ~ **upon** : darse un festín de

feat ['fiːt] *n* : hazaña *f*

feather ['feðər] *n* : pluma *f*

feature ['fiːtʃər] *n* **1** : rasgo *m* (de la cara) **2** CHARACTERISTIC : característica *f* **3** : artículo *m* (en un periódico) **4** ~ **film** : largometraje *m* — *v* **-tured; -turing** *vt* **1** PRESENT : presentar **2** EMPHASIZE : destacar — *vi* : figurar

February ['fɛbjuˌɛri, 'fɛbu-, 'fɛbru-] *n* : febrero *m*

feces ['fiːsiːz] *npl* : excremento *mpl*

federal ['fɛdrəl, -dərəl] *adj* : federal — **federation** [ˌfɛdəˈreɪʃən] *n* : federación *f*

fed up *adj* : harto

fee ['fiː] *n* **1** : honorarios *mpl* **2 entrance** ~ : entrada *f*

feeble ['fiːbəl] *adj* **-bler; -blest 1** : débil **2 a** ~ **excuse** : una pobre excusa

feed ['fiːd] *v* **fed** ['fɛd]; **feeding** *vt* **1** : dar de comer a, alimentar **2** SUPPLY : alimentar — *vi* : comer, alimentarse — ~ *n* : pienso *m*

feel ['fiːl] *v* **felt** ['fɛlt]; **feeling** *vt* **1** : sentir (una sensación, etc.) **2** TOUCH : tocar, palpar **3** BELIEVE : creer — *vi* **1** : sentirse (bien, cansado, etc.) **2** SEEM : parecer **3** ~ **hot/thirsty** : tener calor/sed **4** ~ **like doing** : tener ganas de hacer — ~ *n* : tacto *m*, sensación *f* — **feeling** ['fiːlɪŋ] *n* **1** SENSATION : sensación *f* **2** EMOTION : sentimiento *m* **3** OPINION : opinión *f* **4 hurt s.o.'s** ~**s** : herir los sentimientos de algn

feet → **foot**

feign ['feɪn] *vt* : fingir

feline ['fiːlaɪn] *adj* : felino — ~ *n* : felino *m*, -na *f*

fell[1] → **fall**

fell[2] ['fɛl] *vt* : talar (un árbol)

fellow ['fɛˌloː] *n* **1** COMPANION : compañero *m* **2** MEMBER : socio *m*, -cia *f* **3** MAN : tipo *m* — **fellowship** ['fɛloˌʃɪp] *n* **1** : compañerismo *m* **2** ASSOCIATION : fraternidad *f* **3** GRANT : beca *f*

felon ['fɛlən] *n* : criminal *mf* — **felony** ['fɛləni] *n*, *pl* **-nies** : delito *m* grave

felt[1] → **feel**

felt[2] ['fɛlt] *n* : fieltro *m*

female ['fiːmeɪl] *adj* : femenino — ~ *n* **1** : hembra *f* (animal) **2** WOMAN : mujer *f*

feminine ['fɛmənən] *adj* : femenino — **femininity** [ˌfɛmˈnɪnəti] *n* : femineidad *f* — **feminism** ['fɛməˌnɪzəm] *n* : feminismo *m* — **feminist** ['fɛmənɪst] *adj* : feminista — ~ *n* : feminista *mf*

fence ['fɛnts] *n* : cerca *f*, valla *f*, cerco *m* *Lat* — ~ *v* **fenced; fencing** *vt* *or* ~ **in** : vallar, cercar — *vi* : hacer esgrima — **fencing** ['fɛntsɪŋ] *n* : esgrima *f* (deporte)

fend ['fɛnd] *vt* ~ **off** : rechazar (un enemigo), eludir (una pregunta) — *vi* **for oneself** : valerse por sí mismo — **fender** ['fɛndər] *n* : guardabarros *mpl*

fennel ['fɛnəl] *n* : hinojo *m*

ferment ['fərˌmɛnt] *v* : fermentar — **fermentation** [ˌfərmənˈteɪʃən, -ˌmɛn-] *n* : fermentación *f*

fern ['fərn] *n* : helecho *m*

ferocious [fəˈroːʃəs] *adj* : feroz — **ferocity** [fəˈrɑsəti] *n* : ferocidad *f*

ferret ['fɛrət] *n* : hurón *m* — ~ *vt* ~ **out** : descubrir

Ferris wheel ['fɛrɪs] *n* : noria *f*

ferry ['fɛri] *vt* **-ried; -rying** : transportar — ~ *n*, *pl* **-ries** : ferry *m*

fertile ['fərţəl] *adj* : fértil — **fertility** [fər'tıləţi] *n* : fertilidad *f* — **fertilize** ['fərţəlˌaız] *vt* -**ized**; -**izing** : fecundar (un huevo), abonar (el suelo) — **fertilizer** ['fərţəlˌaızər] *n* : fertilizante *m*, abono *m*

fervent ['fərvənt] *adj* : ferviente — **fervor** *or Brit* **fervour** ['fərvər] *n* : fervor *m*

fester ['festər] *vi* : enconarse

festival ['festəvəl] *n* 1 : fiesta *f* 2 film ~ : festival *m* de cine — **festive** ['festɪv] *adj* : festivo — **festivity** [fes'tɪvəţi] *n*, *pl* -**ties** : festividad *f*

fetch ['fetʃ] *vt* 1 : ir a buscar 2 : venderse por (un precio)

fête ['feɪt, 'fet] *n* : fiesta *f*

fetid ['feţəd] *adj* : fétido

fetish ['feţıʃ] *n* : fetiche *m*

fetters ['feţərz] *npl* : grillos *mpl* — **fetter** ['feţər] *vt* : encadenar

fetus ['fiţəs] *n* : feto *m*

feud ['fjuːd] *n* : enemistad *f* (entre familiares) — ~ *vi* : pelear

feudal ['fjuːdəl] *adj* : feudal — **feudalism** ['fjuːdəlˌɪzəm] *n* : feudalismo *m*

fever ['fiːvər] *n* : fiebre *f* — **feverish** ['fiːvərɪʃ] *adj* : febril

few ['fjuː] *adj* 1 : pocos 2 a ~ **times** : varias veces — ~ *pron* 1 : pocos 2 a ~ : algunos, unos cuantos 3 **quite a** ~ : muchos — **fewer** ['fjuːər] *adj & pron* : menos

fiancé, fiancée [ˌfiːɑnˈseɪ, ˌfiːˈɑnˌseɪ] *n* : prometido *m*, -da *f*; novio *m*, -via *f*

fiasco [fiˈæsˌkoː] *n*, *pl* -**coes** : fiasco *m*

fib ['fɪb] *n* : mentirilla *f* — ~ *vi* **fibbed**; **fibbing** : decir mentirillas

fiber *or fibre* ['faɪbər] *n* : fibra *f* — **fiberglass** ['faɪbərˌglæs] *n* : fibra *f* de vidrio — **fibrous** ['faɪbrəs] *adj* : fibroso

fickle ['fɪkəl] *adj* : inconstante

fiction ['fɪkʃən] *n* : ficción *f* — **fictional** ['fɪkʃənəl] *or* **fictitious** [fɪk'tɪʃəs] *adj* : ficticio

fiddle ['fɪdəl] *n* : violín *m* — ~ *vi* -**dled**; -**dling** 1 : tocar el violín 2 ~ **with** : juguetear con

fidelity [fəˈdeləţi, faɪ-] *n*, *pl* -**ties** : fidelidad *f*

fidget ['fɪʤət] *vi* 1 : estarse inquieto, moverse 2 ~ **with** : juguetear con — **fidgety** ['fɪʤəţi] *adj* : inquieto, nervioso

field ['fiːld] *n* : campo *m* — ~ *vt* : interceptar (una pelota), sortear (una pregunta) — **field glasses** *n* : binoculares *mpl*, gemelos *mpl* — **field trip** *n* : viaje *m* de estudio

fiend ['fiːnd] *n* 1 : demonio *m* 2 FANATIC : fanático *m*, -ca *f* — **fiendish** ['fiːndɪʃ] *adj* : diabólico

fierce ['fɪrs] *adj* **fiercer**; -**est** 1 : feroz 2 INTENSE : fuerte (dícese del viento), acalorado (dícese de un debate) — **fierceness** ['fɪrsnəs] *n* : ferocidad *f*

fiery ['faɪəri] *adj* **fierier**; -**est** 1 BURNING : llameante 2 SPIRITED : ardiente, fogoso — **fieriness** ['faɪərɪnəs] *n* : pasión *f*, ardor *m*

fifteen [fɪf'tiːn] *n* : quince *m* — ~ *adj* : quince — **fifteenth** [fɪf'tiːnθ] *adj* : decimoquinto — ~ *n* 1 : decimoquinto *m*, -ta *f* (en una serie) 2 : quinceavo *m* (en matemáticas)

fifth ['fɪfθ] *n* 1 : quinto *m*, -ta *f* (en una serie) 2 : quinto *m* (en matemáticas) — ~ *adj* : quinto

fiftieth ['fɪftiəθ] *adj* : quincuagésimo — ~ *n* 1 : quincuagésimo *m*, -ma *f* (en una serie) 2 : cincuentavo *m* (en matemáticas)

fifty ['fɪfti] *n*, *pl* -**ties** : cincuenta *m* — ~ *adj* : cincuenta — **fifty–fifty** [ˌfɪfti'fɪfti] *adv* : a medias, mitad y mitad — ~ *adj* a ~ **chance** : un cincuenta por ciento de posibilidades

fig ['fɪg] *n* : higo *m*

fight ['faɪt] *v* **fought** ['fɔt]; **fighting** *vi* 1 BATTLE : luchar 2 QUARREL : pelear 3 ~ **back** : defenderse — *vt* : luchar contra — ~ *n* 1 STRUGGLE : lucha *f* 2 QUARREL : pelea *f* — **fighter** ['faɪţər] *n* 1 : luchador *m*, -dora *f* 2 *or* ~ **plane** : avión *m* de caza

figment ['fɪgmənt] *n* ~ **of the imagination** : producto *m* de la imaginación

figurative ['fɪgjərəţɪv, -gə-] *adj* : figurado

figure ['fɪgjər, -gər] *n* 1 NUMBER : número *m*, cifra *f* 2 PERSON, SHAPE : figura *f* 3 ~ **of speech** : figura *f* retórica 4 **watch one's** ~ : cuidar la línea — ~ *v* -**ured**; -**uring** *vt* : calcular — *vi* 1 : figurar 2 **that** ~**s!** : ¡no me extraña! — **figurehead** ['fɪgjərˌhed, -gər-] *n* : testaferro *m* — **figure out** *vt* 1 UNDERSTAND : entender 2 RESOLVE : resolver

file[1] ['faɪl] *n* : lima *f* (instrumento) — ~ *vt* **filed**; **filing** : limar

file[2] *vt* **filed**; **filing** 1 : archivar (documentos) 2 ~ **charges** : presentar cargos — ~ *n* : archivo *m*

file[3] *n* IN LINE : fila *f* — ~ *vi* ~ **in/out** : entrar/salir en fila

fill ['fɪl] *vt* 1 : llenar, rellenar 2 : cumplir con (un requisito) 3 : tapar (un agujero), empastar (un diente) — *vi* 1 ~ **in for** : reemplazar 2 *or* ~ **up**

: llenarse — **~** *n* **1** eat one's **~**
: comer lo suficiente **2** have one's **~**
of : estar harto de
fillet ['fɪlət, fr'leɪ, 'fɪˌleɪ] *n* : filete *m*
filling ['fɪlɪŋ] *n* **1** : relleno *m* **2** : empaste
m (de dientes) **3 ~ station → service
station**
filly ['fɪli] *n, pl* **-lies** : potra *f*
film ['fɪlm] *n* : película *f* — **~** *vt* : filmar
filter ['fɪltər] *n* : filtro *m* — **~** *vt* : filtrar
filth ['fɪlθ] *n* : mugre *f* — **filthy** ['fɪlθi] *adj*
filthier; -est 1 : mugriento **2** OBSCENE
: obsceno
fin ['fɪn] *n* : aleta *f*
final ['faɪnəl] *adj* **1** LAST : último **2** DE-
FINITIVE : definitivo **3** ULTIMATE : final
— **~** *n* **1** : final *f* (en deportes) **2 ~s**
npl : exámenes *mpl* finales — **finalist**
['faɪnəlɪst] *n* : finalista *mf* — **finalize**
['faɪnəlˌaɪz] *vt* **-ized; -izing** : finalizar
— **finally** ['faɪnəli] *adv* : finalmente
finance [fə'nænts, 'faɪˌnænts] *n* **1** : finanzas *fpl* **2 ~s** *npl* : recursos *mpl* fi-
nancieros — **~** *vt* **-nanced; -nancing**
: financiar — **financial** [fə'nænʧəl,
faɪ-] *adj* : financiero — **financially** [fə-
'nænʧəli, faɪ-] *adv* : económicamente
find ['faɪnd] *vt* **found** ['faʊnd] **finding 1**
LOCATE : encontrar **2** REALIZE : darse
cuenta de **3 ~ guilty** : declarar culpable **4** *or* **~ out** : descubrir — *vi*
out : enterarse — **~** *n* : hallazgo *m* —
finding ['faɪndɪŋ] *n* **1** FIND : hallazgo *m*
2 ~s *npl* : conclusiones *fpl*
fine¹ ['faɪn] *n* : multa *f* — **~** *vt* **fined;
fining** : multar
fine² *adj* **finer; -est 1** DELICATE : fino **2**
EXCELLENT : excelente **3** SUBTLE : sutil
4 : bueno (dícese del tiempo) **5 ~**
print : letra *f* menuda **6 it's ~ with
me** : me parece bien — **~** *adv* OK
: bien — **fine arts** *npl* : bellas artes *fpl*
— **finely** ['faɪnli] *adv* **1** EXCELLENTLY
: excelentemente **2** PRECISELY : con
precisión **3** MINUTELY : fino, menudo
finger ['fɪŋgər] *n* : dedo *m* — **~** *vt*
: tocar, toquetear — **fingernail** ['fɪŋ-
gərˌneɪl] *n* : uña *f* — **fingerprint** ['fɪŋ-
gərˌprɪnt] *n* : huella *f* digital — **fingertip** ['fɪŋgərˌtɪp] *n* : punta *f* del dedo
finicky ['fɪnɪki] *adj* : maniático, mañoso
Lat
finish ['fɪnɪʃ] *v* : acabar, terminar — **~**
n **1** END : fin *m*, final *m* **2** *or* **~ line**
: meta *f* **3** SURFACE : acabado *m*
finite ['faɪˌnaɪt] *adj* : finito
fir ['fər] *n* : abeto *m*
fire ['faɪr] *n* **1** : fuego *m* **2** CONFLAGRA-
TION : incendio *m* **3 catch ~** : incendiarse (dícese de bosques, etc.), pren-

derse (dícese de fósforos, etc.) **4 on
~** : en llamas **5 open ~ on** : abrir
fuego sobre — **~** *vt* **fired; firing 1**
DISMISS : despedir **2** SHOOT : disparar
— *vi* : disparar — **fire alarm** *n* : alarma *f* contra incendios — **firearm** ['faɪr-
ˌɑrm] *n* : arma *f* de fuego — **firecracker** ['faɪrˌkrækər] *n* : petardo *m* — **fire
engine** *n* : carro *m* de bomberos *Lat*,
coche *m* de bomberos *Spain* — **fire
escape** *n* : escalera *f* de incendios —
fire extinguisher *n* : extintor *m* (de
incendios) — **firefighter** ['faɪrˌfaɪtər] *n*
: bombero *m*, -ra *f* — **firefly** ['faɪrˌflaɪ]
n, pl **-flies** : luciérnaga *f* — **firehouse**
→ fire station — **fireman** ['faɪrmən] *n,
pl* **-men** [-mən, -ˌmen] **→ firefighter** —
fireplace ['faɪrˌpleɪs] *n* : hogar *m*,
chimenea *f* — **fireproof** ['faɪrˌpruːf] *adj*
: ignífugo — **fireside** ['faɪrˌsaɪd] *n*
: hogar *m* — **fire station** *n* : estación *f*
de bomberos *Lat*, parque *m* de
bomberos *Spain* — **firewood** ['faɪr-
ˌwʊd] *n* : leña *f* — **fireworks** ['faɪrˌwərk]
npl : fuegos *mpl* artificiales
firm¹ ['fərm] *n* : empresa *f*
firm² *adj* : firme — **firmly** ['fərmli] *adv*
: firmemente — **firmness** ['fərmnəs] *n*
: firmeza *f*
first ['fərst] *adj* **1** : primero **2 at ~ sight**
: a primera vista **3 for the ~ time**
: por primera vez — **~** *adv* **1**
: primero **2 ~ and foremost** : ante
todo **3 ~ of all** : en primer lugar —
~ *n* **1** : primero *m*, -ra *f* **2 at ~** : al
principio — **first aid** *n* : primeros aux-
ilios *mpl* — **first-class** ['fərstˌklæs]
adv : en primera — **~** *adj* : de
primera — **firsthand** ['fərstˈhænd] *adv*
: directamente — **~** *adj* : de primera
mano — **firstly** ['fərstli] *adv* : en
primer lugar — **first name** *n* : nombre
m de pila — **first-rate** ['fərstˈreɪt] *adj*
→ first-class
fiscal ['fɪskəl] *adj* : fiscal
fish ['fɪʃ] *n, pl* **fish** *or* **fishes** : pez *m*
(vivo), pescado *m* (para comer) — **~**
vi **1** : pescar **2 ~ for** SEEK : buscar **3**
go ~ing : ir de pesca — **fisherman**
['fɪʃərmən] *n, pl* **-men** [-mən, -ˌmen]
: pescador *m*, -dora *f* — **fishhook** ['fɪʃ-
ˌhʊk] *n* : anzuelo *m* — **fishing** ['fɪʃɪŋ] *n*
: pesca *f* — **fishing pole** *n* : caña *f* de
pescar — **fish market** *n* : pescadería *f*
— **fishy** ['fɪʃi] *adj* **fishier; -est 1** : a
pescado (dícese de sabores, etc.) **2**
SUSPICIOUS : sospechoso
fist ['fɪst] *n* : puño *m*
fit¹ ['fɪt] *n* **1** : ataque *m* **2 he had a ~**
: le dio un ataque

fit² *adj* **fitter; fittest 1** SUITABLE : apropiado **2** HEALTHY : en forma **3 be ~ for** : ser apto para — **~** *v* **fitted;**
fitting *vt* **1** : encajar en (un hueco, etc.) **2** *(relating to clothing)* : quedar bien a **3** SUIT : ser apropiado para **4** MATCH : coincidir con **5** *or* **~ out** : equipar — *vi* **1** : caber (en una caja, etc.), encajar (en un hueco, etc.) **2** *or* **~ in** BELONG : encajar **3 this dress doesn't ~** : este vestido no me queda bien — **~** *n* **1** it's a good fit : me queda bien — **fitful** ['fɪtfəl] *adj* : irregular — **fitness** ['fɪtnəs] *n* **1** HEALTH : salud *f* **2** SUITABILITY : idoneidad *f* — **fitting** ['fɪt-ɪŋ] *adj* : apropiado

five ['faɪv] *n* : cinco *m* — **~** *adj* : cinco — **five hundred** *n* : quinientos *m* — **~** *adj* : quinientos

fix ['fɪks] *vt* **1** ATTACH : fijar, sujetar **2** REPAIR : arreglar **3** PREPARE : preparar — **~** *n* PREDICAMENT : aprieto *m*, apuro *m* — **fixed** ['fɪkst] *adj* : fijo — **fixture** ['fɪkstʃər] *n* : instalación *f*

fizz ['fɪz] *vi* : burbujear — **~** *n* : efervescencia *f*

fizzle ['fɪzəl] *vi* **-zled; -zling** *or* **~ out** : quedar en nada

flabbergasted ['flæbər,gæstəd] *adj* : estupefacto, pasmado

flabby ['flæbi] *adj* **-bier; -est** : fofo

flaccid ['flæksəd, 'flæsəd] *adj* : fláccido

flag¹ ['flæg] *vi* WEAKEN : flaquear

flag² *n* : bandera *f* — **~** *vt* **flagged; flagging** *or* **~ down** : hacer señales de parada a — **flagpole** ['flæg,poːl] *n* : asta *f*

flagrant ['fleɪgrənt] *adj* : flagrante

flair ['flær] *n* : don *m*, facilidad *f*

flake ['fleɪk] *n* : copo *m* (de nieve), escama *f* (de pintura, de la piel) — **~** *vi* **flaked; flaking** : pelarse

flamboyant [flæm'bɔɪənt] *adj* : extravagante

flame ['fleɪm] *n* **1** : llama *f* **2 burst into ~s** : estallar en llamas **3 go up in ~s** : incendiarse

flamingo [flə'mɪŋgo] *n*, *pl* **-gos** : flamenco *m*

flammable ['flæməbəl] *adj* : inflamable

flank ['flæŋk] *n* : ijada *m* (de un animal), flanco *m* (militar) — **~** *vt* : flanquear

flannel ['flænəl] *n* : franela *f*

flap ['flæp] *n* : solapa *f* (de un sobre, un libro, etc.), tapa *f* (de un recipiente) — **~** *v* **flapped; flapping** *vi* : agitarse — *vt* : batir, agitar

flapjack ['flæp,dʒæk] → pancake

flare ['flær] *vi* **flared; flaring 1 ~ up** BLAZE : llamear **2 ~ up** EXPLODE,

ERUPT : estallar, explotar — **~** *n* **1** BLAZE : llamarada *f* **2** SIGNAL : (luz *f* de) bengala *f*

flash ['flæʃ] *vi* **1** : brillar, destellar **2 ~ past** : pasar como un rayo — *vt* **1** : dirigir (una luz) **2** SHOW : mostrar **3 ~ a smile** : sonreír — **~** *n* **1** : destello *m* **2 ~ of lightning** : relámpago *m* **3 in a ~** : de repente **4 in an hora justa** — **flashlight** ['flæʃ,laɪt] *n* : linterna *f* — **flashy** ['flæʃi] *adj* **flashier; -est** : ostentoso

flask ['flæsk] *n* : frasco *m*

flat ['flæt] *adj* **flatter; flattest 1** LEVEL : plano, llano **2** DOWNRIGHT : categórico **3** FIXED : fijo **4** MONOTONOUS : monótono **5** : bemol (en la música) **6 ~ tire** : neumático *m* desinflado — **~** *n* **1** : bemol *m* (en la música) **2** *Brit* APARTMENT : apartamento *m*, departamento *m* *Lat* **3** PUNCTURE : pinchazo *m* — **~** *adv* **1 ~ broke** : pelado **2 in one hour** : en una hora justa — **flatly** ['flætli] *adv* : categóricamente — **flat-out** ['flæt,aʊt] *adj* **1** : frenético **2** DOWNRIGHT : categórico — **flatten** ['flætən] *vt* **1** LEVEL : aplanar, allanar **2** KNOCK DOWN : arrasar

flatter ['flætər] *vt* **1** : halagar **2** BECOME : favorecer — **flatterer** ['flætərər] *n* : adulador *m*, -dora *f* — **flattering** ['flætərɪŋ] *adj* **1** : halagador **2** BECOMING : favorecedor — **flattery** ['flætəri] *n*, *pl* **-ries** : halagos *mpl*

flaunt ['flɔnt] *vt* : hacer alarde de

flavor *or Brit* **flavour** ['fleɪvər] *n* : gusto *m*, sabor *m* — **~** *vt* : sazonar — **flavorful** *or Brit* **flavourful** ['fleɪvərfəl] *adj* : sabroso — **flavoring** *or Brit* **flavouring** ['fleɪvərɪŋ] *n* : condimento *m*, sazón *f*

flaw ['flɔ] *n* : defecto *m* — **flawless** ['flɔləs] *adj* : perfecto

flax ['flæks] *n* : lino *m*

flea ['fliː] *n* : pulga *f*

fleck ['flɛk] *n* **1** PARTICLE : mota *f* **2** SPOT : pinta *f*

flee ['fliː] *v* **fled** ['flɛd]; **fleeing** *vi* : huir — *vt* : huir de

fleece ['fliːs] *n* : vellón *m* — **~** *vt* **fleeced; fleecing 1** SHEAR : esquilar **2** DEFRAUD : desplumar

fleet ['fliːt] *n* : flota *f*

fleeting ['fliːtɪŋ] *adj* : fugaz

Flemish ['flɛmɪʃ] *adj* : flamenco

flesh ['flɛʃ] *n* **1** : carne *f* **2** PULP : pulpa *f* **3 in the ~** : en persona — **fleshy** ['flɛʃi] *adj* **fleshier; -est 1** : gordo **2** PULPY : carnoso

flew → **fly**

flex ['flɛks] *vt* : flexionar — **flexibility**

[ˌfleksəˈbɪləti] n, pl **-ties** : flexibilidad f
— **flexible** [ˈfleksəbəl] adj : flexible

flick [ˈflɪk] n : golpecito m — ~ vt : dar un golpecito a — vi ~ **through** : hojear

flicker [ˈflɪkər] vi : parpadear — ~ n 1 : parpadeo m 2 **a ~ of hope** : un rayo de esperanza

flier [ˈflaɪər] n 1 AVIATOR : aviador m, -dora f 2 or **flyer** LEAFLET : folleto m, volante m Lat

flight[1] [ˈflaɪt] n 1 : vuelo m 2 TRAJECTORY : trayectoria f 3 ~ **of stairs** : tramo m

flight[2] n ESCAPE : huida f

flimsy [ˈflɪmzi] adj **flimsier; -est 1** LIGHT : ligero 2 SHAKY : poco sólido 3 **a ~ excuse** : una excusa floja

flinch [ˈflɪntʃ] vi ~ **from** : encogerse ante

fling [ˈflɪŋ] vt **flung** [ˈflʌŋ]; **flinging 1** : arrojar 2 ~ **open** : abrir de un golpe — ~ n 1 AFFAIR : aventura f 2 **have a ~ at** : intentar

flint [ˈflɪnt] n : pedernal m

flip [ˈflɪp] v **flipped; flipping** vt 1 or ~ **over** : dar la vuelta a 2 ~ **a coin** : echarlo a cara o cruz — vi 1 or ~ **over** : volcarse 2 ~ **through** : hojear — ~ n SOMERSAULT : voltereta f

flippant [ˈflɪpənt] adj : ligero, frívolo

flipper [ˈflɪpər] n : aleta f

flirt [ˈflərt] vi : coquetear — ~ n : coqueto m, -ta f — **flirtatious** [ˌflərˈteɪʃəs] adj : coqueto

flit [ˈflɪt] vi **flitted; flitting** : revolotear

float [ˈfloɪt] n 1 : flotador m 2 : carroza f (en un desfile) — ~ vi : flotar — vt : hacer flotar

flock [ˈflɑk] n : rebaño m (de ovejas), bandada f (de pájaros) — ~ vi : congregarse

flog [ˈflɑg] vt **flogged; flogging** : azotar

flood [ˈflʌd] n 1 : inundación f 2 : torrente m (de palabras, de lágrimas, etc.) — ~ vt : inundar — **floodlight** [ˈflʌd-ˌlaɪt] n : foco m

floor [ˈflor] n 1 : suelo m, piso m Lat 2 STORY : piso m 3 **dance ~** : pista f de baile 4 **ground ~** : planta f baja — ~ vt 1 KNOCK DOWN : derribar 2 NONPLUS : desconcertar — **floorboard** [ˈflor-ˌbord] n : tabla f del suelo

flop [ˈflɑp] vi **flopped; flopping 1** FLAP : agitarse 2 COLLAPSE : dejarse caer 3 FAIL : fracasar — ~ n FAILURE : fracaso m — **floppy** [ˈflɑpi] adj **-pier; -est** : flojo, flexible — **floppy disk** n : diskette m, disquete m

flora [ˈflorə] n : flora f — **floral** [ˈflorəl]

adj : floral — **florid** [ˈflorɪd] adj 1 FLOWERY : florido 2 RUDDY : rojizo — **florist** [ˈflorɪst] n : florista mf

floss [ˈflos] n → **dental floss**

flounder[1] [ˈflaundər] n, pl **flounder** or **flounders** : platija f

flounder[2] vi 1 or ~ **about** : resbalarse, revolcarse 2 : titubear (en un discurso)

flour [ˈflauər] n : harina f

flourish [ˈflərɪʃ] vi : florecer — vt BRANDISH : blandir — ~ n : floritura f — **flourishing** [ˈflərɪʃɪŋ] adj : floreciente

flout [ˈflaut] vt : desacatar, burlarse de

flow [ˈfloɪ] vi : fluir, correr — ~ n 1 : flujo m, circulación f 2 : corriente f (de información, etc.)

flower [ˈflauər] n : flor f — ~ vi : florecer — **flowered** [ˈflauərd] adj : floreado — **flowerpot** [ˈflauərˌpɑt] n : maceta f — **flowery** [ˈflauəri] adj : florido

flown → **fly**

flu [ˈflu] n : gripe f

fluctuate [ˈflʌktʃuˌeɪt] vi **-ated; -ating** : fluctuar — **fluctuation** [ˌflʌktʃuˈeɪʃən] n : fluctuación f

fluency [ˈfluəntsi] n : fluidez f — **fluent** [ˈfluənt] adj 1 : fluido 2 **be ~ in** : hablar con fluidez — **fluently** [ˈfluəntli] adv : con fluidez

fluff [ˈflʌf] n : pelusa f — **fluffy** [ˈflʌfi] adj **fluffier; -est** : de pelusa, velloso

fluid [ˈfluɪd] adj : fluido — ~ n : fluido m

flung → **fling**

flunk [ˈflʌŋk] vt : reprobar Lat, suspender Spain — vi : ser reprobado Lat, suspender Spain

fluorescence [ˌflurˈesənts, ˌflor-] n : fluorescencia f — **fluorescent** [ˌflurˈesənt, ˌflor-] adj : fluorescente

flurry [ˈfləri] n, pl **-ries 1** GUST : ráfaga f 2 or **snow ~** : nevisca f 3 ~ **of questions** : aluvión m de preguntas

flush [ˈflʌʃ] vi BLUSH : ruborizarse, sonrojarse — vt ~ **the toilet** : tirar de la cadena, jalarle a la cadena Lat — ~ n BLUSH : rubor m, sonrojo m — ~ adj ~ **with** : a nivel con, a ras de — ~ adv : al mismo nivel, a ras

fluster [ˈflʌstər] vt : poner nervioso

flute [ˈflut] n : flauta f

flutter [ˈflʌtər] vi 1 or ~ **about** : ir y venir — ~ n 1 : revoloteo m (de alas) 2 STIR : revuelo m

flux [ˈflʌks] n **be in a state of ~** : cambiar continuamente

fly[1] [ˈflaɪ] v **flew** [ˈflu]; **flown** [ˈfloɪn]; **flying** vi 1 : volar 2 TRAVEL : ir en avión 3 WAVE : ondear 4 RUSH : correr 5 ~

by : pasar volando — *vt* **1** PILOT : pilotar **2** : hacer volar (una cometa), enarbolar (una bandera) — **~** *n, pl* **flies** : bragueta *f* (de un pantalón)

fly² *n, pl* **flies** : mosca *f* (insecto)

flyer → flier

flying saucer *n* : platillo *m* volador *Lat*, platillo *m* volante *Spain*

flyswatter ['flaɪˌswɑtər] *n* : matamoscas *m*

foal ['foɪl] *n* : potro *m*, -tra *f*

foam ['foʊm] *n* : espuma *f* — **~** *vi* : hacer espuma — **foamy** ['foʊmi] *adj* **foamier; -est** : espumoso

focus ['foʊkəs] *n, pl* **-ci** ['foʊˌsaɪ, -ˌkaɪ] **1** : foco *m* **2 be in ~** : estar enfocado **3** **~ of attention** : centro *m* de atención — **~** *v* **-cused** *or* **-cussed; -cusing** *or* **-cussing** *vt* **1** : enfocar **2** : centrar (la atención, etc.) — *vi* : enfocar (con los ojos), concentrarse en (con la mente)

fodder ['fɑdər] *n* : forraje *m*

foe ['foʊ] *n* : enemigo *m*, -ga *f*

fog ['fɔg, 'fɑg] *n* : niebla *f* — **~** *v* **fogged; fogging** *vt* : empañar — *vi or* **~ up** : empañarse — **foggy** ['fɔgi, 'fɑ-] *adj* **foggier; -est** : nebuloso — **foghorn** ['fɔgˌhɔrn, 'fɑg-] *n* : sirena *f* de niebla

foil¹ ['fɔɪl] *vt* : frustrar

foil² *n or* **aluminum ~** : papel *m* de aluminio

fold¹ ['foʊld] *n* **1** : redil *m* (para ovejas) **2** **return to the ~** : volver al redil

fold² *vt* **1** : doblar, plegar **2 ~ one's arms** : cruzar los brazos — *vi* **1** *or* **~ up** : doblarse, plegarse **2** FAIL : fracasar — **~** *n* : pliegue *m* — **folder** ['foʊldər] *n* : carpeta *f*

foliage ['foʊlidʒ, -lɪdʒ] *n* : follaje *m*

folk ['foʊk] *n, pl* **folk** *or* **folks 1** : gente *f* **2 ~s** *npl* PARENTS : padres *mpl* — **~** *adj* **1** : popular **2 ~ dance** : danza *f* folklórica — **folklore** ['foʊkˌlɔr] *n* : folklore *m*

follow ['fɑloʊ] *vt* **1** : seguir **2** UNDERSTAND : entender **3 ~ up** : seguir — *vi* **1** : seguir **2** UNDERSTAND : entender **3 ~ up on** : seguir con — **follower** ['fɑloʊər] *n* : seguidor *m*, -dora *f* — **following** ['fɑloʊɪŋ] *adj* : siguiente — **~** *n* : seguidores *mpl* — **~** *prep* : después de

folly ['fɑli] *n, pl* **-lies** : locura *f*

fond ['fɑnd] *adj* **1** : cariñoso **2 be ~ of sth** : ser aficionado a algo **3 be ~ of s.o.** : tener cariño a algn

fondle ['fɑndəl] *vt* **-dled; -dling** : acariciar

fondness ['fɑndnəs] *n* **1** LOVE : cariño *m* **2** LIKING : afición *f*

food ['fuːd] *n* : comida *f*, alimento *m* — **foodstuffs** ['fuːdˌstʌfs] *npl* : comestibles *mpl*

fool ['fuːl] *n* **1** : idiota *mf* **2** JESTER : bufón *m*, -fona *f* — **~** *vi* **1** JOKE : bromear **2 ~ around** : perder el tiempo — *vt* TRICK : engañar — **foolhardy** ['fuːlˌhɑrdi] *adj* : temerario — **foolish** ['fuːlɪʃ] *adj* : tonto — **foolishness** ['fuːlɪʃnəs] *n* : tontería *f* — **foolproof** ['fuːlˌpruːf] *adj* : infalible

foot ['fʊt] *n, pl* **feet** ['fiːt] *n* : pie *m* — **footage** ['fʊtɪdʒ] *n* : secuencias *fpl* (cinemáticas) — **football** ['fʊtˌbɔl] *n* : fútbol *m* americano — **footbridge** ['fʊtˌbrɪdʒ] *n* : pasarela *f*, puente *m* peatonal — **foothills** ['fʊtˌhɪlz] *npl* : estribaciones *fpl* — **foothold** ['fʊtˌhoʊld] *n* : punto *m* de apoyo — **footing** ['fʊtɪŋ] *n* **1** BALANCE : equilibrio *m* **2 on equal ~** : en igualdad — **footlights** ['fʊtˌlaɪts] *npl* : candilejas *fpl* — **footnote** ['fʊtˌnoʊt] *n* : nota *f* al pie de la página — **footpath** ['fʊtˌpæθ] *n* : sendero *m* — **footprint** ['fʊtˌprɪnt] *n* : huella *f* — **footstep** ['fʊtˌstɛp] *n* : paso *m* — **footstool** ['fʊtˌstuːl] *n* : escabel *m* — **footwear** ['fʊtˌwær] *n* : calzado *m*

for ['fɔr] *prep* **1** (*indicating purpose, etc.*) : para **2** (*indicating motivation, etc.*) : por **3** (*indicating duration*) : durante **4 we walked ~ 3 miles** : andamos 3 millas **5** AS FOR : con respecto a — **~** *conj* : puesto que, porque

forage ['fɔridʒ] *n* : forraje *m* — **~** *vi* **-aged; -aging 1** : forrajear **2 ~ for** : buscar

foray ['fɔrˌeɪ] *n* : incursión *f*

forbid [fər'bɪd] *vt* **-bade** [-'bæd, -'beɪd] *or* **-bad** [-'bæd]; **-bidden** [-'bɪdən]; **-bidding** : prohibir — **forbidding** [fər'bɪdɪŋ] *adj* : intimidante, severo

force ['fɔrs] *n* **1** : fuerza *f* **2 by ~** : por la fuerza **3 in ~** : en vigor, en vigencia **4 armed ~s** : fuerzas *fpl* armadas — **~** *vt* **forced; forcing 1** : forzar **2** OBLIGATE : obligar — **forced** ['fɔrst] *adj* : forzado, forzoso — **forceful** ['fɔrsfəl] *adj* : fuerte, enérgetico

forceps ['fɔrsəps, -ˌsɛps] *ns & pl* : fórceps *m*

forcibly [-bli] *adv* : por la fuerza

ford ['fɔrd] *n* : vado *m* — **~** *vt* : vadear

fore ['fɔr] *n* **come to the ~** : empezar a destacarse

forearm ['fɔrˌɑrm] *n* : antebrazo *m*

foreboding [fɔr'boʊdɪŋ] *n* : premonición *f*, presentimiento *m*

forecast ['for,kæst] *vt* **-cast; -casting** : predecir, pronosticar — **~** *n* : predicción *f*, pronóstico *m*

forefathers ['for,fɑðərz] *n* : antepasados *mpl*

forefinger ['for,fɪŋɡər] *n* : índice *m*, dedo *m* índice

forefront ['for,frʌnt] *n* **at/in the ~** : a la vanguardia

forego [for'ɡoː] → **forgo**

foregone [for'ɡɔn] *adj* **~ conclusion** : resultado *m* inevitable

foreground ['for,ɡraund] *n* : primer plano *m*

forehead ['forəd, 'for,hed] *n* : frente *f*

foreign ['forən] *adj* **1** : extranjero **2 ~ trade** : comercio *m* exterior — **foreigner** ['forənər] *n* : extranjero *m*, -ra *f*

foreman ['formən] *n*, *pl* **-men** [-mən, -,men] : capataz *mf*

foremost ['for,moːst] *adj* : principal — **~** *adv* **first and ~** : ante todo

forensic [fə'rensɪk] *adj* : forense

forerunner ['for,rʌnər] *n* : precursor *m*, -sora *f*

foresee [for'siː] *vt* **-saw; -seen; -seeing** : prever — **foreseeable** [for'siːəbəl] *adj* : previsible

foreshadow [for'ʃædoː] *vt* : presagiar

foresight ['for,saɪt] *n* : previsión *f*

forest ['forəst] *n* : bosque *m* — **forestry** ['forəstri] *n* : silvicultura *f*

foretaste ['for,teɪst] *n* : anticipo *m*

foretell [for'tel] *vt* **-told; -telling** : predecir

forethought ['for,θɔt] *n* : reflexión *f* previa

forever [fər'evər] *adv* **1** ETERNALLY : para siempre **2** CONTINUALLY : siempre, constantemente

forewarn [for'worn] *vt* : advertir, prevenir

foreword ['forwərd] *n* : prólogo *m*

forfeit ['forfət] *n* **1** PENALTY : pena *f* **2** : prenda *f* (en un juego) — **~** *vt* : perder

forge ['fordʒ] *n* : forja *f* — **~** *v* **forged; forging** *vt* **1** : forjar (metal, etc.) **2** COUNTERFEIT : falsificar — *vi* **~ ahead** : avanzar, seguir adelante — **forger** ['fordʒər] *n* : falsificador *m*, -dora *f* — **forgery** ['fordʒəri] *n*, *pl* **-eries** : falsificación *f*

forget [fər'ɡet] *v* **-got** [-'ɡɑt]; **-gotten** [--'ɡɑtən] *or* **-got; -getting** *vt* : olvidar, olvidarse de — *vi* **1** : olvidarse **2 I forgot** : se me olvidó — **forgetful** [fər'ɡetfəl] *adj* : olvidadizo

forgive [fər'ɡɪv] *vt* **-gave** [-'ɡeɪv]; **-given** [-'ɡɪvən]; **-giving** : perdonar — **forgiveness** [fər'ɡɪvnəs] *n* : perdón *m*

forgo *or* **forego** [for'ɡoː] *vt* **-went; -gone; -going** : privarse de, renunciar a

fork ['fork] *n* **1** : tenedor *m* **2** PITCHFORK : horca *f* **3** : bifurcación *f* (de un camino, etc.) — *vi* : ramificarse, bifurcarse — *vt* **~ over** : desembolsar

forlorn [fər'lorn] *adj* : triste

form ['form] *n* **1** : forma *f* **2** DOCUMENT : formulario *m* **3** KIND : tipo *m* — *vt* **1** : formar **2 ~ a habit** : adquirir un hábito — *vi* : formarse

formal ['forməl] *adj* : formal — **~** *n* **1** BALL : baile *m* (formal) **2** *or* **~ dress** : traje *m* de etiqueta — **formality** [for'mæləti] *n*, *pl* **-ties** : formalidad *f*

format ['for,mæt] *n* : formato *m* — **~** *vt* **-matted; -matting** : formatear

formation [for'meɪʃən] *n* **1** : formación *f* **2** SHAPE : forma *f*

former ['formər] *adj* **1** PREVIOUS : antiguo, anterior **2** : primero (de dos) — **formerly** ['formərli] *adv* : anteriormente, antes

formidable ['formədəbəl, for'mɪdə-] *adj* : formidable

formula ['formjələ] *n*, *pl* **-las** *or* **-lae** [-,liː, -,laɪ] **1** : fórmula *f* **2** *or* **baby ~** : preparado *m* para biberón

forsake [fər'seɪk] *vt* **-sook** [-'suk]; **-saken** [-'seɪkən]; **-saking** : abandonar

fort ['fort] *n* : fuerte *m*

forth ['forθ] *adv* **1 and so ~** : etcétera **2 back and ~** → **back 3 from this day ~** : de hoy en adelante — **forthcoming** [forθ'kʌmɪŋ, 'forθ,-] *adj* **1** COMING : próximo **2** OPEN : comunicativo — **forthright** ['forθ,raɪt] *adj* : directo, franco

fortieth ['fortiəθ] *adj* : cuadragésimo — **~** *n* **1** : cuadragésimo *m*, -ma *f* (en una serie) **2** : cuarentavo *m*, cuarentava parte *f*

fortify ['forţə,faɪ] *vt* **-fied; -fying** : fortificar — **fortification** [,forţəfə'keɪʃən] *n* : fortificación *f*

fortitude ['forţə,tuːd, -,tjuːd] *n* : fortaleza *f*

fortnight ['fort,naɪt] *n* : quince días *mpl*, quincena *f*

fortress ['fortrəs] *n* : fortaleza *f*

fortunate ['fortʃənət] *adj* : afortunado — **fortunately** ['fortʃənətli] *adv* : afortunadamente — **fortune** ['fortʃən] *n* : fortuna *f* — **fortune-teller** ['fortʃən,telər] *n* : adivino *m*, -na *f*

forty ['forti] *n*, *pl* **forties** : cuarenta *m* — **~** *adj* : cuarenta

forum ['forəm] n, pl **-rums** : foro m
forward ['forwərd] adj 1 : hacia adelante
(en dirección), delantero (en posición)
2 BRASH : descarado — ~ adv 1
: (hacia) adelante 2 **from this day** ~
: de aquí en adelante — ~ vt : remitir,
enviar — ~ n : delantero m, -ra f (en
deportes) — **forwards** ['forwərdz] adv
→ **forward**
fossil ['fɑsəl] n : fósil m
foster ['fostər] adj : adoptivo — ~ vt
: promover, fomentar
fought → **fight**
foul ['faul] adj 1 REPULSIVE : asqueroso
2 — **language** : palabrotas fpl 3 —
play : actos mpl criminales 4 —
weather : mal tiempo m — ~ n : falta
f (en deportes) — ~ vi : cometer fal-
tas (en deportes) — ~ vt : ensuciar
found¹ ['faund] → **find**
found² vt : fundar, establecer — **foun-**
dation [faun'deɪʃən] n 1 : fundación f 2
BASIS : fundamento m 3 : cimientos
mpl (de un edificio)
founder¹ ['faundər] n : fundador m,
-dora f
founder² vi SINK : hundirse
fountain ['fauntən] n : fuente f
four ['for] n : cuatro m — ~ adj : cuatro
— **fourfold** ['for,fo:ld, -'fo:ld] adj : cua-
druple — **four hundred** adj : cuatrocientos — ~ n : cuatrocientos m
fourteen [for'ti:n] n : catorce m — ~
adj : catorce — **fourteenth** [for'ti:nθ]
adj : decimocuarto — ~ n 1 : decimocuarto m, -ta f (en una serie) 2
: catorceavo m, catorceava parte f
fourth ['forθ] n 1 : cuarto m, -ta f (en una
serie) 2 : cuarto m, cuarta parte f — ~
adj : cuarto
fowl ['faul] n, pl **fowl** or **fowls** : ave f
fox ['fɑks] n, pl **foxes** : zorro m, -ra f —
~ vt TRICK : engañar — **foxy** ['fɑksi]
adj **foxier; -est** SHREWD : astuto
foyer ['foɪər, 'foɪjeɪ] n : vestíbulo m
fraction ['frækʃən] n : fracción f
fracture ['fræktʃər] n : fractura f — ~ vt
-tured; -turing : fracturar
fragile ['frædʒəl, -dʒaɪl] adj : frágil
fragment ['frægmənt] n : fragmento m
fragrant ['freɪgrənt] adj : fragante —
fragrance ['freɪgrəns] n : fragancia f,
aroma m
frail ['freɪl] adj : débil, delicado
frame ['freɪm] vt **framed; framing** 1 EN-
CLOSE : enmarcar 2 COMPOSE, DRAFT
: formular 3 INCRIMINATE : incriminar
— ~ n 1 : armazón mf (de un edificio,
etc.) 2 : marco m (de un cuadro, una
puerta, etc.) 3 or ~s npl : montura f

(para anteojos) 4 ~ **of mind** : estado
m de ánimo — **framework** ['freɪm-
,wɜrk] n : armazón f
franc ['fræŋk] n : franco m
frank ['fræŋk] adj : franco — **frankly** adv
: francamente — **frankness** ['fræŋk-
nəs] n : franqueza f
frantic ['fræntɪk] adj : frenético
fraternal [frə'tərnəl] adj : fraterno, fraternal — **fraternity** [frə'tərnəti] n, pl
-ties : fraternidad f — **fraternize**
['frætər,naɪz] vi **-nized; -nizing** : con-
fraternizar
fraud ['frɔd] n 1 DECEIT : fraude m 2 IM-
POSTOR : impostor m, -tora f — **fraud-**
ulent ['frɔdʒələnt] adj : fraudulento
fraught ['frɔt] adj ~ **with** : lleno de,
cargado de
fray¹ ['freɪ] n 1 **join the** ~ : salir a la
palestra 2 **return to the** ~ : volver a
la carga
fray² vt : crispar (los nervios) — vi
: deshilacharse
freak ['fri:k] n 1 ODDITY : fenómeno m 2
ENTHUSIAST : entusiasta mf — **freak-**
ish ['fri:kɪʃ] adj : anormal
freckle ['frekəl] n : peca f
free ['fri:] adj **freer; freest** 1 : libre 2 or
~ **of charge** : gratuito, gratis 3 LOOSE
: suelto — ~ vt **freed; freeing** 1 : liberar, poner en libertad 2 RELEASE,
UNFASTEN : soltar, desatar — ~ adv or
for ~ : gratis — **freedom** ['fri:dəm] n
: libertad f — **freelance** ['fri:,læns] adj
: por cuenta propia — **freely** ['fri:li]
adv 1 : libremente 2 LAVISHLY : con
generosidad — **freeway** ['fri:,weɪ] n
: autopista f — **free will** n : libre
albedrío m 2 **of one's own** ~ : por su
propia voluntad
freeze ['fri:z] v **froze** ['fro:z]; **frozen**
['fro:zən]; **freezing** vi 1 : congelarse,
helarse 2 STOP : quedarse inmóvil — vt
: helar (agua, etc.), congelar (alimentos, precios, etc.) — **freeze-dry** ['fri:z-
'draɪ] vt **-dried; -drying** : liofilizar —
freezer ['fri:zər] n : congelador m —
freezing ['fri:zɪŋ] adj 1 CHILLY : helado
2 **it's freezing!** : ¡hace un frío espantoso!
freight ['freɪt] n 1 SHIPPING : porte m,
flete m Lat 2 CARGO : carga f
French ['frentʃ] adj : francés — ~ n 1
: francés m (idioma) 2 **the** ~ npl : los
franceses — **Frenchman** ['frentʃmən]
n : francés m — **Frenchwoman**
['frentʃ,wumən] n : francesa f —
french fries ['frentʃ,fraɪz] npl : papas
fpl fritas
frenetic [frɪ'netɪk] adj : frenético

frenzy ['frɛnzi] *n, pl* **-zies** : frenesí *m* — **frenzied** ['frɛnzid] *adj* : frenético

frequent [fri'kwɛnt, 'fri:kwənt] *vt* : frecuentar — ~ ['fri:kwənt] *adj* : frecuente — **frequency** ['fri:kwəntsi] *n, pl* **-cies** : frecuencia *f* — **frequently** *adv* : a menudo, frecuentemente

fresco ['frɛs,ko:] *n, pl* **-coes** : fresco *m*

fresh ['frɛʃ] *adj* **1** : fresco **2** IMPUDENT : descarado **3** CLEAN : limpio **4** NEW : nuevo **5** ~ **water** : agua *m* dulce — **freshen** ['frɛʃən] *vt* : refrescar — *vi* ~ **up** : arreglarse — **freshly** ['frɛʃli] *adv* : recién — **freshman** ['frɛʃmən] *n, pl* **-men** [-mən, -mɛn] : estudiante *mf* de primer año — **freshness** ['frɛʃnəs] *n* : frescura *f*

fret ['frɛt] *vi* **fretted; fretting** : preocuparse — **fretful** ['frɛtfəl] *adj* : nervioso, irritable

friar ['fraɪər] *n* : fraile *m*

friction ['frɪkʃən] *n* : fricción *f*

Friday ['fraɪˌdeɪ, -di] *n* : viernes *m*

friend ['frɛnd] *n* : amigo *m*, -ga *f* — **friendliness** ['frɛndlinəs] *n* : simpatía *f* — **friendly** ['frɛndli] *adj* **-lier; -est** : simpático, amable — **friendship** ['frɛndˌʃɪp] *n* : amistad *f*

frigate ['frɪgət] *n* : fragata *f*

fright ['fraɪt] *n* : miedo *m*, susto *m* — **frighten** ['fraɪtən] *vt* : asustar, espantar — **frightened** ['fraɪtənd] *adj* : asustado, temeroso **2 be** ~ **of** : tener miedo de — **frightening** ['fraɪtənɪŋ] *adj* : espantoso — **frightful** ['fraɪtfəl] *adj* : espantoso, terrible

frigid ['frɪdʒɪd] *adj* : frío, glacial

frill ['frɪl] *n* **1** RUFFLE : volante *m* **2** LUXURY : lujo *m*

fringe ['frɪndʒ] *n* **1** : fleco *m* **2** EDGE : periferia *f*, margen *m* **3** ~ **benefits** : incentivos *mpl*, extras *mpl*

frisk ['frɪsk] *vt* SEARCH : cachear, registrar — **frisky** ['frɪski] *adj* **friskier; -est** : retozón, juguetón

fritter ['frɪtər] *n* : buñuelo *m* — ~ *vt* ~ **away** : malgastar (dinero), desperdiciar (tiempo)

frivolous ['frɪvələs] *adj* : frívolo — **frivolity** [frɪ'vɑləti] *n, pl* **-ties** : frivolidad *f*

frizzy ['frɪzi] *adj* **frizzier; -est** : rizado, crespo

fro ['fro:] *adv* **to and** ~ → **to**

frock ['frɑk] *n* : vestido *m*

frog ['frɔg, 'frɑg] *n* **1** : rana *f* **2 have a** ~ **in one's throat** : tener carraspera

frolic ['frɑlɪk] *vi* **-icked; -icking** : retozar

from ['frʌm, 'frɑm] *prep* **1** : desde **2** (*indicating a starting point*) : desde **2** (*in-

dicating a cause) : de, por **4** ~ **now on** : a partir de ahora

front ['frʌnt] *n* **1** : parte *f* delantera **2** : delantera *f* (de un vestido, etc.), fachada *f* (de un edificio), frente *m* (militar) **3 cold** ~ : frente *m* frío **4 in** ~ **of** : delante de, adelante de *Lat* — ~ *vi or* ~ **on** : dar a, estar orientado a — ~ *adj* **1** : delantero, de adelante **2 the** ~ **row** : la primera fila

frontier [frʌn'tɪr] *n* : frontera *f*

frost ['frɔst] *n* **1** : helada *f* **2** : escarcha *f* (en una superficie) — ~ *vt* ICE : bañar (pasteles) — **frostbite** ['frɔstˌbaɪt] *n* : congelación *f* — **frosting** ['frɔstɪŋ] *n* ICING : baño *m* — **frosty** ['frɔsti] *adj* **frostier; -est 1** : cubierto de escarcha **2** CHILLY : helado, frío

froth ['frɔθ] *n, pl* **froths** ['frɔθs, 'frɔðz] : espuma *f* — **frothy** ['frɔθi] *adj* **frothier; -est** : espumoso

frown ['fraʊn] *vi* **1** : fruncir el ceño, fruncir el entrecejo **2** ~ **at** : mirar con ceño **3** ~ **upon** : desaprobar — ~ *n* : ceño *m* (fruncido)

froze, frozen → **freeze**

frugal ['fru:gəl] *adj* : frugal

fruit ['fru:t] *n* **1** : fruta *f* **2** PRODUCT, RESULT : fruto *m* — **fruitcake** ['fru:tˌkeɪk] *n* : pastel *m* de frutas — **fruitful** ['fru:tfəl] *adj* : fructífero — **fruition** [fru'ɪʃən] *n* **come to** ~ : realizarse — **fruitless** ['fru:tləs] *adj* : infructuoso — **fruity** ['fru:ti] *adj* **fruitier; -est** : (con sabor) a fruta

frustrate ['frʌsˌtreɪt] *vt* **-trated; -trating** : frustrar — **frustrating** ['frʌsˌtreɪtɪŋ] *adj* : frustrante — **frustration** [frʌs'treɪʃən] *n* : frustración *f*

fry ['fraɪ] *vt* **fried; frying** : freír — ~ *n, pl* **fries 1 small** ~ : gente *f* de poca monta **2 fries** *npl* → **french fries** — **frying pan** *n* : sartén *mf*

fudge ['fʌdʒ] *n* : dulce *m* blando de chocolate y leche

fuel ['fjuːəl] *n* : combustible *m* — ~ *vt* **-eled** *or* **-elled; -eling** *or* **-elling 1** : alimentar (un horno), abastecer de combustible (un avión) **2** STIMULATE : estimular

fugitive ['fjuːdʒətɪv] *n* : fugitivo *m*, -va *f*

fulfill *or* **fulfil** [fʊl'fɪl] *vt* **-filled; -filling 1** : cumplir con (una obligación), desarrollar (potencial) **2** FILL, MEET : cumplir — **fulfillment** [fʊl'fɪlmənt] *n* **1** ACCOMPLISHMENT : cumplimiento *m* **2** SATISFACTION : satisfacción *f*

full ['fʊl, 'fʌl] *adj* **1** FILLED : lleno **2** COMPLETE : complete, detallado **3** : redondo (dícese de la cara), amplio (dícese de ropa) **4 at ~ speed** : a toda velocidad **5 in ~ bloom** : en plena flor — **~** *adv* **1** DIRECTLY : de lleno **2 know ~ well** : saber muy bien — **~** *n* **1 pay in ~** : pagar en su totalidad **2 to the ~** : al máximo — **full-fledged** ['fʊl'flɛdʒd] *adj* : hecho y derecho — **fully** ['fʊli] *adv* **1** COMPLETELY : completamente **2** AT LEAST : al menos, por lo menos

fumble ['fʌmbəl] *vi* **-bled; -bling 1** RUMMAGE : hurgar **2 ~ with** : manejar con torpeza

fume ['fjuːm] *vi* **fumed; fuming 1** SMOKE : echar humo, humear **2** RAGE : estar furioso — **fumes** *npl* : gases *mpl*

fumigate ['fjuːməˌgeɪt] *vt* **-gated; -gating** : fumigar

fun ['fʌn] *n* **1** AMUSEMENT : diversión *f* **2 have ~** : divertirse **3 make ~ of** : reírse de, burlarse de — **~** *adj* : divertido

function ['fʌŋkʃən] *n* **1** : función *f* **2** GATHERING : recepción *f*, reunión *f* social — **~** *vi* : funcionar — **functional** ['fʌŋkʃənəl] *adj* : funcional

fund ['fʌnd] *n* **1** : fondo *m* **2 ~s** *npl* RESOURCES : fondos *mpl* — **~** *vt* : financiar

fundamental [ˌfʌndəˈmɛntəl] *adj* : fundamental — **fundamentals** *npl* : fundamentos *mpl*

funeral ['fjuːnərəl] *adj* : funeral, fúnebre — **~** *n* : funeral *m*, funerales *mpl* — **funeral home** *or* **funeral parlor** *n* : funeraria *f*

fungus ['fʌŋgəs] *n*, *pl* **fungi** ['fʌnˌdʒaɪ, 'fʌŋˌgaɪ] : hongo *m*

funnel ['fʌnəl] *n* **1** : embudo *m* **2** SMOKESTACK : chimenea *f*

funny ['fʌni] *adj* **funnier; -est 1** : divertido, gracioso **2** STRANGE : extraño, raro — **funnies** ['fʌniz] *npl* : tiras *fpl* cómicas

fur ['fər] *n* **1** : pelaje *m*, pelo *m* (de un animal) **2** *or* **~ coat** : (prenda *f* de) piel *f* — **~** *adj* : de piel

furious ['fjʊriəs] *adj* : furioso

furnace ['fərnəs] *n* : horno *m*

furnish ['fərnɪʃ] *vt* **1** SUPPLY : proveer **2** : amueblar (una casa, etc.) — **furnishings** ['fərnɪʃɪŋz] *npl* : muebles *mpl*, mobiliario *m* — **furniture** ['fərnɪtʃər] *n* : muebles *mpl*, mobiliario *m*

furrow ['fəroː] *n* : surco *m*

furry ['fəri] *adj* **furrier; -est** : peludo (dícese de un animal), de peluche (dícese de un juguete, etc.)

further ['fərðər] *adv* **1** FARTHER : más lejos **2** MOREOVER : además **3** MORE : más — **~** *vt* : promover, fomentar — **~** *adj* **1** FARTHER : más lejano **2** ADDITIONAL : adicional, más **3 until ~ notice** : hasta nuevo aviso — **furthermore** ['fərðər,mor] *adv* : además — **furthest** ['fərðəst] → **farthest**

furtive ['fərtɪv] *adj* : furtivo

fury ['fjʊri] *n*, *pl* **-ries** : furia *f*

fuse[1] *or* **fuze** ['fjuːz] *n* : mecha *f* (de una bomba, etc.)

fuse[2] *v* **fused; fusing** *vt* **1** MELT : fundir **2** UNITE : fusionar — *vi* : fundirse, fusionarse — **~** *n* **1** : fusible *m* **2 blow a ~** : fundir un fusible — **fusion** ['fjuːʒən] *n* : fusión *f*

fuss ['fʌs] *n* **1** : jaleo *m*, alboroto *m* **2 make a ~** : armar un escándalo — **~** *vi* **1** WORRY : preocuparse **2** COMPLAIN : quejarse — **fussy** ['fʌsi] *adj* **fussier; -est 1** IRRITABLE : irritable **2** ELABORATE : recargado **3** FINICKY : quisquilloso

futile ['fjuːtəl, 'fjuːˌtaɪl] *adj* : inútil, vano — **futility** [fjuˈtɪləti] *n*, *pl* **-ties** : inutilidad *f*

future ['fjuːtʃər] *adj* : futuro — **~** *n* : futuro *m*

fuze → **fuse**[1]

fuzz ['fʌz] *n* : pelusa *f* — **fuzzy** ['fʌzi] *adj* **fuzzier; -est 1** FURRY : con pelusa, peludo **2** BLURRY : borroso **3** VAGUE : confuso

G

g ['dʒiː] *n*, *pl* **g's** *or* **gs** ['dʒiːz] : g *f*, séptima letra del alfabeto inglés

gab ['gæb] *vi* **gabbed; gabbing** : charlar, cotorrear *fam* — **~** *n* CHATTER : charla *f*

gable ['geɪbəl] *n* : aguilón *m*

gadget ['gædʒət] *n* : artilugio *m*

gag ['gæg] *v* **gagged; gagging** *vt* : amordazar — *vi* CHOKE : atragantarse — **~** *n* **1** : mordaza *f* **2** JOKE : chiste *m*

gage → gauge

gaiety ['geɪəti] *n*, *pl* **-eties** : alegría *f* — **gaily** ['geɪli] *adv* : alegremente

gain ['geɪn] *n* **1** PROFIT : ganancia *f* **2** INCREASE : aumento *m* — **~** *vt* **1** OBTAIN : ganar, adquirir **2 ~ weight** : aumentar de peso — *vi* **1** PROFIT : beneficiarse **2** : adelantar(se) (dícese de un reloj) —

gainful ['geɪnfəl] *adj* : lucrativo

gait ['geɪt] *n* : modo *m* de andar

gala ['geɪlə, 'gæ-, 'ga-] *n* : fiesta *f*

galaxy ['gæləksi] *n*, *pl* **-axies** : galaxia *f*

gale ['geɪl] *n* **1** : vendaval *f* **2** **~s of laughter** : carcajadas *fpl*

gall ['gɔl] *n* **have the ~ to** : tener el descaro de

gallant ['gælənt] *adj* **1** BRAVE : valiente **2** CHIVALROUS : galante

gallbladder ['gɔl,blædər] *n* : vesícula *f* biliar

gallery ['gæləri] *n*, *pl* **-leries** : galería *f*

gallon ['gælən] *n* : galón *m*

gallop ['gæləp] *vi* : galopar — **~** *n* : galope *m*

gallows ['gæ,loːz] *n*, *pl* **-lows** or **-lowses** [-,loːzəz] : horca *f*

gallstone ['gɔl,stoːn] *n* : cálculo *m* biliar

galore [gə'lor] *adj* : en abundancia

galoshes [gə'laʃ] *n* : galochas *fpl*, chanclos *mpl*

galvanize ['gælvən,aɪz] *vt* **-nized; -nizing** : galvanizar

gamble ['gæmbəl] *v* **-bled; -bling** *vi* **1** : jugar — *vt* : jugarse — **~** *n* **1** BET : apuesta *f* **2** RISK : riesga *f* — **gambler** ['gæmbələr] *n* : jugador *m*, -dora *f*

game ['geɪm] *n* **1** : juego *m* **2** MATCH : partido *m* **3** or **~ animals** : caza *f* — **~** *adj* READY : listo, dispuesto

gamut ['gæmət] *n* : gama *f*

gang ['gæŋ] *n* : banda *f*, pandilla *f* — **~** *vi* **~ up on** : unirse contra

gangplank ['gæŋ,plæŋk] *n* : pasarela *f*

gangrene ['gæŋ,griːn, 'gæn-; 'gæŋ'-, gæn-'-] *n* : gangrena *f*

gangster ['gæŋstər] *n* : gángster *mf*

gangway ['gæŋ,weɪ] *n* → **gangplank**

gap ['gæp] *n* **1** OPENING : espacio *m* **2** INTERVAL : intervalo *m* **3** DISPARITY : brecha *f*, distancia *f* **4** DEFICIENCY : laguna *f*

gape ['geɪp] *vi* **gaped; gaping 1** OPEN : estar abierto **2** STARE : mirar boquiabierto

garage [gə'rɑʒ, -'rɑdʒ] *n* : garaje *m* — **~** *vt* **-raged; -raging** : dejar en un garaje

garb ['gɑrb] *n* : vestido *m*

garbage ['gɑrbɪdʒ] *n* : basura *f* — **garbage can** *n* : cubo *m* de la basura

garble ['gɑrbəl] *vt* **-bled; -bling** : tergiversar — **garbled** ['gɑrbəld] *adj* : confuso, incomprensible

garden ['gɑrdən] *n* : jardín *m* — **~** *vi* : trabajar en el jardín — **gardener** ['gɑrdənər] *n* : jardinero *m*, -ra *f* — **gardening** ['gɑrdənɪŋ] *n* : jardinería *f*

gargle ['gɑrgəl] *vi* **-gled; -gling** : hacer gárgaras

garish ['gærɪʃ] *adj* : chillón

garland ['gɑrlənd] *n* : guirnalda *f*

garlic ['gɑrlɪk] *n* : ajo *m*

garment ['gɑrmənt] *n* : prenda *f*

garnish ['gɑrnɪʃ] *vt* : guarnecer — **~** *n* : adorno *m*, guarnición *f*

garret ['gærət] *n* : buhardilla *f*

garrison ['gærəsən] *n* : guarnición *f*

garrulous ['gærələs] *adj* : charlatán, parlanchín

garter ['gɑrtər] *n* : liga *f*

gas ['gæs] *n*, *pl* **gases** ['gæsəz] **1** : gas *m* **2** GASOLINE : gasolina *f* — **~** *v* **gassed; gassing** *vt* : asfixiar con gas — *vi* **~ up** : llenar el tanque con gasolina

gash ['gæʃ] *n* : tajo *m* — **~** *vt* : hacer un tajo en, cortar

gasket ['gæskət] *n* : junta *f*

gasoline ['gæsə,liːn, ,gæsə'-] *n* : gasolina *f*

gasp ['gæsp] *vi* **1** : dar un grito ahogado **2** PANT : jadear — **~** *n* : grito *m* ahogado

gas station *n* : gasolinera *f*

gastric ['gæstrɪk] *adj* : gástrico

gastronomy [gæs'trɑnəmi] *n* : gastronomía *f*

gate ['geɪt] *n* **1** DOOR : puerta *f* **2** BARRIER : barrera *f* — **gateway** ['geɪt,weɪ] *n* : puerta *f*

gather ['gæðər] *vt* **1** ASSEMBLE : reunir **2** COLLECT : recoger **3** CONCLUDE : deducir **4** : fruncir (una tela) **5** **~ speed** : acelerar — *vi* : reunirse (dícese de personas), acumularse (dícese de cosas) — **gathering** ['gæðərɪŋ] *n* : reunión *f*

gaudy ['gɔdi] *adj* **gaudier; -est** : chillón, llamativo

gauge ['geɪdʒ] *n* **1** INDICATOR : indicador *m* **2** CALIBER : calibre *m* — **~** *vt* **gauged; gauging 1** MEASURE : medir **2** ESTIMATE : calcular, evaluar

gaunt ['gɔnt] *adj* : demacrado, descarnado

gauze ['gɔz] *n* : gasa *f*

gave → **give**

gawky ['gɔki] *adj* **gawkier; -est** : desgarbado

gay ['geɪ] *adj* **1** : alegre **2** HOMOSEXUAL : gay, homosexual

gaze ['geɪz] *vi* **gazed; gazing** : mirar (fijamente) — **~** *n* : mirada *f*

gazelle [gə'zɛl] *n* : gacela *f*

gazette [gə'zɛt] *n* : gaceta *f*

gear ['gɪr] *n* **1** EQUIPMENT : equipo *m* **2** POSSESSIONS : efectos *mpl* personales

3 : marcha *f* (de un vehículo) 4 *or* ~
wheel : rueda *f* dentada — ~ *vt* : orientar, adaptar — *vi* ~ **up** : prepararse
— **gearshift** ['gɪr,ʃɪft] *n* : palanca *f* de cambio, palanca *f* de velocidades *Lat*
geese → **goose**
gelatin ['dʒelətən] *n* : gelatina *f*
gem ['dʒem] *n* : gema *f*, piedra *f* preciosa
— **gemstone** ['dʒem,sto:n] *n* : piedra *f* preciosa
gender ['dʒendər] *n* 1 SEX : sexo *m* 2
: género *m* (en la gramática)
gene ['dʒi:n] *n* : gen *m*, gene *m*
genealogy [,dʒi:ni'ɑlədʒi, ,dʒe-, -'æ-] *n, pl*
-gies : genealogía *f*
general ['dʒenrəl, 'dʒenə-] *adj* : general
— ~ *n* 1 : general *mf* (militar) 2 **in** ~
: en general, por lo general — **generalize** ['dʒenrə,laɪz, 'dʒenərə-] *v* **-ized;**
-izing : generalizar — **generally**
['dʒenrəli, 'dʒenərə-] *adv* : generalmente, en general — **general practitioner** *n* : médico *m*, -ca *f* de cabecera
generate ['dʒenə,reɪt] *vt* **-ated; -ating**
: generar — **generation** [,dʒenə'reɪʃən]
n : generación *f* — **generator** ['dʒenə-
,reɪtər] *n* : generador *m*
generous ['dʒenərəs] *adj* 1 : generoso *f* 2
AMPLE : abundante — **generosity**
[,dʒenə'rɑsəti] *n, pl* **-ties** : generosidad *f*
genetic [dʒə'netɪk] *adj* : genético — **genetics** [dʒə'netɪks] *n* : genética *f*
genial ['dʒi:niəl] *adj* : afable, simpático
genital ['dʒenətəl] *adj* : genital — **genitals** ['dʒenət̬əlz] *npl* : genitales *mpl*
genius ['dʒi:njəs] *n* : genio *m*
genocide ['dʒenə,saɪd] *n* : genocidio *m*
genteel [dʒen'ti:l] *adj* : refinado
gentle ['dʒentəl] *adj* **-tler; -tlest** 1 MILD
: suave, dulce 2 LIGHT : ligero 3 **a** ~
hint : una indirecta discreta — **gentleman** ['dʒentəlmən] *n, pl* **-men** [-mən,
-,men] 1 MAN : caballero *m*, señor *m* 2
a perfect ~ : un perfecto caballero —
gentleness ['dʒentəlnəs] *n* : delicadeza *f*, ternura *f*
genuine ['dʒenjuwən] *adj* 1 AUTHENTIC
: verdadero, auténtico 2 SINCERE : sincero
geography [dʒi'ɑgrəfi] *n* : geografía *f* — **geographic** [,dʒi:ə'græfɪk]
or **geographical** [-fɪkəl] *adj* : geográfico
geology [dʒi'ɑlədʒi] *n* : geología *f* — **geologic** [,dʒi:ə'lɑdʒɪk] *or* **geological**
[-dʒɪkəl] *adj* : geológico
geometry [dʒi'ɑmətri] *n, pl* **-tries**
: geometría *f* — **geometric** [,dʒi:ə-
'metrɪk] *or* **geometrical** [-trɪkəl] *adj*
: geométrico

geranium [dʒə'reɪniəm] *n* : geranio *m*
geriatric [,dʒeri'ætrɪk] *adj* : geriátrico — **geriatrics** [,dʒeri'ætrɪks] *n* : geriatría *f*
germ ['dʒərm] *n* 1 : germen *m* 2 MICROBE
: microbio *m*
German ['dʒərmən] *adj* : alemán — ~ *n*
: alemán *m* (idioma)
germinate ['dʒərmə,neɪt] *v* **-nated;**
-nating *vi* : germinar — *vt* : hacer germinar
gestation [dʒe'steɪʃən] *n* : gestación *f*
gesture ['dʒestʃər] *n* : gesto *m* — ~ *vi*
-tured; -turing 1 : hacer gestos 2 ~
to : hacer señas a
get ['get] *v* **got** ['gɑt]; **got** *or* **gotten**
['gɑtən]; **getting** *vt* 1 OBTAIN : conseguir, obtener 2 RECEIVE : recibir 3
EARN : ganar 4 FETCH : traer 5 CATCH
: coger, agarrar *Lat* 6 UNDERSTAND
: entender 7 PREPARE : preparar 8 ~
one's hair cut : cortarse el pelo 9 ~
s.o. to do sth : lograr que uno haga
algo 10 **have got** : tener 11 **have got**
to : tener que — *vi* 1 BECOME : ponerse, hacerse 2 GO, MOVE : ir 3
PROGRESS : avanzar 4 ~ **ahead** : progresar 5 ~ **at** MEAN : querer decir 6
~ **away** : escaparse 7 ~ **away with**
: salir impune de 8 ~ **back at**
: desquitarse con 9 ~ **by** : arreglárselas 10 ~ **home** : llegar a casa 11 ~
out : salir 12 ~ **over** : reponerse de,
consolarse de 13 ~ **together** : reunirse 14 ~ **up** : levantarse — **getaway** ['getə,weɪ] *n* : fuga *f*, huida *f* —
get-together *n* : reunión *f*
geyser ['gaɪzər] *n* : géiser *m*
ghastly ['gæstli] *adj* **-lier; -est** : horrible, espantoso
ghetto ['geto:] *n, pl* **-tos** *or* **-toes**
: gueto *m*
ghost ['go:st] *n* : fantasma *f*, espectro *m*
— **ghostly** ['go:stli] *adv* : fantasmal
giant ['dʒaɪənt] *n* : gigante *m*, -ta *f* — ~
adj : gigantesco
gibberish ['dʒɪbərɪʃ] *n* : galimatías *m*,
jerigonza *f*
gibe ['dʒaɪb] *vi* **gibed; gibing** ~ **at**
: mofarse de — ~ *n* : pulla *f*, mofa *f*
giblets ['dʒɪbləts] *npl* : menudillos *mpl*
giddy ['gɪdi] *adj* **-dier; -est** : mareado,
vertiginoso — **giddiness** ['gɪdinəs] *n*
: vértigo *m*
gift ['gɪft] *n* 1 PRESENT : regalo *m* 2 TALENT : don *m* — **gifted** ['gɪftəd] *adj* : talentoso, de talento
gigantic [dʒaɪ'gæntɪk] *adj* : gigantesco
giggle ['gɪgəl] *vi* **-gled; -gling** : reírse
tontamente — ~ *n* : risa *f* tonta

gild ['gɪld] *vt* **gilded** ['gɪldəd] *or* **gilt** ['gɪlt]; **gilding** : dorar

gill ['gɪl] *n* : agalla *f*, branquia *f*

gilt ['gɪlt] *adj* : dorado

gimmick ['gɪmɪk] *n* : truco *m*, ardid *m*

gin ['dʒɪn] *n* : ginebra *f*

ginger ['dʒɪndʒər] *n* : jengibre *m* — **ginger ale** *n* : refresco *m* de jengibre — **gingerbread** ['dʒɪndʒər,brɛd] *n* : pan *m* de jengibre — **gingerly** ['dʒɪndʒərli] *adv* : con cuidado, cautelosamente

giraffe [dʒə'ræf] *n* : jirafa *f*

girder ['gərdər] *n* : viga *f*

girdle ['gərdəl] *n* CORSET : faja *f*

girl ['gərl] *n* 1 : niña *f*, muchacha *f*, chica *f* — **girlfriend** ['gərl,frɛnd] *n* : novia *f*, amiga *f*

girth ['gərθ] *n* : circunferencia *f*

gist ['dʒɪst] *n* **get the ~ of** : comprender lo esencial de

give ['gɪv] *v* **gave** ['geɪv]; **given** ['gɪvən]; **giving** *vt* 1 : dar 2 INDICATE : señalar 3 PRESENT : presentar 4 ~ **away** : regalar 5 ~ **back** : devolver 6 ~ **out** : repartir 7 ~ **up smoking** : dejar de fumar — *vi* 1 YIELD : ceder 2 COLLAPSE : romperse 3 ~ **out** : agotarse 4 ~ **up** : rendirse — ~ *n* : elasticidad *f* — **given** ['gɪvən] *adj* 1 SPECIFIED : determinado 2 INCLINED : dado, inclinado — **given name** *n* : nombre *m* de pila

glacier ['gleɪʃər] *n* : glaciar *m*

glad ['glæd] *adj* **gladder**; **gladdest** 1 : alegre, contento 2 **be ~** : alegrarse 3 ~ **to meet you!** : ¡mucho gusto! — **gladden** ['glædən] *vt* : alegrar — **gladly** ['glædli] *adv* : con mucho gusto — **gladness** ['glædnəs] *n* : alegría *f*, gozo *m*

glade ['gleɪd] *n* : claro *m*

glamor *or* **glamour** ['glæmər] *n* : atractivo *m*, encanto *m* — **glamorous** ['glæmərəs] *adj* : atractivo

glance ['glæns] *vi* **glanced**; **glancing** 1 ~ **at** : mirar, dar un vistazo a 2 ~ **off** : rebotar en — ~ *n* : mirada *f*, vistazo *m*

gland ['glænd] *n* : glándula *f*

glare ['glær] *vi* **glared**; **glaring** 1 : brillar, relumbrar 2 ~ **at** : lanzar una mirada feroz a — ~ *n* 1 : luz *f* deslumbrante 2 STARE : mirada *f* feroz — **glaring** ['glærɪŋ] *adj* 1 BRIGHT : deslumbrante 2 FLAGRANT : flagrante

glass ['glæs] *n* 1 : vidrio *m*, cristal *m* 2 **a ~ of milk** : un vaso de leche 3 ~**es** *npl* SPECTACLES : anteojos *mpl*, lentes *fpl* — ~ *adj* : de vidrio — **glassware** ['glæs,wær] *n* : cristalería *f* — **glassy**

glassi *adj* **glassier**; **-est** 1 : vítreo 2 ~ **eyes** : ojos *mpl* vidriosos

glaze ['gleɪz] *vt* **glazed**; **glazing** 1 : poner vidrios a (una ventana, etc.) 2 : vidriar (cerámica) 3 ICE : glasear — ~ *n* 1 : vidriado *m*, barniz *m* (de cerámica) 2 ICING : glaseado *m*

gleam ['gli:m] *n* 1 : destello *m* 2 **a ~ of hope** : un rayo de esperanza — ~ *vi* : destellar, relucir

glee ['gli:] *n* : alegría *f* — **gleeful** ['gli:fəl] *adj* : lleno de alegría

glib ['glɪb] *adj* **glibber**; **glibbest** 1 : de mucha labia 2 **a ~ reply** : una respuesta simplista — **glibly** ['glɪbli] *adv* : con mucha labia

glide ['glaɪd] *vi* **glided**; **gliding** : deslizarse (en una superficie), planear (en el aire) — **glider** ['glaɪdər] *n* : planeador *m*

glimmer ['glɪmər] *vi* : brillar con luz trémula — ~ *n* : luz *f* trémula, luz *f* tenue

glimpse ['glɪmps] *vt* **glimpsed**; **glimpsing** : vislumbrar — ~ *n* : vislumbre *f*

glint ['glɪnt] *vi* : destellar — ~ *n* : destello *m*

glisten ['glɪsən] *vi* : brillar

glitter ['glɪtər] *vi* : relucir, brillar

gloat ['gloːt] *vi* ~ **over** : regodearse con

globe ['gloːb] *n* : globo *m* — **global** ['gloːbəl] *adj* : global, mundial

gloom ['glu:m] *n* 1 DARKNESS : oscuridad *f* 2 SADNESS : tristeza *f* — **gloomy** ['glu:mi] *adj* **gloomier**; **-est** 1 DARK : sombrío, tenebroso 2 DISMAL : deprimente, lúgubre 3 PESSIMISTIC : pesimista

glory ['glori] *n*, *pl* **-ries** : gloria *f* — **glorify** ['glorə,faɪ] *vt* **-fied**; **-fying** : glorificar — **glorious** ['gloriəs] *adj* : glorioso, espléndido

gloss ['glos, 'glɑs] *n* 1 : lustre *m*, brillo *m* — ~ *vt* ~ **over** : minimizar (la importancia de algo)

glossary ['glosəri, 'glɑ-] *n*, *pl* **-ries** : glosario *m*

glossy ['glosi, 'glɑ-] *adj* **glossier**; **-est** : lustroso, brillante

glove ['glʌv] *n* : guante *m*

glow ['gloː] *vi* 1 : brillar, resplandecer 2 ~ **with health** : rebosar de salud — ~ *n* : resplandor *m*, brillo *m*

glue ['glu:] *n* : pegamento *m*, cola *f* — ~ *vt* **glued**; **gluing** *or* **glueing** : pegar

glum ['glʌm] *adj* **glummer**; **glummest** : sombrío, triste

glut ['glʌt] *n* : superabundancia *f*, exceso *m*

glutton ['glʌtən] n : glotón m, -tona f —
  gluttonous ['glʌtənəs] adj : glotón —
  gluttony ['glʌtəni] n, pl **-tonies** : glotonería f
gnarled ['nɑrld] adj : nudoso
gnash ['næʃ] vt ~ one's teeth : hacer
  rechinar los dientes
gnat ['næt] n : jején m
gnaw ['nɔ] vt : roer
go ['goː] v **went** ['wɛnt]; **gone** ['gɔn,
  'gɑn]; **going**; **goes** ['goːz] vi 1 : ir 2
  LEAVE : irse, salir 3 EXTEND : ir, extenderse 4 SELL : venderse 5 FUNCTION
  : funcionar, marchar 6 DISAPPEAR : desaparecer 7 ~ **back on one's word**
  : faltar a su palabra 8 ~ **crazy** : volverse loco 9 ~ **for** LIKE : gustar 10 ~
  off EXPLODE : estallar 11 ~ **with**
  MATCH : armonizar con 12 ~ **without**
  : pasar sin — v aux **be going to** : ir a
  — ~ n, pl **goes 1 be on the ~** : no
  parar 2 **have a ~ at** : intentar
goad ['goːd] vt : aguijonear (un animal),
  incitar (a una persona)
goal ['goːl] n 1 AIM : meta m, objetivo m
  2 : gol m (en deportes) — **goalkeeper**
  ['goːl,kiːpər] or **goalie** ['goːli] n : portero
  m, -ra f; arquero m, -ra f
goat ['goːt] n : cabra f
goatee [goːˈtiː] n : barbita f de chivo
gobble ['gɑbəl] vt **-bled; -bling** or ~
  up : engullir
goblet ['gɑblət] n : copa f
goblin ['gɑblən] n : duende m
god ['gɑd, 'gɔd] n 1 : dios m 2 **God**
  : Dios m — **goddess** ['gɑdəs, 'gɔ-] n
  : diosa f — **godchild** ['gɑd,tʃaɪld, 'gɔd-]
  n, pl **-children** : ahijado m, -da f —
  godfather ['gɑd,fɑðər, 'gɔd-] n : padrino m — **godmother** ['gɑd,mʌðər, 'gɔd-]
  n : madrina f — **godparents** ['gɑd-
  ,pærənt, 'gɔd-] npl : padrinos mpl —
  godsend ['gɑd,sɛnd, 'gɔd-] n : bendición f (del cielo)
goes → **go**
goggles ['gɑgəlz] npl : gafas fpl (protec-
  toras), anteojos mpl
goings-on [goːˈɪŋz,ɑn, -ˈɔn] npl : sucesos
  mpl
gold ['goːld] n : oro m — **golden**
  ['goːldən] adj 1 : (hecho) de oro 2 : dorado, de color oro — **goldfish** ['goːld-
  ,fɪʃ] n : pez m de colores — **goldsmith**
  ['goːld,smɪθ] n : orfebre mf
golf ['gɑlf, 'goːlf] n : golf m — ~ vi
  : jugar (al) golf — **golf ball** n : pelota
  f de golf — **golf course** n : campo m
  de golf — **golfer** ['gɑlfər, 'goːl-] n
  : golfista mf

gone ['gɔn] adj 1 : ido, pasado 2 DEAD
  : muerto 3 LOST : desaparecido
good ['gʊd] adj **better** ['bɛtər]; **best**
  ['bɛst] 1 : bueno 2 KIND : amable 3 ~
  afternoon (evening) : buenas tardes
  4 **be ~ at** : tener facilidad para 5 **feel**
  ~ : sentirse bien 6 ~ **for a cold**
  : beneficioso para los resfriados 7
  have a ~ time : divertirse 8 ~
  morning : buenos días 9 ~ **night**
  : buenas noches — ~ n 1 : bien m 2
  GOODNESS : bondad f 3 ~**s** npl PROP-
  ERTY : bienes mpl 4 ~**s** npl WARES
  : mercancías fpl, mercaderías fpl 5 **for**
  ~ : para siempre — adv : bien —
  good-bye or **good-by** [gʊdˈbaɪ] n
  : adiós m — **Good Friday** n : Viernes
  m Santo — **good-looking** ['gʊdˈlʊkɪŋ]
  adj : bello, guapo — **goodness**
  ['gʊdnəs] n 1 : bondad f 2 **thank** ~!
  : ¡gracias a Dios!, ¡menos mal! —
  goodwill ['gʊd,wɪl] n : buena voluntad
  f — **goody** ['gʊdi] n, pl **goodies**
  : golosina f
gooey ['guːi] adj **gooier; gooiest** : pegajoso
goof n ['guːf] : pifia f fam — ~ vi 1 or
  ~ **up** : cometer un error 2 ~ **around**
  : hacer tonterías
goose ['guːs] n, pl **geese** ['giːs] : ganso
  m, -sa f; oca f — **goose bumps** or
  goose pimples npl : carne f de gallina
gopher ['goːfər] n : taltuza f
gore[1] ['gor] n BLOOD : sangre f
gore[2] vt **gored; goring** : cornear
gorge ['gɔrdʒ] n RAVINE : cañón m —
  vt **gorged; gorging** ~ **oneself** : hartarse
gorgeous ['gɔrdʒəs] adj : magnífico, espléndido
gorilla [gəˈrɪlə] n : gorila m
gory ['gori] adj **gorier; -est** : sangriento
gospel ['gɑspəl] n 1 : evangelio m 2 **the**
  Gospel : el Evangelio
gossip ['gɑsɪp] n 1 : chismoso m, -sa f
  (persona) 2 RUMOR : chisme m — ~
  vi : chismear, contar chismes — **gossipy** ['gɑsɪpi] adj : chismoso
got → **get**
Gothic ['gɑθɪk] adj : gótico
gotten → **get**
gourmet ['gʊrmeɪ, gʊrˈmeɪ] n : gastrónomo m, -ma f
gout ['gaʊt] n : gota f
govern ['gʌvərn] v : gobernar — **governess** ['gʌvərnəs] n : institutriz f —
  government ['gʌvərmənt] n : gobierno
  m — **governor** ['gʌvənər, 'gʌvərnər] n
  : gobernador m, -dora f

gown ['gaun] n 1 : vestido m 2 : toga f (de magistrados, etc.)

grab ['græb] v grabbed; grabbing vt : agarrar, arrebatar

grace ['greɪs] n 1 : gracia f 2 say ~ : bendecir la mesa — ~ vt graced; gracing 1 HONOR : honrar 2 ADORN : adornar — **graceful** ['greɪsfəl] adj : lleno de gracia, grácil — **gracious** ['greɪʃəs] adj : cortés, gentil

grade ['greɪd] n 1 QUALITY : calidad f 2 RANK : grado m, rango m (militar) 3 YEAR : grado m, año m (a la escuela) 4 MARK : nota f 5 SLOPE : cuesta f — vt graded; grading 1 CLASSIFY : clasificar 2 MARK : calificar (exámenes, etc.) — **grade school** → **elementary school**

gradual ['grædʒuəl] adj : gradual — **gradually** ['grædʒuəli, 'grædʒəli] adv : gradualmente, poco a poco

graduate ['grædʒuət] n : licenciado m, -da f (de la universidad), bachiller mf (de la escuela secundaria) — ~ ['grædʒuˌeɪt] v -ated; -ating vi : graduarse, licenciarse — vt CALIBRATE : graduar — **graduation** [ˌgrædʒu-'eɪʃən] n : graduación f

graffiti [grəˈfiːti, græ-] npl : graffiti mpl

graft ['græft] n : injerto m — ~ vt : injertar

grain ['greɪn] n 1 : grano m 2 CEREALS : cereales mpl 3 : veta f, vena f (de madera)

gram ['græm] n : gramo m

grammar ['græmər] n : gramática f — **grammar school** → **elementary school**

grand ['grænd] adj 1 : magnífico, espléndido 2 FABULOUS, GREAT : fabuloso, estupendo — **grandchild** ['grænd,tʃaɪld] n, pl -children : nieto m, -ta f — **granddaughter** ['grænd,dɔtər] n : nieta f — **grandeur** ['grændʒər] n : grandiosidad f — **grandfather** ['grænd,faðər] n : abuelo m — **grandiose** ['grændiˌos, ˌgrændiˈ-] adj : grandioso — **grandmother** ['grænd,mʌðər] n : abuela f — **grandparents** ['grænd,pærənt] npl : abuelos mpl — **grandson** ['grænd,sʌn] n : nieto m — **grandstand** ['grænd,stænd] n : tribuna f

granite ['grænɪt] n : granito m

grant ['grænt] vt 1 : conceder 2 ADMIT : reconocer, admitir 3 take for granted : dar (algo) por sentado — ~ n 1 SUBSIDY : subvención f 2 SCHOLARSHIP : beca f

grape ['greɪp] n : uva f

grapefruit ['greɪp,fruːt] n : toronja f, pomelo m

grapevine ['greɪp,vaɪn] n 1 : vid f, parra f 2 ~ I heard it through the ~ : me lo dijo un pajarito fam

graph ['græf] n : gráfica f, gráfico m — **graphic** ['græfɪk] adj : gráfico

grapple ['græpəl] vi -pled; -pling ~ with : forcejear con (una persona), luchar con (un problema)

grasp ['græsp] vt 1 : agarrar 2 UNDERSTAND : comprender, captar — ~ n 1 : agarre m 2 UNDERSTANDING : comprensión f 3 REACH : alcance m

grass ['græs] n 1 : hierba f (planta) 2 LAWN : césped m, pasto m Lat — **grasshopper** ['græs,hɑpər] n : saltamontes m — **grassy** ['græsi] adj grassier; -est : cubierto de hierba

grate[1] ['greɪt] v grated; -ing vt 1 : rallar (en cocina) 2 ~ one's teeth : hacer rechinar los dientes — vi RASP : chirriar

grate[2] n GRATING : reja f, rejilla f

grateful ['greɪtfəl] adj : agradecido — **gratefully** ['greɪtfəli] adv : con agradecimiento — **gratefulness** ['greɪtfəlnəs] n : gratitud f, agradecimiento m

grater ['greɪtər] n : rallador m

gratify ['grætəˌfaɪ] vt -fied; -fying 1 PLEASE : complacer 2 SATISFY : satisfacer

grating ['greɪtɪŋ] n : reja f, rejilla f

gratitude ['grætəˌtud, -ˌtjud] n : gratitud f

gratuitous [grəˈtuətəs] adj : gratuito

grave[1] ['greɪv] n : tumba f, sepultura f

grave[2] adj graver; -est : grave

gravel ['grævəl] n : grava f, gravilla f

gravestone ['greɪv,ston] n : lápida f — **graveyard** ['greɪv,jɑrd] n : cementerio m

gravity ['grævəti] n, pl -ties : gravedad f

gravy ['greɪvi] n, pl -vies : salsa f (preparada con jugo de carne)

gray ['greɪ] adj 1 : gris 2 ~ hair : pelo m canoso — ~ n : gris m — ~ vi or turn ~ : encanecer, ponerse gris

graze[1] ['greɪz] vi grazed; grazing : pastar, pacer

graze[2] vt 1 TOUCH : rozar 2 SCRATCH : rasguñarse

grease ['griːs] n : grasa f — ~ ['griːs, 'griːz] vt greased; greasing : engrasar — **greasy** ['griːsi, -zi] adj greasier; -est 1 : grasiento 2 OILY : graso, grasoso

great ['greɪt] adj 1 : grande 2 FANTASTIC : estupendo, fabuloso — **great-grandchild** [greɪt'grænd,tʃaɪld] n, pl

-children [-ˌtʃɪldrən] : bisnieto m, -ta f — **great-grandfather** [ˌɡreɪtˈɡrændˌfaðər] n : bisabuelo m — **great-grandmother** [ˌɡreɪtˈɡrændˌmʌðər] n : bisabuela f — **greatly** [ˈɡreɪtli] adv 1 MUCH : mucho 2 VERY : muy — **greatness** [ˈɡreɪtnəs] n : grandeza f

greed [ˈɡriːd] n 1 : codicia f, avaricia f 2 GLUTTONY : glotonería f — **greedily** [ˈɡriːdəli] adv : con avaricia — **greedy** [ˈɡriːdi] adj **greedier; -est** 1 : codicioso, avaro 2 GLUTTONOUS : glotón

Greek [ˈɡriːk] adj : griego m, -ga f — ~ n : griego m (idioma)

green [ˈɡriːn] adj 1 : verde 2 INEXPERIENCED : novato — ~ n 1 : verde m (color) 2 ~s npl : verduras fpl — **greenery** [ˈɡriːnəri] n, pl **-eries** : vegetación f — **greenhouse** [ˈɡriːnˌhaʊs] n : invernadero m

greet [ˈɡriːt] vt 1 : saludar 2 WELCOME : recibir — **greeting** [ˈɡriːtɪŋ] n 1 : saludo m 2 ~s npl REGARDS : saludos mpl, recuerdos mpl

gregarious [ɡrɪˈɡæriəs] adj : sociable

grenade [ɡrəˈneɪd] n : granada f

grew → **grow**

grey → **gray**

greyhound [ˈɡreɪˌhaʊnd] n : galgo m

grid [ˈɡrɪd] n 1 GRATING : rejilla f 2 NETWORK : red f 3 : cuadriculado m (de un mapa)

griddle [ˈɡrɪdəl] n : plancha f

grief [ˈɡriːf] n : dolor m, pesar m — **grievance** [ˈɡriːvənts] n : queja f — **grieve** [ˈɡriːv] v **grieved; grieving** vt : entristecer — vi ~ **for** : llorar a (algn), lamentar — **grievous** [ˈɡriːvəs] adj : grave, doloroso

grill [ˈɡrɪl] vt 1 : asar a la parrilla 2 INTERROGATE : interrogar — ~ n : parrilla f (para cocinar) — **grille** or **grill** [ˈɡrɪl] GRATING : reja f, rejilla f

grim [ˈɡrɪm] adj **grimmer; grimmest** 1 STERN : severo 2 GLOOMY : sombrío

grimace [ˈɡrɪməs, ɡrɪˈmeɪs] n : mueca f — ~ vi **-maced; -macing** : hacer muecas

grime [ˈɡraɪm] n : mugre f, suciedad f — **grimy** [ˈɡraɪmi] adj **grimier; -est** : mugriento, sucio

grin [ˈɡrɪn] vi **grinned; grinning** : sonreír (abiertamente) — ~ n : sonrisa f (abierta)

grind [ˈɡraɪnd] v **ground** [ˈɡraʊnd]; **grinding** vt 1 : moler (el café, etc.) 2 SHARPEN : afilar 3 ~ **one's teeth** : rechinar los dientes — vi : rechinar — ~ **the daily** ~ : la rutina diaria — **grinder** [ˈɡraɪndər] n : molinillo m

grip [ˈɡrɪp] vt **gripped; gripping** 1 : agarrar, asir 2 INTEREST : captar el interés de — ~ n 1 GRASP : agarre m 2 CONTROL : control m, dominio m 3 HANDLE : empuñadura f 4 **come to** ~**s with** : llegar a entender de

gripe [ˈɡraɪp] vi **griped; griping** : quejarse — ~ n : queja f

grisly [ˈɡrɪzli] adj **-lier; -est** : espeluznante, horrible

gristle [ˈɡrɪsəl] n : cartílago m

grit [ˈɡrɪt] n 1 : arena f, grava f 2 GUTS : agallas fpl fam 3 ~**s** npl : sémola f de maíz — ~ vt **gritted; gritting** ~ **one's teeth** : acorazarse

groan [ˈɡroːn] vi : gemir — ~ n : gemido m

grocery [ˈɡroːsəri, -ʃəri] n, pl **-ceries** 1 or ~ **store** : tienda f de comestibles, tienda f de abarrotes Lat 2 **groceries** npl : comestibles mpl, abarrotes mpl Lat — **grocer** [ˈɡroːsər] n : tendero m, -ra f

groggy [ˈɡrɑɡi] adj **-gier; -est** : atontado, grogui fam

groin [ˈɡrɔɪn] n : ingle f

groom [ˈɡruːm, ˈɡrʊm] n BRIDEGROOM : novio m — ~ vt 1 : almohazar (un animal) 2 PREPARE : preparar

groove [ˈɡruːv] n : ranura f, surco m

grope [ˈɡroːp] vi **groped; groping** 1 : andar a tientas 2 ~ **for:** buscar a tientas

gross [ˈɡroːs] adj 1 SERIOUS : grave 2 OBESE : obeso 3 TOTAL : bruto 4 VULGAR : grosero, basto — ~ n 1 or ~ **income** : ingresos mpl brutos 2 pl ~ : gruesa f (12 docenas) — **grossly** [ˈɡroːsli] adv 1 EXTREMELY : enormemente 2 CRUDELY : groseramente

grotesque [ɡroˈtɛsk] adj : grotesco

grouch [ˈɡraʊtʃ] n : gruñón m, -ñona f fam — **grouchy** [ˈɡraʊtʃi] adj **grouchier; -est** : gruñón fam

ground[1] [ˈɡraʊnd] → **grind**

ground[2] n 1 : suelo m, tierra f 2 or ~**s** LAND : terreno m 3 ~**s** REASON : razón f, motivos mpl 4 ~**s** DREGS : pozo m (de café) — ~ vt 1 BASE : fundar, basar 2 : conectar a tierra (un aparato eléctrico) 3 : restringir (un avión o un piloto) a la tierra — **groundhog** [ˈɡraʊndˌhɑɡ] n : marmota f (de América) — **groundless** [ˈɡraʊndləs] adj : infundado — **groundwork** [ˈɡraʊndˌwərk] n : trabajo m preparatorio

group [ˈɡruːp] n : grupo m — ~ vt : agrupar — vi or ~ **together** : agruparse

grove [ˈɡroːv] n : arboleda f

grovel ['grɑvəl, 'grʌ-] *vi* **-eled** *or* **-elled; -eling** *or* **-elling** : arrastrarse, humillarse

grow ['gro:] *v* **grew** ['gru:]; **grown** ['gro:n]; **growing** *vi* **1** : crecer **2** INCREASE : aumentar **3** BECOME : volverse, ponerse **4** ~ **dark** : oscurecerse **5** ~ **up** : hacerse mayor — *vt* **1** CULTIVATE : cultivar **2** : dejarse crecer (el pelo, etc.) — **grower** ['gro:ər] *n* : cultivador *m*, **-dora** *f*

growl ['graʊl] *vi* : gruñir — ~ *n* : gruñido *m*

grown–up ['gro:nəp] *adj* : mayor — ~ *n* : persona *f* mayor

growth ['gro:θ] *n* **1** : crecimiento *m* **2** INCREASE : aumento *m* **3** DEVELOPMENT : desarrollo *m* **4** TUMOR : tumor *m*

grub ['grʌb] *n* **1** LARVA : larva *f* **2** FOOD : comida *f*

grubby ['grʌbi] *adj* **grubbier; -est** : mugriento, sucio

grudge ['grʌdʒ] *vt* **grudged; grudging** : dar de mala gana — ~ *n* **hold a** ~ : guardar rencor

grueling *or* **gruelling** ['gru:lɪŋ, 'gru:ə-] *adj* : extenuante, agotador

gruesome ['gru:səm] *adj* : horripilante

gruff ['grʌf] *adj* **1** BRUSQUE : brusco **2** HOARSE : bronco

grumble ['grʌmbəl] *vi* **-bled; -bling** : refunfuñar, rezongar

grumpy ['grʌmpi] *adj* **grumpier; -est** : malhumorado, gruñón *fam*

grunt ['grʌnt] *vi* : gruñir — ~ *n* : gruñido *m*

guarantee [ˌgærən'ti:] *n* : garantía *f* — ~ *vt* **-teed; -teeing** : garantizar

guard ['gɑrd] *n* **1** : guardia *f* **2** PRECAUTION : protección *f* — ~ *vt* : proteger, vigilar — *vi* ~ **against** : protegerse contra — **guardian** ['gɑrdiən] *n* **1** : tutor *m*, **-tora** *f* (de niños) **2** PROTECTOR : guardián *m*, **-diana** *f*

guava ['gwɑvə] *n* : guayaba *f*

guerrilla *or* **guerilla** [gə'rɪlə] *n* **1** : guerrillero *m*, **-ra** *f* **2** ~ **warfare** : guerra *f* de guerrillas

guess ['ges] *vt* **1** : adivinar **2** SUPPOSE : suponer, creer — *vi* ~ **at** : adivinar — ~ *n* : conjetura *f*, suposición *f*

guest ['gest] *n* **1** : invitado *m*, **-da** *f* **2** : huésped *mf* (a un hotel)

guide ['gaɪd] *n* **1** : guía *mf* (persona), guía *f* (libro, etc.) — ~ *vt* **guided; guiding** : guiar — **guidance** ['gaɪdənts] *n* : orientación *f* — **guidebook** ['gaɪd-ˌbʊk] *n* : guía *f* — **guideline** ['gaɪdˌlaɪn] *n* : pauta *f*, directriz *f*

guild ['gɪld] *n* : gremio *m*

guile ['gaɪl] *n* : astucia *f*

guilt ['gɪlt] *n* : culpa *f*, culpabilidad *f* — **guilty** ['gɪlti] *adj* **guiltier; -est** : culpable

guinea pig ['gɪni-] *n* : conejillo *m* de Indias, cobaya *f*

guise ['gaɪz] *n* : apariencia *f*

guitar [gə'tɑr, gɪ-] *n* : guitarra *f*

gulf ['gʌlf] *n* **1** : golfo *m* **2** ABYSS : abismo *m*

gull ['gʌl] *n* : gaviota *f*

gullet ['gʌlət] *n* **1** THROAT : garganta *f* **2** ESOPHAGUS : esófago *m*

gullible ['gʌlɪbəl] *adj* : crédulo

gully ['gʌli] *n, pl* **-lies** : barranco *m*

gulp ['gʌlp] *vt* *or* ~ **down** : tragarse, engullir — *vi* : tragar saliva — ~ *n* : trago *m*

gum¹ ['gʌm] *n* : encía *f* (de la boca)

gum² *n* **1** : resina *f* (de plantas) **2** CHEWING GUM : goma *f* de mascar, chicle *m*

gumption ['gʌmpʃən] *n* : iniciativa *f*, agallas *fpl fam*

gun ['gʌn] *n* **1** FIREARM : arma *f* de fuego **2** *or* **spray** ~ : pistola *f* **3** → **cannon, pistol, revolver, rifle** — ~ *vt* **gunned; gunning 1** *or* ~ **down** : matar a tiros, asesinar **2** ~ **the engine** : acelerar (el motor) — **gunboat** ['gʌnˌbo:t] *n* : cañonero *m* — **gunfire** ['gʌnˌfaɪr] *n* : disparos *mpl* — **gunman** ['gʌnmən] *n, pl* **-men** [-mən, -ˌmen] : pistolero *m*, gatillero *m Lat* — **gunpowder** ['gʌnˌpaʊdər] *n* : pólvora *f* — **gunshot** ['gʌnˌʃɑt] *n* : disparo *m*, tiro *m*

gurgle ['gərgəl] *vi* **-gled; -gling 1** : borbotar, gorgotear **2** : gorjear (dícese de un niño)

gush ['gʌʃ] *vi* **1** SPOUT : salir a chorros **2** ~ **with praise** : deshacerse en elogios

gust ['gʌst] *n* : ráfaga *f*

gusto ['gʌsˌto:] *n, pl* **gustoes** : entusiasmo *m*

gusty ['gʌsti] *adj* **gustier; -est** : racheado, ventoso

gut ['gʌt] *n* **1** : intestino *m* **2** ~**s** *npl* INNARDS : tripas *fpl* **3** ~**s** *npl* COURAGE : agallas *fpl fam* — ~ *vt* **gutted; gutting 1** EVISCERATE : destripar (un pollo, etc.), limpiar (un pescado) **2** : destruir el interior de (un edificio)

gutter ['gʌtər] *n* : canaleta *f* (de un techo), cuneta *f* (de una calle)

guy ['gaɪ] *n* : tipo *m fam*

guzzle ['gʌzəl] *vt* **-zled; -zling** : chupar *fam*, tragar

gym ['dʒɪm] *or* **gymnasium** [dʒɪm-'neɪziəm, -ʒəm] *n, pl* **-siums** *or* **-sia** [-ziə, -ʒə] : gimnasio *m* — **gymnast**

H

h ['eɪt∫] *n*, *pl* **h's** *or* **hs** ['eɪt∫əz] : h *f*, octava letra del alfabeto inglés

habit ['hæbɪt] *n* **1** CUSTOM : hábito *m*, costumbre *f* **2** : hábito *m* (religioso)

habitat ['hæbɪˌtæt] *n* : hábitat *m*

habitual [həˈbɪt∫ʊəl] *adj* **1** CUSTOMARY : habitual **2** INVETERATE : empedernido

hack[1] ['hæk] *n* **1** : caballo *m* de alquiler **2** *or* ~ **writer** : escritorzuelo *m*, -la *f*

hack[2] *vt* : cortar — *vi or* ~ **into** : piratear (un sistema informático)

hackneyed ['hæknɪd] *adj* : manido, trillado

hacksaw ['hækˌsɔ] *n* : sierra *f* para metales

had → **have**

haddock ['hædək] *ns & pl* : eglefino *m*

hadn't ['hædənt] (*contraction of* **had not**) → **have**

hag ['hæg] *n* : bruja *f*

haggard ['hægərd] *adj* : demacrado

haggle ['hægəl] *vi* **-gled; -gling** : regatear

hail[1] ['heɪl] *vt* **1** GREET : saludar **2** : llamar (un taxi)

hail[2] *n* : granizo *m* (en meteorología) — ~ *vi* : granizar — **hailstone** ['heɪlˌstoʊn] *n* : piedra *f* de granizo

hair ['hær] *n* **1** : pelo *m*, cabello *m* **2** : vello *m* (en las piernas, etc.) — **hairbrush** ['hærˌbrʌ∫] *n* : cepillo *m* (para el pelo) — **haircut** ['hærˌkʌt] *n* **1** : corte *m* de pelo **2 get a** ~ : cortarse el pelo — **hairdo** ['hærˌduː] *n*, *pl* **-dos** : peinado *m* — **hairdresser** ['hærˌdrɛsər] *n* : peluquero *m*, -ra *f* — **hairless** ['hærləs] *adj* : sin pelo, calvo — **hairpin** ['hærˌpɪn] *n* : horquilla *f* — **hair-raising** ['hærˌreɪzɪŋ] *adj* : espeluznante — **hairstyle** ['hærˌstaɪl] → **hairdo** — **hair spray** *n* : laca *f* (para el pelo) — **hairy** ['hæri] *adj* **hairier; -est** : peludo, velludo

hale ['heɪl] *adj* : saludable, robusto

half ['hæf, 'haf] *n*, *pl* **halves** ['hævz, 'havz] **1** : mitad *f* **2** *or* **halftime** : tiempo *m* (en deportes) **3 in** ~ : por la mitad — ~ *adj* **1** : medio **2** ~ **an hour** : una media hora — ~ *adv* : medio — **half brother** *n* : medio hermano *m*, hermanastro *m* — **halfhearted** ['hæfˈhɑrtəd] *adj* : sin ánimo, poco entusiasta — **half sister** *n* : media her-

mana *f*, hermanastra *f* — **halfway** ['hæfˈweɪ] *adv* : a medio camino — ~ *adj* : medio

halibut ['hælɪbət] *ns & pl* : halibut *m*

hall ['hɔl] *n* **1** HALLWAY : corredor *m*, pasillo *m* **2** AUDITORIUM : sala *f* **3** LOBBY : vestíbulo *m* **4** DORMITORY : residencia *f* universitaria

hallmark ['hɔlˌmɑrk] *n* : sello *m* (distintivo)

Halloween [ˌhæləˈwiːn, ˌhɑ-] *n* : víspera *f* de Todos los Santos

hallucination [həˌluːsənˈeɪ∫ən] *n* : alucinación *f*

hallway ['hɔlˌweɪ] *n* **1** ENTRANCE : entrada *f* **2** CORRIDOR : corredor *m*, pasillo *m*

halo ['heɪˌloʊ] *n*, *pl* **-los** *or* **-loes** : aureola *f*, halo *m*

halt ['hɔlt] *n* **1 call a** ~ **to** : poner fin a **2 come to a** ~ : pararse — ~ *vi* : pararse — ~ *vt* : parar

halve ['hæv, 'hav] *vt* **halved; halving 1** DIVIDE : partir por la mitad **2** REDUCE : reducir a la mitad — **halves** → **half**

ham ['hæm] *n* : jamón *m*

hamburger ['hæmˌbərgər] *or* **hamburg** [-ˌbərg] *n* **1** : carne *f* molida **2** *or* ~ **patty** : hamburguesa *f*

hammer ['hæmər] *n* : martillo *m* — ~ *v* : martillar, martillear

hammock ['hæmək] *n* : hamaca *f*

hamper[1] ['hæmpər] *vt* : obstaculizar, dificultar

hamper[2] *n* : cesto *m*, canasta *f* (para ropa sucia)

hamster ['hæmpstər] *n* : hámster *m*

hand ['hænd] *n* **1** : mano *f* **2** : manecilla *f*, aguja *f* (de un reloj, etc.) **3** HANDWRITING : letra *f*, escritura *f* **4** WORKER : obrero *m*, -ra *f* **5 by** ~ : a mano **6 lend a** ~ : echar una mano **7 on** ~ : a mano, disponible **8 on the other** ~ : por otro lado — ~ *vt* **1** : pasar, dar **2** ~ **out** : distribuir **3** ~ **over** : entregar — **handbag** ['hændˌbæg] *n* : cartera *f* *Lat*, bolso *m* *Spain* — **handbook** ['hændˌbʊk] *n* : manual *m* — **handcuffs** ['hændˌkʌfs] *npl* : esposas *fpl* — **handful** ['hændˌfʊl] *n* : puñado *m* — **handgun** ['hændˌgʌn] *n* : pistola *f*, revólver *m*

handicap ['hændiˌkæp] *n* **1** : minusvalía *f*

(física) 2 : hándicap *m* (en deportes) — **~** *vt* **-capped; -capping 1** : asignar un handicap a (en deportes) **2** HAMPER : obstaculizar — **handicapped** ['hændi,kæpt] *adj* : minusválido

handicrafts ['hændi,kræfts] *npl* : artesanía(s) *f(pl)*

handiwork ['hændi,wərk] *n* : trabajo *m* (manual)

handkerchief ['hæŋkərtʃəf, -,tʃi:f] *n, pl* **-chiefs** : pañuelo *m*

handle ['hændəl] *n* : asa *f* (de una taza, etc.), mango *m* (de un utensilio), pomo *m* (de una puerta), tirador *m* (de un cajón) — **~** *vt* **-dled; -dling 1** TOUCH : tocar **2** MANAGE : tratar, manejar — **handlebars** ['hændəl,barz] *npl* : manillar *m*, manubrio *m* Lat

handmade ['hænd,meid] *adj* : hecho a mano

handout ['hænd,aut] *n* **1** ALMS : dádiva *f*, limosna *f* **2** LEAFLET : folleto *m*

handrail ['hænd,reil] *n* : pasamanos *m*

handshake ['hænd,ʃeik] *n* : apretón *m* de manos

handsome ['hæntsəm] *adj* **-somer; -est 1** ATTRACTIVE : apuesto, guapo **2** GENEROUS : generoso **3** SIZABLE : considerable

handwriting ['hænd,raitiŋ] *n* : letra *f*, escritura *f* — **handwritten** ['hænd,ritən] *adj* : escrito a mano

handy ['hændi] *adj* **handier; -est 1** NEARBY : a mano **2** USEFUL : práctico, útil **3** DEFT : habilidoso — **handyman** ['hændimən] *n, pl* **-men** [-mən, -,mɛn] : hombre *m* habilidoso

hang ['hæŋ] *v* **hung** ['hʌŋ]; **hanging** *vt* **1** : colgar **2** (*past tense often* **hanged**) EXECUTE : ahorcar **3 ~ one's head** : bajar la cabeza — *vi* **1** : colgar, pender **2** : caer (dícese de la ropa, etc.) **3 ~ up on s.o.** : colgar a algn — **~** *n* **1** DRAPE : caída *f* **2 get the ~ of** : agarrar la onda de

hangar ['hæŋər, 'hæŋgər] *n* : hangar *m*

hanger ['hæŋər] *n* : percha *f*, gancho *m* (para ropa) Lat

hangover ['hæŋ,o:vər] *n* : resaca *f*

hanker ['hæŋkər] *vi* **~ for** : tener ansias de — **hankering** ['hæŋkəriŋ] *n* : ansia *f*, anhelo *m*

haphazard [,hæp'hæzərd] *adj* : casual, fortuito

happen ['hæpən] *vi* **1** : pasar, suceder, ocurrir **2 ~ to do sth** : hacer algo por casualidad **3 it so happens that...** : da la casualidad de que... — **happening** ['hæpəniŋ] *n* : suceso *m*, acontecimiento *m*

happy ['hæpi] *adj* **-pier; -est 1** : feliz **2 be ~** : alegrarse **3 be ~ with** : estar contento con **4 be ~ to do sth** : hacer algo con mucho gusto — **happily** ['hæpəli] *adv* : alegremente — **happiness** ['hæpinəs] *n* : felicidad *f* — **happy-go-lucky** ['hæpigo'lʌki] *adj* : despreocupado

harass [hə'ræs, 'hærəs] *vt* : acosar — **harassment** [hə'ræsmənt, 'hærəsmənt] *n* : acoso *m*

harbor *or Brit* **harbour** ['harbər] *n* : puerto *m* — *vt* **1** SHELTER : albergar **2 ~ a grudge against** : guardar rencor a

hard ['hard] *adj* **1** : duro **2** DIFFICULT : difícil **3 be a ~ worker** : ser muy trabajador **4 ~ liquor** : bebidas *fpl* fuertes **5 ~ water** : agua *f* dura — *adv* **1** FORCEFULLY : fuerte **2 work ~** : trabajar duro **3 take sth ~** : tomarse algo muy mal — **harden** ['hardən] *vt* : endurecer — **hardheaded** [,hard'hɛdəd] *adj* : testarudo, terco — **hard-hearted** [,hard'hartəd] *adj* : duro de corazón — **hardly** ['hardli] *adv* **1** : apenas **2 ~ ever** : casi nunca — **hardness** ['hardnəs] *n* **1** : dureza *f* **2** DIFFICULTY : dificultad *f* — **hardship** ['hard,ʃip] *n* : dificultad *f* — **hardware** ['hard,wær] *n* **1** : ferretería *f* **2** : hardware *m* (en informática) — **hardworking** ['hard'wərkiŋ] *adj* : trabajador

hardy ['hardi] *adj* **-dier; -est** : fuerte (dícese de personas), resistente (dícese de las plantas)

hare ['hær] *n, pl* **hare** *or* **hares** : liebre *f*

harm ['harm] *n* : daño *m* — **~** *vt* : hacer daño a (una persona), dañar (una cosa), perjudicar (la reputación de algn, etc.) — **harmful** ['harmfəl] *adj* : perjudicial — **harmless** ['harmləs] *adj* : inofensivo

harmonica [har'manikə] *n* : armónica *f*

harmony ['harməni] *n, pl* **-nies** : armonía *f* — **harmonious** [har'mo:niəs] *adj* : armonioso — **harmonize** ['harmə,naiz] *v* **-nized; -nizing** : armonizar

harness ['harnəs] *n* : arnés *m* — **~** *vt* **1** : enjaezar **2** UTILIZE : utilizar

harp ['harp] *n* : arpa *m* — **~** *vi* **~ on** : insistir sobre

harpoon [har'pu:n] *n* : arpón *m*

harpsichord ['harpsi,kord] *n* : clavicémbalo *m*

harsh ['harʃ] *adj* **1** ROUGH : áspero **2** SEVERE : duro, severo **3** : fuerte (dícese de una luz), discordante (dícese de sonidos) — **harshness** ['harʃnəs] *n* : severidad *f*

harvest ['hɑrvəst] *n* : cosecha *f* — ~ *v*
: cosechar

has → **have**

hash ['hæʃ] *vt* 1 CHOP : picar 2 ~ **over**
DISCUSS : discutir — ~ *n* : picadillo *m*
(comida)

hasn't ['hæzənt] (*contraction of* **has
not**) → **has**

hassle ['hæsəl] *n* : problemas *mpl*, lío *m*
— ~ *vt* **-sled; -sling** : fastidiar

haste ['heɪst] *n* 1 : prisa *f*, apuro *m* *Lat* 2
make ~ : darse prisa, apurarse *Lat* —
hasten ['heɪsən] *vt* : acelerar — *vi*
: apresurarse, apurarse *Lat* — **hasty**
['heɪsti] *adj* **hastier; -est** : precipitado

hat ['hæt] *n* : sombrero *m*

hatch ['hætʃ] *n* : escotilla *f* — ~ *vt* 1
: empollar (huevos) 2 CONCOCT : tra-
mar — *vi* : salir del cascarón

hatchet ['hætʃət] *n* : hacha *f*

hate ['heɪt] *n* : odio *m* — ~ *vt* **hated;
hating** : odiar, aborrecer — **hateful**
['heɪtfəl] *adj* : odioso, aborrecible —
hatred ['heɪtrəd] *n* : odio *m*

haughty ['hɔti] *adj* **-tier; -est** : altanero,
altivo

haul ['hɔl] *vt* : arrastrar, jalar *Lat* — ~ *n*
1 CATCH : redada *f* (de peces) 2 LOOT
: botín *m* 3 **a long** ~ : un trayecto
largo

haunch ['hɔntʃ] *n* : cadera *f* (de una persona), anca *f* (de un animal)

haunt ['hɔnt] *vt* 1 : frecuentar, rondar 2
TROUBLE : inquietar — ~ *n* : sitio *m*
predilecto — **haunted** ['hɔntəd] *adj*
: embrujado

have ['hæv, *in sense 3 as an auxiliary
verb usu* 'hæf] *v* **had** ['hæd]; **having;
has** ['hæz, *in sense 3 as an auxiliary
verb usu* 'hæs] *vt* 1 : tener CONSUME
: comer, tomar 3 ALLOW : permitir 4
: dar (una fiesta, etc.), convocar (una
reunión) 5 ~ **one's hair cut** : cortarse el pelo 6 ~ **sth done** : mandar
hacer algo — *v aux* 1 : haber 2 ~ **just
done sth** : acabar de hacer algo 4
you've finished, haven't you? : has
terminado, ¿no?

haven ['heɪvən] *n* : refugio *m*

havoc ['hævək] *n* : estragos *mpl*

hawk¹ ['hɔk] *n* : halcón *m*

hawk² *vt* : pregonar (mercancías)

hay ['heɪ] *n* : heno *m* — **hay fever** *n*
: fiebre *f* del heno — **haystack** ['heɪ-
ˌstæk] *n* : almiar *m* — **haywire** ['heɪ-
ˌwaɪr] *adj* **go** ~ : estropearse

hazard ['hæzərd] *n* : peligro *m*, riesgo *m*
— ~ *vt* : arriesgar, aventurar — **hazardous** ['hæzərdəs] *adj* : arriesgado,
peligroso

haze ['heɪz] *n* : bruma *f*, neblina *f*

hazel ['heɪzəl] *n* : color *m* avellana —
hazelnut ['heɪzəlˌnʌt] *n* : avellana *f*

hazy ['heɪzi] *adj* **hazier; -est** : nebuloso

he ['hiː] *pron* : él

head ['hɛd] *n* 1 : cabeza *f* 2 END, TOP
: cabeza *f* (de un clavo, etc.), cabecera
f (de una mesa) 3 LEADER : jefe *m*, -fa
f 4 **be out of one's** ~ : estar loco 5
come to a ~ : llegar a un punto crítico 6 ~**s or tails** : cara o cruz 7 **per**
~ : por cabeza — *adj* MAIN : principal — ~ *vt* : encabezar — *vi* : dirigirse — **headache** ['hɛdˌeɪk] *n* : dolor
m de cabeza — **headband** ['hɛdˌbænd]
n : cinta *f* del pelo — **headdress** ['hɛd-
ˌdrɛs] *n* : tocado *m* — **headfirst** ['hɛd-
ˈfərst] *adv* : de cabeza — **heading**
['hɛdɪŋ] *n* : encabezamiento *m*, título *m*
— **headland** ['hɛdlənd, -lænd] *n* : cabo
m — **headlight** ['hɛdˌlaɪt] *n* : faro *m* —
headline ['hɛdˌlaɪn] *n* : titular *m* —
headlong ['hɛdˈlɔŋ] *adv* HEADFIRST
: de cabeza 2 HASTILY : precipitadamente — **headmaster** ['hɛdˌmæstər] *n*
: director *m* — **headmistress** ['hɛd-
ˌmɪstrəs, -ˈmɪs-] *n* : directora *f* —
head-on ['hɛdˈɑn, -ˈɔn] *adv & adj* : de
frente — **headphones** ['hɛdˌfoːnz] *npl*
: auriculares *mpl*, audífonos *mpl Lat*
— **headquarters** ['hɛdˌkwɔrtərz] *ns &
pl* : oficina *f* central (de una compañía), cuartel *m* general (de los militares) — **head start** *n* : ventaja *f* —
headstrong ['hɛdˌstrɔŋ] *adj* : testarudo, obstinado — **headwaiter** ['hɛd-
ˈweɪtər] *n* : jefe *m*, -fa *f* de comedor —
headway ['hɛdˌweɪ] *n* 1 : progreso *m* 2
make ~ : avanzar — **heady** ['hɛdi]
adj **headier; -est** : embriagador

heal ['hiːl] *vt* : curar — *vi* : cicatrizar

health ['hɛlθ] *n* : salud *f* — **healthy**
['hɛlθi] *adj* **healthier; -est** : sano,
saludable

heap ['hiːp] *n* : montón *m* — ~ *vt*
: amontonar

hear ['hɪr] *v* **heard** ['hərd]; **hearing** *vt*
: oír — *vi* 1 : oír 2 ~ **about** : enterarse
de 3 ~ **from** : tener noticias de —
hearing ['hɪrɪŋ] *n* 1 : oído *m* 2 : vista *f*
(en un tribunal) — **hearing aid** *n* : audífono *m* — **hearsay** ['hɪrˌseɪ] *n* : ru-
mores *mpl*

hearse ['hərs] *n* : coche *m* fúnebre

heart ['hɑrt] *n* 1 : corazón *m* 2 **at** ~ : en
el fondo 3 **by** ~ : de memoria 4 **lose**
~ : descorazonarse 5 **take** ~ : animarse — **heartache** ['hɑrtˌeɪk] *n* : pena
f, dolor *m* — **heart attack** *n* : infarto
m, ataque *m* al corazón — **heartbeat**

['hɑrt̩biːt] *n* : latido *m* (del corazón) —
heartbreak ['hɑrt̩breɪk] *n* : congoja *f*,
angustia *f* — **heartbroken** ['hɑrt̩-
,broːkən] *adj* : desconsolado — **heart-
burn** ['hɑrt̩bərn] *n* : acidez *f* estomacal
hearth ['hɑrθ] *n* : hogar *m*
heartily ['hɑrt̩əli] *adv* : de buena gana
heartless ['hɑrt̩ləs] *adj* : de mal corazón, cruel
hearty ['hɑrt̩i] *adj* **heartier; -est 1** : cordial, caluroso **2** : abundante (dícese de
una comida)
heat ['hiːt] *vt* : calentar — *vi or* ~ **up**
: calentarse — ~ *n* **1** : calor *m* **2** HEAT-
ING : calefacción *f* — **heated** ['hiːt̩əd]
adj : acalorado — **heater** ['hiːt̩ər] *n*
: calentador *m*
heath ['hiːθ] *n* : brezal *m*
heathen ['hiːðən] *adj* : pagano — ~ *n*,
pl **-thens** *or* **-then** : pagano *m*, -na *f*
heather ['hɛðər] *n* : brezo *m*
heave ['hiːv] *v* **heaved** *or* **hove** ['hoːv];
heaving *vt* **1** LIFT : levantar (con esfuerzo) **2** HURL : lanzar, tirar **3** ~ **a
sigh** : suspirar — ~ *vi or* ~ **up** : levantarse
heaven ['hɛvən] *n* : cielo *m* — **heavenly** ['hɛvənli] *adj* **1** : celestial **2** ~ **body**
: cuerpo *m* celeste
heavy ['hɛvi] *adj* **heavier; -est 1** : pesado **2** INTENSE : fuerte **3** ~ **sigh** : suspiro *m* profundo **4** ~ **traffic** : tráfico
m denso — **heavily** ['hɛvəli] *adv* **1**
: pesadamente **2** EXCESSIVELY : mucho
— **heaviness** ['hɛvinəs] *n* : peso *m*,
pesadez *f* — **heavyweight** ['hɛvi,weɪt]
n : peso *m* pesado
Hebrew ['hiː,bruː] *adj* : hebreo — ~ *n*
: hebreo *m* (idioma)
heckle ['hɛkəl] *vt* **-led; -ling** : interrumpir (a un orador) con preguntas mo-
lestas
hectic ['hɛktɪk] *adj* : agitado, ajetreado
he'd ['hiːd] (*contraction of* **he had** *or* **he
would**) → **have, would**
hedge ['hɛdʒ] *n* : seto *m* vivo — ~ *v*
hedged; hedging *vt* ~ **one's bets**
: cubrirse — *vi* : contestar con evasi-
vas — **hedgehog** ['hɛdʒ,hɔg, -,hɑg] *n*
: erizo *m*
heed ['hiːd] *vt* : prestar atención a, hacer
caso de — ~ *n* **take** ~ : tener cuidado — **heedless** ['hiːdləs] *adj* **be** ~ **of**
: hacer caso omiso de
heel ['hiːl] *n* : talón *m* (del pie), tacón *m*
(de un zapato)
hefty ['hɛfti] *adj* **heftier; -est** : robusto y
pesado
heifer ['hɛfər] *n* : novilla *f*
height ['haɪt] *n* **1** : estatura *f* (de una per-

sona), altura *f* (de un objeto) **2** PEAK
: cumbre *f* **3 the** ~ **of folly** : el colmo
de la locura **4 what is your** ~ ?
: ¿cuánto mides? — **heighten** ['haɪt̩ən]
vt : aumentar, intensificar
heir ['ær] *n* : heredero *m*, -ra *f* —
heiress ['ærəs] *n* : heredera *f* — **heirloom** ['ær,luːm] *n* : reliquia *f* de familia
held → **hold**
helicopter ['hɛlə,kɑptər] *n* : helicóptero
m
hell ['hɛl] *n* : infierno *m* — **hellish**
['hɛlɪʃ] *adj* : infernal
he'll ['hiːl, 'hɪl] (*contraction of* **he shall**
or **he will**) → **shall, will**
hello [hə'loː, hɛ-] *interj* : ¡hola!
helm ['hɛlm] *n* : timón *m*
helmet ['hɛlmət] *n* : casco *m*
help ['hɛlp] *vt* **1** : ayudar **2** ~ **oneself**
: servirse **3 I can't** ~ **it** : no lo puedo
remediar — ~ *n* **1** : ayuda *f* **2** STAFF
: personal *m* **3 help!** : ¡socorro!, ¡auxilio! — **helper** ['hɛlpər] *n* : ayudante
mf — **helpful** ['hɛlpfəl] *adj* **1** OBLIGING
: servicial, amable **2** USEFUL : útil —
helping ['hɛlpɪŋ] *n* : porción *f* — **helpless** ['hɛlpləs] *adj* **1** POWERLESS : incapaz **2** DEFENSELESS : indefenso
hem ['hɛm] *n* : dobladillo *m* — ~ *vt*
hemmed; hemming ~ **in** : encerrar
hemisphere ['hɛmə,sfɪr] *n* : hemisferio
m
hemorrhage ['hɛmərɪdʒ] *n* : hemorragia
f
hemorrhoids ['hɛmə,rɔɪdz, 'hɛm,rɔɪdz]
npl : hemorroides *fpl*, almorranas *fpl*
hemp ['hɛmp] *n* : cáñamo *m*
hen ['hɛn] *n* : gallina *f*
hence ['hɛnts] *adv* **1** : de aquí, de ahí **2**
THEREFORE : por lo tanto **3 ten years**
~ : de aquí a 10 años — **henceforth**
['hɛnts,forθ, ,hɛnts'-] *adv* : de ahora en
adelante
henpeck ['hɛn,pɛk] *vt* : dominar (al
marido)
hepatitis [,hɛpə'taɪt̩əs] *n*, *pl* **-titides**
[-'tɪt̩ə,diːz] : hepatitis *f*
her ['hər] *adj* : su, sus — ~ ['hər, ər]
pron **1** (*used as direct object*) : la **2**
(*used as indirect object*) : le, se **3**
(*used as object of a preposition*) : ella
herald ['hɛrəld] *vt* : anunciar
herb ['ərb, 'hərb] *n* : hierba *f*
herd ['hərd] *n* : manada *f* — ~ *vt* : conducir (en manada) — *vi or* ~ **together** : reunir
here ['hɪr] *adv* **1** : aquí, acá **2** ~ **you
are!** : ¡toma! — **hereabouts** ['hɪrə-
,baʊts] *or* **hereabout** [-,baʊt] *adv* : por
aquí (cerca) — **hereafter** [hɪr'æftər]

adv : en el futuro — **hereby** [hɪr'baɪ] *adv* : por este medio

hereditary [hə'redə,teri] *adj* : hereditario — **heredity** [hə'redəṭi] *n* : herencia *f*

heresy ['hɛrəsi] *n, pl* **-sies** : herejía *f*

herewith [hɪr'wɪθ] *adv* : adjunto

heritage ['herəṭɪdʒ] *n* **1** : herencia *f* **2** : patrimonio *m* (nacional)

hermit ['hərmət] *n* : ermitaño *m*, -ña *f*

hernia ['hərniə] *n, pl* **-nias** *or* **-niae** [-ni,i:, -ni,aɪ] : hernia *f*

hero ['hi:,ro:, 'hɪr,o:] *n, pl* **-roes** : héroe *m* — **heroic** [hɪ'ro:ɪk] *adj* : heroico — **heroine** ['heroən] *n* : heroína *f* — **heroism** ['hero,ɪzəm] *n* : heroísmo *m*

heron ['herən] *n* : garza *f*

herring ['herɪŋ] *n, pl* **-ring** *or* **-rings** : arenque *m*

hers ['hərz] *pron* **1** : (el) suyo, (la) suya, (los) suyos, (las) suyas **2 some friends of** ~ : unos amigos suyos, unos amigos de ella — **herself** [hər'self] *pron* **1** (*used reflexively*) : se **2** (*used emphatically*) : ella misma

he's ['hi:z] (*contraction of* **he is** *or* **he has**) → **be, have**

hesitant ['hezətənt] *adj* : titubeante, vacilante — **hesitate** ['hezə,teɪt] *vi* **-tated; -tating** : vacilar, titubear — **hesitation** [,hezə'teɪʃən] *n* : vacilación *f*, titubeo *m*

heterosexual [,hetəro'sekʃʊəl] *adj* : heterosexual — ~ *n* : heterosexual *mf*

hexagon ['heksə,gɑn] *n* : hexágono *m*

hey ['heɪ] *interj* : ¡eh!, ¡oye!

heyday ['heɪ,deɪ] *n* : auge *m*, apogeo *m*

hi ['haɪ] *interj* : ¡hola!

hibernate ['haɪbər,neɪt] *vi* **-nated; -nating** : hibernar

hiccup ['hɪkəp] *n* **have the** ~**s** : tener hipo — ~ *vi* **-cuped; -cuping** : tener hipo

hide[1] ['haɪd] *n* : piel *f*, cuero *m*

hide[2] *v* **hid** ['hɪd]; **hidden** ['hɪdən] *or* **hid; hiding** *vt* **1** : esconder **2** : ocultar (motivos, etc.) — *vi* : esconderse — **hide-and-seek** ['haɪdənd'si:k] *n* : escondite *m*, escondidas *fpl Lat*

hideous ['hɪdiəs] *adj* : horrible, espantoso

hideout ['haɪd,aʊt] *n* : escondite *m*, guarida *f*

hierarchy ['haɪə,rɑrki] *n, pl* **-chies** : jerarquía *f* — **hierarchical** [haɪə'rɑrkɪkəl] *adj* : jerárquico

high ['haɪ] *adj* **1** : alto **2** INTOXICATED : borracho, drogado **3 a** ~ **voice** : una voz aguda **4 it's two feet** ~ : tiene dos pies de alto **5** ~ **winds** : fuertes vientos *mpl* — ~ *adv* : alto — ~ *n*

: récord *m*, máximo *m* — **higher** ['haɪər] *adj* **1** : superior **2** ~ **education** : enseñanza *f* superior — **highlight** ['haɪ,laɪt] *n* : punto *m* culminante — **highly** ['haɪli] *adv* **1** VERY : muy, sumamente **2 think** ~ **of** : tener en mucho a — **Highness** ['haɪnəs] *n* **His/Her** ~ : Su Alteza *f* — **high school** *n* : escuela *f* superior, escuela *f* secundaria — **high-strung** ['haɪ'strʌŋ] *adj* : nervioso, excitable — **highway** ['haɪ,weɪ] *n* : carretera *f*

hijack ['haɪ,dʒæk] *vt* : secuestrar — **hijacker** ['haɪ,dʒækər] *n* : secuestrador *m*, -dora *f* — **hijacking** *n* : secuestro *m*

hike ['haɪk] *v* **hiked; hiking** *vi* : ir de caminata — *vt* or ~ **up** RAISE : subir — ~ *n* : caminata *f*, excursión *f* — **hiker** ['haɪkər] *n* : excursionista *mf*

hilarious [hɪ'læriəs, haɪ-] *adj* : muy divertido — **hilarity** [hɪ'lærəṭi, haɪ-] *n* : hilaridad *f*

hill ['hɪl] *n* **1** : colina *f*, cerro *m* **2** SLOPE : cuesta *f* — **hillside** ['hɪl,saɪd] *n* : ladera *f*, cuesta *f* — **hilly** ['hɪli] *adj* **hillier; -est** : accidentado

hilt ['hɪlt] *n* : puño *m*

him ['hɪm, əm] *pron* **1** (*used as direct object*) : lo **2** (*used as indirect object*) : le, se **3** (*used as object of a preposition*) : él — **himself** [hɪm'self] *pron* **1** (*used reflexively*) : se **2** (*used emphatically*) : él mismo

hind ['haɪnd] *adj* : trasero, posterior

hinder ['hɪndər] *vt* : dificultar, estorbar — **hindrance** ['hɪndrənts] *n* : obstáculo *m*

hindsight ['haɪnd,saɪt] *n* **in** ~ : en retrospectiva

Hindu ['hɪn,du:] *adj* : hindú

hinge ['hɪndʒ] *n* : bisagra *f*, gozne *m* — ~ *vi* **hinged; hinging** ~ **on** : depender de

hint ['hɪnt] *n* **1** : indirecta *f* **2** TIP : consejo *m* **3** TRACE : asomo *m*, toque *m* — ~ *vt* : dar a entender — *vi* ~ **at** : insinuar

hip ['hɪp] *n* : cadera *f*

hippopotamus [,hɪpə'pɑṭəməs] *n, pl* **-muses** *or* **-mi** [-,maɪ] : hipopótamo *m*

hire ['haɪr] *n* **1** : alquiler *m* **2 for** ~ : se alquila — ~ *vt* **hired; hiring 1** EMPLOY : contratar, emplear **2** RENT : alquilar

his ['hɪz, ɪz] *adj* : su, sus, de él — ~ *pron* **1** : (el) suyo, (la) suya, (los) suyos, (las) suyas **2 some friends of** ~ : unos amigos suyos, unos amigos de él

Hispanic [hɪ'spænɪk] *adj* : hispano, hispánico

hiss ['hɪs] *vi* : silbar — *n* : silbido *m*

history ['hɪstəri] *n, pl* **-ries 1** : historia *f* **2** BACKGROUND : historial *m* — **historian** [hɪ'stɔriən] *n* : historiador *m*, -dora *f* — **historic** [hɪ'stɔrɪk] *or* **historical** [-ɪkəl] *adj* : histórico

hit ['hɪt] *v* **hit; hitting** *vt* **1** : golpear, pegar **2** : dar (con un proyectil) **3** AFFECT : afectar **4** REACH : alcanzar **5 the car ~ a tree** : el coche chocó contra un árbol — *vi* : pegar — ~ *n* **1** : golpe *m* **2** SUCCESS : éxito *m*

hitch ['hɪtʃ] *vt* **1** ATTACH : enganchar **2** *or* **~ up** RAISE : subirse **3** **~ a ride** : hacer autostop — ~ *n* PROBLEM : problema *m* — **hitchhike** ['hɪtʃ,haɪk] *vi* **-hiked; -hiking** : hacer autostop — **hitchhiker** ['hɪtʃ,haɪkər] *n* : autostopista *mf*

hitherto ['hɪðər,tu:, ,hɪðər'-] *adv* : hasta ahora

HIV [,eɪtʃ,ar'vi:] *n* : VIH *m*, virus *m* del sida

hive ['haɪv] *n* : colmena *f*

hives ['haɪvz] *ns & pl* : urticaria *f*

hoard ['hɔrd] *n* : tesoro *m* (de dinero), reserva *f* (de provisiones) — ~ *vt* : acumular

hoarse ['hɔrs] *adj* **hoarser; -est** : ronco

hoax ['ho:ks] *n* : engaño *m*

hobble ['habəl] *vi* **-bled; -bling** : cojear

hobby ['habi] *n, pl* **-bies** : pasatiempo *m*

hobo ['ho:bo:] *n, pl* **-boes** : vagabundo *m*, -da *f*

hockey ['haki] *n* : hockey *m*

hoe ['ho:] *n* : azada *f* — ~ *vt* **hoed; hoeing** : azadonar

hog ['hɔg, 'hag] *n* : cerdo *m* — ~ *vt* **hogged; hogging** MONOPOLIZE : acaparar

hoist ['hɔɪst] *vt* **1** : izar (una vela, etc.) **2** LIFT : levantar — ~ *n* : grúa *f*

hold¹ ['ho:ld] *n* : bodega *f* (en un barco o un avión)

hold² *v* **held** ['held]; **holding** *vt* **1** GRIP : agarrar **2** POSSESS : tener **3** SUPPORT : sostener **4** : celebrar (una reunión, etc.), mantener (una conversación) **5** CONTAIN : contener **6** CONSIDER : considerar **7** *or* **~ back** : detener **8** **~ hands** : agarrarse de la mano **9** **~ up** ROB : atracar **10** **~ up** DELAY : retrasar — *vi* **1** LAST : durar, continuar **2** APPLY : ser válido — ~ *n* **1** GRIP : agarre *m* **2** **get ~ of** : conseguir **3** **get ~ of oneself** : controlarse — **holder** ['ho:ldər] *n* : tenedor *m*, -dora *f* — **holdup** ['ho:ld-

,ʌp] *n* **1** ROBBERY : atraco *m* **2** DELAY : retraso *m*, demora *f*

hole ['ho:l] *n* : agujero *m*, hoyo *m*

holiday ['halə,deɪ] *n* **1** : día *m* feriado, fiesta *f* **2** *Brit* VACATION : vacaciones *fpl*

holiness ['ho:linəs] *n* : santidad *f*

holler ['halər] *vi* : gritar — ~ *n* : grito *m*

hollow ['halo:] *n* **1** : hueco *m* **2** VALLEY : hondonada *f* — ~ *adj* **-lower; -est 1** : hueco **2** FALSE : vacío, falso — ~ *vt* *or* **~ out** : ahuecar

holly ['hali] *n, pl* **-lies** : acebo *m*

holocaust ['halə,kɔst, 'ho:-, 'hɑ-] *n* : holocausto *m*

holster ['ho:lstər] *n* : pistolera *f*

holy ['ho:li] *adj* **-lier; -est** : santo, sagrado

homage ['amɪdʒ, 'ha-] *n* : homenaje *m*

home ['ho:m] *n* **1** : casa *f* **2** FAMILY : hogar *m* **3** INSTITUTION : residencia *f*, asilo *m* **4 at ~ and abroad** : dentro y fuera del país — ~ *adv* **go ~** : ir a casa — **homeland** ['ho:m,lænd] *n* : patria *f* — **homeless** ['ho:mləs] *adj* : sin hogar — **homely** ['ho:mli] *adj* **-lier; -est 1** DOMESTIC : casero **2** UGLY : feo — **homemade** ['ho:m'meɪd] *adj* : casero, hecho en casa — **homemaker** ['ho:m,meɪkər] *n* : ama *f* de casa — **home run** *n* : jonrón *m* — **homesick** ['ho:m,sɪk] *adj* **be ~** : echar de menos a la familia — **homeward** ['ho:mwərd] *adj* : de vuelta, de regreso — **homework** ['ho:m,wərk] *n* : tarea *f*, deberes *mpl* — **homey** ['ho:mi] *adj* **homier; -est** : hogareño, acogedor

homicide ['hamə,saɪd, 'ho:-] *n* : homicidio *m*

homogeneous [,ho:mə'dʒi:niəs, -njəs] *adj* : homogéneo

homosexual [,ho:mə'sekʃuəl] *adj* : homosexual — ~ *n* : homosexual *mf* — **homosexuality** [,ho:mə,sekʃu'æləti] *n* : homosexualidad *f*

honest ['anəst] *adj* **1** : honrado **2** FRANK : sincero — **honestly** *adv* : sinceramente — **honesty** ['anəsti] *n, pl* **-ties** : honradez *f*

honey ['hʌni] *n, pl* **-eys** : miel *f* — **honeycomb** ['hʌni,ko:m] *n* : panal *m* — **honeymoon** ['hʌni,mu:n] *n* : luna *f* de miel

honk ['haŋk, 'hɔŋk] *vi* : tocar la bocina — ~ *n* : bocinazo *m*

honor *or* *Brit* **honour** ['anər] *n* : honor *m* — ~ *vt* **1** : honrar **2** : aceptar (un cheque, etc.), cumplir con (una promesa) — **honorable** *or* *Brit* **honourable** ['anərəbəl] *adj* : honorable, honroso — **honorary** ['anə,reri] *adj* : honorario

hood ['hʊd] n 1 : capucha f (de un abrigo, etc.) 2 : capó m (de un automóvil)
hoodlum ['hʊdləm, 'huːd-] n : matón m
hoodwink ['hʊd,wɪŋk] vt : engañar
hoof ['hʊf, 'huːf] n, pl **hooves** ['hʊvz, 'huːvz] or **hoofs** : pezuña f (de una vaca, etc.), casco m (de un caballo)
hook ['hʊk] n 1 : gancho m 2 or **and eye** : corchete m 3 → **fishhook** 4 **off the** ~ : descolgado — ~ vt : enganchar — vi : engancharse
hoop ['huːp] n : aro m
hooray [hʊ'reɪ] → **hurrah**
hoot ['huːt] vi 1 : ulular (dícese de un búho) 2 ~ **with laughter** : reírse a carcajadas — ~ n 1 : ululato m (de un búho) 2 **I don't give a** ~ : me importa un comino
hop¹ ['hɑp] vi **hopped; hopping** : saltar a la pata coja — ~ n : salto m a la pata coja
hop² n ~s : lúpulo m (planta)
hope ['hoːp] v **hoped; hoping** vi : esperar — vt : esperar que — ~ n : esperanza f — **hopeful** ['hoːpfəl] adj : esperanzado — **hopefully** adv 1 : con esperanza 2 ~ **it will help** : se espera que ayude — **hopeless** ['hoːpləs] adj : desesperado — **hopelessly** ['hoːpləsli] adv : desesperadamente
horde ['hord] n : horda f
horizon [hə'raɪzən] n : horizonte m — **horizontal** [,hɔrə'zɑntəl] adj : horizontal
hormone ['hɔr,moːn] n : hormona f
horn ['hɔrn] n 1 : cuerno m (de un animal) 2 : trompa f (instrumento musical) 3 : bocina f, claxon m (de un vehículo)
hornet ['hɔrnət] n : avispón m
horoscope ['hɔrə,skoːp] n : horóscopo m
horror ['hɔrər] n : horror m — **horrendous** [hɔ'rendəs] adj : horrendo — **horrible** ['hɔrəbəl] adj : horrible — **horrid** ['hɔrɪd] adj : horroroso, horrible — **horrify** ['hɔrə,faɪ] vt **-fied; -fying** : horrorizar
hors d'oeuvre [ɔr'dərv] n, pl **hors d'oeuvres** [-'dərvz] : entremés m
horse ['hɔrs] n : caballo m — **horseback** ['hɔrs,bæk] n **on** ~ : a caballo — **horsefly** ['hɔrs,flaɪ] n, pl **-flies** : tábano m — **horseman** ['hɔrsmən] n, pl **-men** [-mən, -,men] : jinete m — **horseplay** ['hɔrs,pleɪ] fpl : payasadas fpl — **horsepower** ['hɔrs,paʊər] n : caballo m de fuerza — **horseradish** ['hɔrs,rædɪʃ] n : rábano m picante — **horseshoe** ['hɔrs,ʃuː] n : herradura f — **horse-**

woman ['hɔrs,wʊmən] n, pl **-women** [-,wɪmən] : jinete f
horticulture ['hɔrtə,kʌltʃər] n : horticultura f
hose ['hoːz] n 1 pl **hoses** : manguera f, manga f 2 **hose** pl STOCKINGS : medias fpl — ~ vt **hosed; hosing** : regar (con manguera) — **hosiery** ['hoːʒəri, 'hoːʒə-] n : calcetería f
hospice ['hɑspəs] n : hospicio m
hospital ['hɑs,pɪtəl] n : hospital m — **hospitable** [hɑ'spɪtəbəl, 'hɑs,pɪ-] adj : hospitalario — **hospitality** [,hɑspə-'tæləti] n, pl **-ties** : hospitalidad f — **hospitalize** ['hɑs,pɪtə,laɪz] vt **-ized; -izing** : hospitalizar
host¹ ['hoːst] n **a** ~ **of** : toda una serie de
host² n 1 : anfitrión m, -triona f 2 : presentador m, -dora f (de televisión, etc.) — ~ vt : presentar (un programa de televisión, etc.)
host³ n EUCHARIST : hostia f, Eucaristía f
hostage ['hɑstɪdʒ] n : rehén m
hostel ['hɑstəl] n or **youth** ~ : albergue m juvenil
hostess ['hoːstɪs] n : anfitriona f
hostile ['hɑstəl, -,taɪl] adj : hostil — **hostility** [hɑs'tɪləti] n, pl **-ties** : hostilidad f
hot ['hɑt] adj **hotter; hottest** 1 : caliente, caluroso (dícese del tiempo), cálido (dícese del clima) 2 SPICY : picante 3 **feel** ~ : tener calor 4 **have a** ~ **temper** : tener mal genio 5 ~ **news** : noticias fpl de última hora 6 **it's** ~ **today** : hace calor
hot dog n : perro m caliente
hotel [hoː'tel] n : hotel m
hotheaded ['hɑt'hedəd] adj : exaltado
hound ['haʊnd] n : perro m (de caza) — ~ vt : acosar, perseguir
hour ['aʊər] n : hora f — **hourglass** ['aʊər,glæs] n : reloj m de arena — **hourly** ['aʊərli] adv & adj : cada hora, por hora
house ['haʊs] n, pl **houses** ['haʊzəz, -səz] 1 : casa f 2 : cámara f (del gobierno) 3 **publishing** ~ : editorial f — ~ ['haʊz] vt **housed; housing** : albergar — **houseboat** ['haʊs,boːt] n : casa f flotante — **housefly** ['haʊs,flaɪ] n, pl **-flies** : mosca f común — **household** ['haʊs,hoːld] adj 1 : doméstico 2 ~ **name** : nombre m muy conocido — ~ n : casa f — **housekeeper** ['haʊs,kiːpər] n : ama f de llaves — **housekeeping** ['haʊs,kiːpɪŋ] n : gobierno m de la casa — **housewarming** ['haʊs,wɔrmɪŋ] n : fiesta f de estreno de

una casa — **housewife** ['haʊs,waɪf] *n*, *pl* **-wives** : ama *f* de casa — **housework** ['haʊs,wərk] *n* : faenas *fpl* domésticas — **housing** ['haʊzɪŋ] *n* 1 : viviendas *fpl* 2 CASE : caja *f* protectora

hove → **heave**

hovel ['hʌvəl, 'hɑ-] *n* : casucha *f*, tugurio *m*

hover ['hʌvər, 'hɑ-] *vi* 1 : cernerse 2 ~ **about** : rondar

how ['haʊ] *adv* 1 : cómo 2 *(used in exclamations)* : qué 3 ~ **are you?** : ¿cómo está Ud.? 4 ~ **come** : por qué 5 ~ **much** : cuánto 6 ~ **do you do?** : mucho gusto 7 ~ **old are you?** : ¿cuántos años tienes? — ~ *conj* : como

however [haʊ'ɛvər] *conj* 1 : de cualquier manera que 2 ~ **you like** : como quieras — ~ *adv* 1 NEVERTHELESS : sin embargo, no obstante 2 ~ **difficult it is** : por díficil que sea 3 ~ **hard I try** : por más que me esfuerce

howl ['haʊl] *vi* : aullar — ~ *n* : aullido *m*

hub ['hʌb] *n* 1 CENTER : centro *m* 2 : cubo *m* (de una rueda)

hubbub ['hʌ,bʌb] *n* : alboroto *m*, jaleo *m*

hubcap ['hʌb,kæp] *n* : tapacubos *m*

huddle ['hʌdəl] *vi* **-dled; -dling** *or* ~ **together** : apiñarse

hue ['hju:] *n* : color *m*, tono *m*

huff ['hʌf] *n* **be in a** ~ : estar enojado

hug ['hʌg] *vt* **hugged; hugging** : abrazar — ~ *n* : abrazo *m*

huge ['hju:dʒ] *adj* **huger; hugest** : inmenso, enorme

hull ['hʌl] *n* : casco *m* (de un barco, etc.)

hum ['hʌm] *v* **hummed; humming** *vi* 1 : tararear 2 BUZZ : zumbar — *vt* : tararear (una melodía) — ~ *n* : zumbido *m*

human ['hju:mən, 'ju:-] *adj* : humano — ~ *n* : (ser *m*) humano *m* — **humane** [hju:'meɪn, ju:-] *adj* : humano, humanitario — **humanitarian** [hju:,mænə'terɪən, ju:-] *adj* : humanitario — **humanity** [hju:'mænəṭi, ju:-] *n*, *pl* **-ties** : humanidad *f*

humble ['hʌmbəl] *vt* **-bled; -bling** 1 : humillar 2 ~ **oneself** : humillarse — ~ *adj* **-bler; -blest** : humilde

humdrum ['hʌm,drʌm] *adj* : monótono, rutinario

humid ['hju:məd, 'ju:-] *adj* : húmedo — **humidity** [hju:'mɪdəṭi, ju:-] *n*, *pl* **-ties** : humedad *f*

humiliate [hju:'mɪli,eɪt, ju:-] *vt* **-ated; -ating** : humillar — **humiliating** [hju:-'mɪli,eɪṭɪŋ, ju:-] *adj* : humillante — **humiliation** [hju:,mɪli'eɪʃən, ju:-] *n* : humillación *f* — **humility** [hju:'mɪləṭi, ju:-] *n* : humildad *f*

humor *or Brit* **humour** ['hju:mər, 'ju:-] *n* : humor *m* — ~ *vt* : seguir la corriente a, complacer — **humorous** ['hju:mərəs, 'ju:-] *adj* : humorístico, cómico

hump ['hʌmp] *n* : joroba *f*

hunch ['hʌntʃ] *vi or* ~ **over** : encorvarse — ~ *n* : presentimiento *m*

hundred ['hʌndrəd] *adj* : cien, ciento — ~ *n*, *pl* **-dreds** *or* **-dred** : ciento *m* — **hundredth** ['hʌndrədθ] *adj* : centésimo — ~ *n* 1 : centésimo *m*, -ma *f* (en una serie) 2 : centésimo *m* (en matemáticas)

hung → **hang**

Hungarian [hʌŋ'gæriən] *adj* : húngaro — ~ *n* : húngaro *m* (idioma)

hunger ['hʌŋgər] *n* : hambre *m* — ~ *vi* 1 : tener hambre 2 ~ **for** : ansiar, anhelar — **hungry** ['hʌŋgri] *adj* **-grier; -est** 1 : hambriento 2 **be** ~ : tener hambre

hunk ['hʌŋk] *n* : pedazo *m* (grande)

hunt ['hʌnt] *vt* 1 : cazar 2 ~ **for** : buscar — ~ *n* 1 : caza *f*, cacería *f* 2 SEARCH : búsqueda *f*, busca *f* — **hunter** ['hʌntər] *n* : cazador *m*, -dora *f* — **hunting** ['hʌntɪŋ] *n* 1 : caza *f* 2 **go** ~ : ir de caza

hurdle ['hərdəl] *n* 1 : valla *f* (en deportes) 2 OBSTACLE : obstáculo *m*

hurl ['hərl] *vt* : lanzar, arrojar

hurrah [hʊ'rɑ, -'rɔ] *interj* : ¡hurra!

hurricane ['hərə,keɪn] *n* : huracán *m*

hurry ['həri] *n* : prisa *f*, apuro *f Lat* — *v* **-ried; -rying** *vi* : darse prisa, apurarse *Lat* — *vt* : apurar, dar prisa a — **hurried** ['hərid] *adj* : apresurado — **hurriedly** ['hərədli] *adv* : apresuradamente, de prisa

hurt ['hərt] *v* **hurt; hurting** *vt* 1 INJURE : hacer daño a, lastimar 2 OFFEND : ofender, herir — *vi* 1 : doler 2 **my foot** ~**s** : me duele el pie — ~ *n* 1 INJURY : herida *f* 2 DISTRESS : dolor *m*, pena *f* — **hurtful** ['hərtfəl] *adj* : hiriente, doloroso

hurtle ['hərtəl] *vi* **-tled; -tling** : lanzarse, precipitarse

husband ['hʌzbənd] *n* : esposo *m*, marido *m*

hush ['hʌʃ] *vt* : hacer callar, acallar — ~ *n* : silencio *m*

husk ['hʌsk] *n* : cáscara *f*

husky¹ ['hʌski] *adj* **-kier; -est** HOARSE : ronco

husky² *n*, *pl* **-kies** : perro *m*, -rra *f* esquimal

husky³ adj BURLY : fornido
hustle ['həsəl] v -tled; -tling vt : dar prisa a, apurar Lat — vi : darse prisa, apurarse Lat — n ~ **and bustle** : ajetreo m, bullicio m
hut ['hʌt] n : cabaña f
hutch ['hʌtʃ] n or **rabbit** ~ : conejera f
hyacinth ['haɪə,sɪmθ] n : jacinto m
hybrid ['haɪbrɪd] n : híbrido m — ~ adj : híbrido
hydrant ['haɪdrənt] n or **fire** ~ : boca f de incendios
hydraulic [har'drɔlɪk] adj : hidráulico
hydroelectric [,haɪdroɪ'lektrɪk] adj : hidroeléctrico
hydrogen ['haɪdrədʒən] n : hidrógeno m
hyena [har'iːnə] n : hiena f
hygiene ['haɪ,dʒiːn] n : higiene f — **hygienic** [haɪ'dʒɛnɪk, -'dʒiː-; ,haɪdʒi'ɛnɪk] adj : higiénico
hymn ['hɪm] n : himno m

hyperactive [,haɪpər'æktɪv] adj : hiperactivo
hyphen ['haɪfən] n : guión m
hypnosis [hɪp'noːsɪs] n, pl -noses [-,siːz] : hipnosis f — **hypnotic** [hɪp'nɑ-tɪk] adj : hipnótico — **hypnotism** ['hɪpnə,tɪzəm] n : hipnotismo m — **hypnotize** ['hɪpnə,taɪz] vt -tized; -tizing : hipnotizar
hypochondriac [,haɪpə'kɑndri,æk] n : hipocondríaco m, -ca f
hypocrisy [hɪp'ɑkrəsi] n, pl -sies : hipocresía f — **hypocrite** ['hɪpə,krɪt] n : hipócrita mf — **hypocritical** [,hɪpə-'krɪtɪkəl] adj : hipócrita
hypothesis [har'pɑθəsɪs] n, pl -eses [-,siːz] : hipótesis f — **hypothetical** [,haɪpə'θɛtɪkəl] adj : hipotético
hysteria [hɪs'tɛriːə, -tɪr-] n : histeria f, histerismo m — **hysterical** [hɪs'tɛrɪkəl] adj : histérico

I

i ['aɪ] n, pl **i's** or **is** ['aɪz] : i f, novena letra del alfabeto inglés
I ['aɪ] pron : yo
ice ['aɪs] n : hielo m — ~ v **iced; icing** vt 1 FREEZE : congelar 2 CHILL : enfriar 3 : bañar (pasteles, etc.) — ~ vi or ~ up : helarse, congelarse — **iceberg** ['aɪs,bərg] n : iceberg m — **icebox** ['aɪs-,bɑks] → **refrigerator** — **ice-cold** ['aɪs'koːld] adj : helado — **ice cream** n : helado m — **ice cube** n : cubito m de hielo — **ice-skate** ['aɪs,skeɪt] vi -skated; -skating : patinar — **ice skate** n : patín m de cuchilla — **icicle** ['aɪ,sɪkəl] n : carámbano m — **icing** ['aɪsɪŋ] n : baño m
icon ['aɪ,kɑn, -kən] n : icono m
icy ['aɪsi] adj **icier; -est** 1 : cubierto de hielo (dícese de pavimento, etc.) 2 FREEZING : helado
I'd ['aɪd] (contraction of **I should** or **I would**) → **should, would**
idea [ar'diːə] n : idea f
ideal [ar'diːəl] adj : ideal — ~ n : ideal m — **idealist** [ar'diːəlɪst] n : idealista mf — **idealistic** [aɪ,diːə'lɪstɪk] adj : idealista — **idealize** [ar'diːə,laɪz] vt -ized; -izing : idealizar
identity [ar'dɛntət̬i] n, pl -ties : identidad f — **identical** [ar'dɛntɪkəl] adj : idéntico — **identify** [ar'dɛntə,faɪ] v -fied; -fying vt : identificar — vi ~ with : identificarse con — **identifica-**

tion [aɪ,dɛntəfə'keɪʃən] n 1 : identificación f 2 ~ **card** : carnet m, carné m
ideology [,aɪdi'ɑlədʒi, ,ɪ-] n, pl -gies : ideología f — **ideological** [,aɪdiə-'lɑdʒɪkəl, ,ɪ-] adj : ideológico
idiocy ['ɪdiəsi] n, pl -cies : idiotez f
idiom ['ɪdiəm] n EXPRESSION : modismo m — **idiomatic** [,ɪdiə'mæt̬ɪk] adj : idiomático
idiosyncrasy [,ɪdio'sɪŋkrəsi] n, pl -sies : idiosincrasia f
idiot ['ɪdiət] n : idiota mf — **idiotic** [,ɪdi-'ɑt̬ɪk] adj : idiota
idle ['aɪdəl] adj **idler; idlest** 1 LAZY : haragán, holgazán 2 INACTIVE : parado (dícese de una máquina) 3 UNEMPLOYED : desocupado 4 VAIN : frívolo, vano 5 **out of** ~ **curiosity** : por pura curiosidad — ~ v **idled; idling** vi : andar al ralentí (dícese de un motor) — vt ~ **away the hours** : pasar el rato — **idleness** ['aɪdəlnəs] n : ociosidad f
idol ['aɪdəl] n : ídolo m — **idolize** ['aɪdə,laɪz] vt -ized; -izing : idolatrar
idyllic [ar'dɪlɪk] adj : idílico
if ['ɪf] conj 1 : si 2 THOUGH : aunque, si bien 3 ~ **so** : si es así
igloo ['ɪglu] n, pl -loos : iglú m
ignite [ɪg'naɪt] v -nited; -niting vt : encender — vi : encenderse — **ignition** [ɪg'nɪʃən] n 1 : ignición f 2 or ~ **switch** : encendido m

ignore [ig'nor] *vt* **-nored; -noring** : ignorar, no hacer caso de — **ignorance** [ig'nərənts] *n* : ignorancia *f* — **ignorant** ['ignərənt] *adj* 1 : ignorante 2 **be ~ of** : desconocer, ignorar

ilk ['ilk] *n* : tipo *m*, clase *f*

ill ['il] *adj* **worse** ['wərs]; **worst** ['wərst] 1 SICK : enfermo 2 BAD : malo — *adv* **worse; worst** : mal — **ill-advised** [,ilæd'vaizd, -əd-] *adj* : imprudente — **ill at ease** *adj* : incómodo

I'll ['ail] (*contraction of* **I shall** *or* **I will**) → **shall, will**

illegal [il'li:gəl] *adj* : ilegal

illegible [il'ledʒəbəl] *adj* : ilegible

illegitimate [,ilə'dʒitəmət] *adj* : ilegítimo — **illegitimacy** [,ilə'dʒitəməsi] *n* : ilegitimidad *f*

illicit [il'lisət] *adj* : ilícito

illiterate [il'litərət] *adj* : analfabeto — **illiteracy** [il'litərəsi] *n, pl* **-cies** : analfabetismo *m*

ill-mannered [il'mænərd] *adj* : descortés, maleducado

ill-natured [il'neitʃərd] *adj* : de mal genio

illness ['ilnəs] *n* : enfermedad *f*

illogical [il'lodʒikəl] *adj* : ilógico

ill-treat [il'tri:t] *vt* : maltratar

illuminate [i'lu:mə,neit] *vt* **-nated; -nating** : iluminar — **illumination** [i,lu:mə'neiʃən] *n* : iluminación *f*

illusion [i'lu:ʒən] *n* : ilusión *f* — **illusory** [i'lu:səri, -zəri] *adj* : ilusorio

illustrate ['ilə,streit] *v* **-trated; -trating** : ilustrar — **illustration** [,ilə'streiʃən] *n* 1 : ilustración *f* 2 EXAMPLE : ejemplo *m* — **illustrative** [i'lʌstrətiv, 'ilə,streitiv] *adj* : ilustrativo

illustrious [i'lʌstriəs] *adj* : ilustre, glorioso

ill will *n* : animadversión *f*, mala voluntad *f*

I'm ['aim] (*contraction of* **I am**) → **be**

image ['imidʒ] *n* : imagen *f* — **imaginary** [i'mædʒə,neri] *adj* : imaginario — **imagination** [i,mædʒə'neiʃən] *n* : imaginación *f* — **imaginative** [i'mædʒə,neitiv, -aneitiv] *adj* : imaginativo — **imagine** [i'mædʒən] *vt* **-ined; -ining** : imaginar(se)

imbalance [im'bælənts] *n* : desequilibrio *m*

imbecile ['imbəsəl, -,sil] *n* : imbécil *mf*

imbue [im'bju:] *vt* **-bued; -buing** : imbuir

imitation [,imə'teiʃən] *n* : imitación *f* — ~ *adj* : de imitación, artificial — **imitate** ['imə,teit] *vt* **-tated; -tating** : imitar, remedar — **imitator** ['imə,teitər] *n* : imitador *m*, -dora *f*

immaculate [i'mækjələt] *adj* : inmaculado

immaterial [,imə'tiriəl] *adj* : irrelevante, sin importancia

immature [,imə'tʃur, -,tjur, -,tur] *adj* : inmaduro — **immaturity** [,imə'tʃurəti, -'tjur-, -'tur-] *n, pl* **-ties** : inmadurez *f*

immediate [i'mi:diət] *adj* : inmediato — **immediately** [i'mi:diətli] *adv* : inmediatamente

immense [i'mɛnts] *adj* : inmenso — **immensity** [i'mɛntsəti] *n, pl* **-ties** : inmensidad *f*

immerse [i'mərs] *vt* **-mersed; -mersing** : sumergir — **immersion** [i'mərʒən] *n* : inmersión *f*

immigrate ['imə,greit] *vi* **-grated; -grating** : inmigrar — **immigrant** ['imigrənt] *n* : inmigrante *mf* — **immigration** [,imə'greiʃən] *n* : inmigración *f*

imminent ['imənənt] *adj* : inminente — **imminence** ['imənənts] *n* : inminencia *f*

immobile [im'o:bəl] *adj* : inmóvil — **immobilize** [i'mo:bə,laiz] *vt* **-lized; -lizing** : inmovilizar

immoral [i'mɔrəl] *adj* : inmoral — **immorality** [,imɔ'ræləti, ,imə-] *n, pl* **-ties** : inmoralidad *f*

immortal [i'mɔrtəl] *adj* : inmortal — ~ *n* : inmortal *mf* — **immortality** [,imɔr'tæləti] *n* : inmortalidad *f*

immune [i'mju:n] *adj* : inmune — **immunity** [i'mju:nəti] *n, pl* **-ties** : inmunidad *f* — **immunization** [,imjunə'zeiʃən] *n* : inmunización *f* — **immunize** ['imju,naiz] *vt* **-nized; -nizing** : inmunizar

imp ['imp] *n* RASCAL : diablillo *m*

impact ['im,pækt] *n* : impacto *m*

impair [im'pær] *vt* : dañar, perjudicar

impart [im'part] *vt* : impartir (información), conferir (una calidad, etc.)

impartial [im'parʃəl] *adj* : imparcial — **impartiality** [im,parʃi'æləti] *n, pl* **-ties** : imparcialidad *f*

impassable [im'pæsəbəl] *adj* : intransitable

impasse ['im,pæs] *n* : impasse *m*

impassioned [im'pæʃənd] *adj* : apasionado

impassive [im'pæsiv] *adj* : impasible

impatience [im'peiʃənts] *n* : impaciencia *f* — **impatient** [im'peiʃənt] *adj* : impaciente — **impatiently** [im'peiʃəntli] *adv* : con impaciencia

impeccable [im'pekəbəl] *adj* : impecable

impede [ɪm'piːd] *vt* **-peded; -peding**
: dificultar — **impediment** [ɪm-
'pɛdəmənt] *n* : impedimento *m*, obstáculo *m*

impel [ɪm'pɛl] *vt* **-pelled; -pelling** : impeler

impending [ɪm'pɛndɪŋ] *adj* : inminente

impenetrable [ɪm'pɛnətrəbəl] *adj* : impenetrable

imperative [ɪm'pɛrətɪv] *adj* **1** COM-
MANDING : imperativo **2** NECESSARY
: imprescindible — **~** *n* : imperativo
m

imperceptible [ˌɪmpər'sɛptəbəl] *adj* : imperceptible

imperfection [ˌɪmpər'fɛkʃən] *n* : imperfección *f* — **imperfect** [ɪm'pərfɪkt] *adj*
: imperfecto — **~** *n* **or** **~ tense** : imperfecto *m*

imperial [ɪm'pɪriəl] *adj* : imperial — **imperialism** [ɪm'pɪriəˌlɪzəm] *n* : imperialismo *m* — **imperious** [ɪm'pɪriəs] *adj*
: imperioso

impersonal [ɪm'pərsənəl] *adj* : impersonal

impersonate [ɪm'pərsənˌeɪt] *vt* **-ated;
-ating** : hacerse pasar por, imitar —
impersonation [ˌɪmpərsən'eɪʃən] *n*
: imitación *f* — **impersonator** [ɪm-
'pərsənˌeɪtər] *n* : imitador *m*, -dora *f*

impertinent [ɪm'pərtənənt] *adj* : impertinente — **impertinence** [ɪm'pərtənənts]
n : impertinencia *f*

impervious [ɪm'pərviəs] *adj* **~ to** : impermeable a

impetuous [ɪm'pɛtʃuəs] *adj* : impetuoso, impulsivo

impetus [ˈɪmpətəs] *n* : ímpetu *m*, impulso *m*

impinge [ɪm'pɪndʒ] *vi* **-pinged; -ping-
ing ~ on** : afectara, incidir en

impish [ˈɪmpɪʃ] *adj* : pícaro, travieso

implant [ɪm'plænt] *vt* : implantar

implausible [ɪm'plɔːzəbəl] *adj* : inverosímil

implement [ˈɪmpləmənt] *n* : instrumento
m, implemento *m* *Lat* — **~** [ˈɪmplə-
ˌmɛnt] *vt* : poner en práctica

implicate [ˈɪmpləˌkeɪt] *vt* **-cated; -cating**
: implicar — **implication** [ˌɪmpləˈkeɪ-
ʃən] *n* **1** INVOLVEMENT : implicación *f* **2**
CONSEQUENCE : consecuencia *f* **3 by
~** : de forma indirecta

implicit [ɪm'plɪsət] *adj* **1** : implícito **2**
UNQUESTIONING : absoluto, incondi-
cional

implore [ɪm'plɔr] *vt* **-plored; -ploring**
: implorar, suplicar

imply [ɪm'plaɪ] *vt* **-plied; -plying 1** HINT
: insinuar **2** ENTAIL : implicar

impolite [ˌɪmpə'laɪt] *adj* : descortés,
maleducado

import [ɪm'port] *vt* : importar (mercancías) — **import** [ɪm'portənt] *adj*
: importante — **importance** [ɪm-
'portənts] *n* : importancia *f* — **importation** [ˌɪmpɔr'teɪʃən] *n* : importación *f* —
importer [ɪm'portər] *n* : importador *m*,
-dora *f*

impose [ɪm'poːz] *v* **-posed; -posing** *vt*
: imponer — *vi* **~ on** : importunar,
molestar — **imposing** [ɪm'poːzɪŋ] *adj*
: imponente — **imposition** [ˌɪmpə-
'zɪʃən] *n* **1** ENFORCEMENT : imposición *f*
2 be an ~ on : molestar

impossible [ɪm'pɑsəbəl] *adj* : imposible
— **impossibility** [ɪmpɑsə'bɪləti] *n, pl*
-ties : imposibilidad *f*

impostor *or* **imposter** [ɪm'pɑstər] *n*
: impostor *m*, -tora *f*

impotent [ˈɪmpətənt] *adj* : impotente —
impotence [ˈɪmpətənts] *n* : impotencia
f

impound [ɪm'paʊnd] *vt* : incautar, embargar

impoverished [ɪm'pɑvərɪʃt] *adj* : empo-
brecido

impracticable [ɪm'præktɪkəbəl] *adj* : impracticable

impractical [ɪm'præktɪkəl] *adj* : poco
práctico

imprecise [ˌɪmprɪ'saɪs] *adj* : impreciso
— **imprecision** [ˌɪmprɪ'sɪʒən] *n* : imprecisión *f*

impregnable [ɪm'prɛgnəbəl] *adj* : impenetrable

impregnate [ɪm'prɛgˌneɪt] *vt* **-nated;
-nating 1** : impregnar **2** FERTILIZE : fecundar

impress [ɪm'prɛs] *vt* **1** : causar una
buena impresión a **2** AFFECT : impresionar **3 ~ sth on s.o.** : recalcar algo
a algn — *vi* : impresionar — **impression** [ɪm'prɛʃən] *n* : impresión *f* — **impressionable** [ɪm'prɛʃənəbəl] *adj* : impresionable — **impressive** [ɪm'prɛsɪv]
adj : impresionante

imprint [ɪm'prɪnt, 'ɪm,-] *vt* : imprimir —
~ [ˈɪmˌprɪnt] *n* MARK : impresión *f*,
huella *f*

imprison [ɪm'prɪzən] *vt* : encarcelar —
imprisonment [ɪm'prɪzənmənt] *n* : encarcelamiento *m*

improbable [ɪm'prɑbəbəl] *adj* : improbable — **improbability** [ɪmprɑbə'bɪləti]
n, pl **-ties** : improbabilidad *f*

impromptu [ɪm'prɑmpˌtuː, -ˌtjuː] *adj* : improvisado

improper [ɪm'prɑpər] *adj* **1** UNSEEMLY
: indecoroso **2** INCORRECT : impropio

— **impropriety** [ˌɪmprə'praɪəṭi] n, pl
-eties : inconveniencia f
improve [ɪm'pruːv] v -proved; -proving
: mejorar — **improvement** [ɪm-
'pruːvmənt] n : mejora f
improvise ['ɪmprə,vaɪz] v -vised;
-vising : improvisar — **improvisation** [ɪm,prɑvə'zeɪʃən, ,ɪmprəvə-] n : improvisación f
impudent ['ɪmpjədənt] adj : insolente —
impudence ['ɪmpjədənts] n : insolencia f
impulse ['ɪm,pʌls] n 1 : impulso m 2 on
~ : sin reflexionar — **impulsive** [ɪm-
'pʌlsɪv] adj : impulsivo — **impulsiveness** [ɪm'pʌlsɪvnəs] n : impulsividad f
impunity [ɪm'pjuːnəṭi] n 1 : impunidad f
2 with ~ : impunemente
impure [ɪm'pjʊr] adj : impuro — **impurity** [ɪm'pjʊrəṭi] n, pl -ties : impureza f
in ['ɪn] prep 1 : en 2 DURING : por, en Lat
3 WITHIN : dentro de 4 dressed ~ red
: vestido de rojo 5 ~ the rain : bajo la
lluvia 6 ~ the sun : al sol 7 ~ this
way : de esta manera 8 the best ~
the world : el mejor del mundo 9 written ~ ink/French : escrito con
tinta/en francés — adv 1 INSIDE : dentro, adentro 2 be ~ : estar (en casa) 3
be ~ on : participar en 4 come in!
: ¡entre!, ¡pase! 5 he's ~ for a shock
: se va a llevar una shock — ~ adj : de
moda
inability [ˌɪnə'bɪləṭi] n, pl -ties : incapacidad f
inaccessible [ˌɪnɪk'sesəbəl] adj : inaccesible
inaccurate [ɪn'ækjərət] adj : inexacto
inactive [ɪn'æktɪv] n : inactivo — **inactivity** [ˌɪn,æk'tɪvəṭi] n, pl -ties : inactividad f
inadequate [ɪn'ædɪkwət] adj : insuficiente
inadvertently [ˌɪnəd'vərtəntli] adv : sin
querer
inadvisable [ˌɪnəd'vaɪzəbəl] adj : desaconsejable
inane [ɪ'neɪn] adj inaner; -est : estúpido, tonto
inanimate [ɪn'ænəmət] adj : inanimado
inapplicable [ɪn'æplɪkəbəl, ˌɪnə'plɪkəbəl]
adj : inaplicable
inappropriate [ˌɪnə'proːpriət] adj : impropio, inoportuno
inarticulate [ˌɪnɑr'tɪkjələt] adj : incapaz
de expresarse
inasmuch as [ˌɪnæz'mʌt,fæz] conj : ya
que, puesto que
inattentive [ˌɪnə'tentɪv] adj : poco atento
inaudible [ɪn'ɔdəbəl] adj : inaudible

inaugural [ɪ'nɔgjərəl, -gərəl] adj 1 : inaugural 2 ~ address : discurso m de
investidura — **inaugurate** [ɪ'nɔgjə,reɪt,
-gə-] vt -rated; -rating 1 : investir (a
un presidente, etc.) 2 BEGIN : inaugurar — **inauguration** [ɪ,nɔgjə'reɪʃən,
-gə-] n : investidura f (de una persona), inauguración f (de un edificio,
etc.)
inborn ['ɪn,bɔrn] adj : innato
inbred ['ɪn,bred] adj INNATE : innato
incalculable [ɪn'kælkjələbəl] adj : incalculable
incapable [ɪn'keɪpəbəl] adj : incapaz —
incapacitate [ˌɪnkə'pæsə,teɪt] vt -tated;
-tating : incapacitar — **incapacity**
[ˌɪnkə'pæsəṭi] n, pl -ties : incapacidad f
incarcerate [ɪn'kɑrsə,reɪt] vt -ated;
-ating : encarcelar
incarnate [ɪn'kɑrnət, -,neɪt] adj : encarnado — **incarnation** [ˌɪn,kɑr'neɪʃən] n
: encarnación f
incendiary [ɪn'sendi,eri] adj : incendiario
incense[1] ['ɪn,sents] n : incienso m
incense[2] [ɪn'sents] vt -censed;
-censing : indignar, enfurecer
incentive [ɪn'sentɪv] n : incentivo m
inception [ɪn'sepʃən] n : comienzo m,
principio m
incessant [ɪn'sesənt] adj : incesante
incest ['ɪn,sest] n : incesto m — **incestuous** [ɪn'sestʃʊəs] adj : incestuoso
inch ['ɪntʃ] n : pulgada f — ~ v : avanzar poco a poco
incident ['ɪnsədənt] n : incidente m —
incidence ['ɪnsədənts] n : índice m (de
crímenes, etc.) — **incidental** [ˌɪnsə-
'dentəl] adj 1 MINOR : incidental 2
CHANCE : casual — **incidentally**
[ˌɪnsə'dentəli, -'dentli] adv : a propósito
incinerate [ɪn'sɪnə,reɪt] vt -ated; -ating
: incinerar — **incinerator** [ɪn'sɪnə-
,reɪṭər] n : incinerador m
incision [ɪn'sɪʒən] n : incisión f
incite [ɪn'saɪt] vt -cited; -citing : incitar,
instigar
incline [ɪn'klaɪn] v -clined; -clining vt 1
BEND : inclinar 2 be ~ed to : inclinarse a, tender a — ~ vi : inclinarse
— ~ ['ɪn,klaɪn] n : pendiente f — **inclination** [ˌɪnklə'neɪʃən] n 1 : inclinación f
2 DESIRE : deseo m, ganas fpl
include [ɪn'kluːd] vt -cluded; -cluding
: incluir — **inclusion** [ɪn'kluːʒən] n
: inclusión f — **inclusive** [ɪn'kluːsɪv]
adj : inclusivo
incognito [ˌɪn,kɑg'niːṭo, ɪn'kɑgnə,toː] adv
& adj : de incógnito
incoherent [ˌɪnko'hɪrənt, -'her-] adj : in-

coherente — **incoherence** [ˌɪnko-
'hɪrənts, -'her-] n : incoherencia f
income ['ɪnˌkʌm] n : ingresos mpl — **income tax** n : impuesto m sobre la
renta
incomparable [ɪn'kɑmpərəbəl] adj : incomparable
incompatible [ˌɪnkəm'pæt̬əbəl] adj : incompatible
incompetent [ɪn'kɑmpət̬ənt] adj : incompetente — **incompetence** [ɪn-
'kɑmpət̬ənts] n : incompetencia f
incomplete [ˌɪnkəm'pliːt] adj : incompleto
incomprehensible [ˌɪnˌkɑmprɪ'hɛntsə-
bəl] adj : incomprensible
inconceivable [ˌɪnkən'siːvəbəl] adj : inconcebible
inconclusive [ˌɪnkən'kluːsɪv] adj : no
concluyente
incongruous [ɪn'kɑŋgruəs] adj : incongruente
inconsiderate [ˌɪnkən'sɪdərət] adj : desconsiderado
inconsistent [ˌɪnkən'sɪstənt] adj 1 : inconsecuente 2 **be ~ with** : no concordar con — **inconsistency** [ˌɪnkən-
'sɪstəntsi] n, pl **-cies** : inconsecuencia f
inconspicuous [ˌɪnkən'spɪkjuəs] adj
: que no llama la atención
inconvenient [ˌɪnkən'viːnjənt] adj : incómodo, inconveniente — **inconvenience** [ˌɪnkən'viːnjənts] n 1 BOTHER : incomodidad f, molestia f 2 DRAWBACK
: inconveniente m — ~ vt **-nienced;
-niencing** vt : importunar, molestar
incorporate [ɪn'kɔrpəˌreɪt] vt **-rated;
-rating** : incorporar
incorrect [ˌɪnkə'rɛkt] adj : incorrecto
increase ['ɪnˌkriːs, ɪn'kriːs] n : aumento m
— ~ [ɪn'kriːs, 'ɪnˌkriːs] v **-creased;
-creasing** : aumentar — **increasingly**
[ɪn'kriːsɪŋli] adv : cada vez más
incredible [ɪn'krɛdəbəl] adj : increíble
incredulous [ɪn'krɛdʒələs] adj : incrédulo
incriminate [ɪn'krɪməˌneɪt] vt **-nated;
-nating** : incriminar
incubator ['ɪŋkjuˌbeɪt̬ər, 'ɪn-] n : incubadora f
incumbent [ɪn'kʌmbənt] n : titular mf
incur [ɪn'kər] vt **incurred; incurring**
: provocar (al enojo, etc.), incurrir en
(gastos)
incurable [ɪn'kjurəbəl] adj : incurable
indebted [ɪn'dɛt̬əd] adj 1 : endeudado 2
be ~ to s.o. : estar en deuda con algn
indecent [ɪn'diːsənt] adj : indecente —
indecency [ɪn'diːsəntsi] n, pl **-cies** : indecencia f

indecisive [ˌɪndɪ'saɪsɪv] adj : indeciso
indeed [ɪn'diːd] adv 1 TRULY : verdaderamente, sin duda 2 IN FACT : en
efecto 3 ~? : ¿de veras?
indefinite [ɪn'dɛfənət] adj 1 : indefinido
2 VAGUE : impreciso — **indefinitely**
[ɪn'dɛfənətli] adv : indefinidamente
indelible [ɪn'dɛləbəl] adj : indeleble
indent [ɪn'dɛnt] vt : sangrar (un párrafo)
— **indentation** [ˌɪnˌdɛn'teɪʃən] n DENT,
NOTCH : mella f
independent [ˌɪndə'pɛndənt] adj : independiente — **independence** [ˌɪndə-
'pɛndənts] n : independencia f
indescribable [ˌɪndɪ'skraɪbəbəl] adj : indescriptible
indestructible [ˌɪndɪ'strʌktəbəl] adj : indestructible
index ['ɪnˌdɛks] n, pl **-dexes** or **-dices**
['ɪndəˌsiːz] : índice m — ~ vt : incluir
en un índice — **index finger** n : dedo
m índice
Indian ['ɪndiən] adj : indio m, -dia f
indication [ˌɪndə'keɪʃən] n : indicio m,
señal f — **indicate** ['ɪndəˌkeɪt] vt
-cated; -cating : indicar — **indicative**
[ɪn'dɪkət̬ɪv] adj : indicativo — **indicator** ['ɪndəˌkeɪt̬ər] n : indicador m
indict [ɪn'daɪt] vt : acusar (de un crimen)
— **indictment** [ɪn'daɪtmənt] n : acusación f
indifferent [ɪn'dɪfrənt, -'dɪfə-] adj 1 : indiferente 2 MEDIOCRE : mediocre —
indifference [ɪn'dɪfrənts, -'dɪfə-] n : indiferencia f
indigenous [ɪn'dɪdʒənəs] adj : indígena
indigestion [ˌɪndar'dʒɛstʃən, -dɪ-] n : indigestión f — **indigestible** [ˌɪndaɪ-
'dʒɛstəbəl, -dɪ-] adj : indigesto
indignation [ˌɪndɪg'neɪʃən] n : indignación f — **indignant** [ɪn'dɪgnənt] adj
: indignado — **indignity** [ɪn'dɪgnət̬i] n,
pl **-ties** : indignidad f
indigo ['ɪndɪˌgoː] n, pl **-gos** or **-goes**
: añil m
indirect [ˌɪndə'rɛkt, -daɪ-] adj : indirecto
indiscreet [ˌɪndɪ'skriːt] adj : indiscreto
— **indiscretion** [ˌɪndɪ'skrɛʃən] n : indiscreción f
indiscriminate [ˌɪndɪ'skrɪmənət] adj : indiscriminado
indispensable [ˌɪndɪ'spɛntsəbəl] adj : indispensable, imprescindible
indisputable [ˌɪndɪ'spjuːt̬əbəl, ɪn'dɪspjuː-
t̬ə-] adj : indiscutible
indistinct [ˌɪndɪ'stɪŋkt] adj : indistinto
individual [ˌɪndə'vɪdʒuəl] adj 1 : individual 2 PARTICULAR : particular — ~ n
: individuo m — **individuality** [ˌɪndə-
ˌvɪdʒu'ælət̬i] n, pl **-ties** : individualidad

f — **individually** [ˌɪndəˈvɪdʒuəli, -dʒəli] *adv* : individualmente

indoctrinate [ɪnˈdɑktrəˌneɪt] *vt* **-nated; -nating** : adoctrinar — **indoctrination** [ɪnˌdɑktrəˈneɪʃən] *n* : adoctrinamiento *m*

indoor [ˈɪnˈdor] *adj* 1 : (de) interior 2 ∼ **plant** : planta *f* de interior 3 ∼ **pool** : piscina *f* cubierta 4 ∼ **sports** : deportes *mpl* bajo techo — **indoors** [ˈɪnˈdorz] *adv* : adentro, dentro

induce [ɪnˈduːs, -ˈdjuːs] *vt* **-duced; -ducing** 1 : inducir 2 CAUSE : provocar — **inducement** [ɪnˈduːsmənt, -ˈdjuːs-] *n* : incentivo *m*

indulge [ɪnˈdʌldʒ] *v* **-dulged; -dulging** *vt* 1 GRATIFY : satisfacer 2 PAMPER : consentir — *vi* ∼ **in** : permitirse — **indulgence** [ɪnˈdʌldʒənts] *n* 1 : indulgencia *f* 2 SATISFYING : satisfacción *f* — **indulgent** [ɪnˈdʌldʒənt] *adj* : indulgente

industry [ˈɪndəstri] *n*, *pl* **-tries** 1 : industria *f* 2 DILIGENCE : diligencia *f* — **industrial** [ɪnˈdʌstriəl] *adj* : industrial — **industrialize** [ɪnˈdʌstriəˌlaɪz] *vt* **-ized; -izing** : industrializar — **industrious** [ɪnˈdʌstriəs] *adj* : diligente, trabajador

inebriated [ɪˈniːbriˌeɪtəd] *adj* : ebrio, embriagado

inedible [ˈɪnˈedəbəl] *adj* : no comestible

ineffective [ˌɪnɪˈfɛktɪv] *adj* 1 : ineficaz 2 INCOMPETENT : incompetente — **ineffectual** [ˌɪnɪˈfɛktʃuəl] *adj* : inútil, ineficaz

inefficient [ˌɪnɪˈfɪʃənt] *adj* 1 : ineficiente 2 INCOMPETENT : incompetente — **inefficiency** [ˌɪnɪˈfɪʃəntsi] *n*, *pl* **-cies** : ineficiencia *f*

ineligible [ˈɪnˈelədʒəbəl] *adj* : ineligible

inept [ɪˈnɛpt] *adj* 1 : inepto 2 ∼ **at** : incapaz para

inequality [ˌɪnɪˈkwɑləti] *n*, *pl* **-ties** : desigualdad *f*

inert [ɪˈnərt] *adj* : inerte — **inertia** [ɪˈnərʃə] *n* : inercia *f*

inescapable [ˌɪnɪˈskeɪpəbəl] *adj* : ineludible

inevitable [ɪˈnevəṭəbəl] *adj* : inevitable — **inevitably** [-bli] *adv* : inevitablemente

inexcusable [ˌɪnɪkˈskjuːzəbəl] *adj* : inexcusable

inexpensive [ˌɪnɪkˈspɛntsɪv] *adj* : barato, económico

inexperienced [ˌɪnɪkˈspɪriəntst] *adj* : inexperto

inexplicable [ˌɪnɪkˈsplɪkəbəl] *adj* : inexplicable

infallible [ɪnˈfæləbəl] *adj* : infalible

infamous [ˈɪnfəməs] *adj* : infame

infancy [ˈɪnfəntsi] *n*, *pl* **-cies** : infancia *f* — **infant** [ˈɪnfənt] *n* : bebé *m*; niño *m*, -ña *f* — **infantile** [ˈɪnfənˌtaɪl, -təl, -ˌtiːl] *adj* : infantil

infantry [ˈɪnfəntri] *n*, *pl* **-tries** : infantería *f*

infatuated [ɪnˈfætʃuˌeɪtəd] *adj* be ∼ **with** : estar encaprichado con — **infatuation** [ɪnˌfætʃuˈeɪʃən] *n* : encaprichamiento *m*

infect [ɪnˈfɛkt] *vt* : infectar — **infection** [ɪnˈfɛkʃən] *n* : infección *f* — **infectious** [ɪnˈfɛkʃəs] *adj* : contagioso

infer [ɪnˈfər] *vt* **inferred; inferring** : deducir, inferir — **inference** [ˈɪnfərənts] *n* : deducción *f*

inferior [ɪnˈfɪriər] *adj* : inferior — ∼ *n* : inferior *mf* — **inferiority** [ɪnˌfɪriˈɔrəṭi] *n*, *pl* **-ties** : inferioridad *f*

infernal [ɪnˈfərnəl] *adj* : infernal — **inferno** [ɪnˈfərˌno:] *n*, *pl* **-nos** : infierno *m*

infertile [ɪnˈfərtəl, -ˌtaɪl] *adj* : estéril — **infertility** [ˌɪnfərˈtɪləti] *n* : esterilidad *f*

infest [ɪnˈfɛst] *vt* : infestar

infidelity [ˌɪnfəˈdɛləṭi, -faɪ-] *n*, *pl* **-ties** : infidelidad *f*

infiltrate [ɪnˈfɪlˌtreɪt, ˈɪnfɪl-] *v* **-trated; -trating** *vt* : infiltrar — *vi* : infiltrarse

infinite [ˈɪnfənət] *adj* : infinito

infinitive [ɪnˈfɪnəṭɪv] *n* : infinitivo *m*

infinity [ɪnˈfɪnəṭi] *n*, *pl* **-ties** 1 : infinito *m* 2 an ∼ **of** : una infinidad de

infirm [ɪnˈfərm] *adj* : enfermizo, endeble — **infirmary** [ɪnˈfərməri] *n*, *pl* **-ries** : enfermería *f* — **infirmity** [ɪnˈfərməṭi] *n*, *pl* **-ties** 1 FRAILTY : endeblez *f* 2 AILMENT : enfermedad *f*

inflame [ɪnˈfleɪm] *vt* **-flamed; -flaming** : inflamar — **inflammable** [ɪnˈflæməbəl] *adj* : inflamable — **inflammation** [ˌɪnfləˈmeɪʃən] *n* : inflamación *f* — **inflammatory** [ɪnˈflæməˌtori] *adj* : inflamatorio

inflate [ɪnˈfleɪt] *vt* **-flated; -flating** : inflar — **inflation** [ɪnˈfleɪʃən] *n* : inflación *f* — **inflationary** [ɪnˈfleɪʃəˌneri] *adj* : inflacionario, inflacionista

inflexible [ɪnˈflɛksɪbəl] *adj* : inflexible

inflict [ɪnˈflɪkt] *vt* : infligir

influence [ˈɪnˌfluːənts, ɪnˈfluːənts] *n* 1 : influencia *f* 2 under the ∼ : embriagado — ∼ *vt* **-enced; -encing** : influir en, influenciar — **influential** [ˌɪnfluˈentʃəl] *adj* : influyente

influenza [ˌɪnfluˈenzə] *n* : gripe *f*, influenza *f*

influx [ˈɪnˌflʌks] *n* : afluencia *f*

inform [ɪnˈfɔrm] *vt* 1 : informar 2 keep me ∼ed : manténme al corriente — *vi* ∼ **on** : delatar, denunciar

informal [ɪn'fɔrməl] adj 1 : informal 2 : familiar (dícese del lenguaje) — **informality** [,ɪnfɔr'mæləti, -fər-] n, pl -ties : falta f de ceremonia — **informally** [ɪn'fɔrməli] adv : de manera informal

information [,ɪnfər'meɪʃən] n : información f — **informative** [ɪn'fɔrmətɪv] adj : informativo — **informer** [ɪn'fɔrmər] n : informante mf

infrared [,ɪnfrə'red] adj : infrarrojo

infrastructure ['ɪnfrə,strʌktʃər] n : infraestructura f

infrequent [ɪn'fri:kwənt] adj : infrecuente — **infrequently** [ɪn'fri:kwəntli] adv : raramente

infringe [ɪn'frɪndʒ] v -**fringed**; -**fringing** vt : infringir — vi ~ **on** : violar — **infringement** [ɪn'frɪndʒmənt] n : violación f

infuriate [ɪn'fjʊri,eɪt] vt -**ated**; -**ating** : enfurecer, poner furioso — **infuriating** [ɪn'fjʊri,eɪtɪŋ] adj : exasperante

infuse [ɪn'fju:z] vt -**fused**; -**fusing** : infundir — **infusion** [ɪn'fju:ʒən] n : infusión f

ingenious [ɪn'dʒi:njəs] adj : ingenioso — **ingenuity** [,ɪndʒə'nu:əti, -'nju:-] n, pl -ities : ingenio

ingenuous [ɪn'dʒɛnjʊəs] adj : ingenuo

ingest [ɪn'dʒɛst] vt : ingerir

ingot ['ɪŋgət] n : lingote m

ingrained [ɪn'greɪnd] adj : arraigado

ingratiate [ɪn'greɪʃi,eɪt] vt -**ated**; -**ating** ~ **oneself with** : congraciarse con

ingratitude [ɪn'grætə,tu:d, -,tju:d] n : ingratitud f

ingredient [ɪn'gri:diənt] n : ingrediente m

ingrown ['ɪn,groʊn] adj ~ **nail** : uña f encarnada

inhabit [ɪn'hæbət] vt : habitar — **inhabitant** [ɪn'hæbətənt] n : habitante mf

inhale [ɪn'heɪl] v -**haled**; -**haling** vt : inhalar, aspirar — vi : inspirar

inherent [ɪn'hɪrənt, -'her-] adj : inherente — **inherently** [ɪn'hɪrəntli, -'her-] adv : intrínsecamente

inherit [ɪn'herət] vt : heredar — **inheritance** [ɪn'herətəns] n : herencia f

inhibit [ɪn'hɪbət] vt IMPEDE : inhibir — **inhibition** [,ɪnhə'bɪʃən, ,ɪnə-] n : inhibición f

inhuman [ɪn'hju:mən, -'ju:-] adj : inhumano — **inhumane** [,ɪnhju'meɪn, -ju-] adj : inhumano — **inhumanity** [,ɪnhju'mænəti, -ju-] n, pl -ties : inhumanidad f

initial [ɪ'nɪʃəl] adj : inicial — n : inicial f — vt -**tialed** or -**tialled**; -**tialing** or -**tialling** : poner las iniciales a

initiate [ɪ'nɪʃi,eɪt] vt -**ated**; -**ating** 1 BEGIN : iniciar 2 ~ **s.o. into sth** : iniciar a algn en algo — **initiation** [ɪ,nɪʃi'eɪʃən] n : iniciación f — **initiative** [ɪ'nɪʃətɪv] n : iniciativa f

inject [ɪn'dʒɛkt] vt : inyectar — **injection** [ɪn'dʒɛkʃən] n : inyección f

injure ['ɪndʒər] vt -**jured**; -**juring** 1 : herir 2 ~ **oneself** : hacerse daño — **injurious** [ɪn'dʒʊriəs] adj : perjudicial — **injury** ['ɪndʒəri] n, pl -ries 1 : herida f 2 HARM : perjuicio m

injustice [ɪn'dʒʌstəs] n : injusticia f

ink ['ɪŋk] n : tinta f — **inkwell** ['ɪŋk,wel] n : tintero m

inland ['ɪn,lænd, -lənd] adj : interior — ~ adv : hacia el interior, tierra adentro

in-laws ['ɪn,lɔz] npl : suegros mpl

inlet ['ɪn,let, -lət] n : ensenada f, cala f

inmate ['ɪn,meɪt] n 1 PATIENT : paciente mf 2 PRISONER : preso m, -sa f

inn ['ɪn] n : posada f, hostería f

innards ['ɪnərdz] npl : entrañas fpl, tripas fpl fam

innate ['ɪneɪt] adj : innato

inner ['ɪnər] adj : interior, interno — **innermost** ['ɪnər,moʊst] adj : más íntimo, más profundo

inning ['ɪnɪŋ] n : entrada f

innocent ['ɪnəsənt] adj : inocente — ~ n : inocente mf — **innocence** ['ɪnəsənts] n : inocencia f

innocuous [ɪ'nɑkjəwəs] adj : inocuo

innovate ['ɪnə,veɪt] vi -**vated**; -**vating** : innovar — **innovation** [,ɪnə'veɪʃən] n : innovación f — **innovative** ['ɪnə,veɪtɪv] adj : innovador — **innovator** ['ɪnə,veɪtər] n : innovador m, -dora f

innuendo [,ɪnju'ɛndoʊ] n, pl -**dos** or -**does** : insinuación f, indirecta f

innumerable [ɪ'nu:mərəbəl, -'nju:-] adj : innumerable

inoculate [ɪ'nɑkjə,leɪt] vt -**lated**; -**lating** : inocular — **inoculation** [ɪ,nɑkjə'leɪʃən] n : inoculación f

inoffensive [,ɪnə'fentsɪv] adj : inofensivo

inpatient ['ɪn,peɪʃənt] n : paciente mf hospitalizado

input ['ɪn,pʊt] n 1 : contribución f 2 : entrada f (de datos) — ~ vt -**putted** or -**put**; -**putting** : entrar (datos, etc.)

inquire [ɪn'kwaɪr] v -**quired**; -**quiring** vt : preguntar — vi 1 ~ **about** : informarse sobre 2 ~ **into** : investigar — **inquiry** ['ɪn,kwaɪri, ɪn'kwaɪri; 'ɪn,kwəri, -ɪn-] n, pl -ries 1 QUESTION : pregunta f 2 INVESTIGATION : investigación f — **inquisition** [,ɪnkwə'zɪʃən, ,ɪŋ-] n : inquisición f — **inquisitive** [ɪnˈkwɪzət̬ɪv] adj : curioso

insane [ɪnˈseɪn] adj : loco — **insanity** [ɪnˈsænət̬i] n, pl **-ties** : locura f

insatiable [ɪnˈseɪʃəbəl] adj : insaciable

inscribe [ɪnˈskraɪb] vt **-scribed; -scribing** : inscribir — **inscription** [ɪnˈskrɪpʃən] n : inscripción f

inscrutable [ɪnˈskruːt̬əbəl] adj : inescrutable

insect [ˈɪnˌsekt] n : insecto m — **insecticide** [ɪnˈsektəˌsaɪd] n : insecticida m

insecure [ˌɪnsɪˈkjʊr] adj : inseguro, poco seguro — **insecurity** [ˌɪnsɪˈkjʊrət̬i] n, pl **-ties** : inseguridad f

insensitive [ɪnˈsensət̬ɪv] adj : insensible — **insensitivity** [ɪnˌsensəˈtɪvət̬i] n, pl **-ties** : insensibilidad f

inseparable [ɪnˈsepərəbəl] adj : inseparable

insert [ɪnˈsərt] vt : insertar (texto), introducir (una moneda, etc.)

inside [ˈɪnˌsaɪd, ˌɪnˌsaɪd] n 1 : interior m 2 ~ **out** : al revés — adv : dentro, adentro — ~ adj : interior — ~ prep 1 or ~ **of** : dentro de 2 ~ **an hour** : en menos de una hora

insidious [ɪnˈsɪdiəs] adj : insidioso

insight [ˈɪnˌsaɪt] n : perspicacia f

insignia [ɪnˈsɪgniə] or **insigne** [-niː] n, pl **-nia** or **-nias** : insignia f, enseña f

insignificant [ˌɪnsɪgˈnɪfɪkənt] adj : insignificante

insincere [ˌɪnsɪnˈsɪr] adj : insincero

insinuate [ɪnˈsɪnjuˌeɪt] vt **-ated; -ating** : insinuar — **insinuation** [ɪnˌsɪnjuˈeɪʃən] n : insinuación f

insipid [ɪnˈsɪpəd] adj : insípido

insist [ɪnˈsɪst] v : insistir — **insistent** [ɪnˈsɪstənt] adj : insistente

insofar as [ˌɪnsoˈfɑræz] conj : en la medida en que

insole [ˈɪnˌsoːl] n : plantilla f

insolent [ˈɪnsələnt] adj : insolente — **insolence** [ˈɪnsələns] n : insolencia f

insolvent [ɪnˈsɑlvənt] adj : insolvente

insomnia [ɪnˈsɑmniə] n : insomnio m

inspect [ɪnˈspekt] vt : inspeccionar, revisar — **inspection** [ɪnˈspekʃən] n : inspección f — **inspector** [ɪnˈspektər] n : inspector m, -tora f

inspire [ɪnˈspaɪr] vt **-spired; -spiring** : inspirar — **inspiration** [ˌɪnspəˈreɪʃən] n : inspiración f — **inspirational** [ˌɪnspəˈreɪʃənəl] adj : inspirador

instability [ˌɪnstəˈbɪləti] n, pl **-ties** : inestabilidad f

install [ɪnˈstɔl] vt **-stalled; -stalling** : instalar — **installation** [ˌɪnstəˈleɪʃən] n : instalación f — **installment** [ɪnˈstɔlmənt] n 1 PAYMENT : plazo m, cuota f 2 : entrega f (de una publicación o telenovela)

instance [ˈɪnstənts] n 1 : ejemplo m 2 **for** ~ : por ejemplo 3 **in this** ~ : en este caso

instant [ˈɪnstənt] n : instante m — ~ adj 1 IMMEDIATE : inmediato 2 ~ **coffee** : café m instantáneo — **instantaneous** [ˌɪnstənˈteɪniəs] adj : instantáneo — **instantly** [ˈɪnstəntli] adv : al instante, instantáneamente

instead [ɪnˈsted] adv 1 : en cambio 2 **I went** ~ : fui en su lugar — **instead of** prep : en vez de, en lugar de

instep [ˈɪnˌstep] n : empeine m

instigate [ˈɪnstəˌgeɪt] vt **-gated; -gating** : instigar — **instigation** [ˌɪnstəˈgeɪʃən] n : instigación f — **instigator** [ˈɪnstəˌgeɪtər] n : instigador m, -dora f

instill [ɪnˈstɪl] or Brit **instil** vt **-stilled; -stilling** : inculcar, infundir

instinct [ˈɪnˌstɪŋkt] n : instinto m — **instinctive** [ɪnˈstɪŋktɪv] or **instinctual** [ɪnˈstɪŋktʃuəl] adj : instintivo

institute [ˈɪnstəˌtuːt, -ˌtjuːt] vt **-tuted; -tuting** 1 : instituir 2 INITIATE : iniciar — ~ n : instituto m — **institution** [ˌɪnstəˈtuːʃən, -ˈtjuː-] n : institución f

instruct [ɪnˈstrʌkt] vt 1 : instruir 2 COMMAND : mandar — **instruction** [ɪnˈstrʌkʃən] n : instrucción f — **instructor** [ɪnˈstrʌktər] n : instructor m, -tora f

instrument [ˈɪnstrəmənt] n : instrumento m — **instrumental** [ˌɪnstrəˈmentəl] adj 1 : instrumental 2 **be** ~ **in** : jugar un papel fundamental en

insubordinate [ˌɪnsəˈbɔrdənət] adj : insubordinado — **insubordination** [ˌɪnsəˌbɔrdənˈeɪʃən] n : insubordinación f

insufferable [ɪnˈsʌfərəbəl] adj : insoportable

insufficient [ˌɪnsəˈfɪʃənt] adj : insuficiente

insular [ˈɪnsələr, -sju-] adj 1 : insular 2 NARROW-MINDED : estrecho de miras

insulate [ˈɪnsəˌleɪt] vt **-lated; -lating** : aislar — **insulation** [ˌɪnsəˈleɪʃən] n : aislamiento m

insulin [ˈɪnsələn] n : insulina f

insult [ɪnˈsʌlt] vt : insultar — ~ [ˈɪnˌsʌlt] n : insulto m — **insulting** [ɪnˈsʌltɪŋ] adj : insultante, ofensivo

insure [ɪnˈʃʊr] vt **-sured; -suring** : asegurar — **insurance** [ɪnˈʃʊrənts, ˈɪnˌʃʊr-] n : seguro m

insurmountable [ˌɪnsərˈmaʊntəbəl] adj : insuperable

intact [ɪnˈtækt] adj : intacto

intake ['ɪn,teɪk] *n* : consumo *m* (de alimentos), entrada *f* (de aire, etc.)

intangible [ɪn'tændʒəbəl] *adj* : intangible

integral ['ɪntɪɡrəl] *adj* : integral

integrate ['ɪntə,ɡreɪt] *v* **-grated; -grating** *vt* : integrar — *vi* : integrarse

integrity [ɪn'tɛɡrəti] *n* : integridad *f*

intellect ['ɪntəl,ɛkt] *n* : intelecto *m* — **intellectual** [ˌɪntə'lɛktʃʊəl] *adj* : intelectual — **~** *n* : intelectual *mf* — **intelligence** [ɪn'tɛlədʒənts] *n* : inteligencia *f* — **intelligent** [ɪn'tɛlədʒənt] *adj* : inteligente — **intelligible** [ɪn'tɛlədʒəbəl] *adj* : inteligible

intend [ɪn'tɛnd] *vt* **1 be ~ed for** : ser para **2 ~ to do** : pensar hacer, tener la intención de hacer — **intended** [ɪn'tɛndəd] *adj* : intencionado, deliberado

intense [ɪn'tɛnts] *adj* : intenso — **intensely** [ɪn'tɛntsli] *adv* : sumamente, profundamente — **intensify** [ɪn'tɛntsə,faɪ] *v* **-fied; -fying** *vt* : intensificar — *vi* : intensificarse — **intensity** [ɪn'tɛntsəti] *n, pl* **-ties** : intensidad *f* — **intensive** [ɪn'tɛntsɪv] *adj* : intensivo

intent [ɪn'tɛnt] *n* : intención *f* — **~** *adj* **1** : atento, concentrado **2 ~ on doing** : resuelto a hacer — **intention** [ɪn'tɛntʃən] *n* : intención *f* — **intentional** [ɪn'tɛntʃənəl] *adj* : intencional, deliberado — **intently** [ɪn'tɛntli] *adv* : atentamente, fijamente

interact [ˌɪntər'ækt] *vi* **1** : interactuar **2 ~ with** : relacionarse con — **interaction** [ˌɪntər'ækʃən] *n* : interacción *f* — **interactive** [ˌɪntər'æktɪv] *adj* : interactivo

intercede [ˌɪntər'siːd] *vi* **-ceded; -ceding** : interceder

intercept [ˌɪntər'sɛpt] *vt* : interceptar

interchange [ˌɪntər'tʃeɪndʒ] *vt* **-changed; -changing** : intercambiar — **~** ['ɪntər,tʃeɪndʒ] *n* **1** : intercambio *m* **2** JUNCTION : enlace *m* — **interchangeable** [ˌɪntər'tʃeɪndʒəbəl] *adj* : intercambiable

intercourse ['ɪntər,kors] *n* : relaciones *fpl* (sexuales)

interest ['ɪntrəst, -tə,rɛst] *n* : interés *m* — **~** *vt* : interesar — **interested** [-əd] *adj* : interesado — **interesting** ['ɪntrəstɪŋ, -tə,rɛstɪŋ] *adj* : interesante

interface ['ɪntər,feɪs] *n* : interfaz *mf* (de una computadora)

interfere [ˌɪntər'fɪr] *vi* **-fered; -fering 1 ~ in** : entrometerse en, interferir en **2 ~ with** DISRUPT : afectar (una actividad, etc.) — **interference** [ˌɪntər-'fɪrənts] *n* **1** : interferencia *f* **2** : intromisión *f* (en el radio, etc.)

interim ['ɪntərəm] *n* **1** : interín *m* **2 in the ~** : mientras tanto — **~** *adj* : interino, provisional

interior [ɪn'tɪriər] *adj* : interior — **~** *n* : interior *m*

interjection [ˌɪntər'dʒɛkʃən] *n* : interjección *f*

interlock [ˌɪntər'lɑk] *vt* : engranar

interloper [ˌɪntər'loːpər] *n* : intruso *m*, -sa *f*

interlude ['ɪntər,luːd] *n* **1** : intervalo *m* **2** : interludio *m* (en música, etc.)

intermediate [ˌɪntər'miːdiət] *adj* : intermedio — **intermediary** [ˌɪntər'miːdi,ɛri] *n, pl* **-aries** : intermediario *m*, -ria *f*

interminable [ɪn'tərmənəbəl] *adj* : interminable

intermission [ˌɪntər'mɪʃən] *n* : intervalo *m*, intermedio *m*

intermittent [ˌɪntər'mɪtənt] *adj* : intermitente

intern[1] ['ɪn,tərn, ɪn'tərn] *vt* : confinar

intern[2] ['ɪn,tərn] *vi* : hacer las prácticas — **~** *n* : interno *m*, -na *f*

internal [ɪn'tərnəl] *adj* : interno

international [ˌɪntər'næʃənəl] *adj* : internacional

interpret [ɪn'tərprət] *vt* : interpretar — **interpretation** [ɪnˌtərprə'teɪʃən] *n* : interpretación *f* — **interpreter** [ɪn'tərprətər] *n* : intérprete *mf*

interrogate [ɪn'tɛrə,ɡeɪt] *vt* **-gated; -gating** : interrogar — **interrogation** [ɪnˌtɛrə'ɡeɪʃən] *n* QUESTIONING : interrogatorio *m* — **interrogative** [ˌɪntə-'rɑɡətɪv] *adj* : interrogativo

interrupt [ˌɪntə'rʌpt] *v* : interrumpir — **interruption** [ˌɪntə'rʌpʃən] *n* : interrupción *f*

intersect [ˌɪntər'sɛkt] *vt* : cruzar (dícese de calles), cortar (dícese de líneas) — *vi* : cruzarse, cortarse — **intersection** [ˌɪntər'sɛkʃən] *n* : cruce *m*, intersección *f*

intersperse [ˌɪntər'spərs] *vt* **-spersed; -spersing** : intercalar

interstate [ˌɪntər'steɪt] *n or* **~ highway** : carretera *f* interestatal

intertwine [ˌɪntər'twaɪn] *vi* **-twined; -twining** : entrelazarse

interval ['ɪntərvəl] *n* : intervalo *m*

intervene [ˌɪntər'viːn] *vi* **-vened; -vening 1** : intervenir **2** ELAPSE : transcurrir, pasar — **intervention** [ˌɪntər'vɛn-tʃən] *n* : intervención *f*

interview ['ɪntər,vjuː] *n* : entrevista *f* — **~** *vt* : entrevistar — **interviewer** ['ɪntər,vjuːər] *n* : entrevistador *m*, -dora *f*

intestine [ɪn'tɛstən] n : intestino m — **intestinal** [ɪn'tɛstənəl] adj : intestinal
intimate[1] ['ɪntəˌmeɪt] vt -mated; -mating : insinuar, dar a entender
intimate[2] ['ɪntəmət] adj : íntimo — **intimacy** ['ɪntəməsi] n, pl -cies : intimidad f
intimidate [ɪn'tɪməˌdeɪt] vt -dated; -dating : intimidar — **intimidation** [ɪnˌtɪmə'deɪʃən] n : intimidación f
into ['ɪnˌtu:] prep 1 : en, a 2 bump ~ : darse contra 3 (used in mathematics) 3 ~ 12 : 12 dividido por 3
intolerable [ɪn'tɑlərəbəl] adj : intolerable — **intolerance** [ɪn'tɑlərənts] n : intolerancia f — **intolerant** [ɪn'tɑlərənt] adj : intolerante
intoxicate [ɪn'tɑksəˌkeɪt] vt -cated; -cating : embriagar — **intoxicated** [ɪn'tɑksəˌkeɪtəd] adj 1 : embriagado 2 ~ with : ebrio de
intransitive [ɪn'trænt̬sət̬ɪv, -'trænzə-] adj : intransitivo
intravenous [ˌɪntrə'vi:nəs] adj : intravenoso
intrepid [ɪn'trɛpəd] adj : intrépido
intricate ['ɪntrɪkət] adj : complicado, intrincado — **intricacy** ['ɪntrɪkəsi] n, pl -cies : complejidad f
intrigue ['ɪnˌtri:g, ɪn'tri:g] n : intriga f — ~ [ɪn'tri:g] v -trigued; -triguing : intrigar — **intriguing** [ɪn'tri:gɪŋli] adj : intrigante
intrinsic [ɪn'trɪnzɪk, -'trɪntsɪk] adj : intrínseco
introduce [ˌɪntrə'du:s, -'dju:s] vt -duced; -ducing 1 : introducir 2 : presentar (a una persona) — **introduction** [ˌɪntrə'dʌkʃən] n 1 : introducción f 2 : presentación f (de una persona) — **introductory** [ˌɪntrə'dʌktəri] adj : introductorio
introvert ['ɪntrəˌvərt] n : introvertido m, -da f — **introverted** ['ɪntrəˌvərtəd] adj : introvertido
intrude [ɪn'tru:d] vi -truded; -truding 1 : entrometerse 2 ~ on s.o. : molestar a algn — **intruder** [ɪn'tru:dər] n : intruso m, -sa f — **intrusion** [ɪn'tru:ʒən] n : intrusión f — **intrusive** [ɪn'tru:sɪv] adj : intruso
intuition [ˌɪntu'ɪʃən, -tju-] n : intuición f — **intuitive** [ɪn'tu:ət̬ɪv, -tju-] adj : intuitivo
inundate ['ɪnənˌdeɪt] vt -dated; -dating : inundar
invade [ɪn'veɪd] vt -vaded; -vading : invadir
invalid[1] [ɪn'væləd] adj : inválido
invalid[2] ['ɪnvələd] n : inválido m, -da f

invaluable [ɪn'væljəbəl, -'væljuə-] adj : inestimable, invalorable Lat
invariable [ɪn'væriəbəl] adj : invariable
invasion [ɪn'veɪʒən] n : invasión f
invent [ɪn'vɛnt] vt : inventar — **invention** [ɪn'vɛntʃən] n : invención f — **inventive** [ɪn'vɛntɪv] adj : inventivo — **inventor** [ɪn'vɛntər] n : inventor m, -tora f
inventory ['ɪnvənˌtɔri] n, pl -ries : inventario m
invert [ɪn'vərt] vt : invertir
invertebrate [ɪn'vərt̬əˌbrət, -ˌbreɪt] adj : invertebrado — ~ n : invertebrado m
invest [ɪn'vɛst] vt : invertir
investigate [ɪn'vɛstəˌgeɪt] v -gated; -gating : investigar — **investigation** [ɪnˌvɛstə'geɪʃən] n : investigación f — **investigator** [ɪn'vɛstəˌgeɪtər] n : investigador m, -dora f
investment [ɪn'vɛstmənt] n : inversión f — **investor** [ɪn'vɛstər] n : inversor m, -sora f
inveterate [ɪn'vɛt̬ərət] adj : inveterado
invigorating [ɪn'vɪgəˌreɪt̬ɪŋ] adj : vigorizante
invincible [ɪn'vɪntsəbəl] adj : invencible
invisible [ɪn'vɪzəbəl] adj : invisible
invitation [ˌɪnvə'teɪʃən] n : invitación f — **invite** [ɪn'vaɪt] vt -vited; -viting 1 : invitar 2 SEEK : buscar (problemas, etc.) — **inviting** [ɪn'vaɪt̬ɪŋ] adj : atrayente
invoice ['ɪnˌvɔɪs] n : factura f
invoke [ɪn'vo:k] vt -voked; -voking : invocar
involuntary [ɪn'vɑlənˌtɛri] adj : involuntario
involve [ɪn'vɑlv] vt -volved; -volving 1 CONCERN : concernir, afectar 2 ENTAIL : suponer — **involved** [ɪn'vɑlvd] adj 1 COMPLEX : complicado 2 CONCERNED : afectado — **involvement** [ɪn'vɑlvmənt] n : participación f
invulnerable [ɪn'vʌlnərəbəl] adj : invulnerable
inward ['ɪnwərd] adj INNER : interior, interno — or **inwards** [-wərdz] adv : hacia adentro, hacia el interior
iodine ['aɪəˌdaɪn, -dən] n : yodo m, tintura f de yodo
ion ['aɪən, 'aɪˌɑn] n : ion m
iota [aɪ'o:t̬ə] n : pizca f, ápice m
IOU [ˌaɪˌo:'ju:] n : pagaré m, vale m
Iranian [ɪ'reɪniən, -'ræ-, -'rɑ-; aɪ'-] adj : iraní
Iraqi ['rɑki, -'ræk-] adj : iraquí
ire ['aɪr] n : ira f — **irate** [aɪ'reɪt] adj : furioso
iris ['aɪrəs] n, pl **irises** or **irides** ['aɪrə-

,diːz, 'ɪr-] **1** : iris *m* (del ojo) **2** : lirio *m* (planta)

Irish ['aɪrɪʃ] *adj* : irlandés

irksome ['ərksəm] *adj* : irritante, fastidioso

iron ['aɪərn] *n* **1** : hierro *m*, fierro *m Lat* (metal) **2** : plancha *f* (para la ropa) — ~ *v* : planchar

ironic [aɪ'rɑnɪk] *or* **ironical** [-nɪkəl] *adj* : irónico

ironing board *n* : tabla *f* (de planchar)

irony ['aɪrəni] *n, pl* **-nies** : ironía *f*

irrational [ɪ'ræʃənəl] *adj* : irracional

irreconcilable [ɪˌrekən'saɪləbəl] *adj* : irreconciliable

irrefutable [ɪˌrɪ'fjuːtəbəl, ɪr'refjə-] *adj* : irrefutable

irregular [ɪ'regjələr] *adj* : irregular — **irregularity** [ɪˌregjə'lærəti] *n, pl* **-ties** : irregularidad *f*

irrelevant [ɪ'reləvənt] *adj* : irrelevante

irreparable [ɪ'repərəbəl] *adj* : irreparable

irreplaceable [ɪrɪ'pleɪsəbəl] *adj* : irreemplazable

irresistible [ɪrɪ'zɪstəbəl] *adj* : irresistible

irresolute [ɪ'rezəˌluːt] *adj* : irresoluto

irrespective of [ɪrɪ'spektɪvəv] *prep* : sin tener en cuenta

irresponsible [ɪrɪ'spɑntsəbəl] *adj* : irresponsable — **irresponsibility** [ɪrɪˌspɑntsə'bɪləti] *n, pl* **-ties** : irresponsabilidad *f*

irreverent [ɪ'revərənt] *adj* : irreverente

irreversible [ɪrɪ'vərsəbəl] *adj* : irreversible, irrevocable

irrigate ['ɪrəˌgeɪt] *vt* **-gated; -gating** : irrigar, regar — **irrigation** [ɪrə'geɪʃən] *n* : irrigación *f*, riego *m*

irritate ['ɪrəˌteɪt] *vt* **-tated; -tating** : irritar — **irritable** ['ɪrətəbəl] *adj* : irritable — **irritably** ['ɪrətəbli] *adv* : con irritación — **irritating** ['ɪrəˌteɪtɪŋ] *adj* : irritante — **irritation** [ɪrə'teɪʃən] *n* : irritación *f*

is → **be**

Islam [ɪs'lɑm, ɪz-, -'læm; 'ɪsˌlɑm, 'ɪz-, -ˌlæm] *n* : el Islam — **Islamic** [ɪs'lɑmɪk, ɪz-, -'læ-] *adj* : islámico

island ['aɪlənd] *n* : isla *f* — **isle** ['aɪl] *n* : isla *f*

isolate ['aɪsəˌleɪt] *vt* **-lated; -lating** : aislar — **isolation** [aɪsə'leɪʃən] *n* : aislamiento *m*

Israeli [ɪz'reɪli] *adj* : israelí

issue ['ɪˌʃuː] *n* **1** MATTER : asunto *m*, cuestión *f* **2** : número *m* (de una revista, etc.) **3 make an ~ of** : insistir demasiado sobre **4 take ~ with** : disentir de — ~ *v* **-sued; -suing** *vi* **from** : surgir de — *vt* **1** : emitir (sellos, etc.), distribuir (provisiones, etc.) **2** PUBLISH : publicar

isthmus ['ɪsməs] *n* : istmo *m*

it ['ɪt] *pron* **1** (*as subject*) : él, ella **2** (*as indirect object*) : le, se **3** (*as direct object*) : lo, la **4** (*as object of a preposition*) : él, ella **5 it's raining** : está lloviendo **6 it's 8 o'clock** : son las ocho **7 it's hot out** : hace calor **8 ~ is necessary** : es necesario **9 who is ~?** : ¿quién es? **10 it's me** : soy yo

Italian [ɪ'tæliən, aɪ-] *adj* : italiano — ~ *n* : italiano *m* (idioma)

italics ['ɪtælɪks, aɪ-] *n* : cursiva *f*

itch ['ɪtʃ] *vi* **1** : picar **2 be ~ing to** : morirse por — ~ *n* : picazón *f* — **itchy** ['ɪtʃi] *adj* **itchier; -est** : que pica

it'd ['ɪtəd] (*contraction of* **it had** *or* **it would**) → **have, would**

item ['aɪtəm] *n* **1** : artículo *m* **2** : punto *m* (en una agenda) **3 ~ of clothing** : prenda *f* de vestir **4 news ~** : noticia *f* — **itemize** ['aɪtəˌmaɪz] *vt* **-ized; -izing** : detallar, enumerar

itinerant [aɪ'tɪnərənt] *adj* : ambulante

itinerary [aɪ'tɪnəˌreri] *n, pl* **-aries** : itinerario *m*

it'll ['ɪtəl] (*contraction of* **it shall** *or* **it will**) → **shall, will**

its ['ɪts] *adj* : su, sus

it's ['ɪts] (*contraction of* **it is** *or* **it has**) → **be, have**

itself [ɪt'self] *pron* **1** (*used reflexively*) : se **2** (*used for emphasis*) : (él) mismo, (ella) misma, sí (mismo) **3 by ~** : solo

I've ['aɪv] (*contraction of* **I have**) → **have**

ivory ['aɪvəri] *n, pl* **-ries** : marfil *m*

ivy ['aɪvi] *n, pl* **ivies** : hiedra *f*

J

j ['dʒeɪ] *n*, *pl* **j's** *or* **js** ['dʒeɪz] : j *f*, décima letra del alfabeto inglés

jab ['dʒæb] *vt* **jabbed; jabbing 1** PIERCE : pinchar **2** POKE : golpear (con la punta de algo) — ~ *n* **1** PRICK : pinchazo *m* **2** POKE : golpe *m* abrupto

jabber ['dʒæbər] *vi* : farfullar

jack ['dʒæk] *n* **1** : gato *m* (mecanismo) **2** : sota *f* (de naipes) — ~ *vt or* ~ **up 1** : levantar (con un gato) **2** INCREASE : subir

jackal ['dʒækəl] *n* : chacal *m*

jackass ['dʒækˌæs] *n* : asno *m*, burro *m*

jacket ['dʒækət] *n* **1** : chaqueta *f* **2** : sobrecubierta *f* (de un libro), carátula *f* (de un disco)

jackhammer ['dʒækˌhæmər] *n* : martillo *m* neumático

jackknife ['dʒækˌnaɪf] *n* : navaja *f* — ~ *vi* **-knifed; -knifing** : plegarse (dícese de un camión)

jack-o'-lantern ['dʒækəˌlæntərn] *n* : linterna *f* hecha de una calabaza

jackpot ['dʒækˌpɑt] *n* : premio *m* gordo

jaded ['dʒeɪdəd] *adj* **1** TIRED : agotado **2** BORED : hastiado

jagged ['dʒægəd] *adj* : dentado

jail ['dʒeɪl] *n* : cárcel *f* — ~ *vt* : encarcelar — **jailer** *or* **jailor** ['dʒeɪlər] *n* : carcelero *m*, -ra *f*

jalapeño [ˌhɑləˈpeɪnjo, ˌhæ-, -ˈpino] *n* : jalapeño *m Lat*

jam¹ ['dʒæm] *v* **jammed; jamming** *vt* **1** CRAM : apiñar, embutir **2** BLOCK : atascar, atorar — *vi* : atascarse, atrancarse — ~ *n* **1** *or* **traffic** ~ : embotellamiento *m* (de tráfico) **2** FIX : lío *m*, aprieto *m*

jam² *n* PRESERVES : mermelada *f*

jangle ['dʒæŋgəl] *v* **-gled; -gling** *vi* : hacer un ruido metálico — *vt* : hacer sonar — ~ *n* : ruido *m* metálico

janitor ['dʒænətər] *n* : portero *m*, -ra *f*; conserje *mf*

January ['dʒænjuˌɛri] *n* : enero *m*

Japanese [ˌdʒæpəˈniːz, -ˈniːs] *adj* : japonés — ~ *n* : japonés *m* (idioma)

jar¹ ['dʒɑr] *v* **jarred; jarring** *vi* **1** GRATE : chirriar **2** CLASH : desentonar **3** ~ **on** IRRITATE : crispar, enervar (a algn) — *vt* JOLT : sacudir — ~ *n* : sacudida *f*

jar² *n* : tarro *m*

jargon ['dʒɑrgən] *n* : jerga *f*

jaundice ['dʒɔndɪs] *n* : ictericia *f*

jaunt ['dʒɔnt] *n* : excursión *f*

jaunty ['dʒɔnti] *adj* **-tier; -est** : garboso, desenvuelto

jaw ['dʒɔ] *n* : mandíbula *f* (de una persona), quijada *f* (de un animal) — **jawbone** ['dʒɔˌbon] *n* : mandíbula *f*, quijada *f*

jay ['dʒeɪ] *n* : arrendajo *m*

jazz ['dʒæz] *n* : jazz *m* — ~ *vt or* ~ **up** : animar, alegrar — **jazzy** ['dʒæzi] *adj* **jazzier; -est** FLASHY : llamativo

jealous ['dʒɛləs] *adj* : celoso — **jealousy** ['dʒɛləsi] *n* : celos *mpl*, envidia *f*

jeans ['dʒiːnz] *npl* : jeans *mpl*, vaqueros *mpl*

jeer ['dʒɪr] *vt* **1** BOO : abuchear **2** MOCK : mofarse de — *vi* ~ **at** : mofarse de — ~ *n* : mofa *f*

jell ['dʒɛl] *vi* : cuajar

jelly ['dʒɛli] *n*, *pl* **-lies** : jalea *f* — **jellyfish** ['dʒɛliˌfɪʃ] *n* : medusa *f*

jeopardy ['dʒɛpərdi] *n* : peligro *m*, riesgo *m* — **jeopardize** ['dʒɛpərˌdaɪz] *vt* **-dized; -dizing** : arriesgar, poner en peligro

jerk ['dʒərk] *n* **1** JOLT : sacudida *f* brusca **2** FOOL : idiota *mf* — ~ *vt* : sacudir — *vi* JOLT : dar sacudidas

jersey ['dʒərzi] *n*, *pl* **-seys** : jersey *m*

jest ['dʒɛst] *n* : broma *f* — ~ *vi* : bromear — **jester** ['dʒɛstər] *n* : bufón *m*

Jesus ['dʒiːzəs, -zəz] *n* : Jesús *m*

jet ['dʒɛt] *n* **1** STREAM : chorro *m* **2** *or* ~ **airplane** : avión *m* a reacción, reactor *m* — **jet-propelled** *adj* : a reacción

jettison ['dʒɛtəsən] *vt* **1** : echar al mar **2** DISCARD : deshacerse de

jetty ['dʒɛti] *n*, *pl* **-ties** : desembarcadero *m*, muelle *m*

jewel ['dʒuːəl] *n* **1** : joya *f* **2** GEM : piedra *f* preciosa — **jeweler** *or* **jeweller** ['dʒuːələr] *n* : joyero *m*, -ra *f* — **jewelry** ['dʒuːəlri] *n* : joyas *fpl*, alhajas *fpl*

Jewish ['dʒuːɪʃ] *adj* : judío

jibe ['dʒaɪb] *vi* **jibed; jibing** AGREE : concordar

jiffy ['dʒɪfi] *n*, *pl* **-fies** : santiamén *m*, segundo *m*

jig ['dʒɪg] *n* : giga *f*

jiggle ['dʒɪgəl] *vt* **-gled; -gling** : sacudir, zarandear — ~ *n* : sacudida *f*

jigsaw ['dʒɪg,sɔ] n 1 : sierra f de vaivén 2 or ~ **puzzle** : rompecabezas m

jilt ['dʒɪlt] vt : dejar plantado

jingle ['dʒɪŋgəl] v -gled; -gling vi : tintinear — vt : hacer sonar — ~ n TINKLE : tintineo m

jinx ['dʒɪŋks] n CURSE : maldición f

jitters ['dʒɪṭərz] npl have the ~ : estar nervioso — **jittery** ['dʒɪṭəri] adj : nervioso

job ['dʒɑb] n 1 EMPLOYMENT : empleo m, trabajo m 2 TASK : trabajo m

jockey ['dʒɑki] n, pl -eys : jockey mf

jog ['dʒɑg] v **jogged; jogging** vt ~ **s.o.'s memory** : refrescar la memoria a algn — vi : hacer footing — **jogging** n : footing m

join ['dʒɔɪn] vt 1 UNITE : unir, juntar 2 MEET : reunirse con 3 : hacerse socio de (una organización, etc.) — vi 1 or ~ **together** : unirse 2 : hacerse socio (de una organización, etc.)

joint ['dʒɔɪnt] n 1 : articulación f (en anatomía) 2 JUNCTURE : juntura f, unión f — ~ adj : conjunto — **jointly** ['dʒɔɪntli] adv : conjuntamente

joke ['dʒok] n : chiste m, broma f — ~ vi **joked; joking** : bromear — **joker** ['dʒokər] n 1 : bromista mf 2 : comodín m (en los naipes)

jolly ['dʒɑli] adj -lier; -est : alegre, jovial

jolt ['dʒolt] vt : sacudir — ~ n 1 : sacudida f brusca 2 SHOCK : golpe m (emocional)

jostle ['dʒɑsəl] v -tled; -tling vt : empujar, dar empujones — vi : empujarse

jot ['dʒɑt] vt **jotted; jotting** or ~ **down** : anotar, apuntar

journal ['dʒərnəl] n 1 DIARY : diario m 2 PERIODICAL : revista f — **journalism** ['dʒərnəl,ɪzəm] n : periodismo m — **journalist** ['dʒərnəlɪst] n : periodista mf

journey ['dʒərni] n, pl -neys : viaje m — ~ vi -neyed; -neying : viajar

jovial ['dʒoʊviəl] adj : jovial

joy ['dʒɔɪ] n : alegría f — **joyful** ['dʒɔɪfəl] adj : alegre, feliz — **joyous** ['dʒɔɪəs] adj : jubiloso, alegre

jubilant ['dʒuːbələnt] adj : jubiloso — **jubilee** ['dʒuːbə,liː] n : aniversario m especial

Judaism ['dʒuːdə,ɪzəm, 'dʒuːdi-, 'dʒuːdeɪ-] n : judaísmo m

judge ['dʒʌdʒ] vt **judged; judging** : juzgar — ~ n : juez mf — **judgment** or **judgement** ['dʒʌdʒmənt] n 1 RULING : fallo m, sentencia f 2 VIEW : juicio m

judicial [dʒuˈdɪʃəl] adj : judicial — **judicious** [dʒuˈdɪʃəs] adj : juicioso

jug ['dʒʌg] n : jarra f

juggle ['dʒʌgəl] vi -gled; -gling : hacer juegos malabares — **juggler** ['dʒʌgələr] n : malabarista mf

jugular vein ['dʒʌgjələr-] n : vena f yugular

juice ['dʒuːs] n : jugo m — **juicy** ['dʒuːsi] adj **juicier; -est** : jugoso

jukebox ['dʒuːk,bɑks] n : máquina f de discos

July [dʒʊˈlaɪ] n : julio m

jumble ['dʒʌmbəl] vt -bled; -bling : mezclar — ~ n : revoltijo m

jumbo ['dʒʌm,boʊ] adj : gigante

jump ['dʒʌmp] vi 1 LEAP : saltar 2 START : sobresaltarse 3 RISE : subir de un golpe 4 ~ **at** : no dejar escapar (una oportunidad, etc.) — vt : saltar — ~ n 1 LEAP : salto m 2 INCREASE : aumento m — **jumper** ['dʒʌmpər] n 1 : saltador m, -dora f (en deportes) 2 : jumper m (vestido) — **jumpy** ['dʒʌmpi] adj **jumpier; -est** : nervioso

junction ['dʒʌŋkʃən] n 1 JOINING : unión f 2 : cruce m (de calles), empalme m (de un ferrocarril) — **juncture** ['dʒʌŋktʃər] n : coyuntura f

June ['dʒuːn] n : junio m

jungle ['dʒʌŋgəl] n : selva f

junior ['dʒuːnjər] adj 1 YOUNGER : más joven 2 SUBORDINATE : subalterno — ~ n 1 : persona f de menor edad 2 SUBORDINATE : subalterno m, -na f 3 : estudiante mf de penúltimo año

junk ['dʒʌŋk] n : trastos mpl (viejos) — ~ vt : echar a la basura

junta ['hʊntə, 'dʒʌn-, 'hʌn-] n : junta f (militar)

jurisdiction [,dʒurəsˈdɪkʃən] n : jurisdicción f

jury ['dʒuri] n, pl -ries : jurado m — **juror** ['dʒurər] n : jurado m

just ['dʒʌst] adj : justo — ~ adv 1 BARELY : apenas 2 EXACTLY : exactamente 3 ONLY : sólo, solamente 4 ~ **now** : ahora mismo 5 **she has ~ left** : acaba de salir 6 **we were ~ leaving** : justo íbamos a salir

justice ['dʒʌstɪs] n 1 : justicia f 2 JUDGE : juez mf

justify ['dʒʌstə,faɪ] vt -fied; -fying : justificar — **justification** [,dʒʌstəfəˈkeɪʃən] n : justificación f

jut ['dʒʌt] vi **jutted; jutting** or ~ **out** : sobresalir

juvenile ['dʒuːvə,naɪl, -vənəl] adj 1 YOUNG : juvenil 2 CHILDISH : infantil — ~ n : menor mf

juxtapose ['dʒʌkstə,poːz] vt -posed; -posing : yuxtaponer

K

k ['keɪ] *n*, *pl* **k's** *or* **ks** ['keɪz] : k *f*, undécima letra del alfabeto inglés

kaleidoscope [kə'laɪdə,sko:p] *n* : calidoscopio *m*

kangaroo [,kæŋgə'ru:] *n*, *pl* **-roos** : canguro *m*

karat ['kærət] *n* : quilate *m*

karate [kə'rɑṭi] *n* : karate *m*

keel ['ki:l] *n* : quilla *f* — ~ *vi or* ~ **over** : volcarse (dícese de un barco), desplomarse (dícese de una persona)

keen ['ki:n] *adj* **1** SHARP : afilado **2** PENETRATING : cortante, penetrante **3** ENTHUSIASTIC : entusiasta **4** ~ **eyesight** : visión *f* aguda

keep ['ki:p] *v* **kept** ['kɛpt]; **keeping** *vt* **1** : guardar **2** : cumplir (una promesa), acudir a (una cita) **3** DETAIN : hacer quedar, detener **4** PREVENT : impedir **5** ~ **up** : mantener — *vi* **1** REMAIN : mantenerse **2** LAST : conservarse **3** *or* ~ **on** CONTINUE : no dejar — ~ **1** : para siempre — **keeper** ['ki:pər] *n* : guarda *mf* — **keeping** ['ki:pɪŋ] *n* **1** CARE : cuidado *m* **2 in** ~ **with** : de acuerdo con — **keepsake** ['ki:p,seɪk] *n* : recuerdo *m*

keg ['kɛg] *n* : barril *m*

kennel ['kɛnəl] *n* : caseta *f* para perros, perrera *f*

kept → **keep**

kerchief ['kərtʃəf, -,tʃi:f] *n* : pañuelo *m*

kernel ['kərnəl] *n* **1** : almendra *f* **2** CORE : meollo *m*

kerosene *or* **kerosine** ['kɛrə,si:n, ,kɛrə'-] *n* : queroseno *m*

ketchup ['kɛtʃəp, 'kæ-] *n* : salsa *f* de tomate

kettle ['kɛṭəl] *n* : hervidor *m*, tetera *f* (para hervir)

key ['ki:] *n* **1** : llave *f* **2** : tecla *f* (de un piano o una máquina) — ~ *vt* **be keyed up** : estar nervioso — ~ *adj* : clave — **keyboard** ['ki:,bord] *n* : teclado *m* — **keyhole** ['ki:,ho:l] *n* : ojo *m* (de la cerradura) — **keynote** ['ki:-,no:t] *n* : tónica *f* — **key ring** *n* : llavero *m*

khaki ['kæki, 'kɑ-] *adj* : caqui

kick ['kɪk] *vt* **1** : dar una patada a **2** ~ **out** : echar a patadas — *vi* **1** : dar patadas (dícese de una persona), cocear (dícese de un animal) **2** RECOIL : dar un culatazo — ~ *n* **1** : patada *f*, coz *f* (de un animal) **2** RECOIL : culatazo *m* **3** PLEASURE, THRILL : placer *m*

kid ['kɪd] *n* **1** GOAT : chivo *m*, -va *f*; cabrito *m* **2** CHILD : niño *m*, -ña *f* — ~ *v* **kidded; kidding** *vi or* ~ **around** : bromear — *vt* TEASE : tomar el pelo a — **kidnap** ['kɪd,næp] *vt* **-napped** *or* **-naped** [-,næpt]; **-napping** *or* **-naping** [-,næpɪŋ] : secuestrar, raptar

kidney ['kɪdni] *n*, *pl* **-neys** : riñón *m*

kidney bean *n* : frijol *m*

kill ['kɪl] *vt* **1** : matar **2** DESTROY : acabar con **3** ~ **time** : matar el tiempo — ~ *n* **1** KILLING : matanza *f* **2** PREY : presa *f* — **killer** ['kɪlər] *n* : asesino *m*, -na *f* — **killing** ['kɪlɪŋ] *n* **1** : matanza *f* **2** MURDER : asesinato *m*

kiln ['kɪl, 'kɪln] *n* : horno *m*

kilo ['ki:,lo:] *n*, *pl* **-los** : kilo *m* — **kilogram** ['kɪlə,græm, 'ki:-] *n* : kilogramo *m* — **kilometer** [kɪ'lɑmətər, 'kɪlə,mi:-] *n* : kilómetro *m* — **kilowatt** ['kɪlə,wɑt] *n* : kilovatio *m*

kin ['kɪn] *n* : parientes *mpl*

kind ['kaɪnd] *n* : tipo *m*, clase *f* — ~ *adj* : amable

kindergarten ['kɪndər,gɑrtən, -dən] *n* : jardín *m* infantil, jardín *m* de niños *Lat*

kindhearted [,kaɪnd'hɑrṭəd] *adj* : de buen corazón

kindle ['kɪndəl] *vt* **-dled; -dling 1** : encender (un fuego) **2** AROUSE : despertar

kindly ['kaɪndli] *adj* **-lier; -est** : bondadoso, amable — ~ *adv* **1** : amablemente **2 take** ~ **to** : aceptar de buena gana **3 we** ~ **ask you not smoke** : les rogamos que no fumen — **kindness** ['kaɪndnəs] *n* : bondad *f* — **kind of** *adv* SOMEWHAT : un tanto, algo

kindred ['kɪndrəd] *adj* **1** : emparentado **2** ~ **spirit** : alma *f* gemela

king ['kɪŋ] *n* : rey *m* — **kingdom** ['kɪŋdəm] *n* : reino *m*

kink ['kɪŋk] *n* **1** TWIST : vuelta *f*, curva *f* **2** FLAW : problema *m*

kinship ['kɪn,ʃɪp] *n* : parentesco *m*

kiss ['kɪs] *vt* : besar — *vi* : besarse — ~ *n* : beso *m*

kit ['kɪt] *n* **1** : juego *m*, kit *m* **2 first-aid**

~ : botiquín *m* **3 tool** ~ : caja *f* de herramientas
kitchen ['kɪtʃən] *n* : cocina *f*
kite ['kaɪt] *n* : cometa *f*, papalote *m Lat*
kitten ['kɪtən] *n* : gatito *m*, -ta *f* — **kitty** ['kɪt̮i] *n, pl* **-ties** FUND : fondo *m* común
knack ['næk] *n* : maña *f*, facilidad *f*
knapsack ['næpˌsæk] *n* : mochila *f*
knead ['niːd] *vt* **1** : amasar, sobar **2** MASSAGE : masajear
knee ['niː] *n* : rodilla *f* — **kneecap** ['niːˌkæp] *n* : rótula *f*
kneel ['niːl] *vi* **knelt** ['nɛlt] *or* **kneeled** ['niːld]; **kneeling** : arrodillarse
knew → **know**
knickknack ['nɪkˌnæk] *n* : chuchería *f*
knife ['naɪf] *n, pl* **knives** ['naɪvz] : cuchillo *m* — ~ *vt* **knifed** ['naɪft]; **knifing** : acuchillar
knight ['naɪt] *n* **1** : caballero *m* **2** : caballo *m* (en ajedrez) — **knighthood** ['naɪtˌhʊd] *n* : título *m* de Sir
knit ['nɪt] *v* **knit** *or* **knitted** ['nɪt̮əd]; **knitting** *v* : tejer — ~ *n* : prenda *f* tejida
knob ['nɑb] *n* : tirador *m*, botón *m*, perilla *f Lat*
knock ['nɑk] *vt* **1** : golpear **2** CRITICIZE : criticar **3** ~ **down** : derribar, echar

al suelo — *vi* **1** : dar un golpe, llamar (a la puerta) **2** COLLIDE : darse, chocar — ~ *n* : golpe *m*, llamada *f* (a la puerta)
knot ['nɑt] *n* : nudo *m* — ~ *vt* **knotted**; **knotting** : anudar — **knotty** ['nɑt̮i] *adj* **-tier**; **-est 1** : nudoso **2** : enredado (dícese de un problema)
know ['noː] *v* **knew** ['nuː, 'njuː]; **known** ['noːn]; **knowing** *vt* **1** : saber **2** : conocer (a una persona, un lugar) **3** ~ **how to** : saber — *vi* : saber — **knowing** ['noːɪŋ] *adj* : cómplice — **knowingly** ['noːɪŋli] *adv* **1** : de manera cómplice **2** DELIBERATELY : a sabiendas — **know–it–all** ['noːɪt̮ˌɔl] *n* : sabelotodo *mf fam* — **knowledge** ['nɑlɪdʒ] *n* **1** : conocimiento *m* **2** LEARNING : conocimientos *mpl*, saber *m* — **knowledgeable** ['nɑlɪdʒəbəl] *adj* : informado, entendido
knuckle ['nʌkəl] *n* : nudillo *m*
Koran [kəˈrɑn, -ˈræn] *n* **the Koran** : el Corán *m*
Korean [kəˈriːən] *adj* : coreano *m*, -na *f* — ~ *n* : coreano *m* (idioma)
kosher ['koːʃər] *adj* : aprobado por la ley judía

L

l ['ɛl] *n, pl* **l's** *or* **ls** ['ɛlz] : l *f*, duodécima letra del alfabeto inglés
lab ['læb] → **laboratory**
label ['leɪbəl] *n* **1** TAG : etiqueta *f* **2** BRAND : marca *f* — ~ *vt* **-beled** *or* **-belled**; **-beling** *or* **-belling** : etiquetar
labor ['leɪbər] *n* **1** : trabajo *m* **2** WORKERS : mano *f* de obra **3 in** ~ : de parto — ~ *vi* **1** : trabajar **2** STRUGGLE : avanzar penosamente — *vt* BELABOR : insistir en (un punto)
laboratory ['læbrəˌtori, ləˈbɔrə-] *n, pl* **-ries** : laboratorio *m*
laborer ['leɪbərər] *n* : trabajador *m*, -dora *f*
laborious [ləˈboriəs] *adj* : laborioso
lace ['leɪs] *n* **1** : encaje *m* **2** SHOELACE : cordón *m* (de zapatos), agujeta *f Lat* — ~ *vt* **laced**; **lacing 1** TIE : atar **2 be laced with** : echar licor a (una bebida, etc.)
lacerate ['læsəˌreɪt] *vt* **-ated**; **-ating** : lacerar
lack ['læk] *vt* : carecer de, no tener — *vi* **be lacking** : faltar — ~ *n* : falta *f*, carencia *f*

lackadaisical [ˌlækəˈdeɪzɪkəl] *adj* : apático, indolente
lackluster ['lækˌlʌstər] *adj* : sin brillo, apagado
laconic [ləˈkɑnɪk] *adj* : lacónico
lacquer ['lækər] *n* : laca *f*
lacrosse [ləˈkrɔs] *n* : lacrosse *f*
lacy ['leɪsi] *adj* **lacier**; **-est** : como de encaje
lad ['læd] *n* : muchacho *m*, niño *m*
ladder ['lædər] *n* : escalera *f*
laden ['leɪdən] *adj* : cargado
ladle ['leɪdəl] *n* : cucharón *m* — ~ *vt* **-dled**; **-dling** : servir con cucharón
lady ['leɪdi] *n, pl* **-dies** : señora *f*, dama *f* — **ladybug** ['leɪdiˌbʌg] *n* : mariquita *f* — **ladylike** ['leɪdiˌlaɪk] *adj* : elegante, como señora
lag ['læg] *n* **1** DELAY : retraso *m* **2** INTERVAL : intervalo *m* — ~ *vi* **lagged**; **lagging** : quedarse atrás, rezagarse
lager ['lɑgər] *n* : cerveza *f* rubia
lagoon [ləˈguːn] *n* : laguna *f*
laid *pp* → **lay¹**
lain *pp* → **lie¹**
lair ['lær] *n* : guarida *f*

lake ['leɪk] n : lago m

lamb ['læm] n : cordero m

lame ['leɪm] adj **lamer; lamest 1** : cojo, renco **2 a ~ excuse** : una excusa poco convincente

lament [lə'ment] vt **1** MOURN : llorar **2** DEPLORE : lamentar — ~ n : lamento m — **lamentable** ['læməntəbəl, lə'mentə-] adj : lamentable

laminate ['læmə,neɪt] vt **-nated; -nating** : laminar

lamp ['læmp] n : lámpara f — **lamppost** ['læmp,po:st] n : farol m — **lampshade** ['læmp,ʃeɪd] n : pantalla f

lance ['læns] n : lanza f — ~ vt **lanced; lancing** : abrir con lanceta (en medecina)

land ['lænd] n **1** : tierra f **2** COUNTRY : país m **3** or **plot of ~** : terreno m — ~ vt **1** : desembarcar (pasajeros de un barco), hacer aterrizar (un avión) **2** CATCH : sacar (un pez) del agua **3** SECURE : conseguir (empleo, etc.) — vi **1** : aterrizar (dícese de un avión) **2** FALL : caer — **landing** ['lændɪŋ] n **1** : aterrizaje m (de aviones) **2** : desembarco m (de barcos) **3** : descanso m (de una escalera) — **landlady** ['lænd,leɪdi] n, pl **-dies** : casera f — **landlord** ['lænd,lɔrd] n : casero m — **landmark** ['lænd,mɑrk] n **1** : punto m de referencia **2** MONUMENT : monumento m histórico — **landowner** ['lænd,o:nər] n : hacendado m, -da f; terrateniente mf — **landscape** ['lænd,skeɪp] n : paisaje m — ~ vt **-scaped; -scaping** : ajardinar — **landslide** ['lænd,slaɪd] n **1** : desprendimiento m de tierras **2** or **~ victory** : victoria f arrolladora

lane ['leɪn] n **1** : carril m (de una carretera) **2** PATH, ROAD : camino m

language ['læŋgwɪdʒ] n **1** : idioma m, lengua f **2** SPEECH : lenguaje m

languid ['læŋgwɪd] adj : lánguido — **languish** ['læŋgwɪʃ] vi : languidecer

lanky ['læŋki] adj **lankier; -est** : delgado, larguirucho fam

lantern ['læntərn] n : linterna f

lap ['læp] n **1** : regazo m (de una persona) **2** : vuelta f (en deportes) — ~ v **lapped; lapping** vt or **~ up** : beber a lengüetadas — vi **~ against** : lamer

lapel [lə'pɛl] n : solapa f

lapse ['læps] n **1** : lapsus m, falla f (de memoria, etc.) **2** INTERVAL : lapso m, intervalo m — ~ vi **lapsed; lapsing 1** EXPIRE : caducar **2** ELAPSE : transcurrir, pasar **3 ~ into** : caer en

laptop ['læp,tɑp] adj : portátil

larceny ['lɑrsəni] n, pl **-nies** : robo m

lard ['lɑrd] n : manteca f de cerdo

large ['lɑrdʒ] adj **larger; largest 1** : grande **2 at ~** : en libertad **3 by and ~** : por lo general — **largely** ['lɑrdʒli] adv : en gran parte

lark ['lɑrk] n **1** : alondra f (pájaro) **2 for a ~** : por divertirse

larva ['lɑrvə] n, pl **-vae** [-,vi:, -,vaɪ] : larva f

larynx ['lærɪŋks] n, pl **-rynges** [lə'rɪn-,dʒiːz] or **-ynxes** ['lærɪŋksəz] : laringe f — **laryngitis** [,lærən'dʒaɪtəs] n : laringitis f

lasagna [lə'zɑnjə] n : lasaña f

laser ['leɪzər] n : láser m

lash ['læʃ] vt **1** WHIP : azotar **2** BIND : amarrar — vi **~ out at** : arremeter contra — ~ n **1** BLOW : latigazo m (con un látigo) **2** EYELASH : pestaña f

lass ['læs] or **lassie** ['læsi] n : muchacha f, chica f

lasso ['læ,so:, læ'suː] n, pl **-sos** or **-soes** : lazo m

last ['læst] vi : durar — ~ n **1** : último m, -ma f **2 at ~** : por fin, finalmente — ~ adv **1** : por última vez, en último lugar **2 arrive ~** : llegar el último — ~ adj **1** : último **2 ~ year** : el año pasado — **lastly** ['læstli] adv : por último, finalmente

latch ['lætʃ] n : picaporte m, pestillo m

late ['leɪt] adj **later; latest 1** : tarde **2** : avanzado (dícese de la hora) **3** DECEASED : difunto **4** RECENT : reciente — ~ adv **later; latest** : tarde — **lately** ['leɪtli] adv : recientemente, últimamente — **lateness** ['leɪtnəs] n **1** : retraso m **2** : lo avanzado (de la hora)

latent ['leɪtənt] adj : latente

lateral ['lætərəl] adj : lateral

latest ['leɪtəst] n **at the ~** : a más tardar

lathe ['leɪð] n : torno m

lather ['læðər] n : espuma f — ~ vt : enjabonar — vi : hacer espuma

Latin–American ['lætənə'merɪkən] adj : latinoamericano

latitude ['lætə,tuːd, -,tjuːd] n : latitud f

latter ['lætər] adj **1** : último **2** SECOND : segundo — ~ **pron the ~** : éste, ésta, éstos pl, éstas pl

lattice ['lætəs] n : enrejado m

laugh ['læf] vi : reír(se) — ~ n : risa f — **laughable** ['læfəbəl] adj : risible, ridículo — **laughter** ['læftər] n : risa f, risas fpl

launch ['lɔntʃ] vt : lanzar — ~ n : lanzamiento m

launder ['lɔndər] vt **1** : lavar y planchar (ropa) **2** : blanquear, lavar (dinero) — **laundry** ['lɔndri] n, pl **-dries 1** : ropa f

sucia 2 : lavandería f (servicio) 3 **do the ~** : lavar la ropa
lava ['lɑvə, 'læ-] n : lava f
lavatory ['lævəˌtori] n, pl **-ries** BATH-ROOM : baño m, cuarto m de baño
lavender ['lævəndər] n : lavanda f
lavish ['lævɪʃ] adj 1 EXTRAVAGANT : pródigo 2 ABUNDANT : abundante 3 LUXURIOUS : lujoso — ~ vt : prodigar
law ['lɔ] n 1 : ley f 2 : derecho m (profesión, etc.) 3 **practice ~** : ejercer la abogacía — **lawful** ['lɔfəl] adj : legal, legítimo
lawn ['lɔn] n : césped m — **lawn mower** n : cortadora f de césped
lawsuit ['lɔˌsuːt] n : pleito m
lawyer ['lɔiər, 'lɔjər] n : abogado m, -da f
lax ['læks] adj : poco estricto, relajado
laxative ['læksətɪv] n : laxante m
lay[1] ['leɪ] vt **laid** ['leɪd]; **laying** 1 PLACE, PUT : poner, colocar 2 **~ eggs** : poner huevos 3 **~ off** : despedir (un empleado) 4 **~ out** : presentar, exponer 5 **~ out** DESIGN : diseñar (el trazado de)
lay[2] pp → **lie**[1]
lay[3] adj 1 SECULAR : laico 2 NONPROFESSIONAL : lego, profano
layer ['leɪər] n : capa f
layman ['leɪmən] n, pl **-men** : lego m, laico m (en religión)
layout ['leɪˌaʊt] n ARRANGEMENT : disposición f
lazy ['leɪzi] adj **-zier; -est** : perezoso — **laziness** ['leɪzinəs] n : pereza f
lead[1] ['liːd] v **led** ['led]; **leading** 1 GUIDE : conducir 2 DIRECT : dirigir 3 HEAD : encabezar, ir al frente de — vi : llevar, conducir (a algo) — ~ n 1 : delantera f 2 **follow s.o.'s ~** : seguir el ejemplo de algn
lead[2] ['led] n 1 : plomo m (metal) 2 GRAPHITE : mina f — **leaden** ['ledən] adj 1 : de plomo 2 HEAVY : pesado
leader ['liːdər] n : jefe m, -fa f — **leadership** ['liːdərˌʃɪp] n : mando m, dirección f
leaf ['liːf] n, pl **leaves** ['liːvz] 1 : hoja f 2 **turn over a new ~** : hacer borrón y cuenta nueva — ~ vi **~ through** : hojear (un libro, etc.) — **leaflet** ['liːflət] n : folleto m
league ['liːg] n 1 : liga f 2 **be in ~ with** : estar confabulado con
leak ['liːk] vt 1 : dejar escapar (un líquido o un gas) 2 : filtrar (información) — vi 1 : gotear, escaparse (dícese de un líquido o un gas) 2 : filtrarse (dícese de información) — ~ n 1 : agujero m (de un cubo, etc.), gotera f

(de un techo) 2 : fuga f, escape m (de un líquido o un gas) 3 : filtración f (de información) — **leaky** ['liːki] adj **leakier; -est** : que hace agua
lean[1] ['liːn] v **leaned** or Brit **leant** ['lent]; **leaning** vi 1 BEND : inclinarse 2 **~ against** : apoyarse contra — vt : apoyar
lean[2] adj 1 THIN : delgado 2 : sin grasa (dícese de la carne)
leaning ['liːnɪŋ] n : inclinación f
leanness ['liːnnəs] n : delgadez f (de una persona), lo magro (de la carne)
leap ['liːp] vi **leapt** or **leaped** ['liːpt, 'lept]; **leaping** : saltar, brincar — ~ n : salto m, brinco m — **leap year** n : año m bisiesto
learn ['lərn] v **learned** ['lərnd, 'lərnt]; **learning** : aprender — **learned** ['lərnəd] adj : sabio, erudito — **learner** ['lərnər] n : principiante mf, estudiante mf — **learning** ['lərnɪŋ] n : erudición f, saber m
lease ['liːs] n : contrato m de arrendamiento — ~ vt **leased; leasing** : arrendar
leash ['liːʃ] n : correa f
least ['liːst] adj 1 : menor 2 SLIGHTEST : más mínimo — ~ n 1 **at ~** : por lo menos 2 **the ~** : lo menos 3 **to say the ~** : por no decir más — ~ adv : menos
leather ['leðər] n : cuero m
leave ['liːv] v **left** ['left]; **leaving** vt 1 : dejar 2 : salir(se) de (un lugar) 3 **~ out** : omitir — vi DEPART : irse — ~ n 1 or **~ of absence** : permiso m, licencia f 2 **take one's ~** : despedirse
leaves → **leaf**
lecture ['lektʃər] n 1 TALK : conferencia f 2 REPRIMAND : sermón m, reprimenda f — ~ **-tured; -turing** vi 1 : sermonear — vi : dar clase, dar una conferencia
led pp → **lead**[1]
ledge ['ledʒ] n : antepecho m (de una ventana), saliente m (de una montaña)
leech ['liːtʃ] n : sanguijuela f
leek ['liːk] n : puerro m
leer ['lɪr] vi : lanzar una mirada lasciva — ~ n : mirada f lasciva
leery ['lɪri] adj : receloso
leeway ['liːˌweɪ] n : libertad f de acción, margen m
left[1] → **leave**
left[2] ['left] adj : izquierdo — ~ adv : a la izquierda — ~ n : izquierda f — **left-handed** ['left'hændəd] adj : zurdo
leftovers ['leftˌoːvərz] npl : restos mpl, sobras fpl

leg ['lɛg] n 1 : pierna f (de una persona, de ropa), pata f (de un animal, de muebles) 2 : etapa f (de un viaje)

legacy ['lɛgəsi] n, pl **-cies** : legado m

legal ['li:gəl] adj 1 LAWFUL : legítimo, legal 2 JUDICIAL : legal, jurídico — **legality** [li'gæləti] n, pl **-ties** : legalidad f — **legalize** ['li:gə,laɪz] vt **-ized; -izing** : legalizar

legend ['lɛdʒənd] n : leyenda f — **legendary** ['lɛdʒən,deri] adj : lengendario

legible ['lɛdʒəbəl] adj : legible

legion ['li:dʒən] n : legión f

legislate ['lɛdʒəs,leɪt] vi **-lated; -lating** : legislar — **legislation** [,lɛdʒəs'leɪʃən] n : legislación f — **legislative** ['lɛdʒəs,leɪtɪv] adj : legislativo, legislador — **legislature** ['lɛdʒəs,leɪtʃər] n : asamblea f legislativa

legitimate [lɪ'dʒɪtəmət] adj : legítimo — **legitimacy** [lɪ'dʒɪtəməsi] n : legitimidad f

leisure ['li:ʒər, 'lɛ-] n 1 : ocio m, tiempo m libre 2 **at your** ~ : cuando te venga bien — **leisurely** ['li:ʒərli, 'lɛ-] adj & adv : lento, sin prisas

lemon ['lɛmən] n : limón m — **lemonade** [,lɛmə'neɪd] n : limonada f

lend ['lɛnd] vt **lent** ['lɛnt]; **lending** : prestar

length ['lɛŋkθ] n 1 : largo m 2 DURATION : duración f 3 **at** ~ FINALLY : por fin 4 **at** ~ : EXTENSIVELY : extensamente 5 **go to any** ~s : hacer todo lo posible — **lengthen** ['lɛŋkθən] vt 1 : alargar 2 PROLONG : prolongar — vi : alargarse — **lengthways** ['lɛŋkθ,weɪz] or **lengthwise** ['lɛŋkθ,waɪz] adv : a lo largo — **lengthy** ['lɛŋkθi] adj **lengthier; -est** : largo

lenient ['li:niənt] adj : indulgente — **leniency** ['li:niənsi] n, pl **-cies** : indulgencia f

lens ['lɛnz] n 1 : cristalino m (del ojo) 2 : lente mf (de un instrumento) 3 → **contact lens**

Lent ['lɛnt] n : Cuaresma f

lentil ['lɛntəl] n : lenteja f

leopard ['lɛpərd] n : leopardo m

leotard ['li:ə,tɑrd] n : leotardo m, malla f

lesbian ['lɛzbiən] n : lesbiana f

less ['lɛs] adv (comparative of **little**) : menos — ~ adj (comparative of **little**) : menos — ~ pron : menos — ~ prep MINUS : menos — **lessen** ['lɛsən] v : disminuir — **lesser** ['lɛsər] adj : menor

lesson ['lɛsən] n 1 CLASS : clase f, curso m 2 **learn one's** ~ : aprender la lección

lest ['lɛst] conj ~ **we forget** : para que no olvidemos

let ['lɛt] vt **let; letting** 1 ALLOW : dejar, permitir 2 RENT : alquilar 3 ~**'s go!** : ¡vamos!, ¡vámonos! 4 ~ **down** DISAPPOINT : fallar 5 ~ **in** : dejar entrar 6 ~ **off** FORGIVE : perdonar 7 ~ **up** ABATE : amainar, disminuir

letdown ['lɛt,daʊn] n : chasco m, decepción f

lethal ['li:θəl] adj : letal

lethargic [lɪ'θɑrdʒɪk] adj : letárgico

let's ['lɛts] (contraction of **let us**) → **let**

letter ['lɛtər] n 1 : carta f 2 : letra f (del alfabeto)

lettuce ['lɛtəs] n : lechuga f

letup ['lɛtəp] n : pausa f, descanso m

leukemia [lu'ki:miə] n : leucemia f

level ['lɛvəl] n 1 : nivel m 2 **be on the** ~ : ser honrado — ~ vt **-eled** or **-elled; -eling** or **-elling** 1 : nivelar 2 AIM : apuntar 3 RAZE : arrasar — ~ adj 1 FLAT : llano, plano 2 : nivel (de altura) — **levelheaded** ['lɛvəl'hɛdəd] adj : sensato, equilibrado

lever ['lɛvər, 'li:-] n : palanca f — **leverage** ['lɛvərɪdʒ, 'li:-] n 1 : apalancamiento m (en física) 2 INFLUENCE : influencia f

levity ['lɛvəti] n : ligereza f

levy ['lɛvi] n, pl **levies** : impuesto m — ~ vt **levied; levying** : imponer, exigir (un impuesto)

lewd ['lu:d] adj : lascivo

lexicon ['lɛksɪ,kɑn] n, pl **-ica** [-kə] or **-icons** : léxico m, lexicón m

liable ['laɪəbəl] adj 1 : responsable 2 LIKELY : probable 3 SUSCEPTIBLE : propenso — **liability** [,laɪə'bɪləti] n, pl **-ties** 1 RESPONSIBILITY : responsabilidad f 2 DRAWBACK : desventaja f 3 **liabilities** npl DEBTS : deudas fpl, pasivo m

liaison ['li:ə,zɑn, li'eɪ-] n 1 : enlace m 2 AFFAIR : amorío m

liar ['laɪər] n : mentiroso m, -sa f

libel ['laɪbəl] n : libelo m, difamación f — ~ vt **-beled** or **-belled; -beling** or **-belling** : difamar

liberal ['lɪbrəl, 'lɪbərəl] adj : liberal — ~ n : liberal mf

liberate ['lɪbə,reɪt] vt **-ated; -ating** : liberar — **liberation** [,lɪbə'reɪʃən] n : liberación f

liberty ['lɪbərti] n, pl **-ties** : libertad f

library ['laɪ,breri] n, pl **-braries** : biblioteca f — **librarian** [laɪ'breriən] n : bibliotecario m, -ria f

lice → **louse**

license or **licence** ['laɪsənts] n 1 PERMIT

: licencia f **2** FREEDOM : libertad f **3**
AUTHORIZATION : permiso m — **~** vt
licensed; licensing : autorizar

lick ['lɪk] vt **1** : lamer **2** DEFEAT : dar una
paliza a fam — **~** n : lamida f

licorice ['lɪkərɪʃ, -rəs] n : regaliz m

lid ['lɪd] n **1** : tapa f **2** EYELID : párpado m

lie¹ ['laɪ] vi **lay** ['leɪ]; **lain** ['leɪn]; **lying**
['laɪɪŋ] **1** or — **down** : acostarse,
echarse **2** BE : estar, encontrarse

lie² vi **lied; lying** ['laɪɪŋ] : mentir — **~** n
: mentira f

lieutenant [luːˈtenənt] n : teniente mf

life ['laɪf] n, pl **lives** ['laɪvz] : vida f —
lifeboat ['laɪf,boːt] n : bote m salvavidas — **lifeguard** ['laɪf,gɑrd] n : socorrista mf — **lifeless** ['laɪfləs] adj : sin
vida — **lifelike** ['laɪf,laɪk] adj : natural,
realista — **lifelong** ['laɪflɔŋ] adj : de
toda la vida — **life preserver** n : salvavidas m — **lifestyle** ['laɪf,staɪl] n : estilo m de vida — **lifetime** ['laɪf,taɪm] n
: vida f

lift ['lɪft] vt **1** RAISE : levantar **2** STEAL
: robar — vi CLEAR UP : despejarse **2**
or — **off** : despegar (dícese de un
avión, etc.) — **~** n **1** LIFTING : levantamiento m **2** give s.o. a **~** : llevar en
coche a algn — **liftoff** ['lɪft,ɔf] n : despegue m

light¹ ['laɪt] n **1** : luz f **2** LAMP : lámpara
f **3** HEADLIGHT : faro m **4** do you have
a **~**? : ¿tienes fuego? — **~** adj **1**
BRIGHT : bien iluminado **2** : claro
(dícese de los colores), rubio (dícese
del pelo) — **~** v **lit** ['lɪt] or **lighted**;
lighting vt **1** : encender (un fuego) **2**
ILLUMINATE : iluminar — vi or **~** up
: iluminarse — **lightbulb** ['laɪt,bʌlb] n
: bombilla f, bombillo m Lat — **light-
en** ['laɪtən] vt BRIGHTEN : iluminar —
lighter ['laɪtər] n : encendedor m —
lighthouse ['laɪt,haʊs] n : faro m —
lighting ['laɪtɪŋ] n : alumbrado —
lightning ['laɪtnɪŋ] n : relámpago m,
rayo m — **light-year** ['laɪt,jɪr] n : año
m luz

light² adj : ligero — **lighten** ['laɪtən] vt
: aligerar — **lightly** ['laɪtli] adv **1**
: suavemente **2** let off **~** : tratar con
indulgencia — **lightness** ['laɪtnəs] n
: ligereza f — **lightweight** ['laɪt,weɪt]
adj : ligero

like¹ ['laɪk] v **liked; liking** vt **1** : gustarle
(a uno) **2** WANT : querer — vi if you **~**
: si quieres — **likes** npl : preferencias
fpl, gustos mpl — **likable** or **likeable**
['laɪkəbəl] adj : simpático

like² adj SIMILAR : parecido — **~** prep
: como — **~** conj **1** AS : como **2** AS IF

: como si — **likelihood** ['laɪkli,hʊd] n
: probabilidad f — **likely** ['laɪkli] adj
-lier; -est : probable — **liken** ['laɪkən]
vt : comparar — **likeness** ['laɪknəs] n
: semejanza f, parecido m — **likewise**
['laɪk,waɪz] adv **1** : lo mismo **2** ALSO
: también

liking ['laɪkɪŋ] n : afición f (por una
cosa), simpatía f (por una persona)

lilac ['laɪlək, -,læk, -,lɑk] n : lila f

lily ['lɪli] n, pl **lilies** : lirio m, azucena f
— **lily of the valley** : lirio m de los
valles

lima bean ['laɪmə] n : frijol m de media
luna

limb ['lɪm] n **1** : miembro m (en anatomía) **2** : rama f (de un árbol)

limber ['lɪmbər] vi or **~** up : calentarse,
hacer ejercicios preliminares — **~**
adj : ágil

limbo ['lɪm,boː] n, pl **-bos** : limbo m

lime ['laɪm] n **1** : lima f, limón m verde Lat

limelight ['laɪm,laɪt] n **be in the ~**
: estar en el candelero

limerick ['lɪmərɪk] n : poema m jocoso
de cinco versos

limestone ['laɪm,stoːn] n : (piedra f) caliza f

limit ['lɪmət] n : límite m — **~** vt : limitar, restringir — **limitation** [,lɪmə-
'teɪʃən] n : limitación f, restricción f —
limited ['lɪmətəd] adj : limitado

limousine ['lɪməˌziːn, ,lɪmə'-] n : limusina
f

limp¹ ['lɪmp] vi : cojear — **~** n : cojera
f

limp² adj : flojo, fláccido

line ['laɪn] n **1** : línea f **2** ROPE : cuerda f
3 ROW : fila f **4** QUEUE : cola f **5** WRIN-
KLE : arruga f **6** drop a **~** : mándar
unas líneas — v **lined; lining** vt **1**
: forrar (un vestido, etc.), cubrir (las
paredes, etc.) **2** MARK : rayar, trazar
líneas en **3** BORDER : bordear — vi **~**
up : ponerse in fila, hacer cola

lineage ['lɪniːɪdʒ] n : linaje m

linear ['lɪniər] adj : lineal

linen ['lɪnən] n : lino m

liner ['laɪnər] n **1** LINING : forro m **2** SHIP
: buque m, transatlántico m

lineup ['laɪnˌʌp] n **1** or **police ~** : fila f
de sospechosos **2** : alineación f (en deportes)

linger ['lɪŋgər] vi **1** : quedarse, entretenerse **2** PERSIST : persistir

lingerie [,lɑndʒəˈreɪ, ,lænʒəˈriː] n : ropa f
íntima femenina, lencería f

lingo ['lɪŋgoː] n, pl **-goes** JARGON : jerga f

linguistics [lɪŋˈgwɪstɪks] n : lingüística f
— **linguist** ['lɪŋgwɪst] n : lingüista mf

— **linguistic** [lɪŋ'gwɪstɪk] *adj* : lingüístico

lining ['laɪnɪŋ] *n* : forro *m*

link ['lɪŋk] *n* 1 : eslabón *m* (de una cadena) 2 BOND : lazo *m* 3 CONNECTION : conexión *f* — ~ *vt* : enlazar, conectar — *vi* ~ **up** : unirse, conectar

linoleum [lə'noːliəm] *n* : linóleo *m*

lint ['lɪnt] *n* : pelusa *f*

lion ['laɪən] *n* : león *m* — **lioness** ['laɪənɪs] *n* : leona *f*

lip ['lɪp] *n* 1 : labio *m* 2 EDGE : borde *m* — **lipstick** ['lɪp,stɪk] *n* : lápiz *m* de labios

liqueur [lɪ'kʊr, -'kər, -'kjʊr] *n* : licor *m*

liquid ['lɪkwəd] *adj* : líquido — ~ *n* : líquido *m* — **liquidate** ['lɪkwə,deɪt] *vt* **-dated; -dating** : liquidar — **liquidation** [,lɪkwə'deɪʃən] *n* : liquidación *f*

liquor ['lɪkər] *n* : bebidas *fpl* alcohólicas

lisp ['lɪsp] *vi* : cecear — ~ *n* : ceceo *m*

list[1] ['lɪst] *n* : lista *f* — ~ *vt* 1 ENUMERATE : hacer una lista de, enumerar 2 INCLUDE : incluir (en una lista)

list[2] *vi* : escorar (dícese de un barco)

listen ['lɪsən] *vi* 1 : escuchar 2 ~ **to** HEED : hacer caso de 3 ~ **to reason** : atender a razones — **listener** ['lɪsənər] *n* : oyente *mf*

listless ['lɪstləs] *adj* : apático

lit ['lɪt] *pp* → **light**

litany ['lɪtəni] *n, pl* **-nies** : letanía *f*

liter ['liːtər] *n* : litro *m*

literacy ['lɪtərəsi] *n* : alfabetismo *m*

literal ['lɪtərəl] *adj* : literal — **literally** *adv* : literalmente, al pie de la letra

literate ['lɪtərət] *adj* : alfabetizado

literature ['lɪtərə,tʃur, -tʃər] *n* : literatura *f* — **literary** ['lɪtə,reri] *adj* : literario

lithe ['laɪð, 'laɪθ] *adj* : ágil y grácil

litigation [,lɪtə'geɪʃən] *n* : litigio *m*

litre → **liter**

litter ['lɪtər] *n* 1 RUBBISH : basura *f* 2 : camada *f* (de animales) 3 **or kitty** ~ : arena *f* higiénica — ~ *vt* : tirar basura en, ensuciar — *vi* : tirar basura

little ['lɪtəl] *adj* **littler or less** ['les] *or* **lesser** ['lesər]; **littlest or least** ['liːst] 1 SMALL : pequeño 2 **a** ~ SOME : un poco de 3 **he speaks** ~ **English** : habla poco inglés — ~ *adv* **less** ['les]; **least** ['liːst] : poco — ~ *pron* 1 : poco *m*, -ca *f* 2 **little by** ~ : poco a poco

liturgy ['lɪtərdʒi] *n, pl* **-gies** : liturgia *f* — **liturgical** [lə'tərdʒɪkəl] *adj* : litúrgico

live ['lɪv] *vi* **lived; living** 1 : vivir 2 RESIDE : residir 3 ~ **on** : vivir de — *vt* : vivir, llevar (una vida) — ~ ['laɪv] *adj* 1 : vivo 2 : con corriente (dícese de cables eléctricos) 3 : en vivo, en directo (dícese de programas de televisión, etc.) — **livelihood** ['laɪvli,hud] *n* : sustento *m*, medio *m* de vida — **lively** ['laɪvli] *adj* **-lier; -est** : animado, alegre — **liven** ['laɪvən] *vt or* ~ **up** : animar — *vi* : animarse

liver ['lɪvər] *n* : hígado *m*

livestock ['laɪv,stɑk] *n* : ganado *m*

livid ['lɪvəd] *adj* 1 : lívido 2 ENRAGED : furioso

living ['lɪvɪŋ] *adj* : vivo — ~ *n* **make a** ~ : ganarse la vida — **living room** *n* : living *m*, sala *f* (de estar)

lizard ['lɪzərd] *n* : lagarto *m*

llama ['lɑmə, 'jɑ-] *n* : llama *f*

load ['loːd] *n* 1 CARGO : carga *f* 2 BURDEN : carga *f*, peso *m* 3 ~**s of** : un montón de — ~ *vt* : cargar

loaf[1] ['loːf] *n, pl* **loaves** ['loːvz] : pan *m*, barra *f* (de pan)

loaf[2] *vi* : holgazanear — **loafer** ['loːfər] *n* 1 : holgazán *m*, -zana *f* 2 : mocasín *m* (zapato)

loan ['loːn] *n* : préstamo *m* — ~ *vt* : prestar

loathe ['loːð] *vt* **loathed; loathing** : odiar — **loathsome** ['loːθsəm, 'loːð-] *adj* : odioso

lobby ['lɑbi] *n, pl* **-bies** 1 : vestíbulo *m* 2 *or* **political** ~ : grupo *m* de presión, lobby *m* — ~ *v* **-bied; -bying** *vt* : ejercer presión sobre

lobe ['loːb] *n* : lóbulo *m*

lobster ['lɑbstər] *n* : langosta *f*

local ['loːkəl] *adj* : local — ~ *n* **the** ~**s** : los vecinos del lugar — **locale** [loː'kæl] *n* : escenario *m* — **locality** [loː'kæləti] *n, pl* **-ties** : localidad *f*

locate ['loː,keɪt, loː'keɪt] *vt* **-cated; -cating** 1 SITUATE : situar, ubicar 2 FIND : localizar — **location** [loː'keɪʃən] *n* : situación *f*, lugar *m*

lock[1] ['lɑk] *n* : mechón *m* (de pelo)

lock[2] *n* 1 : cerradura *f* (de una puerta, etc.) 2 : esclusa *f* (de un canal) — ~ *vt* 1 : cerrar (con llave) 2 *or* ~ **up** CONFINE : encerrar — *vi* 1 : cerrarse con llave 2 : bloquearse (dícese de una rueda, etc.) — **locker** ['lɑkər] *n* : armario *m* — **locket** ['lɑkət] *n* : medallón *m* — **locksmith** ['lɑk,smɪθ] *n* : cerrajero *m*, -ra *f*

locomotive [,loːkə'moːtɪv] *n* : locomotora *f*

locust ['loːkəst] *n* : langosta *f*, chapulín *m Lat*

lodge ['lɑdʒ] *v* **lodged; lodging** *vt* 1 HOUSE : hospedar, alojar 2 FILE : presentar — *vi* : hospedarse, alojarse — ~ *n* : pabellón *m* — **lodger** ['lɑdʒər] *n*

: huésped *m*, -peda *f* — **lodging** ['lɑdʒɪŋ] *n* **1** : alojamiento *m* **2** ~s *npl* : habitaciones *fpl*

loft ['lɔft] *n* **1** : desván *m* (en una casa) **2** HAYLOFT : pajar *m* — **lofty** ['lɔfti] *adj* **loftier; -est 1** : noble, elevado **2** HAUGHTY : altanero

log ['lɔg, 'lɑg] *n* **1** : tronco *m*, leño *m* **2** RECORD : diario *m* — *vi* **logged; logging 1** : talar (árboles) **2** RECORD : registrar, anotar **3** ~ **on** : entrar (en el sistema) **4** ~ **off** : salir (del sistema) — **logger** ['lɔgər, 'lɑ-] *n* : leñador *m*, -dora *f*

logic ['lɑdʒɪk] *n* : lógica *f* — **logical** ['lɑdʒɪkəl] *adj* : lógico — **logistics** [lə-'dʒɪstɪks, lo-] *ns & pl* : logística *f*

logo ['lo:go:] *n, pl* **logos** [-go:z] : logotipo *m*

loin ['lɔɪn] *n* : lomo *m*

loiter ['lɔɪtər] *vi* : vagar, holgazanear

lollipop *or* **lollypop** ['lɑli,pɑp] *n* : pirulí *m*, chupete *m Lat*

lone ['lo:n] *adj* : solitario — **loneliness** ['lo:nlinəs] *n* : soledad *f* — **lonely** ['lo:nli] *adj* **-lier; -est** : solitario, solo — **loner** ['lo:nər] *n* : solitario *m*, -ria *f* — **lonesome** ['lo:nsəm] *adj* : solo, solitario

long[1] ['lɔŋ] *adj* **longer** ['lɔŋgər]; **longest** ['lɔŋgəst] : largo — *adv* **1** : mucho tiempo **2 all day** ~ : todo el día **3 as** ~ **as** : mientras **4 no** ~**er** : ya no **5 so** ~**!** : ¡hasta luego!, ¡adiós! — *n* **1 before** ~ : dentro de poco **2 the** ~ **and the short** : lo esencial

long[2] *vi* ~ **for** : anhelar, desear

longevity [lɑn'dʒevəti] *n* : longevidad *f*

longing ['lɔŋɪŋ] *n* : ansia *f*, anhelo *m*

longitude ['lɑndʒə,tu:d, -,tju:d] *n* : longitud *f*

look ['lʊk] *vi* **1** : mirar **2** SEEM : parecer **3** ~ **after** : cuidar (de) **4** ~ **for** EXPECT : esperar **5** ~ **for** SEEK : buscar **6** ~ **into** : investigar **7** ~ **out** : tener cuidado **8** ~ **over** EXAMINE : revisar **9** ~ **up to** : respetar — *vt* : mirar — *n* **1** : mirada *f* **2** APPEARANCE : aspecto *m*, aire *m* — **lookout** ['lʊk,aʊt] *n* **1** : puesto *m* de observación **2** WATCHMAN : vigía *mf* **3 be on the** ~ **for** : estar al acecho de

loom[1] ['lu:m] *n* : telar *m*

loom[2] *vi* **1** APPEAR : aparecer, surgir **2** APPROACH : ser inminente

loop ['lu:p] *n* : lazada *f*, lazo *m* — ~ *vt* : hacer lazadas con — **loophole** ['lu:p,ho:l] *n* : escapatoria *f*

loose ['lu:s] *adj* **looser; -est 1** MOVABLE : flojo, suelto **2** SLACK : flojo **3** ROOMY : holgado **4** APPROXIMATE : libre, aproximado **5** FREE : suelto **6** IMMORAL : relajado — **loosely** ['lu:sli] *adv* **1** : sin apretar **2** ROUGHLY : aproximadamente — **loosen** ['lu:sən] *vt* : aflojar

loot ['lu:t] *n* : botín *m* — ~ *vt* : saquear, robar — **looter** ['lu:tər] *n* : saqueador *m*, -dora *f* — **looting** ['lu:tɪŋ] *n* : saqueo *m*

lop ['lɑp] *vt* **lopped; lopping** : cortar, podar

lopsided ['lɑp,saɪdəd] *adj* : torcido, chueco *Lat*

lord ['lɔrd] *n* **1** : señor *m*, noble *m* **2 the Lord** : el Señor

lore ['lɔr] *n* : saber *m* popular, tradición *f*

lose ['lu:z] *v* **lost** ['lɔst]; **losing** ['lu:zɪŋ] *vt* **1** : perder **2** ~ **one's way** : perderse **3** ~ **time** : atrasarse (dícese de un reloj) — *vi* : perder — **loser** ['lu:zər] *n* : perdedor *m*, -dora *f* — **loss** ['lɔs] *n* **1** : pérdida *f* **2** DEFEAT : derrota *f* **3 be at a** ~ **for words** : no encontrar palabras — **lost** ['lɔst] *adj* **1** : perdido **2 get** ~ : perderse

lot ['lɑt] *n* **1** FATE : suerte *f* **2** PLOT : solar *m* **3 a** ~ **of** *or* ~**s of** : mucho, un montón de

lotion ['lo:ʃən] *n* : loción *f*

lottery ['lɑtəri] *n, pl* **-teries** : lotería *f*

loud ['laʊd] *adj* **1** : alto, fuerte **2** NOISY : ruidoso **3** FLASHY : llamativo — ~ *adv* **1** : fuerte **2 out** ~ : en voz alta — **loudly** ['laʊdli] *adv* : en voz alta — **loudspeaker** ['laʊd,spi:kər] *n* : altavoz *m*

lounge ['laʊndʒ] *vi* **lounged; lounging 1** : repantigarse **2** ~ **about** : holgazanear — ~ *n* : salón *m*

louse ['laʊs] *n, pl* **lice** ['laɪs] : piojo *m* — **lousy** ['laʊzi] *adj* **lousier; -est 1** : piojoso **2** BAD : pésimo, muy malo

love ['lʌv] *n* **1** : amor *m* **2 fall in** ~ : enamorarse — ~ *v* **loved; loving** : querer, amar — **lovable** ['lʌvəbəl] *adj* : adorable, amoroso *Lat* — **lovely** ['lʌvli] *adj* **-lier; -est** : lindo, precioso — **lover** ['lʌvər] *n* : amante *mf* — **loving** ['lʌvɪŋ] *adj* : cariñoso

low ['lo:] *adj* **lower** ['lo:ər]; **-est 1** : bajo **2** SCARCE : escaso **3** DEPRESSED : deprimido — ~ *adv* **1** : bajo **2 turn the lights down** ~ : bajar las luces — ~ *n* **1** : punto *m* bajo **2** *or* ~ **gear** : primera velocidad *f* — **lower** ['lo:ər] *adj* : inferior, más bajo — ~ *vt* : bajar — **lowly** ['lo:li] *adj* **-lier; -est** : humilde

loyal ['lɔɪəl] *adj* : leal, fiel — **loyalty** ['lɔɪəlti] *n, pl* **-ties** : lealtad *f*

lozenge ['lɑzəndʒ] n : pastilla f
lubricate ['lu:brɪˌkeɪt] vt -cated; -cating
: lubricar — **lubricant** ['lu:brɪkənt] n
: lubricante — **lubrication** [ˌlu:brɪ-
'keɪʃən] n : lubricación f
lucid ['lu:səd] adj : lúcido — **lucidity**
[lu:'sɪdəti] n : lucidez f
luck ['lʌk] n 1 : suerte f 2 **good
~!** : ¡buena suerte! — **luckily** ['lʌkəli]
adv : afortunadamente — **lucky** ['lʌki]
adj **luckier; -est 1** : afortunado **2 ~
charm** : amuleto m (de la suerte)
lucrative ['lu:krətɪv] adj : lucrativo
ludicrous ['lu:dəkrəs] adj : ridículo, absurdo
lug ['lʌg] vt **lugged; lugging** : arrastrar
luggage ['lʌgɪdʒ] n : equipaje m
lukewarm ['lu:k'wɔrm] adj : tibio
lull ['lʌl] vt **1** CALM : calmar **2 ~ to
sleep** : adormecer — **~** n : período m
de calma, pausa f
lullaby ['lʌləˌbaɪ] n, pl **-bies** : canción f
de cuna, nana f
lumber ['lʌmbər] n : madera f — **lumberjack** ['lʌmbərˌdʒæk] n : leñador m,
-dora f
luminous ['lu:mənəs] adj : luminoso
lump ['lʌmp] n **1** CHUNK, PIECE : pedazo
m, trozo m **2** SWELLING : bulto m **3**
: grumo m (en un líquido) — **~** vt or
~ together : juntar, agrupar —
lumpy ['lʌmpi] adj **lumpier; -est**
: grumoso (dícese de una salsa), lleno
de bultos (dícese de un colchón)
lunacy ['lu:nəsi] n, pl **-cies** : locura f
lunar ['lu:nər] adj : lunar
lunatic ['lu:nəˌtɪk] n : loco m, -ca f

lunch ['lʌntʃ] n : almuerzo m, comida f
— **~** vi : almorzar, comer — **lunch-
eon** ['lʌntʃən] n : comida f, almuerzo m
lung ['lʌŋ] n : pulmón m
lunge ['lʌndʒ] vi **lunged; lunging 1**
: lanzarse **2 ~ at** : arremeter contre
lurch¹ ['lərtʃ] vi **1** STAGGER : tambalearse
2 : dar bandazos (dícese de un vehículo)
lurch² n **leave in a ~** : dejar en la estacada
lure ['lur] n **1** BAIT : señuelo m **2** AT-
TRACTION : atractivo m — **~** vt **lured;
luring** : atraer
lurid ['lurəd] adj **1** GRUESOME : espeluznante **2** SENSATIONAL : sensacionalista
3 GAUDY : chillón
lurk ['lərk] vi : estar al acecho
luscious ['lʌʃəs] adj : delicioso, exquisito
lush ['lʌʃ] adj : exuberante, suntuoso
lust ['lʌst] n **1** : lujuria f **2** CRAVING
: ansia f, anhelo m — **~** vi **after**
: desear (a una persona), codiciar
(riquezas, etc.)
luster or **lustre** ['lʌstər] n : lustre m
lusty ['lʌsti] adj **lustier; -est** : fuerte,
vigoroso
luxurious [ˌlʌg'ʒurəs, ˌlʌk'ʃur-] adj : lujoso — **luxury** ['lʌkʃəri, 'lʌgʒə-] n, pl
-ries : lujo m
lye ['laɪ] n : lejía f
lying → lie
lynch ['lɪntʃ] vt : linchar
lynx ['lɪŋks] n : lince m
lyric ['lɪrɪk] or **lyrical** ['lɪrɪkəl] adj : lírico
— **lyrics** npl : letra f (de una canción)

M

m ['ɛm] n, pl **m's** or **ms** ['ɛmz] : m f, de-
cimotercera letra del alfabeto inglés
ma'am ['mæm] → **madam**
macabre [mə'kɑb, -'kɑbər, -'kɑbrə] adj
: macabro
macaroni [ˌmækə'roni] n : macarrones
mpl
mace ['meɪs] n **1** : maza f (arma o símbolo) **2** : macis f (especia)
machete [mə'ʃɛti] n : machete m
machine [mə'ʃiːn] n : máquina f — **machinery** [mə'ʃiːnəri] n, pl **-eries 1**
: maquinaria f **2** WORKS : mecanismo
m — **machine gun** n : ametralladora f
mad ['mæd] adj **madder; maddest 1**
INSANE : loco **2** FOOLISH : insensato **3**
ANGRY : furioso

madam ['mædəm] n, pl **mesdames**
[mer'dɑm] : señora f
madden ['mædən] vt : enfurecer
made → make
madly ['mædli] adv : como un loco, locamente — **madman** ['mædˌmæn,
-mən] n, pl **-men** [-mən, -mɛn] : loco
m — **madness** ['mædnəs] n : locura
f
Mafia ['mɑfiə] n : Mafia f
magazine ['mægəˌziːn] n **1** PERIODICAL
: revista f **2** : recámara f (de un arma
de fuego)
maggot ['mægət] n : gusano m
magic ['mædʒɪk] n : magia f — **~** or
magical ['mædʒɪkəl] adj : mágico —
magician [mə'dʒɪʃən] n : mago m, -ga f

magistrate ['mædʒə,streɪt] *n* : magistra-do *m*, -da *f*

magnanimous [mæg'nænəməs] *adj* : magnánimo

magnate ['mæg,neɪt, -nət] *n* : magnate *mf*

magnet ['mægnət] *n* : imán *m* — **magnetic** [mæg'nɛtɪk] *adj* : magnético — **magnetism** ['mægnə,tɪzəm] *n* : magnetismo *m* — **magnetize** ['mægnə,taɪz] *vt* **-tized; -tizing** : magnetizar

magnificent [mæg'nɪfəsənt] *adj* : magnífico — **magnificence** [mæg'nɪfəsənts] *n* : magnificencia *f*

magnify ['mægnə,faɪ] *vt* **-fied; -fying 1** ENLARGE : ampliar **2** EXAGGERATE : exagerar — **magnifying glass** *n* : lupa *f*

magnitude ['mægnə,tuːd, -,tjuːd] *n* : magnitud *f*

magnolia [mæg'noːljə] *n* : magnolia *f*

mahogany [mə'hɑgəni] *n, pl* **-nies** : caoba *f*

maid ['meɪd] *n* : sirvienta *f*, criada *f*, muchacha *f* — **maiden** ['meɪdən] *adj* FIRST : inaugural — **maiden name** *n* : nombre *m* de soltera

mail ['meɪl] *n* **1** : correo *m* **2** LETTERS : correspondencia *f* — ~ *vt* : enviar por correo — **mailbox** ['meɪl,bɑks] *n* : buzón *m* — **mailman** ['meɪl,mæn, -mən] *n, pl* **-men** [-mən, -,mɛn] : cartero *m*

maim ['meɪm] *vt* : mutilar

main ['meɪn] *n* : tubería *f* principal (de agua o gas), cable *m* principal (de un circuito) — ~ *adj* : principal — **mainframe** ['meɪn,freɪm] *n* : computadora *f* central — **mainland** ['meɪn,lænd, -lənd] *n* : continente *m* — **mainly** ['meɪnli] *adv* : principalmente — **mainstay** ['meɪn,steɪ] *n* : sostén *m* (principal) — **mainstream** ['meɪn,striːm] *n* : corriente *f* principal — ~ *adj* : dominante, convencional

maintain [meɪn'teɪn] *vt* : mantener — **maintenance** ['meɪntənənts] *n* : mantenimiento *m*

maize ['meɪz] *n* : maíz *m*

majestic [mə'dʒɛstɪk] *adj* : majestuoso — **majesty** ['mædʒəsti] *n, pl* **-ties** : majestad *f*

major ['meɪdʒər] *adj* **1** : muy importante, principal **2** : mayor (en música) — ~ *n* **1** : mayor *mf*, comandante *mf* (en las fuerzas armadas) **2** : especialidad *f* (universitaria) — ~ *vi* **-jored; -joring** : especializarse — **majority** [mə'dʒɔrəṭi] *n, pl* **-ties** : mayoría *f*

make ['meɪk] *v* **made** ['meɪd]; **making** *vt* **1** : hacer **2** MANUFACTURE : fabricar **3**

CONSTITUTE : constituir **4** PREPARE : preparar **5** RENDER : poner **6** COMPEL : obligar **7** ~ **a decision** : tomar una decisión **8** ~ **a living** : ganar la vida — *vi* **1** ~ **do** : arreglárselas **2** ~ **for** : dirigirse a **3** ~ **good** SUCCEED : tener éxito — ~ *n* BRAND : marca *f* — **make—believe** [,meɪkbə'liːv] *n* : fantasía *f* — ~ *adj* : imaginario — **make out** *vt* **1** : hacer (un cheque, etc.) **2** DISCERN : distinguir **3** UNDERSTAND : comprender — *vi* **how did you ~?** : ¿qué tal te fue? — **maker** ['meɪkər] *n* MANUFACTURER : fabricante *mf* — **makeshift** ['meɪk,ʃɪft] *adj* : improvisado — **makeup** ['meɪk,ʌp] *n* **1** COMPOSITION : composición *f* **2** COSMETICS : maquillaje *m* — **make up** *vt* **1** PREPARE : preparar **2** INVENT : inventar **3** CONSTITUTE : formar — *vi* RECONCILE : hacer las paces

maladjusted [,mælə'dʒʌstəd] *adj* : inadaptado

malaria [mə'lɛriə] *n* : malaria *f*, paludismo *m*

male ['meɪl] *n* : macho *m* (de animales o plantas), varón *m* (de personas) — ~ *adj* **1** : macho **2** MASCULINE : masculino

malevolent [mə'lɛvələnt] *adj* : malévolo

malfunction [mæl'fʌŋkʃən] *vi* : funcionar mal — ~ *n* : mal funcionamiento *m*

malice ['mælɪs] *n* : mala intención *f*, rencor *m* — **malicious** [mə'lɪʃəs] *adj* : malicioso

malign [mə'laɪn] *adj* : maligno — ~ *vt* : calumniar

malignant [mə'lɪgnənt] *adj* : maligno

mall ['mɔl] *n* or **shopping** ~ : centro *m* comercial

malleable ['mæliəbəl] *adj* : maleable

mallet ['mælət] *n* : mazo *m*

malnutrition [,mælnu'trɪʃən, -nju-] *n* : desnutrición *f*

malpractice [,mæl'præktəs] *n* : mala práctica *f*, negligencia *f*

malt ['mɔlt] *n* : malta *f*

mama *or* **mamma** ['mɑmə] *n* : mamá *f*

mammal ['mæməl] *n* : mamífero *m*

mammogram ['mæmə,græm] *n* : mamografía *f*

mammoth ['mæməθ] *adj* : gigantesco

man ['mæn] *n, pl* **men** ['mɛn] : hombre *m* — ~ *vt* **manned; manning** : tripular (un barco o avión), encargarse de (un servicio)

manage ['mænɪdʒ] *v* **-aged; -aging** *vt* **1** HANDLE : manejar **2** DIRECT : administrar, dirigir — *vi* COPE : arreglárselas

— **manageable** ['mænɪdʒəbəl] *adj* : manejable — **management** ['mænɪdʒmənt] *n* : dirección *f* — **manager** ['mænɪdʒər] *n* : director *m*, -tora *f*; gerente *mf* — **managerial** [ˌmænə-'dʒɪriəl] *adj* : directivo

mandarin ['mændərən] *n or* ~ **orange** : mandarina *f*

mandate ['mændeɪt] *n* : mandato *m* — **mandatory** ['mændəˌtori] *adj* : obligatorio

mane ['meɪn] *n* : crin *f* (de un caballo), melena *f* (de un león)

maneuver [mə'nuːvər, -'njuː-] *n* : maniobra *f* — ~ *v* -**vered; -vering** : maniobrar

mangle ['mæŋgəl] *vt* -**gled; -gling** : destrozar

mango ['mæŋgoː] *n, pl* -**goes** : mango *m*

mangy ['meɪndʒi] *adj* **mangier; -est** : sarnoso

manhandle ['mænˌhændəl] *vi* -**dled; -dling** : maltratar

manhole ['mænˌhoːl] *n* : boca *f* de alcantarilla

manhood ['mænˌhʊd] *n* **1** : madurez *f* (de un hombre) **2** VIRILITY : virilidad *f*

mania ['meɪniə, -njə] *n* : manía *f* — **maniac** ['meɪniˌæk] *n* : maníaco *m*, -ca *f*

manicure ['mænəˌkjʊr] *n* : manicura *f* — ~ *vt* -**cured; -curing** : hacer la manicura a

manifest ['mænəˌfest] *adj* : manifiesto, patente — ~ *vt* : manifestar — **manifesto** [ˌmænə'festoː] *n, pl* -**tos** *or* -**toes** : manifiesto *m*

manipulate [mə'nɪpjəˌleɪt] *vt* -**lated; -lating** : manipular — **manipulation** [məˌnɪpjə'leɪʃən] *n* : manipulación *f*

mankind ['mænˌkaɪnd, ˌkaɪnd] *n* : género *m* humano, humanidad *f*

manly ['mænli] *adj* -**lier; -est** : viril — **manliness** ['mænlinəs] *n* : virilidad *f*

man-made ['mænˌmeɪd] *adj* : artificial

mannequin ['mænɪkən] *n* : maniquí *m*

manner ['mænər] *n* **1** : manera *f* **2** KIND : clase *f* **3** ~**s** *npl* ETIQUETTE : modales *mpl*, educación *f* — **mannerism** ['mænəˌrɪzəm] *n* : peculiaridad *f* (de una persona)

manoeuvre *Brit* → **maneuver**

manor ['mænər] *n* : casa *f* solariega

manpower ['mænˌpaʊər] *n* : mano *f* de obra

mansion ['mæntʃən] *n* : mansión *f*

manslaughter ['mænˌslɔtər] *n* : homicidio *m* sin premeditación

mantel ['mæntəl] *or* **mantelpiece** ['mæntəlˌpiːs] *n* : repisa *f* de la chimenea

manual ['mænjuəl] *adj* : manual — ~ *n* : manual *m*

manufacture [ˌmænjə'fæktʃər] *n* : fabricación *f* — ~ *vt* -**tured; -turing** : fabricar — **manufacturer** [ˌmænjə-'fæktʃərər] *n* : fabricante *mf*

manure [mə'nʊr, -'njʊr] *n* : estiércol *m*

manuscript ['mænjəˌskrɪpt] *n* : manuscrito *m*

many ['meni] *adj* **more** ['mor]; **most** ['moːst] **1** : muchos **2 as** ~ : tantos **3 how** ~ : cuántos **4 too** ~ : demasiados — ~ *pron* : muchos *pl*, -chas *pl*

map ['mæp] *n* : mapa *m* — ~ *vt* **mapped; mapping 1** : trazar el mapa de **2** *or* ~ **out** : planear, proyectar

maple ['meɪpəl] *n* : arce *m*

mar ['mar] *vt* **marred; marring** : estropear

marathon ['mærəˌθɑn] *n* : maratón *m*

marble ['marbəl] *n* **1** : mármol *m* **2** ~**s** *npl* : canicas *fpl* (para jugar)

march ['martʃ] *n* : marcha *f* — ~ *vi* : marchar, desfilar

March ['martʃ] *n* : marzo *m*

mare ['mær] *n* : yegua *f*

margarine ['mardʒərən] *n* : margarina *f*

margin ['mardʒən] *n* : margen *m* — **marginal** ['mardʒənəl] *adj* : marginal

marigold ['mærəˌgoːld] *n* : caléndula *f*

marijuana [ˌmærə'hwɑnə] *n* : marihuana *f*

marinate ['mærəˌneɪt] *vt* -**nated; -nating** : marinar

marine [mə'riːn] *adj* : marino — ~ *n* : soldado *m* de marina

marionette [ˌmæriə'net] *n* : marioneta *f*

marital ['mærətəl] *adj* **1** : matrimonial **2** ~ **status** : estado *m* civil

maritime ['mærəˌtaɪm] *adj* : marítimo

mark ['mark] *n* **1** : marca *f* **2** STAIN : mancha *f* **3** IMPRINT : huella *f* **4** TARGET : blanco *m* **5** GRADE : nota *f* — ~ *vt* **1** : marcar **2** STAIN : manchar **3** POINT OUT : señalar **4** : calificar (un examen, etc.) **5** COMMEMORATE : conmemorar **6** CARACTERIZE : caracterizar **7** ~ **off** : delimitar — **marked** ['markt] *adj* : marcado, notable — **markedly** ['markədli] *adv* : notablemente — **marker** ['markər] *n* : marcador *m*

market ['market] *n* : mercado *m* — ~ *vt* : vender, comercializar — **marketable** ['markətəbəl] *adj* : vendible — **marketplace** ['markətˌpleɪs] *n* : mercado *m*

marksman ['marksmən] *n, pl* -**men** [-mən, -ˌmen] : tirador *m* — **marksmanship** ['marksmənˌʃɪp] *n* : puntería *f*

marmalade ['marməˌleɪd] *n* : mermelada *f*

maroon[1] [mə'ruːn] *vt* : abandonar, aislar
maroon[2] *n* : rojo *m* oscuro
marquee [mɑr'kiː] *n* CANOPY : marquesina *f*
marriage ['mærɪdʒ] *n* **1** : matrimonio *m* **2** WEDDING : casamiento *m*, boda *f* — **married** ['mærid] *adj* **1** : casado **2 get ~** : casarse
marrow ['mæroː] *n* : médula *f*, tuétano *m*
marry ['mæri] *v* **-ried; -rying** *vt* **1** : casar **2** WED : casarse con — *vi* : casarse
Mars ['mɑrz] *n* : Marte *m*
marsh ['mɑrʃ] *n* **1** : pantano *m* **2** *or* **salt ~** : marisma *f*
marshal ['mɑrʃəl] *n* : mariscal *m* (en el ejército); jefe *m*, -fa *f* (de policía, de bomberos, etc.) — ~ *vt* **-shaled** *or* **-shalled; -shaling** *or* **-shalling** : poner en orden (los pensamientos, etc.), reunir (las tropas)
marshmallow ['mɑrʃ,meloː, -,mæloː] *n* : malvavisco *m*
marshy ['mɑrʃi] *adj* **marshier; -est** : pantanoso
mart ['mɑrt] *n* : mercado *m*
martial ['mɑrʃəl] *adj* : marcial
martyr ['mɑrtər] *n* : mártir *mf* — ~ *vt* : martirizar
marvel ['mɑrvəl] *n* : maravilla *f* — ~ *vi* **-veled** *or* **-velled; -veling** *or* **-velling** : maravillarse — **marvelous** ['mɑrvələs] *or* **marvellous** *adj* : maravilloso
mascara [mæs'kærə] *n* : rímel *m*
mascot ['mæs,kɑt, -kət] *n* : mascota *f*
masculine ['mæskjələn] *adj* : masculino — **masculinity** [,mæskjə'lɪnəti] *n* : masculinidad *f*
mash ['mæʃ] *vt* **1** CRUSH : aplastar, majar **2** PUREE : hacer puré de — **mashed potatoes** *npl* : puré *m* de patatas, puré *m* de papas *Lat*
mask ['mæsk] *n* : máscara *f* — ~ *vt* : enmascarar
masochism ['mæsə,kɪzəm, 'mæzə-] *n* : masoquismo *m* — **masochist** ['mæsə,kɪst, 'mæzə-] *n* : masoquista *mf* — **masochistic** [,mæsə'kɪstɪk, ,mæzə-] *adj* : masoquista
mason ['meɪsən] *n* : albañil *mf* — **masonry** ['meɪsənri] *n*, *pl* **-ries** : albañilería *f*
masquerade [,mæskə'reɪd] *n* : mascarada *f* — ~ *vi* **-aded; -ading ~ as** : disfrazarse de, hacerse pasar por
mass ['mæs] *n* **1** : masa *f* **2** MULTITUDE : cantidad *f* **3 the ~es** : las masas
Mass ['mæs] *n* : misa *f*
massacre ['mæsɪkər] *n* : masacre *f* — ~ *vt* **-cred; -cring** : masacrar

massage [mə'sɑʒ, -'sɑdʒ] *n* : masaje *m* — ~ *vt* **-saged; -saging** : dar masaje a, masajear — **masseur** [mæ'sər] *n* : masajista *m* — **masseuse** [mæ'sɜz, -'sɔrz, -'suːz] *n* : masajista *f*
massive ['mæsɪv] *adj* **1** BULKY, SOLID : macizo **2** HUGE : enorme, masivo
mast ['mæst] *n* : mástil *m*
master ['mæstər] *n* **1** : amo *m*, señor *m* (de la casa) **2** EXPERT : maestro *m*, -tra *f* **3 ~'s degree** : maestría *f* — ~ *vt* : dominar — **masterful** ['mæstərfəl] *adj* : magistral — **masterpiece** ['mæstər,piːs] *n* : obra *f* maestra — **mastery** ['mæstəri] *n* : maestría *f*
masturbate ['mæstər,beɪt] *v* **-bated; -bating** *vi* : masturbarse — **masturbation** [,mæstər'beɪʃən] *n* : masturbación *f*
mat ['mæt] *n* **1** DOORMAT : felpudo *m* **2** RUG : estera *f*
matador ['mætə,dɔr] *n* : matador *m*
match ['mætʃ] *n* **1** EQUAL : igual *mf* **2** : fósforo *m*, cerilla *f* (para encender) **3** GAME : partido *m*, combate *m* (en boxeo) **4 be a good ~** : hacer buena pareja — ~ *vt* **1** *or* **~ up** : emparejar **2** EQUAL : igualar **3** : combinar con, hacer juego con (ropa, colores, etc.) — *vi* : concordar, coincidir
mate ['meɪt] *n* **1** COMPANION : compañero *m*, -ra *f*; amigo *m*, -ga *f* **2** : macho *m*, hembra *f* (de animales) — ~ *vi* **mated; mating** : aparearse
material [mə'tɪriəl] *adj* **1** : material **2** IMPORTANT : importante — ~ *n* **1** : material *m* **2** CLOTH : tela *f*, tejido *m* — **materialistic** [mə,tɪriə'lɪstɪk] *adj* : materialista — **materialize** [mə'tɪriə,laɪz] *vi* **-ized; -izing** : aparecer
maternal [mə'tərnəl] *adj* : maternal — **maternity** [mə'tərnəti] *n*, *pl* **-ties** : maternidad *f* — ~ *adj* **1** : de maternidad **2 ~ clothes** : ropa *f* de futura mamá
math ['mæθ] → **mathematics**
mathematics [,mæθə'mætɪks] *ns & pl* : matemáticas *fpl* — **mathematical** [,mæθə'mætɪkəl] *adj* : matemático — **mathematician** [,mæθəmə'tɪʃən] *n* : matemático *m*, -ca *f*
matinee *or* **matinée** [,mætən'eɪ] *n* : matiné(e) *f*, fonción *f* de tarde
matrimony ['mætrə,moːni] *n* : matrimonio *m* — **matrimonial** [,mætrə'moːniəl] *adj* : matrimonial
matrix ['meɪtrɪks] *n*, *pl* **-trices** ['meɪtrə,siz, 'mæ-] *or* **-trixes** ['meɪtrɪksəz] : matriz *f*
matte ['mæt] *adj* : mate
matter ['mætər] *n* **1** SUBSTANCE : materia

f **2** QUESTION : asunto *m*, cuestión *f* **3 as a ~ of fact** : en efecto, en realidad **4 for that ~** : de hecho **5 to make ~s worse** : para colmo de males **6 what's the ~?** : ¿qué pasa? — **~** *vi* : importar

mattress ['mætrəs] *n* : colchón *m*

mature [mə'tʊr, -tjʊr, -'tʃʊr] *adj* **-turer; -est** : maduro — **~** *vi* **-tured; -turing** : madurar — **maturity** [mə'tʊrəţi, -tjʊr-, -'tʃʊr-] *n* : madurez *f*

maul ['mɔl] *vt* : maltratar, aporrear

mauve ['moːv, 'mɔv] *n* : malva *m*

maxim ['mæksəm] *n* : máxima *f*

maximum ['mæksəməm] *n, pl* **-ma** ['mæksəmə] *or* **-mums** : máximo *m* — **~** *adj* : máximo — **maximize** ['mæksə,maiz] *vt* **-mized; -mizing** : llevar al máximo

may ['mei] *v aux, past* **might** ['mait]; *present s & pl* **may** **1** : poder **2 come what ~** : pase lo que pase **3 it ~ happen** : puede pasar **4 ~ the best man win** : que gane el mejor

May ['mei] *n* : mayo *m*

maybe ['meibi] *adv* : quizás, tal vez

mayhem ['mei,hem, 'meiəm] *n* : alboroto *m*

mayonnaise ['meiə,neiz] *n* : mayonesa *f*

mayor ['meiər, 'mer] *n* : alcalde *m*, -desa *f*

maze ['meiz] *n* : laberinto *m*

me ['mi] *pron* **1** : me **2 for ~** : para mí **3 give it to ~!** : ¡dámelo! **4 it's ~** : soy yo **5 with ~** : conmigo

meadow ['medoː] *n* : prado *m*, pradera *f*

meager ['miːgər] *or* **meagre** *adj* : escaso

meal ['miːl] *n* **1** : comida *f* **2** : harina *f* (de maíz, etc.) — **mealtime** ['miːl,taim] *n* : hora *f* de comer

mean¹ ['miːn] *vt* **meant** ['ment]; **meaning 1** SIGNIFY : querer decir **2** INTEND : querer, tener la intención de **3 be meant for** : estar destinado a **4 he didn't ~ it** : no lo dijo en serio

mean² *adj* **1** UNKIND : malo **2** STINGY : mezquino, tacaño **3** HUMBLE : humilde

mean³ *adj* AVERAGE : medio — **~** *n* : promedio *m*

meander [mi'ændər] *vi* **-dered; -dering 1** WIND : serpentear **2** WANDER : vagar

meaning ['miːnɪŋ] *n* : significado *m*, sentido *m* — **meaningful** ['miːnɪŋfəl] *adj* : significativo — **meaningless** ['miːnɪŋləs] *adj* : sin sentido

meanness ['miːnnəs] *n* **1** UNKINDNESS : maldad *f* **2** STINGINESS : mezquindad *f*

means ['miːnz] *n* **1** : medio *m* **2 by all ~** : por supuesto **3 by ~ of** : por medio de **4 by no ~** : de ninguna manera

meantime ['miːn,taim] *n* **1** : interín *m* **2 in the ~** : mientras tanto — **~** *adv* → **meanwhile**

meanwhile ['miːn,hwail] *adv* : mientras tanto — **~** *n* → **meantime**

measles ['miːzəlz] *npl* : sarampión *m*

measly ['miːzli] *adj* **-slier; -est** : miserable, misero

measure ['meʒər, 'mei-] *n* : medida *f* — **~** *v* **-sured; -suring** : medir — **measurable** ['meʒərəbəl, 'mei-] *adj* : mensurable — **measurement** ['meʒərmənt, 'mei-] *n* : medida *f* — **measure up** *vi* **~ to** : estar a la altura de

meat ['miːt] *n* : carne *f* — **meatball** ['miːt,bɔl] *n* : albóndiga *f* — **meaty** ['miːţi] *adj* **meatier; -est 1** : carnoso **2** SUBSTANTIAL : sustancioso

mechanic [mi'kænik] *n* : mecánico *m*, -ca *f* — **mechanical** [mi'kænikəl] *adj* : mecánico — **mechanics** [mi'kæniks] *ns & pl* **1** : mecánica *f* **2** WORKINGS : mecanismo *m* — **mechanism** ['mekə,nizəm] *n* : mecanismo *m* — **mechanize** ['mekə,naiz] *vt* **-nized; -nizing** : mecanizar

medal ['medəl] *n* : medalla *f* — **medallion** [mə'dæljən] *n* : medallón *m*

meddle ['medəl] *vi* **-dled; -dling** : entrometerse

media ['miːdiə] *or* **mass ~** *npl* : medios *mpl* de comunicación

median ['miːdiən] *adj* : medio

mediate ['miːdi,eit] *vi* **-ated; -ating** : mediar — **mediation** [,miːdi'eiʃən] *n* : mediación *f* — **mediator** ['miːdi,eitər] *n* : mediador *m*, -dora *f*

medical ['medikəl] *adj* : médico — **medicated** ['medə,keitəd] *adj* : medicinal — **medication** [,medə'keiʃən] *n* : medicamento *m* — **medicinal** [mə'dısənəl] *adj* : medicinal — **medicine** ['medəsən] *n* **1** : medicina *f* **2** MEDICATION : medicina *f*, medicamento *m*

medieval *or* **mediaeval** [mid'iːvəl, mi:-, ,me-, -di'i:vəl] *adj* : medieval

mediocre [,miːdi'oːkər] *adj* : mediocre — **mediocrity** [,miːdi'ɑkrəţi] *n, pl* **-ties** : mediocridad *f*

meditate ['medə,teit] *vi* **-tated; -tating** : meditar — **meditation** [,medə'teiʃən] *n* : meditación *f*

medium ['miːdiəm] *n, pl* **-diums** *or* **-dia** ['miːdiə] **1** MEANS : medio *m* **2** MEAN : punto *m* medio, término *m* medio **3** → **media** — **~** *adj* : mediano

medley ['medli] *n, pl* **-leys 1** : mezcla *f*
2 : popurrí *m* (de canciones)

meek ['miːk] *adj* : dócil

meet ['miːt] *v* **met** ['met]; **meeting** *vt* **1**
ENCOUNTER : encontrarse con **2** SATIS-
FY : satisfacer **3** **pleased to ~ you**
: encantado de conocerlo — *vi* **1** : encontrarse **2** ASSEMBLE : reunirse **3** BE
INTRODUCED : conocerse — **~ *n*** : encuentro *m* — **meeting** ['miːtɪŋ] *n* : reunión *f*

megabyte ['megəˌbaɪt] *n* : megabyte *m*

megaphone ['megəˌfoːn] *n* : megáfono
m

melancholy ['melənˌkɑli] *n, pl* **-cholies**
: melancolía *f* — **~** *adj* : melancólico,
triste

mellow ['meloː] *adj* **1** : suave, dulce **2**
CALM : apacible **3** : maduro (dícese de
frutas), añejo (dícese de vinos) — **~**
vt : suavizar, endulzar — *vi* : suavizarse

melody ['melədi] *n, pl* **-dies** : melodía *f*

melon ['melən] *n* : melón *m*

melt ['melt] *vi* : derretirse, fundirse — *vt*
: derretir

member ['member] *n* : miembro *m* —
membership ['memberˌʃɪp] *n* **1** : calidad *f* de miembro **2** MEMBERS : miem-
bros *mpl*

membrane ['memˌbreɪn] *n* : membrana *f*

memory ['memri, 'memə-] *n, pl* **-ries 1**
: memoria *f* **2** RECOLLECTION : recuerdo *m* — **memento** [mɪˈmenˌtoː] *n, pl*
-tos *or* **-toes** : recuerdo *m* — **memo**
['memoː] *n, pl* **memos** *or* **memorandum** [ˌmeməˈrændəm] *n, pl* **-dums** *or*
-da [-də] : memorándum *m* — **memoirs** ['memˌwarz] *npl* : memorias *fpl* —
memorable ['memərəbəl] *adj* : memorable — **memorial** [məˈmoːriəl] *adj*
: conmemorativo — **~** *n* : monumento *m* (conmemorativo) — **memorize**
['meməˌraɪz] *vt* **-rized; -rizing** : aprender de memoria

men → **man**

menace ['menəs] *n* : amenaza *f* — **~** *vt*
-aced; -acing : amenazar — **menac-
ing** ['menəsɪŋ] *adj* : amenazador

mend ['mend] *vt* **1** : reparar, arreglar **2**
DARN : zurcir — *vi* HEAL : curarse

menial ['miːniəl] *adj* : servil, bajo

meningitis [ˌmenənˈdʒaɪtəs] *n, pl*
-gitides [-ˈdʒɪtəˌdiːz] : meningitis *f*

menopause ['menəˌpɔz] *n* : menopausia
f

menstruate ['menˌstruˌeɪt] *vi* **-ated;
-ating** : menstruar — **menstruation**
[ˌmenstruˈeɪʃən] *n* : menstruación *f*

mental ['mentəl] *adj* : mental — **mentality** [menˈtæləˌti] *n, pl* **-ties** : mentalidad *f*

mention ['mentʃən] *n* : mención *f* —
mention *vt* **1** : mencionar **2 don't ~
it!** : ¡de nada!, ¡no hay de qué!

menu ['menjuː] *n* : menú *m*

meow [miˈaʊ] *n* : maullido *m*, miau *m*
— **~** *vi* : maullar

mercenary ['mersənˌeri] *n, pl* **-naries**
: mercenario *m*, -ria *f* — **~** *adj* : mercenario

merchant ['mertʃənt] *n* : comerciante *mf*
— **merchandise** ['mertʃənˌdaɪz, -ˌdaɪs]
n : mercancía *f*, mercadería *f*

merciful ['mersɪfəl] *adj* : misericordioso, compasivo — **merciless** ['mer-
sɪləs] *adj* : despiadado

mercury ['merkjəri] *n, pl* **-ries** : mercurio *m*

Mercury *n* : Mercurio *m*

mercy ['mersi] *n, pl* **-cies 1** : misericordia *f*, compasión *f* **2 at the ~ of** : a
merced de

mere ['mir] *adj, superlative* **merest**
: mero, simple — **merely** ['mirli] *adv*
: simplemente

merge ['merdʒ] *v* **merged; merging** *vi*
: unirse, fusionarse (dícese de las
compañías), confluir (dícese de los
ríos, las calles, etc.) — *vt* : unir, fusionar, combinar — **merger** ['merdʒər]
n : unión *f*, fusión *f*

merit ['merət] *n* : mérito *m* — **~** *vt*
: merecer

mermaid ['mərˌmeɪd] *n* : sirena *f*

merry ['meri] *adj* **-rier; -est** : alegre —
merry–go–round ['meriɡoˌraʊnd] *n*
: tiovivo *m*

mesa ['meɪsə] *n* : mesa *f*

mesh ['meʃ] *n* : malla *f*

mesmerize ['mezməˌraɪz] *vt* **-ized;
-izing** : hipnotizar

mess ['mes] *n* **1** : desorden *m* **2** MUDDLE
: lío *m* **3** : rancho *m* (militar) — **~** *vt*
1 *or* **~ up** SOIL : ensuciar **2 ~ up** DIS-
ARRANGE : desordenar **3 ~ up** BUN-
GLE : echar a perder — *vi* **1 ~ around**
PUTTER : entretenerse **2 ~ with** PRO-
VOKE : meterse con

message ['mesɪdʒ] *n* : mensaje *m* —
messenger ['mesəndʒər] *n* : mensajero
m, -ra *f*

messy ['mesi] *adj* **messier; -est** : desordenado, sucio

met → **meet**

metabolism [məˈtæbəˌlɪzəm] *n* : metabolismo *m*

metal ['metəl] *n* : metal *m* — **metallic**
[məˈtælɪk] *adj* : metálico

metamorphosis [ˌmetəˈmorfəsɪs] n, pl **-phoses** [-ˌsiːz] : metamorfosis f

metaphor [ˈmetəˌfor, -fər] n : metáfora f

meteor [ˈmiːtiər, -ˌtiːɔr] n : meteoro m — **meteorological** [ˌmiːtiːərəˈlɑdʒɪkəl] adj : meteorológico — **meteorologist** [ˌmiːtiːəˈrɑlədʒɪst] n : meteorólogo m, -ga f — **meteorology** [ˌmiːtiːəˈrɑlədʒi] n : meteorología f

meter or Brit **metre** [ˈmiːtər] n 1 : metro m 2 : contador m (de electricidad, etc.)

method [ˈmeθəd] n : método m — **methodical** [məˈθɑdɪkəl] adj : metódico

meticulous [məˈtɪkjələs] adj : meticuloso

metric [ˈmetrɪk] or **metrical** [-trɪkəl] adj : métrico

metropolis [məˈtrɑpələs] n : metrópoli f — **metropolitan** [ˌmetrəˈpɑlətən] adj : metropolitano

Mexican [ˈmeksɪkən] adj : mexicano

mice → **mouse**

microbe [ˈmaɪkroːb] n : microbio m

microfilm [ˈmaɪkroˌfɪlm] n : microfilm m

microphone [ˈmaɪkrəˌfoːn] n : micrófono m

microscope [ˈmaɪkrəˌskoːp] n : microscopio m — **microscopic** [ˌmaɪkrəˈskɑpɪk] adj : microscópico

microwave [ˈmaɪkrəˌweɪv] n or **~ oven** : microondas m

mid [ˈmɪd] adj 1 **~ morning** : a media mañana 2 **in ~-August** : a mediados de agosto 3 **she is in her mid thirties** : tiene alrededor de 35 años — **midair** [ˈmɪdˌær] n **in ~** : en el aire — **midday** [ˈmɪdˌdeɪ] n : mediodía m

middle [ˈmɪdəl] adj : de en medio, del medio — ~ n 1 : medio m, centro m 2 **in the ~ of** : en medio de (un espacio), a mitad de (una actividad) 3 **in the ~ of the month** : a mediados del mes — **middle-aged** [ˌmɪdəlˈeɪdʒd] adj : de mediana edad — **Middle Ages** npl : Edad f Media — **middle class** n : clase f media — **middleman** [ˈmɪdəlˌmæn] n, pl **-men** [-mən, -ˌmen] : intermediario m, -ria f

midget [ˈmɪdʒət] n : enano m, -na f

midnight [ˈmɪdˌnaɪt] n : medianoche f

midriff [ˈmɪdˌrɪf] n : diafragma m

midst [ˈmɪdst] n 1 **in the ~ of** : en medio de 2 **in our ~** : entre nosotros

midsummer [ˈmɪdˌsʌmər, -ˌsʌ-] n : pleno verano m

midway [ˈmɪdˌweɪ] adv : a mitad de camino, a medio camino

midwife [ˈmɪdˌwaɪf] n, pl **-wives** [-ˌwaɪvz] : comadrona f

midwinter [ˈmɪdˌwɪntər, -ˌwin-] n : pleno invierno m

miff [ˈmɪf] vt : ofender

might¹ [ˈmaɪt] (used to express permission or possibility or as a polite alternative to **may**) → **may**

might² n : fuerza f, poder m — **mighty** [ˈmaɪti] adj **mightier; -est** 1 : fuerte, poderoso 2 GREAT : enorme — **~** adv : muy

migraine [ˈmaɪˌgreɪn] n : jaqueca f, migraña f

migrate [ˈmaɪˌgreɪt] vi **-grated; -grating** : emigrar — **migrant** [ˈmaɪgrənt] n : trabajador m, -dora f ambulante

mild [ˈmaɪld] adj 1 GENTLE : suave 2 LIGHT : leve 3 **a ~ climate** : una clima templada

mildew [ˈmɪlˌduː, -ˌdjuː] n : moho m

mildly [ˈmaɪldli] adv : ligeramente, suavemente — **mildness** [ˈmaɪldnəs] n : apacibilidad f (de personas), suavedad f (de sabores, etc.)

mile [ˈmaɪl] n : milla f — **mileage** [ˈmaɪlɪdʒ] n : distancia f recorrida (en millas), kilometraje m — **milestone** [ˈmaɪlˌstoːn] n : hito m

military [ˈmɪləˌteri] adj : militar — **~ the ~** : las fuerzas armadas — **militant** [ˈmɪlətənt] adj : militante — **~** n : militante mf — **militia** [məˈlɪʃə] n : milicia f

milk [ˈmɪlk] n : leche f — **~** vt 1 : ordeñar (una vaca, etc.) 2 EXPLOIT : explotar — **milky** [ˈmɪlki] adj **milkier; -est** : lechoso — **Milky Way** n **the ~** : la Vía Láctea

mill [ˈmɪl] n 1 : molino m 2 FACTORY : fábrica f 3 GRINDER : molinillo m — **~** vt : moler — vi or **~ about** : arremolinarse

millennium [məˈleniəm] n, pl **-nia** [-niə] or **-niums** : milenio m

miller [ˈmɪlər] n : molinero m, -ra f

milligram [ˈmɪləˌgræm] n : miligramo m — **millimeter** or Brit **millimetre** [ˈmɪləˌmiːtər] n : milímetro m

million [ˈmɪljən] n, pl **millions** or **million** 1 : millón m 2 **a ~ people** : un millón de personas — **~** adj **a ~** : un millón de — **millionaire** [ˌmɪljəˈnær, ˈmɪljəˌnær] n : millonario m, -ria f — **millionth** [ˈmɪljənθ] adj : millonésimo

mime [ˈmaɪm] n 1 : mimo mf 2 PANTOMIME : pantomima f — **~** v **mimed; miming** vt : imitar — vi : hacer la mímica — **mimic** [ˈmɪmɪk] vt **-icked; -icking** : imitar, remedar — **~** n : imitador m, -dora f — **mimicry** [ˈmɪmɪkri] n, pl **-ries** : imitación f

mince ['mɪnts] v **minced; mincing** vt 1 : picar, moler 2 **not to ~ one's words** : no tener pelos en la lengua

mind ['maɪnd] n 1 : mente f 2 INTELLECT : capacidad f intelectual 3 OPINION : opinión f 4 REASON : razón f 5 **have a ~ to** : tener intención de — ~ vt 1 TEND : cuidar 2 OBEY : obedecer 3 WATCH : tener cuidado con 4 **I don't ~ the heat** : no me molesta el calor — vi 1 OBEY : obedecer 2 **I don't ~** : no me importa, me es igual — **mindful** ['maɪndfəl] adj : atento — **mindless** ['maɪndləs] adj 1 SENSELESS : estúpido, sin sentido 2 DULL : aburrido

mine¹ ['maɪn] pron 1 : (el) mío, (la) mía, (los) míos, (las) mías 2 **a friend of ~** : un amigo mío

mine² n : mina f — ~ vt **mined; mining** 1 : extraer (oro, etc.) 2 : minar (con artefactos explosivos) — **minefield** ['maɪnˌfiːld] n : campo m de minas — **miner** ['maɪnər] n : minero m, -ra f

mineral ['mɪnərəl] n : mineral m

mingle ['mɪŋɡəl] v **-gled; -gling** vt : mezclar — vi 1 : mezclarse 2 : circular (a una fiesta, etc.)

miniature ['mɪniəˌtʃʊr, 'mɪnɪˌtʃʊr, -tʃər] n : miniatura f — ~ adj : en miniatura

minimal ['mɪnəməl] adj : mínimo — **minimize** ['mɪnəˌmaɪz] vt **-mized; -mizing** : minimizar — **minimum** ['mɪnəməm] adj : mínimo — ~ n, pl **-ma** ['mɪnəmə] or **-mums** : mínimo m

mining ['maɪnɪŋ] n : minería f

minister ['mɪnəstər] n 1 : pastor m, -tora f (de una iglesia) 2 : ministro m, -tra f (en política) — ~ vi **to ~** : cuidar (de), atender a — **ministerial** [ˌmɪnə-'stɪriəl] adj : ministerial — **ministry** ['mɪnəstri] n, pl **-tries** : ministerio m

mink ['mɪŋk] n, pl **mink** or **minks** : visón m

minnow ['mɪnoː] n, pl **-nows** : pececillo m de agua dulce

minor ['maɪnər] adj 1 : menor 2 INSIGNIFICANT : sin importancia — ~ n 1 : menor mf (de edad) 2 : asignatura f secundaria (de estudios) — **minority** [məˈnɔrəti, maɪ-] n, pl **-ties** : minoría f

mint¹ ['mɪnt] n 1 : menta f (planta) 2 : pastilla f de menta (dulce)

mint² n 1 **the U.S. Mint** : la casa de la moneda de los EE.UU. 2 **be worth a ~** : valer un dineral — ~ vt : acuñar — ~ adj **in ~ condition** : como nuevo

minus ['maɪnəs] prep 1 : menos 2 WITHOUT : sin — ~ n or **~ sign** : signo m de menos

minuscule ['mɪnəsˌkjuːl, mɪˈnʌs-] adj : minúsculo

minute¹ [maɪˈnuːt, mɪ-, -ˈnjuːt] n 1 : minuto m 2 MOMENT : momento m 3 **~s** npl : actas fpl (de una reunión)

minute² ['mɪnət] adj **-nuter; -est** 1 TINY : diminuto, minúsculo 2 DETAILED : minucioso

miracle ['mɪrɪkəl] n : milagro m — **miraculous** [məˈrækjələs] adj : milagroso

mirage [mɪˈrɑʒ, 'mɪrˌɑʒ] n : espejismo m

mire ['maɪr] n : lodo m, fango m

mirror ['mɪrər] n : espejo m — ~ vt : reflejar

mirth ['mərθ] n : alegría f, risas fpl

misapprehension [ˌmɪsˌæprɪˈhɛntʃən] n : malentendido m

misbehave [ˌmɪsbɪˈheɪv] vi **-haved; -having** : portarse mal — **misbehavior** [ˌmɪsbɪˈheɪvjər] n : mala conducta f

miscalculate [mɪsˈkælkjəˌleɪt] v **-lated; -lating** : calcular mal

miscarriage [ˌmɪsˈkærɪdʒ, 'mɪsˌkærɪdʒ] n 1 : aborto m 2 **~ of justice** : error m judicial

miscellaneous [ˌmɪsəˈleɪniəs] adj : diverso, vario

mischief ['mɪstʃəf] n : travesuras fpl — **mischievous** ['mɪstʃəvəs] adj : travieso

misconception [ˌmɪskənˈsɛpʃən] n : concepto m erróneo

misconduct [mɪsˈkɑndəkt] n : mala conducta f

misdeed [mɪsˈdiːd] n : fechoría f

misdemeanor [ˌmɪsdɪˈmiːnər] n : delito m menor

miser ['maɪzər] n : avaro m, -ra f; tacaño m, -ña f

miserable ['mɪzərəbəl] adj 1 UNHAPPY : triste 2 WRETCHED : miserable 3 **~ weather** : tiempo m malo — **miserly** ['maɪzərli] adj : mezquino

misery ['mɪzəri] n, pl **-eries** 1 : sufrimiento m 2 WRETCHEDNESS : miseria f

misfire [mɪsˈfaɪr] vi **-fired; -firing** : fallar

misfit ['mɪsˌfɪt, mɪsˈfɪt] n : inadaptado m, -da f

misfortune [mɪsˈfɔrtʃən] n : desgracia f

misgiving [mɪsˈɡɪvɪŋ] n : duda f

misguided [mɪsˈɡaɪdəd] adj : descaminado, equivocado

mishap ['mɪsˌhæp] n : contratiempo m

misinform [ˌmɪsɪnˈfɔrm] vt : informar mal

misinterpret [ˌmɪsɪnˈtərprət] vt : interpretar mal

misjudge [mɪsˈdʒʌdʒ] vt **-judged; -judging** : juzgar mal

mislay [mɪsˈleɪ] *vt* **-laid** [-leɪd]; **-laying** : extraviar, perder

mislead [mɪsˈliːd] *vt* **-led** [-ˈled]; **-leading** : engañar — **misleading** [mɪsˈliːdɪŋ] *adj* : engañoso

misnomer [mɪsˈnoːmər] *n* : nombre *m* inapropiado

misplace [mɪsˈpleɪs] *vt* **-placed**; **-placing** : extraviar, perder

misprint [ˈmɪsˌprɪnt, mɪs-] *n* : errata *f*, error *m* de imprenta

miss [ˈmɪs] *vt* 1 : errar, faltar 2 OVER-LOOK : pasar por alto 3 : perder (una oportunidad, un vuelo, etc.) 4 AVOID : evitar 5 OMIT : saltarse 6 I **~ you** : te echo de menos — **~** *n* 1 : fallo *m* (de un tiro, etc.) 2 FAILURE : fracaso *m*

Miss [ˈmɪs] *n* : señorita *f*

missile [ˈmɪsəl] *n* 1 : misil *m* 2 PROJEC-TILE : proyectil *m*

missing [ˈmɪsɪŋ] *adj* : perdido, desaparecido

mission [ˈmɪʃən] *n* : misión *f* — **missionary** [ˈmɪʃəˌneri] *n, pl* **-aries** : misionero *m*, -ra *f*

misspell [mɪsˈspel] *vt* : escribir mal

mist [ˈmɪst] *n* : neblina *f*, bruma *f*

mistake [mɪˈsteɪk] *vt* **mistook** [-ˈstʊk]; **mistaken** [-ˈsteɪkən]; **-taking** 1 MISIN-TERPRET : entender mal 2 CONFUSE : confundir — **~** *n* 1 : error *m* 2 **make a ~** : equivocarse — **mistaken** [mɪˈsteɪkən] *adj* : equivocado

mister [ˈmɪstər] *n* : señor *m*

mistletoe [ˈmɪsəlˌtoː] *n* : muérdago *m*

mistreat [mɪsˈtriːt] *vt* : maltratar

mistress [ˈmɪstrəs] *n* 1 : dueña *f*, señora *f* (de una casa) 2 LOVER : amante *f*

mistrust [mɪsˈtrʌst] *n* : desconfianza *f* — **~** *vt* : desconfiar de

misty [ˈmɪsti] *adj* **mistier; -est** : neblinoso, nebuloso

misunderstand [ˌmɪsˌʌndərˈstænd] *vt* **-stood; -standing** : entender mal — **misunderstanding** [ˌmɪsˌʌndərˈstændɪŋ] *n* : malentendido *m*

misuse [mɪsˈjuːz] *vt* **-used; -using** 1 : emplear mal 2 MISTREAT : maltratar — **~** [mɪsˈjuːs] *n* : mal empleo *m*, abuso *m*

mitigate [ˈmɪtəˌɡeɪt] *vt* **-gated; -gating** : mitigar

mitt [ˈmɪt] *n* : manopla *f*, guante *m* (de béisbol) — **mitten** [ˈmɪtən] *n* : manopla *f*, mitón *m*

mix [ˈmɪks] *vt* 1 : mezclar 2 **~ up** : confundir — *vi* : mezclarse — **~** *n* : mezcla *f* — **mixture** [ˈmɪkstʃər] *n* : mezcla *f* — **mix-up** [ˈmɪksˌʌp] *n* : confusión *f*, lío *m fam*

moan [ˈmoːn] *n* : gemido *m* — **~** *vi* : gemir

mob [ˈmɑb] *n* : muchedumbre *f* — **~** *vt* **mobbed; mobbing** : acosar

mobile [ˈmoːbəl, -ˌbiːl, -ˌbaɪl] *adj* : móvil — **~** [ˈmoːbiːl] *n* : móvil *m* — **mobile home** *n* : caravana *f* — **mobility** [moːˈbɪləti] *n* : movilidad *f* — **mobilize** [ˈmoːbəˌlaɪz] *vt* **-lized; -lizing** : movilizar

moccasin [ˈmɑkəsən] *n* : mocasín *m*

mock [ˈmɑk, ˈmɔk] *vt* : burlarse de, mofarse de — **~** *adj* : falso — **mockery** [ˈmɑkəri, ˈmɔ-] *n, pl* **-eries** : burla *f* — **mock-up** [ˈmɑkˌʌp] *n* : maqueta *f*

mode [ˈmoːd] *n* 1 : modo *m* 2 FASHION : moda *f*

model [ˈmɑdəl] *n* 1 : modelo *m* 2 MOCK-UP : maqueta *f* 3 : modelo *mf* (persona) — **~** *v* **-eled** *or* **-elled; -eling** *or* **-elling** *vt* 1 SHAPE : modelar 2 WEAR : lucir — *vi* : trabajar de modelo — **~** *adj* : modelo

modem [ˈmoːdəm, -ˌdem] *n* : módem *m*

moderate [ˈmɑdərət] *adj* : moderado — **~** *n* : moderado *m*, -da *f* — **~** [ˈmɑdəˌreɪt] *v* **-ated; -ating** *vt* : moderar — *vi* : moderarse — **moderation** [ˌmɑdəˈreɪʃən] *n* : moderación *f* — **moderator** [ˈmɑdəˌreɪtər] *n* : moderador *m*, -dora *f*

modern [ˈmɑdərn] *adj* : moderno — **modernize** [ˈmɑdərˌnaɪz] *vt* **-ized; -izing** : modernizar

modest [ˈmɑdəst] *adj* : modesto — **modesty** [ˈmɑdəsti] *n* : modestia *f*

modify [ˈmɑdəˌfaɪ] *vt* **-fied; -fying** : modificar

moist [ˈmɔɪst] *adj* : húmedo — **moisten** [ˈmɔɪsən] *vt* : humedecer — **moisture** [ˈmɔɪstʃər] *n* : humedad *f* — **moisturizer** [ˈmɔɪstʃəˌraɪzər] *n* : crema *f* hidratante

molar [ˈmoːlər] *n* : muela *f*

molasses [məˈlæsəz] *n* : melaza *f*

mold[1] [ˈmoːld] *n* FORM : molde *m* — **~** *vt* : moldear, formar

mold[2] *n* FUNGUS : moho *m* — **moldy** [ˈmoːldi] *adj* **moldier; -est** : mohoso

mole[1] [ˈmoːl] *n* : lunar *m* (en la piel)

mole[2] *n* : topo *m* (animal)

molecule [ˈmɑlɪˌkjuːl] *n* : molécula *f*

molest [məˈlest] *vt* 1 HARASS : importunar 2 : abusar (sexualmente)

molten [ˈmoːltən] *adj* : fundido

mom [ˈmɑm, ˈmʌm] *n* : mamá *f*

moment [ˈmoːmənt] *n* : momento *m* — **momentarily** [ˌmoːmənˈterəli] *adv* 1 : momentáneamente 2 SOON : dentro de poco, pronto — **momentary** [ˈmoːmənˌteri] *adj* : momentáneo

momentous [mo'mentəs] *adj* : muy importante

momentum [mo'mentəm] *n, pl* **-ta** [-tə] *or* **-tums 1** : momento *m* (en física) **2** IMPETUS : ímpetu *m*

monarch ['mɑ,nɑrk, -nərk] *n* : monarca *mf* — **monarchy** ['mɑ,nɑrki, -nər-] *n, pl* **-chies** : monarquía *f*

monastery ['mɑnə,steri] *n, pl* **-teries** : monasterio *m*

Monday ['mʌn,deɪ, -di] *n* : lunes *m*

money ['mʌni] *n, pl* **-eys** *or* **-ies** ['mʌniz] : dinero *m* — **monetary** ['mɑnə,teri, 'mʌnə-] *adj* : monetario — **money order** *n* : giro *m* postal

mongrel ['mɑŋgrəl, 'mʌn-] *n* : perro *m* mestizo

monitor ['mɑnə,tər] *n* : monitor *m* (de una computadora, etc.) — **~** *vt* : controlar

monk ['mʌŋk] *n* : monje *m*

monkey ['mʌŋki] *n, pl* **-keys** : mono *m*, -na *f* — **monkey wrench** *n* : llave *f* inglesa

monogram ['mɑnə,græm] *n* : monograma *m*

monologue ['mɑnə,lɔg] *n* : monólogo *m*

monopoly [mə'nɑpəli] *n, pl* **-lies** : monopolio *m* — **monopolize** [mə'nɑpə,laɪz] *vt* **-lized; -lizing** : monopolizar

monotonous [mə'nɑtənəs] *adj* : monótono — **monotony** [mə'nɑtəni] *n* : monotonía *f*

monster ['mɑntstər] *n* : monstruo *m* — **monstrosity** [mɑn'strɑsəti] *n, pl* **-ties** : monstruosidad *f* — **monstrous** ['mɑntstrəs] *adj* **1** : monstruoso **2** HUGE : gigantesco

month ['mʌnθ] *n* : mes *m* — **monthly** ['mʌnθli] *adv* : mensualmente — **~** *adj* : mensual

monument ['mɑnjəmənt] *n* : monumento *m* — **monumental** [,mɑnjə'mentəl] *adj* : monumental

moo ['muː] *vi* : mugir — **~** *n* : mugido *m*

mood ['muːd] *n* : humor *m* — **moody** ['muːdi] *adj* **moodier; -est 1** GLOOMY : melancólico, deprimido **2** IRRITABLE : malhumorado **3** TEMPERAMENTAL : de humor variable

moon ['muːn] *n* : luna *f* — **moonlight** ['muːn,laɪt] *n* : luz *f* de la luna

moor[1] ['mʊr, 'mɔr] *n* : brezal *m*, páramo *m*

moor[2] *vt* : amarrar — **mooring** ['mʊrɪŋ, 'mɔr-] *n* DOCK : atracadero *m*

moose ['muːs] *ns & pl* : alce *m*

moot ['muːt] *adj* : discutible

mop ['mɑp] *n* **1** : trapeador *m Lat*, fregona *f Spain* **2** *or* **~ of hair** : pelambrera *f* — **~** *vt* **mopped; mopping** : trapear *Lat*, pasar la fregona a *Spain*

mope ['moːp] *vi* **moped; moping** : andar deprimido

moped ['moː,ped] *n* : ciclomotor *m*

moral ['mɔrəl] *adj* : moral — **~** *n* **1** : moraleja *f* (de un cuento, etc.) **2** **~s** *npl* : moral *f*, moralidad *f* — **morale** [mə'ræl] *n* : moral *f* — **morality** [mə'ræləti] *n, pl* **-ties** : moralidad *f*

morbid ['mɔrbɪd] *adj* : morboso

more ['mɔr] *adj* : más — **~** *adv* **1** : más **2** **— and ~** : cada vez más **3** **~ or less** : más o menos **4 once ~** : una vez más — **~** *n* : más *m* — **~** *pron* : más — **moreover** [mɔr'oːvər] *adv* : además

morgue ['mɔrg] *n* : depósito *m* de cadáveres

morning ['mɔrnɪŋ] *n* **1** : mañana *f* **2 good ~!** : ¡buenos días! **3 in the ~** : por la mañana

moron ['mɔr,ɑn] *n* : estúpido *m*, -da *f*; imbécil *mf*

morose [mə'roːs] *adj* : malhumorado

morphine ['mɔr,fiːn] *n* : morfina *f*

morsel ['mɔrsəl] *n* **1** BITE : bocado *m* **2** FRAGMENT : pedazo *m*

mortal ['mɔrtəl] *adj* : mortal — **~** *n* : mortal *mf* — **mortality** [mɔr'tæləti] *n* : mortalidad *f*

mortar ['mɔrtər] *n* : mortero *m*

mortgage ['mɔrgɪdʒ] *n* : hipoteca *f* — **~** *vt* **-gaged; -gaging** : hipotecar

mortify ['mɔrtə,faɪ] *vt* **-fied; -fying 1** : mortificar **2** HUMILIATE : avergonzar

mosaic [mo'zeɪɪk] *n* : mosaico *m*

Moslem ['mɑzləm] → **Muslim**

mosque ['mɑsk] *n* : mezquita *f*

mosquito [mə'skiːto] *n, pl* **-toes** : mosquito *m*, zancudo *m Lat*

moss ['mɔs] *n* : musgo *m*

most ['moːst] *adj* **1** : la mayoría de, la mayor parte de **2 (the) ~** : más — **~** *adv* : más — **~** *n* : más *m*, máximo *m* — **~** *pron* : la mayoría, la mayor parte — **mostly** ['moːstli] *adv* **1** MAINLY : en su mayor parte, principalmente **2** USUALLY : normalmente

motel [mo'tel] *n* : motel *m*

moth ['mɔθ] *n* : palomilla *f*, polilla *f*

mother ['mʌðər] *n* : madre *f* — **~** *vt* **1** : cuidar de **2** SPOIL : mimar — **motherhood** ['mʌðər,hʊd] *n* : maternidad *f* — **mother-in-law** ['mʌðərɪn,lɔ] *n, pl* **mothers-in-law** : suegra *f* — **motherly** ['mʌðərli] *adj* : maternal — **mother-of-pearl** [,mʌðərəv'pərl] *n* : nácar *m*

motif [mo'tiːf] *n* : motivo *m*

motion ['moːʃən] *n* 1 : movimiento *m* 2 PROPOSAL : moción *f* 3 set in ~ : poner en marcha — ~ *vi* ~ to s.o. : hacer una señal a algn — **motionless** ['moːʃənləs] *adj* : inmóvil — **motion picture** *n* : película *f*

motive ['moːtɪv] *n* 1 : motivo *m* — **motivate** ['moːtəˌveɪt] *vt* -vated; -vating : motivar — **motivation** [ˌmoːtəˈveɪʃən] *n* : motivación *f*

motor ['moːtər] *n* : motor *m* — **motorbike** ['moːtərˌbaɪk] *n* : motocicleta *f* (pequeña), moto *f* — **motorboat** ['moːtərˌboːt] *n* : lancha *f* motora — **motorcycle** ['moːtərˌsaɪkəl] *n* : motocicleta *f* — **motorcyclist** ['moːtərˌsaɪkəlɪst] *n* : motociclista *mf* — **motorist** ['moːtərɪst] *n* : automovilista *mf*, motorista *mf Lat*

motto ['moːtoː] *n, pl* **-toes** : lema *m*

mould ['moːld] → **mold**

mound ['maʊnd] *n* 1 PILE : montón *m* 2 HILL : montículo *m*

mount[1] ['maʊnt] *n* 1 HORSE : montura *f* 2 SUPPORT : soporte *m* — ~ *vt* : montar (un caballo, etc.), subir (una escalera) — *vi* INCREASE : aumentar

mount[2] *n* HILL : monte *m* — **mountain** ['maʊntən] *n* : montaña *f* — **mountainous** ['maʊntənəs] *adj* : montañoso

mourn ['morn] *vt* : llorar (por) — *vi* : lamentarse — **mourner** ['mornər] *n* : doliente *mf* — **mournful** ['mornfəl] *adj* : triste — **mourning** ['mornɪŋ] *n* : luto *m*

mouse ['maʊs] *n, pl* **mice** ['maɪs] : ratón *m* — **mousetrap** ['maʊsˌtræp] *n* : ratonera *f*

moustache ['mʌˌstæʃ, məˈstæʃ] → **mustache**

mouth ['maʊθ] *n* : boca *f* (de una persona o un animal), desembocadura *f* (de un río) — **mouthful** ['maʊθˌfʊl] *n* : bocado *m* — **mouthpiece** ['maʊθˌpiːs] *n* : boquilla *f* (de un instrumento musical)

move ['muːv] *v* **moved; moving** *vi* 1 GO : ir 2 RELOCATE : mudarse 3 STIR : moverse 4 ACT : tomar medidas — *vt* 1 : mover 2 AFFECT : conmover 3 TRANSPORT : transportar, trasladar 4 PROPOSE : proponer — ~ *n* 1 MOVEMENT : movimiento *m* 2 RELOCATION : mudanza *f* 3 STEP : medida *f* — **movable** ['muːvəbəl] *or* **moveable** *adj* : movible, móvil — **movement** ['muːvmənt] *n* : movimiento *m*

movie ['muːvi] *n* 1 : película *f* 2 ~s *npl* : cine *m*

mow ['moː] *vt* **mowed; mowed** *or* **mown** ['moːn]; **mowing** : cortar (la hierba) — **mower** ['moːər] → **lawn mower**

Mr. ['mɪstər] *n, pl* **Messrs.** ['mɛsərz] : señor *m*

Mrs. ['mɪsəz, -səs, *esp South* 'mɪzəz, -zəs] *n, pl* **Mesdames** [meɪˈdeɪm, -ˈdæm] : señora *f*

Ms. ['mɪz] *n* : señora *f*, señorita *f*

much ['mʌtʃ] *adj* **more; most** : mucho — ~ *adv* **more** ['mor]; **most** ['moːst] 1 : mucho 2 as ~ as : tanto como 3 how ~? : ¿cuánto? 4 too ~ : demasiado — ~ *pron* : mucho, -cha

muck ['mʌk] *n* 1 DIRT : mugre *f*, suciedad *f* 2 MANURE : estiércol *m*

mucus ['mjuːkəs] *n* : mucosidad *f*

mud ['mʌd] *n* : barro *m*, lodo *m*

muddle ['mʌdəl] *v* **-dled; -dling** *vt* 1 CONFUSE : confundir 2 JUMBLE : desordenar — *vi* ~ **through** : arreglárselas — ~ *n* : confusión *f*, lío *m fam*

muddy ['mʌdi] *adj* **-dier; -est** : fangoso, lleno de barro

muffin ['mʌfən] *n* : mollete *m*

muffle ['mʌfəl] *vt* **-fled; -fling** : amortiguar (un sonido) — **muffler** ['mʌflər] *n* 1 SCARF : bufanda *f* 2 : silenciador *m*, mofle *m Lat* (de un automóvil)

mug ['mʌg] *n* CUP : tazón *m* — ~ *vt* : asaltar, atracar — **mugger** ['mʌgər] *n* : atracador *m*, -dora *f*

muggy ['mʌgi] *adj* **-gier; -est** : bochornoso

mule ['mjuːl] *n* : mula *f*

mull ['mʌl] *vt or* ~ **over** : reflexionar sobre

multicolored [ˌmʌltiˈkʌlərd, ˌmʌltaɪ-] *adj* : multicolor

multimedia [ˌmʌltiˈmiːdiə, ˌmʌltaɪ-] *adj* : multimedia

multinational [ˌmʌltiˈnæʃənəl, ˌmʌltaɪ-] *adj* : multinacional

multiple ['mʌltəpəl] *adj* : múltiple — ~ *n* : múltiplo *m* — **multiplication** [ˌmʌltəpləˈkeɪʃən] *n* : multiplicación *f* — **multiply** ['mʌltəˌplaɪ] *v* **-plied; -plying** *vt* : multiplicar — *vi* : multiplicarse

multitude ['mʌltəˌtuːd, -ˌtjuːd] *n* : multitud *f*

mum ['mʌm] *adj* keep ~ : guardar silencio

mumble ['mʌmbəl] *v* **-bled; -bling** *vt* : mascullar — *vi* : hablar entre dientes

mummy ['mʌmi] *n, pl* **-mies** : momia *f*

mumps ['mʌmps] *ns & pl* : paperas *fpl*

munch ['mʌntʃ] *v* : mascar, masticar

mundane [ˌmʌnˈdeɪn, 'mʌn-] *adj* : rutinario, ordinario

municipal [mju'nɪsəpəl] *adj* : municipal — **municipality** [mju,nɪsə'pælətɪ] *n, pl* **-ties** : municipio *m*

munitions [mju'nɪʃənz] *npl* : municiónes *fpl*

mural ['mjʊrəl] *n* : mural *m*

murder ['mərdər] *n* : asesinato *m*, homicidio *m* — ~ *vt* : asesinar, matar — *vi* : matar — **murderer** ['mərdərər] *n* : asesino *m*, -na *f*; homicida *mf* — **murderous** ['mərdərəs] *adj* : asesino, homicida

murky ['mərki] *adj* **-kier; -est** : turbio, oscuro

murmur ['mərmər] *n* : murmullo *m* — **murmur** *v* : murmurar

muscle ['mʌsəl] *n* : músculo *m* — ~ *vi* **-cled; -cling** *or* ~ **in** : meterse por la fuerza en — **muscular** ['mʌskjələr] *adj* **1** : muscular **2** STRONG : musculoso

muse[1] ['mjuːz] *n* : musa *f*

muse[2] *vi* **mused; musing** : meditar

museum [mju'ziːəm] *n* : museo *m*

mushroom ['mʌʃ,ruːm, -rʊm] *n* **1** : hongo *m*, seta *f* **2** : champiñón *m* (en la cocina) — ~ *vi* GROW : crecer rápidamente, multiplicarse

mushy ['mʌʃi] *adj* **mushier; -est 1** SOFT : blando **2** MAWKISH : sensiblero

music ['mjuːzɪk] *n* : música *f* — **musical** ['mjuːzɪkəl] *adj* : musical — ~ *n* : comedia *f* musical — **musician** [mju-'zɪʃən] *n* : músico *m*, -ca *f*

Muslim ['mʌzləm, 'mʊs-, 'muz-] *adj* : musulmán — ~ *n* : musulmán *m*, -mana *f*

muslin ['mʌzlən] *n* : muselina *f*

mussel ['mʌsəl] *n* : mejillón *m*

must ['mʌst] *v aux* **1** : deber, tener que **2** **you** ~ **come** : tienes que venir **3 you**

~ **be tired** : debes (de) estar cansado — ~ *n* : necesidad *f*

mustache ['mʌ,stæʃ, mʌ'stæʃ] *n* : bigote *m*, bigotes *mpl*

mustang ['mʌ,stæŋ] *n* : mustang *m*

mustard ['mʌstərd] *n* : mostaza *f*

muster ['mʌstər] *vt* **1** : reunir **2** *or* ~ **up** : armarse de, cobrar (valor, fuerzas, etc.)

musty ['mʌsti] *adj* **mustier; -est** : que huele a cerrado

mute ['mjuːt] *adj* **muter; mutest** : mudo — ~ *n* : mudo *m*, -da *f*

mutilate ['mjuːtə,leɪt] *vt* **-lated; -lating** : mutilar

mutiny ['mjuːtəni] *n, pl* **-nies** : motín *m* — ~ *vi* **-nied; -nying** : amotinarse

mutter ['mʌtər] *v* : murmurar

mutton ['mʌtən] *n* : carne *f* de carnero

mutual ['mjuːtʃʊəl] *adj* **1** : mutuo **2** COMMON : común — **mutually** ['mjuːtʃʊəli, -tʃəli] *adv* : mutuamente

muzzle ['mʌzəl] *n* **1** SNOUT : hocico *m* **2** : bozal *m* (para un perro, etc.) **3** : boca *f* (de un arma de fuego) — ~ *vt* **-zled; -zling** : poner un bozal a (un animal)

my ['maɪ] *adj* : mi

myopia [maɪ'oːpiə] *n* : miopía *f* — **myopic** [maɪ'oːpɪk, -'ɑ-] *adj* : miope

myself [maɪ'self] *pron* **1** (*reflexive*) : me **2** (*emphatic*) : yo mismo **3 by** ~ : solo

mystery ['mɪstəri] *n, pl* **-teries** : misterio *m* — **mysterious** [mɪ'strɪəs] *adj* : misterioso

mystic ['mɪstɪk] *adj or* **mystical** ['mɪstɪkəl] : místico

mystify ['mɪstə,faɪ] *vt* **-fied; -fying** : dejar perplejo, confundir

mystique [mɪ'stiːk] *n* : aura *f* de misterio

myth ['mɪθ] *n* : mito *m* — **mythical** ['mɪθɪkəl] *adj* : mítico

N

n ['en] *n, pl* **n's** *or* **ns** ['enz] : n *f*, decimocuarta letra del alfabeto inglés

nab ['næb] *vt* **nabbed; nabbing 1** ARREST : pescar *fam* **2** GRAB : agarrar

nag ['næg] *v* **nagged; nagging** *vi* COMPLAIN : quejarse — *vt* **1** ANNOY : fastidiar, dar la lata a **2** SCOLD : regañar — **nagging** *adj* : persistente

nail ['neɪl] *n* **1** : clavo *m* **2** : uña *f* (de un dedo) — ~ *vt or* ~ **down** : clavar — **nail file** *n* : lima *f* de uñas

naive *or* **naïve** ['nɑ'iːv] *adj* **-iver; -est** : ingenuo — **naïveté** [,nɑ,iːvə'teɪ, nɑ-'iːvə-] *n* : ingenuidad *f*

naked ['neɪkəd] *adj* **1** : desnudo **2 the** ~ **truth** : la pura verdad **3 to the** ~ **eye** : a simple vista

name ['neɪm] *n* **1** : nombre *m* **2** REPUTATION : fama *f* **3 what is your** ~? : ¿cómo se llama? **4** → **first name, surname** — ~ *vt* **named; naming 1** : poner nombre a **2** APPOINT : nombrar **3** — **a price** : fijar un precio — **nameless** ['neɪmləs] *adj* : anónimo — **namely** ['neɪmli] *adv* : a saber — **namesake** ['neɪm,seɪk] *n* : tocayo *m*, -ya *f*

nap[1] ['næp] *vi* **napped; napping** : echarse una siesta — ~ *n* : siesta *f*

nap² *n* : pelo *m* (de una tela)
nape ['neip, 'næp] *n or* ~ **of the neck** : nuca *f*
napkin ['næpkən] *n* 1 : servilleta *f* 2 → **sanitary napkin**
narcotic [nɑr'kɑtɪk] *n* : narcótico *m*, estupefaciente *m*
narrate ['nær,eɪt] *vt* -**rated**; -**rating** : narrar — **narration** [næ'reɪʃən] *n* : narración *f* — **narrative** ['nærətɪv] *n* : narración *f* — **narrator** ['nær,eɪtər] *n* : narrador *m*, -dora *f*
narrow ['nær,oː] *adj* 1 : estrecho, angosto 2 RESTRICTED : limitado — ~ *vi* : estrecharse — *vt* 1 : estrechar 2 *or* ~ **down** : limitar — **narrowly** ['næroli] *adv* : por poco — **narrow-minded** [,næro'maɪndəd] *adj* : de miras estrechas
nasal ['neɪzəl] *adj* : nasal
nasty ['næsti] *adj* -**tier**; -**est** 1 MEAN : malo, cruel 2 UNPLEASANT : desagradable 3 REPUGNANT : asqueroso — **nastiness** ['næstinəs] *n* : maldad *f*
nation ['neɪʃən] *n* : nación *f* — **national** ['næʃənəl] *adj* : nacional — **nationalism** ['næʃənə,lɪzəm] *n* : nacionalismo *m* — **nationality** [,næʃə'næləti] *n*, *pl* -**ties** : nacionalidad *f* — **nationalize** ['næʃənə,laɪz] *vt* -**ized**; -**izing** : nacionalizar — **nationwide** ['neɪʃən-'waɪd] *adj* : por todo el país
native ['neɪtɪv] *adj* 1 : natal (dícese de un país, etc.) 2 INNATE : innato 3 ~ **language** : lengua *f* materna — ~ *n* 1 : nativo *m*, -va *f* 2 be a ~ of : ser natural de — **Native American** : indio *m* americano, india *f* americana — **nativity** [nə'tɪvəti, neɪ-] *n*, *pl* -**ties** the Nativity : la Navidad
nature ['neɪtʃər] *n* 1 : naturaleza *f* 2 KIND : índole *f*, clase *f* 3 DISPOSITION : carácter *m*, natural *m* — **natural** ['nætʃərəl] *adj* : natural — **naturalize** ['nætʃərə,laɪz] *vt* -**ized**; -**izing** : naturalizar — **naturally** ['nætʃərəli] *adv* : naturalmente
naught ['nɔt] *n* 1 NOTHING : nada *f* 2 ZERO : cero *m*
naughty ['nɔti] *adj* -**tier**; -**est** 1 : travieso, pícaro 2 RISQUÉ : picante
nausea ['nɔziə, 'nɔʃə] *n* : náuseas *fpl* — **nauseating** ['nɔzi,eɪtɪŋ] *adj* : nauseabundo — **nauseous** ['nɔʃəs, -ziəs] *adj* 1 feel ~ : sentir náuseas 2 SICKENING : nauseabundo
nautical ['nɔtɪkəl] *adj* : náutico
naval ['neɪvəl] *adj* : naval
nave ['neɪv] *n* : nave *f* (de una iglesia)
navel ['neɪvəl] *n* : ombligo *m*

navigate ['nævə,geɪt] *v* -**gated**; -**gating** *vi* : navegar — *vt* 1 : gobernar (un barco), pilotar (un avión) 2 : navegar por (un río, etc.) — **navigable** ['nævɪgəbəl] *adj* : navegable — **navigation** [,nævə-'geɪʃən] *n* : navegación *f* — **navigator** ['nævə,geɪtər] *n* : navegante *mf*
navy ['neɪvi] *n*, *pl* -**vies** 1 : marina *f* de guerra 2 *or* ~ **blue** : azul *m* marino
near ['nɪr] *adv* : cerca — ~ *prep* : cerca de — ~ *adj* : cercano, próximo — ~ *vt* : acercarse a — **nearby** [nɪr'baɪ, 'nɪr-,baɪ] *adv* : cerca — ~ *adj* : cercano — **nearly** ['nɪrli] *adv* : casi — **nearsighted** ['nɪr,saɪtəd] *adj* : miope, corto de vista
neat ['niːt] *adj* 1 TIDY : muy arreglado 2 CLEVER : hábil, ingenioso — **neatly** ['niːtli] *adv* 1 : ordenadamente 2 CLEVERLY : hábilmente — **neatness** ['niːtnəs] *n* : pulcritud *f*, orden *m*
nebulous ['nɛbjuləs] *adj* : nebuloso
necessary ['nɛsə,seri] *adj* : necesario — **necessarily** [,nɛsə'serəli] *adv* : necesariamente — **necessitate** [nɪ'sɛsə-,teɪt] *vt* -**tated**; -**tating** : exigir, requerir — **necessity** [nɪ'sɛsəti] *n*, *pl* -**ties** 1 : necesidad *f* 2 **necessities** *npl* : cosas *fpl* indispensables
neck ['nɛk] *n* 1 : cuello *m* (de una persona o una botella), pescuezo *m* (de un animal) 2 COLLAR : cuello *m* — **necklace** ['nɛkləs] *n* : collar *m* — **necktie** ['nɛk,taɪ] *n* : corbata *f*
nectar ['nɛktər] *n* : néctar *m*
nectarine [,nɛktə'riːn] *n* : nectarina *f*
need ['niːd] *n* : necesidad *f* 2 if ~ be : si hace falta — ~ *vt* 1 : necesitar, exigir 2 ~ **to** : tener que — *v aux* : tener que
needle ['niːdəl] *n* : aguja *f* — ~ *vt* -**dled**; -**dling** : pinchar
needless ['niːdləs] *adj* 1 : innecesario 2 ~ **to say** : de más está decir
needlework ['niːdəl,wərk] *n* : bordado *m*
needn't ['niːdənt] (*contraction of* **need not**) → **need**
needy ['niːdi] **needier**; -**est** *adj* : necesitado
negative ['nɛgətɪv] *adj* : negativo — ~ *n* 1 : negación *f* (en gramática) 2 : negativo *m* (en fotografía)
neglect [nɪ'glɛkt] *vt* : descuidar — ~ *n* : descuido *m*, abandono *m*
negligee [,nɛglə'ʒeɪ] *n* : negligé *m*
negligence ['nɛglɪdʒənts] *n* : negligencia *f*, descuido *m* — **negligent** ['nɛg-lɪdʒənt] *adj* : negligente, descuidado
negligible ['nɛglɪdʒəbəl] *adj* : insignificante

negotiate [nɪˈgoːʃiˌeɪt] v **-ated; -ating** : negociar — **negotiable** [nɪˈgoːʃəbəl, -ʃiə-] adj : negociable — **negotiation** [nɪˌgoːʃiˈeɪʃən, -siˈeɪ-] n : negociación f — **negotiator** [nɪˈgoːʃiˌeɪtər, -siˌeɪ-] n : negociador m, -dora f

Negro [ˈniːˌgroː] n, pl **-groes** *sometimes considered offensive* : negro m, -gra f

neigh [neɪ] vi : relinchar — ~ n : relincho m

neighbor *or Brit* **neighbour** [ˈneɪbər] n : vecino m, -na f — **neighborhood** *or Brit* **neighbourhood** [ˈneɪbərˌhud] n **1** : barrio m, vecindario m **2 in the ~ of** : alrededor de — **neighborly** *or Brit* **neighbourly** [ˈneɪbərli] adv : amable

neither [ˈniːðər, ˈnaɪ-] conj **1 ~...nor** : ni...ni **2 ~ and/do I** : yo tampoco — ~ pron : ninguno, -na — ~ adj : ninguno (de los dos)

neon [ˈniːˌɑn] n : neón m

nephew [ˈneˌfjuː, *chiefly British* ˈneˌvjuː] n : sobrino m

Neptune [ˈnepˌtuːn, -ˌtjuːn] n : Neptuno m

nerve [ˈnərv] n **1** : nervio m **2** COURAGE : coraje m **3** GALL : descaro m **4 ~s** npl JITTERS : nervios mpl — **nervous** [ˈnərvəs] adj : nervioso — **nervousness** [ˈnərvəsnəs] n : nerviosismo m — **nervy** [ˈnərvi] adj **nervier; -est** : descarado

nest [ˈnest] n : nido m — vi : anidar

nestle [ˈnesəl] vi **-tled; -tling** : acurrucarse

net¹ [ˈnet] n : red f — ~ vt **netted; netting** : pescar, atrapar (con una red)

net² adj : neto — ~ vt **netted; netting** YIELD : producir neto

nettle [ˈnetəl] n : ortiga f

network [ˈnetˌwərk] n : red f

neurology [nʊˈrɑlədʒi, njʊ-] n : neurología f

neurosis [nʊˈroːsɪs, njʊ-] n, pl **-roses** [-ˌsiːz] : neurosis f — **neurotic** [nʊˈrɑtɪk, njʊ-] adj : neurótico

neuter [ˈnuːtər, ˈnjuː-] adj : neutro — vt : castrar

neutral [ˈnuːtrəl, ˈnjuː-] n : punto m muerto (de un automóvil) — ~ adj **1** : neutral **2** : neutro (en electrotecnia o química) — **neutrality** [nuːˈtræləˌti, njuː-] n : neutralidad f — **neutralize** [ˈnuːtrəˌlaɪz, ˈnjuː-] vt **-ized; -izing** : neutralizar

neutron [ˈnuːˌtrɑn, ˈnjuː-] n : neutrón m

never [ˈnevər] adv **1** : nunca, jamás **2** NOT : no **3 ~ again** : nunca más **4 ~ mind** : no importa — **nevermore** [ˌnevərˈmor] adv : nunca jamás — **nevertheless** [ˌnevərðəˈles] adv : sin embargo, no obstante

new [ˈnuː, ˈnjuː] adj : nuevo — **newborn** [ˈnuːˌbɔrn, ˈnjuː-] adj : recién nacido — **newcomer** [ˈnuːˌkʌmər, ˈnjuː-] n : recién llegado m, -da f — **newly** [ˈnuːli, ˈnjuː-] adv : recién, recientemente — **newlywed** [ˈnuːliˌwed, ˈnjuː-] n : recién casado m, -da f — **news** [ˈnuːz, ˈnjuːz] n : noticias fpl — **newscast** [ˈnuːzˌkæst, ˈnjuː-] n : noticiario m, noticiero m Lat — **newscaster** [ˈnuːzˌkæstər, ˈnjuː-] n : presentador m, -dora f (de un noticiario) — **newsletter** [ˈnuːzˌletər, ˈnjuː-] n : boletín m informativo — **newspaper** [ˈnuːzˌpeɪpər, ˈnjuːz-] n : periódico m, diario m — **newsstand** [ˈnuːzˌstænd, ˈnjuːz-] n : puesto m de periódicos

newt [ˈnuːt, ˈnjuːt] n : tritón m

New Year's Day n : día m del Año Nuevo

next [ˈnekst] adj **1** : próximo **2** FOLLOWING : siguiente — ~ adv **1** : la próxima vez **2** AFTERWARD : después, luego **3** NOW : ahora — **next-door** [ˈnekstˈdor] adj : de al lado — **next to** adv ALMOST : casi — ~ prep BESIDE : al lado de

nib [ˈnɪb] n : plumilla f

nibble [ˈnɪbəl] vt **-bled; -bling** : mordisquear

Nicaraguan [ˌnɪkəˈrɑgwən] adj : nicaragüense

nice [ˈnaɪs] adj **nicer; nicest 1** PLEASANT : agradable, bueno **2** KIND : amable — **nicely** [ˈnaɪsli] adv **1** WELL : bien **2** KINDLY : amablemente — **niceness** [ˈnaɪsnəs] n : amabilidad f — **niceties** [ˈnaɪsəˌtiz] npl : detalles mpl, sutilezas fpl

niche [ˈnɪtʃ] n **1** : nicho m **2 find one's ~** : hacerse su hueco

nick [ˈnɪk] n **1** : corte m pequeño, muesca f **2 in the ~ of time** : justo a tiempo — ~ vt : hacer una muesca en

nickel [ˈnɪkəl] n **1** : níquel m (metal) **2** : moneda f de cinco centavos

nickname [ˈnɪkˌneɪm] n : apodo m, sobrenombre m — ~ vt **-named; -naming** : apodar

nicotine [ˈnɪkəˌtiːn] n : nicotina f

niece [ˈniːs] n : sobrina f

niggling [ˈnɪgəlɪŋ] adj **1** PETTY : insignificante **2** PERSISTENT : constante

night [ˈnaɪt] n **1** : noche f **2 at ~** : de noche **3 last ~** : anoche **4 tomorrow ~** : mañana por la noche — **nightclub** [ˈnaɪtˌklʌb] n : club m nocturno — **nightfall** [ˈnaɪtˌfɔl] n : anochecer m — **nightgown** [ˈnaɪtˌgaʊn] n : camisón m (de noche) — **nightly** ['naɪt] *adj* : de todas las noches — ~ *adv* : cada noche — **nightmare** ['naɪt,mær] *n* : pesadilla *f* — **nighttime** ['naɪt,taɪm] *n* : noche *f*

nil ['nɪl] *n* NOTHING : nada *f*

nimble ['nɪmbəl] *adj* -**bler; -blest** : ágil

nine ['naɪn] *adj* : nueve — ~ *n* : nueve *m* — **nine hundred** *adj* : novecientos — ~ *n* : novecientos *m* — **nineteen** [naɪn'tiːn] *adj* : diecinueve — ~ *n* : diecinueve *m* — **nineteenth** [naɪn'tiːnθ] *adj* : decimonoveno, decimonono — ~ *n* 1 : decimonoveno *m*, -na *f*; decimonono *m*, -na *f* (en una serie) 2 : diecinueveavo *m* (en matemáticas) — **ninetieth** ['naɪnti,əθ] *adj* : nonagésimo — ~ *n* 1 : nonagésimo *m*, -ma *f* (en una serie) 2 : noventavo *m* (en matemáticas) — **ninety** ['naɪnti] *adj* : noventa — ~ *n, pl* -**ties** : noventa *m* — **ninth** ['naɪnθ] *adj* : noveno — ~ *n* 1 : noveno *m*, -na *f* (en una serie) 2 : noveno *m* (en matemáticas)

nip ['nɪp] *vt* **nipped; nipping** 1 PINCH : pellizcar 2 BITE : mordisquear 3 ~ **in the bud** : cortar de raíz — ~ *n* 1 PINCH : pellizco *m* 2 NIBBLE : mordisco *m*

nipple ['nɪpəl] *n* 1 : pezón *m* (de una mujer) 2 : tetilla *f* (de un hombre o un biberón)

nitrogen ['naɪtrədʒən] *n* : nitrógeno *m*

nitwit ['nɪt,wɪt] *n* : idiota *mf*

no ['noʊ] *adv* : no — ~ *adj* 1 : ninguno 2 **I have** ~ **money** : no tengo dinero 3 **it's** ~ **trouble** : no es ningún problema 4 ~ **smoking** : prohibido fumar — ~ *n, pl* **noes** *or* **nos** ['noʊz] : no *m*

noble ['noʊbəl] *adj* -**bler; -blest** : noble — ~ *n* : noble *mf* — **nobility** [noʊ'bɪlə,ti] *n* : nobleza *f*

nobody ['noʊ,bɑdi, -,bɑdi] *pron* : nadie

nocturnal [nɑk'tərnəl] *adj* : nocturno

nod ['nɑd] *v* **nodded; nodding** *vi* 1 *or* ~ **yes** : asentir con la cabeza 2 ~ **off** : dormirse — *vt* ~ **one's head** : asentir con la cabeza — ~ *n* : señal *m* con la cabeza

noes → **no**

noise ['nɔɪz] *n* : ruido *m* — **noisily** ['nɔɪzəli] *adv* : ruidosamente — **noisy** ['nɔɪzi] *adj* **noisier; -est** : ruidoso

nomad ['noʊ,mæd] *n* : nómada *mf* — **nomadic** [noʊ'mædɪk] *adj* : nómada

nominal ['nɑmənəl] *adj* : nominal

nominate ['nɑmə,neɪt] *vt* -**nated; -nating** 1 : proponer, postular *Lat* 2 APPOINT : nombrar — **nomination** [nɑmə'neɪʃən] *n* 1 : propuesta *f*, postulación *f Lat* 2 APPOINTMENT : nombramiento *m*

nonalcoholic [nɑn,ælkə'hɔlɪk] *adj* : no alcohólico

nonchalant [nɑnʃə'lɑnt] *adj* : despreocupado

noncommissioned officer [nɑnkə'mɪʃənd] *n* : suboficial *mf*

noncommittal [nɑnkə'mɪtəl] *adj* : evasivo

nondescript [nɑndɪ'skrɪpt] *adj* : anodino, soso

none ['nʌn] *pron* 1 : ninguno, ninguna 2 **there are** ~ **left** : no hay más — ~ *adv* 1 **be** ~ **the worse** : no sufrir daño alguno 2 ~ **too happy** : nada contento 3 ~ **too soon** : a buena hora

nonentity [nɑn'entə,ti] *n, pl* -**ties** : persona *f* insignificante

nonetheless [nʌnðə'les] *adv* : sin embargo, no obstante

nonexistent [nɑnɪg'zɪstənt] *adj* : inexistente

nonfat [nɑn'fæt] *adj* : sin grasa

nonfiction [nɑn'fɪkʃən] *n* : no ficción *f*

nonprofit [nɑn'prɑfət] *adj* : sin fines lucrativos

nonsense ['nɑn,sents, 'nɑntsənts] *n* : tonterías *fpl*, disparates *mpl* — **nonsensical** [nɑn'sentsɪkəl] *adj* : absurdo

nonsmoker [nɑn'smoʊkər] *n* : no fumador *m*, -dora *f*

nonstop [nɑn'stɑp] *adj* : directo — ~ *adv* : sin parar

noodle ['nuːdəl] *n* : fideo *m*

nook ['nʊk] *n* : rincón *m*

noon ['nuːn] *n* : mediodía *m*

no one *pron* : nadie

noose ['nuːs] *n* 1 : dogal *m*, soga *f* 2 LASSO : lazo *m*

nor ['nɔr] *conj* 1 **neither...**~ : ni...ni 2 ~ **I** : yo tampoco

norm ['nɔrm] *n* 1 : norma *f* 2 **the** ~ : lo normal — **normal** ['nɔrməl] *adj* : normal — **normality** [nɔr'mælə,ti] *n* : normalidad *f* — **normally** *adv* : normalmente

north ['nɔrθ] *adv* : al norte — ~ *adj* : norte, del norte — ~ *n* 1 : norte *m* 2 **the North** : el Norte — **North American** *adj* : norteamericano — **northeast** [nɔrθ'iːst] *adv* : hacia el nordeste — ~ *adj* : nordeste, del nordeste — ~ *n* : nordeste *m*, noreste *m* — **northeastern** [nɔrθ'iːstərn] *adj* : nordeste, del nordeste — **northerly** ['nɔrðərli] *adj* : del norte — **northern** ['nɔrðərn] *adj* : del norte, norteño — **northwest** [nɔrθ'wɛst] *adv* : hacia el noroeste —

~ *adj* : noroeste, del noroeste — ~ *n* : noroeste *m* — **northwestern** [nɔrθ-'wɛstərn] *adj* : noroeste, del noroeste

Norwegian [nɔr'wiːdʒən] *adj* : noruego

nose ['noːz] *n* **1** : nariz *f* (de una persona), hocico *m* (de un animal) **2 blow one's ~** : sonarse las narices — ~ *vi* **nosed; nosing** *or* ~ **around** : meter las narices — **nosebleed** ['noːz,bliːd] *n* : hemorragia *f* nasal — **nosedive** ['noːz,daɪv] *n* : descenso *m* en picada

nostalgia [nɑ'stældʒə, nə-] *n* : nostalgia *f* — **nostalgic** [nɑ'stældʒɪk, nə-] *adj* : nostálgico

nostril ['nɑstrəl] *n* : ventana *f* de la nariz

nosy *or* **nosey** ['noːzi] *adj* **nosier; -est** : entrometido

not ['nɑt] *adv* **1** : no **2 he's ~ tired** : no esta cansado **3 I hope ~** : espero que no **4 ~ ... anything** : no...nada

notable ['noːtəbəl] *adj* : notable — ~ *n* : personaje *m* — **notably** ['noːtəbli] *adv* : notablemente

notary public ['noːtəri-] *n, pl* **notaries public** *or* **notary publics** : notario *m*, -ria *f*

notation [noʊ'teɪʃən] *n* : anotación *f*

notch ['nɑtʃ] *n* : muesca *f*, corte *m* — ~ *vt* : hacer un corte en

note ['noʊt] *vt* **noted; noting 1** NOTICE : observar, notar **2** RECORD : anotar — ~ *n* **1** : nota *f* **2 of ~** : destacado **3 take ~ of** : prestar atención a **4 take ~s** : apuntar — **notebook** ['noʊt,bʊk] *n* : libreta *f*, cuaderno *m* — **noted** ['noʊtəd] *adj* : renombrado, célebre — **noteworthy** ['noʊt,wərði] *adj* : notable

nothing ['nʌθɪŋ] *pron* **1** : nada **2 be ~ but** : no ser más que **3 for ~** FREE : gratis — ~ *n* **1** ZERO : zero *m* **2** TRIFLE : nimiedad *f*

notice ['noʊtɪs] *n* **1** SIGN : letrero *m*, aviso *m* **2 at a moment's ~** : sin previo aviso **3 be given one's ~** : ser despedido **4 take ~ of** : prestar atención a — ~ *vt* **-ticed; -ticing** : notar — **noticeable** ['noʊtɪsəbəl] *adj* : perceptible, evidente

notify ['noʊtə,faɪ] *vt* **-fied; -fying** : notificar, avisar — **notification** [,noʊtəfə-'keɪʃən] *n* : notificación *f*, aviso *m*

notion ['noʊʃən] *n* **1** : noción *f*, idea *f* **2 ~s** *npl* : artículos *mpl* de mercería

notorious [noʊ'toːriəs] *adj* : de mala fama — **notoriety** [,noʊtə'raɪəti] *n* : mala fama *f*, notoriedad *f*

notwithstanding [,nɑtwɪθ'stændɪŋ, -wɪð-] *prep* : a pesar de, no obstante — ~ *adv* : sin embargo — ~ *conj* : a pesar de que

nougat ['nuːgət] *n* : turrón *m*

nought ['nɔt, 'nɑt] → **naught**

noun ['naʊn] *n* : nombre *m*, sustantivo *m*

nourish ['nərɪʃ] *vt* : nutrir — **nourishing** ['nərɪʃɪŋ] *adj* : nutritivo — **nourishment** ['nərɪʃmənt] *n* : alimento *m*

novel ['nɑvəl] *adj* : original, novedoso — ~ *n* : novela *f* — **novelist** ['nɑvəlɪst] *n* : novelista *mf* — **novelty** ['nɑvəlti] *n, pl* **-ties** : novedad *f*

November [noʊ'vɛmbər] *n* : noviembre *m*

novice ['nɑvɪs] *n* : novato *m*, -ta *f*; principiante *mf*

now ['naʊ] *adv* **1** : ahora **2** THEN : entonces **3 from ~ on** : de ahora en adelante **4 ~ and then** : de vez en cuando **5 right ~** : ahora mismo — ~ *conj* *or* ~ **that** : ahora que, ya que — **~ n** : a year from ~ : dentro de un año **2 by ~** : ya **3 until ~** : hasta ahora — **nowadays** ['naʊə,deɪz] *adv* : hoy en día

nowhere ['noː,hwer] *adv* **1** (*indicating location*) : por ninguna parte, por ningún lado **2** (*indicating motion*) : a ninguna parte, a ningún lado **3 I'm ~ near finished** : aún me falta mucho para terminar **4 it's ~ near here** : queda bastante lejos de aquí — ~ *n* : ninguna parte *f*

nozzle ['nɑzəl] *n* : boca *f* (de una manguera, etc.)

nuance ['nuː,ɑns, 'nju-] *n* : matiz *m*

nucleus ['nuːkliəs, 'nju-] *n, pl* **-clei** [-kli,aɪ] : núcleo *m* — **nuclear** ['nuːkliər, 'nju-] *adj* : nuclear

nude ['nuːd, 'njuːd] *adj* **nuder; nudest** : desnudo — ~ *n* : desnudo *m*

nudge ['nʌdʒ] *vt* **nudged; nudging** : dar un codazo a — ~ *n* : toque *m* (con el codo)

nudity ['nuːdəti, 'nju-] *n* : desnudez *f*

nugget ['nʌgət] *n* : pepita *f* (de oro, etc.)

nuisance ['nuːsəns, 'nju-] *n* **1** ANNOYANCE : fastidio *m*, molestia *f* **2** PEST : pesado *m*, -da *f* *fam*

null ['nʌl] *adj* **~ and void** : nulo y sin efecto

numb ['nʌm] *adj* **1** : entumecido, dormido **2 ~ with fear** : paralizado de miedo — ~ *vt* : entumecer, adormecer

number ['nʌmbər] *n* **1** : número *m* **2 a ~ of** : varios — ~ *vt* **1** : numerar **2** INCLUDE : contar, incluir **3** TOTAL : ascender a

numeral ['nuːmərəl, 'nju-] *n* : número *m* — **numeric** [nʊ'mɛrɪk, nju-] *or* **numerical** [nʊ'mɛrɪkəl, nju-] *adj* : numérico — **numerous** ['nuːmərəs, 'nju-] *adj* : numeroso

nun ['nʌn] *n* : monja *f*
nuptial ['nʌpʃəl] *adj* : nupcial
nurse ['nərs] *n* **1** : enfermero *m*, -ra *f* **2** → **nursemaid** — ~ *vt* **nursed; nursing 1** : cuidar (de), atender **2** SUCKLE : amamantar — **nursemaid** ['nərs,meɪd] *n* : niñera *f* — **nursery** ['nərsəri] *n, pl* **-eries 1** : cuarto *m* de los niños **2** *or* **day** ~ : guardería *f* **3** : vivero *m* (de plantas) — **nursing home** *n* : asilo *m* de ancianos
nurture ['nərtʃər] *vt* **-tured; -turing 1** NOURISH : nutrir **2** EDUCATE : criar, educar **3** FOSTER : alimentar
nut ['nʌt] *n* **1** : nuez *f* **2** LUNATIC : loco *m*, -ca *f* **3** ENTHUSIAST : fanático *m*, -ca *f* **4** ~**s and bolts** : tuercas y tornillos —

nutcracker ['nʌt,krækər] *n* : cascanueces *m*
nutmeg ['nʌt,mɛg] *n* : nuez *f* moscada
nutrient ['nu:triənt, 'nju:-] *n* : nutriente *m*
nutrition [nu'trɪʃən, nju-] *n* : nutrición *f* — **nutritional** [nu'trɪʃənəl, nju-] *adj* : nutritivo — **nutritious** [nu'trɪʃəs, nju-] *adj* : nutritivo
nuts ['nʌts] *adj* : loco
nutshell ['nʌt,ʃɛl] *n* **1** : cáscara *f* de nuez **2 in a** ~ : en pocas palabras
nutty ['nʌti] *adj* **-tier; -tiest** : loco
nuzzle ['nʌzəl] *v* **-zled; -zling** *vi* : acurrucarse — *vt* : acariciar con el hocico
nylon ['naɪlɑn] *n* **1** : nilón *m* **2** ~**s** *npl* : medias *fpl* de nilón
nymph ['nɪmpf] *n* : ninfa *f*

O

o ['oː] *n, pl* **o's** *or* **os** ['oːz] **1** : o *f*, decimoquinta letra del alfabeto inglés **2** ZERO : cero *m*
O ['oː] → **oh**
oaf ['oːf] *n* : zoquete *m*
oak ['oːk] *n, pl* **oaks** *or* **oak** : roble *m*
oar ['or] *n* : remo *m*
oasis [o'eɪsɪs] *n, pl* **oases** [-,siːz] : oasis *m*
oath ['oːθ] *n, pl* **oaths** ['oːðz, 'oːθs] **1** : juramento *m* **2** SWEARWORD : palabrota *f*
oats ['oːts] *npl* : avena *f* — **oatmeal** ['oːt,miːl] *n* : harina *f* de avena
obedient [o'biːdiənt] *adj* : obediente — **obedience** [o'biːdiənts] *n* : obediencia *f*
obese [o'biːs] *adj* : obeso — **obesity** [o'biːsəti] *n* : obesidad *f*
obey [o'beɪ] *v* **obeyed; obeying** : obedecer
obituary [ə'bɪtʃu̥ɛri] *n, pl* **-aries** : obituario *m*
object ['ɑbdʒɪkt] *n* **1** : objeto *m* **2** AIM : objetivo *m* **3** : complemento *m* (en gramática) — ~ [əb'dʒɛkt] *vt* : objetar — *vi* ~ **to** : oponerse a — **objection** [əb'dʒɛkʃən] *n* : objeción *f* — **objectionable** [əb'dʒɛkʃənəbəl] *adj* : desagradable — **objective** [əb'dʒɛktɪv] *adj* : objetivo — ~ *n* : objetivo *m*
oblige [ə'blaɪdʒ] *vt* **obliged; obliging 1** : obligar **2 be much** ~**d** : estar muy agradecido **3** ~ **s.o.** : hacer un favor a algn — **obligation** [,ɑblə'geɪʃən] *n* : obligación *f* — **obligatory** [ə'blɪgə,tori] *adj* : obligatorio — **obliging** [ə'blaɪdʒɪŋ] *adj* : atento, servicial

oblique [o'bliːk] *adj* **1** SLANTING : oblicuo **2** INDIRECT : indirecto
obliterate [ə'blɪtə,reɪt] *vt* **-ated; -ating 1** ERASE : borrar **2** DESTROY : arrasar
oblivion [ə'blɪviən] *n* : olvido *m* — **oblivious** [ə'blɪviəs] *adj* : inconsciente
oblong ['ɑ,blɔŋ] *adj* : oblongo — ~ *n* : rectángulo *m*
obnoxious [ɑb'nɑkʃəs, əb-] *adj* : odioso
oboe ['oː,boː] *n* : oboe *m*
obscene [ɑb'siːn, əb-] *adj* : obsceno — **obscenity** [ɑb'sɛnəti, əb-] *n, pl* **-ties** : obscenidad *f*
obscurity [ɑb'skjurəti, əb-] *n, pl* **-ties** : oscuridad *f* — **obscure** [ɑb'skjur, əb-] *adj* : oscuro — ~ *vt* **-scured; -scuring 1** DARKEN : oscurecer **2** HIDE : ocultar
observe [əb'zərv] *v* **-served; -serving** *vt* : observar — *vi* WATCH : mirar — **observance** [əb'zərvənts] *n* **1** : observancia *f* **2 religious** ~**s** : prácticas *fpl* religiosas — **observant** [əb'zərvənt] *adj* : observador — **observation** [,ɑbsər'veɪʃən, -zər-] *n* : observación *f* — **observatory** [əb'zərvə,tori] *n, pl* **-ries** : observatorio *m*
obsess [əb'sɛs] *vt* : obsesionar — **obsession** [ɑb'sɛʃən, əb-] *n* : obsesión *f* — **obsessive** [ɑb'sɛsɪv, əb-] *adj* : obsesivo
obsolete [,ɑbsə'liːt, 'ɑbsə,-] *adj* : obsoleto, desusado
obstacle ['ɑbstɪkəl] *n* : obstáculo *m*
obstetrics [əb'stɛtrɪks] *n* : obstetricia *f*
obstinate ['ɑbstənət] *adj* : obstinado
obstruct [əb'strʌkt] *vt* **1** BLOCK : obstru-

ir 2 HINDER : obstaculizar — **obstruction** [əb'strʌkʃən] n : obstrucción f
obtain [əb'teɪn] vt : obtener, conseguir — **obtainable** [əb'teɪnəbəl] adj : asequible
obtrusive [əb'tru:sɪv] adj : entrometido (dícese de las personas), demasiado prominente (dícese de las cosas)
obtuse [ab'tu:s, əb-, -'tju:s] adj : obtuso
obvious ['ɑbviəs] adj : obvio, evidente — **obviously** ['ɑbviəsli] adv 1 CLEARLY : obviamente 2 OF COURSE : claro, por supuesto
occasion [ə'keɪʒən] n 1 : ocasión f on ~ : de vez en cuando — ~ vt : ocasionar — **occasional** [ə'keɪʒənəl] adj : poco frecuente, ocasional — **occasionally** [ə'keɪʒənəli] adv : de vez en cuando
occult [ə'kʌlt, 'ɑ,kʌlt] adj : oculto
occupy ['ɑkjə,paɪ] vt **-pied; -pying** 1 : ocupar 2 ~ **oneself** : entretenerse — **occupancy** ['ɑkjəpəntsi] n, pl **-cies** : ocupación f — **occupant** ['ɑkjəpənt] n : ocupante mf — **occupation** [,ɑkjə'peɪʃən] n : ocupación f — **occupational** [,ɑkjə'peɪʃənəl] adj : profesional
occur [ə'kʌr] vi **occurred; occurring** 1 : ocurrir 2 APPEAR : encontrarse 3 ~ **to s.o.** : ocurrirse a algn — **occurrence** [ə'kərənts] n 1 EVENT : acontecimiento m, suceso m 2 INCIDENCE : incidencia f
ocean ['o:ʃən] n : océano m
ocher or **ochre** ['o:kər] n : ocre m
o'clock [ə'klɑk] adv 1 **at 6** ~ : a las seis 2 **it's one** ~ : es la una 3 **it's ten** ~ : son las diez
octagon ['ɑktə,gɑn] n : octágono m — **octagonal** [ɑk'tægənəl] adj : octagonal
octave ['ɑktɪv] n : octava f
October [ɑk'to:bər] n : octubre m
octopus ['ɑktə,pus, -pəs] n, pl **-puses** or **-pi** [-,paɪ] : pulpo m
oculist ['ɑkjəlɪst] n : oculista mf
odd ['ɑd] adj 1 STRANGE : extraño, raro 2 : sin pareja (dícese de un calcetín, etc.) 3 **forty** ~ **years** : cuarenta y tantos años 4 ~ **jobs** : algunos trabajos mpl 5 ~ **number** : número m impar — **oddity** ['ɑdəti] n, pl **-ties** : rareza f — **oddly** ['ɑdli] adv : de manera extraña — **odds** ['ɑdz] npl 1 CHANCES : probabilidades fpl 2 **at** ~ : en desacuerdo 3 **five to one** ~ : cinco contra uno (en apuestas) — **odds and ends** npl : cosas fpl sueltas
ode ['o:d] n : oda f
odious ['o:diəs] adj : odioso
odor or Brit **odour** ['o:dər] n : olor m —

odorless or Brit **odourless** ['o:dərləs] adj : inodoro
of ['ʌv, 'əv] prep 1 : de 2 **five minutes** ~ **ten** : las diez menos cinco 3 **the eighth** ~ **April** : el ocho de abril
off ['ɔf] adv 1 **be** ~ LEAVE : irse 2 **cut** ~ : cortar 3 **day** ~ : día m de descanso 4 **fall** ~ : caerse 5 **doze** ~ : dormirse 6 **far** ~ : lejos 7 ~ **and on** : de vez en cuando 8 **shut** ~ : apagar 9 **ten miles** ~ : a diez millas de aquí — ~ prep 1 : de 2 **be** ~ **duty** : estar libre 3 ~ **center** : descentrado — ~ adj 1 CANCELED : cancelado 2 OUT : apagado 3 **an** ~ **chance** : una posibilidad remota
offend [ə'fend] vt : ofender — **offender** [ə'fendər] n : delincuente mf — **offense** or **offence** [ə'fents, 'ɔ,fents] n 1 AFFRONT : afrenta f 2 ASSAULT : ataque m 3 : ofensiva f (en deportes) 4 CRIME : delito m 5 **take** ~ : ofenderse — **offensive** [ə'fentsɪv,'ɔ,fent-] adj : ofensivo — ~ n : ofensiva f
offer ['ɔfər] vt : ofrecer — ~ n : oferta f — **offering** ['ɔfərɪŋ] n : ofrenda f
offhand ['ɔf'hænd] adv : de improviso, en este momento — ~ adj : improvisado
office ['ɔfəs] n 1 : oficina f 2 POSITION : cargo m 3 **run for** ~ : presentarse como candidato — **officer** ['ɔfəsər] n 1 : oficial mf 2 or **police** ~ : agente mf (de policía) — **official** [ə'fɪʃəl] n : funcionario m, -ria f — ~ adj : oficial
offing ['ɔfɪŋ] n **in the** ~ : en perspectiva
offset ['ɔf,set] vt **-set; -setting** : compensar
offshore ['ɔf,ʃor] adv : a una distancia de la costa
offspring ['ɔf,sprɪŋ] ns & pl : prole f, progenie f
often ['ɔfən, 'ɔftən] adv 1 : muchas veces, a menudo, con frecuencia 2 **every so** ~ : de vez en cuando
ogle ['o:gəl] vt **ogled; ogling** : comerse con los ojos
ogre ['o:gər] n : ogro m
oh ['o:] interj 1 : ¡oh!, ¡ah! 2 ~ **no!** : ¡ay no! 3 ~ **really?** : ¿de veras?
oil ['ɔɪl] n 1 : aceite m 2 PETROLEUM : petróleo m 3 or ~ **painting** : óleo m — ~ vt : lubricar — **oilskin** ['ɔɪl,skɪn] n : hule m — **oily** ['ɔɪli] adj **oilier; -est** : aceitoso, grasiento
ointment ['ɔɪntmənt] n : ungüento m, pomada f
OK or **okay** [,o:'keɪ] adv 1 : muy bien 2 ~ **!** : ¡de acuerdo!, ¡bueno! — ~ adj 1

ALL RIGHT : bien 2 it's ~ with me : por mí no hay problema — ~ *n* : visto *m* bueno — [oʼkeɪ] *vt* OK'd *or* okayed [oʼkeɪd]; OK'ing *or* okaying : dar el visto bueno a

okra ['oːkrə, *South also* -kri] *n* : quingombó *m*

old ['oːld] *adj* 1 : viejo FORMER : antiguo 3 any ~ : cualquier 4 be ten years ~ : tener diez años (de edad) 5 ~ age : vejez *f* 6 ~ man : anciano *m* 7 ~ woman : anciana *f* — ~ *n* the ~ : los viejos, los ancianos — old-fashioned ['oːld'fæʃənd] *adj* : anticuado

olive ['ɑlɪv, -ləv] *n* 1 : aceituna *f* (fruta) 2 *or* ~ green : verde *m* oliva

Olympic [o'lɪmpɪk] *adj* : olímpico — Olympics [o'lɪmpɪks] *npl* the ~ : las Olimpiadas, las Olimpíadas

omelet *or* omelette ['ɑmlət, 'ɑmə-] *n* : omelette *mf Lat*, tortilla *f* francesa *Spain*

omen ['oːmən] *n* : agüero *m* — ominous ['ɑmənəs] *adj* : ominoso, de mal agüero

omit [o'mɪt] *vt* omitted; omitting : omitir — omission [o'mɪʃən] *n* : omisión *f*

omnipotent [ɑm'nɪpətənt] *adj* : omnipotente

on ['ɑn, 'ɔn] *prep* 1 : en 2 ABOUT : sobre 3 ~ foot : a pie 4 ~ Monday : el lunes 5 ~ the right : a la derecha 6 ~ vacation : de vacaciones 7 talk ~ the phone : hablar por teléfono — ~ *adv* 1 and so ~ : etcétera 2 from that moment ~ : a partir de ese momento 3 keep ~ : seguir 4 later ~ : más tarde 5 ~ and ~ : sin parar 6 put ~ : ponerse (ropa), poner (música, etc.) 7 turn ~ : encender (una luz, etc.), abrir (una llave) — ~ *adj* 1 : encendido (dícese de luces, etc.), abierto (dícese de llaves) 2 be ~ to : estar enterado de

once ['wʌns] *adv* 1 : una vez 2 FORMERLY : antes — ~ *n* 1 at ~ : TOGETHER : al mismo tiempo 2 at ~ IMMEDIATELY : inmediatamente — ~ *conj* : una vez que

oncoming ['ɑn,kʌmɪŋ, 'ɔn-] *adj* : que viene

one ['wʌn] *adj* 1 : un, uno 2 ONLY : único 3 *or* ~ and the same : el mismo — ~ *n* 1 : uno *m* (número) — ~ by ~ : uno a uno — ~ *pron* 1 : uno, una 2 ~ another : el uno al otro 3 ~ never knows : nunca se sabe 4 that ~ : aquél, aquella 5 which ~? : ¿cuál? — oneself [,wʌn'sɛlf] *pron* 1 (*used re-*

flexively) : se 2 (*used after prepositions*) : sí mismo, sí misma 3 (*used emphatically*) : uno mismo, una misma 4 by ~ : solo — one-sided ['wʌn'saɪdəd] *adj* 1 UNEQUAL : desigual 2 BIASED : parcial — one-way ['wʌn'weɪ] *adj* 1 : de sentido único (dícese de una calle) 2 ~ ticket : boleto *m* de ida

ongoing ['ɑn,goɪŋ] *adj* : en curso, corriente

onion ['ʌnjən] *n* : cebolla *f*

only ['oːnli] *adj* : único — ~ *adv* 1 : sólo, solamente 2 if ~ : ojalá, por lo menos — ~ *conj* BUT : pero

onset ['ɑn,sɛt] *n* : comienzo *m*, llegada *f*

onslaught ['ɑn,slɔt, 'ɔn-] *n* : ataque *m*, arremetida *f*

onto ['ɑn,tuː, 'ɔn-] *prep* : sobre

onus ['oːnəs] *n* : responsabilidad *f*

onward ['ɑnwərd, 'ɔn-] *adv & adj* : hacia adelante

onyx ['ɑnɪks] *n* : ónix *m*

ooze ['uːz] *v* oozed; oozing : rezumar

opal ['oːpəl] *n* : ópalo *m*

opaque [o'peɪk] *adj* : opaco

open ['oːpən] *adj* 1 : abierto 2 AVAILABLE : vacante, libre 3 an ~ question : una cuestión pendiente — ~ *vt* : abrir — *vi* 1 : abrirse 2 BEGIN : comenzar — ~ *n* in the ~ 1 OUTDOORS : al aire libre 2 KNOWN : sacado a la luz — open-air ['oːpən'ær] *adj* : al aire libre — opener ['oːpənər] *n* 1 : abridor *m* 2 *or* bottle ~ : abrebotellas *m* 3 *or* can ~ : abrelatas *m* — opening ['oːpənɪŋ] *n* 1 : abertura *f* 2 BEGINNING : comienzo *m*, apertura *f* 3 OPPORTUNITY : opportunidad *f* — openly ['oːpənli] *adv* : abiertamente

opera ['ɑprə, 'ɑpərə] *n* : ópera *f*

operate ['ɑpə,reɪt] *v* -ated; -ating *vi* 1 FUNCTION : funcionar 2 ~ on s.o. : operar a algn — *vt* 1 : hacer funcionar (una máquina) 2 MANAGE : dirigir, manejar — operation [,ɑpə'reɪʃən] *n* 1 : operación *f* 2 FUNCTIONING : funcionamiento *m* — operational [,ɑpə'reɪʃənəl] *adj* : operacional — operative ['ɑpərətɪv, -,reɪ-] *adj* : en vigor — operator ['ɑpə,reɪtər] *n* 1 : operador *m*, -dora *f* 2 *or* machine ~ : operario *m*, -ria *f*

opinion [ə'pɪnjən] *n* : opinión *f* — opinionated [ə'pɪnjə,neɪtəd] *adj* : dogmático

opium ['oːpiəm] *n* : opio *m*

opossum [ə'pɑsəm] *n* : zarigüeya *f*, oposum *m*

opponent [ə'poːnənt] *n* : adversario *m*, -ria *f*; contrincante *mf* (en deportes)

opportunity [ˌɑpərˈtuːnət̬i, -tjuː-] *n, pl* **-ties** : oportunidad *f* — **opportune** [ˌɑpərˈtuːn, -ˈtjuːn] *adj* : oportuno — **opportunist** [ˌɑpərˈtuːnɪst, -ˈtjuː-] *n* : oportunista *mf*

oppose [əˈpoːz] *vt* **-posed; -posing** : oponerse a — **opposed** *adj* ~ **to** : en contra de

opposite [ˈɑpəzət] *adj* **1** FACING : de enfrente **2** CONTRARY : opuesto — ~ *n* **the** ~ : lo contrario, lo opuesto — ~ *adv* : enfrente — ~ *prep* : enfrente de, frente a — **opposition** [ˌɑpəˈzɪʃən] *n* **1** : oposición *f* **2 in** ~ **to** : en contra de

oppress [əˈpres] *vt* : oprimir — **oppression** [əˈpreʃən] *n* : opresión *f* — **oppressive** [əˈpresɪv] *adj* **1** : opresivo **2** STIFLING : agobiante — **oppressor** [əˈpresər] *n* : opresor *m*, -sora *f*

opt [ˈɑpt] *vi* ~ **for** : optar por

optic [ˈɑptɪk] *or* **optical** [-tɪkəl] *adj* : óptico — **optician** [ɑpˈtɪʃən] *n* : óptico *m*, -ca *f*

optimism [ˈɑptəˌmɪzəm] *n* : optimismo — **optimist** [ˈɑptəmɪst] *n* : optimista *mf* — **optimistic** [ˌɑptəˈmɪstɪk] *adj* : optimista

optimum [ˈɑptəməm] *n, pl* **-ma** [-mə] : lo óptimo, lo ideal

option [ˈɑpʃən] *n* **1** : opción *f* **2 have no** ~ : no tener más remedio — **optional** [ˈɑpʃənəl] *adj* : facultativo, opcional

opulence [ˈɑpjələns] *n* : opulencia *f* — **opulent** [ˈɑpjələnt] *adj* : opulento

or [ˈɔr] *conj* **1** (*indicating an alternative*) : o (u *before* o- *or* ho-) **2** (*following a negative*) : ni **3** ~ **else** : si no

oracle [ˈɔrəkəl] *n* : oráculo *m*

oral [ˈɔrəl] *adj* : oral

orange [ˈɔrɪndʒ] *n* **1** : naranja *f* (fruta) **2** : naranja *m* (color)

orator [ˈɔrət̬ər] *n* : orador *m*, -dora *f*

orbit [ˈɔrbət] *n* : órbita *f* — ~ *vt* : girar alrededor de — *vi* : orbitar

orchard [ˈɔrtʃərd] *n* : huerto *m*

orchestra [ˈɔrkəstrə] *n* : orquesta *f*

orchid [ˈɔrkɪd] *n* : orquídea *f*

ordain [ɔrˈdeɪn] *vt* **1** : ordenar (un sacerdote, etc.) **2** DECREE : decretar

ordeal [ɔrˈdiːl, ˈɔrˌdiːl] *n* : prueba *f* dura

order [ˈɔrdər] *vt* **1** : ordenar **2** : pedir (mercancías, etc.) — *vi* : hacer un pedido — ~ *n* **1** ARRANGEMENT : orden *m* **2** COMMAND : orden *f* **3** REQUEST : pedido *m* **4** : orden *f* (religiosa) **5 in** ~ **that** : para que **6 in** ~ **to** : para **7 out of** ~ : averiado, descompuesto *Lat* — **orderly** [ˈɔrdərli] *adj* : ordenado — ~ *n, pl* **-lies 1** : ordenanza *m* (en el

ejército) **2** : camillero *m* (en un hospital)

ordinary [ˈɔrdənˌeri] *adj* **1** : normal, corriente **2** MEDIOCRE : ordinario — **ordinarily** [ˌɔrdənˈerəli] *adv* : generalmente

ore [ˈɔr] *n* : mena *f*

oregano [əˈregəˌnoː] *n* : orégano *m*

organ [ˈɔrgən] *n* : órgano *m* — **organic** [ɔrˈgænɪk] *adj* : orgánico — **organism** [ˈɔrgəˌnɪzəm] *n* : organismo *m* — **organist** [ˈɔrgənɪst] *n* : organista *mf* — **organize** [ˈɔrgəˌnaɪz] *vt* **-nized; -nizing** : organizar — **organization** [ˌɔrgənəˈzeɪʃən] *n* : organización *f* — **organizer** [ˈɔrgəˌnaɪzər] *n* : organizador *m*, -dora *f*

orgasm [ˈɔrˌgæzəm] *n* : orgasmo *m*

orgy [ˈɔrdʒi] *n, pl* **-gies** : orgía *f*

Orient [ˈɔriˌent] *n* **the** ~ : el Oriente — **orient** *vt* : orientar — **oriental** [ˌɔriˈent̬əl] *adj* : del Oriente, oriental — **orientation** [ˌɔriˌenˈteɪʃən] *n* : orientación *f*

orifice [ˈɔrəfəs] *n* : orificio *m*

origin [ˈɔrədʒən] *n* : origen *m* — **original** [əˈrɪdʒənəl] *n* : original *m* — ~ *adj* : original — **originality** [əˌrɪdʒəˈnælət̬i] *n* : originalidad *f* — **originally** [əˈrɪdʒənəli] *adv* : originariamente — **originate** [əˈrɪdʒəˌneɪt] *v* **-nated; -nating** *vt* : originar — *vi* **1** : originarse **2** ~ **from** : provenir de — **originator** [əˈrɪdʒəˌneɪt̬ər] *n* : creador *m*, -dora *f*

ornament [ˈɔrnəmənt] *n* : adorno *m* — ~ *vt* : adornar — **ornamental** [ˌɔrnəˈment̬əl] *adj* : ornamental, de adorno — **ornate** [ɔrˈneɪt] *adj* : elaborado, adornado

ornithology [ˌɔrnəˈθɑlədʒi] *n, pl* **-gies** : ornitología *f*

orphan [ˈɔrfən] *n* : huérfano *m*, -na *f* — ~ *vt* : dejar huérfano — **orphanage** [ˈɔrfənɪdʒ] *n* : orfelinato *m*, orfanato *m*

orthodox [ˈɔrθəˌdɑks] *adj* : ortodoxo — **orthodoxy** [ˈɔrθəˌdɑksi] *n, pl* **-doxies** : ortodoxia *f*

orthopedic [ˌɔrθəˈpiːdɪk] *adj* : ortopédico

oscillation [ˌɑsəˈleɪʃən] *n* : oscilación *f* — **oscillate** [ˈɑsəˌleɪt] *vi* **-lated; -lating** : oscilar

ostensible [ɑˈstensəbəl] *adj* : aparente, ostensible

ostentation [ˌɑstənˈteɪʃən] *n* : ostentación *f* — **ostentatious** [ˌɑstənˈteɪʃəs] *adj* : ostentoso

osteopath [ˈɑstiəˌpæθ] *n* : osteópata *f*

ostracism [ˈɑstrəˌsɪzəm] *n* : ostracismo *m* — **ostracize** [ˈɑstrəˌsaɪz] *vt* **-cized; -cizing** : aislar

ostrich [ˈɑstrɪtʃ, ˈɑs-] *n* : avestruz *m*

other ['ʌðər] *adj* 1 : otro 2 **every ~ day** : cada dos días 3 **on the ~ hand** : por otra parte, por otro lado — **~ pron** 1 : otro, otra 2 **the ~s** : los otros, los otras, los demás, las demás — **other than** *prep* : aparte de, fuera de — **otherwise** ['ʌðər,waiz] *adv* 1 : eso aparte, por lo demás 2 DIFFERENTLY : de otro modo 3 OR ELSE : si no

otter ['ɑtər] *n* : nutria *f*

ought ['ɔt] *v aux* 1 : deber 2 **you ~ to have done it** : deberías haberlo hecho

ounce ['aʊnts] *n* : onza *f*

our ['ɑr, 'aʊr] *adj* : nuestro — **ours** ['aʊrz, 'ɑrz] *pron* 1 : (el) nuestro, (la) nuestra, (los) nuestros, (las) nuestras 2 **a friend of ~** : un amigo nuestro — **ourselves** [ɑr'selvz, aʊr-] *pron* 1 (*used reflexively*) : nos 2 (*used after prepositions*) : nosotros, nosotras 3 (*used for emphasis*) : nosotros mismos, nosotras mismas

oust ['aʊst] *vt* : desbancar

out ['aʊt] *adv* 1 OUTSIDE : fuera, afuera 2 **cry ~** : gritar 3 **eat ~** : comer afuera 4 **go ~** : salir 5 **look ~** : mirar para afuera 6 **run ~ of** : agotar 7 **turn ~** : apagar (una luz) 8 **take ~** REMOVE : sacar — **~ prep ~ out of —** *adj* 1 ABSENT : ausente 2 UNFASHIONABLE : fuera de moda 3 EXTINGUISHED : apagado 4 **the sun is ~** : hace sol

outboard motor ['aʊt,bord] *n* : motor *m* fuera de borde

outbreak ['aʊt,breik] *n* : brote *m* (de una enfermedad), comienzo *m* (de guerra)

outburst ['aʊt,bərst] *n* : arranque *m*, arrebato *m*

outcast ['aʊt,kæst] *n* : paria *mf*

outcome ['aʊt,kʌm] *n* : resultado *m*

outcry ['aʊt,krai] *n*, *pl* -**cries** : protesta *f*

outdated ['aʊt,deitəd] *adj* : anticuado

outdo [aʊt'du:] *vt* -**did** [-'dɪd]; -**done** [-'dʌn]; -**doing**; -**does** [-'dʌz] : superar

outdoor [aʊt'dor] *adj* : al aire libre — **outdoors** [aʊt'dorz] *adv* : al aire libre

outer ['aʊtər] *adj* : exterior — **outer space** *n* : espacio *m* exterior

outfit ['aʊt,fit] *n* 1 EQUIPMENT : equipo *m* 2 CLOTHES : conjunto *m* — **~ vt** -**fitted**; -**fitting** EQUIP : equipar

outgoing ['aʊt,goin] *adj* 1 SOCIABLE : extrovertido 2 **~ mail** : correo *m* (para enviar) 3 **~ president** : presidente *m*, -ta *f* saliente

outgrow [aʊt'gro:] *vt* -**grew** [-'gru:]; -**grown** [-'gro:n]; -**growing** : crecer más que

outing ['aʊtiŋ] *n* : excursión *f*

outlandish [aʊt'lændɪʃ] *adj* : estrafalario

outlast [aʊt'læst] *vt* : durar más que

outlaw ['aʊt,lɔ] *n* : forajido *m*, -da *f* — **~ vt** : declarar ilegal

outlay ['aʊt,lei] *n* : desembolso *m*

outlet ['aʊt,let, -lət] *n* 1 EXIT : salida *f* 2 RELEASE : desahogo *m* 3 *or* **electrical ~** : toma *f* de corriente 4 *or* **retail ~** : tienda *f* al por menor

outline ['aʊt,lain] *n* 1 CONTOUR : contorno *m* 2 SKETCH : bosquejo *m*, boceto *m* 3 SUMMARY : esquema *m* — **~ vt** -**lined**; -**lining** 1 SKETCH : bosquejar 2 EXPLAIN : delinear, esbozar

outlive [aʊt'liv] *vt* -**lived**; -**living** : sobrevivir a

outlook ['aʊt,luk] *n* 1 PROSPECTS : perspectivas *fpl* 2 VIEWPOINT : punto *m* de vista

outlying ['aʊt,laiŋ] *adj* : alejado, distante

outmoded [aʊt'mo:dəd] *adj* : pasado de moda, anticuado

outnumber [aʊt'nʌmbər] *vt* : superar en número a

out of *prep* 1 FROM : de 2 THROUGH : por 3 WITHOUT : sin 4 **~ curiosity** : por curiosidad 5 **~ control** : fuera de control 6 **one ~ four** : uno de cada cuatro — **out-of-date** [aʊtəv'deit] *adj* : anticuado — **out-of-door** [aʊtəv'dor] *or* **out-of-doors** [-'dorz] *adj* → **outdoor**

outpatient ['aʊt,peiʃənt] *n* : paciente *m* externo

outpost ['aʊt,po:st] *n* : puesto *m* avanzado

output ['aʊt,put] *n* 1 : producción *f*, rendimiento *m* 2 : salida *f* (informática) — **~ vt** -**putted** *or* -**put**; -**putting** : producir

outrage ['aʊt,reidʒ] *n* 1 : atrocidad *f*, escándalo *m* 2 ANGER : ira *f*, indignación *f* — **~ vt** -**raged**; -**raging** : ultrajar — **outrageous** [aʊt'reidʒəs] *adj* : escandaloso

outright [aʊt'rait] *adv* 1 COMPLETELY : por completo 2 INSTANTLY : en el acto — **~** ['aʊt,rait] *adj* : completo, absoluto

outset ['aʊt,set] *n* : comienzo *m*, principio *m*

outside [aʊt'said, 'aʊt-] *n* 1 : exterior *m* 2 **from the ~** : desde fuera, desde afuera — **~ adj** 1 : exterior, externo 2 **an ~ chance** : una posibilidad remota — **~ adv** : fuera, afuera — **~ prep** *or* **~ of** : fuera de — **outsider** [aʊt'saidər] *n* : forastero *m*, -ra *f*

outskirts [ˈaʊtˌskərts] *npl* : afueras *fpl*, alrededores *mpl*

outspoken [ˌaʊtˈspoːkən] *adj* : franco, directo

outstanding [aʊtˈstændɪŋ] *adj* 1 UNPAID : pendiente 2 EXCELLENT : excepcional

outstretched [aʊtˈstrɛtʃt] *adj* : extendido

outstrip [aʊtˈstrɪp] *vt* **-stripped** *or* **-stript** [-ˈstrɪpt]; **-stripping** : aventajar

outward [ˈaʊtwərd] *adj* 1 : hacia afuera 2 EXTERNAL : externo, external — **~** *or* **outwards** [-wərdz] *adv* : hacia afuera — **outwardly** [ˈaʊtwərdli] *adv* APPARENTLY : aparentemente

outweigh [aʊtˈweɪ] *vt* : pesar más que

outwit [aʊtˈwɪt] *vt* **-witted; -witting** : ser más listo que

oval [ˈoːvəl] *n* : óvalo *m* — **~** *adj* : ovalado

ovary [ˈoːvəri] *n, pl* **-ries** : ovario *m*

ovation [oˈveɪʃən] *n* : ovación *f*

oven [ˈʌvən] *n* : horno *m*

over [ˈoːvər] *adv* 1 ABOVE : por encima 2 AGAIN : otra vez, de nuevo 3 MORE : más 4 **all ~** : por todas partes 5 **ask ~** : invitar 6 **cross ~** : cruzar 7 **fall ~** : caerse 8 **~ and ~** : una y otra vez 9 **~ here** : aquí 10 **~ there** : allí — **~** *prep* 1 ABOVE, UPON : encima de, sobre 2 ACROSS : por encima de, sobre 3 DURING : en, durante 4 **fight ~** : pelearse por 5 **~ $5** : más de $5 6 **~ the phone** : por teléfono — **~** *adj* : terminado, acabado

overall [ˌoːvərˈɔl] *adv* GENERALLY : en general — *adj* : total, en conjunto — **overalls** [ˈoːvərˌɔlz] *npl* : overol *m Lat*

overbearing [ˌoːvərˈbærɪŋ] *adj* : dominante, imperioso

overboard [ˈoːvərˌbord] *adv* **fall ~** : caer al agua

overburden [ˌoːvərˈbərdən] *vt* : sobrecargar

overcast [ˈoːvərˌkæst] *adj* : nublado

overcharge [ˌoːvərˈtʃɑrdʒ] *vt* **-charged; -charging** : cobrar demasiado

overcoat [ˈoːvərˌkoːt] *n* : abrigo *m*

overcome [ˌoːvərˈkʌm] *v* **-came** [-ˈkeɪm]; **-come; -coming** *vt* 1 CONQUER : vencer 2 OVERWHELM : agobiar — *vi* : vencer

overcook [ˌoːvərˈkʊk] *vt* : cocer demasiado

overcrowded [ˌoːvərˈkraʊdəd] *adj* : abarrotado de gente

overdo [ˌoːvərˈdu:] *vt* **-did** [-ˈdɪd]; **-done** [-ˈdʌn]; **-doing; -does** [-ˈdʌz] 1 : hacer demasiado 2 EXAGGERATE : exagerar 3 → **overcook**

overdose [ˈoːvərˌdoːs] *n* : sobredosis *f*

overdraw [ˌoːvərˈdrɔ] *vt* **-drew** [-ˈdru:]; **-drawn** [-ˈdrɔn]; **-drawing** : girar en descubierto — **overdraft** [ˈoːvərˌdræft] *n* : sobregiro *m*, descubierto *m*

overdue [ˌoːvərˈdu:] *adj* : fuera de plazo (dícese de pagos, libros, etc.)

overeat [ˌoːvərˈi:t] *vi* **-ate** [-ˈeɪt]; **-eaten** [-ˈi:tən]; **-eating** : comer demasiado

overestimate [ˌoːvərˈɛstəˌmeɪt] *vt* **-mated; -mating** : sobreestimar

overflow [ˌoːvərˈfloː] *vt* : desbordar — *vi* : desbordarse — **~** [ˈoːvərˌfloː] *n* : desbordamiento *m* (de un río)

overgrown [ˌoːvərˈgroːn] *adj* : cubierto (de malas hierbas, etc.)

overhand [ˈoːvərˌhænd] *adv* : por encima de la cabeza

overhang [ˌoːvərˈhæŋ] *v* **-hung** [-ˈhʌŋ]; **-hanging** : sobresalir

overhaul [ˌoːvərˈhɔl] *vt* : revisar (un motor, etc.)

overhead [ˌoːvərˈhɛd] *adv* : por encima — **~** [ˈoːvərˌhɛd] *adj* : de arriba — **~** [ˈoːvərˌhɛd] *n* : gastos *mpl* generales

overhear [ˌoːvərˈhɪr] *vt* **-heard; -hearing** : oír por casualidad

overheat [ˌoːvərˈhi:t] *vt* : calentar demasiado — *vi* : recalentarse

overjoyed [ˌoːvərˈdʒɔɪd] *adj* : encantado

overland [ˈoːvərˌlænd, -lənd] *adv & adj* : por tierra

overlap [ˌoːvərˈlæp] *v* **-lapped; -lapping** *vt* : traslapar — *vi* : traslaparse

overload [ˌoːvərˈloːd] *vt* : sobrecargar

overlook [ˌoːvərˈlʊk] *vt* 1 : dar a (un jardín, el mar, etc.) 2 MISS : pasar por alto

overly [ˈoːvərli] *adv* : demasiado

overnight [ˌoːvərˈnaɪt] *adv* 1 : por la noche 2 SUDDENLY : de la noche a la mañana — **~** [ˈoːvərˌnaɪt] *adj* 1 : de noche 2 SUDDEN : repentino

overpass [ˈoːvərˌpæs] *n* : paso *m* elevado

overpopulated [ˌoːvərˈpɑpjəˌleɪtəd] *adj* : superpoblado

overpower [ˌoːvərˈpaʊər] *vt* 1 SUBDUE : dominar 2 OVERWHELM : agobiar, abrumar

overrated [ˌoːvərˈreɪtəd] *adj* : sobreestimado

override [ˌoːvərˈraɪd] *vt* **-rode** [-ˈroːd]; **-ridden** [-ˈrɪdən]; **-riding** 1 : predominar sobre 2 : anular (una decisión, etc.)

overrule [ˌoːvərˈru:l] *vt* **-ruled; -ruling** : anular (una decisión), rechazar (una protesta)

overrun [ˌoːvərˈrʌn] *vt* **-ran** [-ˈræn]; **-running** 1 INVADE : invadir 2 EXCEED : exceder

overseas [o:vər'si:z] *adv* : en el extranjero — ~ ['o:vər,si:z] *adj* : extranjero, exterior

oversee [o:vər'si:] *vt* **-saw** [-'sɔ]; **-seen** [-'si:n]; **-seeing** : supervisar

overshadow [o:vər'ʃæ,do:] *vt* : eclipsar

oversight ['o:vər,saɪt] *n* : descuido *m*

oversleep [o:vər'sli:p] *vi* **-slept** [-'slept]; **-sleeping** : quedarse dormido

overstep [o:vər'step] *vt* **-stepped**; **-stepping** : sobrepasar

overt [o:'vərt, 'o:,vərt] *adj* : manifiesto

overtake [o:vər'teɪk] *vt* **-took** [-'tʊk]; **-taken** [-'teɪkən]; **-taking** **1** PASS : adelantar **2** SURPASS : superar

overthrow [o:vər'θro:] *vt* **-threw** [-'θru:]; **-thrown** [-'θro:n]; **-throwing** : derrocar

overtime ['o:vər,taɪm] *n* **1** : horas *fpl* extras (de trabajo) **2** : prórroga *f* (en deportes)

overtone ['o:vər,to:n] *n* SUGGESTION : tinte *m*, insinuación *f*

overture ['o:vər,tʃʊr, -tʃər] *n* : obertura *f* (en música)

overturn [o:vər'tərn] *vt* **1** : dar la vuelta a **2** NULLIFY : anular — *vi* : volcar

overweight [o:vər'weɪt] *adj* : demasiado gordo

overwhelm [o:vər'hwelm] *vt* **1** : abrumar, agobiar **2** : aplastar (a un enemigo) — **overwhelming** [o:vər'hwelmɪŋ] *adj* : abrumador, apabullante

overwork [o:vər'wərk] *vt* : hacer trabajar demasiado — *vi* : trabajar demasiado

overwrought [o:vər'rɔt] *adj* : alterado, sobreexcitado

owe ['o:] *vt* **owed**; **owing** : deber — **owing to** *prep* : debido a

owl ['aʊl] *n* : búho *m*

own ['o:n] *adj* : propio — ~ *vt* : poseer, tener — *vi* ~ **up** : confesar — ~ *pron* **1** my (your, his/her/their, our) ~ : el mío, la mía; el tuyo, la tuya; el suyo, la suya; el nuestro, la nuestra **2** be on one's ~ : estar solo **3** to each his ~ : cada uno a lo suyo — **owner** ['o:nər] *n* : propietario *m*, -ria *f* — **ownership** ['o:nər,ʃɪp] *n* : propiedad *f*

ox ['aks] *n*, *pl* **oxen** ['aksən] : buey *m*

oxygen ['aksɪdʒən] *n* : oxígeno *m*

oyster ['ɔɪstər] *n* : ostra *f*

ozone ['o:,zo:n] *n* : ozono *m*

P

p ['pi:] *n*, *pl* **p's** or **ps** ['pi:z] : p *f*, decimosexta letra del alfabeto inglés

pace ['peɪs] *n* **1** STEP : paso *m* **2** RATE : ritmo *m* **3** keep ~ with : andar al mismo paso que — ~ *vi* **paced**; **pacing** or ~ **up and down** : caminar de arriba para abajo

pacify ['pæsə,faɪ] *vt* **-fied**; **-fying** : apaciguar — **pacifier** ['pæsə,faɪər] *n* : chupete *m* — **pacifist** ['pæsəfɪst] *n* : pacifista *mf*

pack ['pæk] *n* **1** BUNDLE : fardo *m* **2** BACKPACK : mochila *f* **3** PACKAGE : paquete *m* **4** : baraja *f* (de naipes) **5** : manada *f* (de lobos, etc.), jauría *f* (de perros) — ~ *vt* **1** PACKAGE : empaquetar **2** FILL : llenar **3** : hacer (una maleta) — *vi* : hacer las maletas — **package** ['pækɪdʒ] *vt* **-aged**; **-aging** : empaquetar — ~ *n* : paquete *m* — **packet** ['pækət] *n* : paquete *m*

pact ['pækt] *n* : pacto *m*, acuerdo *m*

pad ['pæd] *n* **1** CUSHION : almohadilla *f* **2** TABLET : bloc *m* (de papel) **3** or **ink** ~ : tampón *m* **4** **launching** ~ : plataforma *f* (de lanzamiento) — ~ *vt* **padded**; **padding** : rellenar — **pad-**

ding ['pædɪŋ] *n* **1** : relleno *m* **2** : paja *f* (en un discurso, etc.)

paddle ['pædəl] *n* **1** : canalete *m* (de una canoa) **2** : pala *f*, paleta *f* (en deportes) — ~ *vt* **-died**; **-dling** : hacer avanzar (una canoa) con canalete

padlock ['pæd,lak] *n* : candado *m* — ~ *vt* : cerrar con candado

pagan ['peɪɡən] *n* : pagano *m*, -na *f* — ~ *adj* : pagano

page[1] ['peɪdʒ] *vt* **paged**; **paging** : llamar por altavoz

page[2] *n* : página *f* (de un libro, etc.)

pageant ['pædʒənt] *n* : espectáculo *m* — **pageantry** ['pædʒəntri] *n* : pompa *f*, boato *m*

paid → **pay**

pail ['peɪl] *n* : cubo *m* Spain, cubeta *f* Lat

pain ['peɪn] *n* **1** : dolor *m* **2** : pena *f* (mental) **3** ~**s** *npl* EFFORT : esfuerzos *mpl* — ~ *vt* : doler — **painful** ['peɪnfəl] *adj* : doloroso — **painkiller** ['peɪn,kɪlər] *n* : analgésico *m* — **painless** ['peɪnləs] *adj* : indoloro, sin dolor — **painstaking** ['peɪn,steɪkɪŋ] *adj* : meticuloso, esmerado

paint ['peɪnt] *v* : pintar — ~ *n* : pintura

f — **paintbrush** ['peɪnt,brʌʃ] n : pincel m (de un artista), brocha f (para pintar casas, etc.) — **painter** ['peɪntər] n : pintor m, -tora f — **painting** ['peɪntɪŋ] n : pintura f

pair ['pær] n 1 : par m 2 COUPLE : pareja f — ~ vt : emparejar

pajamas [pə'dʒɑməz, -'dʒæ-] npl : pijama m, piyama mf Lat

Pakistani [ˌpækɪ'stæni, ˌpɑkɪ'stɑni] adj : paquistaní

pal ['pæl] n : amigo m, -ga f

palace ['pæləs] n : palacio m

palate ['pælət] n : paladar m — **palatable** ['pælətəbəl] adj : sabroso

pale ['peɪl] adj **paler; palest 1** PALLID : pálido **2** : claro (dícese de los colores, etc.) — ~ vi **paled; paling** : palidecer — **paleness** ['peɪlnəs] n : palidez f

Palestinian [ˌpælə'stɪniən] adj : palestino

palette ['pælət] n : paleta f

pallbearer ['pɔl,berər] n : portador m, -dora f del féretro

pallid ['pæləd] adj : pálido — **pallor** ['pælər] n : palidez f

palm[1] ['pɑm, 'pɑlm] n : palma f (de la mano)

palm[2] or ~ **tree** : palmera f — **Palm Sunday** n : Domingo m de Ramos

palpitate ['pælpə,teɪt] vi **-tated; -tating** : palpitar — **palpitation** [ˌpælpə'teɪʃən] n : palpitación f

paltry ['pɔltri] adj **-trier; -est** : mísero, mezquino

pamper ['pæmpər] vt : mimar

pamphlet ['pæmpflət] n : panfleto m, folleto m

pan ['pæn] n 1 SAUCEPAN : cacerola f 2 FRYING PAN : sartén mf — ~ vt **panned; panning** CRITICIZE : poner por los suelos

pancake ['pæn,keɪk] n : crepe mf, panqueque m Lat

panda ['pændə] n : panda mf

pandemonium [ˌpændə'mo:niəm] n : pandemonio m

pander ['pændər] vi ~ **to** : complacer a

pane ['peɪn] n : cristal m, vidrio m

panel ['pænəl] n 1 : panel m 2 GROUP : jurado m 3 or **instrument ~** : tablero m (de instrumentos) — ~ vt **-eled** or **-elled; -eling** or **-elling** : adornar con paneles — **paneling** ['pænəlɪŋ] n : paneles mpl

pang ['pæŋ] n : punzada f

panic ['pænɪk] n : pánico m — ~ v **-icked; -icking** vt : llenar del pánico — vi : ser presa del pánico — **panicky** ['pæniki] adj : presa de pánico

panorama [ˌpænə'ræmə, -'rɑ-] n : panorama m — **panoramic** [ˌpænə'ræmɪk, -'rɑ-] adj : panorámico

pansy ['pænzi] n, pl **-sies** : pensamiento m

pant ['pænt] vi : jadear, resoplar

panther ['pænθər] n : pantera f

panties ['pæntiz] npl : bragas fpl Spain, calzones mpl Lat

pantomime ['pæntə,maɪm] n : pantomima f

pantry ['pæntri] n, pl **-tries** : despensa f

pants ['pænts] npl TROUSERS : pantalón m, pantalones mpl

papa ['pɑpə] n : papá m fam

papal ['peɪpəl] adj : papal

papaya [pə'paɪə] n : papaya f

paper ['peɪpər] n 1 : papel m 2 DOCUMENT : documento m 3 NEWSPAPER : periódico m — ~ vt WALLPAPER : empapelar — ~ adj : de papel — **paperback** ['peɪpər,bæk] n : libro m en rústica — **paper clip** n : clip m, sujetapapeles m — **paperweight** ['peɪpər,weɪt] n : pisapapeles m — **paperwork** ['peɪpər,wərk] n : papeleo m

paprika [pə'pri:kə, pæ-] n : pimentón m

par ['pɑr] n 1 : par m (en golf) 2 **below ~** : debajo de la par 3 **on a ~ with** : al nivel de

parable ['pærəbəl] n : parábola f

parachute ['pærə,ʃu:t] n : paracaídas m — ~ vi **-chuted; -chuting** : lanzarse en paracaídas

parade [pə'reɪd] n 1 : desfile m 2 DISPLAY : alarde m — ~ v **-raded; -rading** vi MARCH : desfilar — vt DISPLAY : hacer alarde de

paradise ['pærə,daɪs, -,daɪz] n : paraíso m

paradox ['pærə,dɑks] n : paradoja f — **paradoxical** [ˌpærə'dɑksɪkəl] adj : paradójico

paraffin ['pærəfən] n : parafina f

paragraph ['pærə,græf] n : párrafo m

Paraguayan [ˌpærə'gwaɪən, -'gweɪ-] adj : paraguayo

parakeet ['pærə,ki:t] n : periquito m

parallel ['pærə,lel, -ləl] adj : paralelo — ~ n 1 : paralelo m (en geografía) 2 SIMILARITY : paralelismo m, semejanza f — ~ vt : ser paralelo a

paralysis [pə'ræləsɪs] n, pl **-yses** [-,si:z] : parálisis f — **paralyze** or Brit **paralise** ['pærə,laɪz] vt **-lyzed** or Brit **-lised; -lyzing** or Brit **-lising** : paralizar

parameter [pə'ræmətər] n : parámetro m

paramount ['pærə,maʊnt] adj **of ~ importance** : de suma importancia

paranoia [ˌpærəˈnɔɪə] n : paranoia f — **paranoid** [ˈpærəˌnɔɪd] adj : paranoico

paraphernalia [ˌpærəfəˈneɪljə, -fər-] ns & pl : parafernalia f

paraphrase [ˈpærəˌfreɪz] n : paráfrasis f — ~ vt **-phrased; -phrasing** : parafrasear

paraplegic [ˌpærəˈpliːdʒɪk] n : parapléjico m, -ca f

parasite [ˈpærəˌsaɪt] n : parásito m

paratrooper [ˈpærəˌtruːpər] n : paracaidista mf (militar)

parcel [ˈpɑrsəl] n : paquete m

parch [ˈpɑrtʃ] vt : resecar

parchment [ˈpɑrtʃmənt] n : pergamino m

pardon [ˈpɑrdən] n 1 : perdón m 2 REPRIEVE : indulto m 3 I beg your ~ : perdone Ud., disculpe Ud. Lat — ~ vt 1 : perdonar 2 REPRIEVE : indultar (a un delincuente)

parent [ˈpærənt] n 1 : madre f, padre m 2 ~s npl : padres mpl — **parental** [pəˈrentəl] adj : de los padres

parenthesis [pəˈrɛnθəsɪs] n, pl **-theses** [-ˌsiːz] : paréntesis m

parish [ˈpærɪʃ] n : parroquia f — **parishioner** [pəˈrɪʃənər] n : feligrés m, -gresa f

parity [ˈpærəţi] n, pl **-ties** : igualdad f

park [ˈpɑrk] n : parque m — ~ v : estacionar, parquear Lat

parka [ˈpɑrkə] n : parka f

parking [ˈpɑrkɪŋ] n : estacionamiento m

parliament [ˈpɑrləmənt, ˈpɑrljə-] n : parlamento m — **parliamentary** [ˌpɑrləˈmentəri, ˌpɑrljə-] adj : parlamentario

parlor or Brit **parlour** [ˈpɑrlər] n : salón m

parochial [pəˈroːkiəl] adj 1 : parroquial 2 PROVINCIAL : de miras estrechas

parody [ˈpærədi] n, pl **-dies** : parodia f — ~ vt **-died; -dying** : parodiar

parole [pəˈroːl] n : libertad f condicional

parrot [ˈpærət] n : loro m, papagayo m

parry [ˈpæri] vt **-ried; -rying** 1 : parar (un golpe) 2 EVADE : eludir (una pregunta, etc.)

parsley [ˈpɑrsli] n : perejil m

parsnip [ˈpɑrsnɪp] n : chirivía f

parson [ˈpɑrsən] n : clérigo m

part [ˈpɑrt] n 1 : parte f 2 PIECE : pieza f 3 ROLE : papel m 4 : raya f (del pelo) — ~ vi 1 or ~ **company** : separarse 2 ~ **with** : dehacerse de — vt SEPARATE : separar

partake [pɑrˈteɪk, pər-] vi **-took; -taken; -taking** ~ **in** : participar en

partial [ˈpɑrʃəl] adj 1 : parcial 2 **be** ~ **to** : ser aficionado a

participate [pərˈtɪsəˌpeɪt, pɑr-] vi **-pated; -pating** : participar — **participant** [pərˈtɪsəpənt, pɑr-] n : participante mf

participle [ˈpɑrţəˌsɪpəl] n : participio m

particle [ˈpɑrţɪkəl] n : partícula f

particular [pɑrˈtɪkjələr] adj 1 : particular 2 FUSSY : exigente — ~ n 1 **in** ~ : en particular, en especial 2 ~**s** npl DETAILS : detalles mpl — **particularly** [pɑrˈtɪkjələrli] adv : especialmente

partisan [ˈpɑrţəzən, -sən] n : partidario m, -ria f

partition [pərˈtɪʃən, pɑr-] n 1 DISTRIBUTION : partición f 2 DIVIDER : tabique m — ~ vt : dividir

partly [ˈpɑrtli] adv : en parte

partner [ˈpɑrtnər] n 1 : pareja f (en un juego, etc.) 2 or **business** ~ : socio m, -cia f — **partnership** [ˈpɑrtnərˌʃɪp] n : asociación f

party [ˈpɑrţi] n, pl **-ties** 1 : partido m (político) 2 GATHERING : fiesta f 3 GROUP : grupo m

pass [ˈpæs] vi 1 : pasar 2 CEASE : pasarse 3 : aprobar (en un examen) 4 or ~ **away** DIE : morir 5 ~ **for** : pasar por 6 ~ **out** FAINT : desmayarse — vt 1 : pasar 2 or ~ **in front of** : pasar por 3 OVERTAKE : adelantar 4 : aprobar (un examen, una ley, etc.) 5 ~ **down** : transmitir — ~ n 1 PERMIT : pase m, permiso m 2 : pase m (en deportes) 3 or **mountain** ~ : paso m de montaña — **passable** [ˈpæsəbəl] adj 1 ADEQUATE : adecuado 2 : transitable (dícese de un camino, etc.) — **passage** [ˈpæsɪdʒ] n 1 : paso m 2 CORRIDOR : pasillo m (dentro de un edificio), pasaje m (entre edificios) 3 VOYAGE : travesía f (por el mar) — **passageway** [ˈpæsɪdʒˌweɪ] n : pasillo m, corredor m

passenger [ˈpæsəndʒər] n : pasajero m, -ra f

passerby [ˌpæsərˈbaɪ, ˈpæsər-] n, pl **passersby** : transeúnte mf

passion [ˈpæʃən] n : pasión f — **passionate** [ˈpæʃənət] adj : apasionado

passive [ˈpæsɪv] adj : pasivo

Passover [ˈpæsˌoːvər] n : Pascua f (en el judaísmo)

passport [ˈpæsˌpɔrt] n : pasaporte m

password [ˈpæsˌwərd] n : contraseña f

past [ˈpæst] adj 1 : pasado 2 FORMER : anterior 3 **the** ~ **few months** : los últimos meses — ~ prep 1 IN FRONT OF : por delante de 2 BEYOND : más allá de 3 **half** ~ **two** : las dos y media — ~ n : pasado m — ~ adv : por delante

pasta ['pastə, 'pæs-] n : pasta f

paste ['peɪst] n 1 : pasta f 2 GLUE : engrudo m — ~ vt **pasted; pasting** : pegar

pastel [pæ'stɛl] n : pastel m — ~ adj : pastel

pasteurize ['pæstʃə,raɪz, 'pæstjə-] vt **-ized; -izing** : pasteurizar

pastime ['pæs,taɪm] n : pasatiempo m

pastor ['pæstər] n : pastor m, -tora f

pastry ['peɪstri] n, pl **-ries** : pasteles mpl

pasture ['pæstʃər] n : pasto m

pasty ['peɪsti] adj **pastier; -est 1** DOUGHY : pastoso **2** PALLID : pálido

pat ['pæt] n 1 : palmadita f **2 a ~ of butter** : una porción de mantequilla — ~ vt **patted; patting** : dar palmaditas a — ~ adv **have down** : saberse de memoria — ~ adj GLIB : fácil

patch ['pætʃ] n 1 : parche m, remiendo m (para la ropa) **2** SPOT : mancha f, trozo m **3** PLOT : parcela f (de tierra) — ~ vt 1 MEND : remendar **2 ~ up** : arreglar — **patchy** ['pætʃi] adj **patchier; -est 1** : desigual **2** INCOMPLETE : parcial, incompleto

patent adj ['pætənt] **1** or **patented** ['pætəntəd] : patentado **2** ['pætənt, 'peɪt-] OBVIOUS : patente, evidente — ~ ['pætənt] n : patente f — ~ ['pætənt] vt : patentar

paternal [pə'tərnəl] adj **1** FATHERLY : paternal **2 ~ grandmother** : abuela f paterna — **paternity** [pə'tərnəti] n : paternidad f

path ['pæθ, 'paθ] n **1** TRACK, TRAIL : camino m, sendero m **2** COURSE : trayectoria f

pathetic [pə'θɛtɪk] adj : patético

pathology [pə'θɑlədʒi] n, pl **-gies** : patología f

pathway ['pæθ,weɪ] n : camino m, sendero m

patience ['peɪʃənts] n : paciencia f — **patient** ['peɪʃənt] adj : paciente — ~ n : paciente mf — **patiently** adv : con paciencia

patio ['pæti,o] n, pl **-tios** : patio m

patriot ['peɪtriət] n : patriota mf — **patriotic** [,peɪtri'ɑtɪk] adj : patriótico

patrol [pə'troːl] n : patrulla f — ~ v **-trolled; -trolling** : patrullar

patron ['peɪtrən] n **1** SPONSOR : patrocinador m, -dora f **2** CUSTOMER : cliente m, -ta f — **patronage** ['peɪtrənɪdʒ, 'pæ-] n **1** SPONSORSHIP : patrocinio m **2** CLIENTELE : clientela f — **patronize** ['peɪtrə,naɪz, 'pæ-] vt **-ized; -izing 1** : ser cliente de (una tienda, etc.) **2** : tratar (a algn) con condescencia

patter ['pætər] n : tamborileo m (de la lluvia), correteo m (de los pies)

pattern ['pætərn] n **1** MODEL : modelo m **2** DESIGN : diseño m **3** STANDARD : pauta f, modo m **4** : patrón m (en costura) — ~ vt : basar (en un modelo)

paunch ['pɔntʃ] n : panza f

pause ['pɔz] n : pausa f — ~ vi **paused; pausing** : hacer una pausa

pave ['peɪv] vt **paved; paving** : pavimentar — **pavement** ['peɪvmənt] n : pavimento m

pavilion [pə'vɪljən] n : pabellón m

paw ['pɔ] n **1** : pata f **2** : garra f (de un gato) — ~ vt : tocar con la pata

pawn¹ ['pɔn] n : peón m (en ajedrez)

pawn² vt : empeñar — **pawnbroker** ['pɔn,broːkər] n : prestamista mf — **pawnshop** ['pɔn,ʃɑp] n : casa f de empeños

pay ['peɪ] v **paid** ['peɪd]; **paying** vt **1** : pagar **2 ~ attention** : prestar atención **3 ~ back** : devolver **4 ~ one's respects** : presentar uno sus respetos **5 ~ a visit** : hacer una visita — vi **1** : pagar **2 crime doesn't ~** : no hay crimen sin castigo — ~ n : paga f — **payable** ['peɪəbəl] adj : pagadero — **paycheck** ['peɪ,tʃɛk] n : cheque m del sueldo — **payment** ['peɪmənt] n **1** : pago m **2** INSTALLMENT : plazo m, cuota f Lat — **payroll** n : nómina f

PC [,pi'si] n, pl **PCs** or **PC's** : PC mf, computadora f personal

pea ['piː] n : guisante m, arveja f Lat

peace ['piːs] n : paz f — **peaceful** ['piːsfəl] adj **1** : pacífico **2** CALM : tranquilo

peach ['piːtʃ] n : melocotón m, durazno m Lat

peacock ['piː,kɑk] n : pavo m real

peak ['piːk] n **1** SUMMIT : cumbre f, cima f, pico m (de una montaña) **2** APEX : nivel m máximo — ~ adj : máximo — ~ vi : alcanzar su nivel máximo

peal ['piːl] n **1** : repique m **2 ~s of laughter** : carcajadas fpl

peanut ['piː,nʌt] n : cacahuete m, maní m Lat

pear ['pær] n : pera f

pearl ['pərl] n : perla f

peasant ['pɛzənt] n : campesino m, -na f

peat ['piːt] n : turba f

pebble ['pɛbəl] n : guijarro m

pecan [pɪ'kɑn, -'kæn, 'piː,kæn] n : pacana f, nuez f Lat

peck ['pɛk] vt : picar, picotear — ~ n **1** : picotazo m (de un pájaro) **2** KISS : besito m

peculiar [pɪ'kjuːljər] adj **1** DISTINCTIVE

: peculiar, característico **2** STRANGE : extraño, raro — **peculiarity** [pɪ,kju:l-'jærəti, -kju:li'ær-] *n, pl* **-ties 1** : peculiaridad *f* **2** ODDITY : rareza *f*

pedal ['pedəl] *n* : pedal *m* — ~ *vi* **-aled** *or* **-alled; -aling** *or* **-alling** : pedalear

pedantic [pɪ'dæntɪk] *adj* : pedante

peddle ['pedəl] *vt* **-dled; -dling** : vender en las calles — **peddler** ['pedlər] *n* : vendedor *m*, -dora *f* ambulante

pedestal ['pedəstəl] *n* : pedestal *m*

pedestrian [pə'destriən] *n* : peatón *m*, -tona *f* — ~ *adj* **crossing** : paso *f* de peatones

pediatrics [,pi:di'ætrɪks] *ns & pl* : pediatría *f* — **pediatrician** [,pi:diə'trɪʃən] *n* : pediatra *mf*

pedigree ['pedə,gri:] *n* : pedigrí *m* (de un animal), linaje *m* (de una persona)

peek ['pi:k] *vi* : mirar a hurtadillas — ~ *n* : miradita *f* (furtiva)

peel ['pi:l] *vt* : pelar (fruta, etc.) — *vi* : pelarse (dícese de la piel), desconcharse (dícese de la pintura) — ~ *n* : piel *f*, cáscara *f*

peep¹ ['pi:p] *vi* CHEEP : piar — ~ *n* : pío *m* (de un pajarito)

peep² *vi* PEEK : mirar a hurtadillas **2** *or* ~ **out** : asomar — ~ *n* GLANCE : mirada *f* (furtiva)

peer¹ ['pɪr] *n* : par *mf*

peer² *vi* : mirar (con atención)

peeve ['pi:v] *vt* : irritar — **peevish** ['pi:vɪʃ] *adj* : malhumorado

peg ['peg] *n* **1** : clavija *f* **2** HOOK : gancho *m*

pelican ['pelɪkən] *n* : pelícano *m*

pellet ['pelət] *n* **1** : bolita *f* **2** SHOT : perdigón *m*

pelt¹ ['pelt] *n* : piel *f* (de un animal)

pelt² *vt* : lanzar (algo a algn)

pelvis ['pelvɪs] *n, pl* **-vises** *or* **-ves** ['pel,vi:z] : pelvis *f* — **pelvic** ['pelvɪk] *adj* : pélvico

pen¹ ['pen] *vt* **penned; penning** ENCLOSE : encerrar — ~ *n* : corral *m*, redil *m*

pen² *n* **1** *or* **ballpoint** ~ : bolígrafo *m* **2** *or* **fountain** ~ : pluma *f*

penal ['pi:nəl] *adj* : penal — **penalize** ['pi:nəl,aɪz, 'pen-] *vt* **-ized; -izing** : penalizar — **penalty** ['penəlti] *n, pl* **-ties 1** : pena *f*, castigo *m* **2** : penalty *m* (en deportes)

penance ['penənts] *n* : penitencia *f*

pencil ['pentsəl] *n* : lápiz *m* — **pencil sharpener** *n* : sacapuntas *m*

pendant ['pendənt] *n* : colgante *m*

pending ['pendɪŋ] *adj* : pendiente — ~ *prep* : en espera de

penetrate ['penə,treɪt] *v* **-trated; -trating** : penetrar — **penetrating** ['penə,treɪ-tɪŋ] *adj* : penetrante — **penetration** [,penə'treɪʃən] *n* : penetración *f*

penguin ['peŋgwɪn, 'pen-] *n* : pingüino *m*

penicillin [,penə'sɪlən] *n* : penicilina *f*

peninsula [pə'nɪntsələ, -'nɪntʃʊlə] *n* : península *f*

penis ['pi:nəs] *n, pl* **-nes** [-,ni:z] *or* **-nises** : pene *m*

penitentiary [,penə'tentʃəri] *n, pl* **-ries** : penitenciaría *f*

pen name *n* : seudónimo *m*

pennant ['penənt] *n* : banderín *m*

penny ['peni] *n, pl* **-nies** *or* **pence** ['pents] : centavo *m* (de los Estados Unidos), penique *m* (del Reino Unido) — **penniless** ['peniləs] *adj* : sin un centavo

pension ['pentʃən] *n* : pensión *f*, jubilación *f*

pensive ['pentsɪv] *adj* : pensativo

pentagon ['pentə,gɑn] *n* : pentágono *m*

penthouse ['pent,haʊs] *n* : ático *m*

pent-up ['pent,ʌp] *adj* : reprimido

people ['pi:pəl] *ns & pl* **1** *people npl* : gente *f*, personas *fpl* **2** *pl* ~ **s** : pueblo *m*

pep ['pep] *n* : energía *f*, vigor *m* — ~ *vt or* ~ **up** : animar

pepper ['pepər] *n* **1** : pimienta *f* (condimento) **2** : pimiento *m* (fruta) — **peppermint** ['pepər,mɪnt] *n* : menta *f*

per ['pər] *prep* **1** : por **2** ACCORDING TO : según **3** ~ **day** : al día **4 miles** ~ **hour** : millas *fpl* por hora

perceive [pər'si:v] *vt* **-ceived; -ceiving** : percibir

percent [pər'sent] *adv* : por ciento — **percentage** [pər'sentɪdʒ] *n* : porcentaje *m*

perception [pər'sepʃən] *n* : percepción *f* — **perceptive** [pər'septɪv] *adj* : perspicaz

perch¹ ['pərtʃ] *n* : percha *f* (para los pájaros) — *vi* : posarse

perch² *n* : perca *f* (pez)

percolate ['pərkə,leɪt] *vi* **-lated; -lating** : filtrarse — **percolator** ['pərkə,leɪtər] *n* : cafetera *f* de filtro

percussion [pər'kʌʃən] *n* : percusión *f*

perennial [pə'reniəl] *adj* : perenne — ~ *n* : planta *f* perenne

perfect ['pərfɪkt] *adj* : perfecto — ~ [pər'fekt] *vt* : perfeccionar — **perfection** [pər'fekʃən] *n* : perfección *f* — **perfectionist** [pər'fekʃ,ənɪst] *n* : perfeccionista *mf*

perforate ['pərfə,reɪt] *vt* **-rated; -rating** : perforar

perform [pər'fɔrm] *vt* **1** CARRY OUT : realizar, hacer **2** : representar (una obra teatral), interpretar (una obra musical) — *vi* **1** FUNCTION : funcionar **2** ACT : actuar — **performance** [pər'fɔrmənts] *n* **1** : realización *f* **2** INTERPRETATION : interpretación *f* **3** PRESENTATION : representación *f* — **performer** [pər'fɔrmər] *n* : actor *m*, -triz *f*; intérprete *mf* (de música)

perfume ['pər,fjuːm, pər'-] *n* : perfume *m*

perhaps [pər'hæps] *adv* : tal vez, quizá, quizás

peril ['perəl] *n* : peligro *m* — **perilous** ['perələs] *adj* : peligroso

perimeter [pə'rɪmətər] *n* : perímetro *m*

period ['pɪriəd] *n* **1** : período *m* (de tiempo) **2** : punto *m* (en puntuación) **3** ERA : época *f* — **periodic** [,pɪri'ɑdɪk] *adj* : periódico — **periodical** [,pɪri'ɑdɪkəl] *n* : revista *f*

peripheral [pə'rɪfərəl] *adj* : periférico

perish ['perɪʃ] *vi* : perecer — **perishable** ['perɪʃəbəl] *adj* : perecedero — **perishables** ['perɪʃəbəlz] *npl* : productos *mpl* perecederos

perjury ['pərdʒəri] *n* : perjurio *m*

perk ['pərk] *vi* ~ **up** : animarse, reanimarse — *n* : extra *m* — **perky** ['pərki] *adj* **perkier; -est** : alegre

permanence ['pərmənənts] *n* : permanencia *f* — **permanent** ['pərmənənt] *adj* : permanente — ~ *n* : permanente *f*

permeate ['pərmi,eɪt] *v* **-ated; -ating** : penetrar

permission [pər'mɪʃən] *n* : permiso *m* — **permissible** [pər'mɪsəbəl] *adj* : permisible — **permissive** [pər'mɪsɪv] *adj* : permisivo — **permit** [pər'mɪt] *vt* **-mitted; -mitting** : permitir — ~ ['pər,mɪt, pər'-] *n* : permiso *m*

peroxide [pə'rɑk,saɪd] *n* : peróxido *m*

perpendicular [,pərpən'dɪkjələr] *adj* : perpendicular

perpetrate ['pərpə,treɪt] *vt* **-trated; -trating** : cometer — **perpetrator** ['pərpə,treɪtər] *n* : autor *m*, -tora *f* (de un delito)

perpetual [pər'petʃuəl] *adj* : perpetuo

perplex [pər'pleks] *vt* : dejar perplejo — **perplexing** [pər'pleksɪŋ] *adj* : desconcertante — **perplexity** [pər'pleksəti] *n, pl* **-ties** : perplejidad *f*

persecute ['pərsɪ,kjuːt] *vt* **-cuted; -cuting** : perseguir — **persecution** [,pərsɪ'kjuːʃən] *n* : persecución *f*

persevere [,pərsə'vɪr] *vi* **-vered; -vering** : perseverar — **perseverance** [,pərsə'vɪrənts] *n* : perseverancia *f*

persist [pər'sɪst] *vi* : persistir — **persistence** [pər'sɪstənts] *n* : persistencia *f* — **persistent** [pər'sɪstənt] *adj* : persistente

person ['pərsən] *n* : persona *f* — **personal** ['pərsənəl] *adj* : personal — **personality** [,pərsən'æləti] *n, pl* **-ties** : personalidad *f* — **personally** ['pərsənəli] *adv* : personalmente, en persona — **personnel** [,pərsən'el] *n* : personal *m*

perspective [pər'spektɪv] *n* : perspectiva *f*

perspiration [,pərspə'reɪʃən] *n* : transpiración *f* — **perspire** [pər'spaɪr] *vi* **-spired; -spiring** : transpirar

persuade [pər'sweɪd] *vt* **-suaded; -suading** : persuadir — **persuasion** [pər'sweɪʒən] *n* : persuasión *f*

pertain [pər'teɪn] *vi* ~ **to** : estar relacionado con — **pertinent** ['pərtənənt] *adj* : pertinente

perturb [pər'tərb] *vt* : perturbar

Peruvian [pə'ruːviən] *adj* : peruano

pervade [pər'veɪd] *vt* **-vaded; -vading** : penetrar — **pervasive** [pər'veɪsɪv, -zɪv] *adj* : penetrante

perverse [pər'vərs] *adj* **1** CORRUPT : perverso **2** STUBBORN : obstinado — **pervert** ['pər,vərt] *n* : pervertido *m*, -da *f*

peso ['peɪ,soː] *n, pl* **-sos** : peso *m*

pessimism ['pesə,mɪzəm] *n* : pesimismo *m* — **pessimist** ['pesəmɪst] *n* : pesimista *mf* — **pessimistic** [,pesə'mɪstɪk] *adj* : pesimista

pest ['pest] *n* **1** : insecto *m* nocivo, animal *m* nocivo **2** : peste *f fam* (persona)

pester ['pestər] *vt* **-tered; -tering** : molestar

pesticide ['pestə,saɪd] *n* : pesticida *m*

pet ['pet] *n* **1** : animal *m* doméstico **2** FAVORITE : favorito *m*, -ta *f* — ~ *vt* **petted; petting** : acariciar

petal ['petəl] *n* : pétalo *m*

petite [pə'tiːt] *adj* : chiquita

petition [pə'tɪʃən] *n* : petición *f* — ~ *vt* : dirigir una petición a

petrify ['petrə,faɪ] *vt* **-fied; -fying** : petrificar

petroleum [pə'troːliəm] *n* : petróleo *m*

petticoat ['peti,koːt] *n* : enagua *f*, fondo *m Lat*

petty ['peti] *adj* **-tier; -est** **1** UNIMPORTANT : insignificante, nimio **2** MEAN : mezquino — **pettiness** ['petinəs] *n* : mezquindad *f*

petulant ['petʃələnt] *adj* : irritable, de mal genio

pew ['pjuː] *n* : banco *m* (de iglesia)

pewter ['pjuːtər] n : peltre m
phallic ['fælɪk] adj : fálico
phantom ['fæntəm] n : fantasma m
pharmacy ['fɑrməsi] n, pl **-cies** : farmacia f — **pharmacist** ['fɑrməsɪst] n : farmacéutico m, -ca f
phase ['feɪz] n : fase f — ~ vt **phased; phasing 1** ~ **in** : introducir progresivamente **2** ~ **out** : retirar progresivamente
phenomenon [fɪ'nɑmənɑn, -nən] n, pl **-na** [-nə] or **-nons** : fenómeno m — **phenomenal** [fɪ'nɑmənəl] adj : fenomenal
philanthropy [fə'lænθrəpi] n, pl **-pies** : filantropía f — **philanthropist** [fə'lænθrəpɪst] n : filántropo m, -pa f
philosophy [fə'lɑsəfi] n, pl **-phies** : filosofía f — **philosopher** [fə'lɑsəfər] n : filósofo m, -fa f
phlegm ['flɛm] n : flema f
phobia ['foːbiə] n : fobia f
phone ['foːn] n → **telephone**
phonetic [fə'nɛtɪk] adj : fonético
phony or **phoney** ['foːni] adj **-nier; -est** : falso — ~ n, pl **-nies** : farsante mf
phosphorus ['fɑsfərəs] n : fósforo m
photo ['foːtoː] n, pl **-tos** : foto f — **photocopier** ['foːtoˌkɑpiər] n : fotocopiadora f — **photocopy** ['foːtoˌkɑpi] n, pl **-copies** : fotocopia f — ~ vt **-copied; -copying** : fotocopiar — **photograph** ['foːtəˌgræf] n : fotografía f, foto f — ~ vt : fotografiar — **photographer** [fə'tɑgrəfər] n : fotógrafo m, -fa f — **photographic** [ˌfoːtə'græfɪk] adj : fotográfico — **photography** [fə'tɑgrəfi] n : fotografía f
phrase ['freɪz] n : frase f — ~ vt **phrased; phrasing** : expresar
physical ['fɪzɪkəl] adj : físico — ~ n : reconocimiento m médico
physician [fə'zɪʃən] n : médico m, -ca f
physics ['fɪzɪks] ns & pl : física f — **physicist** ['fɪzəsɪst] n : físico m, -ca f
physiology [ˌfɪzi'ɑlədʒi] n : fisiología f
physique [fə'ziːk] n : físico m
piano [pi'ænoː] n, pl **-anos** : piano m — **pianist** [pi'ænɪst, 'piːənɪst] n : pianista mf
pick ['pɪk] vt **1** CHOOSE : escoger **2** GATHER : recoger **3** REMOVE : quitar (poco a poco) **4** ~ **a fight** : buscar camorra — vi **1** ~ **and choose** : ser exigente **2** ~ **on** : meterse con — ~ n **1** CHOICE : selección f **2** or **pickax** ['pɪkˌæks] : pico m **3 the** ~ **of** : lo mejor de
picket ['pɪkət] n **1** STAKE : estaca f **2** or ~ **line** : piquete m — v : piquetear
pickle ['pɪkəl] n **1** : pepinillo m (encur-

tido) **2** JAM : lío m fam, apuro m — ~ vt **-led; -ling** : encurtir
pickpocket ['pɪkˌpɑkət] n : carterista mf
pickup ['pɪkˌəp] n **1** IMPROVEMENT : mejora f **2** or ~ **truck** : camioneta f — **pick up** vt **1** LIFT : levantar **2** TIDY : arreglar, ordenar — vi IMPROVE : mejorar
picnic ['pɪkˌnɪk] n : picnic m — ~ vi **-nicked; -nicking** : ir de picnic
picture ['pɪktʃər] n **1** PAINTING : cuadro m **2** DRAWING : dibujo m **3** PHOTO : fotografía f **4** IMAGE : imagen f **5** MOVIE : película f — ~ vt **-tured; -turing 1** DEPICT : representar **2** IMAGINE : imaginarse — **picturesque** [ˌpɪktʃə'rɛsk] adj : pintoresco
pie ['paɪ] n : pastel m (con fruta o carne), empanada f (con carne)
piece ['piːs] n **1** : pieza f **2** FRAGMENT : trozo m, pedazo m **3 a** ~ **of advice** : un consejo — ~ vt **pieced; piecing** or ~ **together** : juntar, componer — **piecemeal** ['piːsˌmiːl] adv : poco a poco — ~ adj : poco sistemático
pier ['pɪr] n : muelle m
pierce ['pɪrs] vt **pierced; piercing** : perforar — **piercing** adj : penetrante
piety ['paɪəti] n, pl **-eties** : piedad f
pig ['pɪg] n : cerdo m, -da f; puerco m, -ca f
pigeon ['pɪdʒən] n : paloma f — **pigeonhole** ['pɪdʒənˌhoːl] n : casilla f
piggyback ['pɪgiˌbæk] adv & adj : a cuestas
pigment ['pɪgmənt] n : pigmento m
pigpen ['pɪgˌpɛn] n : pocilga f
pigtail ['pɪgˌteɪl] n : coleta f, trenza f
pile[1] ['paɪl] n HEAP : montón m, pila f — ~ v **piled; piling** vt : amontonar, apilar — vi ~ **up** : amontonarse, acumularse
pile[2] n NAP : pelo m (de telas)
pilfer ['pɪlfər] vt : robar, hurtar
pilgrim ['pɪlgrəm] n : peregrino m, -na f — **pilgrimage** ['pɪlgrəmɪdʒ] n : peregrinación f
pill ['pɪl] n : pastilla f, píldora f
pillage ['pɪlɪdʒ] n : saqueo m — ~ vt **-laged; -laging** : saquear
pillar ['pɪlər] n : pilar m, columna f
pillow ['pɪloː] n : almohada f — **pillowcase** ['pɪloːˌkeɪs] n : funda f (de almohada)
pilot ['paɪlət] n : piloto mf — ~ vt : pilotar, pilotear — **pilot light** n : piloto m
pimp ['pɪmp] n : proxeneta m
pimple ['pɪmpəl] n : grano m
pin ['pɪn] n **1** : alfiler m **2** BROOCH

: broche *m* 3 *or* **bowling** ~ : bolo *m*
— ~ *vt* **pinned; pinning 1** FASTEN
: prender, sujetar (con alfileres) **2** *or*
~ **down** : inmovilizar
pincers ['pɪntsərz] *npl* : tenazas *fpl*
pinch ['pɪntʃ] *vt* **1** : pellizcar **2** STEAL
: robar — *vi* : apretar — ~ *n* **1** : pellizco *m* **2** BIT : pizca *f* **3 in a** ~ : en
caso necesario
pine[1] ['paɪn] *n* : pino *m* (árbol)
pine[2] *vi* **pined; pining 1** LANGUISH
: languidecer **2** — **for** : suspirar por
pineapple ['paɪn,æpəl] *n* : piña *f*, ananás
m
pink ['pɪŋk] *n* : rosa *m*, rosado *m* — ~
adj : rosa, rosado
pinnacle ['pɪnɪkəl] *n* : pináculo *m*
pinpoint ['pɪn,pɔɪnt] *vt* : localizar, precisar
pint ['paɪnt] *n* : pinta *f*
pioneer [,paɪə'nɪr] *n* : pionero *m*, -ra *f*
pious ['paɪəs] *adj* : piadoso
pipe ['paɪp] *n* **1** : tubo *m*, caño *m* **2** : pipa
f (para fumar) — **pipeline** ['paɪp,laɪn] *n*
1 : conducto *m*, oleoducto *m* (para
petróleo)
piquant ['piːkənt, 'pɪkwənt] *adj* : picante
pique ['piːk] *n* : resentimiento *m*
pirate ['paɪrət] *n* : pirata *mf*
pistachio [pə'stæʃi,o, -'sta-] *n*, *pl* **-chios**
: pistacho *m*
pistol ['pɪstəl] *n* : pistola *f*
piston ['pɪstən] *n* : pistón *m*
pit ['pɪt] *n* **1** HOLE : hoyo *m*, fosa *f* **2** MINE
: mina *f* **3** : hueso *m* (de una fruta) **4** ~
of the stomach : boca *f* del estómago
— ~ *vt* **pitted; pitting 1** : marcar de
hoyos **2** : deshuesar (una fruta) **3** ~
against : enfrentar a
pitch ['pɪtʃ] *vt* **1** : armar (una tienda) **2**
THROW : lanzar — *vi* **1** *or* ~ **forward**
: caerse **2** LURCH : cabecear (dícese de
un barco o un avión) — ~ *n* **1** DE-
GREE, LEVEL : grado *m*, punto *m* **2**
TONE : tono *m* **3** THROW : lanzamiento
m **4** *or* **sales** ~ : presentación *f* (de
un vendedor)
pitcher ['pɪtʃər] *n* **1** JUG : jarro *m* **2** : lan-
zador *m*, -dora *f* (en béisbol, etc.)
pitchfork ['pɪtʃ,fork] *n* : horquilla *f*,
horca *f*
pitfall ['pɪt,fɔl] *n* : riesgo *m*, dificultad *f*
pith ['pɪθ] *n* **1** : médula *f* (de un hueso,
etc.) **2** CORE : meollo *m* — **pithy** ['pɪθi]
adj **pithier; -est** : conciso y sustancioso
pity ['pɪti] *n*, *pl* **pities 1** COMPASSION
: compasión *f* **2 what a** ~**!** : ¡qué lástima! — ~ *vt* **pitied; pitying** : compadecerse de — **pitiful** ['pɪtɪfəl] *adj*

: lastimoso — **pitiless** ['pɪtɪləs] *adj*
: despiadado
pivot ['pɪvət] *n* : pivote *m* — ~ *vi* **1**
: girar sobre un eje **2** — **on** : depender
de
pizza ['piːtsə] *n* : pizza *f*
placard ['plækərd, -,kɑrd] *n* POSTER : cartel *m*, póster *m*
placate ['pleɪ,keɪt, 'plæ-] *vt* **-cated;
-cating** : apaciguar
place ['pleɪs] *n* **1** : sitio *m*, lugar *m* **2**
SEAT : asiento *m* **3** POSITION : puesto *m*
4 ROLE : papel *m* **5 take** ~ : tener
lugar **6 take the** ~ **of** : sustituir a —
~ *vt* **placed; placing 1** PUT, SET
: poner, colocar **2** IDENTIFY : identificar, recordar **3** ~ **an order** : hacer
un pedido — **placement** ['pleɪsmənt] *n*
: colocación *f*
placid ['plæsəd] *adj* : plácido, tranquilo
plagiarism ['pleɪdʒə,rɪzəm] *n* : plagio *m*
— **plagiarize** ['pleɪdʒə,raɪz] *vt* **-rized;
-rizing** : plagiar
plague ['pleɪg] *n* **1** : plaga *f* (de insectos,
etc.) **2** : peste *f* (en medicina)
plaid ['plæd] *n* : tela *f* escocesa — ~ *adj*
: escocés
plain ['pleɪn] *adj* **1** SIMPLE : sencillo **2**
CLEAR : claro, evidente **3** CANDID
: franco **4** HOMELY : poco atractivo **5 in**
~ **sight** : a la vista (de todos) — ~ *n*
: llanura *f*, planicie *f* — **plainly** ['pleɪn-
li] *adv* **1** CLEARLY : claramente **2**
FRANKLY : francamente **3** SIMPLY : sencillamente
plaintiff ['pleɪntɪf] *n* : demandante *mf*
plan ['plæn] *n* **1** : plan *m*, proyecto *m* **2**
DIAGRAM : plano *m* — *v* **planned;
planning** *vt* **1** : planear, proyectar **2**
INTEND : tener planeado — *vi* : hacer
planes
plane[1] ['pleɪn] *n* **1** LEVEL : plano *m*,
nivel *m* **2** AIRPLANE : avión *m*
plane[2] *n* *or* **carpenter's** ~ : cepillo *m*
planet ['plænət] *n* : planeta *m*
plank ['plæŋk] *n* : tabla *f*
planning ['plænɪŋ] *n* : planificación *f*
plant ['plænt] *vt* : plantar (flores, árboles), sembrar (semillas) — ~ *n*
1 : planta *f* **2** FACTORY : fábrica *f*
plantain ['plæntən] *n* : plátano *m* (grande)
plantation [plæn'teɪʃən] *n* : plantación *f*
plaque ['plæk] *n* : placa *f*
plaster ['plæstər] *n* : yeso *m* — ~ *vt* **1**
: enyesar **2** COVER : cubrir — **plaster
cast** *n* : escayola *f*
plastic ['plæstɪk] *adj* **1** : de plástico **2**
FLEXIBLE : plástico, flexible **3** ~ **surgery** : cirugía *f* plástica — ~ *n* : plástico *m*

plate 334 pneumatic

plate ['pleɪt] n 1 SHEET : placa f 2 DISH : plato m 3 ILLUSTRATION : lámina f — ~ vt **plated**; **plating** : chapar (en metal)

plateau [plæ'toː] n, pl **-teaus** or **-teaux** [-'toːz] : meseta f

platform ['plæt,fɔrm] n 1 : plataforma f 2 : andén m (de una estación de ferrocarril) 3 or political ~ : programa m electoral

platinum ['plætənəm] n : platino m

platitude ['plætə,tuːd, -,tjuːd] n : lugar m común

platoon [plə'tuːn] n : sección f (en el ejército)

platter ['plætər] n : fuente f

plausible ['plɔzəbəl] adj : creíble, verosímil

play ['pleɪ] n 1 : juego m 2 DRAMA : obra f de teatro — ~ vi 1 : jugar 2 ~ **in a band** : tocar en un grupo — vt 1 : jugar (deportes, etc.), jugar a (juegos) 2 : tocar (música o un instrumento) 3 ~ **the role of** : representar el papel de — **player** ['pleɪər] n 1 : jugador m, -dora f 2 ACTOR : actor m, actriz f 3 MUSICIAN : músico m, -ca f — **playful** ['pleɪfəl] adj : juguetón — **playground** ['pleɪ,graʊnd] n : patio m de recreo — **playing card** n : naipe m, carta f — **playmate** ['pleɪ,meɪt] n : compañero m, -ra f de juego — **play-off** ['pleɪ,ɔf] n : desempate m — **playpen** ['pleɪ,pɛn] n : corral m (para niños) — **plaything** ['pleɪ,θɪŋ] n : juguete m — **playwright** ['pleɪ,raɪt] n : dramaturgo m, -ga f

plea ['pliː] n 1 : acto m de declararse (en derecho) 2 APPEAL : ruego m, súplica f — **plead** ['pliːd] v **pleaded** or **pled** ['plɛd]; **pleading** vi 1 ~ **for** : suplicar 2 ~ **guilty** : declararse culpable 3 ~ **not guilty** : negar la acusación — vt 1 : alegar, pretextar 2 ~ **a case** : defender un caso

pleasant ['plɛzənt] adj : agradable, grato — **please** ['pliːz] v **pleased**; **pleasing** vt 1 GRATIFY : complacer 2 SATISFY : satisfacer — vi 1 : agradar 2 **do as you** ~ : haz lo que quieras — ~ adv : por favor — **pleased** ['pliːzd] adj : contento — **pleasing** ['pliːzɪŋ] adj : agradable — **pleasure** ['plɛʒər] n : placer m, gusto m

pleat ['pliːt] vt : plisar — ~ n : pliegue m

pledge ['plɛdʒ] n 1 SECURITY : prenda f 2 PROMISE : promesa f — ~ vt **pledged**; **pledging** 1 PAWN : empeñar 2 PROMISE : prometer

plenty ['plɛnti] n 1 : abundancia f 2 ~ **of time** : tiempo m de sobra — **plentiful** ['plɛntɪfəl] adj : abundante

pliable ['plaɪəbəl] adj : flexible

pliers ['plaɪərz] npl : alicates mpl

plight ['plaɪt] n : situación f difícil

plod ['plɑd] vi **plodded**; **plodding** 1 : caminar con paso pesado 2 DRUDGE : trabajar laboriosamente

plot ['plɑt] n 1 LOT : parcela f 2 : argumento m (de una novela, etc.) 3 CONSPIRACY : complot m, intriga f — ~ v **plotted**; **plotting** vt : tramar (un plan), trazar (una gráfica, etc.) — vi CONSPIRE : conspirar

plow or **plough** ['plaʊ] n 1 : arado m 2 → **snowplow** — ~ v : arar

ploy ['plɔɪ] n : estratagema f

pluck ['plʌk] vt 1 : arrancar 2 : desplumar (un pollo, etc.) 3 : recoger (flores) 4 ~ **one's eyebrows** : depilarse las cejas

plug ['plʌg] n 1 STOPPER : tapón m 2 : enchufe m (eléctrico) — ~ vt **plugged**; **plugging** 1 BLOCK : tapar 2 ADVERTISE : dar publicidad a 3 ~ **in** : enchufar

plum ['plʌm] n : ciruela f

plumb ['plʌm] adj : a plomo, vertical — **plumber** ['plʌmər] n : fontanero m, -ra f; plomero m, -ra f Lat — **plumbing** ['plʌmɪŋ] n 1 : fontanería f, plomería f Lat 2 PIPES : cañerías fpl

plume ['pluːm] n : pluma f

plummet ['plʌmət] n : caer en picado

plump ['plʌmp] adj : rechoncho fam

plunder ['plʌndər] vi : saquear, robar — ~ n : botín m

plunge ['plʌndʒ] v **plunged**; **plunging** vt 1 IMMERSE : sumergir 2 THRUST : hundir — vi 1 : zambullirse (en el agua) 2 DESCEND : descender en picada — ~ n 1 DIVE : zambullida f 2 DROP : descenso m abrupto

plural ['plʊrəl] adj : plural — ~ n : plural m

plus ['plʌs] adj : positivo — ~ n 1 or ~ **sign** : signo m (de) más 2 ADVANTAGE : ventaja f — ~ prep : más — ~ conj : y, además

plush ['plʌʃ] n : felpa f — ~ adj 1 : de felpa 2 LUXURIOUS : lujoso

plutonium [pluːˈtoːniəm] n : plutonio m

ply ['plaɪ] vt **plied**; **plying** 1 : ejercer (un oficio) 2 ~ **with questions** : acosar con preguntas

plywood ['plaɪ,wʊd] n : contrachapado m

pneumatic [nʊˈmætɪk, njʊ-] adj : neumático

pneumonia [nʊˈmoːnjə, njʊ-] n : pulmonía f

poach[1] [ˈpoːtʃ] vt : cocer a fuego lento

poach[2] vt or ~ game : cazar ilegalmente — **poacher** [ˈpoːtʃər] n : cazador m furtivo, cazadora f furtiva

pocket [ˈpakət] n : bolsillo m — ~ vt : meterse en el bolsillo — **pocketbook** [ˈpakət͵bʊk] n : cartera f, bolsa f Lat — **pocketknife** [ˈpakət͵naɪf] n, pl -knives : navaja f

pod [ˈpad] n : vaina f

poem [ˈpoːəm] n : poema m — **poet** [ˈpoːət] n : poeta mf — **poetic** [poˈɛt͵ɪk] or **poetical** [-t͵ɪkəl] adj : poético — **poetry** [ˈpoːətri] n : poesía f

poignant [ˈpɔɪnjənt] adj : conmovedor

point [ˈpɔɪnt] n 1 : punto m 2 PURPOSE : sentido m 3 TIP : punta f 4 FEATURE : cualidad f 5 **be beside the** ~ : no venir al caso 6 **there's no** ~ ... : no sirve de nada — ~ vt 1 AIM : apuntar 2 or ~ **out** : señalar, indicar — vi ~ **at** : señalar (con el dedo) — **point–blank** [ˈpɔɪntˈblæŋk] adv : a quemarropa — **pointer** [ˈpɔɪntər] n 1 NEEDLE : aguja f 2 : perro m de muestra 3 TIP : consejo m — **pointless** [ˈpɔɪntləs] adj : inútil — **point of view** n : perspectiva f, punto m de vista

poise [ˈpɔɪz] n 1 : elegancia f 2 COMPOSURE : aplomo m

poison [ˈpɔɪzən] n : veneno m — ~ vt : envenenar — **poisonous** [ˈpɔɪzənəs] adj : venenoso (dícese de una culebra, etc.), tóxico (dícese de una sustancia)

poke [ˈpoːk] vt **poked; poking** 1 JAB : golpear (con la punta de algo), dar 2 THRUST : introducir, asomar — ~ n : golpe m abrupto (con la punta de algo)

poker[1] [ˈpoːkər] n : atizador m (para el fuego)

poker[2] n : póquer m (juego de naipes)

polar [ˈpoːlər] adj : polar — **polar bear** n : oso m blanco — **polarize** [ˈpoːlə͵raɪz] vt **-ized; -izing** : polarizar

pole[1] [ˈpoːl] n : palo m, poste m

pole[2] n : polo m (en geografía)

police [pəˈliːs] vt **-liced; -licing** : mantener el orden en — ~ ns & pl **the** ~ : la policía — **policeman** [pəˈliːsmən] n, pl **-men** [-mən, -͵mɛn] : policía m — **police officer** n : policía mf, agente mf de policía — **policewoman** [pəˈliːs͵wʊmən] n, pl **-women** [-͵wɪmən] : (mujer f) policía f

policy [ˈpaləsi] n, pl **-cies** 1 : política f 2 or **insurance** ~ : póliza f de seguros

polio [ˈpoːli͵oː] or **poliomyelitis** [͵poːli͵oː͵maɪəˈlaɪtəs] n : polio f, poliomielitis f

polish [ˈpalɪʃ] vt 1 : pulir 2 : limpiar (zapatos), encerar (un suelo) — ~ n 1 LUSTER : brillo m, lustre m 2 : betún m (para zapatos), cera f (para suelos y muebles), esmalte m (para las uñas)

Polish [ˈpoːlɪʃ] adj : polaco — ~ n : polaco m (idioma)

polite [pəˈlaɪt] adj **-liter; -est** : cortés — **politeness** [pəˈlaɪtnəs] n : cortesía f

political [pəˈlɪt͵ɪkəl] adj : político — **politician** [͵paləˈtɪʃən] n : político m, -ca f — **politics** [ˈpalə͵tɪks] ns & pl : política f

polka [ˈpoːlkə, ˈpoːkə] n : polka f — **polka dot** [ˈpoːkə͵dat] n : lunar m

poll [ˈpoːl] n 1 : encuesta f, sondeo m 2 **the** ~**s** : las urnas — ~ vt 1 : obtener (votos) 2 CANVASS : encuestar, sondear

pollen [ˈpalən] n : polen m

pollute [pəˈluːt] vt **-luted; -luting** : contaminar — **pollution** [pəˈluːʃən] n : contaminación f

polyester [ˈpali͵ɛstər, ͵pali-] n : poliéster m

polygon [ˈpali͵gan] n : polígono m

pomegranate [ˈpamə͵grænət, ˈpam͵grænət] n : granada f

pomp [ˈpamp] n : pompa f — **pompous** [ˈpampəs] adj : pomposo

pond [ˈpand] n : charca f (natural), estanque m (artificial)

ponder [ˈpandər] vt : considerar — vi ~ **over** : reflexionar sobre

pony [ˈpoːni] n, pl **-nies** : poni m — **ponytail** [ˈpoːni͵teɪl] n : cola f de caballo

poodle [ˈpuːdəl] n : caniche m

pool [ˈpuːl] n 1 PUDDLE : charco m 2 : fondo m común (de recursos) 3 BILLIARDS : billar m 4 or **swimming** ~ : piscina f — ~ vt : hacer un fondo común de

poor [ˈpʊr, ˈpor] adj 1 : pobre 2 INFERIOR : malo 3 **the** ~ : los pobres — **poorly** [ˈpʊrli, ˈpor-] adv : mal

pop[1] [ˈpap] v **popped; popping** vt 1 : hacer reventar 2 ~ **sth into** : meter algo en — vi 1 BURST : reventarse, estallar 2 ~ **in** : entrar (un momento) 3 ~ **out** : saltar (dícese de los ojos) 4 ~ **up** APPEAR : aparecer — ~ n 1 : ruido m seco 2 → **soda pop**

pop[2] n or ~ **music** : música f popular

popcorn [ˈpap͵kɔrn] n : palomitas fpl

pope [ˈpoːp] n : papa m

poplar [ˈpaplər] n : álamo m

poppy [ˈpapi] n, pl **-pies** : amapola f

popular [ˈpapjələr] adj : popular — **pop-**

ularity [ˌpɑpjəˈlærəti] n : popularidad f
— **popularize** [ˈpɑpjələˌraɪz] vt **-ized;**
-izing : popularizar
populate [ˈpɑpjəˌleɪt] vt **-lated; -lating**
: poblar — **population** [ˌpɑpjəˈleɪʃən] n
: población f
porcelain [ˈpɔrsələn] n : porcelana f
porch [ˈpɔrtʃ] n : porche m
porcupine [ˈpɔrkjəˌpaɪn] n : puerco m
espín
pore[1] [ˈpor] vi **pored; poring** ~ **over**
: estudiar esmeradamente
pore[2] n : poro m
pork [ˈpork] n : carne f de cerdo
pornography [pɔrˈnɑgrəfi] n : pornografía f — **pornographic** [ˌpɔrnə
ˈgræfɪk] adj : pornográfico
porous [ˈporəs] adj : poroso
porpoise [ˈpɔrpəs] n : marsopa f
porridge [ˈpɔrɪdʒ] n : avena f (cocida),
gachas fpl (de avena)
port[1] [ˈport] n HARBOR : puerto m
port[2] n or ~ **side** : babor m
port[3] n : oporto m (vino)
portable [ˈpɔrtəbəl] adj : portátil
portent [ˈpɔrˌtɛnt] n : presagio m
porter [ˈpɔrtər] n : maletero m, mozo m
(de estación)
portfolio [pɔrtˈfoːliˌo] n, pl **-lios** : cartera
f
porthole [ˈpɔrtˌhoːl] n : portilla f
portion [ˈpɔrʃən] n : porción f
portrait [ˈpɔrtrət, -ˌtreɪt] n : retrato m
portray [pɔrˈtreɪ] vt 1 : representar, retratar 2 : interpretar (un personaje)
Portuguese [ˌpɔrtʃəˈgiːz, -ˈgiːs] adj : portugués — n 1 : portugués m (idioma)
pose [ˈpoːz] v **posed; posing** vt
: plantear (una pregunta, etc.), representar (una amenaza) — vi 1 : posar 2
~ **as** : hacerse pasar por — n
: pose f
posh [ˈpɑʃ] adj : elegante, de lujo
position [pəˈzɪʃən] n 1 : posición f 2 JOB
: puesto m — ~ vt : colocar, situar
positive [ˈpɑzəˌtɪv] adj 1 : positivo 2
CERTAIN : seguro
possess [pəˈzɛs] vt : poseer — **posses**
sion [pəˈzɛʃən] n 1 : posesión f 2 ~ **s**
npl BELONGINGS : bienes mpl — **pos**
sessive [pəˈzɛsɪv] adj : posesivo
possible [ˈpɑsəbəl] adj : posible — **pos**
sibility [ˌpɑsəˈbɪləti] n, pl **-ties** : posibilidad f — **possibly** [ˈpɑsəbli] adv
: posiblemente
post[1] [ˈpoːst] n POLE : poste m, palo m
post[2] n POSITION : puesto m
post[3] n MAIL : cartas fpl — ~ vt 1
: echar al correo 2 **keep** ~ **ed** : tener
al corriente — **postage** [ˈpoːstɪdʒ] n

: franqueo m — **postal** [ˈpoːstəl] adj
: postal — **postcard** [ˈpoːstˌkard] n
: tarjeta f postal
poster [ˈpoːstər] n : cartel m
posterity [pɑˈstɛrəti] n : posteridad f
posthumous [ˈpɑstʃəməs] adj : póstumo
postman [ˈpoːstmən, -ˌmæn] → **mailman**
— **post office** n : oficina f de correos
postpone [ˌpoːstˈpoːn] vt **-poned;**
-poning : aplazar — **postponement**
[ˌpoːstˈpoːnmənt] n : aplazamiento m
postscript [ˈpoːstˌskrɪpt] n : posdata f
posture [ˈpɑstʃər] n : postura f
postwar [ˌpoːstˈwɔr] adj : de (la) posguerra
pot [ˈpɑt] n 1 : olla f (de cocina) 2 FLOW
ERPOT : maceta f 3 ~ **s and pans**
: cacharros mpl
potassium [pəˈtæsiəm] n : potasio m
potato [pəˈteɪˌto] n, pl **-toes** : patata f,
papa f Lat
potent [ˈpoːtənt] adj 1 POWERFUL : poderoso 2 EFFECTIVE : eficaz
potential [pəˈtɛntʃəl] adj : potencial —
~ n : potencial m
pothole [ˈpɑtˌhoːl] n : bache m
potion [ˈpoːʃən] n : poción f
pottery [ˈpɑtəri] n, pl **-teries** : cerámica f
pouch [ˈpaʊtʃ] n 1 BAG : bolsa f pequeña
2 : bolsa f (de un animal)
poultry [ˈpoːltri] n : aves fpl de corral
pounce [ˈpaʊnts] vi **pounced; pounc**
ing : abalanzarse
pound[1] [ˈpaʊnd] n : libra f (unidad de
dinero o de peso)
pound[2] n or dog ~ : perrera f
pound[3] vt 1 CRUSH : machacar 2 HIT
: golpear — vi : palpitar (dícese del
corazón)
pour [ˈpor] vt : verter — vi 1 FLOW : fluir,
salir 2 it's ~ **ing** : está lloviendo a
cántaros
pout [ˈpaʊt] vi : hacer pucheros — ~ n
: puchero m
poverty [ˈpɑvərti] n : pobreza f
powder [ˈpaʊdər] vt 1 : empolvar 2
CRUSH : pulverizar — ~ n 1 : polvo m
2 or face ~ : polvos mpl — **pow**
dery [ˈpaʊdəri] adj : polvoriento
power [ˈpaʊər] n 1 CONTROL : poder m 2
ABILITY : capacidad f 3 STRENGTH
: fuerza f 4 : potencia f (política) 5 EN
ERGY : energía f 6 ELECTRICITY : electricidad f — ~ vt : impulsar — **power**
ful [ˈpaʊərfəl] adj : poderoso —
powerless [ˈpaʊərləs] adj : impotente
practical [ˈpræktɪkəl] adj : práctico —
practically [ˈpræktɪkli] adv : casi,
prácticamente
practice or **practise** [ˈpræktəs] v **-ticed**

or **-tised;** **-ticing** *or* **-tising** *vt* **1** : practicar **2** : ejercer (una profesión) — *vi* : practicar — **practice** *n* **1** : práctica *f* **2** CUSTOM : costumbre *f* **3** : ejercicio *m* (de una profesión) **4 be out of ~** : no estar en forma — **practitioner** [præk-'tɪʃənər] *n* **1** : profesional *mf* **2 general ~** : médico *m*, -ca *f* de medicina general

pragmatic [præg'mætɪk] *adj* : pragmático

prairie ['præri] *n* : pradera *f*

praise ['preɪz] *vt* **praised; praising** : elogiar, alabar — ~ *n* : elogio *m*, alabanza *f* — **praiseworthy** ['preɪz,wərði] *adj* : loable

prance ['prænts] *vi* **pranced; prancing** : hacer cabriolas

prank ['præŋk] *n* : travesura *f*

prawn ['prɔn] *n* : gamba *f*

pray ['preɪ] *vi* **1** : rezar **2 ~ for** : rogar — **prayer** ['preɪr] *n* : oración *f*

preach ['priːtʃ] *v* : predicar — **preacher** ['priːtʃər] *n* MINISTER : pastor *m*, -tora *f*

precarious [prɪ'kæriəs] *adj* : precario

precaution [prɪ'kɔʃən] *n* : precaución *f*

precede [prɪ'siːd] *vt* **-ceded; -ceding** : preceder a — **precedence** ['presədənts, prɪ'siːdənts] *n* : precedencia *f* — **precedent** ['presədənt] *n* : precedente *m*

precinct ['priː,sɪŋkt] *n* **1** DISTRICT : distrito *m* **2 ~s** *npl* : recinto *m*

precious ['preʃəs] *adj* : precioso

precipice ['presəpəs] *n* : precipicio *m*

precipitate [prɪ'sɪpə,teɪt] *vt* **-tated; -tating** : precipitar — **precipitation** [prɪ,sɪpə'teɪʃən] *n* **1** HASTE : precipitación *f* **2** : precipitaciones *fpl* (en meteorología)

precise [prɪ'saɪs] *adj* : preciso — **precisely** *adv* : precisamente — **precision** [prɪ'sɪʒən] *n* : precisión *f*

preclude [prɪ'kluːd] *vt* **-cluded; -cluding** **1** PREVENT : impedir **2** EXCLUDE : excluir

precocious [prɪ'koːʃəs] *adj* : precoz

preconceived [,priːkən'siːv] *adj* : preconcebido

predator ['predətər] *n* : depredador *m*

predecessor ['predə,sesər, 'priː-] *n* : antecesor *m*, -sora *f*; predecesor *m*, -sora *f*

predicament [prɪ'dɪkəmənt] *n* : apuro *m*

predict [prɪ'dɪkt] *vt* : pronosticar, predecir — **predictable** [prɪ'dɪktəbəl] *adj* : previsible — **prediction** [prɪ'dɪkʃən] *n* : pronóstico *m*, predicción *f*

predispose [,priːdɪ'spoːz] *vt* **-posed; -posing** : predisponer

predominant [prɪ'dɑmənənt] *adj* : predominante

preeminent [pri'emənənt] *adj* : preeminente

preempt [pri'empt] *vt* : adelantarse a (un ataque, etc.)

preen ['priːn] *vt* **1** : arreglarse (las plumas) **2 ~ oneself** : acicalarse

prefabricated [,priː'fæbrə,keɪtəd] *adj* : prefabricado

preface ['prefəs] *n* : prefacio *m*, prólogo *m*

prefer [prɪ'fər] *vt* **-ferred; -ferring** : preferir — **preferable** ['prefərəbəl] *adj* : preferible — **preference** ['prefrənts, 'prefər-] *n* : preferencia *f* — **preferential** [,prefə'rentʃəl] *adj* : preferente

prefix ['priː,fɪks] *n* : prefijo *m*

pregnancy ['pregnəntsi] *n, pl* **-cies** : embarazo *m* — **pregnant** ['pregnənt] *adj* : embarazada

prehistoric [,priːhɪs'tɔrɪk] *or* **prehistorical** [-ɪkəl] *adj* : prehistórico

prejudice ['predʒədəs] *n* **1** BIAS : prejuicio *m* **2** HARM : perjuicio *m* — ~ *vt* **-diced; -dicing** **1** BIAS : predisponer **2** HARM : perjudicar — **prejudiced** ['predʒədəst] *adj* : parcial

preliminary [prɪ'lɪmə,neri] *adj* : preliminar

prelude ['preɪ,luːd, 'preɪ,juːd; 'preɪ,luːd, 'priː-] *n* : preludio *m*

premarital [,priː'mærətəl] *adj* : prematrimonial

premature [,priːmə'tur, -'tjur, -'tʃur] *adj* : prematuro

premeditated [prɪ'medə,teɪtəd] *adj* : premeditado

premier [prɪ'mɪr, -'mjɪr; 'priː,mɪər] *adj* : principal — ~ *n* PRIME MINISTER : primer ministro *m*, primera ministra *f*

premiere [prɪ'mjer, -'mɪr] *n* : estreno *m*

premise ['premɪs] *n* **1** : premisa *f* (de un argumento) **2 ~s** *npl* : recinto *m*, local *m*

premium ['priːmiəm] *n* **1** : premio *m* **2 insurance ~** : prima *f* (de seguro)

preoccupied [prɪ'ɑkjə,paɪd] *adj* : preocupado

prepare [prɪ'pær] *v* **-pared; -paring** *vt* : preparar — *vi* : prepararse — **preparation** [,prepə'reɪʃən] *n* **1** : preparación *f* **2 ~s** *npl* ARRANGEMENTS : preparativos *mpl* — **preparatory** [prɪ'pærə,tori] *adj* : preparatorio

prepay [,priː'peɪ] *vt* **-paid; -paying** : pagar por adelantado

preposition [,prepə'zɪʃən] *n* : preposición *f*

preposterous [prɪ'pɑstərəs] *adj* : absurdo, ridículo

prerequisite [ˌpri'rekwəzət] *n* : requisito *m* previo

prerogative [prɪ'rɑgətɪv] *n* : prerrogativa *f*

prescribe [prɪ'skraɪb] *vt* **-scribed; -scribing 1** : prescribir **2** : recetar (en medicina) — **prescription** [prɪ'skrɪpʃən] *n* : receta *f*

presence ['prezənts] *n* : presencia *f*

present¹ ['prezənt] *adj* **1** CURRENT : actual **2 be ~ at** : estar presente en — **~** *n* **1** : presente *m* **2 at ~** : actualmente

present² ['prezənt] *n* GIFT : regalo *m* — **~** [prɪ'zent] *vt* **1** INTRODUCE : presentar **2** GIVE : entregar — **presentation** [ˌpri:ˌzen'teɪʃən, ˌprezən-] *n* **1** : presentación *f* **2 or ~ ceremony** : ceremonia *f* de entrega

presently ['prezəntli] *adv* **1** SOON : dentro de poco **2** NOW : actualmente

preserve [prɪ'zərv] *vt* **-served; -serving 1** : conservar **2** MAINTAIN : mantener — **~** *n* **1** JAM : confitura *f* **2 or game ~** : coto *m* de caza — **preservation** [ˌprezər'veɪʃən] *n* : preservación *f*, conservación *f* — **preservative** [prɪ'zərvətɪv] *n* : conservante *m*

president ['prezədənt] *n* : presidente *m*, -ta *f* — **presidency** ['prezədənsi] *n, pl* **-cies** : presidencia *f* — **presidential** [ˌprezə'dentʃəl] *adj* : presidencial

press ['pres] *n* : prensa *f* — **~** *vt* **1** : apretar **2** IRON : planchar — *vi* **1** : apretar **2** URGE : presionar — **pressing** ['presɪŋ] *adj* : urgente — **pressure** ['preʃər] *n* : presión *f* — **~** *vt* **-sured; -suring** : presionar, apremiar

prestige [pre'sti:ʒ, -'stɪdʒ] *n* : prestigio *m* — **prestigious** [pre'stɪdʒəs] *adj* : prestigioso

presume [prɪ'zu:m] *vt* **-sumed; -suming** : presumir — **presumably** [prɪ'zu:məbli] *adv* : es de suponer, supuestamente — **presumption** [prɪ'zʌmpʃən] *n* : presunción *f* — **presumptuous** [prɪ'zʌmptʃuəs] *adj* : presuntuoso

pretend [prɪ'tend] *vt* **1** CLAIM : pretender **2** FEIGN : fingir — *vi* : fingir — **pretense** *or* **pretence** [prɪ'tents, 'pri:ˌtents] *n* **1** CLAIM : pretensión *f* **2 under false ~s** : con pretextos falsos — **pretentious** [prɪ'tentʃəs] *adj* : pretencioso

pretext ['pri:ˌtekst] *n* : pretexto *m*

pretty ['prɪti] *adj* **-tier; -est** : lindo, bonito — **~** *adv* FAIRLY : bastante

pretzel ['pretsəl] *n* : galleta *f* salada

prevail [prɪ'veɪl] *vi* **1** TRIUMPH : prevalecer **2** PREDOMINATE : predominar **3 ~ upon** : persuadir — **prevalent** ['prevələnt] *adj* : extendido

prevent [prɪ'vent] *vt* : impedir — **prevention** [prɪ'ventʃən] *n* : prevención *f* — **preventive** [prɪ'ventɪv] *adj* : preventivo

preview ['pri:ˌvju] *n* : preestreno *m*

previous ['pri:viəs] *adj* : previo, anterior — **previously** ['pri:viəsli] *adv* : anteriormente

prey ['preɪ] *n, pl* **preys** : presa *f* — **prey on** *vt* **1** : alimentarse de **2 ~ on one's mind** : atormentar a algn

price ['praɪs] *n* : precio *m* — **~** *vt* **priced; pricing** : poner un precio a — **priceless** ['praɪsləs] *adj* : inestimable

prick ['prɪk] *n* : pinchazo *m* — **~** *vt* **1** : pinchar **2 ~ up one's ears** : levantar las orejas — **prickly** ['prɪkəli] *adj* : espinoso

pride ['praɪd] *n* : orgullo *m* — **~** *vt* **prided; priding ~ oneself on** : enorgullecerse de

priest ['pri:st] *n* : sacerdote *m* — **priesthood** ['pri:stˌhʊd] *n* : sacerdocio *m*

prim ['prɪm] *adj* **primmer; primmest** : remilgado

primary ['praɪˌmeri, 'praɪməri] *adj* **1** FIRST : primario **2** PRINCIPAL : principal — **primarily** [praɪ'merəli] *adv* : principalmente

prime¹ ['praɪm] *vt* **primed; priming 1** : cebar (un arma de fuego, etc.) **2** PREPARE : preparar

prime² *n* **the ~ of one's life** : la flor de la vida — **~** *adj* **1** MAIN : principal, primero **2** EXCELLENT : excelente — **prime minister** *n* : primero ministro *m*, primera ministra *f*

primer¹ ['praɪmər] *n* : base *f* (de pintura)

primer² ['prɪmər] *n* READER : cartilla *f*

primitive ['prɪmətɪv] *adj* : primitivo

primrose ['prɪmˌroz] *n* : primavera *f*

prince ['prɪnts] *n* : príncipe *m* — **princess** ['prɪntsəs, 'prɪnˌses] *n* : princesa *f*

principal ['prɪntsəpəl] *adj* : principal — **~** *n* : director *m*, -tora *f* (de un colegio)

principle ['prɪntsəpəl] *n* : principio *m*

print ['prɪnt] *n* **1** MARK : huella *f* **2** LETTERING : letra *f* **3** ENGRAVING : grabado *m* **4** : estampado *m* (de tela) **5** : copia *f* (en fotografía) **6 out of ~** : agotado — **~** *vt* : imprimir (libros, etc.) — *vi* : escribir con letra de molde — **printer** ['prɪntər] *n* **1** : impresor *m*, -sora *f* (persona) **2** : impresora *f* (máquina) — **printing** ['prɪntɪŋ] *n* **1** : impresión *f* **2**

: imprenta *f* (profesión) **3** LETTERING
: letras *fpl* de molde
prior ['praɪər] *adj* **1** : previo **2** ~ **to**
: antes de — **priority** [praɪ'ɔrət̬i] *n*, *pl*
-ties : prioridad *f*
prison ['prɪzən] *n* : prisión *f*, cárcel *f* —
prisoner ['prɪzənər] *n* **1** : preso *m*, -sa *f*
2 ~ **of war** : prisionero *m*, -ra *f* de
guerra
privacy ['praɪvəsi] *n*, *pl* **-cies** : intimidad
f — **private** ['praɪvət] *adj* **1** : privado **2**
SECRET : secreto — ~ *n* : soldado *m*
raso — **privately** ['praɪvətli] *adv* : en
privado
privilege ['prɪvlɪdʒ, 'prɪvə-] *n* : privilegio
m — **privileged** ['prɪvlɪdʒd, 'prɪvə-] *adj*
: privilegiado
prize ['praɪz] *n* : premio *m* — ~ *adj*
: premiado — ~ *vt* **prized; prizing**
: valorar, apreciar — **prizefighter**
['praɪz,faɪt̬ər] *n* : boxeador *m*, -dora *f*
profesional — **prizewinning** ['praɪz-
,wɪnɪŋ] *adj* : premiado
pro ['pro:] *n* **1** → **professional 2 the** ~**s**
and cons : los pros y los contras
probability [,prɑbə'bɪlət̬i] *n*, *pl* **-ties**
: probabilidad *f* — **probable** ['prɑbə-
bəl] *adj* : probable — **probably** [-bli]
adv : probablemente
probation [pro'beɪʃən] *n* **1** : período *m*
de prueba (de un empleado, etc.) **2**
: libertad *f* condicional (de un preso)
probe ['pro:b] *n* **1** : sonda *f* (en medicina, etc.) **2** INVESTIGATION : investigación *f* — ~ *vt* **probed; probing 1**
: sondar **2** INVESTIGATE : investigar
problem ['prɑbləm] *n* : problema *m*
procedure [prə'si:dʒər] *n* : procedimiento *m*
proceed [pro'si:d] *vi* **1** ACT : proceder **2**
CONTINUE : continuar **3** ADVANCE
: avanzar — **proceedings** [pro'si:dɪŋz]
npl **1** EVENTS : actos *mpl* **2** : proceso *m*
(en derecho) — **proceeds** ['pro:,si:dz]
npl : ganancias *fpl*
process ['prɑ,ses, 'pro:-] *n*, *pl* **-cesses**
['prɑ,sesəz, 'pro:-, -səsəz, -sə,si:z] **1** : proceso *m* **2 in the** ~ **of** : en vías de —
~ *vt* : procesar — **procession** [prə-
'seʃən] *n* : desfile *m*
proclaim [pro'kleɪm] *vt* : proclamar —
proclamation [,prɑklə'meɪʃən] *n* : proclamación *f*
procrastinate [prə'kræstə,neɪt] *vi* **-nated;**
-nating : demorar, aplazar
procure [prə'kjʊr] *vt* **-cured; -curing**
: obtener
prod ['prɑd] *vt* **prodded; prodding**
: pinchar, aguijonear
prodigal ['prɑdɪgəl] *adj* : pródigo

prodigy ['prɑdədʒi] *n*, *pl* **-gies** : prodigio
m
produce [prə'du:s, -'dju:s] *vt* **-duced;**
-ducing 1 : producir **2** CAUSE : causar
3 SHOW : presentar, mostrar **4** : poner
en escena (una obra de teatro) — ~
['prɑ,du:s, 'pro:-, -,dju:s] *n* : productos
mpl agrícolas — **producer** [prə'du:sər,
-'dju:-] *n* : productor *m*, -tora *f* — **product** ['prɑdʌkt] *n* : producto *m* — **productive** [prə'dʌktɪv] *adj* : productivo
profane [pro'feɪn] *adj* **1** : profano **2** IR-
REVERENT : blasfemo — **profanity**
[pro'fænət̬i] *n*, *pl* **-ties** : blasfemia *f*
profess [prə'fes] *vt* : profesar — **profession** [prə'feʃən] *n* : profesión *f* —
professional [prə'feʃənəl] *adj* : profesional — ~ *n* : profesional *mf* —
professor [prə'fesər] *n* : profesor *m*,
-sora *f*
proficiency [prə'fɪʃəntsi] *n* : competencia *f* — **proficient** [prə'fɪʃənt] *adj*
: competente
profile ['pro:,faɪl] *n* **1** : perfil *m* **2 keep a
low** ~ : no llamar la atención
profit ['prɑfət] *n* : beneficio *m*, ganancia
f — ~ *vi* : sacar provecho (de), beneficiarse (de) — **profitable** ['prɑfət̬əbəl]
adj : provechoso
profound [prə'faʊnd] *adj* : profundo
profuse [prə'fju:s] *adj* : profuso — **profusion** [prə'fju:ʒən] *n* : profusión *f*
prognosis [prɑg'no:sɪs] *n*, *pl* **-noses**
[-,si:z] : pronóstico *m*
program ['pro:,græm, -grəm] *n* : programa *m* — ~ *vt* **-grammed** *or*
-gramed; -gramming *or* **-graming**
: programar
progress ['prɑgrəs, -,gres] *n* **1** : progreso
m **2** ADVANCE : avance *m* — ~ [prə-
'gres] *vi* : progresar, avanzar — **progressive** [prə'gresɪv] *adj* **1** : progresista (dícese de la política, etc.) **2**
INCREASING : progresiva
prohibit [pro'hɪbət] *vt* : prohibir — **prohibition** [,pro:ə'bɪʃən, ,pro:hə-] *n* : prohibición *f*
project ['prɑdʒekt, -dʒɪkt] *n* : proyecto *m*
— ~ [prə'dʒekt] *vt* : proyectar — *vi*
PROTRUDE : sobresalir — **projectile**
[prə'dʒektəl, -,taɪl] *n* : proyectil *m* —
projection [prə'dʒekʃən] *n* **1** : proyección *f* **2** PROTRUSION : saliente *m* —
projector [prə'dʒektər] *n* : proyector *m*
proliferate [prə'lɪfə,reɪt] *vi* **-ated; -ating**
: proliferar — **proliferation** [prə,lɪfə-
'reɪʃən] *n* : proliferación *f* — **prolific**
[prə'lɪfɪk] *adj* : prolífico
prologue ['pro:,lɔg] *n* : prólogo *m*
prolong [prə'lɔŋ] *vt* : prolongar

prom ['pram] *n* : baile *m* formal (en un colegio)
prominent ['pramənənt] *adj* : prominente — **prominence** ['pramənənts] *n* 1 : prominencia *f* 2 IMPORTANCE : eminencia *f*
promiscuous [prə'mɪskjuəs] *adj* : promiscuo
promise ['praməs] *n* : promesa *f* — ~ *v* **-ised; -ising** : prometer — **promising** ['praməsɪŋ] *adj* : prometedor
promote [prə'moːt] *vt* **-moted; -moting** 1 : ascender (a un alumno o un empleado) 2 FURTHER : promover, fomentar 3 ADVERTISE : promocionar — **promoter** [prə'moːtər] *n* : promotor *m*, -tora *f*; empresario *m*, -ria *f* (en deportes) — **promotion** [prə'moːʃən] *n* 1 : ascenso *m* (de un alumno o un empleado) 2 ADVERTISING : publicidad *f*, propaganda *f*
prompt ['prampt] *vt* 1 INCITE : provocar (una cosa), inducir (a una persona) 2 : apuntar (a un actor, etc.) — ~ *adj* 1 : rápido 2 PUNCTUAL : puntual
prone ['proːn] *adj* 1 : boca abajo, decúbito prono 2 be ~ to : ser propenso a
prong ['praŋ] *n* : punta *f*, diente *m*
pronoun ['proːnaun] *n* : pronombre *m*
pronounce [prə'naunts] *vt* **-nounced; -nouncing** : pronunciar — **pronouncement** [prə'nauntsmənt] *n* : declaración *f* — **pronunciation** [prə,nʌntsi'eɪʃən] *n* : pronunciación *f*
proof ['pruːf] *n* : prueba *f* — ~ *adj* ~ **against** : a prueba de — **proofread** ['pruːf,riːd] *vt* **-read; -reading** : corregir
prop ['prap] *n* 1 SUPPORT : puntal *m*, apoyo *m* 2 : accesorio *m* (en teatro) — ~ *vt* **propped; propping** 1 ~ **up** SUPPORT : apoyar
propaganda [,prapə'gændə, ,proː-] *n* : propaganda *f*
propagate ['prapəgeɪt] *v* **-gated; -gating** *vt* : propagar — *vi* : propagarse
propel [prə'pel] *vt* **-pelled; -pelling** : propulsar — **propeller** [prə'pelər] *n* : hélice *f*
propensity [prə'pentsəti] *n, pl* **-ties** : propensión *f*
proper ['prapər] *adj* 1 SUITABLE : apropiado 2 REAL : verdadero 3 CORRECT : correcto 4 GENTEEL : cortés 5 ~ **name** : nombre *m* propio — **properly** ['prapərli] *adv* : correctamente
property ['prapərti] *n, pl* **-ties** 1 : propiedad *f* 2 BUILDING : inmueble *m* 3 LAND, LOT : parcela *f*

prophet ['prafət] *n* : profeta *m*, profetisa *f* — **prophecy** ['prafəsi] *n, pl* **-cies** : profecía *f* — **prophesy** ['prafə,saɪ] *vt* **-sied; -sying** *vt* : profetizar — *vi* : hacer profecías — **prophetic** [prə'fetɪk] *adj* : profético
proportion [prə'porʃən] *n* 1 : proporción *f* 2 SHARE : parte *f* — **proportional** [prə'porʃənəl] *adj* : proporcional — **proportionate** [prə'porʃənət] *adj* : proporcional
proposal [prə'poːzəl] *n* : propuesta *f*
propose [prə'poːz] *v* **-posed; -posing** *vt* 1 SUGGEST : proponer 2 ~ **to do sth** : pensar hacer algo — *vi* : proponer matrimonio — **proposition** [,prapə'zɪʃən] *n* : proposición *f*
proprietor [prə'praɪətər] *n* : propietario *m*, -ria *f*
propriety [prə'praɪəti] *n, pl* **-eties** : decencia *f*, decoro *m*
propulsion [prə'pʌlʃən] *n* : propulsión *f*
prose ['proːz] *n* : prosa *f*
prosecute ['prasɪ,kjuːt] *vt* **-cuted; -cuting** : procesar — **prosecution** [,prasrkju:ʃən] *n* 1 : procesamiento *m* 2 the ~ : la acusación — **prosecutor** ['prasɪ,kjuːtər] *n* : acusador *m*, -dora *f*
prospect ['pra,spekt] *n* 1 : perspectiva *f* 2 POSSIBILITY : posibilidad *f* — **prospective** [prə'spektɪv, 'pra,spek-] *adj* : futuro, posible
prosper ['praspər] *vi* : prosperar — **prosperity** [pra'sperəti] *n* : prosperidad *f* — **prosperous** ['praspərəs] *adj* : próspero
prostitute ['prastə,tuːt, -,tjuːt] *n* : prostituta *f* — **prostitution** [,prastə'tuːʃən, -'tjuː-] *n* : prostitución *f*
prostrate ['pra,streɪt] *adj* : postrado
protagonist [pro'tægənɪst] *n* : protagonista *mf*
protect [prə'tekt] *vt* : proteger — **protection** [prə'tekʃən] *n* : protección *f* — **protective** [prə'tektɪv] *adj* : protector — **protector** [prə'tektər] *n* : protector *m*, -tora *f*
protégé ['proːtə,ʒeɪ] *n* : protegido *m*, -da *f*
protein ['proːtiːn] *n* : proteína *f*
protest ['proː,test] *n* : protesta *f* — ~ [proː'test] *vt* : protestar — *vi* ~ **against** : protestar contra — **Protestant** ['pratəstənt] *n* : protestante *mf* — **protester** *or* **protestor** ['proː,testər, prə-] *n* : manifestante *mf*
protocol ['proːtə,kɔl] *n* : protocolo *m*
prototype ['proːtə,taɪp] *n* : prototipo *m*
protract [pro'trækt] *vt* : prolongar
protrude [pro'truːd] *vi* **-truded; -truding** : sobresalir

proud ['praud] *adj* : orgulloso
prove ['pruːv] *v* **proved; proved** *or* **proven** ['pruːvən]; **proving** *vt* : probar — *vi* : resultar
proverb ['prɑˌvərb] *n* : proverbio *m*, refrán *m* — **proverbial** [prə'vərbiəl] *adj* : proverbial
provide [prə'vaid] *v* **-vided; -viding** *vt* : proveer — *vi* **for** SUPPORT : mantener — **provided** [prə'vaidəd] *or* **that** *conj* : con tal (de) que, siempre que — **providence** ['prɑvədənts] *n* : providencia *f*
province ['prɑvɪnts] *n* **1** : provincia *f* **2** SPHERE : campo *m*, competencia *f* — **provincial** [prə'vɪntʃəl] *adj* : provinciano
provision [prə'vɪʒən] *n* **1** : provisión *f*, suministro *m* **2** STIPULATION : condición *f* **3 ~s** *npl* : viveres *mpl* — **provisional** [prə'vɪʒənəl] *adj* : provisional — **proviso** [prə'vaiˌzoː] *n, pl* **-sos** *or* **-soes** : condición *f*
provoke [prə'voːk] *vt* **-voked; -voking** : provocar — **provocation** [ˌprɑvə'keiʃən] *n* : provocación *f* — **provocative** [prə'vɑkətɪv] *adj* : provocador, provocativo
prow ['prau] *n* : proa *f*
prowess ['prauəs] *n* **1** BRAVERY : valor *m* **2** SKILL : habilidad *f*
prowl ['praul] *vi* : merodear, rondar — *vt* : merodear por — **prowler** ['praulər] *n* : merodeador *m*, -dora *f*
proximity [prɑk'sɪməti] *n* : proximidad *f* — **proxy** ['prɑksi] *n, pl* **proxies by ~** : por poder
prude ['pruːd] *n* : mojigato *m*, -ta *f*
prudence ['pruːdənts] *n* : prudencia *f* — **prudent** ['pruːdənt] *adj* : prudente
prune[1] ['pruːn] *n* : ciruela *f* pasa
prune[2] *vt* **pruned; pruning** : podar (arbustos, etc.)
pry ['prai] *v* **pried; prying** *vi* **~ into** : entrometerse en — *vt or* **~ open** : abrir (a la fuerza)
psalm ['sɑm, 'sɑlm] *n* : salmo *m*
pseudonym ['suːdəˌnɪm] *n* : seudónimo *m*
psychiatry [sə'kaiətri, sai-] *n* : psiquiatría *f* — **psychiatric** [ˌsaiki'ætrɪk] *adj* : psiquiátrico — **psychiatrist** [sə'kaiətrɪst, sai-] *n* : psiquiatra *mf*
psychic ['saikɪk] *adj* : psíquico
psychoanalysis [ˌsaikoə'næləsɪs] *n, pl* **-yses** : psicoanálisis *m* — **psychoanalyst** [ˌsaiko'ænəlɪst] *n* : psicoanalista *mf* — **psychoanalyze** [ˌsaiko'ænəlˌaiz] *vt* **-lyzed; -lyzing** : psicoanalizar
psychology [sai'kɑləʤi] *n, pl* **-gies**

: psicología *f* — **psychological** [ˌsaikə'lɑʤɪkəl] *adj* : psicológico — **psychologist** [sai'kɑləʤɪst] *n* : psicólogo *m*, -ga *f*
psychopath ['saikəˌpæθ] *n* : psicópata *mf*
psychotherapy [ˌsaiko'θerəpi] *n, pl* **-pies** : psicoterapia *f*
psychotic [sai'kɑtɪk] *adj* : psicótico
puberty ['pjuːbərti] *n* : pubertad *f*
pubic ['pjuːbɪk] *adj* : púbico
public ['pʌblɪk] *adj* : público — **~** *n* : público *m* — **publication** [ˌpʌblə'keiʃən] *n* : publicación *f* — **publicity** [pə'blɪsəti] *n* : publicidad *f* — **publicize** ['pʌbləˌsaiz] *vt* **-cized; -cizing** : publicitar, divulgar
publish ['pʌblɪʃ] *vt* : publicar — **publisher** ['pʌblɪʃər] *n* **1** : editor *m*, -tora *f* (persona) **2** : casa *f* editorial (negocio)
pucker ['pʌkər] *vt* : fruncir, arrugar — *vi* : arrugarse
pudding ['pudɪŋ] *n* : budín *m*, pudín *m*
puddle ['pʌdəl] *n* : charco *m*
pudgy ['pʌʤi] *adj* **pudgier; -est** : rechoncho *fam*
Puerto Rican [ˌpwertə'riːkən, ˌpɔrtə-] *adj* : puertorriqueño
puff ['pʌf] *vi* **1** BLOW : soplar **2** PANT : resoplar **3 ~ up** SWELL : hincharse — *vt* **~ out** : hinchar — **~** *n* **1** : bocanada *f* (de humo) **2** : chupada *f* (a un cigarrillo) **3** *or* **cream ~** : pastelito *m* de crema **4** *or* **powder ~** : borla *f* — **puffy** ['pʌfi] *adj* **puffier; -est** : hinchado
pull ['pul, 'pʌl] *vt* **1** : tirar de **2** EXTRACT : sacar **3** TEAR : desgarrarse (un músculo, etc.) **4 ~ off** REMOVE : quitar **5 ~ oneself together** : calmarse **6 ~ up** : levantar, subir — *vi* **1** : tirar **2 ~ through** RECOVER : reponerse **3 ~ together** COOPERATE : reunir **4 ~ up** STOP : parar — **~** *n* **1** : tirón *m* **2** INFLUENCE : influencia *f* — **pulley** ['puli] *n, pl* **-leys** : polea *f* — **pullover** ['pulˌoːvər] *n* : suéter *m*
pulp ['pʌlp] *n* **1** : pulpa *f* (de frutas, etc.) **2** *or* **wood ~** : pasta *f* de papel
pulpit ['pulˌpɪt] *n* : púlpito *m*
pulsate ['pʌlˌseit] *vi* **-sated; -sating** : palpitar — **pulse** ['pʌls] *n* : pulso *m*
pulverize ['pʌlvəˌraiz] *vt* **-ized; -izing** : pulverizar
pummel ['pʌməl] *vt* **-meled; -meling** : aporrear
pump[1] ['pʌmp] *n* **1** : bomba *f* — **~** *vt* **1** : bombear **2 ~ up** : inflar
pump[2] *n* SHOE : zapato *m* de tacón
pumpernickel ['pʌmpərˌnikəl] *n* : pan *m* negro de centeno

pumpkin ['pʌmpkɪn, 'pʌŋkən] *n* : calabaza *f*, zapallo *m Lat*

pun ['pʌn] *n* : juego *m* de palabras — ~ *vi* punned; punning : hacer juegos de palabras

punch[1] ['pʌntʃ] *vt* 1 : dar un puñetazo a 2 PERFORATE : perforar (papeles, etc.), picar (un boleto) — ~ *n* 1 : golpe *m*, puñetazo *m* 2 *or* paper ~ : perforadora *f*

punch[2] *n* : ponche *m* (bebida)

punctual ['pʌŋktʃʊəl] *adj* : puntual — **punctuality** [ˌpʌŋktʃʊˈæləti] *n* : puntualidad *f*

punctuate ['pʌŋktʃuˌeɪt] *vt* -ated; -ating : puntuar — **punctuation** [ˌpʌŋktʃʊˈeɪʃən] *n* : puntuación *f*

puncture ['pʌŋktʃər] *n* : pinchazo *m*, ponchadura *f Lat* — ~ *vt* -tured; -turing : pinchar, ponchar *Lat*

pungent ['pʌndʒənt] *adj* : acre

punish ['pʌnɪʃ] *vt* : castigar — **punishment** ['pʌnɪʃmənt] *n* : castigo *m* — **punitive** ['pjuːnətɪv] *adj* : punitivo

puny ['pjuːni] *adj* -nier; -est : enclenque

pup ['pʌp] *n* : cachorro *m*, -rra *f* (de un perro); cría *f* (de otros animales)

pupil[1] ['pjuːpəl] *n* : alumno *m*, -na *f* (de colegio)

pupil[2] *n* : pupila *f* (del ojo)

puppet ['pʌpət] *n* : títere *m*

puppy ['pʌpi] *n, pl* -pies : cachorro *m*, -rra *f*

purchase ['pərtʃəs] *vt* -chased; -chasing : comprar — ~ *n* : compra *f*

pure ['pjur] *adj* purer; purest : puro

puree [pjuˈreɪ, -ˈriː] *n* : puré *m*

purely ['pjurli] *adv* : puramente

purgatory ['pərgəˌtori] *n, pl* -ries : purgatorio *m* — **purge** ['pərdʒ] *vt* purged; purging : purgar — ~ *n* : purga *f*

purify ['pjurəˌfaɪ] *vt* -fied; -fying : purificar — **purification** [ˌpjurəfəˈkeɪʃən] *n* : purificación *f*

puritanical [ˌpjurəˈtænɪkəl] *adj* : puritano

purity ['pjurəti] *n* : pureza *f*

purple ['pərpəl] *n* : morado *m*

purport [pər'port] *vt* ~ to be : pretender ser

purpose ['pərpəs] *n* 1 : propósito *m* 2 RESOLUTION : determinación *f* 3 on ~ : a propósito — **purposeful** ['pərpəsfəl] *adj* : resuelto — **purposely** ['pərpəsli] *adv* : a propósito

purr ['pər] *n* : ronroneo *m* — ~ *vi* : ronronear

purse ['pərs] *n* 1 *or* change ~ : monedero *m* 2 HANDBAG : cartera *f*, bolso *m Spain*, bolsa *f Lat* — ~ *vt* pursed; pursing : fruncir

pursue [pər'suː] *vt* -sued; -suing 1 CHASE : perseguir 2 SEEK : buscar — **pursuer** [pər'suːər] *n* : perseguidor *m*, -dora *f* — **pursuit** [pər'suːt] *n* 1 CHASE : persecución *f* 2 SEARCH : búsqueda *f* 3 OCCUPATION : actividad *f*

pus ['pʌs] *n* : pus *m*

push ['pʊʃ] *vt* 1 SHOVE : empujar 2 PRESS : apretar 3 URGE : presionar — **around** BULLY : mangonear — *vi* 1 : empujar 2 ~ for : presionar para — ~ *n* 1 SHOVE : empujón *m* 2 DRIVE : dinamismo *m* 3 EFFORT : esfuerzo *m* — **pushy** ['pʊʃi] *adj* pushier; -est : mandón, prepotente

pussy ['pʊsi] *n, pl* pussies : gatito *m*, -ta *f*; minino *m*, -na *f*

put ['pʊt] *v* put; putting *vt* 1 : poner 2 INSERT : meter 3 EXPRESS : decir 4 ~ one's mind to sth : proponerse hacer algo — *vi* ~ up with : aguantar — **put away** *vt* 1 STORE : guardar 2 *or* ~ **aside** : dejar a un lado — **put down** *vt* 1 SUPPRESS : aplastar, sofocar 2 ATTRIBUTE : atribuir — **put off** *vt* DEFER : aplazar, posponer — **put on** *vt* 1 ASSUME : adoptar 2 PRESENT : presentar (una obra de teatro, etc.) 3 WEAR : ponerse — **put out** *vt* INCONVENIENCE : incomodar — **put up** *vt* 1 BUILD : construir 2 LODGE : alojar 3 PROVIDE : poner (dinero)

putrefy ['pjuːtrəˌfaɪ] *vi* -fied; -fying : pudrirse

putty ['pʌti] *n, pl* -ties : masilla *f*

puzzle ['pʌzəl] *v* -zled; -zling *vt* : confundir, dejar perplejo — *vi* ~ over : tratar de descifrar — ~ *n* 1 : rompecabezas *m* 2 MYSTERY : enigma *m*

pylon ['paɪlɑn, -lən] *n* : pilón *m*

pyramid ['pɪrəˌmɪd] *n* : pirámide *f*

python ['paɪθɑn, -θən] *n* : pitón *f*

Q

q ['kjuː] *n*, *pl* **q's** *or* **qs** ['kjuːz] : q *f*, decimoséptima letra del alfabeto inglés

quack¹ ['kwæk] *vi* : graznar (dícese del pato) — **∼** *n* : graznido *m*

quack² *n* CHARLATAN : charlatán *m*, -tana *f*

quadruple [kwɑ'druːpəl, -'drʌ-; 'kwɑdrə-] *v* **-pled; -pling** *vt* : cuadruplicar — *vi* : cuadruplicarse

quagmire ['kwæg,maɪr, 'kwɑg-] *n* : atolladero *m*

quail ['kweɪl] *n*, *pl* **quail** *or* **quails** : codorniz *f*

quaint ['kweɪnt] *adj* **1** ODD : curioso **2** PICTURESQUE : pintoresco

quake ['kweɪk] *vi* **quaked; quaking** : temblar — **∼** *n* → **earthquake**

qualify ['kwɑlə,faɪ] *v* **-fied; -fying** *vt* **1** LIMIT : matizar **2** : calificar (en gramática) **3** EQUIP : habilitar — *vi* **1** : titularse (de abogado, etc.) **2** : clasificarse (en deportes) — **qualification** [,kwɑləfə'keɪʃən] *n* **1** REQUIREMENT : requisito *m* **2** **∼s** *npl* ABILITY : capacidad *f* **3** without **∼** : sin reservas — **qualified** ['kwɑlə,faɪd] *adj* : capacitado

quality ['kwɑləṭi] *n*, *pl* **-ties 1** : calidad *f* **2** PROPERTY : cualidad *f*

qualm ['kwɑm, 'kwɑlm, 'kwɔm] *n* **1** DOUBT : duda *f* **2** have no **∼s** about : no tener ningún escrúpulo en

quandary ['kwɑndri] *n*, *pl* **-ries** : dilema *m*

quantity ['kwɑntəṭi] *n*, *pl* **-ties** : cantidad *f*

quarantine ['kwɔrən,tiːn] *n* : cuarentena *f* — *vt* **-tined; -tining** : poner en cuarentena

quarrel ['kwɔrəl] *n* : pelea *f*, riña *f* — **∼** *vi* **-reled** *or* **-relled; -reling** *or* **-relling** : pelearse, reñir — **quarrelsome** ['kwɔrəlsəm] *adj* : pendenciero

quarry¹ ['kwɔri] *n*, *pl* **quarries** PREY : presa *f*

quarry² *n*, *pl* **quarries** EXCAVATION : cantera *f*

quart ['kwɔrt] *n* : cuarto *m* de galón

quarter ['kwɔrṭər] *n* **1** : cuarto *m* (en matemáticas) **2** : moneda *f* de 25 centavos **3** DISTRICT : barrio *m* **4 ∼ after three** : las tres y cuarto **5 ∼s** *npl* LODGING : alojamiento *m* — **∼** *vt* **1**

: dividir en cuatro partes **2** : acuartelar (tropas) — **quarterly** ['kwɔrṭərli] *adv* : cada tres meses — **∼** *adj* : trimestral — **∼** *n*, *pl* **-lies** : publicación *f* trimestral

quartet [kwɔr'tɛt] *n* : cuarteto *m*

quartz ['kwɔrts] *n* : cuarzo *m*

quash ['kwɑʃ, 'kwɔʃ] *vt* **1** ANNUL : anular **2** SUPPRESS : aplastar, sofocar

quaver ['kweɪvər] *vi* : temblar

quay ['kiː, 'keɪ, 'kweɪ] *n* : muelle *m*

queasy ['kwiːzi] *adj* **-sier; -est** : mareado

queen ['kwiːn] *n* : reina *f*

queer ['kwɪr] *adj* ODD : extraño

quell ['kwɛl] *vt* SUPPRESS : sofocar, aplastar

quench ['kwɛntʃ] *vt* **1** EXTINGUISH : apagar **2 ∼ one's thirst** : quitar la sed

query ['kwɪri, 'kwɛr-] *n*, *pl* **-ries** : pregunta *f* — **∼** *vt* **-ried; -rying 1** ASK : preguntar **2** QUESTION : cuestionar

quest ['kwɛst] *n* : búsqueda *f*

question ['kwɛstʃən] *n* **1** QUERY : pregunta *f* **2** ISSUE : cuestión *f* **3** **be out of the ∼** : ser indiscutible **4** **call into ∼** : poner en duda **5 without ∼** : sin duda — **∼** *vt* **1** ASK : preguntar **2** DOUBT : cuestionar **3** INTERROGATE : interrogar — *vi* : preguntar — **questionable** ['kwɛstʃənəbəl] *adj* : discutible — **question mark** *n* : signo *m* de interrogación — **questionnaire** [,kwɛstʃə'nær] *n* : cuestionario *m*

queue ['kjuː] *n* : cola *f* — **∼** *vi* **queued; queuing** *or* **queueing** : hacer cola

quibble ['kwɪbəl] *vi* **-bled; -bling** : discutir, quejarse por nimiedades

quick ['kwɪk] *adj* **1** : rápido **2** CLEVER : agudo — **∼** *n* **to the ∼** : en lo vivo — **∼** *adv* : rápidamente — **quicken** ['kwɪkən] *vt* : acelerar — **quickly** ['kwɪkli] *adv* : rápidamente — **quicksand** ['kwɪk,sænd] *n* : arena *f* movediza — **quick-tempered** ['kwɪk'tɛmpərd] *adj* : irascible — **quick-witted** ['kwɪk-'wɪṭəd] *adj* : agudo

quiet ['kwaɪət] *n* **1** : silencio *m* **2** CALM : tranquilidad *f* — **∼** *adj* **1** : silencioso **2** CALM : tranquilo **3** RESERVED : callado **4** : discreto (dícese de colores, etc.) — **∼** *vt* **1** SILENCE : hacer callar **2** CALM : calmar — *vi* *or* **∼ down** : cal-

marse — **quietly** *adv* **1** : silenciosamente **2** CALMLY : tranquilamente
quilt ['kwɪlt] *n* : edredón *m*
quintet [kwɪn'tet] *n* : quinteto *m*
quip ['kwɪp] *n* : ocurrencia *f*, salida *f* — ~ *vt* **quipped; quipping** : decir bromeando
quirk ['kwərk] *n* : peculiaridad *f*
quit ['kwɪt] *v* **quit; quitting** *vt* **1** LEAVE : dejar, abandonar **2** ~ **doing** : dejar de hacer — *vi* **1** STOP : parar **2** RESIGN : dimitir, renunciar
quite ['kwaɪt] *adv* **1** COMPLETELY : completamente **2** RATHER : bastante

quits ['kwɪts] *adj* **call it** ~ : quedar en paz
quiver ['kwɪvər] *vi* : temblar
quiz ['kwɪz] *n*, *pl* **quizzes** TEST : prueba *f* — ~ *vt* **quizzed; quizzing** : interrogar
quota ['kwoːt̬ə] *n* : cuota *f*, cupo *m*
quotation [kwo'teɪʃən] *n* **1** : cita *f* **2** ESTIMATE : presupuesto *m* — **quotation marks** *npl* : comillas *fpl* — **quote** ['kwoːt] *vt* **quoted; quoting 1** CITE : citar **2** : cotizar (en finanzas) — ~ *n* **1** → **quotation 2** ~**s** *npl* → **quotation marks**
quotient ['kwoːʃənt] *n* : cociente *m*

R

r ['ɑr] *n*, *pl* **r's** *or* **rs** ['ɑrz] : r *f*, decimoctava letra del alfabeto inglés
rabbi ['ræˌbaɪ] *n* : rabino *m*, -na *f*
rabbit ['ræbət] *n*, *pl* **-bit** *or* **-bits** : conejo *m*, -ja *f*
rabble ['ræbəl] *n* : chusma *f*, populacho *m*
rabies ['reɪbiːz] *ns & pl* : rabia *f* — **rabid** ['ræbɪd] *adj* **1** : rabioso **2** FANATIC : fanático
raccoon [ræ'kuːn] *n*, *pl* **-coon** *or* **-coons** : mapache *m*
race[1] ['reɪs] *n* **1** : raza *f* **2 human** ~ : género *m* humano
race[2] *n* : carrera *f* (competitiva) — ~ *vi* **raced; racing 1** : correr (en una carrera) **2** RUSH : ir corriendo — **racehorse** ['reɪs,hors] *n* : caballo *m* de carreras — **racetrack** ['reɪs,træk] *n* : pista *f* (de carreras)
racial ['reɪʃəl] *adj* : racial — **racism** ['reɪ,sɪzəm] *n* : racismo *m* — **racist** ['reɪsɪst] *n* : racista *mf*
rack ['ræk] *n* **1** SHELF : estante *m* **2 luggage** ~ : portaequipajes *m* — ~ *vt* **1** ~**ed with** : atormentado por **2** ~ **one's brains** : devanarse los sesos
racket[1] ['rækət] *n* : raqueta *f* (en deportes)
racket[2] *n* **1** DIN : alboroto *m*, bulla *f* **2** SWINDLE : estafa *f*
racy ['reɪsi] *adj* **racier; -est** : subido de tono, picante
radar ['reɪ,dɑr] *n* : radar *m*
radiant ['reɪdiənt] *adj* : radiante — **radiance** ['reɪdiənts] *n* : resplandor *m* — **radiate** ['reɪdiˌeɪt] *v* **-ated; -ating** *vt* : irradiar — *vi* **1** : irradiar **2** *or* ~ **out** : extenderse (desde un centro) — **radi-**

ation [ˌreɪdi'eɪʃən] *n* : radiación *f* — **radiator** ['reɪdiˌeɪt̬ər] *n* : radiador *m*
radical ['rædɪkəl] *adj* : radical — ~ *n* : radical *mf*
radii → **radius**
radio ['reɪdiˌoː] *n*, *pl* **-dios** : radio *mf* (aparato), radio *f* (medio) — ~ *vt* : transmitir por radio — **radioactive** ['reɪdioˈæktɪv] *adj* : radioactivo, radiactivo
radish ['rædɪʃ] *n* : rábano *m*
radius ['reɪdiəs] *n*, *pl* **radii** [-diˌaɪ] : radio *m*
raffle ['ræfəl] *vt* **-fled; -fling** : rifar — ~ *n* : rifa *f*
raft ['ræft] *n* : balsa *f*
rafter ['ræftər] *n* : cabrio *m*
rag ['ræg] *n* **1** : trapo *m* **2** ~**s** *npl* TATTERS : harapos *mpl*, andrajos *mpl*
rage ['reɪdʒ] *n* **1** : cólera *f*, rabia *f* **2 be all the** ~ : hacer furor — ~ *vi* **raged; raging 1** : estar furioso **2** : bramar (dícese del viento, etc.)
ragged ['rægəd] *adj* **1** UNEVEN : irregular **2** TATTERED : andrajoso, harapiento
raid ['reɪd] *n* **1** : invasión *f* (militar) **2** : asalto *m* (por delincuentes), redada *f* (por la policía) — ~ *vt* **1** INVADE : invadir **2** ROB : asaltar **3** : hacer una redada en (dícese de la policía) — **raider** ['reɪdər] *n* ATTACKER : asaltante *mf*
rail[1] ['reɪl] *vi* ~ **at s.o.** : recriminar a algn
rail[2] *n* **1** BAR : barra *f* **2** HANDRAIL : pasamanos *m* **3** TRACK : riel *m* **4 by** ~ : por ferrocarril — **railing** ['reɪlɪŋ] *n* **1** : baranda *f* (de un balcón), pasamanos *m* (de una escalera) **2**

RAILS : reja f — **railroad** ['reɪlˌroːd] n : ferrocarril m — **railway** ['reɪlˌweɪ] → **railroad**

rain ['reɪn] n : lluvia f — ~ vi : llover — **rainbow** ['reɪnˌboː] n : arco m iris — **raincoat** ['reɪnˌkoːt] n : impermeable m — **rainfall** ['reɪnˌfɔl] n : precipitación f — **rainy** ['reɪni] adj **rainier; -est** : lluvioso

raise ['reɪz] vt **raised; raising** 1 : levantar 2 COLLECT : recaudar 3 REAR : criar 4 GROW : cultivar 5 INCREASE : aumentar 6 : sacar (objeciones, etc.) — ~ n : aumento m

raisin ['reɪzən] n : pasa f

rake ['reɪk] n : rastrillo m — ~ vt **raked; raking** : rastrillar

rally ['ræli] v **-lied; -lying** vi 1 : unirse, reunirse 2 RECOVER : recuperarse — vt : conseguir (apoyo), unir a (la gente) — ~ n, pl **-lies** : reunión f, mitin m

ram n ['ræm] : carnero m (animal) — ~ vt **rammed; ramming** 1 CRAM : meter con fuerza 2 or ~ **into** : chocar contra

RAM ['ræm] n : RAM f

ramble ['ræmbəl] vi **-bled; -bling** 1 WANDER : pasear 2 or ~ **on** : divagar — ~ n : paseo m, excursión f

ramp ['ræmp] n : rampa f

rampage ['ræmˌpeɪdʒ, ræmˈpeɪdʒ] vi **-paged; -paging** : andar arrasando todo — ~ ['ræmˌpeɪdʒ] n : frenesí m (de violencia)

rampant ['ræmpənt] adj : desenfrenado

rampart ['ræmˌpart] n : muralla f

ramshackle ['ræmˌʃækəl] adj : destartalado

ran → **run**

ranch ['ræntʃ] n : hacienda f — **rancher** ['ræntʃər] n : hacendado m, -da f

rancid ['ræntsɪd] adj : rancio

rancor ['ræŋkər] n : rencor m

random ['rændəm] adj 1 : aleatorio 2 at ~ : al azar

rang → **ring**

range ['reɪndʒ] n 1 GRASSLAND : pradera f 2 STOVE : cocina f 3 VARIETY : gama f 4 SCOPE : amplitud f 5 or **mountain** ~ : cordillera f — ~ vi **ranged; ranging** 1 EXTEND : extenderse 2 ~ **from...to...** : variar entre...y... — **ranger** ['reɪndʒər] n or **forest** ~ : guardabosque mf

rank[1] ['ræŋk] adj 1 SMELLY : fétido 2 OUTRIGHT : completo

rank[2] n 1 ROW : fila f 2 : rango m (militar) 3 ~**s** npl : soldados mpl rasos 4 **the** ~ **and file** : las bases — ~ vt RATE : clasificar — vi : clasificarse

rankle ['ræŋkəl] vi **-kled; -kling** : causar rencor, doler

ransack ['rænˌsæk] vt 1 SEARCH : registrar 2 LOOT : saquear

ransom ['rænˌsəm] n : rescate m — ~ vt : rescatar

rant ['rænt] vi or ~ **and rave** : despotricar

rap[1] ['ræp] n KNOCK : golpecito m — ~ v **rapped; rapping** : golpear

rap[2] n or ~ **music** : rap m

rapacious [rəˈpeɪʃəs] adj : rapaz

rape ['reɪp] vt **raped; raping** : violar — ~ n : violación f

rapid ['ræpɪd] adj : rápido — **rapids** ['ræpɪdz] npl : rápidos mpl

rapist ['reɪpɪst] n : violador m, -dora f

rapport [ræˈpor] n **have a good** ~ : entenderse bien

rapt ['ræpt] adj : absorto, embelesado

rapture ['ræptʃər] n : éxtasis m

rare ['rær] adj **rarer; rarest** 1 FINE : excepcional 2 UNCOMMON : raro 3 : poco cocido (dícese de la carne) — **rarely** ['rærli] adv : raramente — **rarity** ['rærəti] n, pl **-ties** : rareza f

rascal ['ræskəl] n : pillo m, -lla f; pícaro m, -ra f

rash[1] ['ræʃ] adj : imprudente, precipitado

rash[2] n : sarpullido m, erupción f

rasp ['ræsp] vt SCRAPE : raspar — ~ n : escofina f

raspberry ['ræzˌbɛri] n, pl **-ries** : frambuesa f

rat ['ræt] n : rata f

rate ['reɪt] n 1 PACE : velocidad f, ritmo m 2 : tipo m, tasa m (de interés, etc.) 3 PRICE : tarifa f 4 **at any** ~ : de todos modos 5 **birth** ~ : índice m de natalidad — ~ vt **rated; rating** 1 REGARD : considerar 2 DESERVE : merecer

rather ['ræðər, 'rɑ-, 'rɒ-] adv 1 FAIRLY : bastante 2 **I'd** ~... : prefiero... 3 **or** ~ : o mejor dicho

ratify ['rætəˌfaɪ] vt **-fied; -fying** : ratificar — **ratification** [ˌrætəfəˈkeɪʃən] n : ratificación f

rating ['reɪtɪŋ] n 1 : clasificación f 2 ~**s** npl : índice m de audiencia

ratio ['reɪʃio] n, pl **-tios** : proporción f

ration ['ræʃən, 'reɪʃən] n 1 : ración f 2 ~**s** PROVISIONS : víveres mpl — ~ vt **rationed; rationing** : racionar

rational ['ræʃənəl] adj : racional — **rationale** [ˌræʃəˈnæl] n : lógica f, razones fpl — **rationalize** ['ræʃənəˌlaɪz] vt **-ized; -izing** : racionalizar

rattle ['rætəl] v **-tled; -tling** vi : traquetear — vt 1 SHAKE : agitar 2 UPSET : desconcertar 3 ~ **off** : decir de corrido — ~ n 1 : traqueteo m 2 or **baby's** ~ : sonajero m — **rattlesnake** ['ræt̬əl,sneɪk] n : serpiente f de cascabel

raucous ['rɔkəs] adj 1 HOARSE : ronco 2 BOISTEROUS : bullicioso

ravage ['rævɪdʒ] vt -**aged**; -**aging** : estragar, asolar — **ravages** ['rævɪdʒəz] npl : estragos mpl

rave ['reɪv] vi **raved; raving** 1 : delirar 2 ~ **about** : hablar con entusiasmo sobre

raven ['reɪvən] n : cuervo m

ravenous ['rævənəs] adj 1 HUNGRY : hambriento 2 VORACIOUS : voraz

ravine [rə'vin] n : barranco m

ravishing ['rævɪʃɪŋ] adj : encantador

raw ['rɔ] adj **rawer; rawest** 1 UNCOOKED : crudo 2 INEXPERIENCED : inexperto 3 CHAFED : en carne viva 4 : frío y húmedo (dícese del tiempo) 5 ~ **deal** : trato m injusto 6 ~ **materials** : materias fpl primas

ray ['reɪ] n : rayo m

rayon ['reɪɑn] n : rayón m

raze ['reɪz] vt **razed; razing** : arrasar

razor ['reɪzər] n : maquinilla f de afeitar — **razor blade** n : hoja f de afeitar

reach ['ritʃ] vt 1 : alcanzar 2 or ~ **out** : extender 3 : llegar a (un acuerdo, un límite, etc.) 4 CONTACT : contactar — vi 1 : extenderse 2 ~ **for** : tratar de agarrar — ~ n 1 : alcance m 2 **within** ~ : al alcance

react [ri'ækt] vi : reaccionar — **reaction** [ri'ækʃən] n : reacción f — **reactionary** [ri'ækʃəˌnɛri] adj : reaccionario — ~ n, pl -**ries** : reaccionario m, -ria f — **reactor** [ri'æktər] n : reactor m

read ['rid] v **read** ['rɛd]; **reading** vt 1 : leer 2 INTERPRET : interpretar 3 SAY : decir 4 INDICATE : marcar — vi 1 : leer 2 **it** ~**s as follows** : dice lo siguiente — **readable** ['ridəbəl] adj : legible — **reader** ['ridər] n : lector m, -tora f

readily ['rɛdəli] adv 1 WILLINGLY : de buena gana 2 EASILY : fácilmente

reading ['ridɪŋ] n : lectura f

readjust [ˌriə'dʒʌst] vt : reajustar — vi : volverse a adaptar

ready ['rɛdi] adj **readier; -est** 1 : listo, preparado 2 WILLING : dispuesto 3 AVAILABLE : disponible 4 **get** ~ : prepararse — ~ vt **readied; readying** : preparar

real ['ril] adj 1 : verdadero, real 2 GENUINE : auténtico — ~ adv VERY : muy — **real estate** n : propiedad f inmobiliaria, bienes mpl raíces — **realism** ['riəˌlizəm] n : realismo m — **realist** ['riəlist] n : realista mf — **realistic** [ˌriə'listɪk] adj : realista — **reality** [ri'æləti] n, pl -**ties** : realidad f

realize ['riəˌlaɪz] vt -**ized**; -**izing** 1 : darse cuenta de 2 ACHIEVE : realizar — **realization** [ˌriələ'zeɪʃən] n 1 : comprensión f 2 FULFILLMENT : realización f

really ['rɪli, 'ri-] adv : verdaderamente

realm ['rɛlm] n 1 KINGDOM : reino m 2 SPHERE : esfera f

ream ['rim] n : resma f (de papel)

reap ['rip] v : cosechar

reappear [ˌriə'pɪr] vi : reaparecer

rear[1] ['rɪr] vt 1 RAISE : levantar 2 : criar (niños, etc.) — vi or ~ **up** : encabritarse

rear[2] n 1 BACK : parte f de atrás 2 BUTTOCKS : trasero m fam — ~ adj : trasero, posterior

rearrange [ˌriə'reɪndʒ] vt -**ranged**; -**ranging** : reorganizar, cambiar

reason ['rizən] n : razón f — ~ vt THINK : pensar — vi : razonar — **reasonable** ['rizənəbəl] adj : razonable — **reasoning** ['rizənɪŋ] n : razonamiento m

reassure [ˌriə'ʃʊr] vt -**sured**; -**suring** : tranquilizar — **reassurance** [ˌriə'ʃʊrənts] n : (palabras fpl de) consuelo m

rebate ['riˌbeɪt] n : reembolso m

rebel ['rɛbəl] n : rebelde mf — ~ [rɪ'bɛl] vi -**belled**; -**belling** : rebelarse — **rebellion** [rɪ'bɛljən] n : rebelión f — **rebellious** [rɪ'bɛljəs] adj : rebelde

rebirth [ˌri'bərθ] n : renacimiento m

rebound ['riˌbaʊnd, ˌri'baʊnd] vi : rebotar — ~ ['riˌbaʊnd] n : rebote m

rebuff [rɪ'bʌf] vt : rechazar — ~ n : desaire m

rebuild [ˌri'bɪld] vt -**built**; -**building** : reconstruir

rebuke [rɪ'bjuk] vt -**buked**; -**buking** : reprender — ~ n : reprimenda f

rebut [rɪ'bʌt] vt -**butted**; -**butting** : rebatir — **rebuttal** [rɪ'bʌt̬əl] n : refutación f

recall [rɪ'kɔl] vt 1 : llamar (al servicio, etc.) 2 REMEMBER : recordar 3 REVOKE : revocar — ~ [rɪ'kɔl, 'riˌkɔl] n 1 : retirada f 2 MEMORY : memoria f

recant [rɪ'kænt] vi : retractarse

recapitulate [ˌrikə'pɪtʃəˌleɪt] v -**lated**; -**lating** : recapitular

recapture [ˌri'kæptʃər] vt -**tured**; -**turing** 1 : recobrar 2 RELIVE : revivir

recede [rɪ'sid] vi -**ceded**; -**ceding** : retirarse

receipt [ri'si:t] n 1 : recibo m 2 ~s npl : ingresos mpl
receive [ri'si:v] vt -ceived; -ceiving : recibir — **receiver** [ri'si:vər] n 1 : receptor m (de radio, etc.) 2 or **telephone** ~ : auricular m
recent ['ri:sənt] adj : reciente — **recently** [-li] adv : recientemente
receptacle [ri'septikəl] n : receptáculo m, recipiente m
reception [ri'sepʃən] n : recepción f — **receptionist** [ri'sepʃənist] n : recepcionista mf — **receptive** [ri'septiv] adj : receptivo
recess ['ri:ses, ri'ses] n 1 ALCOVE : hueco m 2 : recreo m (escolar) 3 ADJOURNMENT : suspensión f de actividades Spain, receso m Lat — **recession** [ri'seʃən] n : recesión f
recharge [ri:'tʃɑrdʒ] vt -charged; -charging : recargar — **rechargeable** [ri:'tʃɑrdʒəbəl] adj : recargable
recipe ['resəpi:] n : receta f
recipient [ri'sipiənt] n : recipiente mf
reciprocal [ri'siprəkəl] adj : recíproco
recite [ri'sait] vt -cited; -citing 1 : recitar (un poema, etc.) 2 LIST : enumerar — **recital** [ri'saitəl] n : recital m
reckless ['rekləs] adj : imprudente — **recklessness** ['rekləsnəs] n : imprudencia f
reckon ['rekən] vt 1 COMPUTE : calcular 2 CONSIDER : considerar — **reckoning** ['rekəniŋ] n : cálculos mpl
reclaim [ri'kleim] vt 1 : reclamar 2 RECOVER : recuperar
recline [ri'klain] vi -clined; -clining : reclinarse — **reclining** adj : reclinable (dícese de un asiento, etc.)
recluse ['re,klu:s, ri'klu:s] n : solitario m, -ria f
recognition [,rekig'niʃən] n : reconocimiento m — **recognizable** ['rekig,naizəbəl] adj : reconocible — **recognize** ['rekig,naiz] vt -nized; -nizing : reconocer
recoil [ri'kɔil] vi : retroceder — ~ ['ri:,kɔil, ri'-] n : culatazo m (de un arma de fuego)
recollect [,rekə'lekt] v : recordar — **recollection** [,rekə'lekʃən] n : recuerdo m
recommend [,rekə'mend] vt : recomendar — **recommendation** [,rekəmən'deiʃən] n : recomendación f
reconcile ['rekən,sail] v -ciled; -ciling vt 1 : reconciliar (personas), conciliar (datos, etc.) 2 ~ **oneself to** : resignarse a — vi MAKE UP : reconciliarse — **reconciliation** [,rekən,sili'eiʃən] n : reconciliación f

reconnaissance [ri'kɑnəzənts, -sənts] n : reconocimiento m (militar)
reconsider [,ri:kən'sidər] vt : reconsiderar
reconstruct [,ri:kən'strʌkt] vt : reconstruir
record [ri'kɔrd] vt 1 WRITE DOWN : anotar, apuntar 2 REGISTER : registrar 3 : grabar (música, etc.) — ~ ['rekərd] n 1 DOCUMENT : documento m 2 REGISTER : registro m 3 HISTORY : historial m 4 : disco m (de música, etc.) 5 **criminal** ~ : antecedentes mpl penales 6 **world** ~ : récord m mundial — **recorder** [ri'kɔrdər] n 1 : flauta f dulce 2 or **tape** ~ : grabadora f — **recording** [-iŋ] n : disco m — **record player** n : tocadiscos m
recount¹ [ri'kaunt] vt NARRATE : narrar, relatar
recount² ['ri:,kaunt, ,ri'-] vt : volver a contar (votos, etc.) — ~ n : recuento m
recourse ['ri:,kors, ri'-] n 1 : recurso m 2 **have** ~ **to** : recurrir a
recover [ri'kʌvər] vt : recobrar — vi RECUPERATE : recuperarse — **recovery** [ri'kʌvəri] n, pl **-eries** : recuperación f
recreation [,rekri'eiʃən] n : recreo m — **recreational** [,rekri'eiʃənəl] adj : de recreo
recruit [ri'kru:t] vt : reclutar — ~ n : recluta mf — **recruitment** [ri'kru:tmənt] n : reclutamiento m
rectangle ['rek,tæŋgəl] n : rectángulo m — **rectangular** [rek'tæŋgjələr] adj : rectangular
rectify ['rektə,fai] vt -fied; -fying : rectificar
rector ['rektər] n 1 : parroco m (clérigo) 2 : rector m, -tora f (de una universidad) — **rectory** ['rektəri] n, pl **-ries** : rectoría f
rectum ['rektəm] n, pl **-tums** or **-ta** [-tə] : recto m
recuperate [ri'ku:pə,reit, -'kju:-] v -ated; -ating vt : recuperar — vi : recuperarse — **recuperation** [ri,ku:pə'reiʃən, -,kju:-] n : recuperación f
recur [ri'kər] vi -curred; -curring : repetirse — **recurrence** [ri'kərənts] n : repetición f — **recurrent** [ri'kərənt] adj : que se repite
recycle [ri'saikəl] vt -cled; -cling : reciclar
red ['red] adj : rojo — ~ n : rojo m — **redden** ['redən] vt : enrojecer — vi : enrojecerse — **reddish** ['rediʃ] adj : rojizo
redecorate [,ri:'dekə,reit] vt -rated; -rating : pintar de nuevo
redeem [ri'di:m] vt 1 SAVE : salvar,

rescatar **2** : desempeñar (de un monte de piedad) **3** : canjear (cupones, etc.) — **redemption** [rɪ'dɛmpʃən] *n* : redención *f*

red–handed ['rɛd'hændəd] *adv or adj* : con las manos en la masa

redhead {'rɛd,hɛd} *n* : pelirrojo *m*, -ja *f*

red–hot ['rɛd'hɑt] *adj* : al rojo vivo

redness ['rɛdnəs] *n* : rojez *f*

redo [,ri:'du:] *vt* -**did** [-'dɪd]; -**done** [-'dʌn]; -**doing** : hacer de nuevo

redouble [rɪ'dʌbəl] *vt* -**bled**; -**bling** : redoblar

red tape *n* : papeleo *m*

reduce [rɪ'du:s, -'dju:s] *v* -**duced**; -**ducing** *vt* : reducir — *vi* SLIM : adelgazar — **reduction** [rɪ'dʌkʃən] *n* : reducción *f*

redundant [rɪ'dʌndənt] *adj* : redundante

reed ['ri:d] *n* **1** : caña *f* **2** : lengüeta *f* (de un instrumento)

reef ['ri:f] *n* : arrecife *m*

reek ['ri:k] *vi* : apestar

reel ['ri:l] *n* : carrete *m* (de hilo, etc.) — ~ *vt* **1** ~ **in** : enrollar (un sedal), sacar (un pez) del agua **2** ~ **off** : enumerar — *vi* **1** SPIN : dar vueltas **2** STAGGER : tambalearse

reestablish [,ri:r'stæblɪʃ] *vt* : restablecer

refer [rɪ'fər] *v* -**ferred**; -**ferring** *vt* **1** DIRECT : enviar, mandar **2** SUBMIT : remitir — *vi* ~ **to 1** MENTION : referirse a **2** CONSULT : consultar

referee [,rɛfə'ri:] *n* : árbitro *m*, -tra *f* — ~ *v* -**eed**; -**eeing** : arbitrar

reference ['rɛfrəns, 'rɛfə-] *n* **1** : referencia *f* **2** CONSULTATION : consulta *f* **3** or ~ **book** : libro *m* de consulta **4** **in** ~ **to** : con referencia a

refill [,ri:'fɪl] *vt* : rellenar — ~ ['ri:,fɪl] *n* : recambio *m*

refine [rɪ'faɪn] *vt* -**fined**; -**fining** : refinar — **refined** [rɪ'faɪnd] *adj* : refinado — **refinement** [rɪ'faɪnmənt] *n* : refinamiento *m* — **refinery** [rɪ'faɪnəri] *n*, *pl* -**eries** : refinería *f*

reflect [rɪ'flɛkt] *vt* : reflejar — *vi* **1** : reflejarse **2** ~ **badly on** : desacreditar **3** ~ **upon** : reflexionar sobre — **reflection** [rɪ'flɛkʃən] *n* **1** : reflexión *f* **2** IMAGE : reflejo *m* — **reflector** [rɪ'flɛktər] *n* : reflector *m*

reflex ['ri:,flɛks] *n* : reflejo *m*

reflexive [rɪ'flɛksɪv] *adj* : reflexivo

reform [rɪ'fɔrm] *vt* : reformar — *vi* : reformarse — ~ *n* : reforma *f* — **reformer** [rɪ'fɔrmər] *n* : reformador *m*, -dora *f*

refrain¹ [rɪ'freɪn] *vi* ~ **from** : abstenerse de

refrain² *n* : estribillo *m* (en música)

refresh [rɪ'frɛʃ] *vt* : refrescar — **refreshments** [rɪ'frɛʃmənts] *npl* : refrigerio *m*

refrigerate [rɪ'frɪdʒə,reɪt] *vt* -**ated**; -**ating** : refrigerar — **refrigeration** [rɪ,frɪdʒə-'reɪʃən] *n* : refrigeración *f* — **refrigerator** [rɪ'frɪdʒə,reɪtər] *n* : nevera *f* Lat, frigorífico *m* Spain

refuel [ri:'fju:əl] *v* -**eled** *or* -**elled**; -**eling** *or* -**elling** *vt* : llenar de carburante — *vi* : repostar

refuge ['rɛ,fju:dʒ] *n* : refugio *m* — **refugee** [,rɛfjʊ'dʒi:] *n* : refugiado *m*, -da *f*

refund [rɪ'fʌnd, 'ri:,fʌnd] *vt* : reembolsar — ~ ['ri:,fʌnd] *n* : reembolso *m*

refurbish [rɪ'fərbɪʃ] *vt* : renovar, restaurar

refuse¹ [rɪ'fju:z] *v* -**fused**; -**fusing** *vt* **1** : rehusar, rechazar **2** ~ **to do sth** : negarse a hacer algo — *vi* : negarse — **refusal** [rɪ'fju:zəl] *n* : negativa *f*

refuse² ['rɛ,fju:s, -,fju:z] *n* : residuos *mpl*, desperdicios *mpl*

refute [rɪ'fju:t] *vt* -**futed**; -**futing** : refutar

regain [ri:'geɪn] *vt* : recuperar, recobrar

regal ['ri:gəl] *adj* : regio, majestuoso — **regalia** [rɪ'geɪljə] *n* : ropaje *m*, insignias *fpl*

regard [rɪ'gɑrd] *n* **1** : consideración *f* **2** ESTEEM : estima *f* **3** **in this** ~ : en este sentido **4** ~**s** *npl* : saludos *mpl* **5** **with** ~ **to** : respecto a — ~ *vt* **1** : mirar (con recelo, etc.) **2** HEED : tener en cuenta **3** ESTEEM : estimar **4** **as** ~**s** : en lo que se refiere a **5** ~ **as** : considerar — **regarding** [rɪ'gɑrdɪŋ] *prep* : respecto a — **regardless** [rɪ'gɑrdləs] *adv* : a pesar de todo — **regardless of** *prep* **1** : sin tener en cuenta **2** IN SPITE OF : a pesar de

regent ['ri:dʒənt] *n* : regente *mf*

regime [reɪ'ʒi:m, rɪ-] *n* : régimen *m* — **regimen** ['rɛdʒəmən] *n* : régimen *m*

regiment ['rɛdʒəmənt] *n* : regimiento *m*

region ['ri:dʒən] *n* : región *f* — **regional** ['ri:dʒənəl] *adj* : regional

register ['rɛdʒəstər] *n* : registro *m* — ~ *vt* **1** : registrar (a personas), matricular (vehículos) **2** SHOW : marcar, manifestar **3** : certificar (correo) — *vi* ENROLL : inscribirse, matricularse — **registrar** ['rɛdʒə,strɑr] *n* : registrador *m*, -dora *f* oficial — **registration** [,rɛdʒə'streɪʃən] *n* **1** : inscripción *f*, matriculación *f* **2** *or* ~ **number** : número *m* de matrícula — **registry** ['rɛdʒəstri] *n*, *pl* -**tries** : registro *m*

regret [rɪ'grɛt] *vt* -**gretted**; -**gretting** : lamentar — ~ *n* **1** REMORSE : arrepentimiento *m* **2** SORROW : pesar *m*

— **regrettable** [ri'gretəbəl] *adj* : lamentable

regular ['regjələr] *adj* **1** : regular **2** CUSTOMARY : habitual — **~** *n* : cliente *mf* habitual — **regularity** [,regjə'lærəṭi] *n*, *pl* **-ties** : regularidad *f* — **regularly** ['regjələrli] *adv* : regularmente — **regulate** ['regjə,leɪt] *vt* **-lated; -lating** : regular — **regulation** [,regjə'leɪʃən] *n* **1** CONTROL : regulación *f* **2** RULE : regla *f*

rehabilitate [,riːhə'bɪlə,teɪt, ,riːə-] *vt* **-tated; -tating** : rehabilitar — **rehabilitation** [,riːhə,bɪlə'teɪʃən, ,riːə-] *n* : rehabilitación *f*

rehearse [ri'hərs] *v* **-hearsed; -hearsing** : ensayar — **rehearsal** [ri'hərsəl] *n* : ensayo *m*

reign ['reɪn] *n* : reinado *m* — **~** *vi* : reinar

reimburse [,riːəm'bərs] *vt* **-bursed; -bursing** : reembolsar — **reimbursement** [,riːəm'bərsmənt] *n* : reembolso *m*

rein ['reɪn] *n* : rienda *f*

reincarnation [,riːɪn,kar'neɪʃən] *n* : reencarnación *f*

reindeer ['reɪn,dɪr] *n* : reno *m*

reinforce [,riːən'fors] *vt* **-forced; -forcing** : reforzar — **reinforcement** [,riːən'forsmənt] *n* : refuerzo *m*

reinstate [,riːən'steɪt] *vt* **-stated; -stating 1** : restablecer **2** : restituir (a algn en su cargo)

reiterate [ri'ɪṭə,reɪt] *vt* **-ated; -ating** : reiterar

reject [ri'dʒekt] *vt* : rechazar — **rejection** [ri'dʒekʃən] *n* : rechazo *m*

rejoice [ri'dʒɔɪs] *vi* **-joiced; -joicing** : regocijarse

rejuvenate [ri'dʒuːvə,neɪt] *vt* **-nated; -nating** : rejuvenecer

rekindle [,riː'kɪndəl] *vt* **-dled; -dling** : reavivar

relapse [,riː'læps, ri'læps] *n* : recaída *f* — **~** [ri'læps] *vi* **-lapsed; -lapsing** : recaer

relate [ri'leɪt] *v* **-lated; -lating** *vt* **1** TELL : relatar **2** ASSOCIATE : relacionar — *vi* **~ to 1** CONCERN : estar relacionado con **2** UNDERSTAND : identificarse con **3** : relacionarse con (socialmente) — **related** [ri'leɪṭəd] *adj* **~ to** : emparentado con — **relation** [ri'leɪʃən] *n* **1** CONNECTION : relación *f* **2** RELATIVE : pariente *mf* **3 in ~ to** : en relación con **4 ~s** *npl* : relaciones *fpl* — **relationship** [ri'leɪʃən,ʃɪp] *n* **1** : relación *f* **2** KINSHIP : parentesco *m* — **relative** ['reləṭɪv] *n* : pariente *mf* — **~** *adj* : relativo — **relatively** *adv* : relativamente

relax [ri'læks] *vt* : relajar — *vi* : relajarse — **relaxation** [,riː,læk'seɪʃən] *n* **1** : relajación *f* **2** RECREATION : esparcimiento *m*

relay ['riː,leɪ] *n* **1** : relevo *m* **2** *or* **~ race** : carrera *f* de relevos — **~** ['riː,leɪ, ri'leɪ] *vt* **-layed; -laying** : transmitir

release [ri'liːs] *vt* **-leased; -leasing 1** FREE : liberar, poner en libertad **2** : soltar (un freno, etc.) **3** EMIT : despedir **4** : sacar (un libro, etc.), estrenar (una película) — **~** *n* **1** : liberación *f* **2** : estreno *m* (de una película), publicación *f* (de un libro) **3** : fuga *f* (de gases)

relegate ['relə,geɪt] *vt* **-gated; -gating** : relegar

relent [ri'lent] *vi* : ceder — **relentless** [ri'lentləs] *adj* : implacable

relevant ['reləvənt] *adj* : pertinente — **relevance** ['reləvənts] *n* : pertinencia *f*

reliable [ri'laɪəbəl] *adj* : fiable (dícese de personas), fidedigno (dícese de información, etc.) — **reliability** [ri,laɪə'bɪlə,ṭi] *n*, *pl* **-ties** : fiabilidad *f* (de una cosa), responsabilidad *f* (de una persona) — **reliance** [ri'laɪənts] *n* **1** : dependencia *f* **2** TRUST : confianza *f* — **reliant** [ri'laɪənt] *adj* : dependente

relic ['relɪk] *n* : reliquia *f*

relief [ri'liːf] *n* **1** : alivio *m* **2** AID : ayuda *f* **3** : relieve *m* (en la escultura) **4** REPLACEMENT : relevo *m* — **relieve** [ri'liːv] *vt* **-lieved; -lieving 1** : aliviar **2** REPLACE : relevar (a algn) **3 ~ s.o. of** : liberar a algn de

religion [ri'lɪdʒən] *n* : religión *f* — **religious** [ri'lɪdʒəs] *adj* : religioso

relinquish [ri'lɪŋkwɪʃ, -'lɪn-] *vt* : renunciar a, abandonar

relish ['relɪʃ] *n* **1** : salsa *f* (condimento) **2 with ~** : con gusto — **~** *vt* : saborear

relocate [,riː'loː,keɪt, ,riːloː'keɪt] *vt* **-cated; -cating** : trasladar — *vi* : trasladarse — **relocation** [,riːloː'keɪʃən] *n* : traslado *m*

reluctance [ri'lʌktənts] *n* : reticencia *f*, desgana *f* — **reluctant** [ri'lʌktənt] *adj* : reacio, reticente — **reluctantly** [ri'lʌktəntli] *adv* : a regañadientes

rely [ri'laɪ] *vi* **-lied; -lying ~ on 1** DEPEND ON : depender de **2** TRUST : confiar (en)

remain [ri'meɪn] *vi* **1** : quedar **2** STAY : quedarse **3** CONTINUE : seguir, continuar — **remainder** [ri'meɪndər] *n* : resto *m* — **remains** [ri'meɪnz] *npl* : restos *mpl*

remark [ri'mark] *n* : comentario *m*, observación *f* — **~** *vt* : observar — *vi* **~**

on : observar — **remarkable** [ri-'markəbəl] *adj* : extraordinario, notable
remedy ['remədi] *n, pl* **-dies** : remedio *m* — ~ *vt* **-died; -dying** : remediar —
remedial [ri'mi:diəl] *adj* : correctivo
remember [ri'membər] *vt* **1** : acordarse de, recordar **2** ~ **to** : acordarse de — *vi* : acordarse, recordar — **remembrance** [ri'membrənts] *n* : recuerdo *m*
remind [ri'maind] *vt* : recordar — **reminder** [ri'maindər] *n* : recordatorio *m*
reminiscence [,remə'nisənts] *n* : recuerdo *m*, reminiscencia *f* — **reminisce** [,remə'nis] *vi* **-nisced; -niscing** : rememorar los viejos tiempos — **reminiscent** [,remə'nisənt] *adj* **be** ~ **of** : recordar
remiss [ri'mis] *adj* : negligente, remiso
remit [ri'mit] *vt* **-mitted; -mitting 1** PARDON : perdonar **2** : enviar (dinero) — **remission** [ri'mifən] *n* : remisión *f*
remnant ['remnənt] *n* **1** : resto *m* **2** TRACE : vestigio *m*
remorse [ri'mors] *n* : remordimiento *m* — **remorseful** [ri'morsfəl] *adj* : arrepentido
remote [ri'mo:t] *adj* **-moter; -est 1** : remoto **2** ALOOF : distante **3** ~ **from** : apartado de, alejado de — **remote control** *n* : control *m* remoto — **remotely** [ri'mo:tli] *adv* SLIGHTLY : remotamente
remove [ri'mu:v] *vt* **-moved; -moving 1** : quitar (una tapa, etc.), quitarse (ropa) **2** EXTRACT : sacar **3** DISMISS : destituir **4** ELIMINATE : eliminar — **removable** [ri'mu:vəbəl] *adj* : separable, de quita y pon — **removal** [ri'mu:vəl] *n* **1** : eliminación *f* **2** EXTRACTION : extracción *f*
remunerate [ri'mju:nə,reit] *vt* **-ated; -ating** : remunerar
render ['rendər] *vt* **1** : rendir (homenaje), prestar (ayuda) **2** MAKE : hacer **3** TRANSLATE : traducir
rendezvous ['randi,vu:, -dei-] *ns & pl* : cita *f*
rendition [ren'difən] *n* : interpretación *f*
renegade ['reni,geid] *n* : renegado *m*, -da *f*
renew [ri'nu:, -'nju:] *vt* **1** : renovar **2** RESUME : reanudar — **renewal** [ri'nu:əl, -'nju:-] *n* : renovación *f*
renounce [ri'naunts] *vt* **-nounced; -nouncing** : renunciar a
renovate ['renə,veit] *vt* **-vated; -vating** : renovar — **renovation** [,renə'veifən] *n* : renovación *f*
renown [ri'naun] *n* : renombre *m* — **renowned** [ri'naund] *adj* : célebre, renombrado

rent ['rent] *n* **1** : alquiler *m*, arrendamiento *m*, renta *f* **2 for** ~ : se alquila — ~ *vt* : alquilar — **rental** ['rentəl] *n* : alquiler *m* — ~ *adj* : de alquiler — **renter** ['rentər] *n* : arrendatario *m*, -ria *f*
renunciation [ri,nʌntsi'eifən] *n* : renuncia *f*
reopen [ri'o:pən] *vt* : volver a abrir
reorganize [ri'orgə,naiz] *vt* **-nized; -nizing** : reorganizar — **reorganization** [ri,orgənə'zeifən] *n* : reorganización *f*
repair [ri'pær] *vt* : reparar, arreglar — ~ *n* **1** : reparación *f*, arreglo *m* **2 in bad** ~ : en mal estado
repay [ri'pei] *vt* **-paid; -paying 1** : devolver (dinero), pagar (una deuda) **2** : corresponder a (un favor, etc.)
repeal [ri'pi:l] *vt* : abrogar, revocar — ~ *n* : abrogación *f*, revocación *f*
repeat [ri'pi:t] *vt* : repetir — ~ *n* : repetición *f* — **repeatedly** [ri'pi:t̬ədli] *adv* : repetidas veces
repel [ri'pel] *vt* **-pelled; -pelling** : repeler — **repellent** [ri'pelənt] *n* : repelente *m*
repent [ri'pent] *vi* : arrepentirse — **repentance** [ri'pentənts] *n* : arrepentimiento *m*
repercussion [,ri:pər'kʌʃən, ,repər-] *n* : repercusión *f*
repertoire ['repər,twar] *n* : repertorio *m*
repetition [,repə'tifən] *n* : repetición *f* — **repetitious** [,repə'tiʃəs] *adj* : repetitivo — **repetitive** [ri'pet̬ət̬iv] *adj* : repetitivo
replace [ri'pleis] *vt* **-placed; -placing 1** : reponer **2** SUBSTITUTE : reemplazar, sustituir **3** EXCHANGE : cambiar — **replacement** [ri'pleismənt] *n* **1** : sustitución *f* **2** : sustituto *m*, -ta *f* (persona) **3 or** ~ **part** : repuesto *m*
replenish [ri'pleniʃ] *vt* **1** : reponer **2** REFILL : rellenar
replete [ri'pli:t] *adj* ~ **with** : repleto de
replica ['replikə] *n* : réplica *f*
reply [ri'plai] *vi* **-plied; -plying** : contestar, responder — ~ *n, pl* **-plies** : respuesta *f*
report [ri'port] *n* **1** : informe *m* **2** RUMOR : rumor *m* **3 or** **news** ~ : reportaje *m* **4 weather** ~ : boletín *m* meteorológico — ~ *vt* **1** RELATE : anunciar **2** ~ **a crime** : denunciar un delito **3** *or* ~ **on** : informar sobre — *vi* **1** : informar **2** ~ **for duty** : presentarse — **report card** *n* : boletín *m* de calificaciones — **reportedly** [ri'port̬ədli] *adv*

: según se dice — **reporter** [rɪ'portər]
n : periodista *mf*; reportero *m*, -ra *f*
repose [rɪ'poːz] *vi* **-posed; -posing** : reposar — ～ *n* : reposo *m*
reprehensible [ˌreprɪ'hensəbəl] *adj*
: reprensible
represent [ˌreprɪ'zent] *vt* **1** : representar
2 PORTRAY : presentar — **representa-**
tion [ˌreprɪzen'teɪʃən, -zən-] *n* : representación *f* — **representative** [ˌreprɪ-
'zentətɪv] *adj* : representativo — ～ *n*
: representante *mf*
repress [rɪ'pres] *vt* : reprimir — **repres-**
sion [rɪ'preʃən] *n* : represión *f*
reprieve [rɪ'priːv] *n* : indulto *m*
reprimand ['reprəˌmænd] *n* : reprimenda
f — ～ *vt* : reprender
reprint [rɪ'prɪnt] *n* : reimprimir — ～
['riːˌprɪnt, rɪ'prɪnt] *n* : reedición *f*
reprisal [rɪ'praɪzəl] *n* : represalia *f*
reproach [rɪ'proːtʃ] *n* **1** : reproche *m* **2**
beyond ～ : irreprochable — ～ *vt*
: reprochar — **reproachful** [rɪ'proːtʃfəl]
adj : de reproche
reproduce [ˌriːprə'duːs, -'djuːs] *v* **-duced;**
-ducing *vt* : reproducir — *vi* : reproducirse — **reproduction** [ˌriːprə'dʌk-
ʃən] *n* : reproducción *f* — **reproduc-**
tive [ˌriːprə'dʌktɪv] *adj* : reproductor
reproof [rɪ'pruːf] *n* : reprobación *f*
reptile ['reptaɪl] *n* : reptil *m*
republic [rɪ'pʌblɪk] *n* : república *f* — **re-**
publican [rɪ'pʌblɪkən] *n* : republicano
m, -na *f* — ～ *adj* : republicano
repudiate [rɪ'pjuːdiˌeɪt] *vt* **-ated; -ating**
: repudiar
repugnant [rɪ'pʌgnənt] *adj* : repugnante,
asqueroso — **repugnance** [rɪ-
'pʌgnənts] *n* : repugnancia *f*
repulse [rɪ'pʌls] *vt* **-pulsed; -pulsing**
: repeler, rechazar — **repulsive** [rɪ-
'pʌlsɪv] *adj* : repulsivo
reputation [ˌrepjə'teɪʃən] *n* : reputación *f*
— **reputable** ['repjətəbəl] *adj* : de confianza, acreditado — **reputed** [rɪ'pjuː-
təd] *adj* : supuesto
request [rɪ'kwest] *n* : petición *f* — ～ *vt*
: pedir
requiem ['rekwiəm, 'reɪ-] *n* : réquiem *m*
require [rɪ'kwaɪr] *vt* **-quired; -quiring 1**
CALL FOR : requerir **2** NEED : necesitar
— **requirement** [rɪ'kwaɪrmənt] *n* **1**
NEED : necesidad *f* **2** DEMAND : requisito *m* — **requisite** ['rekwəzɪt] *adj*
: necesario
resale ['riːˌseɪl, ˌriːˈseɪl] *n* : reventa *f*
rescind [rɪ'sɪnd] *vt* : rescindir (un contrato), revocar (una ley, etc.)
rescue ['reskjuː] *vt* **-cued; -cuing**
: rescatar, salvar — ～ *n* : rescate *m* —

rescuer ['reskjuər] *n* : salvador *m*,
-dora *f*
research [rɪ'sərtʃ, 'riːˌsərtʃ] *n* : investigación *f* — ～ *vt* : investigar — **re-**
searcher [rɪ'sərtʃər, 'riː-] *n* : investigador *m*, -dora *f*
resemble [rɪ'zembəl] *vt* **-sembled;**
-sembling : parecerse a — **resem-**
blance [rɪ'zembləns] *n* : parecido *m*
resent [rɪ'zent] *vt* : resentirse de, ofenderse por — **resentful** [rɪ'zentfəl] *adj*
: resentido — **resentment** [rɪ-
'zentmənt] *n* : resentimiento *m*
reserve [rɪ'zərv] *vt* **-served; -serving**
: reservar — ～ *n* **1** : reserva *f* **2** ～**s**
npl : reservas *fpl* (militares) — **reser-**
vation [ˌrezər'veɪʃən] *n* : reserva *f* —
reserved [rɪ'zərvd] *adj* : reservado —
reservoir ['rezərˌvwar, -ˌvwor, -ˌvor] *n*
: embalse *m*
reset [riːˈset] *vt* **-set; -setting** : volver a
poner (un reloj, etc.)
residence ['rezədənts] *n* : residencia *f* —
reside [rɪ'zaɪd] *vi* **-sided; -siding** : residir — **resident** ['rezədənt] *adj* : residente — ～ *n* : residente *mf* — **resi-**
dential [ˌrezə'dentʃəl] *adj* : residencial
residue ['rezəˌduː, -ˌdjuː] *n* : residuo *m*
resign [rɪ'zaɪn] *vt* **1** QUIT : dimitir **2** ～
oneself to : resignarse a — **resigna-**
tion [ˌrezɪg'neɪʃən] *n* **1** : dimisión *f* **2**
ACCEPTANCE : resignación *f*
resilient [rɪ'zɪljənt] *adj* **1** : resistente
(dícese de personas) **2** ELASTIC : elástico — **resilience** [rɪ'zɪljənts] *n* **1** : resistencia *f* **2** ELASTICITY : elasticidad *f*
resin ['rezən] *n* : resina *f*
resist [rɪ'zɪst] *vt* : resistir — *vi* : resistirse — **resistance** [rɪ'zɪstənts] *n* : resistencia *f* — **resistant** [rɪ'zɪstənt] *adj*
: resistente
resolve [rɪ'zalv] *vt* **-solved; -solving**
: resolver — ～ *n* : resolución *f* —
resolution [ˌrezə'luːʃən] *n* **1** : resolución *f* **2** DECISION, INTENTION : propósito *m* — **resolute** ['rezəˌluːt] *adj* : resuelto
resonance ['rezənənts] *n* : resonancia *f*
— **resonant** ['rezənənt] *adj* : resonante
resort [rɪ'zort] *n* **1** RECOURSE : recurso *m*
2 or **tourist** ～ : centro *m* turístico —
～ *vi* ～ **to** : recurrir a
resounding [rɪ'zaʊndɪŋ] *adj* **1** RESONANT
: resonante **2** ABSOLUTE : rotundo
resource ['riːˌsors, rɪ'sors] *n* : recurso *m*
— **resourceful** [rɪ'sorsfəl, -zors-] *adj*
: ingenioso
respect [rɪ'spekt] *n* **1** ESTEEM : respeto *m*
2 in some ～**s** : en algún sentido **3**
pay one's ～**s** : presentar uno sus re-

spetos **4 with ~ to** : (con) respecto a
— **~** *vt* : respetar — **respectable** [ri-
'spektəbəl] *adj* : respetable — **respectful** [ri'spektfəl] *adj* : respetuoso — **respective** [ri'spektiv] *adj* : respectivo
— **respectively** *adv* : respectivamente
respiration [ˌrespə'reiʃən] *n* : respiración *f* — **respiratory** ['respərəˌtori, ri-
'spairə-] *adj* : respiratorio
respite ['respit, ri'spait] *n* : respiro *m*
response [ri'spɑnts] *n* : respuesta *f* —
respond [ri'spɑnd] *vi* : responder —
responsibility [riˌspɑntsə'bi̇ləti] *n, pl*
-ties : responsabilidad *f* — **responsible** [ri'spɑntsəbəl] *adj* : responsable —
responsive [ri'spɑntsiv] *adj* : sensible,
receptivo
rest[1] ['rest] *n* **1** : descanso *m* **2** SUPPORT
: apoyo *m* **3** : silencio *m* (en música)
— **~** *vi* **1** : descansar **2** LEAN : apoyarse **3 ~ on** DEPEND ON : depender
de — *vt* **1** RELAX : descansar **2** LEAN :
apoyar
rest[2] *n* REMAINDER : resto *m*
restaurant ['restəˌrɑnt, -rənt] *n* : restaurante *m*
restful ['restfəl] *adj* : tranquilo, apacible
restitution [ˌrestə'tuːʃən, -tjuː-] *n* : restitución *f*
restless ['restləs] *adj* : inquieto, agitado
restore [ri'stor] *vt* **-stored; -storing 1**
RETURN : devolver **2** REESTABLISH
: restablecer **3** REPAIR : restaurar —
restoration [ˌrestə'reiʃən] *n* **1** : restablecimiento *m* **2** REPAIR : restauración *f*
restrain [ri'strein] *vt* **1** : contener **2 ~
oneself** : contenerse — **restrained**
[ri'streind] *adj* : comedido, moderado
— **restraint** [ri'streint] *n* **1** : restricción
f **2** SELF-CONTROL : moderación *f*, control *m* de sí mismo
restriction [ri'strikʃən] *n* : restricción *f*
— **restrict** [ri'strikt] *vt* : restringir —
restricted [ri'striktəd] *adj* : restringido
— **restrictive** [ri'striktiv] *adj* : restrictivo
result [ri'zʌlt] *vi* : resultar — **~** *n* **1** : resultado *m* **2 as a ~ of** : como conse-
cuencia de
resume [ri'zuːm] *v* **-sumed; -suming** *vt*
: reanudar — *vi* : reanudarse
résumé *or* **resume** *or* **resumé** ['rezə-
ˌmei, ˌrezə'-] *n* : currículum *m* (vitae)
resumption [ri'zʌmpʃən] *n* : reanuda-
ción *f*
resurgence [ri'sərdʒənts] *n* : resurgimiento *m*
resurrection [ˌrezə'rekʃən] *n* : resurrección *f* — **resurrect** [ˌrezə'rekt] *vt* : resucitar

resuscitate [ri'sʌsəˌteit] *vt* **-tated; -tat-
ing** : resucitar
retail ['riːˌteil] *vt* : vender al por menor
— **~** *n* : venta *f* al por menor — **~**
adj : detallista, minorista — **~** *adv*
: al detalle, al por menor — **retailer**
['riːˌteilər] *n* : detallista *mf*, minorista
mf
retain [ri'tein] *vt* : retener
retaliate [ri'tæliˌeit] *vi* **-ated; -ating** : tomar represalias — **retaliation** [riˌtæli-
'eiʃən] *n* : represalias *fpl*
retard [ri'tɑrd] *vt* : retardar, retrasar —
retarded [ri'tɑrdəd] *adj* : retrasado
retention [ri'tentʃən] *n* : retención *f*
reticence ['retəsənts] *n* : reticencia *f* —
reticent ['retəsənt] *adj* : reticente
retina ['retənə] *n, pl* **-nas** *or* **-nae** [-əni,
-əˌnai] : retina *f*
retinue ['retənˌuː, -ˌjuː] *n* : séquito *m*
retire [ri'tair] *vi* **-tired; -tiring 1** WITH-
DRAW : retirarse **2** : jubilarse, retirarse
(de un trabajo) **3** : acostarse (en la
cama) — **retirement** [ri'tairmənt] *n*
: jubilación *f* — **retiring** [ri'tairin] *adj*
SHY : retraído
retort [ri'tort] *vt* : replicar — **~** *n* : réplica *f*
retrace [ˌriː'treis] *vt* **-traced; -tracing ~
one's steps** : volver sobre sus pasos
retract [ri'trækt] *vt* **1** WITHDRAW : retirar
2 : retraer (garras, etc.) — *vi* : retractarse
retrain [ˌriː'trein] *vt* : reciclar
retreat [ri'triːt] *n* **1** : retirada *f* **2** REFUGE
: refugio *m* — **~** *vi* : retirarse
retribution [ˌretrə'bjuːʃən] *n* : castigo *m*
retrieve [ri'triːv] *vt* **-trieved; -trieving 1**
: cobrar, recuperar **2** RESCUE : salvar
— **retrieval** [ri'triːvəl] *n* : recuperación
f — **retriever** [ri'triːvər] *n* : perro *m* cobrador
retroactive [ˌretro'æktiv] *adj* : retroactivo
retrospect ['retrəˌspekt] *n* **in ~** : miran-
do hacia atrás — **retrospective** [ˌretrə-
'spektiv] *adj* : retrospectivo
return [ri'tərn] *vi* **1** : volver, regresar **2**
REAPPEAR : reaparecer — *vt* **1** : devolver **2** YIELD : producir — **~** *n* **1**
: regreso *m*, vuelta *f* **2** : devolución *f*
(de algo prestado) **3** YIELD
: rendimiento *m* **4 in ~ for** : a cambio
de **5** *or* **tax ~** : declaración *f* de impuestos — **~** *adj* : de vuelta
reunite [ˌriːju'nait] *vt* **-nited; -niting** : reunir — **reunion** [ri'juːmjən] *n* : reunión *f*
revamp [ˌriː'væmp] *vt* : renovar
reveal [ri'viːl] *vt* **1** : revelar **2** SHOW
: dejar ver

revel ['revəl] vi **-eled** or **-elled; -eling** or **-elling ~ in** : deleitarse en

revelation [,revə'leɪʃən] n : revelación f

revelry ['revəlri] n, pl **-ries** : jolgorio m, regocijos mpl

revenge [rɪ'vendʒ] vt **-venged; -venging** : vengar — ~ n 1 : venganza f 2 **take ~ on** : vengarse de

revenue ['revənu:, -nju:] n : ingresos mpl

reverberate [rɪ'vərbə,reɪt] vi **-ated; -ating** : retumbar, resonar

reverence ['revərənts] n : reverencia f, veneración f — **revere** [rɪ'vɪr] vt **-vered; -vering** : venerar — **reverend** ['revərənd] adj : reverendo — **reverent** ['revərənt] adj : reverente

reverie ['revəri] n, pl **-eries** : ensueño m

reverse [rɪ'vərs] adj : inverso, contrario — ~ v **-versed; -versing** vt 1 : invertir 2 : cambiar (una política), revocar (una decisión) 3 : dar marcha atrás a (un automóvil) — vi : invertirse — ~ n 1 BACK : dorso m, revés m 2 or ~ **gear** : marcha f atrás 3 **the ~** : lo contrario — **reversible** [rɪ'vərsəbəl] adj : reversible — **reversal** ['revərsəl] n 1 : inversión f 2 CHANGE : cambio m total 3 SETBACK : revés m — **revert** [rɪ'vərt] vi : revertir

review [rɪ'vju:] n 1 : revisión f 2 OVERVIEW : resumen m 3 CRITIQUE : reseña f, crítica f 4 : repaso m (para un examen) — ~ vt 1 EXAMINE : examinar 2 : repasar (una lección) 3 CRITIQUE : reseñar — **reviewer** [rɪ'vjuːər] n : crítico m, -ca f

revile [rɪ'vaɪl] vt **-viled; -viling** : injuriar

revise [rɪ'vaɪz] vt **-vised; -vising** 1 : modificar (una política, etc.) 2 : revisar, corregir (una publicación) — **revision** [rɪ'vɪʒən] n : corrección f, modificación f

revive [rɪ'vaɪv] v **-vived; -viving** vt 1 : reanimar, reactivar 2 : resucitar (a una persona) 3 RESTORE : restablecer — vi 1 : reanimarse, reactivarse 2 COME TO : volver en sí — **revival** [rɪ'vaɪvəl] n : reanimación f, reactivación f

revoke [rɪ'voːk] vt **-voked; -voking** : revocar

revolt [rɪ'voːlt] vi : rebelarse, sublevarse — vt : dar asco a — ~ n : revuelta f, sublevación f — **revolting** [rɪ'voːltɪŋ] adj : asqueroso

revolution [,revə'luːʃən] n : revolución f — **revolutionary** [,revə'luːʃən,eri] adj : revolucionario — ~ n, pl **-aries** : revolucionario m, -ria f — **revolutionize** [,revə'luːʃən,aɪz] vt **-ized; -izing** : revolucionar

revolve [rɪ'vɑlv] v **-volved; -volving** vt : hacer girar — vi : girar — **revolver** [rɪ'vɑlvər] n : revólver m

revue [rɪ'vju:] n : revista f (teatral)

revulsion [rɪ'vʌlʃən] n : repugnancia f

reward [rɪ'wərd] vt : recompensar — ~ n : recompensa f

rewrite [,riː'raɪt] vt **-wrote; -written; -writing** : volver a escribir

rhetoric ['retərɪk] n : retórica f — **rhetorical** [rɪ'tɔrɪkəl] adj : retórico

rheumatism ['ruːmə,tɪzəm, 'ru-] n : reumatismo m — **rheumatic** [rʊ'mætɪk] adj : reumático

rhino ['raɪnoː] n, pl **-no** or **-nos → rhinoceros** — **rhinoceros** [raɪ'nɑsərəs] n, pl **-noceroses** or **-noceros** or **-noceri** [-,raɪ] : rinoceronte m

rhubarb ['ruːbɑrb] n : ruibarbo m

rhyme ['raɪm] n 1 : rima f 2 VERSE : verso m (en rima) — ~ vi **rhymed; rhyming** : rimar

rhythm ['rɪðəm] n : ritmo m — **rhythmic** ['rɪðmɪk] or **rhythmical** [-mɪkəl] adj : rítmico

rib ['rɪb] n : costilla f — ~ vt TEASE : tomar el pelo a

ribbon ['rɪbən] n : cinta f

rice ['raɪs] n : arroz m

rich ['rɪtʃ] adj 1 : rico 2 ~ **foods** : comidas fpl pesadas — **riches** ['rɪtʃəz] npl : riquezas fpl — **richness** ['rɪtʃnəs] n : riqueza f

rickety ['rɪkəti] adj : desvencijado, destartalado

ricochet ['rɪkə,ʃeɪ, -,ʃɛt] n : rebote m — ~ vi **-cheted** [-,ʃeɪd] or **-chetted** [-,ʃɛtəd]; **-cheting** [-,ʃeɪɪŋ] or **-chetting** [-,ʃɛtɪŋ] : rebotar

rid ['rɪd] vt **rid; ridding** 1 : librar 2 **get ~ of** : deshacerse de — **riddance** ['rɪdənts] n **good ~!** : ¡adiós y buen viaje!

riddle[1] ['rɪdəl] n : acertijo m, adivinanza f

riddle[2] vt **-dled; -dling** 1 : acribillar 2 **riddled with** : lleno de

ride ['raɪd] v **rode** ['roːd]; **ridden** ['rɪdən]; **riding** vt 1 : montar (a caballo, en bicicleta, ir (en autobús, etc.) 2 TRAVERSE : recorrer — vi 1 or ~ **horseback** : montar a caballo 2 : ir (en auto, etc.) — ~ n 1 : paseo m, vuelta f 2 : aparato m (en un parque de diversiones) — **rider** ['raɪdər] n 1 : jinete mf (a caballo) 2 CYCLIST : ciclista mf, motociclista mf

ridge ['rɪdʒ] n : cadena f (de montañas)

ridiculous [rə'dɪkjələs] adj : ridículo — **ridicule** ['rɪdə,kjuːl] n : burlas fpl — ~ vt **-culed; -culing** : ridiculizar

rife ['raɪf] *adj* **1** : extendido **2 be ~ with** : estar plagado de

rifle[1] ['raɪfəl] *vt* **-fled; -fling ~ through** : revolver

rifle[2] *n* : rifle *m*, fusil *m*

rift ['rɪft] *n* **1** : grieta *f* **2** : ruptura *f* (entre personas)

rig[1] ['rɪg] *vt* : amañar (una elección)

rig[2] *vt* **rigged; rigging 1** : aparejar (un barco) **2** EQUIP : equipar **3** *or* **~ out** DRESS : vestir **4** *or* **~ up** CONSTRUCT : construir — **~** *n* **1** : aparejo *m* (de un barco) **2** *or* **oil ~** : plataforma *f* petrolífera — **rigging** ['rɪgɪŋ, -gən] *n* : aparejo *m*

right ['raɪt] *adj* **1** JUST : bueno, justo **2** CORRECT : correcto **3** APPROPRIATE : apropiado, adecuado **4** STRAIGHT : recto **5 be ~** : tener razón **6 → right-hand — ~** *n* **1** GOOD : bien *m* **2** ENTITLEMENT : derecho *m* **3 on the ~** : a la derecha **4** *or* **~ side** : derecha *f* — **~** *adv* **1** WELL : bien **2** PRECISELY : justo **3** DIRECTLY : derecho **4** IMMEDIATELY : inmediatamente **5** COMPLETELY : completamente **6** *or* **to the ~** : a la derecha — **~** *vt* **1** STRAIGHTEN : enderezar **2 ~ a wrong** : reparar un daño — **right angle** : ángulo *m* recto — **righteous** ['raɪtʃəs] *adj* : recto, honrado — **rightful** ['raɪtfəl] *adj* : legítimo — **right-hand** ['raɪt'hænd] *adj* : derecho — **right-handed** ['raɪt'hændəd] *adj* : diestro — **rightly** ['raɪtli] *adv* **1** : justamente **2** CORRECTLY : correctamente — **right-wing** ['raɪt'wɪŋ] *adj* : derechista

rigid ['rɪdʒəd] *adj* : rígido

rigor *or Brit* **rigour** ['rɪgər] *n* : rigor *m* — **rigorous** ['rɪgərəs] *adj* : riguroso

rim ['rɪm] *n* **1** EDGE : borde *m* **2** : llanta *f* (de una rueda) **3** : montura *f* (de anteojos)

rind ['raɪnd] *n* : corteza *f*

ring[1] ['rɪŋ] *v* **rang** ['ræŋ]; **rung** ['rʌŋ]; **ringing** *vi* **1** : sonar (dícese de un timbre, etc.), **2** RESOUND : resonar — **~** *vt* **1** : tocar (un timbre, etc.) — **~** *n* **1** : toque *m* (de un timbre, etc.) **2** CALL : llamada *f* (por teléfono)

ring[2] *n* **1** : anillo *m*, sortija *f* **2** BAND, HOOP : aro *m* **3** CIRCLE : círculo *m* **4** *or* **boxing ~** : cuadrilátero *m* **5** NETWORK : red *f* — **~** *vt* : cercar, rodear — **ringleader** ['rɪŋ,li:dər] *n* : cabecilla *mf*

ringlet ['rɪŋlət] *n* : rizo *m*, bucle *m*

rink ['rɪŋk] *n* : pista *f* (de patinaje)

rinse ['rɪn(t)s] *vt* **rinsed; rinsing** : enjuagar — **~** *n* : enjuague *m*

riot ['raɪət] *n* : disturbio *m* — **~** *vi* : causar disturbios — **rioter** ['raɪətər] *n* : alborotador *m*, -dora *f*

rip ['rɪp] *v* **ripped; ripping** *vt* **1** : rasgar, desgarrar **2 ~ off** : arrancar — *vi* : rasgarse — **~** *n* **1** : rasgón *m*, desgarrón *m*

ripe ['raɪp] *adj* **riper; ripest 1** : maduro **2 ~ for** : listo por — **ripen** ['raɪpən] *v* : madurar — **ripeness** ['raɪpnəs] *n* : madurez *f*

rip-off ['rɪp,ɔf] *n* : timo *m fam*

ripple ['rɪpəl] *v* **-pled; -pling** *vi* : rizarse (dícese de agua) — *vt* : rizar — **~** *n* : onda *f*, rizo *m*

rise ['raɪz] *vi* **rose** ['ro:z]; **risen** ['rɪzən]; **rising 1** GET UP : levantarse **2** : salir (dícese del sol, etc.) **3** ASCEND : subir **4** INCREASE : aumentar **5 ~ up** REBEL : sublevarse — **~** *n* **1** ASCENT : subida *f* **2** INCREASE : aumento *m* **3** SLOPE : cuesta *f* — **riser** ['raɪzər] *n* **1 early ~** : madrugador *m*, -dora *f* **2 late ~** : dormilón *m*, -lona *f*

risk ['rɪsk] *n* : riesgo *m* — **~** *vt* : arriesgar — **risky** ['rɪski] *adj* **riskier; -est** : arriesgado, riesgoso *Lat*

rite ['raɪt] *n* : rito *m* — **ritual** ['rɪtʃuəl] *adj* : ritual — **~** *n* : ritual *m*

rival ['raɪvəl] *n* : rival *mf* — **~** *adj* : rival — **~** *vt* **-valed** *or* **-valled; -valing** *or* **-valling** : rivalizar con — **rivalry** ['raɪvəlri] *n, pl* **-ries** : rivalidad *f*

river ['rɪvər] *n* : río *m*

rivet ['rɪvət] *n* : remache *m* — **~** *vt* **1** : remachar **2** FIX : fijar (los ojos, etc.) **3 be ~ed by** : estar fascinado con

roach ['ro:tʃ] → **cockroach**

road ['ro:d] *n* **1** : carretera *f* **2** STREET : calle *f* **3** PATH : camino *m* — **roadblock** ['ro:d,blak] *n* : control *m* — **roadside** ['ro:d,saɪd] *n* : borde *m* de la carretera — **roadway** ['ro:d,weɪ] *n* : carretera *f*

roam ['ro:m] *vi* : vagar — *vt* : vagar por

roar ['ror] *vi* **1** : rugir **2 ~ with laughter** : reírse a carcajadas — *vt* : decir a gritos — **~** *n* **1** : rugido *m* (de un animal), estruendo *m* (de un avión, etc.)

roast ['ro:st] *vt* : asar (carne, etc.), tostar (café, etc.) — *vi* : asarse — **~** *n* : asado *m* — **~** *adj* : asado — **roast beef** *n* : rosbif *m*

rob ['rab] *v* **robbed; robbing** *vt* **1** : robar **2 ~ of** : privar de — *vi* : robar — **robber** ['rabər] *n* : ladrón *m*, -drona *f* — **robbery** ['rabəri] *n, pl* **-beries** : robo *m*

robe ['ro:b] *n* **1** : toga *f* (de un magistrado, etc.) **2 → bathrobe**

robin ['rabən] *n* : petirrojo *m*

robot ['ro:bʌt, -bət] *n* : robot *m*
robust [ro'bʌst, 'ro:bʌst] *adj* : robusto
rock[1] ['rak] *vt* **1** : acunar (a un niño), mecer (una cuna) **2** SHAKE : sacudir — *vi* : mecerse — ~ *n or* ~ **music** : música *f* rock
rock[2] *n* **1** : roca *f* (sustancia) **2** BOULDER : peña *f*, peñasco *m* **3** STONE : piedra *f*
rocket ['rakət] *n* : cohete *m*
rocking chair *n* : mecedora *f*
rocky ['raki] *adj* **rockier; -est 1** : rocoso **2** SHAKY : tambaleante
rod ['rad] *n* **1** : varilla *f* **2** *or* **fishing** ~ : caña *f* de pescar
rode → **ride**
rodent ['ro:dənt] *n* : roedor *m*
rodeo ['ro:di,o:, ro'de,o:] *n, pl* **-deos** : rodeo *m*
roe ['ro:] *n* : hueva *f*
rogue ['ro:g] *n* : pícaro *m*, -ra *f*
role ['ro:l] *n* : papel *m*
roll ['ro:l] *n* **1** : rollo *m* (de película, etc.) **2** LIST : lista *f* **3** : redoble *m* (de un tambor) **4** SWAYING : balanceo *m* **5** BUN : pancito *m Lat*, panecillo *m Spain* — ~ *vt* **1** : hacer rodar **2** *or* ~ **out** : estirar (masa) **3** ~ **up** : enrollar (papel, etc.), arremangar (una manga) — *vi* **1** : rodar **2** SWAY : balancearse **3** ~ **around** : revolcarse **4** ~ **over** : darse la vuelta — **roller** ['ro:lər] *n* **1** : rodillo *m* **2** CURLER : rulo *m* — **roller coaster** ['ro:lər,ko:stər] *n* : montaña *f* rusa — **roller-skate** ['ro:lər,skeɪt] *vi* **-skated; -skating** : patinar (sobre ruedas) — **roller skate** *n* : patín *m* (de ruedas)
Roman ['ro:mən] *adj* : romano — **Roman Catholic** *adj* : católico
romance [ro'mæns, 'ro:mæns] *n* **1** : novela *f* romántica **2** AFFAIR : romance *m*
Romanian [ru'meɪniən, ro-] *adj* : rumano — ~ *n* : rumano *m* (idioma)
romantic [ro'mæntɪk] *adj* : romántico
romp ['ramp] *n* : retozo *m* — ~ *vi* : retozar
roof ['ru:f, 'ruf] *n, pl* **roofs** ['ru:fs, 'rufs; 'ru:vz, 'ruvz] **1** : tejado *m*, techo *m* **2** ~ **of the mouth** : paladar *m* — **roofing** ['ru:fɪŋ, 'rufɪŋ] *n* : techumbre *f* — **rooftop** ['ru:f,tap, 'ruf-] *n* : tejado *m*, techo *m*
rook[1] ['ruk] *n* : grajo *m* (ave)
rook[2] *n* : torre *f* (en ajedrez)
rookie ['ruki] *n* : novato *m*, -ta *f*
room ['ru:m, 'rum] *n* **1** : cuarto *m*, habitación *f* **2** BEDROOM : dormitorio *m* **3** SPACE : espacio *m* **4** OPPORTUNITY : posibilidad *f* — **roommate** ['ru:m-,meɪt, 'rum-] *n* : compañero *m*, -ra *f* de

cuarto — **roomy** ['ru:mi, 'rumi] *adj* **roomier; -est** : espacioso
roost ['ru:st] *n* : percha *f* — ~ *vi* : posarse — **rooster** ['ru:stər, 'rus-] *n* : gallo *m*
root[1] ['ru:t, 'rut] *n* : raíz *f* — ~ *vt* ~ **out** : extirpar
root[2] *vi* ~ **around in** : hurgar en
root[3] *vi* ~ **for** SUPPORT : alentar
rope ['ro:p] *n* : cuerda *f* — ~ *vt* **roped; roping 1** : atar (con cuerda) **2** ~ **off** : acordonar
rosary ['ro:zəri] *n, pl* **-ries** : rosario *m*
rose[1] → **rise**
rose[2] ['ro:z] *n* : rosa *f* (flor), rosa *f* (color) — ~ *adj* : rosa — **rosebush** ['ro:z,bʊʃ] *n* : rosal *m*
rosemary ['ro:z,meri] *n, pl* **-maries** : romero *m*
Rosh Hashanah [,rɑʃhɑ'ʃɑnə, ,ro:ʃ-] *n* : el Año Nuevo judío
roster ['rastər] *n* : lista *f*
rostrum ['rastrəm] *n, pl* **-tra** *or* **-trums** [-trə] : tribuna *f*
rosy ['ro:zi] *adj* **rosier; -est 1** : sonrosado **2** PROMISING : halagüeno
rot ['rat] *v* **rotted; rotting** *vi* : pudrirse — *vt* : pudrir — ~ *n* : putrefacción *f*
rotary ['ro:təri] *adj* : rotativo — ~ *n* : rotonda *f*, glorieta *f Spain*
rotate ['ro:,teɪt] *v* **-tated; -tating** *vi* : girar — *vt* **1** : girar **2** ALTERNATE : alternar — **rotation** [ro'teɪʃən] *n* : rotación *f*
rote ['ro:t] *n* **by** ~ : de memoria
rotor ['ro:tər] *n* : rotor *m*
rotten ['ratən] *adj* **1** : podrido **2** BAD : malo
rouge ['ru:ʒ, 'ru:dʒ] *n* : colorete *m*
rough ['rʌf] *adj* **1** COARSE : áspero **2** RUGGED : accidentado **3** CHOPPY : agitado **4** DIFFICULT : duro **5** FORCEFUL : brusco **6** APPROXIMATE : aproximado **7** UNREFINED : tosco **8** ~ **draft** : borrador *m* — ~ *vt* **1** ~ **roughen 2** ~ **up** BEAT : dar una paliza a — **roughage** ['rʌfɪdʒ] *n* : fibra *f* — **roughen** ['rʌfən] *vt* : poner áspero — *vi* : ponerse áspero — **roughly** ['rʌfli] *adv* **1** : bruscamente **2** ABOUT : aproximadamente — **roughness** ['rʌfnəs] *n* COARSENESS : aspereza *f*
roulette [ru:'lɛt] *n* : ruleta *f*
round ['raʊnd] *adj* : redondo — ~ *adv* → **around** — ~ *n* **1** : círculo *m* **2** : ronda *f* (de bebidas, negociaciones, etc.) **3** : asalto *m* (en boxeo), vuelta *f* (en juegos) **4** ~ **of applause** : aplauso *m* **5** ~ **s** *npl* : visitas *fpl* (de un médico), rondas *fpl* (de un policía, etc.) — ~ *vt* **1** TURN : doblar **2** ~ **off**

: redondear 3 ~ off or ~ out COM-
PLETE : rematar 4 ~ up GATHER : reunir (personas), rodear (ganado) — ~
prep → around — roundabout
['raʊndəˌbaʊt] adj : indirecto —
round–trip ['raʊndˌtrɪp] n : viaje m de
ida y vuelta — roundup ['raʊndˌʌp] n
: rodeo m (de animales), redada f (de
delincuentes, etc.)
rouse ['raʊz] vt roused; rousing 1
AWAKEN : despertar 2 EXCITE : excitar
rout ['raʊt] n : derrota f aplastante — ~
vt : derrotar
route ['ruːt, 'raʊt] n 1 : ruta f 2 or delivery ~ : recorrido m
routine [ruːˈtiːn] n : rutina f — ~ adj
: rutinario
rove ['roːv] v roved; roving vi : errar,
vagar — vt : errar por
row¹ ['roː] vt 1 : llevar a remo 2 ~ a
boat : remar — vi : remar
row² n 1 : fila f (de gente o asientos),
hilera f (de casas, etc.) 2 in a ~
SUCCESSIVELY : seguido
row³ ['raʊ] n 1 RACKET : bulla f 2 QUAR-
REL : pelea f
rowboat ['roːˌboːt] n : bote m de remos
rowdy ['raʊdi] adj -dier; -est : escandaloso, alborotador — ~ n, pl -dies
: alborotador m, -dora f
royal ['rɔɪəl] adj : real — royalty ['rɔɪəlti]
n, pl -ties 1 : realeza f 2 royalties npl
: derechos mpl de autor
rub ['rʌb] v rubbed; rubbing vt 1 : frotar 2 CHAFE : rozar 3 ~ in : aplicar
frotando — vi 1 ~ against : rozar 2
~ off : salir (al frotar) — ~ n : fro-
tamiento m
rubber ['rʌbər] n 1 : goma f, caucho m 2
~s npl : chanclos mpl — rubber
band n : goma f (elástica) — rubber
stamp n : sello m (de goma) — rub-
bery ['rʌbəri] adj : gomoso
rubbish ['rʌbɪʃ] n 1 : basura f 2 NON-
SENSE : tonterías fpl
rubble ['rʌbəl] n : escombros mpl
ruby ['ruːbi] n, pl -bies : rubí m
rudder ['rʌdər] n : timón m
ruddy ['rʌdi] adj -dier; -est : rubicundo
rude ['ruːd] adj ruder; rudest 1 IMPO-
LITE : grosero, mal educado 2 ABRUPT
: brusco — rudely ['ruːdli] adv
: groseramente — rudeness ['ruːdnəs]
n : mala educación f
rudiment ['ruːdəmənt] n : rudimento m
— rudimentary [ˌruːdəˈmentəri] adj
: rudimentario
rue ['ruː] vt rued; ruing : lamentar —
rueful ['ruːfəl] adj : triste, arrepentido
ruffle ['rʌfəl] vt -fled; -fling 1 : des-

peinar (pelo), erizar (plumas) 2 VEX
: alterar, contrariar — ~ n : volante m
(de un vestido, etc.)
rug ['rʌg] n : alfombra f, tapete m
rugged ['rʌgəd] adj 1 : escabroso (dícese del terreno), escarpado (dícese de
montañas) 2 HARSH : duro 3 STURDY
: fuerte
ruin ['ruːən] n : ruina f — ~ vt : arruinar
rule ['ruːl] n 1 : regla f 2 CONTROL : dominio m 3 as a ~ : por lo general —
~ v ruled; ruling vt 1 GOVERN : gobernar 2 : fallar (dícese de un juez) 3 ~
out : descartar — vi : gobernar, reinar
— ruler ['ruːlər] n 1 : gobernante mf,
soberano m, -na f 2 : regla f (para
medir) — ruling ['ruːlɪŋ] n VERDICT
: fallo m
rum ['rʌm] n : ron m
Rumanian [rʊˈmeɪniən] → Romanian
rumble ['rʌmbəl] vi -bled; -bling 1 : retumbar 2 : hacer ruidos (dícese del estómago) — ~ n : retumbo m, estruendo m
rummage ['rʌmɪdʒ] vi -maged; -maging
: hurgar
rumor ['ruːmər] n : rumor m — ~ vt be
~ed : rumorearse
rump ['rʌmp] n 1 : grupa f (de un animal) 2 ~ steak : filete m de cadera
rumpus ['rʌmpəs] n : lío m, jaleo m fam
run ['rʌn] v ran ['ræn]; run; running vi 1
: correr 2 FUNCTION : funcionar 3 LAST
: durar 4 : desteñir (dícese de colores)
5 EXTEND : correr, extenderse 6 : presentarse (como candidato) 7 ~ away
: huir 8 ~ into ENCOUNTER : tropezar
con 9 ~ into HIT : chocar contra 10
~ late : ir retrasado 11 ~ out of
: quedarse sin 12 ~ over : atropellar
— vt 1 : correr 2 OPERATE : hacer funcionar 3 : hacer correr (agua) 4 MAN-
AGE : dirigir 5 ~ a fever : tener fiebre
— ~ n 1 : carrera f 2 TRIP : viaje m,
paseo m (en coche) 3 SERIES : serie f 4
in the long ~ : a la larga 5 in the
short ~ : a corto plazo — runaway
['rʌnəˌweɪ] n : fugitivo m, -va f — ~
adj : fugitivo — rundown ['rʌnˌdaʊn] n
: resumen m — run–down ['rʌnˈdaʊn]
adj 1 : destartalado 2 EXHAUSTED
: agotado
rung¹ → ring¹
rung² ['rʌŋ] n : peldaño m (de una escalera, etc.)
runner ['rʌnər] n 1 : corredor m, -dora f
2 : patín m (de un trineo), riel m (de un
cajón, etc.) — runner–up [ˌrʌnərˈʌp] n,
pl runners–up : subcampeón m,
-peona f — running ['rʌnɪŋ] adj 1

FLOWING : corriente **2** CONTINUOUS : continuo **3** CONSECUTIVE : seguido

runt ['rʌnt] *n* : animal *m* más pequeño (de una camada)

runway ['rʌn,weɪ] *n* : pista *f* de aterrizaje

rupture ['rʌptʃər] *n* : ruptura *f* — ~ *v* **-tured; -turing** *vt* : romper — *vi* : reventar

rural ['rurəl] *adj* : rural

ruse ['ru:s, 'ru:z] *n* : ardid *m*

rush¹ ['rʌʃ] *n* : junco *m* (planta)

rush² *vi* : ir de prisa — *vt* **1** : apresurar, apurar **2** ATTACK : asaltar **3** : llevar rápidamente (al hospital, etc.) — ~ *n* **1** : prisa *f*, apuro *m* **2** : ráfaga *f* (de aire), torrente *m* (de agua) — ~ *adj* : ur-

gente — **rush hour** *n* : hora *f* punta

russet ['rʌsət] *n* : color *m* rojizo

Russian ['rʌʃən] *adj* : ruso — ~ *n* : ruso *m* (idioma)

rust ['rʌst] *n* : herrumbre *f*, óxido *m* — ~ *vi* : oxidarse — *vt* : oxidar

rustic ['rʌstɪk] *adj* : rústico

rustle ['rʌsəl] *v* **-tled; -tling** *vt* **1** : hacer susurrar **2** : robar (ganado) — *vi* : susurrar — ~ *n* : susurro *m*

rusty ['rʌsti] *adj* **rustier; -est** : oxidado

rut ['rʌt] *n* **1** : surco *m* **2 be in a** ~ : ser esclavo de la rutina

ruthless ['ru:θləs] *adj* : despiadado, cruel

rye ['raɪ] *n* : centeno *m*

S

s ['es] *n*, *pl* **s's** *or* **ss** ['esəz] : s *f*, decimonovena letra del alfabeto inglés

Sabbath ['sæbəθ] *n* **1** : sábado *m* (día santo judío) **2** : domingo *m* (día santo cristiano)

sabotage ['sæbə,tɑʒ] *n* : sabotaje *m* — ~ *vt* **-taged; -taging** : sabotear

saccharin ['sækərən] *n* : sacarina *f*

sack ['sæk] *n* : saco *m* — ~ *vt* **1** FIRE : despedir **2** PLUNDER : saquear

sacrament ['sækrəmənt] *n* : sacramento *m*

sacred ['seɪkrəd] *adj* : sagrado

sacrifice ['sækrə,faɪs] *n* : sacrificio *m* — ~ *vt* **-ficed; -ficing** : sacrificar

sacrilege ['sækrəlɪdʒ] *n* : sacrilegio *m* — **sacrilegious** [,sækrə'lɪdʒəs, -'li:-] *adj* : sacrílego

sad ['sæd] *adj* **sadder; saddest** : triste — **sadden** ['sædən] *vt* : entristecer

saddle ['sædəl] *n* : silla *f* (de montar) — ~ *vt* **-dled; -dling 1** : ensillar (un caballo, etc.) **2** ~ **s.o. with sth** : cargar a algn con algo

sadistic [sə'dɪstɪk] *adj* : sádico

sadness ['sædnəs] *n* : tristeza *f*

safari [sə'furi, -'fær-] *n* : safari *m*

safe ['seɪf] *adj* **safer; safest 1** : seguro **2** UNHARMED : ileso **3** CAREFUL : prudente **4** ~ **and sound** : sano y salvo — ~ *n* : caja *f* fuerte — **safeguard** ['seɪf,gɑrd] *n* : salvaguarda *f* — ~ *vt* : salvaguardar — **safely** ['seɪfli] *adv* **1** : sin peligro **2 arrive** ~ : llegar sin novedad — **safety** ['seɪfti] *n*, *pl* **-ties** : seguridad *f* — **safety belt** *n* : cinturón *m* de seguridad — **safety pin** *n* : imperdible *m*

saffron ['sæfrən] *n* : azafrán *m*

sag ['sæg] *vi* **sagged; sagging 1** : combarse **2** GIVE : aflojarse **3** FLAG : flaquear

saga ['sɑgə, 'sæ-] *n* : saga *f*

sage¹ ['seɪdʒ] *n* : salvia *f* (planta)

sage² *adj* **sager; -est** : sabio — ~ *n* : sabio *m*, -bia *f*

said → **say**

sail ['seɪl] *n* **1** : vela *f* (de un barco) **2 go for a** ~ : salir a navegar **3 set** ~ : zarpar — *vi* : navegar — *vt* : gobernar (un barco), navegar (el mar) — **sailboat** ['seɪl,boʊt] *n* : velero *m* — **sailor** ['seɪlər] *n* : marinero *m*

saint ['seɪnt, *before a name* ,seɪnt *or* sənt] *n* : santo *m*, -ta *f* — **saintly** ['seɪntli] *adj* **saintlier; -est** : santo

sake ['seɪk] *n* **1 for goodness' ~!** : ¡por Dios! **2 for the** ~ **of** : por (el bien de)

salad ['sæləd] *n* : ensalada *f*

salamander ['sælə,mændər] *n* : salamandra *f*

salami [sə'lɑmi] *n* : salami *m*

salary ['sæləri] *n*, *pl* **-ries** : sueldo *m*

sale ['seɪl] *n* **1** : venta *f* **2 for** ~ : se vende **3 on** ~ : de rebaja — **salesman** ['seɪlzmən] *n*, *pl* **-men** [-mən, -,men] : vendedor *m*, dependiente *m* — **saleswoman** ['seɪlz,wumən] *n*, *pl* **-women** [-,wɪmən] : vendedora *f*, dependienta *f*

salient ['seɪljənt] *adj* : saliente

saliva [sə'laɪvə] *n* : saliva *f*

sallow ['sæloʊ] *adj* : amarillento, cetrino

salmon ['sæmən] *ns & pl* : salmón *m*

salon [sə'lɑn, 'sæ,lɑn] *n* → **beauty salon**

saloon [sə'luːn] *n* : bar *m*

salsa ['sɔlsə, 'sɑl-] *n* : salsa *f* mexicana, salsa *f* picante

salt ['sɔlt] *n* : sal *f* — ~ *vt* : salar — **saltwater** ['sɔlt,wɔtər, -,wɑ-] *adj* : de agua salada — **salty** ['sɔlti] *adj* **saltier; -est** : salado

salute [sə'luːt] *v* **-luted; -luting** *vt* : saludar — *vi* : hacer un saludo — ~ *n* : saludo *m*

salvage ['sælvɪdʒ] *n* : salvamento *m* — ~ *vt* **-vaged; -vaging** : salvar

salvation [sæl'veɪʃən] *n* : salvación *f*

salve ['sæv, 'sav] *n* : ungüento *m*

same ['seɪm] *adj* **1** : mismo **2 be the ~ (as)** : ser igual (que) **3 the ~ thing (as)** : la misma cosa (que) — ~ *pron* **1 all the ~** : igual **2 the ~** : lo mismo — ~ *adv* **the ~** : igual

sample ['sæmpəl] *n* : muestra *f* — ~ *vt* **-pled; -pling** : probar

sanatorium [sænə'tɔriəm] *n, pl* **-riums** *or* **-ria** [-iə] : sanatorio *m*

sanctify ['sæŋktə,faɪ] *vt* **-fied; -fying** : santificar

sanction ['sæŋkʃən] *n* : sanción *f* — ~ *vt* : sancionar

sanctity ['sæŋktəti] *n, pl* **-ties** : santidad *f*

sanctuary ['sæŋktʃu,eri] *n, pl* **-aries** : santuario *m*

sand ['sænd] *n* : arena *f* — ~ *vt* : lijar (madera)

sandal ['sændəl] *n* : sandalia *f*

sandpaper ['sænd,peɪpər] *n* : papel *m* de lija — ~ *vt* : lijar

sandwich ['sænd,wɪtʃ] *n* : sandwich *m*, bocadillo *m Spain* — ~ *vt* ~ **between** : meter entre

sandy ['sændi] *adj* **sandier; -est** : arenoso

sane ['seɪn] *adj* **saner; sanest 1** : cuerdo **2 SENSIBLE** : sensato

sang → sing

sanitarium [sænə'teriəm] *n, pl* **-iums** *or* **-ia** [-iə] → **sanatorium**

sanitary ['sænə,teri] *adj* **1** : sanitario **2 HYGIENIC** : higiénico — **sanitary napkin** *n* : compresa *f* (higiénica) — **sanitation** [sænə'teɪʃən] *n* : sanidad *f*

sanity ['sænəti] *n* : cordura *f*

sank → sink

Santa Claus ['sæntə,klɔz] *n* : Papá *m* Noel

sap[1] ['sæp] *n* **1** : savia *f* (de una planta) **2 SUCKER** : inocentón *m*, -tona *f*

sap[2] *vt* **sapped; sapping** : minar (la fuerza, etc.)

sapphire ['sæ,faɪr] *n* : zafiro *m*

sarcasm ['sɑr,kæzəm] *n* : sarcasmo *m* — **sarcastic** [sɑr'kæstɪk] *adj* : sarcástico

sardine [sɑr'diːn] *n* : sardina *f*

sash ['sæʃ] *n* : faja *f* (de un vestido), fajín *m* (de un uniforme)

sat → sit

satanic [sə'tænɪk, seɪ-] *adj* : satánico

satchel ['sætʃəl] *n* : cartera *f*

satellite ['sætə,laɪt] *n* : satélite *m*

satin ['sætən] *n* : raso *m*

satire ['sæ,taɪr] *n* : sátira *f* — **satiric** [sə'tɪrɪk] *or* **satirical** [-ɪkəl] *adj* : satírico

satisfaction [sætəs'fækʃən] *n* : satisfacción *f* — **satisfactory** [sætəs'fæktəri] *adj* : satisfactorio — **satisfy** ['sætəs,faɪ] *v* **-fied; -fying** *vt* **1** : satisfacer **2 CONVINCE** : convencer — **satisfying** *adj* : satisfactorio

saturate ['sætʃə,reɪt] *vt* **-rated; -rating 1** : saturar **2 DRENCH** : empapar — **saturation** [sætʃə'reɪʃən] *n* : saturación *f*

Saturday ['sætər,deɪ, -di] *n* : sábado *m*

Saturn ['sætərn] *n* : Saturno *m*

sauce ['sɔs] *n* : salsa *f* — **saucepan** ['sɔs,pæn] *n* : cacerola *f* — **saucer** ['sɔsər] *n* : platillo *m* — **saucy** ['sɔsi] *adj* **saucier; -est IMPUDENT** : descarado

sauna ['sɔnə, 'saunə] *n* : sauna *mf*

saunter ['sɔntər, 'sɑn-] *vi* : pasear

sausage ['sɔsɪdʒ] *n* : salchicha *f*

sauté [sɔ'teɪ, soː-] *vt* **-téed** *or* **-téd; -téing** : saltear, sofreír

savage ['sævɪdʒ] *adj* : salvaje, feroz — ~ *n* : salvaje *mf* — **savagery** ['sævɪdʒri, -dʒəri] *n, pl* **-ries** : ferocidad *f*

save ['seɪv] *vt* **saved; saving 1 RESCUE** : salvar **2 RESERVE** : guardar **3** : ahorrar (dinero, tiempo, etc.) — ~ *prep* **EXCEPT** : salvo

savior ['seɪvjər] *n* : salvador *m*, -dora *f*

savor ['seɪvər] *vt* : saborear — **savory** ['seɪvəri] *adj* : sabroso

saw[1] → **see**

saw[2] ['sɔ] *n* : sierra *f* — ~ *vt* **sawed; sawed** *or* **sawn; sawing** : serrar — **sawdust** ['sɔ,dʌst] *n* : serrín *m*, aserrín *m*

saxophone ['sæksə,foʊn] *n* : saxofón *m*

say ['seɪ] *v* **said** ['sɛd]; **saying; says** ['sɛz] *vt* **1** : decir **2 INDICATE** : marcar (dícese de relojes, etc.) — *vi* **1** : decir **2 that is to ~** : es decir — ~ *n, pl* **says** ['seɪz] **1 have no ~** : no tener ni voz ni voto **2 have one's ~** : dar su opinión — **saying** ['seɪɪŋ] *n* : refrán *m*

scab ['skæb] *n* **1** : costra *f* (en una herida) **2 STRIKEBREAKER** : esquirol *mf*

scaffold ['skæfəld, -,foʊld] *n* : andamio *m* (en construcción)

scald ['skɔld] *vt* : escaldar

scale[1] ['skeıl] *n* : balanza *f* (para pesar)
scale[2] *n* : escama *f* (de un pez, etc.) —
~ *vt* scaled; scaling : escamar
scale[3] *vt* scaled; scaling 1 CLIMB : escalar 2 ~ down : reducir — ~ *n* : escala *f* (musical, salarial, etc.)
scallion ['skæljən] *n* : cebolleta *f*
scallop ['skɑləp, 'skæ-] *n* : vieira *f*
scalp ['skælp] *n* : cuero *m* cabelludo
scam ['skæm] *n* : estafa *f*, timo *m fam*
scamper ['skæmpər] *vi* ~ away : irse corriendo
scan ['skæn] *vt* scanned; scanning 1
: escandir (versos) 2 EXAMINE : escudriñar 3 SKIM : echar un vistazo a 4 : escanear (en informática)
scandal ['skændəl] *n* 1 : escándalo *m* 2 GOSSIP : habladurías *fpl* — scandalous ['skændələs] *adj* : escandaloso
Scandinavian [ˌskændə'neıviən] *adj* : escandinavo
scant ['skænt] *adj* : escaso
scapegoat ['skeıpˌgoːt] *n* : chivo *m* expiatorio
scar ['skɑr] *n* : cicatriz *f* — ~ *v* scarred; scarring 1 : dejar una cicatriz en — *vi* : cicatrizar
scarce ['skers] *adj* scarcer; -est : escaso — scarcely ['skersli] *adv* : apenas — scarcity ['skersəti] *n, pl* -ties : escasez *f*
scare ['sker] *vt* scared; scaring 1
: asustar 2 be ~d of : tener miedo a — ~ *n* 1 FRIGHT : susto *m* 2 ALARM : pánico *m* — scarecrow ['sker,kroː] *n* : espantapájaros *m*, espantajo *m*
scarf ['skɑrf] *n, pl* scarves ['skɑrvz] *or* scarfs 1 : bufanda *f* 2 KERCHIEF : pañuelo *m*
scarlet ['skɑrlət] *adj* : escarlata — scarlet fever *n* : escarlatina *f*
scary ['skeri] *adj* scarier; -est : que da miedo
scathing ['skeıðıŋ] *adj* : mordaz
scatter ['skætər] *vt* 1 STREW : esparcir 2 DISPERSE : dispersar — *vi* : dispersarse
scavenger ['skævəndʒər] *n* : carroñero *m*, -ra *f* (animal)
scenario [sə'næri,oː, -'nɑr-] *n, pl* -ios 1
: guión *m* (cinemático) 2 the worst-case ~ : el peor de los casos
scene ['siːn] *n* 1 : escena *f* 2 behind the ~s : entre bastidores 3 make a ~
: armar un escándalo — scenery ['siːnəri] *n, pl* -eries 1 : decorado *m* 2 LANDSCAPE : paisaje *m* — scenic ['siːnık] *adj* : pintoresco
scent ['sent] *n* 1 : aroma *m* 2 PERFUME
: perfume *m* 3 TRAIL : rastro *m* — scented ['sentəd] *adj* : perfumado

sceptic ['skeptık] → **skeptic**
schedule ['skeˌdʒuːl, -dʒəl, *esp Brit* 'ʃedˌjuːl] *n* 1 : programa *m* 2 TIMETABLE
: horario *m* 3 behind ~ : atrasado, con retraso 4 on ~ : según lo previsto — ~ *vt* -uled; -uling : planear, programar
scheme ['skiːm] *n* 1 PLAN : plan *m* 2 PLOT : intriga *f* 3 DESIGN : esquema *f* — ~ *vi* schemed; scheming : intrigar
schism ['sızəm, 'skı-] *n* : cisma *m*
schizophrenia [ˌskıtsə'friːniə, ˌskızə-, -'freː-] *n* : esquizofrenia *f* — schizophrenic [ˌskıtsə'frenık, ˌskızə-] *adj* : esquizofrénico
scholar ['skɑlər] *n* : erudito *m*, -ta *f* — scholarly ['skɑlərli] *adj* : erudito — scholarship ['skɑlərˌʃıp] *n* 1 : erudición *f* 2 GRANT : beca *f*
school[1] ['skuːl] *n* : banco *m* (de peces)
school[2] *n* 1 : escuela *f* 2 COLLEGE : universidad *f* 3 DEPARTMENT : facultad *f* — ~ *vt* : instruir — schoolboy ['skuːlˌbɔı] *n* : colegial *m* — schoolgirl ['skuːlˌgərl] *n* : colegiala *f* — schoolteacher ['skuːlˌtiːtʃər] *n* → teacher
science ['saıənts] *n* : ciencia *f* — scientific [ˌsaıən'tıfık] *adj* : científico *m* — scientist ['saıəntıst] *n* : científico *m*, -ca *f*
scissors ['sızərz] *npl* : tijeras *fpl*
scoff ['skɑf] *vi* ~ at : burlarse de, mofarse de
scold ['skoːld] *vt* : regañar
scoop ['skuːp] *n* 1 : pala *f* 2 : noticia *f* exclusiva (en periodismo) — ~ *vt* 1
: sacar (con pala) 2 ~ out : ahuecar 3 ~ up : recoger
scoot ['skuːt] *vi* : ir rápidamente — scooter ['skuːtər] *n* 1 : patinete *m* 2 *or* motor ~ : escúter *m*
scope ['skoːp] *n* 1 RANGE : alcance *m* 2 OPPORTUNITY : posibilidades *fpl*
scorch ['skɔrtʃ] *vt* : chamuscar
score ['skor] *n, pl* scores 1 : tanteo *m* (en deportes) 2 RATING : puntuación *f* 3 : partitura *f* (musical) 4 *or* play score TWENTY : veintena *f* 5 keep ~ : llevar la cuenta 6 on that ~ : en ese sentido — ~ *v* scored; scoring *vt* 1 : marcar, anotarse *Lat* (un tanto) 2 : sacar (una nota) — *vi* : marcar (en deportes)
scorn ['skɔrn] *n* : desdén *m* — ~ *vt*
: desdeñar — scornful ['skɔrnfəl] *adj*
: desdeñoso
scorpion ['skɔrpiən] *n* : alacrán *m*, escorpión *m*
Scot ['skɑt] *n* : escocés *m*, -cesa *f* — Scotch ['skɑtʃ] *adj* → Scottish — ~ *n or* ~ whiskey : whisky *m* escocés — Scottish ['skɑtıʃ] *adj* : escocés

scoundrel ['skaʊndrəl] *n* : sinvergüenza *mf*

scour ['skaʊər] *vt* **1** SCRUB : fregar **2** SEARCH : registrar

scourge ['skərdʒ] *n* : azote *m*

scout ['skaʊt] *n* : explorador *m*, -dora *f*

scowl ['skaʊl] *vi* : fruncir el ceño — **~** *n* : ceño *m* fruncido

scram ['skræm] *vi* **scrammed; scramming** : largarse

scramble ['skræmbəl] *v* **-bled; -bling** *vi* **1** CLAMBER : trepar **2 ~ for** : pelearse por — *vt* : mezclar — **~** *n* : rebatiña *f*, pelea *f* — **scrambled eggs** *npl* : huevos *mpl* revueltos

scrap[1] ['skræp] *n* **1** PIECE : pedazo *m* **2** *or* **~ metal** : chatarra *f* **3 ~s** *npl* : sobras — **~** *vt* **scrapped; scrapping** : desechar

scrap[2] *n* FIGHT : pelea *f*

scrapbook ['skræp,bʊk] *n* : álbum *m* de recortes

scrape ['skreɪp] *v* **scraped; scraping** *vt* **1** : raspar **2** : rasparse (la rodilla, etc.) **3** *or* **~ off** : raspar **4 ~ together** : reunir — *vi* **1** RUB : rozar **2 ~ by** : arreglárselas — **~** *n* **1** : rasguño *m* **2** PREDICAMENT : apuro *m*

scratch ['skrætʃ] *vt* **1** CLAW : arañar **2** MARK : rayar **3** : rascarse (la cabeza, etc.) **4 ~ out** : tachar — **~** *n* **1** : arañazo *m* **2** MARK : rayón *m* **3 start from ~** : empezar desde cero

scrawl ['skrɔl] *v* : garabatear — **~** *n* : garabato *m*

scrawny ['skrɔni] *adj* **scrawnier; -est** : escuálido

scream ['skri:m] *vi* : gritar, chillar — **~** *n* : grito *m*, chillido *m*

screech ['skri:tʃ] *n* **1** : chillido *m* (de personas) **2** : chirrido *m* (de frenos, etc.) — **~** *vi* **1** : chillar **2** : chirriar (dícese de los frenos, etc.)

screen ['skri:n] *n* **1** : pantalla *f* **2** PARTITION : mampara *f* **3** *or* **window ~** : mosquitero *m* — **~** *vt* **1** SHIELD : proteger **2** HIDE : ocultar **3** : seleccionar (candidatos, etc.)

screw ['skru:] *n* **1** : tornillo *m* — **~** *vt* **1** : atornillar **2 ~ up** RUIN : fastidiar — **screwdriver** ['skru:,draɪvər] *n* : destornillador *m*

scribble ['skrɪbəl] *v* **-bled; -bling** : garabatear — **~** *n* : garabato *m*

script ['skrɪpt] *n* **1** HANDWRITING : escritura *f* **2** : guión *m* (de cine, etc.) — **scripture** ['skrɪptʃər] *n* **1** : escritos *mpl* sagrados **2 the Scriptures** *npl* : las Escrituras *fpl*

scroll ['skro:l] *n* : rollo *m* (de pergamino, etc.)

scrounge ['skraʊndʒ] *v* **scrounged; scrounging** *vt* : gorrear *fam* — *vi* **~ around for sth** : andar buscando algo

scrub[1] ['skrʌb] *n* UNDERBRUSH : maleza *f*

scrub[2] *vt* **scrubbed; scrubbing** SCOUR : fregar — **~** *n* : fregado *m*

scruff ['skrʌf] *n* **by the ~ of the neck** : por el pescuezo

scruple ['skru:pəl] *n* : escrúpulo *m* — **scrupulous** ['skru:pjələs] *adj* : escrupuloso

scrutiny ['skru:təni] *n, pl* **-nies** : análisis *m* cuidadoso — **scrutinize** ['skru:tən,aɪz] *vt* **-nized; -nizing** : escudriñar

scuff ['skʌf] *vt* : raspar, rayar

scuffle ['skʌfəl] *n* : refriega *f*

sculpture ['skʌlptʃər] *n* : escultura *f* — **sculpt** ['skʌlpt] *v* : esculpir — **sculptor** ['skʌlptər] *n* : escultor *m*, -tora *f*

scum ['skʌm] *n* **1** FROTH : espuma *f* **2** : escoria *f* (dícese de personas)

scurry ['skəri] *vi* **-ried; -rying** : corretear

scuttle[1] ['skʌtəl] *n* : cubo *m* (para carbón)

scuttle[2] *vt* **-tled; -tling** : hundir (un barco)

scuttle[3] *vi* SCAMPER : corretear

sea ['si:] *n* **1** : mar *mf* **2 at ~** : en el mar — **~** *adj* : del mar — **seafarer** ['si:,færər] *n* : marinero *m* — **seafood** ['si:,fu:d] *n* : mariscos *mpl* — **seagull** ['si:,gʌl] *n* : gaviota *f*

seal[1] ['si:l] *n* : foca *f* (animal)

seal[2] *n* **1** STAMP : sello *m* **2** CLOSURE : cierre *m* (hermético) — **~** *vt* : sellar

seam ['si:m] *n* **1** : costura *f* **2** VEIN : veta *f*

seaman ['si:mən] *n, pl* **-men** [-mən, -,mɛn] : marinero *m*

seamy ['si:mi] *adj* **seamier; -est** : sórdido

seaplane ['si:,pleɪn] *n* : hidroavión *m*

seaport ['si:,port] *n* : puerto *m* marítimo

search ['sərtʃ] *vt* : registrar — *vi* **~ for** : buscar — **~** *n* **1** : registro *m* **2** HUNT : búsqueda *f* — **searchlight** ['sərtʃ,laɪt] *n* : reflector *m*

seashell ['si:,ʃɛl] *n* : concha *f* (marina) — **seashore** ['si:,ʃor] *n* : orilla *f* del mar — **seasick** ['si:,sɪk] *adj* **1** : mareado **2 be ~** : marearse — **seasickness** ['si:,sɪknəs] *n* : mareo *m*

season ['si:zən] *n* **1** : estación *f* (del año) **2** : temporada *f* (en deportes, etc.) — **~** *vt* **1** FLAVOR : sazonar **2** : secar (madera) — **seasonal** ['si:zənəl] *adj*

: estacional — **seasoned** *adj* EXPERI-
ENCED : veterano — **seasoning**
['si:zənɪŋ] *n* : condimento *m*
seat ['si:t] *n* **1** : asiento *m* **2** : fondillos
mpl (de un pantalón) **3** BUTTOCKS
: trasero *m* **4** CENTER : sede *f* — ~ *vt* **1**
be ~ed : sentarse **2 the bus** ~s **30**
: el autobús tiene cabida para 30 —
seat belt *n* : cinturón *m* de seguridad
seaweed ['si:wi:d] *n* : alga *f* marina
secede [sɪ'si:d] *vi* **-ceded; -ceding**
: separarse (de una nación, etc.)
secluded [sɪ'klu:dəd] *adj* : aislado —
seclusion [sɪ'klu:ʒən] *n* : aislamiento
m
second ['sɛkənd] *adj* : segundo — ~ *or*
secondly ['sɛkəndli] *adv* : en segundo
lugar — ~ *n* **1** : segundo *m*, -da *f* **2**
MOMENT : segundo *m* **3 have** ~s
: repetir (en una comida) — ~ *vt* : secundar — **secondary** ['sɛkən,dɛri] *adj*
: secundario — **secondhand** ['sɛkənd-
'hænd] *adj* : de segunda mano — **second–rate** ['sɛkənd'reɪt] *adj* : mediocre
secret ['si:krət] *adj* : secreto — ~ *n*
: secreto *m* — **secrecy** ['si:krəsi] *n*, *pl*
-cies : secreto *m*
secretary ['sɛkrə,tɛri] *n*, *pl* **-taries 1**
: secretario *m*, -ria *f* **2** : ministro *m*, -tra
f (del gobierno)
secretion [sɪ'kri:ʃən] *n* : secreción *f* —
secrete [sɪ'kri:t] *vt* **-creted; -creting**
: secretar
secretive ['si:krətɪv, sɪ'kri:tɪv] *adj*
: reservado — **secretly** ['si:krətli] *adv*
: en secreto
sect ['sɛkt] *n* : secta *f*
section ['sɛkʃən] *n* : sección *f*, parte *f*
sector ['sɛktər] *n* : sector *m*
secular ['sɛkjələr] *adj* : secular
security [sɪ'kjurəti] *n*, *pl* **-ties 1** : seguridad *f* **2** GUARANTEE : garantía *f* **3 securities** *npl* : valores *mpl* — **secure** [sɪ-
'kjur] *adj* **-curer; -est** : seguro — ~ *vt*
-cured; -curing 1 FASTEN : asegurar **2**
GET : conseguir
sedan [sɪ'dæn] *n* : sedán *m*
sedate [sɪ'deɪt] *adj* : sosegado
sedative ['sɛdə,tɪv] *adj* : sedante — ~ *n*
: sedante *m*
sedentary ['sɛdən,tɛri] *adj* : sedentario
sediment ['sɛdəmənt] *n* : sedimento *m*
seduce [sɪ'du:s, -'dju:s] *vt* **-duced; -duc-
ing** : seducir — **seduction** [sɪ'dʌkʃən]
n : seducción *f* — **seductive** [sɪ'dʌktɪv]
adj : seductor
see ['si:] *v* **saw** ['sɔ]; **seen** ['si:n]; **seeing**
vt **1** : ver **2** UNDERSTAND : entender **3**
ESCORT : acompañar **4** ~ **s.o. off** : despedirse de algn **5** ~ **sth through** : ll-

evar algo a cabo **6** ~ **you later!**
: ¡hasta luego! — *vi* **1** : ver **2** UNDER-
STAND : entender **3 let's** ~ : vamos a
ver **4** ~ **to** : ocuparse de
seed ['si:d] *n*, *pl* **seed** *or* **seeds 1**
: semilla *f* **2** SOURCE : germen *m* —
seedy ['si:di] *adj* **seedier; -est** :
SQUALID : sórdido
seek ['si:k] *v* **sought** ['sɔt]; **seeking** *vt* **1**
or ~ **out** : buscar **2** REQUEST : pedir **3**
~ **to** : tratar de — *vi* SEARCH : buscar
seem ['si:m] *vi* : parecer
seep ['si:p] *vi* : filtrarse
seesaw ['si:,sɔ] *n* : balancín *m*
seethe ['si:ð] *vi* **seethed; seething** : rabiar, estar furioso
segment ['sɛgmənt] *n* : segmento *m*
segregate ['sɛgrɪ,geɪt] *vt* **-gated;
-gating** : segregar — **segregation**
[,sɛgrɪ'geɪʃən] *n* : segregación *f*
seize ['si:z] *v* **seized; seizing** *vt* **1**
GRASP : agarrar **2** CAPTURE : tomar **3**
: aprovechar (una oportunidad) — *vi*
or ~ **up** : agarrotarse — **seizure**
['si:ʒər] *n* **1** CAPTURE : toma *f* **2** : ataque
m (en medicina)
seldom ['sɛldəm] *adv* : pocas veces,
raramente
select [sə'lɛkt] *adj* : selecto — ~ *vt*
: seleccionar — **selection** [sə'lɛkʃən] *n*
: selección *f* — **selective** [sə'lɛktɪv]
adj : selectivo
self ['sɛlf] *n*, *pl* **selves** ['sɛlvz] **1** : ser *m*
2 her better ~ : su lado bueno —
self–addressed [,sɛlfə'drɛst] *adj* : con
la dirección del remitente — **self–as-
sured** [,sɛlfə'ʃurd] *adj* : seguro de sí
mismo — **self–centered** [sɛlf'sɛntərd]
adj : egocéntrico — **self–confidence**
[,sɛlf'kɑnfədənt] *n* : confianza *f* en sí
mismo — **self–confident** [sɛlf'kɑn-
fədənt] *adj* : seguro de sí mismo —
self–conscious [,sɛlf'kɑntʃəs] *adj*
: cohibido — **self–control** [sɛlfkən-
'tro:l] *n* : dominio *m* de sí mismo —
self–defense [,sɛlfdɪ'fɛnts] *n* : defensa
f propia — **self–employed** [,sɛlfɪm-
'plɔɪd] *adj* : que trabaja por cuenta
propia — **self–esteem** [,sɛlfɪ'sti:m] *n*
: amor *m* propio — **self–evident** [,sɛlf-
'ɛvədənt] *adj* : evidente — **self–help**
[sɛlf'hɛlp] *n* : autoayuda *f* — **self–
important** [,sɛlfɪm'pɔrtənt] *adj* : presumido — **self–interest** [,sɛlf'ɪntrəst,
-tə,rɛst] *n* : interés *m* personal — **selfish** ['sɛlfɪʃ] *adj* : egoísta — **selfish-
ness** ['sɛlfɪʃnəs] *n* : egoísmo *m* — **self-
less** ['sɛlfləs] *adj* : desinteresado —
self–pity [sɛlf'pɪti] *n*, *pl* **-ties** : autocompasión *f* — **self–portrait** [,sɛlf-

'portrət] *n* : autorretrato *m* — **self-respect** [ˌselfrɪˈspekt] *n* : amor *m* propio — **self-righteous** [ˌselfˈraɪtʃəs] *adj* : santurrón — **self-service** [ˌselfˈsərvɪs] *adj* : de autoservicio — **self-sufficient** [ˌselfsəˈfɪʃənt] *adj* : autosuficiente — **self-taught** [ˌselfˈtɔt] *adj* : autodidacta

sell [ˈsel] *v* **sold** [ˈsoːld]; **selling** *vt* : vender — *vi* : venderse — **seller** [ˈselər] *n* : vendedor *m*, -dora *f*

selves → **self**

semantics [sɪˈmæntɪks] *ns & pl* : semántica *f*

semblance [ˈsembləns] *n* : apariencia *f*

semester [səˈmestər] *n* : semestre *m*

semicolon [ˈsemiˌkoːlən, ˈseˌmaɪ-] *n* : punto y coma *m*

semifinal [ˌsemiˈfaɪnəl, ˌseˌmaɪ-] *n* : semifinal *f*

seminary [ˈseməˌneri] *n, pl* **-naries** : seminario *m* — **seminar** [ˈseməˌnɑr] *n* : seminario *m*

senate [ˈsenət] *n* : senado *m* — **senator** [ˈsenətər] *n* : senador *m*, -dora *f*

send [ˈsend] *vt* **sent** [ˈsent]; **sending** 1 : mandar, enviar 2 **~ away for** : pedir 3 **~ back** : devolver (mercancías, etc.) 4 **~ for** : mandar a buscar — **sender** [ˈsendər] *n* : remitente *mf*

senile [ˈsiːˌnaɪl] *adj* : senil — **senility** [sɪˈnɪləti] *n* : senilidad *f*

senior [ˈsiːnjər] *n* 1 SUPERIOR : superior *m* 2 : estudiante *mf* de último año (en educación) 3 *or* **~ citizen** : persona *f* mayor 4 **be s.o.'s ~** : ser mayor que algn — **~** *adj* 1 : superior (en rango) 2 ELDER : mayor — **seniority** [ˌsiːˈnjɔrəti] *n* : antigüedad *f*

sensation [senˈseɪʃən] *n* : sensación *f* — **sensational** [senˈseɪʃənəl] *adj* : sensacional

sense [ˈsents] *n* 1 : sentido *m* 2 FEELING : sensación *f* 3 COMMON SENSE : sentido *m* común 4 **make ~** : tener sentido — **~** *vt* **sensed**; **sensing** : sentir — **senseless** [ˈsentsləs] *adj* 1 : sin sentido 2 UNCONSCIOUS : inconsciente — **sensible** [ˈsentsəbəl] *adj* : sensato, práctico — **sensibility** [ˌsentsəˈbɪləti] *n, pl* **-ties** : sensibilidad *f* — **sensitive** [ˈsentsətɪv] *adj* 1 : sensible 2 TOUCHY : susceptible — **sensitivity** [ˌsentsəˈtɪvəti] *n, pl* **-ties** : sensibilidad *f* — **sensual** [ˈsentʃuəl] *adj* : sensual — **sensuous** [ˈsentʃuəs] *adj* : sensual

sent → **send**

sentence [ˈsentəns, -ənz] *n* 1 : frase *f* 2 JUDGMENT : sentencia *f* — **~** *vt* **-tenced; -tencing** : sentenciar

sentiment [ˈsentəmənt] *n* 1 : sentimiento *m* 2 BELIEF : opinión *f* — **sentimental** [ˌsentəˈmentəl] *adj* : sentimental — **sentimentality** [ˌsentəˌmenˈtæləti] *n, pl* **-ties** : sentimentalismo *m*

sentry [ˈsentri] *n, pl* **-tries** : centinela *m*

separation [ˌsepəˈreɪʃən] *n* : separación *f* — **separate** [ˈsepəˌreɪt] *v* **-rated; -rating** *vt* 1 : separar 2 DISTINGUISH : distinguir — *vi* : separarse — **~** [ˈseprət, ˈsepə-] *adj* 1 : separado 2 DETACHED : aparte 3 DISTINCT : distinto — **separately** [ˈseprətli, ˈsepə-] *adv* : por separado

September [sepˈtembər] *n* : septiembre *m*, setiembre *m*

sequel [ˈsiːkwəl] *n* 1 : continuación *f* 2 CONSEQUENCE : secuela *f*

sequence [ˈsiːkwənts] *n* 1 ORDER : orden *m* 2 : secuencia *f* (de números o escenas)

Serb [ˈsərb] *or* **Serbian** [ˈsərbiən] *adj* : serbio

serene [səˈriːn] *adj* : sereno — **serenity** [səˈrenəti] *n* : serenidad *f*

sergeant [ˈsɑrdʒənt] *n* : sargento *mf*

serial [ˈsɪriəl] *adj* : seriado — **~** *n* : serial *m* — **series** [ˈsɪrˌiːz] *n, pl* **series** : serie *f*

serious [ˈsɪriəs] *adj* : serio — **seriously** [ˈsɪriəsli] *adv* 1 : seriamente 2 GRAVELY : gravemente 3 **take ~** : tomar en serio

sermon [ˈsərmən] *n* : sermón *m*

serpent [ˈsərpənt] *n* : serpiente *f*

servant [ˈsərvənt] *n* : criado *m*, -da *f*

serve [ˈsərv] *v* **served; serving** *vi* 1 : servir 2 (en deportes) 3 **~ as** : servir de — *vt* 1 : servir 2 **~ time** : cumplir una condena — **server** [ˈsərvər] *n* 1 WAITER : camarero *m*, -ra *f* 2 : servidor *m* (en informática)

service [ˈsərvəs] *n* 1 : servicio *m* 2 CEREMONY : oficio *m* 3 MAINTENANCE : revisión *f* 4 **armed ~s** : fuerzas *fpl* armadas — **~** *vt* **-viced; -vicing** : revisar (un vehículo, etc.) — **serviceman** [ˈsərvəsˌmæn, -mən] *n, pl* **-men** [-mən, -ˌmen] : militar *m* — **service station** *n* : estación *f* de servicio — **serving** [ˈsərvɪŋ] *n* : porción *f*, ración *f*

session [ˈseʃən] *n* : sesión *f*

set [ˈset] *n* 1 : juego *m* (de platos, etc.) 2 : set *m* (en tenis, etc.) 3 *or* **stage ~** : decorado *m* 4 **television ~** : aparato *m* de televisión — **~** *v* set; **setting** *vt* 1 *or* **~ down** : poner 2 : poner en hora (un reloj) 3 FIX : fijar (una fecha, etc.) 4 **~ fire to** : prender fuego a 5 **~ free** : poner en libertad 6 **~ off**

: hacer sonar (una alarma), hacer estallar (una bomba) **7 ~ out to (do sth)** : proponerse (hacer algo) **8 ~ up** ASSEMBLE : montar, armar **9 ~ up** ESTABLISH : establecer — *vi* **1** : cuajarse (dícese de la gelatina, etc.), fraguar (dícese del cemento) **2** : ponerse (dícese del sol, etc.) **3 ~ in** BEGIN : empezar **4 ~ off** *or* **~ out** : salir (de viaje) — **~** *adj* **1** FIXED : fijo **2** READY : listo, preparado — **setback** ['set,bæk] *n* : revés *m* — **setting** ['setɪŋ] *n* **1** : posición *f* (de un control) **2** MOUNTING : engaste *m* (de joyas) **3** SCENE : escenario *m*

settle ['setəl] *v* **settled; settling** *vi* **1** : asentarse (dícese de polvo, colonos, etc.) **2 ~ down** RELAX : calmarse **3 ~ for** : conformarse con **4 ~ in** : instalarse — *vt* **1** DECIDE : fijar, decidir **2** RESOLVE : resolver **3** PAY : pagar **4** CALM : calmar **5** COLONIZE : colonizar — **settlement** ['setəlmənt] *n* **1** PAYMENT : pago *m* **2** COLONY : colonia *f*, poblado *m* **3** AGREEMENT : acuerdo *m* — **settler** ['setələr] *n* : colono *m*, -na *f*

seven ['sevən] *adj* : siete — **~** *n* : siete *m* — **seven hundred** *adj* : setecientos — **~** *n* : setecientos *m* — **seventeen** [,sevən'tin] *adj* : diecisiete — **~** *n* : diecisiete *m* — **seventeenth** [,sevən'tinθ] *adj* : decimoséptimo — **~** *n* **1** : decimoséptimo *m*, -ma *f* (en una serie) **2** : diecisieteavo *m* (en matemáticas) — **seventh** ['sevənθ] *adj* : séptimo — **~** *n* **1** : séptimo *m*, -ma *f* (en una serie) **2** : séptimo *m* (en matemáticas) — **seventieth** ['sevəntiəθ] *adj* : septuagésimo — **~** *n* **1** : septuagésimo *m*, -ma *f* (en una serie) **2** : setentavo *m* (en matemáticas) — **seventy** ['sevənti] *adj* : setenta — **~** *n*, *pl* **-ties** : setenta *m*

sever ['sevər] *vt* **-ered; -ering** : cortar, romper

several ['sevrəl, 'sevə-] *adj* : varios — **~** *pron* : varios, varias

severance ['sevrənts, 'sevə-] *n* : ruptura *f*

severe [sə'vɪr] *adj* **severer; -est** **1** : severo **2** SERIOUS : grave — **severely** *adv* **1** : severamente **2** SERIOUSLY : gravemente — **severity** [sə'verəti] *n* **1** : severidad *f* **2** SERIOUSNESS : gravedad *f*

sew ['soː] *v* **sewed; sewn** ['soːn] *or* **sewed; sewing** : coser

sewer ['suːər] *n* : cloaca *f* — **sewage** ['suːɪdʒ] *n* : aguas *fpl* negras

sewing ['soːɪŋ] *n* : costura *f*

sex ['seks] *n* **1** : sexo *m* **2** INTERCOURSE : relaciones *fpl* sexuales — **sexism** ['sek,sɪzəm] *n* : sexismo *m* — **sexist** ['seksɪst] *adj* : sexista — **sexual** ['sekʃuəl] *adj* : sexual — **sexuality** [,sekʃu'æləti] *n* : sexualidad *f* — **sexy** ['seksi] *adj* **sexier; -est** : sexy

shabby ['ʃæbi] *adj* **shabbier; -est** **1** WORN : gastado **2** UNFAIR : malo, injusto

shack ['ʃæk] *n* : choza *f*

shackle ['ʃækəl] *n* : grillete *m*

shade ['ʃeɪd] *n* **1** : sombra *f* **2** : tono *m* (de un color) **3** NUANCE : matiz *m* **4** *or* **lampshade** : pantalla *f* **5** *or* **window ~** : persiana *f* — **~** *vt* **shaded;** **shading** : proteger de la luz — **shadow** ['ʃædoː] *n* : sombra *f* — **shadowy** ['ʃædowi] *adj* INDISTINCT : vago — **shady** ['ʃeɪdi] *adj* **shadier; -est** **1** : sombreado **2** DISREPUTABLE : sospechoso

shaft ['ʃæft] *n* **1** : asta *f* (de una flecha, etc.) **2** HANDLE : mango *m* **3** AXLE : eje *m* **4** : rayo *m* (de luz) **5** *or* **mine ~** : pozo *m*

shaggy ['ʃægi] *adj* **shaggier; -est** : peludo

shake ['ʃeɪk] *v* **shook** ['ʃuk]; **shaken** ['ʃeɪkən]; **shaking** *vt* **1** : sacudir **2** MIX : agitar **3 ~ hands with s.o.** : dar la mano a algn **4 ~ one's head** : negar con la cabeza **5 ~ up** UPSET : afectar — *vi* : temblar — **~** *n* **1** : sacudida *f* **2** → **handshake** — **shaker** ['ʃeɪkər] *n* **1** salt ~ : salero *m* **2** pepper ~ : pimentero *m* — **shaky** ['ʃeɪki] *adj* **shakier; -est** **1** : tembloroso **2** UNSTABLE : poco firme

shall ['ʃæl] *v aux, past* **should** ['ʃud]; *pres sing & pl* **shall 1** (*expressing volition or futurity*) → **will 2** (*expressing possibility or obligation*) → **should 3 ~ we go?** : ¿nos vamos?

shallow ['ʃæloː] *adj* **1** : poco profundo **2** SUPERFICIAL : superficial

sham ['ʃæm] *n* : farsa *f* — **~** *v* **shammed; shamming** : fingir

shambles ['ʃæmbəlz] *ns & pl* : caos *m*, desorden *m*

shame ['ʃeɪm] *n* **1** : vergüenza *f* **2 what a ~!** : ¡qué lástima! — **~** *vt* **shamed; shaming** : avergonzar — **shameful** ['ʃeɪmfəl] *adj* : vergonzoso — **shameless** ['ʃeɪmləs] *adj* : desvergonzado

shampoo ['ʃæm,puː] *vt* : lavar (el pelo) — **~** *n, pl* **-poos** : champú *m*

shamrock ['ʃæm,rɑk] *n* : trébol *m*

shan't ['ʃænt] (*contraction of* **shall not**) → **shall**

shape ['ʃeɪp] v **shaped; shaping** vt **1** : formar **2** DETERMINE : determinar **3** **be** ~**d like** : tener forma de — vi or ~ **up** : tomar forma de — ~ n **1** : forma f **2 get in** ~ : ponerse en forma — **shapeless** ['ʃeɪpləs] adj : informe

share ['ʃer] n **1** : porción f **2** : acción f (en una compañía) — ~ vt **shared; sharing** vt **1** : compartir **2** DIVIDE : dividir — vi : compartir — **shareholder** ['ʃer,holdər] n : accionista mf

shark ['ʃɑrk] n : tiburón m

sharp ['ʃɑrp] adj **1** : afilado **2** POINTY : puntiagudo **3** ACUTE : agudo **4** HARSH : duro, severo **5** CLEAR : nítido **6** : sostenido (en música) **7 a** ~ **curve** : una curva cerrada — ~ adv **at two o'clock** ~ : a las dos en punto — ~ n : sostenido (en música) — **sharpen** ['ʃɑrpən] vt : afilar (un cuchillo, etc.), sacar punta a (un lápiz) — **sharpener** ['ʃɑrpənər] n **1** or **knife** ~ : afilador m **2** or **pencil** ~ : sacapuntas m — **sharply** ['ʃɑrpli] adv : bruscamente

shatter ['ʃætər] vt **1** : hacer añicos **2** DEVASTATE : destrozar — vi : hacerse añicos

shave ['ʃeɪv] v **shaved; shaved** or **shaven** ['ʃeɪvən]; **shaving** vt **1** : afeitar **2** SLICE : cortar — vi : afeitarse — ~ n : afeitada f — **shaver** ['ʃeɪvər] n : máquina f de afeitar

shawl ['ʃɔl] n : chal m

she ['ʃiː] pron : ella

sheaf ['ʃiːf] n, pl **sheaves** ['ʃiːvz] **1** : gavilla f **2** : fajo m (de papeles)

shear ['ʃɪr] vt **sheared; sheared** or **shorn** ['ʃɔrn]; **shearing** : esquilar — **shears** ['ʃɪrz] npl : tijeras fpl (grandes)

sheath ['ʃiːθ] n, pl **sheaths** ['ʃiːðz, 'ʃiːθs] : funda f, vaina f

shed¹ ['ʃed] v **shed; shedding** vt **1** : derramar (lágrimas, etc.) **2** : mudar (de piel, etc.), quitarse (ropa) **3** ~ **light on** : aclarar

shed² n : cobertizo m

she'd ['ʃiːd] (contraction of **she had** or **she would**) → **have, would**

sheen ['ʃiːn] n : brillo m, lustre m

sheep ['ʃiːp] n, pl **sheep** : oveja f — **sheepish** ['ʃiːpɪʃ] adj : avergonzado

sheer ['ʃɪr] adj **1** THIN : transparente **2** PURE : puro **3** STEEP : escarpado

sheet ['ʃiːt] n **1** : sábana f (de la cama) **2** : hoja f (de papel) **3** : capa f (de hielo, etc.) **4** PLATE : placa f, lámina f

shelf ['ʃelf] n, pl **shelves** ['ʃelvz] : estante m

shell ['ʃel] n **1** : concha f **2** : caparazón m (de un crustáceo, etc.) **3** : cáscara f (de un huevo, etc.) **4** : armazón mf (de un edificio, etc.) **5** POD : vaina f **6** MISSILE : proyectil m — ~ vt **1** : pelar (nueces, etc.) **2** BOMBARD : bombardear

she'll ['ʃiːl, 'ʃɪl] (contraction of **she shall** or **she will**) → **shall, will**

shellfish ['ʃel,fɪʃ] n : marisco m

shelter ['ʃeltər] n **1** : refugio m **2 take** ~ : refugiarse — ~ vt **1** PROTECT : proteger **2** HARBOR : albergar

shelve ['ʃelv] vt **shelved; shelving** DEFER : dar carpetazo a

shepherd ['ʃepərd] n : pastor m — ~ vt GUIDE : conducir, guiar

sherbet ['ʃərbət] n : sorbete m

sheriff ['ʃerɪf] n : sheriff mf

sherry ['ʃeri] n, pl **-ries** : jerez m

she's ['ʃiːz] (contraction of **she is** or **she has**) → **be, have**

shield ['ʃiːld] n : escudo m — ~ vt : proteger

shier, shiest → **shy**

shift ['ʃɪft] vt **1** MOVE : mover **2** SWITCH : transferir — vi **1** CHANGE : cambiar **2** MOVE : moverse **3** or ~ **gears** : cambiar de velocidad — ~ n **1** CHANGE : cambio m **2** : turno m (de trabajo) — **shiftless** ['ʃɪftləs] adj : holgazán — **shifty** ['ʃɪfti] adj **shiftier; -est** : sospechoso

shimmer ['ʃɪmər] vi : brillar, relucir

shin ['ʃɪn] n : espinilla f

shine ['ʃaɪn] v **shone** ['ʃoʊn] or **shined; shining** vi : brillar — vt **1** : alumbrar (una luz) **2** POLISH : sacar brillo a — ~ n : brillo m

shingle ['ʃɪŋgəl] n : teja f plana y delgada (en construcción) — ~ vt **-gled; -gling** : techar — **shingles** ['ʃɪŋgəlz] npl : herpes m

shiny ['ʃaɪni] adj **shinier; -est** : brillante

ship ['ʃɪp] n **1** : barco m, buque m **2** → **spaceship** — ~ vt **shipped; shipping** : transportar, enviar (por barco) — **shipbuilding** ['ʃɪp,bɪldɪŋ] n : construcción f naval — **shipment** ['ʃɪpmənt] n : envío m — **shipping** ['ʃɪpɪŋ] n **1** : transporte m **2** SHIPS : barcos mpl — **shipshape** ['ʃɪp,ʃeɪp] adj : ordenado — **shipwreck** ['ʃɪp,rek] n : naufragio m — ~ vt **be** ~**ed** : naufragar — **shipyard** ['ʃɪp,jɑrd] n : astillero m

shirk ['ʃərk] vt : esquivar

shirt ['ʃərt] n : camisa f

shiver ['ʃɪvər] vi : temblar (del frío, etc.) — ~ n : escalofrío m

shoal ['ʃoʊl] n : banco m

shock ['ʃɑk] *n* 1 IMPACT : choque *m* 2 SURPRISE, UPSET : golpe *m* emocional 3 : shock *m* (en medicina) 4 *or* electric ~ : descarga *f* (eléctrica) — ~ *vt* : escandalizar — **shock absorber** *n* : amortiguador *m* — **shocking** ['ʃɑkɪŋ] *adj* : escandaloso

shoddy ['ʃɑdi] *adj* **shoddier; -est** : de mala calidad

shoe ['ʃuː] *n* : zapato *m* — ~ *vt* **shod** ['ʃɑd]; **shoeing** : herrar (un caballo) — **shoelace** ['ʃuːleɪs] *n* : cordón *m* (de zapato) — **shoemaker** ['ʃuːmeɪkər] *n* : zapatero *m*, -ra *f*

shone → **shine**

shook → **shake**

shoot ['ʃuːt] *v* **shot** ['ʃɑt]; **shooting** *vt* 1 : disparar 2 : echar (una mirada) 3 PHOTOGRAPH : fotografiar 4 FILM : rodar — *vi* 1 : disparar 2 ~ **by** : pasar como una bala — ~ *n* : brote *m*, retoño *m* (de una planta) — **shooting star** *n* : estrella *f* fugaz

shop ['ʃɑp] *n* 1 : tienda *f* 2 WORKSHOP : taller *m* — ~ *vi* **shopped; shopping** 1 : hacer compras 2 **go shopping** : ir de compras — **shopkeeper** ['ʃɑpˌkiːpər] *n* : tendero *m*, -ra *f* — **shoplift** ['ʃɑpˌlɪft] *vi* : hurtar mercancía (en tiendas) — **shoplifter** ['ʃɑpˌlɪftər] *n* : ladrón *m*, -drona *f* (que roba en tiendas) — **shopper** ['ʃɑpər] *n* : comprador *m*, -dora *f*

shore ['ʃor] *n* : orilla *f*

shorn → **shear**

short ['ʃort] *adj* 1 : corto 2 : bajo (de estatura) 3 CURT : brusco 4 **a ~ time ago** : hace poco 5 **be ~ of** : estar corto de — ~ *adv* 1 **stop ~** : parar en seco 2 **fall ~** : quedarse corto — **shortage** ['ʃortɪdʒ] *n* : escasez *f*, carencia *f* — **shortcake** ['ʃortˌkeɪk] *n* : tarta *f* de fruta — **shortcoming** ['ʃortˌkʌmɪŋ] *n* : defecto *m* — **shortcut** ['ʃortˌkʌt] *n* : atajo *m* — **shorten** ['ʃortən] *vt* : acortar — **shorthand** ['ʃortˌhænd] *n* : taquigrafía *f* — **short-lived** ['ʃortˌlɪvd, -ˌlaɪvd] *adj* : efímero — **shortly** ['ʃortli] *adv* : dentro de poco — **shortness** ['ʃortnəs] *n* 1 : lo corto (de una cosa), baja estatura *f* (de una persona) 2 ~ **of breath** : falta *f* de aliento — **shorts** *npl* : shorts *mpl*, pantalones *mpl* cortos — **shortsighted** ['ʃortˌsaɪtəd] → **nearsighted**

shot ['ʃɑt] *n* 1 : disparo *m*, tiro *m* 2 : tiro *m* (en deportes) 3 ATTEMPT : intento *m* 4 PHOTOGRAPH : foto *f* 5 INJECTION : inyección *f* 6 : trago *m* (de licor) — **shotgun** ['ʃɑtˌɡʌn] *n* : escopeta *f*

should ['ʃʊd] *past of* **shall** 1 **if she ~ call** : si llama 2 **i ~ have gone** : debería haber ido 3 **they ~ arrive soon** : deben llegar pronto 4 **what ~ we do?** : ¿qué hacemos?

shoulder ['ʃoːldər] *n* 1 : hombro *m* 2 : arcén *m* (de una carretera) — ~ *vt* : cargar con (la responsabilidad, etc.) — **shoulder blade** *n* : omóplato *m*

shouldn't ['ʃʊdənt] (*contraction of* should not) → **should**

shout ['ʃaʊt] *v* : gritar — ~ *n* : grito *m*

shove ['ʃʌv] *v* **shoved; shoving** : empujar — ~ *n* : empujón *m*

shovel ['ʃʌvəl] *n* : pala *f* — ~ *vt* **-veled** *or* **-velled; -veling** *or* **-velling** 1 : mover (tierra, etc.) con una pala 2 DIG : cavar (con una pala)

show ['ʃoː] *v* **showed; shown** ['ʃoːn] *or* **showed; showing** *vt* 1 : mostrar 2 TEACH : enseñar 3 PROVE : demostrar 4 ESCORT : acompañar 5 : proyectar (una película), dar (un programa de televisión) 6 ~ **off** : hacer alarde de — *vi* 1 : notarse, verse 2 ~ **off** : lucirse 3 ~ **up** ARRIVE : aparecer — ~ *n* 1 : demostración *f* 2 EXHIBITION : exposición *f* 3 : espectáculo *m* (teatral), programa *m* (de televisión, etc.) — **showdown** ['ʃoːˌdaʊn] *n* : confrontación *f*

shower ['ʃaʊər] *n* 1 : ducha *f* 2 : chaparrón *m* (en meteorología) 3 PARTY : fiesta *f* — ~ *vt* 1 SPRAY : regar 2 ~ **s.o. with** : colmar a algn de — *vi* 1 : ducharse 2 RAIN : llover — **showy** ['ʃoːi] *adj* **showier; -est** : llamativo, ostentoso

shrank → **shrink**

shrapnel ['ʃræpnəl] *ns & pl* : metralla *f*

shred ['ʃred] *n* 1 : tira *f* (de tela, etc.) 2 IOTA : pizca *f* — ~ *vt* **shredded; shredding** 1 : hacer tiras 2 GRATE : rallar

shrewd ['ʃruːd] *adj* : astuto

shriek ['ʃriːk] *vi* : chillar — ~ *n* : chillido *m*, alarido *m*

shrill ['ʃrɪl] *adj* : agudo, estridente

shrimp ['ʃrɪmp] *n* : camarón *m*

shrine ['ʃraɪn] *n* 1 TOMB : sepulcro *m* 2 SANCTUARY : santuario *m*

shrink ['ʃrɪŋk] *v* **shrank** ['ʃræŋk]; **shrunk** ['ʃrʌŋk] *or* **shrunken** ['ʃrʌŋkən]; **shrinking** *vt* : encoger — *vi* 1 : encogerse (dícese de ropa), reducirse (dícese de números, etc.) 2 *or* ~ **back** : retroceder

shrivel ['ʃrɪvəl] *vi* **-veled** *or* **-velled; -veling** *or* **-velling** *or* ~ **up** : arrugarse, marchitarse

shroud ['ʃraʊd] *n* **1** : sudario *m*, mortaja *f* **2** VEIL : velo *m* — ~ *vt* : envolver

shrub ['ʃrʌb] *n* : arbusto *m*, mata *f*

shrug ['ʃrʌg] *vi* **shrugged; shrugging** : encogerse de hombros

shrunk → **shrink**

shudder ['ʃʌdər] *vi* : estremecerse — ~ *n* : estremecimiento *m*

shuffle ['ʃʌfəl] *v* **-fled; -fling** *vt* : barajar (naipes), revolver (papeles, etc.) — *vi* : caminar arrastrando los pies

shun ['ʃʌn] *vi* **shunned; shunning** : evitar, esquivar

shut ['ʃʌt] *v* **shut; shutting** *vt* **1** CLOSE : cerrar **2** ~ **off** → **turn off 3** ~ **up** CONFINE : encerrar — *vi* **1** *or* ~ **down** : cerrarse **2** ~ **up!** : ¡cállate! — **shutter** ['ʃʌtər] *n* **1** *or* **window** ~ : contraventana *f* **2** : obturador *m* (de una cámara)

shuttle ['ʃʌtəl] *n* **1** : lanzadera *f* (para tejer) **2** *or* ~ **bus** : autobús *m* (de corto recorrido) **3** → **space shuttle** — ~ *v* **-tled; -tling** *vt* : transportar — *vi* : ir y venir

shy ['ʃaɪ] *adj* **shier** *or* **shyer** ['ʃaɪər]; **shiest** *or* **shyest** ['ʃaɪəst] : tímido — ~ *vi* **shied; shying** *or* ~ **away** : retroceder — **shyness** ['ʃaɪnəs] *n* : timidez *f*

sibling ['sɪblɪŋ] *n* : hermano *m*, hermana *f*

sick ['sɪk] *adj* **1** : enfermo **2 be** ~ VOMIT : vomitar **3 be** ~ **of** : estar harto de **4 feel** ~ : tener náuseas — **sicken** ['sɪkən] *vt* DISGUST : dar asco a — **sickening** ['sɪkənɪŋ] *adj* : nauseabundo

sickle ['sɪkəl] *n* : hoz *f*

sickly ['sɪkli] *adj* **sicklier; -est 1** UNHEALTHY : enfermizo **2** → **sickening** — **sickness** ['sɪknəs] *n* : enfermedad *f*

side ['saɪd] *n* **1** : lado *m* **2** : costado *m* (de una persona), ijada *f* (de un animal) **3** : parte *f* (en una disputa, etc.) **4** ~ **by** ~ : uno al lado de otro **5 take** ~**s** : tomar partido — ~ *vi* ~ **with** : ponerse de parte de — **sideboard** ['saɪd,bɔrd] *n* : aparador *m* — **sideburns** ['saɪd,bərnz] *npl* : patillas *fpl* — **side effect** *n* : efecto *m* secundario — **sideline** ['saɪd,laɪn] *n* : línea *f* de banda (en deportes) — **sidestep** ['saɪd,step] *vt* **-stepped; -stepping** : eludir, esquivar — **sidetrack** ['saɪd,træk] *vt* **get** ~**ed** : distraerse — **sidewalk** ['saɪd,wɔk] *n* : acera *f* — **sideways** ['saɪd,weɪz] *adj & adv* : de lado — **siding** ['saɪdɪŋ] *n* : revestimiento *m* exterior

siege ['siːdʒ, 'siːʒ] *n* : sitio *m*

sieve ['sɪv] *n* : tamiz *m*, cedazo *m*

sift ['sɪft] *vt* **1** : cerner, tamizar **2** *or* ~ **through** : pasar por el tamiz

sigh ['saɪ] *vi* : suspirar — ~ *n* : suspiro *m*

sight ['saɪt] *n* **1** : vista *f* **2** SPECTACLE : espectáculo *m* **3** : lugar *m* de interés (turístico) **4 catch** ~ **of** : avistar — ~ *vt* : avistar — **sightseer** ['saɪt,siːər] *n* : turista *mf*

sign ['saɪn] *n* **1** : signo *m* **2** NOTICE : letrero *m* **3** GESTURE : seña *f*, señal *f* — ~ *vt* : firmar (un cheque, etc.) — *vi* **1** : firmar **2** ~ **up** ENROLL : inscribirse

signal ['sɪgnəl] *n* : señal *f* — ~ *v* **-naled** *or* **-nalled; -naling** *or* **-nalling** *vt* **1** : hacer señas a **2** INDICATE : señalar — *vi* **1** : hacer señas **2** : señalizar (en un vehículo)

signature ['sɪgnətʃər] *n* : firma *f*

significance [sɪg'nɪfɪkənts] *n* **1** : significado *m* **2** IMPORTANCE : importancia *f* — **significant** [sɪg'nɪfɪkənt] *adj* : importante — **signify** ['sɪgnə,faɪ] *vt* **-fled; -fying** : significar

sign language *n* : lenguaje *m* gestual — **signpost** ['saɪn,poːst] *n* : poste *m* indicador

silence ['saɪlənts] *n* : silencio *m* — ~ *vt* **-lenced; -lencing** : silenciar — **silent** ['saɪlənt] *adj* **1** : silencioso **2** MUM : callado **3** : mudo (dícese de películas y letras)

silhouette [sɪlə'wet] *n* : silueta *f* — ~ *vt* **-etted; -etting be** ~**d against** : perfilarse contra

silicon ['sɪlɪkən, -ˌkɑn] *n* : silicio *m*

silk ['sɪlk] *n* : seda *f* — **silky** ['sɪlki] *adj* **silkier; -est** : sedoso

sill ['sɪl] *n* : alféizar *m* (de una ventana), umbral *m* (de una puerta)

silly ['sɪli] *adj* **sillier; -est** : tonto, estúpido

silt ['sɪlt] *n* : cieno *m*

silver ['sɪlvər] *n* **1** : plata *f* **2** → **silverware** — ~ *adj* : de plata — **silverware** ['sɪlvər,wær] *n* : plata *f* — **silvery** ['sɪlvəri] *adj* : plateado

similar ['sɪmələr] *adj* : similar, parecido — **similarity** [ˌsɪmə'lærəti] *n*, *pl* **-ties** : semejanza *f*, parecido *m*

simmer ['sɪmər] *v* : hervir a fuego lento

simple ['sɪmpəl] *adj* **simpler; -plest 1** : simple **2** EASY : sencillo — **simplicity** [sɪm'plɪsəti] *n* : simplicidad *f*, sencillez *f* — **simplify** ['sɪmplə,faɪ] *vt* **-fled; -fying** : simplificar — **simply** ['sɪmpli] *adv* **1** : sencillamente **2** ABSOLUTELY : realmente

simulate ['sɪmjə,leɪt] *vt* **-lated; -lating** : simular

simultaneous [,saɪməl'teɪniəs] *adj* : simultáneo

sin ['sɪn] *n* : pecado *m* — ~ *vi* **sinned; sinning** : pecar

since ['sɪns] *adv* **1** *or* ~ **then** : desde entonces **2 long** ~ : hace mucho — ~ *conj* **1** : desde que **2** BECAUSE : ya que, como **3 it's been years** ~... : hace años que... — ~ *prep* : desde

sincere [sɪn'sɪr] *adj* **-cerer; -est** : sincero — **sincerely** *adv* : sinceramente — **sincerity** [sɪn'serəʈi] *n* : sinceridad *f*

sinful ['sɪnfəl] *adj* : pecador (dícese de las personas), pecaminoso (dícese de las acciones)

sing ['sɪŋ] *v* **sang** ['sæŋ] *or* **sung** ['sʌŋ]; **sung; singing** : cantar

singe ['sɪndʒ] *vt* **singed; singeing** : chamuscar

singer ['sɪŋər] *n* : cantante *mf*

single ['sɪŋgəl] *adj* **1** : solo, único **2** UNMARRIED : soltero **3 every** ~ **day** : cada día, todos los días — ~ *n* **1** : soltero *m*, -ra *f* **2** *or* ~ **room** : habitación *f* individual — ~ *vt* **-gled; -gling** ~ **out 1** SELECT : escoger **2** DISTINGUISH : señalar — **single–handed** ['sɪŋgəl'hændəd] *adj* : sin ayuda, solo

singular ['sɪŋgjələr] *adj* : singular — ~ *n* : singular *m*

sinister ['sɪnəstər] *adj* : siniestro

sink ['sɪŋk] *v* **sank** ['sæŋk] *or* **sunk** ['sʌŋk]; **sunk; sinking** *vi* **1** : hundirse (en un líquido) **2** DROP : bajar, caer — *vt* **1** : hundir **2** ~ **sth into** : clavar algo en — ~ *n* **1** *or* **kitchen** ~ : fregadero *m* **2** *or* **bathroom** ~ : lavabo *m*, lavamanos *m*

sinner ['sɪnər] *n* : pecador *m*, -dora *f*

sip ['sɪp] *v* **sipped; sipping** *vt* : sorber — *vi* : beber a sorbos — ~ *n* : sorbo *m*

siphon ['saɪfən] *n* : sifón *m* — ~ *vt* : sacar con sifón

sir ['sər] *n* **1** (*in titles*) : sir *m* **2** (*as a form of address*) : señor *m* **3 Dear Sir** : Estimado señor

siren ['saɪrən] *n* : sirena *f*

sirloin ['sər,lɔɪn] *n* : solomillo *m*

sissy ['sɪsi] *n*, *pl* **-sies** : mariquita *mf fam*

sister ['sɪstər] *n* : hermana *f* — **sister–in–law** ['sɪstərɪn,lɔ] *n*, *pl* **sisters–in–law** : cuñada *f*

sit ['sɪt] *v* **sat** ['sæt]; **sitting** *vi* **1** *or* ~ **down** : sentarse **2** LIE : estar (ubicado) **3** MEET : estar en sesión **4** *or* ~ **up** : incorporarse — *vt* : sentar

site ['saɪt] *n* **1** : sitio *m*, lugar *m* **2** LOT : solar *m*

sitting room → **living room**

sitter ['sɪtər] → **baby–sitter**

situated ['sɪtʃu,eɪt̬əd] *adj* : ubicado, situado — **situation** [,sɪtʃu'eɪʃən] *n* : situación *f*

six ['sɪks] *adj* : seis — ~ *n* : seis *m* — **six hundred** *adj* : seiscientos — ~ *n* : seiscientos *m* — **sixteen** [sɪks'tiːn] *adj* : dieciséis — ~ *n* : dieciséis *m* — **sixteenth** [sɪks'tiːnθ] *adj* : decimosexto — ~ *n* **1** : decimosexto *m*, -ta *f* (en una serie) **2** : dieciseisavo *m*, dieciseisava parte *f* — **sixth** ['sɪksθ, 'sɪkst] *adj* : sexto — ~ *n* **1** : sexto *m*, -ta *f* (en una serie) **2** : sexto *m* (en matemáticas) — **sixtieth** ['sɪkstiəθ] *adj* : sexagésimo — ~ *n* **1** : sexagésimo *m*, -ma *f* (en una serie) **2** : sesentavo *m* (en matemáticas) — **sixty** ['sɪksti] *adj* : sesenta — ~ *n*, *pl* **-ties** : sesenta *m*

size ['saɪz] *n* **1** : tamaño *m*, talla *f* (de ropa), número *m* (de zapatos) **2** EXTENT : magnitud *f* — ~ *vt* **sized; sizing** ~ **up** : evaluar — **sizable** *or* **sizeable** ['saɪzəbəl] *adj* : considerable

sizzle ['sɪzəl] *vi* **-zled; -zling** : chisporrotear

skate[1] ['skeɪt] *n* : raya *f* (pez)

skate[2] *n* : patín *m* — ~ *vi* **skated; skating** : patinar — **skateboard** ['skeɪt,bord] *n* : monopatín *m* — **skater** ['skeɪt̬ər] *n* : patinador *m*, -dora *f*

skeleton ['skelət̬ən] *n* : esqueleto *m*

skeptic ['skeptɪk] *n* : escéptico *m*, -ca *f* — **skeptical** ['skeptɪkəl] *adj* : escéptico — **skepticism** ['skeptə,sɪzəm] *n* : escepticismo *m*

sketch ['sketʃ] *n* **1** : esbozo *m*, bosquejo *m* **2** SKIT : sketch *m* — ~ *vt* : bosquejar — *vi* : hacer bosquejos — **sketchy** ['sketʃi] *adj* **sketchier; -est** : incompleto

skewer ['skjuːər] *n* : brocheta *f*, broqueta *f*

ski ['skiː] *n*, *pl* **skis** : esquí *m* — ~ *vi* **skied; skiing** : esquiar

skid ['skɪd] *n* : derrape *m*, patinazo *m* — ~ *vi* **skidded; skidding** : derrapar, patinar

skier ['skiːər] *n* : esquiador *m*, -dora *f*

skill ['skɪl] *n* **1** : habilidad *f*, destreza *f* **2** TECHNIQUE : técnica *f* — **skilled** ['skɪld] *adj* : hábil

skillet ['skɪlət] *n* : sartén *mf*

skillful ['skɪlfəl] *adj* : hábil, diestro

skim ['skɪm] *vt* **skimmed; skimming 1** : espumar (sopa, etc.), descremar (leche) **2** : pasar rozando (una superficie) **3** *or* **~ through** : echar un vistazo a — **~** *adj* : descremado

skimp ['skɪmp] *vi* **~ on** : escatimar — **skimpy** ['skɪmpi] *adj* **skimpier; -est 1** : exiguo, escaso **2** : brevísimo (dícese de ropa)

skin ['skɪn] *n* : piel *f* — **~** *vt* **skinned; skinning** : despellejar — **skin diving** *n* : buceo *m*, submarinismo *m* — **skinny** ['skɪni] *adj* **skinnier; -est** : flaco

skip ['skɪp] *v* **skipped; skipping** *vi* : ir brincando — *vt* OMIT : saltarse — **~** *n* : brinco *m*, salto *m*

skipper ['skɪpər] *n* : capitán *m*, -tana *f*

skirmish ['skərmɪʃ] *n* : escaramuza *f*

skirt ['skərt] *n* : falda *f* — **~** *vt* **1** BORDER : bordear **2** EVADE : eludir

skull ['skʌl] *n* : cráneo *m* (de una persona viva), calavera *f* (de un esqueleto)

skunk ['skʌŋk] *n* : mofeta *f*, zorrillo *m* *Lat*

sky ['skaɪ] *n*, *pl* **skies** : cielo *m* — **skylight** ['skaɪ,laɪt] *n* : claraboya *f*, tragaluz *m* — **skyline** ['skaɪ,laɪn] *n* : horizonte *m* — **skyscraper** ['skaɪ,skreɪpər] *n* : rascacielos *m*

slab ['slæb] *n* : bloque *m* (de piedra, etc.)

slack ['slæk] *adj* **1** LOOSE : flojo **2** CARELESS : descuidado — **~** *n* **1 take up the ~** : tensar (una cuerda, etc.) **2 ~s** *npl* : pantalones *mpl* — **slacken** ['slækən] *vt* : aflojar — *vi* : aflojarse

slain → slay

slam ['slæm] *n* : golpe *m*, portazo *m* (de una puerta) — **~** *v* **slammed; slamming** *vt* **1** *or* **~ down** : tirar, plantar **2** *or* **~ shut** : cerrar de golpe **3** — **~ the door** : dar un portazo — *vi* **1** : cerrarse de golpe **2 ~ into** : chocar contra

slander ['slændər] *vt* : calumniar, difamar — **~** *n* : calumnia *f*, difamación *f*

slang ['slæŋ] *n* : argot *m*

slant ['slænt] *n* : inclinación *f* — **~** *vi* : inclinarse

slap ['slæp] *vt* **slapped; slapping 1** : dar una bofetada a **2 ~ s.o. on the back** : dar una palmada en la espalda a algn — **~** *n* : bofetada *f*, cachetada *f* *Lat*

slash ['slæʃ] *vt* **1** : hacer un tajo en **2** : rebajar (precios) drásticamente — **~** *n* : tajo *m*

slat ['slæt] *n* : tablilla *f*

slate ['sleɪt] *n* : pizarra *f*

slaughter ['slɔtər] *n* : matanza *f* — **~** *vt* **1** : matar (animales) **2** MASSACRE : masacrar — **slaughterhouse** ['slɔtər,haus] *n* : matadero *m*

slave ['sleɪv] *n* : esclavo *m*, -va *f* — **~** *vi* **slaved; slaving** : trabajar como un burro — **slavery** ['sleɪvəri] *n* : esclavitud *f*

Slavic ['slɑvɪk, 'slæ-] *adj* : eslavo

slay ['sleɪ] *vt* **slew** ['slu:]; **slain** ['sleɪn]; **slaying** : asesinar

sleazy ['sli:zi] *adj* **sleazier; -est** : sórdido

sled ['sled] *n* : trineo *m*

sledgehammer ['sledʒ,hæmər] *n* : almádena *f*

sleek ['sli:k] *adj* : liso y brillante

sleep ['sli:p] *n* **1** : sueño *m* **2 go to ~** : dormirse — **~** *vi* **slept** ['slept]; **sleeping** : dormir — **sleeper** ['sli:pər] *n* **be a light ~** : tener el sueño ligero — **sleepless** ['sli:pləs] *adj* **have a ~ night** : pasar la noche en blanco — **sleepwalker** ['sli:p,wɔkər] *n* : sonámbulo *m*, -la *f* — **sleepy** ['sli:pi] *adj* **sleepier; -est 1** : somnoliento, soñoliento **2 be ~** : tener sueño

sleet ['sli:t] *n* : aguanieve *f* — **~** *vi* : caer aguanieve

sleeve ['sli:v] *n* : manga *f* — **sleeveless** ['sli:vləs] *adj* : sin mangas

sleigh ['sleɪ] *n* : trineo *m*

slender ['slendər] *adj* : delgado

slew ['slu:] → **slay**

slice ['slaɪs] *vt* **sliced; slicing** : cortar — **~** *n* : trozo *m*, rebanada *f* (de pan, etc.), tajada *f* (de carne)

slick ['slɪk] *adj* SLIPPERY : resbaladizo, resbaloso *Lat*

slide ['slaɪd] *v* **slid** ['slɪd]; **sliding** ['slaɪdɪŋ] *vi* : deslizarse — *vt* : deslizar — **~** *n* **1** : deslizamiento *m* **2** : tobogán *m* (para niños) **3** : diapositiva *f* (fotográfica) **4** DECLINE : descenso *m*

slier, sliest → sly

slight ['slaɪt] *adj* **1** : ligero, leve **2** SLENDER : delgado — **~** *vt* : desairar — **slightly** ['slaɪtli] *adv* : ligeramente, un poco

slim ['slɪm] *adj* **slimmer; slimmest 1** : delgado **2 a ~ chance** : escasas posibilidades *fpl* — **~** *v* **slimmed; slimming** : adelgazar

slime ['slaɪm] *n* **1** : baba *f* (de un caracol, etc.) **2** MUD : limo *m* — **slimy** ['slaɪmi] *adj* **slimier; -est** : viscoso

sling ['slɪŋ] *vt* **slung** ['slʌŋ]; **slinging 1** THROW : lanzar **2** HANG : colgar — **~** *n* **1** : honda *f* **2** : cabestrillo *m* (en medicina) — **slingshot** ['slɪŋ,ʃɑt] *n* : tirachinas *m*

slink ['slɪŋk] *vi* **slunk** ['slʌŋk]; **slinking** : andar furtivamente

slip¹ ['slɪp] *v* **slipped; slipping** *vi* **1** SLIDE : resbalarse **2 let sth ~** : dejar escapar algo **3 ~ away** : escabullirse **4 ~ up** : equivocarse — *vt* **1** : deslizar **2 ~ into** : ponerse (una prenda) **3 it slipped my mind** : se me olvidó — **~** *n* **1** MISTAKE : error *m*, desliz *m* **2 ~ of the tongue** : lapsus *m* **3** PETTICOAT : enagua *f*

slip² *n* **~ of paper** : papelito *m*

slipper ['slɪpər] *n* : zapatilla *f*, pantufla *f*

slippery ['slɪpəri] *adj* **slipperier; -est** : resbaladizo, resbaloso *Lat*

slit ['slɪt] *n* **1** OPENING : rendija *f* **2** CUT : corte *m*, raja *f* — *vt* **slit; slitting** : cortar

slither ['slɪðər] *vi* : deslizarse

sliver ['slɪvər] *n* : astilla *f*

slogan ['sloːgən] *n* : eslogan *m*

slop ['slɑp] *v* **slopped; slopping** *vt* : derramar — *vi* : derramarse

slope ['sloːp] *vi* **sloped; sloping** : inclinarse — **~** *n* : pendiente *f*, declive *m*

sloppy ['slɑpi] *adj* **sloppier; -est 1** CARELESS : descuidado **2** UNKEMPT : desaliñado

slot ['slɑt] *n* : ranura *f*

sloth ['sloθ, 'sloːθ] *n* : pereza *f*

slouch ['slaʊtʃ] *vi* : andar con los hombros caídos (en una silla)

slovenly ['slʌvənli, 'slʌv-] *adj* : desaliñado

slow ['sloː] *adj* **1** : lento **2 be ~** : estar atrasado (dícese de un reloj) — **~** *adv* → **slowly** — **~** *vt* : retrasar, retardar — *vi* **or ~ down** : ir más despacio — **slowly** ['sloːli] *adv* : lentamente, despacio — **slowness** ['sloːnəs] *n* : lentitud *f*

sludge ['slʌdʒ] *n* SEWAGE : aguas *fpl* negras

slug¹ ['slʌg] *n* **1** : babosa *f* (molusco) **2** BULLET : bala *f* **3** TOKEN : ficha *f*

slug² *vt* **slugged; slugging** : pegar un porrazo a

sluggish ['slʌgɪʃ] *adj* : lento

slum ['slʌm] *n* : barrio *m* bajo

slumber ['slʌmbər] *vi* : dormir — **~** *n* : sueño *m*

slump ['slʌmp] *vi* **1** DROP : bajar **2** COLLAPSE : dejarse caer **3** → **slouch** — **~** *n* : bajón *m*

slung → **sling**

slunk → **slink**

slur¹ ['slər] *n* ASPERSION : calumnia *f*, difamación *f*

slur² *vt* **slurred; slurring** : arrastrar (las palabras)

slurp ['slərp] *v* : beber haciendo ruido — **~** *n* : sorbo *m* (ruidoso)

slush ['slʌʃ] *n* : nieve *f* medio derretida

sly ['slaɪ] *adj* **slier** ['slaɪər]; **sliest**

['slaɪəst] **1** : astuto, taimado **2 on the ~** : a escondidas

smack¹ ['smæk] *vi* **~ of** : oler a

smack² *vt* **1** : pegar una bofetada a **2** KISS : besar **3 ~ one's lips** : relamerse — **~** *n* **1** SLAP : bofetada *f* **2** KISS : beso *m* — **~** *adv* : justo, exactamente

small ['smɔl] *adj* : pequeño, chico — **smallpox** ['smɔlpɑks] *n* : viruela *f*

smart ['smɑrt] *adj* **1** : listo, inteligente **2** STYLISH : elegante — **~** *vi* STING : escocer — **smartly** ['smɑrtli] *adv* : elegantemente

smash ['smæʃ] *n* **1** BLOW : golpe *m* **2** COLLISION : choque *m* **3** BANG, CRASH : estrépito *m* — **~** *vt* **1** BREAK : romper **2** DESTROY : aplastar — *vi* **1** SHATTER : hacerse pedazos **2 ~ into** : estrellarse contra

smattering ['smætərɪŋ] *n* : nociones *fpl*

smear ['smɪr] *n* : mancha *f* — **~** *vt* **1** : embadurnar (de pinta, etc.), untar (de aceite, etc.) **2** SMUDGE : manchar

smell ['smɛl] *v* **smelled** *or* **smelt** ['smɛlt]; **smelling** : oler — **~** *n* **1** : (sentido *m* del) olfato *m* **2** ODOR : olor *m* — **smelly** ['smɛli] *adj* **smellier; -est** : maloliente

smelt ['smɛlt] *vt* : fundir

smile ['smaɪl] *vi* **smiled; smiling** : sonreír — **~** *n* : sonrisa *f*

smirk ['smərk] *vi* : sonreír con suficiencia — **~** *n* : sonrisa *f* satisfecha

smitten ['smɪtən] *adj* **be ~ with** : estar enamorado de

smith ['smɪθ] → **blacksmith**

smock ['smɑk] *n* : blusón *m*, bata *f*

smog ['smɑg, 'smɔg] *n* : smog *m*

smoke ['smoːk] *n* : humo *m* — **~** *v* **smoked; smoking** *vi* **1** : humear (dícese de fuegos, etc.) **2** : fumar (dícese de personas) — *vt* **1** : ahumar (carne, etc.) **2** : fumar (cigarrillos) — **smoker** ['smoːkər] *n* : fumador *m*, -dora *f* — **smokestack** ['smoːkˌstæk] *n* : chimenea *f* — **smoky** ['smoːki] *adj* **smokier; -est 1** : lleno de humo **2** : a humo (dícese de sabores, etc.)

smolder ['smoːldər] *vi* : arder (sin llama)

smooth ['smuːð] *adj* **1** : liso (dícese de superficies), suave (dícese de movimientos), tranquilo (dícese del mar) **2** : sin grumos (dícese de salsas, etc.) — **~** *vt* : alisar — **smoothly** ['smuːðli] *adv* : suavemente — **smoothness** ['smuːðnəs] *n* : suavidad *f*

smother ['smʌðər] *vt* : asfixiar (a algn), sofocar (llamas, etc.)

smudge ['smʌdʒ] *v* **smudged; smudg-**

ing vt : emborronar — vi : correrse — ~ n : mancha f, borrón m

smug ['smʌg] adj **smugger; smuggest** : suficiente

smuggle ['smʌgəl] vt **-gled; -gling** : pasar de contrabando — **smuggler** ['smʌgələr] n : contrabandista mf

snack ['snæk] n : refrigerio m, tentempié m fam

snag ['snæg] n : problema m — ~ v **snagged; snagging** vt : enganchar — vi : engancharse

snail ['sneɪl] n : caracol m

snake ['sneɪk] n : culebra f, serpiente f

snap ['snæp] v **snapped; snapping** vi 1 BREAK : romperse 2 ~ **at** : intentar morder (dícese de un perro, etc.) 3 ~ **at** : contestar bruscamente a — vt 1 BREAK : romper 2 ~ **one's fingers** : chasquear los dedos 3 ~ **open/shut** : abrir/cerrar de golpe — ~ n 1 : chasquido m 2 FASTENER : broche m (de presión) 3 **be a** ~ : ser facilísimo — **snappy** ['snæpi] adj **snappier; -est** 1 FAST : rápido 2 STYLISH : elegante — **snapshot** ['snæp,ʃat] n : instantánea f

snare ['snær] n : trampa f — ~ vt **snared; snaring** : atrapar

snarl[1] ['snɑrl] vi TANGLE : enmarañar, enredar — ~ n : enredo m, maraña f

snarl[2] vi GROWL : gruñir — n : gruñido m

snatch ['snætʃ] vt : arrebatar

sneak ['sni:k] vi : ir a hurtadillas — vt : hacer furtivamente — ~ n : soplón m, -plona f fam — **sneakers** ['sni:kərz] npl : tenis mpl, zapatillas fpl — **sneaky** ['sni:ki] adj **sneakier; -est** : solapado

sneer ['snɪr] vi : sonreír con desprecio — ~ n : sonrisa f de desprecio

sneeze ['sni:z] vi **sneezed; sneezing** : estornudar — ~ n : estornudo m

snide ['snaɪd] adj : sarcástico

sniff ['snɪf] vi : oler — vt 1 : oler 2 → **sniffle** — ~ n : aspiración f por la nariz — **sniffle** ['snɪfəl] vi **-fled; -fling** : sorberse la nariz — **sniffles** ['snɪfəlz] npl **have the** ~ : estar resfriado

snip ['snɪp] n : tijeretada f — ~ vt **snipped; snipping** : cortar (con tijeras)

snivel ['snɪvəl] vi **-veled** or **-velled; -veling** or **-velling** : lloriquear

snob ['snɑb] n : esnob mf — **snobbish** ['snɑbɪʃ] adj : esnob

snoop ['snu:p] vi : husmear — ~ n : fisgón m, -gona f

snooze ['snu:z] vi **snoozed; snoozing** : dormitar — ~ n : siestecita f, siestita f

snore ['snor] vi **snored; snoring** : roncar — ~ n : ronquido m

snort ['snɔrt] vi : bufar — ~ n : bufido m

snout ['snaʊt] n : hocico m, morro m

snow ['sno:] n : nieve f — ~ vi : nevar — **snowfall** ['sno:,fɔl] n : nevada f — **snowflake** ['sno:,fleɪk] n : copo m de nieve — **snowman** ['sno:,mæn] n : muñeco m de nieve — **snowplow** ['sno:,plaʊ] n : quitanieves m — **snowshoe** ['sno:,ʃu:] n : raqueta f (para nieve) — **snowstorm** ['sno:,stɔrm] n : tormenta f de nieve — **snowy** ['sno:i] adj **snowier; -est** 1 **a** ~ **day** : un día nevoso 2 ~ **mountains** : montañas fpl nevadas

snub ['snʌb] vt **snubbed; snubbing** : desairar — ~ n : desaire m

snuff ['snʌf] vt or ~ **out** : apagar

snug ['snʌg] adj **snugger; snuggest** 1 : cómodo 2 TIGHT : ajustado — **snuggle** ['snʌgəl] vi **-gled; -gling** : acurrucarse

so ['so:] adv 1 LIKEWISE : también 2 THUS : así 3 THEREFORE : por lo tanto 4 or ~ **much** : tanto 5 or ~ **very** : tan 6 **and** ~ **on** : etcétera 7 **I think** ~ : creo que sí 8 **I told you** ~ : te lo dije — ~ conj 1 THEREFORE : así que 2 or ~ **that** : para que 3 ~ **what?** : ¿y qué? — ~ adj TRUE : cierto — ~ pron or ~ : más o menos

soak ['so:k] vi : estar en remojo — vt 1 : poner en remojo 2 ~ **up** : absorber — ~ n : remojo m

soap ['so:p] n : jabón m — ~ vt or ~ **up** : enjabonar — **soapy** ['so:pi] **soapier; -est** adj : jabonoso

soar ['sor] vi 1 : planear 2 SKYROCKET : dispararse

sob ['sɑb] vi **sobbed; sobbing** : sollozar — ~ n : sollozo m

sober ['so:bər] adj 1 : sobrio 2 SERIOUS : serio — **sobriety** [sə'braɪəti, so-] n 1 : sobriedad f 2 SERIOUSNESS : seriedad f

so-called ['so:,kɔld] adj : supuesto, presunto

soccer ['sɑkər] n : futbol m, fútbol m

social ['so:ʃəl] adj : social — n : reunión f social — **sociable** ['so:ʃəbəl] adj : sociable — **socialism** ['so:ʃə,lɪzəm] n : socialismo m — **socialist** ['so:ʃəlɪst] n : socialista mf — ~ adj : socialista — **socialize** ['so:ʃə,laɪz] v **-ized; -izing** vt : socializar — vi ~ **with** : alternar con — **society** [sə'saɪəti] n, pl **-eties** : sociedad f — **sociology** [,so:si'ɑlədʒi] n : sociología f

sock[1] ['sak] *n, pl* **socks** *or* **sox** ['saks] : calcetín *m*

sock[2] *vt* : pegar, golpear — ~ *n* PUNCH : puñetazo *m*

socket ['sakət] *n* **1** *or* **electric ~** : enchufe *m*, toma *f* de corriente **2** *or* **eye ~** : órbita *f*, cuenca *f* **3** : glena *f* (de una articulación)

soda ['so:də] *n* **1** *or* **~ pop** : refresco *m*, gaseosa *f* **2** *or* **~ water** : soda *f*

sodium ['so:diəm] *n* : sodio *m*

sofa ['so:fə] *n* : sofá *m*

soft ['soft] *adj* **1** : blando **2** SMOOTH : suave — **softball** ['soft,bol] *n* : softbol *m* — **soft drink** *n* : refresco *m* — **soften** ['sofən] *vt* **1** : ablandar **2** EASE, SMOOTH : suavizar — *vi* **1** : ablandarse **2** EASE : suavizarse — **softly** ['softli] *adv* : suavemente — **software** ['soft,wær] *n* : software *m*

soggy ['sagi] *adj* **soggier; -est** : empapado

soil ['soil] *vt* : ensuciar — ~ *n* DIRT : tierra *f*

solace ['saləs] *n* : consuelo *m*

solar ['so:lər] *adj* : solar

sold → **sell**

solder ['sadər, 'so-] *n* : soldadura *f* — ~ *vt* : soldar

soldier ['so:ldʒər] *n* : soldado *mf*

sole[1] ['so:l] *n* : lenguado *m* (pez)

sole[2] *n* : planta *f* (del pie), suela *f* (de un zapato)

sole[3] *adj* : único — **solely** ['so:li] *adv* : únicamente, sólo

solemn ['saləm] *adj* : solemne — **solemnity** [sə'lemnəti] *n, pl* **-ties** : solemnidad *f*

solicit [sə'lisət] *vt* : solicitar

solid ['saləd] *adj* **1** : sólido **2** UNBROKEN : continuo **3 ~ gold** : oro *m* macizo **4 two ~ hours** : dos horas seguidas — ~ *n* : sólido *m* — **solidarity** [salə'dærəti] *n* : solidaridad *f* — **solidify** [sə'lidə,fai] *v* **-fied; -fying** *vt* : solidificar — *vi* : solidificarse — **solidity** [sə'lidəti] *n, pl* **-ties** : solidez *f*

solitary ['salə,teri] *adj* : solitario — **solitude** ['salə,tu:d, -,tju:d] *n* : soledad *f*

solo ['so:,lo:] *n, pl* **solos** : solo *m* — **soloist** ['so:lo:st] *n* : solista *mf*

solution [sə'lu:ʃən] *n* : solución *f* — **soluble** ['saljəbəl] *adj* : soluble — **solve** ['salv] *vt* **solved; solving** : resolver — **solvent** ['salvənt] *n* : solvente *m*

somber ['sambər] *adj* : sombrío

some ['sʌm] *adj* **1** (*of unspecified identity*) : un **2** (*of an unspecified amount*) : algo de, un poco de **3** (*of an unspecified number*) : unos **4** CERTAIN : algunos **5 that was ~ game!** : ¡fue un partidazo! — ~ *pron* **1** SEVERAL : algunos, unos **2** PART : un poco, algo — ~ *adv* **twenty people** : unas veinte personas — **somebody** ['sʌm,badi, -,bədi] *pron* : alguien — **someday** ['sʌm,dei] *adv* : algún día — **somehow** ['sʌm,hau] *adv* **1** : de algún modo **2 ~ or other** : de alguna manera u otra — **someone** ['sʌm,wʌn] *pron* : alguien

somersault ['sʌmər,solt] *n* : voltereta *f*, salto *m* mortal

something ['sʌmθiŋ] *pron* **1** : algo **2 ~ else** : otra cosa — **sometime** ['sʌm,taim] *adv* **1** : algún día, en algún momento **2 ~ next month** : (durante) el mes que viene — **sometimes** ['sʌm,taimz] *adv* : a veces — **somewhat** ['sʌm,hwʌt, -,hwat] *adv* : algo — **somewhere** ['sʌm,hwer] *adv* **1** : en alguna parte, en algún lado **2 ~ around** : alrededor de **3 ~ else** → **elsewhere**

son ['sʌn] *n* : hijo *m*

song ['soŋ] *n* : canción *f*

son-in-law ['sʌnin,lo] *n, pl* **sons-in-law** : yerno *m*

sonnet ['sanət] *n* : soneto *m*

soon ['su:n] *adv* **1** : pronto **2** SHORTLY : dentro de poco **3 as ~ as** : en cuanto **4 as ~ as possible** : lo más pronto posible **5 ~ after** : poco después **6 ~er or later** : tarde o temprano **7 the ~er the better** : cuanto antes mejor

soot ['sut, 'su:t, 'sʌt] *n* : hollín *m*

soothe ['su:ð] *vt* **soothed; soothing 1** CALM : calmar **2** RELIEVE : aliviar

sop ['sap] *vt* **sopped; sopping ~ up** : absorber

sophistication [sə,fistə'keiʃən] *n* : sofisticación *f* — **sophisticated** [sə'fistə,keitəd] *adj* : sofisticado

sophomore ['saf,mor, 'safə,mor] *n* : estudiante *mf* de segundo año

soprano [sə'præ,no:] *n, pl* **-nos** : soprano *mf*

sorcerer ['sorsərər] *n* : hechicero *m*, brujo *m* — **sorcery** ['sorsəri] *n* : hechicería *f*, brujería *f*

sordid ['sordid] *adj* : sórdido

sore ['sor] *adj* **sorer; sorest 1** : dolorido **2** ANGRY : enfadado **3 ~ throat** : dolor *m* de garganta **4 I have a ~ throat** : me duele la garganta — ~ *n* : llaga *f* — **sorely** ['sorli] *adv* : muchísimo — **soreness** ['sornəs] *n* : dolor *m*

sorrow ['sar,o:] *n* : pesar *m*, pena *f* — **sorry** ['sari] *adj* **sorrier; -est 1** PITIFUL : lamentable **2 feel ~ for** : compadecer **3 I'm ~** : lo siento

sort ['sort] n 1 : tipo m, clase f 2 a ~ of : una especie de — vt : clasificar —
sort of adv 1 SOMEWHAT : algo 2 MORE OR LESS : más o menos
SOS [ˌɛsˌoːˈɛs] n : SOS m
so-so ['soːˌsoː] adj & adv : así así fam
soufflé [suːˈfleɪ] n : suflé m
sought → **seek**
soul ['soːl] n : alma f
sound¹ ['saʊnd] adj 1 HEALTHY : sano 2 FIRM : sólido 3 SENSIBLE : lógico 4 a ~ **sleep** : un sueño profundo 5 **safe and** ~ : sano y salvo
sound² n : sonido m — vt : hacer sonar, tocar (una trompeta, etc.) — vi 1 : sonar 2 SEEM : parecer
sound³ n CHANNEL : brazo m de mar — ~ vt 1 : sondar (en navegación) 2 or ~ **out** : sondear
soundly ['saʊndli] adv 1 SOLIDLY : sólidamente 2 DEEPLY : profundamente
soundproof ['saʊndˌpruːf] adj : insonorizado
soup ['suːp] n : sopa f
sour ['saʊər] adj 1 : agrio 2 ~ **milk** : leche f cortada — ~ vt : agriar
source ['sors] n : fuente f, origen m
south ['saʊθ] adv : al sur — ~ adj : (del) sur — ~ n : sur m — **South African** adj : sudafricano — **South American** adj : sudamericano — **southeast** [saʊˈθiːst] adv : hacia el sureste — ~ adj : (del) sureste — ~ n : sureste m, sudeste m — **southeastern** [saʊˈθiːstərn] adj : southeast — **southerly** ['sʌðərli] adv & adj : del sur — **southern** ['sʌðərn] adj : del sur, meridional — **southwest** [saʊθˈwɛst] adv : hacia el suroeste — ~ adj : (del) suroeste — ~ n : suroeste m, sudoeste m — **southwestern** [saʊθˈwɛstərn] adj → **southwest**
souvenir [ˌsuːvəˈnɪr, 'suːvə-] n : recuerdo m
sovereign ['sɑːvərən] n : soberano m, -na f — ~ adj : soberano — **sovereignty** ['sɑːvərənti] n, pl -ties : soberanía f
Soviet ['soːviˌɛt, 'sɑː-, -viət] adj : soviético
sow¹ ['saʊ] n : cerda f
sow² ['soː] vt **sowed; sown** ['soːn] or **sowed; sowing** : sembrar
sox → **sock**
soybean ['sɔɪˌbiːn] n : soya f, soja f
spa ['spɑː] n : balneario m
space ['speɪs] n 1 : espacio m 2 ROOM, SPOT : sitio m, lugar m — ~ vt **spaced; spacing** : espaciar — **spaceship** ['speɪsˌʃɪp] n : nave f espacial — **space shuttle** n : transbordador m espacial — **spacious** ['speɪʃəs] adj : espacioso, amplio
spade¹ ['speɪd] n SHOVEL : pala f
spade² n : pica f (naipe)
spaghetti [spəˈɡɛti] n : espaguetis mpl
span ['spæn] n 1 PERIOD : espacio m 2 : luz f (entre dos soportes) — ~ vt **spanned; spanning** 1 : abarcar (un período) 2 CROSS : extenderse sobre
Spaniard ['spænjərd] n : español m, -ñola f
spaniel ['spænjəl] n : spaniel m
Spanish ['spænɪʃ] adj : español — ~ n : español m (idioma)
spank ['spæŋk] vt : dar palmadas a (en las nalgas)
spar ['spɑr] vi **sparred; sparring** : entrenarse (en boxeo)
spare ['spær] vt **spared; sparing** 1 PARDON : perdonar 2 SAVE : ahorrar 3 **can you** ~ **a dollar?** : ¿me das un dólar? 4 **I can't** ~ **the time** : no tengo tiempo 5 ~ **no expense** : no reparar en gastos 6 **to** ~ : de sobra — ~ adj 1 : de repuesto 2 EXCESS : de más 3 LEAN : delgado — ~ n or ~ **part** : repuesto m — **spare time** : tiempo m libre — **sparing** ['spærɪŋ] adj : parco, económico
spark ['spɑrk] n : chispa f — ~ vi : chispear, echar chispas — vt : despertar (interés), provocar (crítica) — **sparkle** ['spɑrkəl] vi **-kled; -kling** : destellar, centellear — ~ n : destello m, centelleo m — **spark plug** n : bujía f
sparrow ['spæroː] n : gorrión m
sparse ['spɑrs] adj **sparser; -est** : escaso
spasm ['spæzəm] n : espasmo m
spat¹ → **spit**
spat² n QUARREL : disputa f, pelea f
spatter ['spætər] vt : salpicar
spawn ['spɔn] vi : desovar — vt : engendrar, producir — ~ n : hueva f
speak ['spiːk] v **spoke** ['spoːk]; **spoken** ['spoːkən]; **speaking** vi 1 : hablar 2 ~ **out against** : denunciar 3 ~ **up** : hablar más alto 4 ~ **up for** : defender — vt 1 : decir 2 : hablar (un idioma) — **speaker** ['spiːkər] n 1 ORATOR : orador m, -dora f 2 : hablante mf (de un idioma) 3 LOUDSPEAKER : altavoz m
spear ['spɪr] n : lanza f — **spearhead** ['spɪrˌhɛd] n : punta f de lanza — ~ vt : encabezar — **spearmint** ['spɪrmɪnt] n : menta f verde
special ['spɛʃəl] adj : especial — **specialist** ['spɛʃəlɪst] n : especialista mf — **specialization** [ˌspɛʃələˈzeɪʃən] n : especialización f — **specialize** ['spɛʃə-

,laɪz] *vi* -**ized**; -**izing** : especializarse
— **specially** *adv* : especialmente —
specialty ['speʃəlti] *n, pl* -**ties** : especialidad *f*

species ['spiːʃiːz, -siːz] *ns & pl* : especie *f*

specify ['spesəˌfaɪ] *vt* -**fied**; -**fying** : especificar — **specific** [sprˈsɪfɪk] *adj* : específico — **specifically** [sprˈsɪfɪkli] *adv* 1 : específicamente 2 EXPLICITLY : expresamente — **specification** [ˌspesəfəˈkeɪʃən] *n* : especificación *f*

specimen ['spesəmən] *n* : espécimen *m*

speck ['spek] *n* 1 SPOT : mancha *f* 2 BIT : mota *f* — **speckled** ['spekəld] *adj* : moteado

spectacle ['spektɪkəl] *n* 1 : espectáculo *m* 2 ~**s** *npl* GLASSES : gafas *fpl*, lentes *fpl*, anteojos *mpl* — **spectacular** [spekˈtækjələr] *adj* : espectacular — **spectator** ['spekˌteɪtər] *n* : espectador *m*, -dora *f*

specter *or* **spectre** ['spektər] *n* : espectro *m*

spectrum ['spektrəm] *n, pl* -**tra** [-trə] *or* -**trums** 1 : espectro *m* 2 RANGE : gama *f*

speculation [ˌspekjəˈleɪʃən] *n* : especulación *f*

speech ['spiːtʃ] *n* 1 : habla *f* 2 ADDRESS : discurso *m* — **speechless** ['spiːtʃləs] *adj* : mudo

speed ['spiːd] *n* 1 : rapidez *f* 2 VELOCITY : velocidad *f* — ~ *v* **sped** ['sped] *or* **speeded**; **speeding** *vi* 1 : conducir a exceso de velocidad 2 ~ **off** : irse a toda velocidad 3 ~ **up** : acelerarse — *vt* or ~ **up** : acelerar — **speed limit** *n* : velocidad *f* máxima — **speedometer** [sprˈdɑmətər] *n* : velocímetro *m* — **speedy** ['spiːdi] *adj* **speedier**, -**est** : rápido

spell[1] ['spel] *vt* 1 : escribir (las letras de) 2 *or* ~ **out** : deletrear 3 MEAN : significar

spell[2] *n* ENCHANTMENT : hechizo *m*

spell[3] *n* : período *m* (de tiempo)

spellbound ['spelˌbaʊnd] *adj* : embelesado

spelling ['speliŋ] *n* : ortografía *f*

spend ['spend] *vt* **spent** ['spent]; **spending** 1 : gastar (dinero) 2 : pasar (las vacaciones, etc.) 3 ~ **time on** : dedicar tiempo a

sperm ['spərm] *n, pl* **sperm** *or* **sperms** : esperma *mf*

spew ['spjuː] *vt* : vomitar, arrojar (lava, etc.)

sphere ['sfɪr] *n* : esfera *f* — **spherical** ['sfɪrɪkəl, 'sfer-] *adj* : esférico

spice ['spaɪs] *n* : especia *f* — ~ *vt* **spiced**; **spicing** : condimentar, sazonar — **spicy** ['spaɪsi] *adj* **spicier**; -**est** : picante

spider ['spaɪdər] *n* : araña *f*

spigot ['spɪgət, -kət] *n* : grifo *m* Spain, llave *f Lat*

spike ['spaɪk] *n* 1 : clavo *m* (grande) 2 POINT : punta *f* — **spiky** ['spaɪki] *adj* : puntiagudo

spill ['spɪl] *vt* : derramar — *vi* : derramarse

spin ['spɪn] *v* **spun** ['spʌn]; **spinning** *vi* : girar — *vt* 1 : hilar (lana, etc.) 2 TWIRL : hacer girar — ~ *n* 1 : vuelta *f*, giro *m* 2 **go for a** ~ : dar una vuelta (en auto)

spinach ['spɪnɪtʃ] *n* : espinacas *fpl*

spinal cord ['spaɪnəl] *n* : médula *f* espinal

spindle ['spɪndəl] *n* : huso *m* (para hilar) — **spindly** ['spɪndli] *adj* : larguirucho *fam*

spine ['spaɪn] *n* 1 : columna *f* vertebral 2 QUILL : púa *f* 3 THORN : espina *f* 4 : lomo *m* (de un libro)

spinster ['spɪnstər] *n* : soltera *f*

spiral ['spaɪrəl] *adj* : de espiral, en espiral — ~ *n* : espiral *f* — ~ *vi* -**raled** *or* -**railed**; -**raling** *or* -**railing** : ir en espiral

spire ['spaɪr] *n* : aguja *f*

spirit ['spɪrət] *n* 1 : espíritu *m* 2 **in good** ~**s** : animado 3 ~**s** *npl* : licores *mpl* — **spirited** ['spɪrətəd] *adj* : animado — **spiritual** ['spɪrɪtʃʊəl, -tʃəl] *adj* : espiritual — **spirituality** [ˌspɪrɪtʃʊˈæləti] *n, pl* -**ties** : espiritualidad *f*

spit[1] ['spɪt] *n* ROTISSERIE : asador *m*

spit[2] *v* **spit** *or* **spat** ['spæt]; **spitting** : escupir — *n* SALIVA : saliva *f*

spite ['spaɪt] *n* 1 : rencor *m* 2 **in** ~ **of** : a pesar de — ~ *vt* **spited**; **spiting** : fastidiar — **spiteful** ['spaɪtfəl] *adj* : rencoroso

spittle ['spɪtəl] *n* : saliva *f*

splash ['splæʃ] *vt* : salpicar — *vi* 1 : salpicar 2 *or* ~ **about** : chapotear — ~ *n* 1 : salpicadura *f* 2 : mancha *f* (de color, etc.)

splatter ['splætər] → **spatter**

spleen ['spliːn] *n* : bazo *m* (órgano)

splendor ['splendər] *n* : esplendor *m* — **splendid** ['splendəd] *adj* : espléndido

splint ['splɪnt] *n* : tablilla *f*

splinter ['splɪntər] *n* : astilla *f* — *vi* : astillarse

split ['splɪt] *v* **split**; **splitting** *vt* 1 : partir 2 BURST : reventar 3 *or* ~ **up** : dividir — *vi* 1 : partirse, rajarse 2 *or* ~ **up**

: dividirse — **~** n 1 CRACK : rajadura f 2 or **~** seam : descosido m 3 DIVISION : división f

splurge ['splərdʒ] vi **splurged; splurging** : derrochar dinero

spoil ['spɔɪl] vt **spoiled** or **spoilt** ['spɔɪlt]; **spoiling** 1 RUIN : estropear 2 PAMPER : consentir, mimar — **spoils** npl : botín m

spoke[1] ['spo:k] → **speak**

spoke[2] n : rayo m (de una rueda)

spoken → **speak**

spokesman ['spo:ksmən] n, pl **-men** [-mən, -men] : portavoz m — **spokeswoman** ['spo:ks,wumən] n, pl **-women** [-,wimən] : portavoz f

sponge ['spʌndʒ] n : esponja f — **~** vt **sponged; sponging** : limpiar con una esponja — **spongy** ['spʌndʒi] adj **spongier; -est** : esponjoso

sponsor ['spɑntsər] n : patrocinador m, -dora f — **~** vt : patrocinar — **sponsorship** ['spɑntsər,ʃɪp] n : patrocinio m

spontaneity [,spɑntə'ni:əti, -'neɪ-] n : espontaneidad f — **spontaneous** [spɑn'teɪniəs] adj : espontáneo

spooky ['spu:ki] adj **spookier; -est** : espeluzante

spool ['spu:l] n : carrete m

spoon ['spu:n] n : cuchara f — **spoonful** ['spu:n,ful] n : cucharada f

sporadic [spə'rædɪk] adj : esporádico

spore ['spor] n : espora f

sport ['sport] n 1 : deporte m 2 be a good **~** : tener espíritu deportivo — **sportsman** ['sportsmən] n, pl **-men** [-mən, -men] : deportista m — **sportswoman** ['sports,wumən] n, pl **-women** [-,wimən] : deportista f — **sporty** ['sporti] adj **sportier; -est** : deportivo

spot ['spɑt] n 1 : mancha f 2 DOT : punto m 3 PLACE : lugar m, sitio m 4 **in a tight ~** : en apuros 5 **on the ~** INSTANTLY : en ese mismo momento — **~** vt **spotted; spotting** 1 STAIN : manchar — **spotless** ['spɑtləs] adj : impecable — **spotlight** ['spɑt,laɪt] n 1 : foco m, reflector m 2 **be in the ~** : ser el centro de atención — **spotty** ['spɑti] adj **spottier; -est** : irregular

spouse ['spaus] n : cónyuge mf

spout ['spaut] vi : salir a chorros — **~** n 1 : pico m (de una jarra, etc.) 2 STREAM : chorro m

sprain ['spreɪn] n : esguince m — **~** vt : sufrir un esguince en

sprawl ['sprɔl] vi 1 : repantigarse (en un sillón, etc.) 2 EXTEND : extenderse — **~** n : extensión f

spray[1] ['spreɪ] n BOUQUET : ramillete m

spray[2] n 1 MIST : rocío m 2 or **aerosol ~** : spray m 3 or **~ bottle** : atomizador m — **~** vt : rociar (una superficie), pulverizar (un líquido)

spread ['spred] v **spread; spreading** vt 1 : propagar (enfermedades), difundir (noticias, etc.) 2 or **~ out** : extender 3 : untar (con mantequilla, etc.) — vi 1 : propagarse, difundirse 2 or **~ out** : extenderse — **~** n 1 : propagación f, difusión f 2 PASTE : pasta f (para untar) — **spreadsheet** ['spred,ʃi:t] n : hoja f de cálculo

spree ['spri] n **go on a ~** : ir de juerga fam

sprig ['sprɪg] n : ramito m

sprightly ['spraɪtli] adj **sprightlier; -est** : vivo

spring ['sprɪŋ] v **sprang** ['spræŋ] or **sprung** ['sprʌŋ]; **sprung; springing** vi 1 : saltar 2 **~ from** : surgir de 3 **~ up** : surgir — vt 1 ACTIVATE : accionar 2 **~ a leak** : hacer agua 3 **~ sth on s.o.** : sorprender a algn con algo — **~** n 1 : manantial m (de aguas) 2 : primavera f (estación) 3 LEAP : salto m 4 RESILIENCE : elasticidad f 5 : resorte m (mecanismo) 6 or **bedspring** : muelle m — **springboard** ['sprɪŋbord] n : trampolín m — **springtime** ['sprɪŋ,taɪm] n : primavera f — **springy** ['sprɪŋi] adj **springier; -est** : mullido

sprinkle ['sprɪŋkəl] vt **-kled; -kling** 1 : salpicar, rociar 2 DUST : espolvorear — **~** n : llovizna f — **sprinkler** ['sprɪŋkələr] n : aspersor m

sprint ['sprɪnt] vi 1 : correr 2 : esprintar (en deportes) — **~** n 1 : esprint m (en deportes)

sprout ['spraut] vi : brotar — **~** n : brote m

spruce[1] ['spru:s] vt **spruced; sprucing** **~ up** : arreglar

spruce[2] n : picea f (árbol)

spry ['spraɪ] adj **sprier** or **spryer** ['spraɪər]; **spriest** or **spryest** ['spraɪəst] : ágil, activo

spun → **spin**

spur ['spər] n 1 : espuela f 2 STIMULUS : acicate m 3 **on the ~ of the moment** : sin pensarlo — **~** vt **spurred; spurring** or **~ on** 1 : espolear (un caballo) 2 MOTIVATE : motivar

spurn ['spərn] vt : desdeñar, rechazar

spurt[1] ['spərt] vi : salir a chorros — **~** n : chorro m

spurt[2] n 1 : arranque m (de energía, etc.) 2 **work in ~s** : trabajar por rachas

spy ['spaɪ] v **spied; spying** vt : ver, divisar — vi ~ **on s.o.** : espiar a algn — ~ n : espía mf

squabble ['skwabəl] n : riña f, pelea f — vi **-bled; -bling** : reñir, pelearse

squad ['skwad] n : pelotón m (militar), brigada f (de policías)

squadron ['skwadrən] n : escuadrón m (de soldados), escuadra f (de aviones o naves)

squalid ['skwalɪd] adj : miserable

squall ['skwɔl] n : turbión m

squalor ['skwalər] n : miseria f

squander ['skwandər] vt : derrochar (dinero, etc.), desperdiciar (oportunidades, etc.)

square ['skwær] n 1 : cuadrado m 2 : plaza f (de una ciudad) — ~ adj **squarer; -est** 1 : cuadrado 2 HONEST : justo 3 EVEN : en paz 4 a ~ **meal** : una comida decente — ~ vt **squared; squaring** 1 : elevar al cuadrado (un número) 2 : saldar (una cuenta) — **square root** n : raíz f cuadrada

squash¹ ['skwaʃ, 'skwɔʃ] vt 1 : aplastar 2 : acallar (protestas, etc.) — ~ n : squash m (deporte)

squash² n, pl **squashes** or **squash** : calabaza f (vegetal)

squat ['skwat] vi **squatted; squatting** 1 or ~ **down** : ponerse en cuclillas 2 : ocupar un lugar sin derecho — **squatter; squattest** : achaparrado

squawk ['skwɔk] n : graznido m — vi : graznar

squeak ['skwiːk] vi 1 : chillar 2 CREAK : chirriar — ~ n 1 : chillido m 2 CREAK : chirrido m — **squeaky** ['skwiːki] adj **squeakier; -est** : chirriante

squeal ['skwiːl] vi 1 : chillar (dícese de personas, etc.), chirriar (dícese de frenos, etc.) 2 PROTEST : quejarse — ~ n : chillido m (de una persona), chirrido m (de frenos, etc.)

squeamish ['skwiːmɪʃ] adj : impresionable, delicado

squeeze ['skwiːz] vt **squeezed; squeezing** 1 : apretar 2 : exprimir (frutas, etc.) 3 : extraer (jugo, etc.) — ~ n : apretón m

squid ['skwɪd] n, pl **squid** or **squids** : calamar m

squint ['skwɪnt] vi : entrecerrar los ojos — ~ n : estrabismo m

squirm ['skwərm] vi : retorcerse

squirrel ['skwərəl] n : ardilla f

squirt ['skwərt] vt : lanzar un chorro de — vi : salir a chorros — ~ n : chorrito m

stab ['stæb] n 1 : puñalada f 2 ~ **of pain** : pinchazo m 3 **take a** ~ **at** : intentar — ~ vt **stabbed; stabbing** 1 KNIFE : apuñalar 2 STICK : clavar

stable ['steɪbəl] n 1 : establo m (para ganado) 2 or **horse** ~ : caballeriza f — ~ adj **-bler; -blest** : estable — **stability** [stə'bɪlət̬i] n, pl **-ties** : estabilidad f — **stabilize** ['steɪbəˌlaɪz] vt **-lized; -lizing** : estabilizar

stack ['stæk] n : montón m, pila f — ~ vt : amontonar, apilar

stadium ['steɪdiəm] n, pl **-dia** or **-diums** : estadio m

staff ['stæfs, stævz] n, pl **staffs** or **staves** ['stævz, 'steɪvz] 1 : bastón m 2 pl **staffs** PERSONNEL : personal m 3 pl **staffs** : pentagrama m (en música) — ~ ['stæf] vt : proveer de personal

stag ['stæg] n, pl **stags** or **stag** : ciervo m, venado m — ~ adj : sólo para hombres — ~ adv **go** ~ : ir solo

stage ['steɪdʒ] n 1 : escenario m (de un teatro) 2 PHASE : etapa f 3 **the** ~ : el teatro — ~ vt **staged; staging** 1 : poner en escena 2 ARRANGE : montar — **stagecoach** ['steɪdʒˌkoːtʃ] n : diligencia f

stagger ['stægər] vi : tambalearse — vt 1 : escalonar (turnos, etc.) 2 **be** ~**ed by** : quedarse estupefacto por — ~ n : tambaleo m — **staggering** ['stægərɪŋ] adj : asombroso

stagnant ['stægnənt] adj : estancado — **stagnate** ['stægˌneɪt] vi **-nated; -nating** : estancarse

stain ['steɪn] vt 1 : manchar 2 : teñir (madera) — ~ n 1 : mancha f 2 DYE : tinte m, tintura f — **stainless steel** ['steɪnləs-] n : acero m inoxidable

stair ['stær] n 1 STEP : escalón m, peldaño m 2 ~**s** npl : escalera(s) f(pl) — **staircase** ['stær,keɪs] n : escalera(s) f(pl) — **stairway** ['stær,weɪ] n : escalera(s) f(pl)

stake ['steɪk] n 1 POST : estaca f 2 BET : apuesta f 3 INTEREST : intereses mpl 4 **be at** ~ : estar en juego — ~ vt **staked; staking** 1 : estacar 2 BET : jugarse 3 ~ **a claim to** : reclamar

stale ['steɪl] adj **staler; stalest** 1 : duro (dícese del pan) 2 OLD : viejo 3 STUFFY : viciado

stalk¹ ['stɔk] n : tallo m (de una planta)

stalk² vt : acechar — vi or ~ **off** : irse con altivez

stall¹ ['stɔl] n 1 : compartimiento m (de un establo) 2 STAND : puesto m — ~ vt : parar (un motor) — vi : pararse

stall[2] *vt* DELAY : entretener — *vi* : andar con rodeos

stallion ['stæljən] *n* : caballo *m* semental

stalwart ['stɔlwərt] *adj* 1 STRONG : fornido 2 ~ **supporter** : partidario *m* leal

stamina ['stæmənə] *n* : resistencia *f*

stammer ['stæmər] *vi* : tartamudear — ~ *n* : tartamudeo *m*

stamp ['stæmp] *n* 1 SEAL : sello *m* 2 DIE : cuño *m* 3 *or* **postage** ~ : sello *m*, estampilla *f* Lat, timbre *m* Lat — ~ *vt* 1 : franquear (una carta) 2 IMPRINT : sellar 3 MINT : acuñar 4 ~ **one's foot** : dar una patada (en el suelo)

stampede [stæm'pi:d] *n* : estampida *f* — ~ *vi* -**peded; -peding** : salir en estampida

stance ['stæns] *n* : postura *f*

stand ['stænd] *v* **stood** ['stʊd]; **standing** *vi* 1 : estar de pie, estar parado Lat 2 BE : estar 3 CONTINUE : seguir vigente 4 LIE, REST : reposar 5 ~ **aside** *or* ~ **back** : apartarse 6 ~ **out** : sobresalir 7 *or* ~ **up** : ponerse de pie, pararse Lat — *vt* 1 PLACE : poner, colocar 2 ENDURE : soportar 3 ~ **a chance** : tener una posibilidad — **stand by** *vt* 1 : mantener (una promesa, etc.) 2 SUPPORT : apoyar — **stand for** *vt* 1 MEAN : significar 2 PERMIT : permitir — **stand up** *vi* 1 ~ **for** : defender 2 ~ **up to** : resistir a — ~ *n* 1 RESISTANCE : resistencia *f* 2 STALL : puesto *m* 3 BASE : base *f* 4 POSITION : posición *f* 5 ~**s** *npl* : tribuna *f*

standard ['stændərd] *n* 1 : norma *f* 2 BANNER : estandarte *m* 3 CRITERION : criterio *m* 4 ~ **of living** : nivel *m* de vida — ~ *adj* : estándar — **standardize** ['stændər,daɪz] *vt* -**ized; -izing** : estandarizar

standing ['stændɪŋ] *n* 1 RANK : posición *f* 2 DURATION : duración *f*

standpoint ['stænd,pɔɪnt] *n* : punto *m* de vista

standstill ['stænd,stɪl] *n* 1 **be at a** ~ : estar paralizado 2 **come to a** ~ : pararse

stank → **stink**

stanza ['stænzə] *n* : estrofa *f*

staple[1] ['steɪpəl] *n* : producto *m* principal — ~ *adj* : principal, básico

staple[2] *n* : grapa *f* (para papeles) — *vt* -**pled; -pling** : grapar, engrapar Lat — **stapler** ['steɪplər] *n* : grapadora *f*, engrapadora *f* Lat

star ['stɑr] *n* : estrella *f* — *v* **starred; starring** *vt* FEATURE : estar protagonizado por — *vi* ~ **in** : protagonizar

starboard ['stɑrbərd] *n* : estribor *m*

starch ['stɑrtʃ] *vt* : almidonar — ~ *n* 1 : almidón *m* 2 : fécula *f* (comida)

stardom ['stɑrdəm] *n* : estrellato *m*

stare ['stær] *vi* **stared; staring** : mirar fijamente — ~ *n* : mirada *f* fija

starfish ['stɑr,fɪʃ] *n* : estrella *f* de mar

stark ['stɑrk] *adj* 1 PLAIN : austero 2 HARSH : severo, duro 3 SHARP : marcado — ~ *adv* 1 : completamente 2 ~ **naked** : en cueros (vivos)

starlight ['stɑr,laɪt] *n* : luz *f* de las estrellas

starling ['stɑrlɪŋ] *n* : estornino *m*

starry ['stɑri] *adj* **starrier; -est** : estrellado

start ['stɑrt] *vi* 1 : empezar, comenzar 2 SET OUT : salir 3 JUMP : sobresaltarse 4 *or* ~ **up** : arrancar — *vt* 1 : empezar, comenzar 2 CAUSE : provocar 3 *or* ~ **up** ESTABLISH : montar 4 *or* ~ **up** : arrancar (un motor, etc.) — ~ *n* 1 : principio *m* 2 **get an early** ~ : salir temprano 3 **give s.o. a** ~ : asustar a algn — **starter** ['stɑrtər] *n* : motor *m* de arranque (de un vehículo)

startle ['stɑrtəl] *vt* -**tled; -tling** : asustar

starve ['stɑrv] *v* **starved; starving** *vi* : morirse de hambre — *vt* : privar de comida — **starvation** [stɑr'veɪʃən] *n* : inanición *f*, hambre *f*

stash ['stæʃ] *vt* : esconder

state ['steɪt] *n* 1 : estado *m* 2 **the States** : los Estados Unidos — ~ *vt* **stated; stating** 1 SAY : decir 2 REPORT : exponer — **stately** ['steɪtli] *adj* **statelier; -est** : majestuoso — **statement** ['steɪtmənt] *n* 1 : declaración *f* 2 *or* **bank** ~ : estado *m* de cuenta — **statesman** ['steɪtsmən] *n*, *pl* -**men** [-mən, -,mɛn] : estadista *mf*

static ['stætɪk] *adj* : estático — ~ *n* : estática *f*

station ['steɪʃən] *n* 1 : estación *f* (de trenes, etc.) 2 RANK : condición *f* (social) 3 : canal *m* (de televisión), emisora *f* (de radio) 4 → **fire station, police station** — *vt* : apostar, estacionar — **stationary** ['steɪʃə,neri] *adj* : estacionario

stationery ['steɪʃə,neri] *n* : papel *m* y sobres *mpl* (para cartas)

station wagon *n* : camioneta *f* (familiar)

statistic [stə'tɪstɪk] *n* : estadística *f* — **statistical** [stə'tɪstɪkəl] *adj* : estadístico

statue ['stætʃu:] *n* : estatua *f*

stature ['stætʃər] *n* : estatura *f*, talla *f*

status ['steɪtəs, 'stæ-] *n* 1 : situación *f* 2 *or* **social** ~ : estatus *m* 3 **marital** ~ : estado *m* civil

statute ['stæˌtʃuːt] *n* : estatuto *m*
staunch ['stɔntʃ] *adj* : leal
stave ['steɪv] *vt* **staved** *or* **stove** ['stoːv];
  staving 1 ~ in : romper **2 ~ off**
  : evitar
staves → staff
stay[1] ['steɪ] *vi* **1** REMAIN : quedarse, permanecer **2** LODGE : alojarse **3 ~**
  awake : mantenerse despierto **4 ~ in**
  : quedarse en casa — *vt* : suspender
  (una ejecución, etc.) — ~ *n* **1** : estancia *f*, estadía *f Lat* **2** SUSPENSION
  : suspensión *f*
stay[2] *n* SUPPORT : soporte *m*
stead ['stɛd] *n* **1 in s.o.'s ~** : en lugar
  de algn **2 stand s.o. in good ~** : ser
  muy útil a algn — **steadfast** ['stɛd-
  ˌfæst] *adj* **1** FIRM : firme **2** LOYAL : leal,
  fiel — **steadily** ['stɛdəli] *adv* **1** : progresivamente **2** INCESSANTLY : sin
  parar **3** FIXEDLY : fijamente — **steady**
  ['stɛdi] *adj* **steadier; -est 1** FIRM, SURE
  : firme, seguro **2** FIXED : fijo **3** DE-
  PENDABLE : responsable **4** CONSTANT
  : constante — ~ *vt* **steadied; steady-**
  ing 1 : mantener firme **2** : calmar (los
  nervios)
steak ['steɪk] *n* : bistec *m*, filete *m*
steal ['stiːl] *v* **stole** ['stoːl]; **stolen**
  ['stoːlən]; **stealing** *vt* : robar — *vi* **1**
  : robar **2 ~ away** : escabullirse
stealth ['stɛlθ] *n* : sigilo *m* — **stealthy**
  ['stɛlθi] *adj* **stealthier; -est** : furtivo,
  sigiloso
steam ['stiːm] *n* **1** : vapor *m* **2 let off ~**
  : desahogarse — ~ *vi* : echar vapor —
  vt **1** : cocer al vapor **2 ~ up** : empañar
  — **steam engine** *n* : motor *m* de vapor
  — **steamship** ['stiːmˌʃɪp] *n* : (barco *m*
  de) vapor *m* — **steamy** ['stiːmi] *adj*
  steamier; -est 1 : lleno de vapor **2**
  PASSIONATE : tórrido
steel ['stiːl] *n* : acero *m* — ~ *vt* ~ **one-**
  self : armarse de valor — ~ *adj* : de
  acero
steep[1] ['stiːp] *adj* **1** : empinado **2** CON-
  SIDERABLE : considerable **3** : muy alto
  (dícese de precios)
steep[2] *vt* : dejar (té, etc.) en infusión
steeple ['stiːpəl] *n* : aguja *f*, campanario
  m
steer[1] ['stɪr] *n* : buey *m*
steer[2] *vt* : dirigir (un auto, etc.), pilotear
  (un barco) — **steering wheel** *n*
  : volante *m*
stem[1] ['stɛm] *n* : tallo *m* (de una planta),
  pie *m* (de una copa) — ~ *vi* ~ **from**
  : provenir de
stem[2] *vt* **stemmed; stemming** : contener, detener

stench ['stɛntʃ] *n* : hedor *m*, mal olor *m*
stencil ['stɛntsəl] *n* : plantilla *f* (para
  marcar)
step ['stɛp] *n* **1** : paso *m* **2** RUNG, STAIR
  : escalón *m* **3 ~ by ~** : paso por paso
  4 take ~s : tomar medidas **5 watch**
  your ~ : mira por dónde caminas —
  ~ *vi* **stepped; stepping 1** : dar un
  paso **2 ~ back** : retroceder **3 ~ down**
  RESIGN : retirarse **4 ~ in** : intervenir **5**
  ~ out : salir (por un momento) **6 ~**
  this way : pase por aquí — **step up** *vt*
  INCREASE : aumentar
stepbrother ['stɛpˌbrʌðər] *n* : hermanastro *m* — **stepdaughter** ['stɛpˌdɔtər] *n*
  : hijastra *f* — **stepfather** ['stɛpˌfɑðər,
  -fa-] *n* : padrastro *m*
stepladder ['stɛpˌlædər] *n* : escalera *f* de
  tijera
stepmother ['stɛpˌmʌðər] *n* : madrastra *f*
  — **stepsister** ['stɛpˌsɪstər] *n* : hermanastra *f* — **stepson** ['stɛpˌsʌn] *n*
  : hijastro *m*
stereo ['stɛriˌoː, 'stɪr-] *n, pl* **stereos** : estéreo *m* — ~ *adj* : estéreo
stereotype ['stɛriəˌtaɪp, 'stɪr-] *vt* **-typed;**
  -typing : estereotipar — ~ *n* : estereotipo *m*
sterile ['stɛrəl] *adj* : estéril — **sterility**
  [stəˈrɪləti] *n* : esterilidad *f* — **steriliza-**
  tion [ˌstɛrələˈzeɪʃən] *n* : esterilización *f*
  — **sterilize** ['stɛrəˌlaɪz] *vt* **-ized; -izing**
  : esterilizar
sterling ['stərlɪŋ] *adj* : excelente — **ster-**
  ling silver *n* : plata *f* de ley
stern[1] ['stərn] *adj* : severo, adusto
stern[2] *n* : popa *f*
stethoscope ['stɛθəˌskoːp] *n* : estetosco-
  pio *m*
stew ['stuː, 'stjuː] *n* : estofado *m*, guiso *m*
  — ~ *vt* : estofar, guisar — *vi* **1** : cocer
  2 FRET : preocuparse
steward ['stuːərd, 'stjuː-] *n* **1** : administrador *m*, -dora *f* **2** : auxiliar *m* de
  vuelo (en un avión) **3** : camarero *m* (en
  un barco) — **stewardess** ['stuːərdəs,
  'stjuː-] *n* **1** : auxiliar *f* de vuelo, azafata
  f (en un avión) **2** : camarera *f* (en un
  barco)
stick[1] ['stɪk] *n* **1** : palo *m* **2** TWIG : ramita *f* (suelta) **3** WALKING STICK : bastón
  m
stick[2] *v* **stuck** ['stʌk]; **sticking** *vt* **1**
  : pegar **2** STAB : clavar **3** PUT : poner **4**
  ~ out : sacar (la lengua, etc.) — *vi* **1**
  : pegarse **2** JAM : atascarse **3 ~**
  around : quedarse **4 ~ out** PROTRUDE
  : sobresalir **5 ~ out** SHOW : asomar **6**
  ~ up : sobresalir **7 ~ up for** : defender — **sticker** ['stɪkər] *n* : etiqueta *f*

adhesiva — **stickler** ['stɪklər] n **be a ~ for** : insistir mucho en — **sticky** ['stɪki] adj **stickier; -est** : pegajoso

stiff ['stɪf] adj **1** RIGID : rígido, tieso **2** STILTED : forzado **3** STRONG : fuerte **4** DIFFICULT : difícil **5** : entumecido (dícese de músculos) — **stiffen** ['stɪfən] vt : fortalecer, hacer más duro — vi **1** HARDEN : endurecerse **2** : entumecerse (dícese de músculos) — **stiffness** ['stɪfnəs] n : rigidez f

stifle ['staɪfəl] vt **-fled; -fling** : sofocar

stigmatize ['stɪgmətaɪz] vt **-tized; -tizing** : estigmatizar

still ['stɪl] adj **1** : inmóvil **2** SILENT : callado — adv **1** : todavía, aún **2** NEVERTHELESS : de todos modos, aún así **3 sit ~!** : ¡quédate quieto! — ~ n : quietud f, calma f — **stillborn** ['stɪl,bɔrn] adj : nacido muerto — **stillness** ['stɪlnəs] n : calma f, silencio m

stilt ['stɪlt] n : zanco m — **stilted** ['stɪltəd] adj : forzado

stimulate ['stɪmjə,leɪt] vt **-lated; -lating** : estimular — **stimulant** ['stɪmjələnt] n : estimulante m — **stimulation** [,stɪmjə'leɪʃən] n : estimulación f — **stimulus** ['stɪmjələs] n, pl **-li** [-,laɪ] : estímulo m

sting ['stɪŋ] v **stung** ['stʌŋ]; **stinging** : picar — ~ n : picadura f — **stinger** ['stɪŋər] n : aguijón m

stingy ['stɪndʒi] adj **stingier; -est** : tacaño — **stinginess** ['stɪndʒinəs] n : tacañería f

stink ['stɪŋk] vi **stank** ['stæŋk] or **stunk** ['stʌŋk]; **stunk; stinking** : apestar, oler mal — ~ n : hedor m, peste f fam

stint ['stɪnt] vi **~ on** : escatimar — ~ n : período m

stipulate ['stɪpjə,leɪt] vt **-lated; -lating** : estipular

stir ['stər] v **stirred; stirring** vt **1** : remover, revolver **2** MOVE : mover **3** INCITE : incitar **4** or **~ up** : despertar (memorias, etc.), provocar (ira, etc.) — vi : moverse, agitarse — ~ n COMMOTION : revuelo m

stirrup ['stərəp, 'stɪr-] n : estribo m

stitch ['stɪtʃ] n **1** : puntada f **2** PAIN : punzada f (en el costado) — ~ v : coser

stock ['stɑk] n **1** INVENTORY : existencias fpl **2** SECURITIES : acciones fpl **3** ANCESTRY : linaje m, estirpe f **4** BROTH : caldo m **5 out of ~** : agotado **6 take ~ of** : evaluar — ~ vt : surtir, abastecer — vi **~ up on** : abastecerse de — **stockbroker** ['stɑk,broːkər] n : corredor m, -dora f de bolsa

stocking ['stɑkɪŋ] n : media f

stock market n : bolsa f — **stockpile** ['stɑk,paɪl] n : reservas fpl — ~ vt **-piled; -piling** : almacenar — **stocky** ['stɑki] adj **stockier; -est** : robusto, fornido

stodgy ['stɑdʒi] adj **stodgier; -est 1** DULL : pesado **2** OLD-FASHIONED : anticuado

stoic ['stoːɪk] n : estoico m, -ca f — ~ or **stoical** [-ɪkəl] adj : estoico — **stoicism** ['stoːə,sɪzəm] n : estoicismo m

stoke ['stoːk] vt **stoked; stoking** : echar carbón o leña a

stole¹ ['stoːl] → **steal**

stole² n : estola f

stolen → **steal**

stomach ['stʌmɪk] n : estómago m — ~ vt : aguantar, soportar — **stomachache** ['stʌmɪk,eɪk] n : dolor m de estómago

stone ['stoːn] n **1** : piedra f **2** : hueso m (de una fruta) — ~ vt **stoned; stoning** : apedrear — **stony** ['stoːni] adj **stonier; -est 1** : pedregoso **2 a ~ silence** : un silencio sepulcral

stood → **stand**

stool ['stuːl] n : taburete m

stoop ['stuːp] vi **1** : agacharse **2 ~ to** : rebajarse a — ~ n **have a ~** : ser encorvado

stop ['stɑp] v **stopped; stopping** vt **1** PLUG : tapar **2** PREVENT : impedir **3** HALT : parar, detener **4** CEASE : dejar de — vi **1** : detenerse, parar **2** CEASE : cesar, dejar **3 ~ by** : visitar — ~ n **1** : parada f, alto m **2 come to a ~** : pararse, detenerse **3 put a ~ to** : poner fin a — **stopgap** ['stɑp,gæp] n : arreglo m provisorio — **stoplight** ['stɑp,laɪt] n : semáforo m — **stoppage** ['stɑpɪdʒ] n or **work ~** : paro m — **stopper** ['stɑpər] n : tapón m

store ['stɔr] vt **stored; storing** : guardar (comida, etc.), almacenar (datos, mercancías, etc.) — ~ n **1** SUPPLY : reserva f **2** SHOP : tienda f — **storage** ['stɔrɪdʒ] n : almacenamiento m — **storehouse** ['stɔr,haʊs] n : almacén m — **storekeeper** ['stɔr,kiːpər] n : tendero m, -ra f — **storeroom** ['stɔr,ruːm, -,rʊm] n : almacén m

stork ['stɔrk] n : cigüeña f

storm ['stɔrm] n : tormenta f, tempestad f — ~ vi **1** RAGE : ponerse furioso **2 ~ in/out** : entrar/salir furioso — ~ vt ATTACK : asaltar — **stormy** ['stɔrmi] adj **stormier; -est** : tormentoso

story¹ ['stɔri] n, pl **stories 1** TALE : cuento m **2** ACCOUNT : historia f **3** RUMOR : rumor m

story[2] *n* FLOOR : piso *m*, planta *f*
stout ['staut] *adj* 1 BRAVE : valiente 2 RESOLUTE : tenaz 3 STURDY : fuerte 4 FAT : corpulento
stove[1] ['sto:v] *n* 1 : estufa *f* (para calentar) 2 RANGE : cocina *f*
stove[2] → stave
stow ['sto:] *vt* 1 : guardar 2 LOAD : cargar — *vi* ~ away : viajar de polizón — **stowaway** ['sto:ə,weɪ] *n* : polizón *m*
straddle ['strædəl] *vt* -dled; -dling : sentarse a horcajadas sobre
straggle ['strægəl] *vi* -gled; -gling : rezagarse, quedarse atrás — **straggler** ['strægələr] *n* : rezagado *m*, -da *f*
straight ['streɪt] *adj* 1 : recto, derecho 2 : lacio (dícese del pelo) 3 HONEST : franco 4 TIDY : arreglado — ~ *adv* 1 DIRECTLY : derecho 2 EXACTLY : justo 3 CLEARLY : con claridad 4 FRANKLY : con franqueza — **straightaway** ['streɪt,weɪ, -,weɪ] *adv* : inmediatamente — **straighten** ['streɪtən] *vt* 1 : enderezar 2 ~ up : arreglar — **straightforward** [streɪt'fɔrwərd] *adj* 1 FRANK : franco 2 CLEAR : claro, sencillo
strain[1] ['streɪn] *n* 1 LINEAGE : linaje *m* 2 STREAK : veta *f* 3 VARIETY : variedad *f* 4 ~s *npl* : acordes *mpl* (de música)
strain[2] *vt* 1 : forzar (la vista o la voz) 2 FILTER : colar 3 : tensar (relaciones, etc.) 4 ~ a muscle : sufrir un esguince 5 ~ oneself : hacerse daño — *vi* : esforzarse (por) — ~ *n* 1 STRESS : tensión *f* 2 SPRAIN : esguince *m* — **strainer** ['streɪnər] *n* : colador *m*
strait ['streɪt] *n* : estrecho *m* 2 in dire ~s : en grandes apuros
strand[1] ['strænd] *vt* be ~ed : quedar(se) varado
strand[2] *n* 1 : hebra *f* 2 a ~ of hair : un pelo
strange ['streɪndʒ] *adj* **stranger; -est** 1 : extraño, raro 2 UNFAMILIAR : desconocido — **strangely** ['streɪndʒli] *adv* : de manera extraña — **strangeness** ['streɪndʒnəs] *n* 1 : rareza *f* 2 UNFAMILIARITY : lo desconocido — **stranger** ['streɪndʒər] *n* : desconocido *m*, -da *f*
strangle ['stræŋgəl] *vt* -gled; -gling : estrangular
strap ['stræp] *n* 1 : correa *f* 2 or shoulder ~ : tirante *m* — ~ *vt* **strapped; strapping** : sujetar con una correa — **strapless** ['stræpləs] *n* : sin tirantes — **strapping** ['stræpɪŋ] *adj* : robusto, fornido
strategy ['strætədʒi] *n*, *pl* **-gies** : estrate-

gia *f* — **strategic** [strə'ti:dʒɪk] *adj* : estratégico
straw ['strɔ] *n* 1 : paja *f* 2 or drinking ~ : pajita *f* 3 the last ~ : el colmo
strawberry ['strɔ,beri] *n*, *pl* **-ries** : fresa *f*
stray ['streɪ] *n* : animal *m* perdido — ~ *vi* 1 : perderse, extraviarse 2 : apartarse (de un grupo, etc.) 3 DEVIATE : desviarse — ~ *adj* : perdido
streak ['stri:k] *n* 1 : raya *f* 2 VEIN : veta *f* 3 ~ of luck : racha *f* de suerte — *vi* ~ by : pasar como una flecha
stream ['stri:m] *n* 1 : arroyo *m*, riachuelo *m* 2 FLOW : chorro *m*, corriente *f* — *vi* : correr — **streamer** ['stri:mər] *n* 1 PENNANT : banderín *m* 2 : serpentina *f* (de papel) — **streamlined** ['stri:m,laɪnd] *adj* 1 : aerodinámico 2 EFFICIENT : eficiente
street ['stri:t] *n* : calle *f* — **streetcar** ['stri:t,kɑr] *n* : tranvía *m* — **streetlight** ['stri:t,laɪt] *n* : farol *m*
strength ['streŋkθ] *n* 1 : fuerza *f* 2 FORTITUDE : fortaleza *f* 3 TOUGHNESS : resistencia *f*, solidez *f* 4 INTENSITY : intensidad *f* 5 ~s and weaknesses : virtudes y defectos — **strengthen** ['streŋkθən] *vt* 1 : fortalecer 2 REINFORCE : reforzar 3 INTENSIFY : intensificar
strenuous ['strenjuəs] *adj* 1 : enérgico 2 ARDUOUS : duro, riguroso
stress ['stres] *n* 1 : tensión *f* 2 EMPHASIS : énfasis *m* 3 : acento *m* (en lingüística) — ~ *vt* 1 EMPHASIZE : enfatizar 2 or ~ out : estresar — **stressful** ['stresfəl] *adj* : estresante
stretch ['stretʃ] *vt* 1 : estirar (músculos, elástico, etc.) 2 EXTEND : extender 3 ~ the truth : forzar la verdad — *vi* 1 : estirarse 2 EXTEND : extenderse — ~ *n* 1 : extensión *f* 2 ELASTICITY : elasticidad *f* 3 EXPANSE : tramo *m* 4 : período *m* (de tiempo) — **stretcher** ['stretʃər] *n* : camilla *f*
strew ['stru:] *vt* **strewed; strewed** *or* **strewn** ['stru:n]; **strewing** : esparcir (semillas, etc.), desparramar (papeles, etc.)
stricken ['strɪkən] *adj* ~ with : aquejado de (una enfermedad), afligido por (tristeza, etc.)
strict ['strɪkt] *adj* : estricto — **strictly** *adv* ~ speaking : en rigor
stride ['straɪd] *vi* **strode** ['stro:d]; **stridden** ['strɪdən]; **striding** : ir dando zancadas — ~ *n* 1 : zancada *f* 2 make great ~s : hacer grandes progresos
strident ['straɪdənt] *adj* : estridente
strife ['straɪf] *n* : conflictos *mpl*

strike ['straɪk] v **struck** ['strʌk]; **struck;**
striking vt 1 HIT : golpear 2 or ~
against : chocar contra 3 or ~ **out**
DELETE : tachar 4 : dar (la hora) 5 IM-
PRESS : impresionar 6 : descubrir (oro
o petróleo) 7 it ~s me as... : me
parece... 8 ~ **up** START : entablar —
vi 1 : golpear 2 ATTACK : atacar 3 : declararse en huelga 4 : sobrevenir
(dícese de una enfermedad, etc.) — ~
n 1 BLOW : golpe m 2 : huelga f, paro m
Lat (de trabajadores) 3 ATTACK
: ataque m — **strikebreaker** ['straɪk-
‚breɪkər] n : esquirol mf — **striker**
['straɪkər] n : huelguista mf — **striking**
['straɪkɪŋ] adj : notable, llamativo

string ['strɪŋ] n 1 : cordel m 2 : sarta f
(de perlas, insultos, etc.), serie f (de
eventos, etc.) 3 ~s npl : cuerdas fpl
(en música) — ~ vt **strung** ['strʌŋ];
stringing 1 : ensartar 2 or ~ **up** : colgar — **string bean** n : habichuela f
verde

stringent ['strɪndʒənt] adj : estricto,
severo

strip¹ ['strɪp] v **stripped; stripping** vt 1
REMOVE : quitar 2 UNDRESS : desnudar
3 ~ **s.o. of sth** : despojar a algn de
algo — vi UNDRESS : desnudarse

strip² n : tira f

stripe ['straɪp] n : raya f, lista f —
striped ['straɪpt, 'straɪpəd] adj : a rayas,
rayado

strive ['straɪv] vi **strove** ['stroːv]; **striven**
['strɪvən] or **strived**; **striving** 1 ~ **for**
: luchar por 2 ~ **to** : esforzarse por

strode → **stride**

stroke ['stroːk] vt **stroked; stroking**
: acariciar — ~ n 1 : golpe m 2 : derrame m cerebral (en medicina)

stroll ['stroːl] vi : pasearse — ~ n
: paseo m — **stroller** ['stroːlər] n
: cochecito m (para niños)

strong ['strɔŋ] adj : fuerte — **stronghold** ['strɔŋhoːld] n : bastión m —
strongly ['strɔŋli] adv 1 DEEPLY : profundamente 2 WHOLEHEARTEDLY : totalmente 3 VIGOROUSLY : enérgica-
mente

strove → **strive**

struck → **strike**

structure ['strʌktʃər] n : estructura f —
structural ['strʌktʃərəl] adj : estructural

struggle ['strʌgəl] vi **-gled; -gling** 1
: forcejear 2 STRIVE : luchar — ~ n
: lucha f

strum ['strʌm] vt **strummed; strum-
ming** : rasguear

strung → **string**

strut ['strʌt] vi **strutted; strutting** : pavonearse — ~ n : puntal m (en construcción)

stub ['stʌb] n : colilla f (de un cigarrillo),
cabo m (de un lápiz, etc.), talón m (de
un cheque) — ~ vt **stubbed; stub-
bing** ~ **one's toe** : darse en el dedo

stubble ['stʌbəl] n : barba f de varios
días

stubborn ['stʌbərn] adj 1 : terco, obstinado 2 PERSISTENT : tenaz

stucco ['stʌkoː] n, pl **stuccos** or **stuc-
coes** : estuco m

stuck → **stick** — **stuck-up** ['stʌk'ʌp]
adj : engreído, creído fam

stud¹ ['stʌd] n : semental m (animal)

stud² n 1 NAIL, TACK : tachuela f, tachón
m 2 or ~ **earring** : arete m Lat, pendiente m Spain 3 : montante m (en
construcción)

student ['stuːdənt, 'stjuː-] n : estudiante
mf; alumno m, -na f (de un colegio) —
studio ['stuːdi‚oː, 'stjuː-] n, pl **studios**
: estudio m — **study** ['stʌdi] n, pl **studies** : estudio m — ~ v **studied;
studying** : estudiar — **studious** ['stuː-
diəs, 'stjuː-] adj : estudioso

stuff ['stʌf] n 1 : cosas fpl 2 MATTER,
SUBSTANCE : cosa f 3 **know one's** ~
: ser experto — ~ vt 1 FILL : rellenar
2 CRAM : meter — **stuffing** ['stʌfɪŋ] n
: relleno m — **stuffy** ['stʌfi] adj **stuffi-
er; -est 1** STODGY : pesado, aburrido 2
: tapado (dícese de la nariz) 3 ~
rooms : salas fpl mal ventiladas

stumble ['stʌmbəl] vi **-bled; -bling** 1
: tropezar 2 ~ **across** or **upon**
: tropezar con

stump ['stʌmp] n 1 : muñón m (de una
pierna, etc.) 2 or **tree** ~ : tocón m —
~ vt : dejar perplejo

stun ['stʌn] vt **stunned; stunning** 1
: aturdir (con un golpe) 2 ASTONISH
: dejar atónito

stung → **sting**

stunk → **stink**

stunning ['stʌnɪŋ] adj 1 : increíble, sensacional 2 STRIKING : imponente

stunt¹ ['stʌnt] vt : atrofiar

stunt² n : proeza f (acrobática)

stupendous [stʊ'pɛndəs, stjuː-] adj : estupendo

stupid ['stuːpəd, 'stjuː-] adj 1 : estúpido 2
SILLY : tonto, bobo — **stupidity** [stuː-
'pɪdəti, stjuː-] n : tontería f, estupidez f

sturdy ['stərdi] adj **sturdier; -est 1**
: fuerte, resistente 2 ROBUST : robusto

stutter ['stʌtər] vi : tartamudear — ~ n
: tartamudeo m

sty ['staɪ] n 1 pl **sties** PIGPEN : pocilga f

2 *pl* **sties** *or* **styes** : orzuelo *m* (en el ojo)

style ['staɪl] *n* **1** : estilo *m* **2** FASHION : moda *f* **3 be in —** : estar de moda — *vt* **styled; styling** : peinar (pelo), diseñar (vestidos, etc.) — **stylish** ['staɪlɪʃ] *adj* : elegante, chic — **stylist** ['staɪlɪst] *n* : estilista *mf*

suave ['swɑv] *adj* : refinado y afable

sub[1] ['sʌb] *vi* **subbed; subbing → substitute —** ~ *n* → **substitute**

sub[2] *n* → **submarine**

subconscious [sʌb'kɑntʃəs] *adj* : subconsciente — ~ *n* : subconsciente *m*

subdivide [sʌbdə'vaɪd, 'sʌbdə,vaɪd] *vt* **-vided; -viding** : subdividir — **subdivision** ['sʌbdə,vɪʒən] *n* : subdivisión *f*

subdue [səb'du:, -'dju:] *vt* **-dued; -duing 1** CONQUER : sojuzgar **2** CONTROL : dominar **3** SOFTEN : atenuar — **subdued** *adj* : apagado

subject ['sʌbdʒɪkt] *n* **1** : sujeto *m* **2** : súbdito *m*, -ta *f* (de un gobierno) **3** TOPIC : tema *m* — *adj* **1** : sometido **2** ~ **to** : sujeto a — ~ [səb'dʒɛkt] *vt* ~ **to** : someter a — **subjective** [səb'dʒɛktɪv] *adj* : subjetivo

subjunctive [səb'dʒʌŋktɪv] *n* : subjuntivo *m* — **subjunctive** *adj* : subjuntivo

sublime [sə'blaɪm] *adj* : sublime

submarine ['sʌbmə,riːn, ˌsʌbmə'-] *adj* : submarino — ~ *n* : submarino *m*

submerge [səb'mərdʒ] *v* **-merged; -merging** *vt* : sumergir — *vi* : sumergirse

submit [səb'mɪt] *v* **-mitted; -mitting** *vi* **1** YIELD : rendirse **2** ~ **to** : someterse a — *vt* : presentar — **submission** [səb-'mɪʃən] *n* **1** : sumisión *f* **2** PRESENTATION : presentación *f* — **submissive** [səb-'mɪsɪv] *adj* : sumiso

subordinate [sə'bɔrdənət] *adj* : subordinado — ~ *n* : subordinado *m*, -da *f* — ~ [sə'bɔrdən,eɪt] *vt* **-nated; -nating** : subordinar

subpoena [sə'pi:nə] *n* : citación *f*

subscribe [səb'skraɪb] *vi* **-scribed; -scribing** ~ **to** : suscribirse a (una revista, etc.), suscribir (una opinión, etc.) — **subscriber** [səb'skraɪbər] *n* : suscriptor *m*, -tora *f* (de una revista, etc.); abonado *m*, -da *f* (de un servicio) — **subscription** [səb'skrɪpʃən] *n* : suscripción *f*

subsequent ['sʌbsɪkwənt, -sə,kwent] *adj* **1** : subsiguiente **2** ~ **to** : posterior a — **subsequently** ['sʌb,kwentli, -kwənt-] *adv* : posteriormente

subservient [səb'sərviənt] *adj* : servil

subside [səb'saɪd] *vi* **-sided; -siding 1** SINK : hundirse **2** : amainar (dícese de tormentas, pasiones, etc.), remitir (dícese de fiebres, etc.)

subsidiary [səb'sɪdi,eri] *adj* : secundario — ~ *n, pl* **-ries** : filial *f*

subsidy ['sʌbsədi] *n, pl* **-dies** : subvención *f* — **subsidize** ['sʌbsə,daɪz] *vt* **-dized; -dizing** : subvencionar

subsistence [səb'sɪstənts] *n* : subsistencia *f* — **subsist** [səb'sɪst] *vi* : subsistir

substance ['sʌbstənts] *n* : sustancia *f*

substandard [sʌb'stændərd] *adj* : inferior

substantial [səb'stæntʃəl] *adj* **1** CONSIDERABLE : considerable **2** STURDY : sólido **3** : sustancioso (dícese de una comida, etc.) — **substantially** [səb-'stæntʃəli] *adv* : considerablemente

substitute ['sʌbstə,tu:t, -,tju:t] *n* : sustituto *m*, -ta *f* (de una persona); sucedáneo *m* (de una cosa) — ~ *vt* **-tuted; -tuting** : sustituir — **substitution** [ˌsʌbstə'tu:ʃən, -'tju:-] *n* : sustitución *f*

subterranean [ˌsʌbtə'reɪniən] *adj* : subterráneo

subtitle ['sʌb,taɪtəl] *n* : subtítulo *m*

subtle ['sʌtəl] *adj* **-tler; -tlest** : sutil — **subtlety** ['sʌtəlti] *n, pl* **-ties** : sutileza *f*

subtraction [səb'trækʃən] *n* : resta *f* — **subtract** [səb'trækt] *vt* : restar

suburb ['sʌ,bərb] *n* **1** : barrio *m* residencial, suburbio *m* **2 the —s** : las afueras — **suburban** [sə'bərbən] *adj* : de las afueras (de una ciudad)

subversion [səb'vərʒən] *n* : subversión *f* — **subversive** [səb'vərsɪv] *adj* : subversivo

subway ['sʌb,weɪ] *n* : metro *m*

succeed [sək'si:d] *vt* : suceder a — *vi* : tener éxito (dícese de personas), dar resultado (dícese de planes, etc.) — **success** [sək'sɛs] *n* : éxito *m* — **successful** [sək'sɛsfəl] *adj* : de éxito, exitoso *Lat* — **successfully** *adv* : con éxito

succession [sək'sɛʃən] *n* **1** : sucesión *f* **2 in** ~ : sucesivamente, seguidos — **successive** [sək'sɛsɪv] *adj* : sucesivo — **successor** [sək'sɛsər] *n* : sucesor *m*, -sora *f*

succinct [sək'sɪŋkt, sə'sɪŋkt] *adj* : sucinto

succulent ['sʌkjələnt] *adj* : suculento

succumb [sə'kʌm] *vi* : sucumbir

such ['sʌtʃ] *adj* **1** : tal **2** ~ **as** : como **3** ~ **a pity!** : ¡qué lástima! — ~ *pron* **1** : tal **2 and** ~ : y cosas por el estilo **3 as** ~ : como tal — ~ *adv* **1** VERY : muy **2** ~ **a nice man!** : ¡qué hombre tan simpático! **3** ~ **that** : de tal manera que

suck ['sʌk] *vt* **1** *or* ~ **on** : chupar **2** *or* ~ **up** : sorber (bebidas), aspirar (con una máquina) — **sucker** ['sʌkər] *n* **1** SHOOT : chupón *m* **2** FOOL : imbécil *mf* — **suckle** ['sʌkəl] *vt* -**led**; -**ling** : amamantar — **suction** ['sʌkʃən] *n* : succión *f*

sudden ['sʌdən] *adj* **1** : repentino **2 all of a** ~ : de repente — **suddenly** ['sʌdənli] *adv* : de repente

suds ['sʌdz] *npl* : espuma *f* (de jabón)

sue ['su:] *vt* **sued**; **suing** : demandar (por)

suede ['sweɪd] *n* : ante *m*, gamuza *f*

suet ['su:ət] *n* : sebo *m*

suffer ['sʌfər] *vi* : sufrir — *vt* **1** : sufrir **2** BEAR : tolerar — **suffering** ['sʌfərɪŋ] *n* : sufrimiento *m*

suffice [sə'faɪs] *vi* -**ficed**; -**ficing** : bastar — **sufficient** [sə'fɪʃənt] *adj* : suficiente — **sufficiently** [sə'fɪʃəntli] *adv* : (lo) suficientemente

suffix ['sʌ,fɪks] *n* : sufijo *m*

suffocate ['sʌfə,keɪt] *v* -**cated**; -**cating** *vt* : asfixiar — *vi* : asfixiarse — **suffocation** [,sʌfə'keɪʃən] *n* : asfixia *f*

suffrage ['sʌfrɪdʒ] *n* : sufragio *m*

sugar ['ʃʊgər] *n* : azúcar *mf* — **sugarcane** ['ʃʊgər,keɪn] *n* : caña *f* de azúcar — **sugary** ['ʃʊgəri] *adj* : azucarado

suggestion [səg'dʒestʃən, sə-] *n* **1** : sugerencia *f* **2** TRACE : indicio *m* — **suggest** [səg'dʒest, sə-] *vt* **1** : sugerir **2** INDICATE : indicar

suicide ['su:ə,saɪd] *n* **1** : suicidio *m* (acto) **2** : suicida *mf* (persona) — **suicidal** [,su:ə'saɪdəl] *adj* : suicida

suit ['su:t] *n* **1** LAWSUIT : pleito *m* **2** : traje *m* (ropa) **3** : palo *m* (de naipes) — *vt* **1** ADAPT : adaptar **2** BEFIT : ser apropiado para **3** ~ **s.o.** : convenir a algn (dícese de fechas, etc.), quedar bien a algn (dícese de ropa) — **suitable** ['su:təbəl] *adj* : apropiado — **suitcase** ['su:t,keɪs] *n* : maleta *f*, valija *f Lat*

suite ['swi:t, *for 2 also* 'su:t] *n* **1** : suite *f* (de habitaciones) **2** : juego *m* (de muebles)

suitor ['su:tər] *n* : pretendiente *m*

sulfur ['sʌlfər] *n* : azufre *m*

sulk ['sʌlk] *vi* : enfurruñarse *fam* — **sulky** ['sʌlki] *adj* **sulkier**; -**est** : malhumorado

sullen ['sʌlən] *adj* : hosco

sultry ['sʌltri] *adj* **sultrier**; -**est 1** : bochornoso **2** SENSUAL : sensual

sum ['sʌm] *n* : suma *f* — ~ *vt* **summed**; **summing** ~ **up** : resumir — **summarize** ['sʌmə,raɪz] *v* -**rized**; -**rizing** : resumir — **summary** ['sʌməri] *n*, *pl* -**ries** : resumen *m*

summer ['sʌmər] *n* : verano *m*

summit ['sʌmət] *n* : cumbre *f*

summon ['sʌmən] *vt* **1** : llamar (a algn), convocar (una reunión) **2** : citar (en derecho) — **summons** ['sʌmənz] *n*, *pl* **summonses** SUBPOENA : citación *f*

sumptuous ['sʌmptʃuəs] *adj* : suntuoso

sun ['sʌn] *n* : sol *m* — **sunbathe** ['sʌn,beɪð] *vi* -**bathed**; -**bathing** : tomar el sol — **sunbeam** ['sʌn,bi:m] *n* : rayo *m* de sol — **sunburn** ['sʌn,bərn] *n* : quemadura *f* de sol

Sunday ['sʌn,deɪ, -di] *n* : domingo *m*

sundry ['sʌndri] *adj* : varios, diversos

sunflower ['sʌn,flaʊər] *n* : girasol *m*

sung → **sing**

sunglasses ['sʌn,glæsəz] *npl* : gafas *fpl* de sol, lentes *mpl* de sol

sunk → **sink** — **sunken** ['sʌŋkən] *adj* : hundido

sunlight ['sʌn,laɪt] *n* : (luz *f* del) sol *m* — **sunny** ['sʌni] *adj* -**nier**; -**est** : soleado — **sunrise** ['sʌn,raɪz] *n* : salida *f* del sol — **sunset** ['sʌn,set] *n* : puesta *f* del sol — **sunshine** ['sʌn,ʃaɪn] *n* : sol *m*, luz *f* del sol — **suntan** ['sʌn,tæn] *n* : bronceado *m*

super ['su:pər] *adj* : súper *fam*

superb [su'pərb] *adj* : magnífico, espléndido

superficial [,su:pər'fɪʃəl] *adj* : superficial

superfluous [su'pərfluəs] *adj* : superfluo

superimpose [,su:pərɪm'po:z] *vt* -**posed**; -**posing** : sobreponer

superintendent [,su:pərɪn'tendənt] *n* **1** : superintendente *mf* (de policía) **2** *or* **building** ~ : portero *m*, -ra *f* **3** *or* **school** ~ : director *m*, -tora *f* (de un colegio)

superior [su'pɪriər] *adj* : superior — ~ *n* : superior *m* — **superiority** [su,pɪri'ɔrəti] *n*, *pl* -**ties** : superioridad *f*

superlative [su'pərlətɪv] *adj* **1** : superlativo (en gramática) **2** EXCELLENT : excepcional — ~ *n* : superlativo *m*

supermarket ['su:pər,mɑrkət] *n* : supermercado *m*

supernatural [,su:pər'nætʃərəl] *adj* : sobrenatural

superpower ['su:pər,paʊər] *n* : superpotencia *f*

supersede [,su:pər'si:d] *vt* -**seded**; -**seding** : reemplazar, suplantar

supersonic [,su:pər'sɑnɪk] *adj* : supersónico

superstition [,su:pər'stɪʃən] *n* : superstición *f* — **superstitious** [,su:pər'stɪʃəs] *adj* : supersticioso

supervisor ['su:pər,vaɪzər] *n* : supervisor

m, -sora *f* — **supervise** ['suːpər,vaɪz] *vt*
-vised; -vising : supervisar — **supervision** [,suːpər'vɪʒən] *n* : supervisión *f*
— **supervisory** [,suːpər'vaɪzəri] *adj*
: de supervisor
supper ['sʌpər] *n* : cena *f*, comida *f*
supplant [sə'plænt] *vt* : suplantar
supple ['sʌpəl] *adj* **-pler; -plest** : flexible
supplement ['sʌpləmənt] *n* : suplemento *m* — **~** ['sʌplə,ment] *vt* : complementar — **supplementary** [,sʌplə-
'mentəri] *adj* : suplementario
supply [sə'plaɪ] *vt* **-plied; -plying 1**
: suministrar **2 ~ with** : proveer de —
~ *n*, *pl* **-plies 1** : suministro *m*, provisión *f* **2 ~ and demand** : oferta y
demanda **3 supplies** *npl* PROVISIONS
: provisiones *fpl*, víveres *mpl* — **supplier** [sə'plaɪər] *n* : proveedor *m*, -dora *f*
support [sə'port] *vt* **1** BACK : apoyar **2**
: mantener (una familia, etc.) **3** PROP
UP : sostener — **~** *n* **1** : apoyo *m*
(moral), ayuda *f* (económica) **2** PROP
: soporte *m* — **supporter** [sə'portər] *n*
: partidario *m*, -ria *f*
suppose [sə'poːz] *vt* **-posed; -posing 1**
: suponer **2 be ~d to (do sth)** : tener
que (hacer algo) — **supposedly** *adv*
: supuestamente
suppress [sə'pres] *vt* **1** : reprimir **2**
: suprimir (noticias, etc.) — **suppression** [sə'preʃən] *n* **1** : represión *f* **2**
: supresión *f* (de información)
supreme [su'priːm] *adj* : supremo — **supremacy** [su'preməsi] *n*, *pl* **-cies** : supremacía *f*
sure ['ʃur] *adj* **surer; -est 1** : seguro **2**
make ~ that : asegurarse de que —
~ *adv* **1** OF COURSE : por supuesto,
claro **2 it — is hot!** : ¡qué calor! —
surely ['ʃurli] *adv* : seguramente
surfing ['sərfɪŋ] *n* : surf *m*, surfing *m*
surface ['sərfəs] *n* : superficie *f* — **~** *v*
-faced; -facing *vi* : salir a la superficie
— *vt* : revestir
surfeit ['sərfət] *n* : exceso *m*
surfing ['sərfɪŋ] *n* : surf *m*, surfing *m*
surge ['sərdʒ] *vi* **surged; surging 1**
SWELL : hincharse (dícese del mar) **2**
SWARM : moverse en tropel — **~** *n* **1**
: oleaje *m* (del mar), oleada *f* (de gente)
2 INCREASE : aumento *m* (súbito)
surgeon ['sərdʒən] *n* : cirujano *m*, -na *f*
— **surgery** ['sərdʒəri] *n*, *pl* **-geries**
: cirugía *f* — **surgical** ['sərdʒɪkəl] *adj*
: quirúrgico
surly ['sərli] *adj* **surlier; -est** : hosco,
arisco
surmount [sər'maunt] *vt* : superar

surname ['sər,neɪm] *n* : apellido *m*
surpass [sər'pæs] *vt* : superar
surplus ['sər,plʌs] *n* : excedente *m*
surprise [sə'praɪz, sər-] *n* **1** : sorpresa *f* **2**
take by ~ : sorprender — **~** *vt*
-prised; -prising : sorprender — **surprising** [sə'praɪzɪŋ, sər-] *adj* : sorprendente
surrender [sə'rendər] *vt* : entregar,
rendir — *vi* : rendirse — **~** *n* : rendición *m* (de una ciudad, etc.), entrega *f*
(de posesiones)
surrogate ['sərəgət, -geɪt] *n* : sustituto *m*
surround [sə'raund] *vt* : rodear — **surroundings** [sə'raundɪŋz] *npl* : ambiente *m*
surveillance [sər'veɪlənts, -'veɪljənts,
-'veɪənts] *n* : vigilancia *f*
survey [sər'veɪ] *vt* **-veyed; -veying 1**
: medir (un solar) **2** INSPECT : inspeccionar **3** POLL : sondear — **~** ['sər,veɪ]
n, *pl* **-veys 1** INSPECTION : inspección *f*
2 : medición *f* (de un solar) **3** POLL
: encuesta *f*, sondeo *m* — **surveyor**
[sər'veɪər] *n* : agrimensor *m*, -sora *f*
survive [sər'vaɪv] *v* **-vived; -viving** *vi*
: sobrevivir — *vt* : sobrevivir a — **survival** [sər'vaɪvəl] *n* : supervivencia *f* —
survivor [sər'vaɪvər] *n* : superviviente
mf
susceptible [sə'septəbəl] *adj* **~ to**
: propenso a — **susceptibility** [sə-
,septə'bɪləti] *n*, *pl* **-ties** : propensión *f* (a
enfermedades, etc.)
suspect ['sʌs,pekt, sə'spekt] *adj* : sospechoso — **~** ['sʌs,pekt] *n* : sospechoso
m, -sa *f* — **~** [sə'spekt] *vt* : sospechar
(algo), sospechar de (algn)
suspend [sə'spend] *vt* : suspender —
suspense [sə'spents] *n* **1** : incertidumbre *m* **2** : suspenso *m* *Lat*, suspense *m*
Spain (en el cine, etc.) — **suspension**
[sə'spentʃən] *n* : suspensión *f*
suspicion [sə'spɪʃən] *n* : sospecha *f* —
suspicious [sə'spɪʃəs] *adj* **1** QUESTION-
ABLE : sospechoso **2** DISTRUSTFUL
: suspicaz
sustain [sə'steɪn] *vt* **1** : sostener **2** SUF-
FER : sufrir
swagger ['swægər] *vi* : pavonearse
swallow[1] ['swaloː] *v* : tragar — **~** *n*
: trago *m*
swallow[2] *n* : golondrina *f* (pájaro)
swam → swim
swamp ['swɑmp] *n* : pantano *m*, ciénaga
f — **~** *vt* : inundar — **swampy**
['swɑmpi] *adj* **swampier; -est** : pantanoso, cenagoso
swan ['swɑn] *n* : cisne *f*
swap ['swɑp] *vt* **swapped; swapping 1**

: intercambiar **2 ~ sth for sth** : cambiar algo por algo **3 ~ sth with s.o.** : cambiar algo a algn — **~** *n* : cambio *m*

swarm ['sworm] *n* : enjambre *m* — **~** *vi* : enjambrar

swat ['swɑt] *vt* **swatted; swatting** : aplastar (un insecto)

sway ['sweɪ] *n* **1** : balanceo *m* **2** INFLUENCE : influjo *m* — **~** *vi* : balancearse — *vt* : influir en

swear ['swær] *v* **swore** ['swor]; **sworn** ['sworn]; **swearing** *vi* **1** : jurar **2** CURSE : decir palabrotas — *vt* : jurar — **swearword** ['swær,wərd] *n* : palabrota *f*

sweat ['swɛt] *vi* **sweat** *or* **sweated; sweating** : sudar — **~** *n* : sudor *m* — **sweater** ['swɛtər] *n* : suéter *m* — **sweatshirt** ['swɛt,ʃərt] *n* : sudadera *f* — **sweaty** ['swɛti] *adj* **sweatier; -est** : sudado

Swedish ['swiːdɪʃ] *adj* : sueco — **~** *n* : sueco *m* (idioma)

sweep ['swiːp] *v* **swept** ['swɛpt]; **sweeping** *vt* **1** : barrer **2 ~ aside** : apartar **3 ~ through** : extenderse por — *vi* **1** : barrer — **~** *n* **1** : barrido *m* **2** : movimiento *m* circular (de la mano, etc.) **3** SCOPE : alcance *m* — **sweeping** ['swiːpɪŋ] *adj* **1** WIDE : amplio **2** EXTENSIVE : extenso — **sweepstakes** ['swiːp,steɪks] *ns & pl* : lotería *f*

sweet ['swiːt] *adj* **1** : dulce **2** PLEASANT : agradable — **~** *n* : dulce *m* — **sweeten** ['swiːtən] *vt* : endulzar — **sweetener** ['swiːtənər] *n* : endulzante *m* — **sweetheart** ['swiːt,hɑrt] *n* **1** : novio *m*, -via *f* **2** (*used as a form of address*) : cariño — **sweetness** ['swiːtnəs] *n* : dulzura *f* — **sweet potato** *n* : batata *f*, boniato *m*

swell ['swɛl] *vi* **swelled; swelled** *or* **swollen** ['swoːlən, 'swʌl-]; **swelling 1** *or* **~ up** : hincharse **2** INCREASE : aumentar, crecer — **~** *n* : oleaje *m* (del mar) — **swelling** ['swɛlɪŋ] *n* : hinchazón *f*

sweltering ['swɛltərɪŋ] *adj* : sofocante

swept → sweep

swerve ['swərv] *vi* **swerved; swerving** : virar bruscamente

swift ['swɪft] *adj* : rápido — **swiftly** *adv* : rápidamente

swig ['swɪg] *n* : trago *m* — **~** *vi* **swigged; swigging** : beber a tragos

swim ['swɪm] *vi* **swam** ['swæm]; **swum** ['swʌm]; **swimming 1** : nadar **2** REEL : dar vueltas — **~** *n* **1** : baño *m* **2 go for a ~** : ir a nadar — **swimmer** ['swɪmər] *n* : nadador *m*, -dora *f*

swindle ['swɪndəl] *vt* **-dled; -dling** : estafar, timar — **~** *n* : estafa *f*, timo *m fam*

swine ['swaɪn] *ns & pl* : cerdo *m*, -da *f*

swing ['swɪŋ] *v* **swung** ['swʌŋ]; **swinging** *vt* **1** : balancear, hacer oscilar **2** MANAGE : arreglar — *vi* **1** : balancearse, oscilar **2** SWIVEL : girar — **~** *n* **1** : vaivén *m*, balanceo *m* **2** SHIFT : cambio *m* **3** : columpio *m* (para niños) **4 in full ~** : en pleno proceso

swipe ['swaɪp] *v* **swiped; swiping** *vt* STEAL : birlar *fam*, robar — *vi* **~ at** : intentar pegar

swirl ['swərl] *vi* : arremolinarse — **~** *n* **1** EDDY : remolino *m* **2** SPIRAL : espiral *f*

swish ['swɪʃ] *vt* : agitar (haciendo un sonido) — *vi* **1** RUSTLE : hacer frufrú **2 ~ by** : pasar silbando

Swiss ['swɪs] *adj* : suizo

switch ['swɪtʃ] *n* **1** WHIP : vara *f* **2** CHANGE : cambio *m* **3** : interruptor *m*, llave *f* (de la luz, etc.) — **~** *vt* **1** CHANGE : cambiar de **2** EXCHANGE : intercambiar **3 ~ on** : encender, prender *Lat* **4 ~ off** : apagar — *vi* **1** : sacudir (la cola, etc.) **2** CHANGE : cambiar **3** SWAP : intercambiarse — **switchboard** ['swɪtʃ,bord] *n* : centralita *f*, conmutador *m Lat*

swivel ['swɪvəl] *vi* **-veled** *or* **-velled; -veling** *or* **-velling** : girar (sobre un pivote)

swollen → swell

swoon ['swuːn] *vi* : desvanecerse

swoop ['swuːp] *vi* **~ down on** : abatirse sobre — **~** *n* : descenso *m* en picada

sword ['sord] *n* : espada *f*

swordfish ['sord,fɪʃ] *n* : pez *m* espada

swore, sworn → swear

swum → swim

swung → swing

syllable ['sɪləbəl] *n* : sílaba *f*

syllabus ['sɪləbəs] *n*, *pl* **-bi** [-,baɪ] *or* **-buses** : programa *m* (de estudios)

symbol ['sɪmbəl] *n* : símbolo *m* — **symbolic** [sɪm'bɑlɪk] *adj* : simbólico — **symbolism** ['sɪmbə,lɪzəm] *n* : simbolismo *m* — **symbolize** ['sɪmbə,laɪz] *vt* **-ized; -izing** : simbolizar

symmetry ['sɪmətri] *n*, *pl* **-tries** : simetría *f* — **symmetrical** [sə'mɛtrɪkəl] *adj* : simétrico

sympathy ['sɪmpəθi] *n*, *pl* **-thies 1** COMPASSION : compasión *f* **2** UNDERSTANDING : comprensión *f* **3** CONDOLENCES : pésame *m* **4 sympathies** *npl* LOYALTY : simpatías *fpl* — **sympathize** ['sɪmpə,θaɪz] *vi* **-thized; -thizing 1 ~ with** PITY : compadecerse de **2 ~**

with UNDERSTAND : comprender —
sympathetic [,sɪmpə'θetɪk] *adj* 1 COM-
PASSIONATE : compasivo 2 UNDER-
STANDING : comprensivo
symphony ['sɪmfəni] *n, pl* **-nies** : sinfonía *f*
symposium [sɪm'po:ziəm] *n, pl* **-sia**
[-ziə] *or* **-siums** : simposio *m*
symptom ['sɪmptəm] *n* : síntoma *m* —
symptomatic [,sɪmptə'mætɪk] *adj*
: sintomático
synagogue ['sɪnəgɑg, -,gɔg] *n* : sinagoga *f*
synchronize ['sɪŋkrə,naɪz, 'sɪn-] *vt*
-nized; -nizing : sincronizar
syndrome ['sɪn,droːm] *n* : síndrome *m*
synonym ['sɪnə,nɪm] *n* : sinónimo *m* —

synonymous [sə'nɑnəməs] *adj* : sinónimo
synopsis [sə'nɑpsɪs] *n, pl* **-opses** [-,siːz]
: sinopsis *f*
syntax ['sɪn,tæks] *n* : sintaxis *f*
synthesis ['sɪnθəsɪs] *n, pl* **-theses** [-,siːz]
: síntesis *f* — **synthesize** ['sɪnθə,saɪz] *vt*
-sized; -sizing : sintetizar — **synthetic** [sɪn'θetɪk] *adj* : sintético
syphilis ['sɪfələs] *n* : sífilis *f*
Syrian ['sɪriən] *adj* : sirio
syringe [sə'rɪndʒ, 'sɪrɪndʒ] *n* : jeringa *f*,
jeringuilla *f*
syrup ['sərəp, 'sɪrəp] *n* : jarabe *m*
system ['sɪstəm] *n* 1 : sistema *m* 2 BODY
: organismo *m* 3 **digestive ~** : aparato *m* digestivo — **systematic** [,sɪstə-
'mætɪk] *adj* : sistemático

T

t ['tiː] *n, pl* **t's** *or* **ts** ['tiːz] : t *f*, vigésima
letra del alfabeto inglés
tab ['tæb] *n* 1 TAG : etiqueta *f* 2 FLAP
: lengüeta *f* 3 ACCOUNT : cuenta *f* 4
keep ~s on : vigilar
table ['teɪbəl] *n* 1 : mesa *f* 2 LIST : tabla *f*
3 **~ of contents** : índice *m* de materias — **tablecloth** ['teɪbəl,klɔθ] *n*
: mantel *m* — **tablespoon** ['teɪbəl-
,spuːn] *n* 1 : cuchara *f* grande 2 : cucharada *f* (cantidad)
tablet ['tæblət] *n* 1 PAD : bloc *m* 2 PILL
: pastilla *f* 3 *or* **stone ~** : lápida *f*
tabloid ['tæb,lɔɪd] *n* : tabloide *m*
taboo [tə'buː, tæ-] *adj* : tabú — *n*
: tabú *m*
tacit ['tæsɪt] *adj* : tácito
taciturn ['tæsɪ,tərn] *adj* : taciturno
tack ['tæk] *vt* 1 : fijar con tachuelas 2 **~
on** ADD : añadir — *n* 1 : tachuela *f*
2 **change ~** : cambiar de rumbo
tackle ['tækəl] *n* 1 GEAR : aparejo *m* 2
: placaje *m*, tacle *m Lat* (acción) — **~**
vt **-led; -ling** 1 : placar, taclear *Lat* 2
CONFRONT : abordar
tacky ['tæki] *adj* **tackier; -est** 1 : pegajoso 2 GAUDY : de mal gusto
tact ['tækt] *n* : tacto *m* — **tactful**
['tæktfəl] *adj* : diplomático, discreto
tactical ['tæktɪkəl] *adj* : táctico — **tactic**
['tæktɪk] *n* : táctica *f* — **tactics** ['tæk-
tɪks] *ns & pl* : táctica *f*
tactless ['tæktləs] *adj* : indiscreto
tadpole ['tæd,poːl] *n* : renacuajo *m*
tag[1] ['tæg] *n* LABEL : etiqueta *f* — **~** *v*
tagged; tagging *vt* : etiquetar — *vi*

~ along with s.o. : acompañar a algn
tag[2] *vt* : tocar (en varios juegos)
tail ['teɪl] *n* 1 : cola *f* 2 **~s** *npl* : cruz *f*
(de una moneda) — *vt* FOLLOW
: seguir
tailor ['teɪlər] *n* : sastre *m*, -tra *f* — **~** *vt*
1 : confeccionar (ropa) 2 ADAPT : adap-
tar
taint ['teɪnt] *vt* : contaminar
take ['teɪk] *v* **took** ['tʊk]; **taken** ['teɪkən];
taking *vt* 1 : tomar 2 BRING : llevar 3
REMOVE : sacar 4 BEAR : soportar,
aguantar 5 ACCEPT : aceptar 6 **I ~ it
that...** : supongo que... 7 **~ a bath**
: bañarse 8 **~ a walk** : dar un paseo 9
~ back : retirar (palabras, etc.) 10 **~
in** ALTER : achicar 11 **~ in** GRASP : entender 12 **~ in** TRICK : engañar 13 **~
off** REMOVE : quitar, quitarse (ropa) 14
~ on : asumir (una responsabilidad,
etc.) 15 **~ out** : sacar 16 **~ over**
: tomar el poder de 17 **~ place** : tener
lugar 18 **~ up** SHORTEN : acortar 19
~ up OCCUPY : ocupar — *vi* 1 : prender (dícese de una vacuna, etc.) 2 **~
off** : despegar (dícese de aviones, etc.)
3 **~ over** : asumir el mando — **~** 1
PROCEEDS : ingresos *mpl* 2 : toma *f* (en
el cine) — **takeoff** ['teɪk,ɔf] *n* : despegue *m* (de un avión, etc.) —
takeover ['teɪk,oːvər] *n* : toma *f* (de
poder, etc.), adquisición *f* (de una empresa)
talcum powder ['tælkəm] *n* : polvos *mpl*
de talco
tale ['teɪl] *n* : cuento *m*

talent ['tælənt] n : talento m — **talented** ['tæləntəd] adj : talentoso

talk ['tɔk] vi 1 : hablar 2 ~ **about** : hablar de 3 ~ **to/with** : hablar con — vt 1 SPEAK : hablar 2 ~ **over** : hablar de, discutir — ~ n 1 CHAT : conversación f 2 SPEECH : charla f — **talkative** ['tɔkətɪv] adj : hablador

tall ['tɔl] adj 1 : alto 2 **how ~ are you?** : ¿cuánto mides?

tally ['tæli] n, pl **-lies** : cuenta f — ~ v **-lied; -lying** vt RECKON : calcular — vi MATCH : concordar, cuadrar

talon ['tælən] n : garra f

tambourine [tæmbə'riːn] n : pandereta f

tame ['teɪm] adj **tamer; -est** 1 : domesticado 2 DOCILE : manso 3 DULL : insípido, soso — ~ vt **tamed; taming** : domar

tamper ['tæmpər] vi ~ **with** : forzar (una cerradura), amañar (documentos, etc.)

tampon ['tæm,pɑn] n : tampón m

tan ['tæn] v **tanned; tanning** vt : curtir (cuero) — vi : broncearse — ~ n 1 SUNTAN : bronceado m 2 : (color m) café m con leche

tang ['tæŋ] n : sabor m fuerte

tangent ['tændʒənt] n : tangente f

tangerine ['tændʒə,riːn, ,tændʒə'-] n : mandarina f

tangible ['tændʒəbəl] adj : tangible

tangle ['tæŋgəl] v **-gled; -gling** vt : enredar — vi : enredarse — ~ n : enredo m

tango ['tæŋgoː] n, pl **-gos** : tango m

tank ['tæŋk] n 1 : tanque m, depósito m 2 : tanque m (militar) — **tanker** ['tæŋkər] n 1 : buque m tanque 2 or ~ **truck** : camión m cisterna

tantalizing ['tæntə,laɪzɪŋ] adj : tentador

tantrum ['tæntrəm] n **throw a ~** : hacer un berrinche

tap¹ ['tæp] n FAUCET : llave f, grifo m Spain — ~ vt **tapped; tapping** 1 : sacar (un líquido, etc.), sangrar (un árbol) 2 : intervenir (un teléfono)

tap² vt **tapped; tapping** STRIKE : tocar, dar un golpecito en — ~ n : golpecito m, toque m

tape ['teɪp] n : cinta f — ~ vt **taped; taping** 1 : pegar con cinta 2 RECORD : grabar — **tape measure** n : cinta f métrica

taper ['teɪpər] n : vela f (larga) — ~ vi 1 NARROW : estrecharse 2 or ~ **off** : disminuir

tapestry ['tæpəstri] n, pl **-tries** : tapiz m

tar ['tɑr] n : alquitrán m — ~ vt **tarred; tarring** : alquitranar

tarantula [tə'ræntʃələ, -'ræntələ] n : tarántula f

target ['tɑrgət] n 1 : blanco m 2 GOAL : objetivo m

tariff ['tærɪf] n : tarifa f, arancel m

tarnish ['tɑrnɪʃ] vt 1 : deslustrar 2 : empañar (una reputación, etc.) — vi : deslustrarse

tart¹ ['tɑrt] adj SOUR : ácido, agrio

tart² n : pastel m

tartan ['tɑrtən] n : tartán m

task ['tæsk] n : tarea f

tassel ['tæsəl] n : borla f

taste ['teɪst] v **tasted; tasting** vt TRY : probar — vi 1 : saber 2 ~ **like** : saber a — ~ n 1 FLAVOR : gusto m, sabor m 2 **have a ~ of** : probar 3 **in good/bad ~** : de buen/mal gusto — **tasteful** ['teɪstfəl] adj : de buen gusto — **tasteless** ['teɪstləs] adj 1 : sin sabor 2 COARSE : de mal gusto — **tasty** ['teɪsti] adj **tastier; -est** : sabroso

tatters ['tæţərz] npl : harapos mpl — **tattered** ['tæţərd] adj : harapiento

tattle ['tæţəl] vi **-tled; -tling** ~ **on s.o.** : acusar a algn

tattoo [tæ'tuː] vt : tatuar — ~ n : tatuaje m

taught → teach

taunt ['tɔnt] n : pulla f, burla f — ~ vt : mofarse de, burlarse de

taut ['tɔt] adj : tirante, tenso

tavern ['tævərn] n : taberna f

tax ['tæks] vt 1 : gravar 2 STRAIN : poner a prueba — ~ n 1 : impuesto m 2 BURDEN : carga f — **taxable** ['tæksəbəl] adj : imponible — **taxation** [tæk'seɪʃən] n : impuestos mpl — **tax-exempt** ['tæksɪg'zempt, -eg-] adj : libre de impuestos

taxi ['tæksi] n, pl **taxis** : taxi m — ~ vi **taxied; taxiing** or **taxying; taxis** or **taxies** : rodar por la pista (dícese de un avión)

taxpayer ['tæks,peɪər] n : contribuyente mf

tea ['tiː] n : té m

teach ['tiːtʃ] v **taught** ['tɔt]; **teaching** vt : enseñar, dar clases de (una asignatura) — vi : dar clases — **teacher** ['tiːtʃər] n : profesor m, -sora f; maestro m, -tra f (de niños pequeños) — **teaching** ['tiːtʃɪŋ] n : enseñanza f

teacup ['tiː,kʌp] n : taza f de té

team ['tiːm] n : equipo m — ~ vi or ~ **up** : asociarse — **teammate** ['tiːm,meɪt] n : compañero m, -ra f de equipo — **teamwork** ['tiːm,wərk] n : trabajo m de equipo

teapot ['tiː,pɑt] n : tetera f

tear¹ ['tær] v **tore** ['tor]; **torn** ['torn]; **tearing** vt **1** : romper, rasgar **2** ~ **apart** : destrozar **3** ~ **down** : derribar **4** ~ **off** or ~ **out** : arrancar **5** ~ **up** : romper (papel, etc.) — vi **1** : romperse, rasgarse **2** RUSH : ir a toda velocidad — ~ n : desgarro m, rasgón m

tear² ['tɪr] n : lágrima f — **tearful** ['tɪrfəl] adj : lloroso

tease ['tiːz] vt **teased**; **teasing 1** : tomar el pelo a, burlarse de **2** ANNOY : fastidiar

teaspoon ['tiːˌspuːn] n **1** : cucharita f **2** : cucharadita f (cantidad)

technical ['tɛknɪkəl] adj : técnico — **technicality** [ˌtɛknəˈkæləti] n, pl **-ties** : detalle m técnico — **technically** [-kli] adv : técnicamente — **technician** [tɛkˈnɪʃən] n : técnico m, -ca f

technique [tɛkˈniːk] n : técnica f

technological [ˌtɛknəˈladʒɪkəl] adj : tecnológico — **technology** [tɛkˈnalədʒi] n, pl **-gies** : tecnología f

teddy bear ['tɛdi] n : oso m de peluche

tedious ['tiːdiəs] adj : tedioso, aburrido — **tedium** ['tiːdiəm] n : tedio m

tee ['tiː] n : tee m (en deportes)

teem ['tiːm] vi **1** POUR : llover a cántaros **2** be ~**ing with** : estar repleto de

teenage ['tiːnˌeɪdʒ] or **teenaged** [-ˌeɪdʒd] adj : adolescente — **teenager** ['tiːnˌeɪdʒər] n : adolescente mf — **teens** ['tiːnz] npl : adolescencia f

teepee → **tepee**

teeter ['tiːtər] vi : tambalearse

teeth → **tooth** — **teethe** ['tiːð] vi **teethed**; **teething** : echar los dientes

telecommunication [ˌtɛləkəˌmjuːnəˈkeɪʃən] n : telecomunicación f

telegram ['tɛləˌgræm] n : telegrama m

telegraph ['tɛləˌgræf] n : telégrafo m — ~ v : telegrafiar

telephone ['tɛləˌfoʊn] n : teléfono m — ~ v **-phoned**; **-phoning** : llamar por teléfono

telescope ['tɛləˌskoʊp] n : telescopio m

televise ['tɛləˌvaɪz] vt **-vised**; **-vising** : televisar — **television** ['tɛləˌvɪʒən] n : televisión f

tell ['tɛl] v **told** ['toʊld]; **telling** vt **1** : decir **2** RELATE : contar **3** DISTINGUISH : distinguir **4** ~ **s.o. off** : regañar a algn — vi **1** : decir **2** KNOW : saber **3** SHOW : tener efecto **4** ~ **on s.o.** : acusar a algn — **teller** ['tɛlər] n or **bank** ~ : cajero m, -ra f

temp ['tɛmp] n : empleado m, -da f temporal

temper ['tɛmpər] vt MODERATE : temperar — ~ n **1** MOOD : humor m **2 have a bad** ~ : tener mal genio **3 lose one's** ~ : perder los estribos — **temperament** ['tɛmpərmənt, -prə-, -pərə-] n : temperamento m — **temperamental** [ˌtɛmpərˈmɛntəl, -prə-, -pərə-] adj : temperamental — **temperate** ['tɛmpərət] adj **1** : moderado **2** ~ **zone** : zona f templada

temperature ['tɛmpərˌtʃʊr, -prə-, -pərə-, -tʃər] n **1** : temperatura f **2 have a** ~ : tener fiebre

tempest ['tɛmpəst] n : tempestad f

temple ['tɛmpəl] n **1** : templo m **2** : sien f (en anatomía)

tempo ['tɛmpoː] n, pl **-pi** [-ˌpiː] or **-pos 1** : tempo m **2** PACE : ritmo m

temporarily [ˌtɛmpəˈrɛrəli] adv : temporalmente — **temporary** ['tɛmpəˌrɛri] adj : temporal

tempt ['tɛmpt] vt : tentar — **temptation** [tɛmpˈteɪʃən] n : tentación f

ten ['tɛn] adj : diez — ~ n : diez m

tenacity [təˈnæsəti] n : tenacidad f — **tenacious** [təˈneɪʃəs] adj : tenaz

tenant ['tɛnənt] n : inquilino m, -na f; arrendatario m, -ria f

tend¹ ['tɛnd] vt MIND : cuidar

tend² vi ~ **to** : tender a — **tendency** ['tɛndənʦi] n, pl **-cies** : tendencia f

tender¹ ['tɛndər] adj **1** : tierno **2** PAINFUL : dolorido

tender² vt : presentar — ~ n **1** : oferta f **2 legal** ~ : moneda f de curso legal

tenderloin ['tɛndərˌlɔɪn] n : lomo f (de cerdo o vaca)

tenderness ['tɛndərnəs] n : ternura f

tendon ['tɛndən] n : tendón m

tenet ['tɛnət] n : principio m

tennis ['tɛnəs] n : tenis m

tenor ['tɛnər] n : tenor m

tense¹ ['tɛnʦ] n : tiempo m (de un verbo)

tense² v **tensed**; **tensing** vt : tensar — vi : tensarse — ~ adj **tenser**; **tensest** : tenso — **tension** ['tɛnʃən] n : tensión f

tent ['tɛnt] n : tienda f de campaña

tentacle ['tɛntɪkəl] n : tentáculo m

tentative ['tɛntətɪv] adj **1** HESITANT : vacilante **2** PROVISIONAL : provisional

tenth ['tɛnθ] adj : décimo — ~ n **1** : décimo m, -ma f (en una serie) **2** : décimo m (en matemáticas)

tenuous ['tɛnjuəs] adj : tenue, endeble

tepid ['tɛpɪd] adj : tibio

term ['tɜrm] n **1** WORD : término m **2** PERIOD : período m **3 be on good** ~**s** : tener buenas relaciones **4 in** ~**s of** : con respecto a — ~ vt : calificar de

terminal ['tərmənəl] *adj* : terminal — **~** *n* **1** : terminal *m* **2** *or* **bus ~** : terminal *f*

terminate ['tərmə,neɪt] *v* **-nated; -nating** *vi* : terminar(se) — *vt* : poner fin a — **termination** [,tərmə'neɪʃən] *n* : terminación *f*

termite ['tər,maɪt] *n* : termita *f*

terrace ['terəs] *n* : terraza *f*

terrain [tə'reɪn] *n* : terreno *m*

terrestrial [tə'restriəl] *adj* : terrestre

terrible ['terəbəl] *adj* : espantoso, terrible — **terribly** ['terəbli] *adv* : terriblemente

terrier ['teriər] *n* : terrier *mf*

terrific [tə'rɪfɪk] *adj* **1** HUGE : tremendo **2** EXCELLENT : estupendo

terrify ['terə,faɪ] *vt* **-fied; -fying** : aterrar, aterrorizar — **terrifying** ['terə,faɪɪŋ] *adj* : aterrador

territory ['terə,tori] *n, pl* **-ries** : territorio *m* — **territorial** [,terə'toriəl] *adj* : territorial

terror ['terər] *n* : terror *m* — **terrorism** ['terər,ɪzəm] *n* : terrorismo *m* — **terrorist** ['terərɪst] *n* : terrorista *mf* — **terrorize** ['terər,aɪz] *vt* **-ized; -izing** : aterrorizar

terse ['tərs] *adj* **terser; tersest** : seco, lacónico

test ['test] *n* **1** TRIAL : prueba *f* **2** EXAM : examen *m*, prueba *f* **3** : análisis *m* (en medicina) — **~** *vt* **1** TRY : probar **2** QUIZ : examinar **3** : analizar (la sangre, etc.), examinar (los ojos, etc.)

testament ['testəmənt] *n* **1** WILL : testamento *m* **2 the Old/New Testament** : el Antiguo/Nuevo Testamento

testicle ['testɪkəl] *n* : testículo *m*

testify ['testə,faɪ] *v* **-fied; -fying** : testificar

testimony ['testə,moni] *n, pl* **-nies** : testimonio *m*

test tube *n* : probeta *f*, tubo *m* de ensayo

tetanus ['tetənəs] *n* : tétano *m*

tether ['teðər] *vt* : atar

text ['tekst] *n* : texto *m* — **textbook** ['tekst,bʊk] *n* : libro *m* de texto

textile ['tek,staɪl, 'tekstəl] *n* : textil *m*

texture ['tekstʃər] *n* : textura *f*

than ['ðæn] *conj & prep* : que, de (con cantidades)

thank ['θæŋk] *vt* **1** : agradecer, dar (las) gracias a **2 ~ you!** : ¡gracias! — **thankful** ['θæŋkfəl] *adj* : agradecido — **thankfully** ['θæŋkfəli] *adv* **1** : con agradecimiento **2** FORTUNATELY : gracias a Dios — **thanks** ['θæŋks] *npl* **1** : agradecimiento *m* **2 ~!** : ¡gracias!

Thanksgiving [θæŋks'gɪvɪŋ, 'θæŋks,-] *n* : día *m* de Acción de Gracias

that ['ðæt] *pron, pl* **those** ['ðoːz] **1** : ése, ésa, eso **2** (*more distant*) : aquél, aquélla, aquello **3 is ~ you?** : ¿eres tú? **4 like ~** : así **5 ~ is...** : es decir... **6 those who...** : los que... — **~** *conj* : que — **~** *adj, pl* **those 1** : ese, esa **2** (*more distant*) : aquel, aquella **3 ~ one** : ése, ésa — **~** *adv* : tan

thatched ['θætʃt] *adj* : con techo de paja

thaw ['θɔ] *vt* : descongelar (alimentos), derretir (hielo) — *vi* **1** : descongelarse **2** MELT : derretirse — **~** *n* : deshielo *m*

the [ðə, *before vowel sounds usu* ðiː] *art* **1** : el, la, los, las **2** PER : por — **~** *adv* **1 ~ sooner ~ better** : cuanto más pronto, mejor **2 I like this one ~ best** : éste es el que más me gusta

theater *or* **theatre** ['θiːətər] *n* : teatro *m* — **theatrical** [θi'ætrɪkəl] *adj* : teatral

theft ['θeft] *n* : robo *m*, hurto *m*

their ['ðer] *adj* : su, sus, de ellos, de ellas — **theirs** ['ðerz] *pron* **1** : el) suyo, (la) suya, (los) suyos, (las) suyas **2 some friends of ~** : unos amigos suyos, unos amigos de ellos

them ['ðem] *pron* **1** (*used as direct object*) : los, las **2** (*used as indirect object*) : les, se **3** (*used as object of a preposition*) : ellos, ellas

theme ['θiːm] *n* **1** : tema *m* **2** ESSAY : trabajo *m* (escrito)

themselves [ðəm'selvz, ðem-] *pron* **1** (*used reflexively*) : se **2** (*used emphatically*) : ellos mismos, ellas mismas **3** (*used after a preposition*) : sí (mismos), sí (mismas)

then ['ðen] *adv* **1** : entonces **2** NEXT : luego, después **3** BESIDES : además — **~** *adj* : entonces

thence ['ðens, 'θents] *adv* : de ahí (en adelante)

theology [θi'alədʒi] *n, pl* **-gies** : teología *f* — **theological** [,θiə'ladʒɪkəl] *adj* : teológico

theorem ['θiːərəm, 'θɪrəm] *n* : teorema *m* — **theoretical** [,θiə'retɪkəl] *adj* : teórico — **theory** ['θiːəri, 'θɪri] *n, pl* **-ries** : teoría *f*

therapeutic [,θerə'pjutɪk] *adj* : terapéutico — **therapist** ['θerəpɪst] *n* : terapeuta *mf* — **therapy** ['θerəpi] *n, pl* **-pies** : terapia *f*

there ['ðer] *adv* **1** *or* **over ~** : allí, allá **2** *or* **right ~** : ahí **3 in ~** : ahí (dentro) **4 ~, it's done!** : ¡listo! **5 up/down ~** : ahí arriba/abajo **6**

who's ~? : ¿quién es? — ~ *pron* 1
~ is/are : hay 2 ~ are three of us
: somos tres — **thereabouts** *or* **there-
about** [ˌðærəˈbauts, -ˈbaut; ˈðærə-] *adv*
or ~ : por ahí — **thereafter** [ðær-
ˈæftər] *adv* : después — **thereby** [ðær-
ˈbai, ˈðær,bai] *adv* : así — **therefore**
[ˈðær,for] *adv* : por lo tanto

thermal [ˈθərməl] *adj* : térmico

thermometer [θərˈmɑmətər] *n* : termómetro *m*

thermos [ˈθərməs] *n* : termo *m*

thermostat [ˈθərmə,stæt] *n* : termostato
m

thesaurus [θɪˈsɔrəs] *n, pl* **-sauri** [-ˈsɔr,ai]
or **-sauruses** [-ˈsɔrəsəz] : diccionario
m de sinónimos

these → this

thesis [ˈθiːsɪs] *n, pl* **theses** [ˈθiː,siːz]
: tesis *f*

they [ˈðei] *pron* 1 : ellos, ellas 2 where
are ~? : ¿dónde están? 3 as ~ say
: como dicen — **they'd** [ˈðeid] (*contraction of* **they had** *or* **they would**)
→ **have, would** — **they'll** [ˈðeil, ðel]
(*contraction of* **they shall** *or* **they
will**) → **shall, will** — **they're** [ðer]
(*contraction of* **they are**) → **be** —
they've [ˈðeiv] (*contraction of* **they
have**) → **have**

thick [ˈθɪk] *adj* 1 : grueso 2 DENSE : espeso 3 a ~ **accent** : un acento marcado 4 it's two inches ~ : tiene dos
pulgadas de grosor — ~ *n* in the ~
of : en medio de — **thicken** [ˈθɪkən] *vt*
: espesar — *vi* : espesarse — **thicket**
[ˈθɪkət] *n* : matorral *m* — **thickness**
[ˈθɪknəs] *n* : grosor *m*, espesor *m*

thief [ˈθiːf] *n, pl* **thieves** [ˈθiːvz] : ladrón
m, -drona *f*

thigh [ˈθai] *n* : muslo *m*

thimble [ˈθɪmbəl] *n* : dedal *m*

thin [ˈθɪn] *adj* **thinner; -est** 1 : delgado
2 : ralo (dícese del pelo) 3 WATERY
: claro, aguado 4 FINE : fino — ~ *v*
thinned; thinning *vt* DILUTE : diluir
— *vi* : ralear (dícese del pelo)

thing [ˈθɪŋ] *n* 1 : cosa *f* 2 for one ~ : en
primer lugar 3 how are ~s? : ¿qué
tal? 4 it's a good ~ that... : menos
mal que... 5 the **important** ~ **is...**
: lo importante es...

think [ˈθɪŋk] *v* **thought** [ˈθɔt]; **thinking**
vt 1 : pensar 2 BELIEVE : creer 3 ~ **up**
: idear — *vi* 1 : pensar 2 ~ **about** *or*
~ **of** CONSIDER : pensar en 3 ~ **of** RE-
MEMBER : acordarse de 4 what do you
~ **of it?** : ¿qué te parece? — **thinker**
[ˈθɪŋkər] *n* : pensador *m*, -dora *f*

third [ˈθərd] *adj* : tercero — ~ *or* **third-**

ly [-li] *adv* : en tercer lugar — ~ *n* 1
: tercero *m*, -ra *f* (en una serie) 2 :
tercero *m* (en matemáticas) — **Third
World** *n* : Tercer Mundo *m*

thirst [ˈθərst] *n* : sed *f* — **thirsty** [ˈθərsti]
adj **thirstier; -est** 1 : sediento 2 be ~
: tener sed

thirteen [ˌθərˈtiːn] *adj* : trece — ~ *n*
: trece *m* — **thirteenth** [ˌθərˈtiːnθ] *adj*
: décimo tercero — ~ *n* 1 : déci-
motercero *m*, -ra *f* (en una serie) 2
: treceavo *m* (en matemáticas)

thirty [ˈθərti] *adj* : treinta — ~ *n*,
pl **thirties** : treinta *m* — **thirtieth**
[ˈθərtiəθ] *adj* : trigésimo — ~ *n* 1
: trigésimo *m*, -ma *f* (en una serie) 2
: treintavo *m* (en matemáticas)

this [ˈðɪs] *pron, pl* **these** [ˈðiːz] 1 : éste,
ésta, esto 2 **like** ~ : así — ~ *adj, pl*
these 1 : este, esta 2 ~ **one** : éste,
ésta 3 ~ **way** : por aquí — ~ *adv* ~
big : así de grande

thistle [ˈθɪsəl] *n* : cardo *m*

thong [ˈθɔŋ] *n* 1 : correa *f* 2 SANDAL
: chancla *f*

thorn [ˈθɔrn] *n* : espina *f* — **thorny**
[ˈθɔrni] *adj* : espinoso

thorough [ˈθəro] *adj* 1 : meticuloso 2
COMPLETE : completo — **thoroughly**
adv 1 : a fondo COMPLETELY : completamente — **thoroughbred** [ˈθəro-
,bred] *adj* : de pura sangre — **thor-
oughfare** [ˈθəro,fær] *n* : vía *f* pública

those → that

though [ˈðo] *conj* : aunque — ~ *adv* 1
: sin embargo 2 as ~ : como si

thought [ˈθɔt] → **think** — ~ *n* 1 : pensamiento *m* 2 IDEA : idea *f* — **thoughtful** [ˈθɔtfəl] *adj* 1 : pensativo 2 KIND
: amable — **thoughtless** [ˈθɔtləs] *adj*
1 CARELESS : descuidado 2 RUDE : desconsiderado

thousand [ˈθauzənd] *adj* : mil — ~ *n*,
pl **-sands** *or* **-sand** : mil *m* — **thousandth** [ˈθauzənθ] *adj* : milésimo —
~ *n* 1 : milésimo *m*, -ma *f* (en una
serie) 2 : milésimo *m* (en matemáticas)

thrash [ˈθræʃ] *vt* : dar una paliza a — *vi*
or ~ **around** : agitarse, revolcarse

thread [ˈθred] *n* 1 : hilo *m* 2 : rosca *f* (de
un tornillo) — ~ *vt* : enhilar (una
aguja), ensartar (cuentas) — **thread-
bare** [ˈθred,bær] *adj* : raído

threat [ˈθret] *n* : amenaza *f* — **threaten**
[ˈθretən] *v* : amenazar — **threatening**
[ˈθretəniŋ] *adj* : amenazador

three [ˈθriː] *adj* : tres — ~ *n* : tres *m* —
three hundred *adj* : trescientos — ~
n : trescientos *m*

threshold ['θreʃˌhoːld, -ˌoːld] n : umbral m

threw → **throw**

thrift ['θrɪft] n : frugalidad f — **thrifty** ['θrɪfti] adj **thriftier; -est** : económico, frugal

thrill ['θrɪl] vt : emocionar — ~ n : emoción f — **thriller** ['θrɪlər] n : película f de suspense Spain, película f de suspenso Lat — **thrilling** ['θrɪlɪŋ] adj : emocionante

thrive ['θraɪv] vi **throve** ['θroːv] or **thrived; thriven** ['θrɪvən] 1 FLOURISH : florecer 2 PROSPER : prosperar

throat ['θroːt] n : garganta f

throb ['θrɑb] vi **throbbed; throbbing** 1 PULSATE : palpitar 2 VIBRATE : vibrar 3 ~ **with pain** : tener un dolor punzante

throes ['θroːz] npl 1 PANGS : agonía f 2 **in the** ~ **of** : en medio de

throne ['θroːn] n : trono m

throng ['θrɔŋ] n : muchedumbre f, multitud f

throttle ['θrɑtəl] vt **-tied; -tling** : estrangular — ~ n : válvula f reguladora

through ['θruː] prep 1 : por, a través de 2 BETWEEN : entre 3 BECAUSE OF : a causa de 4 DURING : durante 5 → **throughout 6 Monday ~ Friday** : de lunes a viernes — ~ adv 1 : de un lado a otro (en el espacio), de principio a fin (en el tiempo) 2 COMPLETELY : completamente — ~ adj 1 **be** ~ : haber terminado 2 ~ **traffic** : tráfico m de paso — **throughout** ['θruːˌaʊt] prep : por todo (un lugar), a lo largo de (un período de tiempo)

throw ['θroː] v **threw** ['θruː]; **thrown** ['θroːn]; **throwing** vt 1 : tirar, lanzar 2 : proyectar (una sombra) 3 CONFUSE : desconcertar 4 ~ **a party** : dar una fiesta 5 ~ **away** or ~ **out** : tirar, botar Lat — vi ~ **up** VOMIT : vomitar — ~ n : tiro m, lanzamiento m

thrush ['θrʌʃ] n : tordo m, zorzal m

thrust ['θrʌst] vt **thrust; thrusting** 1 : empujar (bruscamente) 2 PLUNGE : clavar 3 ~ **upon** : imponer a — ~ n 1 : empujón m 2 : estocada f (en esgrima)

thud ['θʌd] n : ruido m sordo

thug ['θʌg] n : matón m

thumb ['θʌm] n : (dedo m) pulgar m — ~ vt or ~ **through** : hojear — **thumbnail** ['θʌmˌneɪl] n : uña f del pulgar — **thumbtack** ['θʌmˌtæk] n : tachuela f, chinche f Lat

thump ['θʌmp] vt : golpear — vi : latir con fuerza (dícese del corazón) — ~ n : ruido m sordo

thunder ['θʌndər] n : truenos mpl — ~ vi : tronar — vt SHOUT : bramar — **thunderbolt** ['θʌndərˌboːlt] n : rayo m — **thunderous** ['θʌndərəs] adj : atronador — **thunderstorm** ['θʌndərˌstorm] n : tormenta f eléctrica

Thursday ['θərzˌdeɪ, -di] n : jueves m

thus ['ðʌs] adv 1 : así 2 THEREFORE : por lo tanto

thwart ['θwort] vt : frustrar

thyme ['taɪm, 'θaɪm] n : tomillo m

thyroid ['θaɪˌroɪd] n : tiroides mf

tiara [ti'ærə, -'ɑr-] n : diadema f

tic ['tɪk] n : tic m (nervioso)

tick[1] ['tɪk] n : garrapata f (insecto)

tick[2] n 1 : tictac m (sonido) 2 CHECK : marca f — vi : hacer tictac — vt 1 or ~ **off** CHECK : marcar 2 ~ **off** ANNOY : fastidiar

ticket ['tɪkət] n 1 : pasaje m (de avión), billete m Spain (de tren, avión, etc.), boleto m Lat (de tren o autobús) 2 : entrada f (al teatro, etc.) 3 FINE : multa f

tickle ['tɪkəl] v **-led; -ling** vt 1 : hacer cosquillas a 2 AMUSE : divertir — vi : picar — ~ n : cosquilleo m — **ticklish** ['tɪkəlɪʃ] adj 1 : cosquilloso 2 TRICKY : delicado

tidal wave ['taɪdəl] n : maremoto m

tidbit ['tɪdˌbɪt] n MORSEL : golosina f

tide ['taɪd] n : marea f — ~ vt **tided; tiding** ~ **over** : ayudar a superar un apuro

tidy ['taɪdi] adj **-dier; -est** : ordenado, arreglado — ~ vt **-died; -dying** or ~ **up** : ordenar, arreglar

tie ['taɪ] n 1 : atadura f, cordón m 2 BOND : lazo m 3 : empate m (en deportes) 4 NECKTIE : corbata f — ~ v **tied; tying** or **tieing** vt 1 : atar, amarrar Lat — ~ **a knot** : hacer un nudo — vi : empatar (en deportes)

tier ['tɪr] n : nivel m, piso (de un pastel), grada f (de un estadio)

tiger ['taɪgər] n : tigre m

tight ['taɪt] adj 1 : apretado 2 SNUG : ajustado, ceñido 3 TAUT : tirante 4 STINGY : agarrado 5 SCARCE : escaso 6 **a** ~ **seal** : un cierre hermético 7 **a** ~ **spot** : un aprieto — ~ adv **closed** : bien cerrado — **tighten** ['taɪtən] vt 1 : apretar 2 TENSE : tensar 3 : hacer más estricto (reglas, etc.) — **tightly** ['taɪtli] adv : bien, fuerte — **tightrope** ['taɪtˌroːp] n : cuerda f floja — **tights** ['taɪts] npl : leotardo m, mallas fpl

tile ['taɪl] n 1 : azulejo m, baldosa f (de

piso) **2** *or* **roofing ~** : teja *f* — **~** *vt*
tiled; tiling 1 : revestir de azulejos,
embaldosar (un piso) **2** : tejar (un
techo)
till¹ ['tɪl] *prep & conj* → **until**
till² *vt* : cultivar
till³ *n* : caja *f* (registradora)
tilt ['tɪlt] *n* **1** : inclinación *f* **2 at full ~** : a
toda velocidad — **~** *vt* : inclinar — *vi*
: inclinarse
timber ['tɪmbər] *n* **1** : madera *f* (para
construcción) **2** BEAM : viga *f*
timbre ['tæmbər, 'tɪm-] *n* : timbre *m*
time ['taɪm] *n* **1** : tiempo *m* **2** AGE : época
f **3** : compás *m* (en música) **4 at ~s**
: a veces **5 at a ~** : en este momento **6 for the ~ being** : por el momento **7 from ~ to ~** : de vez en
cuando **8 have a good ~** : pasarlo
bien **9 many ~s** : muchas veces **10
on ~** : a tiempo **11 ~ after ~** : una
y otra vez **12 what ~ is it?** : ¿qué
hora es? — **~** *vt* **timed; timing**
: tomar el tiempo a (algn), cronometrar (una carrera, etc.) — **timeless**
['taɪmləs] *adj* : eterno — **timely** ['taɪm-
li] *adj* **-lier; -est** : oportuno — **timer**
['taɪmər] *n* : temporizador *m*, avisador
m (de cocina) — **times** ['taɪmz] *prep* **3
~ 4 is 12** : 3 por 4 son 12 — **timetable** ['taɪm,teɪbəl] *n* : horario *m*
timid ['tɪmɪd] *adj* : tímido
tin ['tɪn] *n* **1** : estaño *m* **2** CAN : lata *f*,
bote *m Spain* — **tinfoil** ['tɪn,fɔɪl] *n*
: papel *m* (de aluminio)
tinge ['tɪndʒ] *vt* **tinged; tingeing** *or*
tinging ['tɪndʒɪŋ] : matizar — **~** *n* **1**
TINT : matiz *m* **2** TOUCH : dejo *m*
tingle ['tɪŋgəl] *vi* **-gled; -gling** : sentir
(un) hormigueo — **~** *n* : hormigueo
m
tinker ['tɪŋkər] *vi* **~ with** : intentar
arreglar (con pequeños ajustes)
tinkle ['tɪŋkəl] *vi* **-kled; -kling** : tintinear
— **~** *n* : tintineo *m*
tint ['tɪnt] *n* : tinte *m* — **~** *vt* : teñir
tiny ['taɪni] *adj* **-nier; -est** : diminuto,
minúsculo
tip¹ ['tɪp] *v* **tipped; tipping** *vt* **1** TILT : inclinar **2** *or* **~ over** : volcar — *vi* : inclinarse
tip² *n* END : punta *f*
tip³ *n* ADVICE : consejo *m* — **~** *vt* **~
off** : avisar
tip⁴ *vt* : dar una propina a — **~** *n* GRA-
TUITY : propina *f*
tipsy ['tɪpsi] *adj* : achispado
tiptoe ['tɪp,to] *n* **on ~** : de puntillas —
~ *vi* **-toed; -toeing** : caminar de puntillas

tip–top ['tɪp,tap, -,tap] *adj* : excelente
tire¹ ['taɪr] *n* : neumático *m*, llanta *f Lat*
tire² *v* **tired; tiring** *vt* : cansar — *vi*
: cansarse — **tired** ['taɪrd] *adj* **1 ~ of**
: cansado de, harto de **2 ~ out** : agotado — **tireless** ['taɪrləs] *adj* : incansable — **tiresome** ['taɪrsəm] *adj* : pesado
tissue ['tɪ,ʃuː] *n* **1** : pañuelo *m* de papel **2**
: tejido *m* (en biología)
title ['taɪtəl] *n* : título *m* — **~** *vt* **-tled;
-tling** : titular
to ['tuː] *prep* **1** : a **2** TOWARD : hacia **3** IN
ORDER TO : para **4** UP TO : hasta **5 a
quarter ~ seven** : las siete menos
cuarto **6 be nice ~ them** : trátalos
bien **7 ten ~ the box** : diez por caja **8
the mate ~ this shoe** : el compañero de este zapato **9 two ~ four
years old** : entre dos y cuatro años de
edad **10 want ~ do** : querer hacer —
~ *adv* **1 come ~** : volver en sí **2 ~
and fro** : de un lado a otro
toad ['toːd] *n* : sapo *m*
toast ['toːst] *vt* **1** : tostar (pan, etc.) **2**
: brindar por (una persona) — **~** *n*
1 : pan *m* tostado, tostadas *fpl* **2** DRINK
: brindis *m* — **toaster** ['toːstər] *n*
: tostador *m*
tobacco [tə'bækoː] *n, pl* **-cos** : tabaco *m*
toboggan [tə'bagən] *n* : tobogán *m*
today [tə'deɪ] *adv* : hoy — **~** *n* : hoy *m*
toddler ['tadələr] *n* : niño *m* pequeño,
niña *f* pequeña (que comienza a caminar)
toe ['toː] *n* : dedo *m* (del pie) — **toenail**
['toː,neɪl] *n* : uña *f* (del pie)
together [tə'geðər] *adv* **1** : juntos **2 ~
with** : junto con
toil ['tɔɪl] *n* : trabajo *m* duro — **~** *vi*
: trabajar duro
toilet ['tɔɪlət] *n* **1** BATHROOM : baño *m*,
servicio *m* **2** : inodoro *m* (instalación)
— **toilet paper** *n* : papel *m* higiénico
— **toiletries** ['tɔɪlətriz] *npl* : artículos
mpl de tocador
token ['toːkən] *n* **1** SIGN : muestra *f* **2** ME-
MENTO : recuerdo *m* **3** : ficha *f* (para un
tren, etc.)
told → **tell**
tolerable ['talərəbəl] *adj* : tolerable —
tolerance ['talərənts] *n* : tolerancia *f* —
tolerant ['talərənt] *adj* : tolerante —
tolerate ['talə,reɪt] *vt* **-ated; -ating**
: tolerar
toll¹ ['toːl] *n* **1** : peaje *m* **2 death ~**
: número *m* de muertos **3 take a ~ on**
: afectar
toll² *vi* RING : tocar, doblar — **~** *n*
: tañido *m*

tomato [tə'meɪṭo, -'mɑ-] *n, pl* **-toes** : tomate *m*

tomb ['tuːm] *n* : tumba *f*, sepulcro *m* — **tombstone** ['tuːm,stoːn] *n* : lápida *f*

tome ['toːm] *n* : tomo *m*

tomorrow [tə'mɑro] *adv* : mañana — ~ *n* : mañana *m*

ton ['tʌn] *n* : tonelada *f*

tone ['toːn] *n* : tono *m* — ~ *vt* **toned**; **toning** *or* ~ **down** : atenuar

tongs ['tɑŋz, 'tɔŋz] *npl* : tenazas *fpl*

tongue ['tʌŋ] *n* : lengua *f*

tonic ['tɑnɪk] *n* **1** : tónico *m* **2** *or* ~ **water** : tónica *f*

tonight [tə'naɪt] *adv* : esta noche — ~ *n* : esta noche *f*

tonsil ['tɑntsəl] *n* : amígdala *f*

too ['tuː] *adv* **1** ALSO : también **2** EXCESSIVELY : demasiado

took → **take**

tool ['tuːl] *n* : herramienta *f* — **toolbox** ['tuːl,bɑks] *n* : caja *f* de herramientas

toot ['tuːt] *vt* : sonar (un claxon, etc.) — ~ *vi* **1** WHISTLE : pitido *m* **2** HONK : bocinazo *m*

tooth ['tuːθ] *n, pl* **teeth** ['tiːθ] : diente *m* — **toothache** ['tuːθ,eɪk] *n* : dolor *m* de muelas — **toothbrush** ['tuːθ,brʌʃ] *n* : cepillo *m* de dientes — **toothpaste** ['tuːθ,peɪst] *n* : pasta *f* de dientes, pasta *f* dentífrica

top¹ ['tɑp] *n* **1** : parte *f* superior **2** SUMMIT : cima *f*, cumbre *f* **3** COVER : tapa *f*, cubierta *f* **4** on ~ of : encima de — ~ *vt* **topped**; **topping 1** COVER : rematar (un edificio, etc.), bañar (un pastel, etc.) **2** SURPASS : superar **3** ~ **off** : llenar — ~ *adj* **1** : de arriba, superior **2** BEST : mejor **3** a ~ **executive** : un alto ejecutivo

top² *n* : trompo *m* (juguete)

topic ['tɑpɪk] *n* : tema *m* — **topical** ['tɑpɪkəl] *adj* : de interés actual

topmost ['tɑp,moːst] *adj* : más alto

topple ['tɑpəl] *v* **-pled**; **-pling** *vi* : caerse — ~ *vt* **1** OVERTURN : volcar **2** OVERTHROW : derrocar

torch ['tɔrtʃ] *n* : antorcha *f*

tore → **tear¹**

torment ['tɔr,mɛnt] *n* : tormento *m* — ~ [tɔr'mɛnt, 'tɔr-] *vt* : atormentar

torn → **tear¹**

tornado [tɔr'neɪdo] *n, pl* **-does** *or* **-dos** : tornado *m*

torpedo [tɔr'piːdo] *n, pl* **-does** : torpedo *m* — ~ *vt* : torpedear

torrent ['tɔrənt] *n* : torrente *m*

torrid ['tɔrɪd] *adj* : tórrido

torso ['tɔr,soː] *n, pl* **-sos** *or* **-si** [-,siː] : torso *m*

tortilla [tɔr'tiːjə] *n* : tortilla *f*

tortoise ['tɔrtəs] *n* : tortuga *f* (terrestre) — **tortoiseshell** ['tɔrtəs,ʃɛl] *n* : carey *m*, concha *f*

tortuous ['tɔrtʃʊəs] *adj* : tortuoso

torture ['tɔrtʃər] *n* : tortura *f* — ~ *vt* **-tured**; **-turing** : torturar

toss ['tɔs, 'tɑs] *vt* **1** : tirar, lanzar **2** : mezclar (una ensalada) — *vi* ~ **and turn** : dar vueltas — ~ *n* : lanzamiento *m*

tot ['tɑt] *n* : pequeño *m*, -ña *f*

total ['toːtəl] *adj* : total — ~ *n* : total *m* — ~ *vt* **-taled** *or* **-talled**; **-taling** *or* **-talling 1** : ascender a **2** *or* ~ **up** : totalizar, sumar — **totalitarian** [toːˌtælə'tɛriən] *adj* : totalitario

tote ['toːt] *vt* **toted**; **toting** : llevar

totter ['tɑtər] *vi* : tambalearse

touch ['tʌtʃ] *vt* **1** : tocar **2** MOVE : conmover **3** AFFECT : afectar **4** ~ **up** : retocar — *vi* : tocarse — ~ *n* **1** : tacto *m* (sentido) **2** HINT : toque *m* **3** BIT : pizca *f* **4 keep in** ~ : mantenerse en contacto **5 lose one's** ~ : perder la habilidad — **touchdown** ['tʌtʃ,daʊn] *n* : touchdown *m* — **touchy** ['tʌtʃi] *adj* **touchier**; **-est 1** : delicado **2 be** ~ **about** : picarse a la mención de

tough ['tʌf] *adj* **1** : duro **2** STRONG : fuerte **3** STRICT : severo **4** DIFFICULT : difícil — **toughen** ['tʌfən] *vt* *or* ~ **up** : endurecer — *vi* : endurecerse — **toughness** ['tʌfnəs] *n* : dureza *f*

tour ['tʊr] *n* **1** : viaje *m* (por un país, etc.), visita *f* (a un museo, etc.) **2** : gira *f* (de un equipo, etc.) — *vi* **1** TRAVEL : viajar **2** : hacer una gira (dícese de equipos, etc.) — *vt* : viajar por, recorrer — **tourist** ['tʊrɪst, 'tər-] *n* : turista *mf*

tournament ['tərnəmənt, 'tʊr-] *n* : torneo *m*

tousle ['taʊzəl] *vt* **-sled**; **-sling** : despeinar

tout ['taʊt] *vt* : promocionar

tow ['toː] *vt* : remolcar — ~ *n* : remolque *m*

toward ['tord, tə'word] *or* **towards** ['tordz, tə'wordz] *prep* : hacia

towel ['taʊəl] *n* : toalla *f*

tower ['taʊər] *n* : torre *f* — ~ *vi* ~ **over** : descollar sobre — **towering** ['taʊərɪŋ] *adj* : altísimo

town ['taʊn] *n* **1** VILLAGE : pueblo *m* **2** CITY : ciudad *f* — **township** ['taʊn,ʃɪp] *n* : municipio *m*

tow truck ['toː,trʌk] *n* : grúa *f*

toxic ['tɑksɪk] *adj* : tóxico

toy ['tɔɪ] *n* : juguete *m* — **∼** *vi* **∼ with** : juguetear con

trace ['treɪs] *n* **1** SIGN : rastro *m*, señal *f* **2** HINT : dejo *m* — **∼** *vt* **traced; tracing 1** : calcar (un dibujo, etc.) **2** DRAW : trazar **3** FIND : localizar

track ['træk] *n* **1** : pista *f* **2** PATH : sendero *m* **3** *or* **railroad ∼** : vía *f* (férrea) **4 keep ∼ of** : llevar la cuenta de — **∼** *vt* TRAIL : seguir la pista de

tract[1] ['trækt] *n* **1** EXPANSE : extensión *f* **2** : tracto *m* (en anatomía)

tract[2] *n* PAMPHLET : folleto *m*

traction ['trækʃən] *n* : tracción *f*

tractor ['træktər] *n* **1** : tractor *m* **2** *or* **∼ -trailer** : camión *m* (con remolque)

trade ['treɪd] *n* **1** PROFESSION : oficio *m* **2** COMMERCE : comercio *m* **3** INDUSTRY : industria *f* **4** EXCHANGE : cambio *m* — **∼** *v* **traded; trading** *vi* : comerciar — *vt* **∼ sth with s.o.** : cambiar algo a algn — **trademark** ['treɪd,mɑrk] *n* : marca *f* registrada

tradition [trə'dɪʃən] *n* : tradición *f* — **traditional** [trə'dɪʃənəl] *adj* : tradicional

traffic ['træfɪk] *n* : tráfico *m* — **∼** *vi* **trafficked; trafficking ∼ in** : traficar con — **traffic light** *n* : semáforo *m*

tragedy ['trædʒədi] *n*, *pl* **-dies** : tragedia *f* — **tragic** ['trædʒɪk] *adj* : trágico

trail ['treɪl] *vi* **1** DRAG : arrastrar **2** LAG : rezagarse **3 ∼ off** : apagarse — *vt* **1** DRAG : arrastrar **2** PURSUE : seguir la pista de — **∼** *n* **1** : rastro *m*, huellas *fpl* **2** PATH : sendero *m* — **trailer** ['treɪlər] *n* **1** : remolque *m* **2** : caravana *f* (vivienda)

train ['treɪn] *n* **1** : tren *m* **2** : cola *f* (de un vestido) **3** SERIES : serie *f* **4 ∼ of thought** : hilo *m* (de las ideas) — *vt* **1** : adiestrar, entrenar (atletas, etc.) **2** AIM : apuntar — *vi* : prepararse, entrenarse (en deportes, etc.) — **trainer** ['treɪnər] *n* : entrenador *m*, -dora *f*

trait ['treɪt] *n* : rasgo *m*

traitor ['treɪtər] *n* : traidor *m*, -dora *f*

tramp ['træmp] *vi* : caminar (pesadamente) — **∼** *n* VAGRANT : vagabundo *m*, -da *f*

trample ['træmpəl] *vt* **-pled; -pling** : pisotear

trampoline [,træmpə'liːn, 'træmpə,-] *n* : trampolín *m*

trance ['trænts] *n* : trance *m*

tranquillity *or* **tranquility** [træn'kwɪləti] *n* : tranquilidad *f* — **tranquil** ['trænkwəl] *adj* : tranquilo — **tranquilize** ['trænkwə,laɪz] *vt* **-ized; -izing** : tranquilizar — **tranquilizer** ['trænkwə,laɪzər] *n* : tranquilizante *m*

transaction [træn'zækʃən] *n* : transacción *f*

transatlantic [,træntsət'læntɪk, ,trænz-] *adj* : transatlántico

transcend [træn'send] *vt* **1** : ir más allá de **2** OVERCOME : superar

transcribe [træn'skraɪb] *vt* **-scribed; -scribing** : transcribir — **transcript** ['træn,skrɪpt] *n* : transcripción *f*

transfer [træns'fər, 'træns,fər] *v* **-ferred; -ferring** *vt* **1** : transferir (fondos, etc.) **2** : trasladar (a un empleado, etc.) — *vi* **1** : cambiarse (de escuelas, etc.) **2** : hacer transbordo (entre trenes, etc.) — **∼** ['trænts,fər] *n* **1** : transferencia *f* (de fondos, etc.), traslado *m* (de una persona) **2** : boleto *m* (para hacer transbordo) **3** DECAL : calcomanía *f*

transform [trænts'fɔrm] *vt* : transformar — **transformation** [,træntsfər'meɪʃən] *n* : transformación *f*

transfusion [trænts'fjuːʒən] *n* : transfusión *f*

transgression [trænts'greʃən, trænz-] *n* : transgresión *f* — **transgress** [trænts'gres, trænz-] *vt* : transgredir

transient ['træntʃənt, 'træntsiənt] *adj* : pasajero

transit ['træntsɪt, 'træntzɪt] *n* **1** : tránsito *m* **2** TRANSPORTATION : transporte *m* — **transition** [træn'sɪʃən, -'zɪʃ-] *n* : transición *f* — **transitive** ['træntsətɪv, 'trænzə-] *adj* : transitivo — **transitory** ['træntsə,tori, 'trænzə-] *adj* : transitorio

translate ['trænts,leɪt, trænz-,-, 'træns,-] *vt* **-lated; -lating** : traducir — **translation** [trænts'leɪʃən, trænz-] *n* : traducción *f* — **translator** ['trænts,leɪtər, trænz-; 'træntstə,-, 'træns,-] *n* : traductor *m*, -tora *f*

translucent [trænts'luːsənt, trænz-] *adj* : translúcido

transmit [trænts'mɪt, trænz-] *vt* **-mitted; -mitting** : transmitir — **transmission** [trænts'mɪʃən, trænz-] *n* : transmisión *f* — **transmitter** [trænts'mɪtər, trænz-; 'træntsə,-, 'trænsə,-] *n* : transmisor *m*

transparent [trænts'pærənt] *adj* : transparente — **transparency** [trænts'pærəntsi] *n*, *pl* **-cies** : transparencia *f*

transpire [trænts'paɪr] *vi* **-spired; -spiring 1** TURN OUT : resultar **2** HAPPEN : suceder

transplant [trænts'plænt] *vt* : trasplantar — **∼** ['trænts,plænt] *n* : trasplante *m*

transport [trænts'port, 'trænts,-] *vt* : transportar — **∼** ['trænts,port] *n* : transporte *m* — **transportation** [,træntspər'teɪʃən] *n* : transporte *m*

transpose [trænts'poːz] *vt* **-posed;**

-posing 1 : trasponer **2** : transportar (en música)

trap ['træp] *n* : trampa *f* — ~ *vt* **trapped; trapping** : atrapar — **trapdoor** ['træp'dor] *n* : trampilla *f*

trapeze [træ'piːz] *n* : trapecio *m*

trappings ['træpɪŋz] *npl* : adornos *mpl*, atavíos *mpl*

trash ['træʃ] *n* : basura *f*

trauma ['trɔmə, 'trau-] *n* : trauma *m* — **traumatic** [trə'mætɪk, trɔ-, trau-] *adj* : traumático

travel ['trævəl] *vi* **-eled** *or* **-elled; -eling** *or* **-elling 1** : viajar **2** MOVE : desplazarse — ~ *n* : viajes *mpl* — **traveler** *or* **traveller** ['trævələr] *n* : viajero *m*, -ra *f*

traverse [trə'vərs, træ'vərs, 'trævərs] *vt* **-versed; -versing** : atravesar

travesty ['trævəsti] *n, pl* **-ties** : parodia *f*

trawl ['trɔl] *vi* : pescar (con red de arrastre) — **trawler** ['trɔlər] *n* : barco *m* de pesca

tray ['treɪ] *n* : bandeja *f*

treachery ['trɛtʃəri] *n, pl* **-eries** : traición *f* — **treacherous** ['trɛtʃərəs] *adj* **1** : traidor **2** DANGEROUS : peligroso

tread ['trɛd] *v* **trod** ['trɔd]; **trodden** ['trɔdən] *or* **trod; treading** *vt* **1** *or* ~ **on** : pisar **2** ~ **water** : flotar — *vi* **1** STEP : pisar **2** WALK : caminar — ~ *n* **1** STEP : paso *m* **2** : banda *f* de rodadura (de un neumático) — **treadmill** ['trɛd,mɪl] *n* : rueda *f* de andar

treason ['triːzən] *n* : traición *f* (a la patria)

treasure ['trɛʒər, 'treɪ-] *n* : tesoro *m* — ~ *vt* **-sured; -suring** : apreciar — **treasurer** ['trɛʒərər, 'treɪ-] *n* : tesorero *m*, -ra *f* — **treasury** ['trɛʒəri, 'treɪ-] *n, pl* **-suries** : erario *m*, tesoro *m*

treat ['triːt] *vt* **1** : tratar **2** CONSIDER : considerar **3** ~ **s.o. to (dinner, etc.)** : invitar a algn (a cenar, etc.) — ~ *n* **1** : gusto *m*, placer *m* **2 it's my** ~ : invito yo

treatise ['triːtɪs] *n* : tratado *m*

treatment ['triːtmənt] *n* : tratamiento *m*

treaty ['triːti] *n, pl* **-ties** : tratado *m*

treble ['trɛbəl] *adj* **1** TRIPLE : triple **2** : de tiple (en música) — ~ *vt* **-bled; -bling** : triplicar — **treble clef** : clave *f* de sol

tree ['triː] *n* : árbol *m*

trek ['trɛk] *vi* **trekked; trekking** : viajar (con dificultad) — ~ *n* : viaje *m* difícil

trellis ['trɛlɪs] *n* : enrejado *m*

tremble ['trɛmbəl] *vi* **-bled; -bling** : temblar

tremendous [trɪ'mɛndəs] *adj* : tremendo

tremor ['trɛmər] *n* : temblor *m*

trench ['trɛntʃ] *n* **1** : zanja *f* **2** : trinchera *f* (militar)

trend ['trɛnd] *n* **1** : tendencia *f* **2** FASHION : moda *f* — **trendy** ['trɛndi] *adj* **trendier; -est** : de moda

trepidation [,trɛpə'deɪʃən] *n* : inquietud *f*

trespass ['trɛspəs, -,pæs] *vi* : entrar ilegalmente (en propiedad ajena)

trial ['traɪəl] *n* **1** : juicio *m*, proceso *m* **2** TEST : prueba *f* **3** ORDEAL : dura prueba *f* — ~ *adj* : de prueba

triangle ['traɪ,æŋgəl] *n* : triángulo *m* — **triangular** [traɪ'æŋgjələr] *adj* : triangular

tribe ['traɪb] *n* : tribu *f* — **tribal** ['traɪbəl] *adj* : tribal

tribulation [,trɪbjə'leɪʃən] *n* : tribulación *f*

tribunal [traɪ'bjuːnəl, trɪ-] *n* : tribunal *m*

tribute ['trɪbjuːt] *n* : tributo *m* — **tributary** ['trɪbjə,teri] *n, pl* **-taries** : afluente *m*

trick ['trɪk] *n* **1** : trampa *f* **2** PRANK : broma *f* **3** KNACK, FEAT : truco *m* **4** : baza *f* (en naipes) — ~ *vt* : engañar — **trickery** ['trɪkəri] *n* : engaño *m*

trickle ['trɪkəl] *vi* **-led; -ling** : gotear — ~ *n* : goteo *m*

tricky ['trɪki] *adj* **trickier; -est 1** SLY : astuto, taimado **2** DIFFICULT : difícil

tricycle ['traɪsɪkəl, -,sɪkəl] *n* : triciclo *m*

trifle ['traɪfəl] *n* **1** TRIVIALITY : nimiedad *f* **2 a** ~ : un poco — ~ *vi* **-fled; -fling** ~ **with** : jugar con — **trifling** ['traɪflɪŋ] *adj* : insignificante

trigger ['trɪgər] *n* : gatillo *m* — ~ *vt* : causar, provocar

trill ['trɪl] *n* : trino *m* — ~ *vi* : trinar

trillion ['trɪljən] *n* : billón *m*

trilogy ['trɪlədʒi] *n, pl* **-gies** : trilogía *f*

trim ['trɪm] *vt* **trimmed; trimming 1** : recortar **2** ADORN : adornar — ~ *adj* **trimmer; trimmest 1** SLIM : esbelto **2** NEAT : arreglado — ~ *n* **1** : recorte *m* **2** DECORATION : adornos *mpl* **3 in** ~ : en buena forma — **trimming** ['trɪmɪŋ] *npl* **1** : adornos *mpl* **2** GARNISH : guarnición *f*

Trinity ['trɪnəti] *n* : Trinidad *f*

trinket ['trɪŋkət] *n* : chuchería *f*

trio ['triː,oː] *n, pl* **trios** : trío *m*

trip ['trɪp] *v* **tripped; tripping** *vi* **1** : caminar (a paso ligero) **2** STUMBLE : tropezar **3** ~ **up** : equivocarse — *vt* **1** ACTIVATE : activar **2** ~ **s.o.** : hacer una zancadilla a algn **3** ~ **s.o. up** : hacer equivocar a algn — ~ *n* **1** : viaje *m* **2** STUMBLE : traspié *m*

tripe ['traɪp] *n* **1** : mondongo *m*, callos *mpl* **2** NONSENSE : tonterías *fpl*

triple ['trɪpəl] *vt* **-pled; -pling** : triplicar — ~ *n* : triple *m* — ~ *adj* : triple

triplet ['trɪplət] *n* : trillizo *m*, -za *f* — **triplicate** ['trɪplɪkət] *n* : triplicado *m*

tripod ['traɪ,pɑd] *n* : trípode *m*

trite ['traɪt] *adj* **triter; tritest** : trillado

triumph ['traɪəmf] *n* : triunfo *m* — ~ *vi* : triunfar — **triumphal** [traɪˈʌmfəl] *adj* : triunfal — **triumphant** [traɪˈʌmfənt] *adj* : triunfante

trivial ['trɪviəl] *adj* : trivial — **trivia** ['trɪviə] *ns & pl* : trivialidades *fpl* — **triviality** [ˌtrɪviˈæləti] *n, pl* **-ties** : trivialidad *f*

trod, trodden → **tread**

trolley ['trɑli] *n, pl* **-leys** : tranvía *m*

trombone [trɑmˈboːn] *n* : trombón *m*

troop ['truːp] *n* **1** : escuadrón *m* (de caballería), compañía *f* (de soldados) **2** ~s *npl* : tropas *fpl* — ~ *vi* : **in/out** : entrar/salir en tropel — **trooper** ['truːpər] *n* **1** : soldado *m* **2** *or* **state ~** : policía *mf* estatal

trophy ['troːfi] *n, pl* **-phies** : trofeo *m*

tropic ['trɑpɪk] *n* **1** : trópico *m* **2** **the ~s** : el trópico — ~ *or* **tropical** [-pɪkəl] *adj* : tropical

trot ['trɑt] *n* : trote *m* — ~ *vi* **trotted; trotting** : trotar

trouble ['trʌbəl] *v* **-bled; -bling** *vt* **1** WORRY : preocupar **2** BOTHER : molestar — *vi* : molestarse — ~ *n* **1** PROBLEMS : problemas *mpl* **2** EFFORT : molestia *f* **3 be in ~** : estar en apuros **4 get in ~** : meterse en problemas **5 I had ~ doing it** : me costó hacerlo — **troublemaker** ['trʌbəlˌmeɪkər] *n* : alborotador *m*, -dora *f* — **troublesome** ['trʌbəlsəm] *adj* : problemático

trough ['trɔf] *n, pl* **troughs** ['trɔfs, 'trɔvz] **1** : depresión *f* **2** *or* **feeding ~** : comedero *m* **3** *or* **drinking ~** : bebedero *m*

troupe ['truːp] *n* : compañía *f* (de teatro)

trousers ['traʊzərz] *npl* : pantalón *m*, pantalones *mpl*

trout ['traʊt] *n, pl* **trout** : trucha *f*

trowel ['traʊəl] *n* : paleta *f* (de albañil), desplantador *m* (de jardinero)

truant ['truːənt] *n* : alumno *m*, -na *f* que falta a clase

truce ['truːs] *n* : tregua *f*

truck ['trʌk] *vt* : transportar en camión — ~ *n* **1** : camión *m* **2** CART : carro *m* — **trucker** ['trʌkər] *n* : camionero *m*, -ra *f*

trudge ['trʌdʒ] *vi* **trudged; trudging** : caminar a paso pesado

true ['truː] *adj* **truer; truest** **1** : verdadero **2** LOYAL : fiel **3** GENUINE : auténtico **4 be ~** : ser cierto, ser verdad

truffle ['trʌfəl] *n* : trufa *f*

truly ['truːli] *adv* : verdaderamente

trump ['trʌmp] *n* : triunfo *m* (en naipes)

trumpet ['trʌmpət] *n* : trompeta *f*

trunk ['trʌŋk] *n* **1** STEM, TORSO : tronco *m* **2** : trompa *f* (de un elefante) **3** : baúl *m* (equipaje) **4** : maletero *m* (de un auto) **5** ~s *npl* : traje *m* de baño (de hombre)

truss ['trʌs] *n* **1** FRAMEWORK : armazón *m* **2** : braguero *m* (en medicina)

trust ['trʌst] *n* **1** CONFIDENCE : confianza *f* **2** HOPE : esperanza *f* **3** CREDIT : crédito *m* **4** : trust *m* (en finanzas) **5 in ~** : en fideicomiso — ~ *vi* **1** : confiar **2** HOPE : esperar — *vt* **1** : confiar en, fiarse de (en frases negativas) **2 ~ s.o. with sth** : confiar algo a algn — **trustee** [ˌtrʌsˈtiː] *n* : fideicomisario *m*, -ria *f* — **trustworthy** ['trʌstˌwərði] *adj* : digno de confianza

truth ['truːθ] *n, pl* **truths** ['truːðz, 'truːθs] : verdad *f* — **truthful** ['truːθfəl] *adj* : sincero, veraz

try ['traɪ] *v* **tried; trying** *vt* **1** ATTEMPT : tratar (de), intentar **2** : juzgar (un caso, etc.) **3** TEST : poner a prueba **4** *or* **~ out** : probar **5** ~ **on** : probarse (ropa) — *vi* : hacer un esfuerzo — ~ *n, pl* **tries** : intento *m* — **trying** *adj* **1** ANNOYING : irritante, pesado **2** DIFFICULT : duro — **tryout** ['traɪˌaʊt] *n* : prueba *f*

tsar ['zɑr, 'tsɑr, 'sɑr] → **czar**

T-shirt ['tiːˌʃərt] *n* : camiseta *f*

tub ['tʌb] *n* **1** : cuba *f*, tina *f* **2** CONTAINER : envase *m* **3** BATHTUB : bañera *f*

tuba ['tuːbə, 'tjuː-] *n* : tuba *f*

tube ['tuːb, 'tjuːb] *n* **1** : tubo *m* **2** *or* **inner ~** : cámara *f* **3 the ~** : la tele

tuberculosis [tuˌbərkjəˈloːsɪs, tjuː-] *n, pl* **-loses** [-ˌsiːz] : tuberculosis *f*

tubing ['tuːbɪŋ, 'tjuː-] *n* : tubería *f* — **tubular** ['tuːbjələr, 'tjuː-] *adj* : tubular

tuck ['tʌk] *vt* **1** : meter **2** ~ **away** : guardar **3** ~ **in** : meter por dentro (una blusa, etc.) **4** ~ **s.o. in** : arropar a algn — ~ *n* : jareta *f*

Tuesday ['tuːzˌdeɪ, 'tjuːz-, -di] *n* : martes *m*

tuft ['tʌft] *n* : mechón *m* (de pelo), penacho *m* (de plumas)

tug ['tʌg] *vt* **tugged; tugging** *or* ~ **at** : tirar de, jalar de — ~ *n* : tirón *m*, jalón *m* — **tugboat** ['tʌgˌboːt] *n* : remolcador *m* — **tug-of-war** [ˌtʌgəˈwɔr] *n, pl* **tugs-of-war** : tira y afloja *m*

tuition [tuːˈɪʃən, tjuː-] *n* **1** : enseñanza *f* **2** *or* ~ **fees** : matrícula *f*

tulip [ˈtuːlɪp, ˈtjuː-] *n* : tulipán *m*

tumble [ˈtʌmbəl] *vi* -**bled**; -**bling** : caerse — ~ *n* : caída *f* — **tumbler** [ˈtʌmblər] *n* : vaso *m* (sin pie)

tummy [ˈtʌmi] *n, pl* -**mies** : barriga *f*, panza *f*

tumor [ˈtuːmər ˈtjuː-] *n* : tumor *m*

tumult [ˈtuːmʌlt ˈtjuː-] *n* : tumulto *m* — **tumultuous** [tʊˈmʌltʃuəs, tjuː-] *adj* : tumultuoso

tuna [ˈtuːnə ˈtjuː-] *n, pl* -**na** *or* -**nas** : atún *m*

tune [ˈtuːn, ˈtjuːn] *n* **1** MELODY : melodía *f* **2** SONG : tonada *f* **3** *in* ~ : afinado **4** **out of** ~ : desafinado — ~ *v* **tuned**; **tuning** *vt* : afinar — *vi* ~ **in** : sintonizar — **tuner** [ˈtuːnər, ˈtjuː-] *n* **1** : afinador *m*, -dora *f* (de pianos, etc.) **2** : sintonizador *m* (de un receptor)

tunic [ˈtuːnɪk, ˈtjuː-] *n* : túnica *f*

tunnel [ˈtʌnəl] *n* : túnel *m* — ~ *vi* -**neled** *or* -**nelled**; -**neling** *or* -**nelling** : hacer un túnel

turban [ˈtərbən] *n* : turbante *m*

turbine [ˈtərbən, -ˌbaɪn] *n* : turbina *f*

turbulent [ˈtərbjələnt] *adj* : turbulento — **turbulence** [ˈtərbjələnts] *n* : turbulencia *f*

turf [ˈtərf] *n* **1** GRASS : césped *m* **2** SOD : tepe *m*

turgid [ˈtərdʒɪd] *adj* : ampuloso (dícese de prosa, etc.)

turkey [ˈtərki] *n, pl* -**keys** : pavo *m*

turmoil [ˈtərˌmɔɪl] *n* : confusión *f*

turn [ˈtərn] *vt* **1** : hacer girar (una rueda, etc.), volver (la cabeza, una página, etc.) **2** : dar la vuelta a (una esquina) **3** SPRAIN : torcer **4** ~ **down** REFUSE : rechazar **5** ~ **down** LOWER : bajar **6** ~ **in** : entregar **7** ~ **off** : cerrar (una llave), apagar (la luz, etc.) **8** ~ **on** : abrir (una llave), encender, prender *Lat* (la luz, etc.) **9** ~ **out** EXPEL : echar **10** ~ **out** PRODUCE : producir **11** ~ **out** → turn off **12** *or* ~ **over** FLIP : dar la vuelta a, voltear *Lat* **13** ~ **over** TRANSFER : entregar **14** ~ **s.o.'s stomach** : revolver el estómago a algn **15** ~ **sth into sth** : convertir algo en algo **16** ~ **up** RAISE : subir — *vi* **1** ROTATE : girar, dar vueltas **2** BECOME : ponerse **3** SOUR : agriarse **4** RESORT : recurrir **5** *or* ~ **around** : darse la vuelta, volverse **6** ~ **into** : convertirse en **7** ~ **left** : doblar a la izquierda **8** ~ **out** COME : acudir **9** ~ **out** RESULT : resultar **10** ~ **up** APPEAR : aparecer — ~ *n* **1** : vuelta *f* **2**

CHANGE : cambio *m* **3** CURVE : curva *f* **4** **do a good** ~ : hacer un favor **5** **whose** ~ **is it?** : ¿a quién le toca?

turnip [ˈtərnəp] *n* : nabo *m*

turnout [ˈtərnˌaʊt] *n* : concurrencia *f* — **turnover** [ˈtərnˌoːvər] *n* **1** : tartaleta *f* (postre) **2** : volumen *m* (de ventas) **3** : movimiento *m* (de personal) — **turnpike** [ˈtərnˌpaɪk] *n* : carretera *f* de peaje — **turntable** [ˈtərnˌteɪbəl] *n* : plato *m* giratorio

turpentine [ˈtərpənˌtaɪn] *n* : trementina *f*

turquoise [ˈtərˌkɔɪz, -ˌkwɔɪz] *n* : turquesa *f*

turret [ˈtərət] *n* **1** : torrecilla *f* **2** : torreta *f* (de un tanque, etc.)

turtle [ˈtərtəl] *n* : tortuga *f* (marina) — **turtleneck** [ˈtərtəlˌnɛk] *n* : cuello *m* de tortuga

tusk [ˈtʌsk] *n* : colmillo *m*

tussle [ˈtʌsəl] *n* : pelea *f* — ~ *vi* -**sled**; -**sling** : pelearse

tutor [ˈtuːtər, ˈtjuː-] *n* : profesor *m*, -sora *f* particular — ~ *vt* : dar clases particulares a

tuxedo [təkˈsiːˌdoː] *n, pl* -**dos** *or* -**does** : esmoquin *m*, smoking *m*

TV [ˌtiːˈviː, ˈtiːˌviː] → television

twang [ˈtwæŋ] *n* **1** : tañido *m* **2** : acento *m* nasal (de la voz)

tweak [ˈtwiːk] *vt* : pellizcar — ~ *n* : pellizco *m*

tweed [ˈtwiːd] *n* : tweed *m*

tweet [ˈtwiːt] *n* : gorjeo *m*, pío *m* — ~ *vi* : piar

tweezers [ˈtwiːzərz] *npl* : pinzas *fpl*

twelve [ˈtwɛlv] *adj* : doce — ~ *n* : doce *m* — **twelfth** [ˈtwɛlfθ] *adj* : duodécimo — ~ *n* **1** : duodécimo *m*, -ma *f* (en una serie) **2** : doceavo *m* (en matemáticas)

twenty [ˈtwʌnti, ˈtwɛn-] *adj* : veinte — ~ *n, pl* -**ties** : veinte *m* — **twentieth** [ˈtwʌntiəθ, ˈtwɛn-] *adj* : vigésimo — ~ *n* **1** : vigésimo *m*, -ma *f* (en una serie) **2** : veinteavo *m* (en matemáticas)

twice [ˈtwaɪs] *adv* **1** : dos veces **2** ~ **as much/many as** : el doble de (algo), el doble que (algo)

twig [ˈtwɪg] *n* : ramita *f*

twilight [ˈtwaɪˌlaɪt] *n* : crepúsculo *m*

twin [ˈtwɪn] *n* : gemelo *m*, -la *f*; mellizo *m*, -za *f* — ~ *adj* : gemelo, mellizo

twine [ˈtwaɪn] *n* : cordel *m*, bramante *m* *Spain*

twinge [ˈtwɪndʒ] *n* : punzada *f*

twinkle [ˈtwɪŋkəl] *vi* -**kled**; -**kling** **1** : centellear **2** : brillar (dícese de los ojos) — ~ *n* : centelleo *m*, brillo *m* (de los ojos)

twirl ['twərl] *vt* : girar, dar vueltas a — *vi* : girar, dar vueltas — **~** *n* : giro *m*, vuelta *f*
twist ['twist] *vt* **1** : retorcer **2** TURN : girar **3** SPRAIN : torcerse **2** : tergiversar (palabras) — *vi* **1** : retorcerse **2** COIL : enrollarse **3** : serpentear (entre montañas, etc.) — **~** *n* **1** BEND : vuelta *f* **2** TURN : giro *m* **3** — **of lemon** : rodajita *f* de limón — **twister** ['twistər] →
tornado
twitch ['twitʃ] *vi* : moverse (espasmódicamente) — **~** *n* **nervous ~** : tic *m* nervioso
two ['tu:] *adj* : dos — **~** *n, pl* **twos** : dos *m* — **twofold** ['tu:fo:ld] *adj* : doble — **~** ['tu:fo:ld] *adv* : al doble — **two**

hundred *adj* : doscientos — **~** *n* : doscientos *m*
tycoon [tar'ku:n] *n* : magnate *mf*
tying → **tie**
type ['taip] *n* : tipo *m* — **~** *v* **typed; typing** : escribir a máquina — **typewritten** ['taip,ritən] *adj* : escrito a máquina — **typewriter** ['taip,raitər] *n* : máquina *f* de escribir
typhoon [tar'fu:n] *n* : tifón *m*
typical ['tipikəl] *adj* : típico, característico — **typify** ['tipə,fai] *vt* **-fied; -fying** : tipificar
typist ['taipist] *n* : mecanógrafo *m*, -fa *f*
typography [tar'pagrəfi] *n* : tipografía *f*
tyranny ['tirəni] *n, pl* **-nies** : tiranía *f* — **tyrant** ['tairənt] *n* : tirano *m*, -na *f*
tzar ['zar, 'tsar, 'sar] → **czar**

U

u ['ju:] *n, pl* **u's** *or* **us** ['ju:z] : u *f*, vigésima primera letra del alfabeto inglés
udder ['ʌdər] *n* : ubre *f*
UFO [ju:,ef'o:, 'ju:,fo:] (*unidentified flying object*) *n, pl* **UFO's** *or* **UFOs** : ovni *m*, OVNI *m*
ugly ['ʌgli] *adj* **uglier; -est** : feo — **ugliness** ['ʌglinəs] *n* : fealdad *f*
ulcer ['ʌlsər] *n* : úlcera *f*
ulterior [ʌl'tiriər] *adj* **~ motive** : segunda intención *f*
ultimate ['ʌltəmət] *adj* **1** FINAL : final, último **2** UTMOST : máximo **3** FUNDAMENTAL : fundamental — **ultimately** ['ʌltəmətli] *adv* **1** FINALLY : por último, finalmente **2** EVENTUALLY : a la larga
ultimatum [ʌltə'meitəm, -'ma-] *n, pl* **-tums** *or* **-ta** [-ṭə] : ultimátum *m*
ultraviolet [ʌltrə'vaiələt] *adj* : ultravioleta
umbilical cord [ʌm'bilikəl] *n* : cordón *m* umbilical
umbrella [ʌm'brelə] *n* : paraguas *m*
umpire ['ʌm,pair] *n* : árbitro *m*, -tra *f* — **~** *vt* **-pired; -piring** : arbitrar
umpteenth [ʌmp'ti:nθ] *adj* : enésimo
unable [ʌn'eibəl] *adj* **1** : incapaz **2 be ~ to** : no poder
unabridged [ʌnə'bridʒd] *adj* : íntegro
unacceptable [ʌnik'septəbəl] *adj* : inaceptable
unaccountable [ʌnə'kauntəd] *adj* : inexplicable
unaccustomed [ʌnə'kʌstəmd] *adj* **be ~ to** : no estar acostumbrado a
unadulterated [ʌnə'dʌltə,reiṭəd] *adj* : puro

unaffected [ʌnə'fektəd] *adj* **1** : no afectado **2** NATURAL : sin afectación, natural
unafraid [ʌnə'freid] *adj* : sin miedo
unaided [ʌn'eidəd] *adj* : sin ayuda
unanimous [ju'nænəməs] *adj* : unánime
unannounced [ʌnə'naunst] *adj* : sin dar aviso
unarmed [ʌn'armd] *adj* : desarmado
unassuming [ʌnə'su:miŋ] *adj* : modesto, sin pretensiones
unattached [ʌnə'tætʃt] *adj* **1** : suelto **2** UNMARRIED : soltero
unattractive [ʌnə'træktiv] *adj* : poco atractivo
unauthorized [ʌn'ɔθə,raizd] *adj* : no autorizado
unavailable [ʌnə'veiləbəl] *adj* : no disponible
unavoidable [ʌnə'vɔidəbəl] *adj* : inevitable
unaware [ʌnə'wær] *adj* **1** : inconsciente **2 be ~ of** : ignorar — **unawares** [ʌnə'wærz] *adv* **catch s.o. ~** : agarrar a algn desprevenido
unbalanced [ʌn'bæləntst] *adj* : desequilibrado
unbearable [ʌn'bærəbəl] *adj* : inaguantable, insoportable
unbelievable [ʌnbə'li:vəbəl] *adj* : increíble
unbending [ʌn'bendiŋ] *adj* : inflexible
unbiased [ʌn'baiəst] *adj* : imparcial
unborn [ʌn'bɔrn] *adj* : aún no nacido
unbreakable [ʌn'breikəbəl] *adj* : irrompible

unbridled [ʌn'braɪdəld] *adj* : desenfrenado

unbroken [ʌn'broːkən] *adj* **1** INTACT : intacto **2** CONTINUOUS : continuo

unbutton [ʌn'bʌtən] *vt* : desabrochar, desabotonar

uncalled-for [ʌn'kɔld,fɔr] *adj* : inapropiado, innecesario

uncanny [ən'kæni] *adj* **-nier; -est** : extraño, misterioso

unceasing [ʌn'siːsɪŋ] *adj* : incesante

unceremonious [ʌn,serə'moːniəs] *adj* **1** INFORMAL : poco ceremonioso **2** ABRUPT : brusco

uncertain [ʌn'sərtən] *adj* **1** : incierto **2** **in no ~ terms** : de forma vehemente **— uncertainty** [ʌn'sərtənti] *n, pl* **-ties** : incertidumbre *f*

unchanged [ʌn'tʃeɪndʒd] *adj* : igual, sin alterar **— unchanging** [ʌn'tʃeɪdʒɪŋ] *adj* : inmutable

uncivilized [ʌn'sɪvə,laɪzd] *adj* : incivilizado

uncle ['ʌŋkəl] *n* : tío *m*

unclear [ʌn'klɪr] *adj* : poco claro

uncomfortable [ʌn'kʌmpfərtəbəl] *adj* **1** : incómodo **2** DISCONCERTING : inquietante, desagradable

uncommon [ʌn'kɑmən] *adj* : raro

uncompromising [ʌn'kʌmprə,maɪzɪŋ] *adj* : intransigente

unconcerned [ʌnkən'sərnd] *adj* : indiferente

unconditional [ʌnkən'dɪʃənəl] *adj* : incondicional

unconscious [ʌn'kɑntʃəs] *adj* : inconsciente

unconstitutional [ʌn,kɑnstə'tuːʃənəl, -tjuː-] *adj* : inconstitucional

uncontrollable [ʌnkən'troːləbəl] *adj* : incontrolable

unconventional [ʌnkən'ventʃənəl] *adj* : poco convencional

uncouth [ʌn'kuːθ] *adj* : grosero

uncover [ʌn'kʌvər] *vt* **1** : destapar **2** REVEAL : descubrir

undecided [ʌndi'saɪdəd] *adj* : indeciso

undeniable [ʌndi'naɪəbəl] *adj* : innegable

under ['ʌndər] *adv* **1** : debajo **2** LESS : menos **3** *or* **~ anesthetic** : bajo los efectos de la anestesia **— ~** *prep* **1** BELOW, BENEATH : debajo de, abajo de **2 — 20 minutes** : menos de 20 minutos **3 — the circumstances** : dadas las circunstancias

underage [ʌndər'eɪdʒ] *adj* : menor de edad

underclothes ['ʌndər,kloːz, -,kloːðz] → **underwear**

undercover [ʌndər'kʌvər] *adj* : secreto

undercurrent ['ʌndər,kərənt] *n* : tendencia *f* oculta

underdeveloped [ʌndərdɪ'vɛləpt] *adj* : subdesarrollado

underestimate [ʌndər'estə,meɪt] *vt* **-mated; -mating** : subestimar

underfoot [ʌndər'fut] *adv* : bajo los pies

undergo [ʌndər'goː] *vt* **-went** [-'wɛnt;], **-gone** [-'gɔn]; **-going** : sufrir, experimentar

undergraduate [ʌndər'grædʒuət] *n* : estudiante *m* universitario, estudiante *f* universitaria

underground [ʌndər'graund] *adv* **1** : bajo tierra **2 go ~** : pasar a la clandestinidad **— ~** ['ʌndər,graund] *adj* **1** : subterráneo **2** SECRET : secreto, clandestino **— ~** ['ʌndər,graund] *n* : movimiento *m* clandestino

undergrowth ['ʌndər,groːθ] *n* : maleza *f*

underhanded [ʌndər'hændəd] *adj* SLY : solapado

underline ['ʌndər,laɪn] *vt* **-lined; -lining** : subrayar

underlying [ʌndər'laɪŋ] *adj* : subyacente

undermine [ʌndər'maɪn] *vt* **-mined; -mining** : socavar, minar

underneath [ʌndər'niːθ] *adv* : debajo, abajo **— ~** *prep* : debajo de, abajo de *Lat*

underpants ['ʌndər,pænts] *npl* : calzoncillos *mpl*, calzones *mpl Lat*

underpass ['ʌndər,pæs] *n* : paso *m* inferior

underprivileged [ʌndər'prɪvlɪdʒd] *adj* : desfavorecido

underrate [ʌndər'reɪt] *vt* **-rated; -rating** : subestimar

undershirt ['ʌndər,ʃərt] *n* : camiseta *f*

understand [ʌndər'stænd] *v* **-stood** [-'stud]; **-standing** : comprender, entender **— understandable** [ʌndər'stændəbəl] *adj* : comprensible **— understanding** [ʌndər'stændɪŋ] *adj* : comprensivo, compasivo **— ~** *n* **1** : comprensión *f* **2** AGREEMENT : acuerdo *m*

understatement [ʌndər'steɪtmənt] *n* **that's an ~** : decir sólo eso es quedarse corto

understudy ['ʌndər,stʌdi] *n, pl* **-dies** : sobresaliente *mf* (en el teatro)

undertake [ʌndər'teɪk] *vt* **-took** [-'tuk]; **-taken** [-'teɪkən]; **-taking** : emprender (una tarea), encargarse de (una responsabilidad) **— undertaker** ['ʌndər,teɪkər] *n* : director *m*, -tora *f* de una funeraria **— undertaking** ['ʌndər,teɪkɪŋ, ,ʌndər-] *n* : empresa *f*, tarea *f*

undertone ['ʌndər,toːn] *n* **1** : voz *f* baja **2** SUGGESTION : matiz *m*

undertow ['ʌndər,toː] *n* : resaca *f*

underwater [ʌndər'wɔtər, -wɑ-] *adj* : submarino — ~ *adv* : debajo (del agua)

under way [ʌndər'weɪ] *adv* get ~ : ponerse en marcha

underwear ['ʌndər,wær] *n* : ropa *f* interior

underwent → **undergo**

underworld ['ʌndər,wʌrld] *n* the ~ CRIMINALS : la hampa, los bajos fondos

underwriter ['ʌndər,raɪtər, ,ʌndər'-] *n* : asegurador *m*, -dora *f*

undesirable [ʌndɪ'zaɪrəbəl] *adj* : indeseable

undeveloped [ʌndɪ'veləpt] *adj* : sin desarrollar

undignified [ʌn'dɪgnəfaɪd] *adj* : indecoroso

undisputed [ʌndɪ'spjuːtəd] *adj* : indiscutible

undo [ʌn'duː] *vt* **-did** [-'dɪd]; **-done** [-'dʌn]; **-doing 1** UNFASTEN : deshacer, desatar **2** : reparar (daños, etc.)

undoubtedly [ʌn'daʊtədli] *adv* : indudablemente

undress [ʌn'dres] *vt* : desnudar — *vi* : desnudarse

undue [ʌn'duː, -'djuː] *adj* : indebido, excesivo

undulate ['ʌndʒə,leɪt] *vi* **-lated; -lating** : ondular

unduly [ʌn'duːli, -'djuː-] *adv* : excesivamente

undying [ʌn'daɪɪŋ] *adj* : eterno

unearth [ʌn'ərθ] *vt* : desenterrar

unearthly [ʌn'ərθli] *adj* **-lier; -est** : sobrenatural, de otro mundo

uneasy [ʌn'iːzi] *adj* **-easier; -est 1** AWKWARD : incómodo **2** WORRIED : inquieto **3** RESTLESS : agitado — **uneasily** [ʌn'iːzəli] *adv* : inquietamente — **uneasiness** [ʌn'iːzinəs] *n* : inquietud *f*

uneducated [ʌn'edʒə,keɪtəd] *adj* : inculto

unemployed [ʌnɪm'plɔɪd] *adj* : desempleado — **unemployment** [ʌnɪm'plɔɪmənt] *n* : desempleo *m*

unerring [ʌn'erɪŋ, -'ər-] *adj* : infalible

unethical [ʌn'eθɪkəl] *adj* : poco ético

uneven [ʌn'iːvən] *adj* **1** : desigual **2** : impar (dícese de un número)

unexpected [ʌnɪk'spektəd] *adj* : inesperado

unfailing [ʌn'feɪlɪŋ] *adj* **1** CONSTANT : constante **2** INEXHAUSTIBLE : inagotable

unfair [ʌn'fær] *adj* : injusto — **unfairly** [ʌn'færli] *adv* : injustamente — **unfairness** [ʌn'færnəs] *n* : injusticia *f*

unfaithful [ʌn'feɪθfəl] *adj* : infiel — **unfaithfulness** [ʌn'feɪθfəlnəs] *n* : infidelidad *f*

unfamiliar [ʌnfə'mɪljər] *adj* **1** : desconocido **2** be ~ with : desconocer

unfasten [ʌn'fæsən] *vt* **1** : desabrochar (ropa, etc.) **2** UNDO : desatar (una cuerda, etc.)

unfavorable [ʌn'feɪvərəbəl] *adj* : desfavorable

unfeeling [ʌn'fiːlɪŋ] *adj* : insensible

unfinished [ʌn'fɪnɪʃt] *adj* : sin terminar

unfit [ʌn'fɪt] *adj* **1** UNSUITABLE : impropio **2** UNSUITED : no apto, incapaz

unfold [ʌn'foːld] *vt* **1** : desplegar, desdoblar **2** REVEAL : revelar (un plan, etc.) — *vi* **1** : extenderse, desplegarse **2** DEVELOP : desarrollarse

unforeseen [ʌnfor'siː] *adj* : imprevisto

unforgettable [ʌnfər'gɛtəbəl] *adj* : inolvidable

unforgivable [ʌnfər'gɪvəbəl] *adj* : imperdonable

unfortunate [ʌn'fortʃənət] *adj* **1** UNLUCKY : desgraciado, desafortunado **2** INAPPROPRIATE : inoportuno — **unfortunately** [ʌn'fortʃənətli] *adv* : desgraciadamente

unfounded [ʌn'faʊndəd] *adj* : infundado

unfriendly [ʌn'frendli] *adj* **-lier; -est** : poco amistoso

unfurl [ʌn'fərl] *vt* : desplegar

unfurnished [ʌn'fərnɪʃt] *adj* : desamueblado

ungainly [ʌn'geɪnli] *adj* : desgarbado

ungodly [ʌn'gɑdli, -'gɑd-] *adj* **1** : impío **2 an ~ hour** : una hora intempestiva

ungrateful [ʌn'greɪtfəl] *adj* : desagradecido

unhappy [ʌn'hæpi] *adj* **-pier; -est 1** SAD : infeliz, triste **2** UNFORTUNATE : desafortunado — **unhappily** [ʌn'hæpəli] *adv* **1** SADLY : tristemente **2** UNFORTUNATELY : desgraciadamente — **unhappiness** [ʌn'hæpinəs] *n* : tristeza *f*

unharmed [ʌn'hɑrmd] *adj* : salvo, ileso

unhealthy [ʌn'helθi] *adj* **-thier; -est 1** : malsano **2** SICKLY : enfermizo

unheard-of [ʌn'hərdəv] *adj* : sin precedente, insólito

unhook [ʌn'hʊk] *vt* : desenganchar

unhurt [ʌn'hərt] *adj* : ileso

unicorn ['juːnə,korn] *n* : unicornio *m*

unification [juːnəfə'keɪʃən] *n* : unificación *f*

uniform ['juːnə,form] *adj* : uniforme —

~ *n* : uniforme *m* — **uniformity** [ˌjuːnəˈfɔrməti] *n, pl* **-ties** : uniformidad *f*

unify [ˈjuːnəˌfaɪ] *vt* **-fied; -fying** : unificar

unilateral [ˌjuːnəˈlætərəl] *adj* : unilateral

unimaginable [ˌʌnɪˈmædʒənəbəl] *adj* : inconcebible

unimportant [ˌʌnɪmˈpɔrtənt] *adj* : insignificante

uninhabited [ˌʌnɪnˈhæbətəd] *adj* : deshabitado, despoblado

uninjured [ˌʌnˈɪndʒərd] *adj* : ileso

unintentional [ˌʌnɪnˈtentʃənəl] *adj* : involuntario

union [ˈjuːnjən] *n* **1** : unión *f* **2** *or* **labor ~** : sindicato *m*, gremio *m Lat*

unique [jʊˈniːk] *adj* : único — **uniquely** [jʊˈniːkli] *adv* EXCEPTIONALLY : excepcionalmente

unison [ˈjuːnəsən, -zən] *n* **in ~** : al unísono

unit [ˈjuːnɪt] *n* **1** : unidad *f* **2** : módulo *m* (de un mobiliario)

unite [jʊˈnaɪt] *v* **united; uniting** *vt* : unir — *vi* : unirse — **unity** [ˈjuːnəti] *n, pl* **-ties 1** : unidad *f* **2** HARMONY : acuerdo *m*

universe [ˈjuːnəˌvərs] *n* : universo *m* — **universal** [ˌjuːnəˈvərsəl] *adj* : universal

university [ˌjuːnəˈvərsəti] *n, pl* **-ties** : universidad *f*

unjust [ˌʌnˈdʒʌst] *adj* : injusto — **unjustified** [ˌʌnˈdʒʌstəˌfaɪd] *adj* : injustificado

unkempt [ˌʌnˈkempt] *adj* **1** : descuidado, desaseado **2** : despeinado (dícese del pelo)

unkind [ˌʌnˈkaɪnd] *adj* : poco amable, cruel — **unkindness** [ˌʌnˈkaɪndnəs] *n* : falta *f* de amabilidad, crueldad *f*

unknown [ˌʌnˈnoːn] *adj* : desconocido

unlawful [ˌʌnˈlɔfəl] *adj* : ilegal

unless [ənˈles] *conj* : a menos que, a no ser que

unlike [ˌʌnˈlaɪk] *adj* : diferente — **~** *prep* : a diferencia de — **unlikelihood** [ˌʌnˈlaɪkliˌhʊd] *n* : improbabilidad *f* — **unlikely** [ˌʌnˈlaɪkli] *adj* **-lier; -est** : improbable

unlimited [ˌʌnˈlɪmətəd] *adj* : ilimitado

unload [ˌʌnˈloːd] *v* : descargar

unlock [ˌʌnˈlɑk] *vt* : abrir (con llave)

unlucky [ˌʌnˈlʌki] *adj* **-luckier; -est 1** UNFORTUNATE : desgraciado **2** : de mala suerte (dícese de un número, etc.)

unmarried [ˌʌnˈmærid] *adj* : soltero

unmask [ˌʌnˈmæsk] *vt* : desenmascarar

unmistakable [ˌʌnmɪˈsteɪkəbəl] *adj* : inconfundible

unnatural [ˌʌnˈnætʃərəl] *adj* **1** : anormal **2** AFFECTED : afectado, forzado

unnecessary [ˌʌnˈnesəˌseri] *adj* : innecesario — **unnecessarily** [-ˌnesəˈserəli] *adv* : innecesariamente

unnerving [ˌʌnˈnərvɪŋ] *adj* : desconcertante

unnoticed [ˌʌnˈnoːtəst] *adj* : inadvertido

unobtainable [ˌʌnəbˈteɪnəbəl] *adj* : inasequible

unobtrusive [ˌʌnəbˈstruːsɪv] *adj* : discreto

unofficial [ˌʌnəˈfɪʃəl] *adj* : no oficial

unorthodox [ˌʌnˈɔrθəˌdɑks] *adj* : poco ortodoxo

unpack [ˌʌnˈpæk] *vt* **1** : desempaquetar, desempacar *Lat* (un paquete, etc.) **2** : deshacer (una maleta) — *vi* : deshacer las maletas

unparalleled [ˌʌnˈpærəˌleld] *adj* : sin igual

unpleasant [ˌʌnˈplezənt] *adj* : desagradable

unplug [ˌʌnˈplʌg] *vt* **-plugged; -plugging** : desconectar, desenchufar

unpopular [ˌʌnˈpɑpjələr] *adj* : poco popular

unprecedented [ˌʌnˈpresəˌdentəd] *adj* : sin precedente

unpredictable [ˌʌnprɪˈdɪktəbəl] *adj* : imprevisible

unprepared [ˌʌnprɪˈpærd] *adj* **1** : no preparado **2** UNREADY : desprevenido

unqualified [ˌʌnˈkwɑləˌfaɪd] *adj* **1** : no calificado, sin título **2** COMPLETE : absoluto

unquestionable [ˌʌnˈkwestʃənəbəl] *adj* : indiscutible — **unquestioning** [ˌʌnˈkwestʃənɪŋ] *adj* : incondicional

unravel [ˌʌnˈrævəl] *v* **-eled** *or* **-elled; -eling** *or* **-elling** *vt* : desenmarañar — *vi* : deshacerse

unreal [ˌʌnˈriːl] *adj* : irreal — **unrealistic** [ˌʌnˌriːəˈlɪstɪk] *adj* : poco realista

unreasonable [ˌʌnˈriːzənəbəl] *adj* **1** : irrazonable **2** EXCESSIVE : excesivo

unrecognizable [ˌʌnˈrekəgˌnaɪzəbəl] *adj* : irreconocible

unrelated [ˌʌnriˈleɪtəd] *adj* : no relacionado

unrelenting [ˌʌnriˈlentɪŋ] *adj* : implacable

unreliable [ˌʌnriˈlaɪəbəl] *adj* : que no es de fiar

unrepentant [ˌʌnriˈpentənt] *adj* : impenitente

unrest [ˌʌnˈrest] *n* **1** : inquietud *f*, malestar *m* **2** *or* **political ~** : disturbios *mpl*

unripe [ˌʌnˈraɪp] *adj* : verde, no maduro

unrivaled *or* **unrivalled** [ʌn'raɪvəld] *adj* : incomparable, sin par

unroll [ʌn'roʊl] *vt* : desenrollar — *vi* : desenrollarse

unruly [ʌn'ru:li] *adj* : indisciplinado

unsafe [ʌn'seɪf] *adj* : inseguro

unsaid [ʌn'sed] *adj* : sin decir

unsanitary [ʌn'sænəˌteri] *adj* : antihigiénico

unsatisfactory [ʌnˌsætəs'fæktəri] *adj* : insatisfactorio

unscathed [ʌn'skeɪðd] *adj* : ileso

unscrew [ʌn'skru:] *vt* : destornillar

unscrupulous [ʌn'skru:pjələs] *adj* : sin escrúpulos

unseemly [ʌn'si:mli] *adj* **-lier; -est** : indecoroso

unseen [ʌn'si:n] *adj* **1** : no visto **2** UNNOTICED : inadvertido

unselfish [ʌn'selfɪʃ] *adj* : desinteresado

unsettle [ʌn'setəl] *vt* **-tled; -tling** DISTURB : perturbar — **unsettled** [ʌn'setəld] *adj* **1** CHANGEABLE : inestable **2** DISTURBED : agitado, inquieto **3** : variable (dícese del tiempo)

unsightly [ʌn'saɪtli] *adj* : feo

unskilled [ʌn'skɪld] *adj* : no calificado — **unskillful** [ʌn'skɪlfəl] *adj* : torpe, poco hábil

unsociable [ʌn'soʊʃəbəl] *adj* : poco sociable

unsound [ʌn'saʊnd] *adj* **1** : defectuoso, erróneo **2 of ~ mind** : demente

unspeakable [ʌn'spi:kəbəl] *adj* **1** : indecible **2** TERRIBLE : atroz

unstable [ʌn'steɪbəl] *adj* : inestable

unsteady [ʌn'stedi] *adj* **1** : inestable **2** SHAKY : tembloroso

unsuccessful [ʌnsək'sesfəl] *adj* **1** : fracasado **2 be ~** : no tener éxito

unsuitable [ʌn'su:təbəl] *adj* **1** : inadecuado **2** INCONVENIENT : inconveniente

unsure [ʌn'ʃʊr] *adj* : inseguro

unsuspecting [ʌnsə'spektɪŋ] *adj* : confiado

unsympathetic [ʌnˌsɪmpə'θetɪk] *adj* : indiferente

unthinkable [ʌn'θɪŋkəbəl] *adj* : inconcebible

untidy [ʌn'taɪdi] *adj* : desordenado (dícese de una sala, etc.), desaliñado (dícese de una persona)

untie [ʌn'taɪ] *vt* **-tied; -tying** *or* **-tieing** : desatar

until [ʌn'tɪl] *prep* : hasta — *~ conj* : hasta que

untimely [ʌn'taɪmli] *adj* **1** PREMATURE : prematuro **2** INOPPORTUNE : inoportuno

untold [ʌn'toʊld] *adj* : incalculable

untoward [ʌn'tɔrd, -'tɔːrd, -tə'wɔrd] *adj* **1** ADVERSE : adverso **2** IMPROPER : indecoroso

untroubled [ʌn'trʌbəld] *adj* **1** : tranquilo **2 be ~ by** : no estar afectado por

untrue [ʌn'tru:] *adj* : falso

unused [ʌn'ju:zd, *in sense 2 usually* -'ju:st] *adj* **1** NEW : nuevo **2 be ~ to** : no estar acostumbrado a

unusual [ʌn'ju:ʒuəl] *adj* : poco común, insólito — **unusually** [ʌn'ju:ʒuəl, -'ju:ʒəli] *adv* : excepcionalmente

unveil [ʌn'veɪl] *vt* : descubrir, revelar

unwanted [ʌn'wɑntəd] *adj* : superfluo (dícese de un objeto), no deseado (dícese de un niño, etc.)

unwarranted [ʌn'wɔrəntəd] *adj* : injustificado

unwelcome [ʌn'welkəm] *adj* : inoportuno, molesto

unwell [ʌn'wel] *adj* **be ~** : sentirse mal

unwieldy [ʌn'wi:ldi] *adj* : difícil de manejar

unwilling [ʌn'wɪlɪŋ] *adj* : poco dispuesto — **unwillingly** [ʌn'wɪlɪŋli] *adv* : de mala gana

unwind [ʌn'waɪnd] *v* **-wound** [-'waʊnd]; **-winding** *vt* : desenrollar — *vi* **1** : desenrollarse **2** RELAX : relajarse

unwise [ʌn'waɪz] *adj* : imprudente

unworthy [ʌn'wərði] *adj* **be ~ of** : no ser digno de

unwrap [ʌn'ræp] *vt* **-wrapped; -wrapping** : desenvolver

up ['ʌp] *adv* **1** ABOVE : arriba **2** UPWARDS : hacia arriba **3 ten miles farther ~** : diez millas más adelante **4 ~ here/there** : aquí/allí arriba **5 ~ north** : en el norte **6 ~ until** : hasta — *~ adj* **1** AWAKE : levantado **2** FINISHED : terminado **3 be ~ against** : enfrentarse con **4 be ~ on** : estar al corriente de **5 it's ~ to you** : depende de tí **6 prices are ~** : los precios han aumentado **7 the sun is ~** : ha salido el sol **8 what's ~?** : ¿qué pasa? — *~ prep* **1 go ~ the river** : ir río arriba **2 go ~ the stairs** : subir la escalera **3 ~ the coast** : a lo largo de la costa — *~ v* **upped** ['ʌpt]; **upping; ups** *vt* : aumentar — *vi* **she ~ and left** : agarró y se fue

upbringing ['ʌpˌbrɪŋɪŋ] *n* : educación *f*

upcoming [ʌp'kʌmɪŋ] *adj* : próximo

update [ʌp'deɪt] *vt* **-dated; -dating** : poner al día, actualizar — ['ʌpˌdeɪt] *n* : puesta *f* al día

upgrade ['ʌpˌgreɪd, ˌʌp-] *vt* **-graded; -grading** : elevar la categoría de (un puesto, etc.), mejorar (una facilidad, etc.)

upheaval [ʌp'hi:vəl] *n* : trastorno *m*
uphill [ʌp'hɪl] *adv* : cuesta arriba — ~ ['ʌp,hɪl] *adj* **1** : en subida **2 be an ~ battle** : ser muy difícil
uphold [ʌp'ho:ld] *vt* **-held; -holding** : sostener, apoyar
upholstery [ʌp'ho:lstəri] *n, pl* **-steries** : tapicería *f*
upkeep ['ʌp,ki:p] *n* : mantenimiento *m*
upon [ə'pɔn, ə'pɑn] *prep* **1** : en, sobre **2 ~ leaving** : al salir
upper ['ʌpər] *adj* : superior — ~ *n* : parte *f* superior (del calzado, etc.)
uppercase [ʌpər'keɪs] *adj* : mayúsculo
upper class *n* : clase *f* alta
upper hand *n* : ventaja *f*, dominio *m*
uppermost ['ʌpər,mo:st] *adj* : más alto
upright ['ʌp,raɪt] *adj* **1** VERTICAL : vertical **2** ERECT : derecho **3** JUST : recto, honesto — ~ *n* : montante *m*, poste *m*
uprising ['ʌp,raɪzɪŋ] *n* : insurrección *f*, revuelta *f*
uproar ['ʌp,ror] *n* COMMOTION : alboroto *m*
uproot [ʌp'ru:t, -'rʊt] *vt* : desarraigar
upset [ʌp'sɛt] *vt* **-set; -setting 1** OVERTURN : volcar **2** DISTRESS : alterar, inquietar **3** DISRUPT : trastornar — ~ *adj* **1** DISTRESSED : alterado **2 have an ~ stomach** : estar mal del estómago — ~ ['ʌp,sɛt] *n* : trastorno *m*
upshot ['ʌp,ʃɑt] *n* : resultado *m* final
upside down [ʌp,saɪd'daʊn] *adv* **1** : al revés **2 turn ~** : volver — **upside-down** [ʌp,saɪd'daʊn] *adj* : al revés
upstairs [ʌp'stærz] *adv* : arriba — ~ ['ʌp,stærz, ʌp'-] *adj* : de arriba — ~ ['ʌp,stærz, ʌp'-] *ns & pl* : piso *m* de arriba
upstart ['ʌp,stɑrt] *n* : advenedizo *m*, -za *f*
upstream ['ʌp,stri:m] *adv* : río arriba
upswing ['ʌp,swɪŋ] *n* **be on the ~** : estar mejorándose
up-to-date [ʌptə'deɪt] *adj* **1** : corriente, al día **2** MODERN : moderno
uptown ['ʌp'taʊn] *adv* : hacia la parte alta de la ciudad, hacia el distrito residencial
upturn ['ʌp,tərn] *n* : mejora *f*, auge *m* (económico)
upward ['ʌpwərd] *or* **upwards** [-wərdz] *adv* : hacia arriba — **upward** *adj* : ascendente, hacia arriba
uranium [jʊ'reɪniəm] *n* : uranio *m*
urban ['ərbən] *adj* : urbano
urbane [ər'beɪn] *adj* : urbano, cortés
urge ['ərdʒ] *vt* **urged; urging 1** PRESS : instar, exhortar **2 ~ on** : animar — ~ *n* : impulso *m*, ganas *fpl* — **ur-**

gency ['ərdʒəntsi] *n, pl* **-cies** : urgencia *f* — **urgent** ['ərdʒənt] *adj* **1** : urgente **2 be ~** : urgir
urine ['jʊrən] *n* : orina *f* — **urinate** ['jʊrə,neɪt] *vi* **-nated; -nating** : orinar
urn ['ərn] *n* : urna *f*
Uruguayan [ʊrə'gwaɪən, jʊr-, -'gweɪ-] *adj* : uruguayo
us ['ʌs] *pron* **1** (*as direct or indirect object*) : nos **2** (*as object of a preposition*) : nosotros, nosotras **3 both of ~** : nosotros dos **4 it's ~!** : ¡somos nosotros!
usage ['ju:sɪdʒ, -zɪdʒ] *n* : uso *m*
use ['ju:z] *v* **used** ['ju:zd, *the phrase* "used to" *is usually* 'ju:stu:]; **using** *vt* **1** : usar **2** CONSUME : consumir, tomar (drogas, etc.) **3 ~ up** : agotar, consumir — *vi* **1 she ~d to dance** : acostumbraba bailar **2 winters ~d to be colder** : los inviernos solían ser más fríos — ~ ['ju:s] *n* **1** : uso *m* **2 have no ~ for** : no necesitar **3 have the ~ of** : poder usar, tener acceso a **4 it's no ~!** : ¡es inútil! — **used** ['ju:zd, *in sense 2 usually* 'ju:st] *adj* **1** SECONDHAND : usado **2 be ~ to** : estar acostumbrado a — **useful** ['ju:sfəl] *adj* : útil, práctico — **usefulness** ['ju:sfələs] *n* : utilidad *f* — **useless** ['ju:sləs] *adj* : inútil — **user** ['ju:zər] *n* : usuario *m*, -ria *f*
usher ['ʌʃər] *vt* **1** : acompañar, conducir **2 ~ in** : hacer entrar — ~ *n* : acomodador *m*, -dora *f*
usual ['ju:ʒuəl] *adj* **1** : habitual, usual **2 as ~** : como de costumbre — **usually** ['ju:ʒuəli, 'ju:ʒəli] *adv* : usualmente
usurp [jʊ'sərp, -'zərp] *vt* : usurpar
utensil [jʊ'tɛntsəl] *n* : utensilio *m*
uterus ['ju:tərəs] *n, pl* **uteri** [-,raɪ] : útero *m*, matriz *f*
utility [ju:'tɪləţi] *n, pl* **-ties 1** : utilidad *f* **2 or public ~** : empresa *f* de servicio público
utilize ['ju:ţəl,aɪz] *vt* **-lized; -lizing** : utilizar
utmost ['ʌt,mo:st] *adj* **1** FARTHEST : extremo **2 of the ~ importance** : de suma importancia — ~ *n* **do one's ~** : hacer todo lo posible
utopia [jʊ'to:piə] *n* : utopía *f* — **utopian** [jʊ'to:piən] *adj* : utópico
utter¹ ['ʌţər] *adj* : absoluto, completo
utter² *vt* : decir, pronunciar (palabras) — **utterance** ['ʌţərənts] *n* : declaración *f*, expresión *f*
utterly ['ʌţərli] *adv* : completamente, totalmente

V

v ['viː] *n*, *pl* **v's** *or* **vs** ['viːz] : v *f*, vigésima segunda letra del alfabeto inglés

vacant ['veɪkənt] *adj* **1** AVAILABLE : libre **2** UNOCCUPIED : desocupado **3** : vacante (dícese de un puesto) **4** : ausente (dícese de una mirada) — **vacancy** ['veɪkəntsi] *n*, *pl* **-cies 1** : (puesto *m*) vacante *f* **2** : habitación *f* libre (en un hotel, etc.)

vacate ['veɪˌkeɪt] *vt* **-cated; -cating** : desalojar, desocupar

vacation [verˈkeɪʃən, və-] *n* : vacaciones *fpl*

vaccination [ˌvæksəˈneɪʃən] *n* : vacunación *f* — **vaccinate** ['væksəˌneɪt] *vt* **-nated; -nating** : vacunar — **vaccine** [vækˈsiːn, 'væk-] *n* : vacuna *f*

vacuum ['væˌkjuːm, -kjəm] *n*, *pl* **vacuums** *or* **vacua** : vacío *m* — ~ *vt* : pasar la aspiradora por — **vacuum cleaner** *n* : aspiradora *f*

vagina [vəˈdʒaɪnə] *n*, *pl* **-nae** [-ˌniː, -ˌnaɪ] *or* **-nas** : vagina *f*

vagrant ['veɪɡrənt] *n* : vagabundo *m*, -da *f*

vague ['veɪɡ] *adj* **vaguer; -est** : vago, indistinto

vain ['veɪn] *adj* **1** CONCEITED : vanidoso **2 in** ~ : en vano

valentine ['væləntaɪn] *n* : tarjeta *f* del día de San Valentín

valiant ['væljənt] *adj* : valiente, valeroso

valid ['væləd] *adj* : válido — **validate** ['væləˌdeɪt] *vt* **-dated; -dating** : validar — **validity** [vəˈlɪdəti, væ-] *n* : validez *f*

valley ['væli] *n*, *pl* **-leys** : valle *m*

valor ['vælər] *n* : valor *m*, valentía *f*

value ['væljuː] *n* : valor *m* — ~ *vt* **-ued; -uing** : valorar — **valuable** ['væljuəbəl, 'væljəbəl] *adj* : valioso — **valuables** *npl* : objetos *mpl* de valor

valve ['vælv] *n* : válvula *f*

vampire ['væmˌpaɪr] *n* : vampiro *m*

van ['væn] *n* : furgoneta *f*, camioneta *f*

vandal ['vændəl] *n* : vándalo *m* — **vandalism** ['vændəlˌɪzəm] *n* : vandalismo *m* — **vandalize** ['vændəlˌaɪz] *vt* : destrozar, destruir

vane ['veɪn] *n* *or* **weather** ~ : veleta *f*

vanguard ['vænˌɡɑrd] *n* : vanguardia *f*

vanilla [vəˈnɪlə, -ˈne-] *n* : vainilla *f*

vanish ['vænɪʃ] *vi* : desaparecer

vanity ['vænəti] *n*, *pl* **-ties 1** : vanidad *f* **2** *or* ~ **table** : tocador *m*

vantage point ['væntɪdʒ] *n* : posición *f* ventajosa

vapor ['veɪpər] *n* : vapor *m*

variable ['veriəbəl] *adj* : variable — ~ *n* : variable *f* — **variance** ['veriənts] *n* **at** ~ **with** : en desacuerdo con — **variant** ['veriənt] *n* : variante *f* — **variation** [ˌveriˈeɪʃən] *n* : variación *f* — **varied** ['verid] *adj* : variado — **variegated** ['veriəˌɡeɪtəd] *adj* : abigarrado, multicolor — **variety** [vəˈraɪəti] *n*, *pl* **-ties 1** : variedad *f* **2** ASSORTMENT : surtido *m* **3** SORT : clase *f* — **various** ['veriəs] *adj* : varios, diversos

varnish ['vɑrnɪʃ] *n* : barniz *f* — ~ *vt* : barnizar

vary ['veri] *v* **varied; varying** : variar

vase ['veɪs, 'veɪz, 'vɑz] *n* **1** : jarrón *m* **2** *or* **flower** ~ : florero *m*

vast ['væst] *adj* : vasto, enorme — **vastness** ['væstnəs] *n* : inmensidad *f*

vat ['væt] *n* : cuba *f*

vault[1] ['vɔlt] *vi* LEAP : saltar — ~ *n* : salto *m*

vault[2] *n* **1** DOME : bóveda *f* **2** *or* **bank** ~ : cámara *f* acorazada, bóveda *f* de seguridad *Lat* **3** CRYPT : cripta *f*

VCR [ˌviːˌsiːˈɑr] (*videocassette recorder*) *n* : video *m*

veal ['viːl] *n* : (carne *f* de) ternera *f*

veer ['vɪr] *vi* : virar

vegetable ['vedʒtəbəl, 'vedʒətə-] *adj* : vegetal — ~ *n* **1** : vegetal *m* (planta) **2** ~**s** *npl* : verduras *fpl* — **vegetarian** [ˌvedʒəˈteriən] *n* : vegetariano *mf* — **vegetation** [ˌvedʒəˈteɪʃən] *n* : vegetación *f*

vehemence ['viːəmənts] *n* : vehemencia *f* — **vehement** ['viːəmənt] *adj* : vehemente

vehicle ['viːəkəl, 'viːˌhɪkəl] *n* : vehículo *m*

veil ['veɪl] *n* : velo *m* — ~ *vt* **1** : cubrir con un velo **2** CONCEAL : velar

vein ['veɪn] *n* **1** : vena *f* **2** : veta *f* (de un mineral, etc.)

velocity [vəˈlɑsəti] *n*, *pl* **-ties** : velocidad *f*

velvet ['velvət] *n* : terciopelo *m* — **velvety** ['velvəti] *adj* : aterciopelado

vending machine ['vendɪŋ-] *vt* : máquina *f* expendedora

vendor ['vɛndər] n : vendedor m, -dora f
veneer [və'nɪr] n 1 : chapa f 2 FACADE : apariencia f
venerable ['vɛnərəbəl] adj : venerable — **venerate** ['vɛnəˌreɪt] vt -ated; -ating : venerar — **veneration** [ˌvɛnə'reɪʃən] n : veneración f
venereal [və'nɪriəl] adj : venéreo
venetian blind [və'niːʃən-] n : persiana f veneciana
Venezuelan [ˌvɛnə'zweɪlən, -zʊ'eɪ-] adj : venezolano
vengeance ['vɛndʒənts] n 1 : venganza f 2 **take — on** : vengarse de — **vengeful** ['vɛndʒfəl] adj : vengativo
venison ['vɛnəsən, -zən] n : (carne f de) venado m
venom ['vɛnəm] n : veneno m — **venomous** ['vɛnəməs] adj : venenoso
vent ['vɛnt] vt : desahogar — ~ n 1 or **air ~** : rejilla f de ventilación 2 OUTLET : desahogo m — **ventilate** ['vɛntəlˌeɪt] vt -lated; -lating : ventilar — **ventilation** [ˌvɛntəl'eɪʃən] n : ventilación f — **ventilator** ['vɛntəlˌeɪtər] n : ventilador m
ventriloquist [vɛn'trɪləkwɪst] n : ventrílocuo m, -cua f
venture ['vɛntʃər] v -tured; -turing vt 1 RISK : arriesgar 2 ... (una opinión, etc.) — vi : atreverse — ~ n or **business ~** : empresa f
venue ['vɛnjuː] n : lugar m
Venus ['viːnəs] n : Venus m
veranda or **verandah** [və'rændə] n : veranda f
verb ['vərb] n : verbo m — **verbal** ['vərbəl] adj : verbal — **verbatim** [vər'beɪtəm] adv : palabra por palabra — ~ adj : literal — **verbose** [vər'boːs] adj : verboso
verdict ['vərdɪkt] n 1 : veredicto m 2 OPINION : opinión f
verge ['vərdʒ] n 1 : borde m 2 **on the ~ of** : a punto de (hacer algo), al borde de (algo) — ~ vi **verged; verging ~ on** : rayar en
verify ['vɛrəˌfaɪ] vt -fied; -fying : verificar — **verification** [ˌvɛrəfə'keɪʃən] n : verificación f
vermin ['vərmən] ns & pl : alimañas fpl
vermouth [vər'muːth] n : vermut m
versatile ['vərsətəl] adj : versátil — **versatility** [ˌvərsə'tɪləti] n : versatilidad f
verse ['vərs] n 1 LINE : verso m 2 POETRY : poesía f 3 : versículo m (en la Biblia) — **versed** ['vərst] adj **be well ~ in** : ser muy versado en
version ['vərʒən] n : versión f
versus ['vərsəs] prep : versus

vertebra ['vərtəbrə] n, pl **-brae** [-ˌbreɪ, -ˌbriː] or **-bras** : vértebra f
vertical ['vərtɪkəl] adj : vertical — ~ n : vertical f
vertigo ['vərtɪˌgoː] n, pl **-goes** or **-gos** : vértigo m
verve ['vərv] n : brío m
very ['vɛri] adv 1 : muy 2 **at the ~ least** : por lo menos 3 **the ~ same thing** : la misma cosa 4 **~ much** : mucho 5 **~ well** : muy bien — ~ adj **verier; -est** 1 PRECISE, SAME : mismo 2 MERE : solo, mero 3 **the ~ thing** : justo lo que hacía falta
vessel ['vɛsəl] n 1 CONTAINER : recipiente m 2 SHIP : nave f, buque m 3 or **blood ~** : vaso m sanguíneo
vest ['vɛst] n 1 : chaleco m 2 Brit UNDERSHIRT : camiseta f
vestibule ['vɛstəˌbjuːl] n : vestíbulo m
vestige ['vɛstɪdʒ] n : vestigio m
vet ['vɛt] n 1 → **veterinarian** 2 → **veteran**
veteran ['vɛtərən, 'vɛtrən] n : veterano m, -na f
veterinarian [ˌvɛtərə'nɛriən, ˌvɛtə'nɛr-] n : veterinario m, -ria f — **veterinary** ['vɛtərəˌnɛri] adj : veterinario
veto ['viːtoː] n, pl **-toes** : veto m — ~ vt : vetar
vex ['vɛks] vt ANNOY : irritar
via ['vaɪə, 'viːə] prep : por, vía
viable ['vaɪəbəl] adj : viable
viaduct ['vaɪəˌdʌkt] n : viaducto m
vial ['vaɪəl] n : frasco m
vibrant ['vaɪbrənt] adj : vibrante — **vibrate** ['vaɪˌbreɪt] vi -brated; -brating : vibrar — **vibration** [vaɪ'breɪʃən] n : vibración f
vicar ['vɪkər] n : vicario m, -ria f
vicarious [vaɪ'kæriəs, vɪ-] adj : indirecto
vice ['vaɪs] n : vicio m
vice president n : vicepresidente m, -ta f
vice versa [ˌvaɪsɪ'vərsə, ˌvaɪs'vər-] adv : viceversa
vicinity [və'sɪnəti] n, pl **-ties** 1 : inmediaciones fpl 2 **in the ~ of** ABOUT : alrededor de
vicious ['vɪʃəs] adj 1 SAVAGE : feroz 2 MALICIOUS : malicioso
victim ['vɪktəm] n : víctima f
victor ['vɪktər] n : vencedor m, -dora f
victory ['vɪktəri] n, pl **-ries** : victoria f — **victorious** [vɪk'toːriəs] adj : victorioso
video ['vɪdiˌoː] n : video m, vídeo m Spain — ~ adj : de video — **videocassette** [ˌvɪdioʊkə'sɛt] n : videocasete m — **videotape** ['vɪdioˌteɪp] n : video-

cinta f — ~ vt -taped; -taping : videograbar

vie ['vaɪ] vi **vied**; **vying** ['vaɪɪŋ] : competir

Vietnamese [vi‚ɛtnə'miːz, -'miːs] adj : vietnamita

view ['vjuː] n 1 : vista f 2 OPINION : opinión f 3 come into ~ : aparecer 4 in ~ of : en vista de (que) — ~ vt 1 : ver 2 CONSIDER : considerar — **viewer** ['vjuːər] n or television ~ : televidente mf — **viewpoint** ['vjuːˌpɔɪnt] n : punto m de vista

vigil ['vɪdʒəl] n : vela f — **vigilance** ['vɪdʒələnts] n : vigilancia f — **vigilant** ['vɪdʒələnt] adj : vigilante

vigor or Brit **vigour** ['vɪgər] n : vigor m — **vigorous** ['vɪgərəs] adj 1 : enérgico 2 ROBUST : vigoroso

Viking ['vaɪkɪŋ] n : vikingo m, -ga f

vile ['vaɪl] adj **viler**; **vilest** 1 : vil 2 REVOLTING : asqueroso 3 TERRIBLE : horrible

villa ['vɪlə] n : casa f de campo

village ['vɪlɪdʒ] n : pueblo m (grande), aldea f (pequeña) — **villager** ['vɪlɪdʒər] n : vecino m, -na f (de un pueblo); aldeano m, -na f (de una aldea)

villain ['vɪlən] n : villano m, -na f

vindicate ['vɪndəˌkeɪt] vt -cated; -cating 1 : vindicar 2 JUSTIFY : justificar

vindictive [vɪn'dɪktɪv] adj : vengativo

vine ['vaɪn] n 1 : enredadera f 2 GRAPEVINE : vid f

vinegar ['vɪnɪgər] n : vinagre m

vineyard ['vɪnjərd] n : viña f, viñedo m

vintage ['vɪntɪdʒ] n 1 : cosecha f (de vino) 2 ERA : época f — ~ adj 1 : añejo (dícese de un vino) 2 CLASSIC : de época

vinyl ['vaɪnəl] n : vinilo m

viola [vi'oːlə] n : viola f

violate ['vaɪəˌleɪt] vt -lated; -lating : violar — **violation** [ˌvaɪə'leɪʃən] n : violación f

violence ['vaɪələnts, 'vaɪə-] n : violencia f — **violent** ['vaɪələnt, 'vaɪə-] adj : violento

violet ['vaɪələt, 'vaɪə-] n : violeta f (flor), violeta m (color)

violin [ˌvaɪə'lɪn] n : violín m — **violinist** [ˌvaɪə'lɪnɪst] n : violinista mf — **violoncello** [ˌvaɪələn'tʃɛloː, ˌviː-] → **cello**

VIP [ˌviːˌaɪ'piː] n, pl **VIPs** [-'piːz] : VIP mf

viper ['vaɪpər] n : víbora f

virgin ['vərdʒən] n : virgen mf — ~ adj 1 : virgen (dícese de la lana, etc.) 2 CHASTE : virginal — **virginity** [vər'dʒɪnəti] n : virginidad f

virile ['vɪrəl, -ˌaɪl] adj : viril — **virility** [və'rɪləti] n : virilidad f

virtual ['vərtʃʊəl] adj : virtual — **virtually** ['vərtʃʊəli, 'vərtʃəli] adv : prácticamente

virtue ['vərtʃuː] n 1 : virtud f 2 by ~ of : en virtud de

virtuoso [ˌvərtʃu'oːsoː, -zoː] n, pl **-sos** or **-si** [-ˌsiː, -ˌziː] : virtuoso m, -sa f

virtuous ['vərtʃuəs] adj : virtuoso

virulent ['vɪrələnt, 'vɪrjə-] adj : virulento

virus ['vaɪrəs] n : virus m

visa ['viːzə, -sə] n : visado m, visa f Lat

vis-à-vis [ˌviːzə'viː, -sə-] prep : con respecto a

viscous ['vɪskəs] adj : viscoso

vise ['vaɪs] n : torno m de banco

visible ['vɪzəbəl] adj 1 : visible 2 NOTICEABLE : evidente — **visibility** [ˌvɪzə'bɪləti] n, pl **-ties** : visibilidad f

vision ['vɪʒən] n 1 : visión f 2 have ~s of : imaginarse — **visionary** ['vɪʒəˌneri] adj : visionario — ~ n, pl **-ries** : visionario m, -ria f

visit ['vɪzət] vt : visitar — vi 1 : hacer una visita 2 be ~ing : estar de visita — ~ n : visita f — **visitor** ['vɪzətər] n 1 : visitante mf 2 GUEST : visita f

visor ['vaɪzər] n : visera f

vista ['vɪstə] n : vista f

visual ['vɪʒʊəl] adj : visual — **visualize** ['vɪʒʊəˌlaɪz] vt **-ized**; **-izing** : visualizar

vital ['vaɪtəl] adj 1 : vital 2 CRUCIAL : esencial — **vitality** [vaɪ'tæləti] n, pl **-ties** : vitalidad f, energía f

vitamin ['vaɪtəmən] n : vitamina f

vivacious [və'veɪʃəs, vaɪ-] adj : vivaz, animado

vivid ['vɪvəd] adj : vivo (dícese de colores), vívido (dícese de sueños, etc.)

vocabulary [voˈkæbjəˌleri] n, pl **-laries** : vocabulario m

vocal ['voːkəl] adj 1 : vocal 2 OUTSPOKEN : vociferante — **vocal cords** npl : cuerdas fpl vocales — **vocalist** ['voːkəlɪst] n : cantante mf, vocalista mf

vocation [voˈkeɪʃən] n : vocación f — **vocational** [voˈkeɪʃənəl] adj : profesional

vociferous [voˈsɪfərəs] adj : vociferante, ruidoso

vodka ['vɑdkə] n : vodka m

vogue ['voːg] n 1 : moda f, boga f 2 be in ~ : estar de moda, estar en boga

voice ['vɔɪs] n : voz f — ~ vt **voiced**; **voicing** : expresar

void ['vɔɪd] adj 1 INVALID : nulo 2 ~ of : falto de — ~ n : vacío m — ~ vt : anular

volatile ['vɑlətəl] *adj* : volátil — **volatility** [,vɑlə'tɪləti] *n* : volatilidad *f*

volcano [vɑl'keɪ,noː] *n, pl* **-noes** *or* **-nos** : volcán *m* — **volcanic** [vɑl'kænɪk] *adj* : volcánico

volition [voʊ'lɪʃən] *n* of one's own ~ : por voluntad propia

volley ['vɑli] *n, pl* **-leys 1** : descarga *f* (de tiros) **2** : torrente *m* (de insultos, etc.) **3** : volea *f* (en deportes) — **volleyball** ['vɑli,bɔl] *n* : voleibol *m*

volt ['voːlt] *n* : voltio *m* — **voltage** ['voːltɪdʒ] *n* : voltaje *m*

voluble ['vɑljəbəl] *adj* : locuaz

volume ['vɑljəm, -juːm] *n* : volumen *m* — **voluminous** [və'luːmənəs] *adj* : voluminoso

voluntary ['vɑlən,teri] *adj* : voluntario — **volunteer** [,vɑlən'tɪr] *n* : voluntario *m*, **-ria** *f* — ~ *vt* : ofrecer — *vi* ~ **to** : ofrecerse a

voluptuous [və'lʌptʃuəs] *adj* : voluptuoso

vomit ['vɑmət] *n* : vómito *m* — ~ *v* : vomitar

voracious [vɔ'reɪʃəs, və-] *adj* : voraz

vote ['voːt] *n* **1** : voto *m* **2** SUFFRAGE : derecho *m* al voto — ~ *vi* **voted; voting** : votar — **voter** ['voːtər] *n* : votante *mf* — **voting** ['voːtɪŋ] *n* : votación *f*

vouch ['vɑʊtʃ] *vi* ~ **for** : responder de (algo), responder por (algn) — **voucher** ['vɑʊtʃər] *n* : vale *m*

vow ['vɑʊ] *n* : voto *m* — ~ *vt* : jurar

vowel ['vɑʊəl] *n* : vocal *m*

voyage ['vɔɪidʒ] *n* : viaje *m*

vulgar ['vʌlgər] *adj* **1** COMMON : ordinario **2** CRUDE : grosero, vulgar — **vulgarity** [,vʌl'gærəti] *n, pl* **-ties** : vulgaridad *f*

vulnerable ['vʌlnərəbəl] *adj* : vulnerable — **vulnerability** [,vʌlnərə'bɪləti] *n, pl* **-ties** : vulnerabilidad *f*

vulture ['vʌltʃər] *n* : buitre *m*

vying → **vie**

W

w ['dʌbəl,juː] *n, pl* **w's** *or* **ws** [-juːz] : w *f*, vigésima tercera letra del alfabeto inglés

wad ['wɑd] *n* : taco *m* (de papel, etc.), fajo *m* (de billetes)

waddle ['wɑdəl] *vi* **-died; -dling** : andar como un pato

wade ['weɪd] *v* **waded; wading** *vi* : caminar por el agua — *vt or* ~ **across** : vadear

wafer ['weɪfər] *n* : barquillo *m*

waffle ['wɑfəl] *n* : gofre *m Spain*, wafle *m Lat*

waft ['wɑft, 'wæft] *vt* : llevar por el aire — *vi* : flotar

wag ['wæg] *v* **wagged; wagging** *vt* : menear — *vi* : menearse

wage ['weɪdʒ] *n or* **wages** *npl* : salario *m* — ~ *vt* **waged; waging** ~ **war** : hacer la guerra

wager ['weɪdʒər] *n* : apuesta *f* — ~ *v* : apostar

wagon ['wægən] *n* **1** CART : carrito *m* **2** → **station wagon**

waif ['weɪf] *n* : niño *m* abandonado

wail ['weɪl] *vi* : lamentarse — ~ *n* : lamento *m*

waist ['weɪst] *n* : cintura *f* — **waistline** ['weɪst,laɪn] *n* : cintura *f*

wait ['weɪt] *vi* : esperar — *vt* **1** AWAIT : esperar **2** ~ **tables** : servir a la mesa

— ~ *n* **1** : espera *f* **2 lie in** ~ : estar al acecho — **waiter** ['weɪtər] *n* : camarero *m*, mozo *m Lat* — **waiting room** *n* : sala *f* de espera — **waitress** ['weɪtrəs] *n* : camarera *f*, moza *f Lat*

waive ['weɪv] *vt* **waived; waiving** : renunciar a — **waiver** ['weɪvər] *n* : renuncia *f*

wake[1] ['weɪk] *v* **woke** ['woːk] **woken** ['woːkən] *or* **waked; waking** *vi or* ~ **up** : despertarse — *vt* : despertar — ~ *n* : velatorio *m* (de un difunto)

wake[2] *n* **1** : estela *f* (de un barco) **2 in the** ~ **of** : tras, como consecuencia de

waken ['weɪkən] *vt* : despertar — *vi* : despertarse

walk ['wɔk] *vi* **1** : caminar, andar **2** STROLL : pasear **3 too far to** ~ : demasiado lejos para ir a pie — *vt* **1** : caminar por **2** : sacar a pasear (a un perro) — ~ *n* **1** : paseo *m* **2** PATH : camino *m* **3** GAIT : andar *m* — **walker** ['wɔkər] *n* **1** : paseante *mf* **2** HIKER : excursionista *mf* — **walking stick** *n* : bastón *m* — **walkout** ['wɔk,aʊt] *n* STRIKE : huelga *f* — **walk out** *vi* **1** STRIKE : declararse en huelga **2** LEAVE : salir, irse **3** ~ **on** : abandonar

wall ['wɔl] *n* : muro *m* (exterior), pared *f* (interior), muralla *f* (de una ciudad)

wallet ['wɑlət] *n* : billetera *f*, cartera *f*
wallflower ['wɔl,flauər] *n* **be a ~** : comer pavo
wallop ['wɑləp] *vt* : pegar fuerte — **~** *n* : golpe *m* fuerte
wallow ['wɑ,loː] *vi* : revolcarse
wallpaper ['wɔl,peɪpər] *n* : papel *m* pintado — **~** *vt* : empapelar
walnut ['wɔl,nʌt] *n* : nuez *f*
walrus ['wɔlrəs, 'wɑl-] *n, pl* **-rus** *or* **-ruses** : morsa *f*
waltz ['wɔlts] *n* : vals *m* — **~** *vi* : valsar
wan ['wɑn] *adj* **wanner; -est** : pálido
wand ['wɑnd] *n* : varita *f* (mágica)
wander ['wɑndər] *vi* **1** : vagar, pasear **2** STRAY : divagar — *vt* : pasear por — **wanderer** ['wɑndərər] *n* : vagabundo *m*, -da *f* — **wanderlust** ['wɑndər,lʌst] *n* : pasión *f* por viajar
wane ['weɪn] *vi* **waned; waning** : menguar — **~** *n* **be on the ~** : estar disminuyendo
want ['wɑnt, 'wɔnt] *vt* **1** DESIRE : querer **2** NEED : necesitar **3** LACK : carecer de — **~** *n* **1** NEED : necesidad *f* **2** LACK : falta *f* **3** DESIRE : deseo *m* — **wanting** ['wɑntɪŋ, 'wɔn-] *adj* **be ~** : carecer
wanton ['wɑntən, 'wɔn-] *adj* **1** LEWD : lascivo **2** **~ cruelty** : crueldad *f* despiadada
war ['wɔr] *n* : guerra *f*
ward ['wɔrd] *n* **1** : sala *f* (de un hospital, etc.) **2** : distrito *m* electoral **3** : pupilo *m*, -la *f* (de un tutor, etc.) — **~** *vt* — **off** : protegerse contra — **warden** ['wɔrdən] *n* **1** : guardián *m*, -diana *f* **2** *or* **game** : guardabosque *mf* **3** *or* **prison ~** : alcaide *m*
wardrobe ['wɔrd,roːb] *n* **1** CLOSET : armario *m* **2** CLOTHES : vestuario *m*
warehouse ['wær,haus] *n* : almacén *m*, bodega *f* *Lat* — **wares** ['wærz] *npl* : mercancías *fpl*
warfare ['wɔr,fær] *n* : guerra *f*
warily ['wærəli] *adv* : cautelosamente
warlike ['wær,laɪk] *adj* : belicoso
warm ['wɔrm] *adj* **1** : caliente **2** LUKEWARM : tibio **3** CARING : cariñoso **4** **I feel ~** : tengo calor **5** **~ clothes** : ropa *f* de abrigo — **~** *vt* *or* **~ up** : calentar — *vi* **1** *or* **~ up** : calentarse **2** **~ to** : tomar simpatía a (algn), entusiasmarse con (algo) — **warm-blooded** ['wɔrm'blʌdəd] *adj* : de sangre caliente — **warmhearted** ['wɔrm-'hɑrtəd] *adj* : cariñoso — **warmly** ['wɔrmli] *adv* **1** : calurosamente **2** **dress ~** : abrigarse — **warmth** ['wɔrmpθ] *n* **1** : calor *m* **2** AFFECTION : cariño *m*, afecto *m*

warn ['wɔrn] *vt* : advertir, avisar— **warning** ['wɔrnɪŋ] *n* : advertencia *f*, aviso *m*
warp ['wɔrp] *vt* **1** : alabear (madera, etc.) **2** DISTORT : deformar — *vi* : alabearse
warrant ['wɔrənt] *n* **1** : autorización *f* **2** **arrest ~** : orden *f* judicial — **~** *vt* : justificar — **warranty** ['wɔrənti, ,wɔrən'tiː] *n, pl* **-ties** : garantía *f*
warrior ['wɔriər] *n* : guerrero *m*, -ra *f*
warship ['wɔr,ʃɪp] *n* : buque *m* de guerra
wart ['wɔrt] *n* : verruga *f*
wartime ['wɔr,taɪm] *n* : tiempo *m* de guerra
wary ['wæri] *adj* **warier; -est** : cauteloso
was → be
wash ['wɔʃ, 'wɑʃ] *vt* **1** : lavar(se) **2** CARRY : arrastrar **3** **~ away** : llevarse **4** **~ over** : bañar — *vi* : lavarse — **~** *n* **1** : lavado *m* **2** LAUNDRY : ropa *f* sucia — **washable** ['wɔʃəbəl, 'wɑ-] *adj* : lavable — **washcloth** ['wɔʃ,klɔθ, 'wɑʃ-] *n* : toallita *f* (para lavarse) — **washed-out** ['wɔʃ'aut, 'wɑʃ-] *adj* **1** : desvaído (dícese de colores) **2** EXHAUSTED : agotado — **washer** ['wɔʃər, 'wɑ-] *n* **1** → **washing machine 2** : arandela *f* (de una llave, etc.) — **washing machine** *n* : máquina *f* de lavar, lavadora *f* — **washroom** ['wɔʃ-,ruːm, 'wɑʃ-, -,rʊm] *n* : servicios *mpl* (públicos), baño *m*
wasn't ['wɑzənt] (*contraction of* **was not**) → **be**
wasp ['wɑsp] *n* : avispa *f*
waste ['weɪst] *v* **wasted; wasting** *vt* **1** : desperdiciar, derrochar, malgastar **2** **~ time** : perder tiempo — *vi* *or* **~ away** : consumirse — **~** *adj* : de desecho — **~** *n* **1** : derroche *m*, desperdicio *m* **2** RUBBISH : desechos *mpl* **3** **a ~ of time** : una pérdida de tiempo — **wastebasket** ['weɪst,bæskət] *n* : papelera *f* — **wasteful** ['weɪstfəl] *adj* : derrochador — **wasteland** ['weɪst-,lænd, -lənd] *n* : yermo *m*
watch ['wɑtʃ] *vi* **1** : mirar **2** *or* **keep ~** : velar **3** **~ out!** : ¡ten cuidado!, ¡ojo! — *vt* **1** : mirar **2** *or* **~ over** : cuidar **3** **~ what you do** : ten cuidado con lo que haces — **~** *n* **1** : reloj *m* **2** SURVEILLANCE : vigilancia *f* **3** LOOKOUT : guardia *mf* — **watchdog** ['wɑtʃ-,dɔg] *n* : perro *m* guardián — **watchful** ['wɑtʃfəl] *adj* : vigilante — **watchman** ['wɑtʃmən] *n, pl* **-men** [-mən, -,men] : vigilante *m*, guarda *m* — **watchword** ['wɑtʃ,wərd] *n* : santo *m* y seña
water ['wɔtər, 'wɑ-] *n* : agua *f* — **~** *vt* **1**

: regar (el jardín, etc.) 2 ~ **down** DI-
LUTE : diluir, aguar — *vi* 1 : lagrimar
(dícese de los ojos) 2 **my mouth is
~ing** : se me hace agua la boca —
watercolor ['wɔt̮ər,kʌlər, 'wɑ-] *n* : acuarela *f* — **watercress** ['wɔt̮ər,krɛs,
'wɑ-] *n* : berro *m* — **waterfall** ['wɔt̮ər-
,fɔl, 'wɑ-] *n* : cascada *f*, salto *m* de agua
— **water lily** *n* : nenúfar *m* — **water-
logged** ['wɔt̮ər,lɔgd, 'wɑt̮ər,lɑgd] *adj*
: lleno de agua, empapado — **watermelon** ['wɔt̮ər,mɛlən, 'wɑ-] *n* : sandía *f*
— **waterpower** ['wɔt̮ər,pauər, 'wɑ-] *n*
: energía *f* hidráulica — **waterproof**
['wɔt̮ər,pruːf, 'wɑ-] *adj* : impermeable
— **watershed** ['wɔt̮ər,ʃɛd, 'wɑ-] *n* 1
: cuenca *f* (de un río) 2 : momento *m*
crítico — **waterskiing** ['wɔt̮ər,skiːiŋ,
'wɑ-] *n* : esquí *m* acuático — **watertight** ['wɔt̮ər,tait, 'wɑ-] *adj* : hermético
— **waterway** ['wɔt̮ər,wei, 'wɑ-] *n* : vía *f*
navegable — **waterworks** ['wɔt̮ər-
,wərks, 'wɑ-] *npl* : central *f* de abastecimiento de agua — **watery** ['wɔt̮əri,
'wɑ-] *adj* 1 : acuoso 2 DILUTED : aguado, diluido 3 WASHED-OUT : desvaído
(dícese de colores)
watt ['wɑt] *n* : vatio *m* — **wattage** ['wɑt-
,idʒ] *n* : vataje *m*
wave ['weiv] *v* **waved; waving** *vi* 1
: saludar con la mano 2 : flotar (dícese
de una bandera) — *vt* 1 SHAKE : agitar
2 CURL : ondular 3 SIGNAL : hacer
señas a (con la mano) — ~ *n* 1 : ola *f*
(de agua) 2 CURL : onda *f* 3 : onda *f* (en
física) 4 : señal *f* (con la mano) 5
SURGE : oleada *f* — **wavelength**
['weiv,lɛŋkθ] *n* : longitud *f* de onda
waver ['weivər] *vi* : vacilar
wax[1] ['wæks] *vi* : crecer (dícese de la
luna)
wax[2] *n* : cera *f* (para pisos, etc.) — ~ *vt*
: encerar — **waxy** ['wæksi] *adj* **waxier;
-est** : ceroso
way ['wei] *n* 1 : camino *m* 2 MEANS
: manera *f*, modo *m* 3 **by the** ~ : a
propósito, por cierto 4 **by** ~ **of** : vía,
pasando por 5 **come a long** ~ : hacer
grandes progresos 6 **get in the** ~
: meterse en el camino 7 **get one's
own** ~ : salirse uno con la suya 8
mend one's ~**s** : dejar las malas cos-
tumbres 9 **out of the** ~ REMOTE : remoto, recóndito 10 **which** ~ **did he
go?** : ¿por dónde fue?
we ['wiː] *pron* : nosotros, nosotras
weak ['wiːk] *adj* 1 : débil 2 DILUTED
: aguado 3 **a** ~ **excuse** : una excusa
poco convincente — **weaken** ['wiːkən]
vt : debilitar — *vi* : debilitarse —

weakling ['wiːklɪŋ] *n* : debilucho *m*,
-cha *f* — **weakly** ['wiːkli] *adv* : débilmente — ~ *adj* **weakiler; -est** : enfermizo — **weakness** ['wiːknəs] *n* 1
: debilidad *f* 2 FLAW : flaqueza *f*, punto
m débil
wealth ['wɛlθ] *n* : riqueza *f* — **wealthy**
['wɛlθi] *adj* **wealthier; -est** : rico
wean ['wiːn] *vt* : destetar
weapon ['wɛpən] *n* : arma *f*
wear ['wær] *v* **wore** ['wor]; **worn** ['worn];
wearing *vt* 1 : llevar (ropa, etc.),
calzar (zapatos) 2 *or* ~ **away** : desgastar 3 ~ **oneself out** : agotarse 4
~ **out** : gastar — *vi* 1 LAST : durar 2
~ **off** : desaparecer 3 ~ **out** : gastarse — ~ *n* 1 USE : uso *m* 2 CLOTHING
: ropa *f* 3 **be the worse for** ~ : estar
deteriorado — **wear and tear** *n* : desgaste *m*
weary ['wɪri] *adj* **-rier; -est** : cansado —
~ *v* **-ried; -rying** *vt* : cansar — *vi*
: cansarse — **weariness** ['wɪrinəs] *n*
: cansancio *m* — **wearisome** ['wɪri-
səm] *adj* : cansado
weasel ['wiːzəl] *n* : comadreja *f*
weather ['wɛðər] *n* : tiempo *m* — ~ *vt*
1 WEAR : erosionar, desgastar 2 EN-
DURE, OVERCOME : superar — **weath-
er-beaten** ['wɛðər,biːt̮ən] *adj* : curtido
— **weatherman** ['wɛðər,mæn] *n, pl*
-men [-mən, -,mɛn] : meteorólogo *m*,
-ga *f* — **weather vane** *n* : veleta *f*
weave ['wiːv] *v* **wove** ['woːv] *or*
weaved; woven ['woːvən] *or* **weaved;
weaving** *vt* 1 : tejer (tela) 2 INTERLACE
: entretejer 3 ~ **one's way** : abrirse
camino — *vi* : tejer — ~ *n* : tejido *m*
— **weaver** ['wiːvər] *n* : tejedor *m*, -dora
f
web ['wɛb] *n* 1 : telaraña *f* (de araña) 2
: membrana *f* interdigital (de aves) 3
NETWORK : red *f*
wed ['wɛd] *v* **wedded; wedding** *vt*
: casarse con — *vi* : casarse
we'd ['wiːd] (*contraction of* **we had, we
should,** *or* **we would**) → **have,
should, would**
wedding ['wɛdɪŋ] *n* : boda *f*, casamiento
m
wedge ['wɛdʒ] *n* 1 : cuña *f* 2 PIECE : porción *f*, trozo *m* — ~ *vt* **wedged;
wedging** 1 : apretar (con una cuña) 2
CRAM : meter
Wednesday ['wɛnz,dei, -di] *n* : miércoles *m*
wee ['wiː] *adj* 1 : pequeñito 2 **in the** ~
hours : a las altas horas
weed ['wiːd] *n* : mala hierba *f* — ~ *vt* 1
: desherbar 2 ~ **out** : eliminar

week ['wi:k] *n* : semana *f* — **weekday**
['wi:k,deɪ] *n* : día *m* laborable — **weekend** ['wi:k,end] *n* : fin *m* de semana —
weekly ['wi:kli] *adv* : semanalmente
— ~ *adj* : semanal — ~ *n*, *pl* **-lies**
: semanario *m*
weep ['wi:p] *v* **wept** ['wept]; **weeping**
: llorar — **weeping willow** *n* : sauce *m*
llorón — **weepy** ['wi:pi] *adj* **weepier;
-est** : lloroso
weigh ['weɪ] *vt* **1** : pesar **2** CONSIDER
: sopesar **3** ~ **down** : sobrecargar
(con una carga), abrumar (con preocu-
paciones, etc.) — *vi* : pesar
weight ['weɪt] *n* **1** : peso *m* **2 gain** ~
: engordar **3 lose** ~ : adelgazar —
weighty ['weɪti] *adj* **weightier; -est 1**
HEAVY : pesado **2** IMPORTANT : importante, de peso
weird ['wɪrd] *adj* **1** : misterioso **2**
STRANGE : extraño
welcome ['welkəm] *vt* **-comed; -com-
ing** : dar la bienvenida a, recibir — ~
adj **1** : bienvenido **2 you're** ~ : de
nada — ~ *n* : bienvenida *f*, acogida *f*
weld ['weld] *v* : soldar
welfare ['wel,fær] *n* **1** WELL-BEING : bienestar *m* **2** AID : asistencia *f* social
well[1] ['wel] *adv* **better** ['betər]; **best**
['best] **1** : bien **2** CONSIDERABLY : bastante **3 as** ~ : también **4 as** ~ **as**
: además de — ~ *adj* : bien — *interj* **1** (*used to introduce a remark*)
: bueno **2** (*used to express surprise*)
: ¡vaya!
well[2] *n* : pozo *m* — ~ *vi or* ~ **up** : brotar, manar
we'll ['wi:l, wɪl] (*contraction of* **we shall**
or **we will**) → **shall, will**
well–being ['wel'bi:ɪŋ] *n* : bienestar *m* —
well–bred ['wel'bred] *adj* : fino, bien
educado — **well–done** ['wel'dʌn] *adj* **1**
: bien hecho **2** : bien cocido (dícese de
la carne, etc.) — **well–known** ['wel-
'nom] *adj* : famoso, bien conocido —
well–meaning ['wel'mi:nɪŋ] *adj* : bienintencionado — **well–off** ['wel'ɔf] *adj*
: acomodado — **well–rounded** ['wel-
'raundəd] *adj* : completo — **well–to–
do** [,weltə'du:] *adj* : próspero, adinerado
Welsh ['welʃ] *adj* : galés — ~ *n* **1**
: galés *m* (idioma) **2 the** ~ : los gale-
ses
went → **go**
wept → **weep**
were → **be**
we're ['wɪr, 'wər, 'wi:ər] (*contraction of*
we are) → **be**

weren't ['wərənt, 'wərnt] (*contraction of*
were not) → **be**
west ['west] *adv* : al oeste — ~ *adj*
: oeste, del oeste — ~ *n* **1** : oeste *m* **2**
the West : el Oeste, el Occidente —
westerly ['westərli] *adv & adj* : del
oeste — **western** ['westərn] *adj* **1** : del
oeste **2 Western** : occidental — **West-
erner** ['westərnər] *n* : habitante *mf* del
oeste — **westward** ['westwərd] *adv &
adj* : hacia el oeste
wet ['wet] *adj* **wetter; wettest 1** : mojado **2** RAINY : lluvioso **3** ~ **paint** : pintura *f* fresca — ~ *vt* **wet** *or* **wetted;
wetting** : mojar, humedecer
we've ['wi:v] (*contraction of* **we have**)
→ **have**
whack ['hwæk] *vt* : golpear fuertemente
— ~ *n* : golpe *m* fuerte
whale ['hweɪl] *n*, *pl* **whales** *or* **whale**
: ballena *f*
wharf ['hwɔrf] *n*, *pl* **wharves** ['hwɔrvz]
: muelle *m*, embarcadero *m*
what ['hwɑt, 'hwʌt] *adj* **1** (*used in questions and exclamations*) : qué **2** WHAT-
EVER : cualquier — ~ *pron* **1** (*used in
questions*) : qué **2** (*used in indirect
statements*) : lo que, que **3** ~ **does it
cost?** : ¿cuánto cuesta? **4** ~ **for?**
: ¿por qué? **5** ~ **if** : y si — **whatever**
[hwɑt'evər, hwʌt-] *adj* **1** : cualquier **2
there's no chance** ~ : no hay ninguna posibilidad **3 nothing** ~ : nada en
absoluto — ~ *pron* **1** ANYTHING : lo
que **2** (*used in questions*) : qué **3** ~ **it
may be** : sea lo que sea — **whatsoev-
er** [,hwɑtso'evər, 'hwʌt-] *adj & pron* →
whatever
wheat ['hwi:t] *n* : trigo *m*
wheedle ['hwi:dəl] *vt* **-dled; -dling** : engatusar
wheel ['hwi:l] *n* **1** : rueda *f* **2** *or* **steering**
~ : volante *m* (de automóviles, etc.),
timón *m* (de barcos) — ~ *vt* : empujar (algo sobre ruedas) — *vi* **or** ~
around : darse la vuelta — **wheelbarrow** ['hwi:l,bæro:] *n* : carretilla *f* —
wheelchair ['hwi:l,tʃær] *n* : silla *f* de
ruedas
wheeze ['hwi:z] *vi* **wheezed; wheezing**
: resollar — ~ *n* : resuello *m*
when ['hwen] *adv* : cuándo — ~ *conj* **1**
: cuando **2 the days** ~ **I clean the
house** : los días (en) que limpio la
casa — ~ *pron* : cuándo — **whenever** [hwen'evər] *adv* : cuando sea — ~
conj **1** : cada vez que **2** ~ **you like**
: cuando quieras
where ['hwer] *adv* **1** : dónde **2** ~ **are
you going?** : ¿adónde vas? — ~ *conj*

& *pron* : donde — **whereabouts** ['*h*wer,bauts] *adv* : (por) dónde — ~ *ns & pl* : paradero *m* — **wherever** ['*h*wer'ever] *adv* 1 : en cualquier parte 2 WHERE : dónde, adónde — ~ *conj* : dondequiera que

whet ['*h*wet] *vt* **whetted; whetting** 1 : afilar 2 ~ **the appetite** : estimular el apetito

whether ['*h*weðer] *conj* 1 : si 2 **we doubt** ~ **he'll show up** : dudamos que aparezca 3 ~ **you like it or not** : tanto si quieras como si no

which ['*h*wɪtʃ] *adj* 1 : qué, cuál 2 **in** ~ **case** : en cuyo caso — ~ *pron* 1 (*used in questions*) : cuál 2 (*used in relative clauses*) : que, el (la) cual — **whichever** [*h*wɪtʃ'ever] *adj* : cualquier — ~ *pron* : el (la) que, cualquiera que

whiff ['*h*wɪf] *n* 1 PUFF : soplo *m* 2 SMELL : olorcillo *m*

while ['*h*waɪl] *n* 1 : rato *m* 2 **be worth one's** ~ : valer la pena 3 **in a** ~ : dentro de poco — ~ *conj* 1 : mientras 2 WHEREAS : mientras que 3 AL-THOUGH : aunque — ~ *vt* whiled; whiling ~ **away the time** : matar el tiempo

whim ['*h*wɪm] *n* : capricho *m*, antojo *m*

whimper ['*h*wɪmpər] *vi* : lloriquear— ~ *n* : quejido *m*

whimsical ['*h*wɪmzɪkəl] *adj* : caprichoso, fantasioso

whine ['*h*waɪn] *vi* **whined; whining** 1 : gimotear 2 COMPLAIN : quejarse — ~ *n* : quejido *m*, gemido *m*

whip ['*h*wɪp] *v* **whipped; whipping** *vt* 1 : azotar 2 BEAT : batir (huevos, crema, etc.) 3 ~ **up** AROUSE : avivar, despertar — *vi* FLAP : agitarse — ~ *n* : látigo *m*

whir ['*h*wər] *vi* **whirred; whirring** : zumbar — ~ *n* : zumbido *m*

whirl ['*h*wərl] *vi* 1 : dar vueltas, girar 2 *or* ~ **about** : arremolinarse — ~ *n* 1 : giro *m* 2 SWIRL : torbellino *m* — **whirlpool** ['*h*wərl,puːl] *n* : remolino *m* — **whirlwind** ['*h*wərl,wɪnd] *n* : torbellino *m*

whisk ['*h*wɪsk] *vt* 1 : batir 2 ~ **away** : llevarse — ~ *n or* **egg** ~ : batidor *m* — **whisk broom** *n* : escobilla *f*

whisker ['*h*wɪskər] *n* 1 : pelo *m* (de la barba) 2 ~**s** *npl* : bigotes *mpl* (de animales)

whiskey *or* **whisky** ['*h*wɪski] *n, pl* **-keys** *or* **-kies** : whisky *m*

whisper ['*h*wɪspər] *vi* : cuchichear, susurrar — *vt* : susurrar — ~ *n* : susurro *m*

whistle ['*h*wɪsəl] *v* **-tled; -tling** *vi* 1 : silbar, chiflar *Lat* 2 : pitar (dícese de un tren, etc.) — *vt* : silbar — ~ *n* 1 : silbido *m*, chiflido *m* (sonido) 2 : silbato *m*, pito *m* (instrumento)

white ['*h*waɪt] *adj* **whiter; -est** : blanco — ~ *n* 1 : blanco *m* (color) 2 : clara *f* (de huevos) 3 *or* ~ **person** : blanco *m*, -ca *f* — **white-collar** ['*h*waɪt'kɑlər] *adj* 1 : de oficina 2 ~ **worker** : oficinista *mf* — **whiten** ['*h*waɪtən] *vt* : blanquear — **whiteness** ['*h*waɪtnəs] *n* : blancura *f* — **whitewash** ['*h*waɪt,wɔʃ] *vt* 1 : enjalbegar 2 CONCEAL : encubrir (un escándalo, etc.) — ~ *n* 1 : jalbegue *m*, lechada *f* 2 COVER-UP : encubrimiento *m*

whittle ['*h*wɪtəl] *vt* **-tled; -tling** 1 : tallar (madera) 2 *or* ~ **down** : reducir

whiz *or* **whizz** ['*h*wɪz] *vi* **whizzed; whizzing** 1 BUZZ : zumbar 2 ~ **by** : pasar muy rápido — ~ *or* **whizz** *n, pl* **whizzes** : zumbido *m* — **whiz kid** *n* : joven *m* prometedor

who ['huː] *pron* 1 (*used in direct and indirect questions*) : quién 2 (*used in relative clauses*) : que, quien — **whodunit** [hu'dʌnɪt] *n* : novela *f* policíaca — **whoever** [hu'ever] *pron* 1 : quienquiera que, quien 2 (*used in questions*) : quién

whole ['hoːl] *adj* 1 : entero 2 INTACT : intacto 3 **a** ~ **lot** : muchísimo — ~ *n* 1 : todo *m* 2 **as a** ~ : en conjunto 3 **on the** ~ : en general — **wholehearted** ['hoːl'hɑrtəd] *adj* : sincero — **wholesale** ['hoːl,seɪl] *n* : venta *f* al por mayor — ~ *adj* 1 : al por mayor 2 ~ **slaughter** : matanza *f* sistemática — ~ *adv* : al por mayor — **wholesaler** ['hoːl,seɪlər] *n* : mayorista *mf* — **wholesome** ['hoːlsəm] *adj* : sano — **whole wheat** *adj* : de trigo integral — **wholly** ['hoːli] *adv* : completamente

whom ['huːm] *pron* 1 (*used in direct questions*) : a quién 2 (*used in indirect questions*) : de quién, con quién, en quién 3 (*used in relative clauses*) : que, a quien

whooping cough *n* : tos *f* ferina

whore ['hor] *n* : puta *f*

whose ['huːz] *adj* 1 (*used in questions*) : de quién 2 (*used in relative clauses*) : cuyo — ~ *pron* : de quién

why ['*h*waɪ] *adv* : por qué — ~ *n, pl* **whys** : porqué *m* — ~ *conj* : por qué — ~ *interj* (*used to express surprise*) : ¡vaya!, ¡mira!

wick ['wɪk] *n* : mecha *f*

wicked ['wɪkəd] *adj* 1 : malo, malvado 2

MISCHIEVOUS : travieso **3** TERRIBLE : terrible, horrible — **wickedness** ['wɪkədnəs] *n* : maldad *f*

wicker ['wɪkər] *n* : mimbre *m* — ~ *adj* : de mimbre

wide ['waɪd] *adj* **wider; widest 1** : ancho **2** VAST : amplio, extenso **3** *or* ~ **of the mark** : desviado — ~ *adv* **1** ~ **apart** : muy separados **2 far and** ~ : por todas partes **3** ~ **open** : abierto de par en par — **wide-awake** ['waɪd'weɪk] *adj* : (completamente) despierto — **widely** ['waɪdli] *adv* : extensivamente — **widespread** ['waɪd'sprɛd] *adj* : extendido

widow ['wɪdo:] *n* : viuda *f* — ~ *vt* : dejar viuda — **widower** ['wɪdowər] *n* : viudo *m*

width ['wɪdθ] *n* : ancho *m*, anchura *f*

wield ['wiːld] *vt* **1** : usar, manejar **2** EXERT : ejercer

wiener ['wiːnər] → **frankfurter**

wife ['waɪf] *n*, *pl* **wives** ['waɪvz] : esposa *f*, mujer *f*

wig ['wɪg] *n* : peluca *f*

wiggle ['wɪgəl] *v* **-gled; -gling** *vt* : menear, contonear — *vi* : menearse — ~ *n* : meneo *m*

wigwam ['wɪg,wɑm] *n* : wigwam *m*

wild ['waɪld] *adj* **1** : salvaje **2** DESOLATE : agreste **3** UNRULY : desenfrenado **4** RANDOM : al azar **5** FRANTIC : frenético **6** OUTRAGEOUS : extravagante — ~ *adv* **1** → **wildly 2 run** ~ : volver al estado silvestre (dícese de las plantas), desmandarse (dícese de los niños) — **wildcat** ['waɪld,kæt] *n* : gato *m* montés — **wilderness** ['wɪldərnəs] *n* : yermo *m*, desierto *m* — **wildfire** ['waɪld,faɪr] *n* **1** : fuego *m* descontrolado **2 spread like** ~ : propagarse como un reguero de pólvora — **wildflower** ['waɪld,flaʊər] *n* : flor *f* silvestre — **wildlife** ['waɪld,laɪf] *n* : fauna *f* — **wildly** ['waɪldli] *adv* **1** FRANTICALLY : frenéticamente **2** EXTREMELY : locamente

will¹ ['wɪl] *v past* **would** ['wʊd]; *pres sing & pl* **will** *vi* WISH : querer — *v aux* **1 tomorrow we** ~ **go shopping** : mañana iremos de compras **2 he** ~ **get angry over nothing** : se pone furioso por cualquier cosa **3 I** ~ **go despite them** : iré a pesar de ellos **4 I won't do it** : no lo haré **5 that** ~ **be the mailman** : eso ha de ser el cartero **6 the couch** ~ **hold three people** : en el sofá cabrán tres personas **7 accidents** ~ **happen** : los accidentes ocurrirán **8 you** ~ **do as I say** : harás lo que digo

will² *n* **1** : voluntad *f* **2** TESTAMENT : testamento *m* **3 free** ~ : libre albedrío *m* — **willful** *or* **wilful** ['wɪlfəl] *adj* **1** OBSTINATE : terco **2** INTENTIONAL : intencionado — **willing** ['wɪlɪŋ] *adj* **1** : complaciente **2 be** ~ **to** : estar dispuesto a — **willingly** ['wɪlɪŋli] *adv* : con gusto — **willingness** ['wɪlɪŋnəs] *n* : buena voluntad *f*

willow ['wɪlo:] *n* : sauce *m*

willpower ['wɪl,paʊər] *n* : fuerza *f* de voluntad

wilt ['wɪlt] *vi* : marchitarse

wily ['waɪli] *adj* **wilier; -est** : artero, astuto

win ['wɪn] *v* **won** ['wʌn]; **winning** : ganar — *vt* **1** : ganar, conseguir **2** ~ **over** : ganarse a — ~ *n* : triunfo *m*, victoria *f*

wince ['wɪnts] *vi* **winced; wincing** : hacer una mueca de dolor — ~ *n* : mueca *f* de dolor

winch ['wɪntʃ] *n* : torno *m*

wind¹ ['wɪnd] *n* **1** : viento *m* **2** BREATH : aliento *m* **3** FLATULENCE : flatulencia *f* **4 get** ~ **of** : enterarse de

wind² ['waɪnd] *v* **wound** ['waʊnd]; **winding** *vi* : serpentear — *vt* **1** COIL : enrollar **2** ~ **a clock** : dar cuerda a un reloj

windfall ['wɪnd,fɔl] *n* : beneficio *m* imprevisto

winding ['waɪndɪŋ] *adj* : tortuoso

wind instrument *n* : instrumento *m* de viento

windmill ['wɪnd,mɪl] *n* : molino *m* de viento

window ['wɪn,do:] *n* : ventana *f* (de un edificio o una computadora), ventanilla *f* (de un vehículo), vitrina *f* (de una tienda) — **windowpane** ['wɪn,do:,peɪn] *n* : vidrio *m* — **windowsill** ['wɪn,do:,sɪl] *n* : repisa *f* de la ventana

windpipe ['wɪnd,paɪp] *n* : tráquea *f*

windshield ['wɪnd,ʃild] *n* **1** : parabrisas *m* **2** ~ **wiper** : limpiaparabrisas *m*

window-shop ['wɪndo,ʃɑp] *vi* **-shopped; -shopping** : mirar las vitrinas

wind up ['waɪnd,ʌp] *vt* : terminar, concluir — *vi* : terminar, acabar — **windup** *n* : conclusión *f*

windy ['wɪndi] *adj* **windier; -est 1** : ventoso **2 it's** ~ : hace viento

wine ['waɪn] *n* : vino *m* — **wine cellar** *n* : bodega *f*

wing ['wɪŋ] *n* **1** : ala *f* **2 under s.o.'s** ~ : bajo el cargo de algn — **winged** ['wɪŋd, 'wɪŋəd] *adj* : alado

wink ['wɪŋk] *vi* : guiñar — ~ *n* **1** : guiño *m* **2 not sleep a** ~ : no pegar el ojo

winner ['wɪnər] *n* : ganador *m*, -dora *f* —

winning ['wɪnɪŋ] *adj* **1** : ganador **2** CHARMING : encantador — **winnings** ['wɪnɪŋz] *npl* : ganancias *fpl*

winter ['wɪntər] *n* : invierno — ~ *adj* : invernal, de invierno — **wintergreen** ['wɪntər,grin] *n* : gaulteria *f* — **wintertime** ['wɪntər,taɪm] *n* : invierno *m* — **wintry** ['wɪntri] *adj* **wintrier; -est** : invernal, de invierno

wipe ['waɪp] *vt* **wiped; wiping 1** : limpiar **2** ~ **away** : enjugar (lágrimas), borrar (una memoria) **3** ~ **out** : aniquilar, destruir — ~ *n* : pasada *f* (con un trapo, etc.)

wire ['waɪr] *n* **1** : alambre *m* **2** : cable *m* (eléctrico o telefónico) **3** TELEGRAM : telegrama *m* — ~ *vt* **-wired; wiring 1** : instalar el cableado en (una casa, etc.) **2** BIND : atar con alambre **3** TELEGRAPH : enviar un telegrama a — **wireless** ['waɪrləs] *adj* : inalámbrico — **wiring** ['waɪrɪŋ] *n* : cableado *m* — **wiry** ['waɪri] *adj* **wirier; -est 1** : hirsuto, tieso (dícese del pelo) **2** : esbelto y musculoso (dícese del cuerpo)

wisdom ['wɪzdəm] *n* : sabiduría *f* — **wisdom tooth** *n* : muela *f* de juicio

wise ['waɪz] *adj* **wiser; wisest 1** : sabio **2** SENSIBLE : prudente — **wisecrack** ['waɪz,kræk] *n* : broma *f*, chiste *m* — **wisely** ['waɪzli] *adv* : sabiamente

wish ['wɪʃ] *vt* **1** : desear **2** ~ **s.o. well** : desear lo mejor a algn — *vi* **1** : pedir (como deseo) **2 as you** ~ : como quieras — ~ *n* **1** : deseo *m* **2 best** ~**es** : muchos recuerdos — **wishbone** ['wɪʃ,bon] *n* : espoleta *f* — **wishful** ['wɪʃfəl] *adj* **1** : deseoso **2** ~ **thinking** : ilusiones *fpl*

wishy-washy ['wɪʃi,wɔʃi, -,wɑʃi] *adj* : insípido, soso

wisp ['wɪsp] *n* **1** : mechón *m* (de pelo) **2** : voluta *f* (de humo)

wistful ['wɪstfəl] *adj* : melancólico

wit ['wɪt] *n* **1** CLEVERNESS : ingenio *m* **2** HUMOR : agudeza *f* **3 at one's** ~**'s end** : desesperado **4 scared out of one's** ~**s** : muerto de miedo

witch ['wɪtʃ] *n* : bruja *f* — **witchcraft** ['wɪtʃ,kræft] *n* : brujería *f*, hechicería *f*

with ['wɪð, 'wɪθ] *prep* **1** : con **2 I'm going** ~ : voy contigo **3 it varies** ~ **the season** : varía según la estación **4 the girl** ~ **red hair** : la muchacha de pelo rojo **5** ~ **all his work, the business failed** : a pesar de su trabajo, el negocio fracasó

withdraw [wɪð'drɔ, wɪθ-] *v* **-drew** [-'dru:]; **-drawn** [-'drɔn]; **-drawing** *vt* : retirar — *vi* : apartarse — **withdrawal** [wɪð'drɔəl, wɪθ-] *n* **1** : retirada *f* **2** : abandono (de drogas, etc.) — **withdrawn** [wɪð'drɔn, wɪθ-] *adj* : introvertido

wither ['wɪðər] *vi* : marchitarse

withhold [wɪð'hold, wɪθ-] *vt* **-held** [-'held]; **-holding** : retener (fondos), negar (permiso, etc.)

within [wɪð'ɪn, wɪθ-] *adv* : dentro — ~ *prep* **1** : dentro de **2** (*in expressions of distance*) : a menos de **3** (*in expressions of time*) : dentro de, en menos de **4** ~ **reach** : al alcance de la mano

without [wɪð'aut, wɪθ-] *adv* **do** ~ : pasar sin algo — ~ *prep* : sin

withstand [wɪð'stænd, wɪθ-] *vt* **-stood** [-'stud]; **-standing 1** BEAR : aguantar **2** RESIST : resistir

witness ['wɪtnəs] *n* **1** : testigo *mf* **2** EVIDENCE : testimonio *m* **3 bear** ~ : atestiguar — ~ *vt* **1** SEE : ser testigo de **2** : atestiguar (una firma, etc.)

witticism ['wɪtə,sɪzəm] *n* : agudeza *f*, ocurrencia *f*

witty ['wɪti] *adj* **-tier; -est** : ingenioso, ocurrente

wives → **wife**

wizard ['wɪzərd] *n* **1** : mago *m*, brujo *m* **2 a math** ~ : un genio de matemáticas

wizened ['wɪzənd, 'wi:-] *adj* : arrugado

wobble ['wɑbəl] *vi* **-bled; -bling 1** : tambalearse **2** : temblar (dícese de la voz, etc.) — **wobbly** ['wɑbəli] *adj* : cojo

woe ['wo:] *n* **1** : aflicción *f* **2** ~**s** *npl* TROUBLES : penas *fpl* — **woeful** ['wofəl] *adj* : triste

woke, woken → **wake**

wolf ['wulf] *n, pl* **wolves** ['wulvz] : lobo *m*, -ba *f* — ~ *vt or* ~ **down** : engullir

woman ['wumən] *n, pl* **women** ['wɪmən] : mujer *f* — **womanly** ['wumənli] *adj* : femenino

womb ['wu:m] *n* : útero *m*, matriz *f*

won → **win**

wonder ['wʌndər] *n* **1** MARVEL : maravilla *f* **2** AMAZEMENT : asombro *m* — ~ *v* : preguntarse — **wonderful** ['wʌndərfəl] *adj* : maravilloso, estupendo

won't ['wont] (*contraction of* **will not**) → **will**

woo ['wu:] *vt* **1** COURT : cortejar **2** : buscar el apoyo de (clientes, votantes, etc.)

wood ['wud] *n* **1** : madera *f* (materia) **2** FIREWOOD : leña *f* **3** *or* ~**s** *npl* FOREST : bosque *m* — ~ *adj* : de madera — **woodchuck** ['wud,tʃʌk] *n* : marmota *f* de América — **wooded** ['wudəd] *adj* : arbolado, boscoso — **wooden**

['wʊdən] *adj* : de madera — **wood-pecker** ['wʊd,pekər] *n* : pájaro *m* carpintero — **woodshed** ['wʊd,ʃed] *n* : leñera *f* — **woodwind** ['wʊd,wɪnd] *n* : instrumento *m* de viento de madera — **woodwork** ['wʊd,wərk] *n* : carpintería *f*

wool ['wʊl] *n* : lana *f* — **woolen** *or* **woollen** ['wʊlən] *adj* : de lana — ~ *n* 1 : lana *f* (tela) 2 ~**s** *npl* : prendas *fpl* de lana — **woolly** ['wʊli] *adj* **-lier; -est** : lanudo

word ['wərd] *n* 1 : palabra *f* 2 NEWS : noticias *fpl* 3 ~**s** *npl* : letra *f* (de una canción, etc.) 4 **have** ~**s with** : reñir con 5 **just say the** ~ : no tienes que decirlo 6 **keep one's** ~ : cumplir su palabra — ~ *vt* : expresar — **word processing** *n* : procesamiento *m* de textos — **word processor** *n* : procesador *m* de textos — **wordy** ['wərdi] *adj* **wordier; -est** : prolijo

wore → **wear**

work ['wərk] *n* 1 LABOR : trabajo *m* 2 EMPLOYMENT : trabajo *m*, empleo *m* 3 : obra *f* (de arte, etc.) 4 ~**s** *npl* FACTORY : fábrica *f* 5 ~**s** *npl* MECHANISM : mecanismo *m* — ~ *v* **worked** ['wərkt] *or* **wrought** ['rɔt]; **working** *vt* 1 : hacer trabajar (a una persona) 2 : manejar, operar (una máquina, etc.) — *vi* 1 : trabajar 2 FUNCTION : funcionar 3 : surtir efecto (dícese de una droga), resultar (dícese de una idea, etc.) — **worked up** *adj* : nervioso — **worker** ['wərkər] *n* : trabajador *m*, -dora *f*; obrero *m*, -ra *f* — **working** ['wərkɪŋ] *adj* 1 : que trabaja (dícese de personas), de trabajo (dícese de la ropa, etc.) 2 **be in** ~ **order** : funcionar bien — **working class** *n* : clase *f* obrera — **workingman** ['wərkɪŋ,mæn] *n*, *pl* **-men** [-mən, -,men] : obrero *m* — **workman** ['wərkmən] *n*, *pl* **-men** [-mən, -,men] 1 : obrero *m* 2 ARTISAN : artesano *m* — **workmanship** ['wərkmən,ʃɪp] *n* : artesanía *f*, destreza *f* — **workout** ['wərk,aʊt] *n* : ejercicios *mpl* (físicos) — **work out** *vt* 1 DEVELOP : elaborar 2 SOLVE : resolver — *vi* 1 TURN OUT : resultar 2 SUCCEED : lograr, salir bien 3 EXERCISE : hacer ejercicio — **workshop** ['wərk,ʃɑp] *n* : taller *m* — **work up** *vt* 1 EXCITE : ponerse como loco 2 GENERATE : desarrollar

world ['wərld] *n* : mundo *m* 2 **think the** ~ **of s.o.** : tener a algn en alta estima — ~ *adj* : mundial, del mundo — **worldly** ['wərldli] *adj* : mundano —

worldwide ['wərld,waɪd] *adv* : en todo el mundo — ~ *adj* : global, mundial

worm ['wərm] *n* 1 : gusano *m*, lombriz *f* 2 ~**s** *npl* : lombrices *fpl* (parásitos)

worn → **wear** — **worn-out** ['wɔrn'aʊt] *adj* 1 USED : gastado 2 TIRED : agotado

worry ['wəri] *v* **-ried; -rying** *vt* : preocupar, inquietar — *vi* : preocuparse, inquietarse — ~ *n*, *pl* **-ries** : preocupación *f* — **worried** ['wərid] *adj* : preocupado — **worrisome** ['wərisəm] *adj* : inquietante

worse ['wərs] *adv* (*comparative of* **bad** *or of* **ill**) : peor — ~ *adj* (*comparative of* **bad** *or of* **ill**) 1 : peor 2 **from bad to** ~ : de mal en peor 3 **get** ~ : empeorar — ~ *n* 1 **the** ~ : el (la) peor, lo peor 2 **take a turn for the** ~ : ponerse peor — **worsen** ['wərsən] *v* : empeorar

worship ['wərʃəp] *v* **-shiped** *or* **-shipped; -shiping** *or* **-shipping** *vt* : adorar — *vi* : practicar una religión — ~ *n* : adoración *f*, culto *m* — **worshiper** *or* **worshipper** ['wərʃəpər] *n* : adorador *m*, -dora *f*

worst ['wərst] *adv* (*superlative of* **ill** *or of* **bad** *or of* **badly**) : peor — ~ *adj* (*superlative of* **bad** *or of* **ill**) : peor — ~ *n* **the** ~ : lo peor, el (la) peor

worth ['wərθ] *n* 1 : valor *m* (monetario) 2 MERIT : mérito *m*, valía *f* 3 **ten dollars' of gas** : diez dólares de gasolina — ~ *prep* 1 **it's** ~ **$ 10** : vale $ 10 2 **it's** ~ **doing** : vale la pena hacerlo — **worthless** ['wərθləs] *adj* 1 : sin valor 2 USELESS : inútil — **worthwhile** ['wərθ'hwaɪl] *adj* : que vale la pena — **worthy** ['wərði] *adj* **-thier; -est** : digno

would ['wʊd] *past of* **will** 1 **he** ~ **often take his children to the park** : solía llevar a sus hijos al parque 2 **I** ~ **go if I had the money** : iría yo si tuviera el dinero 3 **I** ~ **rather go alone** : preferiría ir sola 4 **she** ~ **have won if she hadn't tripped** : habría ganado si no hubiera tropezado 5 ~ **you kindly help me with this?** : ¿tendría la bondad de ayudarme con esto? — **would-be** ['wʊd'biː] *adj* **a** ~ **poet** : un aspirante a poeta — **wouldn't** ['wʊd-'ənt] (*contraction of* **would not**) → **would**

wound[1] ['wuːnd] *n* : herida *f* — ~ *vt* : herir

wound[2] ['waʊnd] → **wind**

wove, woven → **weave**

wrangle ['ræŋgəl] *vi* **-gled; -gling** : reñir — ~ *n* : riña *f*, disputa *f*

wrap ['ræp] *vt* **wrapped; wrapping 1**
: envolver **2 ~ up** FINISH : dar fin a —
~ n 1 : prenda *f* que envuelve (como
un chal) **2** WRAPPER : envoltura *f* —
wrapper ['ræpər] *n* : envoltura *f*, envoltorio *m* — **wrapping** ['ræpɪŋ] *n*
: envoltura *f*, envoltorio *m*

wrath ['ræθ] *n* : ira *f*, cólera *f* — **wrath-
ful** ['ræθfəl] *adj* : iracundo

wreath ['ri:θ] *n, pl* **wreaths** ['ri:ðz, 'ri:θs]
: corona *f* (de flores, etc.)

wreck ['rɛk] *n* **1** WRECKAGE : restos *mpl*
2 RUIN : ruina *f*, desastre *m* **3 be a
nervous ~** : tener los nervios de-
strozados — **~** *vt* : destrozar (un automóvil), naufragar (un barco) —
wreckage ['rɛkɪdʒ] *n* : restos *mpl* (de
un buque naufragado, etc.), ruinas *fpl*
(de un edificio)

wren ['rɛn] *n* : chochín *m*

wrench ['rɛntʃ] *vt* **1** PULL : arrancar (de
un tirón) **2** SPRAIN, TWIST : torcerse —
~ n 1 TUG : tirón *m*, jalón *m* **2** SPRAIN
: torcedura *f* **3** *or* **monkey ~** : llave *f*
inglesa

wrestle ['rɛsəl] *vi* **-tled; -tling** : luchar
— **wrestler** ['rɛsələr] *n* : luchador *m*,
-dora *f* — **wrestling** ['rɛsəlɪŋ] *n* : lucha
f

wretch ['rɛtʃ] *n* : desgraciado *m*, -da *f* —
wretched ['rɛtʃəd] *adj* **1** : miserable **2**
~ weather : tiempo *m* espantoso

wriggle ['rɪgəl] *vi* **-gled; -gling** : retorcerse, menearse

wring ['rɪŋ] *vt* **wrung** ['rʌŋ]; **wringing 1**
or **~ out** : escurrir (el lavado, etc.) **2**

TWIST : retorcer **3** EXTRACT : arrancar
(información, etc.)

wrinkle ['rɪŋkəl] *n* **1** : arruga *f* — **~** *v*
-kled; -kling *vt* : arrugar — *vi* : arrugarse

wrist ['rɪst] *n* : muñeca *f* — **wristwatch**
['rɪst,watʃ] *n* : reloj *m* de pulsera

writ ['rɪt] *n* : orden *f* (judicial)

write ['raɪt] *v* **wrote** ['ro:t]; **written**
['rɪtən]; **writing** : escribir — **write
down** *vt* : apuntar, anotar — **write off**
vt CANCEL : cancelar — **writer** ['raɪtər]
n : escritor *m*, -tora *f*

writhe ['raɪð] *vi* **writhed; writhing** : retorcerse

writing ['raɪtɪŋ] *n* : escritura *f*

wrong ['rɔŋ] *n* **1** INJUSTICE : injusticia *f*,
mal *m* **2** : agravio *m* (en derecho) **3 be
in the ~** : haber hecho mal — **~** *adj*
1 UNJUST : injusto **2** UNSUITABLE : inadecuado, inapropiado **3** INCORRECT : incorrecto,
equivocado **4 be ~** : no tener razón
— **~** *adv* : mal, incorrectamente —
~ *vt* **wronged; wronging** : ofender,
ser injusto con — **wrongful** ['rɔŋfəl]
adj **1** UNJUST : injusto **2** UNLAWFUL
: ilegal — **wrongly** ['rɔŋli] *adv* **1** UN-
JUSTLY : injustamente **2** INCORRECTLY
: mal

wrote → write

wrought iron ['rɔt] *n* : hierro *m* forjado

wrung → wring

wry ['raɪ] *adj* **wrier** ['raɪər]; **wriest**
['raɪəst] : irónico, sardónico (dícese del
humor)

XYZ

x *n, pl* **x's** *or* **xs** ['ɛksəz] : x *f*, vigésima
cuarta letra del alfabeto inglés

xenophobia [ˌzɛnəˈfoːbiə, ˌzi:-] *n* : xenofobia *f*

Xmas ['krɪsməs] *n* : Navidad *f*

X ray ['ɛks,reɪ] *n* **1** : rayo *m* X **2** *or* **~
photograph** : radiografía *f* — **x–ray**
vt : radiografiar

xylophone ['zaɪlə,fo:n] *n* : xilófono *m*

y ['waɪ] *n, pl* **y's** *or* **ys** ['waɪz] : y *f*,
vigésima quinta letra del alfabeto in-
glés

yacht ['jɑt] *n* : yate *m*

yam ['jæm] *n* **1** : ñame *m* **2** SWEET POTA-
TO : batata *f*, boniato *m*

yank ['jæŋk] *vt* : tirar de, jalar *Lat* — **~**
n : tirón *m*, jalón *m* *Lat*

Yankee ['jæŋki] *n* : yanqui *mf*

yap ['jæp] *vi* **yapped; yapping** : ladrar
— **~** *n* : ladrido *m*

yard ['jɑrd] *n* **1** : yarda *f* (medida) **2**
COURTYARD : patio *m* **3** : jardín *m* (de
una casa) — **yardstick** ['jɑrd,stɪk] *n* **1**
: vara *f* (de medir) **2** CRITERION : criterio *m*

yarn ['jɑrn] *n* **1** : hilado *m* **2** TALE : historia *f*, cuento *m*

yawn ['jɔn] *vi* : bostezar — **~** *n* : bostezo *m*

year ['jɪr] *n* **1** : año *m* **2 she's ten ~s
old** : tiene diez años **3 I haven't seen
them in ~s** : hace siglos que no los
veo — **yearbook** ['jɪr,bʊk] *n* : anuario
m — **yearling** ['jɪrlɪŋ, 'jərlən] *n* : animal *m* menor de dos años — **yearly**
['jɪrli] *adv* **1** : anualmente **2 three**

times ~ : tres veces al año — ~ *adj* : anual

yearn ['jərn] *vi* : anhelar — **yearning** ['jərnɪŋ] *n* : anhelo *m*, ansia *f*

yeast ['jiːst] *n* : levadura *f*

yell ['jɛl] *vi* : gritar, chillar — *vt* : gritar — ~ *n* : grito *m*, chillido *m*

yellow ['jɛlo] *adj* : amarillo — ~ *n* : amarillo *m* — **yellowish** ['jɛloɪʃ] *adj* : amarillento

yelp ['jɛlp] *n* : gañido *m* — ~ *vi* : dar un gañido

yes ['jɛs] *adv* 1 : sí 2 **say** ~ : decir que sí — ~ *n* : sí *m*

yesterday ['jɛstərˌdeɪ, -di] *adv* : ayer — ~ *n* 1 : ayer *m* 2 **the day before** ~ : anteayer

yet ['jɛt] *adv* 1 : aún, todavía 2 **has he come** ~? : ¿ya ha venido? 3 **not** ~ : todavía no 4 ~ **more problems** : más problemas aún 5 NEVERTHELESS : sin embargo — ~ *conj* : pero

yield ['jiːld] *vt* 1 PRODUCE : producir 2 ~ **the right of way** : ceder el paso — *vi* : ceder — ~ *n* : rendimiento *m*, rédito *m* (en finanzas)

yoga ['joːgə] *n* : yoga *m*

yogurt ['joːgərt] *n* : yogur *m*, yogurt *m*

yoke ['joːk] *n* : yugo *m*

yolk ['joːk] *n* : yema *f* (de un huevo)

you ['juː] *pron* 1 (*used as subject—familiar*) : tú; vos (*in some Latin American countries*); ustedes *pl*; vosotros, vosotras *pl Spain* 2 (*used as subject—formal*) : usted, ustedes *pl* 3 (*used as indirect object—familiar*) : te, les *pl* (se *before lo, la, los, las*), os *pl Spain* 4 (*used as indirect object—formal*) : lo (*Spain sometimes* le), la; los (*Spain sometimes* les), las *pl* 5 (*used after a preposition—familiar*) : ti; vos (*in some Latin American countries*); ustedes *pl*; vosotros, vosotras *pl Spain* 6 (*used after a preposition—formal*) : usted, ustedes *pl* 7 **with** ~ (*familiar*) : contigo; con ustedes *pl*; con vosotros, con vosotras *pl Spain* 8 **with** ~ (*formal*) : con usted, con ustedes *pl* 9 ~ **never know** : nunca se sabe — **you'd** ['juːd, 'jʊd] (*contraction of* **you had** *or* **you would**) → **have, would** — **you'll** ['juːl, 'jʊl] (*contraction of* **you shall** *or* **you will**) → **shall, will**

young ['jʌŋ] *adj* **younger** ['jʌŋgər]; **youngest** [-gəst] 1 : joven 2 **my** ~**er brother** : mi hermano menor 3 **she is the** ~**est** : es la más pequeña 4 **the** ~ : los jóvenes — ~ *npl* : jóvenes *mfpl* (de los humanos), crías *fpl* (de

los animales) — **youngster** ['jʌŋkstər] *n* : chico *m*, -ca *f*; joven *mf*

your ['jʊr, 'jɔr, jər] *adj* 1 (*familiar singular*) : tu 2 (*familiar plural*) su, vuestro *Spain* 3 (*formal*) : su 4 **on** ~ **left** : a la izquierda

you're ['jʊr, 'jɔr, jər, 'juːr] (*contraction of* **you are**) → **be**

yours ['jʊrz, 'jɔrz] *pron* 1 (*belonging to one person—familiar*) : (el) tuyo, (la) tuya, (los) tuyos, (las) tuyas 2 (*belonging to more than one person—familiar*) : (el) suyo, (la) suya, (los) suyos, (las) suyas; (el) vuestro, (la) vuestra, (los) vuestros, (las) vuestras *Spain* 3 (*formal*) : (el) suyo, (la) suya, (los) suyos, (las) suyas

yourself [jər'sɛlf] *pron, pl* **yourselves** [-'sɛlvz] 1 (*used reflexively—familiar*) : te, se *pl*, os *pl Spain* 2 (*used reflexively—formal*) : se 3 (*used for emphasis*) : tú mismo, tú misma; usted mismo, usted misma; ustedes mismos, ustedes mismas *pl*; vosotros mismos, vosotras mismas *pl Spain*

youth ['juːθ] *n, pl* **youths** ['juːðz, 'juːθs] 1 : juventud *f* 2 BOY : joven *m* 3 **today's** ~ : los jóvenes de hoy — **youthful** ['juːθfəl] *adj* 1 : juvenil, de juventud 2 YOUNG : joven

you've ['juːv] (*contraction of* **you have**) → **have**

yowl ['jaʊl] *vi* : aullar — ~ *n* : aullido *m*

yucca ['jʌkə] *n* : yuca *f*

Yugoslavian [ˌjuːgo'slɑviən] *adj* : yugoslavo

yule ['juːl] *n* CHRISTMAS : Navidad *f* — **yuletide** ['juːlˌtaɪd] *n* : Navidades *fpl*

z ['ziː] *n, pl* **z's** *or* **zs** : z *f*, vigésima sexta letra del alfabeto inglés

zany ['zeɪni] *adj* -**nier; -est** : alocado, disparatado

zeal ['ziːl] *n* : fervor *m*, celo *m* — **zealous** ['zɛləs] *adj* : entusiasta

zebra ['ziːbrə] *n* : cebra *f*

zenith ['ziːnəθ] *n* 1 : cenit *m* (en astronomía) 2 PEAK : apogeo *m*

zero ['ziːro, 'zɪro] *n, pl* -**ros** : cero *m*

zest ['zɛst] *n* 1 : gusto *m* 2 FLAVOR : sazón *f*

zigzag ['zɪgˌzæg] *n* : zigzag *m* — ~ *vi* -**zagged; -zagging** : zigzaguear

zinc ['zɪŋk] *n* : cinc *m*, zinc *m*

zip ['zɪp] *v* **zipped; zipping** *vt or* ~ **up** : cerrar la cremallera de, cerrar el cierre de *Lat* — *vi* SPEED : pasarse volando — **zip code** *n* : código *m* postal — **zipper** ['zɪpər] *n* : cremallera *f*, cierre *m Lat*

Common Spanish Abbreviations

SPANISH ABBREVIATION AND EXPANSION		ENGLISH EQUIVALENT	
abr.	abril	**Apr.**	April
A.C., a.C.	antes de Cristo	**BC**	before Christ
a. de J.C.	antes de Jesucristo	**BC**	before Christ
admon., admón.	administración	—	administration
a/f	a favor	—	in favor
ago.	agosto	**Aug.**	August
Apdo.	apartado (de correos)	—	P.O. box
aprox.	aproximadamente	**approx.**	approximately
Aptdo.	apartado (de correos)	—	P.O. box
Arq.	arquitecto	**arch.**	architect
A.T.	Antiguo Testamento	**O.T.**	Old Testament
atte.	atentamente	—	sincerely
atto., atta.	atento, atenta	—	kind, courteous
av., avda.	avenida	**ave.**	avenue
a/v.	a vista	—	on receipt
BID	Banco Interamericano de Desarrollo	**IDB**	Interamerican Development Bank
Bo	banco	—	bank
BM	Banco Mundial	—	World Bank
c/, C/	calle	**st.**	street
C	centígrado, Celsius	**C**	centigrade, Celsius
C.	compañía	**Co.**	company
CA	corriente alterna	**AC**	alternating current
cap.	capítulo	**ch., chap.**	chapter
c/c	cuenta corriente	—	current account, checking account
c.c.	centímetros cúbicos	**cu. cm**	cubic centimeters
CC	corriente continua	**DC**	direct current
c/d	con descuento	—	with discount
Cd.	ciudad	—	city
CE	Comunidad Europea	**EC**	European Community
CEE	Comunidad Económica Europea	**EEC**	European Economic Community
cf.	confróntese	**cf.**	compare
cg.	centígramo	**cg**	centigram
CGT	Confederación General de Trabajadores *o* del Trabajo	—	confederation of workers, workers' union
CI	coeficiente intelectual *o* de inteligencia	**IQ**	intelligence quotient
Cía.	compañía	**Co.**	company
cm.	centímetro	**cm**	centimeter
Cnel.	coronel	**Col.**	colonel
col.	columna	**col.**	column
Col. *Mex*	colonia	—	residential area
Com.	comandante	**Cmdr.**	commander
comp.	compárese	**comp.**	compare
Cor.	coronel	**Col.**	colonel
C.P.	código postal	—	zip code

SPANISH ABBREVIATION AND EXPANSION		ENGLISH EQUIVALENT	
CSF, c.s.f.	coste, seguro y flete	**c.i.f.**	cost, insurance, and freight
cta.	cuenta	**ac., acct.**	account
cte.	corriente	**cur.**	current
c/u	cada uno, cada una	**ea.**	each
CV	caballo de vapor	**hp**	horsepower
D.	Don	—	—
Da., D.ª	Doña	—	—
d.C.	después de Cristo	**AD**	anno Domini (in the year of our Lord)
dcha.	derecha	—	right
d. de J.C.	después de Jesucristo	**AD**	anno Domini (in the year of our lord)
dep.	departamento	**dept.**	department
DF, D.F.	Distrito Federal	—	Federal District
dic.	diciembre	**Dec.**	December
dir.	director, directora	**dir.**	director
dir.	dirección	—	address
Dña.	Doña	—	—
do.	domingo	**Sun.**	Sunday
dpto.	departamento	**dept.**	department
Dr.	doctor	**Dr.**	doctor
Dra.	doctora	**Dr.**	doctor
dto.	descuento	—	discount
E, E.	Este, este	**E**	East, east
Ed.	editorial	—	publishing house
Ed., ed.	edición	**ed.**	edition
edif.	edificio	**bldg.**	building
edo.	estado	**st.**	state
EEUU, EE.UU.	Estados Unidos	**US, U.S.**	United States
ej.	por ejemplo	**e.g.**	for example
E.M.	esclerosis multiple	**MS**	multiple sclerosis
ene.	enero	**Jan.**	January
etc.	etcétera	**etc.**	et cetera
ext.	extensión	**ext.**	extension
F	Fahrenheit	**F**	Fahrenheit
f.a.b.	franco a bordo	**f.o.b.**	free on board
FC	ferrocarril	**RR**	railroad
feb.	febrero	**Feb.**	February
FF AA, FF.AA.	Fuerzas Armadas	—	armed forces
FMI	Fondo Monetario Internacional	**IMF**	International Monetary Fund
g.	gramo	**g., gm, gr.**	gram
G.P.	giro postal	**M.O.**	money order
gr.	gramo	**g., gm, gr.**	gram
Gral.	general	**Gen.**	general
h.	hora	**hr.**	hour
Hnos.	hermanos	**Bros.**	brothers
I + D, I & D, I y D	investigación y desarrollo	**R & D**	research and development
i.e.	esto es, es decir	**i.e.**	that is
incl.	inclusive	**incl.**	inclusive, inclusively

SPANISH ABBREVIATION AND EXPANSION		ENGLISH EQUIVALENT	
Ing.	ingeniero, ingeniera	eng.	engineer
IPC	índice de precios al consumo	CPI	consumer price index
IVA	impuesto al valor agregado	VAT	value-added tax
izq.	izquierda	l.	left
juev.	jueves	Thurs.	Thursday
jul.	julio	Jul.	July
jun.	junio	Jun.	June
kg.	kilogramo	kg	kilogram
km.	kilómetro	km	kilometer
km/h	kilómetros por hora	kph	kilometers per hour
kv, kV	kilovatio	kw, kW	kilowatt
l.	litro	l, lit.	liter
Lic.	licenciado, licenciada	—	—
Ltda.	limitada	Ltd.	limited
lun.	lunes	Mon.	Monday
m	masculino	m	masculine
m	metro	m	meter
m	minuto	m	minute
mar.	marzo	Mar.	March
mart.	martes	Tues.	Tuesday
mg.	miligramo	mg	milligram
miérc.	miércoles	Wed.	Wednesday
min	minuto	min.	minute
mm.	milímetro	mm	millimeter
M-N, m/n	moneda nacional	—	national currency
Mons.	monseñor	Msgr.	monsignor
Mtra.	maestra	—	teacher
Mtro.	maestro	—	teacher
N, N.	Norte, norte	N, no.	North, north
n/o	nuestro	—	our
n.º	número	no.	number
N. de (la) R.	nota de (la) redacción	—	editor's note
NE	nordeste	NE	northeast
NN.UU.	Naciones Unidas	UN	United Nations
NO	noroeste	NW	northwest
nov.	noviembre	Nov.	November
N.T.	Nuevo Testamento	N.T.	New Testament
ntra., ntro.	nuestra, nuestro	—	our
NU	Naciones Unidas	UN	United Nations
núm.	número	num.	number
O, O.	Oeste, oeste	W	West, west
oct.	octubre	Oct.	October
OEA, O.E.A.	Organización de Estados Americanos	OAS	Organization of American States
OMS	Organización Mundial de la Salud	WHO	World Health Organization
ONG	organización no gubernamental	NGO	non-governmental organization
ONU	Organización de las Naciones Unidas	UN	United Nations
OTAN	Organización del Tratado del Atlántico Norte	NATO	North Atlantic Treaty Organization

	SPANISH ABBREVIATION AND EXPANSION		ENGLISH EQUIVALENT
p.	página	p.	page
P, P.	padre	Fr.	father
pág.	página	pg.	page
pat.	patente	pat.	patent
PCL	pantalla de cristal líquido	LCD	liquid crystal display
P.D.	post data	P.S.	postscript
p. ej.	por ejemplo	e.g.	for example
PNB	Producto Nacional Bruto	GNP	gross national product
pº	paseo	Ave.	avenue
p.p.	porte pagado	ppd.	postpaid
PP, p.p.	por poder, por poderes	p.p.	by proxy
prom.	promedio	av., avg.	average
ptas., pts.	pesetas		
q.e.p.d.	que en paz descanse	R.I.P.	may he/she rest in peace
R, R/	remite	—	sender
RAE	Real Academia Española	—	—
ref., ref.ª	referencia	ref.	reference
rep.	república	rep.	republic
r.p.m.	revoluciones por minuto	rpm.	revolutions per minute
rte.	remite, remitente	—	sender
s.	siglo	c., cent.	century
s/	su, sus	—	his, her, your, their
S, S.	Sur, sur	S, so.	South, south
S.	san, santo	St.	saint
S.A.	sociedad anónima	Inc.	incorporated (company)
sáb.	sábado	Sat.	Saturday
s/c	su cuenta	—	your account
SE	sudeste, sureste	SE	southeast
seg.	segundo, segundos	sec.	second, seconds
sep., sept.	septiembre	Sept.	September
s.e.u.o.	salvo error u omisión	—	errors and omissions excepted
Sgto.	sargento	Sgt.	sergeant
S.L.	sociedad limitada	Ltd.	limited (corporation)
S.M.	Su Majestad	HM	His Majesty, Her Majesty
s/n	sin número	—	no (street) number
s.n.m.	sobre el nivel de mar	a.s.l.	above sea level
SO	sudoeste/suroeste	SW	southwest
S.R.C.	se ruega contestación	R.S.V.P.	please reply
ss.	siguientes	—	the following ones
SS, S.S.	Su Santidad	H.H.	His Holiness
Sta.	santa	St.	Saint
Sto.	santo	St.	saint
t, t.	tonelada	t., tn	ton
TAE	tasa anual efectiva	APR	annual percentage rate
tb.	también	—	also
tel., Tel.	teléfono	tel.	telephone
Tm.	tonelada métrica	MT	metric ton
Tn.	tonelada	t., tn	ton
trad.	traducido	tr., trans., transl.	translated
UE	Unión Europea	EU	European Union
Univ.	universidad	Univ., U.	university

	SPANISH ABBREVIATION AND EXPANSION		ENGLISH EQUIVALENT
UPC	unidad procesadora central	**CPU**	central processing unit
Urb.	urbanización	—	residential area
v	versus	**v., vs.**	versus
v	verso	**v., ver., vs.**	verse
v.	véase	**vid.**	see
Vda.	viuda	—	widow
v.g., v.gr.	verbigracia	**e.g.**	for example
vier., viern.	viernes	**Fri.**	Friday
V.M.	Vuestra Majestad	—	Your Majesty
V^{o}B^{o}, V.^{o}B.^{o}	visto bueno	—	OK, approved
vol, vol.	volumen	**vol.**	volume
vra., vro.	vuestra, vuestro	—	your

Spanish Numbers

Cardinal Numbers

1	uno	28	veintiocho
2	dos	29	veintinueve
3	tres	30	treinta
4	cuatro	31	treinta y uno
5	cinco	40	cuarenta
6	seis	50	cincuenta
7	siete	60	sesenta
8	ocho	70	setenta
9	nueve	80	ochenta
10	diez	90	noventa
11	once	100	cien
12	doce	101	ciento uno
13	trece	200	doscientos
14	catorce	300	trescientos
15	quince	400	cuatrocientos
16	dieciséis	500	quinientos
17	diecisiete	600	seiscientos
18	dieciocho	700	setecientos
19	diecinueve	800	ochocientos
20	veinte	900	novecientos
21	veintiuno	1,000	mil
22	veintidós	1,001	mil uno
23	veintitrés	2,000	dos mil
24	veinticuatro	100,000	cien mil
25	veinticinco	1,000,000	un millón
26	veintiséis	1,000,000,000	mil millones
27	veintisiete	1,000,000,000,000	un billón

Ordinal Numbers

1st	primero, -ra	17th	decimoséptimo, -ma
2nd	segundo, -da	18th	decimoctavo, -va
3rd	tercero, -ra	19th	decimonoveno, -na; *or*
4th	cuarto, -ta		decimonono, -na
5th	quinto, -ta	20th	vigésimo, -ma
6th	sexto, -ta	21st	vigésimoprimero,
7th	séptimo, -ta		vigésimaprimera
8th	octavo, -ta	30th	trigésimo, -ma
9th	noveno, -na	40th	cuadragésimo, -ma
10th	décimo, -ma	50th	quincuagésimo, -ma
11th	undécimo, -ca	60th	sexagésimo, -ma
12th	duodécimo, -ma	70th	septuagésimo, -ma
13th	decimotercero, -ra	80th	octogésimo, -ma
14th	decimocuarto, -ta	90th	nonagésimo, -ma
15th	decimoquinto, -ta	100th	centésimo, -ma
16th	decimosexto, -ta	1,000th	milésimo, -ma

English Numbers

Cardinal Numbers

1	one	20	twenty
2	two	21	twenty-one
3	three	30	thirty
4	four	40	forty
5	five	50	fifty
6	six	60	sixty
7	seven	70	seventy
8	eight	80	eighty
9	nine	90	ninety
10	ten	100	one hundred
11	eleven	101	one hundred and one
12	twelve	200	two hundred
13	thirteen	1,000	one thousand
14	fourteen	1,001	one thousand and one
15	fifteen	2,000	two thousand
16	sixteen	100,000	one hundred thousand
17	seventeen	1,000,000	one million
18	eighteen	1,000,000,000	one billion
19	nineteen	1,000,000,000,000	one trillion

Ordinal Numbers

1st	first	16th	sixteenth
2nd	second	17th	seventeenth
3rd	third	18th	eighteenth
4th	fourth	19th	nineteenth
5th	fifth	20th	twentieth
6th	sixth	21st	twenty-first
7th	seventh	30th	thirtieth
8th	eighth	40th	fortieth
9th	ninth	50th	fiftieth
10th	tenth	60th	sixtieth
11th	eleventh	70th	seventieth
12th	twelfth	80th	eightieth
13th	thirteenth	90th	ninetieth
14th	fourteenth	100th	hundredth
15th	fifteenth	1,000th	thousandth